ISBN 978-0-266-62643-5
PIBN 10967300

Supplement—Feb. 2, 1894.

CONDUCTED BY

W. JOHN STONHILL,

Author of an Essay on the "Utilization of Wood, Straw and other Fibres in the Manufacture of Paper," which received the Medal of the International Forestry Exhibition, 1884.

VOLUME THE TWENTIETH.

JULY, 1893, TO DECEMBER, 1893.

OFFICES:

58, SHOE LANE, LONDON, E.C.

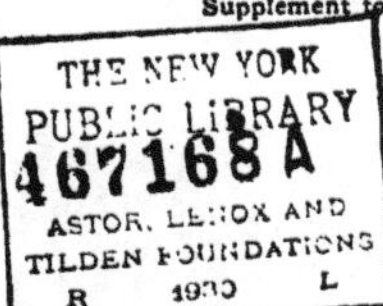

INDEX.

INDEX.

Telegrams: "STONHILL, LONDON." A B C Code. Registered at the General Post Office as a Newspaper.

Vol. XX. No. 1. LONDON, JULY 7, 1893. Price 6d.

LIXIVIATING THE BALL SODA.

The composition of the black ash or crude ball soda as revealed by chemical analysis is very complicated. It contains a great many impurities which affect to a greater or less extent the colour, etc., of the carbonated alkali, which alkali-makers make from it. But the presence of these impurities in the caustic lye does not interfere to any appreciable extent with the work carried on in ordinary pulp mills with probably a few exceptions. In all cases, however, it is desirable to decompose as much of the salt cake or sulphate of soda as possible in order to obtain the maximum yield of alkali.

The following analysis of raw ball soda fairly represents its composition (Lunge):

Carbonate of soda	44·79	per cent.
Silicate "	1·52	"
Aluminate "	1·44	"
Sulphate "	·92	"
Chloride of sodium	1·85	"
Lime	9·68	"
Sulphide of calcium	29·96	"
Carbonate of lime	5·92	"
Ferric oxide	1·21	"
Coal (carbon)	1·20	"
	98·49	

Taken roughly it may be considered to contain 45 per cent. of carbonate of soda, 30 per cent. of sulphide of calcium, 10 per cent. of caustic lime, 5 per cent. of carbonate of lime or undecomposed limestone, and 10 per cent. of carbon and other impurities.

Of these constituents, the sulphide of calcium and the caustic and carbonate of lime, coal, &c., are insoluble, so that when the ball soda is lixiviated in water, one half of it remains behind in the lixiviating vessels as an insoluble residue. This residue is the well-known "waste" of the alkali makers.

The crude soda, after lying exposed to the air for several days, is now broken up and wheeled to the lixiviating vats, where the soluble salts are dissolved out with water. The vessels used are the so-called Shanks' lixiviating vats, although it appears the principle of their construction was first suggested by Buff and Dunlop. The arrangement of the parts of these vats can be best understood from the accompanying sketch, which represents a series of four—the usual number worked. Fig. I. is a plan, Fig. II. a sectional elevation, and Fig. III. a cross section of the arrangement.

Each vat in the illustration is 10-ft. long by 5-ft. wide and 5-ft. deep; formed by placing divisions in a large wrought iron rectangular tank. They are provided with perforated false bottoms of wrought or cast iron plates, resting on supports about six inches from the bottom. An upright pipe (a^{i} a^{ii} a^{iii} a^{iv}), with a branch at right angles, rests over an opening in each false bottom to enable the liquor to flow by displacement from beneath the false bottom into the neighbouring vats. A seating is formed within this pipe immediately below the branch into which a plug fits as shown at a, to arrest the flow of liquor through the pipe whenever it is necessary to do so. It is obvious from this arrangement that if water be allowed to flow into No. 2 vat until it is nearly full, it will overflow into No. 3 by the branch in the pipe a^{ii} if the plug be removed, and that whenever No. 3 vat is in its turn nearly full, the water will overflow through the corresponding pipe a^{iii} into No. 4, but unless a communication is made between No. 4 and No. 1 it is apparent that the circulation from one vat to another will

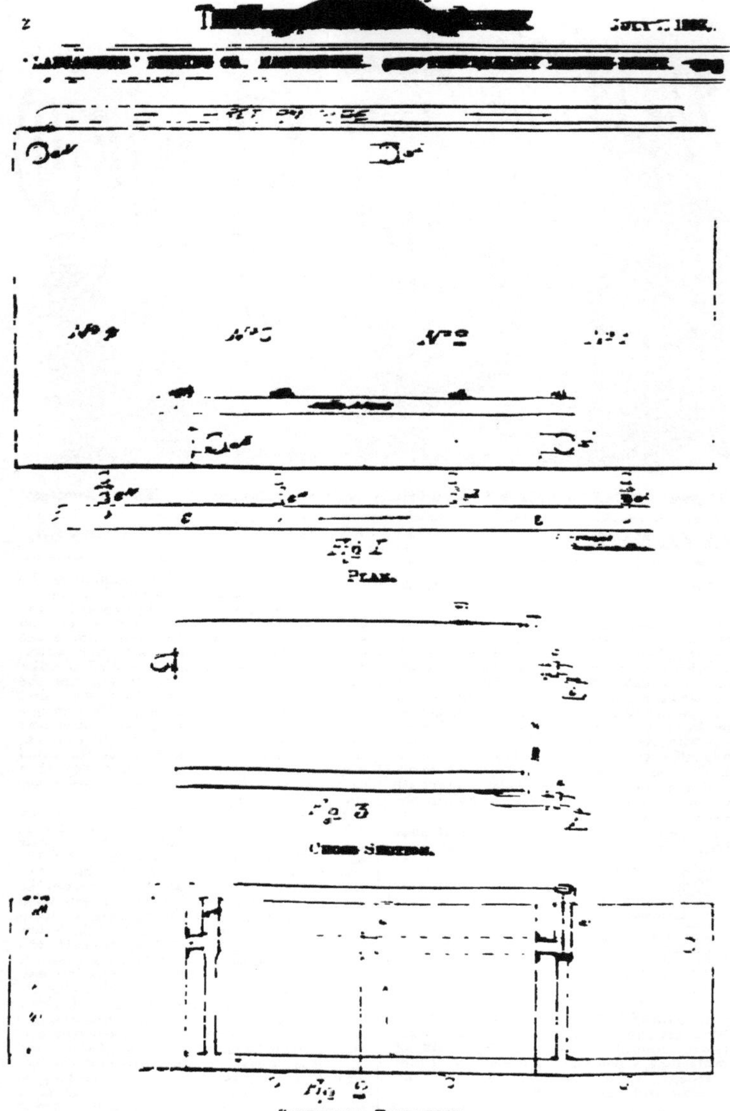

Fig. 1

PLAN.

Fig. 3

CROSS SECTION.

Fig. 2

SECTIONAL ELEVATION.

cease. The pipe b, called the "return pipe," is therefore attached to the apparatus to convey the liquor from No. 4 to No. 1. The pipes in front of the vats are each provided with two branches with cocks attached, and serve two purposes. The top taps, c^{i} c^{ii} c^{iii} c^{iv} are for drawing off the concentrated soda liquors which is conveyed by the shoot E placed beneath them to a large store well, whilst the bottom taps, d^{i} d^{ii} d^{iii} d^{iv}, enable the workmen to empty the vats of weak liquor—when the black ash is thoroughly exhausted of soda—into a well from whence it is pumped into a tank placed on a higher level than the vats, to be used instead of water for lixiviating. With such an arrangement if all the vats are filled with crude soda, either partially exhausted or otherwise, it is obvious that the water will gradually percolate through the solid mass in each vat in succession, and during the journey dissolve the soluble constituents of the crude soda issuing from the last vat of the series as a nearly concentrated solution.

There are usually only three vats of the four in actual operation at one time, the fourth being "off" for emptying and refilling. The *modus operandi* of working them is as follows: We will suppose that No. 2 vat is not working, that the weak liquor in it has been run off by the cock d^{ii} into the weak well, and that the weak liquor is being pumped into the shoot containing the plug holes w^{i}, w^{ii}, w^{iii}, w^{iv}, whence it flows through the plug hole w^{iii} into No. 3 vat. This weak liquor gradually permeates the mass of partially lixiviated ball soda in No. 3, and displaces stronger liquor from beneath the perforated false bottom, through the circulation pipe a^{iii} into No. 4, where it again permeates the mass within this vat, and again rises up the circulation pipe a^{iv}, and is conveyed by the return pipe b to No. 1, which being the last in the series, has been most recently filled with ball soda. The liquor again passes through the body of solid matter in No. 1, but instead of allowing it to flow up the circulation pipe a^{i} into No. 2, its flow in this direction is arrested by inserting the plug, while at the same time the upper cock c^{i} in the front pipe is opened to allow the strong concentrated soda lye to flow into the shoot e, which conveys it to the store vessel. When the supply of weak liquor to No. 3 is exhausted it is replaced with warm water. The water supply and the front cock c^{i} on No. 1, are regulated, so as to obtain the concentrated liquor of a certain strength. The liquors as they flow from one vat to the other are repeatedly tested for density, and whenever that from the "weak vat" is about three or four degrees Twaddell, *i.e.*, the liquor flowing from No. 3 to 4 in the above suppositional case, the supply of water to No. 3 is shut off, the plug inserted into the upright circulation pipe a^{iii}, and after the vat has lain at rest for an hour or so the bottom cock d^{iii} in the front pipe is opened to allow the weak liquor to flow to the weak well. Before this is done, No. 2 vat will have been filled with fresh ball soda, and the liquor running from the top tap c^{i} will have reached its lowest limit in density (about 40° Twaddell). This tap is then shut, and the plug in the upright circulation pipe a^{i} being removed, the liquor flows into No. 2, the top front tap c^{ii} of which is opened. The supply of weak liquor or water to No. 4 is then continued as in the case of No. 3 until the black ash in it is exhausted, after which it is emptied and refilled.

With this system of lixiviating, the ball soda is treated with a lye gradually decreasing in density, until finally water dissolves and removes the last traces of soda from the insoluble residue. The soda is also dissolved out with the least possible quantity of water, and in fulfilling this condition a very important point is secured, namely, the prevention of the formation of sulphide of sodium.

Good lixiviation depends upon the following conditions:—

1st. The concentration of the liquor.
2nd. The duration of the digestion.
3rd. The elevation of the temperature.

The length of time employed to extract the soda, and the quantity and temperature of the water, should all be kept as low as possible, otherwise a proportionately large amount of sulphide of sodium is formed, which in the ordinary run of cases can only be looked upon as a harmful impurity.

When the liquor is first brought into contact with the dry ball soda in the last vat of the series, the lime is converted into hydrate or is slaked, causing the lumps of ash to swell and fall to pieces. The lime thus acts upon the carbonate of soda in solution, converting it into hydrate, so that the strong lye flowing from the strong-liquor-vat contains a large proportion of caustic alkali. The temperature of the water used for lixiviating is usually not allowed to exceed 100 degs. F., there being a considerable amount of heat developed by the slaking of the lime, and as above indicated, elevation of temperature gives rise to the formation of sulphide of sodium. The volume of water should be regulated to yield a concentrated liquor of an average density of 50 degs. Twaddell, tested at 120 degs. F.

The following is the composition of a crude soda liquor obtained by decomposing salt cake with limestone and coal:—

	Grammes per litre.
Carbonate of soda	252·910
Caustic soda	51·680
Chloride of sodium	10·682
Sulphate of soda	2·792
Sulphite of soda	0·291
Hyposulphite of soda	1·327
Sulphide of sodium	4·149
Ferrocyanide of sodium	0·768
Silica, alumina, and ferricoxide ...	4·656
Total soda (Na_2O)	187·980
Soda as carbonate	147·930
Soda as caustic	40·050

From these figures it is evident that nearly 21 per cent. of the alkali (total soda) in the above crude lye consists of caustic, which means that the liquor before it flows from the vats to the store well is causticised to this extent.

The liquor is frequently tested to ascertain its composition, but the analysis carried out in the works laboratory is not so elaborate as to include the determination of all the ingredients above set forth. Manufacturers are content to ascertain the total alkali (Na_2O), the chloride of sodium, sulphide of sodium (Na_2S) and the total sulphate of soda. The latter includes the sulphite, hyposulphite and sulphide of soda as well as the sulphate existing as such. These impurities are also usually calculated on 25 parts of alkali being thus placed on a comparable basis, and the results compared from day to day. Upon this basis the crude ball soda made from the foregoing Lancashire mixing in which limestone alone is used as the calcareous material, will, if properly furnaced in an ordinary hand furnace, yield a liquor of about the following composition:—

ANALYSIS OF VAT LIQUOR.

Twaddell — 50° a 120° Fah. P. C. soda by volume — 23·5.

Sulphide of sodium	—	0·30 to 0·40 on 25 Na_2O.
Total sulphate of soda	—	2·70 to 3·00 ,, ,,
Common salt (Na Cl)	—	2·75 to 3·00 ,, ,,

New Papermaking Machinery

BY

MESSRS. UMPHERSTON & CO., LTD.

This enterprising firm of papermakers' engineers are now introducing several new and important pieces of machinery used in the manufacture of paper. Among these may be mentioned the new rotary strainer and a beating engine of almost mammoth proportions. The inventor of this strainer is Mr. E. W. Goodrick, of Appleton, U.S.A., to whom letters patents have been granted in America and England. The construction of this machine is quite novel, and the term *rotary*, which has been applied to it, is somewhat misleading, owing to the fact that the straining plates are quite stationary, and the principle of its action is entirely different from what are known as *revolving strainers*. The accompanying illustration of this apparatus shows that it consists of a vat having a curved bottom and lateral wings, and being divided into an upper and lower portion by means of the straining plates.

In the lower portion of the vat a series of rotary discs or drums are located and fixed to a horizontal drive shaft which passes through packing boxes in the sides of the vat and rotates in bearings. The lower vat is divided into several compartments of equal size, formed by vertical partitions, which extend transversely to the axis of the drums and also by a longitudinal partition extending parallel with the drive shaft, and hence the axis of the drums. This vertical partition is provided with openings in which the drums revolve, as little space as possible being left between the edges of the partition and these in order to insure tightness and cut off as much communication as possible between the compartments.

All the drums are constructed alike and each are provided with a curved or arc-shaped internal passage, one end of which commences at the vertical side of the drum between its axis and periphery and at a point nearer to the axis than the periphery, while the opposite end of the passage terminates at the periphery and diametrically opposite the axis of the disc. This outlet slopes gradually into the periphery of the disc; and it will be seen that the receiving end of the passage will be within one compartment, while the discharge-opening is within another compartment, for the purpose of drawing the fluid from one compartment and discharging it in the other when the drums are rotating.

The drums are so arranged on the drive-shaft that one half the number will be discharging upon one side of the vertical partition, while the other half of the number are discharging upon the opposite side. The purpose of these rotary drums and their curved passages is to set up active currents in the fluid in the vat, thereby agitating the stock or material as it lands upon the strainer and keeping the latter clear and free from clogging.

When in operation the drums revolve rapidly and the fluid mass of material in the vat is made to enter the receiving end of the passage and by centrifugal force is discharged with great force at the periphery of the wheel through the openings. In this operation each drum acts independently of the other and, as previously stated, the fluid enters the drum from one compartment and is discharged into the opposite compartment, this action taking place alternately as the receiving end of the passage moves from one side of the vertical partition to the other side.

When the drums are revolving at the rate of 500 revolutions a minute the fluid discharges from their peripheries with great force, thereby causing such a pulsation of internal currents that the paper stock is violently agitated and drawn through the strainer, and discharged into the front collecting box and out of the pipe. By this all knots, dirt and extraneous matter are caught on the top of the strainer, from which it can be readily removed from time to time by an attendant or otherwise.

The sole makers of this strainer in Great Britain are Messrs. Umpherston and Co., Ltd., of Leith. The advantages claimed for these strainers are: (1) The plates are stationary. (2) The action is silent, and entirely uniform over the whole plate surface. (3) There are no jog or crank motions, nor any flexible fittings. (4) There are no internal wearing parts, and the only driving gear is *one pulley*. From testimonials which have from time to time reached Messrs. Umpherston and Co., Ltd., it is evident that the very best results are obtained at small cost.

In spite of the patent not yet being one year old, upwards of 40 machines are at work in America. Working drawings showing the details of the construction of this strainer have been supplied to Messrs. Umpherston and Co., and they have completed two and are engaged making others. Special sizes may be made to suit the dimensions of cut plates previously in use; the probable price in this case being about £4 per square foot of plate surface, and worn plates may be reclosed or recut to a different gauge if required at the usual rates.

New Rotary Strainer (Goodrick's Patent).

Messrs. Umpherston and Co., Limited, Leith, have just built to the order of Messrs. Brown, Stewart & Co., Ltd., for their Overton Mill (Greenock), two beaters and two breakers, that may truly be described as mammoth machines. The holding capacity is 20 cwt. These are not the first engines of this size which Messrs. Umpherston have built, as they built one some time since of the same dimensions and for the same firm, and they are so satisfied with the the first one that they have had four more built. In ordering, they insisted on having these exceptional size engines, believing that the work is done better by them than with smaller, and with much more economy. The diameter of the rolls is 4 feet 7 inches, and the length 7 feet 6 inches, and they weigh 6 tons. The beater is 19 feet by 7 feet 9 inches, which equals in capacity 600 cubic feet. The bottom plates each weigh 11½ cwt. The breakers are each fitted with drum washers, 4 feet in diameter and 7-ft. in length, and are made wholly of brass. The cost of each drum washer is upwards of £120. The steel bars in each roll weigh 55 cwt.

Chicago Exhibition.—The Americans are greatly disappointed at the smallness of the number of European visitors. The Germans, it is stated, particularly were frightened at the reports of the very heavy expense of everything in America, and many of them who intended going have now given up the idea.

Sulphite makers in Germany and Austria are so busy now, that of the best makes very little can be had even at greatly raised prices. Paper makers under contract at old prices may consider themselves lucky, as they will have to pay higher rates when these contracts have to be renewed. Several makes which used to be exported regularly are now bought up by neighbouring papermakers at good prices, so that there seems to be no prospect of a cheapening. On the contrary it is expected the price of a couple of years ago will be reached before long.

D. N. BERTRAM'S
Patent REELER

The Special Features of the Machine are:

1.—NO PART OF THE KNIFE BLOCKS or knives, except the cutting edges, comes in contact with the paper, thus avoiding any damage to the web by narrow rings touching it.

2.—There BEING NO BLOCKS between the knives they can be instantly adjusted to any width without taking the spindle from its bearings.

3.—The KNIVES ARE DRIVEN INDEPENDENTLY of the paper at an increased speed ensuring clean cut edges.

4.—The MACHINE IS DRIVEN by belt pulley on drum shaft with fast and slow speeds, worked from front of machine by levers, so arranged that when the fast speed is put on the slow one disengages itself. The change from slow to fast is easily effected, and no jerking takes place.

☞ **THIS PATENT REELER is working in Several Well-known Paper Mills.**

IN THIS MACHINE the paper is slit into widths upon the spindle, which carries the finished webs, thus preventing irregularity of edges; the outside shavings being trimmed before the web passes to the winding-up spindle and slitting-knives.

THE KNIFE CARRIAGE is placed vertically over the web, and fitted with automatic raising gear, to compensate for the increase of web.

THERE IS ALSO AN ARRANGEMENT so that the operator can apply the slitting-knives with any given amount of contact that may be desirable, and it will retain the same position until the whole web is finished.

THE ACTION OF THE PRESSING ROLL on the top of the web ensures the reel being firmly and evenly wound, and there is a shackle at one side of the machine, with screw which can adjust pressing roll to a nicety on the drum upon which the slitting and winding apparatus is carried. This allows webs which may be slightly thicker at one side than another to be wound without creasing.

REFERENCES GIVEN ON APPLICATION.

BERTRAMS LIMITED

(Successors to Geo. & Wm. BERTRAM—ESTABLISHED 1821),

ENGINEERS,

ST. KATHERINE'S WORKS, SCIENNES, EDINBURGH.

EXPORTS OF BRITISH PAPER, &c. DURING 1892.

WRITINGS, PRINTINGS & ENVELOPES.

Countries.	Cwts.	Value.
Russia...	546	£3,603
Sweden and Norway	9,151	12,503
Denmark	1,287	2,068
Germany	3,101	9,192
Holland	8,458	18,372
Belgium	5,863	18,302
France	39,634	72,817
Portugal, Azores and Maderia	657	2,354
Spain and Canaries	2,796	5,870
Turkey	538	2,282
Egypt...	1,855	3,998
China...	3,731	9,640
Japan...	23,082	28,312
United States of America: Atlantic	10,848	28,326
Mexico	1,091	2,727
Central America	2,154	4,518
Republic of Colombia	787	2,068
Peru	1,920	3,654
Chile	5,723	18,270
Brazil...	3,739	9,389
Uruguay	1,255	2,974
Argentine Republic	10,177	24,259
Other Foreign Countries	2,420	7,327
Total to Foreign Countries	140,398	282,810
British Possessions in S. Africa	33,536	61,620
Mauritius	1,637	2,892
British East Indies:		
Bombay and Scinde...	44,605	75,456
Madras...	17,814	31,928
Bengal and Burmah...	23,057	43,266
Straits Settlements...	3,832	8,204
Ceylon	6,857	13,881
Hong Kong...	1,996	4,416
Australasia:		
West Australia	5,143	8,272
South Australia	30,972	43,810
Victoria...	158,389	202,107
New South Wales	94,547	148,228
Queensland	20,357	32,144
Tasmania	8,667	18,855
New Zealand...	52,788	82,669
Fiji Islands	100	252
British N. America	30,644	54,872
British West India Islands and British Guiana...	8,757	19,616
Other British Possessions	3,029	7,260
Total to British Possessions	546,722	848,748
TOTAL	687,120	1,131,558

HANGINGS.

	Cwts.	Value.
Germany	1,788	£6,923
Holland	1,299	4,583
Belgium	1,782	4,928
France	2,670	10,829
Spain and Canaries	1,774	5,854
Italy...	1,190	2,732
China...	1,105	1,531
United States of America: Atlantic...	2,883	10,679
Peru	897	1,957
Chile	2,587	5,200
Brazil...	284	1,036
Other Foreign Countries	1,646	4,737
Total to Foreign Countries	19,880	60,989
Channel Islands	516	1,808
British Possessions in S. Africa	7,475	18,056
British East Indies	1,341	3,295
Australasia:		
South Australia	1,505	4,002
Victoria...	9,360	20,897
New South Wales	6,095	13,090
New Zealand...	6,681	15,156
Other Colonies	978	2,502
British N. America	8,461	6,919
British West India Islands and B. Guiana	539	1,140
Other British Possessions	317	696
Total to British Possessions	37,218	87,501
TOTAL	58,098	148,490

PASTEBOARD, MILLBOARD, &c.

(Including Playing Cards).

	Cwts.	Value.
Germany	779	£1,121
France	984	2,396
Turkey	890	1,045
United States of America: Atlantic..	570	1,981
Chile...	124	767
Brazil...	500	718
Argentine Republic	400	1,250
Other Foreign Countries	1,833	3,845
Total to Foreign Countries	5,580	13,123
British Possessions in S. Africa	1,441	4,719
British East Indies:		
Bombay and Scinde...	1,673	4,886
Madras...	938	3,055
Bengal and Burmah	1,900	4,587
Other Possessions	362	890
Australasia:		
Victoria...	2,732	4,259
New South Wales	3,883	7,380
New Zealand...	1,419	2,896
Other Colonies	1,568	2,634
British North America...	975	1,587
Other British Possessions	476	1,548
Total to British Possessions	17,362	38,441
TOTAL	22,942	51,564

[illegible]

[illegible] exports of "Paper [illegible] as the [illegible] during [illegible]

[illegible]	[illegible]	[illegible]
[illegible]	[illegible]	104.94
[illegible]	[illegible]	4.81
[illegible]	[illegible]	77
[illegible]	11.[illegible]	19.45
[illegible]	[illegible]	8.48
[illegible]	[illegible]	10.92
[illegible]	1.[illegible]	6.41
[illegible]	[illegible]	13
[illegible]	[illegible]	15.44
[illegible]	[illegible]	26.93
[illegible]	[illegible]	[illegible]
[illegible]	[illegible]	3.53
[illegible]	[illegible]	33.37
[illegible]	[illegible]	[illegible]
[illegible]	[illegible]	51.19
[illegible]	[illegible]	[illegible]
[illegible]	[illegible]	[illegible]
[illegible]	[illegible]	70
[illegible]	[illegible]	[illegible]
[illegible]	[illegible]	[illegible]

THE

UNITED ALKALI CO., LTD

G11, EXCHANGE BUILDINGS, LIVERPOOL.

Telegrams: "UBIQUE, LIVERPOOL." Telephone: 1185.

MANUFACTURERS OF

Bleaching Powder,

High-Test SULPHATE of SODA or SALTCAKE, in Bulk or Ground and Packed,
SULPHURIC ACID, RECTIFIED VITRIOL, CHLORIDE of CALCIUM, MONOHYDRATE,
HYDROCHLORIC ACID, Common or Purified, BROWN VITRIOL.

REFINED ALKALI, All Strengths,

CAUSTIC and CARBONATE of POTASH, BICARBONATE of SODA, High Strength,
CHLORATES of POTASH and SODA, CRYSTAL CARBONATE, SAL AMMONIAC,
MURIATE of AMMONIA, SULPHATE of AMMONIA, SULPHATE of ALUMINA.

Soda Crystals,

FERTILIZERS, SALT, Common, White and Rock, CHROMIC ACID,
PEROXIDE of MANGANESE, HYDRATED PEROXIDE of MANGANESE for Gas Purification.
MANGANATE of SODA, SILICATE SODA, PURPLE ORE,

CAUSTIC SODA, 60–77 °/°

Soda Ash,

COPPER PRECIPITATE, S.S. PATENT ROSIN, ROSIN OIL, ULTRAMARINE,
CHLORIDE of MAGNESIUM. STRONTIA SALTS, Oxide, Hydrate, and Carbonate,
GLYCERINE,

SULPHUR, Rock, Roll, Flowers. 

Apparatus to Recover

SODA ASH

(CHAPMAN'S PATENT).

Avoiding POLLUTION of STREAMS, LOSS by LEAKAGE, and NUISANCE to the NEIGHBOURHOOD.

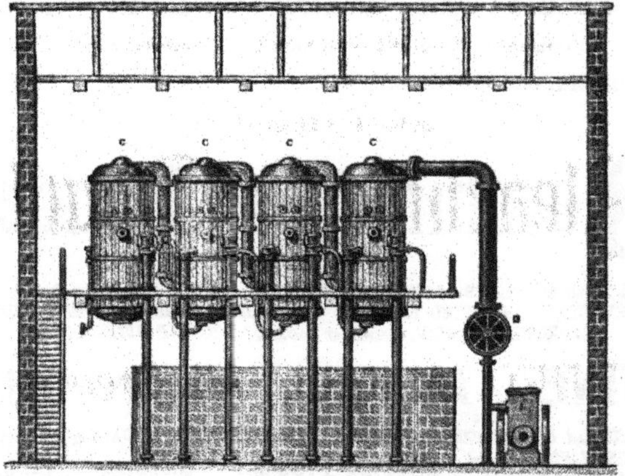

Writing on the 4th April, 1893, the Manager of the WOOLFOLD PAPER MILLS says:—

" We are getting very good work out of our plant. The Evaporator has never worked better than it is now doing. We have been treating our liquor for a month or two at 3½° Tw., and as you are well aware this means a great deal of evaporation for little ash. Many Papermakers would refuse to believe (unless they saw) that we could treat so weak a liquor profitably, but we can."

☛ *The Evaporator at Woolfold is a QUADRUPLE EFFECT (CHAPMAN'S PATENT), working in conjunction with a Thornley's Patent Incinerator, similar to that in use at Gigg Mills, where also the Evaporator is a Quadruple Effect (Chapman's Patent).*

Writing on the 6th March, 1893, the Managing Director of the GIGG MILLS says of this Incinerator:—

" We have now had your Incinerator at work several months, and find it very satisfactory indeed. Since Christmas, for instance, we have recovered from 14 to 16 tons of ash per week, the coal consumed being only a small quantity just for starting up on a Monday morning. It is self-supporting for combustible matter. We can keep good fires all the week and skim constantly, and this, as before stated, without any consumption of coal after starting up. We only used 2 cwts. of coal in the way indicated last week, and recovered 14 tons of ash."

FAWCETT, PRESTON & CO., LIM.,

ENGINEERS,

Phœnix Foundry Liverpool.

THE

United Asbestos Co.,

LIMITED.

DOCK HOUSE, BILLITER STREET, E.C.,

Pioneers

OF THE

Asbestos Trade.

UNITED ASBESTOS NON-CONDUCTING COVERING

(For Steam Boilers & Pipes)

Best and Cheapest in the Market; Will not Injure Boiler Plates.

ASBESTOS GOODS of ALL DESCRIPTIONS

THE UNITED ASBESTOS CO., Limited,

BELTINGS. PACKINGS.

UNITED ASBESTOS A1 MILLBOARDS

(ITALIAN)

Unequalled for Purity, Strength of Fibre, and Uniformity. For Dry Steam Joints it is admitted to be the cleanest, most durable and economical packing in existence.

UNITED ASBESTOS SALAMANDER

Lubricating Cream & Oils,

SPECIALLY ADAPTED TO

PAPERMAKING MACHINERY.

DEPOTS:

MANCHESTER: 34, Deansgate; LIVERPOOL: 33, James Street NEWCASTLE-UPON-TYNE: Quayside; GLASGOW: 54, Robertson Street; CARDIFF: 135, Bute Street; BRISTOL: Provident Buildings HULL: Queen's Dock; ST. PETERSBURG: Gostinoe Dvor (Interior) No. 51

H. WATSON & SONS,

HIGH BRIDGE WORKS, NEWCASTLE-ON-TYNE,

are prepared to

Close Strainer Plates

worn within 2 full Gauges wider than they were when set to work

at $\frac{1}{2}$d. per sq. inch, less 30% discount.

Carriage of all Plates paid by Goods train to Newcastle.

TELEGRAMS "WATSONS, NEWCASTLE." 2568

TURNER BROTHERS,

SPOTLAND, ROCHDALE.

ASBESTOS YARN,
ASBESTOS CLOTH of Every Description.
ASBESTOS METALLIC CLOTH.
ASBESTOS PACKING suitable for all pressures.
ASBESTOS & RUBBER SHEETING.
ASBESTOS & RUBBER TAPE, JOINTS, &c.
ASBESTOS MILLBOARD.
HEMP & COTTON Packings.
CHALK PACKING.
MINERAL PACKING.
ANTI-FRICTION PACKING, &c., &c.

SPINNERS & MANUFACTURERS OF

ASBESTOS

IN ALL ITS FORMS.

SOLE MANUFACTURERS OF THE "GRIPWELL"

HAIR BELTING,

Specially Suitable for Papermakers. 2335

ASBESTOS METALLIC & RUBBER PACKING, SHEETING, TAPE, JOINTS for Manhole and Mudhole Doors.

WORLD'S PAPER TRADE REVIEW OFFICE, 58, SHOE LANE, LONDON, E.C. JULY 6, 1898.

TRADE NOTES.

THE BERGVIK CO., LIM.—The directors of the Bergvik Co., Limited, have declared a dividend of 3 per cent. for the half year on the 6 per cent. preferred shares, payable on and after the 15th inst.

ANNANDALE AND SON, LIM.—REDUCTION OF CAPITAL.—In the Court of Session (Scotland) on the 1st inst., the petition of Messrs. Annandale and Son, papermakers, Polton, Midlothian, came before their lordships. The petitioners sought confirmation of resolution proposing to reduce the capital of the company from £136,000, divided into 6,400 shares of £10 each (of which 1,600 are fully paid-up preference shares, and 4,800 ordinary shares of £25 each, upon which £20 has been paid up), to £64,000, divided into 6,400 shares, of which 1,600 are to be fully paid-up preference shares of £10 each, and 4,800 ordinary shares of £10 each, also fully paid up. No answers having been lodged, their lordships granted the prayer of the petition.

OLIVE BROTHERS, LIM.—Olive Brothers, Limited, has been formed to purchase the business of Messrs. Olive Brothers, paper manufacturers and merchants, now carried on at Woolfold Paper Mills, Bury, and at 19, Cannon-street, Manchester, and to continue the same. The share capital is to be £60,000 (6,000 shares of £10 each), and debenture shares will be issued to the amount of £27,500 (divided into 275 £5 per cent. first mortgage debentures of £100 each). Of the share capital, £20,000 will be issued to the vendors or their nominee in part payment of the purchase price, this being all that, according to the rules of the London and Manchester Stock Exchange, they can take up. They will also take on the same account £12,500 of the debentures and so much of the balance thereof as shall not be otherwise applied for and allotted. The remainder of the shares (4,000) and of the debentures (£15,000) are now offered for subscription. The business now to be managed by a joint-stock company has been carried on at Woolfold Paper Mills for upwards of 20 years by Messrs. Olive Brothers, and the present step is taken in consequence of the death of Mr. William Olive, who had a large capital in the concern which will require to be paid out and which has rendered advisable the bringing of fresh capital into the business so as to secure its proper working. Mr. Thomas Thornley, who has successfully managed the business during the past nine years, is to act as managing director of the new company for five years at least.

MOISTURE IN CHEMICAL WOOD PULP.—The Scandinavian makers of chemical wood pulp, at their last general assembly, stated that the standard atmospheric moisture in chemical wood pulp is 12 per cent., viz., that 100 kg. air-dry pulp contain 88 kg. absolutely dry pulp and 12 kg. moisture.

COMPOUND V. TRIPLE EXPANSION.—Messrs. Scott and Hodgson, of Guide Bridge Ironworks, in referring to the comments made by "A Mill Director" (published in the WORLD'S PAPER TRADE REVIEW, June 23rd) state:—"In these days, if a saving of from 15 to 20 per cent. on the money expended can be realised, we think mill owners are justified in the expenditure. In many instances such results can be attained, even with boiler pressures as low as 100-lbs., and certainly they can with higher pressures. Where new boilers are required, from the present boilers being worn out, the extra cost of boilers required for 'tripling' over compound should only be taken into account, and seeing that a less number of boilers are in most cases sufficient, this will frequently be found to be a further inducement to convert engines to triple expansion. Except with coal of very poor quality indeed, triple engines can, and are, being made to work with considerably less than 2-lbs. of coal per i.h.p. per hour. We know a case where the consumption of South Wales coal is only 1·3-lbs. per i.h.p. per hour, and this with ordinary Lancashire boilers."

C. TOWNSEND HOOK AND CO.'S NEW MACHINE.—Under the heading "Colossal Papermaking Machinery in Edinburgh," the *Scottish Leader* recently published some particulars of the new papermaking machine, being made by Bertrams, Limited, for the Snodland Paper Works. It is capable, says the *Leader*, of turning off sixty tons of lower qualities of printing papers per week, and is specially designed for the manufacture of such papers from wood pulp. It is to run at very high speeds, and to produce a sheet of paper 108 inches wide. The frame of the machine, which carries an endless gauze or wire, is of great strength, and calculated so that the motion imparted to it will weave together the short wood pulp fibres in the best manner, and turn out a strong paper. The couching rolls are of brass, and the pressing rolls of brass and chilled iron. This class of work demands very great precision in adjusting the points of contact of the rolls, and Messrs. Bertrams have all along made this a special feature of their machinery. Very great drying power has been provided, and there are twenty-two drying cylinders, each 48 inches diameter by 114 inches long, mounted on circular framing of the newest designs, and all bound together so as to remain thoroughly rigid when the machine is running at a high speed. Finish to the paper is imparted by twelve calendering rolls of large diameter, and of the very hardest description of chilled iron. Castings for these are now produced in Edinburgh very successfully; hitherto Messrs. Bertrams and other papermaking engineers have had to resort to American makers for such chilled iron, the idea having prevailed that no such rollers could be manufactured in this country. Of late, however, few orders have found their way across the Atlantic. It may be observed that these rolls are harder than any ordinary quality of steel, and the manner in which they are ground—one to fit exactly on the top of the other so as not to admit of the slightest glimmer of light showing between the joints—entails the use of specially constructed machinery. If the joints were not thoroughly true, longitudinally and cylindrically, the paper would be finished in one part and rough in another. The machine is fitted up with all the modern improvements, having two sets of large power steam engines for driving, also vacuum water and pulp pumps all constructed in the Sciennes Works.

A NEW PULP REFINER.—Mr. C. A. Rudolph, Manayunk, Pa., has a new method of producing or refining pulp for papermaking purposes, which, it is said, promises to revolutionise the present method of making mechanical pulp, or refining all other classes of pulp for papermaking purposes.

NATIONAL UNION OF PAPER MILL WORKERS.

HENDON PAPER WORKS DISPUTE.

Since the refusal of the manager to accept the compromise offered by the workers, *i.e.*, half the proposed reduction, no further progress has been made towards a settlement. We are officially informed that the efforts of the firm to fill the places of the workers who are out, have so far been unsuccessful—only twelve men having been secured, eight of whom are firemen.

Donations towards the Lock-out Fund have been received from the following paper mills :—

	£	s.	d.
Oakenholt (North Wales)	1	4	6
Springfield (Bolton,	0	9	0
Spring Grove ...	1	3	0
Lower Darwen ...	1	4	0
Spring Vale	0	6	6
Chafford...	0	3	0
Sherbourne (Birmingham) ...	1	4	6
Rish	0	6	9
Croxley Green ...	1	15	3
Tyne...	0	8	0
Ford (Hylton) ...	4	7	9
Caldergrove	0	16	6
Dalmarnock	0	14	6
Chartham	0	14	4
H. C. & R. J. at D. Mill	0	3	0
Other Donations :—			
Gas Workers Ayres Quay...	0	7	6
Sunderland Compositors	0	12	0
Collected at Hylton meeting	0	10	4
Collected at West Park meeting	0	5	1
Collected at Kensington Sports	0	19	3
Friends & Tradesmen in district	2	13	6
Collected at Labour Party meeting	0	8	5
Hendon Gas Workers	2	0	
R. Edwards, South Hylton	0	2	6
Huddersfield Trades Council	0	10	0
Northampton Boot & Shoe Operatives Society...	1	1	0
Miner's Association (Ryhope)	5	0	0
A. Friend	0	1	6
Wm. B. Reid, Esq.	0	5	0
Wm. Burns, Esq.	0	5	0
Total	£30	1	8

THE HENDON PAPER MILL WORKERS

To the Editor of the WORLD'S PAPER TRADE REVIEW.

SIR,—I trust you will allow me sufficient space in your columns to reply, on behalf of the Hendon Paper Mill Workers, to the letter in your last week's issue, signed by the manager of the above works.

First.—In regard to the hours.—He admits that the hours for shift men on duty are 68 per week, and further asserts that those hours are the lowest worked in the trade. It only needs to be stated that the hours worked in over fifty papermills throughout Lancashire and the Midlands are from 6 to 8 less per week than at Hendon Mill to show who is misleading the public.

Second.—Re Half-Holiday.—While the shift workers at Hendon only got four hours knocked off their Saturday, the shift workers in Lancashire and the Midlands got both the Saturday afternoon and the Sunday night knocked off at once without any reduction in pay.

Third.—As to Rates and Wages.—The machine men and beater men assert that the manager's figures as to their total weekly earnings are overstated by from 2s. to 2s. 6d. per week. They receive 35s. and 30s. respectively for making 30 tons of paper, and 1s. 6d. per ton afterwards, in tonnage or "blood money," as it is more frequently termed. Payment for five tons is deducted for broke—a very unfair deduction, as any practical man would at once admit. When it is considered that these men get no meal hours, and work in an unnatural and unhealthy temperature of 110 deg. Fahrenheit for 12 hours at a stretch, the pay is not by any means excessive.

It would occupy too much of your space to controvert in detail the wages stated to be paid in every separate department, but I should like, sir, by your kind permission, to refer to one other department—the Cuttermen's. Mr. Goodall stated that his table of wages was exclusive of any overtime. Well, according to his statement, the cuttermen's wages are 39s. per week. The men state that their actual wages for an ordinary week of 68 hours were 28s. They have to put in from 80 to 85 hours, however, on an average per week, with overtime, and that is how they get the 39s. per week.

Further, unskilled men never receive higher than 28s., instead of from 30s. to 36s. as he puts it, and many are only paid 21s. It must also be explained that for some time back young lads have been put to do men's work at very low wages. The men also state that they have been considerably reduced in wages during the last twelve months.—

Yours, &c., WM. ROSS, Gen. Sec.
National Union of Paper Mill Workers.

S.O. CONTRACTS.

Tenders for the supply of paper (scheduled below) were invited to be sent in on Wednesday last to the Controller of H.M. Stationery Office, London:—

	Reams.
Antiquarian, wove, 53 by 31, weight per ream 240 lbs....	2
Blotting, demy, white wove, 22½ by 17½ [all rag]; 18 lbs....	2,500
Cap, bag, 24 by 19; 44 lbs.	300
Cap, imperial, 29 by 22½; 75 lbs.	1,000
Copying paper, 18½ by 14; 5 lbs.	2,000
Demy, printing, 22½ by 17½; 17 lbs.	2,500
Demy, blue double, 36 by 23; 48 lbs.	300
Demy, green double, 36 by 23; 48 lbs.	300
Demy, pink double, 36 by 23; 48 lbs.	150
Demy, double second, 31 by 30, 40 lbs.	1,000
Demy, printing double, 35 by 22½; 34 lbs.	1,600
Foolscap, blue wove, 16½ by 13½; 13 lbs	2,000
Foolscap, azure laid, 16½ by 13½ [all rag]; 16 lbs.	500
Foolscap, blue, 24½ by 14; 16 lbs.	400
Foolscap, blue laid double, 27 by 17 [all rag]; 32 lbs.	1,000
Foolscap, cream wove double, 27 by 17; 26 lbs.	2,000
Foolscap, wove [sheet and half], for lithographic printing, 26½ by 13½; 21 lbs.	800
Foolscap, wove double [for lithographic printing], 35½ by 13½; 28 lbs.	300
Imperial, second, 30 by 22; 56 lbs....	600
Imperial, wove [for lithographic printing], 30 by 22; 37 lbs....	400
Medium, second, 23 by 17½; 30 lbs....	3,000
Post, thick blue wove, 19 by 15½ [all rag]; 19 lbs.	800
Post, thick cream wove, 19 by 15½ [all rag]; 22 lbs.	500
Post, thick cream laid, 19 by 15½ [all rag]; 20 lbs.	200
Post, large thick cream laid, 21 by 16½ [all rag]; 22 lbs.	400
Post, buff double, 30½ by 19; 30 lbs.	4,000
Royal, second, 24 by 19½; 33 lbs.	300
Royal, printing, 25 by 20; 28 lbs.	1,000
Royal, large cream wove, "E.O.," 25 by 19½; 25 lbs....	200
Smallhand, double, 30 by 19; 18 lbs.	300
Paper, whitey brown, 44½ by 29½; 34 lbs.	100

HASSENRODER MACHINENPAPIERFABRIK ACTIEN GESELLSCHAFT.—At the last general meeting it was resolved to cancel 25 shares held by the company, thus reducing the nominal capital from M404,000 to M379,000.

SEBNITZER PAPIERFABRIK (formerly Just and Co., Sebnitz, in Saxony), reports a loss of M4,500 in 1892.

THE CHICAGO EXHIBITION.—Herr Henry Villard, a German settled in America, has handed over to the German Chancellor M50,000 for the purpose of allowing assistance in amounts from M1,800 to M2,000 to deserving tradespeople who wish to visit the exhibition.

H. FULLNER, IN WARMBRUNN, the well-known papermakers' engineering firm, has lately supplied the following machines:—Van Gelden Zonen, Wormerveer, near Amsterdam, a paper machine, width, meters 2·150. De Forende Papirfabrikker, Copenhagen, two turbines of 150 to 200-h.p., the appliances for the preparation of rags, two rag engines holding from 300 to 350 kilos, five half-stuff engines holding about 200 kilos; two large bleaching engines, a complete paper machine with meter 1·860 working width, complete with long and cross-cutting machine calender with 10 rollers. All these machines are for the mill at Silkeborg, which will make highest class papers exclusively from rags. For the Granfos Brug Lysaker, near Christiania, one new paper machine with meters 2·100 working width, rebuilding the old paper machine (which was partly destroyed by fire), a long and cross cutting machine, &c. There are further three new paper machines in construction, but the buyers do not wish their names published.

FOCKENDORFER PAPIERFABRIK.—A farewell dinner was given recently to Herr Carl Eichhorn, the late managing director who now retires after an activity of many years at the head of this establishment. The good understanding between employers and work-people and the great love and esteem, which Herr Eichhorn enjoyed, gave occasion to many appropriate speeches. Several presentations took place, and among them a watch was offered as a personal mark of esteem by Herr Eichhorn to the workman Schellenberg, who had been employed in these works for upwards of 33 years.

ACTIEN GESELLSCHAFT FUR PAPPENFABRICATION.—The report of 1892-93 shows that prices have fallen still further, and the general sales were 10 per cent. less than last year. Building operations were very slack and this caused a smaller consumption of roofing boards. Over-production of the last year has not only influenced this class but also binders boards. The gross profits of the three factories belonging to the company only amounted to M135,400 against M185,256 of the previous year. In addition to this unsatisfactory result, various expensive repairs were needed and caused a shut down for six weeks of the Berlin factory. The expense provided for this purpose in the last balance, M4,300, had to be increased by a further M9,000. As the share capital had been reduced by M90,000, and now only amounted to M1,590,000, the gross profits (M154,231), after allowing various amounts, enabled the declaration of a dividend of 4½ per cent.

FIRST HUNGARIAN PAPER INDUSTRY COMPANY.—The general meeting was attended by 18 shareholders, representing 3,500 votes. It was announced that the Nagy-Szlabos Paper Mills, destroyed by fire in July, 1892, were in course of reconstruction, and would be connected by a branch line with the existing railway, the company taking up 100,000 fl. of shares in the railway. The share capital of the Industry Company is of the nominal value of 1,250,000 fl., raised by the distribution of 11,000 new shares of 100 fl. = 200 kr. each.

HERR PETER KATHAN, of the firm Kathan Brothers, in Augsburg, the well-known gold and silver paper manufacturers, died on the 23rd of last month.

WHO'S WHO?

THE PERSONNEL OF THE PAPER, STATIONERY. AND PRINTING TRADES UP-TO-DATE.

RAITHBY, LAWRENCE & Co., Limited, Leicester and London.

The names in the title are those of stationers and printers, who carried on business for several years in Leicester. Desirous of extending their operations, they, on the 1st March, 1890, formed a company, the capital of which was nominally £8,000, with power to increase. This was divided into 1,600 shares of £5 each—600 preference shares and 1,000 ordinary. The preference shares were to bear interest at the rate of 7½ per cent. The first subscribers took up one share each, the names and occupations being:—

Henry Cadney Raithby, Queen-street, Leicester, printer.
Joseph Charles Lawrence, Leicester, printer.
Robert Hilton, 3, Gresham Press-buildings, London, journalist.
Henry Lawrence, Rutland-street, Leicester, accountant.
Robert Grayson, 29, Arundel-street, Leicester, printer.
Alfred Grayson, 59, Coventry-street, Leicester, printer.
William Thomas Knight, Church-road, Harlome, near Birmingham, retired varnish manufacturer.

The Articles of Association contain the following provision:—"The company can from time to time, by special resolution, increase its capital by the creation of any number of new shares." Further, it was provided that every five shares, whether ordinary or preference, should bear one rate. There were not to be less than three directors, nor more than five, subject to special resolution. On this foundation the company was formed, the first directors being A. Raithby, J. C. Lawrence, and Robert Hilton. The qualification of each was fixed at fifty shares, and Mr. Henry Lawrence was appointed the first secretary.

One of the most widely known enterprises of the firm was the journal called the *British Printer*, founded by Mr. Robert Hilton. It was taken over by agreement between Robert Hilton and H. Lawrence, the consideration allowed to the former being 300 fully paid up ordinary shares of £5 each. The company was to receive all the book debts of the journal, which amounted to £219 10s., but any not collected within twelve months were to be charged against Mr. Hilton. The first issue under this arrangement was made on the 25th February, 1890. Mr. Hilton was to retain for ten years in his own name at least two-thirds of the shares, and was not for a similar period to carry on any other journal connected with the printing trade, or be agent thereto, but he was permitted to contribute signed articles to other papers. His salary as manager and editor was fixed at £208 per annum paid weekly.

Regarding the sale of the business to the company, an agreement was drawn up between H. C. Raithby and J. C. Lawrence, of the one part, and J. C. Lawrence of the other part (on behalf of the company). The vendors were to receive 571 fully paid-up ordinary shares, the company paying the debts owing by the concern. The debts payable to the business, amounting to £1,219 13s., were to be taken over by the company. If these debts were not realised in twelve months, the vendors were held liable to make up the difference. Mr. Raithby was to hold for ten years at least 260 shares, and Mr. Lawrence for the same period at least 140. Neither were to engage in any other business. Mr. Raithby's salary was fixed at £155, and Mr. Lawrence's at £200 per annum.

The capital of the company has since been increased to £25,000, by the creation of 3,400 new shares of £5, bringing the total number of shares from 1,600 to 5,000. The new shares consist of 2,400 preferred, and 1,000 ordinary, both to take the same position and rank *pari passu* with those issued on the registration of the company both as to dividend and capital. On the 11th January, 1892, the bookbinding business of Albert Henry Durrad, of King-street, Leiceister, was purchased, the purchase price being £420, paid by the allotment of 84 fully-paid preference shares, with a guaranteed interest of 7½ per cent. per annum. A profit-sharing scheme has been introduced, by which employees can take up a £5 share by paying 2s. per week.

The following are the present names and holdings of shareholders:—

	Ord.	Pref.
Robert Hilton, Marlborough-road, Leicester, journalist	300	—
H. C. Raithby, Queen-street, Leicester, printer...	260	—
J. C. Lawrence, Queen-street, Leicester, printer	160	—
W. T. Knight, Church-road, Harborne, near Birmingham, retired manufacturer ...	140	—
H. Lawrence, 16, Stephens-road, Leicester, accountant	60	60
Mary Raithby, 27, Norfolk-street, Leicester,	20	—
Robert Grayson, Stretton-road, Fosse, Leicester, printer	20	—
A. Bresse, 93, Conduit-street, Leicester, compositor	2	—
J. Clarke, 17, Gopsall-street, Leicester, compositor...	[illegible]	—
C. H. Fisher, 93, Conduit-street, Leicester machine minder	[illegible]	—
E. B. Hutt, 26, Mill Hill-lane, Leicester, compositor	[illegible]	—
A. Hurd, 46, Napier-street, Leicester, compositor	[illegible]	—
T. W. Jackson, 19, Maynard-street, Leicester, machine minder	[illegible]	—
T. Luck, 17, Wilne-street, Highfields, Leicester, machine minder	[illegible]	—
W. Turville, 5, Skipworth-street, Leicester, bookbinder	2	—
H. Whetton, Stretton-road, Fosse, Leicester, clerk	10	—
R. T. Walkington, 91, Twycross-street, Leicester, machine minder	1	—
A. Argyle, 100, Granby-street, Leicester, grocer	—	100
O. Allack, 51, Cobourg-streets, Leeds, compositor	—	2
W. Austin, 19, James-street, Burton-on-Trent, compositor	—	2
A. Buncher, 305, Belgrave-gate, Leicester, agent	—	10

"LANCASHIRE" PATENT BELTS COST LESS THAN SINGLE LEATHER.

	Ord.	Pref.
R. Birdsall, 32, Billing-road, Northampton, bookseller	—	20
G. Brading, 26, High-street, Deptford, stationer	—	100
G. W. Brown, 27, St. Stephen's-road, Leicester, banker's clerk	—	12
Harriet Brown, 27, St. Stephen's-road, Leicester, spinster	—	10
Elizabeth Y. Baker, 38, Market-place, Leicester, wife of W. M. Baker	—	20
A. H. Butler, 124, Newcomen-road, Wellingborough, compositor	—	1
J. F. Bray, 13, Gould's Grounds, Frome, printer's reader	—	10
F. C. Brooks, 11, Devonshire-street, Islington, compositor	—	2
E. P. Brown, Norfolk-road, Maidenhead, printer	—	10
G. Bottoms, 37, Benledi-street, Poplar, compositor	—	1
J. Cunningham, 70, Sparkenhoe-street, Leicester, printer	—	20
J. Calvart, 39, Dover-street, Glasgow, compositor	—	2
J. Davies, 27, Seymour-street, Aberdare, compositor	—	2
A. H. Durrad, 12, Lincoln-street, Leicester, traveller	—	84
Mary A. Freeman, 10, Lincoln-street, Leicester, traveller	—	12
T. S. Freeman, 10, Lincoln-street, Leicester, Bootmaker	—	10
T. Gill, 24, Grasmere-road, Lancaster, assistant reporter	—	4
W. Garnett, 16, Osborne-street, Leeds, compositor	—	2
J. Hollingworth, Millstone-lane, Leicester, wine merchant	—	40
J. Hodges, 2, Highbury-place, N., gentleman	—	30
W. Bextall, 2, Garden-court, Temple, barrister	—	40
J. C. Bextall, 33, Highfield-street, Leicester, gentleman	—	100
Emma Bextall, 33, Highfield-street, Leicester	—	50
J. D. Howarth, 3, Trafalgar-street, Rochdale, letterpress printer	—	2
W. Hedge, 4, Devonshire-villas, Plymouth, compositor	—	3
F. Hackett, 99, Cramner-street, Leicester, bookbinder	—	2
E. A. Higginson, 5, Hobart-street, Leicester, artists' manager	—	20
F. W. Horner, 20, Waterloo-road, Barnsley, printer	—	2
J. H. Harwood, Beaumont-road, Leicester, printers' overseer	—	7
A. Hewitt, 20, Barnett-street, Manchester, printer	—	1
J. Jones, Church Leys, Leicester, wine merchants' assistant	—	26
E. Jackson, Narburgh, near Leicester, spinster	—	10
J. A. Ince, 2, Hadleigh-terrace, Leyton, compositor	—	2
A. Jack, 29, Byerley-street, Seacombe, Cheshire, compositor	—	1
A. Johnson, 11, Arundel-street, Leicester, bookbinder	—	10
W. Lindsay, 10, Wansbeck-street, Newcastle-on-Tyne, printer	—	1
C. T. Mander, John-street, Wolverhampton, varnish maker	—	50
G. H. Mander, Glen-bank, Tettenhall, Wolverhampton, varnish maker	—	60
J. Morley, Buckhurst, Stoneygate, Lancaster, draper	—	80
W. S. Martin, 95, Shardeloe-road, Brockley, printers' traveller	—	20
W. J. Martin, 2, Tressillian-road, Brockley, S.C., gentleman	—	20
P. D. Michael, 96, High-street, Barnstaple, litho printer	—	1
R. R. Morland, 122, Clifton-crescent, Peckham, printers' reader	—	5
C. H. Ottaway, 51, Seymour-street, Hanley, Staffs., compositor	—	2
J. F. Pattison, 55, Banstead-grove, Leeds, printers' manager	—	1
J. J. Rickett, 141, Thorpedale-road, Hornsey, compositor	—	2
G. A. Parker, 76, Stoughton-street, Leicester, compositor	—	20
G. A. F. Pope, 16, Brunswick-terrace, Yeovil, printers' manager...	-	4
A. Parker, 4, Lawn terrace, Cumberland, coal agent	—	20
A. Rust, 30, Market-place, Leicester, stationers' clerk	-	10
T. Rouse, Welbeck-street, Mansfield, Notts, compositor	—	2
G. H. Shuttleworth, 94, King William-street, Coventry, newsagent	—	10
H. Swire, 9, Industrial-street, Bacup, printer	—	2
J. Smith, 15, Brighton-place, Aberdeen, printer	—	[illegible]
G. A. Sykes, 22, Great George-street, Salford, compositor		
W. Stewart, care of S. H. Maden, printer, Crawshaw Booth, compositor	—	[illegible]
J. Stewart, 7, Stewart's-lane, Kirkaldy, litho printer	—	5
H. Smith, 124, Olive-terrace, Accrington, printer	—	2
E. F. D. Stevens, 2, College-street, Leicester, artist	—	10
R. Tarrant, Witney, Oxon, grocer		40
A. J. Tucker, Langford House, Eltham, traveller	—	60
J. Thacker, 167, London-road, Leicester, traveller	—	50
Isaac Underwood, Windsor-street, Chertsey, traveller	—	1
C. V. Vitty, 2, Shaw-street, Ashton-under-Lyne, artist	—	1
Thos. B. Widdowson, 22, Lincoln-street, Leicester	—	10
H. Wilshire, 1, Welford-road, Leicester, accountant	—	4
C. L. Wilson, 29, Seafield road, Brighton, printers' machinist	—	1
A. W. Wrigley, 14, Milk-road, Kettering, printer	—	2
Mark Whiley, 5, Summer-street, Stroud, Gloucester, compositor	—	12
C. Wright, 14, Granby-street, Ilkeston, printer	—	1
W. W. Wild, Percival-street, Rochdale, compositor	—	2
A. W. Wilkie, King-street, Cork, stationer	—	2
	1,371	989

The last summary of the capital and shares of this company to 6th March, 1893, shows that—with a nominal capital of £25,000, divided into 3,000 preference shares, and 2,000 ordinary shares, of £5 each—the number of shares taken up to that date is 1371 preference and 989 ordinary shares. There have been called up on each of 1,371 preference shares £5, also £5 on each of 26 ordinary shares. There is considered as fully paid on each of 963 ordinary shares, £5, making altogether the sum of £4,815, and the total amount of calls received (including payments upon application and allottment) amounts to £8,981. The calls unpaid amount to £4.

RE HENRY THOMAS WEBB.

This bankrupt lately carried on business at 91, Cannon-street, E.C. The statement of affairs shows the liabilities to be £347 17s., and the assets £35 5s., leaving a deficiency of £312 12s. A receiving order was made against the bankrupt on the 12th October, 1885, when trading with another person at 30 and 31, New Bridge-street, Blackfriars, London, under the style of H. T. Webb and Co., paper merchants. The liabilities under those proceedings amounted to £945 11s. 9d., and the assets £258 15s. 8d. A scheme of arrangement was approved by the Court, under which the estate was to be administered as in bankruptcy. A first and final dividend of 1s. 0¼d. in the £ was paid.

The bankrupt, it appears, from 1885 to 1891 was engaged as a commercial traveller in the paper trade. In or about 1891 he took offices at 91, Cannon-street, and commenced business there as a commission agent. This business, as the bankrupt states, proved unremunerative, and, in order to support himself and family, he was compelled to borrow money at a high rate of interest. The liabilities in this respect amount to £118 3s. 2d. The bankrupt attributes his insolvency to loss of income by withdrawal from him of a valuable agency, to high rate of interest on borrowed moneys, to general badness of trade, and insufficiency of income by reason of the small amount of his agency business. No books of account have been produced. The bankrupt admits that he was aware of his insolvency in June, 1892, and the whole of the liabilities have been contracted since that time.

The first meeting of the creditors was held on the 29th June, before Mr. A. H. Wildy, official receiver. No offer was submitted by the debtor, and the case was left in the hands of the official receiver to be wound up in the usual course of bankruptcy. The following are the principal creditors :—

UNSECURED.

	£	s.	d.
C. A. and A. Rose, Glasgow	£100		0
Isaac Gordon, Birmingham	79		6
R. Cobb, 70, Gracechurch-street, E.C.	20		8
Fisher and Stanhope, 16, Finsbury-circus, E.C....	18	[illegible]	6
G. and R. G. Bagshaw, Norwich			4
Bucklmere and Coppard, Macclesfield			9
J. Kempton and Co., London	33	3	0
Adams Bros., Moor-lane, E.C.	26	18	2

The public examination of the bankrupt is appointed to be held on Tuesday, July 11th, at the Court sitting in Bankruptcy, at Bankruptcy-buildings, Carey-street, W.C., at 12.30.

THE INVENTOR OF MECHANICAL WOOD PULP.

The home of Herr Friedrich Gottlob Keller being in that district of the so-called Saxon Switzerland, which is so largely visited by tourists from all countries, the Mountain Tourists' Association have dedicated one of the rocks to the memory of the inventor, and adorned it with a marble plate bearing an appropriate inscription. At the inauguration festival, to which the old benefactor was invited, a great number of friends and acquaintances were assembled and spent a very pleasant time. The spot was very well chosen in most beautiful scenery and will no doubt be visited by thousands, many of whom will thus probably for the first time learn of the invention of mechanical wood pulp.

THE SODA ASH FURNACE at the Singerly Pulp and Paper Company's Works, Elkton, Md., exploded on June 12.

THE *Paper Trade Journal* (New York) states that "the Columbian Exposition is nearly if not quite complete. There is yet something to be done to realise that finish which is essential to its perfection. We regret that the papermaking exhibit stands idle. The gentlemen who have charged themselves with the duty of showing the workings of American paper machinery to the public should not be derelict at this stage, but should get the exhibit under full operation at once. If the great Fair is to become financially successful, the railway passenger rates should be reduced to a minimum. One of the railway companies has announced a reduction in fare between New York and Chicago, and it is to be presumed that other companies will follow; but the reduction so far announced is not sufficient to draw the crowds. If our Chicago friends can succeed in getting the cost of transportation from the seaboard down to a very low figure, they will probably find that a great influx of visitors will be the result."

THE BLACK AND CLAWSON COMPANY are exhibiting at Chicago a patent seamless dryer adjoining the space of the Model Paper Mill to the south. This dryer is one of a lot of ten sold to the Fuji Paper Company, of Tokio, Japan.

EXTENSIVE REPAIRS are to be made to the mill of the Excelsior Fibre Company, Goffstown Centre, N. H., and new machinery will be put in.

THE first step toward giving the tour workers in the Holyoke paper mills Sunday night off has been made by the Massasoit Paper Manufacturing Company. The company began on June 11 to close down on Sunday night and no week's work will begin hereafter until Monday morning at six o'clock.

THE stockholders of the Trenton Falls, N.Y., Lumber Company propose to build a pulp mill at Prospect, N.Y.

MATTERS OF INTEREST.

To business that we love we rise betime
And go to it with delight.
SHAKESPEARE.

Owing to the variable mechanical and other difficulties occasionally arising in paper manufacture, we publish under the above heading (free of charge) questions of trade interest which may be submitted to us. Readers are invited to send queries and also to contribute information in return by sending replies. If our correspondents commit their ideas roughly to paper we will do the rest. People who have great talent for putting words and sentences together sometimes know relatively little, while others who know a great deal can hardly put their knowledge on paper or talk it to others. If a man has really anything to tell he can soon learn to jot it down crudely. If he keeps on doing so, as he becomes fuller and fuller of knowledge he must soon be able to express it properly. No man knows what power is latent in him until he sets to work to dig it out. Of course all communications must bear the writer's name, not necessarily for publication but as a guarantee of good faith, and should be as brief as possible and not take the form of an advertisement on behalf of any particular appliance.

QUERIES.

192.—Would some reader of "Matters of Interest" be good enough to inform me what quantity of soap is employed in a paper mill, say per ton of paper made? Is it more economical for a papermaker to manufacture his own soap than buy it from soapmakers? There are some makers of soap who supply an article said to be specially made for paper. I should be glad to learn what the special requirements of a papermaker's soap are?—W. F. H.

206.—I shall be glad to learn where I can obtain full particulars of the examinations held by the City and Guilds of London Institute; also whether a Science and Arts 1st class certificate (say steam) would be any advantage in such examinations?—YOUNG PAPERMAKER.

207.—Would any reader of "Matters of Interest," who has a chemical knowledge, kindly inform me of the chief properties of aluminium, with special reference to its behaviour in the presence of chemicals such as acids and alkalies? I should also like to know if it has ever been tried as a substitute for lead as a lining for iron vessels in which alkali and acids are employed for digesting paper stock. —PAPERMAKERS' ENGINEER.

208.—Can any reader of this column inform me of some apparatus or simple means with which I can calculate the power absorbed by any particular machine? To take an indication of the steam engine when the machine is running and when stopped is not altogether reliable, and even if it were so it is very inconvenient.—ENGINEER.

209.—By the electrolytic method of producing caustic soda and chlorine from salt, I believe, hydrogen gas is formed. Would some reader kindly inform me what becomes of this in the process of manufacture?—INQUISITIVE.

210.—As the electrolytic method of producing bleach and soda appears to be reaching a stage of practicability, I should like to know whether the cost of a plant requirel to produce sufficient bleach for the average paper mill would be low enough to warrant the outlay by papermakers? What would be about the cost to produce, say 10 tons of bleaching powder weekly?—MILL MANAGER.

211.—I should be extremely obliged if some reader or chemist would kindly inform me how I could test or discover if a sample of some impure salts contained any ammonia salts.—H. W. J.

212.—Will some one be good enough to inform me of the difference between a mineral and a hydrocarbon lubricating oil? I should also esteem it a favour to be informed of the difference between an oil that produces an acid when heated, and one that does not.—A. MILLER.

213.—If two cog wheels, having 82 and 36 cogs respectively, are taken out and replaced with two wheels exactly the same diameter but with 82 and 33 cogs, would there be any difference in the speed obtained?—MACHINEMAN.

214.—What are the usual rates of freight for the shipment of esparto from Spanish ports to the United Kingdom?—FIBRE.

MESSRS. G. LEATHER AND W. H. HORN (trading as Leather, Horn and Co.), paper stock merchants, 27, Cranmer-street, Liverpool, have dissolved partnership.

THE weekly list of paper exports from New York includes the following:—

B. West Indies ...	890 pkgs	Hull	8 cases
Australasia... ...	426 ,,	New Zealand ...	554 ,,
London	104 cases		

BANKRUPTCY PROCEEDINGS IN BOHEMIA.—German crediters greatly complain about the way in which Bohemian estates are managed by the liquidators. A case has lately become known, where an estate showed 10,381 fl. assets and 14,445 fl. debts. After realisation the assets only showed 2,384 fl., which were claimed by the liquidator to pay his expenses. Great indignation is shown at such management, and perhaps the German Government will be asked to put the case before the Central Government of Vienna, and call its attention to the way in which things are managed in Bohemia, very different from what under similar circumstances would have been done in Germany.

AN American lady has conceived the idea of weaving crêpe paper, by which means it is made very strong and durable, and forms an excellent substitute for silk for many purposes. The paper is both braided and woven. The name applied to this manufacture, according to our contemporary, the *Invention*, is "tresse work." Among many other fancy articles that are made may be mentioned fire screens, table mats, bureau scarfs, and lambrequins, which have the charming appearance of Indian silk without the cost.

Printed and Published EVERY FRIDAY
AT 58, SHOE LANE, LONDON, E.C.,
By W. JOHN STONHILL.
ESTABLISHED 1878.

SUBSCRIPTION: £1 PER ANNUM.
POST FREE TO ALL PARTS OF THE GLOBE.
SINGLE COPIES SIXPENCE.

ADVERTISEMENT TARIFF:

Whole Page, per Insertion...	£4
Half Page „	£2
Quarter Page „	£1

SPECIAL POSITIONS, HIGHER RATES.

TELEGRAMS: "STONHILL—LONDON."

FRIDAY, JULY 7, 1893.

WHY the officials of the Stationery Office confine themselves to a certain specified list of firms when inviting tenders for the supply of paper is beyond comprehension, especially as some on the list are foreign paper agents whose interests are antagonistic to those of the British papermaker. It would be more satisfactory if the Controller advertised for tenders from firms having paper mills in the United Kingdom. The present "under cover" method is very mystifying in many respects to say the least.

THOSE firms favoured with the option of tendering evidently know the way of procedure like A B C, and are capable of meeting the requirements of the Stationery Office as easily as working out a sum by rule-of-three. One would think hardly sufficient time was allowed to prepare a fair estimate, as schedules are issued and tenders demanded within the space of a few days. Allowing time for postal service, and the usual official delay in answering enquiries, it is incomprehensible why the statement should be put forth that "samples may be obtained from the examiner of paper, London, and the clerk in charge, Dublin," as a conscientious papermaker in taking the trouble to obtain a specimen of "accepted" paper would assuredly be too late with his tender.

WE refer to the latest requirements of the Stationery Office elsewhere, and may here point out a new clause in the schedule specifying the mode in which the various papers are to be wrapped. This reads as follows: "The paper will be delivered at the Stationery Office, London, correctly put up, well wrapped, and securely tied, end wrappers being used for all papers in the flat. The paper must be of the specified weight per ream, without the wrappers, and the weight per ream must be distinctly marked on each ream."

THE distribution of the exports of British paper is treated fully on page 7. The total value is £1,579,694. Doubtless many of our readers imagined that a much larger trade was done with foreign countries than is really the case. Foreign importation represents only 30 per cent., whilst the remaining 70 per cent. goes to British possessions. The relative difference is as follows:—

	To Foreign Countries.	To British Possessions.
Writings, printings, and envelopes ...	£282,810	£848,748
Hangings	60,989	87,501
Pasteboard, Millboard, &c. ...	13,123	38,441
Other kinds	120,176	127,906
Totals	£477,098	£1,102,596

ANENT British paper importations the principal shipments are from London, the trade last year representing 62 per cent. of the entire value. Liverpool comes next with nearly 13 per cent., and then Glasgow with 10 per cent. Southampton may be credited with 3¼ per cent., Newhaven 2 per cent., Hull 1¾ per cent., and Leith 1¾ per cent. Other ports rank considerably lower.

THE Ford Works Company, Limited, as a name, will soon be buried in oblivion. Mr. Wm. Cash, the liquidator, according to official notification, will, at 99, Cannon-street,

E.C., on the 18th inst., if necessary, be ready to dilate upon the winding-up of the concern. The father of esparto, the late Mr. Thomas Routledge, was identified with the Ford Works, and the flotation of the concern as a limited liability company in 1864 enabled a few prominent papermakers and others to acquire the benefit of the experience of Mr. Routledge in the use of esparto, &c.

MR. ROUTLEDGE sold his business for a sum not exceeding £25,000 in cash and shares, and it was stipulated that he should be managing director, receiving a payment (during the existence of the company or until the 20th of November, 1898) of 30 per cent. of the balance of nett annual profits after deducting a sum equal to a dividend of 10 per cent. upon the paid up capital. Mr. Routledge for his services was also to receive a salary not exceeding £1,500 per annum.

THERE were agreements to the following effect:—

"That the said Thomas Routledge shall use his utmost endeavours to supply to the company at their works for the time being such quantities of esparto, not exceeding ten thousand tons per annum, as the company may require, cost price, the cost of freight, carriage and insurance, brokers' commission, and all incidental expenses being borne by the company, who shall pay to the said Thomas Routledge a bonus, royalty, or profit of 5s. for every ton so supplied as aforesaid; provided always, that the said Thomas Routledge shall not have less than three calendar months notice in writing from the company specifying what quantity of esparto they require, and shall not be required to supply more than ,500 tons thereof quarterly in every year."

"That the said Thomas Routledge shall grant to the company full permission to use his patented processes for the treatment of esparto and other fibres."

"That the company shall until the 20th day of November, 1898, or until the expiration of 10 years from the death of the said Thomas Routledge, be bound to buy upon the terms aforesaid, of or through the said Thomas Routledge or his representatives, all the esparto which they require in their businesses, provided always, that after the death of the said Thomas Routledge, the company shall be at liberty to buy elsewhere in case the representatives of the said Thomas Routledge shall not supply esparto upon the terms aforesaid, or in case the said company shall pay to the said representatives said royalty, bonus, or profit of 5s. for every ton of esparto, which they may so buy elsewhere as aforesaid."

RESOLUTIONS were passed from time to time authorising the directors to borrow certain sums of money, and fresh agreements were entered into with Mr. Routledge, owing to the extension of papermaking plant and the stoppage of half-stuff manufacture. On the 13th June, 1891, the nominal capital was £65,000, of which £39,400 had been called up. It was decided on June 23rd, 1892, to voluntarily wind up and reconstruct, with the result that we now have in place of the "Ford Works Company, Ltd.," the "Ford Works Paper Co., Ltd.," with a nominal capital of £100,000.

THE first subscribers to the old and new Ford Works Companies were as follows:—

FORD WORKS.

Charles Longman, Hemel Hempstead.
F. Pratt Barlow, 65, Old Bailey, E.C.
John Evans, Nash Mills.
George Chater, 86, Cannon-street, E.C.
Thomas Routledge, Ford, Sunderland.
M. Proctor, Newcastle.
C. McAllum, Newcastle.
Will Chater, Newcastle-on-Tyne.
T. B. Barker, South Shields.
R. Benyon, Reading.

FORD PAPER WORKS.

George Chater.	J. Porteus Cornett.
F. P. Barlow.	F. T. P. Barlow.
T. M. Dunster.	R. Benyon.
T. B. Barker.	

WHAT is the recognised moisture in chemical wood pulp is a question which from time to time has been responsible for considerable controversy between buyer and seller. The standard officially adopted by Scandinavian manufacturers is now plainly set forth, and due conformity will bring about a cessation of many a vexatious dispute which generally invokes unpleasantness between the parties concerned. Twelve per cent. is the allowance of atmospheric moisture; therefore 100 kg. air-dry pulp, it is computed, contain 88 kg. absolutely dry pulp and 12 kg. moisture.

WE are glad to hear that the United Alkali Co., Lim., have been successful against the Garstang Union in regard to the rating of salt mines and shafts. The case was of great importance, and raised many interesting and obscure questions as to the correct method of rating brine shafts and beds of salt. Mr. Humphreys-Davies placed the gross value of the property at £618, and the rateable value at £412. Mr. Cross, in support of the respondents, gave the rateable value at £964. Judgment was to the effect that the gross value of the property should be reduced to £639, and the rateable value to £574 10s., the appellants to have their costs.

WORLD'S PAPER TRADE REVIEW OFFICE,
58, SHOE LANE, LONDON, E.C.
JULY 6, 1893.

MARKET REPORT

and RECORD of IMPORTS

Of Foreign Rags, Wood Pulp, Esparto, Paper, Millboards, Strawboards, &c., at the Ports of London Liverpool, Southampton, Bristol, Hull, Fleetwood, Middlesborough, Glasgow, Grangemouth, Granton, Dundee, Leith, Dover, Folkestone, and Newhaven for the WEEK ENDING JULY 5.

From SPECIAL Sources and Telegrams.

Telegrams—"STONHILL, LONDON."

CHEMICALS.—There is a fair amount of business passing in chemicals. CAUSTIC SODA is very firm, and stocks of BLEACHING POWDER low, but the demand for the latter is not great. There is a steady trade being done in SODA CRYSTALS at £2 10s. f.o.b Tyne. SULPHUR stands at from £4 to £4 2s. 6d.

Prices are nominally as follows:

				£	s.	d.
Alkali, 58%	tierces ...	f.o.r. works	2½%	5	10	0
" 58%	bags ...	" "	2½%	5	5	0
58%	... ...	f.o.b. Liverpool	2½%	5	12	6
Alum (Ground),	tierces ...	" Liverpool	2½%	5	7	6
" "	barrels ...	" "	2½%	5	17	6
" "	tierces ...	" Hull	2½%	5	5	0
" "	" ...	Goole	2½%	5	5	0
Alum (Lump)	" ...	f.o.b. Liverpool	2½%	4	17	6
" "	barrels ...	" "	2½%	5	0	0
" "	tierces ...	" Hull	2½%	4	15	0
" "	" ...	Goole	2½%	4	15	0
"	" ...	London	2½%	5	5	0
"	" ...	f.a.s. Glasgow	2½%	5	5	0
Alumina Sulphate,	casks	f.o.b. Tyne		4	2	6
" "	bags	" "		3	17	6
Aluminoferric Cake,	slabs	Liverpool ...	...	2	15	0
" "	tierces	" ...	...	3	2	6
Alumina Cake,	slabs ...	Glasgow	...	2	15	0
" "	tierces ...	"	...	3	2	6
Aluminous Cake,	casks ...	Manchester	3½%	2	7	6
" "	" ...	Newcastle	2½%	2	10	0
" "	" ...	London	2½%	3	0	0
" "	bags ...	"	2½%	2	17	9
Blanc Fixe ...	... ...	f.o.b. Tyne	net	7	10	0
Bleach, 35%	... ...	" "	net	8	5	0
" (soft wood)	...	f.o.r. Lancs.	net	8	0	0
" (hard wood)	...	f.o.b. Liverpool	net	8	10	0
... ...	...	landed London	2½%	9	5	0
Borax (crystals)	... ...	... ...	net	29	0	0
powdered	... ...	... ...	net	30	0	0
Caustic Cream, 60%	...	f.o.r. Lancs.	net	8	7	6
" " 60%	...	f.o.b. Liverpool	net	8	10	0
" Bottoms 58-60%	...	" "	net	5	10	0
" " ...	...	f.o.b. Tyne	net	6	5	0
Carbonat'd Ash 58%	...	" "	3½%	6	10	0
" 48%	...	" "	3½%	5	15	0
" 58%	...	f.o.r. Widnes	3½%	6	7	6
" 48%	...	" "	3½%	5	12	6
Caustic White, 77%	...	f.o.r. Newcastle	net	10	15	0
" " 77%	...	f.o.b. Tyne	net	10	15	0
" " 74%	...	f.o.b. Liverpool	net	10	15	0
" " 70%	...	" "	net	9	15	0
" " 70%	...	" Hull	net	10	0	0
" " 70%	...	f.o.r. London	net	9	15	0
" " 70%	...	" Lancs.,	net	9	12	6
" " 60%	...	" London	net	8	15	0
" " 60%	...	f.o.b. Liverpool	net	8	15	0
Chloride of Barium	...	f.o.b. Tyne	net	7	10	0
Hypo-Sulphite of Soda...		f.o.r Tyne		5	15	0
" "	10-ton lots	ex ship Liverp'l	net	6	10	0
Oxalic Acid ...	... ...	f.o.b. Liverpool	2½%	per lb		¼
Salt Cake	... ...	" works	net	1	10	0
Soda Ash, 52%	... ...	f.o.b. Tyne	net	4	17	6
" 52%	... ...	ex ship Thames	1%	5	5	0
" 52%	... ...	f.o.b. Liverpool	1%	5	0	0
Soda Crystals	... ...	" Tyne	net	2	10	0
" "	... ...	ex ship Thames	2½%	2	17	6
" "	... ...	f.o.b. Liverpool	net	2	17	6
Sulphur, roll	... ...	f.o.r. works	2½%	7	17	6
" flowers	... ...	" "	2½%	9	10	0
" recovered	...	" "	2½%	4	0	0
Sulphate of Ammonia	"	" "	2½%	12	15	0
" of Copper	...	" Liverpool	5%	15	0	0

FOREIGN.—F.o.b. Continental port:

	£	s.	d.
Alkali, 58% 2-cwt. bags £6 10/0; 10-cwt. casks ...	6	15	6
Caustic Soda, 70-72%	11	12	0
Hypo-Sulphite of Soda 10-ton lots 140/0; bags ...	7	10	6
Sulphate of Alumina 7-8 cwt. casks net c.i.f. Ldn	4	7	6
Blanc Fixe (c.i.f. London)	7	12	6

ESPARTO.—There has been some little revival of enquiry for contracts and a moderate extent of business done at about last prices.

Prices c.i.f. London and Leith, or f.o.r. Cardiff, Garston and Tyne Docks are nominally as follows:

		£	s.	d.		£	s.	d.
Spanish—	Fair to Good	£5	10	0	to	5	15	0
"	Fine to Best	5	17	6	"	6	0	0
Oran —	Fair to Good	3	12	6	"	3	17	6
"	First Quality...	4	0	0	"	4	2	6
Tripoli —	Hand-picked	3	17	6	"	4	2	6
"	Fair Average...	3	12	6	"	3	15	0
Bona & Philippeville	... ...	4	0	0	"	4	2	6

IMPORTS of ESPARTO.

Quantity	From	Importer	Port.
730 tons	Carthagena	Reid, Howard & Co	Granton
580 "	Oran	To order	London
4711 bales	"	"	Grangemouth
40 tons	"	"	"
1758 bales	"	"	Liverpool
624 tons	Philippeville	"	London
250 "	Skira	"	Liverpool
1228 "	Sfax	Mackie Koth & Co	Leith

CHEMICAL WOOD PULPS. — British demand for chemical wood pulps is rather quiet. Reports from the continent state that there is every indication of a scarcity of superior grades of SULPHITE, and sales have been made at advanced prices. Notwithstanding, papermakers in Great Britain do not evidence any desire to make future contracts, apparently under the impression that present firmness is only of a temporary nature. The outlook undoubtedly has an upward tendency.

Prices, ex steamer, London, Hull, Newcastle, Leith and, Glasgow are nominally as follows:

	£	s.	d.		£	s.	d.
SODA, Unbleached, Common ...	£10	0	0	to	10	10	0
" " Extra... ...	10	10	0	"	11	0	0
" Half-Bleached	12	10	0	"	14	0	0
SULPHATE, Unbleached, Common	10	10	0	"	11	0	0
" Extra	11	0	0	"	12	0	0
" Half-Bleached	13	10	0	"	14	0	0
" Bleached	15	0	0	"	16	0	0
SULPHITE, Unbleached, Common	10	15	0	to	11	0	0
" Superior	11	10	0	"	12	10	0
" " 50% moisture, d.w.	11	10	0	"	12	2	6
" Extra	13	0	0	"	14	0	0
" Bleached, moist					16	10	0
" Unbleached, English, del. Lancs. ...					10	15	0
" " " No. 1, ex mills, Ldn.					10	10	0
" " " No. 2, " "					9	15	0

MECHANICAL WOOD PULPS.— Arrivals of mechanical have come freely to hand during the past week. Fresh business, however, is reported quiet. Prices are firmly adhered to by the Scandinavian Pulpmakers' Union, although several mills have come forward with offers from 2s. 6d.

to 5s. per ton below the Union prices. There are quotations upon the market for Moist Pine at £2 15s. and Dry Pine at £5 15s. for all next year's delivery.

Prices, ex steamer, London, Hull, Newcastle, Leith and Glasgow are nominally as follows:

MECHANICAL, Aspen, Dry	...	£7 10 0 to 8 0 0
Pine, Dry	...	5 17 6 ,, 6 0 0
Pine, 50% Moist, Spot	...	2 15 0 ,, 2 17 6
Moist Brown (bundles	...	2 15 0 ,, 2 16 3
Dry Brown	...	5 10 0 ,, 5 15 0
Single Sorted... ...	...	2 2 6 ,, 2 5 0

IMPORTS of WOOD PULP.

Quantity	From	Importer	Port.
311 bales	Bergen	To order	Hull
1960 ,,	Christiania	,,	Grangemouth
673 ,,	,,	,,	,,
1148 ,,	,,	,,	Hull
412 ,,	,,	,,	Grangemouth
426 ,,	,,	W. G. Taylor and Co	London
300 ,,	,,	Tough & Henderson	,,
865 ,,	,,	G. Schjoth & Co	Fleetwood
2443 ,,	,,	Christophersen & Co	,,
680 ,,	Christianssand	J. Currie & Co	Leith
258 tons	Drammen	C. Christophersen	London
300 bales	,,	Lloyd & Co	,,
20 ,,	,,	H. Enderson	,,
222 ,,	,,	B. Petersen	,,
1160 ,,	Drontheim	To order	Hull
1100 ,,	,,	,,	Leith
799 ,,	Fiume	A. Guttmann	London
2789 ,,	Gothenburg	Henderson, Craig & Co	,,
162 ,,	,,	To order	Granton
905 ,,	,,	,,	Hull
580 ,,	,,	,,	London
240 ,,	Ghent	,,	,,
2000 ,,	Holmestrand	G. Schjoth and Co	Fleetwood
71 ,,	Hambro	To order	Hull
408 ,,	,,	J. Currie & Co	Leith
187 ,,	,,	To order	London
47 ,,	,,	,,	,,
179 rolls	Harlingen	G. Gibson & Co	Leith
4040 bales	Kotka	To order	London
130 ,,	Norrkoping	Baring Bros & Co	,,
60 ,,	,,	F. Bertuck	,,
3422 ,,	Oxelsund	G. Schjoth & Co	Fleetwood
52 ,,	Rotterdam	To order	Hull
20 rolls	,,	J. Rankin & Son	Grangemouth
360 bales	,,	To order	London
353 ,,	,,	,,	,,
394 ,,	,,	G. Gibson & Co	Leith
712 ,,	Stettin	To order	London
300 ,,	,,	,,	,,
1984 ,,	Skein	G. Schjoth & Co	Fleetwood
1600 ,,	,,	Blydt, Pans & Co	,,
240 ,,	,,	H. Newall & Son	,,
2760 ,,	St. Petersburg	Foy Morgan & Co	,,

Totals from Each Country:

BELGIUM	... 240 bales	NORWAY	... 23173 bales
FINLAND	... 799 ,,	,,	... 258 tons
GERMANY	... 4733 ,,	PRÜSSIA	... 1012 bales
HOLLAND	... 969 ,,	RUSSIA	... 2760 ,,
,,	... 199 rolls	SWEDEN	... 4535 ,,

STRAW.—Market quiet. Prices are very firm.

French Oat (Hand) c.i.f. London ...	55/0;	f.o.r. Hull	55/0
,, Wheat do. do. ...	63/0;	do.	63/0
German Wheat or Rye do. ...	58/0;	do.	58/0

IMPORTS of STRAW

(Purposes unspecified) at principal Ports From

DENMARK	... 917 bales	GERMANY	.. 894 bales
,,	... 14 tons	HOLLAND	... 2104 ,,

STRAW PULP.—Very little demand.

Prices, c.i.f. London, Hull or Leith:

Belgian, 25% moisture	£15 0 0 to 16 0 0
do. dry	16 0 0
German, 50 to 55% moisture	16 10 0
do. dry, ... No. 1 £18 10 0; No. 2	15 0 0

FOREIGN RAGS.—Trade on the continent keeps dull. Prices nominal.

IMPORTS of FOREIGN RAGS.

Quantity	From	Importer	Port.
37 bales	Amsterdam	To order	Liverpool
10 ,,	Adelaide	,,	London
93 ,,	Bremen	,,	Hull
225 ,,	Constantinople	,,	Liverpool
242 ,,	,,	,,	,,
2 ,,	Christiania	,,	Hull
349 ,,	Copenhagen	,,	,,
61 ,,	,,	J. Currie & Co	Leith
191 ,,	Dunkirk	To order	,,
11 ,,	,,	,,	Hull
284 ,,	Genoa	,,	,,
3 ,,	Hiogo	,,	London
41 ,,	Hambro	,,	Hull
198 ,,	Leghorn	,,	,,
48 ,,	Melbourne	,,	,,
13 ,,	Naples	,,	,,
203 ,,	Rouen	,,	London
5 ,,	,,	,,	,,
201 ,,	,,	,,	,,
221 ,,	,,	,,	,,
14 ,,	Rotterdam	,,	,,
80 ,,	,,	,,	,,
100 ,,	Sydney	,,	,,

Totals from Each Country:

AUSTRALIA	... 158 bales	ITALY	... 495 bales
DENMARK	... 410 ,,	JAPAN	... 3 ,,
FRANCE	... 832 ,,	NORWAY	... 2 ,,
GERMANY	... 134 ,,	TURKEY	... 467 ,,
HOLLAND	... 131 ,,		

DUTCH RAGS. f.o.r. Hull:

C.i.f. Thames; Hull 2/6 per ton more; ditto f.o.r. Leith c.i.f. Glasgow 4/-; c.i.f. Liverpool 4/-.

Selected Fines (free from Muslins) ...	17/0	Best Grey Linens ...	9/0
		Common ditto ...	5/6
Selected Outshots	12/0	White Canvas ...	15/0
,, Dirty Fines	7/0	Grey & Brown Canvas	9/9
Light Cottons ...	9/3	Tarred Hemp Rope	8/0
Blue Cottons ...	8/0	Ditto (broken) ...	5/3
Dark Coloured Cottons	2/10½	White Paper Shavings	7/9
New Cuttings (Bleachd)	22/6	Gunny (best) ...	4/9
,, (Unbleached)	19/6	Jute Bagging ...	3/6
,, (Slate) ...	9/0	Ditto (common ...	3/0
Muslins	8/0	Tarpaulins	4/0
Red Cottons (Mixed)	5/9	Cowhair Carpets ...	2/9
Fustians (Light browns	5/0	Hard ditto	3/0

FRENCH RAGS.

Quotations range, per cwt., ex ship London, Southampton, or Hull; 2/0 per ton more at Liverpool, and 10/0 per ton higher at Newcastle, Glasgow or Leith.

French Linens, I ...	22/0	Black Cotton ...	4/0
II 18/6; III ...	14/6	Marseilles Whites, I	16/0
White Cottons, I ...	19/0	II 10/0; III ...	7/6
II 15/0; III ...	12/6	Blue Cotton	11/0
Knitted Cotton ...	11/0	Light Prints... ...	9/0
Light Coloured Cotton	8/0	Mixed Prints ...	6/0
Blue Cotton	9/6	New White Cuttings	23/0
Coloured Cotton ...	6/0	,, Stay ,,	21/0

GERMAN RAGS.

STETTIN: C.i.f. Hull, Leith, Tyne and London.

SPFFF and SPFF	18/6	LFB (Blue)	10/
SPF	12/6	CSPFFF and CSPFF	12/0
FF	11/0	CFB (Blue)	8/0
FG	9/6	CFX (Coloured) ...	5/0
LFX	7/0		

HAMBURG: F.o.b.

NWC	22/0	FF Grey Linens ...	9/0
SPFFF	22/0	LFX Second ditto...	8/0
SPFFF and SPFF	18/0	CSPFFF	17/3
SPFF	16/0	CSPFF	11/3
SPF	12/0	CFB	8/0
CCC	5/6	Dark Blues (selected	11/9
CFX	4/6	Wool Tares... ...	8/0
White Rope... ...	8/0	Jute, No. I 6/0; No. II	5/6

NORWEGIAN RAGS.

C.i.f. London, Hull, Tyne, and Grangemouth.

1st Rope (tarred) ...	8/9-9/0	2nd Canvas ...	8/0
2nd ,, ,, ...	5/9-6/0	Jute Bagging	
Manilla Rope (white)	8/6-8/9	Gunny ...	3/6-3/9
Best Canvas ...	11/9-12/0	Mixed ...	2/6-3/0

RUSSIAN RAGS.

C.i.f. London, Hull, Newcastle or Leith.

SPFF	15/0	CC (Cotton	5/3
SPF	13/6	Jute I	3/6
FG	10/6	,, II...	2/3
LFB	9/6	Rope I...	9/9
FF	8/3	,, II	5/9
LFX	7/3		

For quotations of Belgian Rags see last issue.

HOME RAGS.—Markets are quiet, and prices unaltered. Stocks have not accumulated to any extent.

LONDON:

New White Cuttings	22/0	Canvas No. 1	26/0
Fines (selected)	20/6	,, No. 2 ...	10/0-11/0
,, (good London)...	20/0	,, No. 3	5/6
Outshots (selected) ...	12/6	Mixed Rope	5/3
,, (ordinary) ...	11/0	White Rope	6/0
London Seconds	4/0-4/6	White Manilla Rope	9/0
Country do. ...	6/6-8/0	Coil Rope	8/0
London Thirds ...	1/9-2/0	Bagging...	1/9-2/0
Country do. ...	4/0-5/0	Gunny	3/9-4/0
Light Prints ...	7/0-8/0		

BRISTOL:

Fines	19/0	Clean Canvas ...	15/0
Outshots	13/6	Second Do. ...	9/6-10/6
Seconds	7/0-8/0	Light Prints ...	8/0
Thirds	3/6-4/0	Hemp Coil Rope	9/6-10/0
Mixed Bagging	3/6	Tarred Manilla	7/6

MANCHESTER:

Fines	16/0-17/0	Blues	7/0-7/6
Outshots (best) ...	12/0-12/6	Bagging...	4/3-4/6
,, (ordinary)	11/0-11/6	,, (common)	3/3-3/6
Seconds	7/6-7/9	W. Manilla Rope	10/0-10-6
Thirds	3/9-4/0	Surat Tares... ...	5/0-5/3

EDINBURGH:

Superfines	17/0	Black Cottons	2/9
Outshots	13/0	W. Manilla Rope ...	9/0
Mixed Fines...	14/0	Tarred Ditto	6/9
Common Seconds ...	8/0	,, Hemp Rope...	8/6
First do.	11/0	Rope Ends (new) ...	8/6
Prints	5/6-6/6	,, ,, (old) ...	6/0
Canvas (best)	16/0	Bagging...	2/3-2/6
,, 2nd	10/6	,, (clean) ...	4/6-6/0

DUBLIN.

White Cuttings ...	18/0	Mill Bagging	3/0
Fines	12/0	White Manilla	8/0
Seconds...	6/6	Tarred Hemp	8/0
Light Prints	3/6	Rigging	13/6
Black do.	2/0	Mixed Ropes	3/6
Bagging	2/0		

WASTE PAPERS.—There is a good demand for waste papers.

Cream Shavings ...	12/3	Small Letters	5/.
Fine ,, ...	9/6	Large ,, ...	7/0
Mixed ,, ...	3/6	Brown Paper	2/3
White Printings ...	8/9	Light Browns	3/6
White Waste ...	1/6	Books & Pamphlets ...	6/0
Wood Pulp Cuttings	3/6	Strawboard Cuttings	1/6
Brown Paper	3/0	Jacquards	2/6
Crushed News	2/0		

For Export: 25/- per ton extra.

JUTE.—Cuttings are in fair request.

Good White £16 0 to 17 0		Common ... £10 10 to 11 10	
Good... ...	14 0	Rejections...	£9
Medium ...	13 0	Cuttings ... £5 to 6 0	

STARCH, &c.—There is a steady trade current.

F.o.r. London, less 2½%:

Maize—Crisp, £10 10/-; Powder, £11 0/-; Special £16 0/-
Farina—Prime, £11 0/-; B.K.M.F., £14 0/-

Delivered:

Rice—Special (in chests), £20 10/- (net); Crystal (in bags) £19 10/-; Granulated (in bags) £18 10/-
Dextrine—£16 10/-

ROSIN.—The market is firm with a steady demand.

	Strained.	E.	F.	G.	K.	W.G.	W.W.
Spot—	3/0	4/3	4/6	4/9	7/0	9/6	12/0
To arrive—	3/3	3/6½	3/7½	3/9	6/0	8/0	8/6

SIZING.—Glues are in good demand at firm prices. There is an improved export trade and stocks are reduced.

English Gelatines	per cwt.	70/0 to 140/0
Foreign ,, ...	,,	70/0 ,, 140/0
Fine Skin Glues	,,	45/0 ,, 60/0
Long Scotch Glues	,,	45/0 ,, 60/0
Common ,, ...	,,	30/0 ,, 45/0
"Town" Glues	,,	26/0 ,, 35/0
"Bone" Glues	,,	20/0 ,, 30/0
Foreign Glues	,,	23/0 ,, 40/0
Bone Size	,,	4/0 ,, 10/0
Gelatine Size...	,,	5/0 ,, 10/0
Dry B.A. Pieces	,,	31/6 ,, 33/0
,, English Pieces	,,	24/0 ,, 27/0
Wet ,, ,, ...	,,	7/0 ,, 8/0
,, Sheep Pieces	,,	3/0 ,, 4/0
Buffalo Hide Shavings	,,	26/0 ,, 37/0
,, Picker Waste	,,	27/0 ,, 37/0

COLOURS.—Very little enquiry.

Mineral Black ...	cwt.	3/0	Ultramarine (pure)	
do. superior ...	,,	5/0	... cwt. 40/0 to	45/0
Pure Ivory Black	,,	12/0	PASTE COLOURS with	
Ochre	,,	3/0	60% of colour, as follows:	
French J. C. Ochre	ton	55/0	Orange Pulp ... cwt.	40/0
Chrome (pure) ...	cwt.	40/0	Golden Yellow Pulp	36/0
Red Oxide	,,	4/6	Lemon ,, ,, cwt.	36/0
Umber, Devonshire	,,	30/0	Prussian Yellow ,,	36/0
do. Turkish ...	,,	40/0	Green (free of arsenic	36/0
Lamp Black ...		7/0-10/6	Paste Blue (20-45%)	
Cochineal	lb.	1/3-2/0	... ...	23/6-46/8

MINERALS.—CHINA CLAY is moving much better as regards export trade, and the home demand is fairly good. FRENCH CHALK arrivals are small and prices firm. BARYTES (carbonate) are in better request at previous figures. Finest white sulphate is in demand. IRISH MOSS medium quality is quoted at £12 10s. PATENT HARDENINGS and MINERAL WHITE are in moderate request.

Mineral White (Terra Alba), per ton f.o.r. or boat at works:

Superfine...	28/0	less 2½ %
Pottery Super.... ...	24/0	,,
Ball Seconds	20/0	,,
Seconds	15/0	,,
Thirds	10/6	,,

China Clay, in bulk, f.o.b. Cornwall, 14/0 to 27/6; bags 5/0 and casks 9/6 per ton extra; f.o.b. London, in casks 35/0 to 50/0 per ton.
Superfine Hardening, f.o.r. works, 40/0.
Patent Crystal Hardening, delivered at mills £3 to £3 15/0
Patent Hardening (2 ton lots) f.o.r. Lancs., £3 5/0.
,, ,, (5 ton lots) f.o.b. Liverpool, £3 10/0.
Magnesite (in lump) 32/6 per ton.
Magnesite (containing 98% Carbonate of Magnesia), raw ground, £6 10/0; calcined ground, £12 10/0.
Albarine, £3, del. mills.
Asbestos, best rock, £18; brown grades, £14 to £15
Asbestine Pulp, £4 5/- to £5 c.i.f. London, Liverpool and Glasgow.
Barytes (Carbonate), lump, 90/0 to 95/0; nuts, 72/6 to 85/0.
Barytes (Sulphate), "Angel White," No. 1, 70/0; No. 2, 60/0 to 65/0; No. 3, 45/0. Souheur's Brands: AF, 83/-; BF, 72/-; AB, 33/6; BB, 29/6; CB, 24/3.
French and Italian Chalk (Souheur Brand), per ton in lots of 10 tons, medium, 51/6 c.i.f. London, 56/6 c.i.f. Liverp'l, 58/6 c.i.f. Hull; Swan Brand. 57/6, 72/- & 80/- Blackwell's "Angel White" Brand and "Silvery" 90/- to 92/6; prime quality, 90/- to 95/-; and superfine, 105/-.
Bauxite, Irish Hill Quality, first lump, 20/0; seconds, 16/0; thirds, 12/0; ground, 35/0.
Pyrites (non-cupreous), Liverpool, 5d., 2 %.
Carbonate of Lime (Souheur Brand) Prima 43/-, Secunda 37/-.

LIME. — Best WHITE BUXTON LIME, hand-picked, f.o.t. works, is quoted at 10/0 per ton (less 2½ %).

BALING TWINE.—Prices:

		Thick.	Medium.	Cap.
All Hemp	per lb.	4d.	4¼d.	4¾d
All Jute		3¼d.	3¾d.	4d.

DIRECTORY.

Names and Addresses under this heading will be charged for at the rate of 50/- per annum (52 insertions) for each card of two lines or under. Each additional line £1 extra.

ALUMINOUS CAKE.

The ALUM, CHINA CLAY and VITRIOL Co., Lim., 63, Queen Victoria Street, London, E.C. Works: Rainham-on-Thames. Telegrams—"Chinnock, London.

ANALYTICAL.

WILLIAMS, ROWLAND, F.I.C., F.C.S., 28, Pall Mall, Manchester.

ARTESIAN WELLS.

BATCHELOR, Richard D., Artesian and Consulting Well Engineer, 73, Queen Victoria Street, London, E.C., and at Chatham. 5713

ISLER, C., & Co., Bear Lane, Southwark, S.E.

LE GRAND & SUTCLIFF, Magdala Works, 125, Bunhill Row, E.C.

CHINA CLAY.

The ALUM, CHINA CLAY and VITRIOL Co., Lim., 63, Queen Victoria Street, London, E.C. Mines: Ruddle and Colchester, St. Austell, Cornwall. Telegrams—"Chinnock, London."

ROGERS, J., & Co., Truro, Cornwall.—Agents: Taylor, Sommerville & Co., 83, Queen Victoria Street, E.C., and at 16, Princes Street, Edinburgh.

W. SINGLETON BIRCH & SONS, Lim., 25, Upton Street, Manchester. Mines: Rosevear, St. Austell, Cornwall. 2276

COLOURS.

CARDWELL, J. L., & Co., Commercial Buildings, 15, Cross Street, Manchester. Specialties: Mineral Black, Ven. Red, Ochres and Umbers. 5304

GEMMILL, W. N., & Co., Glasgow, Telegrams "Rube." Starches, Alumina, Antifroths, &c. All Paper Colours.

HINSHELWOOD, THOMAS, & Co., The Glasgow Colour Works, Glasgow. Colours and shades matched exactly.

MULLER, A. E., 9, Fenchurch Street, London, E.C.

Special Prepaid Advertisements

IT IS IMPORTANT that Advertisements under any of the Headings mentioned below should reach us by the FIRST POST on WEDNESDAY Morning to INSURE INSERTION.

Charges for advertisements under the heading Situations Wanted are 1/- for twenty-four words, and One Penny per Word after, Minimum charge ONE SHILLING. Names and addresses to be paid for.

Advertisers by paying an extra fee of 6d. can have the replies addressed to the PAPER TRADE REVIEW under a number, and such replies will then be forwarded Post Free.

Advertisements appearing under the following headings:

Tenders.	Mills Wanted or To Let.
Sales by Auction.	Machinery Wanted or For Sale.
Businesses Wanted.	
Businesses for Disposal.	Situations Vacant.

Miscellaneous.

The charges are 3/- for fifty words or under; 1s. extra for every line or portion after. Ten words to be reckoned for each line. Names and addresses to be paid for. Payment must be made in advance, except where the advertiser has a running account, in which case the cost can be debited thereto.

Legal and Financial Announcements: 1/- per Line.

Cheques and Post-office Orders to be CROSSED —— and Co., and made payable to W. JOHN STONHILL.

Situation Vacant.

WANTED, a Working Millwright; must be capable of taking speeds, indicating steam engines, and erecting new machinery. State wages required and give references.—Address "Millwright," No 5820, office of the WORLD'S PAPER TRADE REVIEW, 58, Shoe Lane, London, E.C. 5820

Situations Wanted.

EXPERIENCED Manager, used to sole charge, good chemist, open to engagement; home or abroad.—Address No. 5750, Office of the WORLD'S PAPER TRADE REVIEW, 58, Shoe-lane, London, E.C. 5750

PRACTICAL Manager open for engagement; 20 years' experience as Manager in several of the best mills in Great Britain, on all classes of paper. Well up in all kinds of modern machinery.—Address No. 5801, office of the WORLD'S PAPER TRADE REVIEW, 58, Shoe Lane, London, E C. 5801

WANTED, a situation in the office of a papermaker or agent as junior traveller and assistant; some years experience of the trade, writings and printings.—Address No. 5818, office of the WORLD'S PAPER TRADE REVIEW, 58, Shoe-lane, London, E.C. 5818

YOUNG MAN seeks situation as Finisher, used to browns and royal hands; good reference.—Address No. 5814, office of the WORLD'S PAPER TRADE REVIEW, 58, Shoe-lane, London, E.C. 5814

Mill to be Let or Sold.

TO be LET or SOLD, a Paper Mill at Stalybridge, called the Higher Mill, containing one large machine and room for another, steam engine and boilers, in good condition.—Apply for further information to the Caretaker on the premises. 2162

Machinery Wanted.

WANTED, new or second-hand Single Cylinder Machine, 9/10 ft. diameter, 84/90 inches on face. State price and where can be seen.—Address No 5817, office of the WORLD'S PAPER TRADE REVIEW, 58, Shoe-lane, London, E.C. 5817

Machinery for Sale.

FOR SALE, One 8-roll Glazing Calender, four iron and four paper rolls, paper rolls 32 inches face; also two sets of 3-roll Friction Glazing Calenders, one iron, one cotton and one steel roll fitted with steam, with or without steam engines. All these calenders made by Robinson, of Salford, Manchester. Also one set of Plate Glazing Rolls 32 inches face.—All the above in good order and condition; can be seen on application to C. Townsend Hook & Co., Snodland. 5815

ON SALE,

ONE

75in. FOURDRINIER

PAPERMAKING MACHINE,

With First and Second Presses.

13 CYLINDERS 3 ft. 6 in. dia., 7 ft. 2 in. on Face.

STUFF and BACK WATER PUMPS.

One STACK of CALENDERS

(BY J. ROBINSON & CO.),

Containing Four Chilled Rolls and Two Paper Rolls.

ALSO

STEAM ENGINE

To Drive Same; 11 inch Cylinder, 18 inch Stroke.

THE MACHINE CAN BE SEEN WORKING

Complete Specifications will be forwarded on application to the

Ramsbottom Paper Mill Co.,

2657 LIMITED,

RAMSBOTTOM, NEAR MANCHESTER.

PAPER & PULP MILL SHARES.

(Report received from Mr. F. D. DEAN, 36, Corporation Street, Manchester.)

Nominal Amnt	Amnt Paid	Name of Company	Last dividend	Price.
7	7	Bury Paper, ord.	nil	5¼—5½
7	7	do. do. 6% pref.	6%	5¼—5¾
100	100	do. do. deb.	5%	103—106
10	10	Bath Paper Mill Co. Lim.	7½%	7—8
10	10	Bergvik Co., def.	15%	13¾
100	100	do. do. 6% cum. pref.	6%	10⅞—11¼
10	10	do. do. deb.	5%	105—110
5	3½	Burnley Paper Co.	3/-	75/0—77/0
5	3½	Darwen Paper Co.	10%	5¾—5⅞
10	10	East Lancashire Co.	nil	5¼—5¾
10	10	do. do. 6% pref.	nil	7—7½
5	5	do. do. bonus	nil	1½—2
5	5	Hyde Paper Co.	4%	4½—5
5	4	North of Ireland Paper Co.	nil	1½—2
10	5	Ramsbottom Paper Co.	17½%	12½—12¾
5	4½	Roach Bridge Paper Co.	5%	3¼—3½
5	5	Star Paper Co.	10%	6¼—6½
5	3	do. do. 10% pref. cum.	10%	4¾—5¼
50	50	do. do. deb.	6%	55—56
5	2½	Kellner Partingt'n Pulp Co	—	56/0—58/0

PAPER EXPORTS & IMPORTS.

FOR THE WEEK ENDING TUESDAY LAST.

EXPORTS TO

Country.	Printings.	Writings.	Other Kinds.
ARABIA	— cwts.	3 cwts.	— cwts.
AUSTRALIA... ...	4845 ,,	1068 ,,	980 ,,
AFRICA	17 ,,	8 ,,	39 ,,
BELGIUM	— ,,	50 ,,	— ,,
B. GUIANA	— ,,	24½ ,,	504 ,,
B. WEST INDIES...	— ,,	8 ,,	— ,,
BRAZIL	— ,,	8 ,,	4 ,,
CANADA	50½ ,,	43½ ,,	28 ,,
CAPE COLONY ...	235 ,,	30 ,,	230 ,,
CHINA	— ,,	15 ,,	8 ,,
DENMARK	— ,,	— ,,	2 ,,
DUTCH GUINEA...	— ,,	— ,,	3 ,,
EGYPT	— ,,	— ,,	3 ,,
FRANCE	1091 ,,	167 ,,	53 ,,
GERMANY	21 ,,	— ,,	18 ,,
HOLLAND	4 ,,	— ,,	12 ,,
INDIA	1522¾ ,,	374 ,,	218½ ,,
JAPAN	369 ,,	18 ,,	85 ,,
MAURITIUS ...	5 ,,	4 ,,	44 ,,
NEW ZEALAND ...	1177 ,,	636 ,,	213 ,,
NEWFOUNDLAND	— ,,	— ,,	4 ,,
PORTUGAL	— ,,	2 ,,	— ,,
RUSSIA	— ,,	10 ,,	2 ,,
SPAIN	— ,,	26 ,,	4 ,,
SWEDEN	— ,,	7 ,,	— ,,
UNITED STATES..	— ,,	121 ,,	45 ,,

IMPORTS FROM

AUSTRIA ...	23 bales	FINLAND ...	250 rolls
BELGIUM ...	1037 ,,	,, ...	27 cases
,, ...	475 cases	GERMANY ...	2213 bales
,, ...	70 rolls	,, ...	153 cases
CHINA	27 cases	HOLLAND ...	12471 bales
CHANNEL I. ...	31 bales	,, ...	76 cases
DENMARK ...	233 ,,	ITALY	28 bales
EGYPT	1 case	NORWAY ...	5414 ,,
FRANCE ...	147 bales	PRUSSIA ...	115 ,,
,, ...	96 cases	SWEDEN ...	1719 ,,
FINLAND ...	349 bales		

Including the Following :

Quantity	From	Importer	Port.
64 bales	Christiania	Ldn. & Rhine Paper Co	London.
41 ,,	,,	Christophersen & Co	,,
3 ,,	,,	E. Lloyd	,,
7 ,,	Copenhagen	Becker & Ulrich	,,
20 ,,	,,	Schenkenwald & Co	,,
63 ,,	,,	Becker & Ulrich	,,
7 ,,	Danzig	H. Huber & Co	,,
8 ,,	Drammen	Fetter & Co	,,
34 ,,	,,	Alsing & Co	,,
259 ,,	,,	Crabb & Co	,,
16 ,,	,,	Cookson & Co	,,
88 ,,	,,	J. Hamilton	,,
72 ,,	,,	J. Spicer & Sons	,,
931 ,,	,,	Green & Co	,,
14 ,,	,,	W. D. Edwards & Co	,,
13 ,,	,,	Smyth & Son	,,
12 ,,	,,	W. E. Bott & Co	,,
20 bales	Gothenburg	Becker & Ulrich	London
12 ,,	,,	Schenkenwald & Co	,,
1 ,,	Hambro	Debenham & Co	,,
928 ,,	Norrkoping	Schenkenwald & Co	,,
158 ,,	,,	J. Spicer & Sons	,,
259 ,,	,,	Prop. Brooks Whf.	,,
40 ,,	Trieste	P. Sabel & Co.	,,
21 ,,	Uddevalle	Hernn, Peron & Co.	,,
367 ,,	,,	D. Gulland	,,

SUMMARY OF IMPORTS & EXPORTS,

FOR THE WEEK ENDING TUESDAY LAST.

London, Liverpool, Bristol, Southampton, Hull, Fleetwood, Harwich, Folkestone, Newhaven, Dover, &c.

IMPORTS.

Paper	19551 bales	Strawboards	1087 bales
,, ...	1834 cases	,, ...	12 cases.
,, ...	250 rolls	Millboards.........	6826 bales
Tissues	159 pkgs.	Stock	483 ,,
,, ...	128 cases	Stationery	69 cases
Pasteboards	5055 ,,		

EXPORTS.

BRITISH GOODS.		Postage Paper...	£215 value
		FOREIGN GOODS.	
Paper	2643 cwt.		
Printing Paper	8247 ,,	Printing Paper...	339 cwts.
Writing Paper ...	2422 ,,	Writing Paper...	26 ,,
Stationery.........	£8719 value	Paper	689 ,,
Stock	172 tons	Stationery..... ...	£189 value
Cardboards	262 cwt.	Strawboards	299 cwt.
Waste	56 tons	Pasteboard	360 ,,
Pasteboards	9 cwt.	Pulp Boards	80 ,,
Strawboards	40 ,,	Wood Pulp	20 tons
Parchment	£145 value	Stock	92 ,,

Glasgow, Greenock, Port-Glasgow, Troon, Grangemouth, &c.

IMPORTS.

Paper	2878 bales	Strawboards	5153 cwts.
,, ...	45 cases	Millboards.........	22 ,,

EXPORTS.

Paper	1824 cwt.	Wrapping Paper	28 cwts.
Writing Paper...	58½ ,,	Stationery	£32 value
Printing Paper..	896½ ,,		

Leith, Granton, Boness, Dundee, &c.

IMPORTS.

Paper	556 bales	Envelopes	530 pkgs
,, ...	11 cases	Tissue	23 ,,
,, ...	70 rolls	Millboard	1050 ,,

NEW PATENTS.

BRITISH.

APPLICATIONS.

11,996. A new or improved construction of paper pulp refining engine. D. Pearson and D. N. Bertram.

12,074. Improvements in obtaining chlorine. A. Vogt and A. R. Scott.

12,420. Improvements in apparatus for mixing and regulating paper stuff. W. Borland.

Taylor's Patent

BEATING and REFINING ENGINE.

THIS BEATER TAKES UP LESS FLOOR SPACE THAN ANY OTHER.

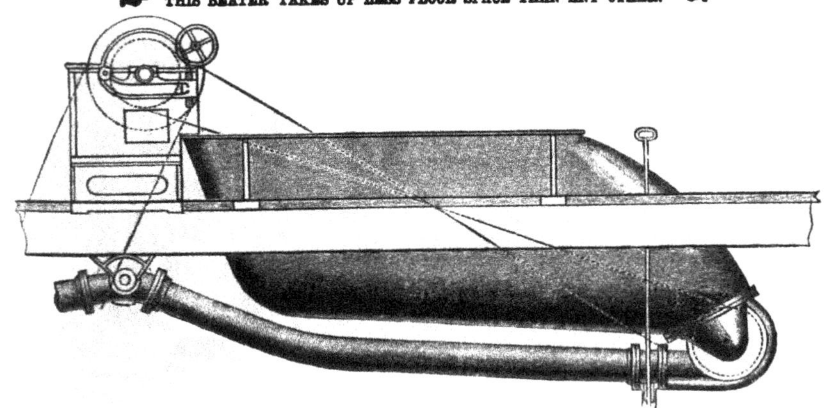

ADVANTAGES:

1.—**GREATLY INCREASED PRODUCTION** over that of the ordinary Beater in use.

2.—**GREAT SAVING IN POWER**, notwithstanding the increased production. This Beater has been proved to beat a given quantity of pulp with less than one-half of the power required by an ordinary beater of good modern construction.

3.—**COMPLETE AND PERFECT CIRCULATION**, which ensures complete uniformity in the length of the fibres.

For Full Particulars and Prices apply to

MASSON, SCOTT & Co., Ltd.,

BATTERSEA, LONDON, S.W

BELL'S ASBESTOS MANUFACTURES

BELL'S

Asbestos Dagger Packing

Every 10 Feet has Label bearing our Name and Trade

BELL'S ASBESTOS

YARN & SOAPSTONE PACKING

Every 10 Feet has Label bearing our Name and Trade Mark

BELL'S ASBESTOS

EXPANSION SHEETING & RINGS

BELL'S ASBESTOS Co., Lim.,

59, SOUTHWARK STREET, LONDON, S.E.

Printed and Published by W. JOHN STONHILL, 58, Shoe Lane, LONDON E.C. July 7, 1893.

OUT AND ABOUT

BEING JOTTINGS IN TOWN AND OUT

SOME GOOD — GOOD FOR NOUT

MESSRS. JOSEPH TOWN AND SONS, of Leeds, of whose frontage we give a sketch below, issue a handsome sample book of their 244 mill tub-sized writings, embracing their well known watermark "J. Town and Sons Superfine." in cream laid and wove, blue laid and wove, azure laid and yellow wove; the J. T. and S. Albion series of "fine" qualities, and also the "seconds." The book also contains examples of the favourite 244 Mill Turkey Mill, Albion, and Sunnydale vellums, and the Albion linears and banks. The finest sheets of the collection are undoubtedly the superfine azure laid double tub-sized all rag papers, which are so well known and appreciated wherever used. They are stocked in the following sizes and weights:—

Imperial	68 lb.
Super royal...	50 ,,
Royal...	42 ,,
Medium	34 lb.
Double medium	66 ,,
,, ,, oblong...	68 ,,
Double large post... ...	48 ,,
Large post	24, 21, 18 ,,
Demy...	25, 24 ,,
Double demy	46 ,,
,, ,, oblong ...	46 ,,
Foolscap	18, 16 ,,
Double foolscap	36, 31 ,,
,, ,, oblong ...	32 ,,
Sheet-and-half foolscap ...	21 ,,
Sheet-and-third ,, ...	49 ,,

TOWN AND SONS' LEEDS WAREHOUSE.

THE accompanying thumb-nail portrait is that of Mr. Frank Forrester, the North of England representative of Messrs. Edward Lloyd, Limited, the widely known papermakers and wholesale stationers. Mr. Forrester founded the *Gloucester Citizen*, is well known in printing and stationery circles throughout the West and North of England, and doubtless has numerous friends and well-wishers in distant parts of the world.

THE Bank Mills, Leeds, have been acquired by Messrs. Roberts, Mart & Co., Ltd., for the purposes of their extensive trade in paper and paper bag making. The mills are of enormous extent, having a frontage of 296 feet, and affording a floor space of nearly 8,000 square yards. No other such imposing premises are devoted to one exclusive branch of the trade in the United Kingdom. The firm carry habitually some £4,000 to £5,000 worth of stock in made-up paper bags, always holding 200 to 300 tons of all sizes ready to meet the urgent requirements of their clients.

The machines relied upon by Messrs. Roberts, Mart and Co. in the production of their bags are those of Messrs. Bumsted and Chandler, of the Cannock Chase Foundry, Hednesford, and Messrs. Strachan and Henshaw, of the Central Engineering Works, Bristol. The machine of Messrs. Bumsted and Chandler, a pen and ink sketch of which we give on page 27, makes a square-bottomed bag, in sizes from a £5 cash bag to a 28-lb. sugar bag. It is wonderfully light running and easy in control; an instance is quoted of a half-horse Otto gas engine driving seven machines, besides two of another make, whilst with a young girl upon each, one man may easily tend half a dozen of them. The square-bottomed bag is very popular. The machine is made in varying sizes, those we have seen being known as No. 1, making from a ½-lb. to a 3½-lb. sugar bag; No. 1½, making up to 4-lb. moist sugar bag; and No. 2, from a 4-lb. to a 12-lb. raw sugar bag. Each machine makes four sizes of bags, at a speed of from 35 to 40 a minute, from the reel of course.

THE machines of Messrs. Strachan and Henshaw in operation at the Bank Mills, a drawing of one of which is annexed, have a capacity of from a 2-oz. sweet to a 14-lb. flour or moist sugar bag, and all intermediate sizes in plain or satchel shapes. But Messrs. Roberts, Mart and Co. use also a larger machine, making the largest milliners' bags, up to 18-in. wide, and plain and satchel bags from 7-in. to 28-in. length. The speed of production is from 9,000 to 12,000 an hour of ordinary bags, and 5,000 to 6,000 an hour of the large millinery bags; or putting it in another way, each machine will make up 8 to 10 cwt. of cap paper, or 15 to 20 cwt. of sugars or browns. They are most economical machines in working, and as an example of their freedom from wearing parts we may mention that Messrs. Roberts, Mart and Co. spoke of two machines having run continuously for seven years without defect and with very trifling cost in repairs.

ON page 28 is a pen and ink drawing of a new appliance for "ripening" litho and other paper, designed and patented by

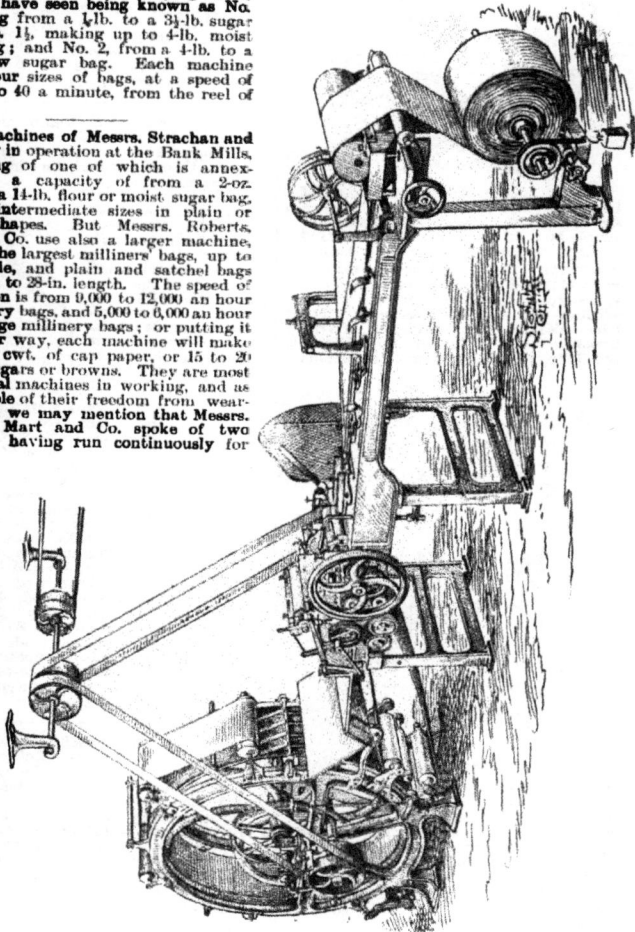

STRACHAN AND HENSHAW'S PAPER BAG MAKING MACHINE, AS SEEN RUNNING AT MESSRS. ROBERTS, MART AND CO.'S WORKS.

Mr. Jennings, who holds the position of foreman in the lithographic works of Messrs. Geo. Philip and Son, Hope-street, Liverpool. The object is to overcome the "stretching" which creates such difficulty for the lithographer in colour work. Hitherto the printer has resorted either to the plan of laying out his paper in trays for a time, hanging the sheets by means of clips or lines, or passing them both ways through the hot rolling machine. Mr. Jennings, however, claims that by feeding the sheets singly once through his "Perfectum" machine they are efficiently "seasoned" and "stretching" entirely overcome. The mechanism and principle of the "Perfectum" are alike simple. It consists only of a series of endless tapes running over cylinders of wood at each end, so that a sheet fed in at the top traverses the width of the machine four times before being delivered at the foot. A current of hot air is maintained by means of a gas stove or other

some new premises at the junction of Railway-road and the High-street, facing the L. and Y. R. Station, at a cost of about £20,000. The building, of which we give a pen and ink drawing, is of red brick with terra cotta dressings. Messrs. Marinoni (Sauvee and Co., 22, Parliament-street, S.W.) are erecting new machines for this journal.

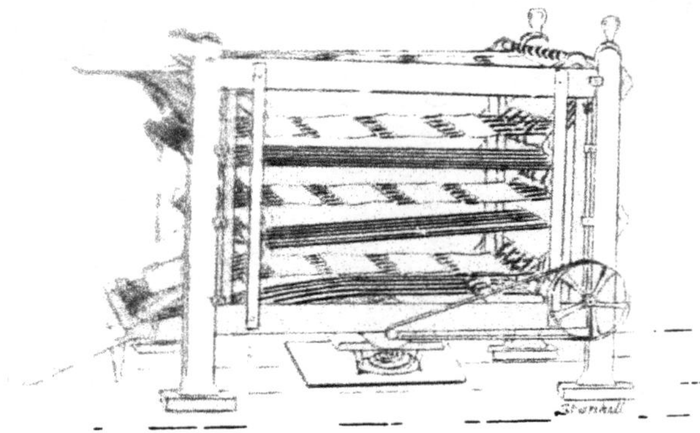

THE "PERFECTUM" PAPER MATURING MACHINE.

OFFICES OF THE "NORTHERN DAILY TELEGRAPH."

Gd for No. 2

[illegible]

[illegible] No. [illegible]

[illegible]

%

[illegible]EST

[illegible]ASS.

[illegible]

Germany	[illegible]	[illegible]
Holland	[illegible]	[illegible]
Belgium	17,295	8,015
France	7,295	1,743
Other Foreign Countries	1,747	1,000
Total from Foreign Countries	1,[illegible]	153,546
Total from British Possessions	7	41
TOTAL	1,[illegible]	153,[illegible]

BRITISH EXPORTS OF FOREIGN PAPER.

PRINTINGS & WRITINGS.

	Cwts.	Value.
United States of America: Atlantic	1,461	4,389
Other Foreign Countries	2,158	3,088
Total to Foreign countries	3,[illegible]	7,[illegible]
Australasia	6,799	7,585
Other British Possessions	2,475	3,533
Total to British Possessions	9,274	11,112
TOTAL	12,878	£19,112

HANGINGS.

	Cwts.	Value.
Foreign Countries	784	1,208
British Possessions	57	277
TOTAL	841	1,485

OTHER KINDS.

	Cwts.	Value.
United States of America	4,280	4,398
Spanish West India Islands	4,747	3,904
Brazil	2,848	2,781
Other Foreign Countries	5,104	9,298
Total to Foreign Countries	18,894	24,171
British East Indies	12,550	13,292
Australasia	8,001	4,727
Canada	1,594	2,380
British West India Islands & British Guiana	6,219	3,012
Other British Possessions	640	1,784
Total to British Possessions	29,014	29,404
TOTAL	47,908	53,575

MILLBOARDS & PASTEBOARDS.

	Cwts.	Value.
Foreign Countries	3,240	2,674
British East Indies	12,049	6,722

Australasia	8,473	3,[illegible]
Other British Possessions	3,286	1,3[illegible]
Total to British Possessions	23,477	11,71[illegible]
TOTAL	2[illegible]	14,3[illegible]

THE GERMAN DAY AT THE CHICAGO EXHIBITION was celebrated on June 15th with a numerous attendance of Germans and Americans of German origin. The latter had requested the well-known American politician, Herr Carl Schurz, to welcome his countrymen from the mother country, and he did this in a masterly speech, which both in the subjects he treated and the happy way and the warm and patriotic feelings he expressed, not only appealed to his audience but also has been reprinted in the leading papers of the fatherland, and everywhere is read with the highest approbation. After showing how the German community had identified themselves with the American Republic, and taken a prominent part in the late Civil War, they had never ceased to take an interest in the great German war when the fatherland had been threatened by its hereditary enemy. The foundation of the German empire at the end of a glorious campaign was nowhere so warmly welcomed as in the States. The Germans there who had known Germany only as a geographical expression now for the first time became proud of the old country, but they are still more pleased now with the German victory in the present exhibition. There are two ways of beating competition, says Herr Schurz, one by underselling, the other by offering a better article. In the old times, and even as far back as the Philadelphia World's Fair the Germans had followed the first policy. This was only natural, as at that time they had hardly realised their improved material position following upon their military victories, but since then they had entirely broken with the past and had taken up the second line by showing at the present exhibition the great superiority of their productions, of which the German-Americans were proud. The "cheap and nasty" have been followed by "good and reasonable prices." This progress is in the first place owing to the high state of education in modern Germany, and to the regained self respect of the nation. When you add steadiness and industry you have every reason to expect that the Germans will keep their present position, and other nations have accepted it, and entertain friendly relations to their mutual advantage.

HERR JOHANN [illegible], ground wood, wood pulp, board and papermaker at Grimburg, near Hermagor, is erecting sulphite works according to a combined system, and hopes to be ready for work in autumn.

THE paper mill at Elmwood, Ill., U.S.A., is to be rebuilt. The citizens raised a bonus of 6,000 dols., including the grounds, and a 30,000 dols. plant will be erected.

MANUF
Los
Nor

TING.
OF
is the

SOCIETY OF CHEMICAL INDUSTRY.

SIR JOHN EVANS, K.C.B., F.R.S., the president, delivered a very able address at the annual meeting of the above society, opened at University College, Liverpool, on Wednesday last week. He expressed a firm belief that only by cordial co-operation among the different industries of this country as that which their society had inaugurated was the commercial position of Great or Greater Britain to be maintained. The more fully the interdependence between one branch of manufacture and another was recognised and acted upon the more likely were they, as a whole, to maintain their place in the keen race of competition with other countries. A merely cursory glance at their journal would at once show how numerous were the departments of British industry more or less dependent on chemical knowledge, the information given on current literature and the specifications of new patents being arranged under no fewer than three and twenty different heads, many of them embracing several varying occupations. Not a few of these headings would, within his memory, have conveyed but little meaning, even to experts. In the domain of electricity it was hard to say whether that science did not owe nearly as much to chemistry as chemistry did to it. The study of heat, irrespective of electricity, has largely reacted on chemistry, and while the Bessemer process has entirely revolutionised the manufacture of steel and almost annihilated the distinction in value between that and other forms of iron, the Siemens's and other furnaces had led to unprecedented economies in the expenditure of fuel, and at the same time had facilitated the application of heat in various chemical processes. In the other direction—absence of heat—Professor Dewar had during the present year made most important advances. Although air had previously been liquefied, he had now been able, by means of intense cold alone, to reduce atmospheric air to the liquid condition. His further results by a combination of enormous pressure and extreme cold were well-known; and now that oxygen and nitrogen had yielded themselves to the advances of science, and had been obtained in quantities in a liquid state, it was hard to say that hydrogen was destined always to remain intractable. What might be the ultimate results of the investigations that could now be carried on in temperatures ranging from 100 degrees to 200 degrees Centigrade below the freezing point of water it was impossible to foresee. From researches already made in this country it would always appear that most substances under extreme cold were, so to speak, dead, and that their ordinary affinities were in abeyance. Possibly what might be termed "glacial chemistry" might eventually enlarge their views as to the various properties of matter. As to the advances in knowledge of the chemistry of light the present condition of photography might testify. Gas ha[illegible] now to compete with electricity as an illuminant, while in many cases it had been superseded by mineral oils which were now [illegible] abundant and cheap. If, however, gas was losing ground as an illuminant, it seemed to be gaining ground as a source of power, [illegible] there were prospects of a considerable increase in the use for this purpose of hydrog[illegible] and its compounds containing far less carb[illegible] than ordinary coal gas. In metallurgy, also, in addition to the improvements in th[illegible] manufacture of steel, many noteworth[illegible] discoveries had been made. Much of the knowledge of the mysterious processes [illegible] fermentation was also of recent date, and was in connection with these [illegible] tha[illegible] the chemist found himself [illegible] clo[illegible] contact with the botanist and physiologis[illegible] Now that so many diseases have been trac[illegible] to pathogenic organisms which are co[illegible] stantly present in water contaminated [illegible] sewage, the question of the vitality of the organisms and their germs had been right[illegible] regarded as one of great importance. T[illegible] remarkable power of light, whether that [illegible] the sun or electricity, in sterilising the ger[illegible] of some micro-organisms already, to so[illegible] extent, previously known, had been co[illegible] clusively demonstrated by Professor Marsh[illegible] Ward. Much had been done of late years [illegible] chemists towards the purification of sew[illegible] with the view of rendering the effluents f[illegible] the ultimate drains of our large municip[illegible] ties as innocuous as possible, and the re[illegible] obtained have been in many instances sa[illegible] factory. They would, no doubt, have b[illegible] even more so had not the imperative dem[illegible] of economy limited the cost. He would [illegible] attempt to discuss the important questio[illegible] the disposal of sewage of great towns, bu[illegible] many it would appear as somewhat of a [illegible] grace to their powers of applying chem[illegible] knowledge that such vast accumulatio[illegible] what were originally highly fertilising [illegible] stances should be discharged into the est[illegible] of the Thames, and not only be absolu[illegible] wasted, but converted into a perp[illegible] nuisance brought up at each tide within [illegible] limits of the metropolis from which [illegible] started. Within the last fifty years we [illegible] imported enormous quantities of g[illegible] phosphates, and nitrates, but of these [illegible] must eventually become a scarcity, if [illegible] end. In the meantime might not che[illegible] do something to reduce the waste of f[illegible] ing agents that was taking place annu[illegible] Agricultural colleges had been fou[illegible] agricultural chemistry was a recog[illegible] branch of science; but with the increa[illegible] knowledge had come increase of foreig[illegible] petition fostered by improved mea[illegible] transit and communication; and it [illegible] the present time a doubtful point w[illegible] many soils, even if rent free, could b[illegible] vated in this country for cereals excep[illegible] loss.

On the motion of PROFESSOR REY[illegible] seconded by DR. CAMPBELL BROWN, [illegible] of thanks was accorded to the presid[illegible] his scholarly and comprehensive addr[illegible]

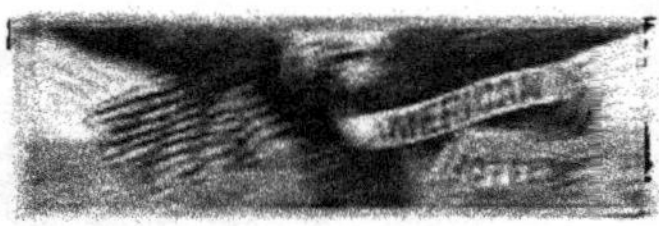

[illegible]

Rags.

[illegible]

Old Papers.

[illegible]

Chemical Fibre.

[illegible]

Manilla Stock.

[illegible]

[illegible]

[illegible]

[illegible]

[illegible]

CANADIAN NOTES.

A Pulp Mill is to be built at [illegible], N.B., where there is said to be a very good water power.

The Maritime Sulphite Fibre Company, Limited, Chatham, N.B., are sending out samples of their fibre.

Mr. Alexander Buntin, son of the late Mr. Alexander Buntin, of Montreal, Canada, succeeds to the interest of the late [illegible] in the wholesale stationery and paper business of Messrs. Buntin, Reid and Co., Toronto, Ont. For the past two years he has been located at Valleyfield, giving his entire time and attention to papermaking, but since acquiring his new interest he has removed to Toronto, and will hereafter give his individual time to the new connection.

WILLIAM LORD,

LORD STREET BOILER WORKS,

BURY, NEAR MANCHESTER.

MAKER OF

Spherical & Cylindrical **BOILERS**

FOR PAPERMAKERS.

THESE BOILERS are FITTED with LORD'S PATENT MANHOLES, which have been adopted by most of the LEADING HOUSES in the PAPER TRADE for EFFICIENCY and SAFETY.

THESE MANHOLES SURPASS ANYTHING YET INVENTED FOR THE PURPOSE.

H. WATSON & SONS,

HIGH BRIDGE WORKS, NEWCASTLE-ON-TYNE,

are prepared to

Close Strainer Plates

worn within 2 full Gauges wider than they were when set to work

at ½d. per sq. inch, less 30% discount.

Carriage of all Plates paid by Goods train to Newcastle.

TELEGRAMS "WATSONS, NEWCASTLE." 3808

PASTING MACHINES

F. H. BANNING,

Manufacturer of Every Kind of DUREN,

MACHINERY FOR PAPERMAKERS.

PASTING MACHINES

For Pasting in Reels of all sorts of Cardboard, Railway Tickets and Duplex Papers. The reels are dried on drying apparatus and finished by the machine after a SPECIAL PROCESS, acknowledged to be

For Pasting of Boards in Sheets with paper in Reels, with drying apparatus; and also for Boards and Paper in Sheets

THE BEST AND CHEAPEST

MACHINES NOW WORKING PRODUCING UP TO 5 TONS IN 24 HOURS

Best of References in England, Scotland, Holland, Germany, and Sweden.

SOLE AGENTS: OTTO KONIG & Co., 27, CROSS STREET, FINSBURY PAVEMENT, LONDON, E.C. 2646

THE ESPARTO TRADE.

Messrs. Ide and Christie, in their monthly circular (dated July 15th), report as follows: The close of the half year has not been marked by any material change in the condition of the market, which has for the majority of descriptions exhibited the same dulness recorded in our last issue. During the past fortnight, however, there have been symptoms of an improvement in tone, and the enquiry for the lower grades has been more active. It is hoped that this is but the beginning of an improved demand which will extend to all other descriptions with the approach of autumn, and that the depression which has hung upon the market for many months will give place to a more cheerful feeling. The imports for June, being 900 tons less than the corresponding month of 1892, swell the total shortage for the half-year to 9,500 tons, while as compared with 1891 the deficiency is over 15,000 tons. In estimating the bearing of these figures, however, it is only fair to keep in mind that the December imports were abnormally heavy, and that under ordinary circumstances of transport a proportion of these would have arrived in January. In this way the total six months' receipts would probably have been more nearly level with those of last year, although still showing a reduction on the year before. The maintenance of the volume of esparto imports, while in itself gratifying as evidence of continued trade vitality, could scarcely fail to be accompanied by some of that shrinkage of market value in which nearly all commodities have shared this year. The question is, however, whether the fall in esparto prices has not been disproportionate and unduly rapid, and rather the result of disorganisation within the trade itself than of the operation of economic conditions. While in the present state of commerce and finance, it would be rash to hazard a statement that the turning point has been already reached, there is still some ground for belief that it is not perhaps entirely distant and obscure.

Spanish imports show a reduction of 2,000 tons as compared with June last year, and the comparative six months' figures now stand as 29,632 tons to 26,157. The enquiry has been very restricted and little new business reported for any position. Advices from Spain somewhat modify the expectations of an abundant new crop. In some early districts already reaped the weight yielded is said to be 25 to 30 per cent. less than last year, and should the results from the latter lands show an equal deficiency the disturbance to calculations of those who have made heavy and distant contracts at low prices may be serious. Meantime sellers for the most part refrain from forcing offers on the market, and quotations remain nominally unchanged.

Algerian receipts have been below the average in quantity, and the total import for the half-year is 40,126, a reduction of 3,000 tons. In spite of this, however, the market is distinctly lacking in strength, and even an indication of lower prices fails to stimulate demand from buyers. There is no news of moment from the shipping ports beyond the repetition that current prices are relatively higher than on this side.

Tunisian arrivals have been small, and bring the total for the six months to 11,000 tons, as against 13,700 last year. Enquiry for new contracts has been slow, but the business done has been carried through without change in price. Susa shipments are again offered under their own name, and consumers who used this description in the past are not indisposed to renew their acquaintance with it.

Tripoli imports have been fairly full, and the total January-June figures stand at 23,399 tons against 30,173 in 1892. A fairly extensive enquiry has been experienced for distant fulfilment, and although buyers' ideas are not always workable, more tone has been imparted to business. The firmness in the market for wood pulp and the advance in straw, combined with the falling off in the Tripoli shipments, are all in the sellers' favour.

DIGESTER LININGS.

The attention of sulphite manufacturers and others is being directed by the New England Sulphite Digester Co., of 125, Kingston-street, Boston, Mass., to what is described by them as "a perfect lining for digesters," the method being that known as the Curtis and Jones artificial stone lining. It is pointed out that scientific investigations confirmed by practical experiments have shown that the main trouble with burnt brick and tile linings, as well as with the different composite mixtures advocated for making acid-resisting cement linings, has been, that the aggregations of particles were mechanically disintegrated by the want of a correct ratio between the linear and the cubical expansion at temperatures far below the maximum or even the average one attained by the contents of a sulphite digester under process. Further, it has been found that while the chemical action of heat and sulphurous acid certainly has considerable disintegrating influence, the above-mentioned mechanical action is a far more potent agent of destruction and requires means different to any hitherto employed to counteract it.

In the Curtis and Jones artificial stone linings it is claimed that the injurious effect produced by want of due proportion between the cubical and linear co-efficients of expansion are obviated by using molded (not burnt) blocks of highly compressed artificial stone which have been rendered hard and dense by a chemico-mechanical treatment with pressure and carbon dioxide, and other gases having the property of rendering the composition of which the moulded blocks are formed very acid-resisting and capable of withstanding sudden changes of temperature. The blocks are made in suitable flasks or moulds, to conform to the shape of the digester to which they are to be applied.

[illegible] of [illegible] will [illegible] of [illegible] lining [illegible] nature [illegible] lining [illegible] addi- [illegible] steel.

THESE MANU[illegible] the artificial stone [illegible] Jones are made:

H[illegible] and entirely acid

[illegible] it saves a great [illegible] condensation and en- [illegible] whole mass.

[illegible] boiling sulphite liquor [illegible] and acid-resisting power, [illegible] of a long life.

[illegible] not required repairs amounting [illegible] year per digester, and hence no loss [illegible] and dropping of production through [illegible] for repairing.

[illegible] the cheapest pulp-making machine [illegible] market. If the cost of the digester [illegible] distributed over the cost of production of [illegible] amount of pulp a digester can produce in, [illegible] or two years (which is the only com- [illegible] and practically correct method of [illegible] the value of a digester lining), this statement will be found strictly accurate.

[illegible] It has a record unequalled for tonnage and durability by anything ever used for this purpose.

ITALY, in regard to the importation of rags and waste products, publishes a ministerial decree which modifies in part the regulations of the 13th February, 1888, 29th December, 1890, 27th August, 1892, and of the 4th October, 1892, and allows the importation into Italy of the under-mentioned goods whatever their origin may be: (a) Rags compressed by hydraulic power, carried as merchandise in bales hooped with iron and bearing the marks or numbers of houses [illegible] by the authorities of the place of [illegible] as carrying on this wholesale trade. (b) Waste and pieces of new tissues [illegible] directly from spinning mills, dyeing [illegible] mills, and tailors' workshops, [illegible] wool, and the cuttings of new paper. The prohibition is still in force for [illegible] wearing apparel or bed-linen, [illegible] for trade.

[illegible] —On Saturday a man named [illegible] residing at 14, Cannon-street, [illegible] while working in the hold of the [illegible] then discharging from Oran, [illegible] injured by a heavy bale of [illegible] falling on him from a height of [illegible] feet. [illegible] was taken to the [illegible] Infirmary.

SULPHATE CELLULOSE.

To the Editor of the WORLD'S PAPER TRADE REVIEW.

SIR,—I beg to thank "An Old Beaterman" for his kind and courteous letter, and hope that he will fully understand that I am not writing in the interests of wood pulp manufacturers, but in the interests of my own craft, which I desire to benefit by my experience in wood paper manufacture.

I did not in my article say that esparto did not need the action to which it is subjected; in fact, when I said that wood was not subjected to the same violent action as esparto, I drew the line between the two fibres.

I certainly do not think that the best brands of wood fibre receive justice if mixed with any other fibre in the beater, as the treatment necessary to bring esparto to its best is so much different to that which develops wood fibre. I do not mean to say that esparto cannot be wrought with wood fibre—that is an every day experience of most paper makers—but I say that to develop wood fibre and make the very best of it, it should be beaten alone.

As to the clay-carrying powers of wood fibre compared with esparto, I will give a few examples—experiments conducted under my own personal superintendence. I have tested a 15-lb. demy fine printing esparto, containing 12 per cent. of China clay, against a 15-lb. demy sulphate of soda fine printing upon the testing machine approved of by the managers of the paper-testing department of the German Laboratory in Charlottenburg, and found 3 per cent. in favour of the wood paper, although it carried 14 per cent. of China clay. But (as I have experienced), much depends upon the intelligent manipulation of the fibre.

I do not wish "An Old Beaterman" to think for one moment that I advocate throwing over esparto. All I wish to say is that my article was written in the interests of my business—papermaking—and that I am sure if we were like other countries, viz., with some go-a-head in us we should have reaped the advantage long ago which our Yankee cousins are doing at the present day.

I again thank "Old Beaterman" for his kind and courteous letter; from such we are enabled to ventilate our views, which must be of benefit to readers generally.

Yours faithfully,

JAMES DUNBAR.

New Cathcart, near Glasgow.

THE annual summer outing of the employees of the *Daily Chronicle* Paper Mills, Sittingbourne, took place this year at Margate and Ramsgate.

World's Paper Trade Review Office,
58, Shoe Lane, London, E.C.
July 20, 1893.

TRADE NOTES.

Mr. Bottomley's Bankruptcy. — An adjourned meeting of creditors was held on Tuesday, before Mr. G. Wreford, senior official receiver. It was announced that the negotiations were proceeding very satisfactorily with the owners of various Austrian businesses which were to be transferred to the Anglo-Austrian Printing and Publishing Unions. The debtor expressed a belief that about £50,000 would eventually be recovered. A further adjournment was made to August 4th.

Manchester Municipal Technical School.—Amongst the results of the technological examinations of the City and Guilds of London Institute held last May the following medals and prizes have been gained by students of the Manchester Municipal Technical School:—W. F. Sutherst, alkali manufacturing, ordinary first, Salters' Company's second prize, value £1, and bronze medal; L. J. Melville, alkali manufacturing, ordinary first, Salters' Company's first prize of £1, and silver medal; H. E. Hunter, mechanical engineering, ordinary first, Skinner's Company's first prize of £2 and silver medal; and F. Southern, paper manufacture, ordinary first, Salters' Company's first prize of £1, and silver medal.

Great Fire in London. — Early on Tuesday morning a fire broke out on the premises of Messrs. W. Brown and Co., wholesale stationers, 38 and 40, St. Mary Axe, City, which spread rapidly in the closely-built area in which it originated, and was not got under until nearly noon, when about 50 buildings, covering an area of almost 100 yards square, had been gutted or destroyed. A firm of wholesale stationers occupied No. 42; Messrs. S. J. Saunders and Co., wholesale stationers, No. 45; and Messrs. Marchant, Singer and Co., No. 47. The premises at 1a, Bevis Marks (Messrs. Doulton, wholesale stationers) were destroyed; also No. 28 (Mr. M. Pearse, wholesale stationer); and great damage was done to buildings in Bishopsgate-avenue. Messrs. Marchant, Singer and Co. advise us that they have taken temporary premises at 22, St. Mary Axe, and have made arrangements to carry on their business as heretofore.

The Commercial Production of Ozone. —M. Emile Andreoli's system of producing ozone on a practical commercial scale is described in the *Times*. In this process, which is in operation at Messrs. Allen and Hanbury's works at Bethnal Green, metallic open ozonizers are used, in contradistinction to the closed and delicately constructed glass apparatus hitherto employed. An alternating current is produced by a dynamo, and is conducted to a transformer which converts it from the ordinary pressure of, say, 100 volts to 8,000 or 10,000 volts. This high tension current is conducted to metallic electrodes, which are constructed with thousands of points, and a condenser charge is obtained by means of which the oxygen around the the points is condensed or ozonized. M. Andreoli found that ozone was generated in far larger quantities by means of point-bearing electrodes than when the electrodes are flat surfaces on which the tension is weak and uniform. The electric tension is at its maximum when there are sharp points from which the discharge escapes, so to speak, in a continuous flow. In one form of ozonizer he uses a series of metallic tapes of small section—each edge of which is serrated like a saw, the tapes being strung, gridiron fashion, in a frame. The points give a much higher percentage of oxygen ozonized, a full 6 per cent. of the oxygen of the air being ozonized, it is stated, at the ordinary temperature and under ordinary conditions by M. Andreoli's apparatus. Other forms of ozonizers are also employed by him for particular purposes, and for utilising a continuous current. The visible effects of the change, as seen in the dark, are manifested by a beautiful violet glow, the presence of ozone being strongly apparent to the sense of smell. It was Van Marum who, in 1785, first detected this smell, which he produced by the passage of electric sparks through the air, and it was Schönhein who, in 1840, gave that odour the name of ozone when he produced it from electrolytic oxygen. Marignac and De la Rive discovered its true elementary composition later on, and Andreoli appears to have solved the question of producing it economically on a commercial scale more than a century after the first detection of its odour.

Patents and the Investing Public.— "One who Knows" writes: "Every now and then a company is floated for working patent rights which are wholly visionary. A glowing prospectus is issued, and, as in nearly every case lately, the money is subscribed, sometimes two or three times over, and then the subscribers find sooner or later that they have been grievously misled. Occasionally it happens that the bulk of the inventive talent of the country is concentrated upon a particular branch of industry, and as a result the Patent Office is flooded with applications, many of which are identical in nature and very few of which reach maturity. Some inventor thinks he has hit upon a good thing. He goes to a patent agent and duly applies for a patent. He makes a specimen, and it appears to act successfully. He looks up some company promoter, comes to an arrangement with him, and his specification (then perhaps four or five months old from the date of application) is submitted to some eminent Q.C. According to the usual formula, the eminent Q.C. certifies that he has carefully examined it and finds that it is valid. This is prominently set out in the prospectus, and this is the particular point I wish to call attention to, because the eminent Q.C. means one thing while the investing public understand him to mean another. All that the certificate means is that the application, specification, and claims are in proper form, and consequently valid until declared invalid in a court of law. The public foolishly understand it to mean, in addition, that the applicant is the first and true inventor, and that no prior application for the same invention is in existence. Every patent agent and every person who has had experience of the practice of the English patent law knows that no application can be fairly certain of being free from anticipation until it is at least from fifteen to sixteen months old. A careful search should then be made, and the prospectus should contain a copy of the certificate of search by a responsible patent agent. Without this any certificate of validity is useless and is simply misleading. The writer is not a patent agent, though he has had considerable experience with patents. Shortly there will be a rude awakening, perhaps for the promoters, certainly for the shareholders. The same thing has happened before, and is likely to occur again. It is impossible to warn the public in any particular case, but I think you will agree with me that it is a subject upon which they may with propriety be cautioned in a general way."

THE PAPER TRADE IN ROUMANIA.—According to a recent report of the Austrian Consul at Bucharest, the introduction of the new customs tariff has had the effect of considerably increasing the volume of Austrian goods imported into Roumania. So far as paper is concerned Austria sends writings of various qualities, drawing paper and white cardboard, straw paper wrappings and an ordinary quality of writings are made in the country itself. Fine drawing papers and wrappings, coloured writings and papers for fancy boxmakers come chiefly from Germany, while France sends some high-class surfaced writings and a thin variety of cardboard, chiefly used as visiting cards, &c. Belgium furnishes all kinds of cardboard, while the United Kingdom supplies the Roumanians with superior writings and drawings. There are but two paper mills in Roumania, and these turn out chiefly account book and envelope papers, playing cards and cardboards.

THE twenty-ninth annual report on alkali, &c., works by the chief inspector, has just been published. It is stated that since the union of the principal alkali manufacturers into one company, considerable changes have been brought about in the various works. A wholesome competition has been established among the managers, and the directors, having the detailed reports before them, have been able to make exact comparison between the different systems of management and working. All that was best in the practical details of manufacture, though found in practice possibly in one of the smaller works, has been adopted in all, and those which were proved on strict comparison to be wasteful have been abandoned. Thus a system of selection has been carried on, which has operated more rapidly and by a less painful method than nature's process of the survival of the fittest. The best of the managers have been promoted to the oversight of districts, and these receive guidance from the central office. Thus a uniformity of method is maintained throughout. One excellent laboratory has been established, and placed under the care of Dr. Hurter and a staff of able chemists. Here all materials are tested, and any new process that is proposed to the company receives a thorough investigation. Doubtless this unity of action has resulted in economy of work; it also affords an additional guarantee for the complete observance of the provisions of the Alkali Act.

THE Salt Union, Limited, and Messrs. Brunner, Mond and Co., chemical manufacturers, have issued notices to the effect that, in consequence of the threatened strike in the coal trade, their employees must consider themselves engaged as from day to day only. This notice affects about 5,000 hands.

ACCORDING to the Labour Correspondent of the Board of Trade the printing and kindred trades are described as being only moderately busy, and reports from some of the larger centres state that the number of unemployed is increasing.

SALES BY AUCTION.

ROCHDALE, LANCASHIRE.

Valuable Three Machine Paper Mill, with about 20 acres of Freehold Land, Water Rights, Reservoirs, and Modern Fixed Plant and Machinery therein, known as Union Paper Works, situate at Belfield, Rochdale, for sale in one lot by order of the Mortgagees.

TO BE SOLD BY AUCTION,

By Messrs.

EDWARD RUSHTON and SON,

at the MITRE HOTEL, CATHEDRAL GATES, MANCHESTER, on TUESDAY, the 1st day of August, 1893, at 3.30 for 4 o'clock in the afternoon, subject to the general conditions of sale of the Manchester Incorporated Law Society, and other conditions:

That Valuable, Well Adapted and Modern PAPER MILL known as

Union Paper Works,

Situate at Belfield, Rochdale, in the county of Lancaster, with modern fixed plant and machinery, water rights, reservoirs, and freehold land thereto belonging, and lately worked by the Union Paper Works Company, Limited. The land forming the estate is freehold and free from chief rent and comprises an area of 98,823 square yards (about 20¼ acres), of which 430 square yards are subject to a lease for 999 years from the 30th June, 1853. The mines and minerals with powers of working same are reserved, also a right to construct and use three tunnels under portion of the estate. Water is stored in six capacious reservoirs, and is obtained from the brook which runs through the estate and from other sources. The buildings are very extensive and are exceedingly well arranged for economical working. They are adapted for containing three papermaking machines and all preparation therefor. They comprise machine house, a fine lofty, well lighted building of one storey (now containing three machines and having vacant space for another machine) 130 ft. 6 in. long by 95 ft. wide; three storied building forming salle, 95 ft. by 30 ft. 6 in.; ditto forming cutting and reeling room, 130 ft. 6 in. by 30 ft. 3 in.; building of one storey forming salle, with glazed roof, 107 ft. by 18 ft.; brick building of two very lofty storeys, forming esparto store, 106 ft. 6 in. long 53 ft. wide; extensive ranges of buildings of one, two and three storeys in height, forming rag, straw and grass boiling houses, rag engine house, presse-pate house, bleach house, boiler and engine houses, mechanics', joiners' and blacksmiths' shops, evaporating house sheds, store houses, offices, lodge, chimney stacks, manager's dwelling house, and other buildings. The motive power, fixed plant and machinery are all of modern construction, a portion having been put in new within the last three or four years. The motive power consists of range of seven Lancashire steam boilers by the Oldham Boiler Works Co., John Petrie and Co., and Messrs. W. and J. Galloway and Sons, all worked at 80 lbs. pressure; two sets fuel economisers, containing 908 pipes; pair compound (tandem) steam engines, with two high-pressure cylinders, 18 in. diameter; two low-pressure cylinders, 36 in. diameter 5 ft. stroke, arranged for strap driving by the North Moor Foundry Co., Limited, 1876; beam compounded steam engine, with 30 in. and 28 in. cylinders, 6 ft. stroke, and the works are well fitted with ranges of main line and cross shafting, with all gearing, pulleys and fixings. The fixed plant and machinery embraces one 90 in. and two 72 in. paper machines, each complete with stuff and service chests, stuff and water pumps, wire and deckle frame, press and couch rolls, steam drying cylinders, damping rolls, Calenders revolving reel, steam piping, etc., by Redfern, Smith and Law and G. and W. Bertram, each machine with separate horizontal steam engine shafts and gearing; three straw and rag chopping machines, shaking machine, straw conveying worm, two 2 ton horizontal revolving rag boilers, by J. and B. [illegible]'s patent vertical grass boiler, 2½ tons c[illegible]sure, by Sinclair, Leith, 1890; verti-[illegible] revolving spherical straw boilers, 12 ft. and 9 ft. 8 in. diameter, by Park, Bury; 25 rag and straw washing, breaking, and beating engines, from 3 to 15 cwt. capacity, by James Park, Bury, Redfern, Smith and Law, and J. and R. Shorrock; two presse-pate machines, each 72 in. wide, with all necessary stuff chests, pumps, strainers, wire deckle frame, couch rolls, etc., by Bentley and Jackson; two American patent "Kingsland" refining engines, two Kollergangs patent edge runners, by Bertram and Son, 1888; J. and R. Wood's patent revolving strainer, 7 ft. 6 in. wide; Wandle's patent ditto, 7 ft. wide; E. Partington's patent duplex revolving paper cutting machine, 82 in. wide, by Walmsley, Bury; three revolving cutting machines, 90 in. and 72 in. wide, by Redfern, Smith and Law; two reeling and slitting machines, 90 in. wide; Lowe's patent single reeling machine, Furnival's patent express guillotine, 41 in. wide; 10 clay mixing, bleaching and rosin pans, complete soda recovery plant, consisting of the Chapman patent quadruple evaporator, with black liquor, by Fawcett, Preston and Co., Limited, Liverpool, 1890, with all requisite store tanks, pumps, incinerating furnaces, etc., on the latest principle; caustic and alum pans, tanks and cisterns, about 20 auxiliary steam engines and pumps, water cisterns and tanks, hoists, 10 ton lurry weighing machine, platform weighing machines, mechanics', joiners' and blacksmiths' tools, benches, partitions, and all fixtures throughout the works. The works are capable of producing over 90 tons of finished paper (printings and news) per week. There is an abundance of good water available, coal is delivered at very low rates, and trained workpeople reside in the vicinity of the works. The purchaser will have the option of taking at a valuation the whole of the loose machinery, loose articles, stock-in-trade, and materials, etc., in and upon the premises. In connection with the estate there is a building occupied as a school, which is let at £25 per annum, also a certain portion of the land is let for farming purposes at £10 per annum.

Descriptive particulars of the works, plant and machinery may be seen at the Auctioneers, 13, Norfolk Street, Manchester; or at the offices of David Smith, Esq. (the liquidator, Messrs. David Smith and Garnett), chartered accountant, Booth Street, Manchester; Messrs. Butcher and Barlow, solicitors, Bury; Messrs. Darbishire, Tatham and Worthington, solicitors, St. James's Square, Manchester; and Messrs. SLATER, HEELIS and CO., solicitors, 71, Princess Street, Manchester.

2863

The Tinfos

Paper & Wood Pulp Mills

WILL BE OFFERED

FOR SALE

AT

NOTODDEN, SKIEN, NORWAY,

ON

FRIDAY, 28TH JULY.

The Paper Mill has

ONE PAPER MACHINE with a STEAM ENGINE.

and the Wood Pulp Mill has

TWO TURBINES OF 275 HORSE-POWER

and a

DRIVING TURBINE OF 160 HORSE-POWER

Further information to be obtained of

ADVOCATE VOGT,
CHRISTIANSAND,

and

MR. G. HARTMANN,
CHRISTIANIA.

2861

Special Prepaid Advertisements

IT IS IMPORTANT that Advertisements [illegible] the Headings mentioned below should reach us by the FIRST POST on WEDNESDAY Morning to ENSURE INSERTION.

[illegible] Wanted [illegible] One Penny per Word after [illegible] ONE SHILLING. [illegible] and addresses to be paid for.

[illegible] replies addressed to the PAPER TRADE REVIEW under a number, and such replies will then be forwarded Post Free.

Advertisements appearing under the following headings:

Tenders. | Mills Wanted or To Let.
Sales by Auction. | Machinery Wanted or
Businesses Wanted. | For Sale.
Businesses for Disposal. | Situations Vacant.
Miscellaneous.

The charges are [illegible] for fifty words or under, [illegible] extra for every line or portion after. Ten words to be reckoned for each line. Names and addresses to be paid for. Payment must be made in advance, except where the advertiser has a running account, in which case [illegible] thereto.

Legal and Financial Announcements: [illegible] per Line.

SUBSCRIPTION [illegible] PER ANNUM POST FREE.

Cheques and Post-office Orders to be CROSSED [illegible] and Co., and made payable to W. JOHN [illegible].

Situation Vacant.

NIGHT FOREMAN wanted for a mill making fine printings and E.S. writings [illegible] per week.—Apply in confidence to No. [illegible], office of the WORLD'S PAPER TRADE REVIEW, 58 Shoe-lane, London, E.C. [illegible]

Situations Wanted.

ADVERTISER open for engagement as Foreman or Under-Manager, over [illegible] years with the [illegible] Paper Co., Maidstone; accustomed to news, printings, E.S. writings, and various other papers; good references.—Address Geo. [illegible], Maidstone, Kent. [illegible]

DRYERMAN, Reelerman or Cutterman seeks situation; disengaged; [illegible] years' character; married, age [illegible].—"[illegible]" [illegible] Street, Maidstone. [illegible]

FOREMAN Papermaker and Leading Millwright.—Advertisers, formerly at [illegible] Mill, Maidstone (destroyed by fire), seek situations as above, either at home or abroad. Excellent references.—Address "Papermaker," No. [illegible], or "Millwright," No. [illegible], office of the WORLD'S PAPER TRADE REVIEW, 58 Shoe Lane, London, E.C. [illegible]

MANAGER, with thorough practical experience of news, printings, [illegible], browns, &c.; also good knowledge of raw materials [illegible] machinery, desires situation. [illegible] references.—Address No. [illegible], office of the PAPER TRADE REVIEW, 58 Shoe Lane, London E.C. [illegible]

WANTED, a situation in the office of a papermaker or agent as junior traveller and [illegible], some years experience of the trade, writings and [illegible].—Address No. [illegible], office of the WORLD'S PAPER TRADE REVIEW, 58 Shoe-lane, London, E.C. [illegible]

YOUNG MAN seeks situation as Finisher, used to browns and royal hands; good references.—Address No. [illegible], office of the WORLD'S PAPER TRADE REVIEW, 58, Shoe-lane, London, E.C. [illegible]

Agencies.

EXPERIENCED Salesman calling regularly upon papermakers throughout Lancashire and the Midlands, desires additional [illegible] agency.—Address No. [illegible], Office of the WORLD'S PAPER TRADE REVIEW, 58 Shoe-lane London E.C. [illegible]

Mill to be Let or Sold.

TO be LET or SOLD, a Paper Mill at [illegible], called the Higher Mill, containing one large machine and room for another, steam engine and boilers, in good condition.—Apply for further information to the Caretaker on the premises. [illegible]

Machinery for Sale.

FOR SALE, One 8-roll Glazing Calender, four iron and four paper rolls, paper rolls [illegible] inches face [illegible] Friction Glazing Calenders, one [illegible] with steam, with or without steam engines. All these calenders made by [illegible], of [illegible], Manchester. Also one set of Plate Glazing Rolls [illegible] inches face.—All the above in good order and condition; can be seen on application to C. Townsend Hook & Co., Snodland. [illegible]

PAPER Machine Drying Cylinders (three [illegible] in. long, [illegible] in. dia., with connections, to be sold cheap.—[illegible] Limited, [illegible]. [illegible]

ON SALE,

ONE

75in. FOURDRINIER

PAPERMAKING MACHINE

With First and Second Presses

15 CYLINDERS 3 ft. 8 in. dia., 7 ft. 2 in. on Face.

STUFF and BACK WATER PUMPS;

AND

One STACK of CALENDERS

BY J. ROBINSON & CO.,

Containing Four Chilled Rolls and Two Paper Rolls;

ALSO

STEAM ENGINE

To Drive Same, 11 inch Cylinder, 18 inch Stroke.

THE MACHINE CAN BE SEEN WORKING

Complete Specifications will be forwarded on application to the

Ramsbottom Paper Mill Co

LIMITED,

RAMSBOTTOM, NEAR MANCHESTER.

MC

[illegible] and Published EVERY FRIDAY
AT [illegible], LONDON, E.C.,
By W. [illegible] STONHILL.
ESTABLISHED 1876.

SUBSCRIPTION: £2 PER ANNUM.
POST FREE TO ALL PARTS OF THE GLOBE.
SINGLE COPIES SIXPENCE.

TELEGRAMS: "STONHILL—LONDON."

FRIDAY, JULY 21, 1893.

THE annual meeting of the Society of Chemical Industry at Liverpool went off with considerable *eclat*. Sir John Evans, K.C.B., F.R.S., as president, gave a very comprehensive address, pointing out how much the various industries and manufactures depended upon chemical knowledge. This important fact has been forced upon papermakers particularly during the last decade, it being found necessary in successful competition to throw over rule-of-thumb methods and work on scientific principles.

ABOUT eighty of the members of the Society visited Widnes, and at the invitation of the United Alkali Company, inspected two important branches of their undertaking, which were formerly owned by Messrs. G. Pilkington and Company, and Messrs. E. Sullivan and Company. The party witnessed the various processes in the manufacture of saltcake, soda ash, caustic soda, bleaching powder, and sulphur by the Chance process. Amongst other places visited were the Sunlight Soap Works (Messrs. Lever Bros.). At the dinner in the evening the president (Sir John Evans) occupied the chair, being supported by Mr. E. C. C. Stamford (the president elect), Mr. H. Brunner, Mr. Ludwig Mond, Dr. Hurter, Messrs. E. K. and S. K. Muspratt, there being altogether 160 guests present.

SOME time ago the idea was mooted in these columns of the advisability of starting a Society of Papermakers' Chemists. Several correspondents were in favour of such an institution. It was contended, however, that as there were not many chemists engaged solely in the paper trade, it would be advisable for engineers and chemists to combine, the idea being to hold periodical meetings, to discuss subjects of importance, and to advance the interests of the trade—by bringing scientific and practical knowledge to bear—in every direction possible. Such a development, we think, would be in the right direction.

BRITISH imports of foreign paper amounted last year to £2,412,001, or £882,307 above the total exports. British exports of paper to the value of £1,162,188 go to the colonies, and as a matter of fact, very little is shipped to foreign countries. The following comparison, no doubt, will prove of interest:—

	Foreign Paper Imported by Great Britain.	British Paper Imported by Foreign Countries.
Writings, printings, and envelopes ...	£435,812	£282,810
Hangings	38,883	60,989
Pasteboard, Millboard, &c. ...	1,482,055	13,123
Other kinds	453,545	120,176
Totals ...	£2,410,245	£477,098

Paper received from British possessions during 1892 is returned at the value of £1,756. To gauge the extent of foreign paper consumption in this country, allowance must be made for the re-exports. In 1892 the British "exports of foreign paper" reached the value of £88,562, the distribution being as follows:—

	To Foreign Countries.	To British Possessions.
Writings, printings, and envelopes ...	£7,994	£11,118
Hangings	1,208	277
Pasteboard, Millboard, &c. ...	24,171	29,404
Other kinds	2,674	11,716
Totals ...	£36,047	£52,515

Deducting £88,562 (for re-exports) from £2,412,001 (the total value of imports), the remainder—£2,323,440—may be taken as representing the annual British consumption of foreign paper.

IT is not believed that the present labour troubles in the coal trade will be of long duration. However, in several districts the miners affected by the proposed reduction of wages have during the past day or two intimated their determination to resist. At a meeting of the executive of the Miners' Federation held at Birmingham on Tuesday in preparation for the following day's conference, it was stated that large numbers of men have not received any notice of a reduction, and it was agreed that in all such cases the men should be allowed to continue at work.

ALTHOUGH the dispute at the Hendon Paper Works was lately settled by mutual conference, there appears to be some hitch in the interpretation of the clause "that all old hands be re-instated as soon as possible." It is to be hoped that the dispute will not be reopened, but satisfactory terms arranged and adhered to for the common good of all concerned.

THE tenth annual outing of the Glasgow Paper Men was a red letter day. Graced with the presence of Mr. John Tod, a host in himself, everything went off in a vivacious and most enjoyable manner. The Manchester Paper Traders held their third annual picnic on Saturday, the 8th inst., and the London Stationers a few weeks ago. These annual re-unions ought to be strongly supported, as they invoke the spirit of good will and hearty co-operation amongst the representatives of the paper and allied trades thus brought together.

M. EMILE ANDREOLI'S process for the commercial production of ozone is described on another page. The value of ozone as a deodoriser and disinfectant is well known, and it is conceded by all who are familiar with its character that it is capable of rendering many valuable services, not only for therapeutic or sanitary purposes, but in chemistry and in several industrial processes. The difficulty, however, has hitherto been the economical production of this valuable agent on a commercial scale. The subject has for many years passed formed the study of most of the leading chemists of this and other countries. Bunsen years ago pointed out that there were hundreds of uses for ozone if only it could be made in large quantities at a low price; while Faraday, in 1851, in a lecture before the Royal Society, pointed out a number of useful results attending its use, and affirmed it to be a most ready and powerful oxidiser. The late Dr. Werner Siemens appears to have been the first, in 1857, to construct an electrical ozonising tube, and he has been followed by Von Babo, Beanes, Ladd, and many others. The practical results, however, appear to have been but limited, and the only outcome, so far as we are aware, is the production of small quantities of ozone in closed tubes and its limited use in some of the hospitals on the Continent. Among others who have long and closely followed up this question is M. Emile Andreoli, whose researches have led to the perfecting by him of a system of producing ozone on a practical commercial scale with, it is stated, marked economy.

COMMERCIAL travellers in Sweden would do well to give attention to the following communication received from the Foreign Office:—"A fresh case has recently been brought to the notice of Her Majesty's Government of an English gentleman being subjected to a heavy fine by the Stockholm Police Court for having merely concluded a contract with a house of business in that city for the supply of certain merchandise for consumption in Great Britain. The gentleman in question had inquired at the hotel where he was staying whether the transaction he contemplated entering into was lawful or otherwise, and he was assured that it was legal. More trustworthy advice should, however, be obtained by persons about to engage in mercantile transactions in Sweden, as it is possible that an opinion in such cases might occasionally be given by persons who were seeking to act as informers, with the view of participating in the reward for notice of a breach of the law on the subject. Her Majesty's Consul at Stockholm urges the importance of gentlemen engaged in business first consulting him if they are in any doubt as to whether a licence is needed or not. The present tendency is for commercial travellers and others to invoke the advice and assistance of Her Majesty's Consul only after some difficulty has arisen, and at a time when his intervention can accordingly be of but little practical service to them."

THE recent fire at Tovil Upper Mills, Maidstone, has proved very unfortunate in cutting off a source of employment. Some 300 hands are thrown out of work, and as far as can be ascertained there is no immediate prospect of a start being made in the near future by the Tovil Paper Company, Limited.

WORLD'S PAPER TRADE REVIEW OFFICE,
58, SHOE LANE, LONDON, E.C.
JULY 20, 1893.

MARKET REPORT

and RECORD of IMPORTS

Of Foreign Rags, Wood Pulp, Esparto, Paper, Millboards, Strawboards, &c., at the Ports of London, Liverpool, Southampton, Bristol, Hull, Fleetwood, Middlesborough, Glasgow, Grangemouth, Granton, Dundee, Leith, Dover, Folkestone, and Newhaven for the WEEK ENDING JULY 19.

From SPECIAL Sources and Telegrams.

Telegrams—"STONEHILL, LONDON."

CHEMICALS.—The market is steady, with a well-maintained demand. BLEACHING POWDER is rather quiet at £8 5s. f.o.b. Tyne; soft-wood, £8 [illegible] to £8 [illegible] f.o.b. Liverpool; and hard-wood £8 10s. to £8 15s. CAUSTIC SODA, 77 per cent., stands at £10 15s. Tyne. SODA CRYSTALS are firm at £2 5s. to £2 10s. SODA ASH is dull. Large forward sales have been made in [illegible], which [illegible] delivery. [illegible] FLAX

Prices are nominally as follows:

				£	s.	d.
Alkali, [illegible]	[illegible]	f.o.b. works	[illegible]	5	10	0
[illegible]	[illegible]		[illegible]	5	5	0
[illegible]		f.o.b. Liverpool	[illegible]	5	12	6
Alum (ground), [illegible]	[illegible]	Liverpool	[illegible]	5	7	6
	[illegible]	" "	[illegible]	5	17	6
" "	[illegible]	Hull	[illegible]	5	5	0
		Goole	[illegible]	5	5	0
Alum (lump)		f.o.b. Liverpool	[illegible]	4	17	6
	[illegible]	"	[illegible]	5	0	0
	[illegible]	Hull	[illegible]	4	15	0
	"	Goole	[illegible]	4	15	0
	"	[illegible]	[illegible]	5	[illegible]	0
		f.o.b. Glasgow	[illegible]	5	[illegible]	[illegible]
Alumina sulphate, [illegible]		f.o.b. Tyne		4	2	6
	[illegible]			3	17	6
Aluminoferric cake, [illegible]		Liverpool		2	15	0
	[illegible]			3	2	6
Aluminous cake, [illegible]		Glasgow		2	15	0
	[illegible]			3	2	6
Aluminous cake, [illegible]		Manchester	[illegible]	4	7	6
		Newcastle	[illegible]	4	10	0
		London	[illegible]	[illegible]	0	0
	bags		[illegible]	4	17	[illegible]
Blanc Fixe		f.o.b. Tyne	net	7	10	0
Bleaching [illegible]			net	8	5	0
(soft wood)		f.o.r. Lancs.	net	8	5	0
(hard wood)		f.o.b. Liverpool	net	8	10	0
		landed London	2½%	9	5	0
Borax (crystals)		" "	net	[illegible]	0	0
powdered		" "	net	30	0	0
[illegible], [illegible]%		f.o.r. Lancs.	net	8	7	6
[illegible]%		f.o.b. Liverpool	net	8	[illegible]	0
[illegible] [illegible]%		" "	net	5	10	0
		f.o.b. Tyne	net	6	5	0
Carbonated Ash, [illegible]%		" "	3½%	6	10	0
[illegible]%		" "	3½%	5	15	0
" [illegible]%		f.o.r. Widnes	3½%	6	7	6
[illegible]%		" "	3½%	5	12	6
Caustic White 77%		f.o.r. Newcastle	net	10	15	0
" " 77%		f.o.b. Tyne	net	10	15	0
" " 74%	...	f.o.b. Liverpool	net	10	15	0
" " 70%	...	" "	net	9	15	0
" " 70%	...	" Hull	net	10	0	0
" " 70%	...	f.o.r. London	net	9	15	0
" " 70%	...	" Lancs.	net	9	17	6
" " 60%	...	" London	net	8	15	0
" " 60%	...	f.o.b. Liverpool	net	8	15	0

				£	s.	d.
Chloride of Barium	...	f.o.b. Tyne	net	7	10	0
Hypo-Sulphite of Soda...		f.o.r. Tyne		5	15	0
" " 10-ton lots		ex ship Liverp'l	net	6	10	0
Oxalic Acid ...	... ...	f.o.b. Liverpool	3½%	per lb		½
Salt Cake	... ...	" works	net	1	10	0
Soda Ash, 58%	... ...	f.o.b. Tyne	net	4	17	6
" 52%	... ...	ex ship Thames	1%	5	5	0
" 52%	... ...	f.o.b. Liverpool	1%	5	0	0
Soda Crystals	... ...	" Tyne	net	2	5	0
" "	... ...	ex ship Thames	2½%	2	17	6
" "	... ...	f.o.b. Liverpool	net	2	17	6
Sulphur, roll	... ...	f.o.r. works	2½%	7	17	6
" flowers	... ...	" "	2½%	9	10	0
" recovered	...	" "	2½%	4	2	6
Sulphate of Ammonia	"	" "	2½%	13	2	6
" of Copper	...	" Liverpool	5%	15	0	0

FOREIGN.—F.o.b. Continental port:

	£	s.	d.
Alkali, 58% 2-cwt. bags £6 10/0; 10-cwt. casks ...	6	15	6
Caustic Soda, 70-72%	11	12	0
Hypo-Sulphite of Soda 10-ton lots 7/10/0; kegs ...	7	10	6
Sulphate of Alumina 7-8 cwt. casks net c.i.f. Ldn	4	7	6
Blanc Fixe (c.i.f. London)	7	12	6

ESPARTO.—The market is quiet, and influenced by the recurrence of the holiday season. Prices are unchanged, and sellers disposed to refuse further reductions.

Prices c.i.f. London and Leith, or f.o.r. Cardiff, Garston and Tyne Docks are nominally as follows:

		£	s.	d.		£	s.	d.
Spanish—	Fair to Good ...	5	10	0	to	5	15	0
"	Fine to Best ...	5	17	6	"	6	0	0
Oran—	Fair to Good ...	3	12	6	"	3	17	6
"	First Quality ...	4	0	0	"	4	2	6
Tripoli—	Hand-picked ...	3	17	6	"	4	2	6
"	Fair Average ...	3	12	6	"	3	15	0
Bona & Philippeville ...		4	0	0	"	4	2	6

IMPORTS of ESPARTO.

Quantity	From	Importer	Port.
3830 bales	Aguilas	Guardbridge Paper Co	Dundee
1050 tons	Oran	F. Brichta & Co	Granton
440 "	"	To order	Boness
269 "	"	C. J. Turcan & Co	Granton
3732 bales	"	Morris & Co.	Fleetwood
50 tons	"	Thin & Sinclair	"

CHEMICAL WOOD PULPS.—SULPHITE is still scarce even at top prices, and SODA which has been easy in price for some time has commenced to move upwards in sympathy with SULPHITE, and still higher prices are anticipated.

Prices, ex steamer, London, Hull, Newcastle, Leith and Glasgow are nominally as follows:

		£	s.	d.		£	s.	d.
SODA, Unbleached, Common	...	10	0	0	to	10	10	0
" " Extra...	...	10	10	0	"	11	0	0
" Half-Bleached	... ...	12	10	0	"	14	0	0
SULPHATE, Unbleached, Common		10	10	0	"	11	0	0
" Extra ...	... ...	11	0	0	"	12	0	0
" Half-Bleached	... ...	13	10	0	"	14	0	0
" Bleached	... ...	15	0	0	"	16	0	0
SULPHITE, Unbleached, Common		10	15	0	to	11	0	0
" Superior	... ...	11	10	0	"	12	10	0
" " 50% moisture, d.w.		11	10	0	"	12	2	6
" Extra ...	... ...	13	0	0	"	14	0	0
" Bleached, moist	... ...					16	10	0
" Unbleached, English, del. Lancs.	...					10	15	0
" " " No. 1, ex mills, Ldn.						10	10	0
" " " No. 2. " "						9	15	0

MECHANICAL WOOD PULPS.—The market on the whole is very firm, most producers being out-sold for this year, consequently nearly all arrivals are due on existing contracts. We hear of one large seller quoting delivered prices which equal 55s. usual discount f.o.r. Fleetwood. This is for moist pine for next year's delivery, and the opinion is current that such a figure will be about the ruling one for contracts for 1894. Dry pine is quoted £6 west coast, and we understand some are willing to sell at a shade less. For prompt delivery or even delivery this year better prices are obtained, but it is a case of speculators being forced to buy to meet engagements.

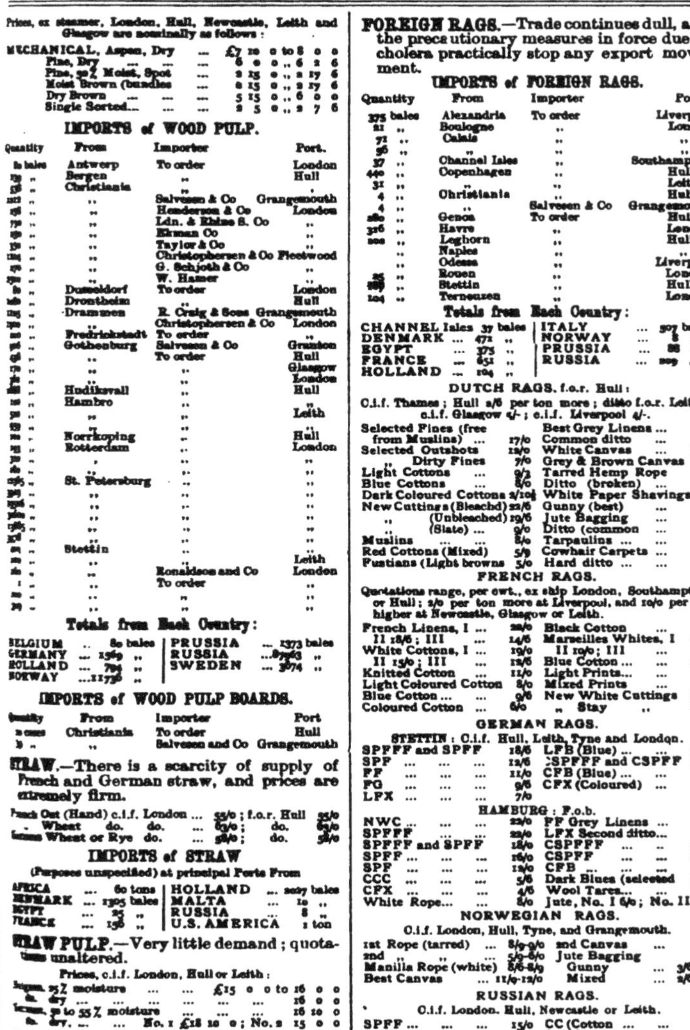

Prices, ex steamer, London, Hull, Newcastle, Leith and Glasgow are nominally as follows :

MECHANICAL, Aspen, Dry	...	£7 10 0	to	8 0 0
Pine, Dry	...	6 0 0	,,	6 2 6
Pine, 50% Moist, Spot	...	2 15 0	,,	2 17 6
Moist Brown (bundles	...	2 15 0	,,	2 17 6
Dry Brown	...	5 15 0	,,	6 0 0
Single Sorted... ...	...	2 5 0	,,	2 7 6

IMPORTS of WOOD PULP.

Quantity	From	Importer	Port.
80 bales	Antwerp	To order	London
[illegible] ,,	Bergen	,,	Hull
[illegible] ,,	Christiania	,,	,,
[illegible] ,,	,,	Salvesen & Co	Grangemouth
[illegible] ,,	,,	Henderson & Co	London
[illegible] ,,	,,	Ldn. & Rhine S. Co	,,
[illegible] ,,	,,	Ekman Co	,,
[illegible] ,,	,,	Taylor & Co	,,
[illegible] ,,	,,	Christophersen & Co	Fleetwood
[illegible] ,,	,,	G. Schjoth & Co	,,
[illegible] ,,	,,	W. Hamer	,,
[illegible] ,,	Dusseldorf	To order	London
[illegible] ,,	Drontheim	,,	Hull
[illegible] ,,	Drammen	R. Craig & Sons	Grangemouth
[illegible] ,,	,,	Christophersen & Co	London
[illegible] ,,	Fredrickstadt	To order	,,
[illegible] ,,	Gothenburg	Salvesen & Co	Granton
[illegible] ,,	,,	To order	Hull
[illegible] ,,	,,	,,	Glasgow
[illegible] ,,	,,	,,	London
[illegible] ,,	Hudiksvall	,,	Hull
[illegible] ,,	Hambro	,,	,,
[illegible] ,,	,,	,,	Leith
[illegible] ,,	,,	,,	,,
[illegible] ,,	Norrkoping	,,	Hull
[illegible] ,,	Rotterdam	,,	London
[illegible] ,,	,,	,,	,,
[illegible] ,,	,,	,,	,,
[illegible] ,,	St. Petersburg	,,	,,
[illegible] ,,	,,	,,	,,
[illegible] ,,	,,	,,	,,
[illegible] ,,	,,	,,	,,
[illegible] ,,	,,	,,	,,
[illegible] ,,	,,	,,	,,
[illegible] ,,	Stettin	,,	,,
[illegible] ,,	,,	,,	Leith
[illegible] ,,	,,	Ronaldson and Co	London
1 ,,	,,	To order	,,
[illegible] ,,	,,	,,	,,
[illegible] ,,	,,	,,	,,

Totals from Each Country:

BELGIUM ..	80 bales	PRUSSIA ...	1373 bales
GERMANY ...	1569 ,,	RUSSIA ...	87963 ,,
HOLLAND ...	794 ,,	SWEDEN ...	3074 ,,
NORWAY ...	11736 ,,		

IMPORTS of WOOD PULP BOARDS.

Quantity	From	Importer	Port
2 cases	Christiania	To order	Hull
3 ,,	,,	Salvesen and Co	Grangemouth

STRAW.—There is a scarcity of supply of French and German straw, and prices are extremely firm.

French Oat (Hand) c.i.f. London ...	55/0	;	f.o.r. Hull	55/0
,, Wheat do. do. ...	63/0	;	do.	63/0
German Wheat or Rye do. ...	58/0	;	do.	58/0

IMPORTS of STRAW

(Purposes unspecified) at principal Ports From

AFRICA ...	60 tons	HOLLAND ...	2027 bales
DENMARK ...	1305 bales	MALTA ...	10 ,,
EGYPT ...	25 ,,	RUSSIA ...	8 ,,
FRANCE ...	156 ,,	U.S. AMERICA	1 ton

STRAW PULP.—Very little demand; quotations unaltered.

Prices, c.i.f. London, Hull or Leith :

Belgian, 25% moisture	£15 0 0	to	16 0 0
do. dry			16 0 0
German, 50 to 55% moisture			16 10 0
do. dry ... ... No. 1 £18 10 0 ; No. 2			15 0 0

JUTE.—Market firmer.

Good White £15 0 to 16 0	Common ...	£10 10 to 11 0
Good — 13 0	Rejections...	8 0 ,, 9 0
Medium — 12 0 ,, 12 10	Cuttings ...	£5 to 6 0

FOREIGN RAGS.—Trade continues dull, and the precautionary measures in force due to cholera practically stop any export movement.

IMPORTS of FOREIGN RAGS.

Quantity	From	Importer	Port.
375 bales	Alexandria	To order	Liverpool
21 ,,	Boulogne	,,	London
71 ,,	Calais	,,	,,
56 ,,	,,	,,	,,
37 ,,	Channel Isles	,,	Southampton
440 ,,	Copenhagen	,,	Hull
31 ,,	,,	,,	Leith
4 ,,	Christiania	,,	Hull
4 ,,	,,	Salvesen & Co	Grangemouth
280 ,,	Genoa	To order	Hull
326 ,,	Havre	,,	London
200 ,,	Leghorn	,,	Hull
,,	Naples	,,	,,
,,	Odessa	,,	Liverpool
25 ,,	Rouen	,,	London
[illegible] ,,	Stettin	,,	Hull
104 ,,	Terneuzen	,,	London

Totals from Each Country:

CHANNEL Isles	37 bales	ITALY ...	507 bales
DENMARK ...	472 ,,	NORWAY ...	8 ,,
EGYPT ...	375 ,,	PRUSSIA ...	88 ,,
FRANCE ...	651 ,,	RUSSIA ...	209 ,,
HOLLAND ...	104 ,,		

DUTCH RAGS. f.o.r. Hull :

C.i.f. Thames ; Hull 2/6 per ton more ; ditto f.o.r. Leith c.i.f. Glasgow 4/- ; c.i.f. Liverpool 4/-.

Selected Fines (free from Muslins) ...	17/0	Best Grey Linens ...	9/0
		Common ditto ...	5/6
Selected Outshots	12/0	White Canvas ...	15/0
,, Dirty Fines	7/0	Grey & Brown Canvas	9/9
Light Cottons ...	9/3	Tarred Hemp Rope	8/0
Blue Cottons ...	8/0	Ditto (broken) ...	5/3
Dark Coloured Cottons	2/10½	White Paper Shavings	7/9
New Cuttings (Bleachd)	22/6	Gunny (best) ...	4/9
,, (Unbleached)	19/6	Jute Bagging ...	3/6
,, (Slate) ...	9/0	Ditto (common ...	3/0
Muslins	8/0	Tarpaulins	4/0
Red Cottons (Mixed)	5/9	Cowhair Carpets ...	2/9
Fustians (Light browns	5/0	Hard ditto	3/0

FRENCH RAGS.

Quotations range, per cwt., ex ship London, Southampton, or Hull ; 2/0 per ton more at Liverpool, and 10/0 per ton higher at Newcastle, Glasgow or Leith.

French Linens, I ...	22/0	Black Cotton ...	4/0
II 18/6 ; III ...	14/6	Marseilles Whites, I	16/0
White Cottons, I ...	19/0	II 10/0 ; III ...	7/6
II 15/0 ; III ...	12/6	Blue Cotton	11/0
Knitted Cotton ...	11/0	Light Prints... ...	9/0
Light Coloured Cotton	8/0	Mixed Prints ...	6/0
Blue Cotton	9/6	New White Cuttings	23/0
Coloured Cotton ...	6/0	,, Stay ,,	21/0

GERMAN RAGS.

STETTIN : C.i.f. Hull, Leith, Tyne and London.

SPFFF and SPFF	18/6	LFB (Blue)	10/
SPF	12/6	CSPFFF and CSPFF	12/0
FF	11/0	CFB (Blue)	8/0
FG	9/6	CFX (Coloured) ...	5/0
LFX	7/0		

HAMBURG : F.o.b.

NWC	22/0	FF Grey Linens ...	9/0
SPFFF	22/0	LFX Second ditto...	8/0
SPFFF and SPFF	18/0	CSPFFF	17/3
SPFF	16/0	CSPFF	11/3
SPF	12/0	CFB	8/0
CCC	5/6	Dark Blues (selected	11/9
CFX	4/6	Wool Tares... ...	8/0
White Rope... ...	8/0	Jute, No. I 6/0 ; No. II	5/6

NORWEGIAN RAGS.

C.i.f. London, Hull, Tyne, and Grangemouth.

1st Rope (tarred) ...	8/9-9/0	2nd Canvas ...	8/0
2nd ,, ,, ...	5/9-6/0	Jute Bagging	
Manilla Rope (white)	8/6-8/9	Gunny ...	3/6-3/9
Best Canvas ...	11/9-12/0	Mixed ...	2/6-3/0

RUSSIAN RAGS.

C.i.f. London, Hull, Newcastle or Leith.

SPFF	15/0	CC (Cotton	5/3
SPF	13/6	Jute I	3/6
FG	10/6	,, II...	2/3
LFB	9/6	Rope I...	9/9
FF	8/3	,, II	5/9
LFX	7/3		

[illegible]

[illegible] FLAX AND HEMP WASTE.

[illegible] Flax Waste, [illegible]; [illegible]

[illegible] RAGS.—LONDON: Trade extremely dull.—BRISTOL: There is only a moderate business passing.—MANCHESTER: Limited enquiry.—EDINBURGH: The demand is rather slow, a good many of the mills being shut down for annual repairs just now. No change in prices.—DUBLIN: Market quiet.

LONDON:

[illegible] White Linens	[illegible]	Canvas No. 1	[illegible]
[illegible]	[illegible]	No. 2	[illegible]
[illegible]	[illegible]	No. 3	[illegible]
[illegible]	[illegible]	Mixed Rope	[illegible]
[illegible]	[illegible]	White Rope	[illegible]
London [illegible]	[illegible]	White Manilla Rope	[illegible]
[illegible]	[illegible]	[illegible] Rope	[illegible]
London Thirds	[illegible]	Bagging	[illegible]
[illegible]	[illegible]	[illegible]	[illegible]
Light Prints	[illegible]		

BRISTOL.

Fines	[illegible]	Clean Canvas	[illegible]
Outshots	[illegible]	[illegible]	[illegible]
Seconds	[illegible]	Light Prints	[illegible]
Thirds	[illegible]	Hemp [illegible] Rope	[illegible]
Mixed Bagging	[illegible]	Tarred Manilla	[illegible]

MANCHESTER.

Fines	[illegible]	Blues	[illegible]
Outshots (best)	[illegible]	Bagging	[illegible]
(ordinary)	[illegible]	(common)	[illegible]
Seconds	[illegible]	W. Manilla Rope	[illegible]
Thirds	[illegible]	[illegible]	[illegible]

EDINBURGH.

Superfines	[illegible]	Black Linens	[illegible]
Outshots	[illegible]	W. Manilla Rope	[illegible]
Mixed Fines	[illegible]	Tarred Ditto	[illegible]
[illegible] Seconds	[illegible]	Hemp Rope	[illegible]
[illegible]	[illegible]	Rope Ends (new)	[illegible]
Prints	[illegible]	old	[illegible]
Linens (best)	[illegible]	Bagging	[illegible]
[illegible]	[illegible]	[illegible]	[illegible]

DUBLIN.

White Linens	[illegible]	Mill Bagging	[illegible]
Fines	[illegible]	White Manilla	[illegible]
Seconds	[illegible]	Tarred Hemp	[illegible]
Light Prints	[illegible]	Bagging	[illegible]
[illegible]	[illegible]	Mixed Ropes	[illegible]
[illegible]	[illegible]		

WASTE PAPERS.—Fair enquiry and prices firmly maintained.

[illegible]

[illegible] Market firm.

[illegible]

STARCH.—Business fairly good, prices rather easier.

F.o.r. London, [illegible]

[illegible]—[illegible], £20 0/-. Powder [illegible]. [illegible] £[illegible]
[illegible]—[illegible], £21 0/-. [illegible]

[illegible]

Rice—[illegible] (in [illegible]), £[illegible]; [illegible] £19 0/-; [illegible]
Dextrine—£16 0/

SIZING.—Glues are in request at well-maintained prices.

English Gelatines			per cwt.	[illegible]
Foreign				[illegible]
Fine [illegible] Glues				[illegible]
Long Scotch Glues				[illegible]
Common				[illegible]
"Town" Glues				[illegible]
"[illegible]" Glues				[illegible]
Foreign Glues				[illegible]
Bone Size				[illegible]
Gelatine Size				[illegible]
Dry S.A. Pieces				[illegible]
English Pieces				[illegible]
Wet				[illegible]
Sheep Pieces				[illegible]
Buffalo Hide Shavings				[illegible]
Picker Waste				[illegible]

COLOURS.—Very small demand.

[illegible]

MINERALS.—CHINA CLAY of the best quality is in fair request. FRENCH CHALK steady. BARYTES are without any noteworthy movement. PATENT HARDENINGS and MINERAL WHITE are in moderate demand.

[illegible] White [illegible]

Superfine	[illegible]
[illegible]	[illegible]
[illegible]	[illegible]
Seconds	[illegible]
Third	[illegible]

China Clay, in bulk, f.o.b. [illegible] [illegible] per ton extra f.o.b. London, in casks [illegible] per ton.
Superior Hardening, f.o.r. works [illegible]
Patent Crystal Hardening, delivered at mills £[illegible] to £[illegible]
Patent Hardening [illegible] f.o.r. London, [illegible]
[illegible] f.o.b. Liverpool, [illegible]
Magnesite [illegible] per ton.
Magnesite (containing [illegible] Carbonate of Magnesia), [illegible] £[illegible]
[illegible], £[illegible]
[illegible] £[illegible]
[illegible] London, Liverpool and Glasgow
Barytes (Carbonate) [illegible]
Barytes (Sulphate), [illegible] White [illegible] No. 1 [illegible]; No. 2 [illegible] No. 3 [illegible]. [illegible] Antwerp, AF, [illegible] AB [illegible], BB [illegible]; CB, [illegible]
French and Italian Chalk ([illegible] Brand, Antwerp), [illegible] Flower O [illegible] c.i.f. London [illegible] Flower OO [illegible] Flower DDL [illegible] Angel White [illegible] prime quality [illegible] superfine [illegible]
Bauxite, [illegible] Quality [illegible]; seconds [illegible], thirds [illegible]
[illegible], Liverpool [illegible]
[illegible] Antwerp) [illegible] Seconds 37/-

LIME.—Best White Buxton Lime, hand-picked, f.o.r. works, is quoted at [illegible] per ton [illegible]

DIRECTORY.

Names and Addresses under this heading will be charged for at the rate of 50/- per annum (52 insertions) for each card of two lines or under. Each additional line £1 extra.

ALUMINOUS CAKE.

The ALUM, CHINA CLAY and VITRIOL Co., Lim., 63, Queen Victoria Street, London, E.C. Works: Rainham-on-Thames. Telegrams—"Chinnock, London."

ANALYTICAL.

WILLIAMS, ROWLAND, F.I.C., F.C.S., 28, Pall Mall, Manchester.

ARTESIAN WELLS.

BATCHELOR, Richard D., Artesian and Consulting Well Engineer, 73, Queen Victoria Street, London, E.C., and at Chatham. 5713

ISLER, C., & Co., Bear Lane, Southwark, S.E.

LE GRAND & SUTCLIFF, Magdala Works, 125, Bunhill Row, E.C.

BOILER COVERING.

LONSDALES, Boiler Coverers, Blackburn, will send a sample cask of their Patent Plastic Cork Covering to any Paper Mill in Great Britain—5 cwt. cask for 25/- (carriage paid).

CHINA CLAY.

The ALUM, CHINA CLAY and VITRIOL Co., Lim., 63, Queen Victoria Street, London, E.C. Mines: Ruddle and Colchester, St. Austell, Cornwall. Telegrams—"Chinnock, London."

ROGERS, J., & Co., Truro, Cornwall.—Agents: Taylor, Sommerville & Co., 83, Queen Victoria Street, E.C., and at 26, Princes Street, Edinburgh.

W. SINGLETON BIRCH & SONS, Lim., 15, Upton Street, Manchester. Mines: Rosevear, St. Austell, Cornwall. 2276

COLOURS.

CARDWELL, J. L., & Co., Commercial Buildings, 15, Cross Street, Manchester. Specialties: Mineral Black, Ven. Red, Ochres and Umbers. 5394

[illegible]

[illegible]

MULLER, A. E., [illegible] Fenchurch Street, London, E.C.

[illegible] MACHINES &c.

[illegible] MACHINES [illegible] the most improved principle [illegible] Paragon [illegible] Turbines [illegible] Manchester. [illegible]

[illegible]

[illegible] Fibre Esparto, and General Produce [illegible] Mark Lane, E.C.

[illegible] or TERRA ALBA.

[illegible] & Co., [illegible] Mills, [illegible] Street, Manchester [illegible] of Aluminous Cake.

[illegible] JOHN, & Co., Carlisle. [illegible]

STEEL.

[illegible] WM., & SONS, Sheffield. [illegible] Bed Irons, Plates, Cutter Knives, Doctor Blades, &c. [illegible]

STRAW.

[illegible] & Co., [illegible] House, [illegible] Street Within, E.C., French, German, and Dutch [illegible], Wheat, Rye, &c., compressed. [illegible]

UNDERWOOD, E., & SON, Limited, [illegible], London, W. Press-packed [illegible], Wheat, or Rye Straw, delivered to the chief British ports or railway stations.

TALC (French and Italian Chalk).

SOUHEUR, JEAN, Antwerp. All Minerals, Silex de Silex, Barytes (superior and common), Carbonate of Lime, Blacklead, &c. British Agent: A. E. Muller, 9, Fenchurch Street, London, E.C. Agent for Liverpool and Manchester: C. M. Austin, [illegible], near Widnes.

RAGS.

CHALMERS, E., & Co., Lim., [illegible], Leith.
MULLER, A. E., 9, Fenchurch Street, London, E.C.
WERTHEIM, A., & Co., Hamburg.

[illegible]

The ALUM, CHINA CLAY and VITROIL Co., Lim. 69, Queen Victoria Street, London, E.C. Telegrams—"[illegible], London."

WOOD PULP.

FRIIS, N., & Co., [illegible], Carl Johans Gade, Christiania, Norway.
GOTTSTEIN, H., & Co., 39, Mark Lane, London, E.C., and at New York.
GRANT, W., & Co., 17, Baltic Street, Leith. Agents for best shippers. Sulphite and Sulphate, Mechanical, Pine, Brown, Aspen.
MATTHIESSEN, CHR., Christiania, Norway.
MULLER, A. E., 9, Fenchurch Street, London, E.C.
The SULPHITE PULP Company, Limited, [illegible], Gordon Street, Glasgow.
WERTHEIM, A., & Co., Hamburg.

PAPER EXPORTS & IMPORTS.

[illegible]

EXPORTS TO

	Printings.	Writings.	Other Kinds.
AUSTRALIA ...	[illegible] cwts	[illegible] cwts	[illegible] cwts.
AFRICA	—	[illegible]	—
BELGIUM	16	—	—
B. GUIANA	—	48	25
B WEST INDIES	[illegible]	21	25
CANADA	[illegible]	[illegible]	4
CAPE COLONY	[illegible]	46	[illegible]
CHANNEL ISLES	27	—	—
CHINA	[illegible]	[illegible]	[illegible]
DENMARK	—	6	—
FRANCE	[illegible]	[illegible]	7
GERMANY	3	—	[illegible]
HOLLAND	[illegible]	—	5
INDIA	[illegible]	[illegible]	[illegible]
JAPAN	[illegible]	—	2
NORWAY	13	—	60
NEW ZEALAND	[illegible]	[illegible]	[illegible]
PORTUGAL	—	—	2
STRAIT Settlements	—	8	—
SPAIN	5	22	175
SWEDEN	—	1	2
TURKEY	—	1	13
UNITED STATES	[illegible]	[illegible]	[illegible]
W. INDIES	18	1	—

IMPORTS FROM

BELGIUM	[illegible] bales	HOLLAND	[illegible] bales
"	1 case	"	[illegible] cases
"	6 rolls	INDIA	5 bales
DENMARK	[illegible] bales	NORWAY	[illegible] "
FRANCE	[illegible] "	PRUSSIA	[illegible] "
"	[illegible] cases	RUSSIA	[illegible] "
"	[illegible] rolls	SWEDEN	[illegible] "
GERMANY	[illegible] bales	"	30 rolls
"	[illegible] cases	U.S.A.	35 cases

Including the Following:

Quantity	From	Importer	Port.
8 bales	Christiania	Tyser & Co	London.
[illegible] "	"	London & Rhine S. Co	"
[illegible] "	"	Green & Co	"
71 "	"	C. Christophersen & Co	"
9 "	"	Crabb & Co	"
[illegible] "	"	W. D. Edwards	"
[illegible] "	Dantzig	H. Huber & Co	"
[illegible] "	"	R. E. Sabel	"
[illegible] "	Drammen	Ahlsing & Co	"
[illegible] "	"	R. L. Lundgren	"
725 "	"	Green & Co	"
[illegible] "	Libau	Becker & Ulrich	"
30 "	New York	S. Maw, Son & Co	"
31 "	Stettin	M. Benscher	"
71 "	"	Becker & Ulrich	"
[illegible] "	"	W. D. Edwards	"
[illegible] "	"	J. Spicer & Sons	"
[illegible] "	"	C. Morgan & Co	"
[illegible] "	"	Becker & Ulrich	"
[illegible] "	"	J. Spicer & Sons	"
[illegible] "	"	Morgan & Co	"
[illegible] "	Uddevalla	J. Hamilton	"
[illegible] "	"	R. L. Lundgren	"
474 "	"	D. Gulland	"

SUMMARY OF IMPORTS & EXPORTS,

FOR THE WEEK ENDING TUESDAY LAST.

London, Liverpool, Bristol, Southampton, Hull, Fleetwood, Harwich, Folkestone, Newhaven, Dover, &c.

IMPORTS.

Paper	18076 bales	Envelopes	90 bdls.
"	136 cases	Strawboards	1637 bales
"	47 rolls	Stationery	48 cases
Tissues	314 pkgs.	Millboards	9316 "
Pasteboards	6950 bales		

EXPORTS.

British Goods.			
		Parchment	£66 value
		Millboards	6 cwt.
Paper	1153 cwt.	*Foreign Goods.*	
Printing Paper	4743 "		
Writing Paper	1893 "	Printing Paper	316 cwts.
Stationery	£7236 value	Paper	285 "
Stock	291½ tons	Stationery	£209 value
Cardboards	292 cwt.	Strawboards	25 cwt.
Waste	118¾ tons		

Glasgow, Greenock, Port-Glasgow, Troon, Grangemouth, &c.

IMPORTS.

Paper	635 bales	Paper	30 rolls
"	11 cases	Strawboards	4829 pkgs.

EXPORTS.

Writing Paper	192¾ cwt.	Stationery	£217 value
Printing Paper	1521¾ "	Envelopes	15 cwt.
Wrapping Paper	101 "	Blotting Paper	£1290 value

Leith, Granton, Bo'ness, Dundee, &c.

IMPORTS.

Paper	465 bales	Envelopes	723 bdls.
"	11 cases		

PAPER & PULP MILL SHARES.

THE market remains in a lifeless condition, and with the exception of Darwen, Ramsbottom and Star pref., which are wanted, the rest of the Companies' shares quoted are offered.

(Report received from Mr. F. D. DEAN, 36, Corporation Street, Manchester.)

Nominal Amnt	Amnt Paid	Name of Company	Last dividend	Price
7	7	Bury Paper, ord.	nil	5¼–5½
7	7	do. do. 6% pref.	6%	5¼–5½
100	100	do. do. deb.	5%	103–106
10	10	Bath Paper Mill Co. Lim.	7½%	6–7
10	10	Bergvik Co., def.	15%	13½
100	100	do. do. 6% cum. pref.	6%	10½–11½
10	10	do. do. deb.	5%	105–110
5	3¾	Burnley Paper Co.	3	76/0–79/0
5	3¾	Darwen Paper Co.	10%	5¼–5¾
10	10	East Lancashire Co.	nil	5–5½
10	10	do. do. 6% pref.	nil	7–7½
5	5	do. do. bonus	nil	1¾–2
5	5	Hyde Paper Co.	4%	4½–5
5	4	North of Ireland Paper Co.	nil	1½–1¾
10	5	Ramsbottom Paper Co.	17½%	12½–13½
5	4½	Roach Bridge Paper Co.	5%	3¼–3½
5	5	Star Paper Co.	10%	6–6½
5	3	do. do. 10% pref. cum.	10%	4¾–5¼
50	50	do. do. deb.	6%	55–56
5	2½	Kellner Partingt'n Pulp Co'	—	56/0–57/0

NEW PATENTS.

APPLICATIONS.

13,175. Improvements in or connected with boilers for boiling or chemically treating and for washing esparto and other grasses, straw, wood, rags, and other fibrous materials for papermaking. G. Sinclair.

13,289. Improvements in or connected with adjustable bearings for dandy rolls. M. Foster and W. Morrison.

National Union of Paper Mill Workers.

The following sums have been received in aid of the Lock-out Fund (re Bamden Dispute): —

	£	s.	d.
Amount previously acknowledged	[illegible]	[illegible]	[illegible]
[illegible]	[illegible]	[illegible]	[illegible]

Total .. [illegible] 13 [illegible]

Wm. [illegible], Secretary.

Head Office: [illegible], Manchester.
17th July, 189[illegible].

BELL'S ASBESTOS MANUFACTURES

BELL'S

Asbestos Dagger Packing

Under this Registered Title are included the inventions of Mr. Field, and experience has proved them to be the Most Efficient, Durable and Economical Packings ever made. They are composed of Rolled Asbestos Cloth, but the India Rubber is placed in two forms to suit various cases. They are Unequalled for Every Kind of Engine, and are being Universally used by the Leading Steamship Companies for ordinary Compound, Triple, and Quadruple Expansion Engines of the Latest Type.

In ordering state whether round or square packing is required.

PATENT No. 15,498.

Every 10 Feet has Label bearing our Name and Trade

BELL'S ASBESTOS

YARN and SOAPSTONE PACKING

SPECIALLY adapted to Locomotive, Traction, and all Engines going at a HIGH SPEED. The Asbestos Fibre of which it is composed is of a Special Quality, which no other firm can obtain, and this gives to it such Efficiency and Durability as is not obtained by the Packing of the same description produced by other makers.

Every 10 Feet has Label bearing our Name and Trade Mark

BELL'S ASBESTOS

EXPANSION SHEETING AND RINGS,

PATENT No. 640, 1884,

COMPOSED of a Specially-prepared India-Rubber Compound, protected by a covering of Vulcani Asbestos Sheeting, and the only jointing material which adequately combines PERMANENT ELASTICI WITH HEAT RESISTANCE. For Manhole, Mudhole, Steampipe, and Mash Tun Door joints it unequalled, and if applied as directed, a Ring can be used many times over.

Made from 1-ply for Cylinder, and Faced Joints to any Thickness for Uneven Surfaces.

BELL'S ASBESTOS Co., Lim.,

59½, SOUTHWARK STREET, LONDON, S.E.

AGENCIES:

BIRMINGHAM: Bell & Co., 19, Summer Row.
BRISTOL: Robert Stotesbury, 114, Redcliff Street.
CARDIFF: Bell & Co., West Bute Street.
HULL: T. Clough, Humber Dock Basin.
LIVERPOOL: Puts, Curphey & Co., 2, Strand Street James Street.
MANCHESTER: F. R. Puts, South Parade.
NEWCASTLE-on-TYNE: W. F. Snowdon, 32, Side.
RUSSIA: J. M. Sumner & Co., Moscow.

THE

HORNE REFINING Engine

Acting as a Partial Beater thus Saves **25** *per cent. of the Time Occupied by the Stuff in the Beating Engine.*

No Paper Mill Should be Without One.

HUNDREDS IN USE.

FREDERIC NELL,

16, MARK LANE, LONDON. E.C.

Printed and Published by W. JOHN STONHILL, 58, Shoe Lane, LONDON E.C. July 21, 1898.

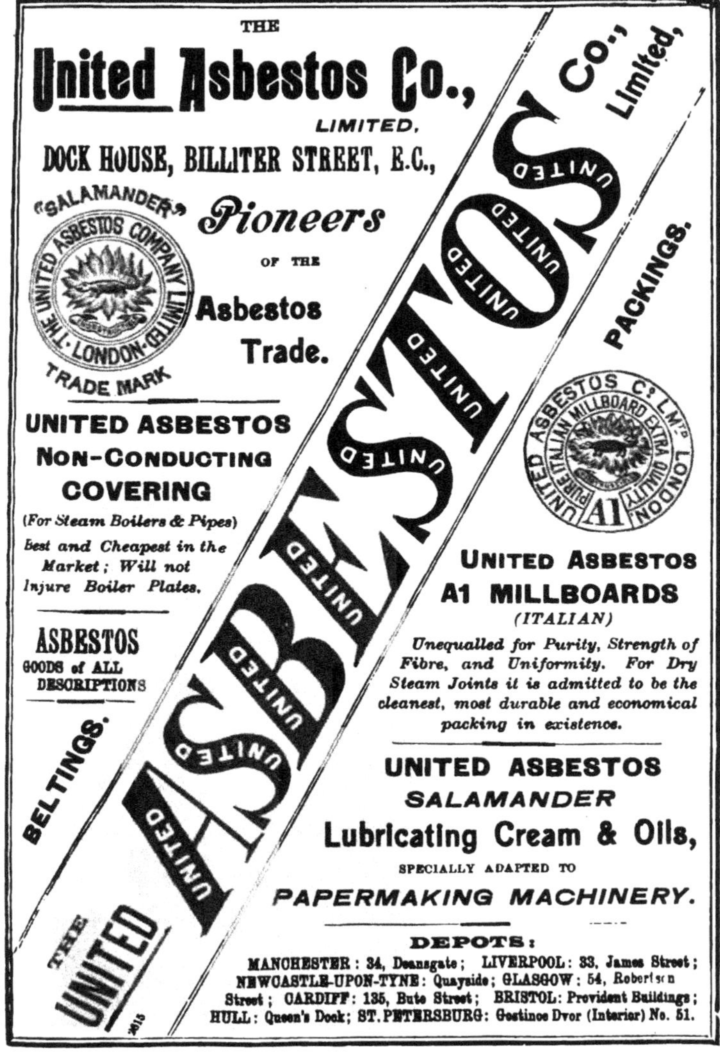
THE
United Asbestos Co.,
LIMITED.
DOCK HOUSE, BILLITER STREET, E.C.,
"SALAMANDER"
THE UNITED ASBESTOS COMPANY LIMITED · LONDON ·
TRADE MARK
Pioneers
OF THE
Asbestos
Trade.
UNITED ASBESTOS
NON-CONDUCTING
COVERING
(For Steam Boilers & Pipes)
Best and Cheapest in the
Market; Will not
Injure Boiler Plates.
ASBESTOS
GOODS of ALL
DESCRIPTIONS
BELTINGS.
THE UNITED ASBESTOS CO., Limited,
PACKINGS.
UNITED ASBESTOS Co. LTD. LONDON
PURE ITALIAN MILLBOARD EXTRA QUALITY
A1
UNITED ASBESTOS
A1 MILLBOARDS
(ITALIAN)
Unequalled for Purity, Strength of
Fibre, and Uniformity. For Dry
Steam Joints it is admitted to be the
cleanest, most durable and economical
packing in existence.
UNITED ASBESTOS
SALAMANDER
Lubricating Cream & Oils,
SPECIALLY ADAPTED TO
PAPERMAKING MACHINERY.
DEPOTS:
MANCHESTER: 34, Deansgate; LIVERPOOL: 33, James Street;
NEWCASTLE-UPON-TYNE: Quayside; GLASGOW: 54, Robertson
Street; CARDIFF: 135, Bute Street; BRISTOL: Provident Buildings;
HULL: Queen's Dock; ST. PETERSBURG: Gostinoe Dvor (Interior) No. 51.

THE GLASGOW PAPER MEN AT ROSSLYN.
Reproduced by the Meisenbach Company from a Photograph by Maclure, Macdonald & Co., Glasgow.

TENTH ANNUAL EXCURSION OF THE GLASGOW PAPER MEN.

(BY OUR OWN REPRESENTATIVE.)

This annual outing, always eagerly looked forward to by those privileged to participate, took place recently, and fine weather fortunately favoured the occasion.

The committee of arrangement are to be congratulated on their choice of a locality in which to spend the day. They have during the last ten years arranged to visit many beautiful spots, but it was agreed on all hands that charming Hawthornden, and the equally lovely valley of the Esk beat the record. Then was there not too the far-famed Rosslyn Chapel to be visited. Having reached Auld Reekie by train, says our representative, we started at once on our drive to Rosslyn, and few—if any—who were among the party (which numbered forty-four all told) will ever forget that drive. What a merry lot we were as we rattled along the road, first through Newington, then along the foot of the lovely Pentland Hills, into the charming village of Lasswade. Many a song was sung, many a joke was cracked, and yarns good, bad and indifferent were spun. The time seemed to fly, and our ten mile drive was over all too quickly: however, the programme had to be carried out, and we arrived at our destination, Hawthornden, in splendid spirits. Of this place Sir Thos. Chambers wrote: "In all Scotland there is no spot more varied, more rich, graceful, or luxuriant than the cliffs, caves, and wooded banks of the river Esk and the classic shades of Hawthornden." Such is the spot that the Glasgow paper men had chosen to visit for their annual outing, and we who had the privilege and pleasure of being present could not but admire their choice. Mr. John Tod—John Strathesk as he is familiarly known to his friends—who had been prevailed upon to preside at the day's proceedings, met the party on its arrival at the entrance to Hawthornden, and living as he does in the very heart of the district he was an invaluable guide. He at once took the paper men under his charge, in his usual jolly and hearty style, and conducted them through the place, explaining each and every point of interest as we came upon them. They saw Bruce's Cave, his sword, and even looked over his "library." The latter, it must be confessed, was rather poorly supplied with books, but then one has to go back a long time (even before the celebrated St. Leonard's and Springfield Paper Mills were first built, and that's a good time back) to get at the time when Bruce could have occupied his library chair or used the sword which is shown—if he ever did use it. However, after spending some considerable time in this truly charming retreat, and admiring the lovely scenery with which it is surrounded, the party at last sighted the Royal Hotel, Rosslyn, where a good dinner awaited them, and on their arriving it was immediately announced. At the table were Mr. John Tod (chairman), Mr. G. Beith (Alex. Cowan and Sons, Ltd.), and Mr. W. Calder (J. and E. Reid), who acted as croupier, as well as Messrs. D. Burnett (Jas. Stewart and Co.), D. McFarlane (Clyde Paper Co.), John Cruikshanks (J. and E. Cruikshanks), D. Goodall (Hendon Paper Co.), — Law (Hill, Craig and Co.), R. Whyte (P. and W. McNiven), —Rutherford (Smith and Ritchie), D. McPherson (R. and J. Cooper), T. B. Greig (Andrew White and Son), — Potter (J. and E. Cruikshanks), J. A. Stewart (Stewart and Sons), — Anderson (Smith, Anderson and Co.), N. Green (Scottish Wholesale Co-operative), Jas. Stewart (Stewart Bros.), A. Paterson (J. and E. Cruikshanks), W. Scott (Farrel and Scott), D. McFarlane (McFarlane and Dickson), John Wood (Robert Craig and Sons), —Suttle (Felber, Jucker and Co.), R. Milne (Alex. Pirie and Sons, Limited), Jas. Smith (J. and J. Smith), —Marshall (Maclure, Macdonald and Co.), — Agnew (Maclure, Macdonald and Co.), P. Spence (Geo. Waterston and Sons), P. Craik (R. Fletcher and Sons), W. Dall (Wrigley and Sons, Limited), — Fairbairn (Loch Mill Linlithgow), — Gilmour (Govanhaugh Paper Co., Limited), —Christie (Geo. Stark and Sons), —R. Watt (Dixon, Horsburgh, and Co., Limited), J. L. Ramage (Craigside Envelope Co., Limited), T. Kennedy (Begg, Kennedy and Harper), —McKenzie (Henry, Bruce and Co.), Thos. Ross (Jas. Hamilton), J. M. Hutchison (Lipton's), J. Harper (Begg, Kennedy and Harper), — Bell (A. R. Bell and Co.), — Ashbury (J. and W. Mitchell, Birmingham), — McFadzen (Olive and Partington), and P. G. Cracknell (*B. and C.* and *P. T. R.*). The assembly made good play with the knife and fork for some time, doing ample justice to the good things which had been supplied for their comfort.

Their appetites were at last appeased, and the CHAIRMAN then rose to propose the usual loyal and patriotic toasts.

The next toast was "The Paper Men of Glasgow," which was proposed in a most inimitable style by the genial Chairman, who was the very soul of the party all day long. The toast could not have been in better hands than those of John Strathesk. He was brimful of fun from beginning to end of his short but really "fetching" speech. He had fairly convulsed the guests during dinner by his quite unique way of making the entire company know each other. This he accomplished by calling on each guest to give his name and the name of the firm with which he was connected, a kind of "who's who" style of getting everybody introduced to everybody else. In the course of his remarks. Mr. Tod expressed the great pleasure he felt at being present at this, the tenth annual outing of the Glasgow Paper Men. They were that day taking their holiday in the very heart of the paper trade of Scotland. Edinburgh was, as they all knew, a great publishing centre, and consequently there was an immense amount of paper required. Then again, were they not in the heart of the district where paper was made. Along the banks of the lovely Esk, which they had just been admiring, there were some dozen mills, beginning with his own (St. Leonard's) and ending with the Inveresk mill at Musselburgh. He was extremely pleased to see the paper men there that day, and he would do his best to give them a right good welcome. They were now in the very "Heart of Midlothian." They had seen the spot where their great novelist and poet Scott had spent his honeymoon, and where he had written many of his best books. He (the Chairman) was out for the day to enjoy himself, and they could not expect him to make a long speech. He hoped the day would be a happy one to each and all, and that they would remember it with pleasure in years to come. The Chairman concluded by asking the company to drink to "The Glasgow Paper Men," and prosperity to them all, and God bless them.

The toast was received with great enthusiasm, and when silence was again restored, Mr. McFadane was called upon to give an original song, which he had composed for the occasion. This we have pleasure in giving in *extenso* :—

Ye brethren o' the paper trade,
Collected here in mony a grade,
I wat ye've a' a tribute paid
　　To the beauties rare, o' Roslyn.

There's glorious grandeur in the west,
That ye hae shown to mony a guest,
But ye'll a' gang hame this nicht wi zest
　　Frae the shady dells o' Roslyn.

But this district as ye'll a' weel ken
Is ca'd Strathesk richt doon the glen,
And our chief here is that king o' men
　　That has added fame to Roslyn.

Wha disna ken o' our John Tod—
In Scotland he's a demi god;
But mair than Scotch folk ken the road
　　Thro' Strathesk up to Roslyn.

But what about his place o' birth,
What tho' he's kent owre a' the earth—
The paper folks best ken his worth,
　　And they're here this nicht at Roslyn.

Nell o' the Manse, ye ken her name,
Her author she's filled fou o' fame,
Weel, Nell puir lass has her last hame
　　Just doon the glen frae Roslyn.

What can I say about Lamlash,
Or Whiting Bay and western trash?
This day ye've got Midlothian hash,
　　Cooked by John Tod at Roslyn.

Past Masters o' the paper corps,
That's hossed ye aft by lake and shore,
This nicht ye'll hae a glorious splore
　　Wi' John Tod here at Roslyn.

But Gillanders aye has our regards,
And tho' his special forte is cards,
We'll hear him turn Othello-wards
　　On the green haugh doon by Roslyn.

Midlothian boasts o' Calders three—
And o' them she's prood as prood can be;
But the Glasgow Calder bears the gree,
　　And we're proud he's here at Roslyn.

My auld friend Bob, I mind ye fine,
Tho' 30 years has passed sin syne—
But what tho' a' thing else we tine
　　If we're Good-all here at Roslyn.

Then Kennedy, that rhymin' chiel,
Wha's got your programme up sae weel,
Wi' him, what pleasure I wad feel
　　Just swappin rhyme at Roslyn.

But what aboot my brother Celt?
I ken na hoo his name is spelt,
But his Celtic power is this day felt,
　　For McFadzen's here at Roslyn.

Our dinner past wi' mickle glee,
And tho' I'm sober as ye see,
I hope y'are a' as fou as we
　　O' nature's joys at Roslyn.

I canna' further mak' words clink,
But only tell ye a' to think,
There's nacht like paper, pens, and ink
　　When we gang hame frae Roslyn.

MR. JOHN CRUIKSHANKS replied to the toast. He said he was pleased to see so many faces present on this occasion, as it showed that these outings were much appreciated. He begged to thank them for the kind manner in which they had received the toast of the "Paper Men of Glasgow," and expressed a hope that the day would prove a happy one for all of them. Next followed a song, "The Twins," by Mr. R. White.

MR. DALL proposed the toast of "Our Friends," to which MR. RAMAGE and MR. BURNETT responded.

MR. GOODALL afterwards rose to propose the health of "Our Chairman," Mr. Tod. He had known that gentleman almost all his life, and in the circumstances he did not think he need ask leave to propose a "vote of thanks" to Mr. Tod for the kind manner in which he had treated the party that day, and acted as guide, philosopher, and friend. He did not think it was possible to find a better chairman. His love of Scottish poets and his perfect knowledge of the country they were in, made him simply invaluable. It was one of his (Mr. Goodall's) earliest recollections that on Wednesdays—before the advent of railways—the whole paper fraternity made their appearance in Edinburgh early in the forenoon in "gigs," "Whitechapel" carts, and other vehicles, sometimes with their wives and buxom daughters (when these latter were for sale), and on these occasions the monotony of the week wes broken, and the social and commercial intercourse thereby en-

produced was supposed to add to the perfection of their apprenticeship. These days unfortunately would never return, and in order to put something in their place to enliven this uneventful life, they had arranged these little annual pilgrimages. This year they had come to the banks of the Esk, and he thought they would admit with him that they had had the pleasure of being ciceroned that day over some of the finest scenery in Scotland, and as he said before, by one of the best guides that could have been found—their distinguished chairman, Mr. Tod. His knowledge of the early Scottish poets and the delight in which he revels amongst the finer strains of our noble Burns, endears him not only to us, but to a wider circle of those lovers of our native doric, to whom the genius of Burns almost amounts to a worship. There he sits, as Milton aptly puts it, like "Laughter holding both his sides," and amusing us with his—

> "Quips and cranks and wanton wiles,
> And nods and becks and wreathed smiles,
> And sport that wrinkled care derides"

till we are shouting with pure delight. I will therefore ask you, gentlemen, to join me in this toast, and I am sure that the mention of Mr. Tod will make you fill up and pledge his health, and that of his fireside in a veneer, full 500 sheets and all insides. The toast was drank with *musical honours and Kentish fire amidst great enthusiasm.*

Song: "The Lea Rig," Mr. Gillanders.

MR. TOD, in reply, said he could hardly find words to express his feelings and thanks for the kind manner in which his health had been proposed and received on this occasion. It had given him the greatest possible pleasure to take the chair at this, their tenth annual dinner, and to act as their guide round the neighbourhood. He was pleased to see such a goodly company present; he trusted that all of them would enjoy the trip, and he hoped that all might be spared to meet again next year on the occasion of the trip of 1894.

A recitation by Mr. Suttie followed.

MR. KENNEDY, in proposing the health of the committee of arrangement, said that he must be a *privileged* man who at that hour would seek to encroach further on their time, but when he asked to be allowed to propose the health of the committee, he was sure the company would indulge him for a moment. They were deeply indebted to these gentlemen, who had shown great tact and skill in making and carrying out all the necessary arrangements, and that they had eclipsed all former committees was not to be wondered at, as each of them were men of great capacity, so much so, that it would not be fair to refer to them either in general terms or in a collective manner. Mr. Calder, the bard of Kirkintilloch, the author of "Away Ye Gay Landscapes," had most certainly distinguished himself for generalship and diplomacy, particularly in the manner in which he had handled his men, and they, as business men who know the value of time, must highly appreciate the great sacrifice Mr. Calder had made in attending so many meetings and prospecting the land, but he had his reward that day. There was an old saying often quoted as a term of reproach when anything connected with numbers is a failure—that "this is a poor turn out for Kirkintilloch"—but that did not apply here, and if on the great day of the genuine general rising, Mr. Calder should mount the "golden stairs" at the head of such a numerous band, he will be certainly greeted with the shout which applies to-day, "Well done, Kirkintilloch." Then there was Mr. McFayden, the Laird of Birdstane, a record committee man. In him they had a rare combination of talent, experience, and enthusiasm, none of which had he spared. He was as obliging as he was versatile, and they could always look to him for a good story, a good song, or if excitement were wanted, an acrobatic entertainment of the highest order. Mr. McFadyen being a Kirkintilloch man, was also entitled to share in the "Well done." Modest John Wood had been wooed into the committee, and who *would* have thought it, he was such an acquisition too. His general knowledge of the district eminently qualified him for the position of cicerone. He had done well in leading the wild men of the West—or the men of the "Wild West"—into this classic district of surpassing interest and beauty, and providing them with such good cheer. "Our fathers did eat manna in the wilderness, but here our mouths are satisfied with good things, and our youth is renewed like the Eagles." He must also mention Mr. Ross, the last but not the least—"the proverbial mustard seed of this great tree." He had raised this day phoenix-like from the dying embers of [illegible]. He (the speaker) was pleased that they appreciated it, for in Mr. Ross they had spirit, energy and perseverance, and he was delighted to be able to congratulate that gentleman on attaining from small beginnings to the happy and enjoyable position of a paper agent. Still, he was not content, as he was seen going to London, where he would find that someone had been there before him, and that there was no room unless at the top; but Mr. Ross would soon find the top position, and he predicted that in a few years they would hear of him not as a paper agent but as a papermaker, with a reputation not second rate like that of the Cowans, or the Annandales, or the Tods, but world-wide like the Balstons and the Hollingsworths, especially when he came to introduce his "Excelsior" brand of papers, which is to beat "Record," and knock "Hercules" into a dying gladiator. He was glad to see that they appreciated the ability of Mr. Ross, and desired to honour him. He could say more, but time was flying, so he asked them to join him in drinking to the health of the "Bard," the "Laird," "Spongia," and "Excelsior."

The toast was enthusiastically received, and after Mr. White had sung the "Low Back Car" in excellent style,

MR. ROSS rose to reply. He thanked Mr. Kennedy for the handsome manner in which he had proposed the health of the committee, and thanked the company for the way in which the toast had been received. He assured them that it had been a great pleasure to the committee to do what they had done to make the day a success. He hoped it would be a big success, and that all would thoroughly enjoy themselves. He thought it would be a pity if these annual outings were to be allowed to drop out; he did not think that would be the case.

The "Trade Press" was then proposed by MR. HARPER, in felicitious terms, and MR. P. G. CRACKNELL, of the *British and Colonial Printer and Stationer* and the *Paper Trade Review*, replied.

The CHAIRMAN then announced that tea would be ready in the same room at 6 o'clock, and called on the entire company to join in singing "Auld Lang Syne." This was given in a very hearty manner, and the party then rose from table.

It had been arranged that the company be photographed in a group; this was done, and we have pleasure in reproducing the picture, which was taken by Messrs. Maclure Macdonald and Co., of 2, Bothwell-circus, Glasgow. After the photo had been successfully secured, the party, under the guidance of Mr. Tod, visited the beautiful Roslyn Chapel, and spent a considerable time in admiring its truly magnificent architectural details. After this had been accomplished, the paper men got back to the hotel and tea was announced. Mr. Tod was again in the chair and kept the company amused the whole time with his fun and frolic, and actually to finish with said he would sing them a song. This he did, giving them a thorough old-fashioned Scotch ditty. Soon after 7 p.m. the company started for the drive back to Edinburgh by quite another route to that by which they came, and one which gave them a view of the South side of the Pentlands, and as they rattled along in the beautiful summer evening the countryside rang again and again with their songs and laughter. The road took them through several country villages and the people, standing at their doors in the cool of the evening, joined in the paper men's merry strains as they passed by. They were back in Edinburgh by 8.30 (good time), and the "Glasgow Boys" were accompanied to the train and seen off. A few of those who were left were staying over Sunday in Edinburgh and some were inhabitants of the city and district. These joined together in an improvised "smoker," and spent the rest of the evening in song and merry chat. Everything comes to an end some time, and the day of the Tenth Annual Excursion of the Glasgow Paper Men was no exception to the rule. As the last survivors separated none of them could help saying that they had had a REAL GOOD DAY, and all joined in the hope that although it had been the first time some of them had met, they would do their best to make sure that it would not be the last. In concluding our report we must not forget to mention that the handsome programme was specially designed by Mr. Thos. Kennedy, and produced by his firm, Messrs. Begg, Kennedy and Harper, of Glasgow. It is certainly one that for design and workmanship it would be hard to beat.

PATENT SPECIFICATIONS.

23,735 (92).—Improvements in the Method of and Apparatus for Binding Strawboards, Pasteboards, and the like to an acute or other Angle without previous Scoring.—T. REMUS. Accepted 18th February, 1893.

The present patent is a further improvement upon Mr. Remus's patent, No. 12,043 (92), and in order to strengthen the joint of the scoring plates in apparatus for binding cardboard, &c., to acute and other angles without scoring or incising, an open joint is used, according to the specification, instead of a closed hinge-like joint described in the former patent. This open joint is the main feature of the specification.

7,221 (93).—Paper Board.—G. C. MARKS. (Communicated by Robert B. McEwan, Jessie L. McEwan, and R. W. McEwan, paper manufacturers, Whippany, New Jersey, U.S.A.) Accepted 13th May, 1893.

The invention relates to the manufacture of paper board, box board, and the like from newspapers and other similar printed white paper, and the object is to obtain a quality of board superior to the varieties now on the market, at less cost. In manufacture the inventors use, on account of its cheapness, freedom from size, and softness, printed newspaper. The process of manufacture is as follows: The stock is first cleansed from dust, &c., and soaked in hot water till it is thoroughly soft. Before it is cool it is transferred to the beating engine, and when sufficiently beaten it is allowed to pass to the stuff chest, from which it is pumped to the making cylinder vat, and at all times it is kept as hot as possible. The result it is claimed is a board which has the permanent particles of printers' ink minutely sub-divided and uniformly distributed throughout its body to produce a smooth and even tint throughout, while the strength of the fibres has not been impaired by attempts to bleach out the ink. In practice, if so desired for special purpose, there may be mixed with the newspapers a slight proportion of other paper or of raw fibre.

Apparatus to Recover

SODA ASH

(CHAPMAN'S PATENT).

Avoiding POLLUTION of STREAMS, LOSS by LEAKAGE, and NUISANCE to the NEIGHBOURHOOD.

... PAPER MILLS says:—

... has never worked ... month or two at 3½° ... for little ash. ... treat so weak

... (CHAPMAN'S PATENT), ... that in use at ...

... MILLS says of this

... it very satis- ... tons of ash ... on a Mon- ... fires all ... of coal ... and re-

...rpool.

Telegrams: "STONHILL, LONDON." A B C Code. Registered at the General Post Office as a Newspaper.

Vol. XX. No. 4. LONDON, JULY 28, 1893. Price 6d.

Alkali Works.

REPORT BY MR. ALFRED E. FLETCHER.

As an indication of the extent of the soda manufacture under the Leblanc process, the following statement is given in the 29th annual report on Alkali Works, by the Chief Inspector. It shows the amount of salt decomposed, as that is an index of the whole amount of soda made, whether it be in the form of ash, crystal, or caustic soda :—

SALT CONSUMED IN THE LEBLANC SODA PROCESS.

District.	Tons Salt, 1892.	Tons Salt, 1891.	Tons Salt, 1890.
Ireland...	3,365	3,252	5,232
North of England	93,200	91,400	124,000
Cheshire, North Wales, and part of Lancashire ...	96,351	125,000	144,350
Widnes...	179,204	198,857	224,203
East Lancashire and Yorkshire	40,600	39,850	37,650
South Midland	25,705	30,747	24,549
South-West of England ..	34,471	32,000	32,000
South-East of England ...	6,973	6,627	6,700
Total ...	479,869	527,733	598,684

The manufacture of soda by the Leblanc process, which has held its ground for a full century, has now for several years diminished in extent, owing to the advance of the ammonia-soda process. The amount produced by each process is shown in the following table :—

SALT DECOMPOSED IN THE LEBLANC AND AMMONIA-SODA PROCESSES (including Scotland).

—	1892.	1891.	1890.
	Tons.	Tons.	Tons.
Leblanc process	519,593	567,863	602,769
Ammonia-soda	304,897	278,528	252,260
Total ...	824,490	846,391	855,029

Although the Leblanc process is thus receding, yet two new large works have been built during the year. One of them is at Irvine, in Scotland, and the other at Felling-on-Tyne. The former has already been started, the other is expected to be in operation shortly. The vitality of the process has been mainly due to its important by-products, bleaching powder, and chlorate of potash. The chlorine required for these has hitherto been produced by the action of the binoxide of manganese on hydrochloric acid. During the past year, however, two works have been erected with a view to the production of chlorine by the use of nitric acid in place of manganese.

In the meantime, continued efforts are put forth to produce chlorine in connection with the ammonia-soda process. Messrs. Brunner, Mond and Co., at Winnington, have now a large plant at work in which bleaching powder is made, but it is too early to report as to its commercial success. The result is watched anxiously by all those interested in the trade.

The amount of soda made by the amm[illegible] soda process itself is continually o[illegible]

increase, as shown in the tabular statement which we give above. This growth will now be still further augmented, as during the last year two large works have been started, and are already in full operation. A large work is also in course of erection by the United Alkali Company, near Fleetwood. There will thus shortly be eight works in operation for carrying on the ammonia-soda process.

Efforts are made in another direction to modify the present processes for the production of soda. This is more in line with the old Leblanc method. Mr. [illegible], [illegible] in mind the attempts made by his [illegible] to improve the soda manufacture, and the wonderful power he showed of [illegible] many of the advances that have since been made, has worked out a process for the production of carbonate of soda from the sulphate without the intervention of lime, as in the Leblanc method. [illegible]

[illegible]

the other sources of [illegible] a continued increase.

THE A[illegible] ACT OF [illegible]

During the last session of Parliament an Act was passed to amend the Act of [illegible], and to bring certain processes of manufacture within its scope which had not hitherto been named in the schedule. [illegible] had become necessary in consequence of the growth of the chemical [illegible] the introduction of new processes.

It may be interesting to mention that on the passing of the first Alkali Act in [illegible], only [illegible] works were at first registered under it. The number of these increased in after years to about [illegible], and the [illegible] of the inspection went no further than the [illegible] of the hydrochloric acid gas evolved in the manufacture.

The limit fixed, beyond which the escape of that acid rendered the manufacturer liable to a penalty, was five per cent. of the amount [illegible]. [illegible]

[illegible]

After the year 1863, when the condensation of the muriatic acid of alkali works had become compulsory, the task was found to be not very difficult, and moreover, it was distinctly remunerative. To condense 95 per cent. of that which passed through the condensers was easy, but, owing to the faulty construction of furnaces and flues, much of it escaped without reaching them and found its way to the outer air. An amended Alkali Act was passed in 1874, by which, though the five per cent. standard was maintained unaltered, a new mode of measuring the escaping acid was adopted, and it was made penal to allow the air passing up the chimney of the work to carry with it more than two-tenths of a grain muriatic acid in the cubic foot. Power was also given to the inspector to insist on the adoption of the best practicable means for preventing the escape of all other noxious gases evolved in the alkali manufacture. About this time the manufacture of alkali was greatly developed, many new works were set up, and, although the escape of acid gases was kept in check, still the damage done to lands in the neighbourhood where they were established did not cease. A royal commission was accordingly appointed to inquire into the conditions of the alkali manufacture, and the effect of past legislation. On their report an amended Act was passed in 1881, which gave the inspectors more power in controlling the noxious gases with which they had hitherto dealt, and also brought the gases of some other chemical manufactures under the Act. The number of the additional processes thus brought under inspection was six; they are named in a schedule to the Act.

To describe all the various processes of manufacture which give rise to certain noxious gases is difficult, and even if at any time the list can be made complete, it is soon rendered imperfect by the establishment of new processes. Thus, in a short time the schedule to the Act of 1881 was found to be incomplete, so that in the last session of Parliament an amended Act was passed, bringing a further group of 13 processes under the provisions of the Alkali Act.

TRADE TABLES.*

ATOMIC WEIGHTS & SYMBOLS OF THE CHEMICAL ELEMENTS.

Element	Symbol.	Atomic Weight.
Aluminium	Al	27·02
Antimony	Sb	119·6
Arsenic	As	74·9
Barium	Ba	136·84
Bismuth	Bi	207·5
Boron	B	10·9
Bromine	Br	79·76
Cadmium	Cd	111·7
Cæsium	Cs	132·7
Calcium	Ca	39·90
Carbon	C	11·97
Cerium	Ce	138·24
Chlorine	Cl	35·37
Chromium	Cr	52·06
Cobalt	Co	58·6
Copper	Cu	63·12
Didymium	D	142·44
Erbium	E	166·9
Fluorine	F	18·96
Gallium	Ga	68·8
Gold	Au	196·2
Hydrogen	H	1·0
Indium	In	113·4
Iodine	I	126·54
Iridium	Ir	192·5
Iron	Fe	55·9
Lanthanum	La	138·22
Lead	Pb	206·39
Lithium	Li	7·0
Magnesium	Mg	23·94
Manganese	Mn	54·8
Mercury	Hg	199·8
Molybdenum ...	Mo	95·9
Nickel	Ni	58·6
Niobium	Nb	93·7
Nitrogen	N	14·01
Osmium	Os	190·0
Oxygen	O	16·0
Palladium	Pd	106·2
Phosphorus	P	30·96
Platinum	Pt	194·38
Potassium	K	39·04
Rhodium	Rh	104·1
Rubidium	Rb	85·2
Ruthenium	Ru	103·5
Scandium	Sc	44·0
Selenium	Se	78·9
Silver	Ag	107·67
Silicon	Si	28·0
Sodium	Na	23·0
Strontium	Sr	87·34
Sulphur	S	32·0
Tellurium	Te	125·0
Thallium	Tl	203·5
Thorium	Th	231·44
Tin	Sn	117·4
Titanium	Ti	48·0
Tungsten	W	183·6
Uranium	U	239·8
Vanadium	V	51·0
Yttrium	Y	88·9
Zinc	Zn	64·7
Zirconium	Zr	90·4

CALCULATIONS RELATING TO PUMPS.

Useful numbers in connection with water:—

Cubic feet per minute × 9,000 = gallons per 24 hours.
Head in feet × ·434 = pounds per square inch.
Tons of water × 224 = gallons.

Power required to raise water with ordinary well pumps may be estimated as follows:

Multiply the quantity of water to be raised in gallons per minute by 10 (the weight in lbs. of one gallon of water), and by the height to be lifted in feet, divide the result by 33,000. This will give the horse power without allowing for friction or "slip." For this loss allow ⅓ or ½ more.

Thus 100 gallons to be raised per minute from a depth of 50 feet :—

$$\frac{100 \times 100 \times 50}{33{,}000} = 1{\cdot}5 \text{ horse power}$$

Add for friction and slip ⅓ of 1·5 = ·5. 1·5 + ·5 = 2 h.p.

Pressure on pump bucket :

The bucket of a pump supports a weight, independent of frictional resistance, equal to that of a column of water having a base equal in area to that of the bucket, of a height equal to the difference in level of the supply water and point of delivery.

Let H = height in feet the water is lifted (difference in level);
D = diameter of bucket in feet ;
P = weight or pressure on bucket in pounds.
Then $P = D^2 \times {\cdot}7854 \times H \times 62{\cdot}43$ lbs.

Discharge of pumps:

If bucket of single acting pump is covered with water at each stroke, ¾ the stroke, and
D = diameter of bucket in inches;
L = length of stroke in inches;
R = number of revolutions of crank shaft;
Then the capacity of pump = $D^2 \times {\cdot}7854 \times L$;
The quantity of water raised each stroke = $D^2 \times {\cdot}7854 \times L \times \frac{3}{4}$;
The quantity of water raised per hour in cubic feet = $(D^2 \times {\cdot}7854 \times L \times \frac{3}{4} \times R \times 60 \text{ minutes}) \div 1728$.

The capacity of a pump with piston or bucket is area of barrel multiplied by length of stroke.

The capacity of pump with ram is area of end of ram multiplied by length of stroke.

To find the gallons of water delivered per stroke of pump:

Square the diameter of the pump bucket or ram, multiply by ·034 and the product multiplied by the length of stroke in feet. This is the quantity delivered, provided the barrel is filled at each stroke. All pumps, however, throw less than their capacity owing to leakage and "slip." For this loss deduct ⅕ from the number of gallons.

Horse-power required for pumping engines:

Let G = the number of gallons to be raised every twenty-four hours;
Let H = the height in feet the water has to be raised.

The actual horse-power required equals G multiplied by H, and the product divided by 4,752,000. 20 per cent. must be added to this to overcome friction, and 50 per cent. more for contingencies. Thus 70 per cent. additional power should be allowed.

CARTBRIDGE PAPER MILLS, POLLOKSHAWS.—Mr. Walter J. Buchanan has received instructions to offer for sale by public auction the whole modern plant of the above mills at Pollokshaws, near Glasgow, on the 5th Sept. The lots include one single cylinder papermaking machine 90 inches wide (by Messrs. George and William Bertram), and one Fourdrinier papermaking machine 86 inches wide, beating and washing engines, glazing calenders, rag boilers, rag cutters, steam engines, steam boilers, &c. Catalogues giving full particulars may be obtained from the auctioneer, 72, Renfield-street, Glasgow.

* [illegible].—Specially Prepared for this Journal.

WOOD PULPS

HERTHEIMO, HAMBURG.

AUGUST 25, 1898.

L. DESTRÉE, A. WIESCHER & CO.,

Exporters

CHEMISTS EMPLOYED FOR TESTING THE MOST SUITABLE DYES and the Most ECONOMICAL Method of Employment.

SPECIAL CARE IN PACKING FOR EXPORTATION.

ADVICE GIVEN TO OUR CUSTOMERS.

Chr. Christophersen and Co.,

39, LOMBARD STREET, LONDON, E.C.

Sulphite, Soda and Mechanical

WOOD PULPS.

"ARBORIFERUS, LONDON." 2141

SOCIETE INDUSTRIELLE de MIOS,

MIOS, GIRONDE, FRANCE.

Bleached Chemical Pine Wood Pulp,

Manufacture of Fine Papers. 2066

J. & A. JENSEN OG DAHL,

CHRISTIANIA.

Makers of Wood Working Machinery, Wood Pulp and Paper Mill Machinery.

Saw and Planing Mills in Norway and Sweden. Russia, France, Holland and Spain. Wood Pulp for Paper. Mills in Norway, and some in Sweden.

CHRISTIANIA, FREDRIKSTAD, PARIS.

STARCH MANUFACTURE
AT
CARROW WORKS, NORWICH.

The manufactures of Messrs. J. and J. Colman, Carrow Works, Norwich, have, as is well known, a world-wide reputation, and not the least important is their starch for papermakers. Rice starch is highly esteemed in England by the manufacturers of fine papers, as well as for sizing all kinds of fine fabrics. It gives a finish and a feel which cannot be attained by the use of any other kind of starch." Messrs. Colman's specially prepared starch for fine writings and printings has met with great apprecia-

STARCH FACTORY.

tion, and the same may be said of the [illegible] starch in crystals and granulated starch, the various grades being applicable for every use in papermaking.

In a "Souvenir of Carrow Works," particulars and illustrations are published of the various departments. The starch factory has nine acres of flooring. Messrs. J. and J. Colman manufacture entirely from rice chiefly grown in Bengal and Madras. Great care and experience are required in the selection and grouping of the various qualities of rice, in order that the product may be of a uniformly good quality and colour. The rice arrives in bags made of gunny, weighing from one to two cwts. It is at once carefully dressed and winnowed through sieves properly arranged for this purpose, to free it from every particle of dust and dirt contracted during the somewhat careless process of harvesting. It then finds its way to a room, where, in order to soften it, and thus to render the operation of grinding more easy, it is subjected to a steeping process. After some hours the rice in its softened condition is finely ground by ordinary mill stones, similar to those generally used for grinding flour. From fifty to one hundred pairs of these are constantly at work night and day in the starch department. The ground rice issues from the stones in a thin stream of about the consistency of cream, its constituent parts being starch, cellulose, or, as it is technically called "fibre," and gluten.

In order to separate the starch from the other substances the ground rice is run into large wooden vats, where it is agitated in water for some time and allowed to stand, when the cellulose, or "fibre," and gluten gradually settle to the bottom of the vessel, leaving the starch in suspension in the water above. By means of valves this is then drawn off, and the starch is allowed to deposit in large [illegible]. The cellulose or fibre and the gluten, which are [illegible], are carefully washed and the water removed from the [illegible]

... Works afford the interesting ... trades being carried on in ... to each other. Here may be ... well-appointed premises, com... smithies, tinmen's work... carpenters' shops, cooper... works, skilled artisans and ... upon some special work, ... results of their efforts being ... and labels bearing the name ... With all these resources at ... order can be executed with ... and punctuality which nothing extraordinary circumstance out... calculations can prevent, ... has that superiority only at... the constant application to one ... description of labour.

... paper mill the firm manufacture ... wrapping and packing papers, and ... way of utilisation of ... old paper, rice bags, fibre, ... sold to the trade.

... publishes the text of ... regard to the registra... authorities of ... within eight days ... Committee for the ... any profession ...

Messrs. Paper Trade Review Office,
58, Shoe Lane, London, E.C.
August 24, 1893.

Trade Notes.

The Universal Barrel Company, Ltd., ... winding up.

Babcock and Wilcox.—For the first half of the current year the directors propose a distribution of 10 per cent. per annum.

Errata.—In the article "Yellow Aniline Dyes for Enamelled Papers," published on the first page, "arsenic" acid by a printer's error appears in the ninth line instead of carbolic acid, and in the fifth line of the second column "quercitron" should read quercitron.

G. E. Belliss and Co., Limited.—This company is registered with a capital of £150,000, in 10,000 ord. and 5,000 £6 per cent. pref. shares of £10 each, to acquire the business of engineers and boiler-makers, now carried on by G. E. Belliss and A. Morcom, under the name of "G. E. Belliss and Co.," at the premises known as Ledram-street Works, Birmingham; and to continue the concern undertaken.

Re Dalziel Brothers.—At the London bankruptcy court on Monday, the usual summary of accounts was issued under the failure of Messrs. Dalziel Brothers, printers, publishers, and engravers, of Fleet-street. The gross liabilities are returned at £39,146, of which £29,580 is expected to rank, and the assets at £10,247. The debtors were proprietors of two comic publications, and also possess the copyright of several books. They attribute their failure chiefly to losses on publishing transactions extending over many years, to bad debts, to the extinction of their wood-engraving business, owing to the introduction of automatic processes, and to loss by colour-printing through foreign competition. In addition to the assets mentioned, a surplus appears on the separate estate of each debtor which, if realised, will be available for the creditors of the joint estate.

Re H. R. Marks.—In the House of Commons on Tuesday, Mr. Barrow asked the Attorney General whether his attention had been called to the failure of H. R. Marks, as reported in the *World's Paper Trade Review*, of August 18th, in which the Official Receiver (Mr. Hough) appeared to have said that about five or six weeks before the receiving order was made certain debentures, amounting to about £15,000, had been issued by W. Wilfred Head and Marks, Limited, under which the assets of the business were charged in favour of the debenture holders; how were these debentures disposed of, and for what consideration, whether the trade creditors, presuming that they had knowledge of the debtors' intention to charge their security, had any lawful means of protecting themselves; and whether, with a view to increasing the safety of the position of creditors of limited liability companies, he would consider the advisability of introducing a bill to provide that debenture bonds should be registered in the same way as bills of sale. The Attorney General said that he knew nothing of the facts of the case, except so far as they appeared on the paper. He could express no opinion upon the three branches of the question, but as to the concluding inquiry, he thought that there was a great deal to be said in favour of debenture bonds being registered in the same way as bills of sale, and he would consult the Lord Chancellor on the subject.

THE LIGHTING OF CRANSTONHILL ENGINEERING WORKS.—The new works of Messrs. Harper, Limited, were lighted up by electricity for the first time on the 15th inst. The effect was very fine, there being no less than 35 arc lamps, aggregating 35,000 candle power and absorbing three-fourths of the available power of the dynamo, which has a capacity of 100 amperes and a voltage of 200 when run at 725 revolutions per minute. The dynamo is driven by a large Tangye gas engine, which assists a duplicate engine to drive the main shafting for the whole works. The gas required to drive the dynamo when the whole place is lighted up is only 3[illegible] feet per hour. This economy seems incredible, but is nevertheless a fact. It is probably due to the particular arrangement of installation and the careful selection of the apparatus and lamps, all of which are of the most modern design and manufacture. This trifling amount of gas would only light up a corner of the works were it put through burners in the usual way, instead of being converted into electricity through the engine and dynamo. The installation is a great success, and is the largest of the kind in Scotland, the Glasgow Central Station having little more than half the number of lamps. Notwithstanding its extent, it has been arranged and erected with much economy, due in great part to the skill of Mr. F. Heppert, electrical engineer from London, who fitted it up. The offices are also nicely lighted up by 35 incandescent lamps so that no gas is used throughout, except for driving engines, of which there are three altogether, to the total exclusion of steam.

DEATH OF MR. ABEL HEYWOOD.—We regret to record the death of Mr. Abel Heywood, aged 84, of Manchester. For the past 52 years the deceased gentleman carried on the business of stationer and bookseller, and during his long life has been identified with every movement for the public good or for the improvement of his adopted city, Manchester, and probably no man has ever died more unanimously honoured in his own locality.

THE COAL CRISIS.—The conference of delegates of the National Miners' Federation was concluded on Wednesday at the Westminster Palace Hotel. Resolutions were carried affirming the decision of the Birmingham conference that no reduction of wages be submitted to; declaring the readiness of the miners to resume work at once on the withdrawal of the notice for 25 per cent. reduction, and pledging them not to ask for an advance till prices reach the 1890 level; and directing representatives of the federation to be sent into the counties of Durham and Northumberland with a view to informing the miners there of the advantages of national federation. The coalmasters of Lanarkshire and Ayrshire on Wednesday made a second concession of 1s. per day advance to the men. Prices of coal have been raised in consequence, and the ironmasters have decided to damp down their furnaces. The colliers' strike in South Wales shows signs of terminating. The men continue to return to work in large numbers.

SCHEME FOR LABOUR EXCHANGES IN PORTUGAL.—Sir H. G. MacDonell, H.M. Minister at Lisbon, forwards a royal decree sanctioning regulations for Labour Exchanges. The Exchanges are to be subject to the Department of Public Works, Commerce and Industry, and are to serve as intermediaries for offering and procuring labour, and as agencies for collecting and publishing accurate information regarding the state of the labour market. Each Exchange will have a waiting room for those seeking work, a library, and reading and other rooms for meetings of unions, &c. The administrative committee will consist of a president appointed by the Government, and four members elected by the delegates of local unions. The committee, among other duties, is to issue a weekly bulletin of the wages of various trades, based chiefly, but not entirely, on the transactions of the Labour Exchange. Each Exchange will be divided into sections, and will be open free every day. Applications for work and for workmen are to be made to the agents of the various sections, by whom, if no corresponding offer be registered, they will be posted in frames in the waiting room. Should a corresponding offer be registered, the agent will furnish the applicant with a way bill, directing him to the proper quarter. The agent will draw up weekly schedules of applications which could not be met during the week. The committee will decide with reference to each case whether, in view of the state of the labour market in other industrial centres, notice of these applications should be sent further. Such notices, if sent to another centre where there is no Labour Exchange, are to be posted in the waiting room of the postal telegraph station, and on the parish church or other public building. Sir H. G. MacDonell also transmits some remarks furnished to him by an important English firm stating that the decrees of the Government with regard to labour, children's employment, &c., though mostly enlightened and beneficial, are not being carried into effect owing to the apathy [illegible] and apathy of the people.

STARCH MANUFACTURE AT CARROW WORKS, NORWICH.

The manufactures of Messrs. J. and J. Colman, Carrow Works, Norwich, have, as is well known, a world-wide reputation, and not the least important is their starch for papermakers. Rice starch is highly esteemed in England by the manufacturers of fine papers, as well as for sizing all kinds of fine fabrics. It gives a finish and a feel which cannot be attained by the use of any other kind of starch. Messrs. Colman's specially prepared starch for fine writings and printings has met with great apprecia-

STARCH FACTORY.

tion, and the same may be said of the firm's starch in crystals and granulated starch, the various grades being applicable to every use in papermaking.

In a "Souvenir of Carrow Works," particulars and illustrations are published of the various departments. The starch factory has nine acres of flooring. Messrs. J. and J. Colman manufacture entirely from rice, chiefly grown in Bengal and Madras. Great care and experience are required in the selection and grouping of the various qualities of rice, in order that the product may be of a uniformly good quality and colour. The rice arrives in bags made of gunny, holding from one to two cwts. It is at once carefully dressed and winnowed through sieves properly arranged for this purpose, to free it from every particle of dust and dirt contracted during the somewhat careless process of harvesting. It then finds its way to a room, where, in order to soften it, and thus to render the operation of grinding more easy, it is subjected to a steeping process. After some hours the rice in its softened condition is finely ground by ordinary mill stones, similar to those generally used for grinding flour. From fifty to one hundred pairs of these are constantly at work night and day in the starch department. The ground rice issues from the stones in a thin stream of about the consistency of cream, its constituent parts being starch, cellulose, or, as it is technically called "fibre," and gluten. In order to separate the starch from the other substances, the ground rice is run into large wooden vats, where it is agitated in water for some time and allowed to stand, when the cellulose, or "fibre," and gluten gradually settle to the bottom of the vessel, leaving the starch in suspension in the water above. By means of valves this is then drawn off, and the starch is allowed to deposit in large shallow zinc vats. The cellulose, or fibre, and the gluten, which are regarded as by-products, are carefully washed, and the water removed from the material by pressure. Square cakes are thus formed, which are sold as cattle food, containing as they do excellent flesh and muscle-forming properties. To return to the starch. As soon as the deposition has taken place in the zinc vats, the water is drawn off, and the starch is found in a thick layer on the floor of the vat in a semi-solid and pure state. It is then placed in long narrow boxes made of wood, perforated with numerous holes, and lined with a cloth of fine texture, specially made for the purpose. Here it remains until the moisture drains out and the starch has become quite solid, although still retaining a considerable quantity of water. As soon as it has become sufficiently hard it is removed from the boxes, and each long block is equally divided into eleven smaller ones, measuring about six inches each way. The shaping and cleaning is performed by means of a broad sharp knife, and it takes the girls some weeks before they are able to turn out the cubes clean, of the proper shape, and at the same time in a rapid manner. The cubes are next transferred to the benches seen on the right half of the illustration. Here they are rapidly papered (an operation requiring considerable dexterity), bound up with specially made twine, labelled, and placed in kilns for the completion of the drying process. The doors of some of these kilns may be seen open on the extreme right. In the process of drying, which takes several days to complete, a contraction takes place, which has received the technical misnomer of "crystallising," and when the cube has, so to speak, crystallised quite through, the starch is ready for the warehouse. There are three of these, each capable of holding, if required, about one thousand tons. To them the papers containing the dried blocks of starch are now removed, and placed in large stacks or piles, each stack representing from ten to fifteen tons.

Starch is sent out in various ways to suit customers. If the papered cubes are required, they are neatly labelled, and placed in strong deal packing cases—the larger quantity of starch sent out being in this form. For the fancy trade, handsomely made cardboard boxes, decorated with tasteful wrappers, and pictures of an ornamental character, are produced in all sizes and weights from 4 lbs down. to 1 oz. Our illustration gives a peep into the cardboard box department, and the various operations required to produce the boxes. Girls only are employed. On the left the lids are being prepared, whilst in the centre the bodies and bottoms are being rapidly manipulated. On the right will be seen the finished boxes and lids placed in stacks for drying before being fitted together. A record is made of the number of bodies or lids made by each girl. Ingenious machinery is in use for cutting and shaping the cardboards, wood pulp boards, etc., which very materially contributes to the rapidity with which the boxes are turned out. When once the boxes are thoroughly dry, they are passed on to the store room, where they are

CARDBOARD BOX DEPARTMENT.

packed in stacks. An illustration is given of this room, and it may be stated that during the busy season from 600,000 to 1,000,000 boxes of various sizes are always in stock. Every size is kept by itself, and on each pile is a label showing the number of boxes it contains. Girls from the adjoining packing room remove them as required. Both the box-making and filing rooms are lighted by electricity, some hundreds of the Swan incandescent lamps being used. The steam power absorbed by the starch department is supplied by four very large steel boilers of the newest type, fitted with automatic self-feeding and stoking apparatus, and actuating two large horizontal steam engines,

Starch Packing Room.

capable of giving out some six or seven hundred horse-power. The total number of hands employed in the manufacture of starch varies from eight hundred to one thousand. The following illustration shows the girls working in the starch-packing room. On the right the starch is being weighed, boxes filled and labelled, the finishing touches being given by the girls on the left. The dried boxes are being removed by the workman in the centre of the picture. The following medals have been obtained by this firm at exhibitions in recognition of the excellence of their starch:—London, 1851; London, 1862; Dublin, 1865; Paris, 1867; Only Grand Gold Medal, Moscow, 1872; First Class Prize Medal, Vienna, 1873; Only Gold Medal, Paris, 1878; Only Gold Medal, Edinburgh, 1886.

The works at Carrow consist of a range of lofty mills (sending up five chimney shafts from 100 to 140 feet high), granaries, warehouses, stores, factories, workshops, wharves, timber and coal yards, covering nearly twenty-six acres of ground. A double line of railway (with sidings and turn-tables) is laid in direct connection with the main lines of the Great Eastern Railway system. By means of a private wire between the works and 108, Cannon-street, London, a distance of one hundred and twenty miles, communication is always open between the manufactory and the large warehouses in the heart of the metropolis of Great Britain. These works are the growth of only thirty-seven years, though the industry itself and the firm are of far older date, the business having been transplanted from Stoke—a few miles distant—to Carrow, where greater facilities were afforded for its development. The works are unrivalled, at any rate in Eastern England, for the concentration in a corresponding area and on such an enormous scale, of the varied industrial pursuits of a great manufacturing centre. Four times each day the broad avenue through the works wears for a brief interval the lively bustle of a thoroughfare in the heart of a big city, as the 2,300 operatives enter upon or leave work.

CARDBOARD BOX STORE.

The Carrow Works afford the interesting spectacle of many trades being carried on in close proximity to each other. Here may be seen in large well-appointed premises, comprising a foundry, smithies, tinmen's workshops, saw mills, carpenters' shops, cooperages, and printing works, skilled artisans and labourers employed upon some special work, the combined results of their efforts being the tins, boxes, and labels bearing the name of "Colman." With all these resources at hand the largest order can be executed with a promptness and punctuality which nothing but some extraordinary circumstance outside all business calculations can prevent, and the work has that superiority only attained by the constant application to one particular description of labour.

In a large paper mill the firm manufacture their own wrapping and packing papers, and so effect a saving in the way of utilisation of waste material—old paper, rice bags, fibre, &c. Surplus stock is sold to the trade.

THE *Journal Official* publishes the text of a law just passed providing for the registration by the Communal authorities of foreigners not naturalised within eight days of their entry into any Commune for the purpose of carrying on any profession, trade, or industry.

WORLD'S PAPER TRADE REVIEW OFFICE,
58, SHOE LANE, LONDON, E.C.
AUGUST 24, 1893.

TRADE NOTES.

THE UNIVERSAL BARREL COMPANY, LTD., is being wound up.

BABCOCK AND WILCOX.—For the first half of the current year the directors propose a distribution of 10 per cent. per annum.

ERRATA.—In the article "Yellow Aniline Dyes for Enamelled Papers," published on the first page, "carbonic" acid (by a printer's error) appears in the ninth line instead of carbolic acid, and in the fifth line of the second column "gaercitron" should read quercitron.

G. E. BELLISS AND CO., LIMITED.—This company is registered with a capital of £150,000, in 10,000 ord. and 5,000 £6 per cent. pref. shares of £10 each, to acquire the business of engineers, and boiler-makers, now carried on by G. E. Belliss and A. Morcam, under the name of "G. E. Belliss and Co.," at the premises known as Ledram-street Works, Birmingham; and to continue the concern undertaken.

RE DALZIEL BROTHERS.—At the London bankruptcy court on Monday, the usual summary of accounts was issued under the failure of Messrs. Dalziel Brothers, printers, publishers, and engravers, of Fleet-street. The gross liabilities are returned at £39,146, of which £20,580 is expected to rank, and the assets at £19,247. The debtors were proprietors of two comic publications, and also possess the copyright of several books. They attribute their failure chiefly to losses on publishing transactions extending over many years, to bad debts, to the extinction of their wood-engraving business, owing to the introduction of automatic processes, and to loss by colour-printing through foreign competition. In addition to the assets mentioned, a surplus appears on the separate estate of each debtor which, if realised, will be available for the creditors of the joint estate.

RE H. R. MARKS.—In the House of Commons on Tuesday, Mr. Barrow asked the Attorney General whether his attention had been called to the failure of H. R. Marks, as reported in the *World's Paper Trade Review*, of August 18th, in which the Official Receiver (Mr. Hough) appeared to have said that about five or six weeks before the receiving order was made certain debentures, amounting to about £15,000, had been issued by W. Wilfred Head and Marks, Limited, under which the assets of the business were charged in favour of the debenture holders; how were these debentures disposed of, and for what consideration, whether the trade creditors, presuming that they had knowledge of the debtors' intention to charge their security, had any lawful means of protecting themselves; and, whether, with a view to increasing the safety of the position of creditors of limited liability companies, he would consider the advisability of introducing a bill to provide that debenture bonds should be registered in the same way as bills of sale. The Attorney General said that he knew nothing of the facts of the case, except so far as they appeared on the paper. He could express no opinion upon the three branches of the question; but, as to the concluding inquiry, he thought that there was a great deal to be said in favour of debenture bonds being registered in the same way as bills of sale, and he would consult the Lord Chancellor on the subject.

THE LIGHTING OF CRAIGINCHES ENGINEERING WORKS.—The new works of Messrs. Harper, Limited, were lighted up by electricity for the first time on the 14th inst. The effect was very fine, there being no less than 55 arc lamps, aggregating 75,000 candle power and absorbing three-fourths of the available power of the dynamo, which has a capacity of 100 amperes and a voltage of 260 when run at 725 revolutions per minute. The dynamo is driven by a large Tangye gas engine, which assists a duplicate engine to drive the main shafting for the whole works. The gas required to drive the dynamo when the whole place is lighted up is only 550 feet per hour. This economy seems incredible, but is nevertheless a fact. It is probably due to the particular arrangement of installation and the careful selection of the apparatus and lamps, all of which are of the most modern design and manufacture. This trifling amount of gas would only light up a corner of the works were it put through burners in the usual way, instead of being converted into electricity through the engine and dynamo. The installation is a great success, and is the largest of the kind in Scotland, the Glasgow Central Station having little more than half the number of lamps. Notwithstanding its extent, it has been arranged and erected with much economy, due in great part to the skill of Mr. F. Hoppert, electrical engineer from London, who fitted it up. The offices are also nicely lighted up by 35 incandescent lamps so that no gas is used throughout except for driving engines, of which there are three altogether, to the total exclusion of steam.

DEATH OF MR. ABEL HEYWOOD.—We regret to record the death of Mr. Abel Heywood, aged 84, of Manchester. For the past 52 years the deceased gentleman carried on the business of stationer and bookseller, and during his long life has been identified with every movement for the public good, or for the improvement of his adopted city, Manchester, and probably no man has ever died more unanimously honoured in his own locality.

THE COAL CRISIS.—The conference of delegates of the National Miners' Federation was concluded on Wednesday at the Westminster Palace Hotel. Resolutions were carried affirming the decision of the Birmingham conference that no reduction of wages be submitted to; declaring the readiness of the miners to resume work at once on the withdrawal of the notice for 25 per cent. reduction, and pledging them not to ask for an advance till prices reach the 1890 level; and directing representatives of the federation to be sent into the counties of Durham and Northumberland with a view to informing the miners there of the advantages of national federation. The coalmasters of Lanarkshire and Ayrshire on Wednesday made a second concession of 1s. per day advance to the men. Prices of coal have been raised in consequence, and the ironmasters have decided to damp down their furnaces. The colliers' strike in South Wales shows signs of terminating. The men continue to return to work in large numbers.

SCHEME FOR LABOUR EXCHANGES IN PORTUGAL. — Sir H. G. MacDonnell, H.M. Minister at Lisbon, forwards a royal decree sanctioning regulations for Labour Exchanges. The Exchanges are to be subject to the Department of Public Works, Commerce and Industry, and are to serve as intermediaries for offering and procuring labour, and as agencies for collecting and publishing accurate information regarding the state of the labour market. Each Exchange will have a waiting room for those seeking work, a library, and reading and other rooms for meetings of unions, &c. The administrative committee will consist of a president appointed by the Government, and four members elected by the delegates of local unions. The committee, among other duties, is to issue a weekly bulletin of the wages of various trades, based chiefly, but not entirely, on the transactions of the Labour Exchange. Each Exchange will be divided into sections, and will be open free every day. Applications for work and for workmen are to be made to the agents of the various sections, by whom (if no corresponding offer be registered) they will be posted in frames in the waiting room. Should a corresponding offer be registered, the agent will furnish the applicant with a way bill, directing him to the proper quarter. The agent will draw up weekly schedules of applications which could not be met during the week. The committee will decide with reference to each case whether, in view of the state of the labour market in other industrial centres, notice of these applications should be sent thither. Such notices, if sent to another centre where there is no Labour Exchange, are to be posted in the waiting room of the postal telegraph station, and on the parish church or other public building. Sir H. G. MacDonnell also transmits some remarks furnished to him by an important English firm stating that the decrees of the Government with regard to labour, children's employment, &c., though mostly enlightened and beneficial, are not being carried into effect owing to the ignorance and apathy of the people.

Special Prepaid Advertisements

☞ IT IS IMPORTANT that Advertisements under any of the Headings mentioned below should reach us by the FIRST POST on WEDNESDAY Morning to INSURE INSERTION.

Situations Vacant.

AN Important firm of German Rag Merchants wants a steady and experienced Agent for paper mills.—Address No. 5860, office of the World's Paper Trade Review, 58, Shoe-lane, London, E.C. 5860

WANTED, a Junior Clerk, accustomed to the routine of a paper mill office.—Apply, stating age and salary required, to C. Anderson, Thames Paper Mills, Purfleet, Essex. 5861

Situations Wanted.

FOREMAN is open to Engagement; well up in coloured shops, browns, and caps; last three-and-a-half years foreman at Brook Mills, Little Eaton, Derby.—Apply, J. C. Brown, Holme Cottage, Little Eaton, Derby. 5857

MANAGER, thorough practical experience in cartridges, manillas, caps and browns, desires change (good reasons given); 12 years present situation; well up in materials and machinery.—Address No. 5849, office of the World's Paper Trade Review, 58, Shoe Lane, E.C. 5849

SMITH, accustomed to paper mill, requires situation; good references.—Address Wm. Fursdon, 6, Albert Square, Auvie Street, Bristol. 5864

TO PAPERMAKERS.—Finisher requires situation; well-up in small hands, groceries, caps and browns; good references.—Address No. 5862, office of the World's Paper Trade Review, 58, Shoe-lane, London, E.C. 5862

Machinery Wanted.

WANTED, a good second-hand Refining Engine, must be as good as new; also, a Guillotine Cutting Machine, about 25 in. wide.—State full particulars and price to No. 5856, office of the World's Paper Trade Review, 58, Shoe-lane, London, E.C. 5856

Machinery for Sale.

ONE Annandale's Spray Damping Machine, mahogany box, extreme width 66 inches, with suitable air-compressor; also, a number of good second-hand Strainer Plates, 24 in. × 18 in., from No. 5 cut and upwards.—Scott and Graham, Engineers, Denny, N.B. 5855

TWO CALENDERS, second-hand, each with four hard-grained rolls, about 69 inches by 11½ inches diam., with Frames, Pressure Levers, and Driving Gear.

ONE KOLLERGANG, new, Stones 52 inches by 14 inches, C.I. Pan, Scrapers, and Driving Gear.

ONE HYDRAULIC PRESS, second-hand, with Press Box 38 inches diam. by 32 inches deep, with wheels; all parts strong, Ram 2 feet 6 inches by 8 inches diam.

ONE 2-cwt. STEAM HAMMER, second-hand, for Roller Bars or General Forgings, Cylinder 7 inches diam. by 12 inch Stroke, with heavy Anvil Block.

Apply 5859

BERTRAMS LIMITED, SCIENNES, EDINBURGH.

Mill to be Let or Sold.

TO be LET or SOLD, a Paper Mill at Stalybridge, called the Higher Mill, containing one large machine and room for another, steam engine and boilers, in good condition.—Apply for further information to the Caretaker on the premises. 2160

For Sale.

A DANISH Firm wishes to enter into relations with a paper mill, for the purpose of selling their collections of Original Coloured Cotton, Half White Cotton, I. and II. Baggings, Small Hemp Rope, and Linsey for Pasteboard Manufacturing.—Address "S.S.," No. 6386, care of Aug. J. Wolff & Co., Annoncenbureau, Copenhagen, K. 5863

MECHANICAL WOOD PULP.—Two Waterfalls, very well situated in the best timber districts of Norway, to be sold, or partner wanted to build pulp mills by experienced pulp manufacturer. Good opportunity for papermakers or pulp merchants.—Address "W.," Heydahl Ohmes' Advertising Office, Christiania, Norway. 5851

DAMPING MACHINES

On the most Improved Principle;

VENTILATION for all purposes;

Improved FANS or AIR PROPELLERS;

Patent SUSPENDING CLIPS to hold from one up to 50 sheets of paper or cardboard;

TURBINES; SMOKE CONSUMING APPARATUS;

Patent Life Protecting HOIST PLATFORMS;

New System of HYDRAULIC POWER for Lifts, Hoists, and Motive Power;

New Process of WIRE WEAVING by Steam Power.

For particulars of all the above address 5812

E. BREADNER

(Ventilator to the Manchester Royal Exchange),

134, DEANSGATE, MANCHESTER.

HENRY G. DAVIES,

Accountant and Auditor,

73, LUDGATE HILL, LONDON, E.C.

Periodical Audits; Special Investigations; Occasional Services; Entire Charge of Accounts Undertaken,

Defective Systems of Bookkeeping Revised.

New Books Planned, etc. 2671

MODERATE FEES. REFERENCES.

Complaints

Concerning Late Delivery of Newspapers are useless, unless the Wrappers accompany the complaint at head quarters of the Post Office.

Our Subscribers' Copies are duly posted before 5.30 p.m. on Friday, and should reach every postal address in the United Kingdom by SATURDAY MORNING'S POST.

We have complaints again of irregular delivery last week, some copies not being delivered until Monday and Tuesday, but our correspondents omit to forward us the wrappers, without which the General Post Office are unable to trace where the delay occurs. The postal marks will enable them to do this.

Printed and Published EVERY FRIDAY

AT 58, SHOE LANE, LONDON, E.C.,
By W. JOHN STONHILL.
ESTABLISHED 1878.

FRIDAY, AUGUST 25, 1893.

THERE appears to be considerable justification in the cry of "much over-production" of paper in the United States, and, in anticipating the rocks ahead, it is not to be wondered at that the American Papermakers' Association desire to discuss the problem at their next annual meeting at Chicago on September 6th. Short time at a number of mills, owing to slackness of orders, is very general, and in some cases employees have agreed to a reduction in wages being made rather than be thrown out of employment in case of a shut-down. The difficulties of the situation will no doubt prove very harassing when brought under discussion, and no remedial measure seems likely as, notwithstanding recognised over-production, new mills are constantly being erected and supplemental plant put in existing works. Much competition may be expected to follow much over-production.

IT is noteworthy that the conditions of trade are not lost sight of by the American Paper Manufacturers' Association, and in their laudable desire to grapple with them they exhibit considerable more activity than the Papermakers' Association of Great Britain, which body only wakes up when some question or suggested measure is put forward likely to interfere with manufacturing industries generally, and even then action is oftentimes delayed until influenced by the efforts of non-members, who from time to time have certainly shown more enterprise in protecting the interests of the paper trade than the Association itself.

WITHOUT casting the slightest reflection on the high capacity of those intimately connected with the Association, it is not too much to say that the organisation, as at present constituted, is almost useless in its bearing upon the welfare of the paper industry. If the Association is one having for its only object the promotion of conviviality amongst papermakers, let it be so recognised, but if it takes unto itself the unction of protecting trade interests then something more ought to be expected than anniversary meetings, where officers are elected or re-elected, and a few complimentary toasts submitted.

INFORMATION, statistical and otherwise, if accurately compiled by the Association, and brought before the trade, would prove of value. Analyses of import and export figures should also have attention, and likely markets abroad for British paper noted. There is legitimate ground for complaining that the Association does very little to bring about an expansion of trade, and considering the dull state of the industry such apathy is simply deplorable. On another page of this paper particulars, supplied by one of Her Majesty's Consuls, are given of the supply of paper to Persia, and as samples were submitted to the Papermakers' Association with the intimation of the possibility of developing a market in that country, it would be interesting to know if any notice has been taken of the matter.

THAT exportations of British paper are in a very bad way may be seen from the official statistics dealing with the past five years' trade. In 1888 the total value was £1,674,908, whereas last year the total only reached £1,431,204. A comparison shows a decrease of 14½ per cent. Surely a decline in British paper exportation is a subject of sufficient importance to merit observation from the Papermakers' Association of Great Britain?

THERE is no decline, however, in British importations of foreign paper. Indeed, during the past five years the value increased 34 per cent. Britishers paid foreign paper manufacturers £1,770,439 in 1888, and as much as £2,372,558 in 1892. What does the Papermakers' Association of Great Britain say to that?

In the High Court of Justice.

Chancery Division.

Mr. Justice Kekewich.

Between MASSON, SCOTT & BERTRAM, on behalf of themselves and all other the Holders of Debentures in the Defendant Company - - - - - - - - Plaintiffs.

AND

THE OTTOMAN PAPER MANUFACTURING COMPANY, LIMITED, THE HONOURABLE EDWARD WILLIAM DOUGLAS, and HENRY WILLIAM COBB - - Defendants.

I,

of

hereby tender, subject to the Conditions attached hereto, for the property comprised in the within Particulars of Sale, at the price of £ , having already sent a cheque to Ernest Cooper, the Receiver appointed in the above action, for £ , being ten per cent. on the amount of my Tender, and I agree with the said Ernest Cooper that in the event of my Tender being accepted I wil complete the purchase of the property comprised in the within Conditions in accordance with the said Conditions, by which I hereby agree to be bound in all respects.

Dated the day of , 1893.

CONDITIONS OF SALE of the said Shares.

1.—The Chief Clerk will open the Tenders on the 19th day of September, 1893, at twelve o'clock at noon, or at such adjourned appointment as he shall then make (at which time the bidders by Tender may, if they think fit, attend in person, or by their Solicitors, at the Chambers of the Vacation Chief Clerk at the Royal Courts of Justice), and, if any Tender be accepted, will in due course certify the result of the sale. Upon the Certificate of Sale (if any) being signed and filed, the same will be binding without further notice or expense to the Purchaser, and in the meantime no tender, unless refused, shall be withdrawn.

2.—Neither the highest nor any other tender will necessarily be accepted. In case none of the Tenders received be deemed sufficient, any bid may, with the sanction of the Chief Clerk, be made or increased so soon as the Tenders have been opened.

3.—The person who is certified to be the Purchaser shall upon receipt of notice of the Certificate having been signed pay, as the Chief Clerk may direct, a sum equal to fifteen per cent. on the purchase-money by way of deposit in addition to the deposit previously paid with the Tender.

4.—Notice shall be given to the bidder whose Tender may be accepted of the filing of the Chief Clerk's Certificate of the result of the sale, and such bidder shall within thirty days from the service of such notice pay the purchase-money (after deducting the amount paid by way of deposit) into Court to the credit of the action, "Masson, Scott and Bertram *v.* The Ottoman Paper Manufacturing Company, Limited, and others—1891.—M.—No. 3411," and in accordance with a direction to be obtained from the Chief Clerk, and, if the same is not so paid, shall pay interest thereon at the rate of seven per cent. per annum from the expiration of the said period of thirty days to the day on which the same is actually paid, deducting income tax.

5.—The statements in the Particulars are believed to be true, but are not warranted, and the Purchaser is to take the said Shares, with all the profits accruing in respect of the same.

6.—On completion of the purchase the receiver will deliver to the purchaser a transfer of the Shares.

7.—If the purchaser shall not pay his purchase-money at the time above specified, or at any other time which may be named in any order or direction for that purpose, and in all other respects perform these Conditions, an order may be made by the said Judge upon application at Chambers for the re-sale of the Shares, and for forfeiture of the amount deposited in respect thereof, and for payment by the Purchaser of the deficiency (if any) in the price which may be obtained upon such re-sale, and of all costs and expenses occasioned by such default.

8.—Notice of the filing of the Chief Clerk's Certificate and every other written Notice, Communication and Summons are to be deemed to be duly delivered to and served upon a Purchaser by being left for him at the address given in his Form of Tender, or upon his Solicitor, if represented by one.

9.—In the event of a Tender being refused, the deposit made in respect thereof will be returned in full.

Printed and Published by W. JOHN STONHILL 58, Shoe Lane, LONDON, E.C. August 25, 1893.

CONCERNING new daily papers we last week suggested that papermakers might do well to keep their eyes upon the growth of special organs amongst trade unionists. Mention was made of the establishment of the *Glasgow Echo* and the *Newcastle Evening News*, both of which have been founded in the direct interests of workers. Great dissatisfaction is felt at what is considered the inefficiency of the London leaders in expressing the views of union workers in the halfpenny evening papers which claim to be running in their interests. Meetings have been held by men who are in a position to guide this movement, and an effort is now being made to establish another half-penny evening London paper. The position of *The Sun* is ridiculed by those it is supposed to represent, and unless a little more activity and considerably more management is shown in the future working of Tay Pay's new paper it will neither gain the respect nor confidence of the general body of workers. Hence the present efforts to negotiate the financial arrangements for the founding of another halfpenny London evening paper to be run upon strong trade union lines.

THE *Labour Gazette* for August notifies the following among its recorded changes in wages as affecting the papermakers in Hendon, the figures within parenthesis showing the number of hands affected:—Machine men (4), change from piece work to time work (piece rates from 44s. to 49s. 6d.; time rates, 32s. to 37s. per week); beater men (32), 2s. per week (39s. and 44s. 6d. to 37s. and 42s. 6d.); potcher men (30), 2s. per week (32s. 9d. to 30s. 9d.); firemen (16), 9d. per week (30s. to 29s. 3d.); paper-cutter men (50), 2s. per week (39s. to 37s.); labourers at roasters (10), 2s. per week (36s. and 40s. to 34s. and 38s.); calender men (4), 2s. per week (30s. to 28s.); other unskilled men (50), 1s. or 2s. per week (30s. and 36s. to 29s. and 34s.).

THE short supplies of fuel and salt have curtailed the production of chemicals, and, upon reference to our Market Report this week, prices of caustic and bleach show an advance of 10s.

THE coal crisis is seriously affecting the paper mills in the Lancashire district, and it is pretty certain that unless the strike terminates at an early date the mills will simply work out their engagements and then close for a period.

SEVERAL fresh cases of cholera are reported at Rotterdam, and the epidemic continues to spread in Galicia and Hungary. The disease is also prevalent in Italy. A year ago—when cholera threatened to visit our shores—the importation of rags from foreign countries was only allowed under many restrictions. These have been considerably relaxed, and rags may now be brought into the country. This is felt to be a source of great danger, and the attention of the Local Government Board is to be drawn to the matter. Mr. Fowler will be urged to revert to the old order of things, and, in view of the possible introduction of infection by rags, to make the restrictions put upon their importation last year permanent.

THE firm tone of the Scandinavian mechanical wood pulp market is well maintained, and judging from the steady increase in consumption, no drop in prices is likely to be realised. Large orders for prompt shipment now come from Germany, particularly for dry pulp as moist is subjected to higher duty and is inconvenient for shipment. Many contracts for 1894 have already been concluded. Under present circumstances it seems strange that some dealers and speculators are still selling for the fall. No doubt they have burnt their fingers this year, and it is to be hoped that the lesson taught them will tend to do away with a system that looks very much like gambling.

BUT for the gross financial mismanagement at the initiation of the Ottoman Company, it would have been one of the finest commercial undertakings ever carried out with English capital. Wiping out these early transactions, and having the four papermaking machines at work, there is a bright future for those who have done so much to make these mills a successful industry in a country of such natural resources. A valuable concession, the personal influence of His Majesty the Sultan, and the well-known fact that the Sultan takes a large amount of interest in the development of manufactures in the great Empire are greatly to the advantage of the enterprise. We purpose giving some interesting particulars in an early issue.

WORLD'S PAPER TRADE REVIEW OFFICES,
58, SHOE LANE, LONDON, E.C.
AUGUST 24, 1893.

MARKET REPORT

and RECORD of IMPORTS

Of Foreign Rags, Wood Pulp, Esparto, Paper, Millboards, Strawboards, &c., at the Ports of London, Liverpool, Southampton, Bristol, Hull, Fleetwood, Middlesborough, Glasgow, Grangemouth, Granton, Dundee, Leith, Dover, Folkestone, and Newhaven for the WEEK ENDING AUGUST 23

From SPECIAL Sources and Telegrams.

Telegrams—"STONEHILL, LONDON."

CHEMICALS.—The market is irregular, both demand and price being affected by the curtailment of production owing to the coal strike. Stocks are getting cleared off. CAUSTIC SODA and BLEACH have been advanced 10/- by makers. Revised quotations are given below. SODA CRYSTALS are scarce, and vary from £2 15/- to £2 17/6. SULPHUR has advanced to £4 5s.

Prices are nominally as follows:

					£	s.	d.
Alkali, 58%	tierces	...	f.o.r. works	2½%	5	10	0
" 58%	bags	...	" "	2½%	5	5	0
58%	...	...	f.o.b. Liverpool	2½%	5	12	6
Alum (Ground),	tierces	...	" Liverpool	2½%	5	7	6
" "	barrels	...	"	2½%	5	17	6
" "	tierces	...	" Hull	2½%	5	5	0
" "	"	...	Goole	2½%	5	5	0
Alum (Lump)	"	...	f.o.b. Liverpool	2½%	4	17	6
" "	barrels	...	"	2½%	5	0	0
" "	tierces	...	" Hull	2½%	4	15	0
" "	"	...	Goole	2½%	4	15	0
" "	"	...	London	2½%	5	5	0
" "	"	...	f.a.s. Glasgow	2½%	5	5	0
Alumina Sulphate, casks			f.o.b. Tyne		4	2	6
" " bags			" "		3	17	6
Aluminoferric Cake, slabs			Liverpool ...	...	2	15	0
" " tierces			" ...	...	3	2	6
Alumina Cake, slabs		...	Glasgow	...	2	15	0
" "	tierces	...	"	...	3	2	6
Aluminous Cake, casks		...	Manchester	3½%	2	7	6
" "	"	...	Newcastle	2½%	2	10	0
" "	"	...	London	2½%	3	0	0
" "	bags	...	"	2½%	2	17	9
Blanc Fixe ...	...	...	f.o.b. Tyne	net	7	10	0
Bleach, 35%	...	...	" "	net	8	15	0
" (soft wood)		...	f.o.r. Lancs.	net	8	10	0
" (hard wood)		...	f.o.b. Liverpool	net	9	0	0
...	...	...	landed London	2½%	9	15	0
Borax (crystals)	...	...	... ...	net	29	0	0
powdered	...	...	... ...	net	30	0	0
Caustic Cream, 60%		..	f.o.r. Lancs.	net	8	12	6
" " 60%		...	f.o.b. Liverpool	net	8	17	6
" Bottoms		...	" "	net	6	15	0
" "	...	...	f.o.b. Tyne	net	6	15	0
Caustic White	77%	...	f.o.r. Newcastle	net	11	5	0
" "	77%	...	f.o.b. Tyne	net	11	5	0
" "	74%	...	f.o.b. Liverpool	net	11	5	0
" "	70%	...	" "	net	10	5	0
" "	70%	...	" Hull	net	10	10	0
" "	70%	...	f.o.r. London	net	10	5	0
" "	70%	...	" Lancs.	net	10	2	6
" "	60%	...	" London	net	9	5	0
" "	60%	...	f.o.b. Liverpool	net	9	5	0
Carbonat'd Ash	58%	...	" "	net	6	0	0
	48%	...	"	net	5	10	0
"	58%	..	f.o.r. Widnes	net	5	15	0
"	48%	...	" "	net	5	5	0
Chloride of Barium		...	f.o.b. Tyne	net	7	10	0
Hypo-Sulphite of Soda...			f.o.r Tyne		5	15	0
" "	10-ton lots		ex ship Liverp'l	net	6	10	0
Oxalic Acid ...	...	...	f.o.b. Liverpool	3½%	per lb		3
Salt Cake ...	...	...	" works	net	1	10	0
Soda Ash, 52%	...	...	f.o.b. Tyne	net	4	10	0
" 52%	...	...	ex ship Thames	1%	4	15	0
" 52%	...	...	f.o.b. Liverpool	1%	5	0	0
Soda Crystals	...	...	" Tyne	net	2	15	0
" "	...	...	ex ship Thames	2½%	3	5	0
" "	...	...	f.o.b. Liverpool	net	3	0	0
Sulphur, roll	...	...	f.o.r. works	2½%	7	17	6
" flowers	...	...	" "	2½%	9	10	0
" recovered	...	...	" "	2½%	4	5	0
Sulphate of Ammonia		"	" "	2½%	13	2	6
" of Copper		...	" Liverpool	5%	15	0	0

FOREIGN.—F.o.b. Continental port:

	£	s.	d.
Alkali, 58% 2-cwt. bags £6 10/0; 10-cwt. casks ...	6	15	6
Caustic Soda, 70-72%	11	12	0
Hypo-Sulphite of Soda 10-ton lots 140/0; bags ...	7	10	6
Sulphate of Alumina 7-8 cwt. casks net c.i.f. Ldn	4	7	6
Blanc Fixe (c.i.f. London)	7	12	6

ESPARTO.—The market is quiet, but fairly steady in tone, and the present low range in values is still attracting buyers' enquiries for distant supplies. Freights advancing and some boats taken up at high rates.

Prices c.i.f. London and Leith, or f.o.r. Cardiff, Garston and Tyne Docks are nominally as follows:

Spanish—Fair to Good ...	£5	10	0	to	5	15	0
" Fine to Best ...	5	17	6	..	6	0	0
Oran — Fair to Good ...	3	12	6	..	3	17	6
" First Quality ...	4	0	0	..	4	2	6
Tripoli — Hand-picked ...	3	17	6	..	4	2	6
" Fair Average ...	3	12	6	..	3	15	0
Bona & Philippeville ...	4	0	0	..	4	2	6

STRAW.—Quotations are nominal for Straw. Supplies from Germany are still stopped, and prices of French are higher than buyers are prepared to give.

IMPORTS of STRAW

(Purposes unspecified) at principal Ports From

CHANNEL Isles	1 bale	HOLLAND ...	897 bales
DENMARK ...	[illegible] bales	RUSSIA ...	10 "

STRAW PULPS.—Straw Pulps are quiet.

Prices, c.i.f. London, Hull or Leith:

Belgian, 25% moisture	£15	0	0	to	16	0	0
do. dry					16	0	0
German, 50 to 55% moisture ...					16	10	0
do. dry ... ... No. 1 £18 10 0; No. 2					15	0	0

CHEMICAL WOOD PULPS.—There is a good enquiry for Chemical Wood Pulps, SULPHITE particularly being in good request at firm prices. SODA and SULPHATE pulps appear to be more appreciated than formerly.

Prices, ex steamer, London, Hull, Newcastle, Leith and Glasgow are nominally as follows:

SODA, Unbleached, Common ...	£10	0	0	to	10	10	0
" " Extra ...	10	10	0	..	11	0	0
" Half-Bleached ...	12	10	0	..	14	0	0
SULPHATE, Unbleached, Common	10	10	0	..	11	0	0
" Extra ...	11	0	0	..	12	0	0
" Half-Bleached ...	13	10	0	..	14	0	0
" Bleached ...	15	0	0	..	16	0	0
SULPHITE, Unbleached, Common	10	15	0	to	11	0	0
" Superior ...	11	10	0	..	12	10	0
" " 50% moisture, d.w.	11	10	0	..	12	2	6
" Extra ...	13	0	0	..	14	0	0
" Bleached, moist ...					16	10	0
" Unbleached, English, del. Lancs. ...					10	15	0
" " " No. 1, ex mills, Ldn.					10	10	0
" " " No. 2. " "					9	15	0

MECHANICAL WOOD PULPS.—Advices from Scandinavia state that the market is exceedingly firm, and prices well-maintained. There is an exceedingly good demand for dry pulp for Germany. Dry Pine of good quality is also in fair British enquiry, and a considerable business is in progress for delivery in 1894.

Prices, ex steamer, London, Hull, Newcastle, Leith and Glasgow are nominally as follows ·

MECHANICAL, Aspen, Dry	...	£7 10 0 to 8 0 0
Pine, Dry	...	6 0 0 ,, 6 2 6
Pine, 50% Moist, Spot	...	2 15 0 ,, 2 17 6
Moist Brown (bundles	...	2 15 0 ,, 2 17 6
Dry Brown	...	5 15 0 ,, 6 0 0
Single Sorted... ...	...	2 5 0 ,, 2 6

IMPORTS of WOOD PULP.

Quantity	From	Importer	Port.
562 bales	Christiania	To order	London
647 ..	,,	,,	Grangemouth
1725 ..	,,	E. J. & W. Goldsmith	London
300 ..	,,	,,	,,
300 ..	,,	,,	,,
219 .	,,	W. G. Taylor and Co	,,
283 ..	,,	Alsing and Co	,,
542 ..	,,	Christophersen & Co	Fleetwood
500 ..	Drammen	London Paper Mills Co	London
250 ..	,,	Ekman Co	,,
290 ,,	,,	H. B. Wood	Fleetwood
480 ..	,,	G. Schjoth & Co	,,
1000 ..	,,	C. Christophersen	London
400 ..	,,	To order	,,
100 ..	,,	C. Christophersen	,,
40 ..	Drontheim	To order	,,
260 ..	Dusseldorf	,,	,,
809 ..	Gothenburg	,,	,,
150 ..	,,	,,	Liverpool
372 ..	,,	Salvesen & Co	Granton
24 ..	,,	G. Schenkenwald & Co	London
254 ..	,,	Christophersen & Co	,,
121 ..	,,	Taylor & Co	,,
476 ..	,,	H. Pearson	,,
1015 ..	Hambro	To order	,,
202 ,,	,,	,,	Grangemouth
54 .	,,	,,	Hull
265 ..	Helsingfors	,,	,,
2694 ..	Kotka	,,	London
80 .	Norrkoping	,,	,,
300 ..	Oporto	,,	,,
250 ..	,,	T. Aitken	Leith
1180 ..	Rotterdam	To order	London
50 ..	,,	,,	,,
12 ..	,,	,,	,,
80 ..	,,	,,	Liverpool
43 ..	,,	,,	London
450 ..	Stettin	,,	,,
250 ..	Stockholm	,,	,,
200 ..	Skein	H. B. Wood	Fleetwood
2448 ..	,,	G. Schjoth & Co	,,

Totals from Each Country:

DENMARK ...	250 bales	PORTUGAL ...	550 bales
GERMANY ...	1431 ,,	PRUSSIA ...	450 ,,
HOLLAND ...	2364 ,,	SWEDEN ...	2471 ,,
NORWAY ...	13080 ,,		

IMPORTS of WOOD PULP BOARDS.

Quantity	From	Importer	Port
150 bales	Copenhagen	L. Henle	London

HOME RAGS.—LONDON: Market dull, prices unchanged.—MANCHESTER: There is only a fair amount of business passing.—EDINBURGH: Trade quiet, prices steady.

LONDON:

New White Cuttings	22/0	Canvas No. 1	17/0
Fines (selected)	20/6	,, No. 2 ...	10/0-11/0
,, (good London)...	20/0	,, No. 3	5/6
Outshots (selected) ...	12/6	Mixed Rope	5/3
,, (ordinary) ...	11/0	White Rope	6/6
London Seconds	4/0-4/6	White Manilla Rope	9/0
Country do. ...	6/6-8/0	Coil Rope	8/0
London Thirds ...	1/9-2/0	Bagging...	1/9-2/0
Country do. ...	4/0-5/0	Gunny	3/6-3/9
Light Prints ...	7/0-8/0		

BRISTOL:

Fines	19/0	Clean Canvas ...	15/0
Outshots	13/6	Second Do. ...	9/6-10/6
Seconds	7/0-8/0	Light Prints ...	8/0
Thirds	3/6-4/0	Hemp Coil Rope	9/6-10/0
Mixed Bagging	3/6	Tarred Manilla	7/6

MANCHESTER:

Fines	16/0-17/0	Blues	7/0-7/6
Outshots (best) ...	12/0-12/6	Bagging...	4/3-4/6
,, (ordinary)	11/0-11/6	,, (common)	3/3-3/6
Seconds	7/6-7/9	W. Manilla Rope	10/0-10-6
Thirds	3/9-4/0	Surat Tares... ...	5/0-5/3

EDINBURGH:

Superfines	17/0	Black Cottons	2/9
Outshots	13/0	W. Manilla Rope ...	9/0
Mixed Fines...	14/0	Tarred Ditto	6/9
Common Seconds ...	8/0	,, Hemp Rope...	8/6
First do.	11/0	Rope Ends (new) ...	8/6
Prints	5/6-6/6	,, ,, (old) ...	6/0
Canvas (best)	16/0	Bagging...	2/0-3/0
,, 2nd	10/6	,, (clean) ...	4/3-6/0

DUBLIN.

White Cuttings ...	18/0	Mi'l Bagging	3/0
Fines	11/0	White Manilla	8/0
Seconds...	5/0	Tarred Hemp	8/0
Light Prints	3/0	Rigging	13/6
Black do.	2/0	Mixed Ropes	3/6
Bagging	2/0		

FOREIGN RAGS.—Merchants are not very pleased with the present regulations in regard to the admittance of foreign rags into Great Britain. The customs have the authority to order the disinfection of any parcel alleged to contain dirty rags or in default to be returned or destroyed. Notwithstanding there has been a fair enquiry, and arrivals have been moderately heavy.

IMPORTS of FOREIGN RAGS.

Quantity	From	Importer	Port.
426 bales	Amsterdam	To order	Hull
743 ,,	,,	,,	,,
321 ..	Alexandria	,,	Liverpool
435 ,,	,,	,,	,,
32 ..	Antwerp	,,	Leith
80 ..	Bremen	,,	Hull
246 ,,	,,		,,
32 .	Barcelona	,,	Liverpool
130 ..	Bordeaux	,,	Hull
4 ,,	Christiania	,,	,,
16 ,,	,,	,,	Grangemouth
390 ..	Copenhagen	,	Hull
60 ..	Constantinople	,,	Liverpool
58 ..	,,	,,	,,
34 ..	Dunkirk	,,	London
350 ..	Harlingen	,,	Hull
309 ,,	,,	,,	,,
42 ,,	Hambro	,,	,,
135 ,,	,,	,,	,,
22 ,,	,,		,,
218 ,,	Konigsberg	,,	London
65 ,,	Rotterdam	,,	Hull
140 ,,	,,	,,	,,
90 ,,	,,	,,	London
48 ,,	,,	,,	Hull
306 ,,	St. Malo	,,	London
102 ,,	,,	,,	,,

Totals from Each Country:

BELGIUM ...	32 bales	HOLLAND ...	2171 bales
DENMARK ...	390 ,,	NORWAY ...	20 ,,
EGYPT ...	756 ,,	PRUSSIA ...	218 ,,
FRANCE ...	632 ,,	SPAIN ...	32 ,,
GERMANY ..	525 ,,	TURKEY ...	118 ,,

DUTCH RAGS. f.o.r. Hull:

C.i.f. Thames; Hull 2/6 per ton more; ditto f.o.r. Leith c.i.f. Glasgow 4/-; c.i.f. Liverpool 4/-.

Selected Fines (free from Muslins) ...	17/0	Best Grey Linens ...	9/0
		Common ditto ...	5/6
Selected Outshots	12/0	White Canvas ...	15/0
,, Dirty Fines	7/0	Grey & Brown Canvas	9/9
Light Cottons ...	9/3	Tarred Hemp Rope	8/0
Blue Cottons ...	8/0	Ditto (broken) ...	5/3
Dark Coloured Cottons	2/10½	White Paper Shavings	7/9
New Cuttings (Bleachd)	22/6	Gunny (best) ...	4/9
,, (Unbleached)	19/6	Jute Bagging ...	3/6
,, (Slate) ...	9/0	Ditto (common ...	3/0
Muslins	8/0	Tarpaulins	4/0
Red Cottons (Mixed)	5/9	Cowhair Carpets ...	2/9
Fustians (Light browns)	5/0	Hard ditto	3/0

RUSSIAN RAGS.

C.i.f. London, Hull, Newcastle or Leith.

SPFF	15/0	CC (Cotton	5/3
SPF	13/6	Jute I	3/6
FG	10/6	,, II...	2/3
LFB	9/6	Rope I...	9/9
FF	8/3	,, II	5/9
LFX	7/3		

GERMAN RAGS.

STETTIN : C.i.f. Hull, Leith, Tyne and London.

SPFFF and SPFF	18/6	LFB (Blue)	10/
SPF	12/6	CSPFFF and CSPFF	12/0
FF	11/0	CFB (Blue)	8/0
FG	9/6	CFX (Coloured) ...	5/0
LFX	7/0		

HAMBURG : F.o.b.

NWC	22/0	FF Grey Linens ...	9/0
SPFFF	22/0	LFX Second ditto...	8/0
SPFFF and SPFF	18/0	CSPFFF	17/3
SPFF	16/0	CSPFF	11/3
SPF	12/0	CFB	8/0
CCC	5/6	Dark Blues (selected	11/9
CFX	4/6	Wool Tares... ...	8/0
White Rope... ...	8/0	Jute, No. I 6/0; No. II	5/6

FRENCH RAGS.

Quotations range, per cwt., ex ship London, Southampton, or Hull; 2/0 per ton more at Liverpool, and 10/0 per ton higher at Newcastle, Glasgow or Leith.

French Linens, I ...	22/0	Black Cotton ...	4/0
II 18/6; III ...	14/6	Marseilles Whites, I	16/0
White Cottons, I ...	19/0	II 10/0; III ...	7/6
II 15/0; III ...	12/6	Blue Cotton	11/0
Knitted Cotton ...	11/0	Light Prints... ...	9/0
Light Coloured Cotton	8/0	Mixed Prints ...	6/0
Blue Cotton	9/6	New White Cuttings	23/0
Coloured Cotton ...	6/0	,, Stay ,,	21/0

NORWEGIAN RAGS.

C.i.f. London, Hull, Tyne, and Grangemouth.

1st Rope (tarred) ...	8/9-9/0	2nd Canvas ...	8/0
2nd ,, ,, ...	5/9-6/0	Jute Bagging	
Manilla Rope (white)	8/6-8/9	Gunny ...	3/6 3/9
Best Canvas ...	11/9-12/0	Mixed ...	2/6-3/0

BELGIAN RAGS.

F.o.b. Ghent. Freights: London, 5/0; Hull and Goole, 7/6 Liverpool and Leith, 10/0; Newcastle, 12/6; Dundee and Aberdeen, 15/0; Glasgow, 16/8.

White Linens No. 1	22/6	Fustians (Light) ...	6/0
,, ,, No. 2	16/6	,, (Dark) ...	4/0
,, ,, No. 3	13/0	Thirds...	3/0
Fines (Mixed) ...	12/0	Black Cottons ...	3/9
Grey Linens (strong)	10/0	Hemp Strings (unt'r'd)	2/0
,, ,, (extra)	14/0	House Cloths ...	5/0
Blue Linens... ...	8/6	Old Bagging (solid)	3/6
White Cottons S'p'fine	18/0	,, ,, (common)	2/6
,, ,, No. 2	15/0	NEW.	
Outshots No. 3 ...	11/0	White & Cream Linens	35/0
Seconds No. 4 ...	8/0	White Cuttings ...	22/0
Prints (Light) ...	8/6	Unbleached Cuttings	21/0
,, (Old)	4/6	Print Cuttings ..	8/0

BELGIAN FLAX and HEMP WASTE.

Best washed and dried Flax Waste, 10/0; Fair ditto 9/0
Flax Spinners' Waste (grease boiled out)... ... 14/0
Hemp Waste, No. 1 9/0; No. 2 ... ... 7/6
Flax Spinners' Waste, No. 1 (Flax Rove) 10/0: No. 2 8/6

WASTE PAPERS.—There is a moderate demand for Waste Papers, which keep firm in value.

Cream Shavings ...	12/3	Small Letters	5/0
Fine ,, ...	9/6	Large ,, ...	7/0
Mixed ,, ...	3/6	Brown Paper	2/3
White Printings ...	8/9	Light Browns	3/6
White Waste ...	1/6	Books & Pamphlets ...	5/0
Wood Pulp Cuttings	3/6	Strawboard Cuttings	1/6
Brown Paper	3/0	Jacquards	2/6
Crushed News	2/0		

For Export: 25/- per ton extra.

JUTE.—Cuttings are in request.

Good White £16 0 to 17 0		Common ... £10 10 to 11 0	
Good... ... 15 0		Rejections... 8 0 ,, 9 0	
Medium .. 0 ,, 13 0		Cuttings ... £5 to 6 0	

COLOURS.—There is a steady enquiry.

Mineral Black ... cwt.	3/0	Ultramarine (pure)	
do. superior ... ,,	5/0	... cwt. 40/0 to 45/0	
Pure Ivory Black ,,	12/0	PASTE COLOURS with 60% of colour, as follows:	
Ochre ... ... ,,	3/0		
French J. C. Ochre ton	55/0	Orange Pulp ... cwt.	40/0
Chrome (pure) ... cwt.	40/0	Golden Yellow Pulp	36/0
Red Oxide ... ... ,,	4/6	Lemon ,, ,, cwt.	36/0
Umber, Devonshire ,,	50/0	Prussian Yellow ,,	36/0
do. Turkish ... ,,	40/0	Green (free of arsenic	36/0
Lamp Black ...	7/0-10/6	Paste Blue (20-45%)	
Cochineal ... ... lb.	1/3-2/0	.. ...	23/6-26/8

SIZING.—Market fairly busy at former figures.

English Gelatines	per cwt.	70/0 to 140/0
Foreign ,, ...	,,	70/0 ,, 140/0
Fine Skin Glues	,,	45/0 ,, 60/0
Long Scotch Glues	,,	45/0 ,, 60/0
Common ,, ...	,,	30/0 ,, 45/0
"Town" Glues	,,	26/0 ,, 36/0
"Bone" Glues	,,	20/0 ,, 30/0
Foreign Glues	,,	23/0 ,, 40/0
Bone Size	,,	4/0 ,, 10/0
Gelatine Size...	,,	5/0 ,, 10/0
Dry B.A. Pieces	,,	31/6 ,, 33/0
,, English Pieces	,,	24/0 ,, 27/0
Wet ,, ,, ...	,,	7/0 ,, 8/0
,, Sheep Pieces	,,	3/0 ,, 4/0
Buffalo Hide Shavings	,,	26/0 ,, 37/0
.. Picker Waste	,,	27/0 ,, 33/0

ROSIN.—Demand slightly better; prices unchanged.

Strained.	E.	F.	G.	K.	W.G.	W.W.
Spot— 3/9	4/0	4/3	4/6	7/0	9/6	10/0
To arrive—3/3	3/6½	3/7½	3/9	6/0	8/0	8/6

STARCH.—Business fairly good at firm prices.

F.o.r. London, less 2½%:

Maize—Crisp, £10 5/-; Powder, £10 10/-; Special £15 0/-
Farina—Prime, £10 15/-; B.K.M.F., £13 10/-

Delivered:

Rice—Special (in chests), £20 0/- (net); Crystal (in bags) £19 0/-; Granulated (in bags) £18 0/- less 2½%.
Dextrine—£16 0/-

MINERALS.—The market on the whole is fairly brisk. CHINA CLAY is steady, a good medium quality being quoted at 22/6 to 25/-. FRENCH CHALK is in better demand at unchanged values. BARYTES (carbonate) are still scarce, while finest white sulphate is in demand. IRISH MOSS (common quality) is freely offered at low prices; the best is scarce at advanced figures.

Mineral White (Terra Alba), per ton f.o.r. or boat at works:

Superfine...	28/0	less 2½%
Pottery Super.... ...	24/0	,,
Ball Seconds	20/0	,,
Seconds	15/0	,,
Thirds	10/6	,,

China Clay, in bulk, f.o.b. Cornwall, 14/0 to 27/6; bags 5/0 and casks 9/6 per ton extra; f.o.b. London, in casks 35/0 to 50/0 per ton.

Superfine Hardening, f.o.r. works, 40/0.

Patent Crystal Hardening, delivered at mills £3 to £3 15/0

Patent Hardening (2 ton lots) f.o.r. Lancs., £3 5/0.
,, ,, (5 ton lots) f.o.b. Liverpool, £3 10/0.

Magnesite (in lump) 32/6 per ton.

Magnesite (containing 98% Carbonate of Magnesia), raw ground, £6 10/0; calcined ground, £12 10/0.

Albarine, £3, del. mills.

Asbestos, best rock, £18; brown grades, £14 to £15

Asbestine Pulp, £4 5/- to £5 c.i.f. London, Liverpool and Glasgow.

Barytes (Carbonate), lump, 90/0 to 95/0; nuts, 72/6 to 85/0.

Barytes (Sulphate), "Angel White," No. 1, 70/0; No. 2, 60/0 to 65/0; No. 3, 45/0. Souheur's Brands (Antwerp): AF, 83/-; BF, 71/-; AB, 33/6; BB, 29/6; CB, 24/3.

French and Italian Chalk (Souheur Brand, Antwerp), per ton in lots of 10 tons: Flower O, 64/6 c.i.f. London, 69/6 c.i.f. Liverp'l, 71/0 c.i.f. Hull; Flower OO, 60/0, 65/0 and 66/6; Flower OOO, 51/6, 56/6 and 58/0, Swan Brand, 57/0, 62/0 and 63/6. Blackwell's "Angel White" Brand and "Silvery" 90/- to 92/6; prime quality, 90/- to 95/-; and superfine, 105/-.

Bauxite, Irish Hill Quality, first lump, 20/0; seconds, 16/0; thirds, 12/0; ground, 35/0.

Pyrites (non-cupreous), Liverpool, 5d., 2 %.

Carbonate of Lime (Souheur Brand, Antwerp) Prima 43/-, Secunda 37/-.

LIME.—Best WHITE BUXTON LIME, hand-picked, f.o.t. works, is quoted at 10/0 per ton (less 2½%).

DIRECTORY.

Names and Addresses under this heading will be charged for at the rate of 50/- per annum (52 insertions) for each card of two lines or under. Each additional line £1 extra.

ALUMINOUS CAKE.

The ALUM, CHINA CLAY and VITRIOL Co., Lim., 63, Queen Victoria Street, London, E.C. Works: Rainham-on-Thames. Telegrams—"Chinnock, London.

ANALYTICAL.

WILLIAMS, ROWLAND, F.I.C., F.C.S., 28, Pall Mall, Manchester.

ARTESIAN WELLS.

BATCHELOR, Richard D., Artesian and Consulting Well Engineer, 73, Queen Victoria Street, London, E.C., and at Chatham. 5713

ISLER, C., & Co., Bear Lane, Southwark, S.E.

LE GRAND & SUTCLIFF, Magdala Works, 125, Bunhill Row, E.C.

BOILER COVERING.

LONSDALES, Boiler Coverers, Blackburn, will send a sample cask of their Patent Plastic Cork Covering to any Paper Mill in Great Britain—5 cwt. cask for 25/- (carriage paid).

CHINA CLAY.

The ALUM, CHINA CLAY and VITRIOL Co., Lim., 63, Queen Victoria Street, London, E.C. Mines: Ruddle and Colchester, St. Austell, Cornwall. Telegrams—"Chinnock, London."

ROGERS, J., & Co., Truro, Cornwall.—Agents: Taylor, Sommerville & Co., 83, Queen Victoria Street. E.C., and at 16, Princes Street, Edinburgh.

W. SINGLETON BIRCH & SONS, Lim., 15, Upton Street, Manchester. Mines: Rosevear, St. Austell, Cornwall. 2276

COLOURS.

CARDWELL, J. L., & Co., Commercial Buildings, 15, Cross Street, Manchester. Specialties: Mineral Black, Ven. Red, Ochres and Umbers. 5304

COLOURS (Continued).

GEMMILL, W. N., & Co., Glasgow, Telegrams "Ruhe." Starches, Alumina, Antifroths, &c. All Paper Colours

HINSHELWOOD, THOMAS, & Co., The Glasgow Colour Works, Glasgow. Colours and shades matched exactly.

MULLER, A. E., 9, Fenchurch Street, London, E.C.

ESPARTO.

IDE & CHRISTIE, Fibre, Esparto, and General Produce Brokers, 72, Mark Lane, E.C.

MINERAL WHITE or TERRA ALBA.

WINSER & Co., Portland Mills, Princess Street, Manchester. Also manufacturers of Aluminous Cake.

HOWE, JOHN, & Co., Carlisle. 2112

STEEL.

MAKIN, WM., & SONS, Sheffield. Established 1736. Roll Bars, Plates, Cutter Knives, Doctor Blades, &c. 5369

STRAW.

GUNTER & Co., Ethelburga House, Bishopsgate Street Within, E.C., French, German, and Dutch Oat, Wheat, Rye, &c., compressed. 2114

UNDERWOOD, E., & SON, Limited, Brentford, London, W. Press-packed Oat, Wheat, or Rye Straw, delivered to the chief British ports or railway stations.

TALC (French and Italian Chalk).

SOUHEUR, JEAN, Antwerp. All Minerals, Blanc de Silex, Barytes (superior and common), Carbonate of Lime, Blacklead, &c. British Agent: A. E Muller, 9, Fenchurch Street, London, E.C. Agent for Liverpool and Manchester: C. H. Austin, Ditton, near Widnes.

RAGS.

CHALMERS, E., & Co., Lim., Bonnington, Leith.

MULLER, A. E., 9, Fenchurch Street, London, E.C.

WERTHEIM, A., & Co., Hamburg.

UMBER.

The **ALUM, CHINA CLAY and VITROIL Co., Lim.** 63, Queen Victoria Street, London, E.C. Telegrams—"Chinnock, London."

WOOD PULP.

FRIIS, N., & Co., 18, Carl Johans Gade, Christiania, Norway.

GOTTSTEIN, H., & Co., 59, Mark Lane, London, E.C., and at New York.

GRANT, W., & Co., 17, Baltic Street, Leith. Agents for best shippers, Sulphite and Sulphate, Mechanical, Pine, Brown, Aspen.

MATTHIESSEN, CHR., Christiania, Norway.

MULLER, A. E., 9, Fenchurch Street, London, E.C.

The **SULPHITE PULP Company, Limited**, 83, Gordon Street, Glasgow.

WERTHEIM, A., & Co., Hamburg.

PAPER EXPORTS & IMPORTS.

FOR THE WEEK ENDING TUESDAY LAST.

EXPORTS TO

	Printings.	Writings.	Other Kinds.
AUSTRALIA	9350¼ cwts	1474½ cwts.	573 cwts.
AFRICA	5 ,,	15 ,,	142 ,,
ARGENTINE ...	— ,,	— ,,	2 ,,
BELGIUM	29 ,,	44 ,,	— ,,
B. GUIANA	— ,,	9 ,,	— ,,
B. WEST INDIES...	29 ,,	3 ,,	8 ,,
CHANNEL ISLES	18 ,,	— ,,	— ,,
CANADA	41 ,,	360¼ ,,	4 ,,
CAPE COLONY ...	268 ,,	120 ,,	361 ,,
CHINA	— ,,	33 ,,	16 ,,
DENMARK	60 ,,	10 ,,	10 ,,
EGYPT	— ,,	— ,,	7 ,,
FRANCE	5 ,,	60 ,,	22 ,,
GERMANY	— ,,	— ,,	11 ,,
HOLLAND	18 ,,	87 ,,	24 ,,
INDIA	461 ,,	201¾ ,,	44 ,,
JAPAN	80 ,,	6 ,,	— ,,
MADAGASCAR ...	3 ,,	— ,,	— ,,
NEW ZEALAND ...	730 ,,	385 ,,	373 ,,
NORWAY	2 ,,	— ,,	— ,,
PORTUGAL	— ,,	6 ,,	— ,,
PRUSSIA	4 ,,	— ,,	— ,,
RUSSIA	3 ,,	1 ,,	— ,,
SPAIN	— ,,	33 ,,	— ,,
TURKEY	— ,,	2 ,,	— ,,
UNITED STATES..	6 ,,	255½ ,,	17 ,,

IMPORTS FROM

AUSTRIA ...	2 cases	HOLLAND ...	40 cases
BELGIUM ...	1355 bales	,, ...	346 rolls
,, ...	470 cases	NORWAY ...	5211 bales
DENMARK ...	269 bales	,, ...	352 rolls
FRANCE ...	453 ,,	PRUSSIA ...	23 bales
,, ...	44 cases	SWEDEN ...	1232 ,,
GERMANY ...	3227 bales	U.S.A.	11 cases
,, ...	137 cases	,, ...	91 rolls
HOLLAND ...	1923 bales		

Including the Following:

Quantity	From	Importer	Port.
24 rolls	Christiania	Lon. & Rhine S. Co	London.
58 bales	,,	,, ,,	
15 ,,	,,	Christophersen & Co	,,
20 ,,	,,	J. Hamilton	,,
20 ,,	Christiansand	J. Spicer & Sons	,,
140 ,,	,,	R. L. Lundgren	,,
17 ,,	,,	J. Hamilton	,,
109 ,,	Copenhagen	Becker & Ulrich	,,
75 ,,	Danzig	H. Huber & Co	,,
7 cases	,,	H. J. Stockton	,,
128 bales	Drammen	Crabb & Co	,,
25 ,,	,,	G. F. Green & Co	,,
21 ,,	,,	Schenkenwald & Co	,,
39 ,,	,,	W. D. Edwards	,,
37 ,,	,,	J. Holloway	,,
191 ,,	,,	F. E. Foulger	,,
46 ,,	,,	Alsing & Co	,,
5 ,,	,,	J. Spicer & Sons	,,
182 ,,	Gothenburg	Schenkenwald & Co	,,
117 ,,	,,	E. E. Sabel	,,
27 ,,	,,	Becker & Co	,,
30 ,,	,,	Green & Co	,,
35 ,,	,,	R. L. Lundgren	,,
64 ,,	,,	Alsing & Co	,,
16 ,,	,,	C. Morgan	,,
21 ,,	,,	Simmons & Co	
2179 ,,	Norrkoping	Schenkenwald & Co	,,
29 ,,	,,	J. S. English & Co	,,
95 ,,	,,	Brooks Whf.	,,
1072 ,,	,,	Dowgate Dk.	,,
2 cases	Trieste	Grosvenor, Chater & Co	,,

SUMMARY OF IMPORTS & EXPORTS,

FOR THE WEEK ENDING TUESDAY LAST.

London, Liverpool, Bristol, Southampton, Hull, Fleetwood, Harwich, Folkestone, Newhaven, Dover, &c.

IMPORTS.

Paper	12112 bales	Millboards	7390 pkgs.
,, ...	602 cases	Tissues	131 bales
,, ...	437 rolls	Strawboards	943 ,,
Pasteboards	8177 pkgs.	Stationery	23 cases

EXPORTS.

BRITISH GOODS.		Strawboard Cuttings	52 tons
Paper	1333 cwt.	FOREIGN GOODS.	
Printing Paper	7604 ,,	Paper	118 cwt.
Writing Paper ...	1829 ,,	Writing Paper...	5 ,,
Stationery	£9679 value	Printing Paper...	418 ,,
Pasteboards	89 cwt.	,, ,, ...	£11 value
Stock	174 tons	Stationery	£280 value
,, ...	42 cases	Cigarette Paper	£11 ,,
Parchment	£125 value	Strawboards	130 cwt.
Strawboards	34 cwt.	Parchment	60 ,,
Millboards	2 ,,	Pasteboards	300 ,,
Waste	160 tons		
Cardboards	188 cwt.		

Glasgow, Greenock, Port-Glasgow, Troon, Grangemouth, &c.

IMPORTS.

Paper	893 bales	Tissues	4 pkgs.
,, ...	3 cases	Strawboards	4339 ,,

EXPORTS.

Writing Paper...	1273¾ cwt.	Stationery	£314 value
Printing Paper..	3000¼ ,,	Envelopes	150 cwt.
Paper	71 ,,	Blotting Paper ..	32 ,,
Brown Paper ...	79½ ,,	Pulp Boards	10 ,,
Stock	60¼ ,,		

Leith, Granton, Boness, Dundee, &c.

IMPORTS.

Paper	255 bales	Envelopes	25 pkgs
,, ...	6 cases	Tissues	5 ,,
,, ...	352 rolls		

BRUNNER, MOND AND CO.—The half-yearly meeting of Brunner, Mond & Co., Ltd., was held on Monday at Liverpool. Mr. J. T. Brunner, M.P., who presided, moved the adoption of the report and accounts, together with a dividend on the preference capital at the rate of 7 per cent. per annum, and a dividend on the ordinary capital at the rate of 100 per cent. per annum. He remarked that that was their twenty-fifth general meeting and on an occasion like that, which was like a silver wedding, a dividend of the character indicated was quite appropriate to the circumstances. The shareholders were this year informed by the auditors that they had examined the securities, and he thought it was right the shareholders should know what had been done, for it was a matter of great importance, and he trusted they would be all satisfied with it. Mr. H. Coghill seconded the motion, and it was agreed to. Another motion was passed that the directors other than the managing directors, be paid £500 for their services during the half-year. In acknowledging a vote of thanks, the chairman said when he saw the same faces around him meeting after meeting, they were very pleasant occasions to him.

THE AFFAIRS OF MESSRS. GUNTER & CO.

A meeting of the creditors of Messrs. Gunter and Co., straw merchants, &c., of Ethelburga-house, Bishopsgate-street Within, E.C., was called on the 18th inst., by Messrs. Spencer, Gibson and Son, the debtors' solicitors, when a statement of affairs was submitted. The names of the creditors, and the amounts owing to them, as far as can be ascertained, are:—

Creditor	£	s.	d.
Allnutt Bros., White Swan Wharf, S.W. ...	£226	6	0
Adams Bros., 17, Gracechurch-street, E.C. ...	2	5	0
F. M. Duhne, Hamburg	108	0	0
Gosschalk and Themans, Zivolle	513	19	10
Theodore Jenson, Copenhagen	583	3	9
Klegman and Hoogewerff, Rotterdam	50	0	0
Ernest Lesueur, Rochfort-sur-Mer	100	0	0
Paper Trade Review (W. John Stonhill)	1	10	9
Prauschkaur, 109, Fenchurch-street, E.C. ...	60	0	0
Phillips and Graves, Botolph-house, E.C. ...	10	11	6
Rohde and Co., Hamburg	4	0	0
Sollas and Sons, 52, Gracechurch-street, E.C. ...	14	0	7
Spencer, Gibson and Son, 68, Cheapside, E.C. ...	85	9	1
J. Lunhalt Ubbricht, Cy., Chemnitz	55	0	0
J. Ward and Sons, 22, Beer-lane, E.C.	85	16	0

At the meeting (Messrs. Gosschalk's, solicitor, in the chair) Mr. Gibson observed that it had been made out almost entirely from information given by Mr. Gunter, whose books had not been written up for the last year. The amount owing to unsecured creditors was £1,662, and to creditors partly secured £2,023. Deducting from this last-mentioned amount the sum of £151 for less estimated value of securities—being £80 for estimated value of book debts assigned, and £70 for a life policy of £2,000—a total of £1,872 6s. 6d. remained to rank for dividend. The liabilities on bills receivable under discount were £300. There was a balance at the bank of £50 4s. 2d. The total amount of liabilities was £3,835 4s. 6d., and the deficiency was £3,767 0s. 4d. There was some straw lying at Newcastle sold to a customer. It was invoiced at £90, but there were disputes over it, and he (Mr. Gibson) was afraid it would realise nothing, so that he could not take it at any value in the statement of affairs. There was also some straw lying at London, but there was only a balance of £10 to come to Mr. Gunter, and there were only two book debts, of £4 and £7 each, altogether £11. The office furniture was not worth more than £12, £15 was owing for two quarters' rent, and this of course was a preferential claim, so according to the statement there was £83 of assets subject to the bills running off when they were due, and assuming that they did run off, after paying the rent, £15, a balance of £68 would remain for dividend.

Much dissatisfaction was expressed with the statement made, and Mr. Gunter was called before the meeting and subjected to a cross-examination regarding how the liabilities of £3,000 were made up. It was said that all monies received had been paid at once into the bank, but later on Mr. Gunter admitted that after so paying the money into the bank he had afterwards paid off other liabilities. His private expenditure was £300 a year. He commenced business in 1881 upon nothing.

Subsequently Mr. Gibson made an offer of 2s. in the £, to be paid by two instalments of 1s. a year. It was the best offer, he remarked, that the statement would allow. After long discussion it was decided not to accept the offer then, and eventually the meeting was adjourned till Wednesday afternoon, the 13th September, at three o'clock.

J. ZUBER AND CO., Commandit-Gesellschaft auf Actien, in Rixheim, Upper Alsatia, Germany, wall paper makers, in their balance sheet just issued show a gross profit of M154,961 on a share capital of M600,000. A dividend of 8 per cent. will be declared.

HERR LOUIS STAFFEL, JUNR., has retired from the firm of W. and Louis Staffel, in Cassel, in order to undertake the management of the Unterschmitten Paper Mills, belonging to his father, Herr Louis Staffel, senr., Witzenhausen. Herr Wilhelm Staffel will continue on his own account the above firm of W. and Louis Staffel, in Cassel.

PASSAUER MECHANISCHE PAPIER FABRIK, AN DER ERLD.—Commencing with a balance of M1,500 from 1892 profits, on April 30th, 1893, a loss of M4,183 had to be carried forward. The share capital consists of M263,700.

MASCHINENPAPIER UND HOLZSTOFF-FABRIKEN UNTERKOCHEN have sold their Bruckmühl branch to Herren Leiss and Co., in Westerham for the sum of M370,000, but without stock. As mortgages for M230,110 are entered upon this branch, the sum of M130,000 will give great strength to the financial position of the firm, and enable it to make important alterations and improvements in their Unterkochen establishment.

THE FIRM OF SPEISEBECHER AND CO., Fabrik Falkenhorst, near Wolkenstein, has been changed into a limited liability company. The production of wood pulp and glazed boards and coloured and fancy papers will be carried on on a larger scale than hitherto.

PATENT PAPIER FABRIK ZU PENIG.—Privy Councillor Herr Julius Vogel, after 25 years' successful activity, has resigne his position as general manager an member of the board of directors. Th directors are now Herr Adolf Schinkel fo the technical, and Herr Heinr Castorf for th commercial management. The technic manager, Herr Friedrich Mosel, has receive collective procuration.

THE Town Council of Lahr in Baden, h arranged with the Baden Sickness and O Age Insurance Fund for an advance by th latter of £7,500 at 3½ per cent., and repayab in 50 years, on behalf of workman desirou of building their own houses. Applican must pay one-fifth of the purchase and buil ing costs, and the houses which they propo to build must be for their own occupation.

Telegrams: "*PUMPS, BURY.*" *Telephone: 64, BURY.*

CHARLES WALMSLEY & Co.,

LIMITED,

ATLAS IRON WORKS, BURY, NEAR MANCHESTER,

Engineers, Millwrights,

ESTABLISHED 1844. **Paper Machinists,**

BRASS & IRON FOUNDERS.

PAPER BRUSH DAMPING MACHINE.

SPECIALTIES:

HIGH - CLASS STEAM ENGINES.

Simple, Double, Triple, and Quadruple Compound,
from 10 to 1,000 i.h.p., fitted with Automatic Cut-off Gears.

ALL TYPES OF PUMPING MACHINERY:

DEEP WELL PUMPS,	BOILER PUMPS,	PAPERMAKERS'
BORE HOLE PUMPS,	VACUUM PUMPS,	CHEMIC & CAUSTIC Pumps,
STATIONARY FIRE Pumps,	HYDRAULIC PUMPS,	STUFF & WATER PUMPS.

SOLE MAKERS OF 2513

PARTINGTON'S Patent DUPLEX CUTTING MACHINE.

COMMERCIAL INTELLIGENCE.

WILLIAM RIPLEY.—Trading as Read, Brooks and Co., printer and publisher, 25, Newberry-street, Cloth Fair, E.C. A schedule of liabilities under a trust deed contains the following names of creditors:—

Taylor Bros., Leeds	£147
Baddeley Bros., London	32
Bibbie, Hobson & Co., London	34
B. Dellagana & Co., Ltd., London	10
J. Dickinson & Co., Ltd., London	18
Grosvenor, Chater & Co., London	79
Harrild & Sons, London	27
Joshua Jones & Co., London	15
W. Jones, London	15
Lepard & Smiths, London	38
A. Pirie & Sons, Ltd., London	24
Slater & Palmer, London	17
J. Spicer & Sons, London	15
Wilmott & Sons, London	16
Jas. Wrigley & Son, London	20

CHARLES DICKENS AND FREDERICK M. EVANS, printers and publishers, 12, St. Bride-street, E.C., and the Crystal Palace Press, Sydenham. Under a registered deed the following firms are scheduled as creditors:—

J. Bartholomew & Co., Edinburgh	£296
T. J. Caldicott, London	100
Chappell & Co., London	92
William Clowes & Son, London	62
Dryden & Foord, London	296
Fisher & Sons, London	732
Harrild & Sons, London	1,134
Miller & Richard, London	56
Novello & Co., London	68
Richardson, Koolman & Isger, London	103
Shackell, Edwards & Co., London	226
Spalding & Hodge, London	424
Strong & Hanbury, London	606
Winterbottom Book Cloth Co.	66
T. Beecham, St. Helen's	97
Crystal Palace, Ltd., Sydenham	832

The total amounts to under £22,000, of which £1,691 is fully secured, and the nett assets are recorded at £4,917.

DAVEY M. BARRON.—Stationer and bookseller, 17, Narrow-street, Peterborough. Under a recently registered deed the following are scheduled as creditors:—

Allan and Stow	£23
Banner of Faith	15
William Clowes and Son	11
Cond Bros.	11
John Dickinson and Co.	23
Eyre and Spottiswoode	52
Frankau and Co.	32
Marden and Co.	22
Oxford University Press	37
Poulton and Sons	32
J. N. Powell and Co.	15
Walmsley and Son	12
Whitaker and Co.	88
Woolff and Son	11

VERY SOCRATIC DIALOGUES UP-TO-DATE.

I.

Dramatis Personæ—Two "GREEKS."

IMPECUNIARIUS.—In conversation over our billiards last night you said, "The most powerful impulse operating in the breast of modern man is the desire to get on—at some one else's expense." I was deeply impressed with the truthfulness of the statement. I have been for years trying to get on—in that way—but though I have adhered closely to the principle my efforts have not been attended with much success hitherto.

CYNICUS.—It is not always given to man to succeed, even though his aims be all right and his methods O.K. I made very little over our little flutter last night for example, though I account myself forty in a hundred better than you.

IMP.—Yes, whilst I esteemed you a "soft thing."

CYN.—It only goes to show the vanity of all human desires, unless one has a lot up one's sleeve.

IMP.—A two to one chance and six to four against, is what the Modern Schools inculcate as the true line of acceptance.

CYN.—In truth I see you have sat at the feet of a philosopher with a large head.

IMP.—I wish to give to this our dialogue a practical turn, and with that end in view will submit my own as an illustrative case, and doubtless you will be able to show to me how it is that attainment has not waited upon effort.

CYN.—To reduce the proposition to its ultima simplicima (to adopt the expressive language of the Latin philosophers), I am to demonstrate, first, why, though a known trier, you fail to get on; and, second, to point out the path by which success may yet be yours.

IMP.—You have found the pin first time. Well, I am a manufacturer of pilulæ crumbæ et saponacæ, warranted to cure warts, corns, or bunions, coughs, colds, pains in the head and chest—

CYN.—Avoidance of verbosity in the laying down of a premise is commendable. But propel your barrow in your own unsightly fashion.

IMP.—In brief, I am a pillmonger. I make and sell many pills, at the expenditure of great effort, but parting with little 'oof on the raw material. But although always striving, with the leading principle, "That which man wants man must have," always in view, the spondulics don't accumulate. In truth, though vending that which costs me little, I realise no profit for my labours, but am out of keck. I pray you, as an erudite Schoolman, expound to me the reason and the remedy.

CYN.—That which costs nought, sold for "ready," should result in profit to the vendor. There is something wrong in your premise. The Schoolman would deduce from this the syllogism,

> That which costs nothing and sells for something must realise a profit:
>
> Impecuniarius sells for something pills which cost him nothing:
>
> Ergo, Impecuniarius must be raking in the shekels.

But if the deduction from the premise be wrong, we must introduce a postulate, and my postulate would be that you are guying me.

IMP.—The assumption would be wrong in fact, and therefore untenable. I'll take my davy what I say is right. I vend pilulæ, crumbæ et saponacæ, the raw material of which costs me next to nix, I collect the dibs, and yet I'm pretty well stoney.

CYN.—The facts are irreconcilable. We will reverse the reasoning, and say,

> Impecuniarius should have profit from his pills:
>
> Impecuniarius has no profit:
>
> Ergo, Impecuniarius is doing it in somehow else.

Your predicative is that you are stoney. My deduction is that you blew in your profits over the Cain-and-Abel, or on geegees.

IMP.—Your reasoning, O Sage, is close and accurate.

CYN.—Accepting your assertion, then, that you are in a state of bankruptcy, how can this condition, which the world calls a misfortune, be turned into a blessing? In this way: Go into the highways and call unto you six other students as "stoney" as yourself, and together draw up articles of association, to acquire and carry on the business of manufacturing and vending pilulæ crumbæ et saponacæ. Register the new undertaking as a Limited Company, and then, my son, there lies before you the fulfilment of your honest desire to get on—at someone else's cost.

IMP.—It sounds simple and delightful. But pray you, Cynicus, expound to me further how, with a business which is "broke," and seven "Greeks" a little more so, the operation of manipulating the mopusses is to be achieved.

CYN.—Have you ever seen the gentle shepherd shear the offspring of the tender and uncomplaining sheep?

IMP.—Truly, I have assisted the husbandman in relieving the wanton young thing of its superfluous fleece, and the fledgling of its ultimate feathers.

CYN.—Then you will prove an apt pupil. But I must reserve for a future dialogue the minuter details of the system of turning a bankrupt business into a little gold mine.

IMP.—Gargle?

CYN.—Why cert'nly!

THE
United Asbestos Co.,
LIMITED,
DOCK HOUSE, BILLITER STREET, E.C.,
"SALAMANDER"
THE UNITED ASBESTOS COMPANY LIMITED · LONDON ·
TRADE MARK
Pioneers
OF THE
Asbestos
Trade.
UNITED ASBESTOS
NON-CONDUCTING
COVERING
(For Steam Boilers & Pipes)
Best and Cheapest in the Market; Will not Injure Boiler Plates.
ASBESTOS
GOODS of ALL DESCRIPTIONS
BELTINGS.
THE UNITED ASBESTOS CO., Limited,
UNITED
PACKINGS.
UNITED ASBESTOS Cº LMTD LONDON
PURE ITALIAN MILLBOARD EXTRA QUALITY
A1
UNITED ASBESTOS
A1 MILLBOARDS
(ITALIAN)
Unequalled for Purity, Strength of Fibre, and Uniformity. For Dry Steam Joints it is admitted to be the cleanest, most durable and economical packing in existence.
UNITED ASBESTOS
SALAMANDER
Lubricating Cream & Oils,
SPECIALLY ADAPTED TO
PAPERMAKING MACHINERY.
DEPOTS:
MANCHESTER: 34, Deansgate; LIVERPOOL: 33, James Street; NEWCASTLE-UPON-TYNE: Quayside; GLASGOW: 54, Robertson Street; CARDIFF: 135, Bute Street; BRISTOL: Provident Buildings; HULL: Queen's Dock; ST. PETERSBURG: Gostinoe Dvor (Interior) No. 51.

Taylor's Patent

BEATING and REFINING ENGINE.

THIS BEATER TAKES UP LESS FLOOR SPACE THAN ANY OTHER.

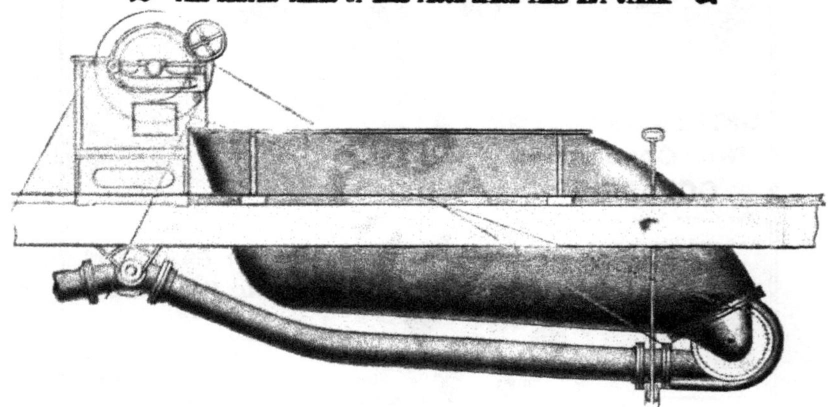

ADVANTAGES:

1.—**GREATLY INCREASED PRODUCTION** over that of the ordinary Beater in use.

2.—**GREAT SAVING IN POWER**, notwithstanding the increased production. This Beater has been proved to beat a given quantity of pulp with less than one-half of the power required by an ordinary beater of good modern construction.

3.—**COMPLETE AND PERFECT CIRCULATION**, which ensures complete uniformity in the length of the fibres.

For Full Particulars and Prices apply to

MASSON, SCOTT & Co., LTD.,

BATTERSEA, LONDON, S.W.

CONCERNING PATENTS.

Some people have curious ideas as to what is and what is not worth patenting, or as to what can be made the subject of a patent. As a rule it is sufficient for a man to conceive an idea: however crude and ill-digested, to him it represents something at least remarkable, generally wonderful. If one could picture the surprise of old Zeus when Minerva sprang fully armed from his brain-pan, it would probably approximate to that of the average applicant for provisional protection. There is a moment of intense surprise that the inspiration should have found birth in his mind, and then a wild rush, sovereign in hand, to secure the fabulous advantages and emoluments that he understands attends the possession of a patent of any kind whatever. He seldom pauses to inquire with himself (1) whether the idea is original, or (2) whether it is a fit subject for a patent, or (3) whether if patented it is likely to prove remunerative. After the first wild rush he as often as not regrets the expenditure of his sovereign and proceeds no further. The succeeding twelve months allow of calmer consideration, and because his conception does not affirmatively answer one or other of the foregoing questions he abandons his infant, and the Patent Office retains his twenty shillings as a contribution towards the expenses of the department. We have used the masculine pronoun, for it is remarkably rare to find a female applicant for protection. Either the ladies have not the inventive faculty, or they commit their ideas to male relatives, or they are more economical as regards expenditure on preliminary fees. Which is it?

That we are not speaking without the book is shown by the number of applications in any given year, and the comparative number of patents carried through. The number of patents sealed bears about the average proportion of one-half of the applications. Taking the eight years succeeding the passing of the Patents Act of 1883 (that is 1884 to 1891), the number of applications was 152,734, while the number sealed was 79,291—a trifle more than one-half. Of the full number, 72,379 were abandoned, only 118 being refused. Is it not Horace who recommends the aspirant for literary fame to hide away his M.S. for seven years, implying that if he re-read it at that interval of time he would certainly not publish it? From the figures given above it is evident that if the would-be patentee followed that course with his "ideas" for a much less period, there would be considerably less work to do in the Patent Office.

An examination of the records of the Patent Office reveals several curious calculations. To begin with, since the passing of the Patent Act of 1852 there has been a steady increase in the number of applications and sealings. Dividing the 40 years from 1852 to 1891 (both inclusive) into five periods of eight years each, we obtain the following figures:—

Years.		No. of Applications.		No. of Patents Sealed.
1852 to 1859	......	22,291	......	15,078
1860 to 1867	......	27,093	......	17,013
1868 to 1875	......	32,028	......	21,472
1876 to 1883	......	44,201	......	29,775
1884 to 1891	......	152,734	......	79,291

Although the tendency has been steadily upwards, the last eight years, following upon the reduction of fees—the introduction of the "easy payment system" under the Act of 1883—show a tremendous jump. Regarded as a business speculation, the "easy payment system" has been a stupendous success. But there is this further curious fact shown in the figures just given, that under the Act of 1852 the number of patents sealed was steadily preserved throughout at the proportion of about two-thirds of the applications, whilst in the eight years under the Act of 1883 the proportion is equally steady at a little over one-half, as witness the totals:—

From.		No. of Applications.		Patents Sealed.
1852 to 1883	......	125,313	......	83,208
1884 to 1891	......	152,734	......	79,291

That the tendency is still upwards is shown by an examination of the figures for each of the years since 1884:—

Year.		No. of Applications.		Patents Sealed.
1884	......	17,110	......	9,984
1885	......	16,101	......	8,775
1886	......	17,176	......	9,105
1887	......	18,051	......	9,457
1888	......	19,103	......	9,820
1889	......	21,008	......	10,664
1890	......	21,307	......	10,599
1891	......	22,888	......	10,887

In the last year quoted the number of applications abandoned was more than 50 per cent. of those sent in, so that we are led to the conclusion that the ratio of abandonments is higher than the increase of applications. In 1892 the applications rose to 24,171, but the abandonments are not yet scheduled, of course.

The total cost of administration of the Patent Office for 1892 (including Trade Marks and Designs) was £93,522 17s. 6d. Taking the probable abandonments at one half the applications, the sovereigns paid upon abortive attempts to become patentees paid about one-eighth of the whole cost. Taking this view of it, it would be a mistake to put any impediment in the way of such applications. With encouragement they might be made to pay the whole of the salaries: they will about cover one-fourth of the sum in 1892. These sovereigns just about paid for the expenditure on new offices and buildings, figuring at £13,000.

By-the-bye, the "Compositor of the *Trade Marks' Journal*" figures in the salaries list for £260 19s. 4d.

The total amount received in fees for patents in 1892 was £180,566 14s. The surplus over cost of administration was £103,036 7s. 9d. The printers' bill was

£19,000, and the value of paper supplied to the printers by H.M. Stationery Office was £1,500. The sale of publications amounted to £5,900 17s. 6d.

The applications for patents in 1892 are distributed throughout the world in the following order:—The United Kingdom, 17,927; the British Colonies and possessions, 418 (Canada coming first with 137, then Victoria 65, New South Wales and New Zealand 52 each, and India 51); European States, 3,453 (Germany taking a heavy lead with 1,791, France coming next with 847, Austria third with 259, and Belgium fourth with 152); the United States, 2,308, and the remaining American States 24; Africa 28, 21 of which emanate from South Africa; whilst the whole of Asia only contributes 12. One application from the Sandwich Islands makes up the total of 24,171.

NEW COMPANIES.

WARD and CO., Ltd.

Registered with a nominal capital of £5,000, in £5 shares of £1 each, to acquire as a going concern the business of newspaper proprietors, printers, &c., hitherto carried on by William Ward and G. Bush, at Forest-gate, and to develop and extend the same. The first directors—to be not less than three nor more than five—are W. Ward, G. Bush and J. Stack. Director's qualification, one share. Remuneration to be fixed by the company in general meeting.

REPORTS CO., Limited.

Registered with a capital of £10,000, in 940 ten per cent. cumulative preference shares, and 640 ordinary shares of £10 and £1 each respectively, to compile, print, publish, bind, and sell law reports, and to enter into an agreement with Herbert G. Sweet. There shall not be less than two nor more than five directors. The first are W. A. Maxwell and W. F. Laurie. Qualification, 10 shares. Remuneration, £500 per annum divisible. Managing director, H. G. Sweet.

"PRINTERS' WEEKLY ADVERTISER," Ltd.

Registered by H. C. Morris, 2, Walbrook, E.C., with a capital of £1,000 in £1 shares, to acquire the copyright of the weekly periodical known as the *Printers and Kindred Traders' Weekly Advertiser*, and to print and publish the same. There shall not be less than three nor more than seven directors. The first are Dr. J. Gale, T. Baker, J. L. Henderson, and J. Henderson. Qualification, 50 shares. Remuneration, £100 per annum. divisible.

"ST. HELENS CHRONICLE" AND PRINTING AND PUBLISHING CO., Limited.

Registered with a capital of £3,000, in £1 shares, sufficiently indicated by the title. Registered without articles of association.

Printed and Published by W. JOHN STONHILL, 58, Shoe Lane, LONDON, E.C. August 25, 1893.

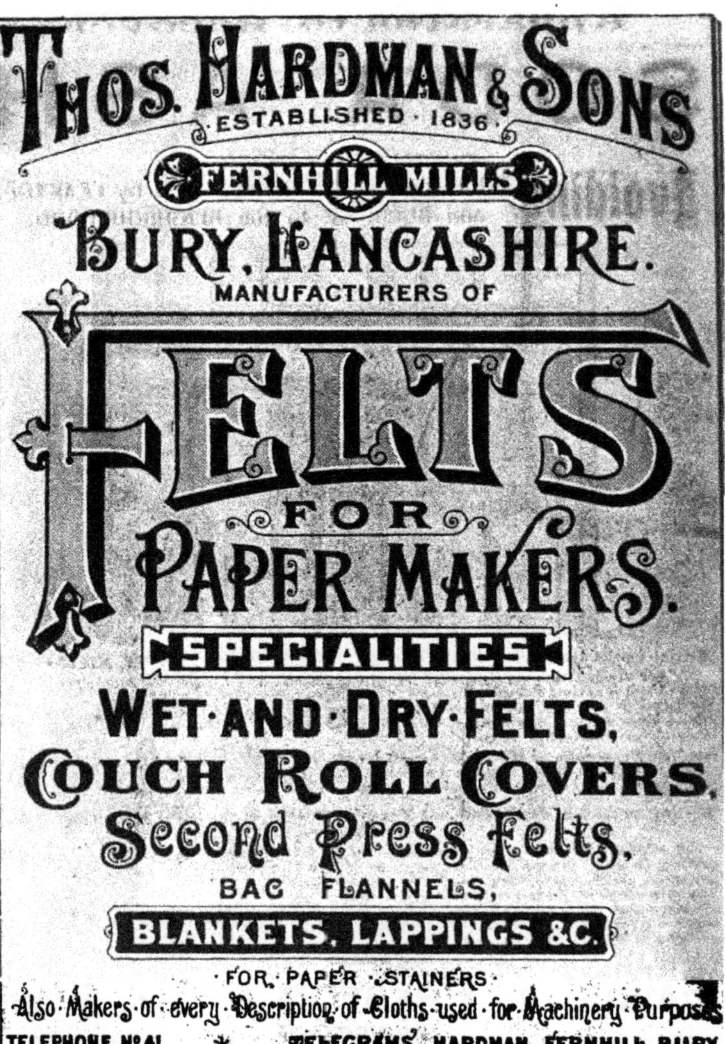

Printed and Published by W. JOHN STONHILL 58, Shoe Lane, LONDON, E.C. August 25, 1893.

Telegrams: "STONHILL, LONDON." A B C Code. Registered at the General Post Office as a Newspaper.

Vol. XX. No. 9. LONDON, SEPTEMBER 1, 1893. Price 6d.

PULP FROM DIFFERENT KINDS OF WOOD.

The different species of wood are known to yield various quantities of pulp when treated chemically by any of the well-known methods. It appears that the yield of fibre from the same kind of wood also varies in amount in proportion to its age, and also with the part of the tree. Young trees give less pulp than those which are full grown, and the branches usually yield less than the stem. The difference in quantitative yield between old and young trees, or between the stem and the branches of the same tree, is oftentimes very small.

The most elaborate experiments yet made on the relative quantities of pulp it is possible to get from different kinds of timber were performed some years ago by Zeigelmeyer, a German wood pulp maker, who placed his results before the German Wood Pulp Society. The proceedings of this society contain Zeigelmeyer's figures, which we reproduce below. These figures are interesting as showing the amount of loss incurred in peeling and cutting the wood as well as the percentage yield of fibre given in the last column of the table. The wood in each case was freshly cut, and the soda process was employed to reduce it to fibre:—

YIELD OF PULP FROM DIFFERENT SORTS OF WOOD.—SODA PROCESS.

Kind of Wood.		Weight of one C. Metre of Fresh Cut Wood	Loss in Peeling and Cleaning.		Loss in Drying at 212° Fah.		Yield of Pulp from one C. Metre of Wood.	Weight of Clean Dry Wood per C. Metre	Yield of Pulp on Dry Wood.
German Name.	Botanical Name.	Kilos	Kilos	%	Kilos	%	Kilos	Kilos	%
[illegible]	Pinus Picea ...	617·5	80	12·9	230	37·2	108·2	307·5	35·1
[illegible]	do. Abies...	566·0	136	24·0	191·7	33·8	88·2	235·3	37·0
[illegible]	do. Sylvestris	697·5	170	24·3	252·2	36·1	105·7	275·3	35·4
[illegible]	do. Austriaca	707·5	147	20·7	285·6	40·3	89	274·9	32·3
[illegible]	do. Larix...	597·5	90	15·0	160·3	26·8	116·8	347·1	33·7
[illegible]	do. Pumilio	449·3	55·1	12·2	118·4	23·5	99·8	265·8	37·5
[illegible]	Fagus Silvatica	865·0	70	8·1	327·5	37·8	130·8	437·4	29·9
[illegible]	Betula Alba ...	623·5	111	17·8	215·5	34·4	85·6	250·9	28·8
[illegible]	Populus Tremula	695·0	135	19·4	227·3	31·7	108·4	332·6	32·9
[illegible]	do. Alba ...	655·0	175	26·9	225·5	34·8	88·1	245·5	35·4
[illegible]	Sorbus Aucuparia	735·5	131·5	18·1	259·0	37·1	100·6	324·3	31·0
[illegible]	do. Tominalis	756·5	166	22·0	224·2	29·6	103·9	365·8	28·4
[illegible]	Salix Capre ...	572·5	80·5	14·0	241·0	42·1	85·7	251	34·1
[illegible]	do. Fragilis	583·5	111	19·0	181·4	31·1	104·8	291·1	36·0
[illegible]	Fraxinus Excelsior	593·5	91	15·3	100·1	16·8	103·9	402·4	35·8
[illegible]	Alnus Glutinosa ...	516·5	97·5	18·8	181·0	35·0	81·3	238	34·3

NORWEGIAN ENTERPRISE.

MR. O. TOBIESEN,
ENGINEER, LYSAKER.

Continuing our series of articles on "Norwegian Enterprise," we take as the subject for the present sketch Mr. O. Tobiesen, an engineer of considerable repute, of Granfos Brug, Lysaker, near Christiania. Our previous biography was that of the champion of the Norwegian wood pulp enterprise, Mr. Chr. Christophersen, Consul-General, whose name, owing to his extensive business connections, is well known not only in Scandinavia but in papermaking countries generally. Mr. Tobiesen, whose portrait we present herewith, has been less before the public, and his endeavours, unfortunately for himself, have not met with that pecuniary success which they seem to have deserved. He has, however, a just claim to be mentioned among the pioneers of the Norwegian pulp and paper industry, and, as a real benefactor to his country.

Mr. Otto Munthe Claudius Tobiesen was born on October 11th, 1845, at Christiania, and after being educated at a middle-class school, he passed the first five classes of the Cathedral School at Christiania. Although intended for the law, an accident, in conjunction with delicate health generally, became the means of procuring him permission to follow his own desire, viz., to study technology, a vocation at that time by no means in high esteem. Greek and Latin having ostensibly been thrown away, a year was devoted to the study of mathematics which had hitherto been neglected. Thus qualified, he went through a three years' course at the Chalmerska Institute, at Gothenburg, Sweden. Having in that way completed his theoretical studies, young Mr. Tobiesen launched into practical life and got a situation at Motala mek. Werkstad, the famous Swedish engineering works. Here Capt. Karlsund at that time held the sway, and it was no easy job to obtain a pupil's situation and wages too. For the first week Captain Karlsund only glared at Mr. Tobiesen when he, as a supplicant, took position outside the works, but he dared not make application too frequently for a place. Then Midsummer Day arrived, and with it all the mirth and festivities that accompany that day in Sweden. All the engineers of the works were invited to a "spleen," and being a Norwegian, Mr. Tobiesen was also invited. At one o'clock in the morning Capt. Karlsund came to see if he could detect some little weakness in the guests, and suddenly addressing Mr. Tobiesen, he said: "Hwarför är inte herren full, som de andra?" ("Why are you not drunk, like the rest, sir?")—and continued: "Come to me to-morrow," and was then engaged. As a common mechanic Mr. Tobiesen now laboured in the workshop all the day long, filing and fitting machines. After the lapse of two years he went to Berlin, where he obtained a situation as a fitter of locomotives with Schwartzkopf. Having been there for two months he advanced to the situation of a draughtsman in the office, and from the chief clerk, for the first time, heard of what was destined to constitute the subject of his future life work, viz., wood pulp.

At this time (1867) wood pulp was in its pure infancy, and Volter may be said to have presented it to the public for the first time at the Paris Exhibition of 1868. Returning home in the autumn of 1868 Mr. Tobiesen commenced the construction of the first Norwegian wood pulp mill, mainly built for the purpose of exporting its produce, thus practically inaugurating that industry which has since become of such importance to Norway, and is becoming so more and more every day. This early mill, driven by a 80-h.p. turbine, was located at Bagaas, in Christiania, the premises belonging to Mr. Tobiesen, senr. The business prospered so well that in 1869 Mr. Tobiesen bought a waterfall with grounds at Lysaker, and there built a wood pulp mill calling the place Granfos Brug. As a fact of historical note it may be mentioned that he invoiced his first parcel (sent to Mr. J. A. Reid) at £8 4s. per ton moist 50 per cent. (the pulp actually containing 56 per cent. moisture). In 1870 the price fell to £7 10s. per ton (50 per cent. moisture).

As the years advanced the infant industry grew, and wood pulp mills of considerable capacity were built, and prices constantly fell. It was found that the mill at Granfos did not command sufficient water power to allow of an extension of the pulp mill enabling it to compete with mills with more water. Mr. Tobiesen therefore decided to add a paper mill to the pulp mill, and in 1878 he erected a paper machine constructed by himself and built by various native engineering firms. The machine, 60-in. in width, at first produced nature browns, but during the years 1879 and 1880 the production was gradually developed to the manufacture of news and wall papers, thus being also one of the very earliest mills in the country making the papers named. In 1880 to 1881 another machine was added, of small dimensions, making tissue papers of various colours, and a few years later a Yankee machine was put into operation. During the years immediately succeeding the erection of his own wood pulp mill, Mr. Tobiesen built a series of other pulp and paper mills in Norway and Sweden, the number of mills built by him being no less than twelve.

History shows us that the pioneers of progress in almost every department of human enterprise very often miss the personal benefit of their endeavours. Mr. Tobiesen has shared that fate. In the early part of 1892 he found it necessary to make arrangements with his creditors, and this he did in an admirable manner, they forming a joint stock company out of his business, for which he naturally became the managing director. As our readers will remember, a fire quite recently destroyed part of the mill. It is expected that it will be in full working order again within a few months.

THE DEATH OF MR. JOHN MASSON.

The death, in New Zealand, of Mr. John Masson was briefly referred to in our issue of August 11th. Cut off at the early age of 23, at a time when he was full of activity and apparently had before him a most brilliant career, the sad circumstance by which he met his end has called forth feelings of deep regret and sympathy from a very wide circle. We have received a copy of the *Mataura Ensign*, containing further particulars of the deplorable occurrence and a report of the evidence given at the inquest. During the progress of the game (between teams representing the paper mills and freezing works), which appears to have been a friendly one, though a trifle rough, more particularly in the forward division, owing to a number of the players being ignorant of the rules, Mr. Masson who was playing three-quarter-back on the mill side, sustained a nasty fall. It was observed that he walked about afterwards with his hands to his head a few minutes, but he was able to continue playing to the end and walk home, though he complained of his head paining him. Upon reaching home (he was residing with Mr. Wyllie, manager of the mill) he again complained of his head and was unable to eat, soon lapsing into an unconscious state. A doctor was sent for, but the case was pronounced hopeless from the first. Though the treatment adopted in the most severe cases of concussion of the brain was resorted to, the poor fellow never regained consciousness. The deceased was the eldest son of Mr. Andrew Masson (Masson, Scott and Co., Limited, Battersea, London), and went to the colony about three months ago to superintend the erection of the machinery purchased by Mr. Culling from his firm for the new works at Mataura. He proved himself a thoroughly capable engineer, and the work progressed satisfactorily under his supervision. Socially he was a great favourite, and his sudden and deplorable end greatly shocked the many friends he has made at Mataura. Mr. Culling cabled the sad news to the relations at home. At the inquest, the evidence of Mr. Walter McLord, an employee at the paper mill, and captain of their team, was to the effect that play was rougher than usual owing to the lack of knowledge of the game by some of the players—about half his team knew the game—but deceased was not worse treated than anyone else. He mentioned to witness towards the end of the game that he had got a knock on the head but did not say how he came by it. Witness warned one player for throwing a boy rather heavily. There was no intentionally rough or dangerous play. Deceased did not complain of being roughly treated and seemed all right at half-time. The game was "Rugby" and Mr. Masson seemed to know the play. Mr. Arthur Wyllie, papermaker, also gave evidence. He said he had known deceased since Good Friday last. He said Mr. Masson, upon returning from the football match, went to his bedroom and witness, thinking he was rather a long time in coming to tea, enquired after him and received the reply, "All right, presently," in a sort of semi-conscious way. Some few minutes later witness went back again and asked him what was the matter. He said he had got a knock on the head and that it was painful, remarking that he had got into collision in the football field. Witness took him a cup of tea, which he did not drink, and then asked him if he would not undress and go to bed. Mr. Wyllie took off his boots and helped him into bed, but as he seemed insensible he thought the case serious and consulted Mr. Culling and a medical man was sent for. Witness stated that decease had no illness while at Mataura and appeared in good health. The Rugby game of football was strongly condemned by the jury, who returned a verdict to the effect that deceased died from concussion of the brain, no blame being attached to anyone.

BABCOCK AND WILCOX, LIM.—The directors recommend that the following dividends be paid for the half-year ended June 30th, 1893:—At the rate of 6 per cent. per annum on the preference shares, £3,000; at the rate of 10 per cent. per annum on the ordinary shares, £7,000; leaving a balance to be carried forward of £9,547 11s. 11d.

NORWEGIAN ENTERPRISE.

... feature of the work consists in the man... in which the various machines are illus... The old and useless method of ... machines by a mere machine ... and substituted ... of photographs ... and the ... can be ... illustrations taken

MR. O. ...

HYDRAULIC PUMP.

...kers' engineers of Great Britain are ...to-date in all the latest and most modern ...es and improvements connected with ... class of machinery. The work itself is ...plete, and got up in a style that makes it ...anual of the subject worthy of study by ...ry papermaker. An important and valu-

from drawings are also coloured and shaded according to draughtsman's rules, and the lithographs are excellent and artistic productions.

According to the preface the firm, after referring to various recent improvements call special attention to their improve...

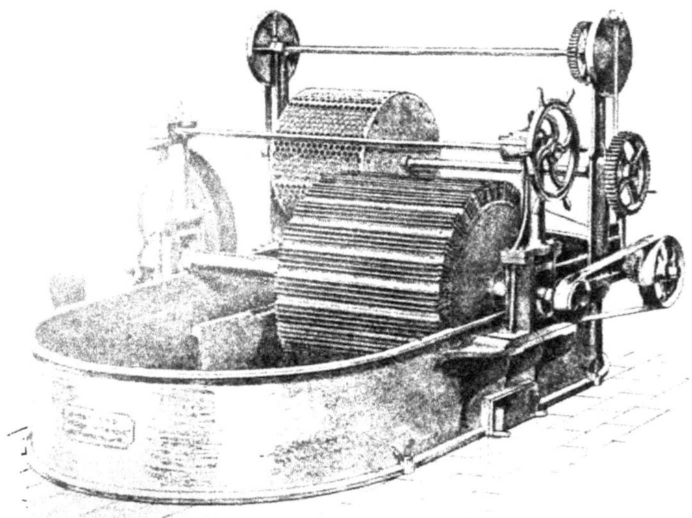

BREAKING AND WASHING ENGINE.

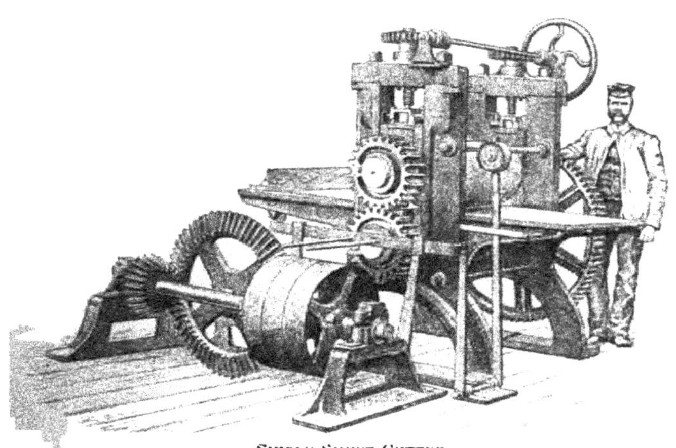

SINGLE SHEET CUTTER.

THE WEST END ENGINE WORKS CO., EDINBURGH.

A copy of the new catalogue of paper-making machinery issued by this enterprising firm has just come to hand, a glance at which will immediately show that paper-

able feature of the work
ner in which the variou
trated. The old an
illustrating machine
drawing has been ab
by perfect reprod
whereby the detail
principles and n
readily seen. Th

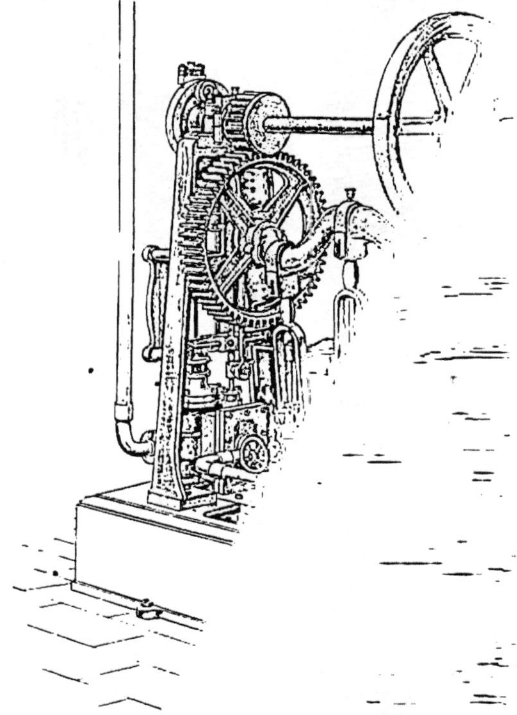

makers' engineers
up-to-date in all the
types and improv
this class of machin
complete, and got u
a manual of the
every papermaker

shifting deckle, automatic wire guide, rag engine roll and drum washer lifting gear, grass duster, hydraulic machinery, square and angle cutters, calenders and reeling machines. Among the more important machines constructed by this firm, and illustrated in the catalogue, may be mentioned the following:—Rag and rope chopper, rag willow and duster, grass duster, causticising plant, consisting of large cast iron vats for dissolving the incinerated soda ash, with wrought iron perforated drums or baskets to hold the same while melting; strong agitator gear, draw-off pipe, water service and sludge valve; settling and storage tanks, pumps, measuring cisterns, etc. Lime mixers of octagon or circular shape with all modern improvements. Rag and grass boilers of cast iron for low pressures and of wrought iron or steel for high pressures; made to revolve, or of the vertical type, with filling and emptying doors; with false bottom, vomit pipe, or with separate pump for circulating the lye and washing the grass in the boilers. Washing and bleaching engines for grass, and breaking and washing engines for rags; hydraulic stuff presses and hydraulic hoists with all fittings complete; cage hoists, with cages of any desired size and also double acting quick lift friction hoists for grass bales, sacks, etc.; double acting horizontal pumps of all sizes f[illegible]

REVOLVING ANGLE SHEET CUTTER.

water, caustic, or bleach and well pumps, to draw from any depth and to throw to any required height. The illustrations and description of the complete paper machine show a beautifully designed and well-built piece of mechanism, with all the most recent improvements. The Presse Pâte, and Yankee webbing machines for special grades of paper are also constructed to any desired design. Flat breast-strainers or knotters and revolving strainers are a great specialty of this firm, and are made to meet the requirements of every class of papermaking fibre. A great variety of cutters is also made by this firm and illustrated and described in their catalogue, the chief being the revolving knife paper cutter of specially strong construction, with framing, drawing-in rolls, five pairs of ripping knives, tube rolls, revolving knife, expanding pulley, delivery felt and full set of change wheels and pulleys to cut from the longest to the shortest sheets required. The expanding pulley may be arranged for altera-

BOARDING CALENDER.

tion of diameter while cutter is working. Reel frame to hold from six to twelve reels, either plain or of new and improved designs, with separate adjustment for each reel and capable of taking in reels of different lengths. Revolving angle sheet cutter; single sheet cutters and board cutters are also extensively made to suit every requirement; friction burnishing calenders, glazing and boarding calenders; ripping and winding machines with slip motion, for slitting and winding at one operation, two, three, four or more webs, and specially adapted for thin papers; ripping and winding machines with winding drum, edge runners or kollergangs; hydraulic press and pumps and hydraulic pumps combined with steam engine; pulp save-alls; felt washers; steam engines and many other important pieces of machinery connected with the manufacture of paper by this firm. Taking the catalogue as a whole it is undoubtedly a first-rate production, and clearly indicates the capabilities of this firm as papermakers' engineers, and also does justice to the firm of Messrs. McLagan and Cumming, the well-known Edinburgh lithographers.

ECONOMIC AIDS IN STEAM GENERATION.

FIRE BARS.

The object of the steam-user being to get the highest possible generation of steam with the smallest possible consumption of fuel, to be entirely successful he needs first to see that the fuel he is using is of the highest calorific value, and then that every appurtenance of the boiler is the best that can be got. Economy in use begins at the furnace door. It is not a bit of use putting in the best of coal if you do not ensure that the mechanical aids to perfect combustion are as perfect as possible. For example, the best British steam coal commercially available is the Welsh, and the lowest the soft seams of Derbyshire or Yorkshire; the relative calorific values of these being as 100 to 83. But where the furnace fittings are crude, 30 per cent. of the value of Welsh coal may be sacrificed through imperfect combustion or other causes. With complete combustion the softer coal will generate more steam than a hard coal without it. The first essential is to ensure an efficient air draught. This the ordinary straight fire bar does not provide. There are numerous devices to overcome the defects of the straight bar. One of the most effective with which we have had to do has been Bamforth's patented bars, which were (and probably now are) in use at Olive and Partington's paper mills at Glossop. These bars are constructed to afford a corrugated air space; such air space being in these equal to three times that of the ordinary straight bars, and the draught of air well diffused, the combustion is brought proportionably nearer to perfection, and a correspondingly higher ratio of the total energy stored in the coal is brought into utilisation. Moreover, they produce less ash than the ordinary bars, and it is claimed that the increased draught, by keeping the bars cool, adds materially to their life.

UNIVERSAL EXHIBITION AT MADRID.—The Consul-General for Spain has issued the prospectus of a Universal Exhibition, to be held at Madrid from April 1st to October 31st, 1894, under the patronage of Her Majesty the Queen Regent of Spain. The prospectus, which may be obtained at the Spanish Consulate, 23, Billiter-street, contains a list of the council, the general regulations, the charges for space, and a specification of the different classes of exhibits which will be accepted. All communications should be sent to the secretary's offices, Palacio de la Industria y de las Artes, Madrid.

[illegible]

[illegible] from injury. [illegible]

[illegible] a dividend of 2 per [illegible].

[illegible], attorney in Vienna, [illegible] Chairman of the Board of Directors of [illegible] Paper Mills and Publishing Company, died recently in his 58th year. His funeral was attended by deputations of the directors, staff and workmen of the concern, to which the deceased had given all his best efforts and intelligence.

HERR [illegible], SCHULTE, papermaker, in Dusseldorf, has gone into bankruptcy. Public examination will take place on September 2nd. Herr [illegible], attorney, has been appointed trustee, and will receive claims on or before September 12th.

CHEMNITZER PAPIERFABRIK ZU EINSIEDEL.—It is stated that the directors intend proposing at the next general meeting, a dividend of 8½ per cent. A large amount will also be allowed for various purposes.

A COMMITTEE under the chairmanship of the Minister of Commerce has reported in favour of the establishment of "Central workshops" in Buda-Pesth. The object is to furnish accommodation under one roof to the smaller artisans, and to place machine power, lighting and heat at their disposal at a moderate cost. It is proposed to entrust their erection and management to a joint stock company.

Apparatus to Recover

SODA ASH

(CHAPMAN'S PATENT).

Avoiding POLLUTION of STREAMS, LOSS by LEAKAGE, and NUISANCE to the NEIGHBOURHOOD.

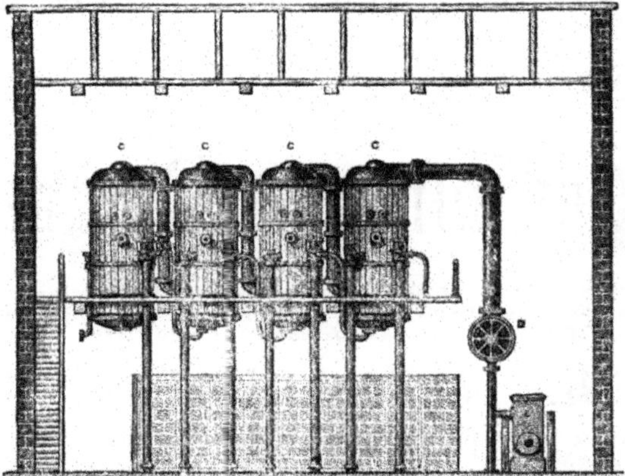

Writing on the 4th April, 1893, the Manager of the WOOLFOLD PAPER MILLS says:—

"*We are getting very good work out of our plant. The Evaporator has never worked better than it is now doing. We have been treating our liquor for a month or two at 3½° Tw., and as you are well aware this means a great deal of evaporation for little ash. Many Papermakers would refuse to believe (unless they saw) that we could treat so weak a liquor profitably, but we can.*"

☞ *The Evaporator at Woolfold is a QUADRUPLE EFFECT (CHAPMAN'S PATENT), working in conjunction with a Thornley's Patent Incinerator, similar to that in use at Gigg Mills, where also the Evaporator is a Quadruple Effect (Chapman's Patent).*

Writing on the 6th March, 1893, the Managing Director of the GIGG MILLS says of this Incinerator:—

"*We have now had your Incinerator at work several months, and find it very satisfactory indeed. Since Christmas, for instance, we have recovered from 14 to 16 tons of ash per week, the coal consumed being only a small quantity just for starting up on a Monday morning. It is self-supporting for combustible matter. We can keep good fires all the week and skim constantly, and this, as before stated, without any consumption of coal after starting up. We only used 2 cwts. of coal in the way indicated last week, and recovered 14 tons of ash.*"

FAWCETT, PRESTON & CO., LIM.,

ENGINEERS,

Phœnix Foundry Liverpool.

CKSON

'Y, near

MANCHESTER

PERFECTING ENGINE

(Made in three Sizes).

... will produce a Better Finished, Stronger and More Even Sheet of Paper from the same ... can be produced by any other Mechanical Process, and at the same time will Reduce the Power required for Beating.

... these Engines on approval subject to our accomplishing the above results.

... FOR ALL CLASSES OF STOCK AND EVERY QUALITY OF PAPER.

OVER 100 NOW IN USE AND ON ORDER.

n Application.

ESTABLISHED A.D. 1736.

WILLIAM MAKIN & SONS,

Attercliffe Steel Works, Sheffield, England.

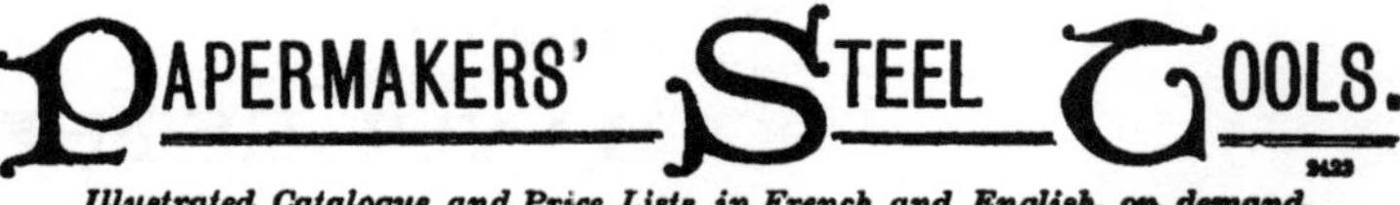

2423

Illustrated Catalogue and Price Lists, in French and English, on demand.

H. WATSON & SONS,

HIGH BRIDGE WORKS, NEWCASTLE-ON-TYNE,

are prepared to

Close Strainer Plates

worn within 2 full Gauges wider than they were when set to work

at $\frac{1}{2}$d. per sq. inch, less 30% discount.

Carriage of all Plates paid by Goods train to Newcastle.

TELEGRAMS "WATSONS, NEWCASTLE." 3606

RICHARD ENGLAND,

(Successor to JAMES PARROTT.) Brown Street, SALFORD.

MAKER OF ALL TYPES AND POWERS OF STEAM ENGINES

Super Calenders, Friction Calenders, Emboss Calenders,

And CALENDERS of all descriptions for PAPER, COTTON, LINEN, WOOLLEN and SILK GOODS

CHILLED IRON, HARD-CAST IRON, STEEL, BRASS & BRASS COVERED ROLLS

Superior Cotton and Paper Bowls,

HAVING THE MOST POWERFUL PLANT IN THE WORLD FOR THEIR MANUFACTURE.

ROLL GRINDING MACHINES. ALL CLASSES OF ROLLS REGROUND.

HYDRAULIC PRESSES and PUMPS. 2408

THE
United Asbestos Co.,
LIMITED.
DOCK HOUSE, BILLITER STREET, E.C.,
"SALAMANDER"
THE UNITED ASBESTOS COMPANY LIMITED · LONDON ·
TRADE MARK
Pioneers
OF THE
Asbestos
Trade.
UNITED ASBESTOS
NON-CONDUCTING
COVERING
(For Steam Boilers & Pipes)
Best and Cheapest in the
Market; Will not
Injure Boiler Plates.
ASBESTOS
GOODS of ALL
DESCRIPTIONS
BELTINGS.
THE UNITED ASBESTOS CO., Limited,
UNITED UNITED UNITED UNITED UNITED UNITED UNITED UNITED
PACKINGS.
UNITED ASBESTOS Cº LMTD LONDON
PURE ITALIAN MILLBOARD EXTRA QUALITY
A1
UNITED ASBESTOS
A1 MILLBOARDS
(ITALIAN)
Unequalled for Purity, Strength of
Fibre, and Uniformity. For Dry
Steam Joints it is admitted to be the
cleanest, most durable and economical
packing in existence.
UNITED ASBESTOS
SALAMANDER
Lubricating Cream & Oils,
SPECIALLY ADAPTED TO
PAPERMAKING MACHINERY.
DEPOTS:
MANCHESTER: 34, Deansgate; LIVERPOOL: 33, James Street;
NEWCASTLE-UPON-TYNE: Quayside; GLASGOW: 54, Robertson
Street; CARDIFF: 135, Bute Street; BRISTOL: Provident Buildings;
HULL: Queen's Dock; ST. PETERSBURG: Gostinoe Dvor (Interior) No. 51.

D. N. BERTRAM'S
Patent REELER

The Special Features of the Machine are :

1.—NO PART OF THE KNIFE BLOCKS or knives, except the cutting edges, comes in contact with the paper, thus avoiding any damage to the web by narrow rings touching it.

2.—There BEING NO BLOCKS between the knives they can be instantly adjusted to any width without taking the spindle from its bearings.

3.—The KNIVES ARE DRIVEN INDEPENDENTLY of the paper at an increased speed ensuring clean cut edges.

4.—The MACHINE IS DRIVEN by belt pulley on drum shaft with fast and slow speeds, worked from front of machine by levers, so arranged that when the fast speed is put on the slow one disengages itself. The change from slow to fast is easily effected, and no jerking takes place.

☞ THIS PATENT REELER is working in Several Well - known Paper Mills.

IN THIS MACHINE the paper is slit into widths upon the spindle, which carries the finished webs, thus preventing irregularity of edges; the outside shavings being trimmed before the web passes to the winding-up spindle and slitting-knives.

THE KNIFE CARRIAGE is placed vertically over the web, and fitted with automatic raising gear, to compensate for the increase of web.

THERE IS ALSO AN ARRANGEMENT so that the operator can apply the slitting-knives with any given amount of contact that may be desirable, and it will retain the same position until the whole web is finished.

THE ACTION OF THE PRESSING ROLL on the top of the web ensures the reel being firmly and evenly wound, and there is a shackle at one side of the machine, with screw which can adjust pressing roll to a nicety on the drum upon which the slitting and winding apparatus is carried. This allows webs which may be slightly thicker at one side than another to be wound without creasing.

REFERENCES GIVEN ON APPLICATION.

BERTRAMS LIMITED

(Successors to Geo. & Wm. BERTRAM—ESTABLISHED 1821).

ENGINEERS,

ST. KATHERINE'S WORKS, SCIENNES, EDINBURGH.

Photo by Berry & Co., Moorgate, near Bolton.

MR. JOHN ALMOND.

British capital and experience have for some years past, in a more or less degree, been identified with the development of the Scandinavian pulp and paper trades. We have frequently recorded the departure from this country of papermakers to take up positions in mills in both Norway and Sweden. The subject of the above portrait, Mr. John Almond, is the latest to transfer his abilities and knowledge in this respect. He is a native of Blackburn, Lancashire, and his first acquaintance with papermaking was with the Grimshaw Bridge Papermaking Co. (under the old firm), making caps, small hand, etc. He was engaged there until about ten years ago, when the mill was closed. Subsequently he was employed at Messrs. Robert Fletcher and Sons, Stoneclough, and it may here be stated that he practically served his apprenticeship. He was fortunate in gaining private instruction from Mr. Joseph Fielding, the late manager at Stoneclough. Mr. Almond has had experience with all the classes of paper for which Messrs. Robert Fletcher and Sons have such a high-class reputation, viz., white and coloured tissues, cigarette, copying papers, etc. He now goes to the mill at Munksjö, Sweden, as under manager, and we wish him every success in his new sphere of labour. The mill contains eleven machines, and the makes include all grades of paper from common browns to fine tissues.

To the Editor of the WORLD'S PAPER TRADE REVIEW.

SIR,—I observe that in your issue of the 25th inst., you quote from the *Labour Gazette*, re change in wages at Hendon. I wish to point out, in the interests of our Society, that the statement you quote is rather misleading and inaccurate. To prove that, I need only ask who ever heard of 32 beatermen being employed at a mill with only four (?) machinemen? The machinemen (of whom there are eight) *have not* been reduced 12s. per week, as the *Labour Gazette* states. To show the correct method of settlement I forward you a copy of the agreement drawn up and duly signed by the representatives of the Hendon Co. and the workers, on the terms of which work was resumed.

COPY OF AGREEMENT.

1.—All old workers to be reinstated as soon as possible.

2.—No victimising to be carried out.

3.—Reduction to be taken off in three months if trade has sufficiently improved to allow it.

4.—Secretaries to be allowed to examine mill reports at end of that time if they think it desirable.

5.—That papermill workers agree to accept a TONNAGE reduction of 3d. per ton for machinemen and beatermen, others to be reduced in proportion. Roastermen and other time workers accept the reduction proposed. Finishers to be put on time wages at the rate of 32s. per week for chargemen, 30s. for 1st hands, 28s. for others.

6.—Tonnage to be *divided equally* over the four machines, starting from the same standard as at present.

7.—Firemen's wages to be reduced 9d. per week, enginemen's to remain as they are.

Signed { THOS. GOODALL.
WM. ROSS.
J. WHITBURN.

Hendon Works, July 7th, 1893.

Hoping you can afford space for above, and thanking you in anticipation,

Yours sincerely,

WM. ROSS,

General Secretary,

National Union of Papermill Workers.

August 28th, 1893.

RELATIVE BRITISH AND BELGIAN TRADE. —The following figures show the trade of the past five years:—

	British Paper Exported to Belgium.		British Imports of Paper from Belgium.	
1888	15,389 cwts.	£33,379	170,668 cwts.	£271,824
1889	12,552 ,,	32,230	195,235 ,,	293,424
1890	12,839 ,,	30,116	195,932 ,,	295,052
1891	11,623 ,,	30,838	221,593 ,,	311,964
1892	10,787 ,,	25,018	189,762 ,,	284,611

Belgium imported alkali from Great Britain in 1892 to the value of £10,087; the value in 1888 was £13,346. Rags, &c., were shipped to Great Britain from Belgium last year to the value of £159,658, the sum in 1888 being £188,012.

GERMAN PAPER AND ALLIED TRADES.

ANNUAL REPORTS FROM CHAMBERS OF COMMERCE.

PRUSSIA.

LIEGNITZ.—The wood pulp industry of this district has not so much suffered from the general badness of trade as from want of water, which greatly hampered production. Prices went up, but not to the advantage of many makers, as they had contracted ahead. Scandinavian makers during the time of over-production brought prices down to the lowest ebb, and since the scarcity of water supplied from their stocks at rising prices. A rectification of the import duty would be desirable to protect home makers. The paper industry has had a very bad year, prices have fallen so much that many mills had to protect themselves against sales with a loss by either working for stock or reducing their production. The Customs' treaties with other countries and particularly with France and Austria are often carried out by ignorant officials to the disadvantage of German makers, as their goods are mostly placed into higher classes than those to which they are entitled.

CASSEL.—Fancy paper, glue and gelatine works were able in 1892 by special efforts to keep up their production at the highest figure. The exportations go to all civilised countries. Relations with France are made difficult by high import duties, and have gone back in consequence. English business suffers by the competition of the Belgians, who enjoy very low freights from Antwerp to all British ports. The prices of the manufactured articles have gone down. Raw materials are steady, and have even become dearer lately. Paper and stationery suffers from reckless competition, particularly school articles. Some of the high schools allow their caretakers to keep stocks and thus compete against dealers. The report adds that though there are some first rate stationery firms, still some of the authorities place larger contracts in other towns from where travellers solicit their orders. These purchases do not seem to offer them any advantage.

WURTTEMBERG.

Nearly all the papermills in the districts of Heilbronn, Reutlingen, Calw, Heidenheim, and Ravensburg complain about difficulties of sales and unremunerative prices, slow remittances and increasing Austrian competition. During the summer business was quite inanimate; it revived in autumn, but prices left no margin. Woodpulp has become scarce, and ground pulp makers justly demand higher prices. Chemical pulp likewise is dearer, but still higher prices for paper cannot be obtained, which show that the trade still suffers from overproduction, and that the treaty with Austria has created an unexpected competition. There is a want of confidence which makes the struggle for existence more difficult from year to year.

HEIDENHEIM.—The Chamber of Commerce considers 1892 the worst year for the chemical pulp industry that has ever been known. In the second half an increased demand took place, but prices did not improve, and chemicals were run up by a convention of makers.

CALW.—The Chamber reports that in ground wood and wood pulp boards the situation has gone from bad to worse. The exportation to France has been made impossible by raising duties several years ago, and a recent treaty has done the same for Switzerland. The new commercial treaty with Austria, by reducing the import duty, has assisted the Austrian competition, which has in its favour cheaper wood and lower wages without having to contribute to workmen's insurance funds. These treaties have therefore injured local industry. In the third quarter slightly better prices could be obtained, as the production fell off through want of water. Wood has become dearer, as the forest managers took steps to enhance the price.

RAVENSBURG.—The Chamber cannot report any improvement in the ground wood industry, prices having gone down so much that no margin of profit seems to be left. The exportation to France and Switzerland is prevented by higher duties. At the end of the year from the North a greater demand for wood pulp took place in consequence of a scarcity of water, but heavy carriage prevented this district from deriving any advantage. Wood prices went up towards the end of the year by 10 to 15 per cent. The Schaal's works in Scheer have been enlarged by increasing the water power and erecting an additional ground wood factory.

The Foreign Chambers of Commerce have also published special reports dealing with specified subjects, and the following no doubt will interest our readers:

SULPHITE PULPS.—Complaints are general concerning Swedish and Austrian competition and the wish is expressed that greater carriage facilities should be given in order to prevent competition from those countries.

MILLBOARDS.—Sales have been difficult, and prices cut down by competition. Fortunately exportation to Austria has been reopened by the new Treaty of Commerce, but it is anticipated that some time will elapse before the position of the past can be regained.

ROOFING BOARD AND WOOD CEMENT.—Reports do not show any fluctuation. Building operations appear to have been slack, and foreign competition apparently has influenced prices.

GLAZING BOARDS, JACQUERD BOARDS, &C.—These productions also appear difficult to sell, and it is complained that they are not so easily exported to Switzerland in consequence of higher duties.

FANCY PAPER TRADE.—According to reports from Stuttgart, the exportation to France which was very considerable, has almost ceased. Owing to competition, profits appear to be vanishing.

WHOLESALE PAPER BUSINESS.—The report issued by the Stuttgart Chamber of Commerce shows that the low level of prices of 1891 have been current for most articles, business has been slack, and only in the best grades of makes has there been any uniformity of price. Common papers descended in price until the increase in value of ground wood pulp, which put a stop to any further downward movement. Low water compelled wood pulp manufacturers either to cease working or to reduce their production, and as a result higher prices were agreed to. The wholesale trade suffers from the efforts of papermakers to deal direct with the consumers.

THE RAG TRADE.—The conditions of trade have for some time past been satisfactory, but owing to the cholera epidemic, exportation to foreign countries became impossible. Business is reported as being difficult to carry through, and prices on the whole unsatisfactory. Mixed rags are quoted lower in price than ever before. Labour conditions are reported as normal, and wages fairly good.

PUBLIC COMPANIES.

BRUSH ELECTRICAL ENGINEERING COMPANY, LIMITED.—The annual general meeting took place on August 25th, in London, Mr. Braithwaite, jun., in the chair. The report for the year ended June 30th, stated that the profit-and-loss account showed a gross profit of £50,158, including the amount brought forward from last account. After providing the full dividend on the 6 per cent. preference shares for the year and an interim dividend at the rate of 5 per cent. per annum, which had already been paid on the ordinary shares, the directors recommended that the whole amount standing to the debt of preliminary expenses account, amounting to £1,575, be written off, and that a further dividend at the rate of 7 per cent. per annum be paid on the ordinary shares for the six months ending 30th June, leaving £815 to be carried forward. The chairman referred with great satisfaction to the progress made by the company in the past year. They owed £37,000 less than they owed last year, and they were owed £14,000 more. They were getting their fair share of all central station work. In the past two years the growth of electric lighting business in London had been very great, and the fact that the subscribed capital of the companies supplying electricity in the metropolis was now about £3,500,000 showed that the industry had emerged from the experimental stage. The report was agreed to.

THE MANCHESTER SHIP CANAL.—The half-yearly meeting of the Manchester Ship Canal Company was held at Manchester on Monday, Lord Egerton of Tatton, the chairman, presiding. In moving the adoption of the report, he complimented the shareholders and also the Corporation of Manchester upon the fortitude with which they had faced the difficulties of the undertaking. He believed the main difficulties were now overcome and that a period of success had begun. As to the present condition of the works, he pointed out that at the eastern entrance to the canal there was a greater depth of water than at the entrance to any of the Liverpool docks, and a still further depth would be reached, for operations with that object were being continued there. The directors who accompanied him on Wednesday last saw a vessel of 4,000 tons at the entrance inside the canal at Eastham, which vessel, he understood, had since left, taking 4,000 tons of salt for India, drawing about 21-ft. of water. At Ellesmere port they found the new pontoon which was to form a dry dock, and was moored in the finished portion of the canal. At Saltport they saw several large vessels in the American trade bringing cargoes of timber, and on the 11th of August the vessels there had a carrying capacity of about 20,000 tons. The work in front of Runcorn had been completed since July, 1892. The recent arbitration proceedings in connection with the deviation railways had turned out very satisfactory to the company. They could not by any agreement beforehand have obtained the same terms, and he was sure no one could have given greater attention or exercised greater patience, discretion, and fairness than had been exercised by the arbitrator, Lord Balfour of Burleigh. The chairman detailed the rapid progress which had been made all along the uncompleted sections of the canal. The dredging had been done within the estimates. Progress was being made in freeing the rivers, and thereby the canal, of polluted matter. Considerable progress has been made with the arrangements necessary for dealing with the traffic expected between Manchester and other places as soon as the canal was opened. He had written to Lord Rosebery, the Foreign Secretary, asking him to make known to Her Majesty's representatives all over the world that the canal would be open for traffic early next year. The erection of warehouses and construction of barges would be left to private enterprise. A syndicate was being formed for developing passenger traffic. The motion was seconded by Sir J. Harwood and passed unanimously.

JOHN PICKTHALL & SONS, Ltd.—This company has been registered with a nominal capital of £10,000 in £1 shares. An agreement has been made between W. Pickthall and W. G. Matthews for the purchase of the several businesses of hemp, flax, paper, and asbestos dealers. One of the objects set forth is to develop the working of asbestos mines. Mr. W. G. Matthews is a paper merchant residing at Nunhead. The registered office of the company is 18, Appold-street, Finsbury.

WORLD'S PAPER TRADE REVIEW OFFICE,
58, SHOE LANE, LONDON, E.C.
AUGUST 31, 1893.

TRADE NOTES.

MESSRS. JOYNSON AND SONS of St. Mary's Cray Paper Mills, are having extensive alterations effected. The work now going on, which is expected to last some six weeks, has temporarily thrown a number of hands out of employment.

THE DARWEN PAPER MILL COMPANY, LIMITED, have now acquired the mill formerly worked by Messrs. Dimmock & Son. At a recent meeting of shareholders held for the purpose of considering the acquisition of the works, the purchase was unanimously sanctioned, and the directors and officials complimented upon their business capacity.

THE workpeople employed at the paper mills at Bury, and employees at other works, commenced their usual "wakes" holiday on Saturday last, the stoppage of business usually extending over three or four days.

DEATHS OF MILL EMPLOYEES.—We regret to record the death of Mr. William Lucas, for over fifty years in the employ of Messrs. Wrigley & Son, Bridge Hall Mills, in the capacity of foreman blacksmith. He was 75 years of age and was only ill a few days. Mr. Lucas was well known in the town of Bury.—On Wednesday, last week, while an engineer named James Wells, of Edinburgh, was erecting some machinery at Westfield Paper Mills, he was seized with an apoplectic fit and expired an hour afterwards. He was about 50 years of age and leaves a large family.

BRIDGE HALL PAPER MILLS, BURY.—On Saturday last the workpeople employed at Messrs. James Wrigley and Sons, Ltd., Bridge Hall Paper Mills, Bury, to the number of about 500, accompanied by their wives and sweethearts, had their annual trip, Blackpool being their destination on this occasion. The train left the Heap Bridge siding at six o'clock in the morning, and Blackpool was reached about two hours later. The day being beautifully fine, the visitors had a thoroughly enjoyable time of it, notwithstanding the crowded state of the town. The party left Blackpool a few minutes before eight o'clock at night, arriving at Heap Bridge about ten minutes past eleven. The firm very generously contributed the greater part of the cost of the outing, the workpeople having to each pay a shilling for his or her ticket, and the same amount for the wife's or husband's, while children's tickets were provided for those who wanted them at half-price.

"NEWSPAPER GAMBLING IN A NEW GUISE."—Under this heading in its issue of August 24th, the *British and Colonial Printer and Stationer* strongly condemned the "Weather Forecast" competition inaugurated by *Pearson's Weekly*. The *British and Colonial Printer and Stationer* was the first to direct official attention to the "Missing Word" craze and its attendant evils, and we are glad to recognise that its latest effort has received the prompt attention of Sir Augustus K. Stevenson, director of public prosecutions, who, in writing to the proprietor (Mr. W. John Stonhill), under date of 25th August, says: "I agree with you as to the mischief of this particular scheme, and am taking steps to obtain a judicial decision as to its legality."

THE IMPORTATION OF RAGS.—In the House of Commons on Friday Mr. Macdona asked the President of the Local Government Board whether the prohibition of the importation of rags, enacted on July 11th and 13th, August 11th, and December 14th, 1892, was on the 9th inst. revoked; and, if so, what other precautions the Local Government Board proposed to take to prevent the introduction of and spread of cholera and other noxious diseases in this country. In reply, Mr. H. Fowler said so much of the order as prohibited the importation of rags packed in bales as merchandise had been revoked. The Local Government Board would act as they had hitherto done under the advice of their medical department with respect to taking all precautions to prevent the introduction and spread of cholera in this country. Mr. Fowler, in further response to a question by Mr. Macdona, said he was not aware that there had been several cases of cholera since the revocation of the order.

THE NEW TARIFF IN VICTORIA.—Up to the present time news and printing paper and writing paper (uncut in mill reams) have been admitted free of duty. The Victoria Government have decided, in view of the great falling off in revenue, to impose an *ad valorem* duty of 3 per cent. on the paper named above. The newspaper proprietors can well afford to pay this duty, considering the low price that news is selling at. Importers of every class of goods and manufactures which are shipped to Victoria now have to pay an additional duty of 3 per cent. This additional impost will doubtless be very inconvenient for those firms who have now shipments in transit, and will be particularly felt by those firms having consignments of almanacs and calendars now on order or in transit.

A BARGAIN in the form of a 75-inch Fourdrinier papermaking machine in good condition is offered for sale in another column, by the Ramsbottom Paper Mill Co., Ltd. The space it occupies is immediately required, and any reasonable offer is preferable to having to "scrap" the machine, which is inevitable, unless some purchaser applies early.

PAPER EXPORTS & IMPORTS.

FOR THE WEEK ENDING TUESDAY LAST.

EXPORTS TO

	Printings.	Writings.	Other Kinds.
AUSTRALIA	1691 cwts	587 cwts.	948 cwts.
AFRICA	195 ,,	10 ,,	14 ,,
ARGENTINE ...	— ,,	123 ,,	2 ,,
BELGIUM	— ,,	96 ,,	1 ,,
B. GUIANA	— ,,	— ,,	165 ,,
B. WEST INDIES...	7 ,,	— ,,	23 ,,
CHANNEL ISLES	29 ,,	— ,,	— ,,
CANADA	343¼ ,,	180 ,,	75½ ,,
CAPE COLONY ...	84 ,,	49 ,,	139½ ,,
CHINA	6 ,,	9 ,,	41 ,,
CHILI	— ,,	— ,,	5 ,,
D. E. INDIES ...	— ,,	— ,,	10 ,,
DENMARK	86¾ ,,	4 ,,	18 ,,
EGYPT	— ,,	— ,,	2 ,,
FRANCE	1293 ,,	19 ,,	4 ,,
GERMANY	— ,,	— ,,	5 ,,
HOLLAND	39 ,,	— ,,	28 ,,
INDIA	721 ,,	457 ,,	765½ ,,
ITALY	— ,,	2 ,,	— ,,
JAPAN	2557 ,,	3 ,,	300 ,,
MADAGASCAR ...	39 ,,	4 ,,	2 ,,
NEW ZEALAND ...	695 ,,	144 ,,	433 ,,
NORWAY	32 ,,	— ,,	— ,,
PORTUGAL	— ,,	1 ,,	— ,,
RUSSIA	20 ,,	6 ,,	— ,,
SPAIN	— ,,	17 ,,	2 ,,
STRAIT Settlements	— ,,	6 ,,	— ,,
SWEDEN	8 ,,	— ,,	10 ,,
TURKEY	— ,,	2 ,,	— ,,
UNITED STATES..	52 ,,	6 ,,	66 ,,
W. INDIES	— ,,	3 ,,	1 ,,

IMPORTS FROM

AUSTRIA ...	357 bales	HOLLAND ...	24 cases
BELGIUM ...	1513 ,,	,, ...	51 rolls
,, ...	62 cases	INDIA	17 cases
DENMARK ...	336 bales	JAPAN	7 ,,
FRANCE ...	443 ,,	NORWAY ...	3009 bales
,, ...	10 cases	,, ...	427 rolls
FINLAND ...	539 bales	PRUSSIA ...	247 bales
,, ...	85 cases	SWEDEN ...	1570 ,,
,, ...	329 rolls	SPAIN	30 cases
GERMANY ...	2944 bales	U.S.A.	9 bales
,, ...	57 cases	,, ...	55 cases
HOLLAND ...	10297 bales		

Including the Following:

Quantity	From	Importer	Port.
54 bales	Christiania	F. E. Foulger	London.
[illegible] ,,	,,	Lon. & Rhine S. Co	,,
8 ,,	,,	Hernu, Peron & Co	,,
4 ,,	,,	Christophersen & Co	,,
4 ,,	,,	Crabb & Co	,,
[illegible] ,,	,,	Alsing & Co	,,
[illegible] ,,	Copenhagen	Becker & Ulrich	,,
166 ,,	Drammen	Alsing & Co	,,
17 ,,	,,	R. L. Lundgren	,,
[illegible] rolls	,,	,, ,,	,,
17 bales	,,	W. D. Edwards	,,
53 ,,	,,	J. Spicer & Sons	,,
47 ,,	,,	Crabb & Co	,,
33 ,,	,,	L. & Rhine Co	,,
39 rolls	,,	Calleys & Co	,,
[illegible] cases	New York	Maw Son & Co	,,
[illegible] bales	Norrkoping	Pro. Dowgate Dk.	,,
[illegible] ,,	,,	Schenkenwald & Co	,,
57 ,,	,,	Pro. Brooks Whf.	,,
[illegible] ,,	,,	J. S. Spicer & Sons	,,
39 ,,	Stettin	B. Beer	,,
[illegible] ,,	,,	Becker & Ulrich	,,
[illegible] ,,	,,	J. Spicer & Son	,,
15 ,,	,,	Morgan & Co	,,
[illegible] ,,	,,	M. Benscher	,,
[illegible] ,,	Trieste	Sabel & Co	,,
[illegible] ,,	Uddevalla	R. L. Lundgren	,,
124 ,,	,,	D. Gulland	,,
[illegible] ,,	,,	Hummel & Co	,,

SUMMARY OF IMPORTS & EXPORTS,

FOR THE WEEK ENDING TUESDAY LAST.

London, Liverpool, Bristol, Southampton, Hull, Fleetwood, Harwich, Folkestone, Newhaven, Dover, &c.

IMPORTS.

Paper	18418 bales	Leather Paper ...	7 cases
,, ...	263 cases	Strawboards	1100 pkgs.
,, ...	756 rolls	Waste	10 ,,
Stationery	13 pkgs.	Straw Paper......	1054 bales
Millboards.........	23600 bales	Tissues	95 ,,
,, ...	15 cases	,, ...	53 cases
Pasteboards	8245 pkgs.	Stock	1286 pkgs.

EXPORTS.

BRITISH GOODS.			
Paper	2081 cwt.	Stationery.........	£9039 value
Writing Paper ...	1433 ,,	Strawboards	10 tons
		FOREIGN GOODS.	
Printing Paper	6947 ,,	Paper	252 cwt.
Parchment	£114 value	Writing Paper...	6 ,,
Waste	37 tons	Printing Paper...	77 ,,
Cardboards	961 cwt.	Stationery	£229 value
Pulp Boards	3 ,,	Packing Paper ...	£70 ,,
Stock	334 tons	Strawboards	237 cwt.
Strawboard Cuttings	84 ,,	Wood Pulp	158 tons
		Stock	17 ,,
Rags.................	10 ,,	Parchment	18 cwt.

Glasgow, Greenock, Port-Glasgow, Troon, Grangemouth, &c.

IMPORTS.

Paper	763 bales	Strawboards	678 cwt.
,, ...	17 cases		

EXPORTS.

Writing Paper...	416 cwt.	Stock	163 cwt.
Printing Paper..	850 ,,	Litho Paper	58 ,,
Paper	641½ ,,	Wrapping Paper	13½ ,,
Stationery	£136 value	Packing Paper...	14½ ,,

Leith, Granton, Boness, Dundee, &c.

IMPORTS.

Paper	744 bales	Pasteboards	441 pkgs.
,, ...	4 cases	Millboards.........	1245 bales
,, ...	84 rolls	Tissues	10 ,,
Envelopes	612 pkgs		

PAPER & PULP MILL SHARES.

The market still remains quiet, with very few buyers of anysort, and where there are buyers they bid very low prices.

(Report received from Mr. F. D. DEAN, 36, Corporation Street, Manchester.)

Nominal Amnt	Amnt Paid	Name of Company	Last dividend	Price.
7	7	Bury Paper, ord.	nil	4½—5
7	7	do. do. 6% pref.	6%	4¾—5¼
100	100	do. do. deb.	5%	103—106
10	10	Bath Paper Mill Co. Lim.	7½%	6—7
10	10	Bergvik Co., def.	15%	13¾
100	100	do. do. 6% cum. pref.	6%	10⅞—11½
10	10	do. do. deb.	5%	105—110
5	3⅛	Burnley Paper Co.	3/-	77/0—78/0
5	3¾	Darwen Paper Co.	10%	5¼—5¾
10	10	East Lancashire Co.	nil	4¾—5
10	10	do. do. 6% pref.	nil	6¾—7
5	5	do. do. bonus	nil	1½—2
5	5	Hyde Paper Co.	4%	4¾—5
5	4	North of Ireland Paper Co.	nil	1⅞—2
10	5	Ramsbottom Paper Co.	17½%	12¼—12½
5	4½	Roach Bridge Paper Co.	5%	3¼—3¾
5	5	Star Paper Co.	10%	6—6¼
5	3	do. do. 10% pref. cum.	10%	4¾—5¼
50	50	do. do. deb.	6%	55—56
5	2½	Kellner Partingt'n Pulp Co	—	56/0—57/0

Greek Customs Tariff.

The new tariff shows for the first time the actual amount of duty leviable upon each class in the forced paper currency of the country, whether under the general or conventional tariff, in parallel columns with the nominal duty in gold. Another column shows the convention (if any) applicable to the class. Another change that has been made is the substitution, in most cases, of 100 okes for 1 oke or 1 quintal as the unit on which duty is calculated:

Number of Class in Tariff.	Description of Class.	Unit of Weight or Measure on which Duty is Charged.	Duty in Metallic Money.		Duty in Bank Notes.		Convention.
			General Tariff.	Conventional Tariff.	General Tariff.	Conventional Tariff.	
	CATEGORY XIX. PRODUCTS OF PAPER MANUFACTURE IN GENERAL.		Dr. l.	Dr. l.	Dr. l.	Dr. l.	
297	Paper paste of whatsoever material, bleached or not, as well as paste coagulated into sheets or rolls, in the form of cardboard, but easily distinguishable from cardboard by the irregularity of its two surfaces and its uneven thickness ...	100 okes	Free	...	Free	...	...
298	Roofing paper, emery paper, glass paper, and tarred paper...	"	Free	...	Free	...	...
299	Coarse paper, blue, grey or yellow, in large or small sheets, cut and prepared, not of cotton, linen or hemp, but of other materials, such as wood, &c., cardboard, and paper telegraph tapes ...	"	40 00	20 00	52 90	26 45	...
300	Printing paper:						
	a. Common, unglazed ...	"	40 00	20 00	52 90	26 45	...
	b. Glazed ...	"	60 00	30 00	79 35	39 68	...
301	Letter paper of all shapes, parchment paper, and wall paper...	"	200 00	100 00	264 50	132 25	...
302	*a.* Paper for registers and account books; drawing paper; paper for the outer covers of stitched books; blank books, ruled or not; books or sheets of paper having printed words on them, suitable for diaries, &c.; and sheets of paper for copying, provided that the paper is unsuitable for making cigarettes ...	"	100 00	60 00	132 25	79 35	...
	b. Account books and copy books, of paper unsuitable for making cigarettes ...	"	120 00	...	158 70	...	...
303	Writing papers of any colours:						
	a. Unglazed ...	"	50 00	30 00	66 13	39 68	...
	b. Glazed ...	"	60 00	40 00	79 35	52 90	...
304	Paper for various uses:						
	a. Paper of one colour for the outer covers of unstitched books, for tobacco wrappers, hat cases, &c., of any thickness, glazed or not, and blue paper for wrappers of "papier timbre," or official documents ...	"	50 00	30 00	66 13	39 68	...
	b. Blotting paper; grey or blue packing paper, glazed or not; canvas; and tissue paper for wrapping lemons, oranges, and other fruits, transparent and porous, in which the pores and the irregularity of the coagulation can be distinguished with the naked eye, and which has not, like cigarette paper, horizontal or vertical watermarks...	"	30 00	20 00	39 68	26 45	...
305	Cigarette paper (monopoly) ...	"	Prohibit'd	...	Prohibit'd	...	...
306	Paper for cheques, bonds, shares, &c.; envelopes, fancy paper, coloured, or wholly or partially silvered or gilt; paper for bouquets or sweetmeats with lace work or other patterns ...	Oke	3 00	2 00	3 97	2 65	...
307	Paper for use as stamped paper (papier timbre) ...	"	Prohibit'd	...	Prohibit'd	...	...
308	Hat cases, and boxes in general, not of papier-mache, nor of fancy paper ...	"	1 00	...	1 32	...	...
309	Articles similar to the above, of fancy paper; paper toys of all kinds, with or without pictures; paper collars and cuffs; and paper ornaments covered with tinfoil for coffins, &c. ...	"	8 00	5 00	10 58	6 61	...
310	Bonbon boxes, plain (that is to say, without admixture of metals, tissues, or precious wood, or bone, &c., otherwise they are included in Category XX.—Mixed materials) ...	"	5 00	...	6 61	...	...
311	Tracing paper; silver paper; design paper ruled in millims.; music paper, without notes, or stitched in books; photographic, phototypic, and lithographic paper; and paper for visiting cards ...	100 okes	80 00	60 00	105 80	79 35	...
312	Papier-mache and articles made thereof (except buttons, which are included in Category XX.) ...	"	300 00	...	396 75	...	...

Table showing the principal articles, the duty on which has been altered in the New Greek Tariff; or against which a New Maximum Duty has been inscribed, the Minimum Duty remaining unchanged. The latter are marked thus *:

Number of Class in New Tariff.	Description of Class (in brief).		Old Duty.		New Duty.		+ Duty Raised. * See above.
			General	Conventional.	General	Conventional.	
			Dr. l.	Dr. l.	Dr. l.	Dr. l.	
299	Coarse paper	100 okes	10 00	...	40 00	20 00	+
300a	Printing paper, unglazed	,,	20 00	...	40 00	20 00	*
300b	,, glazed	,,	20 00	...	60 00	30 00	+
301	Letter paper	,,	100 00	...	200 00	100 00	*
302a	Paper for "proces-verbaux," for account books, &c.	,,	60 00	...	100 00	60 00	*
302b	Account and copy books	,,	60 00	...	120 00	...	+
303a	Writing paper (new class) unglazed	,,	...	...	50 00	30 00	...
303b	,, ,, glazed	,,	...	...	60 00	40 00	...
304a	Paper for covers of unstitched books, for hat cases, &c. ...	,,	20 00	...	50 00	30 00	+
304b	Blotting and packing paper...	,,	16 00	...	30 00	20 00	+
309	Fancy articles, &c.	Oke	5 00	...	8 00	5 00	*
311	Tracing paper, &c.	100 okes	60 00	...	80 00	60 00	*

Coins Accepted as Legal Tender in Greece.

	Nominal Value.		Value Accepted.
	Dr. l.		Dr. l.
£5 piece	126 11	...	125 80
£2 ,, ...	50 44	...	50 32
Sovereign	25 22	...	25 16
Half-Sovereign	12 61	...	12 58

Equivalent of Money, Weights and Measures.

100 lepta	= 1 drachme	= 9 4/10 d.
	1 dramion	0·111 ozs. avoirdupois
400 dramia	1 oke	2·8 lbs.
44 okes	1 quintal	123·2 lbs.
	1 oke of capacity	2·34 pints.

Printed and Published EVERY FRIDAY
AT 58, SHOE LANE, LONDON, E.C.,
By W. JOHN STONHILL.
ESTABLISHED 1878.

FRIDAY, SEPTEMBER 1, 1893.

JUDGING from the annual reports issued by the Chambers of Commerce in the German Empire, the paper trade during the past year or more has been on the decline. Sales have been difficult, over-production gigantic, competition severe, and profits, if not *nil*, very small. In regard to wood pulp, the competition sustained at the hands of the Scandinavian and Austrian manufacturers seems to have paralysed German trade. The higher prices current during the present year have not been of material benefit owing to existing contracts at low prices. Loud complaints are made concerning the conditions under which manufacturers are bound in relation to workmen's insurance, &c., and it is pointed out that they are heavily handicapped in many respects compared with other countries.

GERMAN papermakers for some time have been talking about the wisdom of establishing higher prices, and, preliminarily, have discussed the various causes which have brought about the present unsatisfactory position. They ignore their motto of the past, *viz.*, to sell at any price, and without attributing to themselves any blame, complain that the low prices at present in force have been brought about by the action of agents. German papermakers accuse agents of pushing sales for the sole object of obtaining commission, caring little whether their principals incurred a loss or not. It is also alleged that some of the agents represent more than one maker of the same class of paper, and are guilty of working one against the other in running the market down.

ONE of the latest proposals made is to keep a list of agents for official circulation amongst German papermakers. The idea is that each mill should have a different agent, and that no agent should be allowed to represent two mills. In some quarters the opinion is expressed that this project would meet with considerable difficulty in practical execution; for instance, say there were 500 mills, the consequence would be that 500 paper agents would have to be established in every trade centre, and competition, it is contended, would be keener than before.

PAPERMAKERS in search of agents should use common prudence and make careful enquiries. There are unprincipled persons connected with almost every trade or profession. A good agent would naturally possess a fair connection, and in his own interest would obtain the highest possible prices. The appointment of a separate agent for each mill would tend to multiply competition rather than lessen it. A correspondent writing on this subject says:—"If one agent sold for two mills, he would, for his own personal benefit, not bring the two mills into conflict, but would endeavour to find orders for both; on the other hand if the two mills were represented by two men, the natural consequence would be that one would try to undersell the other." In any case it would be desirable for manufacturers to have a clear understanding with agents concerning terms under which sales could profitable be effected, and to be firm in not descending lower than a certain fixed price. Many makers have special arrangements regarding their so-called "over prices" with extra commission, and this policy seems to work very well. Such pessimistic alarm as ventilated above seems not to be borne out by facts, and the whole, we believe, need not be taken seriously.

CONSIDERABLE opposition is being shown in regard to the "Berliner Vormesse" (Berlin preliminary fair). The Leipzig Chamber of Commerce—according to the president (Mr. A. Thieme) and Dr. Pohle—has been authorised by a large number of influential firms regularly represented at the Leipzig Fair, to declare that the said firms, both in their own interest and in those of their clients have bound themselves not to take part in any manner whatsoever in the so-called Preliminary Fair, which several firms intend to hold in Berlin at this period of the year. It is hoped that this declaration, the promulgation of which has been undertaken by the Chamber of Commerce at the request of a great many important firms in the ceramic trade, will nip in the bud the idea of the formation of another fair at Berlin, which would be equally disastrous to manufacturers and consumers. Otherwise the unavoidable consequences would be, firstly, that the fair would be broken up into a number of subsidiary fairs, each representing a special trade. This would entail the loss of all advantages accruing from the simultaneous representation of all business branches at the Fair. Secondly, the attendance of visitors would be divided between the two fairs, which would compel the manufacturers to exhibit both at Berlin and Leipzig, thereby doubling their outlay, without a corresponding increase of profits.

THERE is an additional reason which has induced the firms interested to issue this declaration, viz.,—various communications received from the Chamber of Commerce have convinced them that the Town Council of Leipzig and the Leipzig Chamber of Commerce are paying every attention to the legitimate wishes and grievances of visitors with regard to several evils that have become more and more prominent during the last few years. In this connection the resolution of the Town Council to turn the old "Gewandhaus" into an Exhibition Hall for the Fair, a change entailing extensive structural alterations at a very heavy outlay, has been specially well received. These alterations will probably be sufficiently advanced by the time of holding the next Easter Fair to allow of a great number of suitable rooms being placed at the disposal of intending exhibitors against a reasonable charge. The most favourable feature of this new measure—viz., prevention of overcharging for space to strangers will be supplemented by the re organisation of the Committee for assisting visitors in finding lodgings.

THE paper trade of the United States of America, according to latest reports, is in a very unsatisfactory condition. A great number of mills are shut down and others running short time, and the outlook is certainly discouraging. The raw material market is also in a depressed condition. Employees are affected, and in several instances wages have been reduced 10 to 15 per cent. millowners pointing out that they are compelled to do this or else close their works.

To the lackadaisical condition of the Papermakers' Association of Great Britain, writes a correspondent, may be attributed the formation of an association for North-East Lancashire, and it is predicted with the present officers at the head of affairs subjects of trade interest will not be neglected, and that consequently the parent society will fall in the background.

THE coal strike is having a disastrous effect upon the chemical trade of Widnes. The supply of fuel and salt running short is likely to affect the employment of about 7,000 men in that district. Several paper mills find the increased price of 2s. 6d. to 6s. per ton for steam coal too much for them, and the outlook is very gloomy just now.

PRIVY-COUNCILLOR NASSE, of Berlin, has just published a statistical account of the probable amount of coal at the disposal of the coming generations in the chief industrial States of Europe and America. He reckons that the Saar district is capable of delivering twelve million tons a year for the next 833 years, and that the Ruhr basin will render thirty-seven millions yearly for 806 years. His speculations as to our own prospects are less favourable. So immense is the English demand for coal in proportion to the extent of our coalfields that he only allows 628 years before the exhaustion of our stock. France is still less fortunate, and will come to the end of her supply in 520 years. Belgium, on the contrary, can reckon upon seven, or possibly eight, centuries. Herr Nasse predicts that the coal competition in Europe in the distant future will be between Belgium and Germany. But he anticipates that North America, which is incomparably richer in coal than Central Europe, may eventually beat them both, and that the Old World will be largely supplied with fuel from the mines of the New.

WORLD'S PAPER TRADE REVIEW OFFICE, 58, SHOE LANE, LONDON, E.C.
AUGUST 31, 1893.

MARKET REPORT

and RECORD of IMPORTS

Of Foreign Rags, Wood Pulp, Esparto, Paper, Millboards, Strawboards, &c., at the Ports of London Liverpool, Southampton, Bristol, Hull, Fleetwood, Middlesborough, Glasgow, Grangemouth, Granton, Dundee, Leith, Dover, Folkestone, and Newhaven for the WEEK ENDING AUGUST 30.

From SPECIAL Sources and Telegrams.

Telegrams—"STONHILL, LONDON."

CHEMICALS.—The curtailment in the production of chemicals owing to the want of fuel has caused an advance in prices. In our last issue we recorded the official intimation of 10s. per ton advance in BLEACH and CAUSTIC and 5s. in SODA CRYSTALS. SODA ASH is unaltered, owing to the present competition in that article. Sales at full prices, viz., £8 15s., have been made in BLEACHING POWDER. CAUSTIC SODA 77% is quoted £11 10s. Tyne, and SODA CRYSTALS £2 17/6. SULPHUR is quiet at £4 2s. 6d. to £4 5s. ALUM unchanged.

Prices are nominally as follows :

Article			Terms		£	s.	d.
Alkali, 58%	tierces	...	f.o.r. works	2½%	5	10	0
" 58%	bags	...	" "	2½%	5	5	0
58%	...	...	f.o.b. Liverpool	2½%	5	12	6
Alum (Ground),	tierces	...	" Liverpool	2½%	5	7	6
" "	barrels	...	"	2½%	5	17	6
" "	tierces	...	" Hull	2½%	5	5	0
" "	"	...	Goole	2½%	5	5	0
Alum (Lump)	"	...	f.o.b. Liverpool	2½%	4	17	6
" "	barrels	...	"	2½%	5	0	0
" "	tierces	...	" Hull	2½%	4	15	0
" "	"	...	Goole	2½%	4	15	0
" "	"	...	London	2½%	5	5	0
" "	"	...	f.a.s. Glasgow	2½%	5	5	0
Alumina Sulphate,	casks		f.o.b. Tyne		4	2	6
" "	bags		" "		3	17	6
Aluminoferric Cake,	slabs		Liverpool ...	...	2	15	0
" "	tierces		" ...	...	3	2	6
Alumina Cake,	slabs	...	Glasgow	...	2	15	0
" "	tierces	...	"	...	3	2	6
Aluminous Cake,	casks	...	Manchester	3½%	2	7	6
" "	"	...	Newcastle	2½%	2	10	0
" "	"	...	London	2½%	3	0	0
" "	bags	...	"	2½%	2	17	9
Blanc Fixe ...	...	...	f.o.b. Tyne	net	7	10	0
Bleach, 35%	...	...	" "	net	8	15	0
" (soft wood)		...	f.o.r. Lancs.	net	8	10	0
" (hard wood)		...	f.o.b. Liverpool	net	9	0	0
...	...	...	landed London	2½%	9	15	0
Borax (crystals)	...	...	... ...	net	29	0	0
powdered	...	...	... ...	net	30	0	0
Caustic Cream, 60%		...	f.o.r. Lancs.	net	8	12	6
" " 60%		...	f.o.b. Liverpool	net	8	17	6
" Bottoms		...	" "	net	6	15	0
" "	...	...	f.o.b. Tyne	net	6	15	0
Caustic White 76-77%		...	f.o.r. Newcastle	net	11	5	0
" " 77%		f.o.r. or	f.o.b. Tyne	net	11	10	0
" " 74%		...	f.o.b. Liverpool	net	11	5	0
" " 70%		...	" "	net	10	5	0
" " 70%		...	" Hull	net	10	10	0
" " 70%		...	f.o.r. London	net	10	5	0
" " 70%		...	" Lancs.,	net	10	2	6
" " 60%		...	" London	net	9	5	0
" " 60%		...	f.o.b. Liverpool	net	9	5	0
Carbonat'd Ash 58%		...	" "	net	6	0	0
48%		...	" "	net	5	10	0
" 58%		...	f.o.r. Widnes	net	5	15	0
48%		...	" "	net	5	5	0
Chloride of Barium		...	f.o.b. Tyne	net	7	10	0
Hypo-Sulphite of Soda...			f.o.r Tyne		5	15	0
" "	10-ton lots		ex ship Liverp'l	net	6	10	0
Oxalic Acid ...	...	...	f.o.b. Liverpool	3½%	per lb		¼
Salt Cake	..	...	" works	net	1	10	0
Soda Ash, 52%	...	...	f.o.b. Tyne	net	4	10	0
" 52%	...	...	ex ship Thames	1%	4	15	0
" 52%	...	...	f.o.b. Liverpool	1%	5	0	0
Soda Crystals	...	...	" Tyne	net	2	17	6
" "	...	...	ex ship Thames	2½%	3	5	0
" "	...	...	f.o.b. Liverpool	net	3	0	0
Sulphur, roll	...	...	f.o.r. works	2½%	7	17	6
" flowers	...	..	" "	2½%	9	10	0
" recovered		...	" "	2½%	4	2	6
Sulphate of Ammonia		"	" "	2½%	13	2	6
" of Copper		...	" Liverpool	5%	15	0	0

FOREIGN.—F.o.b. Continental port :

Article	£	s.	d.
Alkali, 58% 2-cwt. bags £6 10/0; 10-cwt. casks ...	6	15	6
Caustic Soda, 70-72%	11	12	0
Hypo-Sulphite of Soda 10-ton lots 140/0; kegs ...	7	10	6
Sulphate of Alumina 7-8 cwt. casks net c.i.f. Ldn	4	7	6
Blanc Fixe (c.i.f. London)	7	12	6

ESPARTO.—The enquiry is maintained, and a fair amount of business for the season of the year is being carried through at former prices for near but rather lower rates again for distant positions.

Prices c.i.f. London and Leith, or f.o.r. Cardiff, Garston and Tyne Docks are nominally as follows :

		£	s.	d.		£	s.	d.
Spanish—	Fair to Good	£5	10	0	to	5	15	0
"	Fine to Best	5	17	6	"	6	0	0
Oran —	Fair to Good	3	12	6	"	3	17	6
"	First Quality...	4	0	0	"	4	2	6
Tripoli —	Hand-picked	3	17	6	"	4	2	6
"	Fair Average	3	12	6	"	3	15	0
Bona & Philippeville	... ...	4	0	0	"	4	2	6

IMPORTS of ESPARTO.

Quantity	From	Importer	Port.
717½ tons	Aguilas	L. Jacobs Marcus & Co	Granton
18650 "	"	Guardbridge Paper Co	Dundee
17600 cwts.	Almeria	H. Ottomann	Leith
2484 bales	Oran	Morris & Co.	Fleetwood
709 tons	"	Henderson, McIntosh	Granton

CHEMICAL WOOD PULPS.—Users do not seem anxious to conclude contracts. Producers are very firm in upholding prices, especially in regard to best grades of SULPHITE. SODA and SULPHATE pulps are in better enquiry.

Prices, ex steamer, London, Hull, Newcastle, Leith and Glasgow are nominally as follows :

	£	s.	d.		£	s.	d.
SODA, Unbleached, Common ...	£10	0	0	to	10	10	0
" " Extra... ...	10	10	0	"	11	0	0
" Half-Bleached	12	10	0	"	14	0	0
SULPHATE, Unbleached, Common	10	10	0	"	11	0	0
" Extra	11	0	0	"	12	0	0
" Half-Bleached	13	10	0	"	14	0	0
" Bleached	15	0	0	"	16	0	0
SULPHITE, Unbleached. Common	10	15	0	to	11	0	0
" Superior	11	10	0	"	12	10	0
" " 50% moisture, d.w.	11	10	0	"	12	2	6
" Extra	13	0	0	"	14	0	0
" Bleached, moist					16	10	0
" Unbleached, English, del. Lancs. ...					10	15	0
" " " No. 1, ex mills, Ldn.					10	10	0
" " " No. 2, " "					9	15	0

MECHANICAL WOOD PULPS.—The market is extremely firm, and a fair amount of business has been negotiated of late for next year's delivery. Heavy shipments have come to hand this week. Advices from Norway intimate that a moderate amount of business is being done with Germany, and the future outlook is very satisfactory.

Prices, ex steamer, London, Hull, Newcastle, Leith and Glasgow are nominally as follows :

MECHANICAL, Aspen, Dry ...	£7 10 0 to 8 0 0
Pine, Dry	6 0 0 ,, 6 2 6
Pine, 50% Moist, Spot ...	2 15 0 ,, 2 17 6
Moist Brown (bundles ...	2 15 0 ,, 2 17 6
Dry Brown	5 15 0 ,, 6 0 0
Single Sorted...	2 5 0 ,, 2 6

IMPORTS of WOOD PULP.

Quantity	From	Importer	Port.
120 bales	Abo	To order	Hull
273 ,,	Bergen	,,	,,
50 ,,	Christiania	Bott and Co	London
100 ,,	,,	Hummel & Co	,,
426 ,,	,,	Taylor & Co	,,
800 ,,	,,	G. Skramnes	,,
786 ,,	,,	To order	Hull
364 ,,	,,	,,	Grangemouth
800 ,,	,,	,,	,,
1324 ,,	Christiansand	,,	Leith
480 ,,	Copenhagen	J. Currie & Co	,,
2385 ,,	Drammen	E. Lloyd	London
585 ,,	,,	E. J. & W. Goldsmith	,,
2500 ,,	,,	C. Christophersen	,,
320 ,,	Dusseldorf	To order	,,
16 ,,	Drontheim	,,	Hull
400 ,,	Fiume	,,	London
699 ,,	Gothenburg	Salvesen & Co	Leith
977 ,,	,,	To order	Hull
170 ,,	,,	,,	Glasgow
2894 ,,	,,	Henderson & Co	London
540 ,,	,,	To order	,,
303 ,,	,,	,,	,,
44 casks	Ghent	,,	,,
23 bales	,,	,,	,,
408 ,,	Hambro	J. Currie & Co	Leith
54 ,,	,,	,,	,,
202 ,,	,,	To order	London
100 ,,	,,	,,	Hull
204 ,,	,,	,,	Leith
150 ,,	Norrkoping	Baring Bros	London
134 ,,	,,	Tegner, Price & Co	,,
240 ,,	Rotterdam	To order	,,
228 rolls	,,	,,	,,
640 bales	,,	,,	Liverpool
512 ,,	Stettin	,,	London
400 ,,	,,	,,	,,
100 ,,	,,	,,	Leith
200 ,,	,,	,,	Hull
260 ,,	,,	Ronaldson and Co	,,

Totals from Each Country:

BELGIUM ..	44 casks	HOLLAND ...	228 rolls
,, ...	23 bales	,, ...	880 bales
DENMARK ...	480 ,,	NORWAY ...	10823 ,,
FINLAND ...	500 ,,	PRUSSIA ...	1472 ,,
GERMANY ...	1177 ,,	SWEDEN ...	5589 ,,

IMPORTS of WOOD PULP BOARDS.

Quantity	From	Importer	Port
30 bales	Gothenburg	Salvesen & Co	Granton

STRAW.—Very little Straw is obtainable; prices nominal.

IMPORTS of STRAW

(Purposes unspecified) at principal Ports From

BELGIUM ...	12 bales	FRANCE ...	3 bales
DENMARK ...	900 ,,	HOLLAND ...	1192 ,,

STRAW PULPS.—The demand is rather quiet.

Prices, c.i.f. London, Hull or Leith :

Belgian, 25% moisture	£15 0 0 to 16 0 0
do. dry	16 0 0
German, 50 to 55% moisture	16 10 0
do. dry, ... No. 1 £18 10 0; No. 2	15 0 0

IMPORTS of STRAW PULP.

Quantity	From	Importer	Port.
54 bales	Hambro	To order	Hull

JUTE.—Market firm. Cuttings are in fair request.

Good White	£16 0 to 17 0	Common ...	£10 10 to 11 0
Good... ...	15 0	Rejections...	8 0 ,, 9 0
Medium	0 ,, 14 0	Cuttings ...	£5 to 6 0

FOREIGN RAGS.—Trade is in a very unsettled condition, as the removal of restrictions on the importation of rags is likely to be only temporary. The Local Government Board have been urged to revert to the old order of things, and it is further contended previous precautionary measures are quite insufficient for the destruction of the cholera microbe. Arrivals, however, have come well to hand this week.

IMPORTS of FOREIGN RAGS.

Quantity	From	Importer	Port.
36 bales	Amsterdam	To order	Leith
22 ,,	,,	,,	,,
74 ,,	,,	,,	Hull
36 ,,	Antwerp	,,	Leith
28 ,,	,,	,,	,,
84 ,,	Boulogne	,,	London
219 ,,	Bremen	,,	Hull
40 ,,	Buenos Ayres	,,	Liverpool
33 ,,	Christiansand	,,	Leith
56 ,,	,,	,,	,,
96 ,,	Constantinople	,,	Southampton
110 ,,	,,	,,	Liverpool
7 ,,	Christiania	,,	Hull
380 ,,	Ghent	,,	Leith
12 ,,	Gothenburg	,,	Hull
160 ,,	Harlingen	,,	,,
48 ,,	,,	,,	,,
25 ,,	,,	,,	Leith
102 ,,	Hambro	,,	Hull
85 ,,	,,	,,	,,
48 ,,	,,	,,	,,
204 ,,	,,	,,	,,
1 ,,	Kobe	,,	London
134 ,,	Konigsberg	,,	Hull
50 ,,	Rotterdam	,,	Leith
107 ,,	,,	,,	Hull
60 ,,	,,	,,	Leith
50 ,,	,,	,,	Hull
74 ,,	,,	,,	Leith
49 ,,	Rouen	,,	London
99 ,,	,,	,,	,,
97 ,,	Sydney	,,	,,
52 ,,	St. Malo	,,	Southampton
10 ,,	Stettin	,,	Hull

Totals from Each Country:

ARGENTINA	40 bales	JAPAN ...	1 bale
AUSTRALIA ...	97 ,,	NORWAY ...	96 bales
BELGIUM ...	424 ,,	PRUSSIA ...	144 ,,
FRANCE ...	284 ,,	SWEDEN ...	12 ,,
GERMANY ..	718 ,,	TURKEY ...	206 ,,
HOLLAND ...	706 ,,		

DUTCH RAGS, f.o.r. Hull:

C.i.f. Thames; Hull 2/6 per ton more; ditto f.o.r. Leith c.i.f. Glasgow 4/-; c.i.f. Liverpool 4/-..

Selected Fines (free from Muslins) ...	17/0	Best Grey Linens ...	9/0
Selected Outshots	12/0	Common ditto ...	5/6
,, Dirty Fines	7/0	White Canvas ...	15/0
Light Cottons ...	9/3	Grey & Brown Canvas	9/9
Blue Cottons ...	8/0	Tarred Hemp Rope	8/0
Dark Coloured Cottons	2/10½	Ditto (broken) ...	5/3
New Cuttings (Bleachd)	22/6	White Paper Shavings	7/9
,, (Unbleached)	19/6	Gunny (best) ...	4/9
,, (Slate) ...	9/0	Jute Bagging ...	3/6
Muslins	8/0	Ditto (common ...	3/0
Red Cottons (Mixed)	5/9	Tarpaulins	4/0
Fustians (Light browns)	5/0	Cowhair Carpets ...	2/9
		Hard ditto	3/0

RUSSIAN RAGS.

C.i.f. London, Hull, Newcastle or Leith.

SPFF	15/0	CC (Cotton	5/3
SPF	13/6	Jute I	3/6
FG	10/6	,, II...	2/3
LFB	9/6	Rope I...	9/9
FF	8/3	,, II	5/9
LFX	7/3		

GERMAN RAGS.

STETTIN: C.i.f. Hull, Leith, Tyne and London.

SPFFF and SPFF	18/6	LFB (Blue)	10/
SPF	12/6	CSPFFF and CSPFF	12/0
FF	11/0	CFB (Blue)	8/0
FG	9/6	CFX (Coloured) ...	5/0
LFX	7/0		

HAMBURG : F.o.b.

NWC	22/0	FF Grey Linens ...	9/0
SPFFF	22/0	LFX Second ditto...	8/0
SPFFF and SPFF	18/0	CSPFFF	17/3
SPFF	16/0	CSPFF	12/3
SPF	12/0	CFB	8/0
CCC	5/6	Dark Blues (selected	11/9
CFX	4/6	Wool Tares... ...	8/0
White Rope... ...	8/0	Jute, No. I 6/0; No. II	5/6

FRENCH RAGS.

Quotations range, per cwt., ex ship London, Southampton, or Hull; 2/0 per ton more at Liverpool, and 10/0 per ton higher at Newcastle, Glasgow or Leith.

French Linens, I ...	22/0	Black Cotton ...	4/0
II 18/6; III ...	14/6	Marseilles Whites, I	16/0
White Cottons, I ...	19/0	II 10/0; III ...	7/6
II 15/0; III ...	12/6	Blue Cotton	11/0
Knitted Cotton ...	11/0	Light Prints... ...	6/0
Light Coloured Cotton	8/0	Mixed Prints ...	6/0
Blue Cotton	9/6	New White Cuttings	25/0
Coloured Cotton ...	6/0	,, Stay ,,	21/0

NORWEGIAN RAGS.

C.i.f. London, Hull, Tyne, and Grangemouth.

1st Rope (tarred) ...	8/9-9/0	2nd Canvas ...	8/0
2nd ,, ,, ...	5/9-6/0	Jute Bagging	
Manilla Rope (white)	8/6-8/9	Gunny ...	3/6 3/9
Best Canvas ...	11/9-12/0	Mixed ...	2/6-3/0

BELGIAN RAGS.

F.o.b. Ghent. Freights: London, 5/0; Hull and Goole, 7/6 Liverpool and Leith, 10/0; Newcastle, 12/6; Dundee and Aberdeen, 15/0; Glasgow, 16/8.

White Linens No. 1	22/6	Fustians (Light) ...	6/0
,, ,, No. 2	16/6	,, (Dark) ...	4/0
,, ,, No. 3	13/0	Thirds...	3/0
Fines (Mixed) ...	12/0	Black Cottons ...	3/9
Grey Linens (strong)	10/0	Hemp Strings (unt'r'd)	2/0
,, ,, (extra)	14/0	House Cloths ...	5/0
Blue Linens... ...	8/6	Old Bagging (solid)	5/6
White Cottons S'p'fine	18/0	,, ,, (common)	2/6
,, ,, No. 2	15/0	NEW.	
Outshots No. 3 ...	11/0	White & Cream Linens	35/0
Seconds No. 4 ...	8/0	White Cuttings ...	25/0
Prints (Light) ...	8/6	Unbleached Cuttings	21/0
,, (Old)	4/6	Print Cuttings ..	8/0

BELGIAN FLAX and HEMP WASTE.

Best washed and dried Flax Waste, 10/0; Fair ditto	9/0
Flax Spinners' Waste (grease boiled out)... ...	10/0
Hemp Waste, No. 1 9/0; No. 2	7/6
Flax Spinners' Waste, No. 1 (Flax Rove) 10/0: No. 2	8/6

HOME RAGS.—LONDON: Trade is reported as being very dull, and stocks are accumulating. Very little demand is experienced for mills just now.—BRISTOL: There is scarcely any movement in this district, the coal strike tending to minimise business.—MANCHESTER: Trade depressed.—EDINBURGH: Business quiet; prices unchanged.—DUBLIN: Market dull.

LONDON:

New White Cuttings	21/6	Canvas No. 1	15/6
Fines (selected)	20/6	,, No. 2 ...	10/0-10/6
,, (good London)...	20/0	,, No. 3	5/6
Outshots (selected) ...	12/6	Mixed Rope	5/3
,, (ordinary) ...	11/0	White Rope	6/6
London Seconds	3/6-4/0	White Manilla Rope	8/6
Country do. ...	6/6-8/0	Coil Rope	3/6
London Thirds ...	1/9-2/0	Bagging...	1/6
Country do. ...	4/0-5/0	Gunny	3/6
Light Prints ...	7/0-8/0		

BRISTOL:

Fines	19/0	Clean Canvas ...	15/0
Outshots	13/6	Second Do. ...	9/6-12/6
Seconds	7/0-8/0	Light Prints ...	3/0
Thirds	3/6-4/0	Hemp Coil Rope	9/6-10/0
Mixed Bagging	3/6	Tarred Manilla	7/6

MANCHESTER:

Fines	15/0-16/0	Blues	7/0-7/6
Outshots (best) ...	11/6-12/0	Bagging...	4/3-4/6
,, (ordinary)	10/6-11/0	,, (common)	3/3-3/6
Seconds	7/3-7/6	W. Manilla Rope	10/0-12-6
Thirds	3/6-3/9	Surat Tares... ...	5/0-5/3

EDINBURGH:

Superfines	17/0	Black Cottons	2/9
Outshots	13/0	W. Manilla Rope ...	9/0
Mixed Fines...	14/0	Tarred Ditto	6/9
Common Seconds ...	8/0	,, Hemp Rope...	8/6
First do.	11/0	Rope Ends (new) ...	8/6
Prints	5/6-6/6	,, ,, (old) ...	6/0
Canvas (best)	16/0	Bagging...	2/0-3/0
,, 2nd	10/6	,, (clean) ...	4/3-6/0

DUBLIN.

White Cuttings ...	18/0	Mi'l Bagging	3/0
Fines	11/0	White Manilla	8/0
Seconds...	5/0	Tarred Hemp	8/0
Light Prints	3/0	Rigging	13/6
Black do.	2/0	Mixed Ropes	3/6
Bagging	2/0		

WASTE PAPERS.—There is a good demand for Waste Papers at well maintained prices.

Cream Shavings ...	12/3	Small Letters	5/2
Fine ,, ...	9/6	Large ,, ...	7/0
Mixed ,, ...	3/6	Brown Paper	2/3
White Printings ...	8/9	Light Browns	3/6
White Waste ...	1/6	Books & Pamphlets ...	6/0
Wood Pulp Cuttings	3/6	Strawboard Cuttings	1/6
Brown Paper	3/0	Jacquards	2/6
Crushed News	2/0		

For Export: 25/- per ton extra.

COLOURS.—Trade quiet.

Mineral Black ...	cwt.	3/0	Ultramarine (pure)	
do. superior ...	,,	5/0	... cwt. 40/0 to	45/0
Pure Ivory Black	,,	12/0	PASTE COLOURS with	
Ochre	,,	3/0	60% of colour, as follows:	
French J. C. Ochre	ton	55/0	Orange Pulp ... cwt.	40/0
Chrome (pure) ...	cwt.	40/0	Golden Yellow Pulp	36/0
Red Oxide	,,	4/6	Lemon ,, ,, cwt.	36/0
Umber, Devonshire	,,	50/0	Prussian Yellow ,,	36/0
do. Turkish ...	,,	40/0	Green (free of arsenic	36/0
Lamp Black ...		7/0-10/6	Paste Blue (20-45%)	
Cochineal	lb.	1/3-2/0	.. ...	23/6-46/8

FLOCKS.—Cotton Flocks continue in brisk demand; prices firm.

SIZING.—Fair demand.

English Gelatines	per cwt.	70/0	to	140/0
Foreign ,, ...	,,	70/0	,,	140/0
Fine Skin Glues	,,	45/0	,,	60/0
Long Scotch Glues	,,	45/0	,,	60/0
Common ,, ...	,,	30/0	,,	45/0
"Town" Glues	,,	26/0	,,	36/0
"Bone" Glues	,,	20/0	,,	30/0
Foreign Glues	,,	23/0	,,	40/0
Bone Size	,,	4/0	,,	10/0
Gelatine Size...	,,	5/0	,,	10/0
Dry B.A. Pieces	,,	31/6	,,	33/0
,, English Pieces	,,	24/0	,,	27/0
Wet ,, ,, ...	,,	7/0	,,	8/0
,, Sheep Pieces	,,	3/0	,,	4/0
Buffalo Hide Shavings	,,	26/0	,,	37/0
,, Picker Waste	,,	27/0	,,	33/0

ROSIN.—Market quiet, and prices easier. Imports have been large during the past month.

	Strained.	E.	F.	G.	K.	W.G.	W.W.
Spot—	3/7½	4/0	4/3	4/6	6/6	9/6	10/6
To arrive—	3/2	3/5	3/6	3/7½	6/0	8/6	9/0

STARCH.—Prices:

F.o.r. London, less 2½%:

Maize—Crisp, £9 10/-; Powder, £9 15/-; Special £14 10/-
Farina—Prime, £10 10/-; B.K.M.F., £13 10/-

Delivered:

Rice—Special (in chests), £20 0/- (net); Crystal (in bags) £19 0/-; Granulated (in bags) £18 0/- less 2½%.
Dextrine—£16 0/-

MINERALS.—The best grades of CHINA CLAY are in fair demand. In FRENCH CHALK a good business has been carried through at full figures. MINERAL WHITE quiet; prices well-maintained. A steady enquiry is current for PATENT and SUPERFINE HARDENINGS. BARYTES (carbonate) scarce ; finest White Sulphate in demand. Blackwell's MINERALINE is quoted £10, and IRISH MOSS of medium quality is offered at £12 10s.

Mineral White (Terra Alba), per ton f.o.r. or boat at works :

Superfine...	28/0 less 2½ %	
Pottery Super.... ...	24/0	,,
Ball Seconds	20/0	,,
Seconds	15/0	,,
Thirds	10/6	,,

China Clay, in bulk, f.o.b. Cornwall, 14/0 to 27/6; bags 5/0 and casks 9/6 per ton extra ; f.o.b. London, in casks 35/0 to 50/0 per ton.

Superfine Hardening, f.o.r. works, 40/0.

Patent Crystal Hardening, delivered at mills £3 to £3 15/0

Patent Hardening (2 ton lots) f.o.r. Lancs., £3 5/0.
,, ,, (5 ton lots) f.o.b. Liverpool, £3 10/0.

Magnesite (in lump) 32/6 per ton.

Magnesite (containing 98 % Carbonate of Magnesia), raw ground, £6 10/0 ; calcined ground, £12 10/0.

Albarine, £3. del. mills.

Asbestos, best rock, £18 ; brown grades, £14 to £15

Asbestine Pulp, £4 5/- to £5 c.i.f. London, Liverpool and Glasgow.

Barytes (Carbonate), lump, 90/0 to 95/0 ; nuts, 72/6 to 85/0.

Barytes (Sulphate), "Angel White," No. 1, 70/0 ; No. 2, 60/0 to 65/0 ; No. 3, 45/0. Souheur's Brands (Antwerp) : AF, 83/- ; BF, 71/- ; AB, 33/6 ; BB, 29/6 ; CB, 24/3.

French and Italian Chalk (Souheur Brand, Antwerp), per ton in lots of 10 tons : Flower O, 64/6 c.i.f. London, 69/6 c.i.f. Liverp'l, 71/0 c.i.f. Hull ; Flower OO, 60/0, 65/0 and 66/6 ; Flower OOO, 51/6, 56/6 and 58/0, Swan Brand, 57/0, 62/0 and 63/6. Blackwell's "Angel White" Brand and "Silvery" 90/- to 92/6 ; prime quality, 90/- to 95/- ; and superfine, 105/-.

Bauxite, Irish Hill Quality, first lump, 20/0 ; seconds, 16/0 ; thirds, 12/0 ; ground, 35/0.

Pyrites (non-cupreous), Liverpool, 5d., 2 %.

Carbonate of Lime (Souheur Brand, Antwerp) Prima 43/-, Secunda 37/-.

LIME. — Best WHITE BUXTON LIME, hand-picked, f.o.t. works, is quoted at 10/0 per ton (less 2½ %).

[illegible] SOLE MANUFACTURERS.

DIRECTORY.

[illegible] card [illegible]

[illegible]

[illegible] and VITRIOL Co., Lim., [illegible] E.C. Works: [illegible] —"Chinnock, London.

ANALYTICAL.

[illegible] ROWLAND, F.I.C., F.C.S., 28, Pall [illegible]

ARTESIAN WELLS.

[illegible] Richard D., Artesian and Consulting [illegible] 73, Queen Victoria Street, London, E.C., [illegible] 5713

[illegible] C., & Co., Bear Lane, Southwark, S.E.

[illegible] GRAND & SUTCLIFF, Magdala Works, 125, Bunhill Row, E.C.

BOILER COVERING.

LONSDALES, Boiler Coverers, Blackburn, will send a sample cask of their Patent Plastic Cork Covering to any Paper Mill in Great Britain—5 cwt. cask for 25/- (carriage paid).

CHINA CLAY.

The ALUM, CHINA CLAY and VITRIOL Co., Lim., 63, Queen Victoria Street, London, E.C. Mines: Ruddle and Colchester, St. Austell, Cornwall. Telegrams—"Chinnock, London."

ROGERS, J., & Co., Truro, Cornwall.—Agents: Taylor, Sommerville & Co., 83, Queen Victoria Street, E.C., and at 16, Princes Street, Edinburgh.

W. SINGLETON BIRCH & SONS, Lim., 25, Upton Street, Manchester. Mines: Rosevear, St. Austell, Cornwall. 2276

COLOURS.

CARDWELL, J. L., & Co., Commercial Buildings, 15, Cross Street, Manchester. Specialties: Mineral Black, Ven. Red, Ochres and Umbers. 5304

GEMMILL, W. N., & Co., Glasgow, Telegrams "Rube." Starches, Alumina, Antifroths, &c. All Paper Colours

HINSHELWOOD, THOMAS, & Co., The Glasgow Colour Works, Glasgow. Colours and shades matched exactly.

MULLER, A. E., 9, Fenchurch Street, London, E.C.

ESPARTO.

IDE & CHRISTIE, Fibre, Esparto, and General Produce Brokers, 72, Mark Lane, E.C.

MINERAL WHITE or TERRA ALBA.

WINSER & Co., Portland Mills, Princess Street, Manchester. Also manufacturers of Aluminous Cake.

HOWE, JOHN, & Co., Carlisle. 2112

STEEL.

MAKIN, WM., & SONS, Sheffield. Established 1796. Roll Bars, Plates, Cutter Knives, Doctor Blades, &c. [illegible]

STRAW.

UNDERWOOD, E., & SON, Limited, Brentford, London, W. Press-packed Oat, Wheat, or Rye Straw, delivered to the chief British ports or railway stations.

TALC (French and Italian Chalk).

SOUHEUR, JEAN, Antwerp. All Minerals, Blanc de Silex, Barytes (superior and common), Carbonate of Lime, Blacklead, &c. British Agent: A. E. Muller, 9, Fenchurch Street, London, E.C. Agent for Liverpool and Manchester: C. H. Austin, Ditton, near Widnes.

RAGS.

CHALMERS, E., & Co., Lim., Bonnington, Leith.

MULLER, A. E., 9, Fenchurch Street, London, E.C.

WERTHEIM, A., & Co., Hamburg.

UMBER.

The ALUM, CHINA CLAY and VITROIL Co., Lim. 63, Queen Victoria Street, London, E.C. Telegrams—"Chinnock, London."

WOOD PULP.

FRIIS, N., & Co., 28, Carl Johans Gade, Christiania, Norway.

GOTTSTEIN, H., & Co., 59, Mark Lane, London, E.C. and at New York.

GRANT, W., & Co., 17, Baltic Street, Leith. Agents for best shippers, Sulphite and Sulphate, Mechanical, Pine, Brown, Aspen.

MATTHIESSEN, CHR., Christiania, Norway.

MULLER, A. E., 9, Fenchurch Street, London, E.C.

The SULPHITE PULP Company, Limited, 82, Gordon Street, Glasgow.

WERTHEIM, A., & Co., Hamburg.

NEW PATENTS.

BRITISH.

APPLICATIONS.

15,047. Improvements in machinery for drying rags and other materials or fibrous substances. J. Illingworth.

15,331. Improvements in apparatus used in the manufacture of paper pulp. W. H. Coldwell.

15,396. Improvements in or connected with apparatus for the manufacture of chlorate of potash by electrolysis. F. Hurter.

SPECIFICATIONS PUBLISHED.

(7½d. each. By post 8d.)

1892.

25,113. Caustic soda and potash, &c. Boubertie and Cie.

1893.

11,936. Paper pulp refining engine. Pearson and Bertram.

AMERICAN.

500,617. Method of and apparatus for producing paper stock. Sidney W. Rowell, Albany, N.Y.

50[illegible],607. Method of making twine from paper. John F. Steward, Chicago, Ill.

500,915. Machine for making vegetable parchment paper. Gottlieb T. Leonhard, Paterson, N.J.

"LANCASHIRE" BELTS WORK IN HOT OR COLD WATER.

ON SALE,

ONE

75in. FOURDRINIER

PAPERMAKING MACHINE

With First and Second Presses
13 CYLINDERS 3 ft. 6 in. dia., 7 ft. 2 in. on Face,
STUFF and BACK WATER PUMPS;

AND

One STACK of CALENDERS

(BY J. ROBINSON & CO.),

Containing Four Chilled Rolls and Two Paper Rolls;

ALSO

STEAM ENGINE

To Drive Same; 11 inch Cylinder, 18 inch Stroke.

The Machine is just being taken out to make room for larger one.

Complete Specifications will be forwarded on application to the

Ramsbottom Paper Mill Co.,
LIMITED,
RAMSBOTTOM, NEAR MANCHESTER.

2659

SALE BY AUCTION.

At POLLOKSHAWS, near GLASGOW,

on

TUESDAY, 5th SEPTEMBER, at 12 o'clock noon.

IMPORTANT AND EXTENSIVE

PUBLIC SALE

of the

Whole Modern Plant

of the

CARTBRIDGE PAPER MILLS,

POLLOKSHAWS.

Amounting in Value to Over £8,000.

WALTER J. BUCHANAN

has received instructions to Sell by Public Auction as above, including Single Cylinder Papermaking Machine 90 in. wide by Messrs. Geo. and Wm. Bertram, Fourdrinier Papermaking Machine 85 in. wide, 16 Beating and Washing Engines, one Friction 5-roll Glazing Calender 90 in. wide by Herbert and Co., one Angle Paper Cutting Machine 86 in. wide by G. and W. Bertram, two Square Paper Cutting Machines 70 in. and 90 in. wide, one Reeling Machine 90 in. wide, Revolving and Upright Rag Boilers, one Coburn-Taylor Rag Cutter, one Rope Chopper by G. and W. Bertram, one 48 in. Guillotine by Greig, 7 Steam Engines 7 in. to 30 in. cylinders, two Penman's Steam Boilers 30 ft. long by 8 ft. diameter, working to 80 lbs. pressure, one Sinclair's Boiler 22 ft. by 6 ft., one Green's Economiser with 160 pipes, Steam Pumps, Double-Gear Turning Lathe, Planing Machine, vertical, large quantity of Shafting, Steam and Water Pipes, Platform Weighing Machine, 180 Y.P. Reels 6 in. diameter, about 40 tons Old Metal—brass and copper, Machine Felts, two Press Rolls of Rubber 90 in. and 58 in., Rubber and Leather Belting, Milner's Fireproof Safe, Counting House Furniture, etc.

On view on Saturday 2nd and on Monday 4th September from 10 till 4.

Full details in catalogues, to be had on application to the Auctioneer, 72, Renfield Street, Glasgow.

NOTE.—The above machinery is all of Modern Construction and in good order.

72, Renfield Street, Glasgow, 15 August, 1893. 2670

TO BE SOLD

(BY PRIVATE TENDER).

Pursuant to an Order of Mr. Justice Kekewich, made in an Action of

MASSON, SCOTT & BERTRAM,

against the

OTTOMAN PAPER MANUFACTURING COMPANY, LIMITED,

1892 M. No. 3411.

29,940 Shares of T.£10 Each

(FULLY PAID)

in the

Societe Anonyme de la Fabrique Hamidie de Papeterie

The Share Capital of the Societe is T.£300,000, in 30,000 shares of T.£10 each.

The Societe are the owners of LARGE PAPER MILLS, at Beicos, on the Bosphorus, also of a VALUABLE CONCESSION.

TENDERS are to be sent to the Chief Clerk of Mr Justice Chitty, at his Chambers, situate at the Royal Courts of Justice, London, not later than the 18TH DAY OF SEPTEMBER, 1893.

Particulars and Conditions of Sale and Forms of Tender may be obtained gratis of Ernest Cooper, Esq., 14, George Street, Mansion House, London, E.C.; Messrs. McDiarmid & Teather, 5, Newman's Court, Cornhill, London, E.C.; Messrs. Shepheards, 31 & 32, Finsbury Circus, London, E.C.; Messrs. Robins, Cameron, Kemm and Pothecary, Gresham House, Old Broad Street, London, E.C.; Messrs. Linklater and Co., Bond Court, Walbrook, London, E.C.; and Edwin Pears, Esq., 10, Rue Mertchany, Constantinople.

Dated the 17th day of August, 1893.

C. BURNEY,
Chief C

2673

Special Prepaid Advertisements

IT IS IMPORTANT that Advertisements under any of the Headings mentioned below should reach us by the FIRST POST on WEDNESDAY Morning to INSURE INSERTION.

Charges for advertisements under the heading Situations Wanted are 1/- for twenty-four words, and One Penny per Word after, Minimum charge ONE SHILLING. Names and addresses to be paid for.

Advertisers by paying an extra fee of 6d. can have the replies addressed to the PAPER TRADE REVIEW under a number, and such replies will then be forwarded Post Free

Situations Vacant.

AN Important firm of German Rag Merchants wants a steady and experienced Agent for paper mills.—Address No. 5860, office of the WORLD'S PAPER TRADE REVIEW, 58, Shoe-lane, London, E.C. 5860

CLERK Wanted.—Materials' Clerk for counting house in paper mill (Somersetshire) short hand writer preferred.—Apply, stating experience, salary expected, and references, No. 5869, office of the WORLD'S PAPER TRADE REVIEW, 58, Shoe Lane, London' E.C. 5869

Situations Wanted.

FOREMAN is open to Engagement; well up in coloured shops, browns, and caps; last three-and-a-half years foreman at Brook Mills, Little Eaton, Derby.—Apply, J. C. Brown, Holme Cottage, Little Eaton, Derby. 5857

MANAGER, thorough practical experience in cartridges, manillas, caps and browns, desires change (good reasons given); 12 years present situation; well up in materials and machinery.—Address No. 5849, office of the WORLD'S PAPER TRADE REVIEW, 58, Shoe Lane, E.C. 5849

TO PAPERMAKERS.—Finisher requires situation; well-up in small hands, groceries, caps and browns; good references.—Address No. 5862, office of the WORLD'S PAPER TRADE REVIEW, 58, Shoe-lane, London, E.C. 5862

WORKING MILLWRIGHT (good) seeks situation; 20 years' experience in paper mills.—Address No. 5867, Office of the WORLD'S PAPER TRADE REVIEW, 58, Shoe-lane, London, E.C. 5867

Agencies Wanted.

TO MAKERS of NEWS and PRINTING PAPERS.—Wanted, an Agency for the whole of Australia and New Zealand from makers of web news who could supply twenty to thirty tons weekly, and sheet news about five tons weekly. Makers who can supply this quantity and can compete are requested to send samples.

Also open for an Agency for T.S. and E.S. writings, fine and superfine printings, and coloured printings.

Address "Orient," No. 5866, office of the WORLD'S PAPER TRADE REVIEW, 58, Shoe-lane, London, E.C. 5866

Machinery Wanted.

WANTED, a good second-hand Refining Engine, must be as good as new; also, a Guillotine Cutting Machine, about 25 in. wide.—State full particulars and price to No. 5856, office of the WORLD'S PAPER TRADE REVIEW, 58, Shoe-lane, London, E.C. 5856

WANTED, a pair second-hand Press Rolls for a 60 inch machine.—Particulars and lowest price to "A.B.," No. 5868, office of the WORLD'S PAPER TRADE REVIEW, 58, Shoe Lane, London, E.C. 5868

WANTED, for a Sulphite Pulp Mill, a Dryer, width 58-in., production 5 tons per day of dry stuff.—Address offers to Pietro Micali, 147, Grosvenor-road, Pimlico, London. 5853

WANTED, second-hand Circular Cutter, to be put at the end of machine; width from 50 in. to 60 in.—Offers to Sub. C. D., No. 5865, office of the WORLD'S PAPER TRADE REVIEW, 58, Shoe Lane, London, E.C. 5865

Machinery for Sale.

ONE Annandale's Spray Damping Machine, mahogany box, extreme width 66 inches, with suitable air-compressor; also, a number of good second-hand Strainer Plates, 24 in. × 18 in., from No. 5 cut and upwards.—Scott and Graham, Engineers, Denny, N.B. 5855

TWO CALENDERS, second-hand, each with four hard-grained rolls, about 69 inches by 11½ inches diam., with Frames, Pressure Levers, and Driving Gear.

ONE KOLLERGANG, new, Stones 51 inches by 14 inches, C.I. Pan, Scrapers, and Driving Gear.

ONE HYDRAULIC PRESS, second-hand, with Press Box 38 inches diam. by 32 inches deep, with wheels; all parts strong, Ram 2 feet 6 inches by 8 inches diam.

ONE 2-cwt. STEAM HAMMER, second-hand, for Roller Bars or General Forgings, Cylinder 7 inches diam. by 12 inch Stroke, with heavy Anvil Block.

TWELVE REVOLVING STRAINER PLATES, 18½ inches by 11 inches, class B2, 3½ cut.

Apply 5859

BERTRAMS LIMITED, SCIENNES, EDINBURGH.

Mill to be Let or Sold.

TO be LET or SOLD, a Paper Mill at Stalybridge, called the Higher Mill, containing one large machine and room for another, steam engine and boilers, in good condition.—Apply for further information to the Caretaker on the premises. 2162

For Sale.

MECHANICAL WOOD PULP.—Two Waterfalls, very well situated in the best timber districts of Norway, to be sold, or partner wanted to build pulp mills by experienced pulp manufacturer. Good opportunity for papermakers or pulp merchants.—Address "W.," Heydahl Ohmes' Advertising Office, Christiania, Norway. 5851

Complaints

Concerning Late Delivery of Newspapers are useless unless the Wrappers accompany the complaint at head quarters of the Post Office.

Our Subscribers' Copies are duly posted before 5.30 p.m. on Friday, and should reach every postal address in the United Kingdom by SATURDAY MORNING'S POST.

We have complaints again of irregular delivery last week, some copies not being delivered until Monday and Tuesday, but our correspondents omit to forward us the wrappers, without which the General Post Office are unable to trace where the delay occurs. The postal marks will enable them to do this.

Taylor's Patent

BEATING *and* REFINING

ENGINE.

THIS BEATER TAKES UP LESS FLOOR SPACE THAN ANY OTHER.

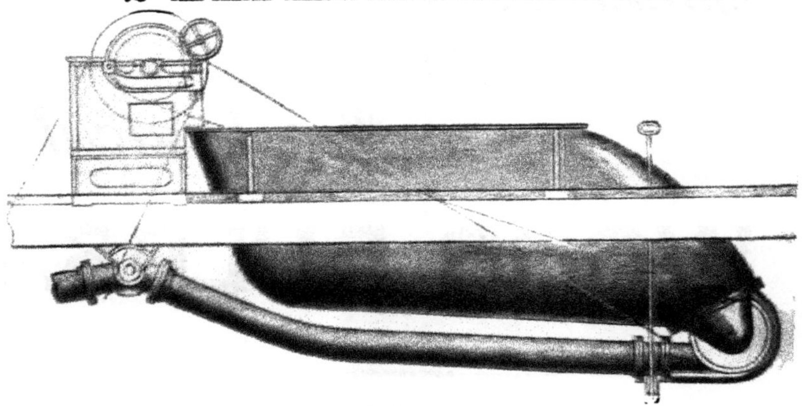

ADVANTAGES:

1.—**GREATLY INCREASED PRODUCTION** over that of the ordinary Beater in use.

2.—**GREAT SAVING IN POWER,** notwithstanding the increased production. This Beater has been proved to beat a given quantity of pulp with less than one-half of the power required by an ordinary beater of good modern construction.

3.—**COMPLETE AND PERFECT CIRCULATION,** which ensures complete uniformity in the length of the fibres.

For Full Particulars and Prices apply to

MASSON, SCOTT & Co., Ltd.

BATTERSEA, LONDON, S.W

LONSDALE'S Boiler Coverer & Paper Hair & Cork NON-CONDUCTING CEMENT.

Extract from the *World's Paper Trade Review*, August 2nd, 1889 :—

The "DAILY CHRONICLE" Mills : "The Steam Mains are covered with a Non-Conducting Composition supplied by *LONSDALE BROS., of BLACKBURN*, which HAS BEEN FOUND TO ADHERE VERY WELL, and to EFFECT A CONSIDERABLE SAVING."

"It has Stood the Test of an EIGHT YEARS' TRIAL."

Improvement in Cork Covering. Patent No. 19,906, 1889. 2666

PASTING MACHINES

F. H. BANNING,

Manufacturer of Every Kind of DUREN,

MACHINERY FOR PAPERMAKERS.

PASTING MACHINES

For Pasting in Reels of all sorts of Cardboard, Railway Tickets and Duplex Papers. The reels are dried on drying apparatus and finished by the machine after a SPECIAL PROCESS, acknowledged to be | For Pasting of Boards in Sheets with paper in Reels, with drying apparatus; and also for Boards and Paper in Sheets

THE BEST AND CHEAPEST *MACHINES NOW WORKING PRODUCING UP TO* **5** *TONS IN* **24** *HOURS*

Best of References in England, Scotland, Holland, Germany, and Sweden.

SOLE AGENTS : **OTTO KONIG & Co.,** 27, CROSS STREET, FINSBURY PAVEMENT, LONDON, E.C. 2546

SOCIÉTÉ INDUSTRIELLE de MIOS,

MIOS, GIRONDE, FRANCE.

Bleached Chemical Pine Wood Pulp,

OF GREAT PURITY,

Especially Adapted for Use in the Manufacture of Fine Papers. 2666

HERMANN MARIA SCHOELLER & CO.

Bleached Sulphate STRAW PULP.

DUEREN,

Manufacturers of BLEACHED SULPHATE

Bleached Sulphate STRAW PULP.

Straw Pulp,

UNEQUALLED FOR COLOUR, STRENGTH AND PURITY.

PACKED IN BALES.

For Samples, &c., apply to the Sole Agents :

Bleached Sulphate STRAW PULP.

HENDERSON, CRAIG & Co., *LIMITED,*

116, QUEEN VICTORIA STREET, LONDON, and at Manchester and Edinburgh.

E. BRAMWELL & Son,

HYPOSULPHITE of SODA, SULPHITE of SODA, | Special Quality for Photographers

Navigation Chemical Works, ST. HELENS, Lancashire. | GLAUBER SALTS, EPSOM SALTS. 2566

YATES & THOM
(Late Wm. & Jno. YATES),
BLACKBURN,

HIGH SPEED ECONOMICAL
COMPOUND ENGINES. | **MODERN MILL GEARING**
IN ALL ITS BRANCHES.

STEEL BOILERS with 2 and 3 FURNACES up to 200 lbs. WORKING PRESSURE

H. GOTTSTEIN & Co.,
59, MARK LANE, LONDON, AND AT NEW YORK.
PAPERMAKING MATERIALS,
CHEMICALS, AND
FOREIGN PRODUCE.

2582

Furnival & Co.'s
SELF-CLAMP GUILLOTINE
IN USE IN MANY MILLS
AND IN EVERY LARGE BRITISH TOWN.

References, Price Lists, &c., on Application.

REDDISH IRON WORKS,
STOCKPORT.

STRAW PULP
The VEREINIGTE STROHSTOFF-FABRIKEN (Dresden)
United Straw Pulp Manufacturing Co., Limited.,
COSWIG, SACHSEN.

Recommend their First-class Bleached Dry STRAW PULP, Brands V.S.T. and V.S.R. Unequalled in Whiteness and Purity. Strong and Felty. Warranted Free from clays and colours. Used by Leading Paper Mills in Europe and U.S.A.

For Samples, &c., please apply to

ROBERT H. HAY & Co., 26, GEORGE STREET, EDINBURGH, Sole Agents for Scotland, Ireland, and the Newcastle district of England; and

CHR. CHRISTOPHERSEN & Co., 39, LOMBARD STREET, LONDON, E.C., Sole Agents for England (except the Newcastle District).

2333

ROBT. McFARLANE AND SON,
MANUFACTURERS OF
PAPER MACHINE WIRES
DANDY ROLLS, BRASS, COPPER & IRON WIRE CLOTH. 2060

ALSO MAKERS OF
TWISTED PRESSE PATE WIRES,
These Wires are coupled with **OUR IMPROVED SEAM**, and are now making the LONGEST RUNS ON RECORD

DINA WORKS, LEITH WALK, EDINBURGH.

London, 1851.

London, 1862.

Dublin, 1865.

Paris, 1867.

Moscow, 1872.

GREEN'S IMPROVED PATENT FUEL ECONOMISER

FOR UTILISING THE WASTE HEAT FROM STEAM BOILERS.

Vienna, 1873.

Bradford, 1882.

THIS ECONOMISER, after having been applied to UPWARDS of 130,000 Boilers, and subjected to Every Variety of Test through a Long Period of Years, still Holds its Position as the

BEST and MOST EFFECTUAL

Means of Heating the Feed Water with the Waste or Residual Heat from the flues of steam boilers, furnaces, &c. Can be

FIXED WITHOUT STOPPAGE.

ILLUSTRATED PAMPHLET ON APPLICATION.

Manchester, 1875. Leeds, 1875.

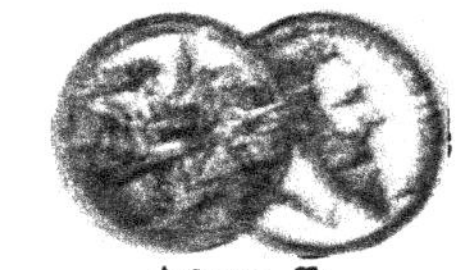

Philadelphia, 1876. Paris, 1878. Antwerp, 1885. Calcutta, 1884.

These Economisers are now made from New Strengthened Models for High Pressures, and are Suitable for ANY Boiler Pressure.

SPECIAL IMPROVEMENTS and NEW PATENTS for TRIPLE and QUADRUPLE EXPANSION.

ORIGINAL INVENTORS, PATENTEES & SOLE MAKERS:

E. GREEN & SO

2, [illegible] STREET, MANCHESTER Works: [illegible]

Telegrams: ECONOMISER Manchester
ECONOMISER [illegible]

SEPT. 1, [illegible]

JAMES MILNE & SON, Lim.,

Makers of

HORSBURGH & LUMSDEN'S

Patent Roller Vacuum Box.

... the Wire is eliminated by ... this Box, and is a necessity for all Paper Machines.

Makers of

REED'S Patent

BEATING ENGINE.

Beats the same class of Stuff in half the time and with one-third less power than any existing Engine.

Papermakers' Engineers,

BRUCE'S

Patent Flat Strainers

WITH INVERTED PLATES and UPWARD FLOW of PULP.

Most Effective Flat Strainer in the Market, with least wear and tear. Can be easily and quickly cleaned. Makes clean pulp ... all dirt, &c., in Vat passing to Auxiliary Strainer.

STEAM ENGINES

AND GEARING

OF ALL KINDS.

TELEGRAMS—"MILNE, EDINBURGH."

MILTON HOUSE WORKS, ABBEYHILL,

EDINBURGH.

Specifications and Estimates on Application.

... OF PAPERMAKERS IS RESPECTFULLY CALLED TO THE ABOVE SPECIALTIES.

... Published by W. JOHN STONHILL 58, Shoe Lane, LONDON, E.C. Sept. 1, 1893.

Employers' Liability 1880—1893.

In view of the very considerable changes that will be effected in the relations between employers and workmen, in respect to compensation for injuries, by the measure now before Parliament, introduced and backed by Mr. Asquith, the Attorney-General, Mr. Herbert Gladstone, and Mr. Burt, we reproduce below in parallel columns the principal provisions of the Employers' Liability Act of 1880, and the new Bill as amended by the Standing Committee on Law. The Bill of 1893 (which is intended to operate from the 1st of January, 1894) entirely repeals the Act of 1880 (43 and 44 Vic., cap 42).

THE PROVISIONS OF THE ACT OF 1880.

THE LIABILITY.

1. Where after the commencement of this Act personal injury is caused to a workman

(1) By reason of any defect in the condition of the ways, works, machinery, or plant connected with or used in the business of the employer; or

(2) By reason of the negligence of any person in the service of the employer who has any superintendence entrusted to him whilst in the exercise of such superintendence; or

(3) By reason of the negligence of any person in the service of the employer to whose orders or directions the workman at the time of the injury was bound to conform, and did conform, where such injury resulted from his having so conformed; or

(4) By reason of the act or omission of any person in the service of the employer done or made in obedience to the rules or bye-laws of the employer, or in obedience to particular instructions given by any person delegated with the authority of the employer in that behalf; or

(5) By reason of the negligence of any person in the service of the employer who has the charge or control of any signal, points, locomotive engine, or train upon a railway;

the workman, or in case the injury results in death the legal representatives of the workman, and any persons entitled in case of death, shall have the same right of compensation and remedies against the employer as if the workman had not been a workman of, nor in the service of the employer, nor engaged in his work.

EXCEPTIONS AS TO LIABILITY.

2. A workman shall not be entitled under this Act to any right of compensation or remedy against the employer in any of the following cases; that is to say:

(1) Under sub-section 1 of section 1, unless the defect therein mentioned arose from, or had not been discovered or remedied owing to the negligence of the employer, or of some person in the service of the employer and entrusted

THE NEW BILL AS AMENDED BY THE STANDING COMMITTEE ON LAW.

THE LIABILITY.

1. (1) Where, after the commencement of this Act, personal injury is caused to a workman by reason of the negligence of any person in the service of the workman's employer, the workman, or in case of death his representatives, shall have the same right to compensation and remedies against the employer as if the workman had not been a workman of nor in the service of the employer, nor engaged in his work.

(2) A workman shall not be deemed to have accepted any risk incident to his employment by reason only of his having entered upon or continued in the employment after he knew of the risk.

EXCEPTIONS AS TO LIABILITY.

(3) No exceptions whatever are set forth in the Bill.

[illegible] THE "LANCASHIRE" [illegible]

LIABILITY 1880—1893.

The New Bill as Amended by the Standing Committee on Law.

[illegible] where the workman [illegible] negligence which [illegible] and failed within a [illegible] to give, or cause to be [illegible] thereof to the em[illegible] person superior to him[illegible] service of the employer, un[illegible] aware that the employer or [illegible] already knew of the said [illegible] negligence.

AGAINST CONTRACTING OUT.

[illegible] was no provision against con[illegible] out of the Act in the Act of [illegible]

AGAINST CONTRACTING OUT.

2. A contract whereby a workman relinquishes any right to compensation to himself or his representatives for personal injury caused to the workman by reason of the negligence of the employer or of any person in the service of the employer, shall not, if made before the accrual of the right, constitute a defence to any action brought for the recovery of such compensation.

EMPLOYER'S CONTRIBUTIONS TO BENEFIT FUNDS.

[There is no corresponding clause under the Act of 1880.]

EMPLOYER'S CONTRIBUTIONS TO BENEFIT FUNDS.

3. Where an employer has contributed to a fund providing any benefit for a workman or his representatives in case of injury or death, the court, or, where there is a jury, the jury, in assessing the amount of compensation payable to a workman or his representatives in case of injury or death, shall treat as a payment on account of the employer's liability so much of any money which has been or will be paid to the workman or his representatives out of the fund as is in the opinion of the court or jury attributable to the employer's contribution.

DEDUCTIONS FROM COMPENSATION.

5. There shall be deducted from any compensation awarded to any workman, [illegible] representatives of a workman, or [illegible] claiming by, under, or through a [illegible] in respect of any cause of action [illegible] under this Act, any penalty or [illegible] a penalty which may have been [illegible] pursuance of any other Act of [illegible] to such workman, represen-

DEDUCTIONS FROM COMPENSATION.

[This section is entirely eliminated.]

EMPLOYERS' LIABILITY [illegible]

The Provisions of the Act of 1880.

tatives, or persons in respect of the same cause of action; and where an action has been brought under this Act by any workman, or the representatives of any workman, or any persons claiming by, under, or through such workman, for compensation in respect of any cause of action arising under this Act, and payment has not previously been made of any penalty or part of a penalty under any other Act of Parliament in respect of the same cause of action, such workman, representatives, or person shall not be entitled thereafter to receive any penalty or part of a penalty under any other Act of Parliament in respect of the same cause of action.

JURISDICTION.

[Actions were removable from the County Court to the High Court under similar conditions to those of any other actions.]

LIMIT OF COMPENSATION.

3. The amount of compensation recoverable under this Act shall not exceed such sum as may be found to be equivalent to the estimated earnings, during the three years preceding the injury, of a person in the same grade employed during those years in the like employment and in the district in which the workman is employed at the time of the injury.

LIMIT OF TIME FOR NOTICE AND ACTION.

4. An action for the recovery under this Act of compensation for an injury shall not be maintainable unless notice that injury has been sustained is given within six weeks, and the action is commenced within six months from the occurrence of the accident causing the injury, or, in case of death, within twelve months from the time of death. Provided always, that in case of death the want of such notice shall be no bar to the maintenance of such action if the judge shall be of opinion that there was reasonable excuse for such want of notice.

Section 7 sets out the manner in which the notice above alluded to shall be given.

SERVANTS OF THE CROWN.

[This provision does not exist.]

The New Bill as Amended by the Standing Committee on Law.

JURISDICTION.

4. Any action by a workman or his representatives against the workman's employer for injury caused to the workman by reason of the negligence of the employer, whether brought under this Act or not, may be brought in a county court, but if in any action so brought the amount claimed exceeds three hundred pounds, the action shall, on the application of either party, be removed into the High Court in like manner and on the same conditions as any other action commenced in a county court may by law be so removed.

LIMIT OF COMPENSATION.

[There is no limit imposed under the Bill to the amount of compensation recoverable.]

LIMIT OF TIME FOR NOTICE AND ACTION.

There is no limit of time specified for any [illegible] under the Bill.

SERVANTS OF THE CROWN.

[Under Section [illegible] the Bill [illegible] workmen in the employ of the Crown in like manner [illegible]

...e as a Newspaper.

Price 6d.

...as rags, chemicals, ...chemicals and coal fell in ... the price to

...ION OF OTHER

...of German papermakers ...m year to year, and only such ... were able to produce special... ...vidends from 5 per cent. to 7 per ...nwhile the Scandinavians devel... ...paper industry out of their wood pulp ... in a similar way as the Germans. ...they had cheap wood, easy communi... ...by water, and no benevolent work... ...legislation, they competed in all ...markets against the Germans, and ...d their productions to German export ...houses in Bremen, Hamburg, &c., to the detriment of German mills. The United

EMPLOYERS' LIABILITY 1880—1893.

The Provisions of the Act of 1880.	*The New Bill as Amended by the Standing Committee on Law.*
	employer of the workman were a private person," but not to persons in the naval or military service of the Crown.
DEFINITIONS.	DEFINITIONS.
8. For the purpose of this Act, unless the context otherwise requires, The expression "person who has superintendence entrusted to him" means a person whose sole or principal duty is that of superintendence, and who is not ordinarily engaged in manual labour; The expression "employer" includes a body of persons corporate or unincorporate; The expression "workman" means a railway servant and any person to whom the Employers and Workmen Act, 1875, applies.	7. In this Act— (1) The expression "workman" includes every person who has entered into or works under a contract of service or apprenticeship with an employer in the United Kingdom or on board a British ship, whether the contract is express or implied, or is verbal or in writing; (2) The expression "employer" includes a body of persons corporate or incorporate, and the representatives of a deceased employer; (3) The expression "ship" includes every description of sea-going vessel not propelled by oars; (4) The expression "representatives" means legal personal representatives, and expressions referring to the representatives of a deceased workman shall be construed as including the persons entitled to compensation in case of his death.
INVESTMENT FOR INFANTS.	INVESTMENT FOR INFANTS.
[No such power was conferred.]	Section 6 gives power to udges to order the investment in trust of any sums recovered under the Act on behalf of infants or persons under disability.
ABROGATION OF EXISTING CONTRACTS.	ABROGATION OF EXISTING CONTRACTS.
[Nil.]	10. Any contract existing at the commencement of this Act, whereby a workman relinquishes any right to compensation to himself or his representatives for personal injury caused to the workman by reason of the negligence of the employer, or of any person in the service of the employer, shall not, for the purpose of this Act, be deemed to continue after the time at which the workman's contract of service would determine if notice of the determination thereof were given at the commencement of this Act.

TRADES UNIONISM:

Its Past Achievements, Present Labours, Position, Dangers, and Possibilities.

The following remarks are extracted from a report of the "Staff Conference," published in the *British and Colonial Printer and Stationer*, August 24th:—

I have been powerfully struck (says one of the speakers) with the immense power which is now wielded by what I may call the democratic organisations of the labouring or industrial population. I do not speak of this power simply as directly affecting the relations between capital and labour, in such matters as wages, hours, and conditions of labour, but also in the much wider sense of political power. My years permit of my going back in memory to the early days of Trades Unionism—its days of struggle for bare existence, for legal sanction. I have, though never intimately mixed up with such efforts in any way, had peculiar opportunities for tracing and examining its growth from the dark days when it stood, as it were, alone against the world, looked upon askance alike by Capital, and the friends and well-wishers of Capital and Labour. In such times the labour organisation was regarded as a purely Ishmaelitish force, with its hand against everybody, and everybody's hand against it. It was essentially a militant organisation, looking upon everything outside of itself as opposed to itself. It was bred of oppression and ignorance, and like all such products, it took its baptism in violence, hatred, and bloodshed. But the progression of half-a-century has eliminated these darker lines, and left us the fabric as it stands in 1893. I have thought, then, that the concrete subject of Trades Unionism was one which we could well and profitably entertain in Conference, and hence my jotting down these few notes or thoughts. As briefly as I can, I will glance at each of the divisions of the subject as I have arranged them, beginning with

Past Achievements.

It would be very difficult indeed to name any important movement having for its object the advancement and amelioration of the labourer and his condition during the last thirty years more particularly, in which Trades Unionism has not borne a leading part. Look where we like—at such subjects as education, sanitation, reforms of the political and economic conditions of our country's life; look at the great ameliorative measures of the past quarter of a century—our Factory Acts, our laws affecting the direct relations of masters and workmen, whether on land or sea, our social and moral legislation, all democratic measures, and the hand of the Trades Unionist is apparent in them all. Pursue the investigation further, in the direction of all intellectual, material, and political progress, and into the widest questions of national and international polity, and we must always recognise the voice and influence of the industrial classes, made manifest through their trade organisations. The tendency of all recent legislation—right back from the present to the time of the Chartist movement—has been the levelling of distinctions between the classes and the masses, not by the pulling down of the former, but by the elevation of the latter. All such movements have begun from the bottom, and they would never have become more than mere dreams of the enthusiast had not labour banded itself in the organisations which we speak of as Trades Unions—its only means of making its voice heard and its power felt. Therefore in speaking of the past achievements of Trades Unionism, I do not think I am attributing to it any too great a share when I say it has influenced and rendered possible every movement having for its result the improvement of the material, social and moral welfare of the population of our country at large.

Its Present Labours.

I look upon it that the present labours of Trades Unionism are being directed to the consolidation of its own forces rather than pushing out its arms in new directions. In this opinion I may be at variance with greater and more reliable thinkers upon the subject. Not being a worker in the ranks, neither a private nor an officer in the great army, but simply an interested on-looker, it is more than possible that I form an erroneous estimate of what I see in progress. To me it seems, however, that the forces of Trades Unionism are marshalling themselves or being marshalled much in the same manner as a responsible general who foresees in the early future a decisive struggle would review and marshal his resources—that is, by adding to his strength every available arm, perfecting his commissariat and ordnance arrangements, securing his bases, pre-arranging his future movements and providing for contingencies. Great efforts are being made in almost every industrial occupation to build up the membership and to strengthen the various organisations financially. The most far-seeing leaders of the Unionists seem to me to advocate the conservation of what has been won rather than any immediate forward movement, and I deduce from this the fact that the best and strongest labours of Trades Unionism at present are being directed to strengthening the various organisations numerically and financially. I am greatly strengthened in this opinion by an examination of the accounts sent in of prevailing disputes and the number of persons affected by them. Not losing sight of the late trial of strength between employers and workpeople in the great textile industries, and the extensive coal strike now proceeding, generally speaking there is an absence of important contests in the principal trades of the country, coincident with the general marked efforts at extension to which I have referred.

The Position of Trades Unionism.

Anyone who gives thought to it will recognise that Trades Unionism in this country occupies a unique position. Glance the world over and nothing like it will be seen. We see a solid army of something like two millions of persons, each corps of which has its separate interests, but all with one united aim. It is calculated that this great army embraces two-sevenths of the entire industrial population of the country: it may safely be affirmed that this two-sevenths embodies a selection of the best, the most vigorous, the most thoughtful, the most provident among the industrial population. These two millions have erected for themselves a Parliament whose weight is acknowledged throughout the world. I refer of course to the Trades Union Congress, meeting this year in Belfast, with its 600 or more delegates. But these two millions have acquired a direct political influence which now outweighs that of any other class or "estate"; not numerically perhaps, counting parliamentary or municipal votes, but actually because it is the only class which is banded closely together for offence and defence. Political parties of whatever shade cannot ignore, but must and do conciliate the two millions as a prime factor in their hopes of success. Upon any question affecting their own material welfare, they possess a casting vote, whose influence will be seen plainly in all Home legislation of the day, and only less plainly in Imperial questions. Now this brings me at once to the consideration of the next division of my subject, namely,

The Dangers

which threaten Trades Unionism. I might sum up the dangers in one phrase —*that the unionists may endeavour to push their advantages too far.* It is by their enthusiasm that they have earned success, and this success may, unless wise counsels prevail in an uncommon degree, induce enthusiasm to take the bit in its teeth and rush to extreme and regrettable lengths. Success has spoiled many noble achievements, as history tells us. The first palpable danger is that the class which was for centuries dominated may in its turn seek to dominate. That the danger is real and palpable might be illustrated by an enumeration of some of the causes of disputes between men and masters. Desiring to avoid all disputatious matter, I will not indicate precisely to what my thoughts point, but content myself with saying that there are evidences, and growing evidences, of an inclination to coerce the employer on the one hand and the non-unionist on the other. Such disputes when they arise, it may be conceded, are small in importance individually, but their frequent recurrences render them important, breed irritation, revivify the dying spirit of opposition to the principle of Unionism, and not infrequently result in actual retrogression for the society which attempts to impose its will. If the danger is obvious when the numerical strength is that of two to five, it will become greater as the relative proportion alters, as alter it will. There is the danger, too, that backed by labour organisations and their political power, democratic legislation may be pushed so far as to subvert the order of things that existed in past years, and to render the position of the employing and other classes unbearable. I am not inferring that such a point has been reached, or is even in sight, but industrial legislation has been pushed forward at so rapid a rate, and succeeding Governments have found themselves so reliant upon the employee, that I at all events recognise a danger here whenever the two-sevenths shall have become four-sevenths. Whenever the numerical strength of Trades Unionism is lifted up so far as to turn the scale—that is when half the industrial population is enrolled in such organisations, there will be an increased impetus, and the absorption will be much more rapid, and with this increased speed of absorption will come the legislative danger I apprehend. There is a danger attending increased financial strength also. It was the remark of a once prominent official of a great miners' organisation in the North, that "when funds were low, the men might be led by a thread; but when the treasury was full, pit chains would not hold them in." Increase of members means increase of resources, and there is the danger of these funds being applied to unwise purposes, and inducing resort to physical contests upon trivial occasions.

Possibilities.

My last word is as to the Possibilities which attend the fuller development of Trades Unionism. I mean of course wise possibilities. When the organisation of industrial resources has been carried to its preponderating degree of strength that is, when there are more labourers inside than there are outside of its control, if wisdom keep pace with growth the era of trade struggles should be over. Strikes now arise owing to the non-existence of permanent means of conciliation and arbitration. Sometimes it is the master, sometimes the men, who hesitate to embrace arbitration to-day. The comparative strength between Capital and Labour in 1893 is so fairly equal that each has confidence in its own physical power. When the balance of power was with Capital it neglected its opportunity of insisting on arbitration in all trade disputes, as it might have done. When the balance inclines to the side of Labour, as it surely will do, theirs will be the opportunity of insistence. They will possess the strength of the giant; if they use it *as* a giant, theirs will be the ultimate loss, as Capital depends for its existence and employment upon confidence in the permanence of things. Permanent and compulsory boards of arbitration for all trade disputes is one of the first grand possibilities that lie before Trades Unionism for achievement. Co-operative industrial enterprise is a second great possibility. Under a peaceful *regime* there must be a great accumulation of funds —otherwise capital. The legitimate outlets for the employment of this accumulated capital will be:—(1) Benefits in sickness and death; (2) pensions in disablement and superannuations in old age; (3) relief under lack of employment; (4) grants in unmerited affliction. Beyond these the great outlet must be in employing the surplus funds in industrial cooperative schemes for the benefit of trade members.

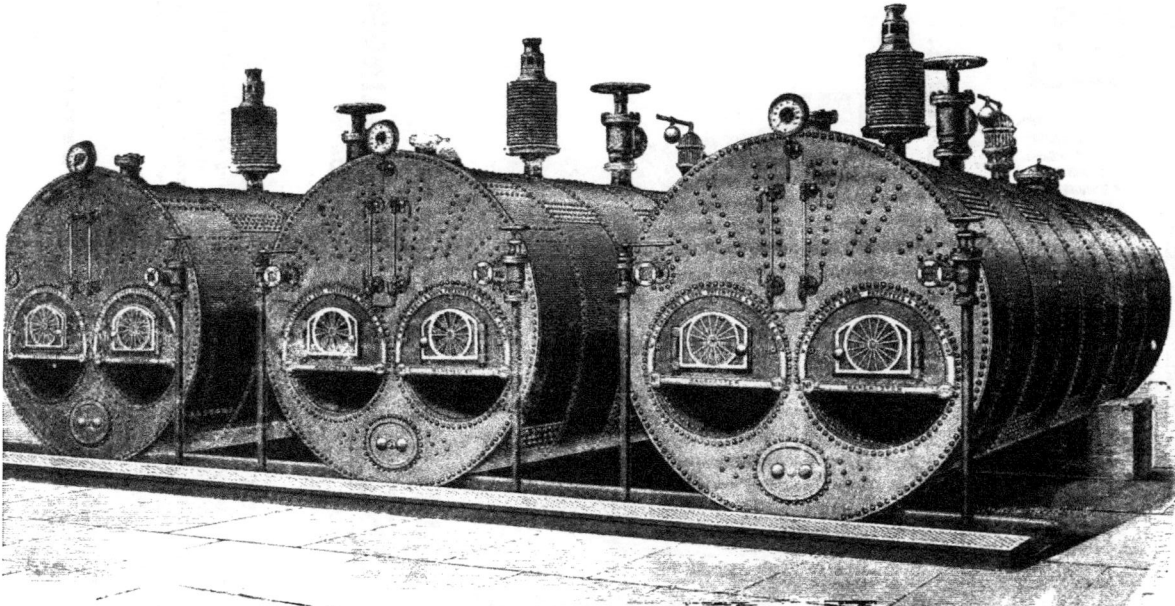

Printed and Published by

Telegrams: "STONHILL, LONDON." A B C Code. Registered at the General Post Office as a Newspaper.

Vol. XX. No. 10. LONDON, SEPTEMBER 8, 1893. Price 6d.

THE GERMAN PAPER INDUSTRY.

Quite a plethora of reports are issued during the year by various bodies in Germany on the paper and allied trades. One of the latest is by the "Elders" of Merchants in Berlin, and from this we learn that an adequate import duty during a number of years has strengthened the paper industry. The German market would have been supplied far beyond its needs had not a large exportation taken place.

Causes of Over-Production.

Like mushrooms, ground wood factories multiplied wherever there seemed to be wood and water enough, and by competition prices were cut down until no margin of profit was left. To save their position many ground pulp-makers were compelled to put up paper machines and to work their pulp into paper. As these new mills did not require much capital, they were able to work cheaper than older establishments, and the latter saw their only safety was in an increased production, which reduced the general working expenses. Thus the paper production soon became so enormously increased that sales could only be effected with the greatest difficulty, and the fall of prices grew chronic, as the following comparison shows:—

	[illegible]	[illegible]
News ...	[illegible]	[illegible]
Printings (free from ground wood) ...	[illegible]	[illegible]
Writings (free from ground wood) ...	[illegible]	[illegible]

(100 Pfennig = 1 Mark.)

Raw materials, such as rags, chemicals, straw pulp, also chemicals and coal fell in price, and enabled the price of paper to follow.

The Competition of Other Countries.

The troubles of German papermakers increased from year to year, and only such companies as were able to produce specialties paid dividends from 5 per cent. to 7 per cent. Meanwhile the Scandinavians developed a paper industry out of their wood pulp factories, in a similar way as the Germans. But as they had cheap wood, easy communications by water, and no benevolent workmen's legislation, they competed in all foreign markets against the Germans, and sold their productions to German export houses in Bremen, Hamburg, &c., to the detriment of German mills. The United States (N.A.) by protective duties strengthened their home industry to such an extent that the medium and lower sorts could be produced there in sufficient quantities, and fresh legislation also prevented the German importation of best sorts, such as drawing, book, post, copying and cigarette papers; the Berlin manufacture of albums, consuming large quantities of paper, came to a standstill. The political difficulties and financial losses in South America stopped exportation in that direction. The increased French duty impeded any further exportation of paper and paper articles to France. The difficult financial position of Spain made great caution necessary. All this proved that the greater difficulty and frequent impossibility of exportation forces Germany to bear the consequences of paper over-production. In the beginning of 1892 the Austrian Treaty invited Austrian makers to com-in the German market, and to make use of their facilities by the favourable rate of exchange, low wages, cheap wood, cheap rags and rag export duty, nor do they have any restriction of the working hours. The general badness of trade has checked the consumption of paper, as every person more or less curtailed his expenses for stationery, books, etc.

MANUFACTURING DIFFICULTIES.

As a special aggravation of existing difficulties the great drought in 1892 must be mentioned. Rivers dried almost entirely up in the summer, and the severe frost of the winter made things worse. Many German ground wood pulp factories had to be closed and the material had to be imported from Sweden. Prices of wood papers, therefore, rose from 22 pf. to 25-26 pf. per kilo, but this rise did not cover the increased cost of production; possibly former prices may rule again with improved water supply, unless the sales have meanwhile become easier again. The new regulations requiring water marks bearing the name of the maker of all papers (so-called "normal" papers) bought by the Government, have restricted the number of competitors, but even in these sorts, which are subject to very onerous conditions, competition was keen and prices were forced down. The laws for workmen's protection cause great hardship to this industry, depending so much upon the employment of female labour in many of its manipulations. The question of Sunday rest occupies the attention of leading men. Though there must be less over-production in consequence, still those expenses going on over the Sunday have now to be divided into six days instead of seven, the cost price per daily production being higher in proportion. This increased cost cannot be put on the price, as long as other nations do not enforce the same restrictions of labour. The Cabinet Secretary (Herr von Berlepsch) lately acknowledged the obligation of the Government to see that the industries of the country suffered no loss. Many industries complain that the situation is becoming worse through restrictions of their free movement, and increased demands on the part of the workers.

A FEW THINGS WANTED.

The desires formulated by the German paper industry are:—To protect their interests more effectually in new commercial treaties than seems to have been possible with Austria; to instruct all German Consulates to facilitate commercial relations by advice, information, and support; to protect the German rag supply like Austria does, and not allow the exportation of rags to countries not buying German paper; to provide low through rates *via* Belgium and Holland at times when seaports are closed; to modify the strictest regulations of the workmen's protective laws, particularly also in the interest of female workers; to restrict the Sunday rest to the lowest limits.

THE IMPORTATION OF RAGS.

In the House of Commons on Thursday, Mr. MACDONA asked the President of the Local Government Board whether the Senate of Hamburg had issued an order to prevent the importation into Hamburg, and prohibited transit over territory under its control, of rags and bedding imported from Russia, actuated by the experience of what the people of Hamburg suffered in 1892; and whether he would consider the advisability of adopting a similar course in this country.

Mr. H. FOWLER said the only information he had as to the order referred to was contained in a telegram from Berlin to the effect that the Senate of Hamburg had issued orders "prohibiting the importation into or transport through Hamburg of old clothes and dirty body and bed linen from Russia. Passengers' luggage is excepted." The order of the Local Government Board of August 5 deals with articles of a similar character. The order prohibits the landing in England of "dirty bedding or disused or filthy clothing, whether belonging to emigrants or otherwise," except under certain specified conditions as to disinfection.

Mr. MACDONA asked whether the importation of rags was not prohibited in New York.

Mr. H. FOWLER said that he had no information upon the point. There were rags called rags of merchandise in bales which had been collected during a long series of years, and the importation of such rags was not prohibited in any country.

On Friday Mr. MACDONA asked the President of the Local Government Board whether he was aware that there were now lying on the wharves at London Bridge over 300 tons of rags imported from cholera-stricken places in Europe, which the rag merchants of London refuse to touch or take from a fear of introducing cholera into our midst; whether the Local Government Board would immediately issue an order to have these bales of rags shipped back to the ports from whence they came, or have them at once destroyed by burning; and whether, in consideration of the fact of Asiatic cholera having already been imported into Grimsby, the Local Government Board would forthwith rescind the order of 9th August, and prohibit the further introduction of rags.

Mr. H. H. FOWLER said the question had only been put down that morning, and the day had been devoted to making enquiry as to whether the statement it contained was correct. Enquiry had been made at the Custom House and of Dr. Collingridge, the medical officer of the port of London, but the Local Government Board were unable to learn anything with reference to this alleged deposit of 300 tons of rags. No doubt the hon. member had satisfied himself that these rags were imported from cholera-stricken places, and if he would give him privately the information he possessed the matter should be thoroughly investigated. He must act on the advice of the competent medical officers of the Local Government Board, in whom he had perfect confidence. He had, moreover, the advantage of the distinguished services of the Parliamentary Secretary (Sir W. Foster). It was on the advice of medical experts that the order of the 9th August was made. That advice had the full approval of the Parliamentary Secretary, and they saw no reason to alter it.

Mr. MACDONA gave notice that he would call attention to the subject on an early occasion.

BRITISH TRADE WITH SPAIN.

The following figures show the quantities and values of British paper of all sorts exported to Spain during the past five years :—

1888	5,078 cwts.	£12,452
1889	5,236 ,,	13,344
1890	5,081 ,,	12,119
1891	4,817 ,,	12,473
1892	6,231 ,,	14,632

British exports to Barcelona of paper, cardboard and prints last year amounted to 213 tons of the value of £12,478. The quantity received from other foreign countries amounted to 2,342 tons of the value of £80,222.

Last year the value of cigarette paper exported from Barcelona to Great Britain amounted to £987, to other countries £125,386. Paper cardboard and prints exported to Great Britain reached the value of £1,120, and to other countries £5,488.

The imports at Barcelona last year included 2,136 tons of wood pulp of the value of £15,365. No wood pulp was received from Great Britain.

The Spanish demand for British Alkali amounted to £123,388 last year, the value in 1888 being only £86,266.

British imports of rags, esparto and other vegetable fibres from Spain during the past five years were :—

1888	64,859 tons	£390,012
1889	67,893 ,,	408,490
1890	68,104 ,,	393,407
1891	63,202 ,,	374,878
1892	59,883 ,,	358,725

SULPHITE FIBRE MILLS IN THE UNITED STATES & CANADA.

MILLS IN OPERATION JULY 1, 1893.

UNITED STATES.

PLACE AND OWNER.	Output per day in lbs.
Birmingham, Conn., Wilkinson Bros. & Co. ...	4,500
Augusta, Me., Cushnoc Fibre Co.	20,000
Howland, Me., Howland Falls Pulp Co.	50,000
Lisbon Falls, Me., Lisbon Falls Fibre Co.	24,000
Madison, Me., Manufacturing Investment Co. ...	40 000
Orono, Me., Orono Pulp and Paper Co.	40,000
South Brewer, Me., Eastern Manufacturing Co. ...	32,000
Conowingo, Md., Susquehanna Waterproof and Paper Co., of Harford Co.	20,000
Cumberland, Md., Cumberland Paper Co.	12,000
Lawrence, Mass., Russell Paper Co.	20,000
Mt. Tom, Mass., Mt. Tom Sulphite Pulp Co. ...	25,000
Turner's Falls, Mass., New England Fibre Co. ...	12,000
Alpena, Mich., Alpena Sulphite Fibre Co.	30,000
Detroit, Mich., Detroit Sulphite Fibre Co.... ...	30,000
Port Huron, Mich., Michigan Sulphite Fibre Co....	24,000
Ypsilanti, Mich., Ypsilanti Paper Co.	4,000
Goffstown Centre, N.H., Excelsior Fibre Co. ...	10,000
Dexter, N.Y., Dexter Sulphite Pulp and Paper Co.	40,000
Mechanicsville, N.Y., Hudson River Water Power Co.	16,000
Palmer's Falls, N.Y., Hudson River Pulp and Paper Co.	30,000
Saugerties, N.Y., Barclay Fibre Co.	20,000
Watertown, N.Y., Remington Paper Co.	36,000
Hamilton, Ohio, Louis Snider's Sons Co.	15,000
West Carrollton, Ohio, Alpha Fibre Co.	24,000
Oregon City, Ore., Willamette Pulp and Paper Co.	20,000
Yorkhaven, Pa., Yorkhaven Paper Co	10,000
Bellows Falls, Vt., Fall Mountain Paper Co. ...	24,000
Davis, W. Va., West Virginia Pulp Co.	30,000
Piedmont, W. Va., Piedmont Pulp and Paper Co.	50,000
Appleton, Wis., Atlas Paper Co.	10,000
Appleton, Wis., Manufacturing Investment Co....	65,000
Kaukauna, Wis., Badger Paper Co.	10,000
Kimberly, Wis., Kimberly and Clark Co.	26,000
Marinette, Wis., Marinette and Menominee Paper Co.	10,000
Oconto Falls, Wis., Falls Manufacturing Co. ...	16,000

CANADA.

Cornwall, Ont., Toronto Paper Manufacturing Co.	10,000
Merritton, Ont., Riordan Paper Mills, Ltd. ...	10,000
Chatham, N.B., Maratime Sulphite Fibre Co., Ltd	24,000
Sheet Harbour, N.S., Halifax Wood Fibre Co. ...	16,000
Hull, Que., The E. B. Eddy Manufacturing Co. Ltd.	26,000

		Pounds.
Total mills in operation in United States ...	35	849,500
Total mills in operation in Canada	5	86,000
	40	935,500

MILLS PROJECTED AND IN PROCESS OF ERECTION JULY 1, 1893.

Denver, Col., Pusey and Jones Co.	20,000
Rumford Falls, Rumford Falls Sulphite Pulp Co...	60,000
Lincoln, Me., Katahdin Pulp and Paper Co. ...	40,000
Berlin Falls, N.H., Burgess Sulphite Pulp Co. ...	60,000
Berlin Falls, N.H., Glen Manufacturing Co. ...	40,000
Au Sable, N.Y., J. and J. Rogers Iron Co.... ...	40,000
Port Edward, N.Y., Glens Falls Paper Co.... ...	60,000
Forestport, N.Y., Wendler and Spiro	30,000
High Falls, N.Y., High Falls Sulphite Pulp and Mining Co.	40,000
Hinckley, N.Y., Warner Miller and Co.	60,000
Niagara Falls, N.Y., Niagara Falls Paper Co. ...	50,000
Potsdam, N.Y., Racquette River Paper and Pulp Co.	20,000
Ticonderoga N.Y., Lake George Pulp and Paper Co.	40,000
Appleton, Wis., Riverside Paper Co....	16,000
Ashland, Wis., Ashland Sulphite Fibre Co... ...	12,000
Combined Locks, Wis., Combined Locks Paper Co.	20,000

Total, 16 mills, 608,000 pounds.

MILLS DESTROYED BY FIRE OR ABANDONED UP TO JULY 1, 1893.

Louisville, Ky., Old Kentucky Paper Co.	10,000
Shawmut, Me., Shawmut Fibre Co.	20,000
South Gardiner, Me., Richards Paper Co.	25,000
Weymouth, N.J., Weymouth Sulphite Paper and Pulp Co.	5,000
Newberne, N.C., Newberne Pulp Co...	4,000
Providence, R.I., Richmond Paper Co.	40,000
Hartsville, S.C., Carolina Fibre Co.	10,000
Kaukauna, Wis., Kaukauna Fibre Co.	16 000
Monico, Wis., Wisconsin Sulphite Fibre Co. ...	20,000

Total, 9 mills, 150,000 pounds.

TOTAL MILLS ALL CLASSES.

Mills in operation	40	Capacity pounds ...	935,500
Mills projected or under construction	16	,, ,, ...	608,000
Total	56	,, ,, ...	1,543,500
Mills destroyed or abandoned	9	,, ,, ...	150,000
Total, all classes...	65	,, ,, ...	1,693,500

ADRESSBUCH DER MASCHINEN-PAPIER UND PAPPEN-FABRIKEN, SOWIE DER HOLZSTOFF UND HOLZPAPPEN, STROHSTOFF- UND CELLULOSE-FABRIKEN DES DEUTSCHEN REICHES, OESTERREICH-UNGARNS UND DER SCHWEIZ. By GUNTTER STAIB, Biberach, Württemberg.

We have received a copy of the 16th edition of the "Directory of Machine Paper and Pulp Board Mills, also Wood Pulp and Wood Pulp Boards, Straw-Stuff and Cellulose Makers of the German Empire, Austro-Hungary, and Switzerland," just published. The work has been compiled by Herr Guntter Staib, editor of the *Wochenblatt* (the organ of the association of German paper and pulp makers). Alphabetical arrangement has been kept up, and facilitated by a list of countries immediately after the introductory remarks. The text has been enlarged by the fact that the 67 papermakers who registered their water marks at the Charlottenburg Paper-Testing Office, are given on pages 147-152, with full indication of the water marks. On page 153 the parchment and tracing papermakers are classified, the names formerly being found among papermakers generally. The statistical comparisons on pages 156-157 show a great increase, particularly of the number of paper machines. At the same time the falling off of straw pulp makers has continued in all the three countries, Germany now having only 34 against 50 some few years ago. Paper mills are also fewer in number, which is explained by the bad state of business; on the other hand, many of the larger mills have increased their productions by putting up their third and fourth machine. In Germany there are 495 paper and 365 pulp board mills with 1,009 machines, 556 ground wood pulp and wood pulp board factories, 34 straw pulp and 67 cellulose makers. On reference to the previous edition a decrease is shown of 6 paper and 4 straw stuff mills, and an increase of 21 pulp board, 26 ground wood pulp, and 4 cellulose makers, with 34 more machines. In Switzerland there are 19 paper and 19 pulp board mills with a total of 48 machines, also 13 ground wood pulp and 7 cellulose makers; there is a decrease of 2 paper and 1 straw stuff mills, and an increase of 2 pulp board and 1 ground wood makers and 2 machines. In Austro-Hungary there are 161 paper and 74 pulp board mills with 330 machines, also 228 ground wood, 9 straw stuff, and 32 cellulose makers; the decrease is 5 paper mills, 3 ground wood, and 2 straw stuff makers, whilst there is an increase of 5 pulp board makers and 13 machines. The directory is printed on 32 different kinds of paper, the name of the papermaker appearing on top and bottom of the various pages. In Great Britain it is generally supposed that German papers are made from ground wood alone, or perhaps here and there with a little cellulose added. The list of papers on which this directory is printed, however, shows that many papers are made in Germany from rags alone, others again from rags and cellulose, or from cellulose and mechanical wood. The compiler of the directory has evidently taken pains to make the work as complete and accurate as possible, and those having relations with papermakers in the countries referred to will find the publication of great service.

THE LEYKAM-JOSEPHSTHALER CELLULOSE FABRIK, in Podgora, near Gorz, has been partly destroyed by fire. The damage is estimated at 40,000fl., which is covered by insurance.

PAPIER AND ZELLSTOFF FABRIKEN UNTERKOCHEN WOLFACH have shown a gross profit of M204,109 on a share capital of M1,200,000. After writing off various amounts a dividend of 4 per cent. is recommended.

MR. FRIEDRICH SCHILDE, former director of the Dresden Paper Mills and Bautzen Mills, which he managed for over 26 years, died suddenly at Port Huron, on a visit to his son, who is the director of the Michigan Fibre Co.

MR. CHRISTOF FRIEDRICH FRENZEL, machine maker in Altchemnitz, has suspended payment. Claims must be sent in before the 15th September.

MR. GOTTL. HEERBRANDT, in Raguhn (Anhalt), papermakers' wire manufacturer, has lately supplied some wire sieves for a foreign millboard factory of the size of 20·10 by 2·45 meters. Each sieve weighed 100 kilos.

FIRE AT WEISSENFELS.—On August 25th the paper mills of Gebrüder Dietrich were the scene of a disastrous fire, which broke out in the rag sorting rooms, and at once extended to the whole of the upper floor of the factory. Although ten fire engines were quickly in action, the fire was not got under for many hours. Fortunately the lower floor, containing a greater part of the machinery, was not reached by the fire. No lives were lost. The owner, Herr Dietrich, had just left an hour before by train for the Reichenhall springs, but on receiving a telegram at Gira came back immediately. The damage done is very considerable, but as only the upper floor has been destroyed, it is hoped to resume work in about a fortnight. All the pressing orders will be executed meanwhile at one or other of the other mills belonging to the firm. The pulp board factory was not reached by the fire, and as it is worked by a turbine, it is not interfered with in the slightest degree.

NEW GROUND WOOD PULP FACTORY.—In the valley of Schwarzenberg a new pulp factory is being erected by the firm of Herren Nestler and Breitfeld, the owners of the iron works Erla, Pfeilhammer and Wittigsthal, the ground pulp works at Erla and a wood pulp board factory at Ottenstein. The new factory takes the place of some old iron works, which are being pulled down for that purpose, after having been in existence since the 15th century, being in fact one of the oldest establishments in the Saxon "Erzgebirge." These iron works have been given up one after the other because the price of iron did not pay any longer, the costs getting heavier and the wood for the charcoal more difficult and expensive to obtain, for in the olden times the works had a privilege for cutting wood in the forest, which however was finally abolished in 1857, by compromise.

CUSTOMS WAR BETWEEN RUSSIA AND GERMANY.—The absorbtion of Finland into the Russian State, as far as customs and duties are concerned, affects the Russian papermakers more than the Finnish. As Finland does a large business with Germany, the Russians no doubt thought they would injure the Germans by driving the Finnish manufacturers into seeking their market in Russia. Much capital, great intelligence, and modern ideas being found to prevail more among the Finnish papermakers than among the Russian mills, the latter may experience a very heavy and unexpected competition against them, coming from a quarter where prohibitive duties will no longer be possible. The failure of the Moscow Exhibition has shown how little the French understand Russian requirements, and it is thought that Russia will be compelled to come to terms with Germany much sooner than the French will be able to supply the Russian market.

THE exports of paper at New York, according to the latest weekly list received, included the following:

Australasia ...	733 pkgs	Liverpool	65 cases
London	2 cases	Southampton ...	1 pkge
B. West Indies ...	1578 pkgs	Cardiff	2 cases
B. Guiana... ...	1 case		

THE INTERNATIONAL PULP CO., whose talc mills and mines are near Gouverneur, N.Y., are pushing forward improvements on two of their mills. These improvements, although they have been contemplated and worked at for some time, are being pushed vigorously since the burning of one of the mills. When repairs, &c., are completed the company will keep up the output to about the same volume as prior to the fire. The company are mining about 125 tons per day at present, and are grading and adapting the output from the different mines to the varied requirements of papermaking. The superintendent, Mr. McDonald, reports that paper mills which had in former years discontinued using talc pulp are now using the blended product of different mines, which exactly meets their requirements. This result is easily understood to be obtainable under a combined ownership of different mines, each of which gives slightly different shades and quality of product. This careful blending, with the uniformity in milling, seems to be the real reason for the much wider use of talc in papermaking and the success which has attended the operations of the company.

THE NEW PULP MILL of Messrs. Bart and Johnson, Chateaugay, N. Y., will be completed within a week and ready to run. It is situated on the Chateaugay River, and the water power is secured by throwing a dam across the river at a narrow gorge, and connecting it with the water wheels is a wooden flume 7 feet square. Forty-five feet head is obtained and about 900-h.p. is developed by the three "Victor" turbines employed. The entire plant is neat and compact and will, it is stated, readily turn out from 10 to 12 tons of pulp per day with the proper amount of power applied.

THE plant of the High Falls Sulphite Pulp and Mining Company at High Falls, N. Y., a point about 6 miles from Canton, N. Y., is nearing completion. The supervising architect and engineer at the works believes that operations will be fully under way by October 1st. Both the pyrites plant and sulphite fibre plants are being built. The pyrites plant will be the first of its kind in America built in connection with sulphite fibre production. The location of the works is upon the Grass River, which has been dammed at a convenient point to give the necessary power. The sulphite mill is built on the lines of "slow burning construction," following much upon the system brought into the papermaking industry by the building of the mills of the Frontenac Paper Company at Dexter, N. Y. It is 268 by 50 feet, built upon a stone foundation, and in looking down upon it has the appearance of a glass building. About midway from each end a section is set apart for the three digesters, two of which will be set at present, and the third added when needed. This division leaves the wood preparing department at one end, while the other end is devoted to the manipulation of the pulp preparatory to shipment. The mill will contain when completed machinery of the various makes, as indicated: One "Trevor" splitter and cut-off saw, two "Ticonderoga" barkers, one "Sturtevant" blower, two "Russell" digesters, four "Gotham" screens, four "Gotham" centrifugal pumps, one "Wendler" chipper two wet machines from the late firm of Wendler, Spiro and Munro, and all of the pyrites plant, including furnaces and sublimators, from the same firm. Mr. Julius Spiro is at present supervising the construction, but will be succeeded after completion by Mr. A. Wendler, his late partner, as supervisor of operations.

AMERICAN PAPER INDUSTRY.

A GENERAL DULNESS.

The following reports from correspondents of the New York *Paper Trade Journal* show that trade is in a very depressed condition:—

HOLYOKE.

The business situation in this city has undergone very little change. Some of the mills are running and some are not, while a few are on half time. Orders are scarce and ready money is scarcer. Finished goods have continued to pile up in uncomfortable quantities, and it will take some of the mills some time to work off the stock now filling the store houses. Some of the manufacturers are of the opinion that it would be better for all of the mills to shut down for a short time, thus affording an opportunity to work off the stock of finished goods and to reduce the production, which would ease up on the market.

FOX RIVER VALLEY.

It would be idle to attempt to make out that business is not suffering in this valley. The plain truth of the matter is that manufacturers are very blue. The state of things in a nutshell is this: There are forty-five machines in this valley, and of this number fifteen are now running and thirty are shut down. Even with machines which are running no particular effort is being made to get large product, and business is practically at a standstill.

PHILADELPHIA.

The paper trade in Philadelphia is characterised by more than the usual midsummer dulness. With few exceptions the mills are shut down; some of them, like the Megargee Mill at Modena, running spasmodically from time to time, and others being closed for a longer or shorter period. Balfour's mill is still running and so are the Jessup and Moore Paper Company's mills; but there is no certainty as to the future.

BOSTON.

Everybody knows that trade is flat and has been so for some weeks; but then, everybody is not discouraged or disappointed thereat. Better times are coming, and it keeps the trade cheerful in figuring out when the beginning of the better times will come. Many mills are shut down; but it is better that they shall shut down than keep running full blast and piling up paper when there is no call for it. In paper mill supplies there is not enough doing to pay office rent. Rags cannot be given away; all orders for foreign pulp have been cancelled and many of the home pulp mills are shut down. Packers of domestic rags are reported to have discharged their assorters, and decline to take supplies from street collectors. Chemicals are subject to the same conditions, and nothing is doing in the chemical market.

CHICAGO.

The business situation continues in a depressed condition, the financial question being now the absorbing topic. It is stated that Col. J. H. Frambach has taken the helm at the Model Paper Mill, and a more animated condition is manifest about this exhibit than at any time since the Exposition opened. It is rumoured here that the entire financial burden of the enterprise has fallen on the colonel's shoulders. When questioned as to this rumour the colonel was non-committal, but was emphatic in proclaiming that the exhibit would be kept alive during the remainder of the Fair.

THE LATE MR. THOMAS ARCHER.

The August publication of the *Papermakers' Monthly Journal* (dated the 26th ult.) is well up to time, considering the many difficulties that have had to be contended with. In addition to the destruction of premises by fire and the loss of files and other valuable data, the gentleman who conducted the paper from the commencement—for the past 31 years—was suddenly taken away by death on the 5th ult. Mr. Thomas Archer (says our contemporary), as an author and journalist, had attained a high reputation for his varied work during a long life. He was at one time editor of the *Citizen*, and a constant contributor to the London press. His special articles in the *Standard* on "Old London" attracted much notice; he was an occasional contributor to the *Graphic*, while he compiled the conceivable illustrated copy of the *Times*, a century since, which appeared in the preliminary number of the *Daily Graphic* in 1889. He was an original member and one of the founders of the Savage Club, and a prominent member of the Whitefriars Club, of which latter community he was compiling the chronicles at the time of his death. Mr. Archer's works included "The Highway of Letters," "Gladstone and his Contemporaries," "Life of the Queen," "Pictures and Royal Portraits," "Workshops of England;" a contribution to the first and subsequent volumes of the Savage Club papers, and several novels and other works. His loss to letters and journalism is immense, to the friends who knew and loved him it is irreparable. He had attained the age of 63. It may be truly said of him that he never had an enemy; all respected and revered "Tom Archer." Even among the humblest circles he made friends by his kindness of heart, of which astonishing proof was afforded in the poor pensioners of the French Hospital, in which he took a great interest, who attended with a wreath at his funeral at Abney Park Cemetery on the 9th. The members of the Savage Club were represented at his funeral by Alderman Treloar, Mr. Geo. M. Fenn, and Mr. Edward Draper. Professor P. L. Simmonds, an old friend, would have attended, but had only just returned the day after the funeral from his holiday tour in Scandinavia.

CRESCENT BRAND. TRADE MARK.

Pure Alkali

Guaranteed 58 Degrees.

EQUAL TO **98 %** CARBONATE OF SODA.

THE STRONGEST AND PUREST

Form of the Article in the Market, and, therefore the Most Economical for the Use of Papermakers, Printers, Bleachers, Wool Scourers, Dyers, Glass, and Soap Makers.

BICARBONATE OF SODA,

Refined and Recrystallised. The Purest and Cheapest in the Market.

CONCENTRATED

CRYSTAL SODA

(Sesqui Carbonate),

By far the Purest and Cheapest Form of Washing Soda. Only 1lb. of Concentrated Crystal Soda required to do the work of 2lbs. of Washing Soda.

SODA CRYSTALS 3089

Of the Finest Quality.

BRUNNER, MOND & Co., Limited,

NORTHWICH, CHESHIRE.

ENTLE

Papermakers'

Engineer

NUTTALL'S IMPROVED RAG CUTT

This Machine has now been Greatly Strengthened and Simplified, and its Output Capacity It is Equally Effective upon the Strongest and Lightest Materials, and will cut Every Cla Used in Paper Mills.

OVER 50 NOW IN USE.

Full Particula

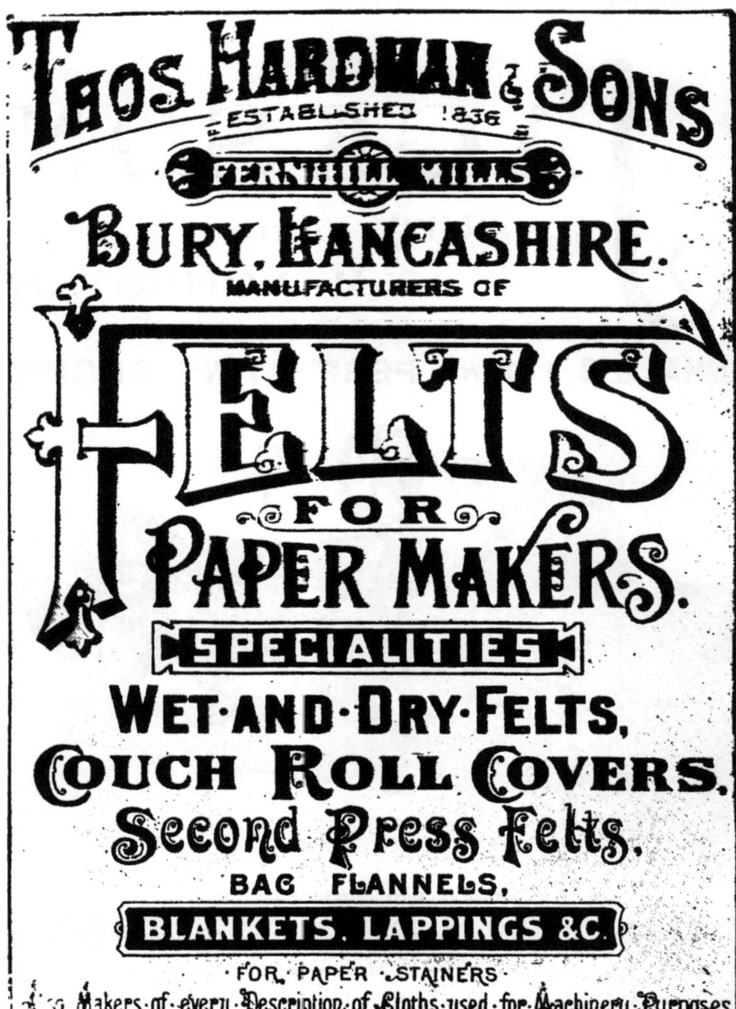
THOS HARDMAN & SONS
ESTABLISHED 1836
FERNHILL MILLS
BURY, LANCASHIRE.
MANUFACTURERS OF
FELTS
FOR
PAPER MAKERS.
SPECIALITIES
WET·AND·DRY·FELTS,
COUCH ROLL COVERS.
Second Press Felts.
BAG FLANNELS,
BLANKETS, LAPPINGS &C.
·FOR, PAPER ·STAINERS·
Also Makers·of·every·Description·of·Cloths·used·for·Machinery·Purposes.
TELEPHONE Nº 41
TELEGRAMS, HARDMAN, FERNHILL, BURY.

INVALUABLE TO PAPERMAKERS.

STEAM TRAPS

For High or Low Pressures. Are working at 200-lbs. Valve opening equal to area of Inlet and Outlet. Cannot Stick. Requires no Attention. Perfectly Automatic. Solid Tile Float. Can be Tested whilst at Work.

STEAM DRYER, WATER & DIRT SEPARATOR

Fixed in and forms part of Main Steam Piping. Intercepts all water carried in suspension with the steam. Prevents dirt and other rubbish passing into Digesters, &c.; Priming Water returned to Boiler. Splendid results. Successful wherever applied.

ANTI-PRIMER.

Is fixed inside the boiler and effectually prevents the water being lifted out along with the steam. The steam issues from the boiler in a perfectly dry state. Indispensable for the economical and efficient working of steam boilers.

MECHANICAL STOKER

The most complete system of firing for all steam boilers. Specially adapted for paper makers. Less mechanism and working parts than any other Mechanical Stoker. Repeat orders have been executed for firms who have had Twenty years' experience of our stoker. Extract from one of reports, "Coal Bill reduced **25** *per cent. less labour in stoking, an entire absence of smoke, no trouble whatever with the apparatus."*

Thousands of the above specialties may be found at work both in this and other countries, and have been adopted by the leading Papermakers, Engineering Firms, Electric Lighting Stations, Collieries, Houses of Parliament, The London County Council, British Museum, National Galliery and many departments of H.M. Government, as well as manu facturies representing every branch of Industrial Art.

McDOUGALL'S PATENT OIL EXTRACTOR FOR PREVENTING OIL AND OTHER DELETERIOUS MATTER FROM THE HOT WELL PASSING IN TO THE BOILER ALONG WITH THE FEED WATER, ALSO SIGHT FEED LUBRICATORS FOR BOTH HIGH AND LOW PRESSURE CYLINDERS. THE ONLY SIGHT FEED FOR THE LOW PRESSURE CYLINDER.

APPLY TO 2562

CHADDERTON IRON WORKS Co., Ltd.

NEAR MANCHESTER.

GENERAL ENGINEERS.

LONDON:	Telegrams:	MANCHESTER:
10, MARK LANE.	"DISINFECT" { MANCHESTER. LONDON.	68, PORT STREET.

CAUSTIC SODA MANUFACTURE.

Messrs. Jean Paul Roubertie Victor Lapeyre, and Ulysse Grenier, of France, give the following description of a process they have protected in this country for the manufacture of caustic soda and potash, and hydrochloric acid by electrolytic treatment of chloride of sodium and chloride of potassium, and apparatus for this purpose:—When a solution of chloride of sodium is treated by electrolysis, there is produced, firstly at the negative pole, sodium (which in combining with the elements of water, forms caustic soda) and hydrogen; secondly, at the positive pole, chlorine is generated, which afterwards forms compounds with oxygen. In the processes heretofore employed, endeavours have been made to utilise the chlorine which is given off at the positive pole, but it is found that the presence of this gas and its oxygen compounds operates detrimentally upon the proper working of the electrolytic action. This invention has for its object to bind the chlorine as it is generated and to transform it into hydrochloric acid, employing by preference for this purpose the hydrogen which is given off at the negative pole. The patentees avoid not only the formation of the oxygen compounds of the chlorine, but also the presence of the latter in a free state in the electrolytic apparatus. They utilise for this purpose the affinity of hydrogen for chlorine, such affinity being so energetic when these substances are produced by electrolysis that the combination can be effected in diffused light. The hydrochloric acid formed in this manner will not mix with the solution of the chloride of sodium or potassium in the electrolytic bath, but will form a supernatant layer on its surface, which can readily be decanted. The apparatus employed for the purposes of the invention may be variously arranged, but in all constructions it consists essentially of two chambers separated from each other at the upper part and resting upon a bottom vessel containing the chloride of sodium, with which they both communicate, the chambers being either rectangular and formed in one piece with an intervening partition, or they may be separate vessels, either of cylindrical or other form. The chambers may be made of wood lined with a material that is not acted upon by acids or alkalies, such as cement, glass, &c. The bottom vessel is charged with sea salt or with chloride of potassium. The one chamber has placed within it the iron negative electrodes situated above the layer of sea salt, and connected with the iron negative pole of the electric generator employed; they are formed of a series of vertical iron plates connected together. The other chamber contains the positive electrodes, which are placed in slanting positions and connected to the positive pole of the generator. They are of any suitable metal silvered, or of lead, or of silvered glass. They might also be of carbon. The negative chamber is closed hermetically, with an escape pipe for leading off the hydrogen gas, the withdrawal of which may be accelerated by a pump, which forces the gas into the positive compartment through a pipe opening underneath the positive electrodes, so that the gas, issuing in small bubbles through perforations, passes up along the inclined surfaces of the electrodes and combines with the nascent chlorine as this forms on the electrodes, thus producing hydrochloric acid, which rises to the top of the electrolyte and flows off through a lateral opening. The soda or potash solution formed in the negative chamber also passes up to the surface of the electrolyte with the hydrogen gas and flows off through a lateral passage, to be concentrated elsewhere. A discharge pipe for the spent electrolyte is provided at the bottom of the negative chamber. The supply and discharge of the liquids is regulated according to the intensity of the electric current employed. The flow may be arranged to take place either continuously or intermittently. In some cases the supply of the salt solution can take place from the top of the negative chamber and the caustic soda or potash solution be discharged at bottom. The negative electrode may also be formed by a helically coiled plate, when the chambers are of cylindrical form, and the positive electrode may be made of funnel shape, leaving an annular space between its upper edge and the sides of the chamber for the escape of the hydrochloric acid. In order to facilitate the combination of the hydrogen and chlorine gases, it is advantageous to subject them to the influence of a strong light, for which purpose the apparatus may be made of glass and the daylight projected into it by means of strong reflectors, or one or more electric lamps may be placed within the negative chamber when this is of opaque material.

WADDING MADE FROM SULPHITE PULP is being greatly appreciated in German hospitals. A firm in the Taunus has prepared sheets of sulphite wadding which looks exactly like cotton wadding, and by anybody except an expert would be taken for such. The sheets consist of several fine layers of cellulose, which at the top and bottom are held together by thin muslin. It can be easily compressed, absorbs moisture readily, its use is easy, clean, and effective, and experiments with it were so successful, that many hospitals have already taken it up according to the prospectus sent out with it. A chemical test of air-dry wadding shows only 0·297 per cent. of a clean white ash, which beside a trace of iron only contains oxyde of calcium, a proof that it has been made from sulphite. A surgeon compared its power of absorbtion of water with other substances and found the following results:—The complete absorbtion of sulphite wadding takes 5 seconds, cotton wadding free from grease 25 minutes, and wood wool bandages 45 minutes. Therefore the sulphite wadding acts 300 times more quickly than the wood-wool wadding. From the financial point of view the sulphite wadding also is a great success, for it only costs M1·60 per kilo, whereas the kilo cotton wadding free from grease comes to M4 at least.

WORLD'S PAPER TRADE REVIEW OFFICE,
58, SHOE LANE, LONDON, E.C.
SEPTEMBER 7, 1893.

TRADE NOTES.

DANDY ROLL AND PAPERMAKERS' ENGINEERING COMPANY, LIMITED.—This company is registered with a nominal capital of £2,000 in £10 shares. Object, to acquire and carry on the business of a dandy roll maker and papermakers' machinist, as hitherto carried on by W. K. Trotman at 29A, Dumont-road, Stoke Newington, N., and, with a view thereto, to carry into effect an agreement, made August 15, 1893, between W. K. Trotman of the one part and this company of the other part. With slight modifications the regulations contained in Table A apply.

THE SALVATION ARMY PRINTING DEPARTMENT.—Statements of a sensational character, concerning the printing department of this organisation were current in Fleet-street last week, some of them being to our mind exceedingly unjustifiable. We therefore visited the department to make personal enquiry as to its position and progress. We are able to report a satisfactory outlook, and to record that thousands of pounds worth of good paying profitable work is being turned out weekly, and in the opinion of the management there can be no better paying branch than the printing section in the entire work and connections of the Army.—*British and Colonial Printer and Stationer.*

AT the Trade Union Congress, held at Belfast, Mr. Monro, the president, on Tuesday, delivered his address, which dealt chiefly with the problem of the relation of the State to the labouring classes. He deprecated resort to strikes until every other expedient had been exhausted, and expressed the hope that the labours of the Royal Commission on Labour might result in the formulation of such a system of conciliation and arbitration as would make the resort to industrial warfare much more rare than it is at present.

PAPER MILL WORKERS' ANNUAL TRIP.—The annual trip of the workpeople employed at the Ramsbottom Paper Mill took place recently, when about 370 employees and friends went to Blackpool. The firm defrayed expenses by giving each married worker two tickets and 3s. and each single worker one ticket and 1s. 6d.; and also ensured each person for the journey as follows:—Killed, £200; partially disabled, 6s. per week; totally disabled, 15s. per week. The train left Ramsbottom about 6.30 in the morning, and on arrival at Blackpool the excursionists dispersed to enjoy themselves in their own way. A pleasant day was spent.

WE understand that the Cleveland Salt Company have completed sinking another brine well at their Middlesbrough works. A bed of rock salt, which was struck at a depth of about 1,300 feet, is now being passed through.

MR. C. MILLBOURN, papermakers' agent, of 156, Upper Thames-street, London, E.C., has been appointed sole agent for Messrs. Salomon Bros., Harburg (Elbe), a firm of rag merchants having very extensive connections.

NOTICE OF REMOVAL.—Messrs. Babcock and Wilcox, Limited, have removed their registered office from 114, Newgate-street, E.C., to more convenient premises at 147, Queen Victoria-street, E.C.

ART AND INDUSTRIAL EXHIBITION.—At Bristol, on Monday last, an Art and Industrial Exhibition was opened. The exhibition was primarily started in order to give the public an opportunity of seeing what is done in connection with local industries.

THE central agricultural committee of the district of the Sologne (France) in the course of a recent report on the commercial possibilities of the neighbourhood, lays particular stress on the desirability of utilising the extensive supplies of timber for the purpose of paper manufacture, especially the pines (*pinus sylvestre*). If the matter is properly taken up there is considered to be a great future for the papermaking industry in the Sologne. Hitherto the excess of resin in the wood has constituted the principal difficulty to its utilisation for wood pulp, but the committee think that this difficulty might be overcome if a prize were offered to the inventor of the best method of economically converting the local timber into pulp of good quality and practical value.

PRICES OF PRINTING PAPER IN GERMANY.—Complaints are freely made that the publishers of large newspapers are really paying prices now for their paper which do not refund the papermaker. The paper is frequently very bad, and it is stated almost falls to pieces after being read and refolded. Yet for all that the only person who makes a profit is the publisher. The price of the papers sold to the public is exactly the same now as in 1875, but the publisher pays for the kilo (= 2-lbs. German) now less than he did for the German lb. in 1875. Then the news produced in Germany was generally made from

45% soda pulp at M24 cwt.	M10·80
50% ground wood at M8 cwt. (equal to ½ meter cwt)	4
N.B.—Half a meter cwt. only.	
	M14·80

Now the news is made from

20% sulphite or less at M15 cwt. ...	M3
75% ground wood at M4·50 cwt. ...	3 37
	M6·37

The addition and cost of chemicals and fillings is about the same in both cases, Therefore the price is now less than half of the price paid for the lb. in 1875. Under such circumstances, if the makers of news in the empire would only keep together, they could form a convention upon a reasonable basis, and it only depends upon them to make a fair margin of profit.

BRITISH PAPER EXPORTS TO AUSTRALASIA.

FIVE YEAR'S TRADE.

The following figures show the respective quantities and values of paper of British manufacture distributed during the past five years in Australasia:—

WEST AUSTRALIA.

1888	2,698 cwts	£4,513
1889	3,079 ,,	5,468
1890	2,675 ,,	4,571
1891	5,892 ,,	9,958
1892	6,645 ,,	10,237

SOUTH AUSTRALIA.

1888	38,144 cwts	£58,341
1889	35,274 ,,	55,193
1890	43,410 ,,	69,496
1891	50,718 ,,	77,961
1892	41,702 ,,	55,766

VICTORIA.

1888	263,473 cwts	£400,183
1889	197,682 ,,	302,040
1890	193,532 ,,	280,366
1891	209,918 ,,	302,812
1892	183,047 ,,	242,870

NEW SOUTH WALES.

1888	217,809 cwts	£298,363
1889	163,513 ,,	232,191
1890	152,198 ,,	215,516
1891	148,184 ,,	217,550
1892	129,806 ,,	188,485

QUEENSLAND.

1888	48,066 cwts	£66,890
1889	43,863 ,,	65,658
1890	43,932 ,,	60,363
1891	43,858 ,,	58,645
1892	29,557 ,,	40,488

TASMANIA.

1888	11,600 cwts	£19,766
1889	12,981 ,,	22,152
1890	12,731 ,,	21,081
1891	13,929 ,,	23,959
1892	11,615 ,,	17,747

NEW ZEALAND.

1888	65,825 cwts	£101,506
1889	74,840 ,,	119,665
1890	72,115 ,,	110,125
1891	66,531 ,,	109,147
1892	68,950 ,,	109,745

Paper of "foreign manufacture" was re-exported by Great Britain to Victoria as follows:—

1888	12,565 cwts	£10,000
1889	11,831 ,,	9,764
1890	6,107 ,,	5,290
1891	7,027	[illegible]
1892	[illegible]	[illegible]

THE BRITISH PAPER CO., LTD.

This company have recently put down a complete installation of electric light at Frogmore Mill, Two Waters. The whole of the work has been carried out by the London and Lancashire Electric and General Engineering Co., Limited, of Dalston, N.E., one of the features of the installation being an improved system of watertight mains, joint boxes, and lamp fittings, the electric wires being drawn into wrought iron tubes with screwed joints, the whole of which has been specially designed by Mr. C. N. Russell, A.M.I.C.E., engineer to the Company, with a view of resisting the effects of steam and moisture so common to paper mills. This system has, we understand, been found to answer admirably, and has received the sanction of the various fire insurance companies. The generator consists of a shunt wound over-type slow speed dynamo, with soft wrought iron magnets, and is capable of giving a current of about 60 amperes, at a pressure of 65 volts, the dynamo being so arranged as to be driven by either steam or water power. The electric current is led from the dynamo to a special main switchboard, having a base of white marble, and set in polished walnut, this being fixed to the wall of the dynamo room. The lamps are arranged in four circuits, which can each be separately controlled from the main switchboard, which is provided with double pole safety fuses, and quick break switches. Incandescent lamps of 16 candle power each, have been introduced throughout the whole of the various departments, including the offices, and foreman's house, separate switches being provided for turning off individual lights, as may be required, while a special arc lamp of 2,000 nominal candle power, is fixed in the beater house, and is intended to be used for colour testing at night time. When the electric current was switched on for the first time the arrangements were under the superintendence of Mr. Russell, assisted by Mr. A. T. Tomlins, the electrician engaged in fitting up the plant, and Mr. E. Talbot, dynamo attendant. Among those who witnessed these interesting proceedings were Mr. H. P. Sanguinetti, the managing director; Mr. J. Pitts, foreman, and Mrs. Pitts. The inauguration of the electric light at this mill is, doubtless a step of no little importance in keeping pace with the times. In connection with this up-to-date lighting arrangement, it is worthy of note that, under the proprietorship of the British Paper Co., Limited, Frogmore Mill bids fair to uphold the reputation of the district as a papermaking centre—a reputation that was gained in the early years of the present century. It was at Two Waters that Messrs. Fourdrinier erected and ran the first machine upon which paper was made in England, this event occurring about the year 1809; the second place where machine-made paper was produced in this country being Nash Mills, where Mr. John Dickinson invented and ran, in the face of great opposition from the hand papermakers, his patent cylinder machine.

CHROMO PAPERS.

The principal fields for the consumption of German chromo and colour print articles are Great Britain, France, and the United States. Last year trade appears to have been very bad, and for the purpose of a remunerative business large sales have to be effected. The restriction of the latter by prohibitive duties in various states has seriously affected this industry, and compelled many manufacturers to give up production, and others only worked with greatly reduced profits, leaving barely a margin.

The exportation to Great Britain decreased, and prices were cut down. The consumption only remained unimpaired in the cheapest sorts.

The exportation to France has become almost impossible, as lower sorts cannot stand the heavy import duty, and the consumption of higher class goods is small. In consequence of the high duty several German manufacturers have removed to France, to supply the French market free from duty, and to compete in Germany against home manufacturers easily, as the import duty to their former fields of operation is only small.

The business with the United States was almost unchanged. The preparations for the Chicago Exhibition brought good business to makers of articles in the advertisement line, but competition cut down the prices of larger orders. An improvement of this branch can only be expected when the import difficulties through excessive duties in foreign countries are removed, or at any rate lessened.

TENDERS for the supply of paper to Her Majesty's Stationery Office, London, were received yesterday (Thursday). A rather large item in the schedule was 22,000 reams of cap double small 23 by 17, weight per ream 10 lbs. Other lots were from 20 to 9,000 reams, the total quantity being 50,230 reams.

MR. C. J. CLAY, of the great printing firm, has been appointed a magistrate for Cambridge.

THE PRINTING WORKS AND LABOUR HOME, begun some two years ago by the Church of England Association, at Burwood Mews, Edgware-road, W., has been closed. This institution was a large buyer of paper, but although they undertook the miscellaneous printing in connection with their numerous organisations, yet the long runs were never transferred to their own printing office, and remained at Eyre and Spottiswoode, who probably now may get the entire work of the association. The premises at Burwood Mews are closed, and our representative, after a clang of the bell much the same as at a convent, learned from Sister Agatha that the printing was a purely private proprietary, and the branch was closed by the wish of its own management.

NEWSPAPER GAMBLING IN A NEW GUISE. —At Bow-street on Wednesday, Arthur Pearson, the proprietor of *Pearson's Weekly*, appeared in answer to three summonses charging him with carrying on an illegal lottery, in the shape of a "Weather Forecast Competion." Sir A. K. Stephenson, Public Prosecutor, appeared for the prosecution, and contended that the proposed competition was one into which the element of skill did not really enter. Mr. Muir Mackenzie, for the defence, argued that the scheme was a perfectly legitimate project for the exercise of skill, but Sir John Bridge expressed the opinion that the proposed competition was a pure lottery, and one of a mischievous character, and he imposed a penalty of £20, with £5 costs.

COSMOPOLITANISM, LIMITED.

Your Briton is a fine cosmopolitan fellow. He has been wrongly accused of possessing insular prejudices, and some have gone so far as to say he is clannish in his social and business habits. But nothing could possibly be more unjust or further away from the facts. It may have been true of the period of Addison and Steele. Even a short generation ago there might have been ground for asserting that the Englishman looked down upon or avoided the foreigner. But all that sort of feeling gradually died out after the French wars. The Briton has travelled since then, and hordes of foreign travellers, commercial and otherwise, have been among us. The brotherhood of nations has been preached to us and among us with such effect, that really and truly we have gone a trifle beyond the scriptural injunction to love our neighbour as ourselves, and have learned in business as well as in honour to prefer one another. In the year 1893 we just dote on the foreigner. We welcome him open armed to our island shores, without scrip or purse, though all the world beside reject him. He cuts the ground from beneath the feet of our native workers, but what of that? As a kind of return visit, when we find ourselves with a week or two of leisure and a spare ten pound note we go on the "continong"—as we call it on our return—to spend both. There is no sort of pride about us. We especially like to buy of him; we go out of our way to do it. He does not reciprocate more than he can help, but that is because he is not the same whole-souled cosmopolitan that we are. We not only buy from him all that we can for ourselves, but also for all our friends and relations abroad; but such is our good nature that we allow him—nay we insist, that he shall put his national trade mark upon his goods, in order that our distant friends and customers may not be misled into the belief that we can or do make such goods for them or wish to monopolise their dealings. This is "preferring one another" in an international way—pointing the way for the Indians and the Australasians, and the Americans to do their buying direct. It is in the highest degree commendable, and the Western nations appreciate our goodness, but do not generally follow our example. They are not educated up to it. We have heard of a great British paper house, supplying a prominent daily with reels of paper, stretching its courtesy so far as to give its client a line of introduction to the directorate of a foreign mill, to enhance the interest of a continental sojourn. This good nature was repaid by the foreign directorate promptly securing the future favours of the client. Delightful instance of the Briton's trustful regard for his foreign competitor! British paper exports in five years have fallen nearly fifteen per cent., and imports have gone up thirty-four per cent. We help them to cut us out in other markets while buying from them ourselves more and more largely. The cry of certain of our paper consumers is all for foreign makes. To secure a sixteenth of a penny reduction in price they will order months in advance and in such "makings" as they would not give to a home mill. It may be all true that the home mill or the home agent gives us "spot" advantages which the foreigner cannot give; it may be true enough that the British house is willing to constitute itself our warehouse, and our warehouse staff; to put itself to infinite trouble to meet our smallest needs, extending to retail lots if necessary at wholesale prices; but our cosmopolitan preference steps in with ton lots, and we send our large orders abroad. We may gain only a problematical advantage in price; we may have to wait long and incur disappointments and risks, but we give indisputable proof of our broad-minded love of our neighbour. Not our next door neighbour; there is no credit in that; but our most distant neighbour. Our home manufacturers may suffer loss through this policy, workmen may live from hand to mouth; mills may even shut down through their inability to further oblige the consumer, and operatives may starve. What then?—so long as we vindicate our cosmopolitanism. A fig for the charity that begins at home! But what a howl goes up from these same consumers when it is rumoured that a mercenary Government has followed out the principle and bought a few reams of paper, or sent a few pound's worth of work to our foreign brethren! That is quite another sort of cosmopolitanism. We have heard a certain daily journal in the North held up to ridicule for putting boldly on its face the words "Printed on paper made in England." How many papers dare tell the truth as boldly by affixing the line, "Printed on paper made in Belgium," or Germany, or Sweden, or elsewhere? A list of papers qualified to use the line would be useful and instructive. We suggest as an addition to "country of origin" legislation that a close wire mark be demanded upon all sheets and reels of foreign origin, as the most effective present means of improving the home industry of papermaking. Our cosmopolitan love for the distant neighbour would instantly show a much greater shrinkage even than our exports have recently done were such a proposal put into practical shape.

Printed and Published EVERY FRIDAY
AT 58, SHOE LANE, LONDON, E.C.,
By W. JOHN STONHILL.
ESTABLISHED 1878.

FRIDAY, SEPTEMBER 8, 1893.

GERMAN papermakers appear to be in a very unhappy mood. They are discontented with certain legislation, which, according to the opinions expressed, greatly hampers progress and development. Whatever may have been the reduction in exportation to other countries, German papermakers were very active during the year of 1892 in flooding the British market, and the following figures giving three years' trade show that instead of any decrease there was an increase:

1892	687,835 cwts.	£672,880
1891	651,489 ,,	610,846
1890	598,855 ,,	562,863

A comparison of the values evidences an increase of 10·1 per cent. in 1892 over the preceding year, and an incease of 19·5 per cent. over 1890.

PRINTINGS and writings from Germany fell materially, however, during the first half of 1893 compared with the corresponding period of the two previous years. The respective quantities and values were:

Jan.-June,	1893	33,227 cwts.	£37,381
,,	1892	51,724 ,,	62,563
,,	1891	41,037 ,,	48,196

In "other kinds" the value was lower for the half-year of 1893 as the following statistics show:

Jan.-June,	1893	259,120 cwts.	£224,515
,,	1892	288,671 ,,	272,438
,,	1891	256,787 ,,	233,804

Germany and Holland are the two chief countries exporting paper to Great Britain, the dual value in 1892 amounting to over one-and-a-quarter million pounds sterling.

THE frequent publication of reports on the condition of the German paper and pulp industries by Chambers of Commerce and other bodies gives manufacturers the opportunity of ventilating their grievances. In this respect, modesty is not one of their many virtues, as a reference to page 2 of the current issue will indicate to our readers. German papermakers want their interests more effectually protected in new commercial treaties, and consider it only right and proper to receive prompt official intimation of opportunities to develop trade in the world's markets. Those countries not importing German paper, ought not to have the privilege of importing German rags, or at least such a course is suggested. The Germans, however, probably more in patriotism than in selfishness, think low through rates *via* Belgium and Holland should be provided when seaports are closed; and, we understand, they would not be averse to a modification of duties in several countries where German sales have declined. Legislation restricting the employment of female workers and imposing Sunday rest are also matters regarded as inimical to the interests of the German paper industry.

IN many respects German papermakers are to be commended for the activity they display in tracing the causes of depression and in advocating remedial measures. The Papermakers' Association of Great Britain would do well to emulate their example. Surely it would interest the trade to have an annual statement on the condition of the home paper industry, the effect of foreign competition, and whether production is declining or otherwise. The prolonged suspension of useful functions by the Association is to be greatly deplored.

CANADIAN exports of wood pulp to Great Britain during August amounted to 17,285 bales, 9,700 bales being received from Halifax, and 7,585 bales from Montreal. The parcels were mostly to order and were landed at Southampton, Liverpool, and Glasgow. There was one lot of 2,000 bales imported by Messrs. W. E. Bott and Co., of London.

ADVICES from Scandinavia state that mechanical wood pulp is decidedly stiffening, in conjunction with chemical pulp. Papermakers, however, object to pay the higher prices demanded. It is calculated that dry pulp will reach £6 per ton, and the moist pine pulp £3 to £3 2s. 6d. per ton before the close of the year. In consequence of the drought in Germany papermakers in that country have again to resort to Scandinavia for supplies.

RAG importation represents to many cholera importation. Several questions have been asked in the House of Commons in regard to allowing rags to be landed at British ports, and it has been urged that speedy restrictions should be enforced. Probably the Local Government Board will rescind the order of the 9th August at an early date, as deaths from cholera have occurred at Grimsby, and 300 tons of rags are alleged to be lying on wharves at London Bridge, imported from cholera-stricken places in Europe. Whether it be true or not that London merchants refuse to handle these goods, a correspondent writes that on Tuesday last 400 bales of rags, weighing about 200 tons, were despatched in railway vans from the St. Katharine Docks. The destination of the greater part of them is stated to be Yorkshire. The recent order of the Local Government Board empowering Custom House officials to disinfect or destroy any dirty clothing or bedding does not include rags packed in bales and imported as merchandise. The West Hartlepool Sanitary Authority, at a meeting on Tuesday afternoon, placed on record a strong protest against the importation of foreign rags as calculated to propagate disease, and decided to memorialise the Local Government Board in favour of prohibiting such imports unless the rags are thoroughly disinfected before shipment.

PAPERMAKERS, in common with other large consumers of coal, are experiencing considerable inconvenience owing to the continued strike. A large number of works are closing, and business is consequently disorganised. The strike in South Wales, however, is steadily coming to an end. It is estimated that not more than 20 per cent. of the men now remain out. The refusal of the North Staffordshire coalowners to allow their men to resume work, except at the reduction of 25 per cent., has caused consternation throughout the district. The men are disposed to continue their resistance, and there is no immediate prospect of a settlement. There was serious rioting and disturbance on Tuesday at Alfreton and elsewhere in the Derbyshire coalfield, and also at Barnsley, in West Yorkshire. The Mid and East Lothian miners decided by ballot in favour of referring their claim for a 20 per cent. advance to arbitration, instead of seeking to enforce it by a strike.

THE high opinion in which the late Mr. John Masson was held may be gathered from the following extract sent to us by a London correspondent, who recently received a letter from his son in New Zealand:—"The accident at Mataura, of which you were advised, has thrown a pall over everything with us just now. Mr. Masson was such a splendid young fellow, and had won not the respect only, but the affection of every one who had come in contact with him. To his poor father and others it would, I am sure, in the midst of their great grief, have been a source of deep consolation to witness how thoroughly all felt and acted, and spoke, as if a friend and brother had been taken away from them; even the poor fellow with whose frame Mr. Masson came into fatal collision, goes about as if demented: he really loved the one whose decease he innocently caused, and it seems as if the life of the young men around was being perceptibly raised in tone and aim by the cordial sympathy and manly bearing of one who as heartily entered into their amusement, as he faithfully strove to enlist them in the highest service of life through the varied agencies of the Christian church. This is the stamp of life we want among us. That one so promising should be so early cut off is one of the things about which we can only say, 'Our Father knoweth.' Dear Masson has not lived in vain, his three short months in New Zealand have been fruitful of the right kind of influence; his memory will be long precious in New Zealand."

THE Australian Government have consented to modify their proposals for imposing a 3 per cent. primage duty on imports not already paying 25 per cent. *ad valorem* duty. As now amended the new financial scheme imposes a primage duty of one per cent. on all imported goods, with the exception of a limited number of specially exempted articles.

WORLD'S PAPER TRADE REVIEW OFFICE,
58, SHOE LANE, LONDON, E.C.
SEPTEMBER 7, 1893.

MARKET REPORT

and RECORD of IMPORTS

Of Foreign Rags, Wood Pulp, Esparto, Paper, Millboards, Strawboards, &c., at the Ports of London, Liverpool, Southampton, Bristol, Hull, Fleetwood, Middlesborough, Glasgow, Grangemouth, Granton, Dundee, Leith, Dover, Folkestone, and Newhaven for the WEEK ENDING SEPTEMBER 6.

From SPECIAL Sources and Telegrams.

Telegrams—"STONHILL, LONDON."

CHEMICALS.—Chemicals are rather quiet. Owing to the scarcity of fuel, many of the chemical works in the neighbourhood of Manchester are stopped in several departments. Manufacturers, however, having large stocks in hand, have been able to supply contracts, but orders for prompt delivery are booked at higher prices. CAUSTIC SODA is £11 5s. for 77 per cent., and BLEACHING POWDER varies from £8 15s. to £9. SODA CRYSTALS show a decline at £2 15s. SODA ASH, 52 per cent. is quoted, £4 10s. f.o.b. Liverpool. CARBONATED ASH, f.o.b. Liverpool, is priced £5 10s. for 58 per cent., and £4 7s. 6d. for 48 per cent.; f.o.r. Widnes, £5 5s. for 58 per cent., and £5 2s. 6d. for 48 per cent. SULPHUR is steady at from £4 2s. 6d. to £4 5s. SULPHATE OF ALUMINA and BLANC FIXE are unchanged, and GERMAN SULPHATE OF ALUMINA is offered at £4 7s. 6d. c.i.f. London.

Prices are nominally as follows:

Article	Packing	Delivery	Terms	£	s.	d.
Alkali, 58%	tierces ...	f.o.r. works	2½%	5	10	0
" 58%	bags ...	" "	2½%	5	5	0
58%	... ...	f.o.b. Liverpool	2½%	5	12	6
Alum (Ground),	tierces ...	" Liverpool	2½%	5	7	6
" "	barrels ...	" "	2½%	5	17	6
" "	tierces ...	" Hull	2½%	5	5	0
" "	" ...	Goole	2½%	5	5	0
Alum (Lump)	" ...	f.o.b. Liverpool	2½%	4	17	6
" "	barrels ...	" "	2½%	5	0	0
" "	tierces ...	" Hull	2½%	4	15	0
" "	" ...	Goole	2½%	4	15	0
"	" ...	London	2½%	5	5	0
"	" ...	f.a.s. Glasgow	2½%	5	5	0
Alumina Sulphate,	casks	f.o.b. Tyne		4	2	6
" "	bags	" "		3	17	6
Aluminoferric Cake,	slabs	Liverpool ...	...	2	15	0
" "	tierces	" ...	...	3	2	6
Alumina Cake,	slabs ...	Glasgow	...	2	15	0
" "	tierces ...	"	...	3	2	6
Aluminous Cake,	casks ...	Manchester	3½%	2	7	6
" "	" ...	Newcastle	2½%	2	10	0
" "	" ...	London	2½%		0	0
" "	bags ...	"	2½%	2	17	9
Blanc Fixe ...	... ...	f.o.b. Tyne	net	7	10	0
Bleach, 35%	... ...	" "	net	8	15	0
" (soft wood)	...	f.o.r. Lancs.	net	8	10	0
" (hard wood)	...	f.o.b. Liverpool	net	9	0	0
...	... ...	landed London	2½%	9	15	0
Borax (crystals)	... ...	... ...	net	29	0	0
powdered ...	...	... ...	net	30	0	0
Caustic Cream, 60%	...	f.o.r. Lancs.	net	8	12	6
" " 60%	...	f.o.b. Liverpool	net	8	17	6
" Bottoms	...	" "	net	6	15	0
" "	... ...	f.o.b. Tyne	net	6	15	0

Article	Strength	Delivery	Terms	£	s.	d.
Caustic White	76 77% ...	f.o.r. Newcastle	net	11	5	0
" "	77%	f.o.r. or f.o.b. Tyne	net	11	10	0
" "	74% ...	f.o.b. Liverpool	net	11	5	0
" "	70% ...	" "	net	10	5	0
" "	70% ...	" Hull	net	10	10	0
" "	70% ..	f.o.r. London	net	10	5	0
" "	70% ...	" Lancs.,	net	10	2	6
" "	60% ...	" London	net	9	5	0
" "	60% ...	f.o.b. Liverpool	net	9	5	0
Carbonat'd Ash	58% ...	" "	net	5	10	0
	48% ...	" "	net	4	7	6
"	58% ..	f.o.r. Widnes	net	5	5	0
	48% ...	" "	net	5	2	6
Chloride of Barium	...	f.o.b. Tyne	net	7	10	0
Hypo-Sulphite of Soda...		f.o.r Tyne		5	15	0
" "	10-ton lots	ex ship Liverp'l	net	6	10	0
Oxalic Acid ...	... ...	f.o.b. Liverpool	3½%	per lb		½
Salt Cake ...	.. ...	" works	net	1	10	0
Soda Ash, 52%	... ..	f.o.b. Tyne	net	4	10	0
" 52%	... ...	ex ship Thames	1%	4	15	0
" 52%	... ...	f.o.b. Liverpool	1%	4	10	0
Soda Crystals	... ...	" Tyne	net	2	15	0
" "	... ...	ex ship Thames	2½%	3	5	0
" "	... ...	f.o.b. Liverpool	net	3	0	0
Sulphur, roll	... ...	f.o.r. works	2½%	7	17	6
" flowers ...	...	" "	2½%	9	10	0
" recovered	...	" "	2½%	4	2	6
Sulphate of Ammonia	"	" "	2½%	13	2	6
" of Copper	...	" Liverpool	5%	15	0	0

FOREIGN.—F.o.b. Continental port:

Article	£	s.	d.
Alkali, 58% 2-cwt. bags £6 10/0; 10-cwt. casks ...	6	15	6
Caustic Soda, 70-72%	11	12	0
Hypo-Sulphite of Soda 10-ton lots 140/0; kegs ...	7	10	6
Sulphate of Alumina 7-8 cwt. casks net c.i f. Ldn	4	7	6
Blanc Fixe (c.i.f. London)	7	12	6

ESPARTO.—Enquiry continues fairly well sustained for next year's shipment and buyers and sellers' ideas of value are not far apart. Imports for the past month have only been on a moderate scale and barely equal to consumption. Many mills, however, are undergoing repairs at this season and consequently using less material.

Prices c.i.f. London and Leith, or f.o.r. Cardiff, Garston and Tyne Docks are nominally as follows:

Spanish—	Fair to Good ...	£5 10 0 to 5 15 0
"	Fine to Best ...	5 17 6 " 6 0 0
Oran —	Fair to Good ...	3 12 6 " 3 17 6
"	First Quality...	4 0 0 " 4 2 6
Tripoli —	Hand-picked ...	3 17 6 " 4 2 6
"	Fair Average ...	3 12 6 " 3 15 0
Bona & Philippeville ...		4 0 0 " 4 2 6

IMPORTS of ESPARTO.

Quantity	From	Importer	Port.
738 tons	Almeria	Morris & Co	Granton
555 bales	Arzew	L. Jacobs & Co	London
48 "	"	Marcus & Co	"
401 "	Oran	To order	"
20 "	"	"	"

STRAW.—Straw is very scarce and very high prices ruling. Wheat and Oat Straw is offered at 67s. 6d. per ton c.i.f. London.

IMPORTS of STRAW

(Purposes unspecified) at principal Ports From

DENMARK ...	923 bales	HOLLAND ..	775 bales
FRANCE ...	270 "		

STRAW PULPS.—Market dull.

Prices, c.i.f. London, Hull or Leith:

Belgian, 25% moisture	£15 0 0 to 16 0 0
do. dry	16 0 0
German, 50 to 55% moisture	16 10 0
do. dry, ... No. 1 £18 10 0; No. 2	15 0 0

CHEMICAL WOOD PULPS.—SULPHITE has been in good enquiry during the past few weeks, and prices are firmly maintained by manufacturers. Papermakers are inclined to hold off in closing contracts, but apparently there is no likelihood of a drop in the prices of the best qualities. More attention of late has been paid to certain brands of SODA and SULPHATE PULPS.

Prices, ex steamer, London, Hull, Newcastle, Leith and Glasgow are nominally as follows:

SODA, Unbleached, Common ...	£10	0	0	to	10	10	0
,, ,, Extra... ...	10	10	0	,,	11	0	0
,, Half-Bleached	12	10	0	,,	14	0	0
SULPHATE, Unbleached, Common	10	10	0	,,	11	0	0
,, Extra	11	0	0	,,	12	0	0
,, Half-Bleached	13	10	0	,,	14	0	0
,, Bleached	15	0	0	,,	16	0	0
SULPHITE, Unbleached, Common	10	15	0	to	11	0	0
,, Superior	11	10	0	,,	12	10	0
,, ,, 50% moisture, d.w.	11	10	0	,,	12	2	6
,, Extra	13	0	0	,,	14	0	0
,, Bleached, moist					16	10	0
,, Unbleached, English, del. Lancs. ...					10	15	0
,, ,, ,, No. 1, ex mills, Ldn.					10	10	0
,, ,, ,, No. 2. ,, ,,					9	15	0

MECHANICAL WOOD PULPS.—The market continues firm, there being an excellent demand for makes of good quality. A fair amount of business has been negotiated for the German market. Prices have a strong upward tendency; in fact, some Scandinavian makers have had under discussion a further increase.

Prices, ex steamer, London, Hull, Newcastle, Leith and Glasgow are nominally as follows ·

MECHANICAL, Aspen, Dry ...	£7	10	0	to	8	0	0
Pine, Dry	6	0	0	,,	6	2	6
Pine, 50% Moist, Spot ...	2	15	0	,,	2	17	6
Moist Brown (bundles ...	2	15	0	,,	2	17	6
Dry Brown	5	15	0	,,	6	0	0
Single Sorted...	2	5	0	,,	2		6

IMPORTS of WOOD PULP.

Quantity	From	Importer	Port.
21 casks	Bremen	To order	London
1 bale	Boston	W. Friedluender	,,
1090 bales	Christiania	To order	Hull
465 ..	..	,,	Grangemouth
400 ..	..	Tough & Henderson	,,
240 ..	,,	E. J. & W. Goldsmith	,,
406 .	..	W. G. Taylor and Co	,,
1245 ..	..	Blydt, Pans & Co	Fleetwood
400 ,.	Drammen	M. G. Skramnes	London
80 ..	..	W. G. Taylor & Co	,,
500 ..	..	London Paper Mills Co	,,
250 .	,,	C. Anderson	,,
400 ..	,,	To order	..
2400 ..	Drontheim	,,	Glasgow
160 ..	..	,,	Hull
1198 rolls	Fiume	A. Guttmann	London
329 bales	,,	J. A. Reid	,,
65 ,.	Gothenburg	To order	Liverpool
68 ..	..	,,	,,
200 ,.	..	Salvesen & Co	Leith
827 ..	,,	To order	Hull
177 ..	..	,,	,,
250 ,,	..	Tough & Henderson	London
120 ,.	,,	Green & Co	,,
488 ..	,.	Henderson & Co	,,
50 ..	,,	To order	..
33 casks	Ghent	,,	,,
47 ,,	..	..	,,
102 bales	Hambro	,.	Grangemouth
63 ,.	..		Hull
205 ..	..	,.	Leith
358 .,	Helsingfors	..	Hull
183 tons	Halmstadt	,,	,,
400 lbs.	Montreal	..	Liverpool
268 ..	Rotterdam	,,	London
1452 rolls	,,	,,	,,
400 bales	,,	,,	,,
374 ..	,,	,.	,,
1000 ..	Skein	Blydt, Pans & Pace	Fleetwood
1719 ,.	..	G. Schjoth & Co	,,
400 ..	Stettin	J. Currie & Co	Leith
1000 ..	Trieste	To order	London

Totals from Each Country:

AUSTRIA	... 1000 bales	HOLLAND	... 1042 boles
BELGIUM	. 80 casks	,,	... 1452 rolls
CANADA	... 400 bales	NORWAY	...10355 bales
FINLAND	... 1198 rolls	PRUSSIA	... 400 ,,
,,	... 687 bales	SWEDEN	... 2245 ,,
GERMANY	.. 371 ,,	,,	... 183 tons
,,	... 21 casks	U.S. AMERICA	1 bale

IMPORTS of WOOD PULP BOARDS.

Quantity	From	Importer	Port
22 bales	Gothenburg	To order	Liverpool

FOREIGN RAGS.—The importation of foreign rags has given rise to several questions being asked in the House of Commons, it being alleged that their arrival in this country tends to introduce cholera. The official answer was that the medical officers of the Local Government Board thought importation might be done with safety. Now that cases of cholera have occurred at Grimsby it is thought probable that measures will shortly be adopted entirely prohibiting foreign rags being brought to British ports. Since the removal of restrictions a fair amount of business has been carried through; prices, however, have remained without any material fluctuation.

IMPORTS of FOREIGN RAGS.

Quantity	From	Importer	Port.
55 bales	Amsterdam	To order	Leith
103 ..	,,	..	Hull
153 ,,	,,	..	,,
23 ..	Antwerp	.,	Leith
50 ,,	,,		,,
299 ,,	Bordeaux	..	Liverpool
80 ,,	..		Hull
27 ..	Calais		London
424 ..	Copenhagen	.	Hull
11 ..	Christiania	..	,,
21 ..	,,	..	Grangemouth
19 ..	Dunkirk	.,	Hull
49 ..	,,	,,	Leith
146 ..	,,	,,	,,
45 ..	Flushing	,,	Hull
398 ..	Ghent	G. Gibson & Co	Leith
12 .,	Guernsey	To order	Southampton
127 ,,	Harlingen	,,	Hull
69 ..	,,	,,	,,
70 ..	Havre	,,	London
23 ..	Hambro	..	Leith
88 ..	,,	.	Hull
24 ..	Jersey	..	Southampton
414 ..	Konigsberg	..	,,
160 ,,	,,		London
590 ,,	,,		Leith
7 ..	New York	.	London
60 ..	Rotterdam	..	Hull
64 ..	,,	,,	,,
61 ..	,,	,,	..
24 .,	,,	..	,,
92 ..	,,	..	Leith
8 ..	..		,,
2 ..	Rouen	..	Hull
24 .,	Stettin	..	,,
398 ..	St. Nazaire	.,	Liverpool
17 ..	,,	..	Newhaven
155 ..	Terneuzen	,.	,,

Totals from Each Country:

BELGIUM	... 421 bales	HOLLAND	... 998 bales
CHANNEL Isles	36 ,,	NORWAY	... 32 ,,
DENMARK	... 424 ,,	PRUSSIA	... 598 ,,
FRANCE	... 1107 ,,	SWEDEN	... 590 ,,
GERMANY	.. 111 ,,	U.S.A.	... 7 ,,

DUTCH RAGS. f.o.r. Hull:

C.i.f. Thames; Hull 2/6 per ton more; ditto f.o.r. Leith c.i.f. Glasgow 4/-; c.i.f. Liverpool 4/-.

Selected Fines (free from Muslins) ...	17/0	Best Grey Linens ...	9/0
		Common ditto ...	5/6
Selected Outshots	12/0	White Canvas ...	15/0
,, Dirty Fines	7/0	Grey & Brown Canvas	9/0
Light Cottons ...	9/3	Tarred Hemp Rope	8/0
Blue Cottons ...	8/0	Ditto (broken) ...	5/3
Dark Coloured Cottons	2/10½	White Paper Shavings	7/9
New Cuttings (Bleachd)	22/6	Gunny (best) ...	4/9
,, (Unbleached)	19/6	Jute Bagging ...	3/6
,, (Slate) ...	9/0	Ditto (common ...	3/0
Muslins	8/0	Tarpaulins	4/0
Red Cottons (Mixed)	5/9	Cowhair Carpets ...	2/9
Fustians (Light browns)	5/0	Hard ditto	3/0

NORWEGIAN RAGS.

C.i.f. London, Hull, Tyne, and Grangemouth.

1st Rope (tarred) ...	8/9-9/0	2nd Canvas ...	8/0
2nd ,, ,, ...	5/9-6/0	Jute Bagging	
Manilla Rope (white)	8/6-8/9	Gunny ...	3/6 3/9
Best Canvas ...	11/9-12/0	Mixed ...	2/6-3/0

RUSSIAN RAGS.

C.i.f. London, Hull, Newcastle or Leith.

SPFF	15/0	CC (Cotton	4/9
SPF	13/6	Jute I	3/6
FG	10/6	,, II...	2/3
LFB	9/6	Rope I	9/6
FF	8/3	,, II .. .	5/3
LFX	7/3		

GERMAN RAGS.

STETTIN: C.i.f Hull, Leith, Tyne and London.

SPFFF and SPFF	18/6	LFB (Blue)	10/
SPF	12/6	CSPFFF and CSPFF	12/0
FF	11/0	CFB (Blue)	8/0
FG	9/6	CFX (Coloured) ...	[illegible]
LFX	7/0		

HAMBURG: F.o.b.

NWC	22/0	FF Grey Linens ...	9/0
SPFFF	22/0	LFX Second ditto...	8/0
SPFFF and SPFF	18/0	CSPFFF	17/3
SPFF	16/0	CSPFF	11/3
SPF	12/0	CFB	8/0
CCC	5/6	Dark Blues (selected	11/9
CFX	4/6	Wool Tares... ...	8/0
White Rope... ...	8/0	Jute, No. I 6/0; No. II	5/6

FRENCH RAGS.

Quotations range, per cwt., ex ship London, Southampton, or Hull; 2/0 per ton more at Liverpool, and 10/0 per ton higher at Newcastle, Glasgow or Leith.

French Linens, I ...	22/0	Black Cotton ...	4/0
II 18/6; III ...	14/6	Marseilles Whites, I	16/0
White Cottons, I ...	19/0	II 10/0; III ...	7/6
II 15/0; III ...	12/6	Blue Cotton	11/0
Knitted Cotton ...	11/0	Light Prints... ...	9/0
Light Coloured Cotton	8/0	Mixed Prints ...	6/0
Blue Cotton	9/6	New White Cuttings	23/0
Coloured Cotton ...	6/0	,, Stay ,,	21/0

BELGIAN RAGS.

F.o.b. Ghent. Freights: London, 5/0; Hull and Goole, 7/6 Liverpool and Leith, 10/0; Newcastle, 12/6; Dundee and Aberdeen, 15/0; Glasgow, 16/6.

White Linens No. 1	22/6	Fustians (Light) ...	6/0
,, ,, No. 2	16/6	,, (Dark) ...	4/0
,, ,, No. 3	13/0	Thirds...	3/0
Fines (Mixed) ...	12/0	Black Cottons ...	3/9
Grey Linens (strong)	10/0	Hemp Strings (unt'r'd)	2/0
,, ,, (extra)	14/0	House Cloths ...	5/0
Blue Linens... ...	8/6	Old Bagging (solid)	3/6
White Cottons S'p'fine	18/0	,, ,, (common)	2/6
,, ,, No. 2	15/0	NEW.	
Outshots No. 3 ...	11/0	White & Cream Linens	35/0
Seconds No. 4 ...	8/0	White Cuttings ...	22/0
Prints (Light) ...	8/6	Unbleached Cuttings	2[illegible]/0
,, (Old)	4/6	Print Cuttings ..	8/0

BELGIAN FLAX and HEMP WASTE.

Best washed and dried Flax Waste, 10/0; Fair ditto	9/0
Flax Spinners' Waste (grease boiled out)... ...	12/0
Hemp Waste, No. 1 9/0; No. 2	7/6
Flax Spinners' Waste, No. 1 (Flax Rove) 10/0: No. 2	8/6

HOME RAGS.—Reports from London, Bristol, Manchester, Edinburgh and Dublin show that trade remains exceedingly quiet. Prices nominal.

LONDON:

New White Cuttings	1/6	Canvas No. 1	13/6
Fines (selected)	20/6	,, No. 2 ...	10/0-10/6
,, (good London)...	20/0	,, No. 3	5/6
Outshots (selected) ...	12/6	Mixed Rope	5/3
,, (ordinary) ...	11/0	White Rope	5/6
London Seconds	3/6-4/0	White Manilla Rope	3/6
Country do. ...	6/6-8/0	Coil Rope	3/6
London Thirds ...	1/9-2/0	Bagging...	1/6
Country do. ...	4/0-5/0	Gunny	3/6
Light Prints ...	7/0-8/0		

BRISTOL:

Fines	19/0	Clean Canvas ...	15/0
Outshots	13/6	Second Do. ...	9/6-10/6
Seconds	7/0-8/0	Light Prints ...	8/0
Thirds	3/6-4/0	Hemp Coil Rope	9/6-10/0
Mixed Bagging	3/6	Tarred Manilla	7/6

MANCHESTER:

Fines	15/0-16/0	Blues	7/0-7/6
Outshots (best) ...	11/6-12/0	Bagging...	4/3-4/6
,, (ordinary)	10/6-11/0	,, (common)	3/3-3/6
Seconds	7/3-7/6	W. Manilla Rope	10/0-10-6
Thirds	3/6-3/9	Surat Tares... ...	5/0-5/3

EDINBURGH:

Superfines	17/0	Black Cottons	2/9
Outshots	13/0	W. Manilla Rope ...	9/0
Mixed Fines...	14/0	Tarred Ditto	6/9
Common Seconds ...	8/0	,, Hemp Rope...	8/6
First do.	11/0	Rope Ends (new) ...	8/6
Prints	5/6-6/6	,, ,, (old) ...	6/0
Canvas (best)	16/0	Bagging...	2/0-3/0
,, 2nd	10/6	,, (clean) ...	4/3-6/0

DUBLIN.

White Cuttings ...	18/0	Mill Bagging	3/0
Fines	11/0	White Manilla	8/0
Seconds...	5/0	Tarred Hemp	8/0
Light Prints	3/0	Rigging	13/6
Black do.	2/0	Mixed Ropes	3/6
Bagging	2/0		

WASTE PAPERS.—The market for Waste Papers is steady at former quotations.

Cream Shavings ...	12/3	Small Letters	5/0
Fine ,, ...	9/6	Large ,, ...	7/0
Mixed ,, ...	3/6	Brown Paper	2/3
White Printings ...	8/9	Light Browns	3/6
White Waste ...	1/6	Books & Pamphlets ...	6/0
Wood Pulp Cuttings	3/6	Strawboard Cuttings	1/6
Brown Paper	3/0	Jacquards	2/6
Crushed News	2/0		

For Export: 25/- per ton extra.

JUTE.—There is a fair business passing in Cuttings.

Good White £16 0 to 17	0	Common ... £10 10 to 11	0
Good... ... 15	0	Rejections .. 8 0 ,, 9	0
Medium .. 0 ,, 13	0	Cuttings ... £5 to 6	0

COLOURS.—Demand quiet.

Mineral Black ...	cwt.	3/0	Ultramarine (pure)	
do. superior ...	,,	5/0	... cwt. 40/0 to	45/0
Pure Ivory Black	,,	12/0	PASTE COLOURS with	
Ochre	,,	3/0	60% of colour, as follows:	
French J. C. Ochre	ton	55/0	Orange Pulp ... cwt.	40/0
Chrome (pure) ...	cwt.	40/0	Golden Yellow Pulp	36/0
Red Oxide	,,	4/6	Lemon ,, ,, cwt.	36/0
Umber, Devonshire	,,	50/0	Prussian Yellow ,,	36/0
do. Turkish ...	,,	40/0	Green (free of arsenic	36/0
Lamp Black ...		7/0-10/6	Paste Blue (20-45%)	
Cochineal	lb.	1/3-2/0	.. ...	23/6-46/8

SIZING.—Enquiries unsettled. Owing to the continued coal strike and consequent closing of works, trade is in a hopeless condition and quite stagnant.

English Gelatines	per cwt.	70/0 to 140/0
Foreign ,, ...	,,	70/0 ,, 140/0
Fine Skin Glues	,,	45/0 ,, 60/0
Long Scotch Glues	,,	45/0 ,, 60/0
Common ,, ...	,,	30/0 ,, 45/0
"Town" Glues	,,	26/0 ,, 36/0
"Bone" Glues	,,	20/0 ,, 30/0
Foreign Glues	,,	23/0 ,, 40/0
Bone Size	,,	4/0 ,, 10/0
Gelatine Size...	,,	5/0 ,, 10/0
Dry B.A. Pieces	,,	31/6 ,, 33/0
,, English Pieces	,,	24/0 ,, 27/0
Wet ,, ,, ...	,,	7/0 ,, 8/0
,, Sheep Pieces	,,	3/0 ,, 4/0
Buffalo Hide Shavings	,,	26/0 ,, 37/0
,, Picker Waste	,,	27/0 ,, 33/0

ROSIN.—There is a moderate trade being transacted in Rosin at unaltered figures.

	Strained.	E.	F.	G.	K.	W.G.	W.W.
Spot—	3/7½	4/0	4/3	4/6	6/6	9/6	10/6
To arrive—	3/2	3/5	3/6	3/7½	6/0	8/6	9/0

STARCH.—Prices:

F.o.r. London, less 2½%:

Maize—Crisp, £9 10/-; Powder, £9 15/-; Special £14 10/-
Farina—Prime, £10 10/-; B.K.M.F., £13 10/-

Delivered:

Rice—Special (in chests), £20 0/- (net); Crystal (in bags) £19 0/-; Granulated (in bags) £18 0/- less 2½%.
Dextrine—£16 0/- to £17.

MINERALS.—The market for CHINA CLAY is steady, with a demand for best grades. FRENCH CHALK is in fairly good request at unchanged values. BARYTES (sulphate and carbonate) are in request and there is a moderate amount of business passing in PATENT HARDENINGS and MINERAL WHITE. Best grades of IRISH MOSS scarce.

Mineral White (Terra Alba), per ton f.o.r. or boat at works:

Superfine...	28/0 less 2½ %	
Pottery Super.... ...	24/0	,,
Ball Seconds	20/0	,,
Seconds	15/0	,,
Thirds	10/6	,,

China Clay, in bulk, f.o.b. Cornwall, 14/0 to 27/6; bags 5/0 and casks 9/6 per ton extra; f.o.b. London, in casks 35/0 to 50/0 per ton.

Superfine Hardening, f.o.r. works, 40/0.

Patent Crystal Hardening, delivered at mills £3 to £3 15/0

Patent Hardening (2 ton lots) f.o.r. Lancs., £3 5/0.
,, ,, (5 ton lots) f.o.b. Liverpool, £3 10/0.

Magnesite (in lump) 32/6 per ton.

Magnesite (containing 98 % Carbonate of Magnesia), raw ground, £6 10/0; calcined ground, £12 10/0.

Albarine, £3. del. mills.

Asbestos, best rock, £18; brown grades, £14 to £15

Asbestine Pulp, £4 5/- to £5 c.i f. London, Liverpool and Glasgow.

Barytes (Carbonate), lump, 90/0 to 95/0; nuts, 72/6 to 85/0.

Barytes (Sulphate), "Angel White," No. 1, 70/0; No. 2, 60/0 to 65/0; No. 3, 45/0. Souheur's Brands (Antwerp): AF, 83/-; BF, 71/; AB, 33/6; BB, 29/6; CB, 24/3.

French and Italian Chalk (Souheur Brand, Antwerp), per ton in lots of 10 tons: Flower O, 64/6 c.i.f. London, 69/6 c.i f. Liverp'l, 71/0 c.i.f. Hull; Flower OO, 60/0, 65/0 and 66/6; Flower OOO, 51/6, 56/6 and 58/0, Swan Brand, 57/0, 62/0 and 63/6 Blackwell's "Angel White" Brand and "Silvery" 90/- to 92/6; prime quality, 90/- to 95/-; and superfine, 105/.

Bauxite, Irish Hill Quality, first lump, 20/0; seconds, 16/0; thirds, 12/0; ground, 35/0.

Pyrites (non-cupreous), Liverpool, 5d., 2 %.

Carbonate of Lime (Souheur Brand, Antwerp) Prima 43/-, Secunda 37/-.

LIME.—The lime trade, like many others, is somewhat disorganised by the coal strike, and prices vary considerably. Bleach Lime is to be had at about 11s. per ton at the works.

RUSSIAN RAGS.

C.i.f. London, Hull, Newcastle or Leith.

SPFF	15/0	CC (Cotton	4/9
SPF	13/6	Jute I	3/6
FG	10/6	,, II	2/3
LFB	9/6	Rope I	9/0
FF	8/3	,, II	5/3
LFX	7/3		

GERMAN RAGS.

STETTIN: C.i.f. Hull, Leith, Tyne and London.

SPFFF and SPFF	18/6	LFB (Blue)	10/[illegible]
SPF	12/6	CSPFFF and CSPFF	12/0
FF	11/0	CFB (Blue)	8/0
FG	9/6	CFX (Coloured)	[illegible]
LFX	7/0		

HAMBURG; F.o.b.

NWC	22/0	FF Grey Linens	9/0
SPFFF	22/0	LFX Second ditto	8/0
SPFFF and SPFF	18/0	CSPFFF	17/3
SPFF	16/0	CSPFF	11/3
SPF	12/0	CFB	8/0
CCC	5/6	Dark Blues (selected	11/9
CFX	4/6	Wool Tares	8/0
White Rope	8/0	Jute, No. I 6/0; No. II	5/6

FRENCH RAGS.

Quotations range, per cwt., ex ship London, Southampton, or Hull; 2/0 per ton more at Liverpool, and 10/0 per ton higher at Newcastle, Glasgow or Leith.

French Linens, I	22/0	Black Cotton	4/0
II 18/6; III	14/6	Marseilles Whites, I	16/0
White Cottons, I	19/0	II 10/0; III	7/6
II 15/0; III	12/6	Blue Cotton	11/0
Knitted Cotton	11/0	Light Prints	9/0
Light Coloured Cotton	8/0	Mixed Prints	6/0
Blue Cotton	9/6	New White Cuttings	2[illegible]/0
Coloured Cotton	6/0	,, Stay	21/0

BELGIAN RAGS.

F.o.b. Ghent. Freights: London, 5/0; Hull and Goole, 7/6 Liverpool and Leith, 10/0; Newcastle, 12/6; Dundee an[d] Aberdeen, 15/0; Glasgow, 16/8.

White Linens No. 1	22/6	Fustians (Light)	6/
,, ,, No. 2	16/6	,, (Dark)	4/
,, ,, No. 3	13/0	Thirds	3
Fines (Mixed)	12/0	Black Cottons	3
Grey Linens (strong)	10/0	Hemp Strings (unt'r'd)	[illegible]
,, ,, (extra)	14/0	House Cloths	[illegible]
Blue Linens	8/6	Old Bagging (solid)	[illegible]
White Cottons S'p'fine	18/0	,, ,, (common)	[illegible]
,, ,, No. 2	15/0	NEW.	
Outshots No. 3	11/0	White & Cream Linens	3
Seconds No. 4	8/0	White Cuttings	2
Prints (Light)	8/6	Unbleached Cuttings	2
,, (Old)	4/6	Print Cuttings	

BELGIAN FLAX and HEMP WASTE.

Best washed and dried Flax Waste, 10/0; Fair ditto
Flax Spinners' Waste (grease boiled out)...
Hemp Waste, No. 1 9/0; No. 2 ... ...
Flax Spinners' Waste, No. 1 (Flax Rove) 10/0: No.

HOME RAGS.—Reports from London, B[ris]tol, Manchester, Edinburgh and Du[ndee] show that trade remains exceedingly q[uiet]. Prices nominal.

LONDON:

New White Cuttings	22/6	Canvas No. 1	
Fines (selected)	20/6	,, No. 2	10
,, (good London)	20/0	,, No. 3	
Outshots (selected)	12/6	Mixed Rope	
,, (ordinary)	11/0	White Rope	
London Seconds	3/6-4/0	White Manilla Rope	
Country do.	6/6-8/0	Coil Rope	
London Thirds	1/9-2/0	Bagging	
Country do.	4/0-5/0	Gunny	
Light Prints	7/0-8/0		

BRISTOL:

Fines	19/0	Clean Canvas	
Outshots	13/6	Second Do.	
Seconds	7/0-8/0	Light Prints	
Thirds	3/6-4/0	Hemp Coil Rope	
Mixed Bagging	3/6	Tarred Manilla	

MANCHESTER:

'TS.

ST.

Other Kinds.	
482 cwts.	
78	..
60	..
—	..
11	..
—	..
—	..
—	..
457	..
70	..
—	..
—	..
45	..
1	..
2	..
416½	..
—	..
—	..
1:9	..
32	..
—	..
—	..
1	..
—	..
21	..
—	..
15	..
—	..

...14346 bales
... 52 cases
... 52 rolls
... 1397 bales
... 924 rolls
... 23 bales
... 1021 ..
... 405 rolls
... 25 cases
... 163 bales
... 217 cases

ny:

	Port.
	London.
	..
& Co	..
Co	..
..	
	..
	..
	..
	..
n	..
	..
& Co	..
	..
Co	..
Co	..
	..
	..
& Co	..
en & Co	..
	..
ey & Co	..
	..
	..
	..
gren	..
Co	..

y informed and well- to exporters for of Raw Material.— tion, Dresden.

SUMMARY OF

IMPORTS & EXPOR

FOR THE WEEK ENDING TUESDAY LAS

London, Liverpool, Bristol, Southam Hull, Fleetwood, Harwich, Folkestone, haven, Dover, &c.

IMPORTS.

Paper	20143 bales	Pasteboards	100
"	667 cases	"	1(
"	1381 rolls	Strawboards	23
Stock	52 bales	Millboards	118
Tissues	299 ..	Stationery..... ...	
"	5 cases	"	1
Cardboards	756 pkgs.	Leather Paper ...	

EXPORTS.

British Goods.			
		Strawboards	1
Paper	1437 cwt.	Strawboard Cuttings	11
Writing Paper ...	2371 "	Parchment	£1
Printing Paper	4923 ..	Foreign Goods	
Stationery	£8378 value		
Packing Paper ...	£12 ..	Paper	4
Stock	182 tons	Wrapping Paper	5
Waste	151 "	Stationery	£1
Millboards	27 cwt.	Wood Pulp	2
"	£13 value	Strawboards	46
Cardboards	124 cwt.		

Glasgow. Greenock, Port-Glasgow, T Grangemouth, &c.

IMPORTS.

Paper	639 bales	Paper	

EXPORTS.

Paper	3(2½ cwt.	Stationery	£1
Printing Paper..	1564½ "	Envelopes	3
Writing Paper...	242½ "		

Leith, Granton, Boness, Dundee, &

IMPORTS.

Paper	465 bales	Envelopes	17
"	1 case	Tissues	
Millboards	263 pkgs.	Stationery	

NEW PATENTS.

APPLICATIONS.

15,466. A new or improved process for obtaini monium chloride and carbonate or bicarbonate from blast furnace or producer gases. J. Cumin and J. Addie.

15,669. Apparatus for the electrolytic treatment of N. Browne.

15,735. Improvements in obtaining chloride. W. P. and J. Jack.

PAPER & PULP MILL SHAR

(Report received from Mr. F. D. Dean, 36, Corp Street, Manchester.)

Nominal Amnt	Amnt Paid	Name of Company	Last dividend	Pri
7	7	Bury Paper, ord.	nil	4¼—4¾
7	7	do. do. 6% pref.	6%	4½—5
100	100	do. do. deb.	5%	103—
10	10	Bath Paper Mill Co. Lim.	7½%	6 7
10	10	Bergvik Co, def.	15%	13½
100	100	do. do. 6% cum. pref.	6%	106—1
10	10	do. do. deb.	5%	105—1
5	3¾	Burnley Paper Co.	3%	7 0—
5	3¼	Darwen Paper Co.	10%	5¾—6¼
15	10	East Lancashire Co.	nil	4¼—4¾
10	10	do. do. 6% pref.	nil	6½—7
5	5	do. do. bonus	nil	1½—2
5	5	Hyde Paper Co.	4%	4½—5
5	4	North of Ireland Paper Co.	nil	[illegible]—8
15	5	Ramsbottom Paper Co	17½%	12, —
5	4½	Roach Bridge Paper Co.	5%	3—3½
5	5	Star Paper Co.	10%	6—6¼
5	3	do. do. 10% pref. cum	10%	4¾ 5
50	50	do. do. deb.	6%	55—56
5	2½	Kellner Partingt'n Pulp Co	—	5¾6—

DIRECTORY.

Names and Addresses under this heading will be charged for at the rate of 50/- per annum (52 insertions) for each card of two lines or under. Each additional line £1 extra.

ALUMINOUS CAKE.

The ALUM, CHINA CLAY and VITRIOL Co., Lim., 63, Queen Victoria Street, London, E.C. Works: Rainham-on-Thames. Telegrams—"Chinnock, London.

ANALYTICAL.

WILLIAMS, ROWLAND, F.I.C., F.C.S., 28, Pall Mall, Manchester.

ARTESIAN WELLS.

BATCHELOR, Richard D., Artesian and Consulting Well Engineer. 73. Queen Victoria Street, London, E.C., and at Chatham. 5713

ISLER, C., & Co., Bear Lane, Southwark, S.E

LE GRAND & SUTCLIFF, Magdala Works, 125, Bunhill Row, E.C.

BOILER COVERING.

LONSDALES, Boiler Coverers, Blackburn, will send a sample cask of their Patent Plastic Cork Covering to any Paper Mill in Great Britain—5 cwt. cask for 25/- (carriage paid).

CHINA CLAY.

The ALUM, CHINA CLAY and VITRIOL Co., Lim., 63, Queen Victoria Street, London, E.C. Mines: Ruddle and Colchester, St. Austell, Cornwall. Telegrams—"Chinnock, London."

ROGERS, J., & Co., Truro, Cornwall.—Agents: Taylor, Sommerville & Co., 83, Queen Victoria Street. E.C., and at 16, Princes Street, Edinburgh.

W. SINGLETON BIRCH & SONS, Lim., 15, Upton Street, Manchester. Mines: Rosevear, St. Austell, Cornwall. 2276

COLOURS.

CARDWELL, J. L., & Co., Commercial Buildings, 15, Cross Street, Manchester. Specialities: Mineral Black, Ven. Red, Ochres and Umbers. 5204

GEMMILL, W. N., & Co., Glasgow, Telegrams "Ruhe." Starches, Alumina, Antifroths, &c. All Paper Colours

HINSHELWOOD, THOMAS, & Co., The Glasgow Colour Works, Glasgow. Colours and shades matched exactly.

MULLER, A. E., 9, Fenchurch Street, London, E.C.

ESPARTO.

IDE & CHRISTIE, Fibre, Esparto, and General Produce Brokers, 72, Mark Lane, E.C.

MINERAL WHITE or TERRA ALBA.

WINSER & Co., Portland Mills, Princess Street, Manchester. Also manufacturers of Aluminous Cake.

HOWE, JOHN, & Co., Carlisle. 2112

STEEL.

MAKIN, WM., & SONS, Sheffield. Established 1736. Roll Bars, Plates, Cutter Knives, Doctor Blades, &c. 5369

STRAW.

UNDERWOOD, E., & SON, Limited, Brentford, London, W. Press-packed Oat, Wheat, or Rye Straw, delivered to the chief British ports or railway stations.

TALC (French and Italian Chalk).

SOUHEUR, JEAN, Antwerp. All Minerals, Blanc de Silex, Barytes (superior and common), Carbonate of Lime, Blacklead, &c. British Agent: A. E. Muller, 9, Fenchurch Street, London, E.C. Agent for Liverpool and Manchester: C. H. Austin, Ditton, near Widnes.

RAGS.

CHALMERS, E., & Co., Lim., Bonnington, Leith.

MULLER, A. E., 9, Fenchurch Street, London, E.C.

WERTHEIM, A., & Co., Hamburg.

UMBER.

The ALUM, CHINA CLAY and VITROIL Co., Lim. 63, Queen Victoria Street, London, E.C. Telegrams—"Chinnock, London."

WOOD PULP.

FRIIS, N., & Co., 18, Carl Johans Gade, Christiania, Norway.

GOTTSTEIN, H., & Co., 59, Mark Lane, London, E.C., and at New York.

GRANT, W., & Co., 17, Baltic Street, Leith. Agents for best shippers, Sulphite and Sulphate, Mechanical, Pine, Brown, Aspen.

MATTHIESSEN, CHR., Christiania, Norway.

MULLER, A. E., 9, Fenchurch Street, London, E.C.

The SULPHITE PULP Company, Limited, 82, Gordon Street, Glasgow.

WERTHEIM, A., & Co., Hamburg.

PAPER EXPORTS & IMPORTS.

FOR THE WEEK ENDING TUESDAY LAST.

EXPORTS TO

	Printings.	Writings.	Other Kinds.
AUSTRALIA	2049 cwts	432 cwts	482 cwts.
AFRICA	— ,,	16 ,,	78 ,,
ARGENTINE ...	24 ,,	317 ,,	60 ,,
BELGIUM	— ,,	49 ,,	— ,,
B. WEST INDIES...	24 ,,	74½ ,,	11 ,,
B. GUIANA	35 ,,	— ,,	— ,,
CHANNEL ISLES	15 ,,	— ,,	— ,,
CANADA	334½ ,,	244 ,,	— ,,
CAPE COLONY .	217 ,,	159 ,,	457 ,,
CHINA	205 ,,	97 ,,	70 ,,
CHILI	107 ,,	9 ,,	— ,,
EGYPT	— ,,	3 ,,	— ,,
FRANCE	— ,,	20 ,,	45 ,,
GERMANY	40 ,,	— ,,	1 ,,
HOLLAND	65 ,,	8 ,,	2 ,,
INDIA	1730 ,,	1038 ,,	416½ ,,
JAPAN	963 ,,	5 ,,	— ,,
MAURITIUS ...	66 ,,	— ,,	— ,,
NEW ZEALAND ..	149 ,,	19 ,,	129 ,,
N. AMERICA... ...	— ,,	— ,,	32 ,,
PORTUGAL	25 ,,	— ,,	— ,,
PERSIA	— ,,	2 ,,	— ,,
RUSSIA	— ,,	2 ,,	1 ,,
SYRIA	14 ,,	— ,,	— ,,
SPAIN	2 ,,	25 ,,	21 ,,
TURKEY . ..	— ,,	5 ,,	— ,,
U.S.A.	310½ ,,	12 ,,	15 ,,
W. INDIES	106 ,,	23 ,,	— ,,

IMPORTS FROM

AUSTRIA ...	256 bales	HOLLAND ...	14346 bales
BELGIUM ...	2200 ,,	,, ...	52 cases
,, ...	22 cases	,, ...	52 rolls
CAÑADA ...	5 ,,	NORWAY ...	1397 bales
CHINA	43 ,,	,, ...	924 rolls
DENMARK ...	193 bales	PRUSSIA ...	23 bales
FINLAND ...	445 ,,	SWEDEN ...	1021 ,,
,, ...	54 cases	,, ...	405 rolls
FRANCE ...	753 bales	,, ...	25 cases
,, ...	91 cases	U.S.A.	163 bales
GERMANY ...	1715 bales	,, ...	217 cases
,, ...	194 cases		

Including the Following:

Quantity	From	Importer	Port.
12 cases	Boston	B. Galloway	London.
96 bales	Christiania	F. E. Foulger	,,
33 ,,	,,	Christophersen & Co	,,
113 ,,	,,	Lon. & Rhine S. Co	,,
41 rolls	,,	,, ,,	,,
56 bales	,,	Alsing & Co	,,
71 ,,	,,	Crabb & Co	,,
830 rolls	Christiansand	R. L. Lundgren	,,
1 bale	,,	,, ,,	,,
123 ,,	Drammen	Crabb & Co	,,
176 ,,	Gothenberg	Hummel & Co	,,
26 ,,	,,	R. L. Lundgren	,,
67 ,,	,,	J. Hamilton	,,
124 ,,	,,	Schenkenwald & Co	,,
57 ,,	,,	Becker & Co	,,
35 ,,	,,	C. Morgan & Co	,,
10 ,,	,,	C. Burnett & Co	,,
55 ,,	,,	Smythe & Co	,,
24 ,,	,,	Asling & Co	,,
33 ,,	,,	J. Hamilton & Co	,,
9 ,,	,,	Christophersen & Co	,,
6 cases	Hong Kong	Berrick Bros	,,
29 ,,	Marseilles	Williams, Torey & Co	,,
5 ,,	New York	F. Hawk	,,
252 rolls	Uddevalla	D. Gulland	,,
143 ,,	,,	R. L. Lundgren	,,
90 bales	,,	Hummel & Co	,,

THE PAPER TRADE REVIEW is a widely informed and well-managed enterprise, of great value to exporters for its exact Market Reports and statistics of Raw Material.—*Central-Blatt fur die Papier-Fabrikation*, Dresden.

SUMMARY OF

IMPORTS & EXPORTS,

FOR THE WEEK ENDING TUESDAY LAST.

London, Liverpool, Bristol, Southampton, Hull, Fleetwood, Harwich, Folkestone, Newhaven, Dover, &c.

IMPORTS.

Paper	20143 bales	Pasteboards	10021 pkgs.
,, ...	667 cases	,, ...	105 rolls
,, ...	1381 rolls	Strawboards	2331 pkgs.
Stock	52 bales	Millboards	11823 ,,
Tissues	299 ,,	Stationery...... ...	34 cases
,, ...	5 cases	,, ...	10 pkgs.
Cardboards	756 pkgs.	Leather Paper ...	4 cases

EXPORTS.

British Goods.			
Paper	1437 cwt.	Strawboards	10 cwt.
Writing Paper ...	2371 ,,	Strawboard Cuttings	113 tons
Printing Paper	4923 ,,	Parchment	£175 value
Stationery.........	£8878 value	**Foreign Goods.**	
Packing Paper ...	£12 ,,	Paper	40 cwt.
Stock	182 tons	Wrapping Paper	50 ,,
Waste	151 ,,	Stationery	£158 value
Millboards.........	27 cwt.	Wood Pulp	206 tons
,, ...	£13 value	Strawboards	465 cwt.
Cardboards	124 cwt.		

Glasgow, Greenock, Port-Glasgow, Troon, Grangemouth, &c.

IMPORTS.

Paper	639 bales	Paper	3 cases

EXPORTS.

Paper	3522½ cwt.	Stationery	£13 value
Printing Paper..	1564½ ,,	Envelopes	36 pkgs.
Writing Paper...	242½ ,,		

Leith, Granton, Boness, Dundee, &c.

IMPORTS.

Paper	465 bales	Envelopes	175 pkgs.
,, ...	1 case	Tissues	8 ,,
Millboards	263 pkgs.	Stationery	1 case

NEW PATENTS.

APPLICATIONS.

15,466. A new or improved process for obtaining ammonium chloride and carbonate or bicarbonate of soda from blast furnace or producer gases. J. Cuninghame and J. Addie.

15,669. Apparatus for the electrolytic treatment of liquids. N. Browne.

15,735. Improvements in obtaining chloride. W. Paterson and J. Jack.

PAPER & PULP MILL SHARES.

(Report received from Mr. F. D. DEAN, 36, Corporation Street, Manchester.)

Nominal Amnt	Amnt Paid	Name of Company	Last dividend	Price.
7	7	Bury Paper, ord.	nil	4½—4¾
7	7	do. do. 6% pref.	6%	4¾—5
100	100	do. do. deb.	5%	103—106
10	10	Bath Paper Mill Co. Lim.	7½%	6 7
10	10	Bergvik Co., def.	15%	13½
100	100	do. do. 6% cum. pref.	6%	10⅝—11⅛
10	10	do. do. deb.	5%	105—110
5	3⅞	Burnley Paper Co.	3/-	77/0—78/0
5	3¼	Darwen Paper Co.	10%	5⅞—6⅛
10	10	East Lancashire Co.	nil	4½—4⅝
10	10	do. do. 6% pref.	nil	6½—7
5	5	do. do. bonus	nil	1½—2
5	5	Hyde Paper Co.	4%	4½—5
5	4	North of Ireland Paper Co.	nil	1⅝—2
10	5	Ramsbottom Paper Co.	17½%	12¼—12½
3	4½	Roach Bridge Paper Co.	5%	3¼—3¾
5	5	Star Paper Co.	10%	6—6¼
5	3	do. do. 10% pref. cum	10%	4¾—5¼
50	50	do. do. deb.	6%	55—56
5	2½	Kellner Partingt'n Pulp Co	—	56/6—58/6

SEPT. 5 [illegible]

[illegible] Prepaid Advertisements

[illegible] IMPORTANT [illegible] advertisements [illegible] PAPER POST or WEDNES[illegible] [illegible]

[illegible]

[illegible] Wanted.

[illegible]

[illegible] Wanted.

[illegible]

Wanted.

TO MAKERS OF NEWS and PRINTING PAPERS.—[illegible]

[illegible]

DEBENISE Wanted to Papermakers: [illegible]

WANTED to PURCHASE [illegible] WOOD PULP [illegible]

WANTED [illegible] Pulp Mill [illegible]

For Sale.

ONE [illegible]

[illegible] CALENDERS [illegible]

ONE [illegible]

ONE [illegible] PRESS [illegible]

ONE [illegible] STEAM HAMMER [illegible]

[illegible] REVOLVING STRAINER [illegible]

Apply [illegible]

[illegible] LIMITED [illegible] EDINBURGH.

Mill to be Let or Sold.

TO be LET or SOLD a Paper Mill [illegible] good condition.—Apply for further information [illegible]

Complaints

Concerning Late Delivery of Newspapers are useless unless the Wrappers accompany the complaint at head quarters of the Post Office.

Our Subscribers Copies are [illegible] before 5.30 p.m. on Friday, and should reach every postal address in the United Kingdom by SATURDAY MORNING'S POST.

We have complaints again of irregular delivery last week, some copies not being delivered until Monday and Tuesday, but our correspondents omit to forward us the wrappers, without which the General Post Office are unable to trace where the delay occurs. The postmarks will enable them to do this.

Special Prepaid Advertisem...

IT IS IMPORTANT ... under any of the Headings ... should reach us by the FIRST POST ... DAY Morning to INSURE INSERTION.

Charges for advertisements under the ... Wanted are 1/- for twenty-four words ... Word after, Minimum charge ... and addresses to be paid for.

Advertisers by paying ... replies addressed to the Press ... number, and such replies will then ...

Advertisements appearing under the ...

Tenders.
Sales by Auction.
Businesses Wanted.
Businesses for Disposal.

The charges are 1/- for fifty ... every line or portion after ... each line. Names and addresses ... must be made in advance ... has a running account ...

Legal and Financial ...

Cheques and ...

Taylor's Patent

BEATING *and* REFINING ENGINE.

THIS BEATER TAKES UP LESS FLOOR SPACE THAN ANY OTHER.

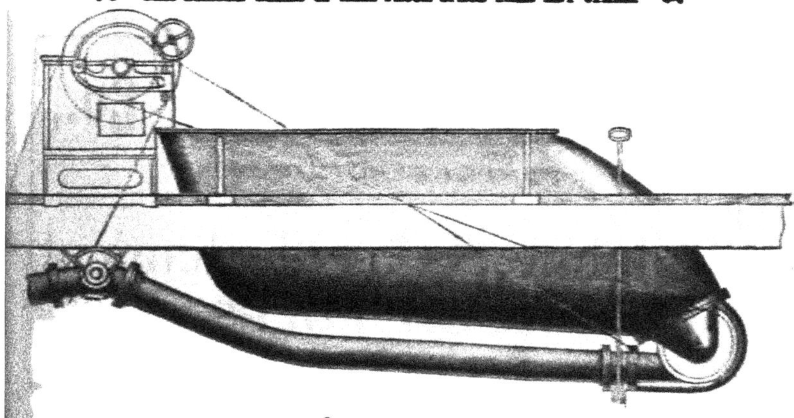

ADVANTAGES:

1.—**GREATLY INCREASED PRODUCTION over that of the** ordinary Beater in use.

2.—**GREAT SAVING IN POWER**, notwithstanding the increased production. This Beater has been proved to beat a given quantity **of pulp with less than one-half of** the power required by an ordinary beater of good modern construction.

3.—**COMPLETE AND PERFECT CIRCULATION**, which ensures complete uniformity in the length of the fibres.

For Full Particulars and Prices apply to

MASSON, SCOTT & Co., Ltd.,

BATTERSEA, LONDON, S.W.

OUR CATALOGUE
BELT PULLEYS.
ROPE PULLEYS.
GEAR WHEELS.
SHAFTING.
PEDESTALS.
FIXINGS.
HARPERS ... ABERDEEN.

LONSDA

The "DAIL
LONSDALE BR

DA ASH

Writing on the 6th March, 1893, the Managing Director of the GIGG MILLS says of the Incinerator:—

"We have now had your Incinerator at work several months, and find it very satisfactory indeed. Since Christmas, for instance, we have recovered from 14 to 16 tons of ash per week, the coal consumed being only a small quantity just for starting up on a Monday morning. It is self supporting for combustible matter. We can keep good fires all the week and steam constantly, and this, as before stated, without any consumption of coal after starting up. We only used 2 cwts. of coal in the way indicated last week, and recovered 14 tons of ash."

WCETT, PRESTON & CO., LIM.

ENGINEERS,

oenix Foundry Liverpool

nted and Published by W. JOHN STONHILL 58, Shoe Lane, LONDON, E.C. Sept. 8, 1893.

THE FILTERING OF WASTE OILS

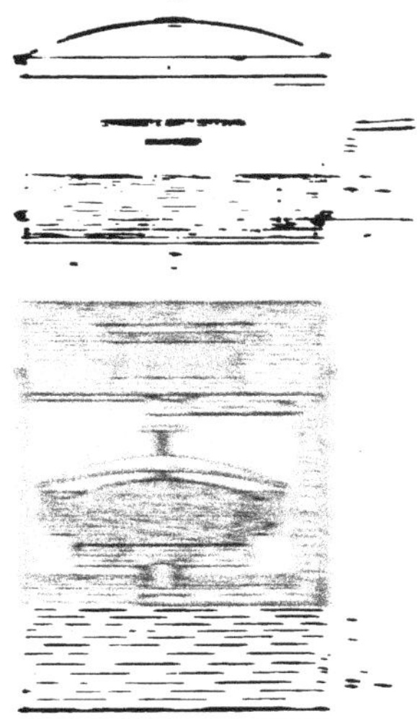

Apparatus to

SODA

(CHAPMAN'...

Avoiding POLLUTION ... and NUIS...

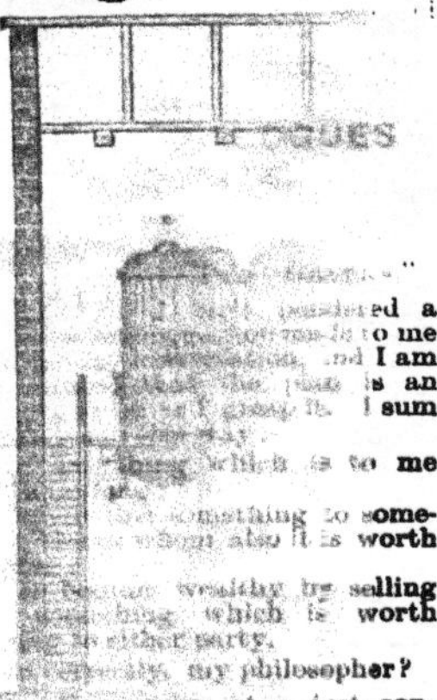

...ed a ...o me ...I am ...s an ... I sum

... to me

... something to some- ... also it is worth

... wealthy by selling ... which is worth ... either party.

... my philosopher?

... arrive at a just con-

Writing on the ... wrong methods of

"We ...

better than ... me then, O Sage. Your ... "Go into the highways ... you six other students as ... yourself, and together draw ... association to acquire and ... the business of manufacturing ... pilulæ crumbæ et saponacæ. ... the new undertaking as a ... Company, and then there lies ... on the fulfilment of your honest ... to get on—at someone else's cost."

... I pray you, explain to me, what is ... Limited Company?

CYN.—"Limited Company," my son, literally read, is a term used to express a trading partnership in which the liability of the partners to payment of its debts is limited to an agreed sum. As for example, ... partner may agree to subscribe a ... in shares, and his liability for ... of the partnership will cease so ... he has paid that specified sum ... treasury of the company, or per- ... someone else to take over his ... by purchasing his shares. Or, as ... native, the partners may agree to ... each so much ooftish, and no

... the event of the company going ... the nick—I beg pardon, proceeding ... dation.

...—I think I tumble to that, but I ... see my "cop."

CYN.—Because, my son, your vision is "limited" also. I have given you only the literal meaning of the term, as accepted by those disciples of Apollonius to whom a spade is an agricultural implement, naught more, naught less, and which could not by any possibility be used by a navvy to dash out his fellow's brains. But in a broader sense the constitution of Limited Companies is a kindly provision made by the State to meet the case of those "Greeks" who have a soul at once above "cly-faking" or pocket-picking, but too timorous for burglary or highway robbery.

IMP.—My mind is lost in the depth of your superior knowledge. I cannot follow your meaning.

CYN.—Because your intellect has grovelled and confined itself to the finding of "jays" and "mugs" in petty gambles, and never soared to the heights of legalised robbery upon a comprehensive scale. I realise that I must make my demonstration with A B C simplicity to meet your weak understanding. The system of dialectics is best adapted to this end. You have propounded to me one question which I have endeavoured to answer. Take the literal meaning of the term "Limited Company," which is clear and simple, and now get on with your game—that is, ask me another keeping your mind strictly to your own business and your own necessities or desires.

IMP.—Then, if I am to free myself from the liabilities of my bankrupt business and at the same time to rake in the shekels, I must sell that business. But being a bankrupt business, who will put down the "dibs" for it? To whom must ... sell it?

CYN.—Can you command the six other students for whom I specified?

IMP.—Surely.

CYN.—Then is it very simple. You must sell your bankrupt business to yourself.

IMP.—To myself?

CYN.—To yourself. I will show the beautiful simplicity of the transaction. A, B, C, D, E, F, and G shall represent A yourself, and the remainder six co-operating impecuniarii. Under signed articles of association you seven shall agree to acquire the business, and conduct it henceforth as a joint stock limited liability company. This new company being registered under the Companies Acts of 1862 to 1890, whose provisions are as loose as any "Greek" could desire, you are at once relieved from the responsibilities of your present bankrupt business. So much for the first half of your thesis.

[illegible]

Cyn.—Not having a single tangible [illegible]

Inf.—Except the [illegible]

Cyn.—But, as I understand, a [illegible]

[illegible]

not see your way to getting rid of a large proportion of your twenty thousand pounds' worth of paper? My son, if you only show yourself one-half as "cute" in this undertaking as I have seen you with a "rigging" of the produce market [illegible] you have a brilliant future before you, and may attain to the dignities of a Lord Mayor.

Inf.—The prospect is fascinating. But tell me further——

Cyn.—Not another word. I have given you sufficient food for thought for one day; more would tend to repletion and stupidity. Besides, I'm due at a [illegible].

Inf.—Where shall we go?

[illegible]

The case of the debtor, described as a printer at [illegible], [illegible] trading under the style of W. W. [illegible] and [illegible], came before Mr. Registrar Brougham, at the London Bankruptcy Court, on Tuesday, August [illegible], it being on the list of the day's public examinations. Upon the case being called, Mr. [illegible], official receiver, reported that it was a most complicated one. The statement of affairs was [illegible], and very little time was allowed for investigation before he could be prepared to conduct the public examination. Under these circumstances he asked for an adjournment of a month. His Honour granted the application, and ordered the case to stand over until the 27th September. The following are the principal creditors disclosed by the statement of affairs, viz.:—

[illegible]

users of machinery, and we understand from the makers that up to the present they have scarcely been able to keep pace with their sales. The latest patent is a syphon feed floating on the oil in the top chamber. The worst of the dirt in the oil settles naturally by gravitation and the syphon only brings over the best surface of the oil delivering it to the filtering pads in the chamber below. The cleaning is effected in two pads of specially prepared filtering cotton. The whole apparatus is most simple and easy to cle[illegible] while the low price of the article plac[illegible] within reach of any one. The pate[illegible] are Messrs. A. C. Wells and Co., M[illegible] Road, St. Pancras, N.W.

VERY SOCRATIC DIALOG[illegible] UP-TO-DATE.

II.

Dramatis Personæ—Tw[illegible]

IMPECUNIARIUS.—I ha[illegible] good deal over the sugge[illegible] by you in our last conve[illegible] bound to confess tha[illegible] alluring one, so far as [illegible] up your scheme in th[illegible] [illegible]topped

I have somethin[illegible] [illegible] the worth nothing: [illegible] the clamping

I am to sell this [illegible] machine is as body else to [illegible] and the cutter nothing: [illegible] on the attend-

I am to bec[illegible] material, say for ex- this som[illegible]pamphlets upon the table nothing t[illegible] against the gauge the

Do I reason cor[illegible] under the cutter and [illegible] the ridge on the disc.

CYNICUS.—Y[illegible] pile also with the back clusion. [illegible] but with the head deduction [illegible] and the tail towards or

IMP.—[illegible] He then, by moving a [illegible] releases a catch [illegible] the clamping disc, and [illegible] is therefore forced down by its [illegible] the two piles of pamphlets. [illegible] is then started, the usual [illegible] the cutter descend and the cut- [illegible] these edges of the two piles [illegible] beneath it, viz., the head of the [illegible] and the tail of the second. The [illegible] and clamp next rise through the [illegible] action of the machine, and [illegible] they are clear of the piles [illegible] are given a quarter revolution together with the discs between which they are held. The clamp and [illegible] then again descend and cut the [illegible] of one of the piles. The cutter [illegible] having again risen, the piles [illegible] receive another quarter turn, so [illegible] the third descent of the cutter the [illegible] first pile and the head of the [illegible] are cut. The clamp and cutter again risen, and the piles and discs [illegible] received another quarter turn, the [illegible] its fourth descent cuts the fore- [illegible] other pile. When the clamp

mor[illegible] [illegible] fourth time, the piles do[illegible] [illegible] another quarter turn, t[illegible] [illegible] back to the starting [illegible] gear is automatic- [illegible]mping disc lifted [illegible] piles, which have [illegible] three sides, can [illegible] attendant and [illegible] in their places. [illegible] feed table [illegible] forwards [illegible] work in [illegible] [illegible]ated ac- [illegible] [illegible]ngth [illegible] [illegible]

[illegible] Letter Card.—H. [illegible] February, 1893. [illegible] present constructed [illegible] letter book owing [illegible] them. The inventor [illegible] over the difficulty in his [illegible] by the peculiar arrangement of [illegible].

[illegible] Improved Means for Indicating the Length of Material in Rolls of Paper or Fabrics.—J. H. DALTON. Accepted 25th February, 1893.

A check measurer to assist in stock-taking, checking, measurement of material from manufacturers, and to show the yards, &c., that may be required, and consists of a table or paper slip measured out in inches, feet, &c., which is rolled up conjointly with the material, so that pieces can be cut off by inspection of sight and the amount remaining unused be shown.

23,663.—Improvements in Perpetual Calendars.—GEORGE DREYFUS. Accepted 4th February, 1893.

A perpetual calendar constructed of rotating and sliding cards, which have to be adjusted in order to get the date required.

CIGAR AND CIGARETTE CASES FROM WOOD PULP.—The firm of Willner Brothers, in Teplitz, in Bohemia, is sending out cigar and cigarette cases made from brown leather pulp, which looks exactly like cases made from real leather. They consist of two parts, which fit into each other, so that they can be drawn out and pushed back again. The outsides have imitation embossed leather paper neatly pasted on, representing all kinds of leather from russia and calf leather to crocodile and serpent skins, in fact anything that the leather trade has brought out lately. Seams are fixed on to mak[illegible] the deception perfect. These cases ar[illegible] certainly a great improvement upon th[illegible] old paper bags, and give also occasion t[illegible] advertise the firm of the cigar mercha[illegible] by a neatly executed gold print which ca[illegible] be affixed to the side.

PATENTED INVENTIONS.

14,194 (92).—**Improvements in Guillotine Machines.**—HERBERT JAMES SALMON, JOHN CAPPER, and WILLIAM HENRY DUFFETT. Accepted June 2nd, 1893.

This patent relates to improvements [illegible] automatically actuating the part of [illegible] machine that acts upon and hold[illegible] material while being cut by the guillo[illegible] knife.

15 495 (92).—**Improvements in Guil[illegible] Machines.** — ROBERT C. A[illegible] Accepted July 1st, 1893.

This invention relates to the [illegible] tion of cutting machines that [illegible] matically trim the edges of [illegible] papers, etc. The first table [illegible] forwards or backwards, and [illegible] of it a revolving disc is [illegible] the upper surface there[illegible] centre of the disc is a [illegible] placed edgewise, and [illegible] this ridge is an adjust[illegible] the disc is a clamping [illegible] vertical rod, which [illegible] down, and can al[illegible] its disc. When [illegible] the upper disc or cl[illegible] the pile of pap[illegible] a spring; when [illegible] the mechanism [illegible] driving pow[illegible] disc. The op[illegible] follows: [illegible] being in the[illegible] ant plac[illegible] ample [illegible] with the [illegible] "head [illegible] the b[illegible] He p[illegible] [illegible]

[illegible]nd Published by W. JOHN STONHILL, 58, Shoe Lane, LONDON, E.C.; Sept. 8, 1893.

[illegible] "[illegible], LONDON." A B C Code. Registered at the General Post Office as a Newspaper.

Vol. [illegible] No. 17. LONDON, SEPTEMBER 15, 1893. Price 6d.

SWEDISH WOOD PULP AND PAPER TRADES.

Much of the value of the reports for last year on the trade of the consular districts of Gothenburg and Stockholm is lost owing to late publication. The condition of the market has materially changed since the views expressed in regard to trade during 1892. Mr Vice-Consul [illegible], in referring to the district of [illegible], states that wood pulp fetched a very low price throughout the year, and the latter article therefore to a great extent was turned into paper at the neighbouring paper mills. At Halmstad there was an increase in the exportation of wood pulp, and at Gefle the export of wood pulp (included under miscellaneous) showed a remarkable advance last year, the total value amounting to [illegible], of which more than four-fifths went to England. Cardboard was exported from Gothenburg in 1892 to the extent of [illegible] cwts., the quantity in 1891 being [illegible] cwts. At Stockholm [illegible] cwts. of rags were exported in 1892, showing a decrease compared with 1891, when the quantity was [illegible] cwts. At the various ports the exports of wood pulp and paper for the past two years were as follows:—

EXPORTS OF WOOD PULP.

	1892	1891
Gothenburg	[illegible] tons	[illegible] tons
Halmstad	[illegible] "	[illegible] "
Malmo ...	[illegible] "	—
Stockholm	[illegible] cwts.	[illegible] cwts.
Soderhamn	[illegible]	[illegible]
Oscarshamn ...	[illegible] cwts.	—

EXPORTS OF PAPER.

	1892	1891
Gothenburg ...	[illegible] tons	[illegible] tons
[illegible] ...	[illegible] cwts.	[illegible] cwts.

At Gothenburg [illegible] tons of alkali were imported during 1892, against [illegible] tons in 1891; the imports of envelopes were [illegible] cwts. in 1892, and [illegible] cwts. in 1891. The following figures show the

IMPORTS OF PAPER.

	1892	1891
Gothenburg ...	[illegible] tons	[illegible] tons
Hudiksvall ...	[illegible] cwts.	[illegible] cwts.
[illegible] ...	[illegible] "	314 "

NOTE.—1 ton = [illegible] kilos.; cwt. = [illegible] kilos. £1 = [illegible] kroner.

The first wood pulp mill in Sweden, according to Mr [illegible], managing director of the [illegible] Export Association, was erected in 1857, and up to [illegible] remained the only one of its kind in the country. In [illegible] the number of mills had reached [illegible], with a production of [illegible] kg. pulp, valued at [illegible] kroner; in [illegible] the pulp mills were [illegible], turning out [illegible] kg. of stuff, estimated at [illegible] kroner, and notwithstanding the downward tendency of the prices of late years the number of Swedish wood pulp manufactories had increased in 1891 to [illegible], with an annual output of nearly [illegible] kg. Most of the Swedish pulp manufactories are based on the mechanical or grinding process; lately, however, the chemical processes have been more and more appreciated even in Sweden. The Swedish export of wood pulp has during the last year increased [illegible] [illegible] mills are still the larger [illegible]

The s
made a st
than in the
sluced, and
consequence.
[illegible] 1892. Higher cost of
and wages and reduced
a loss instead of a profit.
2,237 boils took place, producing
kilos dry pulp, of which 1,143,892
were sold for M276,384. The sulphite
at Porschendorf are dissatisfied, as
they had heavy repairs, and a consequently
smaller production. The Pirna Sulphite
Factory reports that the slackness experienced in 1891 continued up to 1892. Sales
were made only at falling prices; some new
relations were opened with Great Britain.
Then a sudden change took place; the
cholera epidemic induced the United States
(N.A.) to prohibit the importation of rags,
thus compelling the American paper mills to
buy better class sulphite, which caused an
increased demand and higher prices. Improved bleach arrangements and a more
perfect production generally gave upon the
whole a better result than the previous ye
A desire is expressed for a drawback on th
duties on wood.

OWING to the persistent drought and th
consequent high price of straw, the pape
makers in the neighbourhood of Lyons ha
decided to raise the price of their stra
paper to the extent of three francs per 10
kilos, or about 1s. 3d. per cwt.

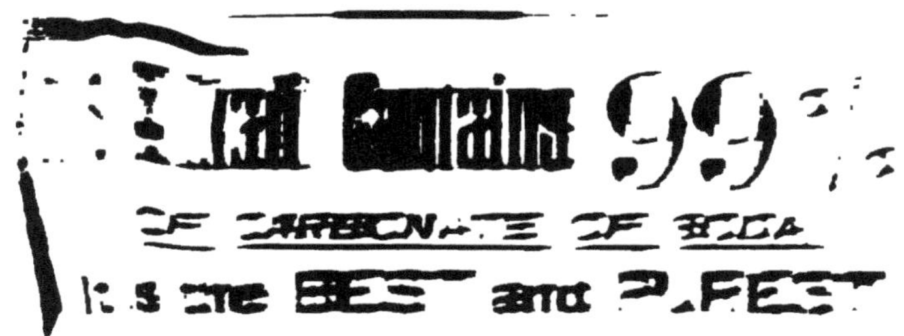

COLOURS.

LAST MONTH'S PAPER TRADE.

Imports, Re-Exports, and Exports.

TOTAL IMPORTS.

Printings and Writings	1893	39,313 cwts	£41,702
	1892	32,412 ,,	37,811
	1891	21,587 ,,	32,517
Other Kinds	1893	230,948 cwts	£173,537
	1892	205,899 ,,	158,140
	1891	181,916 ,,	134,983

From GERMANY.

Printings and Writings	1893	6,650 cwts	£6,643
	1892	13,600 ,,	15,147
	1891	7,632 ,,	10,369
Other Kinds	1893	44,872 cwts	£39,904
	1892	47,640 ,,	44,584
	1891	54,134 ,,	46,008

From BELGIUM.

Printings and Writings	1893	7,047 cwts	£9,081
	1892	4,898 ,,	6,633
	1891	6,102 ,,	7,648
Other Kinds	1893	13,087 cwts	£18,112
	1892	10,375 ,,	15,861
	1891	12,074 ,,	16,571

From HOLLAND.

Printings and Writings	1893	4,959 cwts	£6,841
	1892	4,479 ,,	5,069
	1891	3,353 ,,	5,905
Other Kinds	1893	113,111 cwts	£59,013
	1892	89,373 ,,	46,509
	1891	71,085 ,,	34,337

From SWEDEN.

Printings and Writings	1893	8,048 cwts	£7,601
	1892	4,740 ,,	4,889
	1891	3,727 ,,	3,616

("Other Kinds" are not tabulated).

From FRANCE.

Other Kinds	1893	2,700 cwts	£6,384
	1892	4,095 ,,	7,486
	1891	3,108 ,,	8,352

From OTHER COUNTRIES.

Printings and Writings	1893	12,609 cwts	£11,536
	1892	4,620 ,,	6,073
	1891	3,713 ,,	4,979
Other Kinds	1893	57,178 cwts	£50,124
	1892	54,416 ,,	43,700
	1891	41,515 ,,	29,715

TOTAL RE-EXPORTS.

Printings and Writings	1893	1,828 cwts	£2,187
	1892	1,546 ,,	1,761
	1891	1,308 ,,	1,413
Other Kinds	1893	2,496 cwts	£2,150
	1892	6,161 ,,	5,330
	1891	9,305 ,,	6,914

TOTAL EXPORTS.

Printings and Writings	1893	52,080 cwts	£82,317
	1892	57,834 ,,	93,635
	1891	54,825 ,,	91,816
Other Kinds	1893	12,987 cwts	£21,835
	1892	16,753 ,,	26,774
	1891	19,333 ,,	30,243

To FRANCE.

Printings and Writings	1893	2,976 cwts	£5,176
	1892	4,984 ,,	8,221
	1891	3,146 ,,	5,603
Other Kinds	1893	642 cwts	£3,076
	1892	645 ,,	3,045
	1891	989 ,,	4,010

To the UNITED STATES.

Printings and Writings	1893	673 cwts	£1,960
	1892	417 ,,	1,274
	1891	940 ,,	3,158
Other Kinds	1893	660 cwts	£2,175
	1892	883 ,,	2,821
	1891	1,014 ,,	3,218

To SOUTH AFRICA.

Printings and Writings	1893	3,124 cwts	£5,418
	1892	2,794 ,,	5,158
	1891	2,173 ,,	4,635
Other Kinds	1893	2,829 cwts	£2,785
	1892	2,210 ,,	2,405
	1891	2,456 ,,	2,388

To the EAST INDIES.

Printings and Writings	1893	7,283 cwts	£12,071
	1892	7,525 ,,	14,029
	1891	6,627 ,,	11,740
Other Kinds	1893	693 cwts	£1,348
	1892	1,527 ,,	2,673
	1891	2,092 ,,	2,853

To AUSTRALASIA.

Printings and Writings	1893	23,989 cwts	£31,400
	1892	30,209 ,,	42,514
	1891	29,302 ,,	48,525
Other Kinds	1893	4,305 cwts	£5,209
	1892	7,716 ,,	8,596
	1891	8,942 ,,	10,615

To BRITISH NORTH AMERICA

Printings and Writings	1893	2,971 cwts	£5,415
	1892	3,221 ,,	5,423
	1891	3,355 ,,	5,826
Other Kinds	1893	256 cwts	£600
	1892	288 ,,	702
	1891	76 ,,	178

To OTHER COUNTRIES.

Printings and Writings	1893	11,064 cwts	£20,847
	1892	8,684 ,,	17,016
	1891	9,282 ,,	17,329
Other Kinds	1893	3,602 cwts	£6,642
	1892	3,484 ,,	6,532
	1891	3,764 ,,	6,981

TOTALS FOR JAN.-AUGUST.

	Year	Quantity	Value
Imports..	1893	1,877,961 cwts	£1,512,720
	1892	1,832,187 ,,	1,533,948
	1891	1,653,075 ,,	1,366,'09
Re-Exports	1893	53,895 cwts	£49,242
	1892	59,389 ,,	57,227
	1891	68,137 ,,	60,646
Exports..	1893	567,066 cwts	£896,038
	1892	591,823 ,,	967,221
	1891	614,566 ,,	1,012,044

RAW MATERIALS.

IMPORTS AND EXPORTS FOR AUGUST.

EXPORTS.

	Year	Quantity	Value
Alkali ...	1893	447,084 cwts	£147,332
	1892	500,228 ,,	176,474
	1891	428,053 ,,	158,344

	1891.	1892.	1893.
Russia	£2,504	£7,645	£16,388
Sweden and Norway ...	4,013	2,542	3,947
Germany	2,006	4,219	6,858
Holland	1,864	2,284	2,105
France	1,014	824	1,654
Spain and Canaries	11,204	9,591	8,799
Italy	6,486	8,428	7.931
United States...	84,883	97,878	62,655
Australasia	6,106	7,661	3,357
British North America ...	8,240	6,066	5,988
Other countries	28,011	29,336	27,652

	Year	Quantity	Value
Bleaching Materials	1893	87,050 cwts	£35,781
	1892	150,624 ,,	59,807
	1891	114,739 ,,	39,615

	1891.	1892.	1893.
United States...	£26,147	£33,578	£19,440
Other Countries	13,468	26,229	16,341

	Year	Quantity	Value
Rags ...	1893	3,318 tons	£19,638
	1892	4,054 ,,	26,666
	1891	3,799 ,,	26,689

IMPORTS.

	Year	Quantity	Value
Alkali ...	1893	9,612 cwts	£8,103
	1892	5,639 ,,	3,553
	1891	6,579 ,,	4,120
Esparto	1893	15,130 tons	£67,481
	1892	18,333 ,,	88,969
	1891	19,114 ,,	91,155

	1891.	18 2.	1893.
Spain	£31,070	£28,974	£29,329
Algeria	37,226	29,801	17,762
Other Countries	22,859	30,194	20,390

	Year	Quantity	Value
Wood Pulp	1893	16,731 tons	£98,289
	1892	15,101 ,,	80,714
	1891	15,155 ,,	78,017

	1891.	1892.	1893.
Norway	£38,820	£44,485	£44,250
Other Countries	39,197	36,229	54,039

	Year	Quantity	Value
Rags ...	1893	1,145 tons	£11,297
	1892	2,071 ,,	21,120
	1891	3,322 ,,	33,745

TOTALS FOR JAN.-AUGUST.

EXPORTS.

	Year	Quantity	Value
Alkali ...	1893	4,183,545 cwts	£1,363,253
	1892	3,604,513 ,,	1,329,455
	1891	3,944,105 ,,	1,480,782
Bleaching Materials	1893	1,020,140 cwts	£423,654
	1892	932,148 ,,	370,248
	1891	973,606 ,,	329,783
Rags ...	1893	38,617 tons	£277,889
	1892	35,229 ,,	242,006
	1891	31,927 ,,	230,999

IMPORTS.

	Year	Quantity	Value
Alkali ..	1893	53,513 cwts	£48,129
	1892	34,357 ,,	25,146
	1891	53,087 ,,	31,678
Esparto	1893	133,995 tons	£633,166
	1892	146,056 ,,	691,583
	1891	158,600 ,,	762,394
Wood Pulp	1893	129,481 tons	£709,735
	1892	120,437 ,,	601,027
	1891	98,016 ,,	520,546
Rags ...	1893	15,287 tons	£146,710
	1892	20,688 ,,	194,802
	1801	21,198 ,,	203,779

EXPORTS OF PAPER HANGINGS.

	Year	Quantity	Value
August ...	1893	3,561 cwts	£8,929
	1892	4,485 ,,	10,750
	1891	4,664 ,,	11,720
January to August ...	1893	41,448 cwts	£103,427
	1892	43,758 ,,	112,169
	1891	40,451 ,,	127,855

AN annual report recently issued states that German mills making paper free from ground wood maintained a normal position. The prices of the manufactured articles as well as raw materials remained generally the same as last year, though half a million meter cwt. of chemical pulp and straw pulp were exported. The exportation has increased satisfactorily, and will no doubt still further expand as soon as the political, financial and social conditions of South America improve. The exportation of blotting, tissue, fancy and photographic paper was without material fluctuation. In straw paper a falling off took place of 7,300 meter cwt. in millboards, about 10,000 meter cwt., in glazed, and leather boards about 750 meter cwt. Glazed packing papers were exported more largely, the increase, compared with the previous year, being 11,000 meter cwt.; writings and printings showed an increase of 47,000 meter cwt.; other kinds (not specified) 1,000 meter cwt. Ground wood pulp was imported in 1891 to the extent of 64,000 meter cwt., and in 1892, 134,000 meter cwt., or 70,000 meter cwt. more in consequence of the continued drought in the second half of 1892.

[illegible] —The barque "Henry K. Lauchburg" cleared from Bangor, Me., for Fleetwood, England, on August [illegible] carrying a full cargo of pulp from the Penobscot Pulp and Paper Company's mill at Veazie and the one at [illegible].

Paper Exports at New York for the week reported upon were:—

Australasia	[illegible] pkgs.	[illegible]	[illegible] cases
London	[illegible] cases	[illegible]	case
B. West Indies	[illegible] pkgs.	[illegible]	[illegible] pkgs.
Liverpool	[illegible] cases		

The buildings of the Raquette River Paper Company, Potsdam, N.Y., include a paper mill, a pulp mill, and a sulphite fibre mill. The main building is 56 by 200 feet, two storeys; the machine room is 36 by 180 feet, one storey, with basement; the boiler house is 35 by 65 feet; the sulphite fibre mill is 40 by 111 feet, its centre being 60 feet high; this mill contains two upright digesters built in Dayton, Ohio, which are 10 by 32 feet each. All of the acid plant, sulphite blowers, gas coolers, tanks, &c., are sufficient for a 10 ton sulphite mill. The whole outfit complete was furnished by Messrs. Friend and Stebbins, of West Carrolton, Ohio. In one end of the main building is situated the wash room, which contains a large knotting machine, with several hundred feet of settling troughs, at the end of which is located a large stuff chest, with washers on top to keep the pulp of the right consistency to go to the wet machines, two in number, made by the Bagley and Sewall Company, of Watertown, N.Y. There is also a refining engine, through which the fibre is passed. The sulphite mill is run by water power, which was formerly used for the machine, and the company has just started a new 100 h.p. high speed automatic engine, made by the Watertown Steam Engine Company, the first of the kind which has ever been put on a paper machine, and which the company says has started off with success, and promises to be a "dandy" for this business. The wood chipper was furnished by Messrs. Friend and Stebbins along with the blower for blowing chips. The former was made by the Holyoke Machine Company, and the latter was made by the Sturtevant Company. The paper mill is running well, and also the ground wood mill. Two new 125 h.p. boilers have been started; these were furnished by the Watertown Steam Engine Company, and are rigged with the Brightman stoker, which is so constructed that it feeds the edgings (used for fuel) into the furnace automatically, which secures an even fire and an even pressure of steam. While most of the streams around the country have been suffering with low [illegible]ter, this company has had considerably [illegible] than it could use right along. The [illegible]pany is officered by men of excellent [illegible] judgment and financial standing. Mr. [illegible] A. [illegible], who has done so much towards the organization, construction and equipment, now becomes superintendent of operations.

The United Paper Mills Co., in Copenhagen give [illegible] per cent. dividend for last year, and have placed [illegible] Kr. into the reserve fund.

The Paper Mills at [illegible], o/Rhine, have made extensive alterations and put up additional machinery, among which a steam engine of 120-h.p., several boilers, engines and edge runners will enable these mills to work as specialities, cellulose packing, manilla and other packing papers. The steam engine was supplied by Gebrüder Sulzer, the boilers by Wagner and Co. in Cothen, and other machinery by the firm J. W. Erkens, in Düren.

A Rare Jubilee.—Herr Chr. Drewsen, the owner of the Strandmöllen paper works, near Copenhagen, celebrated on the 30th August, his 90th birthday, and at the same time the 200th anniversary of the opening of these papermills, in which year the ancestors of the present Drewsen family came from Celle, in Germany. The United Papermills, to which the Strandmöllen belong, had erected a bust of Herr Chr. Drewsen, as an acknowledgment of his distinguished merits for the extension of the Danish paper industry. This was also the 71st wedding day, which the old gentleman spent in good health with his wife.

Calculations for the Paper Trade.—Under the title of "Einige ins Papierfach schlagende Berechnungen," Herr Jos Baudisch has published a useful little pamphlet. The Germans have lately introduced a uniform ream of 1,000 sheets, which, with the decimal weights and measures, make it very easy to find price or weight per ream and per sheet without any troublesome calculations. The object of the pamphlet is to show how in the simplest and easiest way the old fashioned reams of 480, 500, etc., sheets can be expressed in the new style. Another uniform rule in the fatherland is to give the weight of paper by the square meter of the sheet in grammes, and some of these tables give the comparative weights in various sizes. There are also instructions how to calculate the production of a paper machine, and also the speed of the machine necessary to produce a certain quantity. All these calculations are very useful and interesting to buyers in the foreign markets, but of course as long as we keep our inconvenient weights and measures we shall not be able to use these tables for any calculations requisite in this country.

PULP FOR ENGLAND.—The barque "Henry K. Litchfield" cleared from Bangor, M for Fleetwood, England, on August carrying a full cargo of pulp from the Pen scot Pulp and Paper Company's n Venzie and the one at Solon.

PAPER EXPORTS at New York fo week reported upon were:—

Australasia	... 127 pkgs	B. Guiana .	
London ...	... 91 cases	B. South Afr	
B. West Indies	... 357 pkgs	Hull...	
Liverpool ...	... 15 cases		

THE buildings of the Rac Paper Company, Potsdam, N.Y paper mill, a pulp mill, and a mill. The main building is two storeys; the machine room feet, one storey, with basem house is 35 by 65 feet; th is 40 by 111 feet, its centr this mill contains two n

which the 6 is run by wa used for the just start matic Steam which and w with for mi w

bus Mr.

URY, near

MANCHESTER

LL'S PATENT PERFECTING ENGINE

NUTTALL'S IM

ALL MATERIALS USED
IN
ACTURE OF PAPER.

ER & SONS,

General Metal Wor

DENNY, N.B. Telegrams: "HUNTER—DEN

FOR PAPER MILLS

ZINC PIPES.

VES & STOP
GATES.

The above Pipes can be erected by workmen, if so desired.

TED & COUNTER-
ZINC PLATES.

Hydraulic Presses,

Holes from No. 18

INFUSERS FOR ANY SIZE,

Made to any dimensions, with Cast Iron piece, and Copper or Galvanized Iron Casi with Steam Connections and Draw-off

GALVANIZED IRON BOX OR TRUCKS,

Fitted with Wheels and Axles, for conveying from and to different departments in Mills, can be so fixed as to suit any gauge of rails, hoist, where such are used, or to allow the turned easily, and in small space, on any kind

COPPER HAND-LADLES, SHO
BUCKETS, STARCH VESSELS,
&c., &c.

This Machine
It is Equally

of Copper and Brass Work, Brass, Bronze, and White Metal Castings, &c.
Every Description of General Plumber Work.

PAPER MILLS are USED by Many of the PRINCIPAL PAPERMAKERS in United Kingdom, and also in several of our Colonies and other Foreign Countries.

and Further Particulars Given for any of the above.

sons were taken into partnership about three years ago, and they will now conduct the business, which it may be stated is the oldest of the kind in Glasgow, and one of the oldest in Scotland. The deceased was highly respected by his employees, and his thorough upright character was the admiration of all who knew him. His many kindly acts, performed in a quiet and unostentatious manner, will long be remembered by those benefited thereby.

MR. ALDERMAN MARSDEN.

[illegible] regret to announce the sudden death [illegible] Alderman Marsden, of Cliffe-house, Monk [illegible] head of the firm of Charles Marsden [illegible] Sons, paper manufacturers, of Dearne Works, Barnsley; Calder Grove, Wakefield; [illegible] Works, Sheffield; and Tamworth. He was 62 years of age, and a [illegible]. He [illegible] a West Riding Magistrate, and held many local public offices. On the West Riding Bench assembling at Barnsley on Wednesday, the sad intelligence was communicated that Alderman Marsden had been found dead in bed.

In regard to the Employers' Liability B[illegible] the chief difficulty, say the *Times*, [illegible] to be raised by supporters of the Government in connection with the question of contracting out. [illegible] the good deal [illegible] the [illegible] Opposition [illegible] the House of Lords into conflict with the Lower Chamber.

MR. [illegible] [illegible]

MR. W[illegible] [illegible]

WILLIAM WILSON.

[illegible] We record the death [illegible] of Lilybank Boiler [illegible]. He died on the 6th [illegible] 24, Princes-square, [Glasgow]. He was born in [the] year 1830, and early in life was [illegible] At Glasgow, where he [illegible] had to keep himself on [illegible] per week, and he even saved [illegible]. After years of self-[illegible] at the age of 22, started in [illegible] boiler maker in [illegible] known as [illegible] Works, where success [illegible] year 18[illegible] he retired and set [illegible]. He then [illegible] and [illegible] William Wilson [illegible]

[illegible] Paper Trade Review Office,
58, Shoe Lane, London, E.C.
September 14, 1893.

Trade Notes.

[illegible] Strike.—At conferences of the [illegible] and Lancashire miners, held at [illegible] and Manchester on Wednesday, [illegible] the recent ballots was reported, [illegible] the men to be practically unani[illegible] resistance to a reduction of wages [illegible] arbitration, while only small minori[illegible] in favour of returning to work, [illegible] a settlement at the old rate of wages. [illegible] the distress among the colliers [illegible] families is increasing. The cost of [illegible] strike in South Wales is estimated at a [illegible] sterling.

[illegible] Accident.—A sad accident occurred [illegible] named John Taggart at the [illegible] Paper Mill, Feniscowles, near Black[illegible] on Monday night, the 11th inst. Tag[illegible] had allowed one of the beating engines [illegible] "run over" on to the driving belt, and to [illegible] the belt from coming off the pulley, [illegible] stepped down into the strap race, and [illegible] against the driving pulley, which [illegible] him against the wall with great [illegible]. He was got up immediately, but [illegible] poor fellow only lived a few minutes. He [illegible] a large family.

[illegible] Bruc, Lysaker, near Chris[illegible].—This mill, which was destroyed by [illegible] the [illegible] April last, has been rebuilt, [illegible] is now in running order. There [illegible] machine, [illegible]-in. wide, for the [illegible] better sorts of news; two one[illegible], [illegible] in. wide, for the pro[illegible] sulphite paper; and there is also [illegible], 84-in. wide, supplied by [illegible] Limited, Edinburgh. Mr. [illegible], the managing director, is [illegible] commended for his enterprise [illegible] mill into working order with[illegible] after the occurrence of [illegible] fire.

[illegible] of Messrs Gunter and [illegible] meeting of the creditors [illegible] held on Wednesday last, [illegible]. It will be remembered that [illegible] the first meeting (held on [illegible]) that an offer of 2s. in [illegible] made, in two instalments [illegible] the best offer that the [illegible] would allow. This [illegible] accepted, and the adjourn[illegible] in order to trace the where[illegible] received and monies paid [illegible]. At the adjourned [illegible] stated that the money [illegible] away in the ordinary [illegible] and the accountant [illegible] been carefully through [illegible] successfully traced the [illegible]. Mr. Gibson then [illegible] an offer of 2s. 6d. [illegible] as follows: 1s. to be paid 14 days after the execution of a deed of composition, 1s. in twelve months after the execution, and another 6d. eighteen months after such execution. Under this arrangement Mr. Gunter was to be released of his liabilities, and would recommence business, Messrs. Gardner and Co. looking after his books on behalf of the creditors, and Mr. Gunter undertook not to draw more than £5 per week during such period. After a discussion upon this offer, those present, with the exception of one creditor, decided not to sign the resolution embodying the offer until they had consulted their firms upon the advisability of so doing. The proceedings then terminated.

Judd's Paper and Stationery Co., Lim.—This company has recently been registered with a nominal capital of £10,000, divided into 2,000 shares of £5, to acquire the goodwill of the business carried on at 17, Charterhouse-buildings, Aldersgate-street, London, under the style or firm of Judd, Lindsay and Company, and to acquire or undertake the whole or any of the assets of the proprietor or proprietors of the business, or in connection therewith; also to enter into and carry into effect an agreement between Frederick Charles Matusch of the one part, and the company of the other part, dated 31st August, 1893, and to carry on the business of publishers, booksellers, printers, bookbinders, typefounders, lithographers, papermakers, stationers, fancy stationers, paper merchants and importers, toy dealers, bon-bon manufacturers, and dealers in confectioners' sundries, advertising agents, or to establish and maintain in London or elsewhere circulating libraries, and any other business (manufacturing or otherwise) which may be of a character similar or analogous to the above, or which may seem to the company to be capable of being carried on conveniently in connection with any of its objects, or calculated (directly or indirectly) to render productive or enhance the value of any of its property or rights, &c., &c., &c. The names of the first subscribers to the articles of association (who hold one share each) are:—Alexander Brown, 9, Warwick-court, W.C., patent agent; Louis Schramm, electrical engineer, 1, Parkville-road, Fulham, S.W.; Francis Jefferys, music publisher, 67, Berners-street, London, W.; Charles Henry Sheard, music publisher, 192, High Holborn, W.C.; Leonard Howell, 301, King's-road, Chelsea, S.W.; Frank Morgan, publisher, 48, Whitcombe-street, Cockspur-street, W., and Albert Heron, watchmaker and jeweller, 12, Brondesbury-road, Kilburn, N. There are not to be more than seven nor less than three directors, and a directors qualification is the holding of shares of the value of £100; and £1 1s. is paid as remuneration for each directors meeting. The memorandum of association does not give the names of any officials of the company, whose registered offices are at 17, Charterhouse-buildings, Clerkenwell-road, E.C.

Mr. G. Nicholson, we are glad to learn, has partially recovered from a long and serious illness which followed a severe accident. He has now resumed business as a rag and waste paper merchant under the style of G. Nicholson and Co., having taken into partnership Mr. J. F. Greller and Mr. W. Badger, who were with the late firm of Messrs. Jacob and Nicholson. Mr. Nicholson has had forty years experience in the trade, and his thorough knowledge of the business will no doubt lead to a continuance of that support accorded to him in the past. The address of the firm is Riley-street, Bermondsey, S.E.

FIRE AT A LONDON RAG WAREHOUSE.—A fire broke out on the premises of Mr. R. Hough, London-street, Ratcliffe, doing considerable damage to the second floor of the large rag warehouse. Automatic sprinklers, however, materially aided the firemen in the work of extinction.

PRESENTATION TO MR. THOMAS SQUIRES.—On Saturday evening last, the members of the Darwen and district branch of the National Union of Paper Mill Workers, and a few friends from the Fenniscowles branch, met at the Crown Hotel for the purpose of making a presentation to Mr. Thomas Squires, of Newton-le-Willows. After full justice had been done to an excellent meat tea, Mr. John Norris, who presided, referred to the excellent services rendered by Mr. Squires in his late capacity of president of the Union. Mr. Haworth, the branch treasurer, said he had pleasure in asking Mr. Squires to accept a handsome timepiece as a testimony of their appreciation. The recipient suitably responded. Various speeches were then given pointing out the benefits to be derived from membership, and a comparison made of their present position with that of former years. Subsequent proceedings included singing and dancing.

THE ABBEY PAPER MILL ANNUAL EXCURSION.—On Saturday last, through the kindness of Messrs. Grosvenor, Chater and Co., Limited, the employees at the Abbey Paper Mill, Greenfield, were given their annual trip. The place decided upon to visit was Liverpool, and great numbers availed themselves of the opportunity of joining the excursion. Among the attractions at Liverpool was notably the opening of the Everton football season with their first league match. The train left Holywell Station at about 7.15 being crowded with excursionists. The journey proved to be a most enjoyable one, the railway officials having made excellent arrangements, as is testified by the fact that the train steamed up at Lime-street station at 9.30, completing the journey in two hours. The return journey was commenced at [illegible], and the passengers were enabled to alight at the Holywell Station at about 12.5 a.m., fully satisfied with the long day's outing. Mr. Petrie, the manager of the Paper Mill, accompanied the excursion, and made every provision for the comfort of the workpeople under his charge.

FATHER KILLED, SON INJURED.—Whilst a man named Hemsley was taking off a band from machinery at the Chu[illegible] paper mill, Ashford, on Monday night, the pole he was using penetrated his chest, causing immediate death. His son was seriously injured in another part of the building.

CHINESE PAPER TRADE.—Paper was exported from Swatow in 1890 to the value of £6[illegible] and during the previous year £[illegible]. From P[illegible] paper second quality exported in 1891 was valued at £[illegible] and in 1890 £[illegible]. The most valuable item is that of [illegible] the [illegible] of playing cards. It may be of interest to note that taking the Haikwan tael at [illegible], these last are valued at an average of a little over 2d. per lb.

THE AMERICAN PAPER MANUFACTURERS' ASSOCIATION.—Mr. Wm. T. Barker, secretary of the American Paper Manufacturers' Association, has issued official notice of the postponement of the annual convention which was to have been held in Chicago early in September. This has been brought about by promises to attend being under a dozen. Papermakers find it necessary owing to depression in trade, not to leave their business.

THE IMPORTATION OF RAGS.

Further questions were asked in the House of Commons on Thursday last week by Mr. Macdona in reference to the importation of rags. He asked the President of the Local Government Board whether cholera was now prevalent in Smyrna, and whether he was aware that one of the largest importers of rags in England had received a telegram, dated September 2nd, offering 500 bales of cotton rags to be delivered forthwith in Liverpool, and if this were so, what steps the Government proposed to take to prevent so serious a risk and danger to the lives of so largely a populated place as Liverpool.

Mr. H. FOWLER replied that he was not aware that cholera was prevalent at Smyrna. The medical officer of health of Liverpool had informed the medical department of the Local Government Board that no difficulty had arisen there in connection with the regulations as to the importation of rags packed in bales and imported as merchandise, and no difficulty was anticipated by him. The hon. member on September 1st asked him whether he was aware that there were lying in the wharves at Lo[illegible] over 300 tons of rags imported from cholera-stricken places in Europe which the rag merchants of London refused to touch or take from the fear of introducing cholera. As he was unable to obtain any information which supported this statement in the question, the hon. member subsequently informed him that the 300 tons of rags were then lying at [illegible] Wharf, London-bridge. An inspector of the Local Government Board immediately [illegible] that wharf, but found no rags there, and he was assured by the superintendent that there had not

WORLD'S PAPER TRADE REVIEW OFFICE,
58, SHOE LANE, LONDON, E.C.,
SEPTEMBER 14, 189[illegible]

TRADE NOTES

THE COAL CRISIS.—At conference [illegible] Yorkshire and Lancashire miner[illegible] Barnsley and Manchester [illegible] the result of the recent ballot [illegible] and showed the men to be pra[illegible] mous in resistance to a reduc[illegible] and to arbitration, while only [illegible] ties are in favour of retu[illegible] pending a settlement at the [illegible] Meanwhile the distress an[illegible] and their families is incre[illegible] the strike in South Wales [illegible] million sterling.

[illegible] FRIDAY
[illegible]ON, E.C.
[illegible] 15, 1893.

FATAL ACCIDENT.—A s[illegible] to a beaterman named [illegible] Star Paper Mill, Fe[illegible] burn, on Monday ni[illegible] gart had allowed one [illegible] to "run over" on to th[illegible] prevent the belt from [illegible] he stepped down [illegible] slipped against th[illegible] threw him agai[illegible] violence. He w[illegible] the poor fellow o[illegible] leaves a large fa[illegible]

GRANFOS B[illegible] TIANIA.—This [illegible] fire on the 2[illegible] and the plan[illegible] is a Fourdri[illegible] cellulose an[illegible] cylinder m[illegible] duction of [illegible] a ten-roll [illegible] Messrs. I[illegible] O. Tol[illegible] certain[illegible] in gett[illegible] in so s[illegible] such [illegible]

Th[illegible] Co. in t[illegible] the [illegible] in [illegible] th[illegible] tl[illegible]

[illegible] processes now be-[illegible] [illegible] discussed in [illegible] journals devoted to [illegible] occasionally we [illegible] several of our [illegible] teaching, in their [illegible] importance to the [illegible] electrolysis. We may [illegible] Professor Lunge, of [illegible] greatest living authorities [illegible] confirms our views. [illegible] experiments and data [illegible] the notice of public [illegible] and command the [illegible] very wide circle. Pro-[illegible] to his pioneering work [illegible] developments, has a recog-[illegible] amongst the wealthy chemical [illegible] Europe, therefore more [illegible] attention will, no doubt, be [illegible] to his connection, in con-[illegible] Mr. Lyte, with another enter-[illegible] Chemical and Electrolytic Syndi-[illegible] recently formed with a [illegible] capital of £30,000, in £5 shares, to [illegible] patents from Professor Lunge [illegible] connected with the manufac-[illegible] bleaching powder, caustic soda, &c. [illegible] that these new patents may [illegible] alter the value of the work done [illegible] country by Greenwood, Holland, [illegible]son, Andreoli and others, not forget-[illegible] Sueur in America, and Hermite in [illegible]

[illegible] the heading of "Much Ado About [illegible] we referred to the criticism on the [illegible] electrolytic process, which ap-[illegible] "Necessary Correction" in the [illegible] *Trade Journal*, edited by Mr. [illegible] Davis. The whole "fable" was based upon the omission of a cypher (which occurred through a printer's error), in a paragraphic reference in these pages to certain calculations as to cost of plant set forth by the inventor. It did not serve the purpose of the *Chemical Trade Journal* to extract from the article which appeared in the REVIEW about a month previous to the paragraph containing the printer's error. The omission, however, was apparent to most of our readers, and particularly to those who have taken a lively interest in the question of electrolysis. It is surprising that the *Chemical Trade Journal* has not had the good grace up to the present to admit that the remarks published in its columns were based upon a wrong foundation. We also understand that the patentee of the process criticised wrote a letter to the paper in question mildly pointing out that the conclusions were erroneous, but for some reason the letter has not had any publicity. We find that one of our London contemporaries has reprinted the article from the *Chemical Trade Journal*, but we hope, in justice to its readers, and in the interests of truth and common honesty, that reference will be made to the reply under "Much Ado About Nothing," published in No. 5, Vol. XX., of the WORLD'S PAPER TRADE REVIEW (August 4th), which the *Chemical Trade Journal* for some reason of its own has not thought proper to notice.

DURING the past six weeks of brig[illegible] weather papermakers, in common wi[illegible] others, have more or less been on the holid[illegible] track. Holidays, perhaps, this year ha[illegible] with many people been less enjoyable th[illegible] usual, owing to the stringency of mone[illegible] and the difficulty of meeting engagement[illegible] and in collecting monies due. There is, ho[illegible] ever, a gleam of sunshine which brighte[illegible] the outlook of the future, inasmuch as the[illegible] must be a very large amount of capital ly[illegible] dormant, and which in the ordinary way [illegible] trade will surely be let loose upon legitim[illegible] industry. Therefore the present time is [illegible] as most men consider, a very risky one [illegible] the development of new industries, but [illegible] the contrary it is a time when honest w[illegible] may well be taken in hand by though[illegible] and experienced capitalists, always pro[illegible] ing they are not too anxious to unduly w[illegible] the backbone of any undertaking.

IN days of old the spread of education [illegible] greatly handicapped in various ways, [illegible] with the growth of knowledge amon[illegible]

were gradually swept away. Nowadays the producers of wretched scrappy magazines tax manufacturers of paper by introducing special clauses in regard to purchases, which ought never to be entertained for one moment. The result is that papermakers are taxed in a way that is iniquitous and thoroughly unsound as a commercial policy, and to those who sin in this way, by submitting to conditions of contract, as well as novel contingencies respecting printing and "averages," etc., we say—halt!

THE importations of printings last month, compared with August, 1892, were 6,[illegible] cwts. and £3,[illegible] higher: other kinds show an advance of 25,0[illegible] cwts. and £15,3[illegible]. The exportation of paper of all descriptions decreased 10,444 cwts., and in value £25,[illegible]. Relative total values:—

	Imports.	Re-Exports.	Exports.
August, 1893	£[illegible]	£[illegible]	£1[illegible]
— 1892	1[illegible]	[illegible]	1[illegible]
— 189[illegible]	1[illegible]	[illegible]	1[illegible]
Jan.-Aug. 1893	£[illegible]	£[illegible]	£[illegible]
— 1892	[illegible]	[illegible]	[illegible]
— 189[illegible]	1,[illegible]	[illegible]	1,[illegible]

COMPARING August trade with that of the corresponding month of last year it will be seen upon reference to the statistical compilation on page 4 that German paper supplies to the British market materially decreased, but arrivals from Belgium, Holland, and Sweden were of much higher value. British paper was in good request for South Africa, and an increased exportation of printings and writing was made to the States and in "other kinds" to France. To Australasia and East Indies there was a heavy drop.

IN raw materials, wood pulp showed an increased importation during the month of August compared with the corresponding period of the preceding year. The difference in quantity was 6[illegible] tons, and in value £17,575. Esparto decreased 3,[illegible] tons and £21,488; linen and cotton rags, [illegible] tons and £9,832. There was an increase of 3,[illegible] cwts. in the importation of alkali, and the value was £4,550 higher. The exports of alkali show a decrease of 53,[illegible] cwts. and £2[illegible]; and bleaching materials 6[illegible] cwts. and £24,026. The exports of rags decreased 7[illegible] tons and £7,028.

RAGS packed in bales and imported as merchandise are not subject to any restrictions under cholera regulations. The term "merchandise," however, being open to misconstruction, a general order [illegible] has been issued, stating that rags which are to be considered as included in the term are "rags compressed by hydraulic force, transported as wholesale merchandise, in bales surrounded by iron bands, and with marks and numbers showing their origin, and accepted as such by the authorities of the country of destination."

FROM a table, prepared by Messrs. Howard, Lockwood and Co., of New York, for submission to the annual meeting of the American Papermakers' Association, the daily capacity not production of the paper mills of the United States now running is [illegible] lbs., an increase of [illegible] lbs. compared with the previous year. The percentage of gain since 1881 is stated to be [illegible] per cent.

The outlook for trade brightens slowly but surely. The almost unprecedented high official Bank rate of 5 per cent. in September is explainable by the fact that very large shipments of gold from Adelaide, Australia, cabled as being for London use, have been surreptitiously diverted en route for re-shipment to the United States, where the terrible stringency of money and credit is ten-fold worse than in Europe, and consequently the bullion dealers find there an immediately more profitable market, money in gold earning as much as [illegible] per cent. for temporary use. The remunerative nature of diverting gold is thus explained:—Two important banking institutions have purchased considerable shipments of gold from Australia, and have arranged for their delivery at Egyptian ports of call, with the results that shipments nominally made to London have never arrived here. A certain well-known private firm of exchange bankers has been engaged in the same business to a considerable extent. The remunerative nature of such a deal needs explanation. A in Australia is sending gold to his London office or agent, B in London, and occasion to send gold to Egypt, India, Malta, or Ceylon. If B can intercept the gold at the place where he requires it, he saves freight, insurance, and [illegible] while A's London representative, by selling the gold in transit and getting immediate payment therefor, gains the interest on the money for the time occupied by the passage between the port of [illegible] and London.

[illegible]

Printed and Published EVERY FRIDAY
AT 58, SHOE LANE, LONDON, E.C.,
By W. JOHN STONHILL.
ESTABLISHED 1878.

FRIDAY, SEPTEMBER 15, 189

THE various electrolytic process... fore the trade have been fully di... these pages, as well as in journals ... the chemical industry, and occ... have been taken to task by se... contemporaries for attaching ... opinion, too much importan... future possibilities of electrol... point out, however, that Pro... Zurich, one of the greatest ... in the alkali trade, conti... As is well known, his exp... frequently come under the ... bodies and institution... closest attention of a ... fessor Lunge, owing to ... and successful developmen... nised position amongst ... manufacturers of E... than ordinary atte... directed in respect to ... junction with Mr. Lyt... prise—the Chemi... cate, Limited ... nominal capital ... acquire certai... and Mr. Lyte, ... ture of bleach... It is possible ... materially al... in this coun... Richardson ... ting Le S... France.

... ESPARTO.

Importer	Port.
To order	Liverpool
J. Cormack	Leith
Love, Stewart & Co	Bo'ness

...AL WOOD PULPS.—SULPHITE con... firm, and prices of best qualities are well maintained. Users, however, seem reluctant to close contracts in the belief that quotations may fall later on. This view, however, is opposite to those of producers. SODA and SULPHATE pulps are steady.

Prices, ex steamer, London, Hull, Newcastle, Leith and Glasgow are nominally as follows:

		£	s.	d.		£	s.	d.
SULPHITE, Unbleached, Common		£10	15	0	to	11	0	0
,,	Superior	11	10	0	,,	12	10	0
,,	,, 50% moisture, d.w.	11	10	0	,,	12	2	6
,,	Extra	13	0	0	,,	14	0	0
,,	Bleached, moist					16	10	0
,,	Unbleached, English, del. Lancs. ...					10	15	0
,,	,, ,, No. 1, ex mills, Ldn.					10	10	0
,,	,, ,, No. 2, ,, ,,					9	15	0
SODA, Unbleached, Common ...		10	0	0	to	10	10	0
,,	,, Extra... ...	10	10	0	,,	11	0	0
,,	Half-Bleached	12	10	0	,,	14	0	0
SULPHATE, Unbleached, Common		10	10	0	,,	11	0	0
,,	Extra	11	0	0	,,	12	0	0
,,	Half-Bleached	13	10	0	,,	14	0	0
,,	Bleached	15	0	0	,,	16	0	0

MECHANICAL WOOD PULPS. — Reports from Scandinavia intimate a general firmness, and higher quotations are now on the market. MOIST PINE, for prompt delivery, is quoted at £3 5s. to £3 10s., and for next year's delivery, £2 17s. 6d. to £3. DRY PINE, for prompt delivery, £6 10s. to £7, and for next year's delivery, £6 to £6 2s. 6d. A good business is being negotiated for the supply of Scandinavian pulp to the German market. The sale of a few odd parcels is reported, but the quality cannot be relied upon. In several instances higher prices have been obtained.

WORLD'S PAPER TRADE REVIEW OFFICE,
58, SHOE LANE, LONDON, E.C.
SEPTEMBER 14, 1893.

MARKET REPORT

and RECORD of IMPORTS

Of Foreign Rags, Wood Pulp, Esparto, Paper, M[illegible] boards, Strawboards, &c., at the Ports of Lon[illegible] Liverpool, Southampton, Bristol, Hull, Fleetw[illegible] Middlesborough, Glasgow, Grangemouth, Gra[illegible] Dundee, Leith, Dover, Folkestone, and N[illegible] for the WEEK ENDING SEPTEMBER [illegible]

From SPECIAL Sources and Tel[illegible]

Telegrams—"STONHILL, LOND[illegible]"

CHEMICALS.—The market is [illegible] demand is not very brisk. The [illegible] fuel has caused works to [illegible] closed, and trade generally [illegible] been at a standstill had it [illegible] large stocks. BLEACHING [illegible] quoted at from £8 10s. to £8 [illegible] SODA (77 per cent.) at £11 [illegible] is easier. SODA CRYSTALS [illegible] £2 15s. SULPHUR is [illegible] enquiry at about £1 [illegible] AMMONIA has advanced [illegible]

Prices are nominal [illegible]

Alkali, 58%	tierces	[illegible]
" 58%	bags	[illegible]
58%		[illegible]
Alum (Ground),	tierces	[illegible]
" "	barrels	[illegible]
" "	tierces	[illegible]
" "	"	[illegible]
Alum (Lump)	"	[illegible]
" "	barrels	[illegible]
" "	tierces	[illegible]
" "	"	4/6
Alumina Sulphate		[illegible]
Aluminoferric		[illegible]
Alumina Cake		[illegible]
Alum [illegible]		[illegible]

[illegible] (Light) ...	6/0
[illegible] (Dark) ...	4/0
[illegible]	3/0
[illegible] Cottons ...	3/9
[illegible]p Strings (untr'd)	2/0
[illegible] House Cloths ...	5/0
[illegible] Bagging (solid)	3/6
" " (common)	2/6
NEW.	
White & Cream Linens	35/0
White Cuttings ...	22/0
Unbleached Cuttings	21/0
Print Cuttings ...	8/0

RAGS.—LONDON: Trade slack; stocks [illegible] heavy, and a better business [illegible] shortly.—BRISTOL: Very [illegible] MANCHESTER: Trade quiet; [illegible] steady.—EDINBURGH: There is practically no change in price, and the demand [illegible] of country rags is rather [illegible] DUBLIN: Market dull.

LONDON:

[illegible] White Cuttings	21/6	Canvas No. 1	15/6
[illegible]	20/6	" No. 2 ...	10/0-10/6
[illegible] (London)...	20/0	" No. 3	5/6
[illegible] (selected) ..	12/6	Mixed Rope	5/3
[illegible] (ordinary) ...	11/0	White Rope	6/6
[illegible] Seconds	3/6-4/0	White Manilla Rope	8/6
[illegible]	6/6-8/0	Coil Rope	8/6
[illegible] Thirds	1/9-2/0	Bagging...	1/6
Country do.	4/0-5/0	Gunny	3/6
Light Prints ..	7/0-8/0		

BRISTOL:

[illegible] ...	19/0	Clean Canvas ...	15/0
[illegible] ...	13/6	Second Do. ...	9/6-10/6
[illegible]	7/0-8/0	Light Prints ...	8/0
Thirds	3/6-4/0	Hemp Coil Rope	9/6-10/0
[illegible] bagging	3/6	Tarred Manilla	7/6

MANCHESTER:

[illegible] ...	15/0-16/0	Blues	7/0-7/6
[illegible] (best) ...	11/6-12/0	Bagging...	4/3-4/6
(ordinary)	10/6-11/0	" (common)	3/3-3/6
[illegible] ...	7/3-7/6	W. Manilla Rope	10/0-10/6
[illegible]	3/0-3/9	Surat Tares... ...	5/0-5/3

[illegible]

EDINBURGH:

[illegible]	17/0	Black C[illegible]	[illegible]
[illegible]	13/0	W. M[illegible]	[illegible]
[illegible]	14/0	Tarred [illegible]	[illegible]
[illegible]	8/0	Rope Ends	[illegible]
[illegible]	11/0	Bagging	[illegible]

[illegible] Waste Papers [illegible] keep [illegible]

[illegible] ...	1/3	Small Letters	[illegible]
[illegible]	2/6	Large "	— — [illegible]
[illegible] ...	3/6	Brown Paper	— — [illegible]
[illegible] ...	8/9	Light Browns	— — [illegible]
[illegible]	1/0	Books & Pamphlets	— — [illegible]
[illegible] Cuttings	3/6	Strawboard Cuttings	— [illegible]
[illegible]	3/0	Jacquards	— [illegible]
[illegible] News	2/0		— — [illegible]

For Export: 25/- per ton extra.

JUTE.—Cuttings are in request.

Good White	£16 0 to 17 0	Common ...	£10 [illegible] to 11 [illegible]
Good	15 0	Rejections...	[illegible]
Medium ..	0 " 13 0	Cuttings ...	£5 to [illegible]

COLOURS.—Trade dull.

Mineral Black ...	cwt.	3/0	Ultramarine (pure)	
do. superior ...	"	5/0	... cwt.	[illegible] to [illegible]
Pure Ivory Black	"	12/0	PASTE COLOURS with	
Ochre	"	3/0	60% of colour, as follows:—	
French J. C. Ochre	ton	55/0	Orange Pulp ... cwt.	[illegible]
Chrome (pure) ...	cwt.	40/0	Golden Yellow Pulp	[illegible]
Red Oxide	"	4/6	Lemon " ... cwt.	[illegible]
Umber, Devonshire	"	50/0	Prussian Yellow "	[illegible]
do. Turkish ...	"	40/0	Green (free of arsenic	[illegible]
Lamp Black ...		7/0-10/6	Paste Blue (20-25%)	
Cochineal	lb.	1/3-2/0	" —	[illegible]

SIZING.—Business quiet; values unaltered.

English Gelatines	per cwt.	70/0	to 140
Foreign "	"	70/0	" [illegible]
Fine Skin Glues	"	45/0	" [illegible]
Long Scotch Glues	"	45/0	" [illegible]
Common "	"	30/0	" 45
"Town" Glues	"	[illegible]	" [illegible]
"Bone" Glues	"	[illegible]	" [illegible]
Foreign Glues	"	23/0	" [illegible]
Bone Size	"	[illegible]	" [illegible]
Gelatine Size...	"	5/0	" [illegible]
Dry B.A. Pieces	"	31/6	" [illegible]
" English Pieces	"	24/0	" [illegible]
Wet " "	"	7/0	" [illegible]
" Sheep Pieces	"	[illegible]	" [illegible]
Buffalo Hide Shavings	"	[illegible]	" [illegible]
" Picker Waste	"	27/0	" [illegible]

ROSIN.—Trade is fairly good at former quotations.

	Strained.	E.	F.	G.	K.	W.G.	W.W.
Spot—	3/7½	4/0	4/3	4/6	6/6	9/6	[illegible]
To arrive—	3/2	3/5	3/6	3/7½	6/0	8/6	[illegible]

STARCH.—Maize shows an advance at [illegible] for Crisp, and £10 5s. for Powder.

F.o.r. London, less 2½%:

Maize—Crisp, £10 0/-; Powder, £10 5/-; Special £24 10/-
Farina—Prime, £10 10/-; B.K.M.F., £13 10/-

Delivered:

Rice—Special (in chests), £20 0/- (net); Crystal (in bags) £19 0/-; Granulated (in bags) £18 0/- less 2½%.
Dextrine—£16 0/- to £17.

MINERALS.—Business in CHINA CLAY h[illegible] been quiet of late, but there seems to be [illegible] better demand just now at previous quot[illegible]

[illegible] having carried [illegible] unchanged [illegible] carton- [illegible] PATENT HAR- [illegible]

Albarine, £3 del. mills.

Asbestos, best rock, £18 ; inferior grades, £12 to £15.

Asbestine Pulp, £4 5/- to £[illegible] c.i.f. London, Liverpool and Glasgow.

Barytes Carbonate, lump, [illegible]; [illegible] to [illegible].

Barytes Sulphate, "Angel White," No. 1 [illegible] No. 2 [illegible]. No. 3 [illegible]. Sommer's Brands Antwerp AP, [illegible]. BF [illegible]. AB, [illegible] BB [illegible] CB [illegible].

French and Italian Chalk (Sommer Brand, Antwerp) per ton in lots of 10 tons. Flower O [illegible] c.i.f. London [illegible] c.i.f. Liverpool [illegible] c.i.f. Hull ; Flower OO [illegible] and [illegible]. Flower OOO, [illegible] [illegible] [illegible]. Swan Brand [illegible], [illegible] and [illegible]. Blackwell's "Angel White" Brand and "Silvery," [illegible] to [illegible] prime quality, [illegible] to [illegible], and superfine, [illegible].

Bauxite (Irish Hill Quality), first lump, [illegible]; seconds [illegible]; thirds, [illegible]; ground, [illegible].

Pyrites non-cupreous, Liverpool, [illegible].

Carbonate of Lime (Sommer Brand) Antwerp. Prima 43/-, Seconda 37/-.

LIME.—Bleach Lime is quoted at about [illegible] per ton at works.

RUSSIAN RAGS

C.i.f. London, Hull, Newcastle [illegible]

SPFF	15/0	CC (Cotton [illegible]	
SPF	13/6	Jute I [illegible]	
FG	10/6	„ II	
LFB	9/6	Rope I	
FF	8/3	„ [illegible]	
LFX	7/3		

GERMAN [illegible]

STETTIN · C.i.f. Hull, Leith [illegible]

SPFFF and SPFF	[illegible]	[illegible]
SPF	[illegible]	CSP [illegible]
FF	[illegible]	
FG	[illegible]	CF [illegible]
LFX	[illegible]	

[illegible]

NWC	[illegible]
SPFFF	[illegible]
SPFFF and SPFF	[illegible]
SPFF	[illegible]
SPF ..	[illegible]
CCC	
CFX	
White Rope	

[illegible] and Consulting [illegible] Street, London, E.C., 5713

[illegible] Southwark, S.E.

[illegible] Works, [illegible] Bun-

Quotations [illegible]

[illegible] COVERING.

[illegible] Blackburn, will send a [illegible] Plastic Cork Covering to [illegible] Britain—5 cwt. cask for 25/-

CHINA CLAY.

[illegible] CHINA CLAY and VITRIOL Co., Lim., [illegible] Victoria Street, London, E.C. Mines: Rud- [illegible], St. Austell, Cornwall. Telegrams— [illegible] London."

[illegible], & Co., Truro, Cornwall.—Agents: Taylor, [illegible] & Co., 83, Queen Victoria Street, E.C., and [illegible] Princes Street, Edinburgh.

SINGLETON BIRCH & SONS, Lim., 15, Upton Street, Manchester. Mines: Reservoir, St. Austell, Cornwall. 2276

COLOURS.

CARDWELL, J. L., & Co., Commercial Buildings, 15, Cross Street, Manchester. Specialities: Mineral Black, Ven. Red, Ochres and Umbers. 5304

GEMMILL, W. N., & Co., Glasgow, Telegrams "Rube." Starches, Aluminas, Antifrothe, &c. All Paper Colours

HINSHELWOOD, THOMAS, & Co., The Glasgow Colour Works, Glasgow. Colours and shades matched exactly

MULLER, A. E., 9, Fenchurch Street, London, E.C.

ESPARTO.

[illegible]DE & CHRISTIE, Fibre, Esparto, and General Produce Brokers 72 Mark Lane, E.C.

MINERAL WHITE or TERRA ALBA.

W[illegible]NSER & Co. [illegible] Mills, Princess Street, Manchester [illegible] Manufacturers of Aluminous Cake.

HOWE JOHN & Co., Carlisle. 2113

STEEL.

MARIN, WM. & SONS, Sheffield. Established 1776. [illegible] Knives, Doctor Blades, &c. [illegible]

STRAW.

UNDERWOOD [illegible] & SON, Limited, Brentford, London [illegible] Wheat, or Rye Straw, de- [illegible] British ports or railway stations.

TALC (French and Italian Chalk).

SOUHAGE JEAN [illegible] All Minerals, Blanc de [illegible] and common), Carbonate of [illegible] British Agent: A. E. Muller, 9, [illegible] Agent for Liverpool [illegible], near Widnes.

RAGS.

CHALMERS, E., & Co., Lim., [illegible], Leith.

MULLER, A. E., 9, Fenchurch Street, London, E.C.

WERTHEIM, A., & Co., Hamburg.

UMBER.

The ALUM, CHINA CLAY and VITRIOL Co., Lim. 63, Queen Victoria Street, London, E.C. Telegrams—"Chinnock, London."

WOOD PULP.

FRIIS, N., & Co., 18, Carl Johans Gade, Christiania, Norway.

GOTTSTEIN, H., & Co., 59, Mark Lane, London, E.C., and at New York.

GRANT, W., & Co., 27, Baltic Street, Leith. Agents for best shippers, Sulphite and Sulphate, Mechanical, Fine, Brown, Aspen.

MATTHIESSEN, CHR., Christiania, Norway.

MULLER, A. E., 9, Fenchurch Street, London, E.C.

The SULPHITE PULP Company, Limited, 84, Gordon Street, Glasgow.

WERTHEIM, A., & Co., Hamburg.

PAPER EXPORTS & IMPORTS.

FOR THE WEEK ENDING [illegible] LAST.

EXPORTS TO

	[illegible]	Writings	Other Kinds
AUSTRALIA	[illegible]	[illegible]	[illegible]
AFRICA	[illegible]	[illegible]	[illegible]
ARGENTINE	—	[illegible]	5
B. WEST INDIES	—	[illegible]	—
B. GUIANA	[illegible]	[illegible]	[illegible]
BRAZIL	[illegible]	[illegible]	—
BELGIUM	[illegible]	[illegible]	[illegible]
CAPE COLONY	[illegible]	[illegible]	[illegible]
CANADA	—	[illegible]	[illegible]
CHINA	[illegible]	[illegible]	[illegible]
CEN. AMERICA	—	—	[illegible]
DUTCH GUIANA	—	—	[illegible]
EGYPT	—	[illegible]	[illegible]
FRANCE	[illegible]	[illegible]	[illegible]
GERMANY	—	—	[illegible]
GREECE	—	[illegible]	—
HOLLAND	[illegible]	—	[illegible]
INDIA	[illegible]	[illegible]	[illegible]
JAPAN	[illegible]	—	[illegible]
MAURITIUS	—	—	[illegible]
NEW ZEALAND	[illegible]	[illegible]	[illegible]
NEWFOUNDLAND	—	[illegible]	—
RUSSIA	—	[illegible]	—
S. SETTLEMENTS	[illegible]	—	[illegible]
SPAIN	5	[illegible]	[illegible]
TURKEY	—	[illegible]	—
U.S.A.	[illegible]	8	—
W. INDIES	[illegible]	—	[illegible]

IMPORTS FROM

AUSTRALIA	[illegible]	HOLLAND	[illegible]
BELGIUM	[illegible]	FINLAND	[illegible]
—	[illegible]	NORWAY	[illegible]
DENMARK	[illegible]	—	[illegible]
FRANCE	[illegible]	PRUSSIA	[illegible]
—	[illegible]	SWEDEN	[illegible]
GERMANY	[illegible]	—	[illegible]
—	[illegible]	U.S.A.	[illegible]
HOLLAND	[illegible]	—	[illegible]
—	[illegible]	—	[illegible]

Including the Following:

Quantity	From	Importer	Port
[illegible] bales	Copenhagen	[illegible]	London
[illegible]	Christiania	[illegible]	
[illegible]	[illegible]	[illegible]	
[illegible]	New York	[illegible]	
[illegible] bales	Stettin	[illegible]	
[illegible]	[illegible]	[illegible]	

SUMMARY OF IMPORTS & EXPORTS.

FOR THE WEEK ENDING [illegible] LAST.

London, Liverpool, Bristol, Southampton, Hull, [illegible], Harwich, Folkestone, Newhaven, Dover, &c.

IMPORTS.

Paper	[illegible] bales	Millboards	[illegible] bales
"	[illegible] cases	Pasteboards	[illegible]
"	[illegible] rolls	Strawboards	[illegible]
Tissues	[illegible] bales	Rags	[illegible]
Stationery	[illegible] cases	Board	[illegible] bales
"	[illegible] pkgs.		

EXPORTS.

British Goods.		Foreign Goods.	
Paper	[illegible] cwt.	Millboards	5 cwt.
Writing Paper	[illegible] "	Cuttings	[illegible]
Printing Paper	[illegible] "	Paper	[illegible] cwt.
Stationery	[illegible] value	Printing Paper	[illegible]
Bags	[illegible]	Writing Paper	[illegible]
[illegible]	[illegible] tons	[illegible]	[illegible] tons
[illegible]	[illegible] cwt.	Stationery	[illegible] value
[illegible]	[illegible]	Strawboard	[illegible] cwt.
Parchment	[illegible] value		
Strawboards	[illegible] cwt.		

Glasgow, Greenock, Port-Glasgow, Troon, [illegible], &c.

IMPORTS.

Paper	[illegible] bales	Paper	[illegible]

EXPORTS.

Paper	[illegible] cwt.	Stationery	[illegible] value
Writing Paper	[illegible] "	Envelopes	[illegible] cwt.
Printing Paper	[illegible] "		

Leith, Granton, Bo'ness, Dundee, &c.

IMPORTS.

Paper	[illegible] bales	Envelopes	[illegible] pkgs.
"	[illegible]	[illegible]	[illegible]
[illegible]	[illegible]		

PAPER & PULP MILL SHARES.

Report received from Mr. [illegible], [illegible] Street, Manchester.

[illegible]

NEW PATENTS.

APPLICATIONS.

[illegible]

DIRECTORY.

Names and Addresses under this heading will be charged for at the rate of 50/- per annum (52 insertions) for each entry of two lines or under. Each additional line £1 extra

ALUMINOUS CAKE.

The ALUM, CHINA CLAY and VITRIOL Co., [illegible] 63, Queen Victoria Street, London, E.C., [illegible] Mainham-on-Thames. Telegrams—"Chinnock[illegible]

ANALYTICAL.

WILLIAMS, ROWLAND, F.I.C., F.C.[illegible] Mall, Manchester.

ARTESIAN WELLS.

BATCHELOR, Richard D., Artesian [illegible] Well Engineer, 73, Queen Victoria [illegible] and at Chatham.

ISLER, C., & Co., Bear Lane, Southwark [illegible]

LE GRAND & SUTCLIFF, Ma[illegible] hill Row, E.C.

BOILER COVE[illegible]

LONSDALES, Boiler Cover[illegible] sample cask of their Patent [illegible] any Paper Mill in Great Brit[illegible] (carriage paid).

CHINA C[illegible]

The ALUM, CHINA CLAY [illegible] 63, Queen Victoria Str[illegible] [illegible]dle and Colchester, S[illegible] "Chinnock, London."

ROGERS, J., & Co., [illegible] Sommerville & Co., [illegible] at 16, Princes Street, [illegible]

W. SINGLETON [illegible] Street, Manchester[illegible] Cornwall.

Wanted.

[illegible] present managing a [illegible] printings, desirous of a [illegible] similar position, or as [illegible] experience in browns, [illegible] thoroughly the paper [illegible] references.—Apply No. [illegible] PAPER TRADE REVIEW, 58, 5875

[illegible] open to engagement; five [illegible] mill work, good knowledge [illegible] experience in soda recovery, [illegible] preparation of raw ma[illegible] Good references.—Address [illegible] WORLD'S PAPER TRADE REVIEW, 5877

[illegible]MAN, expert in Machine and [illegible] and Specifications, patent draw[illegible] occasional work or a permanency; [illegible] knowledge of general machinery.—G. K. [illegible] road, Finsbury-park, N. 5879

[illegible] is open to engagement; is [illegible] of paper made from rags, also wood [illegible] parchment, and paraffin [illegible] and chemical knowledge. Best [illegible] No 5844, office of the WORLD'S PAPER [illegible] Shoe lane, London, E.C. 5844

[illegible]PAPERMAKERS.—Finisher requires [illegible] in small hands, groceries, caps [illegible] references. Address No. 5862, office of [illegible] PAPER TRADE REVIEW, 58, Shoe-lane, London. 5862

[illegible] MILLWRIGHT (good) seeks [illegible] years experience in paper mills.—[illegible] office of the WORLD'S PAPER TRADE [illegible] London, E.C. 5867

Agency Wanted.

[illegible] of NEWS and PRINTING [illegible] an Agency for the [illegible] from makers of [illegible] tons weekly, and [illegible] who can supply [illegible] to send samples. [illegible] and E.S. writings, [illegible] printings. [illegible] the WORLD'S PAPER [illegible], E.C. 58[illegible]

[illegible] for Sale.

[illegible] Knife Paper [illegible] change pulleys, new [illegible] gear; if sold at once [illegible] Cartbridge Paper Mills, [illegible] 58[illegible]

[illegible] CALENDERS, second-hand, each [illegible] hand-grained rolls, about 69 inches by [illegible] with Frames, Pressure Levers, and Driving [illegible]

[illegible] KOLLERGANG, new, Stones 51 inches by 24 inches, [illegible] Scrapers, and Driving Gear.

ONE HYDRAULIC PRESS, second-hand, with Press Box 38 inches diam. by 32 inches deep, with wheels; all parts strong, Ram 2 feet 6 inches by 8 inches diam.

ONE 2-cwt. STEAM HAMMER, second-hand, for Roller Bars or General Forgings, Cylinder 7 inches diam. by 12 inch Stroke, with heavy Anvil Block.

TWELVE REVOLVING STRAINER PLATES, second-hand, 18½ inches by 21 inches, class B2, 3½ cut.

REFINING ENGINE, new, Conical Type; same as one working in a large printing mill.

Any reasonable offer will be considered by 58[illegible]

BERTRAMS LIMITED, SCIENNES, EDINBURGH.

Mill to be Let or Sold.

TO be LET or SOLD, a Paper Mill at Stalybridge, called the Higher Mill, containing one large machine and room for another, steam engine and boilers, in good condition.—Apply for further information to the Caretaker on the premises. 58[illegible]

THE

World's Paper Trade Review.

SUBSCRIPTION, £1 PER ANNUM, Post Free to all Countries.

Workmen's Edition, 2/6 per Volume, or 5/- Yearly.

W. JOHN STONHILL, 58, Shoe Lane, E.C.

Complaints

Concerning Late Delivery of Newspapers are useless unless the Wrappers accompany the complaint at head quarters of the Post Office.

Our Subscribers' Copies are duly posted before 5.30 p.m. on Friday, and should reach every postal address in the United Kingdom by SATURDAY MORNING'S POST.

We have complaints again of irregular delivery last week, some copies not being delivered until Monday and Tuesday, but our correspondents omit to forward us the wrappers, without which the General Post Office are unable to trace where the delay occurs. The postal marks will enable them to do this.

Special Prepaid Advertis...

...and Published by W. JOHN STONHILL 58, Shoe Lane, LONDON, E.C. Sept. 15, 1893.

SIR JOHN GORST on the LABOUR DISPUTES Arbitration Bill.

[illegible] appears in the published [illegible] Staff Conference. [illegible] & Stationer [illegible]

[illegible] bring about [illegible] propounding of a [illegible] questions, such as how [illegible] to be chosen? What is to be [illegible] jurisdiction? What powers shall it possess? How are its awards to be enforced? These are of course the essential points in the labour problem, which have been put over and over again. One would expect that if a right honourable statesman of the standing of Sir John Gorst puts pen to paper to deal with so important a question, he would do more than reiterate what everyone is asking.

Potens: I read his article, and I see that he is at one with your sentiments upon Mr. Mundella's Arbitration Bill, expressed at a previous Conference.

Lithographica: Yes. That Bill, I contended, does nothing whatever to advance the solution, and no bill that does not confer compulsory powers—that does not compel the submission of trade disputes to arbitration—will ever help the matter. Sir John says "it is not a bill to avert strikes." "Its provisions are crude and ill-digested." The "Member for New Ireland" imports party politics into the matter, in which of course we cannot follow him. The Bill, regarded from a perfectly independent standpoint, effects nothing for which machinery does not already exist. I repeat my own words: "The Government has not yet risen, and I see no signs of it rising, that will dare to legislate in favour of compulsory resort to arbitration in all trade disputes. And even if they did, I fail to see the means of enforcing the decisions of the arbitration board upon a body of [illegible] workmen. This would be simply putting the arbitrators or the Board of Trade in the place of the employers, without any power to enforce their decisions. They will not compel the horse to drink." Supposing, for the sake of argument, we imagine the existence of a board of compulsory arbitration at the present time. We will suppose that it has intervened between the coal owners and the colliers of Yorkshire and elsewhere; we will suppose that its decision was unfavourable for the men. Could all the forces of the Crown compel acceptance of that decision, and drive the thousands of labourers [illegible] again? If Sir John Gorst believes in the possibility of creating a board with compulsory powers, as seems to be indicated by his words in *Tall*, it becomes his duty to put his views into practical shape, and to show us the lines upon which an Act for that purpose should be drafted. I contend that it is an impossibility.

Typographer: When we discussed the Arbitration Bill of Mr. Mundella, I expressed the view that it was a well-intentioned measure, and I have seen no reason to modify that opinion. In effect [illegible] of arbitration [illegible] anything of [illegible] the Labour Committee of Arbitration, which has a magnificent field of labour before it. I cannot conceive how anyone [illegible] whose object is [illegible] great [illegible] from it. It is all very well to preach conciliation and arbitration to the bodies of men whose interests conflict or appear to conflict, [illegible] there does not exist [illegible] which both of them have confidence [illegible] of the dispute. It [illegible] is not the time [illegible] for a [illegible] Bill given a permanent board created [illegible] there is reasonable ground for hoping that both will be willing and even eager to submit their dispute to its decision. The creation of such a board is precisely what the Labour Disputes Arbitration Bill aims at.

GERMAN RETALIATORY LEGISLATION.

The new Law framed for the [illegible] [illegible] for the Trade Marks Protection Act of 1894 contains among others the following clauses which affect this country:—

Section 16.—If anyone, with intent to create a misapprehension as to the [illegible] or quality of the goods, by means of an incorrect [illegible] [illegible] goods, their cases or wrappings, in business letters, [illegible] advertisements, invoices, bills, or the like, the armorial bearings [illegible] of the name of armorial bearings [illegible] [illegible] [illegible] [illegible], shall be punishable with a fine of from 150 marks to [illegible] marks, or with imprisonment for a term not exceeding six months.

[illegible] no [illegible] lay [illegible] of the [illegible], ware- [illegible] upon [illegible] State in [illegible] marks on [illegible] pub- [illegible] to en-

[illegible] trade mark [illegible] registration [illegible] agent resident in [illegible] be entitled to [illegible] respect of the [illegible] within the scope of [illegible] of any municipal [illegible] trade mark in question, [illegible] prosecute criminally. [illegible] such agent has his [illegible] this, the place where [illegible] located, shall count, [illegible] Section 24 of the Civil [illegible], as the place where [illegible] qualification exists.

[illegible] applying for the registra- [illegible] trade mark is bound to [illegible] that he has fulfilled, in the [illegible] which he is established, the [illegible] conditions to enable him to lay [illegible] protection there for his mark.

THE MERCHANDISE MARKS ACTS AMENDMENT BILL.

The following are the two principal sections of the short Bill to amend the Merchandise Marks Acts of 1887, introduced and backed by Mr. Seton-Karr, Colonel Howard Vincent, Mr. Tomlinson, Mr. Stock, Mr. Cayzer, and Mr. Ernest Spencer:—

2. All imported goods, except such [illegible] as may be specially exempted from [illegible] time from the provisions of this [illegible] the published regulations of the [illegible] sioners of Customs, on the ground [illegible] are incapable of being marked as in this Act provided, which do not bear in a legible and conspicuous form a definite indication of the country in which such goods were made or produced, are hereby prohibited to be imported into the United Kingdom, as if they were specified in section 42 of the Customs Consolidation Act, 1876.

3. From and after the passing of this Act no goods imported into the United Kingdom which do not bear a definite indication of the country in which such goods were made or produced, or from which they were so imported, shall be exposed or offered for sale in any part of the United Kingdom unless by means either of express notice, or by a board, card, label, ticket, invoice, or other document, the purchaser be made aware that such goods have been imported, and are not of home production.

MORE ABOUT MOLTEN WOOD.

A recent issue of *L'Intermediaire des Imprimeurs* contains a large illustration with a certificate signed by Léon Sézanne to prove that it was cast from melted wood by the process which was described by us some time ago. The picture has every appearance of having been printed from an ordinary electrotype, and speaking of it the editor of *L'Intermediaire* says: "We have received from the inventors new specimens of melted wood that are absolutely marvellous. The illustration shown has been reproduced in melted wood from a wood engraving. Everything has been reproduced with marvellous fidelity, even to an imperfection in the sky in the original which is equally distinct in the cast. We have tried specimens with circular and band saws and find them work remarkably well in the cast wood which takes a polish like agate and can be sawed or bored without splintering. It appears to us that most marvellous articles can be cast from melted wood. E. Desormes, who has followed with much interest this process of manufacturing printing material from molten wood will publish an article in detail in the next number with proofs of their correctness. From what we have seen, it now appears absolutely certain that M. Desormes was quite correct in his article published in *L'Intermediaire* stating that a process had been discovered by which wood could be melted and cast like lead. The inventors, Messrs. Bizouard and Lenoir have offered to allow an opportunity to make the experiment under their directions, the results of which we hope to place before our readers.

REGISTERED TRADE MARKS, according to German Law, always go to a new owner in case a firm is sold, and no stipulations have been made in the contrary that this is not to be so.

THE TROUBLESOME "BERLINER VORMESSE."

[illegible]

[illegible]

NEW COMPANIES.

[illegible]

[illegible] to acquire the [illegible] of pro[illegible] [illegible] newspaper called *The* [illegible] [illegible] S.W. [illegible] [illegible] The subscribers are:—W. A. [illegible] [illegible] L. Barnes [illegible] [illegible] East Dulwich [illegible] [illegible] The number of directors [illegible] not less than three [illegible] qualification [illegible] remuneration to be determined in general meeting. [illegible] S.W.

[illegible]

Registered with a capital of [illegible] in [illegible] shares to carry into effect an agreement made August 10th, between W. Hobson [illegible] of the one part, and this company of the other part, for the acquisition of the undertaking of the *Derbyshire Advertiser and North Staffordshire Journal*; to print and publish the same; and as printers and stationers generally. The first directors—to be not less than two nor more than five—are W. Hobson, H. M. Hobson, H. W. Hobson, C. H. Atkinson, and A. H. Hobson. Qualification, [illegible]. Remuneration to be fixed by the company.

"INDIAN ENGINEER" CO., Ltd.

Registered with a capital of [illegible] in [illegible] shares, to acquire the undertaking of a printer and publisher, hitherto carried on by W. H. Booth, sen., and others at 2, [illegible]-mansions, Westminster, S.W., and at 5 and 6, Government-place, Calcutta; to print and publish the *Indian Engineer*, and to carry on business as printers and publishers generally. The first directors—to be not more than seven—are F. J. Ainsworth and A. J. Ulrich. Qualification, 50 shares. Remuneration, £2 2s. each for each board attendance.

Registered at the General Post Office as a Newspaper.

No. 12. LONDON, SEPTEMBER 22, 1893. Price 6d.

INATIONS ABROAD

Printed and Published by W. JOH

Telegrams: "STONHILL, LONDON." A B C Code. Registered at the General Post Office as a Newspaper.

Vol. XX. No. 12. LONDON, SEPTEMBER 22, 1898. Price 6d.

COMBINATIONS ABROAD.

Central Union of German Mechanical Wood Pulp Syndicates.

At Dresden, Saxony, on Sunday, September 10th, a meeting took place of the delegates of the four German Syndicates of mechanical wood pulp makers. It was determined to institute a Central Union of German Pulp Syndicates, including the Syndicates of Western Germany, Saxony, Silesia, and South Germany, with their selling offices at Cologne, Dresden, and Munich. The Union dispose of an annual production of about 160,000 tons of moist pulp. The meeting resolved to fix a price for the whole of Germany, which would be in unison with the actual prices in force in neighbouring countries. It is expected that this movement will create more firmness and steadiness in the paper market.

A Union of Spanish Papermakers.

A union is being formed with the object of promoting the interests of the trade, not only by representing them to the Government and seeing that commercial treaties are so framed as not to injure the paper trade, but also for discussing questions of general interest. The *Mercado del Papel*, a leading Spanish trade paper, takes a great interest in this question and suggests that one of the first things to do for the association would be to form a syndicate for obtaining cellulose and chemicals for papermakers at remunerative prices. It is rather interesting to note that chemical wood pulp is considered indispensable in the country which exports its esparto to England. Hitherto it appears the prices which Spanish papermakers have had to pay for their pulp were so high as to seriously hamper the Spanish paper industry. According to the motto "Union is Strength" Spanish makers no doubt will succeed in obtaining some of the objects set forth. Many of the cheaper classes of paper, particularly news, are being largely imported from Continental countries, which work under cheaper conditions than Spanish papermakers.

Proposed Consolidation of Strawboard and Wood Pulp Board Interests in U.S.A.

At Niagara Falls an attempt is to be made to consolidate the strawboard and wood pulp board interests in a large corporation. Such a combination, if effected, will, says the New York *Paper Trade Journal*, hardly be able to overcome competition. The history of the strawboard industry has been a record of combinations formed to control production and maintain prices. The company which holds sway over so many mills throughout the country has been the strongest organisation yet formed in this branch of the papermaking industry, but it has encountered the difficulties which its success was expected to develop. The output has increased, and independent manufacturers have helped to complicate the situation in respect to the strawboard output, probably to as great an extent as ever. What the outcome of the effort at Niagara will be may possibly be revealed within a few days. A big consolidation of capital and mills may be effected; but after that, what? Can competition be barred, and will such a combination operate to prevent the extension of competing mills or the entrance of other manufacturers into the field?

THE UNEMPLOYED. — Under the heading "Social Problems in America," a special correspondent of the *Daily Chronicle* writes from New York on the labour question. He attended a conference at which the alarming statement was made that two-thirds of the working classes of New York were out of employment. He was inclined to think that this was exaggeration, but in conversation with a New York journalist, who had investigated the facts, he found it to be quite true. Two-thirds of the workmen of America's greatest city without any work to do! The meeting on the whole was in favour of public provision of work for the unemployed and the New York *World* expressed its approval of this demand. A large number of people are out of employment in all parts of the United States, but New York appears to be hit especially hard.

THE mechanical wood pulp industry, according to Mr. Hugh J. Chisholm, of Portland, Me., "is suffering and is feeling the effects of the present stagnation of business as keenly as any other paper industry, and more especially this has shown itself in the last sixty or ninety days, and there is at the present time anything but a pleasant outlook for the future."

MR. WM. WHITING, of Holyoke, Mass., writes: "The production of writing paper is fully as great if not in excess of the demand, and it is wise on the part of paper manufacturers not to force any paper upon the market beyond what is taken easily. If such is the case prices must decline, and the point has been reached where the profits are not especially remunerative. The forcing of the sales would deprive the manufacturer of all profit. This situation is aggravated at present by the general business depression throughout the country, and there is not likely to be a demand for some months for the full production of the paper mills. As far as my observation goes, the manufacturers have considered the subject thoroughly and are determined that no surplus product shall be placed upon the market, but that the production shall be kept well within the demand, so as to allow the dealers to work off the papers they have on hand without loss."

ALL of the paper mills at Lambertville, N.J., shut down for a week recently.

THE wood pulp mill of Dr. F. E. Robinson, Carthage, N.Y., will be ready for operations about the latter part of this month. This mill is located on a large water-power within the corporation of Carthage, and on a tract of land (68 acres) owned by the proprietor. There has been about $100,000 spent on the water-power and mill by Dr. Robinson at this point, and the mill promises to be one of the finest pulp mills in the country. It will be 130 by 40 feet, and will have five of the Bagley and Sewall Company's pulp grinders. Seven water wheels of S. Morgan Smith's make will give power, and all other appliances are described as of the best.

FIRES.—The chemical building of the Jackson Pulp Company, Jackson, Mich., was burned on August 24. The fire caught from a burning pile of straw and chemicals on the west side of the structure. Loss, $5,000; fully insured.—The pulp mill at South Londonderry, Vt., owned by the Montague Paper Company, of Turner's Falls, Mass., was totally destroyed by fire on August 20. A freight car loaded with pulp wood ready for shipment and standing on a side track was also consumed. The fire is believed to have been of incendiary origin, as the engine was shut down and fire drawn at noon the day before, and there was no other source from which it could accidentally catch.

PAPER STOCK IMPORTS.—The imports of rags and other papermaking fibres—jute butts excepted—at the port of New York during the month ending August 31, according to the *Paper Trade Journal*, amounted to 9,415 bales and 1,331 tons, the difference in quantities compared with the corresponding month of 1892 being a decrease in rags of 3,978 bales, in old papers a decrease of 329 bales, and in manilla stocks a decrease of 7,719 bales. There was no wood pulp imported during August, and of chemical fibre 2,165 tons less than the July imports were brought in. The appended tabulation shows the quantities of papermaking materials of the kind mentioned which were reported as having been imported during the month of August during five years:

	1893.	1892.	1891.	1890.	1889.
Rags.........bales	3,823	7,701	7,172	7,939	17,571
Old Papers	646	975	498	1,395	940
Manilla Stocks..	4,946	12,665	10,981	16,203	3,962
Wood Pulp tons	—	—	215	—	—
Wood Fibre......	1,331	3,000	1,344	1,002	1,381

The arrivals from the different ports were as follows: Antwerp, 80 bales rags, 835 bales manillas; Bordeaux, 463 bales rags; Calcutta, 1,252 bales manillas; Central America, 60 bales rags; Christiania, 40 tons chemical fibre; Copenhagen, 285 tons chemical fibre; Dundee, 75 bales manillas; Fiume, 50 tons chemical fibre; Glasgow, 178 bales old papers; Hamburg, 145 bales rags, 34 bales old papers, 265 tons chemical fibre, 506 bales manillas; Hull, 110 tons chemical fibre, 500 bales manillas; Leghorn, 100 bales rags; Liverpool, 321 bales manillas; London, 211 bales rags, 434 bales old papers, 20 tons chemical fibre, 718 bales manillas; Newcastle, 73 bales manillas; Rotterdam, 487 tons chemical fibre: and Stettin, 2,764 bales rags, 74 tons chemical fibre, 575 bales manillas.

WINTERSCHE PAPIER FABRIKEN, HAMBURG.—The balance sheet of June 30th, 1893, shows a profit of M173,812, of which a sum of M75,477 was written off for various purposes, M4,916 placed in the reserve fund, and M13,041 used for bonuses. The remaining profit of M80,377 is to be used for writing off against participation in the Niederkaufungen mill, so that these shares are now reduced to 60 per cent. of the nominal value. The unsatisfactory position of the paper trade has not improved, and all attempts to improve prices were useless owing to competition. The company did a good home trade, but exportation was so slack that at times concessions had to be made. Chemicals, mechanical and cellulose wood pulps were dearer in the second half, and profits would have been still more reduced, had not improvements in the management and saving of cost in the production been introduced. The share of the company in the Niederkaufungen mill had been increased by M171,678, partly caused by taking up a mortgage of M60,000. Of assets the balance shows: Paper mills at Altkloster M1,271,119; paper mills Wertheim, M1,061,053; shares in Niederkaufungen, M648,117; debtors, M299,788; savings bank and stocks and shares, M174,357; participation in Niederkaufungen, M400,500. Against these assets are the following liabilities: Preference shares A, M1,701,000; shares B, M1,276,500; mortgages in Altkloster and Wertheim, M621,981; reserve fund, M174,357; creditors, M313,657. The branch establishment Niederkaufungen, near Cassel, did not realise the hopes and expectations of the directors and resulted in a loss of M380,894. A change in the directors took place in the last year and somewhat reduced the loss in the latter part of the year, the last few months even showing a decided improvement.

PAPIER FABRIK, BAIENFURT.—From the twentieth report we give the following extracts:—The large increase in the paper and chemical pulp productions brought the gross profits of 1892-93 to M140,040, against M113,268 of the previous year, and this in spite of a very unsatisfactory state of the water supply. The re-building of the somewhat antiquated ground pulp works, which took place during the winter, has also borne fruit in producing an increased quantity and an improved quality. The expense was comparatively small, only M38,044. Other new constructions cost M12,684, and an iron roof in place of a wooden one over the engine room comes to M4,629. To meet the latter amount and the reconstruction, of the ground pulp works M24,000 will be written off, though this whole amount is not necessarily to be considered as a total loss. At the end of last year an increased demand for paper and chemical pulp took place after a long period of constantly falling prices and resulted in a suitable advance in the value of chemical pulp. Duties and taxes, &c., were very considerable, there being paid for taxes M9,745; for accident insurance, M3,429; for old age and invalids insurance, M1,540; for the infirmary, M1,688, and for insurance, M3,448, making a total of M19,850, or nearly 2 per cent. of the share capital. From the gross profit of M140,040, M75,990 will be written off for various purposes, leaving M64,050. This allows a dividend of 5 per cent., 5 per cent. to the reserve fund, 10 per cent. bonus to directors, and 10 per cent. to the staff. After amortisation of 80 shares of M100 each of the railway loan, and 1 per cent. super-dividend, and special bonus to workmen, a balance is carried forward. The meeting unanimously carried all these proposals.

BERLIN AUTUMN FAIR.—The *Tagliche Rundschau* states that the rivalry between Berlin and Leipzig appears to have had its first cause in "Anti-Semitism." It appears that Leipzig is upon the whole in favour of a moderate Anti-Semitism, which is based upon German patriotism against international Judaism, such as is greatly found among many of the Berlin industrials. The latter, therefore, tried a propaganda against Leipzig, and were very careful in not disclosing this motive. However, it was soon discovered that some of the papers supporting the Berlin fair are so-called "Jewish papers," and one of them, *Das Kleine Journal*, has now let the cat out of the bag in a very sharp article against Leipzig. It seems a pity that this question cannot be left alone in matters which ought to be judged upon their own merits.

ULTRAMARINE PRODUCTION IN GERMANY.—The following little table shows the progress of this important industry:—

Years.	Number of Works.	Tons Produced.	Value in Mks.	Value per ton in Mks.
1830				50,000
1840	3			
1855	11			1,750
1862	18	2,755	3,300,000	1,215
1872	23	6,580	7,300.000	1,115
1878	21	7,000	6,100,000	856
1881	21	7,500	6,100,000	813
1885	21	8,000	5,300,600	663
1890	17	8,000	5.000,000	625

Thus the value sank gradually to its present figure, which though fallen very much still seems to leave a margin to the maker. The total quantity went up to 8,000 tons, and has remained at that figure. The number of works went down since 1872.

FRENCH CUSTOMS DECISIONS.—Cylinders for paper, of cast-iron, covered with hardened caoutchouc not representing more than 10 per cent. of the total weight of the articles, pay duty under category 620 at the rate of 70 frs. per 100 kilos. for 10 per cent. of the total weight, and under category 532 at rates varying from 12 to 20 frs. per 100 kilos. on the difference, that is on the remaining 90 per cent.

THE LATE MR. ALDERMAN MARSDEN, J.P.

In our last issue we briefly referred to the sudden death of Mr. Alderman Marsden, J.P., which occurred at his residence, Banks Hall, Cawthorn. At the inquest the evidence showed deceased was in the habit of taking sleeping mixture as he suffered from restless nights, and a verdict of death from misadventure was returned. Although Mr. Marsden had been in delicate health for several years, he had been able to attend to his business daily. His father, Mr. Charles Marsden, was a farmer, but finding that calling was not a lucrative one, he took in 1887 a hand-made paper mill up the river Rivelin, near Sheffield, and it was there that young Thomas learnt the art and mystery of papermaking. He used to be at work with the men at five o'clock in the morning, and mastered every department of the trade—the sorting of rags or ropes, the various stages of manufacturing the paper, finishing it, tying it up, and selling it. The hand-made papers produced were of a special character, and were largely used in the Sheffield cutlery trade, and celebrated for preserving bright steel goods, such as razors, cutlery, table knives, saws, files, &c. They developed a large trade for this class of paper in Sheffield, and the late Mr. Thomas Marsden, who became partner with his father at the age of 22, perceived that it could be made equally pure, and have the same rust-proof qualities, if made by machinery as by hand. He therefore induced his father to allow him first to put down one machine, and afterwards to take another mill, and put down another machine. The works there have been extended from time to time, and are now amongst the largest and best equipped of their kind in the kingdom. Towards the close of 1867 Messrs. Charles Marsden and Sons—that is the designation by which the firm has long been known—entered upon the possession of the Dearne Works, Barnsley, formerly carried on by Mr. Toothill. That was just after the great fire of September 2nd, by which the premises had been almost totally destroyed. The place was then a scene of desolation, but under the direction mainly of deceased the waste places were restored, and order was speedily evolved out of chaos. The buildings which had been destroyed were restored in a form better adapted to meet modern requirements, and since then extensive additions have from time to time been made until the works may now be said to be almost new. But this was not all. After the opening of the Ingbirchworth Waterworks early in 1868, the old waterworks premises at Smithies, belonging to the Board of Health, were no longer necessary for town uses, and early in 1809 Mr. Marsden entered into negotiation with the Waterworks Committee for the leasing of these premises. Terms were agreed upon, subject to the confirmation of the Board, which was readily granted. The terms were £75 a year rent, and a 14 years' lease, renewable at the expiration of that time. These works, which give employment to a large number of hands, both male and female, have since been carried on by deceased on his own account, they being entirely distinct from the firm of Charles Marsden and Sons. Some time afterwards they bought the Calder Grove Mills, Crigglestone, near Wakefield, formerly owned by Messrs. W. and J. Bayldon, and have since practically rebuilt the premises. Some years' ago they purchased the tenants' interest at Alders Mills, Tamworth, which have since been completely renovated and extended. The works are now among the largest of the kind in the kingdom. The firm have seven paper mills, with eleven machines in all, engaged in the manufacture of cultery papers, browns, grocers, news, small hand and glazed casings, &c., the weekly production being over three hundred tons. Deceased was also a colliery owner on a small scale. The Winter Colliery, near Smithies, has been carried on by him for a large number of years, chiefly for the supply of coals to the works, though there was also a considerable house coal trade done. He never had any wage or other disputes with his men. He was among the first to give the advance of 10 per cent. in 1888, and he was one of those owners who gave no notice for a reduction six weeks ago. His men, however, were ordered to come out, and as a consequence part of the paper works had to be shut down. The useful part he has taken in bringing about an improved position for the makers of those classes of papers in which he was chiefly interested is well known. The movement, which at its commencement was viewed with suspicion and incredulity by many, may claim the achievement of complete success. Deceased was a splendid man of business, and it is commercial ability of the highest order, with steady perseverance, which has brought the firm to the first rank of the papermaking industry. Mr. Marsden has been heard to say that the experience he gained during over forty years of commercial life had taught him to live as much as possible within one's income; to treat those he employed as of similar flesh and blood with himself; to try to inculcate habits of thrift, sobriety, and industry among them; and to never get into a law suit if such could possibly be avoided. When he entered into partnership with his father, the latter divided the business into three parts, and said to his son, "One of these parts is your share; you must only draw thirty shillings a week, and leave the rest until you have paid back the whole of the capital." For at least five years the son and his wife lived upon twelve shillings a week over and above the rent, until, between savings and profits, the whole of the capital had been refunded. Mr. Marsden, senr., died at his residence, Moore Oaks, Sheffield, March 23rd, 1879, aged 71 years. Prior to coming to Barnsley the late Mr. Marsden had resided for some time at Pickering, where the firm carried on a branch for several years. According to the *Barnsley Chronicle* he first entered public life in the former district as a member of the Board of Guardians in 1872. Upon being appointed a West Riding magistrate he became an *ex officio* guardian until the expiration of the period for which he had been elected. He entered the Town Council in 1881, and was an active member of several of the committees. In 1886 he was elected as an alderman, and in November of the same year was called upon to fill the office of Mayor, being re-elected to the office in 1887 and again in 1888, on each occasion unanimously. It may be mentioned that immediately after his election as Mayor, a movement was set on foot with a view to presenting him with his portrait, painted in oil. The artist chosen was Mr. Ernest Moore, now of Sheffield, who depicted him in full civic robes, holding in his hand a scroll. The presentation was made at an entertainment given to the workpeople in the Public Hall on the evening of November 9th, 1889, immediately after his vacating the civic chair. The duty of spokesman devolved upon Mr. James Gregg, manager of Calder Grove Works, he being followed by Mr. Chapman, of the Rivelin Works, who had been in the employ of the firm over thirty years. As a member of the Chamber of Commerce Mr. Marsden has from time to time rendered valuable service to the community, more particularly in connection with the question of railway rates. At Monk Bretton he also held several public offices. He was one of the directors of the Barnsley Banking Co., Ltd. In religion deceased was a churchman, and in politics a Conservative, though not of a very pronounced type. Mr. Marsden married, at the age of 22, Lucy Mary, eldest daughter of the late Rev. William Gill, vicar of Stannington. This lady, by whom he had no family, died March 4, 1874, aged 38 years, and was interred at Stannington. He is survived by his youngest brother, Mr. Horatio Marsden, who is, we regret to say, an invalid; by a sister, Mrs. Ingleby, of Chesterfield; and a nephew, Mr. James Marsden, of Tamworth. One of his sisters, who died some years ago, was the wife of Mr. A. H. Green, of the Yorkshire College, Leeds, the distinguished geologist. The funeral took place on Saturday last at Monk Bretton Cemetery, several public bodies being represented, as well as officials and workpeople employed by the firm.

THE AUSTRALIAN-CANADIAN MAIL LINE.—A difficulty has arisen between the Governments of New South Wales and Queensland, which may prevent the Premier of the latter Colony from fulfilling his intention to ask Parliament to vote a subsidy of £5,000 for one year towards Messrs. Huddart, Parker and Co's. new line of steamers from Sydney to Vancouver. Sir Thomas M'Ilwraith desires that the steamers should call at Moreton Bay (Brisbane) and Keppel Bay for Rockhampton, while Sir George Dibbs is only agreeable to their calling at one of the Queensland ports. Brief telegrams have been exchanged between the two Premiers, and it is probable that the result will be that the steamers will not touch at any port in Queensland.

THE BRITISH ASSOCIATION.

SPONTANEOUS COMBUSTION.

At the Nottingham meeting on Saturday Professor Vivian Lewes gave a lecture on the above subject to working men. In considering special cases of spontaneous combustion, he showed that freshly burnt charcoal, especially when powdered, absorbed oxygen from the air with considerable rapidity and with a rise of temperature, which with a large mass was, in some cases, sufficient to set it on fire. The important bearing of this was that beams, skirting, boards, &c., in contact with flues and heating pipes were liable to become charred at a comparatively low temperature, and this form of charcoal was very liable to spontaneous ignition when air came in contact with it. In the same way coal had the power of absorbing oxygen from the air, and when in masses of a thousand tons or more, especially when much broken and moist, would undergo heating and even ignition, this was due to the absorbed oxygen setting up chemical action with the hydrocarbons of the coal, and not, as was generally supposed, from the oxidation of the coal brasses. Nearly all the vegetable and animal oils had the power of absorbing and combining with oxygen, and this gave them the power of drying, and one of the most usual causes of spontaneous ignition in workshops and factories was to be found in oily waste or rags, as the oil being spread on the surface of the material offered a large surface for oxidation, whilst the rags or waste, being excellent non-conductors of heat, allowed the temperature to rise until ignition took place. Well-authenticated cases were known in which sparrows building their nests of oily waste in the eaves of houses had caused serious fires. Hayricks which had been built from grass improperly dried before stacking were also very liable to spontaneous ignition, this being due to the sap of the grass taking up oxygen during a process of fermentation which evolved heat, and the heat being kept in by the surrounding hay rose until the ignition point was reached. If grass once well dried then became wetted by a shower it became mouldy in the stack, but did not heat. The lecturer then concluded by emphasising the fact that the so-called spontaneous combustion was merely an increase in the rate of chemical combination from the slow stage which was hardly noticeable to active combustion, and showed the fallacy of supposing that the living body could undergo any such action. The demonstrations were interesting, and the conclusion of the lecture was followed by prolonged cheering.

ELECTRICITY AND WATER POWER.

On Monday, Mr. A. T. Snell read a paper on "The Utilisation of Waste-Water Power by Electricity." He said that on the Continent water-power was extensively used for driving electric plants, but in Great Britain, for a similar purpose, power was usually derived from the combustion of coal. This difference in practice was partly the result no doubt, of the relative supply of water-power in the neighbourhood of places where electric plants would prove commercially profitable; but it was also largely due to the relative cost of fuel. We did not possess abundant natural sources of water-power in or near our large manufacturing districts, and even if we did it was not probable that with coal at the average price of the last ten years water-power would prove much cheaper when the capital invested, interest, and cost of maintenance of the electric plant were taken into consideration. But would coal at such a price be always obtainable? And was the most made of such water-power as we had and could profitably use? Liverpool was supplied with water from Lake Vyrnwy, in North Wales, the total difference of head being about 500-ft. There must be a considerable quantity of power in the conduit. Was any of it utilised? And if not, did the reason lie in the fact that fuel at present was so cheap? Could the Manchester Waterworks, which formed a magnificent series of artificial lakes, be utilised to drive turbines and give electric energy for lighting the various towns in their vicinity? Again, the watershed behind Greenock had a fall of many hundred feet, and the water was only partly utilised to drive mills. These were only a few instances in which water-power might, perhaps, be advantageously used for driving turbine-dynamos. There were, of course, numerous mountain streams which could be dammed, and thus be converted into reservoirs for feeding turbines. Would it not be wise to make the most of such water-power as we had by using it as an adjunct to, if not as a substitute for, coal? This was quite possible in many places, since power could be transmitted electrically at high pressure for distances of 20 miles or so with a loss not exceeding from 15 to 20 per cent.

THE ESPARTO TRADE.

Messrs. Ide and Christie, in their Monthly Circular (dated September 15th), state that during the last fortnight of August the market ruled very quiet, and there was little or no enquiry for any description or position. Since the beginning of the present month, however, the demand has revived, and a fair extent of business in African has already been negotiated at about sellers' quotations, with further orders pending. The enquiry is still not extensive enough to cause an upward movement in prices, but it has been sufficient to impart a slightly steadier tone to the market. With few exceptions the business done has been for next year's fulfilment, and buyers would appear to be confirmed in the belief that the present range of values is safe for operations for twelve months ahead or longer. The arrivals last month were again below the average consumption, but with many mills undergoing their annual over-hauling and repair the reduced receipts caused little or no inconvenience. It will be observed that the total imports for the eight months of this year show a diminution of 12,000 tons as compared with 1892, and 24,600 tons as compared with 1891. In order to afford a comparison over a longer period we have stated the figures for twelve months ending August 1891-2 and 3, and from this it is seen that the supply during the second and third term is about equal, but falls short of the first by over 21,000 tons. The reduction in last month's arrival was probably attributable to the scarcity of steamers—one of the results of the coal strike in this country—and the much enhanced rates of freights demanded by ready boats. Although the stringency is not quite so severe the difficulty regarding transport is not yet over, and may again be reflected in the imports of the current month.

Spanish arrivals have been of full extent, and brought the eight months total up to 37,862 tons, or an increase of 4,800 tons over last year. Contract deliveries have been fully met, and but little opportunity presents itself of moving off any landed parcels. The distant demand has been very restricted, but there has been less pressure in making offers and in the absence of important business prices remain nominally unchanged. The quality of the new season's grass is very satisfactory, and bears out the estimate formed of it. The destruction by fire of a *fabrica* at Garrucha is reported, but the quantity of esparto consumed is too small to affect the market.

Algerian imports have been considerably below the average in extent, and the total receipts for the two-thirds of this year amount to 51,597 tons against 54,967 in 1892. The reduction has, however, not helped the market, which does not manifest any increase of strength, but remains dull and depressed. It would almost appear as if fair average Oran were about to be placed, as regards price, at the bottom of the list of esparto quotations.

Tunisian has been in small supply and was represented by only one cargo during the past month. There has been a fair enquiry for next year's shipment, and a moderate extent of business carried through at very steady prices.

Tripoli arrivals, although full, were 1,500 tons less than in the corresponding month of last year, and the eight months' total of 30,375 tons marks a shortage of 10,000 tons. The business done this month includes one or two transactions for early delivery, and a few contracts for fulfilment down to the autumn of next year, all of them at about sellers' quotations. The quality of the new season's grass is generally good, and in the higher grade evidences of increased care in selection are apparent.

ANTWERP will venture upon another "Universal Exhibition" in 1894. A special feature of it will be the Congo Exhibition, designed to show the work so successfully carried out in South Africa under the auspices of the King of the Belgians.

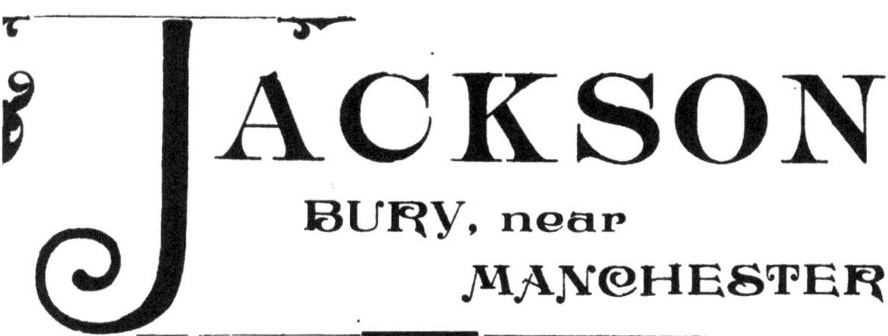

RSHALL'S PATENT PERFECTING ENGINE

(Made in three Sizes).

Engine will produce a Better Finished, Stronger and More Even Sheet of Paper from the same rials than can be produced by any other Mechanical Process, and at the same time will Reduce the Power required for Beating.

We supply these Engines on approval subject to our accomplishing the above results.

ITABLE FOR ALL CLASSES OF STOCK AND EVERY QUALITY OF PAPER.

OVER 100 NOW IN USE AND ON ORDER.

n Application.

THE Rossendale Belting Co.,

ISAAC JACKSON, **GLOSSOP.** REPRESENTATIVE.

Telegrams—"FASTENER, GLOSSOP."

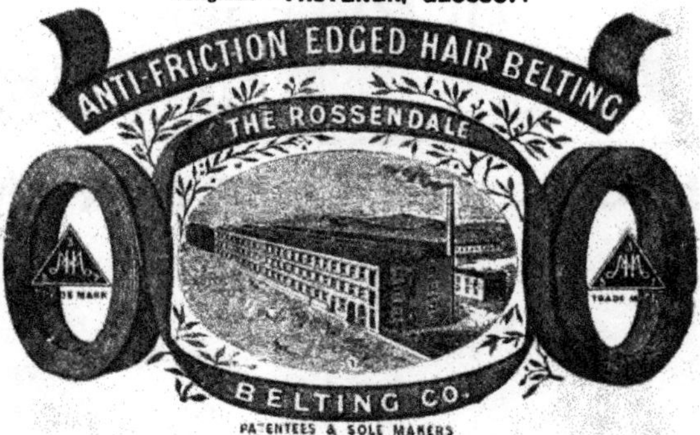

Makers of PATENT EDGED

HAIR BELTING

ALSO PATENT

Cylinder and Beater Belts SPECIALLY PREPARED to RESIST WATER and ACIDS; Made in DIFFERENT PLIES to SUIT HEAVY and LIGHT RUNNING.

JACKSON'S

PATENT CONCAVE AND CONVEX PLATE FASTENER.

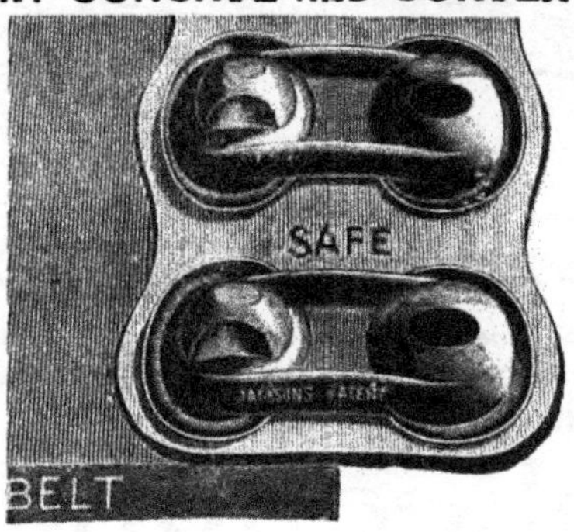

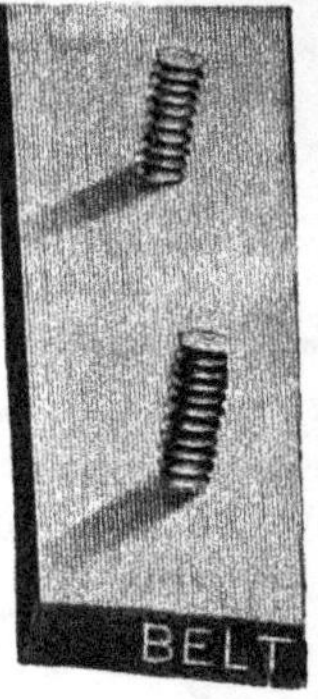

We Recommend JACKSON'S CONCAVE and CONVEX PLATE FASTENER for all BELTS in PAPER MILLS.

WHO'S WHO?

THE PERSONNEL OF THE PAPER, STATIONERY, PRINTING AND ALLIED TRADES.

Everyone must have observed that of late there has been a remarkable change in the style of a very large proportion of the oldest and largest paper, stationery, and printing concerns. The word "Limited" has become quite familiar as an integral part of their nomenclature. This affix was, as we all know, made obligatory by the provisions of "The Companies Act" (25 and 26 Vict. c. 89), which was passed in 1862. Our own Legislature, foreseeing the inconveniences which might be caused by the names of the acting responsible members of a firm not being given, provided for compulsory publication of the names of the shareholders in such companies. These returns are, as a rule, accurately and regularly made up and issued. But they are in a form which to the great majority of the public is quite unavailable. Not one person in a thousand knows "Who's Who" in a concern of even general repute. Yet for many reasons, and on divers occasions it is desirable to know the personnel of the company in question. This information we are about to supply. We shall do it from official and authentic data, and in no merely prying spirit. No reflection on the stability of any firm will be implied. The names of the parties constituting it will be given, and their shares in its capital stated, so far as official documents disclose them. The information we think will be both useful and interesting. Readers will know whom they have to deal with when transacting business with a limited liability company, and a contribution will be made to current trade history which the future annalist may greatly appreciate.

THE WALLIS CHLORINE SYNDICATE, LIMITED.

The frequency of dealings being recorded in the above syndicate by the tape on the Stock Exchange has caused enquiries to reach us from members of the trade as to the objects of the company. The following is the latest available official data:—

The syndicate was floated on the 10th of August, 1892, with a nominal capital of £75,000, divided into 75,000 shares of £1 each. It was established to acquire by purchase or otherwise all patent or other privileges in the nature of patents, to be issued in the United Kingdom or any colony or dependency thereof or any foreign country for protecting or working a process invented by H. W. Wallis for making chlorine, nitric, and sulphuric acids, and bleaching powder or other substances, according to provisional specifications then granted for the United Kingdom and numbered 12,294, 13,047, and 13,822, series 1892, and any improvements on such specified patents, and, with a view thereto to enter into agreements, and especially an agreement dated 29th July, 1892, made between H. W. Wallis of the one part, and H. T. Grant Marston as trustee of the company of the other part, and to carry all or any of such agreements into effect, with or without modification as may be arranged. Also to undertake the manufacture of chlorine-nitric acid and sulphuric bleaching powders and of anything which is usually or can be usefully manufactured together with or without any of the above mentioned materials, or which it may hereafter be found practicable to manufacture out of any or all of them, and the sale of all such materials or substances and of any product or bi-product thereof, whether in a manufactured state or otherwise. Also to purchase either in consideration of the issue of the fully paid up shares of the company or otherwise any patents or privileges in the nature of a patent which the company may consider would be useful or beneficial in working or manufacturing any of the above substances or products, or would otherwise benefit the company, and to do all such things as may be deemed expedient for obtaining the full benefit of the patents or inventions for the time being belonging to the company, or in which it is interested, with full power to grant licences, and to manufacture, sell, and let apparatus for the application of the said inventions, or any of them. The company is also empowered to carry on the trades or businesses of manufacturers of chemicals of every kind, and to buy, sell, and deal in all articles and things which the company is empowered to manufacture or produce, or which may be capable of being used in any business which the company is authorised to carry on, and to carry on any business which may seem to the company to be capable of being conveniently carried on in connection with the above, or calculated directly or indirectly to enhance the value or render profitable any of the company's property or rights, and to do all things necessary for the carrying on of the business above referred to.

The names and addresses of the first subscribers are: — H. W. Appleby, 23, Quested-buildings, Brett-road, E., clerk; T. H. Robinson, 16, Ockenham-road, N., clerk; A. E. Way, 3, Crosby-square, E.C., accountant; Rowland Morford, Ashcroft, Staines, clerk; W. H. Robinson, 33, Baxter-road, N., clerk; A. E. Hill, 41, Baxter-road, N., clerk; and W. Parkins, 46, Hempstall-road, West Hampstead, cashier.

No directors were appointed by the memorandum of association, which document provided that directors were to be appointed subsequently by the first subscribers. A directors qualification is the holding of shares of the nominal value of £250. The question of remuneration is not dealt with by the memorandum.

According to the agreement already mentioned, H. W. Wallis sold his patents to the company for £50 in cash and the issue of 50,000 fully paid up shares of £1 in the company. By another agreement filed at the Registry, dated 9th June, 1893, it appears that the syndicate have purchased the provisional patents of a process for the manufacture of chlorine invented by Archibald Brown. Payment was arranged by this agreement to be made by the allotment of

5,000 shares in the company. The last summary of the capital and shares is dated 13th September, 1892, and is as follows:—

Shares taken up, 50,507.
Called up on each of 507 shares, 1s.
Total amount received in calls, &c., £25 7s.
Agreed to be considered as paid on 50,000 shares, £50,000.

The shareholders list at present stands as follows:—

Shareholder	Shares
H. Weston Wallis, 8, Gt. Winchester-street, E.C., analytical chemist	300
Francis Ellershausen, 7, Gt. Winchester-street, E.C. engineer	29,043
C G. Wagner, Glyndhurst, Ealing-common gentleman	11,250
*N. R. Dyer, Red Hill, Surrey, postmaster	300
*F. W. Berk, 1, Fenchurch-avenue, E.C., merchant	1,000
*W. Hedges, 28, Grange-road, Ealing, merchant ...	300
*H. R. Angel, 7, St. Helen's-place, E.C., shipowner	4,400
†Minnie M. Wallis, 24, Glengarry-road, E. Dulwich	1,700
*J. R. Anderson, 4, St. Mary-axe, E.C., shipowner	367
*W. H. Cope, 7, St. Helen's-place, E.C., ship master	200
*W. G. Elder, 7, St. Helen's-place, E.C., merchant	440
*R. W. Weston, Perrymead, Bath, civil engineer ...	100
*W. B. M. Bird, *E. Strode, 5, Gray's-inn-square, W.C., solicitors	1,100
‡H. W. Appleby, 23, Quested-buildings, Hackney, clerk	1
‡T. H. Robinson, 33, Baxter-road, N., clerk	1
A. E. Way, 3, Crosby-square, E.C., accountant ...	1
R. Morford, Ashcroft, Staines, clerk	1
W. F. Robinson, 33, Baxter-road, N.	1
‡A. E. Hill, 41, Baxter road, N., clerk	1
‡W. Parkins, 46, Hempstall-road, West Hampstead, N.W., clerk	1

† Transferred from H. W. Wallis.
* ,, ,, F. Ellershausen.
‡ First subscribers.

Messrs. Ellershausen and Wagner are directors.

The registered office of the company is situated at 99, Gresham-street, London, E.C.

———o———

SPARRE PATENTS CO., LTD.

This company was registered on the 29th of March, 1888, to purchase and acquire the patent rights and privileges of a like nature in the United Kingdom, United States of America, and elsewhere, in respect of certain inventions of Count Peter Ambjorn-Sparre, of 16, Place de la Madeline, Paris, relating to (1) machine for preparing cards used in Jacquard looms (2) machine for lacing such cards (3) a new system of making military and sporting cartridges (4) a new system of making writing paper, and a new system of moulds, affording protection against imitation of banknotes and securities, and with a view thereto to enter into, adopt, and carry into effect, either with or without modification, an agreement between the company of the one part, and Count Peter Ambjorn Sparre of the other part, also an agreement between Jacob Lloyd of the one part, and the company of the other part, also to purchase and acquire such patent rights and privileges in respect of any other inventions relating to similar matters, or of any mechanical or manufacturing process capable of being used in the manufactures to which any such inventions as aforesaid are applicable or conveniently associated therewith, also to carry on the business of manufacturing and preparing cards for the Jacquard looms, and of manufacturing military and sporting cartridges and paper and moulds and appliances, and any other trade or business connected with the utilisation of any invention or manner of manufacture, the subject of any patent rights and privileges which shall be acquired by the company, either in the United Kingdom or in any part of the world, &c., &c., &c. The capital of the company is £400,000, divided into 80,000 shares of £5 each.

The signatories to the articles of association were:—A. Stanley Felton, 187, Brixton-road, S.W., secretary; Geo. Andrew, 3, Patshull-place, London, N.W.; Ernest T. Booth, 49, Arlington-road, Tulse-hill, gentleman; G. E. Holman, 14, St. Helen's-place, E.C.; W. A. Harrison, 90, Royal road, S.E., reporter; E. W. Francis, 38, Kimberley-road, Clapham, S.W., shorthand writer; J. E. Wood, 16, Matham-grove, East Dulwich, S.E., solicitor's clerk.

Of the original share capital 20,000 shares are termed A shares, and the remaining 60,000 are called B shares, and they are issued and held on the following terms:

(1) The A shares are issued and held upon the terms that the profits of the company available for dividend shall be applied in payment of a cumulative preferential dividend at the rate of 10 per cent. per annum, and the amount credited as paid up on the A shares from the time of the issue thereof in priority of payment of any dividend on the B shares.

(2) The B shares are issued and held on the terms that the profits of the company available for dividend in any year after payment of the said cumulative preferential dividend on the A shares, and the arrears (if any) thereof, shall be applied in payment of dividends for that year, and the amounts credited as paid up on the B shares at the rate of 10 per cent. per annum, or such less rate as such profits shall be sufficient to pay in priority of payment of any further dividend for that year on the A shares.

(3) The surplus profits, if any, available for dividend in any year after payment of such dividends on the A and B shares respectively according to the priorities aforesaid, shall be applied to dividends for that year on the amount credited as paid up on the A and B shares respectively, without preference or priority.

(4) No holder of B shares is liable to refund a dividend paid on B shares for any year by reason of a deficiency in the profits of the subsequent year, to pay the dividends on the A shares at the rate of £10 per cent. per annum.

(5) If and so long as there are any arrears of the cumulative preferential dividend to be paid up on the A shares, the available profits of any year shall be applicable to the dividends for that year on the A shares, at the rate aforesaid, in priority of the arrears of dividends on the A shares for the previous year. The monies available for arrears of dividends for previous years shall be applied to the arrears of more recent previous years, in priority of the arrears of more remote previous years.

(6) On the winding-up of the company, the surplus assets shall be applicable as follows:—In making good arrears of dividends at the cumulative preferential rate on the A shares; in returning to holders of all A shares the amount credited as paid upon their shares; in returning to the holders of the B shares the amount credited as paid up on their shares, and in payment to the holders of A shares and B shares *pari passu*, in proportion to the number of shares held.

The first directors appointed were:—

Hon. Evelyn Ashley.
Major-General T. E. Bryne.
Colonel W. C. Nangle.
Berkeley Paget Esq.
A. H. Henry, Esq.

The number of directors is limited to ten, but there are not to be less than five, and a director's qualification is the holding of 100 shares. The directors are paid their travelling expenses, and are entitled, by way of remuneration, to the following annual sums, to be divided amongst them as they so resolve, and in default of such resolution equally, that is to say:—A fixed annual sum of £2,000, and in every year in which the profits distributed for dividend (ascertained after charging this extra sum as an outgoing) shall exceed the amount required to pay dividend at the rate of 8 per cent. for that year on the total paid up capital, an additional sum equal to 10 per cent. of such excess. But the total remuneration for any one year paid to the directors under this clause (and exclusive of managing directors otherwise remunerated) shall not exceed the amount of £1,000 per director (other than managing directors); the said additional sum shall be reducible so as to prevent this limit being exceeded. The managing directors' remuneration, under another clause is restricted to the sum of £1,000 per annum. By agreement Count Sparre received 60,000 B shares as the price of his inventions.

The last summary of capital and shares is dated 14th July, 1893, and is as follows:—

Number of A shares taken up	10,489
Number of B shares issued	60,000

There has been called upon each of the preference shares £5, but the 60,000 ordinary shares are issued as fully paid. The total amount of calls received, including payments on application and allotment is £50,395. The total amount agreed to be considered as paid on

400 A shares is	£2,000
60,000 B shares is	£300,000

Total amount of calls unpaid, £50. Total amount paid on two shares forfeited £1.

Following are the names of shareholders:

E. J. Allcard, 54, Threadneedle-street, E.C. ...	127
Right Hon. E. Ashley, 62, Lowndes-square, W., privy councillor	100
Florence Mary Bagster, 48, Brenfield-road, S.W...	382
L. S. Baxendale, Junior United Service Club, major	96
C. F. Blackett, Ovel House, Widcombe, major ...	20
Selina Mary Bright, 23, Bayley-lane, Coventry ...	66
F. E. Bryne, Camberley, major-general	4938
T. Ganter, 31, Chalk Farm-road, N.W., jeweller...	38
A. K. George, 43, Sussex-square, Brighton... ...	191
C. W. C. Givens, 2, Morder-road, S.E.	96
Sir Julian Goldsmid, 105, Piccadilly, W.	191
E. E. Grubbe, 7, Great George-street, Parliamentary agent	96
A. H. Henry, 73, Redcliffe-gardens	148
F. R. Haster, 7, Highbridge Walk, Aylesbury ...	2
S. H. Hinde, Windham Club	200
H. Hoare, 24, Norfolk-square, W.	100
A. B. Hollond, Ashfield, Bury St. Edmunds ...	200
F. E. Hollond, Satin House, Oxford	500
J. Lloyd, Talbot House, Manchester, card maker	400
R. Morton, 32, St. John's Park, Blackheath, civil engineer	100
F. S. Nepean, St. 8, George's-road, S.W.	22
May I. Nepean, 8, St. George's-road, S.W... ...	24
C. J. P. Oakes, Yaldhurst, Lymington, lieut.-col.	191
Geraldue O. Mears, 39, Rue de Councillers, Paris	60
Berkley Paget, 2, Lawrence Pountney Hill, E.C...	100
Victor Paley, Freckenham	1,000
W. Owen Robinson, Throgmorton House, E.C. ...	64
F. Smith, Crawley Mansions, S.W.	144
Hon. R. Strutt, 70, Eccleston-square, S.W... ...	120
C. M. Tatham, 10, Old-square, W.C., barrister ...	191
C. R. Tatham, 2, Cambridge-gate, N.W.	191
H. E. Tatham, 3, Tokenhouse-buildings, stockbroker	191
R. E. Tatham, Portman Chambers, W.	191
L. Tillotson, Silkmore, Stafford, lieut.-colonel ..	16
H. Burchall, 52, Chester-terrace, S.W., solicitor ...	84
W. Burchall, 62, Sloane-street, S.W., solicitor ...	166
A. D. Butler, 39, Lombard-street, E.C.	1,500
Thos. E. Bryne, Tekel's Castle, Cambridge, major-general	40
P. Chappelier, 46, Faubourg Poissionniere, Paris	35
Cumberland Union Banking Co., Carlisle	5,000
Anne Fakete, 45, Rue desptc. Ecuries, Paris	80
Elsa Fakete, 45, Rue desptc. Ecuries, Paris ...	40
Irene Fakete, 45, Rue desptc. Ecuries, Paris ...	40
Mor Fakete, 45, Rue desptc. Ecuries, Paris ...	400
Olga Fakete, 45, Rue desptc. Ecuries, Paris ...	40
Paul Fakete, 45, Rue desptc. Ecuries, Paris ...	40
C. S. Hall, 4, Rue de la Paix, Paris	250
H. A. Hankey, 28, Park-crescent, W.	400
W. B. Hawkins, 39, Lombard-street, E.C.	400
E. Ancean Hendebert, 12, Avenue de la Alna, Paris	1,020
Ellen Hinde, New Malden	2,000
H. Hoare, 24, Norfolk-square, W.	5,710
W. Hoare, Staplehurst, Kent	2,000
J. L. A. Hope, 52, Green street, W.	600
Bertha A. Kleman, Queen Anne's Mansions, S.W.	4,000
Pontus Kleman, Queen Anne's Mansions, S.W. ...	1,940
R. Stuart Lane, 3, Aldford-street, W.	100
F. Mention, 45, Boulevard Hensmann, Paris ...	80
Eleanor J. Monro, 4, Wyndham-place, W.... ...	1,850
Hector F. Monro, 4, Wyndham-place, W.	50
A. Pollet, "Les Blenets," Cannes	2,400
H. F. Pollock, 14, St. Helen's-place, E.C., solicitor	200
R. C. Ponsonby, 1, Great George-street, S.W. solicitor...	100
Frederick Power, 11, Hyde Park-gardens, W. ...	800
A. Ragoneaux, 91, Rue de la Victoria, Paris ...	80
C. G. Rayne, Shakespear-street, Newcastle-on-Tyne	120
Julia M. Roberts, 39, Cheapside, E.C.	600
L. Smerling, Stockholm...	600
C. F. Smith, Lancaster House, Savoy-street, W.C. solicitor...	130
Louis Sparre, 39, Rue de la Douai, Paris, ...	7,000
Peter Ambjorn Sparre, 16, Place de la Madeline, Paris	9,625
Mary E. Stuart, 2, Crown Hill Villas, Harlesden...	80
W. Steele Tomkins, 28, Victoria-street, S.W., civil engineer	100
Rosa Welton, Grove House, Clapham	10,000
Edwin Wallerding, Gothenberg, Sweden	300

In reply to enquiries made of the secretary of the Sparre Patent Company, Limited, at 28, Victoria Street, Westminster, we are informed that the works at Northampton, known as Rush Mill, No. 231, are at present shut down for alterations, and further information is not at present available, except that the alterations may be expected to be completed in a few weeks.

THE WORLD'S FAIR.—A proposal to prolong the Chicago World's Fair till the end of the year is being considered, and is said to be favoured by several of the commissioners of foreign nations.

WORLD'S PAPER TRADE REVIEW OFFICE,
58, SHOE LANE, LONDON, E.C.
SEPTEMBER 21, 1893.

TRADE NOTES.

THE directors of C. Townsend Hook and Co. (Limited) declare an annual interim dividend at the rate of 5 per cent. per annum for the half-year ending June 30th last. Dividend warrants will be posted on the 25th inst.

IN *re* PICKTHALL.—This debtor, William Pickthall, trading as a hemp, flax, and paper merchant in Appold-street, Finsbury, under the style of "John Pickthall and Sons," has presented his petition. The liabilities amount to about £11,000, and it is stated that the assets show a surplus. Upon the application of Mr. Ralph Raphael, solicitor to the proceedings, the usual receiving order was made.

REDUCTION OF A COMPANY'S CAPITAL.—In the Chancery Division on Wednesday, in the matter of the Anglo-American Self-Opening Square Paper Bag Company, Ltd., the company petitioned for a reduction of its capital. It was incorporated with a capital of £100,000, divided into £44,000 in "A" shares and £56,000 "B" shares, the whole of the "A" shares being allotted to the vendors in payment of the purchase-money. The vendors had agreed to a return of these shares, and the object of the present application was that they might be cancelled. Mr. Justice Kennedy made the order, but intimated that it would be necessary to add the words "and reduced" to the title of the company for a month longer.

MACHINERY TRUST, LTD.—This company has been registered with a nominal capital of £50,000 in £5 shares. Object, to carry on in the United Kingdom, or in any part of the world, the business of dealers in machines, articles, and things of every description adapted for or capable of being used by manufacturers and others; to construct, lay down, maintain, and deal in machinery, apparatus, and mechanical appliances, also in shares, mortgages, bonds, obligations, &c. The first signatories to the memorandum of association are:—F. Lewes Gower, Home-field-lodge, Warlingham, Surrey; W. D. Ross, 15, Lebanon-gardens, Wandsworth, S.W.; A. M. Haines, Meadowcroft, Horley; J. Place, M.I., M.I.M.E., 4, Chesterfield-street, King's-cross, W.C.; A. E. Nash, 49, Elms-road, Clapham-common, S.W.; E. S. Booty, 31, Addison-gardens, Kensington, W.; W. J. Parmenter, 33, Liverpool-street, King's-cross, W.C. There shall not be less than three nor more than 12 directors; the first are to be elected by the signatories to the memorandum of association. Qualification, £500. Remuneration: Chairman £500 per annum, deputy-chairman £400 per annum, and ordinary directors £100 per annum each. Registered office, 155, Fenchurch-street, E.C.

MESSRS. MESSER AND THORPE'S FIRE BUCKETS.—Amongst the awards in the section of the machinery department of the World's Fair for fire engines and apparatus and appliances for quenching fires, Messrs. Messer and Thorpe, of London, have received an award for fire buckets and cases for storing the same. An illustration of the invention will be found on page 26 of the current issue.

FIRE AT THE ATLAS PAPER WORKS.—The firemen in South London had a troublesome and dangerous fire to deal with on Friday night in the Borough, where the Atlas Paper Works were discovered to have become ignited shortly before eight o'clock. The premises are very extensive, and the outbreak, originating in the basement, was most difficult to reach. Private hydrants fitted to the premises were brought into action while the brigade were being called up, and nearly a dozen steamers were despatched to the scene, but it was upwards of an hour before the firemen could get at the fire. The smoke was very dense, and the task of extinction a difficult one, but the building was saved from destruction and the outbreak was overcome by half-past nine.

THE FATAL ACCIDENT AT CHARTHAM PAPER MILLS.—At the inquest held concerning the death of James Beasley, aged 39 years, who died on the 10th inst. at the Kent and Canterbury Hospital from the effect of an accident received on the previous day whilst endeavouring to remove a large belt from a revolving wheel by means of a pole at Chartham Paper Mills, a verdict was returned of accidental death. The coroner sympathised with the widow of the deceased. He said Beasley bore an excellent character, having gained a good reputation whilst an employee of the old-established Chartham paper mills, and the widow, through his great loss, had parted with a good and affectionate husband, and the children likewise a good father. He (the Coroner) understood that the deceased had no less than eight or nine little children to care for, and to the widow and to them it was a loss that could never be repaired. A correspondent points out that the reference to the son being injured in another part of the building is incorrect. It appears that young Beasley met with an accident in an oast-house, two miles away from the mill, on the 8th inst.

A DISHONEST CASHIER.—James Adam, 25 years of age, a young man of respectable appearance, pleaded guilty to a charge of embezzling £250 between 1st October, 1892, and 6th August, 1893, while cashier to Messrs. John Craig and Sons, Dawsholm Paper Works. It was stated that prisoner's salary was at first £1 a week, but he rose to be cashier at £85 a year. One of the prisoner's masters interceded on his behalf. Sheriff Guthrie said he hoped the prisoner would find a career in some other place which would redeem his character. There must, however, be a term of imprisonment, and he would make it three months.

NASH MILLS.—A complimentary letter has been received by Mr. L. W. Loveitt, secretary to the Nash Mills Steam Fire Brigade (Messrs. John Dickinson and Co., Limited), to the effect that a bronze medal has been awarded to the brigade, by the general council of "The National Fire Brigades Union," for services rendered at the Fire Brigades Tournament and Exhibition, held at the Agricultural Hall, Islington, in June last. The medal, bearing the inscription on the one side "For Services," and on the obverse the arms of the union standing out in bold relief, was enclosed in a handsome morocco case, and will be added to the trophies already collected in the engine house at Nash Mills.

CANADA.—The No. 3 Paper Mill at Hull, Que., is being pushed to completion. It is expected to be ready to start up by December.—The Milton Pulp Company, Milton, N.S., is about to build a pulp mill.

DAILY AMERICAN SERVICE FROM SOUTHAMPTON.—Although great reticence is observed by officials, the *Liverpool Journal of Commerce* gives currency to the impression that "negotiations are proceeding which will result in a daily service of steamers between Southampton and New York. At present there are four steamers a week, leaving three days open, and it is believed that within a comparatively short time, and before the present English mail contract expires, there will be sailings on those days."

ESTIMATED LOSS ON THE WORLD'S FAIR.—The Chicago Exhibition has cost 23,867,752 dols. to August 7th for construction and administration. The gate receipts to the same date were 3,447,037 dols., and from concessions 1,178,546 dols. The daily receipts from all sources are about 80,000 dols., and the average daily expenses 15,000 dols., leaving a net daily revenue of 65,000 dols. Auditor Ackerman, in his condensed balance-sheet of July 31, charges to construction account a total of 18,819,196 dols.; to general and operating expenses, 4,957,879 dols.; and to preliminary organisation, 90,674 dols. Assuming (says the *Engineer*) that the Exhibition will remain open for 60 days from the 7th of August, this leaves a profit of about 4,000,000 dols.; adding 4,600,000 dols. previously received, we have a total net profit of 8,600,000 dols.; deducting this from the cost, we see that a balance of about 15,000,000 dols.; or nearly £3,000,000, remains to be met. The Chicago Exhibition represents the largest money loss ever incurred by an exhibition. The greater number of the Chicago hotels have gone into liquidation or been closed. The insurance companies have withdrawn their policies on several of the caravanseries, specially constructed to accommodate a countless crowd of visitors who have never arrived. The insurance companies assert that in the interests of morality it is wrong to tempt the hotel-keepers to commit arson, the average of visitors to these hotels being from 7 to 10 per cent. only of that expected and provided for. The visitors are, indeed, mostly country folk, coming from a radius of about 300 to 500 miles.

MILL CAPACITY IN U.S.A.

The following statistics (prepared by Messrs. Howard Lockwood and Co., of New York) show the daily capacity in pounds of the paper mills of the United States now running as reported by manufacturers. The respective capacities of the various States are given as follows:—

	Daily Capacity.
California	104,000 pounds
Colorado	114,000 "
Connecticut	497,600 "
Delaware	155,480 "
Georgia...	37,500 "
Illinois	763,280 "
Indiana...	1,127,000 "
Iowa	125,000 "
Kansas	59,000 "
Kentucky	66,500 "
Maine	1,957,500 "
Maryland	333,200 "
Massachusetts ...	1,830,400 "
Michigan	597,000 "
Minnesota	86,000 "
Missouri	40,200 "
Nebraska	38,000 "
New Hampshire ...	925,600 "
New Jersey	417,200 "
New York	4,761,750 "
North Carolina ...	25,000 "
Ohio	1,422,000 "
Oregon	136,500 "
Pennsylvania... ...	1,495,800 "
South Carolina ...	16,000 "
Tennessee	16,000 "
Texas	16,000 "
Vermont	620,700 "
Virginia	146,000 "
Washington	58,000 "
West Virginia ...	269,000 "
Wisconsin	1,701,500 "

The productive capacity of the various grades is classified as follows:—

	Daily Capacity.
Binders' board ..	214,300 pounds
Blotting	63,500 "
Book and news ...	4,622,400 "
Building, roofing and sheathing... ...	590,500 "
Card	178,000 "
Chemical fibre ...	2,210,000 "
Coloured paper ...	178,000 "
Hanging and curtain	270,500 "
Leather board ...	95,000 "
Manilla...	1,908,100 "
Press board	27,800 "
Straw board	1,671,580 "
Straw wrapping ...	1,063,650 "
Tissue	111,700 "
Tissue manilla ...	96,180 "
Wood pulp	4,285,400 "
Wood pulp board ..	372,000 "
Wrapping	755,700 "
Writing	863,900 "
Miscellaneous ...	80,500 "

The total amounts to 19,958,710 pounds, daily capacity, against 16,970,380 pounds in the previous year—a gain of 17⅝ per cent. Compared with 1881 the increase in daily capacity is returned at 275½ per cent.

'ORLD'S PAPER TR
58, SHOE LA
SE

RADE

directors of C.
imited) declar
nd at the rate of
half-year endin
warrants will b

e PICKTHALL.—
all, trading as a
ant in Appold-s
yle of "John Pi
ted his petition.
ut £11,000, an
show a surplus.
Ralph Rapha
gs, the usual

UCTION OF A
Chancery Div
natter of the
ng Square Pa
mpany petitio
d. It was inc
00,000, divid
s and £56,000
A" shares bei
yment of the
rs had agre
s, and the obj
as that they
e Kennedy
that it wou
"and reduc
for a month

HINERY T
en register
,000 in £5 s
United K
orld, the
, articles, a
dapted for
facturers a
maintain
atus, and
res, mortg
st signat
ation are
dge, W
15, Leb
A. M. H
ce, M.I.
King's-
oad, Cla
31, A
V. J. Pa
-cross, W
ree nor
e to be
morand
500. R
num,
, and
each.
-street,

Sept. 22, 1893

PAPER EXPORTS & IMPORTS.

FOR THE WEEK ENDING TUESDAY LAST

EXPORTS TO

SUMMARY OF IMPORTS & EXPORTS,

FOR THE WEEK ENDING TUESDAY LAST.

...ndon, Liverpool, Bristol, Southampton, Hull, Fleetwood, Harwich, Folkestone, Newhaven, Dover, &c.

IMPORTS.

...	12027 bales	Millboards	5353 pkgs.
...	623 cases	,, ...	184 cases
...	233 rolls	Pasteboards	49491 bales
...	1226 pkgs	,, ...	8 cases
...	2 cases	Strawboards	9396 bales
...k ...	234 bales	,, ...	55 rolls
...nery	15 cases	Cardboards	1193 cases
...	25 pkgs.		

EXPORTS.

BRITISH GOODS.			
		Stock	116 tons
...	1388 cwt.	,, ...	632 cwt.
...ing Paper ...	1103 ,,	FOREIGN GOODS.	
...ing Paper	6464 ,,	Paper	171 cwt.
...nery	£9446 value	Printing Paper...	272 ,,
...	80 tons	Writing Paper...	6 ,,
...rds	52 cwt.	Parchment	£55 value
...	3 ,,	Strawboards	30 cwt.
...boards	20 ,,	Stock	4 tons
...ard		Wood Pulp	37 ,,
...ings	438 ,,	Stationery	£314 value
Pulp	5 tons		

...gow, Greenock, Port-Glasgow, Troon, Grangemouth, &c.

IMPORTS.

...	862 bales	Paper	7 cases
...	280 rolls	Stationery	1 case

EXPORTS.

Writing Paper...	213 cwt.	Envelopes	26 cwt.
Printing Paper..	1254¾ ,,	Stationery	£31 value
Paper	53 ,,	Paper Stock	127¾ cwt.
,, ...	£174 value		

Leith, Granton, Boness, Dundee, &c.

IMPORTS.

Paper	83 bales	Tissues	2 bales
,, ...	3 cases		

PAPER & PULP MILL SHARES.

(Report received from Mr. F. D. DEAN, 36, Corporation Street, Manchester.)

Nominal Amnt	Amnt Paid	Name of Company	Last dividend	Price.
7	7	Bury Paper, ord.	nil	4¼—4¾
7	7	do. do. 6% pref.	6%	4¾—5
100	100	do. do. deb.	5%	103—106
10	10	Bath Paper Mill Co. Lim.	7½%	6—7
10	10	Bergvik Co., def.	15%	13¾
100	100	do. do. 6% cum. pref.	6%	10⅞—11¼
10	10	do. do. deb.	5%	105—110
5	3½	Burnley Paper Co.	3/-	77/6—80/0
5	3¾	Darwen Paper Co.	10%	5¾—6¼
10	10	East Lancashire Co.	nil	4¼—4¾
10	10	do. do. 6% pref.	nil	6¾—7
5	5	do. do. bonus	nil	1¾—2
5	5	Hyde Paper Co.	4%	4¾—5
5	4	North of Ireland Paper Co.	nil	2¼—2¾
10	5	Ramsbottom Paper Co.	17½%	12¼—12¾
5	4½	Roach Bridge Paper Co.	5%	3¼—3¾
5	5	Star Paper Co.	10%	6—6¼
5	3	do. do. 10% pref. cum.	10%	4¾—5¼
50	50	do. do. deb.	6%	55—56
5	2½	Kellner Partingt'n Pulp Co.	—	57/6—58/6

"PAPER: ITS HISTORY."

Mr. John Kay, in his booklet on "Paper: Its History" has not made the most of the subject. He admits leaving out technicalities in order to make the work as little like a treatise as possible, and in this he has succeeded. It is true the book is published at the low price of 1s., but considering the significant title there is much omitted of interest, and unnecessary space occupied with extracts that could have well been summarised. At the outset he mentions some of the materials which served the purpose of paper before the latter commodity was invented, and then attention is given to papyrus, parchment, rice paper, &c. The most ancient manuscript on cotton paper appears to have been written in 1050, and then the author discusses Spielmann's and Tate's connection with the introduction of paper-making in this country. The years of 1760-1765 are given as the period before paper-making arrived at any degree of perfection. The remarks on fibrous materials are not likely to interest practical papermakers, and probably the author intends his booklet for general readers, who, though continually using and manipulating paper, have never given a thought as to its history or manufacture. Taking this view the work contains something fresh and instructive for the lay mind. The manufacture of hand-made paper is briefly discribed, and also paper-making machinery, several pages being occupied with a reprint of the description of the mammoth machine at Star Mills which appeared in the local press. The paper industry is next looked at from a social point of view, and the opinions of Gladstone and other prominent men on newspapers quoted. In reference to the uses of paper we find rails, wheels, casks, &c., familiarly to the front. Special productions are also mentioned, and in the appendix the sizes, weights, and prices of various grades of paper are given. Mr. Kay is evidenty conscious that he has not treated the subject in a thoroughly comprehensive manner, as, in conclusion, he facetiously remarks: "I have endeavoured to avoid wearying you more than absolutely necessary, by boiling down, as it were, 'pulping' the many details and technicalities connected with this subject, to do without altogether being unavoidable, so I trust that in passing my 'pulp' through the 'deckle' of your criticism you will not shake it too hard, and that the 'watermark' on the 'mould' may be one of approval, and when it reaches the 'rolling' and 'glazing' stages, may you be gentle with the 'pressure' of your condemnation in the former, and as heavy over my shortcomings with the latter as you can."

PAPER EXPORTS & IMPORTS

FOR THE WEEK ENDING TUESDAY LAST

EXPORTS TO

	Printings.	Writings.	Other Kinds
AUSTRALIA	5555 cwts	243 cwts.	371 cw
AFRICA	— ,,	58 ,,	114 .
AUSTRIA	6 ,,	— ,,	10 .
ARGENTINE ...	— ,,	36 ,,	— .
BELGIUM	13 ,,	77 ,,	1 .
B. WEST INDIES...	85 ,,	8 ,,	22 .
B. GUIANA	— ,,	2 ,,	3 .
CHANNEL ISLES	— ,,	— ,,	6 .
CANADA	99½ ,,	109 ,,	98 .
CAPE COLONY ...	114 ,,	86 ,,	450 .
CHINA	33 ,,	26 ,,	267 .
DENMARK	56 ,,	2 ,,	4 .
FRANCE	44 ,,	17 ,,	72 .
GERMANY	— ,,	— ,,	1 .
HOLLAND	108 ,,	— ,,	3 .
INDIA	615 ,,	481 ,,	104½ .
JAPAN	673 ,,	— ,,	4 .
MAURITIUS ...	— ,,	— ,,	7 .
NEW ZEALAND ...	417 ,,	142 ,,	37 .
NORWAY	— ,,	18 ,,	— .
NEWFOUNDLAND	— ,,	— ,,	15 .
PORTUGAL	— ,,	2 ,,	— .
RUSSIA	— ,,	1 ,,	2 .
SYRIA	— ,,	— ,,	2
SPAIN	— ,,	1 ,,	5 .
S. SETTLEMENTS	— ,,	6 ,,	12 .
U.	500 ,,	5 ,,	9 .

IMPORTS FROM

ARGENTINE...	36 bales	GERMANY ...	104 ca.
AUSTRALIA ...	10 ,,	HOLLAND ...	2221 ba.
,, ...	5 cases	,, ...	257 ca.
BELGIUM ...	2841 bales	INDIA	2 ba
,, ...	143 cases	,, ...	29 ca
,, ...	232 rolls	NORWAY ...	4418 ba
DENMARK ...	93 bales	PRUSSIA ...	321 ,
FINLAND ...	184 ,,	,, ...	42 ca.
FRANCE ...	365 ,,	SWEDEN ...	1299 ba
,, ...	93 cases	U.S.A.	100 ,
GERMANY ...	1907 bales	,, ...	281 r

Including the Following:

Quantity	From	Importer	Port
1 bale	Christiania	Crabb & Co	Lond
100 bales	,,	J. Hamilton	,,
51 ,,	,,	London & Rhine Co	,,
9 ,,	,,	Alsing & Co	,,
435 ,,	Christiansand	R. L. Lundgren	,,
38 ,,	Drammen	Cookson & McDonald	,,
15 ,,	,,	G. F. Green & Co	,,
142 ,,	,,	Crabb & Co	,,
14 ,,	,,	Lon. & Rhine Co	,,
95 ,,	,,	Alsing & Co	,,
175 ,,	Gothenberg	Schenkenwald & Co	,,
39 ,,	,,	Hummell & Co	,,
8 ,,	,,	D. Gulland	,,
17 ,,	,,	Brown & Brough	,,
36 ,,	Marseilles	J. Pollock & Son	,,
1653 ,,	Norrkoping	Schenkenwald & Co	,,
15 ,,	,,	Beronius, King & Co	,,
77 ,,	,,	O. Konig & Co	
29 ,,	,,	Hummell & Co	.
28 ,,	,,	J. Spicer & Sons	,,
1007 ,,	,,	Prop. Dowgate Dk.	,,
9 ,,	,,	,, Brooks Whf.	,,
5 ,,	Stettin	Spicer & Son	
20 ,,	,,	W. D. Edwards	,,
82 ,,	,,	Becker & Ulrich	,,
42 cases	,,	B. Beer	,,
50 bales	,,	Lon. & Rhine Co	,,
3 ,,	,,	E. & E. Sabel	,,
76 ,,	,,	Gun Shot & Griffins Whf.	,,
23 ,,	,,	Benscher	,,
212 ,,	Uddevalla	R. L. Lundgren	,,
256 ,,	,,	D. Gulland	,,

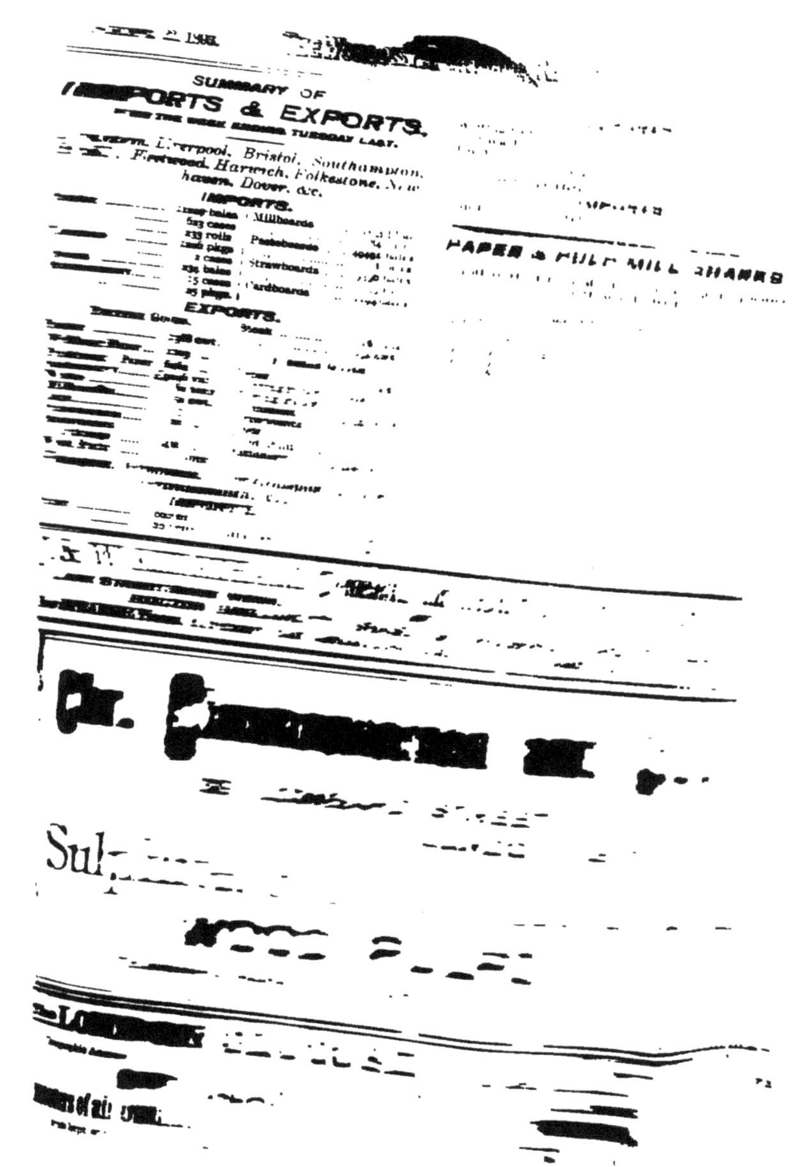

SUMMARY OF

IMPORTS & EXPORTS.

TUESDAY LAST.

Liverpool, Bristol, Southampton, Fleetwood, Harwich, Folkestone, New haven, Dover, &c.

IMPORTS.

bales | Millboards
523 cases |
233 rolls | Pasteboards
pkgs |
2 cases | Strawboards
236 bales |
cases | Cardboards
25 pkgs. |

EXPORTS.

Paper

PAPER & PULP MILL SHARES

Printed and Published EVERY FRIDAY
AT 58, SHOE LANE, LONDON, E.C.,
By W. JOHN STONHILL.
ESTABLISHED 1878.

FRIDAY, SEPTEMBER 22, 1893.

NOTHING calls so much attention to a new enterprise as the ever-lively "tape" of the Stock Exchange. Transactions thus indicated suggest extremely active dealings, but occasionally when matters are fully investigated, it is explained by the sale of vendors' or directors' shares. This appears to be the case with the dealings in the Wallis Chlorine Syndicate, as may be judged from the details published in another column.

THE indisputable success which has attended the Scandinavian Wood Pulp Makers' Association has created a spirit of emulation amongst German manufacturers. For a long time past they have looked with envy upon the prosperity of the Scandinavians, and whilst forming several small unions complete unanimity, apparently, was not achieved. They have, however, been roused to further action, and advices from the Continent state that a Central Union of German Mechanical Wood Pulp Syndicates has been formed. The idea is to fix a uniform price that will bear comparison with the prices of other countries, and it is further maintained that the paper industry will be placed in a better position from the fact that there will be no fluctuation in the prices of German mechanical wood pulp.

THE reason of the low prices for paper in Germany is, it is stated, because German manufacturers are susceptible to the persuasive influence of buyers. Our correspondent goes so far as to say that they do not for one moment look at the cost of raw material or the difficulties of manufacture, but at once fall in with the views of buyers, who make out that paper is on the market at such and such a price and that they cannot afford to pay more. We are not inclined to believe that German papermakers have a weakness to work for nothing, and British buyers of German wood pulp will certainly bear us out in saying that their experience is the very opposite so far as the raw material is concerned.

SOME difference of opinion is shown by German papermakers about the way in which retree papers should be sorted. In some of the best papers some three or four different kinds are sometimes sent out at different prices, while in lower class papers the best retree is left among the so-called good paper, and actually torn papers are thrown back into the engine. The improvement in paper machinery and better half-stuffs such as chemical pulp, allow a more uniform result in the paper coming from the machine, so that the opinion is gaining ground that in best papers only one class of retree should be allowed, and in cheaper sorts only the really useful paper should be sent out.

WHERE retree is sent out, it should be of the same class as the good, and while slight blemishes, for which 10 per cent. reduction in price is allowed, may be accepted, the surface, the sizing, and the general character should be the same. If a writing paper is so badly sized that it will not take the ink, such sheets according to recent judgments in law courts need not be accepted, the same would be the case if blotting paper contained some sheets on which one could write. In both cases the object for which the paper had been ordered, could not be accomplished. As for really inferior and torn sheets, it would save a great deal of friction, and in the end save expense, if those were to go back to the beaters at once. When hand-made and primitive machine-made papers were the rule, the faults now complained of could not in some cases be avoided, and therefore they were sorted out in these various classes, and sometimes sold by themselves for inferior purposes, but now with improved materials and improved machinery a little care and attention will enable papermakers easily to fall in with reasonable views.

It will be some time before the American paper industry recovers from its depressed condition. Reports to hand, however, while not of a very encouraging nature, point to a slight movement in the right direction. Mr. William Whiting advises papermakers to keep down production as there is not likely to be a demand for some months for the full production of the paper mills. Workers in many instances have accepted a reduction of wages from 10 per cent. to 30 per cent. Evidently American papermakers have been too fully occupied with affairs at home to give exportation any material consideration —notwithstanding large accumulated stocks.

Our list of imports of wood pulp this week includes a heavy consignment from Canada, the parcel being one of 5,146 bales from Montreal, per the s.s. Siberian. The port of landing was Glasgow. Some 19,862 packages were also received from Maine, U.S.A., and landed to the order of Messrs. G. Schjoth and Co., at Fleetwood.

Regarding the importation of rags, general order $\frac{111}{1893}$ states that bales, not hydraulically compressed, iron-hooped and marked, must be dealt with under the Local Government Board Order of the 5th August, and not allowed to enter except under the conditions contained in Article 2 of that Order. As regards the requirement that there should be marks and numbers showing the origin of the bales, officers are to note that such origin is not necessarily that of the collection of the rags, *but the place of shipment of the bales*; and that the marks and numbers placed on the bales, or, in the absence of marks, the information usually furnished by the importer on the free entry, must constitute such evidence of origin as is ordinarily accepted for purposes of Customs record.

The scarcity of fuel has not only caused an advance in chemicals, but has greatly hampered many paper mills, where production has had to be curtailed and a certain amount of labour dispensed with. The situation as regards the coal strike, however, is certainly not worse. An increasing number of men are getting to work, and Mr. Pickard, the president of the Federation, recognises that the policy of a universal strike should be abandoned—expressing himself in favour of work being resumed where the masters were willing to give the old rate of wages. More, too, is heard in favour of a meeting of the representatives of the owners and of the workmen. The belief seems to be that if this Conference could be arranged a compromise might be effected.

How to make a living in London, or elsewhere for that matter, is a subject that merits attention in these competitive times. According to an interview published in the *British Weekly* there are some good berths as travellers in the paper trade, and no doubt the salaries mentioned will be sufficient to fire the ambition of youth. Country experience in a stationer's and printer's business, and then a position as counter assistant in London, help to make a good traveller. Advice to beginners is: "If you find a customer who won't deal without drinking, leave him alone, and let the business go." It is stated that "a good traveller will earn from the first at least £150, and as the older travellers of the house drop away, he will get a larger and better connection, and largely increase his income. Travellers are not usually paid by commission, but at fixed rates. £250 to £350 may be taken as a fair average income. Expenses are allowed for, but in London these are much smaller than in the country. At the present time many travellers are leaving their firms to become paper agents to the largest makers. Each great mill-owner has an agent in London, who sells entirely by commission. He will probably confine himself to the wholesale trade and a few of the leading printers, selling only in large quantities. It is by no means easy to get posts of this sort, in which incomes vary from £400 to £1,000 a year. The more mills an agent can represent, the larger his commission."

In spite of all warnings, British traders still seem to fall a victim to the wiles of swindling firms in continental ports. The Consul at Amsterdam mentions that the number of such fraudulent firms in that city is rapidly increasing, and trade with Great Britain is suffering in consequence. The Consul says it has apparently been found impossible to check or punish the impudent robberies of these scoundrels; and we can only hope that repetition of the warning to look well into the antecedents of any firms offering to act as correspondents to British houses may have practical results. Our consular officers are generally willing to deal with questions of the kind—within reasonable limits of course.

WORLD'S PAPER TRADE REVIEW OFFICE,
58, SHOE LANE, LONDON, E.C.
SEPTEMBER 21, 1893.

MARKET REPORT

and RECORD of IMPORTS

Of Foreign Rags, Wood Pulp, Esparto, Paper, Millboards, Strawboards, &c., at the Ports of London Liverpool, Southampton, Bristol, Hull, Fleetwood, Middlesborough, Glasgow, Grangemouth, Granton, Dundee, Leith, Dover, Folkestone, and Newhaven for the WEEK ENDING SEPTEMBER 20.

From SPECIAL Sources and Telegrams.

Telegrams—"STONHILL, LONDON."

CHEMICALS. — The market is quiet, the fuel question being a very serious matter, interfering with production. A good deal of the chemical plant is stopped. An advance of about 10s. has again been made in CAUSTIC SODA, 77% being quoted at £12 f.o.r. Newcastle and f.o.b. Tyne; 74% £11 15s. f.o.b. Liverpool; 70% £10 15s. f.o.b. Liverpool; and 60% £9 15s. The supply of 60% CAUSTIC SODA is stated to be exhausted. BLEACHING POWDER stands at £8 10s. and SODA CRYSTALS at £2 15s. Competition in SODA ASH continues, and prices have a lowering tendency. SULFHUR is in good demand at from £4 2s. 6d. to £4 5s.

Prices are nominally as follows :

					£	s.	d.
Alkali, 58%	tierces	...	f.o.r. works	2½%	5	10	0
,, 58%	bags	...	,, ,,	2½%	5	5	0
58%	...	...	f.o.b. Liverpool	2½%	5	12	6
Alum (Ground),	tierces	...	,, Liverpool	2½%	5	7	6
,, ,,	barrels	...	,, ,,	2½%	5	17	6
,, ,,	tierces	...	,, Hull	2½%	5	5	0
,,	,,	...	Goole	2½%	5	5	0
Alum (Lump)	,,	...	f.o.b. Liverpool	2½%	4	17	6
,, ,,	barrels	...	,, ,,	2½%	5	0	0
,, ,,	tierces	...	,, Hull	2½%	4	15	0
,, ,,	,,	...	Goole	2½%	4	15	0
,,	,,	...	London	2½%	5	5	0
,,	,,	...	f.a.s. Glasgow	2½%	5	5	0
Alumina Sulphate,	casks		f.o.b. Tyne		4	2	6
,, ,,	bags		,, ,,		3	17	6
Aluminoferric Cake,	slabs		Liverpool ...	...	2	15	0
,, ,,	tierces		,, ...	...	3	2	6
Alumina Cake,	slabs	...	Glasgow	...	2	15	0
,, ,,	tierces	...	,,	...	3	2	6
Aluminous Cake,	casks	...	Manchester	2½%	2	7	6
,, ,,	,,	...	Newcastle	2½%	2	10	0
,, ,,	,,	...	London	2½%	3	0	0
,, ,,	bags	...	,,	2½%	2	17	9
Blanc Fixe ...	...	...	f.o.b. Tyne	net	7	10	0
Bleach, 35%	...	...	,, ,,	net	8	10	0
,, (soft wood)		...	f.o.r. Lancs.	net	8	10	0
,, (hard wood)		...	f.o.b. Liverpool	net	9	0	0
...	...	...	landed London	2½%	9	15	0
Borax (crystals)	...	...	... ...	net	29	0	0
powdered ...		...	... .	net	30	0	0
Caustic Cream, 60%		..	f.o.r. Lancs.	net	8	12	6
,, ,, 60%		...	f.o.b. Liverpool	net	8	17	6
,, Bottoms		...	,, ,,	net	6	15	0
,,	...	...	f.o.b. Tyne	net	6	15	0
Caustic White 76-77%		...	f.o.r. Newcastle	net	12	0	0
,, ,, 77%		f.o.r. or	f.o.b. Tyne	net	12	0	0
,, ,, 74%		...	f.o.b. Liverpool	net	11	15	0
,, ,, 70%		...	,, ,,	net	10	15	0
,, ,, 70%		...	,, Hull	net	11	0	0
,, ,, 70%		...	f.o.r. London	net	10	15	0
,, ,, 70%		...	,, Lancs.,	net	10	12	6
,, ,, 60%		...	,, London	net	9	15	0
,, ,, 60%		...	f.o.b. Liverpool	net	9	15	0
Carbonat'd Ash 58%		...	,, ,,	net	5	10	0
48%		...	,, ,,	net	4	7	6
,, 58%		..	f.o.r. Widnes	net	5	5	0
48%		...	,, ,,	net	5	2	6
Chloride of Barium		...	f.o.b. Tyne	net	7	10	0
Hypo-Sulphite of Soda...			f.o.r Tyne		5	15	0
,, ,,	10-ton lots		ex ship Liverp'l	net	6	10	0
Oxalic Acid ...	...	...	f.o.b. Liverpool	3½%	per lb		¼
Salt Cake ...	...	...	,, works	net	1	10	0
Soda Ash, 52%	...	...	f.o.b. Tyne	net	4	10	0
,, 52%	...	...	ex ship Thames	1%	4	15	0
,, 52%	...	...	f.o.b. Liverpool	1%	4	10	0
Soda Crystals	...	...	,, Tyne	net	2	15	0
,, ,,	...	...	ex ship Thames	2½%	3	5	0
,, ,,	...	...	f.o.b. Liverpool	net	3	0	0
Sulphur, roll	...	...	f.o.r. works	2½%	7	17	6
,, flowers	...	...	,, ,,	2½%	9	10	0
,, recovered		...	,, ,,	2½%	4	2	6
Sulphate of Ammonia		,,	,, ,,	2½%	15	0	0
,, of Copper		...	,, Liverpool	5%	15	0	0

FOREIGN.—F.o.b. Continental port :

	£	s.	d.
Alkali, 58% 2-cwt. bags £6 10/0; 10-cwt. casks ...	6	15	6
Caustic Soda, 70-72%	11	12	0
Hypo-Sulphite of Soda 10-ton lots 140/0; kegs ...	7	10	6
Sulphate of Alumina 7-8 cwt. casks net c.i.f. Ldn	4	7	6
Blanc Fixe (c.i.f. London)	7	12	6

ESPARTO.—A fair enquiry prevails for next year's fulfilment, chiefly in African descriptions. Oran is still inclined to weakness, but Sfax and Tripoli are pretty steady. Spanish is very slow, and little new business is passing, but quotations are nominally unaltered.

Prices c.i.f. London and Leith, or f.o.r. Cardiff, Garston and Tyne Docks are nominally as follows :

Spanish—	Fair to Good	£5 10 0	to 5 15 0
,,	Fine to Best	5 17 6	,, 6 0 0
Oran —	Fair to Good	3 12 6	,, 3 17 6
,,	First Quality...	3 17 6	,, 4 0 0
Tripoli —	Hand-picked	3 17 6	,, 4 0 0
,,	Fair Average	3 0 0	,, 3 12 6
Bona & Philippeville	... ...	3 17 6	,, 4 0 0

IMPORTS of ESPARTO.

Quantity	From	Importer	Port.
600 tons	Aguilas	T. Kennedy & Son	Dundee
1800 ,,	Tripoli	To order	London
4366 bales	,,	W. C. Creighton & Sons	,,

STRAW.—The market dull, and supplies are scarce. Imports this week are from France and Holland only.

IMPORTS of STRAW

(Purposes unspecified) at principal Ports From

FRANCE ... 185 bales | HOLLAND ... 826 bales

STRAW PULPS.—Trade quiet.

Prices, c.i.f. London, Hull or Leith :

Belgian, 25% moisture	£15 0 0	to 16 0 0
do. dry		16 0 0
German, 50 to 55% moisture		16 10 0
do. dry, ... No. 1 £18 10 0; No. 2		15 0 0

IMPORTS of STRAW PULP.

Quantity	From	Importer	Port.
107 bales	Hambro	To order	Hull

CHEMICAL WOOD PULPS. — Users are rather slow in making contracts; prices, however, are well-maintained all round, and judging from the firm attitude shown by manufacturers there is not much likelihood of lower prices being realised.

Prices, ex steamer, London, Hull, Newcastle, Leith and Glasgow are nominally as follows :

SULPHITE,	Unbleached, Common	£10 15 0	to 11 0 0
,,	Superior	11 10 0	,, 12 10 0
,,	,, 50% moisture, d.w.	11 10 0	,, 12 2 6
,,	Extra	13 0 0	,, 14 0 0
,,	Bleached, moist		16 10 0
,,	Unbleached, English, del. Lancs. ...		10 15 0
,,	,, ,, No. 1, ex mills, Ldn.		10 10 0
,,	,, ,, No. 2. ,, ,,		9 15 0
SODA,	Unbleached, Common ...	10 0 0	to 10 10 0
,,	,, Extra... ...	10 10 0	,, 11 0 0
,,	Half-Bleached	12 10 0	,, 14 0 0
SULPHATE,	Unbleached, Common	10 10 0	,, 11 0 0
,,	Extra	11 0 0	,, 12 0 0
,,	Half-Bleached	13 10 0	,, 14 0 0
,,	Bleached	15 0 0	,, 16 0 0

MECHANICAL WOOD PULPS.—The market is very firm, and best qualities of pulp scarce, deliveries on contracts coming forward slowly and causing great inconvenience. Very little pulp is obtainable for prompt delivery or for later shipments this year. Prices have an upward tendency, as will be seen from the revised list below.

Prices, ex steamer, London, Hull, Newcastle, Leith and Glasgow are nominally as follows:

MECHANICAL, Aspen, Dry	...	£7 10 0 to 8 0
Pine, Dry	... ...	6 12 6 .. 7 0
Pine, Moist	... ...	3 7 6 .. 3 10
Moist Brown	... ...	3 2 6 .. 3 5
Single Sorted	... ...	2 7 6 .. 2 10
Dry Brown	... ...	6 5 0 .. 6 10 0

IMPORTS of WOOD PULP.

Quantity	From	Importer	Port.
19862 bales	Bangor	G. Schjoth & Co	Fleetwood
500 cases	Barcelona	To order	Liverpool
430 ..	..	..	London
1581 bales	Christiania	..	Hull
204 ..	..	Henderson, Craig & Co	London
199 ..	..	Christophersen & Co	..
1638 ..	..	To order	Grangemouth
102 ..	..	..	..
200 ..	Drammen	Christophersen & Co	London
250 ..	..	G. Schenkenwald & Co	..
500 ..	..	London Paper Mills Co	..
250 ..	..	Ekman Co	..
800 ..	..	Skramnes	..
40 ..	Drontheim	To order	Hull
83 ..	Dusseldorf	..	London
200 tons	Fredrickstadt	..	..
200 bales	Gothenburg	..	Southampton
170 ..	..	..	..
593 ..	..	..	..
908 ..	..	Salvesen & Co	Granton
476 ..	..	H. Pearsall	London
34 ..	..	W. Friedlaender	..
145 ..	..	Henderson Craig & Co	..
21 casks	Ghent	To order	..
102 bales	Hambro	..	..
1280 ..	Helgenaes	..	..
780 ..	Helsingfors	..	Hull
5146 ..	Montreal	..	Glasgow
120 ..	Norrkoping	..	London
250 ..	Oporto	..	Liverpool
500 ..	..	..	London
480 rolls	Rotterdam	..	..
105 bales	..	..	..
160 ..	..	..	..
50 ..	..	..	..
163 ..	Stettin	O. Herrlich	..
176 ..	..	Tough & Henderson	..
200 ..	..	To order	..

Totals from Each Country:

BELGIUM	21 casks	NORWAY	... 5884 bales
CANADA	... 5146 bales	..	... 200 tons
FINLAND	... 780 ..	PRUSSIA	... 539 bales
GERMANY	... 1464 ..	PORTUGAL	... 750 ..
HOLLAND	... 315 ..	SPAIN	... 930 cases
..	... 480 rolls	U.S.AMERICA	19862 bales

IMPORTS of WOOD PULP BOARDS.

Quantity	From	Importer	Port
170 cases	Drammen	F. E. Foulger	London
82 ..	Christiania	To order	Grangemouth

WASTE PAPERS.—The market for Waste Papers is fairly good, and quotations for Mixed Shavings and Light Browns are lower.

Cream Shavings ...	12/3	Small Letters	5/0
Fine	9/6	Large	7/0
Mixed	3/0	Brown Paper	2/3
White Printings ...	8/9	Light Browns	2/9
White Waste ...	1/6	Books & Pamphlets ...	6/0
Wood Pulp Cuttings	3/6	Strawboard Cuttings	1/6
Brown Paper	3/0	Jacquards	2/6
Crushed News	2/0		

For Export: 25/- per ton extra.

JUTE.—There is a moderate trade passing in Cuttings.

Good White £16 0 to 18 0		Common ...	£10 10 to 11 0
Good... ...	15 0	Rejections...	8 0 .. 9 0
Medium ..	0 .. 13 0	Cuttings ...	£5 to 7 0

FOREIGN RAGS.—Apparently no restrictive order will be made by the Local Government Board in regard to the importation of rags. Various grades are now coming into the market more freely, especially for Scotch mills. Prices are nominal. Continental packers anticipate a fair business with the United States shortly.

IMPORTS of FOREIGN RAGS.

Quantity	From	Importer	Port.
133 bales	Amsterdam	To order	Hull
77 ..	Antwerp	..	..
31 ..	Buenos Ayres	..	Liverpool
336 ..	Copenhagen	..	Hull
20 ..	..	..	..
106 ..	Dunkirk	..	..
50 ..	..	..	Leith
102 ..	..	..	Hull
62 ..	Danzig	..	..
69 ..	Ghent	G. Gibson & Co	Leith
27 ..	..	To order	Hull
126 ..	..	..	Liverpool
8 ..	Guernsey	..	Southampton
69 ..	Hambro	..	Hull
63 ..	Harlingen	..	..
4 ..	Jersey	..	Southampton
781 ..	Konigsberg	..	Hull
303 ..	New York	..	..
106 ..	Rotterdam	..	..
9 ..	..	..	..
53 ..	..	..	..
70 ..	Rouen	..	London
20 ..	..	..	Hull
711 ..	Stockholm	..	..
126 ..	St. Malo	..	Southampton
24 ..	Stettin	..	..

Totals from Each Country:

ARGENTINA	31 bales	GERMANY ..	69 bales
BELGIUM ...	299 ..	HOLLAND ...	364 ..
CHANNEL Isles	12 ..	PRUSSIA ...	807 ..
DENMARK ...	1067 ..	U.S.A. ...	303 ..
FRANCE ...	564 ..		

DUTCH RAGS. f.o.r. Hull:

C.i.f. Thames; Hull 2/6 per ton more; ditto f.o.r. Leith c.i.f. Glasgow 4/-; c.i.f. Liverpool 4/-.

Selected Fines (free from Muslins) ...	17/0	Best Grey Linens ...	9/0
		Common ditto ...	5/6
Selected Outshots	9/9	White Canvas ...	15/0
.. Dirty Fines	5/9	Grey & Brown Canvas	9/9
Light Cottons ...	9/3	Tarred Hemp Rope	8/0
Blue Cottons ...	7/6	Ditto (broken) ...	5/3
Dark Coloured Cottons	2/10	White Paper Shavings	7/9
New Cuttings (Bleachd)	22/6	Gunny (best) ...	4/9
.. (Unbleached)	19/6	Jute Bagging ...	3/6
.. (Slate) ...	9/0	Ditto (common ...	3/0
Muslins	8/0	Tarpaulins	4/0
Red Cottons (Mixed)	5/9	Cowhair Carpets ...	2/9
Fustians (Light browns)	5/0	Hard ditto	3/0

GERMAN RAGS.

STETTIN: C.i.f. Hull, Leith, Tyne and London.

SPFFF and SPFF	18/0	LFB (Blue)	9/0
SPF	11/0	CSPFFF and CSPFF	10/0
FF	8/6	CFB (Blue)	7/6
FG	9/0	CFX (Coloured) ...	4/6
LFX	7/0		

HAMBURG: F.o.b.

NWC	22/0	FF Grey Linens ...	9/0
SPFFF	22/0	LFX Second ditto...	8/0
SPFFF and SPFF	18/0	CSPFFF	17/3
SPFF	16/0	CSPFF	11/3
SPF	12/0	CFB	8/0
CCC	5/6	Dark Blues (selected	11/9
CFX	4/6	Wool Tares... ...	8/0
White Rope... ...	8/0	Jute, No. I 6/0; No. II	5/6

FRENCH RAGS.

Quotations range, per cwt., ex ship London, Southampton, or Hull; 2/0 per ton more at Liverpool, and 10/0 per ton higher at Newcastle, Glasgow or Leith.

French Linens, I ...	22/0	Black Cotton ...	4/0
II 18/6; III ...	14/6	Marseilles Whites, I	16/0
White Cottons, I ...	19/0	II 10/0; III ...	7/6
II 15/0; III ...	12/6	Blue Cotton	11/0
Knitted Cotton ...	11/0	Light Prints... ...	9/0
Light Coloured Cotton	8/0	Mixed Prints ...	6/0
Blue Cotton	9/6	New White Cuttings	22/0
Coloured Cotton ...	6/0	.. Stay ..	21/0

BELGIAN RAGS.

F.o.b. Ghent. Freights: London, 5/0; Hull and Goole, 7/5 Liverpool and Leith, 10/0; Newcastle, 12/6; Dundee and Aberdeen, 15/0; Glasgow, 16/6.

White Linens No. 1	22/6	Fustians (Light) ...	6/0
,, ,, No. 2	16/0	,, (Dark) ...	4/0
,, ,, No. 3	13/0	Thirds...	3/0
Fines (Mixed) ...	12/0	Black Cottons ...	3/9
Grey Linens (strong)	9/6	Hemp Strings (unt'r'd)	2/0
,, ,, (extra)	14/0	House Cloths ...	4/9
Blue Linens... ...	8/6	Old Bagging (solid)	3/6
White Cottons S'p'fine	18/0	,, ,, (common)	2/6
,, ,, No. 2	15/0	NEW.	
Outshots No. 3 ...	10/0	White & Cream Linens	35/0
Seconds No. 4 ...	8/0	White Cuttings ...	22/0
Prints (Light) ...	8/6	Unbleached Cuttings	22/0
,, (Old)	4/6	Print Cuttings ..	8/0

BELGIAN FLAX and HEMP WASTE.

Best washed and dried Flax Waste, 10/0; Fair ditto 9/0
Flax Spinners' Waste (grease boiled out)... ... 10/0
Hemp Waste, No. 1 9/0; No. 2 ... ... 7/6
Flax Spinners' Waste, No. 1 (Flax Rove) 10/0: No. 2 8/6

NORWEGIAN RAGS.

C.i.f. London, Hull, Tyne, and Grangemouth.

1st Rope (tarred) ...	8/9-9/0	2nd Canvas ...	8/9
2nd ,, ,, ...	5/9-6/0	Jute Bagging	
Manilla Rope (white)	8/6-8/9	Gunny ...	3/6 3/0
Best Canvas ...	11/9-12/0	Mixed ...	2/6-3/0

RUSSIAN RAGS.

C.i.f. London, Hull, Newcastle or Leith.

SPFF	15/0	CC (Cotton	4/9
SPF	13/6	Jute I	3/6
FG	10/6	,, II...	2/3
LFB	9/6	Rope I...	9/0
FF	8/3	,, II	5/3
LFX	7/3		

HOME RAGS.—LONDON: Demand quiet.—BRISTOL: Trade dull; prices unchanged.—MANCHESTER: The market is in a very depressed condition for all grades of stock, and prices for Seconds, Blues, Bagging and Surat Tares evidence a decrease in value.—EDINBURGH: The demand is small at former quotations. — DUBLIN: Market quiet.

LONDON:

New White Cuttings	21/6	Canvas No. 1	15/0
Fines (selected)	20/6	,, No. 2 ...	9/6-10/6
,, (good London)...	20/0	,, No. 3	5/6
Outshots (selected) ...	12/6	Mixed Rope	5/3
,, (ordinary) ...	11/0	White Rope	6/3
London Seconds	3/6-4/0	White Manilla Rope	8/6
Country do. ...	6/6-8/0	Coil Rope	8/5
London Thirds ...	1/9	Bagging...	1/5
Country do. ...	4/0-3/6	Gunny	3/6
Light Prints ...	7/0-8/0		

BRISTOL:

Fines	19/0	Clean Canvas ...	15/0
Outshots	13/6	Second Do. ...	9/6-10/6
Seconds	7/0-8/0	Light Prints ...	8/0
Thirds	3/6-4/0	Hemp Coil Rope	9/6-10/0
Mixed Bagging	3/6	Tarred Manilla	7/6

MANCHESTER:

Fines	15/0-16/0	Blues	6/6-7/0
Outshots (best) ...	11/6-12/0	Bagging...	4/0-4/3
,, (ordinary)	10/6-11/0	,, (common)	3/0-3/3
Seconds	7/0-7/3	W. Manilla Rope	10/0-10-6
Thirds	3/6-3/9	Surat Tares... ...	4/9-5/0

EDINBURGH:

Superfines	17/0	Black Cottons	2/9
Outshots	13/0	W. Manilla Rope ...	9/-
Mixed Fines...	14/0	Tarred Ditto	6/-
Common Seconds ...	8/0	,, Hemp Rope...	8/-
First do.	11/0	Rope Ends (new) ...	8/-
Prints	5/6-6/6	,, ,, (old) ...	6/-
Canvas (best)	16/0	Bagging...	2/0-3/-
,, 2nd	10/6	,, (clean) ...	4/3-6/-

DUBLIN.

White Cuttings ...	18/0	Mill Bagging	3/-
Fines	11/0	White Manilla	8/-
Seconds...	5/0	Tarred Hemp	8/-
Light Prints	3/0	Rigging	13/6
Black do.	2/0	Mixed Ropes	3/6
... .	2/0		

SIZING. — Prices are steady and firmer, although the demand is somewhat limited.

English Gelatines	per cwt.	70/0 to	140/0
Foreign ,, ...	,,	70/0 ,,	140/0
Fine Skin Glues	,,	45/0 ,,	60/0
Long Scotch Glues	,,	45/0 ,,	60/0
Common ,, ...	,,	30/0 ,,	45/0
"Town" Glues	,,	26/0 ,,	36/0
"Bone" Glues	,,	20/0 ,,	30/0
Foreign Glues	,,	23/0 ,,	40/0
Bone Size	,,	4/0 ,,	10/0
Gelatine Size...	,,	5/0 ,,	10/0
Dry B.A. Pieces	,,	31/6 ,,	32/0
,, English Pieces	,,	24/0 ,,	27/0
Wet ,, ,, ...	,,	7/0 ,,	8/0
,, Sheep Pieces	,,	3/0 ,,	4/0
Buffalo Hide Shavings	,,	26/0 ,,	37/0
,, Picker Waste	,,	27/0 ,,	31/0

ROSIN.—Prices have an upward tendency.

	Strained.	E.	F.	G.	K.	W.G.	W.W.
Spot—	3/7½	4/0	4/3	4/6	6/9	9/9	10/3
To arrive—	3/2	3/5	3/7	3/9	5/6	9/0	9/6

STARCH. — The market for Farina is weaker, and Prime at from 10s. 3d. to 10s. 9d. per cwt., according to quality, is rather lower.

F.o.r. London, less 2½%:

Maize—Crisp, £10 0/-; Powder, £10 5/-; Special £14 10/-
Farina—Prime, £10 5/-; B.K.M.F., £13 10/-

Delivered:

Rice—Special (in chests), £20 0/- (net); Crystal (in bags) £19 0/-; Granulated (in bags) £18 0/- less 2½%.
Dextrine—£16 0/- to £17.

MINERALS.—The market for CHINA CLAY is steady, with a fair demand for best grades. FRENCH CHALK is in request at former quotations. BARYTES (sulphate and carbonate) are in good demand and there is a moderate amount of business passing in PATENT HARDENINGS and MINERAL WHITE. Best grades of IRISH MOSS are scarce.

Mineral White (Terra Alba), per ton f.o.r. or boat at works:

Superfine...	28/0	less 2½ %
Pottery Super.... ...	24/0	,,
Ball Seconds	20/0	,,
Seconds	15/0	,,
Thirds	10/6	,,

China Clay, in bulk, f.o.b. Cornwall, 14/0 to 27/6; bags 5/0 and casks 9/6 per ton extra; f.o.b. London, in casks 35/0 to 50/0 per ton.

Superfine Hardening, f.o.r. works, 40/0.

Patent Crystal Hardening, delivered at mills £3 to £3 15/0

Patent Hardening (2 ton lots) f.o.r. Lancs., £3 5/0.
,, ,, (5 ton lots) f.o.b. Liverpool, £3 10/0.

Magnesite (in lump) 32/6 per ton.

Magnesite (containing 98% Carbonate of Magnesia), raw ground, £6 10/0; calcined ground, £12 10/0.

Albarine, £3. del. mills.

Asbestos, best rock, £18; brown grades, £14 to £15

Asbestine Pulp, £4 5/- to £5 c.i.f. London, Liverpool and Glasgow.

Barytes (Carbonate), lump, 90/0 to 95/0; nuts, 72/6 to 85/0.

Barytes (Sulphate), "Angel White," No. 1, 70/0; No. 2, 60/0 to 65/0; No. 3, 45/0. Souheur's Brands: AF, 83/-; BF, 71/-; AB, 33/6; BB, 29/6; CB, 24/3.

French and Italian Chalk (Souheur Brand), per ton in lots of 10 tons: Flower O, 64/6 c.i.f. London; Flower OO, 60/0, Flower OOO, 51/6. Swan White, 57/0; Snow White, 90/0. Blackwell's "Angel White" Brand and "Silvery" 90/- to 92/6; prime quality, 90/- to 95/-; and superfine, 105/-.

Bauxite, Irish Hill Quality, first lump, 20/0; seconds, 16/0; thirds, 12/0; ground, 35/0.

Pyrites (non-cupreous), Liverpool, 5d., 2 %.

Carbonate of Lime (Souheur Brand), Prima 43/-. Secunda 37/-.

LIME.—Bleach Lime is quoted at about 11s. per ton at works.

DIRECTORY.

Names and Addresses under this heading will be charged for at the rate of 50/- per annum (52 insertions) for each card of two lines or under. Each additional line £1 extra.

ALUMINOUS CAKE.

The ALUM, CHINA CLAY and VITRIOL Co., Lim., 63, Queen Victoria Street, London, E.C. Works: Rainham-on-Thames. Telegrams—"Chinnock, London.

ANALYTICAL.

WILLIAMS, ROWLAND, F.I.C., F.C.S., 28, Pall Mall, Manchester.

ARTESIAN WELLS.

BATCHELOR, Richard D., Artesian and Consulting Well Engineer, 73, Queen Victoria Street, London, E.C., and at Chatham. 5713

ISLER, C., & Co., Bear Lane, Southwark, S.E.

LE GRAND & SUTCLIFF, Magdala Works, 125, Bunhill Row, E.C.

BOILER COVERING.

LONSDALES, Boiler Coverers, Blackburn, will send a sample cask of their Patent Plastic Cork Covering to any Paper Mill in Great Britain—5 cwt. cask for 25/- (carriage paid).

CHINA CLAY.

The ALUM, CHINA CLAY and VITRIOL Co., Lim., 63, Queen Victoria Street, London, E.C. Mines: Ruddle and Colchester, St. Austell, Cornwall. Telegrams—"Chinnock, London."

ROGERS, J., & Co., Truro, Cornwall.—Agents: Taylor, Sommerville & Co., 83, Queen Victoria Street, E.C., and at 16, Princes Street, Edinburgh.

W. SINGLETON BIRCH & SONS, Lim., 15, Upton Street, Manchester. Mines: Rosevear, St. Austell, Cornwall. 2476

COLOURS.

CARDWELL, J. L., & Co., Commercial Buildings, 15, Cross Street, Manchester. Specialties: Mineral Black, Ven. Red, Ochres and Umbers. 5304

GEMMILL, W. N., & Co., Glasgow, Telegrams "Ruhe." Starches, Alumina, Antifroths, &c. All Paper Colours

LONSDALE'S Boiler Coverer AND Paper Hair AND Cork NON-CONDUCTING CEMENT.

Extract from the *World's Paper Trade Review*, August 2nd, 1889 :—

The "DAILY CHRONICLE" Mills: "The Steam Mains are covered with a Non-Conducting Composition supplied by LONSDALE BROS., OF BLACKBURN, which HAS BEEN FOUND TO ADHERE VERY WELL, and to EFFECT A CONSIDERABLE SAVING."

"It has Stood the Test of an EIGHT YEARS' TRIAL."

Improvement in Cork Covering. Patent No. 19,906, 1889. 2058

SOCIÉTÉ INDUSTRIELLE de MIOS,

MIOS, GIRONDE, FRANCE.

Bleached Chemical Pine Wood Pulp,

OF GREAT PURITY,

Especially Adapted for Use in the Manufacture of Fine Papers. 2646

PATENT SPHINCTER GRIP

Flexible Indiarubber ARMOURED Hose

Durability of Steel with Flexibility of Indiarubber Warranted and Guaranteed.

PRACTICABLY INDESTRUCTIBLE.

Made to withstand internal or external pressures up to 5 tons on square inch.

For WATER, STEAM, GAS, AIR-SUCTION, HYDRAULIC, &c.

NEWLY REGISTERED BRAND

'Hercules Special Delivery'

H.S.D. 2514

GUARANTEED 10 YEARS

ECLIPSES ALL HOSES. OVER 5,000,000 Ft. in Actual Use.

Paris Exhibition, 1889, 1st Prize and Medal. American Exhibition London, 1887, Highest Award; Special Mention; Certificate of Merit.

BEWARE OF WORTHLESS IMITATIONS.

REGISTERED TRADE MARK.

SAMPLES and PRICE LISTS POST FREE.

SPHINCTER HOSE & ENGINEERING Co., Lim., OFFICES: 9, MOORFIELDS, LONDON, E.C.

F. MARTEN HALE, General Manager and Secretary.

PAPERMAKERS SHOULD ADVERTISE IN THE

British & Colonial Printer & Stationer,

In Order to Keep their Mills and Makes before the Home and Colonial Trade.

W. JOHN STONHILL, 58, SHOE LANE, LONDON, E.C.

YATES & THOM

(Late Wm. & Jno. YATES),

BLACKBURN,

HIGH SPEED ECONOMICAL **COMPOUND ENGINES.** | **MODERN MILL GEARING** IN ALL ITS BRANCHES.

STEEL BOILERS with 2 and 3 FURNACES up to 200 lbs. WORKING PRESSURE

Special Prepaid Advertisements

IT IS IMPORTANT that Advertisements under any of the Headings mentioned below should reach us by the FIRST POST on WEDNESDAY Morning to INSURE INSERTION.

Charges for advertisements under the heading Situations Wanted are 1/- for twenty-four words, and One Penny per Word after, Minimum charge ONE SHILLING. Names and addresses to be paid for.

Advertisers by paying an extra fee of 6d. can have the replies addressed to the Paper Trade Review under a number, and such replies will then be forwarded Post Free.

Advertisements appearing under the following headings:

Tenders.	Mills Wanted or To Let.
Sales by Auction.	Machinery Wanted or For Sale.
Businesses Wanted.	
Businesses for Disposal.	Situations Vacant.

Miscellaneous.

The charges are 3/- for fifty words or under; 1s. extra for every line or portion after. Ten words to be reckoned for each line. Names and addresses to be paid for. Payment must be made in advance, except where the advertiser has a running account, in which case the cost can be debited thereto.

Legal and Financial Announcements: 1/- per Line.

Cheques and Post-office Orders to be CROSSED ——and Co., and made payable to W. JOHN STONHILL.

Situation Vacant.

WANTED, for a Hand-made Paper Mill, an experienced Foreman.—Apply No. 5886, office of the World's Paper Trade Review, 58, Shoe Lane, London, E.C. 5886

Situations Wanted.

ADVERTISER, at present managing a mill making news and printings, desirous of a change, is open to re-engagement in similar position, or as traveller; has also had several years' experience in browns, caps, and shop papers, and knows thoroughly the paper trade throughout the U.K.; highest references.—Apply No. 5875, office of the World's Paper Trade Review, 58, Shoe Lane, London, E.C. 5875

CHEMIST is open to engagement; five years' experience in paper mill work, good knowledge of papermaking materials, experience in soda recovery, Yaryan and Porion, causticising preparation of raw materials, boiling, bleaching, &c. Good references.—Address No. 5877, office of the World's Paper Trade Review, 58, Shoe Lane, E.C. 5877

CLERK (18), used to Paper Mill work, invoicing, orders, &c., &c.; good references; open for engagement; moderate salary.—Apply No. 5885, office of the World's Paper Trade Review, 58, Shoe-lane, London, E.C. 5885

DRAUGHTSMAN, expert in Machine and Pattern Drawings and Specifications, patent drawings, plans, &c., seeks occasional work or a permanency; has a thorough knowledge of general machinery.—G. E. Jones, 89, Woodstock-road, Finsbury-park, N. 5879

FOREMAN is open to Engagement; well up in coloured shops, browns, and caps; last three-and-a-half years foreman at Brook Mills, Little Eaton, Derby.—Apply, J. C. Brown, Holme Cottage, Little Eaton, Derby. 5857

MANAGER is open to engagement; is well up in all kinds of paper made from rags, also wood pulp, vegetable parchment, imt. parchment, and paraffin paper; good engineering and chemical knowledge. Best references.—Address No. 5844, office of the World's Paper Trade Review, 58, Shoe Lane, London, E.C. 5844

TO PAPERMAKERS.—Finisher requires situation; well up in shops and brown caps; good references.—Address W. H. Organ, 2, Aylmer Cottages, Watchet, near Bridgwater, Somerset. 5880

TO PAPERMAKERS.—Finisher requires situation; well up in small hands, groceries, cartridges, and browns; or could run paper bag machine; good character on leaving.—Address No. 5882, office of the World's Paper Trade Review, 58, Shoe Lane, London, E.C. 5882

Agency Wanted.

TO MAKERS of NEWS and PRINTING PAPERS.—Wanted, an Agency for the whole of Australia and New Zealand from makers of web news who could supply twenty to thirty tons weekly, and sheet news about five tons weekly. Makers who can supply this quantity and can compete are requested to send samples.

Also open for an Agency for T.S. and E.S. writings, fine and superfine printings, and coloured printings.

Address "Orient," No. 5866, office of the World's Paper Trade Review, 58, Shoe-lane, London, E.C. 5866

Machinery for Sale.

72-inch PAPER CUTTING MACHINE FOR SALE, By James Bertram, Edinburgh.
Complete with guillotine cutters, pulleys, &c. Cost £130. Price to clear £25—a bargain.

Every description of Machinery, Engines, Boilers, Pumps, at low prices. Wrought iron Pulleys a Specialty. J. W. PERKIN, 3, Spring Grove Terrace, Alexandra Road, LEEDS. 5883

TWO CALENDERS, second-hand, each with four hard-grained rolls, about 69 inches by 11¼ inches diam., with Frames, Pressure Levers, and Driving Gear.

ONE KOLLERGANG, new, Stones 51 inches by 14 inches, C.I. Pan, Scrapers, and Driving Gear.

ONE HYDRAULIC PRESS, second-hand, with Press Box 38 inches diam. by 32 inches deep, with wheels; all parts strong, Ram 2 feet 6 inches by 8 inches diam.

ONE 2-cwt. STEAM HAMMER, second-hand, for Roller Bars or General Forgings, Cylinder 7 inches diam. by 12 inch Stroke, with heavy Anvil Block.

TWELVE REVOLVING STRAINER PLATES, second-hand, 18⅜ inches by 21 inches, class B2, 3½ cut.

REFINING ENGINE, new, Conical Type; same as one working in a large printing mill.

Any reasonable offer will be considered by 5859
BERTRAMS LIMITED, SCIENNES, EDINBURGH.

Mill to be Let or Sold.

TO be LET or SOLD, a Paper Mill at Stalybridge, called the Higher Mill, containing one large machine and room for another, steam engine and boilers, in good condition.—Apply for further information to the Caretaker on the premises. 2162

NEW PATENTS.

APPLICATIONS.

16,286. Improvements in machines for decorticating ramie and other fibrous plants. J. A. Lacote.

16,854. Improvements in the manufacture of wood pulp and the like. E. Mense.

16,947. Improvements in the manufacture or treatment of paper. A. Yockney.

17,005. Improvements in the manufacture of paper. A. Beckwith.

SPECIFICATIONS PUBLISHED.

(7½d. each. By post 8d.)

1892.

15,346. Obtaining ammonia, hydrochloric acid, &c. Bale.
15,197. Electrolytic apparatus. Andreoli.
15,720. Treating peat for making paper pulp. Brin.

THE
United Asbestos Co.,
LIMITED,
DOCK HOUSE, BILLITER STREET, E.C.,
"SALAMANDER"
THE UNITED ASBESTOS COMPANY LIMITED · LONDON ·
TRADE MARK
Pioneers
OF THE
Asbestos
Trade.
UNITED ASBESTOS
NON-CONDUCTING
COVERING
(For Steam Boilers & Pipes)
Best and Cheapest in the Market; Will not Injure Boiler Plates.
ASBESTOS
GOODS of ALL DESCRIPTIONS
BELTINGS.
THE UNITED ASBESTOS CO., Limited,
PACKINGS.
UNITED ASBESTOS Co LMD LONDON
PURE ITALIAN MILLBOARD EXTRA QUALITY
A1
UNITED ASBESTOS
A1 MILLBOARDS
(ITALIAN)
Unequalled for Purity, Strength of Fibre, and Uniformity. For Dry Steam Joints it is admitted to be the cleanest, most durable and economical packing in existence.
UNITED ASBESTOS
SALAMANDER
Lubricating Cream & Oils,
SPECIALLY ADAPTED TO
PAPERMAKING MACHINERY.
DEPOTS:
MANCHESTER: 34, Deansgate; LIVERPOOL: 33, James Street; NEWCASTLE-UPON-TYNE: Quayside; GLASGOW: 54, Robertson Street; CARDIFF: 135, Bute Street; BRISTOL: Provident Buildings; HULL: Queen's Dock; ST. PETERSBURG: Gostinoe Dvor (Interior) No. 51.

Printed and Published by W. JOHN STONHILL 58, Shoe Lane, LONDON, E.C. Sept. 22, 1893.

VERY SOCRATIC DIALOGUES UP-TO-DATE.

III.

Dramatis Personæ—Two "GREEKS."

CYNICUS.—Have you digested the substance of our last dialogue, IMPECUNIARIUS?

IMPECUNIARIUS.—Yes, O Sage. The "digest" amounts to this. Being in debt and insolvent, I transfer my business to myself, under the style or firm of A, B, C, D, E, F and G, Limited, accepting as consideration therefor ten thousand pounds in shares, and ten thousand pounds in cash—but there being no cash forthcoming I accept in lieu thereof ten thousand pounds' worth of debentures. After that my mark is to rush somebody with these shares and debentures.

CYN.—And you are prepared with your six confed—— I should say your six subordinates?

IMP.—They are on view outside—carrying sandwich boards setting forth the merits of pilulæ crumbæ et saponacæ as a preventive of cholera. Take a squint at them. Ain't they a lovely lot!

CYN.—A villanous crew indeed. They should make model directors. Have you explained to them that they are to become shareholders and directors in the company to be formed?

IMP.—Fully.

CYN.—And they are all willing to join the board?

IMP.—Two boards——forty boards, at the same price I've paid: twos of unsweetened all round, and ninepence apiece each "board" day. This is "board" day, as you see.

CYN.—It is important to have good and high-sounding names and addresses for first subscribers. Have you thought of that?

IMP.—Truly, I once thought it might be worth while to graft a county councillor, or an M.P., or a lord mayor upon the show; but after reflection, and conceiving that respectability—— Eh! Oh, yes, it *would* be playing it too low down, as you say. You smile, most sapient of philosophers.

CYN.—I am led to smile at my pupil's aptitude in grasping great first principles and applying them in the construction of details. The inaptitude of the pupil is the general curse of a teacher's labours.

IMP.—Nature has been beneficent in her gifts to your servant. I take the "griff" easily.

CYN.—I commend you thereon. Then as to these contributaries before us?

IMP.—That nobleman with a boss eye and an empty cutty in his lips is Earl Sir Prince Fitz-Ginhot, of The Arches, Surrey, whose portrait by Harry Furniss (painted by commission for the Punch-Pears Club) is one of the pictures of the season. The eccentric individual next to him, with vacancy in his eye and another in his nether sartorial integuments, is Hookem Pursey, Esquire, of The Dials, Middlesex, a well-known conveyancer.

CYN.—Enough, my son; "Greeks" of noble name every one, beyond doubt, and of "good address:" commercial acquisitions. You have learned your lesson fully: go and apply it, and as you prosper, don't forget your benefactor, guide, philosopher, and friend.

IMP.—But pray thee, Cynicus, expound to me how it can be that such a lovely scheme as this company fake is openly permitted whilst less noxious lays, such as thuggism, burglary, long-firm swindling, and even such gentle grafts as the confidence game, the purse and three-card tricks, or thimble rigging, are treated as criminal offences?

CYN.—The question is a very natural one to arise in the mind of one brought into contact with it for a first time. But it argues a very one-sided knowledge of human nature, or perhaps I should rather say of your day and generation. Who are our law-givers? A body of notables, you would say perhaps, who are sent to the senate, chosen of the people for their high qualities of mind, their virtues, and general attainments; men gifted with profound acumen, knowledge of their species, and of the habits and customs, the frailties and the foibles of their countrymen, whose ken extends from the heights of heavenly virtue to the lowest depths of human depravity. But you would fall into grievous error. The senate is composed of a collection of six hundred or more respectabilities who can see no further than the end of their noses, and not half so far through a brick wall as you or I, who have to bustle round for our "bit." Some have intellects, but most have pet axes to grind. A few have passed through a course of training which fits them to look upon two sides of a problem, but the great bulk would argue syllogistically: the world is made up of men: I am a man: the world is filled with beings precisely like myself. Or, men are wholly virtuous: virtuous men may be trusted in all things: therefore legislation may be all of a trustful character. Or, men are wholly vicious: vice must be repressed: therefore all legislation must be repressive. So all legislation is either optimistic or pessimistic. Senator Optimus legislates for the best of all worlds with the best of all people in it, who need no preventive legislation. Senator Pessimus frames measures for the worst of all humanities, and prescribes fines, scourges, prison walls, and capital punishment. The two views of the condition of the law which so much surprise you are to be attributed to this division of labour. The one has been framed by Senator Optimus, the other by Senator Pessimus: the one is all trust and belief in the virtuous impulses of his fellowman; the other refuses credence to the possibility of any such good impulses existing. The two never by any chance co-operate. The few whose perceptive faculties, as I have said, are large enough to encompass both views, eschew the drudgery of domestic or commercial legislation, and confine themselves to high or imperial politics.

IMP.—What a one-eyed lot of chunks! I would like to study for myself the particular laws which thus legalise the spoiling of the Egyptians. I begin to look back with shame upon my ill-spent youth, which, however, is entirely attributable to the limited opportunities which I possessed, which gave a wrong bent to my intellect. I very early learned the art of putting up a hand at cards, to work the oracle in the science of tossing for mopusses; I acquired a reputation for my skill in manipulating three cards upon the circumference of an umbrella on the skirts of a crowd, or finding a merchant for a purse with a dener in it instead of three half-crowns; and I have practised a thousand other methods of working upon the weaknesses and follies and self-delusions of the genus "flat." But in that sort of cross game the police are everywhere, the risks are great and the profits precarious. Oh! had I had the advantage of your instruction in my early career, I had now been a millionaire, building almshouses, and drawing designs for my own monument!

CYN.—As you say, in such petty schemes as you have been hitherto engaged in, the police are everywhere; but in the path upon which I now set your feet the police are nowhere. Your wish to study for yourself is laudable, and will help you to devise schemes for obtaining boodle. Begin with the Act Anno Vicesimo Quinto et Vicesimo Sexto Victoriæ Reginæ, cap. 89.

IMP.—What is that, pray? Latin? I never heard that sort of Latin around Cable-street, nor yet in Soho, where a good deal of Latin is spoken, and where I learned my own bit.

CYN.—The "Greeks" of those quarters do indeed speak with a dialect and an idiom differing from the pure and impressive language of the law offices and the Pharmaceutical Society, and more nearly approaching that of Psalmanasar—

"In hoc est hoax, cum quiz et jokeses,
Et smokem, toastem, roastem folkses,
Fee, faw, fum."

But I will write down for you in plain translation the chapters to which you should apply yourself to become a proficient in the art of bleeding the public generally instead of a limited section of it. You begin in a humble way with your Pilulæ Company, Limited ——

IMP.—Twenty thousand quid!

CYN.—A trifle! To quote a now forgotten dramatic writer—"There's millions in it!" In a future dialogue I will instruct you upon the curious value which lies in those debentures of yours. Meantime, how about a lubricator?

IMP.—I'll go with you.

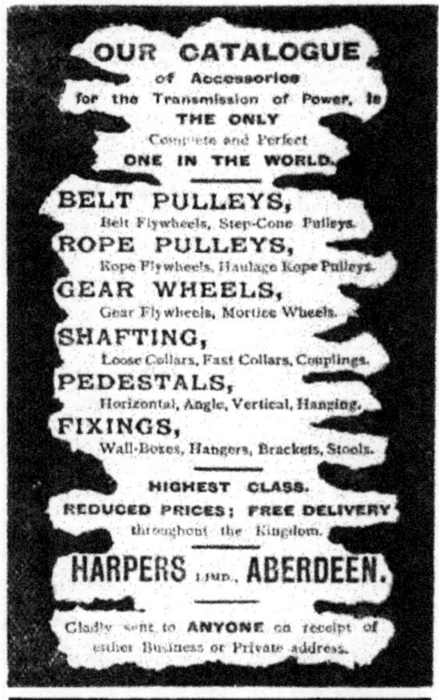

Telegrams: "*PUMPS, BURY.*" *Telephone:* 64, *BURY.*

CHARLES WALMSLEY & Co.,

LIMITED,

ATLAS IRON WORKS, BURY, NEAR MANCHESTER,

Engineers, Millwrights,

ESTABLISHED 1844.

Paper Machinists,

BRASS & IRON FOUNDERS.

PAPER BRUSH DAMPING MACHINE.

SPECIALTIES:

HIGH-CLASS STEAM ENGINES.

Simple, Double, Triple, and Quadruple Compound, from 10 to 1,000 i.h.p., fitted with Automatic Cut-off Gears.

ALL TYPES OF PUMPING MACHINERY:

DEEP WELL PUMPS,	BOILER PUMPS,	PAPERMAKERS'
BORE HOLE PUMPS,	VACUUM PUMPS,	CHEMIC & CAUSTIC Pumps,
STATIONARY FIRE Pumps,	HYDRAULIC PUMPS,	STUFF & WATER PUMPS.

SOLE MAKERS OF 2513

PARTINGTON'S Patent DUPLEX CUTTING MACHINE.

THE CRYSTAL PALACE ANTI-BURGLAR AND FIRE EXHIBITION.

An interesting exhibition of fire extinguishing appliances and devices to frustrate the designs of the burgling fraternity was opened at the Crystal Palace last week, and will be continued during the present month. The exhibits are not many in number, but are full of interest in many respects. Notably the collection of antiquated fire engines, one of which bears the date 1736, while another, shown by Messrs. Shand, Mason and Co., and at one time belonging to the borough of Dunstable, was constructed in 1570. Among the modern fire extinguishing appliances is shown the Patent Bucket Fire Extinguisher of Messrs. Messer and Thorpe, Quality-court, Chancery-lane, E.C. This useful and readily got at arrangement consists of a covered iron tank in the shape of a pedestal, standing about three feet high, with a square of eighteen inches. It is full of water in which is submerged a 'nest of buckets,' telescoped one within the other, which can be withdrawn in a moment filled and ready for use. Mr. E. Marriott, Russell-road, Kensington, shows specimens of "Cyanite" fireproof paints and stains. The anti-burglar section of the exhibition consists principally of fire and thief proof safes. Milners Safe Company, Limited, show plate safes, jewel safes, and strong room doors, in addition to their ordinary office safes. Antcliffs safes are shown by A. Ardley and Co., 17, Great St. Helens, who have also an exhibit of office furniture, copying presses, and other requisites. The Chancery-lane Safe Deposit Co., show sections of their safe corridors, while the Northern Assurance Co., and the Goldsmiths and General Burglary Insurance Association, Limited, have also interesting exhibits. The show is well worth a visit, and although, as we have said, it is not extensive, it contains much that is of interest, and shows the precautions that the ingenuity of man has had to produce for the baffling of those two great evils fire and thieves. The palace grounds are very beautiful just now, and the interior itself most attractive, several additions having recently been made to the art collections.

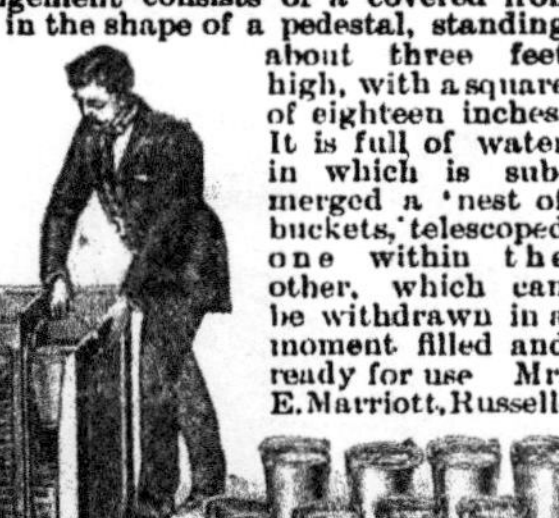

ABRIDGED PATENT SPECIFICATIONS.

13,524 (92).—Improvements in Paper Folding Machines.—LEONARD W. GILL and ALFRED BRADLEY. Accepted 8th July, 1893.

This invention has reference to folding machines such as are used for folding newspapers, pamphlets, etc., of eight or sixteen pages, and where the sheets are fed to adjustable gauges. The chief objects of the invention are to avoid curling the edges of the sheet whilst being fed, and also to enable the sheets to be evenly piled or knocked up direct from the folding rollers without the use of tapes or the necessity of turning the sheet.

16,150 (92).—Improvements in Perforating Machines.—ALFRED PARTRIDGE. Accepted 15th July, 1893.

This invention relates to machines that are employed for perforating paper, cardboard, and the like material, and is simple in construction, being worked by a treadle that operates the perforator by means of a cam.

9,457 (93).—Improvements in Machinery for the Manufacture of Paper Bags.—ACHILLE J. DENOYER. Accepted 2nd June, 1893.

This invention relates to machinery for the manufacture of square or satchel-bottomed paper bags, having an advertisement or other device printed upon them if required.

THE WORLD'S PAPER TRADE REVIEW.

Printed and Published by W. JOHN STONHILL, 58, Shoe Lane, LONDON, E.C. Sept 22, 1893.

Telegrams: "STONHILL, LONDON." A B C Code. Registered at the General Post Office as a Newspaper.

Vol. XX. No. 13. LONDON, SEPTEMBER 29, 1893. Price 6d.

BRIN'S PEAT PULP PROCESS.

In the mechanical and chemical treatment of peat for the manufacture of paper pulp, several improvements are claimed by Mr. Arthur Brin, to cover which a patent has been secured. The object is to effect a thorough bleaching of the material, other processes, according to the patentee, failing in this respect. It is also claimed that an economy is effected in time and materials.

The peat is first brought to a loose fibrous condition, free from the accompanying sand and decomposed vegetable matter, by being passed between a pair of opening rollers, such as shown at A, armed with teeth by which the fibres are opened out or loosened at the same time that the earthy and soluble matters are washed away by a copious stream of water. For this purpose the rollers A may be contained in a chamber B and provided with strainers *b* beneath the rollers to retain the fibres and allow the water to pass away, combs *a* being provided for detaching the fibres from the teeth of the rollers A.

The fibres, having been thus opened out and cleaned, are charged, through a suitable valve, into a vessel C containing a pair of squeezing rollers D made of hard wood or other material not acted on by the reagents employed, whereby the colouring matter contained in the capillary fibres of the peat is expressed, in order that it may be replaced by the liquors used for the treatment of the peat, which by being thus brought into the most intimate contact with the cellulose of the peat are enabled to exert a much more effectual decolourising action without affecting prejudicially the physical qualities of the fibres. The rollers D are mounted in spring-pressed bearings, and the peat fibres are caused to pass between them by an Archimedean screw E, and are at same time subjected to the action of a hot solution of caustic soda at, say, 2½ degs. Baumé, and to a steam pressure of, say, five atmospheres contained in vessel C, the apparatus being so arranged as to admit of a continual circulation of the matters under treatment, so that the fibres shall be caused to pass repeatedly between the rollers.

After being subjected for a sufficient time, say 1½ hour, to this treatment, the fibrous mass is discharged into a tank E[1] where it is washed with cold water sprayed from a rose F, the dirty water being run off through a wire cloth strainer at the bottom of the tank. From this tank the mass, which is kept agitated by a wheel G, is conveyed by a jet of steam and gas issuing at a nozzle *h* immersed therein, through a pipe I to the bleaching vessel K, which contains a pair of squeezing rollers between which the mass is caused to pass repeatedly whilst being subjected to the bleaching action, the arrangement being similar to that of the vessel C. The gas is supplied by a pipe H, and is caused to mingle with the steam supplied by pipe L by the action of the steam issuing from a nozzle within the chamber *l*. The gas employed is what the patentee terms active oxygen or oxychloride of hydrogen, being a mixture of oxygen and chlorine resulting from the passage of oxygen over binoxide of manganese in the presence of liquid hydrochloric acid. The gaseous mixture thus supplied to the vessel K forms hypochlorous acid, which exercises a powerful bleaching action on the pulp, any gas in excess passing on and being caught as hereafter mentioned.

When the charge had been sufficiently bleached it is run off from vessel K into a tank M, whence it is transferred by a pump P or by other means, into a closed vessel N,

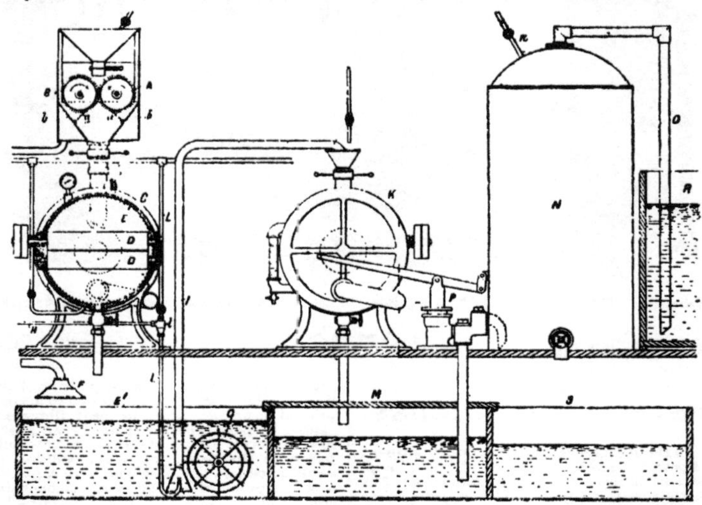

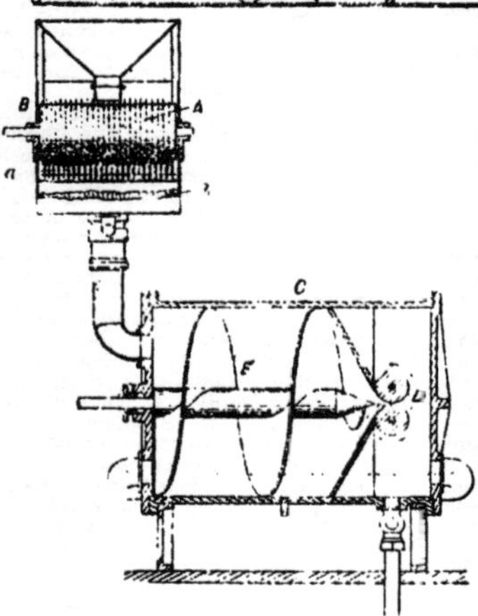

containing a solution of caustic soda at about five or six degrees Baumé, and into which is run, through pipe *n*, water acidulated with two or three per cent. of hydrochloric or sulphuric acid for the purpose of disengaging chlorine, which passes off through a dip-pipe O into a fourth vessel R containing a solution of caustic soda at, say, five degrees Baumé. The pulp now completely bleached is run off from vessel N into a tank S ready for papermaking, whilst the hypochlorous acid formed in the vessel R may be used for bleaching another charge in vessel K, the strength of the bleaching solution being maintained by the injection of gas along with the steam, as before described.

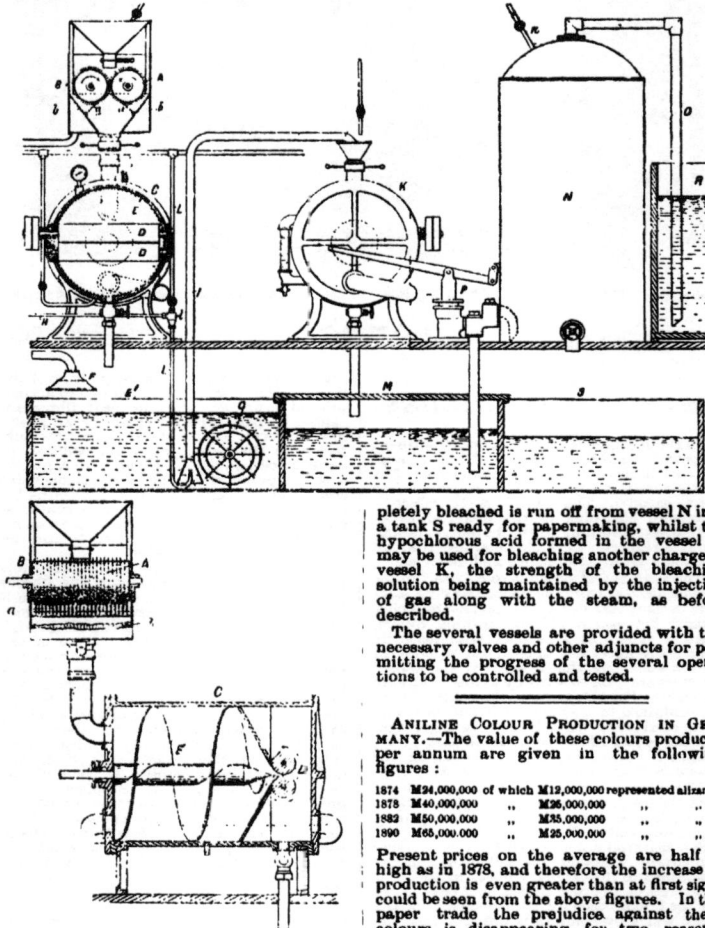

The several vessels are provided with the necessary valves and other adjuncts for permitting the progress of the several operations to be controlled and tested.

ANILINE COLOUR PRODUCTION IN GERMANY.—The value of these colours produced per annum are given in the following figures :

1874	M24,000,000	of which	M12,000,000	represented	alizarine
1878	M40,000,000	,,	M26,000,000	,,	,,
1882	M50,000,000	,,	M35,000,000	,,	,,
1890	M65,000,000	,,	M25,000,000	,,	,,

Present prices on the average are half as high as in 1878, and therefore the increase of production is even greater than at first sight could be seen from the above figures. In the paper trade the prejudice against these colours is disappearing for two reasons, firstly, because the saving is very considerable, and secondly, because fast colours can be found among them when required.

WHO'S WHO?

THE PERSONNEL OF THE PAPER, STATIONERY, PRINTING AND ALLIED TRADES.

Everyone must have observed that of late there has been a remarkable change in the style of a very large proportion of the oldest and largest paper, stationery, and printing concerns. The word "Limited" has become quite familiar as an integral part of their nomenclature. This affix was, as we all know, made obligatory by the provisions of "The Companies Act" (25 and 26 Vict. c. 89), which was passed in 1862. Our own Legislature, foreseeing the inconveniences which might be caused by the names of the acting responsible members of a firm not being given, provided for compulsory publication of the names of the shareholders in such companies. These returns are, as a rule, accurately and regularly made up and issued. But they are in a form which to the great majority of the public is quite unavailable. Not one person in a thousand knows "Who's Who" in a concern of even general repute. Yet for many reasons, and on divers occasions it is desirable to know the personnel of the company in question. This information we are about to supply. We shall do it from official and authentic data, and in no merely prying spirit. No reflection on the stability of any firm will be implied. The names of the parties constituting it will be given, and their shares in te capital stated, so far as official documents disclose them. The information we think will be both useful and interesting. Readers will know whom they have to deal with when transacting business with a limited liability company, and a contribution will be made to current trade history which the future annalist may greatly appreciate.

ANGLO-AMERICAN SELF-OPENING SQUARE PAPER BAG CO., LIMITED.

INCORPORATED CAPITAL:

£100,000 (44,000 "A" and 56,000 "B" SHARES).

REDUCTION OF CAPITAL:

CANCELMENT OF "A" (OR VENDORS') SHARES.

In the WORLD'S PAPER TRADE REVIEW of September 22nd we stated that the vendors had agreed to the cancelment of their shares which had been allotted to them as "A" shares. Mr. Justice Kennedy, in making the order for this reduction of the company's capital said it was necessary to add the words "and reduced" to the title of the concern for a month longer. The company was registered on the 13th April, 1888, the principal specified objects being:

(a) To purchase and acquire patent rights and privileges of a like nature in the United Kingdom and elsewhere, in respect of certain inventions in connection with the manufacture and construction of paper bags by machinery, and with a view thereto to enter into, adopt, and carry into effect, either with or without modification, an agreement made between the International Paper Bag Machine Company of the City of New York, U.S.A., of the one part, and Henry Fricker, trustee for the company, of the other part, and to acquire such patent rights and privileges in respect of any other inventions relating to similar matters, or to any mechanical or manufacturing process capable of being used in turning to account any such inventions as aforesaid or conveniently associated therewith, and to turn all or any such patent rights and privileges as aforesaid into account by working thereunder, granting licenses, sale or otherwise.

(b) To purchase or acquire any other patent rights or privileges whatsoever which the company may by special resolution determine to purchase or acquire, and to turn the same to account by user thereof, or by granting licenses, sale or otherwise.

(c) To carry on the business of constructing manufacturing and preparing machines for the manufacture of paper bags, and of manufacturing paper bags, and any other trade or business connected with the utilisation of any invention or manner of manufacture, the subject of any patent rights and privileges, which shall have been acquired by the company, and either in the United Kingdom or in any part of the world.

The nominal capital of this company at the time of registration was £100,000 divided into 100,000 shares of £1 each, whereof 44,000 are called A shares and the remaining 56,000 are called B shares. The A shares, or so many as were issued, were held upon the terms that they should be entitled to 44 per cent. of the profits of the company, available for dividends in any year, and the B shares were entitled to 56 per cent. of the profits available for dividends in any year.

The signatories to the memorandum of association (holding one B share each) were: William Philip Fricker, 3, Woodley-terrace, Tottenham, commercial clerk; Edward Racine Fricker, Lammas-house, South Hackney Common, commercial clerk; Henry Fricker, 4, Gt. Portland-street, W., manager, Wanzer Sewing Machine Co.; William Henry Whaite, 17, Ospringe-road, Brecknock-road, N.W., solicitors clerk; Alfred Wright, 23, Huddart-street, Burdett-road, E., solicitors clerk; Thomas Hackett, 4, Raddington-road, W., solicitors clerk.

A shareholder had one vote for every 100 A shares held by him, and had one vote for such number of B shares held by him as would allow to the holders of the B shares for the time being issued 560 votes between them so that when all the B shares had been issued, each 100 shares whether A or B, would be entitled to one vote.

There were, at the time of the incorporation, to be only two directors, and the names of the first two were Henry Fricker and Henry Forbes Wetherly. A director's qualification is the holding of B shares in the company in his own right of the value of £1,000. The above-named gentlemen were appointed managing directors for a term of five years from 1st June, 1888. A special resolution, however, passed 25th February, 1890, added the name of Charles Saunderson to the directors, and the number of directors was fixed at three.

[illegible] particulars [illegible] agreements [illegible] registered [illegible]

[illegible] 1888. between International [illegible] Machine Company of New York, [illegible] and the present company [illegible] Agreement for sale of patent [illegible] the present company, the purchase [illegible] satisfied by the issue to the American company of [illegible] fully paid shares.

[illegible] September 1888. Between H. [illegible] [illegible] Henry Tucker and the company [illegible] agreement dated [illegible] May 188[illegible] made between the English and American Company for the purchase of letters patent [illegible] and states that part of the consideration therein stated was payment to the American company of £6,[illegible] by cash and bills in the following proportions, that is to say the sum of £[illegible] in cash, the sum of [illegible] by the set off and allowance [illegible] referred to, and the balance by the promissory notes of Henry Tucker for £1200. This agreement records the performance of these obligations, and states that in consideration of Messrs. Tucker and Wetherby carrying out this arrangement, they were entitled to receive one B share for every one pound subscribed by them, and the agreement therefore gives the authority for such transfer of shares.

10 February 1890. Agreement between Charles Sunderland and the company, whereby the company purchase ten machines for making paper bags, for the sum of £[illegible] payable by the allotment of 4,000 B shares fully paid.

The latest summary filed is dated 30th December, 1892. According to this document [illegible] and 21,500 B shares are taken up. The total amount of calls received amount to £[illegible] and the 41,000 A shares are considered fully paid.

The holders of the A shares [illegible]

[illegible]

The following hold the B shares:

[illegible]

COLLAPSE OF THE PROPOSED SYNDICATE OF CANADIAN PAPERMAKERS.

The Canadian syndicate of paper manufacturers, which was to have [illegible] and which gave promise at the [illegible] of being a [illegible] considerable [illegible] and collapsed before it was [illegible]. It was a bitter disappointment to the [illegible] of this scheme. It was [illegible] by those back of this [illegible] the leading [illegible] paper and [illegible] [illegible] The smaller mills would be [illegible] down, and the [illegible] the demand, and [illegible] [illegible] [illegible] other agreements were [illegible] effect that the [illegible] Canada mills [illegible] after the [illegible] Dominion, while the [illegible] Canada mills [illegible] from the others. [illegible] the [illegible] travelling all over the Dominion, and there was [illegible] cutting of rates. [illegible] fell through [illegible] is believed to have been [illegible] by the [illegible] [illegible] competition. The trade of [illegible] and lower Canada is also so widely different that it was almost impossible to arrange matters satisfactory to all parties, and so the combination never materialised, and the paper business of Canada is conducted on the old lines.

BRITISH NORTH AMERICA.

The following figures show the exportation of British paper and alkali during the past five years.

CANADA.

Paper.

1888	37,357 cwts.	£[illegible]
1889	33,971 ..	[illegible]
1890	31,170 ..	[illegible]
1891	39,282 ..	[illegible]
1892	35,180 ..	[illegible]

Alkali.

1888	271,000 cwts.	£66,186
1889	246,800 ..	55,576
1890	211,100 ..	61,036
1891	215,200 ..	70,[illegible]
1892	239,300 ..	73,629

NEWFOUNDLAND AND COAST OF LABRADOR.

Paper.

[illegible]	[illegible] cwts.	£5,030
[illegible]	[illegible] ..	5,676
[illegible]	[illegible] ..	5,733
[illegible]	[illegible] ..	5,967
[illegible]	[illegible] ..	6,247

WILLIAM LORD,

Lord Street Boiler Works,

BURY, near MANCHESTER.

MAKER OF

SPHERICAL and CYLINDRICAL BOILERS

FOR PAPERMAKERS.

These Boilers are Fitted with LORD'S PATENT MANHOLES, which have been adopted by most of the Leading Houses in the Paper Trade for EFFICIENCY and SAFETY. [illegible]

THESE MANHOLES SURPASS ANYTHING YET INVENTED FOR THE PURPOSE.

H. WATSON & SONS,

HIGH BRIDGE WORKS, NEWCASTLE-ON-TYNE,

are prepared to

Close Strainer Plates

worn within 2 full Gauges wider than they were when set to work

at ½d. per sq. inch, less 30% discount.

Carriage of all Plates paid by Goods train to Newcastle.

TELEGRAMS "[illegible], NEWCASTLE." [illegible]

L. DESTREE, A. WIESCHER & CO.,

HAREN, near BRUSSELS, Belgium.

Manufacturers

Specially for Papermakers

ANILINE COLOURS,

ULTRAMARINE BLUES,

Possessing the Highest Acid Resisting and Colour Giving Properties.

Exporters

CHEMISTS EMPLOYED FOR TESTING THE MOST SUITABLE DYES and the Most ECONOMICAL Method of Employment.

SPECIAL CARE IN PACKING FOR EXPORTATION. [illegible]

EVERY ADVICE GIVEN TO OUR CUSTOMERS.

JACKSON

BURY, near MANCHESTER

SHALL'S PATENT PERFECTING ENGINE

OVER 100 NOW IN USE AND ON ORDER.

Application.

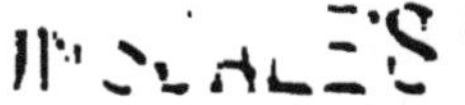

Boiler Coverer Paper Hair Cork
NON-CONDUCTING CEMENT.

Paper Trade Review, August 2nd, 1889:—

"The Steam ... are covered with a Non-Conducting Composition supplied by ... which HAS BEEN FOUND TO ADHERE VERY WELL, and to ... A CONSIDERABLE SAVING."

... the Test of an EIGHT YEARS' TRIAL."

... in Cork Covering. Patent No. 19,906, 1889.

TURNER BROTHERS,

SPOTLAND, ROCHDALE,

SPINNERS and MANUFACTURERS of

ASBESTOS,

IN ALL ITS FORMS.

SOLE MANUFACTURERS OF THE

"GRIPWELL"

SOLID WOVEN HAIR BELTING

FOR MAIN and OTHER DRIVING,

SPECIALLY SUITABLE for PAPERMAKERS.

Bleached Sulphate STRAW PULP.

Bleached Sulphate STRAW PULP.

Bleached Sulphate STRAW PULP.

HERMANN MARIA SCHOELLER & CO.

DUEREN,

Manufacturers of BLEACHED SULPHATE

Straw Pulp,

UNEQUALLED FOR COLOUR, STRENGTH AND PURITY.
PACKED IN BALES.

For Samples, &c., apply to the Sole Agents:

HENDERSON, CRAIG & CO.

LIMITED,

116, QUEEN VICTORIA STREET, LONDON, and at Manchester and Edinburgh

TURKEY.

The [illegible] of Constantinople shows imports of goods from British ports during the [illegible] Turkish financial year of the value of £[illegible].

New Tariff.

It is some years now since new tariffs were [illegible], by which the present ad valorem duty of [illegible] per cent. on imports will be replaced by specific duties calculated to be equivalent to [illegible] duty of [illegible] per cent. on the average on the total value of imports at present prices, while the internal duties and the transit and export duties will be abolished. There is, however, no sign of the new tariffs coming into force for many a day. [illegible] warehouses have been built at the large ports, but many points still remain to be settled in the new commercial treaties between Turkey and the various powers to which the new tariff will be annexed.

British Chamber of Commerce.

Attention is directed to the useful work done by the British Chamber of Commerce in Constantinople. The Chamber, unlike its foreign colleagues, enjoys no Government subvention, and is not accorded as much support as it would seem to deserve by firms at home. The terms of membership are very easy, [illegible] entrance fee and [illegible] annual subscription, for which, it is said, subscribers may rely on getting trustworthy information as to [illegible], &c., when required. It is true that the Chamber does not publish the extensive annual and monthly reports which form a feature of the French Chamber of Commerce's work, but the writer [illegible] that reports on subjects on which information is specially requested are frequently drawn up and sent home to the applicants.

Trade Marks.

Merchants are again warned against [illegible] for goods intended for the Turkish market trade marks which bear similar official [illegible] of any particular [illegible]. Difficulties frequently arise at the custom house from [illegible] of this nature, and in such case it is most difficult to overcome official scruples.

The Custom House.

The custom house is the Turkish department which perhaps causes the foreign merchant the greatest amount of difficulty. A council of so-called experts has been formed, whose functions are to analyse various importations, and report on them before they are allowed to enter the country.

The Hamidiah Paper Works.

No new enterprise in which British capital is involved have been started in Constantinople since last year. The paper mill at Beicos is working under [illegible] conditions, notwithstanding it is still in its infancy.

[illegible]

The following importations of [illegible] stationery, cardboard, &c., for the two years mentioned were as follows:

	1901.		1902.	
[illegible]	70 quintals	[illegible]	191 quintals	£[illegible]
[illegible]	[illegible] cwts.	[illegible]	[illegible] cwts.	[illegible]
[illegible]	[illegible]	[illegible]	[illegible]	[illegible]
[illegible]	50 cases	[illegible]	[illegible] cases	[illegible]
[illegible]	—	—	[illegible] bales	[illegible]

The paper for wrapping is chiefly supplied by Austria-Hungary and Germany, whilst that for writing purposes and for making cigarettes France and Austria-Hungary take the lead.

Paper Exports to Turkey.

During last year the following exports of British goods to Turkey took place:—

Writings, Printings and Envelopes	[illegible] cwts.	£[illegible]
Pasteboard, &c.	[illegible]	[illegible]
Other kinds of Paper	[illegible]	[illegible]
Total	[illegible]	[illegible]

Turkish Rags.

Great Britain imports rags to the annual value of about £[illegible].

Customs Tariff between Austria and Russia.—The negotiations between Austria and Russia in respect of the customs tariff have resulted in a favourable understanding being arrived at.

A new mineral, the properties of which bear some resemblance to those of asbestos, has recently been discovered in the [illegible]. This mineral is [illegible], transparent, and non-combustible. Experiments have been carried out at [illegible], which tend to prove that the new substance can be utilised in the manufacture of bank notes.

Filters [illegible] from Glazed Clay.—The firm of Wilhelm [illegible], Wurtemberg, has for some years given to the production of the same material for filters, [illegible] great attention. By very [illegible] conducted experiments this firm has obtained great success, for not only a [illegible] but also [illegible]. The latter offers greater advantages to the user through greater [illegible]. [illegible]

iv.—Supp[illegible]

LONS[illegible]

The "DAILY [illegible]
LON[illegible]

[illegible]

[illegible] ares [illegible] drawn [illegible]

[illegible] PAPER [illegible] EGYPT. [illegible] names [illegible] in [illegible]. The cigar- [illegible] manufacture. [illegible] In consequence [illegible] which ex- [illegible] receive [illegible] The Government [illegible] that [illegible] great [illegible] not only in Europe [illegible] Asia, America and Australia. [illegible] that the use [illegible] will [illegible] permanent expansion [illegible]. The paper is imported [illegible] books. The amount imported [illegible] was [illegible] France [illegible] Austria [illegible] longer bring [illegible] from [illegible] but also from Bohemia and [illegible] France generally imports [illegible] paper [illegible] book [illegible]. The [illegible] is much [illegible]. Considering the amount [illegible] paper-makers should [illegible] advantage in the trade.

THE SAXON PAPER TRADE.—[illegible] the scarcity of water, the [illegible] industry shows [illegible] better [illegible] in the first six months of [illegible] than in the corresponding period of the previous year. Steam power, which [illegible] mostly, of course increased [illegible] production, but, notwithstanding [illegible] could not be obtained. [illegible] were made within the first six months [illegible] follows:

	[illegible]	[illegible]	[illegible]
	Metre [illegible]	[illegible]	[illegible]
Roofing and asphalt [illegible]	[illegible]	[illegible]	[illegible]
[illegible] bottling and [illegible] paper	[illegible]	[illegible]	[illegible]
[illegible] paper	[illegible]	[illegible]	[illegible]
[illegible] paper	[illegible]	[illegible]	[illegible]
[illegible] packing paper	[illegible]	[illegible]	[illegible]
[illegible] board and [illegible] board	[illegible]	[illegible]	
[illegible] paper	[illegible]	[illegible]	[illegible]
Photographic paper	[illegible]	[illegible]	[illegible]
[illegible] paper	[illegible]	[illegible]	[illegible]
[illegible] and tissue paper	[illegible]	[illegible]	[illegible]
Writing, printing and drawing	[illegible]	[illegible]	[illegible]
[illegible]	[illegible]	[illegible]	[illegible]
[illegible] paper	[illegible]		
Total	[illegible]	[illegible]	[illegible]

The export [illegible] shown [illegible] per cent [illegible] the first half [illegible] per cent [illegible] greater [illegible] South and [illegible] America [illegible] and [illegible] United States. The [illegible] American [illegible] the Argentine Republic [illegible] more considerable [illegible]

THE exports of paper at New York, according to the last weekly list received, include the following items:

Australia	17 [illegible]	Liverpool	[illegible]
London	3[illegible]	New Zealand	[illegible]
B. West Indies	[illegible]		

THE PAPER TRADE.—There is a more cheerful feeling in trade circles, and some mills which have been idle for several weeks have started up. None of the grades show any special or marked features, and of course many machines are yet down, so that production is not up to capacity by a good deal. The demand for news keeps up very well.

A REDUCTION of wages is one of the suggested means of relief [illegible] among manufacturers in the East, and in a few cases it has been acted upon to the extent of [illegible] per cent., but manufacturers admit that it will not effect such a reduction in the cost of production as will justify them in producing anything more than present actual demands. Other manufacturers have reduced the time of running; some to five days and some to three in the week, rates of wages being untouched. In most cases the latter course is most acceptable to the wage-earner. If, however, Congressional action should be such as to withdraw present protection from American manufacturers, then the wages of operatives will, according to the *Paper Trade*, go down beyond question.

SIMONET'S TRITURATEUR.—Messrs. Wandel and Company, [illegible], N.Y., exhibit one of their Simonet's triturateurs for the preparation of paper stock in the French section of Machinery Hall at the Chicago Exhibition, and considerable attention has been directed to the invention.

PROPOSED STRAWBOARD AND WOOD-PULP BOARD COMBINATION.—Now that the manufacturers of straw and wood pulp boards have been endeavouring to harmonise and to enter into a combination, it will be of interest to review the figures which show the growth of these branches of the paper-board industry. Taking the returns from the various mills as submitted for insertion in Lockwood's Directory last year, and comparing them with like returns sent in this year, the New York *Paper Trade* Journal finds that during the twelve months the capacity of the strawboard mills has increased over [illegible] per cent. This is not a startling increase in production. The figures of the wood pulp board output show the most surprising exhibit. In this the increase for the year has been [illegible] in a fraction of [illegible] per cent. Since [illegible] the percentage of gain in proportion has been 28 per cent. for strawboard and [illegible] per cent. in wood pulp board. Although these figures may not be particularly gratifying to the owners of mills engaged in the manufacture of these products, they nevertheless bear testimony to the energy and enterprise which [illegible] of the paper-making. The [illegible] of strawboard [illegible] large proportions [illegible] in [illegible] combination. The [illegible] annual production of the mills under ordinary circumstances may be estimated as follows: Strawboard, [illegible] tons; wood pulp board, [illegible] tons.

JAPAN.

The following statistics show [illegible] exports [illegible]:

PAPER.

[illegible]	[illegible]	[illegible]
[illegible]	[illegible]	[illegible]
[illegible]	[illegible]	[illegible]
[illegible]	[illegible]	[illegible]
1892	[illegible]	[illegible]

[illegible]

[illegible]	[illegible]	[illegible]
[illegible]	[illegible]	[illegible]
[illegible]	1[illegible]	[illegible]
1891	[illegible]	[illegible]
1892	[illegible]	[illegible]

Returns dealing with the trade of Yokohama, Hiogo and Osaka during 1892 show the value of paper exported to be [illegible] and that imported [illegible]. Rags were exported to the value of [illegible] and [illegible] were imported to the extent of [illegible].

The American firm of papermakers' engineers, Black & Clawson [illegible], of Hamilton, Ohio, recently shipped a large and well-equipped Fourdrinier machine for the [illegible] Paper Company, of Tokio, Japan. This makes the fourth paper machine which the company has shipped to Japan. The machine is one of the largest and best manufactured by the Black & Clawson [illegible]. It weighs [illegible] tons and is highly finished. It has a capacity of ten tons a day. The machine is divided into about 250 sections, each being securely boxed. All polished parts of the machine are greased and the boxes are bound with hoop iron. An inventory is taken of what goes in each and every box, and the boxes are marked, numbered and weighed, and the dimensions taken. The inventory with the plans will be sent by mail to Tokio, and upon the arrival of the machine as each box is opened it must correspond in size, weight, number and contents with the inventory. [illegible] a cablegram to the Black and Clawson [illegible] giving the number of the box, would be sufficient for that company to supply the missing parts.

THE death [illegible] founder of the [illegible] Works of [illegible] W. [illegible] and Sons [illegible] is announced.

At [illegible] where the works of the [illegible] Paper Manufacturing [illegible] Ltd., are located, [illegible] discoveries are reported to have been made.

WORLD'S PAPER TRADE REVIEW OFFICE,
58, SHOE LANE, LONDON, E.C.
SEPTEMBER 28, 1893.

TRADE NOTES.

THE order for the new machine for the London Paper Mill Co., at Dartford, has been placed with Messrs. Bertrams Limited, Sciennes, Edinburgh.

SLATEFORD PAPER MILL, MIDLOTHIAN.—This mill, formerly worked by Mr. John Plummer, has been acquired by Mr. William Laughton, late manager of the Gordon's Mill Co. A start is expected to be made in the course of a few days on high-class browns, caps and grocery papers. Messrs. James Bertram and Son, of Leith Walk Foundry, have had in hand the re-arrangement of plant.

THE COLONIAL PAPER COMPANY, LTD.—This company has been registered with a nominal capital of £10,000 in £1 shares. Objects: To carry on the business of manufacturers and dealers in paper and stationery, general machinery connected therewith; also the business of printers and dealers in printing machinery and materials. Amongst the subscribers are Messrs. H. P. Ansell, 65, Kellett-road, S.W., paper merchant; G. R. Punlott, 56, Crewdson-road, S.W., printer; and P. O. Hare Wyllie, The Limes, Montague-road, N., stationer.

SALE OF NEW BRIDGE PAPER WORKS, RADCLIFFE, NEAR MANCHESTER.—For some time past it has been rumoured in the trade that Messrs. John Wild and Sons were about to dispose of their New Bridge Paper Mill. We may now state that the purchasers are Messrs. Bibby, the well-known paper bag makers, of Rochdale. Paper bag manufacture has long been a specialty of New Bridge Works, and with the patented machinery of Messrs. Bibby no doubt this branch will be considerably extended in the future.

THE IMPORTATION OF RAGS AT THE HARTLEPOOLS.—It was stated at last week's meeting of the Hartlepool Port Sanitary Authority, Councillor Yeoman, J.P., presiding, that the rags which had been imported into West Hartlepool, and which were not hydraulically pressed and iron bound, had been returned to Hamburg. Mr. Vitty thought that the matter should be brought before Parliament by the local members, seeing that the Local Government Board had simply acknowledged receipt of this Authority's letter on the subject. The Chairman replied that Mr. Furness would be glad to do so if the letter had not the desired effect. Mr. Hastings, the Inspector, said that the number of bales of rags imported was 536, but 70 of these being disused clothing were returned to Hamburg.

THE most important feature of Wednesday's meeting of the Associated Chambers of Commerce at Plymouth was a statement made by Sir Courtenay Boyle, permanent secretary to the Board of Trade, who said that although trade was not making gigantic strides, it was steadily progressive. He tested that by a comparison of the imports and exports, and the inward and outward tonnage, savings banks deposits, and the increase in the annual product of a penny in the pound on the income-tax. There was a remarkable growth under every head. The dangers which threatened commerce, he went on to say, arose from the spirit of over-speculation, perpetual trade disputes, the tendency to lock capital up in securities which, however sound, could not be readily realised, and the floating of bubble companies which were not intended to last. Such organisations as that Chamber could do more to counteract existing evils than any other body or State department. Resolutions in favour of adopting a decimal system and of strengthening the navy for the protection of commerce were passed.

MR. EMIL ANDREOLI is prolific in patenting modifications in electrolytic apparatus. He now claims (1) the construction of porous conducting diaphragms or septa in the form of narrow baskets of metallic gauze filled with conducting material in fragments more or less minute; (2) an electrolytic apparatus consisting of an outer metallic tank directly connected with the negative pole of an electric generator and an inner tank (containing an anode or anodes) made of metallic gauze or of panels of metallic gauze and granular conducting material, or other porous conducting material, connected with the outer tank by a wire and which is completely closed, excepting inlet and outlet tubes, and submerged in the electrolyte contained in the outer tank; and (3) the construction of anodes, which may be of plain or perforated platinum, or of strips or trellis of platinum, or of retort carbon, or other substance not readily attacked, and are usually fixed parallel with and near to the porous conducting diaphragm or to the sides of the porous conducting tank by being attached to the lid.

THE ELECTROLYSIS OF SALT.—Mr. Thomas Craney, of Michigan, U.S.A., has taken out a patent in this country for several modifications in apparatus for the manufacture of caustic soda by electrolytic decomposition of chloride of sodium. The main object appears to be to adapt the apparatus for continuous work, to facilitate the collection of the products, and to control its operation. The patentee claims: (1) the combination with an electrolytic cell, of a receiver connected to the bottom of the cell by a valve-controlled connection and means for discharging the liquid from the receiver; (2) the combination in an electrolytic cell, of the tank containing the electrolyte, the receiver connected to the bottom thereof, the overflow pipe from the receiver, a weighing receptacle flexibly connected to said overflow, and an overflow from said receptacle; (3) the combination in an electrolytic cell, of a tank containing the electrolyte, the perforated false bottom or grating, the receiver connected to the bottom thereof, the overflow pipe from the receiver extending up the height of the electrolyte in the tank, the weighing receptacle flexibly connected to said overflow pipe and the overflow from the receptacle; (4) the combination with an electrolytic cell of an overflow pipe, through which the liquid is discharged from the bottom of the cell, and a weighing receptacle flexibly connected thereto and into which said overflow pipe discharges.

COLLINS PAPER MILL CO., LTD.—For the quarter ending August 31st a profit is shown of £68. Certain allowances have been made, reducing the adverse balance to £239.

H.M. STATIONERY OFFICE, DUBLIN.—Tenders for the supply of paper to be delivered at the Stationery Office, Dublin, are invited to be sent in to the controller of H.M. Stationery Office, Princes-street, London, S.W., before noon Wednesday next.

RE H. R. MARK.—The whole of Wednesday's sitting of the London Bankruptcy Court was occupied by the public examination of Henry Robert Mark, of the Dr. Johnson Press, Fleet-lane, Old Bailey, trading as W. Wilfred Head and Mark. The debtor filed his petition on the 21st July, the accounts showing total liabilities £16,108 10s. 11d., of which £13,267 13s. 11d. is expected to rank against assets £18,105 13s. He was questioned at some length respecting the circumstances attending the formation of a limited company promoted with a view to taking over the business, and stated that an agreement to sell the business to a Mr. Fairlee for £14,000 in cash having fallen to the ground, he agreed to take debentures for £15,000 in the company in lieu of the cash. Witness had occasionally been pressed for money, and he admitted that the object of converting the business into a limited company was to raise money on the debentures, that course being preferable to giving a bill of sale over the property, which might have injuriously affected the value of the business. The examination was concluded.

THE PROPOSED COAL TRUST.—The prospectus of the proposed coal trust, according to *Echo*, has been published. It states that the company has been formed for the purpose of consolidating the various colliery interests throughout the United Kingdom. Its object is not to create a monopoly for the benefit of the colliery proprietors, but to form a combination which it is believed will be equally advantageous to the coalowners, colliery proprietors, workmen and purchasers and consumers of all classes, and, therefore, permanently beneficial to the nation at large. With regard to the royalty owners, it is intended to purchase their interests from time to time, as opportunities occur. Every colliery proprietor in the United Kingdom will be invited to join the company. The workmen are to take, in addition to their wages, a share of the profits after paying 5 per cent. on the debentures and a fair dividend, not exceeding 10 per cent., on the ordinary stock. It is anticipated that the proposed consolidation will effect considerable saving in the cost of management and working. £120,000,000 is the amount of capital which it is estimated will be needed to carry on the scheme.

M. TIMIRJASEFF, the Russian delegate to the Berlin Conference, is reported to have stated in the course of a conversation that little confidence is entertained in Russia with regard to the conclusion of a commercial treaty between Russia and Germany, the latter power being suspected of wishing to protract the negotiations with the object of inflicting as much injury as possible on Russian commerce in order to obtain terms which Russia could never grant.

UNITED STATES.

CHICAGO AND DISTRICT.—According to a recent consular report on the wholesale trade of Chicago, the following comparative figures relate to books, stationery and wall paper: 1889, £4,268,000; 1890, £4,536,000; 1891, £4,536,000; and 1892, £5,155,000. The stationery and book publishing business and all industries connected with printing had a prosperous time in 1892. The following were the

IMPORTS.

	1889.	1890.	1891.	1892.
Caustic Soda ...	£13,280	£18,888	£11,998	£13,769
Paper Manufactures	4,266	4,504	12,589	17,377

The custom-house transactions for 1892 show that paper was imported into St. Louis of the value of £5,699 16s., the duty being £1,699 14s. Two important enterprises have been added to the manufacturing industries of Denver during the past two years, viz., papermaking and the manufacture of cotton goods. The paper is prepared from the pulp obtained from the white spruce wood of the Rocky Mountains, grown at an elevation of from 8,000 to 11,000 feet; it is said to produce a very superior paper.

NEW YORK AND DISTRICT.—A return of the principal articles of import to New York during the years 1892-91 shows the following:

IMPORTS.

	1892.	1891.
Paper Stock...	£592,667	£498,055
Soda Ash	438,330	369,596
" Caustic..	157,749	189,950

SAN FRANCISCO AND DISTRICT. — The manufactures of paper imported to Portland, Oregon, were of the value of £1,571 in 1892. At Astoria, Oregon, paper pulp still continues to be made in increasing quantities, all of it going to a paper manufacturing concern in California.

BALTIMORE AND DISTRICT.—Amongst the articles of import into Baltimore during 1891 and 1892 were the following:

IMPORTS.

	1892.	1891.
Soda Ash	63,507 casks	39,929 casks.
" Caustic.. ..	9,877 "	2,120 "
Sulphur	15,077 tons	14,996 tons.
Bleaching Powder...	8,825 tierces	5,102 tierces.

At Norfolk, manufactures of paper were imported during the year to the value of £104. At the port of Richmond during 1892 cigarette paper was imported to the value of 1,105 dollars.

NORWEGIAN WOOD PULP INDUSTRY.

MECHANICAL.

Reporting upon mechanical wood pulp, Consul-General Michell states that there was a rise in 1892 on the average prices of 1891, to the extent of about 4s. 5d. to 8s. 11d. per ton dry pulp; the average prices for wet fir pulp having been quite £1 17s. 9d., and for dry £3 18s. 11d. per ton f.o.b. This rise can be considered as very satisfactory, since it represents a gain of £30,000 to £44,500 to the country. Although few of the mills made any very large profits, yet the greater part of them obtained a reasonable return on their capital, considering the depressed condition of the paper trade. The mill owners have all the more reason to be satisfied, for only a short while ago the business was on the verge of ruin.

Although at the beginning of the year the French market, in view of an increased customs rate, had stored a considerable quantity of wood pulp (the yearly demand having thus, to a great extent been, secured), the sales from Norway remained in keeping with the rate of production. Stocks were evenly low.

The quotations of the wood pulp association are not binding on its members, who can sell at any price they like. They are destined to indicate only the state of the market, in order to render it less unstable. In the autumn of 1891 sales for 1892 opened with prices almost corresponding with the association quotations. In the early part of last year buyers held back very obstinately, and under this pressure some of the wood pulp manufacturers accepted so low a price as 33s. 4d. per ton f.o.b. Thereupon, at a meeting of the association, on February 27th, 1892, a large majority of the millowners resolved to stop working, a resolution which, before having been carried out, resulted in several thousand tons being sold at the association quotations. There were, however, vacillations in the market during the summer, and it was only in the autumn that it became quite firm, £2 2s. 3d. f.o.b. having been obtained for small shipments of wet pulp. Owing to a scarcity of water in Germany, dry pulp came into strong demand, and the prices realised in Germany exceeded £4 8s. 11d. f.o.b. The association has given the same quotations for deliveries in 1893 as in 1892, and adopted the same limitations. Many large contracts were already made in the early part of 1893.

There was increased exportation to Great Britain, and also, but in a smaller degree, to Germany, while the export to France fell off. During the first 11 months of 1892 England imported about 28,000 tons of chemical and mechanical pulp more than during the same period of 1891, a considerable portion of the excess being under the head of mechanical pulp. Germany purchases almost exclusively dry pulp.

No new mills were established in 1892, their number remaining at 53. Of these one is connected with the production of wood pulp (competing for a few years past with iron pails from Great Britain), 3 with pasteboard manufactories, and 10 with paper mills.

CELLULOSE.

There was an improvement in this industry also last year. Prices, which threatened to fall when the year opened, rose not inconsiderably. This is attributable to a factor which generally is not a fortunate one, but which, as regards the prices for cellulose pulp, is of great importance, namely, the visitation of cholera.

The importation of rags from many quarters having been prohibited in paper-producing countries, the paper mills were compelled to use cellulose instead. This increased the consumption and steadied the market. It is not improbable that previous opponents of cellulose pulp will, after the trials of 1892, continue to use it in the manufacture of paper.

In November, 1891, the Cellulose Association quoted the following prices for delivery in 1892:—1st class dry sulphite, £10 11s. 1d. per ton f.o.b.; 2nd class dry sulphite, per ton, £9 14s. 5d. f.o.b., and somewhat lower for wet pulp. On September 26th, 1892, the quotations of the Norwegian manufacturers were per ton f.o.b.:

1st class dry sulphite ...	£10 6s. 8d. to £11 2s. 3d.
2nd class dry sulphite ...	£10 0s. 0d. to £10 5s. 7d.

These quotations were maintained at a meeting of Swedish and Norwegian manufacturers held at Gothenburg in November, 1892. Those for dry unmixed sulphate pulp were:

1st class sulphate... ...	£9 14s. 5d. to £10 0s. 0d.
2nd class sulphate ...	£9 3s. 4d. to £9 8s. 11d.

The greater part of the production in 1893 is stated to be already sold.

There are at present 11 mills that produce sulphite and 4 sulphate cellulose; 3 of the sulphite and 2 of the sulphate cellulose mills are connected with paper mills.

Including Swedish goods, the quantity of cellulose exported from Norway in 1892 (up to December 1st) was:

Dry (about)	20,000 tons.
Wet (about)	8,500 tons.

against, respectively, about 17,500 tons and 9,500 tons in 1891.

NORWEGIAN PAPER INDUSTRY.—Consul-General Michell reports that the paper industry made great progress in Norway during 1892. Six new machines have been set going, one of them, however, replacing old machinery. There appears to be a tendency towards a further extension and establishment of paper mills, notwithstanding the present low prices for paper. No new mill is, however, being built, if a small one for the production of pasteboard be excluded. The value of the aggregate production in 1892 is estimated at 25,000 tons. Some of the mills are reported to have already sold all they can produce in 1893. An association of paper manufacturers is being formed in connection with the one lately established in Sweden. It appears that Finland is willing to join the combination.

PAPER EXPORTS & IMPORTS.

FOR THE WEEK ENDING TUESDAY LAST

EXPORTS TO

	Printings.	Writings.	Other Kinds.
AUSTRALIA	4284 cwts	321 cwts	854 cwts.
AFRICA	4 ,,	10 ,,	— ,,
ARGENTINE	— ,,	211 ,,	41 ,,
BELGIUM	19 ,,	6 ,,	— ,,
B. WEST INDIES	— ,,	— ,,	8 ,,
B. GUIANA	— ,,	24 ,,	491 ,,
CANADA	52 ,,	153½ ,,	21½ ,,
CHINA	174 ,,	27 ,,	169 ,,
CHILI	— ,,	41 ,,	10 ,,
CHANNEL ISLES	7 ,,	— ,,	40 ,,
CAPE COLONY	62 ,,	141 ,,	291 ,,
DENMARK	2 ,,	— ,,	— ,,
EGYPT	— ,,	73 ,,	— ,,
FRANCE	— ,,	71 ,,	31 ,,
GERMANY	18 ,,	2 ,,	7 ,,
HOLLAND	25 ,,	— ,,	13 ,,
INDIA	984 ,,	299 ,,	173½ ,,
JAPAN	42 ,,	1550 ,,	2 ,,
MADAGASCAR	— ,,	— ,,	7 ,,
NEW ZEALAND	1148 ,,	348 ,,	323 ,,
RUSSIA	— ,,	13 ,,	40 ,,
SPAIN	— ,,	54 ,,	1 ,,
S. SETTLEMENTS	— ,,	6 ,,	— ,,
S. AMERICA	153 ,,	63 ,,	— ,,
SWEDEN	— ,,	4 ,,	— ,,
U.S.A.	— ,,	81 ,,	45 ,,

IMPORTS FROM

AUSTRIA	72 bales	NORWAY	4220 bales
BELGIUM	1393 ,,	,,	50 rolls
,,	125 cases	PRUSSIA	283 ,,
DENMARK	396 bales	SWEDEN	1892 bales
FRANCE	154 ,,	,,	86 rolls
,,	77 cases	,,	1 case
FINLAND	12 ,,	SPAIN	8 ,,
GERMANY	1549 bales	U.S.A.	904 bales
,,	167 cases	,,	48 cases
HOLLAND	14352 bales	,,	234 rolls
,,	54 cases		

Including the Following:

Quantity	From	Importer	Port.
24 cases	Boston	B. Galloway	London.
116 bales	Copenhagen	Becker & Ulrich	,,
61 ,,	,,	,, ,,	,,
46 ,,	,,	G. Schenkenwald & Co	,,
229 ,,	Christiania	Christophersen & Co	,,
4 ,,	,,	Tyser & Co.	,,
106 ,,	,,	G. F. Green & Co	,,
103 ,,	,,	E. Saunders & Co	,,
43 ,,	,,	Crabb & Co	,,
13 ,,	,,	C. Morgan & Co	,,
42 ,,	,,	J. Hamilton	,,
37 ,,	,,	Alsing & Co	,,
26 ,,	,,	J. Holloway	,,
9 ,,	,,	J. Spicer & Co	,,
5 ,,	,,	F. E. Foulger	,,
191 ,,	Christiansand	R. L. Lundgren	,,
70 ,,	Danzig	H. Huber & Co	,,
32 ,,	,,	E. & E. Sable	,,
169 ,,	Norrkoping	J. Spicer & Son	,,
1792 ,,	,,	Dowgate Dk.	,,
83 ,,	,,	Brooks Whf.	,,
171 rolls	New York	Mfg. Paper Co	,,
14 bales	Stettin	Spicer & Sons	,,
99 ,,	,,	Becker & Ulrich	,,
10 ,,	,,	W. D. Edwards	,,
24 ,,	,,	E. & E. Sabel	,,
52 ,,	,,	B. Beer	,,
69 ,,	Trieste	P. Sabel & Co	,,

THE PAPER TRADE REVIEW is a widely informed and well-managed enterprise, of great value to exporters for its exact Market Reports and statistics of Raw Material.—*Central-Blatt fur die Papier-Fabrikation*, Dresden.

SUMMARY OF IMPORTS & EXPORTS,

FOR THE WEEK ENDING TUESDAY LAST.

London, Liverpool, Bristol, Southampton, Hull, Fleetwood, Harwich, Folkestone, Newhaven, Dover, &c.

IMPORTS.

Paper	22865 bales	Millboards	14717 pkgs.
,,	370 rolls	,,	67 cases
,,	482 cases	Pasteboards	4277 pkgs.
Tissues	187 pkgs	Stock	1041 bales
Strawboards	1127 ,,	Envelopes	5 cases
Stationery	55 cases		

EXPORTS.

BRITISH GOODS			
Paper	2236 cwt.	Waste	58 tons
Writing Paper	3277 ,,	Strawboards	6 ,,
Printing Paper	6741 ,,	Pasteboards	22 cwt.
Stationery	£10949 value		
Cardboards	60 cwt.		
Millboards	16 ,,		
Stock	206 tons		
Rags	9 cwt.		
,,	£49 value		
Strawboard Cuttings	tons		

FOREIGN GOODS.	
Paper	714 cwt.
Printing Paper	275 ,,
Writing Paper	82 ,,
Pasteboards	198 ,,
Strawboards	200 ,,
Parchment	20 ,,
Stationery	£619 value

Glasgow, Greenock, Port-Glasgow, Troon, Grangemouth, &c.

IMPORTS.

Paper	817 bales	Stock	64 bales
,,	4 cases	Strawboards	5490 pkgs.
Tissues	1 case	Cardboards	4 cases

EXPORTS.

Writing Paper	148½ cwt.	Paper Stock	401½ cwt.
Printing Paper	188 ,,	Rags	23 ,,
Paper	121½ ,,	Envelopes	7 ,,
Stationery	£86 value		

Leith, Granton, Boness, Dundee, &c.

IMPORTS.

Paper	1141 bales	Millboards	936 pkgs.
,,	1 case	Tissues	14 ,,
Envelopes	975 pkgs.		

NEW PATENTS.

BRITISH.

SPECIFICATION PUBLISHED.

(7½d. each. By post 8d.)

9,296. Electrolysis of salt. Craney.

AMERICAN.

502,337. Process of ornamenting paper. Seth Wheeler, Albany, N.Y.

502,635. Inlet valve for digesters. Julius E. Rettig, Washington, D.C.

502,400. Roll paper cutter and holder. James S. Hays, Washington, D.C.

502,415. Paper Cutter. John S. Flowers, Three Oaks, Mich., assignor of one-half to Marvin H. Nye, Washington, D.C.

502,457. Paper box. Joseph T. Craw, Jersey City, N.J.

502,560. Safety envelope. Joseph J. Gleason, New York, N.Y.

502,784. Paper bag machine. Arthur L. Stevens, Philadelphia, Pa., assignor to the Diamond Paper Bag Company, Wilmington, Del.

502,847. Paper Bag machine. Edward E. Claussen, Hartford, Conn., assignor to the Union Paper Bag Machine Company, Philadelphia, Pa.

502,966. Package envelope. Martin Hess, New York, N.Y.

503,069. Pulp beating and mixing engine. Edwin W. Barton, Lawrence, Mass.

503,077. Paper box. William Forsyth, Fresno, Cal.

Printed and Published EVERY FRIDAY
AT 58, SHOE LANE, LONDON, E.C.,
By W. JOHN STONHILL.
ESTABLISHED 1878.

FRIDAY, SEPTEMBER 29, 1893.

THE CAUSTIC SODA MARKET is just now in a very "tricky" condition. Established agents who make special dealings and contracts in this product have lately been urging consumers to contract very far ahead. This apparent disinterestedness looks peculiar, and reminds us of Bret Hart's famous Chinee, whose "ways were dark," etc. A little daylight may enlighten our traders, and also save their pockets being unduly lightened. The anxiety of dealers to get buyers on contract not only for next year, but also for 1895—think of it, 1895—is probably inspired by a knowledge that Brunner, Mond and Co., of Northwich renown, have decided to erect large works for the manufacture of caustic soda! With an increased supply almost within sight, the desire of dealers to secure contracts long ahead is at least understandable.

TO THE scarcity of Scandinavian mechanical wood pulp and the higher prices now in force, compared with last year, may be attributed the attention which is being paid to the English market by other producing countries. Quite recently lots of 400 bales, 5,146 bales, and 13,259 bales have been received from Montreal, Canada. Some 958 bales have also been received from Halifax. From the United States a sample was received from Boston, and the enormous quantity of 19,862 bales from Bangor (Maine).

A MOVEMENT is on foot among the Canadian pulp manufacturers to agitate with the United States Government for the removal of the duty on wood pulp. This is an old question, and has been discussed many times. A letter in circular form has been sent to a large number of the pulp manufacturers in Canada and papermakers in the United States asking to have a small contribution, say $25 a firm, to establish a fund to defray all expenses of such a campaign at Washington.

THE prolonged coal strike is beginning to be severely felt in the chemical and paper trades. It has been found necessary to greatly curtail production, and at several chemical works plant has been altogether stopped. As a result of this our readers, upon reference to our Market Report, will find higher quotations for caustic soda and other materials. Many paper mills are on short time, and in some instances have shut down, consequently a large number of employees have been thrown out of employment. The feeling in favour of the resumption of work at the old rates by the colliers who can do so is increasing in the strike districts.

ANOTHER general order ($\frac{1}{1893}$) concerning foreign rags, has been issued by the Customs House authorities. Officers to whom the Local Government Board's Order of the 13th inst. has, by General Order $\frac{1}{1893}$ been communicated for guidance, are hereby further informed for guidance: (1) That bales of rags pressed by steam-force will be equally admissible with those hydraulically pressed, for the purposes of the Local Government Board Order of September 13th. (2) That for the purposes of the same Order, bales of rags bound with iron wire will be accepted as sufficiently meeting the requirement that such bales be "surrounded by iron bands." (3) That two or more bags of rags bound together by iron hoops or wire will, if sufficiently meeting the defined requirements as to "pressing" and "marking," be deemed as admissible under the Order.

CONSUL J. MICHELL, speaking in reference to Russian paper mills, regrets to say that very little or no machinery came from Great Britain in 1892; a small quantity however was imported from Germany. The respective merits of British and continental papermaking machinery have been previously discussed in these pages. On the one side solidity, strength, and durability are marked characteristics, whilst on the other, lightness of construction, less finish, and cheapness, are points which sometimes find favour with purchasers.

A CORRESPONDENT, writing from St. Petersburg, states that the services of foreign mill managers are being dispensed with in Russia, natives being appointed in their stead. He thinks the latter, however, have not sufficient knowledge to carry out the various duties in a satisfactory manner, and therefore does not think the present system of ousting out foreigners will be one of long duration. Consequently he sounds a note of warning to those who later on may have an offer open to them to take a position in Russia, to make sure that they are not made a tool of and thrown over when opportunity presents itself. So many years engagement our correspondent does not think of much use, and suggests that the least the foreigner should insist upon is that the full sum of his salary, covering the time of engagement, be deposited at the Consulate of the nation to which he belongs.

DEPRESSION, like a huge wave, seems to have spread over almost every country during the past year or two. The Home Country has suffered heavily, though at no time can it be said that anything like a crisis has been reached. Trade has been simply continuously dull, and there has been in all industrial enterprises a severe stagnation and monetary strain. Yet speaking of the printing and stationery and allied trades in especial, we have witnessed a surprisingly small number of disasters. Several large houses are known to have been tottering on the brink of bankruptcy for months, and have not yet recovered their footing, though a brightening of trade prospects has assisted them materially. Even such houses as we commonly regard as thoroughly substantial have necessarily felt the strain of continually falling securities. Still, the number and amount of actual stoppages is small comparatively. The contributory trades—such as papermaking and engineering and stationery manufacturing—have felt the effects of dull trade greatly. It would be hard to name a firm dependent upon the general printing and stationery trades that has been able to find anything like full employment for hands and engineering tools. The annual report of the Inspector-General in Bankruptcy, just issued, shows that the losses in trade through failures for the last year were £1,200,000 more than in 1891. The gross amount of "bad debts" is over ten and a half millions. This represents a tax in bankruptcy of something like 6s. per head of population. Adding to this 5s. per head, the amount arising from companies' liquidations, we have a gross tax of 11s. per head.

THE competitive conditions of the printing and publishing trades in London are compelling large firms to consider localities out of town for their works. This migratory element is a feature of the times. Much work has of late been lost to London owing to heavy rentals, higher wages, and other incidental expenses which weigh heavily in competition. An item to be noted is that the shares of Messrs. Waterlow and Son, Ltd., have been steadily rising, since it has become known that they have resolved to have extensive works at Dunstable. The ordinary £10 shares now stand at £25. *Per contra* the shares of Messrs. Cassell and Co. continue to be sold, recent dealings being registered at $16\frac{1}{4}$, $16\frac{1}{2}$, $16\frac{5}{8}$ and $16\frac{11}{16}$. We observe that there has been a small fall in Brunner, Mond and Co.'s shares, although shareholders surely have nothing to grumble at when they receive 100 per cent. dividend. The price of £10 ordinary shares is 57-62, fortunately a margin deterent to speculators. There is more firmness in the shares of the United Alkali Co., the £10 pref. having changed hands at $11\frac{1}{4}$. Wood pulp and papermaking shares have been more looked after, and in Lancashire the shares of the Kellner-Partington Paper and Pulp Co. (£2 15s. paid up) are scarcely purchasable at £3. There has been a hardening in the shares of the Burnley Paper Co. Slight advances have been registered in the Salt Union, George Angus, and Babcock and Wilcox. In Waterlow Bros. and Layton, at 21-22, a slight fall has taken place, due perhaps to the application to the Stock Exchange for a special settling day for the 5 per cent. pref. and ord. shares.

DOUBLE-WIDTH printing presses for newspaper work are necessitating the use of wider reels. Quite lately such newspapers as the *Times*, *Morning Post*, and *Daily News* have all put down double-width presses, adandoning the old type of single-width web rotary machines. There is some talk now of quadruple printing presses being built at prices which will come within the reach of smaller newspaper proprietors. Therefore, before long, it may be a question for the papermakers to consider catering for the supply of such wide width reels of news. The success of the wide machine at the Star mill is, we are informed, undoubted.

WORLD'S PAPER TRADE REVIEW OFFICE,
58, SHOE LANE, LONDON, E.C.
SEPTEMBER 28, 1893.

MARKET REPORT

and RECORD of IMPORTS

Of Foreign Rags, Wood Pulp, Esparto, Paper, Millboards, Strawboards, &c., at the Ports of London, Liverpool, Southampton, Bristol, Hull, Fleetwood, Middlesborough, Glasgow, Grangemouth, Granton, Dundee, Leith, Dover, Folkestone, and Newhaven for the WEEK ENDING SEPTEMBER 27.

From SPECIAL Sources and Telegrams.

Telegrams—"STONHILL, LONDON."

CHEMICALS.—Chemicals quiet. Production in some districts is almost entirely stopped. Very little CAUSTIC SODA is being made, and prices evidence a further increase, 77% f.o.b. Tyne being quoted £12 5s; 70% f.o.b. Liverpool £11, f.o.b. Hull and f.o.r. London £11 5s., f.o.r. Lancs. £10 17s. 6d.; 60% f.o.r. London £10 5s., f.o.b. Liverpool, £10; and 60% Cream £9 2s. 6d. f.o.r. Lancs., and £9 7s. 6d. f.o.b. Liverpool. BLEACHING POWDER is uncertain, and the present high rates show no sign of abating. SODA ASH is lower, prices being from £4 7s. 6d. to £4 12s. 6d., and SODA CRYSTALS f.o.b. Liverpool show an advance of 7s. 6d. SULPHUR remains at from £4 2s. 6d. to £4 5s.

Prices are nominally as follows:

Article		Terms		£	s.	d.
Alkali, 58%	tierces ...	f.o.r. works	2½%	5	10	0
,, 58%	bags ...	,, ,,	2½%	5	5	0
58%	... ...	f.o.b. Liverpool	2½%	5	12	6
Alum (Ground),	tierces ...	,, Liverpool	2½%	5	7	6
,, ,,	barrels ...	,, ,,	2½%	5	17	6
,, ,,	tierces ...	,, Hull	2½%	5	5	0
,, ,,	,, ...	Goole	2½%	5	5	0
Alum (Lump)	,, ...	f.o.b. Liverpool	2½%	4	17	6
,, ,,	barrels ...	,, ,,	2½%	5	0	0
,, ,,	tierces ...	,, Hull	2½%	4	15	0
,, ,,	,, ...	Goole	2½%	4	15	0
,,	,, ...	London	2½%	5	5	0
,,	,, ...	f.a.s. Glasgow	2½%	5	5	0
Alumina Sulphate, casks		f.o.b. Tyne		4	2	6
,, ,, bags		,, ,,		3	17	6
Aluminoferric Cake, slabs		Liverpool ...	...	2	15	0
,, ,, tierces		,, ...	...	3	2	6
Alumina Cake, slabs	...	Glasgow	...	2	15	0
,, ,, tierces	...	,,	...	3	2	6
Aluminous Cake, casks	...	Manchester	3¾%	2	7	6
,, ,, ,,	...	Newcastle	2½%	2	10	0
,, ,, ,,	...	London	2½%	3	0	0
,, ,, bags	...	,,	2½%	2	17	9
Blanc Fixe	...	f.o.b. Tyne	net	7	10	0
Bleach, 35% ...	...	,, ,,	net	8	15	0
,, (soft wood)	...	f.o.r. Lancs.	net	8	10	0
,, (hard wood)	...	f.o.b. Liverpool	net	9	0	0
... ...	...	landed London	2½%	10	0	0
Borax (crystals) ...	...	... ...	net	29	0	6
powdered ...	...	... .	net	30	0	0
Caustic Cream, 60%	..	f.o.r. Lancs.	net	9	2	6
,, ,, 60%	...	f.o.b. Liverpool	net	9	7	6
,, Bottoms	...	,, ,,	net	6	15	0
,, ,, ...	...	f.o.b. Tyne	net	6	15	0
Caustic White 76-77%	...	f.o.r. Newcastle	net	12	0	0
,, ,, 77%	f.o.r. or	f.o.b. Tyne	net	12	5	0
,, ,, 74%	...	f.o.b. Liverpool	net	12	0	0
,, ,, 70%	...	,, ,,	net	11	0	0
,, ,, 70%	...	,, Hull	net	11	5	0
,, ,, 70%	...	f.o.r. London	net	11	5	0
,, ,, 70%	...	,, Lancs.,	net	10	17	6
,, ,, 60%	...	,, London	net	10	5	0
,, ,, 60%	...	f.o.b. Liverpool	net	10	0	0
Carbonat'd Ash 58%	...	,, ,,	net	4	10	0
48%	...	,, ,,	net	4	0	0
,, 58%	...	f.o.r. Widnes	net	4	7	6
48%	...	,, ,,	net	3	17	6
Chloride of Barium	...	f.o.b. Tyne	net	7	10	0
Hypo-Sulphite of Soda...		f.o.r Tyne		5	15	0
,, ,, 10-ton lots		ex ship Liverp'l	net	6	10	0
Oxalic Acid ...	... ...	f.o.b. Liverpool	3½%	per lb		[illegible]
Salt Cake ...	... ...	,, works	net	1	10	0
Soda Ash, 52%	... ..	f.o.b. Tyne	net	4	7	6
,, 52%	... ...	ex ship Thames	1%	4	12	6
,, 52%	... ...	f.o.b. Liverpool	1%	4	5	0
Soda Crystals	... ...	,, Tyne	net	2	15	0
,, ,,	... ...	ex ship Thames	2½%	3	5	0
,, ,,	... ...	f.o.b. Liverpool	net	3	7	6
Sulphur, roll	... ...	f.o.r. works	2½%	7	17	6
,, flowers	... ..	,, ,,	2½%	9	10	0
,, recovered	...	,, ,,	2½%	4	2	6
Sulphate of Ammonia	,,	,, ,,	2½%	15	0	0
,, of Copper	...	,, Liverpool	5%	15	0	0

FOREIGN.—F.o.b. Continental port:

Article	£	s.	d.
Alkali, 58% 2-cwt. bags £6 10/0; 10-cwt. casks ...	6	15	6
Caustic Soda, 70-72%	11	12	0
Hypo-Sulphite of Soda 10-ton lots 140/0; kegs ...	7	10	6
Sulphate of Alumina 7-8 cwt. casks net c.i.f. Ldn	4	7	6
Blanc Fixe (c.i.f. London)	7	12	6

ESPARTO.—The market is generally quiet again, with no great extent of business going through. Quotations practically unaltered for all positions.

Prices c.i.f. London and Leith, or f.o.r. Cardiff, Garston and Tyne Docks are nominally as follows:

		£	s.	d.		£	s.	d.
Spanish—	Fair to Good	£5	10	0	to	5	15	0
,,	Fine to Best	5	17	6	,,	6	0	0
Oran—	Fair to Good	3	12	6	,,	3	17	6
,,	First Quality...	3	17	6	,,	4	0	0
Tripoli—	Hand-picked	3	17	6	,,	4	0	0
,,	Fair Average...	3	0	0	,,	3	12	6
Bona & Philippeville	... ...	3	17	6	,,	4	0	0

IMPORTS of ESPARTO.

Quantity	From	Importer	Port.
799 tons	Carthagena	R. H. Hay & Co	Granton
3383 bales	Garrucha	Guardbridge Paper Co	Dundee
539 ,,	,,	Carrongrove Paper Co	,,
3060 ,,	Oran	To order	Liverpool
29 tons	,,	,,	,,

STRAW.—Foreign Straw still remains very scarce, and difficult to obtain. Wheat and Oat Straw have realised much higher rates during the past week.

IMPORTS of STRAW

(Purposes unspecified) at principal Ports From

DENMARK	... 157 bales	HOLLAND	.. 2290 bales
FRANCE	... 155 ,,		

STRAW PULPS.—Market dull.

Prices, c.i.f. London, Hull or Leith:

		£	s.	d.
Belgian, 25% moisture	£15 0 0 to	16	0	0
do. dry		16	0	0
German, 50 to 55% moisture		16	10	0
do. dry, ...	No. 1 £18 10 0; No. 2	15	0	0

CHEMICAL WOOD PULPS.—Mills on the continent producing the best grades of SULPHITE are inclined to quote higher prices. The present demand for supplies to Great Britain is rather quiet, and users hold back from contracting at current prices. SULPHATE pulps keep steady.

Prices, ex steamer, London, Hull, Newcastle, Leith and Glasgow are nominally as follows:

		£	s.	d.		£	s.	d.
SULPHITE.	Unbleached. Common	£10	15	0	to	11	0	0
,,	Superior	11	10	0	,,	12	10	0
,,	,, 50% moisture, d.w.	11	10	0	,,	12	2	6
,,	Extra	13	0	0	,,	14	0	0
,,	Bleached, moist					16	10	0
,,	Unbleached, English, del. Lancs. ...					10	15	0
,,	,, ,, No. 1, ex mills, Ldn.					10	10	0
,,	,, ,, No. 2, ,, ,,					9	15	0
SODA,	Unbleached, Common ...	10	0	0	to	10	10	0
,,	,, Extra... ...	10	10	0	,,	11	0	0
,,	Half-Bleached	12	10	0	,,	14	0	0

SULPHATE, Unbleached, Common	10 10 0 ,, 11 0 0	
,, Extra	11 0 0 ,, 12 0 0	
,, Half-Bleached	13 10 0 ,, 14 0 0	
Bleached	15 0 0 ,, 16 0 0	

MECHANICAL WOOD PULPS.—The tone of the market continues firm, and owing to the scarcity of best grades prices are well maintained, and if anything have a further upward tendency.

Prices, ex steamer, London, Hull, Newcastle, Leith and Glasgow are nominally as follows:—

MECHANICAL, Aspen, Dry ...	£7 10 0 to 8 0 0
Pine, Dry	6 12 6 ,, 7 0 0
Pine, Moist	3 7 6 ,, 3 10 0
Moist Brown	3 2 6 ,, 3 5 0
Single Sorted	2 7 6 ,, 2 10 0
Dry Brown	6 5 0 ,, 6 10 0

IMPORTS of WOOD PULP.

Quantity	From	Importer	Port.
160 bales	Antwerp	To order	Hull
300 ,,	,,	,,	Glasgow
459 ,,	Bergen	,,	Hull
1040 ,,	Copenhagen	J. Currie & Co	Leith
707 ,,	Christiania	To order	Hull
1129 ,,	,,	,,	Grangemouth
200 ,,	,,	Christophersen & Co	London
406 ,,	,,	Taylor & Co	,,
80 ,,	,,	Skramnes & Co	,,
436 ,,	,,	Green & Co	,,
1950 ,,	,,	H. B. Wood	Fleetwood
5135 ,,	Drontheim	G. Schjoth & Co	,,
500 ,,	Fredrikstadt	To order	London
57 casks	Ghent	,,	,,
18 ,,	,,	,,	,,
597 bales	Gothenburg	C. Salvesen & Co	Granton
190 ,,	,,	To order	Glasgow
70 ,,	,,	,,	London
203 ,,	,,	,,	,,
938 rolls	Halifax	,,	Liverpool
93 bales	Hambro	,,	London
102 ,,	,,	,,	,,
701 ,,	Helsingfors	,,	,,
13259 ,,	Montreal	,,	Glasgow
500 ,,	Norrkoping	Christophersen & Co	London
250 ,,	Oporto	T. Aitken	Leith
81 ,,	Rotterdam	J. Rankin & Son	Grangemouth
81 ,,	,,	J. Currie & Co	Leith
50 ,,	,,	To order	London
893 ,,	,,	,,	,,
55 ,,	,,	,,	,,
450 ,,	Stettin	,,	Hull
350 ,,	,,	Tough & Henderson	London
800 ,,	Sannesund	Kellner-Partington	Fleetwood
1955 ,,	Skein	G. Schjoth & Co	,,
160 ,,	,,	Blydt, Pans & Co	,,

Totals from Each Country:

AUSTRIA ...	200 bales	GERMANY ..	195 bales
BELGIUM .	45 casks	HOLLAND ...	1160 ,,
,, ...	480 bales	NORWAY ...	14417 ,,
CANADA ...	13259 bales	PORTUGAL ...	250 ,,
,, ...	938 rolls	PRUSSIA ...	800 ,,
DENMARK ...	1040 bales	SWEDEN ...	1741 ,,

IMPORTS of WOOD PULP BOARDS.

Quantity	From	Importer	Port
326 bales	Gothenburg	To order	Glasgow

WASTE PAPERS.—Waste Papers are in moderate request.

Cream Shavings ...	12/3	Small Letters	5/0
Fine ,, ...	9/6	Large ,, ...	7/0
Mixed ,, ...	3/0	Brown Paper	2/3
White Printings ...	8/9	Light Browns	2/9
White Waste ...	1/6	Books & Pamphlets ...	6/0
Wood Pulp Cuttings	3/6	Strawboard Cuttings	1/6
Brown Paper	3/0	Jacquards	2/6
Crushed News	2/0		

For Export: 25/- per ton extra.

JUTE.—Cuttings are firm.

Good White ...	£16 to 18	Common ...	£10 10 to £11
Good	£15	Rejections ...	£8 0 ,, £9
Medium ...	£13	Cuttings ...	£5 10 ,, £7

FLOCKS.—Cotton Flocks are in demand; there being no heavy stocks, prices are well maintained.

FOREIGN RAGS.—The market for Cotton and Linen grades is steady. French, Dutch, and Belgian stock is in fair request. The demand for lower grades, however, is very slack. Prices of Norwegian show a slight decline.

IMPORTS of FOREIGN RAGS.

Quantity	From	Importer	Port.
52 bales	Antwerp	G. Gibson & Co	Leith
26 ,,	,,	,,	,,
536 ,,	Alexandria	To order	Southampton
305 ,,	,,	,,	Liverpool
28 ,,	Bordeaux	,,	,,
15 ,,	Buenos Ayres	,,	London
15 ,,	Bremen	,,	Hull
21 ,,	Copenhagen	J. Currie & Co	Leith
52 ,,	Christiania	To order	Hull
4 ,,	,,	,,	Grangemouth
3 ,,	,,	Feyer & Stave	London
8 ,,	,,	R. Hanch	,,
62 ,,	Constantinople	To order	Liverpool
49 ,,	Caen	,,	Harwich
49 ,,	,,	,,	Newhaven
93 ,,	Calais	,,	London
113 ,,	Dunkirk	,,	Liverpool
153 ,,	,,	,,	Hull
64 ,,	,,	G. Gibson & Co	Leith
48 ,,	Guernsey	To order	Southampton
26 ,,	Ghent	G. Gibson & Co	Leith
108 ,,	,,	To order	Liverpool
131 ,,	Hambro	,,	Hull
11 ,,	,,	,,	,,
34 ,,	Harlingen	G. Gibson & Co	Leith
64 ,,	,,	To order	Hull
28 ,,	Havre	,,	Southampton
75 ,,	Leghorn	,,	London
47 ,,	New York	,,	Hull
36 ,,	Rotterdam	,,	,,
30 ,,	,,	,,	,,
64 ,,	,,	G. Gibson & Co	Leith
19 ,,	St. Malo	To order	Southampton
93 ,,	,,	,,	,,
142 ,,	Stettin	G. Gibson & Co	Leith

Totals from Each Country:

ARGENTINA	15 bales	HOLLAND ...	228 bales
BELGIUM ...	212 ,,	NORWAY ...	67 ,,
CHANNEL Isles	48 ,,	PRUSSIA ...	142 ,,
DENMARK ...	21 ,,	SPAIN ...	75 ,,
EGYPT ...	841 ,,	TURKEY ...	62 ,,
FRANCE ...	677 ,,	U.S.A. ...	47 ,,
GERMANY .	157 ,,		

DUTCH RAGS, f.o.r. Hull:

C.i.f. Thames; Hull 2/6 per ton more; ditto f.o.r. Leith c.i.f. Glasgow 5/-; c.i.f. Liverpool 4/-.

Selected Fines (free from Muslins) ...	17/0	Best Grey Linens ...	9/0
		Common ditto ...	5/6
Selected Outshots	9/9	White Canvas ...	15/0
,, Dirty Fines	5/9	Grey & Brown Canvas	9/9
Light Cottons ...	9/3	Tarred Hemp Rope	8/0
Blue Cottons ...	7/6	Ditto (broken) ...	5/3
Dark Coloured Cottons	2/10	White Paper Shavings	7/9
New Cuttings (Bleachd)	22/6	Gunny (best) ...	4/9
,, (Unbleached)	19/6	Jute Bagging ...	3/6
,, (Slate) ...	9/0	Ditto (common ...	3/0
Muslins	8/0	Tarpaulins	4/0
Red Cottons (Mixed)	5/9	Cowhair Carpets ...	2/9
Fustians (Light browns)	5/0	Hard ditto	3/0

BELGIAN RAGS.

F.o.b. Ghent. Freights: London, 5/0; Hull and Goole, 7/6 Liverpool and Leith, 10/0; Newcastle, 12/6; Dundee and Aberdeen, 15/0; Glasgow, 16/8.

White Linens No. 1	22/6	Fustians (Light) ...	6/0
,, ,, No. 2	16/0	,, (Dark) ...	4/0
,, ,, No. 3	13/0	Thirds...	3/0
Fines (Mixed) ...	12/0	Black Cottons ...	3/9
Grey Linens (strong)	9/6	Hemp Strings (unt'r'd)	2/0
,, ,, (extra)	14/0	House Cloths ...	4/9
Blue Linens... ...	8/6	Old Bagging (solid)	3/6
White Cottons S'p'fine	18/0	,, ,, (common)	2/6
,, ,, No. 2	15/0	NEW.	
Outshots No. 3 ...	10/0	White & Cream Linens	35/0
Seconds No. 4 ...	8/0	White Cuttings ...	22/0
Prints (Light) ...	8/6	Unbleached Cuttings	21/0
,, (Old)	4/6	Print Cuttings ..	8/0

BELGIAN FLAX and HEMP WASTE.

Best washed and dried Flax Waste, 10/0; Fair ditto 9/0
Flax Spinners' Waste (grease boiled out)... ... 10/0
Hemp Waste, No. 1 9/0; No. 2 ... ... 7/6
Flax Spinners' Waste, No. 1 (Flax Rove) 10/0: No. 2 8/6

GERMAN RAGS.

STETTIN : C.i.f. Hull, Leith, Tyne and London.

SPFFF and SPFF	18/0	LFB (Blue)	9/0
SPF	11/0	CSPFFF and CSPFF	10/0
FF	8/6	CFB (Blue)	7/6
FG	9/0	CFX (Coloured) ...	4/6
LFX	7/0		

HAMBURG : F.o.b.

NWC	22/0	FF Grey Linens ...	9/0
SPFFF	22/0	LFX Second ditto...	3/0
SPFFF and SPFF	18/0	CSPFFF	17/3
SPFF	16/0	CSPFF	11/3
SPF	12/0	CFB	3/0
CCC	5/6	Dark Blues (selected	11/9
CFX	4/6	Wool Tares... ...	3/0
White Rope... ...	8/0	Jute, No. I 6/0; No. II	5/6

FRENCH RAGS.

Quotations range, per cwt., ex ship London, Southampton, or Hull; 2/0 per ton more at Liverpool, and 10/0 per ton higher at Newcastle, Glasgow or Leith.

French Linens, I ...	22/0	Black Cotton ...	4/0
II 18/6; III ...	14/6	Marseilles Whites, I	16/0
White Cottons, I ...	19/0	II 10/0; III ...	7/6
II 15/0; III ...	12/6	Blue Cotton	11/0
Knitted Cotton ...	11/0	Light Prints... ...	9/0
Light Coloured Cotton	8/0	Mixed Prints ...	6/0
Blue Cotton	9/6	New White Cuttings	13/0
Coloured Cotton ...	6/0	,, Stay ,,	11/0

NORWEGIAN RAGS.

C.i.f. London, Hull, Tyne, and Grangemouth.

1st Rope (tarred) ...	8/6-9/0	2nd Canvas ...	8/0
2nd ,, ,, ...	5/6-6/0	Jute Bagging	
Manilla Rope (white)	8/0-8/9	Gunny ...	3/0-3/6
Best Canvas ...	11/0-12/0	Mixed ...	2/6-2/9

RUSSIAN RAGS.

C.i.f. London, Hull, Newcastle or Leith.

SPFF	15/0	CC (Cotton	4/9
SPF	13/6	Jute I	3/6
FG	10/6	,, II...	2/3
LFB	9/6	Rope I	9/0
FF	8/3	,, II	5/3
LFX	7/3		

HOME RAGS. — LONDON: The market at present is not very brisk, owing to mills working short time; prices unaltered.—BRISTOL: Trade quiet at previous quotations.—MANCHESTER: Market is dull and depressed for all grades of stock; Seconds, Blues, Bagging and Surat Tares are easier. —EDINBURGH: There is very little business moving.—DUBLIN: Market dull.

LONDON:

New White Cuttings	21/6	Canvas No. 1	15/0
Fines (selected)	20/6	,, No. 2 ...	9/6-10/6
,, (good London)...	20/0	,, No. 3	5/6
Outshots (selected) ...	12/6	Mixed Rope	5/3
,, (ordinary) ...	11/0	White Rope	6/6
London Seconds	3/6-4/0	White Manilla Rope	8/6
Country do. ...	6/6-8/0	Coil Rope	8/6
London Thirds ...	1/9-2/0	Bagging...	1/6
Country do. ...	4/0-5/0	Gunny	3/6
Light Prints ...	7/0-8/0		

BRISTOL:

Fines	19/0	Clean Canvas ...	15/0
Outshots	13/6	Second Do. ...	9/6-10/6
Seconds	7/0-8/0	Light Prints ...	8/0
Thirds	3/6-4/0	Hemp Coil Rope	9/6-10/0
Mixed Bagging	3/6	Tarred Manilla	7/6

MANCHESTER:

Fines	15/0-16/0	Blues	6/6-7/0
Outshots (best) ...	11/6-12/0	Bagging...	4/0-4/3
,, (ordinary)	10/6-11/0	,, (common)	3/0-3/3
Seconds	7/0-7/3	W. Manilla Rope	10/0-10/6
Thirds	3/6-3/9	Surat Tares... ...	4/9-5/0

EDINBURGH:

Superfines	17/0	Black Cottons	2/9
Outshots	13/0	W. Manilla Rope ...	9/0
Mixed Fines...	14/0	Tarred Ditto	6/9
Common Seconds ...	8/0	,, Hemp Rope...	8/6
First do.	11/0	Rope Ends (new) ...	8/6
Prints	5/6-6/6	,, ,, (old) ...	6/0
Canvas (best)	16/0	Bagging...	2/9-3/0
,, 2nd	10/6	,, (clean) ...	4/3-6/0

DUBLIN.

White Cuttings ...	18/0	Mill Bagging	3/0
Fines	11/0	White Manilla	8/0
Seconds...	5/0	Tarred Hemp	8/0
Light Prints	3/0	Rigging	13/6
Black do.	2/0	Mixed Ropes	3/6
Bagging	2/0		

SIZING.—"B.A." and English Pieces are in better demand, otherwise there is no alteration.

English Gelatines	per cwt.	70/0 to	140/0
Foreign ,, ...	,,	70/0 ,,	140/0
Fine Skin Glues	,,	45/0 ..	60/0
Long Scotch Glues	,,	45/0 ..	60/0
Common ,, ...	,,	30/0 ..	45/0
"Town" Glues	,,	26/0 ..	36/0
"Bone" Glues	,,	20/0 ,,	30/0
Foreign Glues	..	23/0 ,,	40/0
Bone Size	,,	4/0 ,,	10/0
Gelatine Size...	..	5/0 ..	10/0
Dry B.A. Pieces	..	31/6 ,,	33/0
,, English Pieces ...	..	24/0 ,,	27/0
Wet ,, ,, ...	..	7/0 ,,	8/0
,, Sheep Pieces	..	3/0 ..	4/0
Buffalo Hide Shavings	..	26/0 ,,	37/0
.. Picker Waste	..	27/0 ,,	37/0

ROSIN.—A moderate trade passing.

	Strained.	E.	F.	G.	K.	W.G.	W.W.
Spot—	3/7½	4/0	4/3	4/6	6/9	9/9	10/3
To arrive—	3/2	3/5	3/7	3/9	5/6	9/0	9/6

STARCH.—Prices:

F.o.r. London, less 2½%:

Maize—Crisp, £10 0/-; Powder, £10 5/-; Special £14 10/-
Farina—Prime, £10 5/-; B.K.M.F., £13 10/-

Delivered:

Rice—Special (in chests), £20 0/- (net); Crystal (in bags) £19 0/-; Granulated (in bags) £18 0/- less 2½%.
Dextrine—£16 0/- to £17.

MINERALS. — CHINA CLAY and FRENCH CHALK are in demand at firm prices. BARYTES (carbonate) continue scarce; Finest White Sulphate is in fair request. Business in PATENT HARDENINGS and MINERAL WHITE keeps steady.

Mineral White (Terra Alba), per ton f.o.r. or boat at works:

Superfine...	28/0	less 2½ %
Pottery Super.... ...	24/0	,,
Ball Seconds	20/0	,,
Seconds	15/0	,,
Thirds	10/6	,,

China Clay, in bulk, f.o.b. Cornwall, 14/0 to 27/6; bags 5/0 and casks 9/6 per ton extra; f.o.b. London, in casks 35/0 to 50/0 per ton.

Superfine Hardening, f.o.r. works, 40/0.

Patent Crystal Hardening, delivered at mills £3 to £3 15/0

Patent Hardening (2 ton lots) f.o.r. Lancs., £3 5/0.
,, ,, (5 ton lots) f.o.b. Liverpool, £3 10/0.

Magnesite (in lump) 32/6 per ton.

Magnesite (containing 98 % Carbonate of Magnesia), raw ground, £6 10/0; calcined ground, £12 10/0.

Albarine, £3. del. mills.

Asbestos, best rock, £18; brown grades, £14 to £15

Asbestine Pulp, £4 5/- to £5 c.i.f. London, Liverpool and Glasgow.

Barytes (Carbonate), lump, 90/0 to 95/0; nuts, 72/6 to 85/0.

Barytes (Sulphate), "Angel White," No. 1, 70/0; No. 2, 60/0 to 65/0; No. 3, 45/0. Souheur's Brands: AF, 83/-; BF, 71/-; AB, 33/6; BB, 29/6; CB, 24/3.

French and Italian Chalk (Souheur Brand), per ton in lots of 10 tons: Flower O, 64/6 c.i.f. London; Flower OO, 60/0, Flower OOO, 51/6. Swan White, 57/0; Snow White, 90/0. Blackwell's "Angel White" Brand and "Silvery" 90/- to 92/6; prime quality, 90/- to 95/-; and superfine, 105/-.

Bauxite, Irish Hill Quality, first lump, 20/0; seconds, 16/0; thirds, 12/0; ground, 35/0.

Pyrites (non-cupreous), Liverpool, 5d., 2 %.

Carbonate of Lime (Souheur Brand), Prima 43/-, Secunda 37/-.

LIME.—Bleach Lime is quoted at about 11s. per ton at works.

DIRECTORY.

Names and Addresses under this heading will be charged for at the rate of 50/- per annum (52 insertions) for each card of two lines or under. Each additional line £1 extra.

ALUMINOUS CAKE.

The ALUM, CHINA CLAY and VITRIOL Co., Lim., 63, Queen Victoria Street, London, E.C. Works: Rainham-on-Thames. Telegrams—"Chinnock, London."

ANALYTICAL.

WILLIAMS, ROWLAND, F.I.C., F.C.S., 28, Pall Mall, Manchester.

ARTESIAN WELLS.

BATCHELOR, Richard D., Artesian and Consulting Well Engineer, 73, Queen Victoria Street, London, E.C., and at Chatham. 5713

ISLER, C., & Co., Bear Lane, Southwark, S.E

LE GRAND & SUTCLIFF, Magdala Works, 125, Bunhill Row, E.C.

BOILER COVERING.

LONSDALES, Boiler Coverers, Blackburn, will send a sample cask of their Patent Plastic Cork Covering to any Paper Mill in Great Britain—5 cwt. cask for 25/- (carriage paid).

CHINA CLAY.

The ALUM, CHINA CLAY and VITRIOL Co., Lim., 63, Queen Victoria Street, London, E.C. Mines: Ruddle and Colchester, St. Austell, Cornwall. Telegrams—"Chinnock, London."

ROGERS, J., & Co., Truro, Cornwall.—Agents: Taylor, Sommerville & Co., 83, Queen Victoria Street, E.C., and at 16, Princes Street, Edinburgh.

W. SINGLETON BIRCH & SONS, Lim., 15, Upton Street, Manchester. Mines: Rosevear, St. Austell, Cornwall. 2276

COLOURS.

CARDWELL, J. L., & Co., Commercial Buildings, 15 Cross Street, Manchester. Specialties: Mineral Black, Ven. Red, Ochres and Umbers. 5304

GEMMILL, W. N., & Co., Glasgow, Telegrams "Rube." Starches, Alumina, Antifroths, &c. All Paper Colours

COLOURS (Continued).

HINSHELWOOD, THOMAS, & Co., The Glasgow Colour Works, Glasgow. Colours and shades matched exactly.

MULLER, A. E., 9, Fenchurch Street, London, E.C.

ESPARTO.

IDE & CHRISTIE, Fibre, Esparto, and General Produce Brokers, 72, Mark Lane, E.C.

MINERAL WHITE or TERRA ALBA.

WINSER & Co., Portland Mills, Princess Street, Manchester. Also manufacturers of Aluminous Cake.

HOWE, JOHN, & Co., Carlisle. 2112

STEEL.

MAKIN, WM., & SONS, Sheffield. Established 1756. Roll Bars, Plates, Cutter Knives, Doctor Blades, &c. 6389

STRAW.

UNDERWOOD, E., & SON, Limited, Brentford, London, W. Press-packed Oat, Wheat, or Rye Straw, delivered to the chief British ports or railway stations.

TALC (French and Italian Chalk).

SOUHEUR, JEAN, Antwerp. All Minerals, Blanc de Silex, Barytes (superior and common), Carbonate of Lime, Blacklead, &c. British Agent: A. E. Muller, 9, Fenchurch Street, London, E.C. Agent for Liverpool and Manchester: O. H. Austin, Ditton, near Widnes.

RAGS.

CHALMERS, E., & Co., Lim., Bonnington, Leith.

MULLER, A. E., 9, Fenchurch Street, London, E.C.

WERTHEIM, A., & Co., Hamburg.

UMBER.

The ALUM, CHINA CLAY and VITROIL Co., Lim. 63, Queen Victoria Street, London, E.C. Telegrams—"Chinnock, London."

WOOD PULP.

FRIIS, N., & Co., 18, Carl Johans Gade, Christiania, Norway.

GOTTSTEIN, H., & Co., 59, Mark Lane, London, E.C., and at New York.

GRANT, W., & Co., 17, Baltic Street, Leith. Agents for best shippers. Sulphite and Sulphate, Mechanical, Pine, Brown, Aspen.

MATTHIESSEN, CHR., Christiania, Norway.

MULLER, A. E., 9, Fenchurch Street, London, E.C.

The SULPHITE PULP Company, Limited, 82, Gordon Street, Glasgow.

WERTHEIM, A., & Co., Hamburg.

DAMPING MACHINES

On the most Improved Principle;

VENTILATION for all purposes;

Improved FANS or AIR PROPELLERS;

Patent SUSPENDING CLIPS to hold from one up to 50 sheets of paper or cardboard;

TURBINES; SMOKE CONSUMING APPARATUS;

Patent Life Protecting HOIST PLATFORMS;

New System of HYDRAULIC POWER for Lifts, Hoists, and Motive Power;

New Process of WIRE WEAVING by Steam Power.

For particulars of all the above address 5812

E. BREADNER

(Ventilating Engineer to the Manchester Royal Exchange),

134, DEANSGATE, MANCHESTER.

English and Foreign Rags.

A. E. MULLER,

9, FENCHURCH STREET, LONDON, E.C.

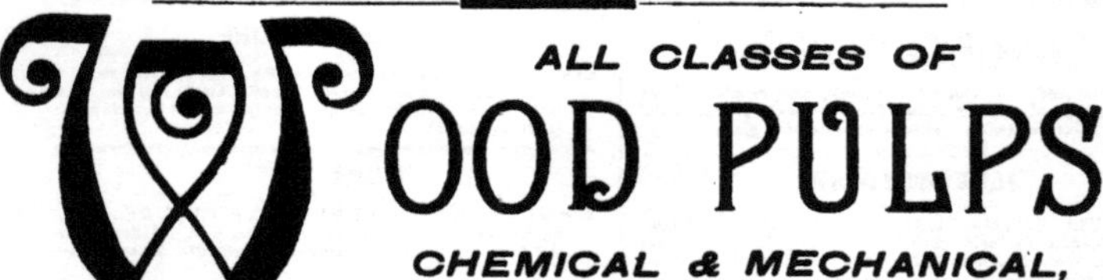

Particularly Finest Brands of Sulphite, Bleached and Unbleached, Unrivalled for Fibre, Colour and Cleanliness.

PAPERMAKERS' CHEMICALS & COLOURS.

ULTRAMARINES, &c.

Special Prepaid Advertisements

IT IS IMPORTANT that Advertisements under any of the Headings mentioned below should reach us by the FIRST POST on WEDNESDAY Morning to INSURE INSERTION.

Charges for advertisements under the heading Situations Wanted are 1/- for twenty-four words, and One Penny per Word after, Minimum charge ONE SHILLING. Names and addresses to be paid for.

Advertisers by paying an extra fee of 6d. can have the replies addressed to the PAPER TRADE REVIEW under a number, and such replies will then be forwarded Post Free.

Advertisements appearing under the following headings:

Tenders.	Mills Wanted or To Let.
Sales by Auction.	Machinery Wanted or For Sale.
Businesses Wanted.	
Businesses for Disposal.	Situations Vacant.

Miscellaneous.

The charges are 2/- for fifty words or under; 1s. extra for every line or portion after. Ten words to be reckoned for each line. Names and addresses to be paid for. Payment must be made in advance, except where the advertiser has a running account, in which case the cost can be debited thereto.

Legal and Financial Announcements: 1/- per Line.

Cheques and Post-office Orders to be CROSSED ——and Co., and made payable to W. JOHN STONHILL.

Situations Vacant.

COMPETENT Clerk for Paper Mill. State salary desired and previous experience.—A. Cannon, Sandford-on-Thames, Oxford. 5888

WANTED, a Machineman; must be tall and thoroughly used to fast speeded news machines, to run a machine 100 inches wide.—Apply, with full particulars of past experience, &c., to "A.Z," No 5887, Office of the WORLD'S PAPER TRADE REVIEW, 58, Shoe-lane, London, E.C. 5887

Situations Wanted.

ADVERTISER, at present managing a mill making news and printings, desirous of a change, is open to re-engagement in similar position, or as traveller; has also had several years' experience in browns, caps, and shop papers, and knows thoroughly the paper trade throughout the U.K.; highest references.—Apply No. 5875, office of the WORLD'S PAPER TRADE REVIEW, 58, Shoe Lane, London, E.C. 5875

CHEMIST is open to engagement; five years' experience in paper mill work, good knowledge of papermaking materials, experience in soda recovery, Yaryan and Porion, causticising preparation of raw materials, boiling, bleaching, &c. Good references.—Address No. 5877, office of the WORLD'S PAPER TRADE REVIEW, 58, Shoe Lane, E.C. 5877

CLERK (18), used to Paper Mill work, invoicing, orders, &c., &c.; good references; open for engagement; moderate salary.—Apply No. 5885, office of the WORLD'S PAPER TRADE REVIEW, 58, Shoe-lane, London, E.C. 5885

CLERK, 5 years' experience in coloured paper, pasteboard and card trade, desires re-engagement; having thorough knowledge of the trade could travel, manage warehouse, or buy for wholesale trade. Undeniable references.—Address No. 5890, office of the WORLD'S PAPER TRADE REVIEW, 58, Shoe-lane, London, E.C. 5890

DRAUGHTSMAN, expert in Machine and Pattern Drawings and Specifications, patent drawings, plans, &c., seeks occasional work or a permanency; has a thorough knowledge of general machinery.—G. K. s, 89, Woodstock-road, Finsbury-park, N. 5879

EXPERIENCED Chemist desires appointment as Chemist or Assistant Manager; experienced in all tests and analyses, causticizing, cellulose, wood and straw pulps, soda recovery, &c.—W. J. Lovett, Sydney House, St. Anne's-on-Sea. 5889

FOREMAN is open to Engagement; well up in coloured shops, browns, and caps; last three-and-a-half years foreman at Brook Mills, Little Eaton, Derby.—Apply, J. C. Brown, Holme Cottage, Little Eaton, Derby. 5857

MANAGER is open to engagement; is well up in all kinds of paper made from rags, also wood pulp, vegetable parchment, imt. parchment, and paraffin paper; good engineering and chemical knowledge. Best references.—Address No. 5844, office of the WORLD'S PAPER TRADE REVIEW, 58, Shoe Lane, London, E.C. 5844

TO PAPERMAKERS.—Finisher requires situation; well up in shops and brown caps; good references.—Address W. H. Organ, 2, Aylmer Cottages, Watchet, near Bridgwater, Somerset. 5880

TO PAPERMAKERS.—Finisher requires situation; well up in small hands, groceries, cartridges, and browns; or could run paper bag machine; good character on leaving.—Address No. 5882, office of the WORLD'S PAPER TRADE REVIEW, 58, Shoe Lane, London, E.C. 5882

Machinery for Sale.

ONE KOLLERGANG, new, Stones 51 inches by 14 inches, C.I. Pan, Scrapers, and Driving Gear.

ONE HYDRAULIC PRESS, second-hand, with Press Box 38 inches diam. by 32 inches deep, with wheels; all parts strong, Ram 2 feet 6 inches by 8 inches diam.

ONE 2-cwt. STEAM HAMMER, second-hand, for Roller Bars or General Forgings, Cylinder 7 inches diam. by 12 nch Stroke, with heavy Anvil Block.

TWELVE REVOLVING STRAINER PLATES, second-hand, 18½ inches by 21 inches, class B2, 3½ cut.

REFINING ENGINE, new, Conical Type; same as one working in a large printing mill.

Any reasonable offer will be considered by 5859

BERTRAMS LIMITED, SCIENNES, EDINBURGH.

Mill to be Let or Sold.

TO be LET or SOLD, a Paper Mill at Stalybridge, called the Higher Mill, containing one large machine and room for another, steam engine and boilers, in good condition.—Apply for further information to the Caretaker on the premises. 2162

PAPER & PULP MILL SHARES.

(Report received from Mr. F. D. DEAN, 36, Corporation Street, Manchester.)

Nominal Amnt	Amnt Paid	Name of Company	Last dividend	Price.
7	7	Bury Paper, ord.	nil	4½—4¾
7	7	do. do. 6% pref.	6%	4¾—5
100	100	do. do. deb.	5%	103—106
10	10	Bath Paper Mill Co. Lim.	7½%	6—7
10	10	Bergvik Co., def.	15%	13½
100	100	do. do. 6% cum. pref.	6%	10½—11½
10	10	do. do. deb.	5%	105—110
5	3½	Burnley Paper Co.	3/-	77/6—80/0
5	3¾	Darwen Paper Co.	10%	5¾—6¼
10	10	East Lancashire Co.	nil	4¼—4¾
10	10	do. do. 6% pref.	nil	6½—7
5	5	do. do. bonus	nil	1½—2
5	5	Hyde Paper Co.	4%	4½—5
5	4	North of Ireland Paper Co.	nil	2¼—2¾
10	5	Ramsbottom Paper Co.	17½%	12¼—12¾
5	4½	Roach Bridge Paper Co.	5%	3½—3¾
5	5	Star Paper Co.	10%	6—6¼
5	3	do. do. 10% pref. cum.	10%	4¾—5¼
50	50	do. do. deb.	6%	55—56
5	2½	Kellner Partingt'n Pulp Co	—	57/6—[illegible]

THE
United Asbestos Co.,
LIMITED.
DOCK HOUSE, BILLITER STREET, E.C.,
"SALAMANDER"
THE UNITED ASBESTOS COMPANY LIMITED · LONDON ·
TRADE MARK
Pioneers
OF THE
Asbestos
Trade.
UNITED ASBESTOS
NON-CONDUCTING
COVERING
(For Steam Boilers & Pipes)
Best and Cheapest in the
Market; Will not
Injure Boiler Plates.
ASBESTOS
GOODS of ALL
DESCRIPTIONS
BELTINGS.
THE
UNITED
ASBESTOS
Co., Limited,
PACKINGS.
UNITED ASBESTOS Cº LIMᴰ
PURE ITALIAN MILLBOARD EXTRA QUALITY
A1
LONDON
UNITED ASBESTOS
A1 MILLBOARDS
(ITALIAN)
Unequalled for Purity, Strength of
Fibre, and Uniformity. For Dry
Steam Joints it is admitted to be the
cleanest, most durable and economical
packing in existence.
UNITED ASBESTOS
SALAMANDER
Lubricating Cream & Oils,
SPECIALLY ADAPTED TO
PAPERMAKING MACHINERY.
DEPOTS:
MANCHESTER: 34, Deansgate; LIVERPOOL: 33, James Street;
NEWCASTLE-UPON-TYNE: Quayside; GLASGOW: 54, Robertson
Street; CARDIFF: 135, Bute Street; BRISTOL: Provident Buildings;
HULL: Queen's Dock; ST. PETERSBURG: Gostinoe Dvor (Interior) No. 51.

Printed and Published by W. JOHN STONHILL 58, Shoe Lane, LONDON, E.C. Sept. 29, 1893.

NEWSOME'S HOIST GUARD.

Messrs. M. Newsome, Sons and Speddings, of the Anchor Foundry, Dewsbury, have introduced a patented hoist guard deserving of attention wherever a hoist is in operation. We give herewith two sketches exhibiting its action. It consists of a flexible metal guard extending from top to bottom of the hoist shaft at both sides as shown at A in Fig. 1. The guard is formed of link chains stretched close to the front and over the full depth of the shaft, except immediately in front of the cage, where instead the chains are made to pass be-

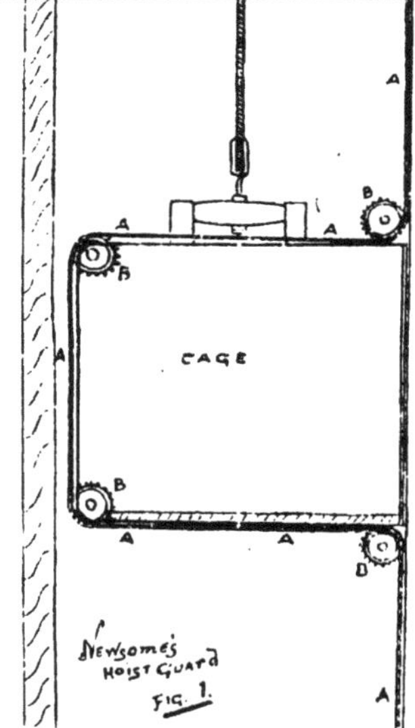

neath the floor of the cage, upwards behind and close to the cage, and over the top, passing over eight pitch wheels, as shown at B. Between the two lines of chains at positions corresponding to the floor stages of every storey iron rods are fixed, as shown in Fig. 2 (C). When the cage is at the floor level these bars are upon the top and behind the cage, but as the latter recedes by ascending or descending they occupy the opening automatically, and perfectly protect it. The main merit of the appliance in our eyes is the fact that it leaves nothing to the care of the operator. It is as secure in its action as an automatically closing door, with the advantage that it is open to the eye or for speech. In fact it leaves the power to operate the cage from any floor as though no guard were interposed, yet with absolute safety. It is in use at

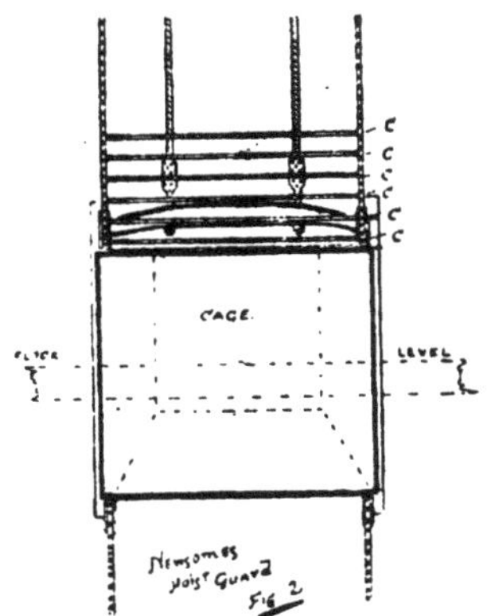

the large works of Messrs. McCorquodale and Co., and also at the Bank Mills, Leeds, and has been largely adopted by the Admiralty and other Government offices.

BRITISH PAPER EXPORTED DURING 1888-92 TO INDIA.

	British India.	
1888	98,869 cwts	£167,995
1889	95,333 ,,	162,027
1890	102,170 ,,	179,083
1891	112,548 ,,	190,012
1892	102,577 ,,	179,315
	Bombay and Scinde.	
1888	55,111 cwts	£88,181
1889	57,026 ,,	88,068
1890	52,596 ,,	86,142
1891	66,109 ,,	103,626
1892	53,743 ,,	89,788
	Madras.	
1888	14,226 cwts	£28,255
1889	13,386 ,,	26,323
1890	17,533 ,,	36,859
1891	16,252 ,,	31,298
1892	19,390 ,,	36,260
	Bengal.	
1888	26,648 cwts	£46,393
1889	22,279 ,,	43,231
1890	28,618 ,,	49,389
1891	27,984 ,,	50,337
1892	27,610 ,,	49,284
	Ceylon.	
1888	7,880 cwts	£15,751
1889	6,873 ,,	13,104
1890	6,419 ,,	12,146
1891	7,938 ,,	15,472
1892	7,807 ,,	15,016

FOREIGN PAPER DISPATCHED FROM U.K. PORTS TO INDIA.

	British India.	
1888	17,889 cwts	£16,893
1889	25,093 ,,	24,457
1890	23,196 ,,	17,371
1891	37,970 ,,	26,738
1892	25,555 ,,	21,467
	Bombay and Scinde.	
1888	8,194 cwts	£7,533
1889	18,097 ,,	17,012
1890	12,622 ,,	8,357
1891	31,973 ,,	22,407
1892	22,045 ,,	17,949
	Madras.	
1888	1,124 cwts	£1,362
1889	1,472 ,,	1,610
1890	965 ,,	1,122
1891	1,239 ,,	983
1892	805 ,,	1,042
	Bengal.	
1888	6,659 cwts	£5,577
1889	3,549 ,,	3,116
1890	5,279 ,,	3,801
1891	3,668 ,,	2,019
1892	2,268 ,,	1,687
	Burmah.	
1888	1,912 cwts	£2,421
1889	1,975 ,,	2,719
1890	4,310 ,,	4,091
1891	1,090 ,,	1,328
1892	437 ,,	789

Printed and Published by W. JOHN STONHILL, 58, Shoe Lane, LONDON, E.C. Sept. 29, 1893.

Telegrams: "STONHILL, LONDON." A B C Code. Registered at the General Post Office as a Newspaper.

Vol. XX. No. 14. LONDON, OCTOBER 6, 1893. Price 6d.

The Treatment of Fibrous Materials.

J. P. CORNETT CLAIMS A SAVING IN BLEACH BY HIS PATENTED KNOTTERING PROCESS.

We illustrate a machine, designed by Mr. J. P. Cornett, mill manager, of Sunderland, which, it is claimed, effectively performs the operations of breaking up esparto, straw, and similar papermaking fibres without materially reducing the roots, weeds and similar noxious materials, the result of which is that the roots and weeds can be easily extracted by knottering before bleaching, as they practically remain in their original unbroken state or condition. By this improved process, it is stated, no bleach is wasted on useless materials.

Figure 1 shows a general side elevational view, Figure 2 being a horizontal sectional plan view of the same, and Figure 3 shows a cross-sectional view, but in the latter the position of the inner cone is shown turned through one-eighth of a revolution for the better elucidation of the construction, and in the following description like marks of reference designate like parts.

Referring to the drawings it will be observed that the machine consists of an outer fixed, or stationary conical cylinder a, and an inner open-ended rotary conical cylinder a^1 mounted on a shaft a^2. Both ends of the outer cone are closed with cover-pieces a^3, through which the shaft a^2 is carried, saddle bearings 4 being provided to form bearings for the shafting at each end; P is a pulley on the shaft, which can be driven by belting or otherwise; 5 is an inlet or feeding hopper for water, and the esparto, straw, or other similar fibrous material after it has been boiled; 6 is an outlet from the conical cylinders to a trough or vessel 7, which is furnished with an overflow outlet 8, which is kept at a sufficient height to maintain a constant body of water or aqueous pulp within the conical cylinders.

The bodies of the conical cylinders may be constructed in any suitable manner; the particular construction is immaterial, and in the drawings they are shown constructed of longitudinal iron bars 9, transverse hoops 10, and wooden linings 11. The outer conical cylinder is furnished on its inside with (as illustrated) four rows of fixed teeth 12, and the inner conical cylinder is similarly furnished on its outside with four rows of teeth 12a the teeth being so arranged that when the inner cone is revolved its teeth shall pass or rotate beween the teeth on the outer cone.

The operation of the machine is as follows: The boiled esparto or other fibre is fed into the machine at the hopper 5 together or in conjunction with a large volume of water or spent liquor from the bleaching and other processes, and as the inner cone rotates the required papermaking fibres are broken up or reduced within the cones but the roots and weeds and other like impurities remain unbroken or comparatively uninjured. The broken up paper-making fibres and the unreduced roots and weeds pass out through outlet pipe 6 to the trough 7. The whole mass is then screened through knotters which readily retain the roots and weeds in their entirety, and in this manner the paper-making fibres are cleaned and purified before being finally cut up or beaten in the "Hollander" or bleaching engine.

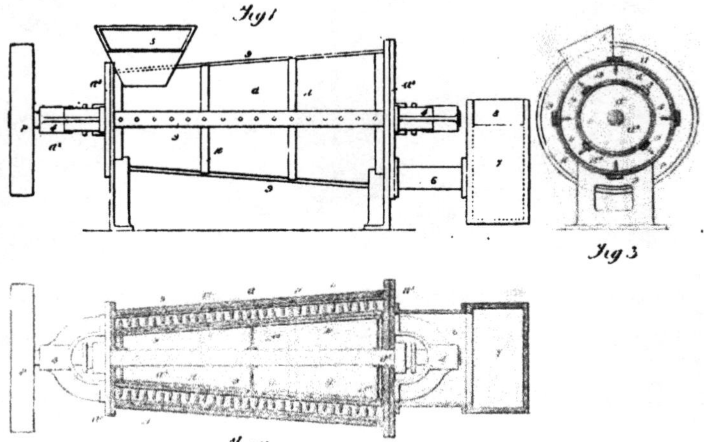

CORNETT'S MACHINE.

The pulp, it is claimed, is consequently improved and more thoroughly cleaned for its subsequent treatment than has hitherto been the case.

WOOD PULP SYNDICATES IN GERMANY.

In the *World's Paper Trade Review* of September 22nd we announced the formation of a Central Union of the four German syndicates of mechanical wood pulp makers, with chief selling offices at Munich. According to the *Wochenblatt* if the water supply improves and a normal rainfall takes place, about 75 per cent. of the total production of white pine or 58,000 tons dry pulp will be obtainable at the various selling places of the association.

Half of the 25 per cent. of the total production, which stands outside of the convention, comes from factories spread over districts far away from the territory of the association. The other half is composed of many very small and a few larger concerns, which either are bound to certain paper mills by local circumstances, or else whose production is subject to great fluctuations, because their water power is also used for brown pulp and wood pulp boards, or for flour and other mills.

The first duty of the association is to arrive at a price for white pine—(1) which causes no loss to the producers, when the production is decreased by a scanty water supply (2) which secures full productive power with a normal water supply, and (3) last not least, which enables German papermakers to hold their own against foreign competition. This price should serve as a basis to the various syndicates for contracts over 1894, and should be kept up for the whole empire with the smallest possible modifications.

From the sale statistics of the Scandinavian Wood Pulp Union it is estimated there will be a production in 1893 of—

90,462	dry tons in Norway.
42,783	,, ,, ,, Sweden.

or 133,245 dry tons in all, representing—

Norway ...	18% dry	...	82% wet (50% moisture).	
Sweden ...	41% ,,	...	49% ,,	,,
All Scandinavia	26% ,,	...	74% ,,	,,

The following quantities, sold on July for delivery 1894, have to be deducted:

Norway	43,950 dry tons or	48·7%
Sweden	17,850 ,, ,, ,,	38·7%

a total of 61,800 dry tons (46·4 per cent.), nearly half the total production.

In the months of July, August and September further large sales have been made in Great Britain, France and Belgium for delivery 1894, also German firms have gone in, so that 75 per cent. of the Scandinavian production for 1894 is sold. Finland, whose production is from 18,000 to 20,000 dry tons, finds itself in a similar position. The Scandinavian Union has worked under a considerable restriction of the production from January 1st to July 1st. This restriction has now been removed, in order to satisfy the strong demand, particularly from Germany. This increased production has been taken into consideration in the above calculations.

The Scandinavians obtained for wet pulp delivered free on truck to English ports from £5 15s. to £6 2s. 6d. the dry ton, which comes to M13·50 to M14 per meter cwt. at the British paper mills. The Belgians pay at their mills from 16·75 f. to 17·50 f., the French duty paid 17·50 f. to 18·50 f. at the mills, according to the distance from the port, and in accordance to the fact, whether the pulp is dry or wet, but it is mostly wet. In Austria 7·80 fl. to 8 fl. per meter cwt. free paper mill is asked for next year. German mills have to pay the highest duty and the heaviest carriage for pulp coming from Scandinavia. At an approximate price to £6 Hull, or 15·50 fr. Antwerp, dry pulp would come to M12 or M12·50 at German port, or duty paid free German paper mill to M14 to M15, according to greater or smaller carriage from the ports.

As the Central Union will have to take the importation from Scandinavia into consideration, the price suggested for next year is from M14·50 to M15 the meter cwt. But in order to enable papermakers to compete in foreign markets they may consider the advisability of a lower rate. According to the sale statistics of the Central Union the German normal total production does not suffice to cover the increased demand brought about by the installation of new papermaking machines. As there are no stocks, and still many unfulfilled contracts, there can be no doubt that a considerable quantity will have to be imported from Scandinavia.

RUSSIAN TRADE.

Great Britain does not do a very extensive trade with Russia. The paper exported evidently comprises special descriptions, as a comparison of the average value per cwt. is much higher compared with paper supplied to other countries. During the past five years the exports of British paper to Russia were as follows:—

1888	808 cwts.	£4,893
1889	1,155 „	5,798
1890	1,199 „	6,306
1891	832 „	4,556
1892	952 „	4,876

British importations of rags from Russia have greatly increased during the past few years, as the following figures show:—

1888	1,703 tons.	£22,419
1889	1,340 „	13,904
1890	1,182 „	11,609
1891	2,484 „	22,559
1892	4,002 „	34,080

In regard to papermaking machinery, there is very little sent to Russia from this country. Our Consul, in deploring this state of things points out that a small quantity is received from Germany.

Speaking of the Nijni Novgorod Fair in 1892, the supply of writing paper was 50 per cent. smaller than in 1891. At first hardly any business was done in it, but towards the end of the Fair a brisk trade followed in the lower sorts, which constitute 75 per cent. of the whole demand for the article. Finnish paper was in great requisition, as was also that of the Howard Mill in Russia.

A new Export Society has been established in Helsingfors, and with a view to promoting its work the Finnish Government has decreed a subsidy of £1,000 per annum towards its expenses for three years. Its object is to further in various ways the export trade of the land by sending out, principally to England, duly qualified persons as enquiry agents, &c. It endeavours so far to augment the export of paper, wooden goods, &c. Paper and paper pulp exported from Helsingfors in 1892, amounted to 1,067,912 Finnish marks, against 734,033 Finnish marks in 1891.

Finland exported 21,734,468 kilos of paper pulp in 1892, against 21,005,949 kilos in 1891. In 1892, 14,050,561 kilos of paper were exported, and in 1891, 13,131,101 kilos.

The Vice-Consul at Moscow, in his report for 1892, states that the machine works and iron foundries owned by British subjects, with English foremen and draughtsmen, did a great amount of work, and a large shop, started a few years ago by enterprising Scotchmen on the same system as the stores in England, has proved an immense success, employing over 800 hands. It is pleasing to note that, contrary to the universal practise in this town, the last-named undertaking is closed on Sundays, thereby setting an example highly approved by the better classes, who wish to see Sunday closing rendered compulsory.

Hangö exported in 1892, 2,401,486 kilos of wood pulp and pasteboard, the value being £20,000. In the previous year the quantity was 1,039,022 kilos, of the value of £13,000. Paper was exported in 1892 to the extent of 2,521,793 kilos, the value being £30,000. In 1891, 1,502,148 kilos of paper were exported, the value being £18,000.

The exports at Kotka included the following:—In 1892, 8,907,851 kilos of wood pulp of the value of 1,021,742 marks; paper, 108,523 kilos, 38,243 marks. In 1891, 8,810,580 kilos of wood pulp of the value of 1,541,851 marks; paper, 267,653 kilos, 49,519 marks.

The exports at Uleaborg in 1892 included 14,253 cubic metres of timber and wood pulp of the value of £2,860. In 1891, 11,208 cubic metres of £1,874 value were exported.

The exports in 1892 of wood pulp, pasteboard, and paper from Wiborg were, 1,520,883, 1,143,766, and 133,997 kilos respectively. In 1891, the comparative figures were 1,616,624, 1,250,747, and 125,075 kilos.

COL. H. A. FRAMBACH

(President of the Badger Paper Co., First National Bank of Kaukauna, and of the Papermaking Exhibit Co.)

BY A CORRESPONDENT.

Few outside of those identified with the paper industry have ever been inside a paper mill, and very few indeed of the great mass of people have any conception of the many manipulations and the machinery required to produce the paper used for writing, printing, and packing purposes. The Chicago Paper Trade Club, consisting of the prominent manufacturers and dealers of the Western States, had this in mind when they organised the American Paper Making Exhibit Company, in order to show at the Columbian Exposition of 1893 a typical American paper mill plant running and making paper. At the Paris Exposition of 1889, a paper machine built by Messrs. Darblay and Cie, and one by De Naeyer, were kept running right along, and one built by Mons. Debiè was operated part of the time. The idea of the Paper Making Exhibit Company was to have a complete plant making paper and run on entirely sulphite wood pulp, ground wood and white shavings. This plant was to be a type of a number quite recently built in the West, Pennsylvania, and Maine, and it was justly supposed that such an exhibit would be of great interest, not only to the trade, but also to visitors in general. The American Paper Making Exhibit Company very wisely argued that if anything like a success was to be attained, the most popular and the most energetic and practical paper manufacturer of the Western States ought to be the president of the company, and be the organising head. This idea resulted in the choice for president falling on Colonel H. A. Frambach, of Kaukauna, Wisconsin, the subject of this sketch. In this manner the company not only gained as president a man whose name is a household word in the paper trade of the great Western country, but one whose indomitable energy would seem to give the best possible guarantee that everything would be done that could possibly be done to make the Fair's paper mill a success. It is not the object of the writer to describe either the machine or the model paper mill beyond mentioning that the machine was built by the Beloit Iron-Works, of Beloit, Wisconsin, 106in. wide and that the accessory parts and the rest of the plant such as calender, pumps, beating engines, filters, steam engines, conveyers, &c., were selected among the machine shops of the United States. The request of the *World's Paper Trade Review* to furnish a sketch of the life of Colonel Frambach was a pleasing assignment for your correspondent, but the second request to furnish a good photograph was a difficult one, owing to the very great modesty of the gallant Colonel, to whom it was necessary to apply a ruse in order to obtain the coveted picture. The town of Kaukauna, Wis., is a striking example of how quickly manufactories in U.S.A. spring up in what was shortly before a comparative wilderness. The water power of Kaukauna is about double that of the world-renowned Lowell, Mass., power, and is the second or third in the U.S. Space does not allow the description of the marvellous development of Kaukauna, the site of which was bought from the Indians for two barrels of rum, and where, in 1832, there were only a couple of very small saw mills, and Colonel Frambach's career must now claim our attention.

Among all the men who have figured prominently before the public in the town and city of Kaukauna during the past twenty years, Colonel H. A. Frambach has without doubt been most conspicuous, he having been honoured—and justly so too—with some of the highest places of trust in the gift of the people. Mr. Frambach was born in Syracuse, N.Y., November 21, 1840, and is of German descent, both of his parents having come from Germany. His father was a linguist of some note, his life having been devoted to the teaching of languages in some of the best colleges. In 1846, soon after the death of Colonel Frambach's mother, the family, consisting then of the father and four children, moved to Racine, Wis., where, after eight years of mourning for his beloved wife, the father also passed away, leaving the subject of this sketch an orphan at the age of fourteen years to battle with the world alone. Colonel Frambach's early life was an humble one indeed, spent in working on a farm during the summer and doing chores for his board and going to school in the winter time. Thus in the little country school house, of which he still holds the most tender recollections, the Colonel laid the foundation for that exellent business education which has served him so well ever since. Just before the war broke out Colonel Frambach was operating a wood boat on the Illinois river, and when the first news of hostilities swept over the country he disposed of his boat and enlisted at once in Company G, 61st Illinois volunteer infantry. He was with Grant in the campaign down the Mississippi river in 1862, serving as a private till after the battle of Shiloh, when he was detailed to that most responsible and dangerous department of army work—the secret service. He served gallantly in this capacity in the department of Tennessee under Generals Logan, Brayman and some others till 1863, when he received the appointment as chief of the secret service in the department of Arkansas, with the rank of Colonel. After the close of the war he retained his connection with the secret service, engaging at the same time in the mercantile business in St. Louis, Mo. In 1872 Colonel Frambach came to Kaukauna where he and his brother John Stovekin joined forces and built the first paper mill in Kaukauna, located where the Kaukauna paper mill now stands. While operating this mill he was engaged to some extent in mercantile business, and in 1876 was chairman of the board of supervisors of Kaukauna. From 1878 to 1880 he operated the Menasha Paper and Pulp Co.'s mills at Menasha, returning to Kaukauna in 1880. Upon his return to this place he operated the Eagle paper mill, in which he was formerly interested, till it was burned down in August 1880. Colonel Frambach rebuilt the mill himself, and it was run under the name of the Frambach Paper Mill. In 1881 he organised the Union Pulp Company with Mr. Rogers of Appleton and the Van Nortwicks of Batavia, Ill. In 1884 he sold his interest in both of the above establishments to the Van Nortwick Syndicate, and in company with Hon. Jos. Villas, of Manitowoc, organised the Badger Paper Company and began building the plant, which was ready for work in 1885.

The great energy and business foresight of this remarkable American papermaker may be best illustrated by describing some of the enterises of which he is the life and soul.

The Badger Paper Co.'s mill is the largest mill in Kaukauna, and runs two Harper machines and one Fourdrinier. With it are connected extensive ground pulp works both at Kaukauna and at Quinnesee Falls, also a three digester sulphite plant of which Colonel Frambach is justly proud, as it is one of the most practical and compact plants in the States, and contrary to the rule there turns out a good quality of fibre daily, which is all used by the Badger Paper Co. The paper made by these mills goes chiefly to Chicago dailies and to the Pacific coast. In 1885 the Manufacturer's Bank was organised by Colonel Frambach, and this in 1887 became the first National Bank of Kaukauna, which to-day stands under the management of Colonel Frambach and the Honorable Joseph Vilas, of Manitowoc.

For some time Colonel Frambach and his son, Mr. Henry Frambach, have conducted a very extensive wall paper manufactory in Kaukauna, which a few weeks ago was incorporated with the National Wall Paper Trust, of New York. They will relieve the Frambachs of the trouble attending the

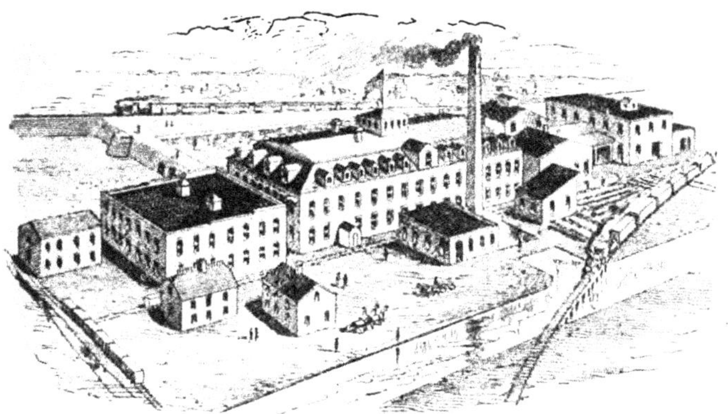

THE BADGER PAPER MILL.

carrying on of the works, will sell the product, paying the Badger Paper Co. for the use of the buildings, power, materials, &c.

Besides the above, Colonel Frambach is interested actively or otherwise in various other enterprises, and quite lately not finding the exhibit of the Model Paper Mill run with enough vim for his liking, has taken the helm himself and licked things into shape in a surprising manner. It is said in Chicago that owing to the backing out of those who ought to have been of assistance, the entire financial burden of the exhibit has fallen on Colonel Frambach's shoulders, which is quite likely, and will be readily believed by anyone conversant with the petty bickerings and mismanagement which seems to have prevailed all along with the World's Columbian Exposition. Should any paper trade reader of this sketch ever strike the Fox River Valley, he will be well repaid by a visit to the Badger Paper Co.'s mills, and what is more pleasant, will receive a welcome which in its genuineness and cordiality will make him think for a moment that he is again in "Merrie England."

APPLICATIONS FOR TRADE MARKS.

RELATING TO PAPER ONLY (CLASS 39).

Published from July to September, 1893.

172,887.—Cigarette papers. "THE HANDY." A combination of devices and the *facsimile* of the signature of the applicant. Firmin Brousse, 14, Rue des Lions, St. Paul, Paris, cigarette paper manufacturer. Applied for 19th May, 1893. Date of publication, July 26th, 1893. Address for service in the United Kingdom, c/o W. P. Thompson and Co., 6, Lord-street, Liverpool.

173,322.—A newspaper. The mark is the familiar title page of *Punch*, which has been used by applicants and predecessors in business thirty-four years before August 13th, 1875. Bradbury Agnew and Co., Limited, 10, Bouverie-street, Whitefriars, London, newspaper proprietors. Applied for June 10th, 1893. Date of publication July 26th, 1893.

166,707.—Cigarette wrapper papers. A device and *facsimile* signature to go upon the wrapper. Leon Duc, trading as Duc Fils, 25, Rue d' Hautville, Paris, paper manufacturer. By consent. Applied for August 26th, 1892. Date of publication August 2nd, 1893. Address for service in the United Kingdom, c/o Paddison and Fullilove, 14, Gray's-inn-square, London.

173,384 A newspaper. Mark consists of title page heading of *The Athenæum*. The Right Hon. Sir Charles Wentworth Dilke, Bart., M.P., 76, Sloane-street, London, S.W., newspaper proprie for June 14th, 1893. Mark u cant and predecessors in b seven years before August 13t of publication August 2nd, 18

173,385.—A newspaper. This n of the title page heading o *Queries*. The Right Hon. Wentworth Dilke, Bart., M.P. street, London, S.W., newspa tors. Applied for June 14th, used by applicant and predeces ness twenty-six years before A 1875. Date of publication A 1893.

166,706.—Cigarette wrapping Figure of a horse in co with a shield device bearing t gram D.F. Leon Duc., tradin Sons, 25, Rue d' Hauteville, Pa manufacturer. Applied for Au 1892. By consent. Date of pu August 9th, 1894. Address for s the United Kingdom, c/o Pattis and Fullilove, 14, Grays-inn London.

171,829.—Paper, including envelop combination of a castle, sword a and the word "RAVENSWOOD." Cowan and Sons, Limited, 38, West ter-street, Edinburgh, papermaker consent. Applied for 1st April, 1893. of publication, August 9th, 1893.

173,122.—A newspaper. The headi *Lloyd's Weekly Newspaper.*" Ed Lloyd, Limited, 12, Salisbury-square, F street, London, E.C., newspaper pro tors. Mark used by applicants and decessors in business upwards of twe years before the 13th August, 1875. App for 31st May, 1893. Date of publicati August 9th, 1893.

173,213.—Postal tubes of paper or cardbo for protecting papers, catalogues or oth documents when passing through the po A *fac simile* signature of the applica forms the essential particular mark. Alla Ransome, Stanley Works, King's-road Chelsea, London, engineer. Applied fo June 5th, 1893. Date of publication, August 9th, 1893.

173,803.—A newspaper. The heading of *The Lancet*. Thomas Henry Wakley, F.R.C.S., and Thomas Wakley, the younger, L.R.C.P., 1, Bedford-street, Strand, and 423, Strand, W.C., newspaper proprietors. Marks used by applicants and predecessors in business fifty-one years before the 13th August, 1875. Applied for 8th July, 1893. Date of publication, August 9th, 1893.

173,834.—Show cards, catalogues, labels, and other articles of stationery, all being included in Class 39, consists of a shield, bearing three crosses and a crescent, surmounted by a groteeque design of a head, and running up the shield in an oblique direction is the word "RELIABLE." Wm.

Ritchie and Sons, 16, Elder-street, Edinburgh, wholesale stationers. Applied for 11th July, 1893. Date of publication, August 9th, 1893.

173,277.—Albumenised Sensitised Paper for use in Photography. A crescent encircled by a ring, around which ring appear the words, "THE 'CRESCENT' BRAND." The firm trading as George Morrish, 20, Paternoster-square, London, printers and publishers. By consent. Applied for 8th June, 1893. Date of publication, August 16th, 1893.

172,100.—Cigarette Paper. A combination of designs for the wrapper. Jacques Braunstein and Maurice Braunstein, trading as Braunstein Freres, 63, 65, Boulevard Exelmans, Paris, and Gassecourt, Seine et Oise, cigarette paper manufacturers. Applied for 14th April, 1893. Date of publication, August 23rd, 1893. Address for service in the United Kingdom, 32, Hamsell-street, London, E.C.

173,435.—A Newspaper. The title heading of *The Chemical News*. William Crooker, 7, Kensington Park-gardens, Middlesex, and Boy - court, Ludgate - hill, London, newspaper proprietor. Mark used since fifteen years and eight months before the 13th August, 1872. Applied for 16th June, 1893. Date of publication, August 23rd, 1893.

172,904.—A journal. The title heading of the *Builder*. Edward Webster Cox and Alfred Stunt, 46, Catherine-street, Covent-garden, London, proprietors of the *Builder* journal. Mark used by applicants and predecessors in business twenty-seven years before the 13th August, 1874. Applied for 19th May, 1893. Date of publication August 23, 1893.

173,816.—Paper clips and fasteners, being articles of stationery. A device containing the word "PHASTGRYP." Samuel Hudson Wright, 6, Castle-market, Dublin, Ireland, umbrella manufacturer. Applied for 10th July, 1893. Date of publication September 6th, 1893.

173,817.—Paper clips and fasteners, being articles of stationery. A device including the word "TENAX." Samuel Hudson Wright, 6, Castle-market, Dublin, Ireland, umbrella manufacturer. Applied for 10th July, 1893. Date of publication September 6th, 1893.

173,445.—Cigarette papers. A design for a wrapper containing the heads and shoulders of four girls. Jac Schnabl and Co., the Predigerstrasse, No. 5, Vienna, Austria. Applied for 16th June, 1893. Date of publication September 20th, 1893. Address for service in the United Kingdom c/o G. F. Redfern and Co., 4, South-street, Finsbury, London.

173,896.—Prints and engravings. The word APIS. Thomas Brooks Brown, 163, Queen-Victoria-street, London, E.C., advertising contractor. By consent. Applied for 14th July, 1893. Date of publication September 20th, 1893.

174,362.—A newspaper. The title heading of *The Morning Advertiser*. Society of Licensed Victuallers, 127, Fleet-street, E.C., newspaper proprietors and publishers. Mark used by applicants and predecessors in business, since twenty years before the 13th August, 1875. Applied for 5th August, 1893. Date of publication September 20th, 1893.

173,448.—Cigarette papers. Design for wrapper, of a lady's hand bearing a fan, which bears the words "PAPIER DELICIEUX." Jac Schnabl and Co., the Predigerstrasse, No. 5, Vienna, Austria, cigarette paper manufacturers. Applied for 16th June, 1893. Date of publication September, 1893. Address for service in the United Kingdom, c/o G. F. Redfern and Co., 4, South-street, Finsbury, London.

173,447.—Cigarette papers. This mark consists of a picture of a fête, or other such occasion, in the sixteenth century, bearing the word "GRANDEZZA." Jac Schnabl and Co., the Predigerstrasse, No. 5, Vienna, Austria, cigarette paper manufacturers. Applied for 16th June, 1893. Date of publication September 27th, 1893. Address for service in the United Kingdom c/o G. F. Redfern and Co., 4, South-street, Finsbury, London.

THE trade carried on by British papermakers with the Argentine Republic has had a very chequered career during the past year or so. In 1888 the value of British paper exported reached £51,000, in 1890 £22,000, and in 1892 £29,000.

PROPOSED MEXICAN PAPER MILL.—Gen. A. G. Greenwood, of Mexico, recently visited Appleton, writes an American correspondent, to look over paper manufactories, and to interest capitalists and operatives in the plan of building a paper mill in Mexico. The general is a man of varied experience. He served in the Southern army during the late war, and afterward went to Mexico, where he served in the revolution there on the side of the republic. This naturally brought him into close relations with the Government, and until two years ago he was engaged as Government contractor for Mexico. For the past two years he has been located in Chicago, but proposes to return to Mexico at the close of the World's Fair. General Greenwood says that there is no mill in Mexico making fine papers, and he wants to establish one. His official relations are such that he would be able to secure valuable concessions and Government contracts which would make the enterprise very profitable, as the Government is itself anxious to secure such an industry. He would like to interest both capital and skilled labour in the enterprise, and there is a prospect that he will not be unsuccessful.

D. N. BERTRAM'S
Patent REELER

London 1862.

Edinburgh 1886.

Edinburgh 1890.

The Special Features of the Machine are:

1.—NO PART OF THE KNIFE BLOCKS or knives, except the cutting edges, comes in contact with the paper, thus avoiding any damage to the web by narrow rings touching it.

2.—There BEING NO BLOCKS between the knives they can be instantly adjusted to any width without taking the spindle from its bearings.

3.—The KNIVES ARE DRIVEN INDEPENDENTLY of the paper at an increased speed ensuring clean cut edges.

4.—The MACHINE IS DRIVEN by belt pulley on drum shaft with fast and slow speeds, worked from front of machine by levers, so arranged that when the fast speed is put on the slow one disengages itself. The change from slow to fast is easily effected, and no jerking takes place.

☞ THIS PATENT REELER is working in Several Well-known Paper Mills.

IN THIS MACHINE the paper is slit into widths upon the spindle, which carries the finished webs, thus preventing irregularity of edges; the outside shavings being trimmed before the web passes to the winding-up spindle and slitting-knives.

THE KNIFE CARRIAGE is placed vertically over the web, and fitted with automatic raising gear, to compensate for the increase of web.

THERE IS ALSO AN ARRANGEMENT so that the operator can apply the slitting-knives with any given amount of contact that may be desirable, and it will retain the same position until the whole web is finished.

THE ACTION OF THE PRESSING ROLL on the top of the web ensures the reel being firmly and evenly wound, and there is a shackle at one side of the machine, with screw which can adjust pressing roll to a nicety on the drum upon which the slitting and winding apparatus is carried. This allows webs which may be slightly thicker at one side than another to be wound without creasing.

REFERENCES GIVEN ON APPLICATION.

BERTRAMS LIMITED

(Successors to Geo. & Wm. BERTRAM—ESTABLISHED 1821),

ENGINEERS,

ST. KATHERINE'S WORKS, SCIENNES, EDINBURGH.

Thos. Hardman & Sons
Established 1836.
Fernhill Mills
Bury, Lancashire.
Manufacturers of
Felts
for
Paper Makers.
Specialities
Wet and Dry Felts,
Couch Roll Covers,
Second Press Felts,
Bag Flannels,
Blankets, Lappings &c.
for Paper Stainers
Also Makers of every Description of Cloths used for Machinery Purposes.
Telephone No 41
Telegrams, Hardman, Fernhill, Bury.

JACKSON

gineers,

ANCHESTER.

RSHALL'S PATENT PERFECTING ENGINE.

ABLE FOR ALL CLASSES OF STOCK AND EVERY QUALITY OF PAPER.

MADE IN THREE SIZES.

Engine will ***produce*** *a Better Finished, Stronger and More Even Sheet of* ***Paper from*** *... materials* ***than can*** *be produced by any other Mechanical Process, and* ***at the same*** *time will* ***REDUCE*** *the* ***TIME*** *and* ***POWER*** *required for Beating.*

We supply these ***Engines*** *on approval subject to our accomplishing the* ***above results.***

hine—NO WELL-EQUIPPED PAPER MILL SHOULD BE WITHOUT.

APPLICATION.

Special Prepaid Advertisements

IT IS IMPORTANT that Advertisements under any of the Headings mentioned below should reach us by the FIRST POST on WEDNESDAY Morning to INSURE INSERTION.

Charges for advertisements under the heading Situations Wanted are 1/- for twenty-four words, and One Penny per Word after, Minimum charge ONE SHILLING. Names and addresses to be paid for.

Advertisers by paying an extra fee of 6d. can have the replies addressed to the PAPER TRADE REVIEW under a number, and such replies will then be forwarded Post Free.

Advertisements appearing under the following headings:

Tenders.	Mills Wanted or To Let.
Sales by Auction.	Machinery Wanted or For Sale.
Businesses Wanted.	Situations Vacant.
Businesses for Disposal.	

Miscellaneous.

The charges are 3/- for fifty words or under; 1s. extra for every line or portion after. Ten words to be reckoned for each line. Names and addresses to be paid for. Payment must be made in advance, except where the advertiser has a running account, in which case the cost can be debited thereto.

Legal and Financial Announcements: 1/- per Line.

Cheques and Post-office Orders to be CROSSED ——and Co., and made payable to W. JOHN STONHILL.

Situations Vacant.

WANTED, a Machineman; must be tall and thoroughly used to fast-speeded news machines, to run a machine 100 inches wide.– Apply, with full particulars of past experience, &c., to "A.Z.," No 5887, Office of the WORLD'S PAPER TRADE REVIEW, 58, Shoe-lane, London, E.C. 5887

WANTED, Head-Foreman for Shotley Grove Paper Works.—Apply by letter, with references, stating age, experience, and salary expected, to John Annandale and Sons, Shotley Bridge, Co. Durham. 589[illegible]

Situations Wanted.

ASSISTANT-MANAGER or Foreman desires an appointment in a sulphite pulp or paper mill in England or abroad; practical engineer and mechanic, fair knowledge of chemistry, speaks several languages, satisfactory references.—Address No. 5892, office of the WORLD'S PAPER TRADE REVIEW, 58, Shoe-lane, London, E.C. 5892

ADVERTISER, at present managing a mill making news and printings, desirous of a change, is open to re-engagement in similar position, or as traveller; has also had several years' experience in browns, caps, and shop papers, and knows thoroughly the paper trade throughout the U.K.; highest references.—Apply No. 5875, office of the WORLD'S PAPER TRADE REVIEW, 58, Shoe Lane, London, E.C. 5875

CLERK (18), used to Paper Mill work, invoicing, orders, &c., &c.; good references; open for engagement; moderate salary.—Apply No. 5885, office of the WORLD'S PAPER TRADE REVIEW, 58, Shoe-lane, London, E.C. 5885

DRAUGHTSMAN, expert in Ma[illegible] Pattern Drawings and Specifications, [illegible] ings, plans, &c., seeks occasional work or a [illegible] has a thorough knowledge of general machi[illegible] Jones, 89, Woodstock-road, Finsbury-park, N.

FOREMAN is open to Enga[illegible] well up in coloured shops, browns, and [illegible] three-and-a-half years foreman at Brook Mills, L[illegible] Derby.—Apply, J. C. Brown, Holme Cottage, L[illegible] Derby.

TO PAPERMAKERS.—Finisher [illegible] situation; well up in shops and brown c[illegible] references.—Address W. H. Organ, 2, Aylmer [illegible] Watchet, near Bridgwater, Somerset.

TO PAPERMAKERS.—Finisher r[illegible] situation; well up in small hands, groce[illegible] ridges, and browns; or could run paper bag machi[illegible] character on leaving.—Address No. 58[illegible], office [illegible] WORLD'S PAPER TRADE REVIEW, 58, Shoe Lane, E.C.

Wanted.

WANTED to PURCHASE, One hu[illegible] tons DRY WOOD PULP, good quality. [illegible] Liverpool or Galveston, Texas.—Send samples and pr[illegible] Oak Cliff Paper Mills, Oak Cliff, Texas, U.S.A.

Machinery for Sale.

ONE KOLLERGANG, new, Stone[illegible] inches by 24 inches, C.I. Pan, Scrapers, and Dri[illegible] Gear.

ONE HYDRAULIC PRESS, second-hand, with [illegible] Box 38 inches diam. by 32 inches deep, with wheels, [illegible] parts strong, Ram 2 feet 6 inches by 8 inches diam.

ONE 2-cwt. STEAM HAMMER, second-hand, for Ro[illegible] Bars or General Forgings, Cylinder 7 inches diam. by [illegible] nch Stroke, with heavy Anvil Block.

TWELVE REVOLVING STRAINER PLATES, secon[illegible] hand, 18¾ inches by 21 inches, class B2, 3½ cut.

REFINING ENGINE, new, Conical Type; same as o[illegible] working in a large printing mill.

Any reasonable offer will be considered by 5859

BERTRAMS LIMITED, SCIENNES, EDINBURGH.

Mill to be Let or Sold.

TO be LET or SOLD, a Paper Mill at Stalybridge, called the Higher Mill, containing one large machine and room for another, steam engine and boilers, in good condition.—Apply for further information to the Caretaker on the premises. 2162

WORLD'S PAPER TRADE REVIEW OFFICE,
58, SHOE LANE, LONDON, E.C.
OCTOBER 5, 1893.

TRADE NOTES.

MESSRS. ROTH, SCHMIDT AND CO. advise us that they have removed from 120, Queen Victoria-street, E.C., into larger and more convenient offices, at 6, Crosby-square, E.C.

DISSOLUTION OF PARTNERSHIP.—The firm of Messrs. John Jackson and Co., rag merchants, of Horbury, Yorks, has dissolved, and the business in future will be carried on by Mr. W. Dews in his own name.

SALT EXPORTS.—Probably for the first time in the history of commerce, says the *Liverpool Journal of Commerce*, the salt exports from the Mersey to the East were overstepped last month by the exports from Hamburg. As compared with the first nine months of last year, this year's exports from the Mersey show a falling off of something like 25 per cent.

HIGH BRIDGE WORKS, NEWCASTLE-ON-TYNE.—Papermakers requiring good second-hand strainer plates will do well to obtain particulars of several sets which Messrs. Henry Watson and Son, of High Bridge Works, Newcastle-on-Tyne, have on hand. They are particularly suitable for makers of coarse papers. The reasonable terms upon which Messrs. Watson and Son close strainer plates merit attention. Plates worn two full gauges wider than they were when first set to work are closed at ½d. per square inch less 35 per cent. discount, carriage being paid by goods train to Newcastle.

RE W. PICKTHALL.—At the London Bankruptcy Court, under the failure of William Pickthall, a first meeting of creditors has been held. The debtor was a hemp, flax and paper merchant, trading in Appold-street, Finsbury, under the style of John Pickthall and Sons. His gross liabilities amount to about £12,300, of which £9,500 are expected to rank, and the assets are estimated at about £9,400, subject to realisation.—Mr. R. Raphael attended on behalf of the debtor, and said that at present he was not in a position to lay a scheme before the creditors, but hoped to do so at a later period.—Resolutions were thereupon passed for the appointment of Mr. Percy Mason, chartered accountant, as trustee under the proceedings, together with a committee of inspection.

TAXATION OF MACHINERY.—The prolonged contest at Chesterfield over the rating of machinery is at last concluded. Messrs. Hewitt, Bunting and Company were not satisfied with the reduction offered by the Assessment Committee from £460 gross (Mr. Hedley's valuation) to £168, and therefore gave notice of appeal to sessions. Acting under the advice of Mr. Humphreys-Davies, who, as Surveyor to the Machinery Users' Association, has been conducting all the appeals, a compromise was offered in order to avoid further expensive litigation. This was accepted by the Board of Guardians, and the result is that the assessment is further reduced to £126. The total figures of the nine manufacturing firms and companies who acted together show the unwarrantable nature of the attack on machinery and how signally it has failed in this instance. The old rateable value of these firms was £8,036. Messrs. Hedley, Mason and Hedley, in their revaluation on behalf of the Union, increased this by £7,382. The Assessment Committee on hearing the objections reduced this increase by £6,062, and on appeal to sessions a further £620 was knocked off, the net result being an increase of £700 in the aggregate assessments of the nine appellants. Thus only 10 per cent. of the increase was finally sustained. These figures show conclusively how machinery users can, by combination, defeat the efforts to tax the productive power of the country.

"FACTS ABOUT DISINFECTANTS."—In "Facts about Disinfectants," by Mr. H. Helbing and Dr. F. W. Passmore, it is stated that nothing is of greater importance amongst the social questions of the present day than the problem of efficient disinfection. In discussing the value of disinfectants, the means of determining the value employed by scientists are bacteriological, chemical, or practical. The properties of a good effective disinfectant is easy distribution, activity against bacteria, activity against spores, deodorising properties, relative strength and cheapness, and innocuousness to human life. The chemical composition and classification are grouped in the pamphlet, and in referring to coal-tar disinfectants it is stated that Jeyes' Fluid is typical in this class. Mr. H. Helbing and Dr. F. W. Passmore say: "We have for more than a year analysed each bulk of Jeyes' Fluid that has been sold for use in this country, and when compared with the analyses we have made during the same period of other similar preparations and imitations, Jeyes' Fluid has proved to be of much more concentrated and uniform composition than any other coal-tar disinfectant we have had in hand. We do not say that there are not other disinfectants equally good and effective, but, whilst we cannot speak of any of those which have come before us as equal to Jeyes', we have convinced ourselves as to the advantages of Jeyes' Fluid, and we do not hesitate to recommend it to all who wish to be sure that disinfection is reliably and successfully carried out. Coal-tar disinfectants are made from coal-tar oils that vary in composition, not only according to the source from which each is prepared, but in each batch prepared from the same source. It is this unreliability of the crude products that makes it so difficult to procure a coal-tar fluid that always contains the same proportions of disinfectants, just as it is difficult to obtain wines or spirits always with the same bouquet, composition and strength." Mr. H. Helbing and Dr. Passmore further state: "We will analyse and advise free of charge on any coal-tar preparation submitted to us by a medical man, sanitary officer or vestry inspector who receives this treatise, on the understanding that such analysis is used for the benefit and safeguard of the general public and community, as we have no doubt, and indeed, sincerely hope, that our publication of 'Facts about Disinfectants' will open the eyes of many, emphasise the importance of greater scientific knowledge in connection with disinfectants, and advance the interests of hygiene and public welfare."

"THE ENGLISH ILLUSTRATED MAGAZINE," for October, well maintains its high reputation in regard to the excellence of its illustrations and literary matter. The frontispiece is a portrait of Lord Aberdeen, Percy A. Hurd contributing an article on "Canada and her New Governor." Lady Colin Campbell, Mrs. Lyn Linton, Robert Barr and Barry Pain are amongst the writers, the contents being varied, instructive, and pleasingly artistic. London: 198, Strand, *Illustrated London News* office.

THE exports of British paper to Mauritius average £3,500 annually.

EXPORTS of paper from New York, according to the last weekly list to hand, include the following:

London	87 pkgs	B. South Africa ...	2 cases
B. West Indies ...	293 ,,	New Zealand ...	2 pkgs
Liverpool	11 cases	Glasgow	100 ,,

THE PAPER TRADE.—Some more mills have started up, but in a good many cases manufacturers are not very certain that the demand will warrant them in keeping machines moving. They hope for the best, and the expectation is that there will soon be more activity displayed in the market. The call for news keeps up very steadily and the product is being placed in very good shape. Some book manufacturers report orders as more plentiful, but this is not so as a rule. None of the other grades have any unusual attention.

WORK on the new paper and pulp mill at Nekoosa, Wis., is progressing rapidly. The dam is half completed, and the boiler, machine and finishing rooms are built. The pulp mill will have fourteen pulp grinders, and there will be four machines in the paper mill. The capacity of the pulp mill will be about 35 tons and the paper mill 30 tons daily. The mill will give employment to about 200 hands. It will be ready to start up by January 1.

CHEMICAL FIBRE PRODUCTION.—The York *Paper Trade Journal* states that 1881 the production of chemical fibre i United States, basing figures upon th ducing capacity of the mills in operatio increased within a very small fraction per cent. In the year mentioned the daily capacity of the fibre mills amoun 129¾ tons; on July 1st of the current y was 1,105 tons. To-day it is more. If t is added the output of the Canadian (63¼ tons) it will be seen that the progr the wood fibre making industry on the American continent within the last d has been very great, and probably n passed in the industrial annals of any country. The following tabulation sho

DAILY PRODUCING CAPACITY (IN POUNDS) OF IN THE UNITED STATES MAKING CHEMICAL

States.	1892.	1893.
Colorado	—	8,000
Connecticut	12,000	12,000
Delaware	50,000	50,000
Indiana	60,000	70,000
Kentucky	—	20,000
Maine	466,000	562,000
Maryland	65,000	66,000
Massachusetts	45,000	49,000
Michigan	78,000	92,000
New Hampshire	100,000	120,000
New Jersey	—	12,000
New York	238,000	330,000
Ohio	78,000	90,000
Oregon	—	20,000
Pennsylvania	293,000	283,000
South Carolina	10,000	10,000
Vermont	24,000	24,000
Virginia	—	40,000
Washington	5,000	5,000
West Virginia	50,000	90,000
Wisconsin	141,000	237,000
Totals	1,730,000	2,210,000

* Increase. † Decrease.

The output for the year ended June was not of course equal to the full ca of the mills. It may be estimated t been equal to, say, 250,000 tons.

THE AMERICAN TALC COMPANY.—T newcomer in the field of mineral pulp facture. This corporation, with an a ized capital of 500,000 dols., was forme number of Providence, R. I., busines and capitalists in the fall of 1891, and s a lease of one of the talc mines near G neur, St. Lawrence County, N.Y. Its are Messrs. I. B. Lawton, president; Darling, treasurer; O. C. Derrieux, Gray, H. C. Luther, I. B. Lawton and Ray, directors. The erection of the pany's mill plant, boarding house, h works, &c., was begun in the spring c This of necessity was slow work, as machinery was made for each depar it being the intention of the comp spare neither time nor money in the ment of the plant. The mill is provide a condensing engine of the latest ty ample battery of boilers for trans power, and with the various other m and appliances for grinding. It is a n parture in the talc business to use ste motive power, but it is claimed that t sures a uniformity of product which has hitherto been impossible under the old systems. The mine is said to be the largest yet discovered in St. Lawrence County; it is now down 240 feet on the incline, about 75 feet from the surface, and has a breast exceeding 22 feet. The colour of the material is said to be the whitest which St. Lawrence County has ever produced. The mine is operated by power drills, the motive power being compressed air, as being the best adapted to mining, the exhaust air affording ample ventilation in the shaft. The talc is taken from the mine in a cable car run by steam, which dumps automatically when the surface is reached into a second car, which is then run into the dry shed. After the talc has lain in this shed for several months it is sorted and reloaded into another cable car, which is also run by steam power and which dumps automatically into the crusher room in the mill, from whence it passes through the crushers and various other processes into the bags, when it is ready for shipment.

PAPIERFABRIK HEGGE. — This concern shows a gross profit of M114,600, against M89,400 in the previous year. A dividend of 8 per cent. is proposed against 7½ per cent. of last year.

POMMERSCHE PAPIERFABRIK HOHENKRUG, after writing off large amounts, proposes to pay a dividend of 2 per cent.

HERR GEORG PAUL KOHLER, in Guben, will continue on his own account the business of the firm "Gubener Papier und Pappenfabrik Weiss und Köhler."

HERR J. G. LANTZKE NACHFOLGER'S paper mills in Falkenberg, near Freienwalde, have been burnt down.

A NEW SULPHITE MILL is about to be erected at Forshagen near Karlstadt, in Sweden, with a capital of 300,000 kronor, and an annual production of 4,000 tons.

HERR IGNAZ SPIRO, the head of the papermaking firm of Ignaz Spiro and Söhne, in Bohm, Krumau, recently celebrated his 50 years' jubilee as a papermaker.

THE CROLLWITZER ACTIEN PAPIERFABRIK propose a dividend of 10 per cent. for 1892-93. Last year 7½ per cent. was paid.

THE ROBSCHUTZER PAPIERFABRIK shows a loss in 1892-93, increasing the previous loss by M12,800, the total now standing at M65,800. During the year 1,924,456 kilos. paper were produced and invoiced out at a total of M458,100.

THE MACHINENBAU ANSTALT GOLZERN proposes a dividend of 11 per cent. (10 per cent. last year).

THE ERNST WICKERT'SCHE PAPPENFABRIK, in Wildenau, near Schwarzenburg, was burnt down on September 14th. As the greater part of the buildings were of wood, there was not much chance of arresting the conflagration. It is understood that the loss is covered by insurance.

THE PAPER TRADE OF JAPAN.—The exportation of paper in 1891 was 422,976 yen, against 379,575 in 1890. Books of all kinds 54,242 yen, against 59,153 yen in 1890. Paper was imported in 1891 for 400,378 yen, against 705,571 yen in 1890. Books came in for 194,485 yen in 1891 and 254,728 yen in 1890—(1 yen = 4s. 1d.)

SWISS PAPER TRADE.—The 64% decrease in the importation of French paper to Switzerland in the first three months of the Customs war has been kept up, the average in the first six months showing 62%. The average of 528,000f. in 1890 and 1891 fell to 199,000f. in the corresponding period of 1892. Germany has taken the greater part of the supply since. The figures are as follows:—

IMPORTATION IN METRE CWT.

	Total.	From France.	From Germany.	From Austria
PRINTINGS & WRITINGS:				
1st Half, 1893	5,551	421	3,560	920
,, 1892	5,582	938	3,331	728
WALL PAPERS, &C.:				
1st Half, 1893	2,378	360	1,736	11
,, 1892	2,518	894	1,472	17
BOOKBINDERS & BOX-MAKERS WORK:				
1st Half, 1893	801	53	677	19
,, 1892	1,853	355	1,423	13
BOOKS:				
1st Half, 1893	6,033	1,839	4,009	42
,, 1892	6,194	2,150	3,843	48
WRITING & DRAWING UTENSILS:				
1st Half, 1893	859	106	597	[illegible]6
,, 1892	919	249	590	51

The demand for printing and writing paper was about the same in both years. The French supply was replaced by 100 metre cwts. from Great Britain, and by the corresponding figures in the above table from Germany and Austria. Otherwise Austria has not much profited by the situation. In wall papers, &c., Germany now supplies about three-quarters of the demand. In this class, and also in bookbinders and fancy boxmakers' work, the Swiss home industry seems to go ahead. The relations between Switzerland and France have so far changed that the exportation from France has gone down 70·6 per cent., and the importation 35·3 per cent. France of course does not lose so much in proportion by a loss of 30,000,000 francs. Switzerland feels its loss of 23,000,000 francs far more. Switzerland has found other markets, and we think English papermakers ought to be able still more to increase their sales. The carriage at any rate is much lower than from remote parts of Germany and Austria.

NORWEGIAN TRADE.

Although papermaking is not regarded as being so profitable as wood pulp manufacture in Norway, yet the industry has developed amazingly during the past five years, as the following exports of paper and pasteboard to Great Britain will show:—

1888	69,024	cwts.	£48,394
1889	79,165	,,	57,363
1890	116,894	,,	81,215
1891	166,570	,,	124,735
1892	231,261	,,	172,671

Increasing quantities of rags are now being shipped from Norway to Great Britain, and a great fillip was given to trade at the time rags were not allowed to be imported from the Continent. The following figures relate to the past five years:—

1888	77,906	tons.	£394,752
1889	90,117	,,	431,146
1890	97,878	,,	443,960
1891	104,248	,,	442,224
1892	122,069	,,	492,019

Norwegian imports of British paper are gradually declining, as will be seen from the values in 1890 to 1892:—

1888	6,770	cwts.	£9,390
1889	8,194	,,	10,900
1890	13,350	,,	17,210
1891	11,527	,,	14,741
1892	9,435	,,	12,010

Alkali is not imported from Great Britain so freely as in former years. The average price per cwt. in 1888 was 3s. 1d., and 1892 5s. 11d. Five years' figures:—

1888	49,200	cwts.	£7,714
1889	45,700	,,	7,509
1890	25,200	,,	6,309
1891	28,600	,,	8,602
1892	22,200	,,	6,575

The export of mechanical pulp (dry) from Christiania in 1892 was 8,512 tons (including 5,057 tons Swedish); wet, 24,655 tons (including 5,371 tons Swedish); cellulose (dry), 12,667 tons (including 558 Swedish); wet, 3,822 tons (including 10 tons Swedish). The total value in 1892 was £234,967, against £184,470 in 1891. Packing paper exported from Christiania was of the value of £90,350 in 1892, and £81,010 in 1891; wood pulp boards, £8,150 and £6,910 respectively.

At Christiansand prices for wood pulp were low in 1892, but the export was about the same as in 1891. The export of paper was considerably smaller than in 1891. The machinery in the mills underwent alteration, while a very serious flood in the rivers during the autumn did considerable damage, and stopped the production for some time. During 1892 some 7,048 tons of wood pulp were [illegible]ported, of which quantity 5,034 tons went [illegible]eat Britain. Of paper 1,125 tons went [illegible]eat Britain out of a total exportation [illegible]0 tons.

The export of wood pulp at Drammen is somewhat increasing, and prices for mechanical, and especially for chemical, pulp were satisfactory, and left a reasonable profit. In 1892 some 255 tons of dry mechanical were exported, against 3,021 tons in 1891; wet, 77,404 tons and 83,308 tons respectively. In chemical (dry), 22,66 tons in 1892, and 830 tons in 1891 were exported; wet, 4,650 tons and 3,682 tons respectively. The export of paper is increasing, several powerful mills being now in full work. Exports in 1892 were 3,900 tons, against 1,583 tons in 1891.

At Fredrikshald the production of the local wood pulp mills was reduced to about 9,000 tons; prices advanced at the end of the year.

Last year the port of Sarpsborg was visited by 11 British steamers with a tonnage of 8,835 reg. tons. They all loaded pulp-wood from the Kellner-Partington Paper Pulp Company, Limited. This company has a large export of this kind of wood, as well as of wood pulp, the latter being mostly shipped by the regular liners hence to London.

The wood pulp trade at Kragero during 1892 was very satisfactory. The value of exports was £9,000, against £7,500 in 1891.

The export of wood pulp also increased a little at Risor. The whole quantity of wet pulp went to the English market, which took only a small part of the dry pulp. The greater part of this was shipped to France. In 1892 472 tons of dry and 200 tons of wet were exported, the quantity in 1891 being 279 tons, and 335 tons respectively.

A report dealing with the trade of Skein and Porsgrund states that the Loveid Paper Works, started up some time ago, are of great magnitude, probably the most extensive and complete in Europe. Prices of wood pulp have been kept up owing to reduced production and combination still existing among the exporters. The outlook for this trade seems fairly encouraging.

The exports at Trondhjem for 1892 shows an increase in cellulose and paper, but a decrease in mechanical. The exports were: Norwegian mechanical, 2,135 tons (2,979 tons in 1891); Swedish mechanical, 3,622 tons (3,832 tons in 1891); cellulose, 2,335 tons against 1,825 tons; paper, 511 tons, against 140 tons.

NEW PATENTS.

BRITISH.

APPLICATION.

17,558. Improvements in machinery for cutting or slitting and winding or reeling paper and the like. J. R. Bertram.

SPECIFICATIONS PUBLISHED.

(7½d. each. By post 8d.)

1893.

12,074. Obtaining chlorine. Vogt and Scott.
14,191. Pulp for papermaking. Cornett.

AMERICAN.

503,304. Wood pulp grinding machine. Friedrich Andre, Hildesheim, Germany.
503,553. Paper pulp beating engine. Albert E. Reed Gravesend, England.

SUMMARY OF
IMPORTS & EXPORTS,

London, Liverpool, Bristol, Southampton, Hull, Fleetwood, Harwich, Folkestone, Newhaven, Dover, &c.

IMPORTS.

FOR THE WEEK ENDING TUESDAY LAST.

Paper	8542 bales	Millboards	7197 pkgs.
"	971 cases	"	77 cases
"	1716 rolls	Pasteboards	12147 pkgs.
Stock	237 pkgs	Strawboards	11182 "
Tissues	262 "	Cardboards	400 "
Bags	38 "	Envelopes	25 "
Stationery	34 cases		

FOR LAST MONTH:

Paper	86935 bales	Strawboards	14155 pkgs.
"	2919 cases	"	55 rolls
"	1992 rolls	Waste	10 pkgs.
Stationery	48 pkgs.	Tissues	3101 "
"	88 cases	"	60 cases
Millboards	63983 pkgs.	Stock	3658 pkgs.
"	266 cases	Cardboards	736 "
Pasteboards	78801 pkgs.	"	1193 cases
"	8 cases	Bags	7 "
"	105 rolls	Envelopes	5 "
Leather Paper	11 cases		

EXPORTS.

FOR THE WEEK ENDING TUESDAY LAST:

BRITISH GOODS.			
Paper	1796 cwt.	Waste	180 tons
Writing Paper	2445 "	"	10 cases
Printing Paper	5129 "	Strawboards	42 cwt.
		FOREIGN GOODS.	
Stationery	£13349 value	Paper	309 cwt.
Stock	143 tons	Writing Paper	70 "
Strawboard Cuttings	10 "	Printing Paper	197 "
Cardboards	32 cwt.	"	£34 value
Millboards	42 "	Strawboards	81 cwt.
Parchment	£28 value	Stationery	£407 value

FOR LAST MONTH:

BRITISH GOODS.			
		Strawboards	18 tons 8 cwt.
Paper	9208 cwt.	Packing Paper	£12 value
Writing Paper	10447 "	FOREIGN GOODS.	
Printing Paper	30964 "	Paper	1593 cwt.
Parchment	£399 value	Writing Paper	111 "
Waste	567 tons	Printing Paper	1196 "
Cardboards	1204 cwt.	Wrapping Paper	50 "
Wood Pulp	5 tons	Packing Paper	£70 value
Wood Pulp Boards	3 cwt.	Stationery	£1350 "
Paper Stock	1097 tons	Strawboards	1248 cwt.
Strawboard Cuttings	687 "	Wood Pulp	401 tons
Rags	10 tons 9 cwt.	Stock	31 "
"	£12 value	Parchment	£55 value
Stationery	£46936 "	"	38 cwt.
		Pasteboards	198 "

Glasgow, Greenock, Port-Glasgow, Troon, Grangemouth, &c.

IMPORTS.

FOR THE WEEK ENDING TUESDAY LAST:

Paper	603 bales	Paper	15 cases
"	280 rolls	Pasteboards	4 "

FOR LAST MONTH:

Paper	3964 bales	Stationery	1 case
"	32 cases	Tissues	1 "
"	280 rolls	Stock	64 bales
Strawboards	6168 cases	Cardboards	4 cases

EXPORTS.

FOR THE WEEK ENDING TUESDAY LAST:

Printing Paper	£164 value	Bags	115 cwt.
"	5938½ cwt.	Pulp Boards	£105 value
Writing Paper	£146 value	Blotting Paper	76½ cwt.
"	1705 cwt.	Stationery	£105 value
Paper	316 "	Stock	10 tons
Envelopes	65½ "		

FOR LAST MONTH:

Paper	1198 cwt.	Litho Paper	58 cwt.
"	£174 value	Wrapping Paper	13½ "
Writing Paper	1111½ cwt.	Packing Paper	14½ "
Printing Paper	4071½ "	Envelopes	119 "
Stationery	£427 value	Rags	23 "
Stock	692½ "		

Leith, Granton, Boness, Dundee, &c.

IMPORTS.

FOR THE WEEK ENDING TUESDAY LAST:

Paper	389 bales	Envelopes	300 pkgs.
"	5 cases	Pasteboards	856 "

FOR LAST MONTH:

Paper	3475 bales	Millboards	2241 pkgs.
"	13 cases	Tissues	26 bales
"	84 rolls	Stationery	1 case
Envelopes	1812 pkgs.	Stock	134 bales
Pasteboards	441 "	Strawboards	1022 pkgs.

PAPER & PULP MILL SHARES.

Kellners have been very much in demand this week and show a rise of about 10s. per share. Darwen, North of Ireland, and Ramsbottom are enquired for. Star are rather offered.

(Report received from Mr. F. D. DEAN, 36, Corporation Street, Manchester.)

Nominal Amnt	Amnt Paid	Name of Company	Last dividend	Price.
7	7	Bury Paper, ord.	nil	4½—4¾
7	7	do. do. 6% pref.	6%	4¾—5
100	100	do. do. deb.	5%	103—106
10	10	Bath Paper Mill Co., Lim.	7½%	6—7
10	10	Bergvik Co., def.	15%	13¾
100	100	do. do. 6% cum. pref.	6%	10⅞—11¼
10	10	do. do. deb.	5%	105—110
5	3½	Burnley Paper Co.	3/-	77/6—80/0
5	3¾	Darwen Paper Co.	10%	5¾—6¼
10	10	East Lancashire Co.	nil	4¼—4½
10	10	do. do. 6% pref.	nil	6¾—7
5	5	do. do. bonus	nil	1½—2
5	5	Hyde Paper Co.	4%	4¾—5
5	4	North of Ireland Paper Co.	nil	2¼—2½
10	5	Ramsbottom Paper Co.	17½%	12¼—12½
5	4½	Roach Bridge Paper Co.	5%	3—3¼
5	5	Star Paper Co.	10%	6—6¼
5	3	do. do. 10% pref. cum.	10%	4¾—5¼
50	50	do. do. deb.	6%	55—56
5	2½	Kellner Partingt'n Pulp Co	—	65/0—66/0

GREAT BRITAIN & GERMANY.

RELATIVE TRADE.

The following statistics show British importations from and exportations to Germany:—

	GERMAN PAPER IMPORTED BY GREAT BRITAIN.			BRITISH PAPER EXPORTED TO GERMANY.		
1888	648,345	cwts.	£597,586	7,841	cwts.	£23,322
1889	686,276	"	595,646	9,586	"	28,284
1890	599,640	"	564,564	11,114	"	27,833
1891	651,844	"	611,943	9,437	"	26,308
1892	688,226	"	673,940	10,844	"	28,170

	GERMAN RAGS DISPATCHED TO GREAT BRITAIN.			BRITISH ALKALI SHIPPED TO GERMANY.		
1888	45,415	tons.	£373,063	159,000	cwts.	£41,301
1889	22,372	"	243,332	143,700	"	39,026
1890	19,614	"	204,303	116,600	"	39,193
1891	19,369	"	194,771	87,100	"	34,311
1892	17,010	"	168,044	98,300	"	42,971

Printed and Published EVERY FRIDAY
AT 58, SHOE LANE, LONDON, E.C.,
By W. JOHN STONHILL.
ESTABLISHED 1878.

FRIDAY, OCTOBER 6, 1893.

IN this issue our readers will notice that we have introduced a new feature in supplementing our usual weekly statistical information relating to the importation and exportation of raw materials, paper, &c., by giving a summary of the specially compiled data published in the *World's Paper Trade Review* during the preceding month. The sources from which we obtain supplies, and also the foreign markets for British goods, so concisely arranged, will no doubt be appreciated, as will also the comparison of prices of principal articles. It may be pointed out that owing to the export of rags being classified under the heading "paper stock," correct figures are unobtainable. We have, however, received official intimation that the export of rags will be properly designated very shortly, and then we shall be in a position to give more details.

THE use of mechanical wood pulp has increased enormously during the past few years. In the infancy of the industry considerable competition was created owing to the constant erection of mills and the disposition shown by manufacturers to cut one another out in the market. This policy was brought to a close by the formation of the Scandinavian Wood Pulp Association, and during the existence of this body prices have been more in accordance with profitable working. The success attending the Scandinavian Union led to several syndicates being formed in Germany, and these have now consolidated with the view of establishing central offices for the sale of their product, to regulate production, and to agree to uniform prices. As German papermakers import large quantities of Scandinavian mechanical wood pulp it prices will have to bear fav son with those adopted by t Union.

THAT combination has l influence from the manufac view, will be seen from the present quotations of pine pu last year. To-day the price £7 for dry pine, an advance with the quotation in Octob pine is quoted £3 7s. 6d. to £3 of £1 compared with the period last year.

WHILST on the subject of m pulp our readers will do well statistical information publ Market Report this week. I that large quantities of w received from Canada and U.S month of September. The 18,805 bales and 938 rolls from 19,808 bales from the Unite the current week's list large recorded from Montreal, Halifa (Maine). The charterers fro place are the Penobscot Pulp a Another firm cultivating busin country is the Manufacturers of New York, who control t of the Laurentide Pulp C Canada.

COALOWNERS are showing a f doubt feeling too near victory the refusal of the Miners' Feder template any reduction is met refusal to discuss any terms whi include it. The word is now witl and we shall be very much surp are not obliged to yield. The mines reopening is insignificar levies will make no impression wide area of starvation and m Mayors of Sheffield and other offered to act in the way of The difficulties in the coal trade, quent high prices of fuel, great with manufacturing industries. I trade the aspect is becoming ve News from Lancashire is to the the Hollins Paper Mill is already the Darwen Paper Mill, which h been purchased by the Darwen Paper Mill Company, also contemplates a shut down. Messrs. Yates, Duxbury and Sons, proprietors of the Hal-i'-th'-Wood Paper Mills, have also found it necessary to suspend work for an indefinite period until an adequate supply of coal can be found. The works have previously been closed for brief periods for a similar reason.

Although the coal strike has had a serious effect on the chemical industry, in many instances necessitating the stoppage of plant, yet prices are not, as some people think, comparatively higher than in former years. Take caustic white 77 per cent. the present price is £11 10s., being 5s. lower than in 1892, and 10s. lower than in 1891. Soda crystals are cheaper by 5s. to 7s. 6d. Bleach 35 per cent. f.o.b Tyne is now quoted at £8 5s., whereas in 1892 it was £9, but in 1891 only £7 5s. Alkali is £5 10s. against £6 15s. last year, and £6 12s. 6d. in 1891. Sulphur shows a big reduction, the present price being £4 2s. 6d., and that last year £4 15s., against £6 5s. in October, 1891.

OVERPRODUCTION! COMPETITION! Such exclamations are common in the paper trade. Meetings of manufacturers to avert such conditions are also of frequent occurrence. The spirit of combination has now manifested itself amongst French manufacturers of thin papers (*papiers minces mousselines*, etc.), carrying on business in central France, who recently held a meeting at Avignon, when it was decided in view of the present condition of the market for these makes, to close each mill (30 were represented at the conference), six days per month for a time, in the hope that diminished production will improve prices. The new arrangement came into force on the 1st inst.

MR. GEORGE ROBERT TYLER, the Lord Mayor elect, is the present Master of the Stationers' Company, son of the late Mr. William Tyler, of Queenhithe, and was born in 1835. He is the head of the firm of Messrs. Venables, Tyler, and Company, papermakers, Queenhithe, which has already supplied a Lord Mayor to the City in the person of Mr. Alderman Venables, who was Chief Magistrate in 1826. Mr. Tyler has served every civic office. He was elected a common councilman in 1877, and was afterwards deputy of his ward. He succeeded as Alderman of Queenhithe Ward Mr. Herbert J. Waterlow, who retired in 1887, and he served the office of Sheriff in 1891-2 in the Mayoralty of Sir David Evans.

THERE is in electrolysis something more than the production of chlorine and soda, hence the necessity of filing several applications for patents of apparatuses, devices, &c., which separately constitute valid patents, capable of being worked in combination one with the other, but which together would not be patentable, and would resemble a patent filed a few weeks ago under the title of "electric motors, dynamos, electrolysis of solutions, manufacture of sodium, potassium, cyanide, gold extraction, and recovery of tin from scrap." It will be readily understood why we constantly see the names of Andreoli, Greenwood, Richardson, Kellner, and others associated with new patents relating to electrolysis. The object of Andreoli, for instance, is to produce oxygen and hydrogen, to manufacture chlorates, &c., and not to make only chlorine and caustic soda. The charateristic novelty of his patent (which we briefly referred to in our last issue) is the conducting diaphragm, &c., which we understand has been adopted by Kellner and others. In the manufacture of chlorine, this arrangement would not prevent the diffusion of liquids; in Andreoli's new electrolytic tank one hardly finds chlorine in the negative and soda in the positive compartments.

HALF-AN-HOUR spent in the Patent Office Library looking up the word "Motors" will, even to this day, reveal a curious crop of "perpetual motion machines." Anybody might think that if there was one fallacy more completely threshed out than others it was the old dream of trying to get more energy out of an engine than was originally put into it. Yet the *Illustrated Journal* is strewn with the wrecks of innumerable vain attempts, of which the following are some recent specimens :—

"Engine, worked by water-power, returns water back to the supply reservoir.

"Propelling ships: stern paddle wheel driven by surrounding water and current through from bows. A charming device for utilising the speed of the vessel before it has been obtained."

"Driving screw-propeller by paddles driven by motion of ship."

Compressing air for compressed air engine by screw fan driven by engine itself."

"A drum fitted with blades is rotated in a vessel of water. The rebound of the water from the sides of the vessel on to the blades accelerates the rotation."

These are but a few hopeless instances out of many, the object of all being to produce energy without any corresponding output of energy. There is no sadder sight on earth than one of the authors of these wild schemes for defrauding nature. They are always poor and nearly always sanguine, till one day the mechanism of the overwrought body, which has been working too long without fuel on the same uneconomic principle, gives way, and the inventor joins his weary fellows in the land of dreams.

PAPER EXPORTS.

FOR THE WEEK ENDING TUESDAY LAST;

	Printings.	Writings.	Other Kinds.
AUSTRALIA	5312 cwts.	2465 cwts.	927 cwts.
ARABIA...	—	6 "	— "
AFRICA	134 "	79 "	1 "
ARGENTINE ...	— "	66 "	— "
BELGIUM	— "	16 "	27 "
B. WEST INDIES...	— "	42 "	2 "
BRAZIL	232 "	3 "	21 "
B. GUIANA	19 "	— "	2 "
CHANNEL ISLES...	— "	44 "	— "
CEN. AMERICA ...	— "	26 "	— "
CANADA	4622½ "	2256 "	3 "
CAPE COLONY .	154 "	38 "	227 "
CHILI	— "	— "	95 "
CHINA	299 "	75 "	12 "
DENMARK	37 "	3 "	— "
DUTCH GUIANA...	— "	— "	3 "
D. E. INDIES ...	17 "	— "	— "
FRANCE	61 "	104 "	41 "
EGYPT	7 "	3 "	22 "
GERMANY	— "	— "	45 "
HOLLAND	— "	— "	7 "
INDIA	744¼ "	345¼ "	745 "
JAPAN	— "	7 "	— "
ITALY	— "	— "	2 "
MAURITIUS ...	— "	25 "	2 "
MADAGASCAR ...	16 "	— "	— "
NEW ZEALAND ...	739 "	471 "	182 "
NORWAY	— "	22 "	1 "
S. AMERICA... ...	— "	20 "	— "
SPAIN	— "	40 "	11 "
SYRIA	— "	3 "	— "
TURKEY	— "	16 "	— "
U.S.A.	— "	554 "	4 "
W. INDIES	— "	— "	2 "

LAST MONTH'S SUMMARY.

AUSTRALIA	22501 cwts.	HOLLAND ...	408 cwts.
AFRICA ...	721 "	INDIA	7615½ "
ARGENTINE	862 "	ITALY	2 "
AUSTRIA ...	16 "	JAPAN	6408 "
BELGIUM ...	567 "	MAD'GASCAR	52 "
B. W. INDIES	2724 "	MAURITIUS	119 "
B GUIANA ...	874½ "	N. ZEALAND	5580 "
BRAZIL ...	161 "	NORWAY ...	34½ "
CANADA ...	18391½ "	NEWF'NDL'D	22 "
CHINA	1592 "	N. AMERICA	32 "
CHILI	172 "	PORTUGAL ...	28 "
CHANN'L Isles	97 "	PERSIA ...	2 "
CAPE COLONY	31922 "	RUSSIA ...	88 "
Cen. AMERICA	2 "	SPAIN	313 "
D. E. INDIES	10 "	SYRIA	16 "
DENMARK ...	1722 "	S. SETTL'M'TS	68 "
D. GUIANA ...	2 "	SWEDEN ...	18 "
EGYPT	116 "	S. AMERICA ..	216 "
FRANCE ...	1989 "	TURKEY ...	12 "
GERMANY ...	87 "	U.S.A.	14084 "
GREECE ...	3 "	W. INDIES ...	282 "

PAPER IMPORTS.

FOR THE WEEK ENDING TUESDAY LAST:

BELGIUM ...	1472 bales	HOLLAND ...	19 rolls
"	398 cases	JAPAN	6 cases
DENMARK ...	16 bales	NORWAY ...	492 bales
FINLAND ...	482 "	PRUSSIA ...	246 "
FRANCE ...	475 "	SWEDEN ...	592 "
" ...	60 cases	"	504 rolls
GERMANY ...	3433 bales	SPAIN	6 bales
"	196 cases	U.S.A.	765 "
HOLLAND ...	1676 bales	"	86 cases
"	376 cases	" ...	428 rolls

Including the Following:

Quantity	From	Importer	Port.
21 bales	Danzig	E. & E. Sabel	London.
36 "	"	H. Huber & Co	"
100 "	Gothenberg	E. & E. Sabel	"
36 "	"	Schenkenwald & Co	"
254 rolls	"	" "	"
17 bales	"	Hummell & Co	"
132 "	"	Becker & Co	
36 "	"	Alsing & Co	
72 "	"	Hundgrew	"
5 "	Marseilles	Wooley & Cowley	"
8 cases	New York	Rottman Stone & Co	"
50 "	"	May, Roberts & Co	"
8 "	"	J. Dickinson & Co	"
95 bales	Stettin	Becker & Ulrich	"
6 "	"	J. Dickinson	"
45 "	"	J. Spicer & Son	"
52 "	"	B. Beer	"
526 "	Uddevalla	R. L. Lundgren	"
519 "	"	D. Gulland.	"

LAST MONTH'S SUMMARY.

AUSTRIA ...	685 bales	HOLLAND ...	533 cases
AUSTRALIA ...	10 "	" .	314 rolls
" ...	6 cases	INDIA	2 bales
ARGENTINA...	36 bales	" .. .	46 cases
BELGIUM ...	6041 "	JAPAN	7 "
" ...	859 cases	NORWAY ...	13568 bales
CANADA ...	5 "	" ..	1509 rolls
CHINA	43 "	PRUSSIA	924 bales
DENMARK ...	1203 bales	" ...	42 cases
FINLAND ...	1168 "	" .	283 rolls
" ...	152 cases	SWEDEN ..	7576 bales
" ...	329 rolls	" ...	26 cases
FRANCE ...	1805 bales	" ..	546 rolls
" ...	391 cases	SPAIN ...	33 cases
GERMANY ..	10235 bales	U.S.A.	1195 bales
" ...	529 cases	"	426 cases
HOLLAND ..	48342 bales	"	595 rolls

PAPER IMPORTERS

WHERE NOT "TO ORDER."

Grabb & Co.
J. Hamilton
Lon. & Rhine Co.
Alsing & Co.
R. L. Lundgren
Cookson & McDonald
G. F. Green & Co.
Schenkenwald & Co.
Hummell & Co.
D. Gulland
Brown & Brough
J. Pollock & Son
Beronius, King & Co.
O. Konig & Co.
J. Spicer & Sons
Prop. Dowgate Dk.
Prop. Brooks Whf.
W. D. Edwards
Becker & Ulrich
B Beer
E. & E. Sabel
Gun Shot & Griffin's Whf.
Beuscher
F. E. Foulger
Hernu, Peron & Co.
Christophersen & Co.
Calleys & Co.
Maw, Son & Co.
B. Galloway
C. Morgan & Co.
C. Burnett & Co.
Smythe & Co.
Berrick Bros.
Williams, Torrey & Co.
F. Hawk
W. E. Bott & Co.
Pukert & Co.
J. Holloway
C. R. Briggs
G. E. Koenigsfield
C. Saunder & Son
L. Henle
Bulter & Crisp
F. W. Fagge
Kaul & Hainlin
Tyser & Co.
Mfg. Paper Co.

WORLD'S PAPER TRADE REVIEW OFFICE,
58, SHOE LANE, LONDON, E.C.
OCTOBER 5, 1893.

MARKET REPORT

and RECORD of IMPORTS

Of Foreign Rags, Wood Pulp, Esparto, Paper, Millboards, Strawboards, &c., at the Ports of London Liverpool, Southampton, Bristol, Hull, Fleetwood, Middlesborough, Glasgow, Grangemouth, Granton, Dundee, Leith, Dover, Folkestone, and Newhaven, for the WEEK ENDING OCTOBER 4.

From SPECIAL Sources and Telegrams.

Telegrams—"STONHILL, LONDON."

CHEMICALS.—The market is quiet and in one or two instances prices have a lowering tendency. CAUSTIC SODA, for instance, is easier, although scarce, 77% f.o.r. Newcastle being quoted at about £11 10s. Increased quantities, however, will be put upon the market when Brunner, Mond & Co. commence the manufacture of this article, and, consequently, consumers hold back from contracting. BLEACHING POWDER remains at from £8 5s. to £10, and SODA CRYSTALS at £2 12s. 6d. SODA ASH is being freely sold for next year. SULPHUR is unaltered at £4 2s. 6d. Prices of BLANC FIXE and SULPHATE OF ALUMINA are without change. In foreign chemicals prices are easier, 58% ALKALI is offered in 2-cwt. bags at £4 10s. or 10-cwt. casks at £5, CAUSTIC SODA 70-72% at £10 12s. 6d., and HYPO-SULPHITE OF SODA in casks of 10 tons at £6.

Prices are nominally as follows:

Article		Terms		£	s.	d.
Alkali, 58%	tierces ...	f.o.r. works	2½%	5	10	0
" 58%	bags ...	" "	2½%	5	5	0
58%	... ...	f.o.b. Liverpool	2½%	5	12	6
Alum (Ground),	tierces ...	" Liverpool	2½%	5	7	6
" "	barrels ...	" "	2½%	5	17	6
" "	tierces ...	" Hull	2½%	5	5	0
" "	" ...	Goole	2½%	5	5	0
Alum (Lump)	" ...	f.o.b. Liverpool	2½%	4	17	6
" "	barrels ...	" "	2½%	5	0	0
" "	tierces ...	" Hull	2½%	4	15	0
" "	" ...	Goole	2½%	4	15	0
" "	" ...	London	2½%	5	5	0
" "	" ...	f.a.s. Glasgow	2½%	5	5	0
Alumina Sulphate,	casks	f.o.b. Tyne		4	2	6
" "	bags	" "		3	17	6
Aluminoferric Cake,	slabs	Liverpool ...	...	2	15	0
" "	tierces	" ...	...	3	2	6
Alumina Cake,	slabs ...	Glasgow	...	2	15	0
" "	tierces ...	"	...	3	2	6
Aluminous Cake,	casks ...	Manchester	3½%	2	7	6
" "	" ...	Newcastle	2½%	2	10	0
" "	" ...	London	2½%	3	0	0
" "	bags ...	"	2½%	2	17	9
Blanc Fixe ...	... ...	f.o.b. Tyne	net	7	10	0
Bleach, 35%	... ...	" "	net	8	5	0
" (soft wood)	...	f.o.r. Lancs.	net	8	10	0
" (hard wood)	...	f.o.b. Liverpool	net	9	0	0
... ...	...	landed London	2½%	10	0	0
Borax (crystals)	... ...	... ...	net	29	0	6
powdered	... ...	... .	net	30	0	0
Caustic Cream, 60%	...	f.o.r. Lancs.	net	9	2	6
" " 60%	...	f.o.b. Liverpool	net	9	7	6
" Bottoms	...	" "	net	6	15	0
" "	... ...	f.o.b. Tyne	net	6	15	0
Chloride of Barium	...	f.o.b. Tyne	net	7	10	0

Article		Terms		£	s.	d.
Caustic White 76 77%	...	f.o.r. Newcastle	net	11	10	0
" " 77%	f.o.r. or	f.o.b. Tyne	net	12	5	0
" " 74%	...	f.o.b. Liverpool	net	12	0	0
" " 70%	...	" "	net	11	0	0
" " 70%	...	" Hull	net	11	5	0
" " 70%	...	f.o.r. London	net	11	5	0
" " 70%	...	" Lancs.,	net	10	17	6
" " 60%	...	" London	net	10	5	0
" " 60%	...	f.o.b. Liverpool	net	10	0	0
Carbonat'd Ash 58%	...	" "	net	4	10	0
" 48%	...	" "	net	4	0	0
" 58%	..	f.o.r. Widnes	net	4	7	6
" 48%	...	" "	net	3	17	6
Hypo-Sulphite of Soda...		f.o.r Tyne		5	15	0
" " 10-ton lots		ex ship Liverp'l	net	6	10	0
Oxalic Acid ...	... ...	f.o.b. Liverpool	3½%	per lb		½
Salt Cake ...	... ...	" works	net	1	10	0
Soda Ash, 52%	... ...	f.o.b. Tyne	net	4	7	6
" 52%	... ...	ex ship Thames	1%	4	12	6
" 52%	... ...	f.o.b. Liverpool	1%	4	5	0
Soda Crystals	... ...	" Tyne	net	2	12	6
" "	... ...	ex ship Thames	2½%	3	5	0
" "	... ...	f.o.b. Liverpool	net	3	7	6
Sulphur, roll	... ...	f.o.r. works	2½%	7	17	6
" flowers	... ...	" "	2½%	9	10	0
" recovered	...	" "	2½%	4	2	6
Sulphate of Ammonia	"	" "	2½%	15	0	0
" of Copper	...	" Liverpool	5%	15	0	0

FOREIGN.—F.o.b. Continental port:

Article	£	s.	d.
Alkali, 58% 2-cwt. bags £4 10/0; 10-cwt. casks ...	5	0	0
Caustic Soda, 70-72%	10	12	6
Hypo-Sulphite of Soda 10-ton lots casks	6	0	0
Sulphate of Alumina 7-8 cwt. casks net c.i f. Ldn	4	7	6
Blanc Fixe (c.i.f. London)	7	12	6

COMPARATIVE PRICES:

Caustic White 77% f.o.r. Newcastle.	Oct., 1893	£11 10 0 nett.
	" 1892	£11 15 0 nett.
	" 1891	£12 0 0 nett.
Bleach 35% f.o.b. Tyne.	Oct., 1893	£8 5 0 nett.
	" 1892	£9 0 0 nett.
	" 1891	£7 5 0 2½%
Soda Crystals f.o.b. Tyne.	Oct., 1893	£2 12 6 nett.
	" 1892	£2 17 6 nett.
	" 1891	£3 0 0 nett.
Sulphur Recovered f.o.r. Works.	Oct., 1893	£4 2 6 nett.
	" 1892	£4 15 0 2½%
	" 1891	£6 5 0 2½%
Alkali 58% tierces f.o.r. Works.	Oct., 1893	£5 10 0 2½%
	" 1892	£6 15 0 2½%
	" 1891	£6 12 6 2½%

ESPARTO.—Market quiet at about former currencies. A fair enquiry for quotations of distant shipments, but without much actual business resulting. Early delivery neglected and parcels in this position difficult to sell.

Prices c.i.f. London and Leith, or f.o.r. Cardiff, Garston and Tyne Docks are nominally as follows:

Kind	Quality	£	s.	d.		£	s.	d.
Spanish—	Fair to Good	£5	7	6	to	5	12	6
"	Fine to Best	5	10	0	"	5	15	0
Oran —	Fair to Good	3	7	6	"	3	10	0
"	First Quality...	3	15	0	"	3	17	6
Tripoli —	Hand-picked	3	15	0	"	3	17	6
"	Fair Average...	3	7	6	"	3	10	0
Bona & Philippeville	... ...	3	15	0	"	3	17	

COMPARATIVE PRICES
("Fair to Good" Quality):

Spanish	Oct., 1893	£5 10 0	to	£5 15 0
	" 1892	£5 10 0	"	£6 0 0
	" 1893	£5 15 0	"	£6 0 0
Oran	Oct., 1893	£3 12 6	"	£3 17 6
	" 1892	£4 0 0	"	£4 5 0
	" 1891	£3 17 6	"	£4 2 6
Tripoli	Oct., 1893	£3 0 0	"	£3 12 6
	" 1892	£3 15 0	"	£4 0 0
	" 1891	£3 17 6	"	£4 0 6

WEEK'S IMPORTS.

Quantity	From	Importer	Port.
220 tons	Almeria	Morris & Co	Dundee
4736 bales	Aguilas	Guardbridge Paper Co	"
735 tons	Sfax	To order	Liverpool

LAST MONTH'S IMPORTS.

Where From:

AGUILAS ...	19967½ tons	ORAN	5985 bales
ALMERIA ...	895 ,,	,, ...	1963 tons
ARZEW ...	6063 bales	TRIPOLI ...	1800 ,,
CARTHAGENA	799 tons	,, ...	4366 bales
GARRUCHA..	3921 bales		

Port of Landing:

BONESS ...	700 tons	LEITH... ...	682 tons
DUNDEE ...	19250 ,,	LIVERPOOL..	29 ,,
,, ...	3921 bales	,, ...	8740 bales
FLEETWOOD	2484 ,,	LONDON ...	1800 tons
GRANTON ...	29634½ tons	,, ...	5390 bales

Importers (Where not "To Order"):

R. H. Hay and Co	Morris and Co
Guardbridge Paper Co	Henderson and McIntosh
Carrongrove Paper Co	J. Cormack
T. Kennedy and Son	Love, Stewart and Co
L. Jacobs, Marcus and Co	W. C. Creighton and Sons
H. Ottomann	

JUTE.—Cuttings are in moderate request.

Good White ...	£16 to 18	Common ...	£10 10 to £1[illegible]
Good	£15	Rejections...	£8 0 ,, £9
Medium ...	£13	Cuttings ...	£5 10 ,, £7

CHEMICAL WOOD PULPS.—The firm tone of the Chemical Wood Pulp market is well maintained. There is not a great deal of business, however, being carried through, as users do not readily fall in with the views of sellers, who, for recognised brands, demand higher prices. SULPHITE is in good enquiry, but contracts are being slowly negotiated. SODA and SULPHATE pulps are receiving more attention.

Prices, ex steamer, London, Hull, Newcastle, Leith and Glasgow are nominally as follows:

SULPHITE, Unbleached, Common	£10 15 0	to	11 0 0
,, Superior	11 10 0	,,	12 10 0
,, ,, 50% moisture, d.w.	11 10 0	,,	12 2 6
,, Extra	13 0 0	,,	14 0 0
,, Bleached, moist			16 10 0
,, Unbleached, English, del. Lancs. ...			10 15 0
,, ,, ,, No. 1, ex mills, Ldn.			10 10 0
,, ,, ,, No. 2, ,, ,,			9 15 0
SODA, Unbleached, Common ...	10 0 0	to	10 10 0
,, ,, Extra... ...	10 10 0	,,	11 0 0
,, Half-Bleached	12 10 0	,,	14 0 0
SULPHATE, Unbleached, Common	10 10 0	,,	11 0 0
,, Extra	11 0 0	,,	12 0 0
,, Half-Bleached	13 10 0	,,	14 0 0
Bleached	15 0 0	,,	16 0 0

MECHANICAL WOOD PULPS.—There is an excellent demand for Scandinavian Mechanical Wood Pulps of good quality, and prices are well maintained, especially for early delivery. Arrivals of Canadian pulp are coming more freely to hand. More regularity of prices is reported in Germany, owing to the establishment of a Central Union of the four syndicates.

Prices, ex steamer, London, Hull, Newcastle, Leith and Glasgow are nominally as follows:

MECHANICAL, Aspen, Dry ...	£7 10 0	to	8 0 0
Pine, Dry	6 12 6	,,	7 0 0
Pine, Moist	3 7 6	,,	3 10 0
Moist Brown	3 2 6	,,	3 5 0
Single Sorted	2 7 6	,,	2 10 0
Dry Brown	6 5 0	,,	6 10 0

COMPARATIVE PRICES:

Pine, Dry	Oct., 1893	£6 12 6	to	£7 0 0
	,, 1892	£4 12 6	,,	£5 0 0
	,, 1891	£4 5 0	,,	£4 10 0
Pine, Moist	Oct., 1893	£3 7 6	,,	£3 10 0
	,, 1892	£2 6 6	,,	£2 10 0
	,, 1891	£2 7 6	,,	£2 10 0

WEEK'S IMPORTS.

Quantity	From	Importer	Port
1484 bales	Abo	To order	Hull
24442 ,,	Bangor	G. Schjoth & Co	Fleetwood
40 ,,	Copenhagen	To order	Leith
50 ,,	Christiania	G. Schjoth & Co	Fleetwood
1150 ,,	,,	Christophersen & Co	,,
1718 ,,	,,	To order	Grangemouth
2528 ,,	,,	,,	Hull
200 ,,	Drontheim	,,	,,
570 ,,	Drammen	G. Schjoth & Co	Fleetwood
400 ,,	,,	Blydt, Pans & Pace	,,
250 ,,	,,	Christophersen & Co	,,
105 ,,	Fiume	To order	Leith
64 ,,	Gothenburg	C. Salvesen & Co	Granton
200 ,,	,,	To order	Southampton
5 ,,	,,	Green & Co	London
444 ,,	,,	To order	Hull
67 casks	Ghent	,,	London
4480 ,,	Halifax	Steinhoff & Son	,,
99 bales	,,	To order	,,
20 brls	,,	,,	Liverpool
175 rolls	Hambro	,,	Leith
78 bales	,,	,,	,,
772 rolls	Montreal	,,	Glasgow
8705 bales	,,	,,	,,
3076 ,,	,,	,,	Liverpool
207 ,,	Rotterdam	,,	Hull
80 ,,	,,	,,	,,
52 ,,	,,	,,	,,
400 ,,	,,	,,	London
85 ,,	,,	,,	,,
185 ,,	,,	,,	Liverpool
237 ,,	,,	,,	London
6570 ,,	Soderhamn	,,	,,
10 ,,	Stettin	J. Currie & Co	Leith
510 ,,	,,	To order	Hull
121 ,,	,,	,,	,,
1429 ,,	Sannesund	G. Schjoth and Co	Fleetwood
54 cks	Terneuzen	To order	London

Totals from Each Country:

AUSTRIA ...	105 bales	GERMANY ...	6648 bales
BELGIUM ...	67 casks	,, ...	175 rolls
CANADA ...	24442 bales	HOLLAND ...	1335 bales
,, ...	20 brls	,, ...	54 casks
,, ...	774 rolls	NORWAY ...	8085 bales
DENMARK ...	40 bales	PRUSSIA ...	641 ,,
FINLAND ...	1484 ,,	SWEDEN ...	713 ,,

LAST MONTH'S IMPORTS.

Where From:

AUSTRIA ...	1200 bales	HOLLAND ...	2160 rolls
BELGIUM ...	571 ,,	NORWAY ...	54347 bales
,, ...	190 casks	,, ...	100 tons
CANADA ...	18805 bales	PORTUGAL ...	1300 bales
,, ...	938 rolls	PRUSSIA ...	4203 ,,
DENMARK ...	1520 bales	,, ...	179 rolls
FINLAND ...	3052 ,,	SWEDEN ...	11300 bales
,, ...	1198 rolls	,, ...	183 tons
GERMANY ...	4721 bales	SPAIN	930 cases
HOLLAND ...	3737 ,,	U.S.A.	19863 bales

Port of Landing:

FLEETWOOD	38132 bales	LIVERPOOL.	938 rolls
GLASGOW ...	20465 ,,	LEITH... ...	6590 bales
GRANTON ...	2427 ,,	LONDON ...	36544 ,,
GRANG'M'TH	8450 ,,	,, ...	4[illegible]0 cases
HULL	11707 ,,	,, ...	241 casks
,, ...	183 tons	,, ...	100 tons
LIVERPOOL.	1723 bales	,, ...	3537 rolls
,, ...	500 cases	SOUTHAMP'N	963 bales

Importers (Where not "To Order"):

Bott and Co	C. Anderson
Hummell and Co	A. Guttmann
Taylor and Co	J. A. Reid
G. Skramnes	Green and Co
J. Currie and Co	G. Schjoth and Co
E. Lloyd	H. B. Wood
E. J. and W. Goldsmith	La Cour and Watson
Christophersen	Alsing and Co
Salvesen and Co	Steinhoff and Son
Henderson and Co	G. Schenkenwald and Co
Baring Bros	Ekman Co
Tegner, Price and Co	H. Pearsall
Ronaldson and Co	Henderson, Craig and Co

W. Friedlaender	O. Herrlich
Tough and Henderson	T. Aitken
Blydt, Pans and Co	J. Rankin and Son
London Paper Mill Co	Kellner-Partington Paper Co

WEEK'S IMPORTS of WOOD PULP BOARDS.

Quantity	From	Importer	Port
14 bales	Christiania	To order	Grangemouth
52 "	Gothenburg	"	Southampton
100 "	"	"	"

MONTH'S IMPORTS WOOD PULP BOARDS.

Where From:

CHRISTIANIA	162 cases	HAMBRO ...	946 bales
DRAMMEN...	170 "	HELSINGFORS	466 "
GOTHENBURG	558 "		

Port of Landing:

GRANG'M'TH	162 cases	LIVERPOOL .	20 cases
GRANTON ...	30 "	LONDON ...	946 bales
GLASGOW ...	326 "	"	352 cases

Importers (Where not "To Order"):

J. Holloway	Salveeen and Co
M. Schules and Co	F. E. Foulger

STRAW.—Supplies are very scarce.

WEEK'S IMPORTS.

(Purposes unspecified) at principal Ports From

DENMARK ...	99 bales	U.S.A.	14 bales
HOLLAND ...	759 "		

MONTH'S IMPORTS.

ALGERIA ...	20 tons	DENMARK ...	5544 bales
BELGIUM ...	12 bales	FRANCE ...	1009 "
CANADA ...	102 "	HOLLAND ...	7040 "

STRAW PULPS.—Market quiet. During the month of September 161 bales from Hambro were registered as being imported.

Prices, c.i.f. London, Hull or Leith:

Belgian, 25% moisture	£15 0 0 to 16 0 0
do. dry	16 0 0
German, 50 to 55% moisture	16 10 0
do. dry, ... No. 1 £18 10 0; No. 2	15 0 0

FOREIGN RAGS.—The market on the Continent evidences little change. The coal strike and Jewish holidays combined have tended to make business quiet all round. Stocks of best grades are not heavy; and there is little demand for lower qualities. In some cases, however, common grades have been in request to replace wood pulp.

FRENCH RAGS.

Quotations range, per cwt., ex ship London, Southampton, or Hull; 2/0 per ton more at Liverpool, and 10/0 per ton higher at Newcastle, Glasgow or Leith.

French Linens, I ...	22/0	Black Cotton ...	4/0
II 18/6; III ...	14/6	Marseilles Whites, I	16/0
White Cottons, I ...	19/0	II 10/0; III ...	7/6
II 15/0; III ...	12/6	Blue Cotton	11/0
Knitted Cotton ...	11/0	Light Prints... ...	9/0
Light Coloured Cotton	8/0	Mixed Prints ...	6/0
Blue Cotton	9/6	New White Cuttings	23/0
Coloured Cotton ...	6/0	" Stay "	21/0

DUTCH RAGS. f.o.r. Hull:

C.i.f. Thames; Hull 2/6 per ton more; ditto f.o.r. Leith c.i.f. Glasgow 4/-; c.i.f. Liverpool 4/-.

Selected Fines (free from Muslins) ...	17/0	Best Grey Linens ...	9/0
		Common ditto ...	5/6
Selected Outshots	9/9	White Canvas ...	15/0
" Dirty Fines	5/9	Grey & Brown Canvas	9/9
Light Cottons ...	9/3	Tarred Hemp Rope	8/0
Blue Cottons ...	7/6	Ditto (broken) ...	5/3
Dark Coloured Cottons	2/10	White Paper Shavings	7/9
New Cuttings (Bleachd)	22/6	Gunny (best) ...	4/9
" (Unbleached)	19/6	Jute Bagging ...	3/6
" (Slate) ...	9/0	Ditto (common ...	3/0
Muslins	8/0	Tarpaulins	4/0
Red Cottons (Mixed)	5/9	Cowhair Carpets ...	2/9
Fustians (Light browns)	5/0	Hard ditto	3/0

BELGIAN RAGS.

F.o.b. Ghent. Freights: London, 5/0; Hull and Goole, 7/6 Liverpool and Leith, 10/0; Newcastle, 12/6; Dundee and Aberdeen, 15/0; Glasgow, 16/8.

White Linens No. 1	22/6	Fustians (Light) ...	6/0
" " No. 2	16/0	" (Dark) ...	4/0
" " No. 3	13/0	Thirds...	3/0
Fines (Mixed) ...	12/0	Black Cottons ...	3/9
Grey Linens (strong)	9/6	Hemp Strings (unt'r'd)	2/0
" " (extra)	14/0	House Cloths ...	4/9
Blue Linens... ...	8/6	Old Bagging (solid)	3/6
White Cottons S'p'fine	18/0	" " (common)	2/6
" " No. 2	15/0	NEW.	
Outshots No. 3 ...	10/0	White & Cream Linens	35/0
Seconds No. 4 ...	8/0	White Cuttings ...	22/0
Prints (Light) ...	8/6	Unbleached Cuttings	21/0
" (Old)	4/6	Print Cuttings ..	8/0

BELGIAN FLAX and HEMP WASTE.

Best washed and dried Flax Waste, 10/0; Fair ditto
Flax Spinners' Waste (grease boiled out)... ... 1
Hemp Waste, No. 1 9/0; No. 2 ... ... 9/0
Flax Spinners' Waste, No. 1 (Flax Rove) 10/0: No. 2 8/6

GERMAN RAGS.

STETTIN: C.i.f. Hull, Leith, Tyne and London.

SPFFF and SPFF	18/0	LFB (Blue)	9/0
SPF	11/0	CSPFFF and CSPFF	10/0
FF	8/6	CFB (Blue)	7/6
FG	9/0	CFX (Coloured) ...	4/6
LFX	7/0		

HAMBURG: F.o.b.

NWC	22/0	FF Grey Linens ...	9/0
SPFFF	22/0	LFX Second ditto...	8/0
SPFFF and SPFF	18/0	CSPFFF	17/3
SPFF	16/0	CSPFF	11/3
SPF	12/0	CFB	8/0
CCC	5/6	Dark Blues (selected	11/9
CFX	4/6	Wool Tares... ...	8/0
White Rope... ...	8/0	Jute, No. I 6/0; No. II	5/6

NORWEGIAN RAGS.

C.i.f. London, Hull, Tyne, and Grangemouth.

1st Rope (tarred) ...	8/6-9/0	2nd Canvas ...	8/0
2nd " " ...	5/6-6/0	Jute Bagging	
Manilla Rope (white)	8/0-8/9	Gunny ...	3/0 3/6
Best Canvas ...	11/9-12/0	Mixed ...	2/6-2/9

RUSSIAN RAGS.

C.i.f. London, Hull, Newcastle or Leith.

SPFF	15/0	CC (Cotton	4/9
SPF	13/6	Jute I	3/6
FG	10/6	" II...	2/3
LFB	9/6	Rope I...	9/0
FF	8/3	" II	5/3
LFX	7/2		

WEEK'S IMPORTS.

Quantity	From	Importer	Port.
46 bales	Antwerp	To order	London
45 "	Amsterdam	"	"
32 "	"	"	Hull
14 "	Boston	"	Southampton
33 "	Christiansand	"	Leith
4 "	Christiania	"	Hull
63 "	Cadiz	"	Leith
10 "	Dieppe	"	Newhaven
17 "	Hambro	"	London
88 "	"	"	Hull
18 "	Harlingen	"	"
25 "	Jersey	"	Southampton
101 "	Konigsberg	"	Hull
80 "	"	"	"
66 "	Lisbon	"	Southampton
300 "	Melbourne	"	Hull
1 "	Rouen	"	London
106 "	St. Nazaire	"	Newhaven
10 "	"	"	Southampton
237 "	Ternuzen	"	Liverpool

Totals from Each Country:

AUSTRALIA...	300 bales	NORWAY ...	37 bales
BELGIUM ...	46 "	PRUSSIA ...	101 "
CHANNEL Isles	25 "	SWEDEN ...	80 "
FRANCE ...	117 "	SPAIN ...	129 "
GERMANY ..	27 "	U.S.A. ...	14 "
HOLLAND ...	332 "		

MONTH'S IMPORTS.

Where From:

AUSTRALIA	97 bales	ITALY	199 bales
ARGENTINE	86 „	JAPAN... ...	1 bale
BELGIUM ...	1452 „	NORWAY ...	164 bales
CHANNEL Isles	124 „	PRUSSIA ...	2003 „
DENMARK ...	1889 „	SPAIN	75 „
EGYPT ...	141 „	SWEDEN ...	602 „
FRANCE ...	5418 „	TURKEY ...	369 „
GERMANY ...	1317 „	U.S.A.	657 „
HOLLAND ...	2751 „		

Port of Landing:

HARWICH ...	49 bales	LIVERPOOL.	1825 bales
HULL ...	10201 „	LONDON ...	1460 „
GRANG'M'TH	55 „	NEWHAVEN	221 „
LEITH... ...	3314 „	SOUTH'MPT'N	1573 „

Importers (Where not "To Order"):

G. Gibson and Co	Feyer and Stave
J. Currie and Co	R. Hanch

HOME RAGS.—Reports to hand from London, Bristol, Edinburgh, Manchester and Dublin, indicate a quiet market. The enquiry for some grades, however, is encouraging.

LONDON:

New White Cuttings	21/6	Canvas No. 1	15/0
Fines (selected)	20/6	„ No. 2 ...	9/6-10/6
„ (good London)...	20/0	„ No. 3	5/6
Outshots (selected) ...	12/6	Mixed Rope	5/3
„ (ordinary) ...	11/0	White Rope	6/6
London Seconds	3/6-4/0	White Manilla Rope	8/6
Country do. ...	6/6-8/0	Coil Rope	8/6
London Thirds ...	1/9-2/0	Bagging...	2/6
Country do. ...	4/0-5/0	Gunny	3/6
Light Prints ...	7/0-8/0		

BRISTOL:

Fines	19/0	Clean Canvas ...	15/0
Outshots	13/6	Second Do. ...	9/6-10/6
Seconds	7/0-8/0	Light Prints ...	8/0
Thirds	3/6-4/0	Hemp Coil Rope	9/6-10/0
Mixed Bagging	3/6	Tarred Manilla	7/6

MANCHESTER:

Fines	15/0-16/0	Blues	6/6-7/0
Outshots (best) ...	11/6-12/0	Bagging...	4/0-4/3
„ (ordinary)	10/6-11/0	„ (common)	3/0-3/3
Seconds	7/0-7/3	W. Manilla Rope	10/0-10-6
Thirds	3/6-3/9	Surat Tares... ...	4/9-5/0

EDINBURGH:

Superfines	17/0	Black Cottons	2/9
Outshots	13/0	W. Manilla Rope ...	9/0
Mixed Fines...	14/0	Tarred Ditto	6/9
Common Seconds ...	8/0	„ Hemp Rope...	8/6
First do.	11/0	Rope Ends (new) ...	8/6
Prints	5/6-6/6	„ „ (old) ...	6/0
Canvas (best)	16/0	Bagging...	2/0-3/0
„ 2nd	10/6	„ (clean) ...	4/3-6/0

DUBLIN.

White Cuttings ...	18/0	Mill Bagging	3/0
Fines	11/0	White Manilla	8/0
Seconds...	5/0	Tarred Hemp	8/0
Light Prints	3/0	Rigging	13/6
Black do.	2/0	Mixed Ropes	3/6
Bagging	2/0		

WASTE PAPERS.—There is a fair business passing in Waste Papers.

Cream Shavings ...	12/3	Small Letters	5/0
Fine „ ...	9/6	Large „	7/0
Mixed „ ...	2/0	Brown Paper	2/9
White Printings ...	8/9	Light Browns	2/9
White Waste ...	1/6	Books & Pamphlets ...	6/0
Wood Pulp Cuttings	3/6	Strawboard Cuttings	1/6
Brown Paper	3/0	Jacquards	2/6
Crushed News	2/0		

For Export: 25/- per ton extra.

ROSIN. — Demand fairly good at former quotations.

	Strained.	E.	F.	G.	K.	W.G.	W.W.
Spot—	3/7½	4/0	4/3	4/6	6/9	9/9	10/3
To arrive—	3/2	3/5	3/7	3/9	5/6	9/0	9/6

SIZING.—The coal strike has effected t demand, many manufactories being clos Stocks of Glues are nil and prices harde ing. Foreign Glues are very scarce a dear.

English Gelatines	per cwt.	70/0	to 14
Foreign „	„	70/0	„ 14
Fine Skin Glues	„	45/0	„ 6
Long Scotch Glues	„	45/0	„ 6
Common „	„	30/0	„ 4
"Town" Glues	„	26/0	„ 3
"Bone" Glues	„	20/0	„ 30
Foreign Glues	„	23/0	„ 40
Bone Size	„	4/0	„ 10
Gelatine Size...	„	5/0	„ 10
Dry B.A. Pieces	„	31/6	„ 33/
„ English Pieces	„	24/0	„ 27/
Wet „ „	„	7/0	„ 8/
„ Sheep Pieces	„	3/0	„ 4/
Buffalo Hide Shavings	„	26/0	„ 37/
„ Picker Waste	„	27/0	„ 33/

STARCH.—Prices:

F.o.r. London, less 2½%:

Maize—Crisp, £10 0/-; Powder, £10 5/-; Special £14 10/-
Farina—Prime, £10 5/-; B.K.M.F., £13 10/-

Delivered:

Rice—Special (in chests), £20 0/- (net); Crystal (in bags) £19 0/-; Granulated (in bags) £18 0/- less 2½%.
Dextrine—£16 0/- to £17.

MINERALS.—The market for CHINA CLAY is steady, with a fair demand for best grades. FRENCH CHALK is in request at previous figures. BARYTES (carbonate and sulphate) are in demand, and there is a moderate amount of business passing in PATENT HARDENINGS and MINERAL WHITE. Best grades of IRISH MOSS scarce.

Mineral White (Terra Alba), per ton f.o.r. or boat at works:

Superfine...	28/0	less 2½ %
Pottery Super.... ...	24/0	„
Ball Seconds	20/0	„
Seconds	15/0	„
Thirds	10/6	„

China Clay, in bulk, f.o.b. Cornwall, 14/0 to 27/6; bags 5/0 and casks 9/6 per ton extra; f.o.b. London, in casks 35/0 to 50/0 per ton.

Superfine Hardening, f.o.r. works, 40/0.

Patent Crystal Hardening, delivered at mills £3 to £3 15/0

Patent Hardening (2 ton lots) f.o.r. Lancs., £3 5/0.
„ „ (5 ton lots) f.o.b. Liverpool, £3 10/0.

Magnesite (in lump) 32/6 per ton.

Magnesite (containing 98 % Carbonate of Magnesia), raw ground, £6 10/0; calcined ground, £12 10/0.

Albarine, £3. del. mills.

Asbestos, best rock, £18; brown grades, £14 to £15

Asbestine Pulp, £4 5/- to £5 c.i.f. London, Liverpool and Glasgow.

Barytes (Carbonate), lump, 90/0 to 95/0; nuts, 72/6 to 85/0.

Barytes (Sulphate), "Angel White," No. 1, 70/0; No. 2, 60/0 to 65/0; No. 3, 45/0. Souheur's Brands: AF, 83/-; BF, 71/-; AB, 33/6; BB, 29/6; CB, 24/3.

French and Itallan Chalk (Souheur Brand), per ton in lots of 10 tons: Flower O, 64/6 c.i.f. London; Flower OO, 60/0, Flower OOO, 51/6. Swan White, 57/0; Snow White, 90/0. Blackwell's "Angel White" Brand and "Silvery" 90/- to 92/6; prime quality, 90/- to 95/-; and superfine, 105/-.

Bauxite, Irish Hill Quality, first lump, 20/0; seconds, 16/0; thirds, 12/0; ground, 35/0.

Pyrites (non-cupreous), Liverpool, 5d., 2 %.

Carbonate of Lime (Souheur Brand), Prima 43/-, Secunda 37/-.

LIME.—Bleach Lime is quoted at 12s. 6d. per ton at works.

BALING TWINE.—Prices:

		Thick.	Medium.	Cap.
All Hemp ...	per lb.	4d.	4¼d.	4¾d.
All Jute ...		3½d.	3¾d.	4d.

DIRECTORY.

Names and Addresses under this heading will be charged for at the rate of 50/- per annum (52 insertions) for each card of two lines or under. Each additional line £1 extra.

ALUMINOUS CAKE.

The ALUM, CHINA CLAY and VITRIOL Co., Lim., 63, Queen Victoria Street, London, E.C. Works: Rainham-on-Thames. Telegrams—"Chinnock, London.

ANALYTICAL.

WILLIAMS, ROWLAND, F.I.C., F.C.S., 28, Pall Mall, Manchester.

ARTESIAN WELLS.

BATCHELOR, Richard D., Artesian and Consulting Well Engineer, 73, Queen Victoria Street, London, E.C., and at Chatham. 5713

ISLER, C., & Co., Bear Lane, Southwark, S.E

LE GRAND & SUTCLIFF, Magdala Works, 125, Bunhill Row, E.C.

BOILER COVERING.

LONSDALES, Boiler Coverers, Blackburn, will send a sample cask of their Patent Plastic Cork Covering to any Paper Mill in Great Britain—5 cwt. cask for 25/- (carriage paid).

CHINA CLAY.

The ALUM, CHINA CLAY and VITRIOL Co., Lim., 63, Queen Victoria Street, London, E.C. Mines: Ruddle and Colchester, St. Austell, Cornwall. Telegrams—"Chinnock, London."

ROGERS, J., & Co., Truro, Cornwall.—Agents: Taylor, Sommerville & Co., 83, Queen Victoria Street, E.C., and at 16, Princes Street, Edinburgh.

W. SINGLETON BIRCH & SONS, Lim., 15, Upton Street, Manchester. Mines: Rosevear, St. Austell, Cornwall. 2276

COLOURS.

CARDWELL, J. L., & Co., Commercial Buildings, 15, Cross Street, Manchester. Specialties: Mineral Black, Ven. Red, Ochres and Umbers. 5304

GEMMILL, W. N., & Co., Glasgow, Telegrams "Ruhe." Starches, Alumina, Antifroths, &c. All Paper Colours

COLOURS (Continued).

HINSHELWOOD, THOMAS, & Co., The Glasgow Colour Works, Glasgow. Colours and shades matched exactly.
MULLER, A. E., 9, Fenchurch Street, London, E.C.

ESPARTO.

IDE & CHRISTIE, Fibre, Esparto, and General Produce Brokers, 72, Mark Lane, E.C.

MINERAL WHITE or TERRA ALBA.

WINSER & Co., Portland Mills, Princess Street, Manchester. Also manufacturers of Aluminous Cake.
HOWE, JOHN, & Co., Carlisle. 2112

STEEL.

MAKIN, WM., & SONS, Sheffield. Established 1776. Roll Bars, Plates, Cutter Knives, Doctor Blades, &c. 63e0

STRAW.

UNDERWOOD, E., & SON, Limited, Brentford, London, W. Press-packed Oat, Wheat, or Rye Straw, delivered to the chief British ports or railway stations.

TALC (French and Italian Chalk).

SOUHEUR, JEAN, Antwerp. All Minerals, Blanc de Silex, Barytes (superior and common), Carbonate of Lime, Blacklead, &c. British Agent: A. E. Muller, 9, Fenchurch Street, London, E.C. Agent for Liverpool and Manchester: C. H. Austin, Ditton, near Widnes.

RAGS.

CHALMERS, E., & Co., Lim., Bonnington, Leith.
MULLER, A. E., 9, Fenchurch Street, London, E.C.
WERTHEIM, A., & Co., Hamburg.

UMBER.

The ALUM, CHINA CLAY and VITROIL Co., Lim. 63, Queen Victoria Street, London, E.C. Telegrams—"Chinnock, London."

WOOD PULP.

FRIIS, N., & Co., 18, Carl Johans Gade, Christiania, Norway.
GOTTSTEIN, H., & Co., 59, Mark Lane, London, E.C., and at New York.
GRANT, W., & Co., 17, Baltic Street, Leith. Agents for best shippers, Sulphite and Sulphate, Mechanical, Pine, Brown, Aspen.
MATTHIESSEN, CHR., Christiania, Norway.
MULLER, A. E., 9, Fenchurch Street, London, E.C.
The SULPHITE PULP Company, Limited, 82, Gordon Street, Glasgow.
WERTHEIM, A., & Co., Hamburg.

G11, EXCHANGE BUILDINGS, LIVERPOOL.

Telegrams: "UBIQUE, LIVERPOOL." Telephone: 1185.

MANUFACTURERS OF

Bleaching Powder,

High-Test SULPHATE of SODA or SALTCAKE, in Bulk or Ground and Packed, SULPHURIC ACID, RECTIFIED VITRIOL, CHLORIDE of CALCIUM, MONOHYDRATE, HYDROCHLORIC ACID, Common or Purified, BROWN VITRIOL.

REFINED ALKALI, All Strengths,

CAUSTIC and CARBONATE of POTASH, BICARBONATE of SODA, High Strength, CHLORATES of POTASH and SODA, CRYSTAL CARBONATE, SAL AMMONIAC, MURIATE of AMMONIA, SULPHATE of AMMONIA, SULPHATE of ALUMINA.

Soda Crystals,

FERTILIZERS, SALT, Common, White and Rock, CHROMIC ACID, PEROXIDE of MANGANESE, HYDRATED PEROXIDE of MANGANESE for Gas Purification. MANGANATE of SODA, SILICATE SODA, PURPLE ORE,

CAUSTIC SODA, 60–77 °/o

Soda Ash,

COPPER PRECIPITATE, S.S. PATENT ROSIN, ROSIN OIL, ULTRAMARINE, CHLORIDE of MAGNESIUM. STRONTIA SALTS, Oxide, Hydrate, and Carbonate, GLYCERINE,

SULPHUR, Rock, Roll, Flowers.

ESTABLISHED A.D. 1736.

WILLIAM MAKIN & SONS

Attercliffe Steel Works, Sheffield, England.

PAPERMAKERS' STEEL TOOLS

2422

Illustrated Catalogue and Price Lists, in French and English, on demand.

The LONDON GLUCOSE & FARINA Co.,

Telegraphic Address: "SNOWWHITE, LONDON." *72, MARK LANE, LONDON, E.C.*

"AJAX" Brand (Registered.)

Importers of all Qualities of FARINAS, STARCHES, GLUES DEXTRINE, &c

Stock kept at all important places in U.K. Contracts made for any period at Special Prices. 2638

Furnival & Co.'s

SELF-CLAMP GUILLOTINE

IN USE IN MANY MILLS

AND IN EVERY LARGE BRITISH TOWN.

References, Price Lists, &c., on Application.

REDDISH IRON WORKS,

STOCKPORT.

SOCIÉTÉ INDUSTRIELLE de MIOS,

MIOS, GIRONDE, FRANCE.

Bleached Chemical Pine Wood Pulp,

OF GREAT PURITY,

Especially Adapted for Use in the Manufacture of Fine Papers. 2646

STRAW PULP

The VEREINIGTE STROHSTOFF-FABRIKEN (Dresden)

United Straw Pulp Manufacturing Co., Limited.,

COSWIG, SACHSEN.

Recommend their First-class Bleached Dry STRAW PULP, Brands V.S.T. and V.S.R. Unequalled in Whiteness and Purity. Strong and Felty. Warranted Free from clays and colours. Used by Leading Paper Mills in Europe and U.S.A.

For Samples, &c., please apply to

ROBERT H. HAY & Co., 26, GEORGE STREET, EDINBURGH, Sole Agents for Scotland, Ireland, and the Newcastle district of England; and

CHR. CHRISTOPHERSEN & Co., 39, LOMBARD STREET, LONDON, E.C., Sole Agents for England (except the Newcastle District). [illegible]

E. BRAMWELL & Son,

HYPOSULPHITE of SODA, SULPHITE of SODA, } Special Quality for Photographers

Navigation Chemical Works, ST. HELENS, Lancashire. | GLAUBER SALTS, EPSOM SALTS.

2696

LONSDALE'S Boiler Coverer and Paper Hair and Cork NON-CONDUCTING CEMENT.

Extract from the *World's Paper Trade Review*, August 2nd, 1889 :—

The "DAILY CHRONICLE" Mills: "The Steam Mains are covered with a Non-Conducting Composition supplied by *LONSDALE BROS., OF BLACKBURN*, which HAS BEEN FOUND TO ADHERE VERY WELL, and to EFFECT A CONSIDERABLE SAVING."

"It has Stood the Test of an EIGHT YEARS' TRIAL."

Improvement in Cork Covering. Patent No. 19,906, 1889. 2058

Chr. Christophersen and Co.,

39, LOMBARD STREET, LONDON, E.C.

Sulphite, Soda and Mechanical WOOD PULPS.

Telegraphic Address: "ARBORARIUS, LONDON." 2141

RICHARD ENGLAND, Brown Street, SALFORD.

(Successor to JAMES PARROTT.)

Maker of all Types and Powers of STEAM ENGINES

Super Calenders, Friction Calenders, Emboss Calenders,

And CALENDERS of all descriptions for PAPER, COTTON, LINEN, WOOLLEN and SILK GOODS

CHILLED IRON, HARD-CAST IRON, STEEL, BRASS & BRASS COVERED ROLLS

Superior Cotton and Paper Bowls,

HAVING THE MOST POWERFUL PLANT IN THE WORLD FOR THEIR MANUFACTURE.

ROLL GRINDING MACHINES. *All Classes of Rolls Reground.*

HYDRAULIC PRESSES and PUMPS.

H. GOTTSTEIN & Co.,

59, MARK LANE, LONDON, AND AT NEW YORK.

PAPERMAKING MATERIALS, CHEMICALS, AND FOREIGN PRODUCE.

PAPERMAKERS SHOULD ADVERTISE IN THE

British & Colonial Printer & Stationer,

In Order to Keep their Mills and Makes before the Home and Colonial Trade.

W. JOHN STONHILL, 58, SHOE LANE, LONDON, E.C.

J. Kenyon & Son,
DERBY STREET MILLS,
BURY,
NEAR MANCHESTER.
FELTS for Papermakers.
Couch Roll Covers,
WET & DRY FELTS,
OF ALL KINDS, INCLUDING (976)
PATENT COTTON DRY FELT, WITH NEW AND IMPROVED SEAM.
Woollen, Linen & Cotton Cloths for Machinery.

Printed and Published by W. JOHN STONHILL 58, Shoe Lane, LONDON, E.C. October 6, 1893.

Taylor's Patent

BEATING and REFINING ENGINE.

☛ THIS BEATER TAKES UP LESS FLOOR SPACE THAN ANY OTHER. ☚

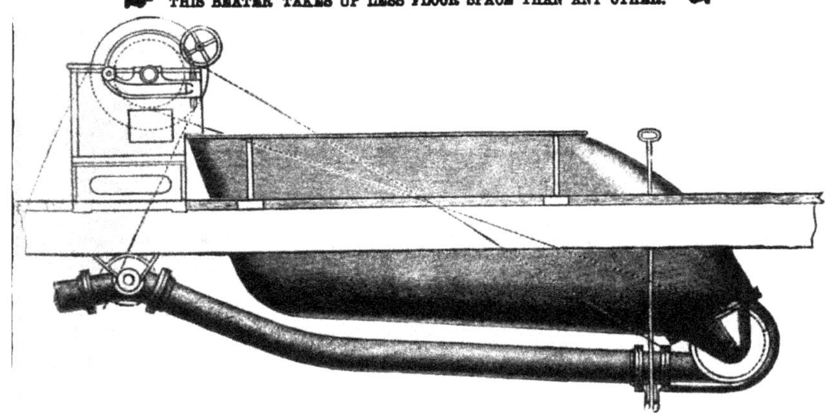

ADVANTAGES:

1.—**GREATLY INCREASED PRODUCTION** over that of the ordinary Beater in use.

2.—**GREAT SAVING IN POWER**, notwithstanding the increased production. This Beater has been proved to beat a given quantity of pulp with less than one-half of the power required by an ordinary beater of good modern construction.

3.—**COMPLETE AND PERFECT CIRCULATION**, which ensures complete uniformity in the length of the fibres.

For Full Particulars and Prices apply to

MASSON, SCOTT & CO., LTD.,

BATTERSEA, LONDON, S.W

A VISIT TO THE

Britannia Engineering Works.

MESSRS. DICK, KERR & CO., LIMITED, KILMARNOCK.

Travellers on the main line of the Glasgow and South Western Railway will have noticed on the right hand side of the line, not far from Kilmarnock Station, an extensive block of buildings, topped by a huge chimney shaft. This forms the Britannia Engineering Works of Messrs. Dick, Kerr and Co., Limited, a firm who occupy a prominent position in the engineering industry, and who are, amongst other things, specially noted as manufacturers of gas engines.

Kilmarnock is not the original home of the business, as when it was founded, under the title of W. B. Dick and Co., the headquarters were in London, where they still have an office at 101, Leadenhall-street, E.C. This was about twenty years since, but about 1873 the firm acquired the land on which their extensive works are now situate. Previous to that date the title of the firm had been changed to Dick, Kerr and Co., and in 1890 the concern was formed into a limited company, of which the present managing director is Mr. John Kerr.

We have on two or three previous occasions called attention to the merits of the "Griffin" gas engine, but hitherto—outside the trades we represent—we have only had the opportunity of seeing the engine at work in London exhibitions and places of that kind. Being however in Glasgow a short time since, we took the opportunity of going to Kilmarnock for the purpose of visiting the Britannia Works. On arriving there we were cordially received by the works manager, Mr. Hartley, who showed us round the extensive works of which he has the active control.

We first visited the general machine shop, which is about 120-ft. long and 70-ft. broad. This building is fitted with a very extensive plant. Nearly all the machines in use have been obtained from firms of the highest standing in the machine tool-making trade, and the names of Messrs. Hetherington, Messrs. Craven Bros., and Messrs. Coventry, all of Manchester, occurred very frequently as makers of some of the machines we saw there. Messrs. Lang and Son, of Johnston, are responsible for a portion of the plant, as are also Messrs. Sharp, Stewart and Co., of Glasgow, and several other leading firms. Messrs. Dick, Kerr and Co. are not, however, entirely dependent on external sources for the tools they use, a considerable proportion of them being made on the premises to suit their own requirements, and these, it is needless to say, are of the highest finish. In all about 300 machines are running in their shops. We particularly noticed an apparatus for boring the beds of gas engines: the construction of this appliance is such that the bed can be put in its rough state, and requires no after setting. The barrels are bored out, the ends faced, and the crank shaft seating machined at one and the same time. The driving power for separate operations carried out in the shop is entirely independent.

As we have already stated, the firm are probably best known in the paper and printing trades for their patent "Griffin" gas engine. The chief points in this engine are no doubt familiar to many of our readers. First amongst them perhaps is the double action in the cylinder. In most gas engines the impulse is imparted to only *one* side of the piston, so that the engine has to make two revolutions before it is possible to obtain a second impulse, or if it be working under full power an even greater interval frequently elapses. In the "Griffin" engine this inconvenience is entirely overcome, the impulse being divided so as to obtain two explosions in the same interval, one in the front and the other at the back of the piston. By this means it will be readily understood that much easier running is secured than under the conditions which prevail in some other types of gas engines.

Recent improvements in the "Griffin" have made it possible for the maximum effort obtained from the combustion of the gas to be imparted to the crank, so as to obtain the most efficient turning power. This not only conduces to considerable economy in the consumption of gas, but also ensures that uniformity of speed which renders the "Griffin" specially suited to cases in which steady running is of paramount importance, as in paper mills, electric lighting plant, etc.

Messrs. Dick, Kerr and Co. are now engaged in building what may perhaps be described as the largest gas engine yet made. It is being constructed for a well-known English firm, and is to be of six hundred indicated horse power, and will, when finished, work with varying load from one third to full power, with not exceeding 2½ per cent. variation in speed. As far as we know nothing approaching this power has ever been constructed in the way of a gas engine, nor with present construction is such steadiness as this possible. We may instance, as showing the confidence that some of our best firms have in Messrs. Dick, Kerr and Co.'s capacity to turn out gas engines of abnormal power, that whilst at the Britannia Works we were shown a letter asking for an estimate for the building of a "Griffin" to indicate 2,000 h.p. We may be permitted to say that the magnitude of the proposition *did* somewhat surprise the Kilmarnock firm, used as they are to big orders. They however, in reply, expressed their readiness to build a 1,000 h.p. gas engine, not caring at present to go beyond that figure: not that they anticipated any difficulty in construction, but simply because they would not just at present like to absolutely guarantee that 2,000 h.p. could be obtained from a gas engine. No doubt, before very long, engines of 500 or even 1,000 h.p. will become fairly common, and then no doubt the larger order can be fulfilled with comparative ease. These engines are now at work in a considerable number of printing offices throughout the kingdom and, as far as our knowledge goes, with perfect satisfaction to the users. This firm is now making a special electric light engine, which is automatically controlled in steadiness of running with a variation of not exceeding three per cent. from one third load to nearly full load.

them called into question at any time, even by makers of opposition types. Every engine sent out by this firm has previously been thoroughly tested, and when the engines leave the makers' hands they are guaranteed in every respect. As an instance of the progress being made by this firm we were shown a gas engine which has given the extraordinarily low consumption of less than eleven cubic feet of gas per 1-h.p. per hour.

The firm under notice are not only manufacturers of gas engines, but general engineers in a very large way of business. They have put down the two systems of cable tramways at present in use at Edinburgh, as well as the one at Matlock, and they have also just completed one of the most important tramway systems in the metropolis, *i.e.*, that of Brixton. Messrs. Dick, Kerr and Co. are also makers of tramway engines.

THE "GRIFFIN" GAS ENGINE.

There are many types of gas engines in the market, and it is usual with makers to instance comparative tests between their own and other firm's engines. Sometimes the user of a certain type of engine consider it to be the *only* good one on the market, and those put in by others to be of little or no use. One or two such cases we have had occasion to look into, and have generally found that a very old type of engine was referred to as being the less useful of the two; this is well enough in its way, but quite useless as a means of comparison; in fact it would be as logical to compare the old steeple engine of half a century ago with the triple or quadruple expansion engines of to-day.

The merits of the Messrs. Dick, Kerr and Co.'s gas engines are practically indisputable; in fact we have never heard

A large building some distance from the main erection is set apart as a pattern room. It is thus isolated owing to the inflammable nature of the materials used, and to minimise the possibility of accidents the driving power here is arranged under the floor. We saw patterns in stock in this shop for engines from ½ to 500 h.p. Next we came to the railway department, where the firm make switches, crossings, turntables, etc., for which they have an excellent reputation, their railway plant being in use on a number of British and foreign railways. Many Government contracts have been secured by them. They make a specialty of supplying light railways for mills, sugar estates, etc., and also manufacture the rolling stock needed to work them. In the waggon shop, to which we were next taken, we saw a large number of

INTERIOR OF THE BRITANNIA ENGINEERING WORKS.

waggons of various sizes in progress of construction. They are made here for almost every purpose to which such vehicles can be put. A complete installation of railway was being built for the shipyard and workshops of Messrs. J. and G. Thomson, the well-known Clyde ship builders, constructors of the City of Paris, the Ramillies, also many first class Atlantic steam ships.

One of our illustrations shows the gas engine store, a very extensive apartment about 300 feet long by 100 broad. At the time of our visit there were some 300 gas engines in stock, varying in sizes from ½ to 500 h.p. It will be seen from the picture we give that engines, partly made and in pieces, are literally stacked in piles throughout this shop. At the extreme end of the store is the testing department where, as we have already mentioned, each engine is tested before being sent out from the works.

Before quitting this subject it may be useful to point out that Messrs. Dick, Kerr and Co., while recognising the advantages, and, within certain limits, the economy, of using ordinary gas from the mains, advocate and have in many instances arranged their engines to work by gas produced by the Dowson or Mansfield processes. Both of these have been previously described in the columns of our journal, and we must refer our readers for particulars to our former articles on this subject. An extensive gas plant is in operation, and the largest-sized engines can be tested on the works. In the recent additions to these works the machinery is being driven with a gas engine operated by this cheap gas. After being cooled and cleansed it is led directly to the engine, and the Dowson Company claim that by the use of their process 1-h.p. can be obtained from the consumption of less than ¾-lb. of fuel per hour.

Since the Britannia Works were started the business has steadily increased. At the commencement about 150 hands were employed, now there are from three to four hundred in regular work, and if the firm are exceptionally busy these figures are largely exceeded. Notwithstanding the general dulness of trade during the past winter, Messrs. Dick, Kerr and Co. have had plenty of work, and have had their hands quite full executing orders.

Within a few weeks the entire premises will be lit by the electric light, an installation having been in use for some time past for the purpose of lighting the offices.

In concluding we must express our thanks to Mr. Hartley for his kindness in giving us the opportunity of going over this interesting establishment, and to Mr. Connor, the chief draughtsman, for the courtesy and attention he displayed in explaining the technical terms and details of the various processes and appliances we saw in the course of our tour of the works.

A USEFUL MACHINE.

Mr. Friedheim's (of 7, Water-lane, Ludgate-circus, London, E.C.) speciality is a combined rotary card cutting and scoring machine, which may be used either separately or simultaneously for each purpose, turning out as many as 100,000 visiting cards per day, and which can be supplied to cut the thickest card-

board or thinnest ivories with equal ease. Among other classes of machines supplied by Mr. Friedheim are gold blocking, card punching, and round cornering machines, lever presses, card shears, &c., in addition to a special machine for cutting railway tickets, in which the strips are automatically fed in and delivered out ready packed in bundles of 500 tickets, all of which actions are performed by a special movement. Most of the machines in use at the present time for cutting and scoring the boxes used in automatic machines are supplied by this gentleman, and nearly all the leading firms in this country, including Messrs. J. Dickinson and Co., Spicer and Sons, Spicer Brothers, Spottiswoode and Co., Eyre and Spottiswoode, have been using for years Mr. Friedheim's machine with great success.

Messrs. Richard Hornsby and Sons, Limited, of Spittlegate Ironworks, Grantham, have commenced to manufacture water-tube boilers under the patents of the Mills Patent Sectional Boiler Company, Limited, of Pendleton, Manchester. Messrs. Hornsby will in future carry on the manufacture of these boilers under the title of the "Hornsby water-tube boilers." These well-known boilers are made with patent water-lined furnaces (single and double flues), for bituminous and smoky coal, effecting great economy in fuel, and with large brick-lined furnaces for inferior and bulky fuel, or for any fuel requiring large grate area. They are specially adapted for export, as they can be handled in sections where transport is difficult.

TARIFF CHANGES AND CUSTOMS REGULATIONS.

Russia.

According to some recent decisions of the Russian Customs department articles of celluloid intended to be used as a substitute for paper, such as sheets for binding, &c., are dutiable under category 177, section 6, at the rate of 10 roubles 60 copecks per poud. Toys and small fancy articles when made of one common metal, but covered with other common metals, painted or trimmed with ordinary materials, are dutiable under category 215, section 2, at the rate of 50 copecks per Russian pound.

The poud = 36 lbs. avoirdupois. The Russian pound = ·902 lbs. avoirdupois, and the gold rouble = 3s. 2d.

Italy.

Toys of tinned ware fastened on cardboard will in future be dutiable under category 329a, the duty being 100 lire per quintal.

Wrapping paper of asbestos comes under category 183f, the duty being 3 lire per quintal.

Cards for time tables come under category 185, and pay duty at the rate of 100 lire per quintal.

Kodak cameras and similar detective photographic apparatus are scheduled under category 228a, the duty being 125 lire per quintal.

The quintal = 220·4 lbs. avoirdupois. The lire = 9 $\frac{6}{10}$d., about 25 being equal to £1 sterling.

United States.

Paper made to imitate stained window glass, with representations of rural scenes and flowers, and other designs printed on it, and made by lithographic process from stone or zinc, is dutiable at 35 per cent. *ad valorem*, under paragraph 420 N.T.

Newfoundland.

Parchment or waxed paper when imported direct for wrapping boneless fish for export, will in future be admitted into this colony duty free. The import duty previously levied was 25 per cent. *ad valorem*.

Some curious figures are revealed by the returns of the Patent Office for a year. From the figures there given it appears that at present the number of patents carried through are somewhere near one-half of the number applied for. During the eight years which have elapsed since the passing of the Patents Act of 1883 (1884 to 1891), the number of applications was 152,734, while the number sealed was 79,291, only 118 being refused, and 72,379 abandoned. The effect of the Act of 1883 is strikingly shown by the tabulated returns for the last 40 years. Dividing them into five periods of eight years each, we have the following:—

Years.	Number of Applications.	Patents Sealed.
1852 to 1859	22,291	15,078
1860 „ 1867	27,093	17,013
1868 „ 1875	32,028	21,472
1876 „ 1883	44,201	29,775
1884 „ 1891	152,734	79,291

The applications for patents in 1892 numbered 24,171 as against 22,888 in 1891. The applications were distributed as follows:—

United Kingdom	17,927
British Colonies and Possessions	418
European States	3,453
United States...	2,306
American States outside the Union	24
Africa	28
Asia	12
Sandwich Islands	1

The total amount received from fees in 1892 was £180,566 14s. The cost of administration (including Trade Marks and Designs, was £90,822 17s. 6d.

A manufacturing and export stationery house that is rapidly coming to the front is that of Messrs. Begg, Kennedy and Harper, 25—33, Hope-street, Glasgow. Established in a small and unpretentious way just ten years ago, in Union-street, they outgrew their borders in about six years, and are now located in extensive premises at the address first given. In addition to their Glasgow house they have established a branch in Kirkcaldy. The principal export connections of the firm lie with India, Ceylon, Newfoundland, and the West Indies. Their lines in manufactured stationery command growing attention, and we confidently look to it that they will at no distant date take rank among the most prominent of the Scotch houses.

In journalistic circles much comment is being made upon the enterprise of Mr. W. T. Emmott, of Manchester, the proprietor of the *Umpire* weekly newspaper, the *Textile Manufacturer*, and other established technical newspapers, in acquiring the *Examiner and Times* of Manchester, which was the first daily newspaper in England sold at the popular price of one penny. Everything connected with the transfer of the *Examiner and Times* to Mr. Emmott's Blackfriars Printing Works, Manchester, has now been completed, and before long we anticipate the pleasure of describing and illustrating what is claimed to be the very finest machine room and best equipped offices in England. The further progress and development of the *Examiner and Times* under Mr. Emmott's management, will be watched with interest.

Printed and Published by W. JOHN STONHILL, 58, Shoe Lane, E.C. Oct. 6, 18[illegible].

Telegrams: "[illegible]HILL, LONDON." A B C Code. Registered at the General Post Office as a Newspaper.

Vol. XX, No. 15. LONDON, OCTOBER 13, 1893. Price 6d.

CHLORINE PRODUCTION ON A CONTINUOUS SYSTEM.

An improved continuous process for obtaining chlorine is jointly claimed by Mr. A. Vogt, chemical engineer, and Mr. A. R. Scott, manufacturing chemist, of Carntyne Chemical Works, Parkhead, Lanark, N.B. Hydrochloric acid, preferably dry, is made to flow through channel apparatus over and in the same direction with a stream of sulphuric acid, with which there also flows nitric acid, the process being capable of modification by using aqueous hydrochloric acid with an increased proportion of sulphuric acid, or by introducing the nitric acid in a vaporised condition.

Figure 1 is a diagrammatic plan, and Figure 2 is a corresponding sectional elevation, whilst Figure 3 is an enlarged vertical section as taken along a part of the channel and transversely to Figures 1 and 2.

In the left-hand parts of Figures 1 and 2 a furnace, 4, is shown, arranged for heating a set of pans, 5, for reconcentrating the sulphuric acid, which becomes diluted in the process. From the pans, 5, the concentrated sulphuric acid is transferred by means of a [illegible], *a*, to a reservoir or tank, 6, from which it is supplied by means of a [illegible] 7, to the channel apparatus in which the process is in operation. This channel apparatus consists of a rectangular lead or [illegible] structure, 8, divided into four [illegible] lengths by vertical partitions, 9, [illegible] one is shown separately in Figure [illegible] spaces thereby formed are subdivided by partitions, 10, none of which reach the bottom, but which are formed and placed in a manner to allow gases to flow alternately under and over each in succession. The partitions, 9, are made each with lower and upper openings, 11, 12, at one end, the lower opening being for the passage of the liquids and the upper one for the gases: and these openings, 11, 12, are at opposite ends of the alternate partitions, 9, the dotted lines in Figure 3, indicating the positions of the openings in the next partition. With these arrangements the liquids and gases flow from the inlet part, 13, along the spaces formed by the partitions, 9, alternately in opposite directions to the outlet part, 14, the partitions, 10, at right angles to the partitions, 9, being for the purpose of keeping the gases well mixed, and of preventing portions passing along the tops of the spaces without approaching the liquids.

The sulphuric acid is caused to flow through the apparatus in a stream having a small depth of, for example, 2 to 4 centimetres. The nitric acid is supplied from a reservoir or tank, 15, by a pipe, *b*, and inlet trap, *c*, which prevents escape of gas, and is introduced at the inlet part, 13, at the surface of the sulphuric acid, so that it may flow along that surface with as little mixing as possible. The hydrochloric acid is supplied at the inlet part, 13, by a pipe, 16. The gaseous chlorine and nitrogen compounds formed in the process by the reactions between the three acids, leave the channel apparatus, 8, at the outlet part, 14, by a pipe, 17, communicating with the bottom of a tower, 18, up which the gases pass whilst sulphuric acid passes downwards to absorb the nitrogen compounds. Fr the top of the tower, 18, the chlorine ha mixed with it some hydrochloric acid, pa by a pipe, 19, to the bottom of a sec

... 0, down which water is passed to ... th the hydrochloric acid. Finally the ... me is led by a pipe, 21, to the bottom of ... d tower, 22, in which it is acted on by ... huric acid to absorb moisture; and it ... then be passed to lime chambers or used ... desired manner.

... en the sulphuric acid leaves the channel ... aratus, 8, at the outlet part, 18, it is still ... ng enough for dehydrating hydrochloric ... s that acid comes from the ordinary ... decomposing furnace, and it is used for ... t purpose in supplementary channel ... aratus, 23, which is internally divided ... the main channel apparatus, 8, the fresh ... drochloric acid gas entering by a pipe, *d*, ... the part, 24, at which the sulphuric acid

28, transferred to the concentrating pans, 5. The channel apparatus, 8, and, 23, is heated by means of a furnace, 29, from which flues, 30, extend under the apparatus.

THE BOHEMIAN PAPER INDUSTRY.—The Chamber of Commerce, in Eger (Bohemia), have issued a report of the progress of trade in the Eger district. The production of ground wood pulp is principally represented in the parishes of Salmthal, Liditzau, and Breitenbach, Neudek, Thierbach, and Voigtegrun. In recent times chemical wood pulp has been manufactured in Josefihutte, where some old iron works have been converted into a large sulphite factory. Ten concerns exclusively produce pulp, nine by

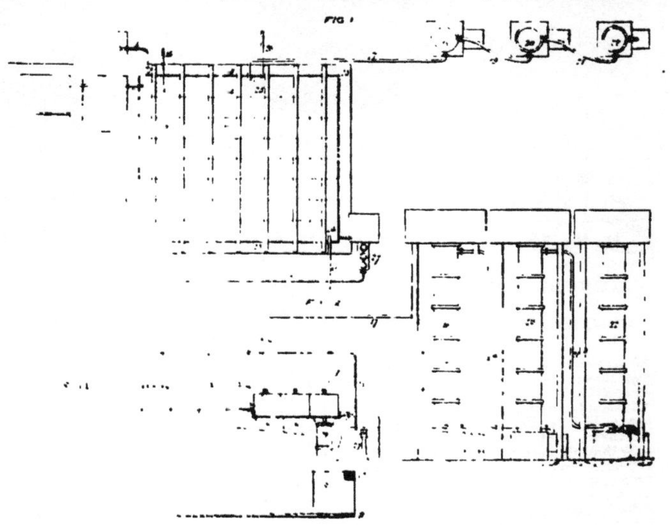

... VOGT & SCOTT'S PROCESS.

... [illegible] ... the ... hydro... 23, ... passed ... apparatus ... to the ... the ... acid ... to ... the ...

mechanical and one by chemical means. The power is supplied by 7 turbines of 810-h.p., 4 water wheels of 175-h.p.; total, 11 motors with 985-h.p., 11 circular saws, 11 defibreurs, 31 refiners, and 4 boilers, are employed by these works. There are 3 directors, 9 foremen, 144 males, and 14 female workers. Ten paper mills are in Platten, Breitenbach, Salmthal, Merkelsgrun, Neudek, Pirken, Neuberg, and Grun. They are driven by 3 steam engines of 125-h.p., 8 turbines of 1,000-h.p., 9 water wheels of 88-h.p.; total, 20 motors of 1,213-h.p. Appliances: 4 rag boilers, 20 engines, 2 paper machines, 20 millboard machines, 13 glazing machines. There are 5 clerks, 6 foremen, 179 male, 45 female workers.

Pure

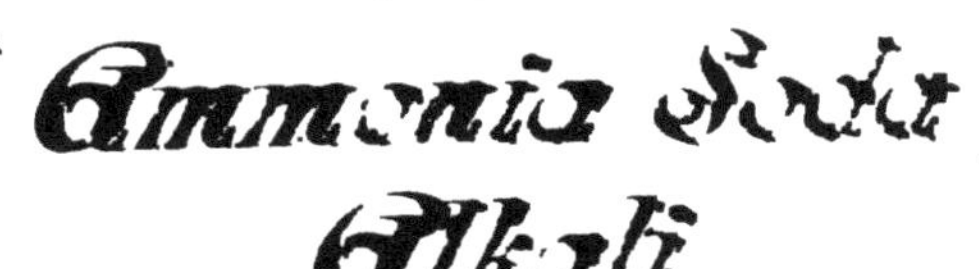

Ammonia Soda Alkali

MANUFACTURED BY

BRUNNER, MOND & CO.

LIMITED

Lostock Alkali Works,

NORTHWICH, CHESHIRE.

Telegrams: "FIRST," NORTHWICH.

This Alkali Contains 99%

OF CARBONATE OF SODA.

It is the BEST and PUREST

For the Manufacture of PAPER, WOOD PULP, SOAP, GLASS, COLOURS, and for the use of BLEACHERS, PRINTERS, &c.

[illegible] MONTH'S PAPER TRADE.

[illegible] EXPORTS.

TOTAL IMPORTS.

	Year	Quantity	Value
[illegible]	1893	[illegible] cwts	£41,230
	1892	[illegible] ,,	35,141
	1891	[illegible]7,712 ,,	31,978
[illegible] Kinds	1893	[illegible] cwts	£144,583
	1892	[illegible] ,,	154,776
	1891	191,[illegible] ,,	140,655

From GERMANY.

	Year	Quantity	Value
[illegible]ings and Writings	1893	6,125 cwts	£8,051
	1892	9,844 ,,	9,695
	1891	8,933 ,,	9,636
Other Kinds	1893	40,786 cwts	£34,536
	1892	39,950 ,,	38,306
	1891	43,218 ,,	37,576

From BELGIUM.

	Year	Quantity	Value
Printings and Writings	1893	6,622 cwts	£10,059
	1892	6,535 ,,	7,494
	1891	6,584 ,,	7,282
Other Kinds	1893	12,409 cwts	£15,299
	1892	10,865 ,,	15,828
	1891	13,447 ,,	16,534

From HOLLAND.

	Year	Quantity	Value
Printings and Writings	1893	5,276 cwts	£7,502
	1892	2,382 ,,	2,914
	1891	1,546 ,,	2,405
Other Kinds	1893	96,678 cwts	£47,807
	1892	93,316 ,,	48,128
	1891	85,933 ,,	41,114

From SWEDEN.

	Year	Quantity	Value
Printings and Writings	1893	7,771 cwts	£7,667
	1892	10,224 ,,	10,168
	1891	6,384 ,,	6,371

("Other Kinds' are not tabulated).

From FRANCE.

	Year	Quantity	Value
Other Kinds	1893	2,983 cwts	£7,564
	1892	2,748 ,,	7,258
	1891	1,712 ,,	5,902

From OTHER COUNTRIES.

	Year	Quantity	Value
Printings and Writings	1893	9,085 cwts	£9,951
	1892	5,098 ,,	6,870
	1891	5,485 ,,	6,284
Other Kinds	1893	47,579 cwts	£39,577
	1892	[illegible] ,,	45,256
	1891	47,539 ,,	38,629

TOTAL RE-EXPORTS.

	Year	Quantity	Value
Printings [illegible]	1893	1,7[illegible] cwts	£2,083
	1892	1,066 ,,	2,224
	1891	1,141 ,,	1,388
[illegible]	1893	3,8[illegible] cwts	£2,801
	1892	4,240 ,,	3,801
	1891	8,700 ,,	6,887

TOTAL EXPORTS.

	Year	Quantity	Value
Printings and Writings	1893	58,813 cwts	£90,595
	1892	55,691 ,,	92,350
	1891	64,439 ,,	106,537
Other Kinds	1893	13,928 cwts	£23,228
	1892	14,965 ,,	23,473
	1891	19,515 ,,	31,642

To FRANCE.

	Year	Quantity	Value
Printings and Writings	1893	2,569 cwts	£4,625
	1892	3,349 ,,	5,765
	1891	3,298 ,,	6,353
Other Kinds	1893	842 cwts	£4,259
	1892	523 ,,	2,684
	1891	1,343 ,,	5,178

To the UNITED STATES.

	Year	Quantity	Value
Printings and Writings	1893	589 cwts	£1,779
	1892	1,463 ,,	4,274
	1891	605 ,,	2,390
Other Kinds	1893	437 cwts	£1,418
	1892	924 ,,	2,491
	1891	1,044 ,,	2,703

To SOUTH AFRICA.

	Year	Quantity	Value
Printings and Writings	1893	3,622 cwts	£5,888
	1892	3,027 ,,	5,161
	1891	2,296 ,,	4,576
Other Kinds	1893	2,594 cwts	£2,558
	1892	2,823 ,,	2,990
	1891	2,417 ,,	2,685

To the EAST INDIES.

	Year	Quantity	Value
Printings and Writings	1893	7,260 cwts	£12,297
	1892	6,907 ,,	12,836
	1891	6,961 ,,	12,155
Other Kinds	1893	2,231 cwts	£3,125
	1892	1,701 ,,	2,805
	1891	2,798 ,,	3,860

To AUSTRALASIA.

	Year	Quantity	Value
Printings and Writings	1893	30,400 cwts	£38,139
	1892	25,779 ,,	37,845
	1891	37,467 ,,	54,985
Other Kinds	1893	3,761 cwts	£4,118
	1892	5,519 ,,	6,146
	1891	7,605 ,,	8,641

To BRITISH NORTH AMERICA

	Year	Quantity	Value
Printings and Writings	1893	2,488 cwts	£5,295
	1892	3,098 ,,	5,810
	1891	4,766 ,,	8,324
Other Kinds	1893	633 cwts	£1,442
	1892	463 ,,	1,090
	1891	698 ,,	1,365

To OTHER COUNTRIES.

	Year	Quantity	Value
Printings and Writings	1893	11,885 cwts	£22,572
	1892	11,468 ,,	20,659
	1891	9,046 ,,	17,804
Other Kinds	1893	3,490 cwts	£6,308
	1892	2,952 ,,	5,267
	1891	3,670 ,,	7,210

TOTALS FOR JAN.-SEPT.

Imports	[illegible]	[illegible] cwts.	£1,[illegible]
	1892	[illegible]	1,7[illegible]
	[illegible]	[illegible]	1,5[illegible]
Re-Exports	[illegible]	[illegible] cwts.	£[illegible]
	[illegible]	[illegible]	[illegible]
	[illegible]	[illegible]	[illegible]
Exports	[illegible]	[illegible] cwts.	£[illegible]
	[illegible]	[illegible]	1,[illegible]
	[illegible]	[illegible]	1,1[illegible]

RAW MATERIALS.

IMPORTS AND EXPORTS FOR SEPTEMBER.

EXPORTS.

Alkali	[illegible]	[illegible] cwts.	£114,[illegible]
	[illegible]	[illegible]	[illegible]
	[illegible]	[illegible]	[illegible]

	[illegible]	[illegible]	[illegible]
Russia	[illegible]	[illegible]	[illegible]
Sweden and Norway	[illegible]	[illegible]	[illegible]
Germany	[illegible]	[illegible]	[illegible]
Holland	[illegible]	1,[illegible]	[illegible]
France	[illegible]	[illegible]	[illegible]
Spain and Canaries	[illegible]	[illegible]	[illegible]
Italy	[illegible]	[illegible]	[illegible]
United States	[illegible]	[illegible]	[illegible]
Australasia	[illegible]	[illegible]	[illegible]
British North America	[illegible]	[illegible]	[illegible]
Other countries	[illegible]	[illegible]	[illegible]

Bleaching Materials	[illegible]	[illegible] cwts.	£[illegible]
	[illegible]	[illegible]	[illegible]
	[illegible]	[illegible]	[illegible]

	[illegible]	[illegible]	[illegible]
United States	[illegible]	[illegible]	[illegible]
Other Countries	[illegible]	[illegible]	[illegible]

Rags	1893	2,7[illegible] tons	£16,5[illegible]
	1892	4,3[illegible]	[illegible]
	1891	3,945	[illegible]

IMPORTS.

Alkali	1893	6,0[illegible] cwts.	£5,[illegible]
	1892	4,341	3,2[illegible]
	1891	6,5[illegible]	4,21[illegible]
Esparto	1893	11,706 tons	£53,61[illegible]
	1892	14,14[illegible]	71,1[illegible]
	1891	8,7[illegible]	45,[illegible]

	1891.	1892	1893.
Spain	£[illegible]	£[illegible]	£1[illegible]
Algeria	[illegible]	[illegible]	14,[illegible]
Other Countries	—	[illegible]	[illegible]

Wood Pulp	1893	19,054 tons	£1[illegible]
	1892	12,[illegible]	[illegible]
	1891	14,3[illegible]	[illegible]

	1891	[illegible]	189[illegible].
Norway	£4[illegible]	£[illegible]	£[illegible]
Other Countries	[illegible]	[illegible]	[illegible]

Rags	1893	1,776 tons	£1[illegible],067
	1892	61[illegible]	4,242
	1891	2,258	22,615

TOTALS FOR JAN.-SEPT.

EXPORTS.

Alkali	[illegible]	4,[illegible] cwts.	£[illegible]
	[illegible]	4,[illegible]	1,[illegible]
	[illegible]	[illegible]	1,[illegible]
Bleaching Materials	[illegible]	[illegible] cwts.	£[illegible]
	[illegible]	1,[illegible]	[illegible]
	[illegible]	1,[illegible]	[illegible]
Rags	[illegible]	[illegible] tons	£[illegible]
	[illegible]	[illegible]	[illegible]
	[illegible]	[illegible]	[illegible]

IMPORTS.

Alkali	[illegible]	[illegible] cwts.	[illegible]
	[illegible]	[illegible]	[illegible]
	[illegible]	[illegible]	[illegible]
Esparto	[illegible]	1[illegible] tons	£[illegible]
	[illegible]	[illegible]	[illegible]
	[illegible]	[illegible]	[illegible]
Wood Pulp	[illegible]	[illegible] tons	£[illegible]
	[illegible]	1[illegible] 449	[illegible]
	[illegible]	11[illegible]	[illegible]
Rags	[illegible]	1[illegible] tons	£[illegible]
	[illegible]	[illegible]	[illegible]
	1891	[illegible]	[illegible]

EXPORTS OF PAPER HANGINGS.

Sept.	[illegible]	[illegible] cwts.	£[illegible]
	[illegible]	[illegible]	[illegible]
	[illegible]	[illegible]	11,316
January to Sept.	[illegible]	[illegible] cwts.	£112,[illegible]
	[illegible]	[illegible]	11[illegible]
	[illegible]	[illegible]	1[illegible]

The consumption of British paper has [illegible] fluctuated to any great extent in Malta and Gozo during the past five years. In 18[illegible] [illegible] cwts. of the value of £1,7[illegible] were exported, and in 1888 [illegible] cwts. of the value of £[illegible].

The Channel Islands pay Great Britain over £[illegible] yearly for paper. Five years ago the amount was £[illegible].

During 1892 British Guiana was supplied by Great Britain with paper of its own manufacture to the value of £[illegible], and that of foreign manufacture £[illegible].

Strawpaper and Strawboards [illegible] shown an upward movement for some time, not only because all the prices of straw have risen very much, but also the production has been greatly reduced by the continued scarcity of water. The makers of strawboards and strawpaper have been working with a loss, and as the causes of dearer production are not likely to be removed for a long time to come, but, on the contrary, will be felt still more later on, a further [illegible] only a question of time and it is not [illegible] that the former prices, unsatisfactory [illegible] makers, can be brought on again.

JACKSON

gineers,

ANCHESTER.

RSHALL'S PATENT PERFECTING ENGINE.

BLE FOR ALL CLASSES OF STOCK AND EVERY QUALITY OF PAPER.

MADE IN THREE SIZES.

gine will produce a Better Finished, Stronger and More Even Sheet of Paper from materials than can be produced by any other Mechanical Process and at the same time will REDUCE the TIME and POWER required for Beating.

supply these Engines on approval subject to our accomplishing the above results.

ine NO WELL-EQUIPPED PAPER MILL SHOULD BE WI

APPLICATION.

... ... and in order to recover this ... ... passed through a layer of cotton ... other fibrous material (such as slag ... ... possessing the quality of filtering ... ... solid particles out of a gas. In ... ... economise the inert gas used in the ... ... to obtain it as free as possible ... ... ingredients, the same inert ... ... after it has been treated over and ... again.

... ... gas, obtained in the second ... described in Mr. Ludwig Mond's ... ... frequently contains small ... ... of hydrochloric acid gas. To ... and to recover this hydrochloric ... proposes to wash the chlorine gas ... concentrated solution of chloride of ... which only absorbs traces of chlorine ... completely retains the hydrochloric ... ... part of his invention he carries ... stone towers packed with fire bricks, ... or the like, such as are frequently used ... absorption of acid gases. By subsequently ... heating the chloride of calcium solution ... containing hydrochloric acid, the latter ... as dry or almost dry hydrochloric ... gas, which can be condensed by water ... commercial hydrochloric acid, or ... may be directly treated for the manufacture of chlorine. For the latter purpose it is preferred to send it directly into ... apparatus in which the oxides or salts ... treated with ammonium chloride vapour. ... chloride of calcium solution, after being ... ... used again for washing the ... gas.

The LONDON GLUCOSE & FARINA Co.,

Telegraphic Address: "SNOWWHITE, LONDON." 72, MARK LANE. LONDON. E.C.

"AJAX" Brand (Registered.)

Importers of all Qualities of FARINAS, STARCHES, GLUES DEXTRINE, &c

Stock kept at all important places in U.K. Contracts made for any period at Special Prices. 2638

TURNER BROTHERS,

SPOTLAND, ROCHDALE.

ASBESTOS YARN,
ASBESTOS CLOTH of Every Description.
ASBESTOS METALLIC CLOTH.
ASBESTOS PACKING suitable for all pressures.
ASBESTOS & RUBBER SHEETING.
ASBESTOS & RUBBER TAPE, JOINTS, &c.
ASBESTOS MILLBOARD.
HEMP & COTTON Packings.
CHALK PACKING.
MINERAL PACKING.
ANTI-FRICTION PACKING, &c., &c.

SPINNERS & MANUFACTURERS OF

ASBESTOS

IN ALL ITS FORMS.

SOLE MANUFACTURERS OF THE "GRIPWELL"

HAIR BELTING,

Specially Suitable for Papermakers. 2335

ASBESTOS METALLIC & RUBBER PACKING, SHEETING, TAPE, JOINTS for Manhole and Mudhole Doors.

Bleached Sulphate STRAW PULP.

Bleached Sulphate STRAW PULP.

Bleached Sulphate STRAW PULP.

HERMANN MARIA SCHOELLER & CO.

DUEREN,

Manufacturers of BLEACHED SULPHATE

Straw Pulp,

UNEQUALLED FOR COLOUR, STRENGTH AND PURITY.
PACKED IN BALES.

For Samples, &c., apply to the Sole Agents:

HENDERSON, CRAIG & Co., LIMITED,

116, QUEEN VICTORIA STREET, LONDON, and at Manchester and Edinburgh.

PRESTON & Co, Ltd.

WORLD'S PAPER TRADE REVIEW OFFICE,
58, SHOE LANE, LONDON, E.C.
OCTOBER 19, 1893.

TRADE NOTES.

THE UNIVERSAL BARREL CO., LIM.—The first meeting of creditors and contributories is called for the 26th inst., at 33, Carey-street, Lincoln's-inn, London, W.C.

UNDER the failure of the Springfield Chemical Co., Lim., the first and final dividend of 3½d. is payable on the 25th inst., at the official receiver's office, 14, Chapel-street, Preston.

ST. NEOTS PAPER MILL CO.—We have received the following circular, dated October 16th:—"The directors beg to announce that arrangements have been concluded with the landlord for the re-equipment of the mill. The necessary new shares and debentures for the reconstitution of the company's capital have been provided. The alterations will be commenced at once, and it is hoped will be concluded very early in the new year. It will not be necessary to shut down both machines, and the directors will use their best endeavours to meet the convenience of customers during alterations. Mr. O. Bricknall retains charge of the manufacturing department of the company's business. Mr. J. A. Kidd, 120, Queen Victoria-street, E.C., is London agent."

THE COAL CRISIS.—The Birley pits, near Sheffield, which employ 2,200 men, were opened on Thursday at the old rate of wages. The manager thinks the coalowners cannot now do better than accept the proposals of the Miners' Federation, and form a Board of Conciliation. The colliery near Wigan which was to have opened on Wednesday at the old rate did not, after all, resume operations, the notice being withdrawn. A meeting of coalowners, held on Wednesday, at Manchester, decided that the men's proposal to resume work at the old rate of wages could not be accepted, but reiterated their offer to open the pits at a reduction of 15 per cent., and added that they did not propose this as a final settlement of the dispute, but as a means of ending the present deadlock, and were quite willing to submit the whole question to a joint representative committee with an independent chairman.

OIL AS A SUBSTITUTE FOR COAL.—The exorbitant prices asked for coal have directed attention to some other means of driving machinery, and Messrs. W. Holt and Co., Bark-street Mill, are the first in Bolton to adopt oil as a substitute for coal. The patent is that of Mr. William Allen, Manchester. The oil is conveyed into the boiler by means of pipes and steam pressure, and cleanliness and ease of manipulation are two striking features in connection with this new fuel.

RUSSIAN CERTIFICATES OF ORIGIN.—The following communication on certificates of origin for Russia has been received at the Liverpool Chamber of Commerce:—"Foreign Office, October 16, 1893. Sir,—Numerous complaints having been made respecting the requirement of the Russian Customs authorities that all articles, with the exception of a few especially named, sent to Russia after transhipment or discharge in a German port shall be accompanied by manufacturers invoices or letters, properly legalised by certified copies of these documents, her Majesty's Chargé d'Affairs at St. Petersburg has, under instructions from the Earl of Rosebery, made several representations on the subject to the Russian Government. I am, however, directed by his lordship to express to you his regret that no relaxation of this requirement could be obtained, except that the manufacturers' letters or invoices need not give the price of the articles they refer to. Care should therefore be taken not to send through a German port goods for which it is not wished to produce invoices. I am, Sir, your obedient humble servant, T. V. LISTER."

MR. J. T. BRUNNER, M.P., chairman of Brunner, Mond and Co., Limited, has intimated to the relief committee assisting the Salt Union employees thrown out of work at Winsford, Cheshire, by the coal strike, that he is prepared to contribute £50 a week to the relief fund as long as the strike lasts.

MESSRS. JOHN DICKINSON AND CO. have just opened up telephonic communication between the Apsley Mills and their London warehouse in the Old Bailey. It is anticipated that in the course of time the same means will have to be resorted to for the purpose of direct intercourse with some of the firm's principal customers.

"SKYTOGEN."—The modern art of papermaking has produced an article "Skytogen," which not only looks like leather, but is also in the feel and touch hardly to be distinguished from it. The raw material is made from sulphite pulp, and goes then to the fancy papermaker, who dyes and rolls the surface and embosses it with patterns, which so closely resemble the texture of the various kinds of tanned hides that none but an expert can distinguish one from the other. If "Skytogen" has perhaps not quite reached the durability of real leather, it at any rate is so tough and pliable that it finds an extensive use in the bookbinding and fancy box trades, supplying an infinity of elegant articles produced at a comparatively moderate cost.

WE have received the October numbers of the "Strand Magazine," and the "Picture Magazine," published by George Newnes, Limited. The former well maintains its reputation in providing reading matter and illustrations of an interesting character, and the variety of the subjects in the "Picture Magazine" makes this publication popular amongst all classes. *Tit Bits* for October 14th contains several announcements of novel competitions.

Mr. Josiah Montague Goodall, head of the firm of Charles Goodall and Son, Camden Works, N.W., and St. Bride-street, E.C., died on Sunday, the 15th inst., at Hastings, aged 65. The decease of Mr. Goodall will be heard of with regret by a very large circle of business and private friends, not only in this country, but the world over.

SALES BY AUCTION.

Tuesday, October 24th:
Broughton Grove Paper Works.

Messrs. William Wilson and Son will offer under the hammer at the Mitre Hotel, Cathedral Gates, Manchester, on Tuesday next, the Broughton Grove Paper Works and adjoining building estate, by order of the mortgagee; also the extensive machinery. Catalogues and conditions of sale may be obtained from the auctioneers, 29, Fountain-street, Manchester, and of Messrs. W. H. Hewitt and Son, Solicitors, 32, St. Ann-street, Manchester.

Friday, October 27th:
Soyland Paper Mill and Cottages.

At the "White Swan" Hotel, Halifax, York, Mr. J. Shoesmith (of Messrs. Davis and Shoesmith) will submit for sale on Friday next, the Soyland Paper Mill and other property; also plant and machinery. Catalogues may be had of the auctioneers, Barum Top, Halifax, and on application at the offices of the *World's Paper Trade Review*. See advertisement on page 15.

German Exportations of paper and paper articles to Uruguay have held their own during recent years. The total importation into Uruguay has gone down very much, but Germany's participation, according to recently published statistics, has become larger. The endeavours of German manufacturers to fall in with the requirements of the consumer have shown a marked success, and will no doubt pay still more with a revival of the trade, which has been stagnant since 1890. The Uruguayan income from foreign import duties has not gone down, and as production has increased in that country, and prices become better, an improvement in business is confidently expected. The impediments in the shipping from Hamburg through cholera restrictions were only temporary, and did not affect the export trade to the advantage of other countries.

"Trade with Egypt."—In reporting upon the importation of paper goods at Alexandria, in our last issue, "Egyptian pound sterling" should have appeared instead of "Egyptian lb."

SPAIN.

The Spanish trade returns for the first quarter of this year, recently published in the *Madrid Gazette*, show a decrease in the totals both of the import and export trade when compared with the figures of the two preceding years, though there has been, in spite of the present high tariff, a slight rise in certain branches of commerce. Compared with the same period of 1892 there is a decreased exportation of paper.

The following imports of paper were registered at the port of Huelva from the countries named: Great Britain 5,961 kilos., France 228 kilos., Germany 714 kilos., Austria 34 kilos., and Japan 98 kilos.

The importations at Bilbao in 1892 included: Pasteboard—772 tons from Norway, 264 tons from Belgium, 61 tons from Germany. Printings—1 ton from France, 3 tons from England, 22 tons from Belgium, 18 tons from Germany, and ½ ton from Holland. Other papers—¼ ton from France, 51 tons from England, 15¼ tons from Belgium, 13 tons from Germany. Cardboard—8 tons from France, 19 tons from England, 33 tons from Belgium, 49 tons from Germany, 5 tons from Holland.

The exportations of cigarette paper were 95 tons to France, 7 tons 3 cwts. to England, 1 ton 10 cwt. to Belgium, 19 tons 15 cwts. to Germany.

Paper and its appliances were imported at the ports of Santander to the quantity of 471,390 lbs. of the value of £17,175 in 1892, and 483,463 lbs. of £18,000 value in 1891. Paper and its appliances exported to Santander from European countries during 1892 were: England 105,000 lbs., France 8,135 lbs., Belgium, 78,114 lbs., and Germany 278,500 lbs. It will be seen that Germany comes first, Great Britain second, Belgium third, and France fourth.

China.—A report on last year's trade of Shanghai, recently published, gives a comparative table of principal exports since the year 1870. Paper in 1870 averaged 260,000 Haikwan taels; 1875, 429,000; 1880, 512,000; 1885, 595,000; 1890, 1,359,000; and in 1892, 1,592,000. Shanghai imports included foreign paper to the extent of 6,019 piculs of the value of 179,703 taels. No statistics are given for 1892. Native paper was imported at Shanghai in 1891 to the extent of 151,315 piculs, of the value of 1,654,431 taels. Last year's figures were 161,876 piculs, of the value of 1,876,254 taels. Paper was exported from Shanghai in 1891 to the extent of 131,304 piculs, of the value of 1,425,061 taels; in 1892, 157,639 piculs, of the value of 1,583,230 taels. The exchange may be reckoned to be at 4s. 4d. to the tael. The return of the principal articles of export, including re-exports, from Canton shows 2,435,644-lbs. of paper, of the value of £17,549 in 1892; and 1,865,721-lbs., of the value of £42,827 in 1891. The imports into Tientsin in 1892 included first quality papers of the quantity of 3,354,800-lbs. of the value of £96,975; in 1891, 3,920,800-lbs., of the value of £136,003.

WHO'S WHO?

THE PERSONNEL OF THE PAPER, STATIONERY, PRINTING AND ALLIED TRADES.

Everyone must have observed that of late there has been a remarkable change in the style of a very large proportion of the oldest and largest paper, stationery, and printing concerns. The word "Limited" has become quite familiar as an integral part of their nomenclature. This affix was, as we all know, made obligatory by the provisions of "The Companies Act" (25 and 26 Vict. c. 89), which was passed in 1862. Our own Legislature, foreseeing the inconveniences which might be caused by the names of the acting responsible members of a firm not being given, provided for compulsory publication of the names of the shareholders in such companies. These returns are, as a rule, accurately and regularly made up and issued. But they are in a form which to the great majority of the public is quite unavailable. Not one person in a thousand knows "Who's Who" in a concern of even general repute. Yet for many reasons, and on divers occasions it is desirable to know the personnel of the company in question. This information we are about to supply. We shall do it from official and authentic data, and in no merely prying spirit. No reflection on the stability of any firm will be implied. The names of the parties constituting it will be given, and their shares in its capital stated, so far as official documents disclose them. The information we think will be both useful and interesting. Readers will know whom they have to deal with when transacting business with a limited liability company, and a contribution will be made to current trade history which the future annalist may greatly appreciate.

TOVIL PAPER Co., Limited.

The registration of this company dates back to the 15th January, 1873. Nominal capital £60,000, divided into 6,000 shares of £10 each. Objects: The acquisition by purchase, taking in exchange or on lease or agreement, or otherwise under any absolute or conditional contract deed or agreement of lands, buildings, mills, &c., &c., and in the first instance the acquisition of the Tovil Paper Mills, situate at Tovil, Maidstone, with its business buildings, machinery, plant, utensils, and other property and effects, of every or any description, together with the business, rights, trade marks, patent and other rights and privileges, and to carry on the main business of manufacturers of paper, millboard, cardboard, and all the branches of such business, including the importing and exporting of linen and other rags, straw, esparto grass, palm leaves, size, and other articles of commerce of every description, whether required for the manufacture of paper or otherwise, &c., &c., &c.

The names of the first subscribers were: L. D. Wigan, Oakwood, Maidstone, banker; W. F. Mercer, Boxley, Maidstone, banker; A. Cooper, Park-road, Twickenham, accountant; H. Cooper, Hope Lodge, Woodford, manufacturer; Francis Cooper, 14, George-street, Mansion House, E.C., accountant; E. H. Fletcher, 32, Lorn-road, Brixton, accountant; W. Milward, Osmond-row, Richmond. The first directors were: L. D. Wigan, W. F. Mercers, and Francis Cooper.

The number of directors was limited to three and was not to be more than seven. The holding of one share was sufficient qualification for a directorship.

By a memorandum of agreement dated 13th September 1887, made between Messrs. Wigan and Mercers (of Maidstone, bankers) of the one part and the company of the other part, it is stated that the company purchased what are therein referred to as "certain premises at or near Maidstone" for the price of 1,000 shares in the company, which shares were alloted as follows:

Samuel Mercers	200
Henry Tasker	200
W. F. Mercers...	200
J. A. Wigan	200
Randall Mercer	200

The last summary issued is dated 15th November, 1892, and the document states that 3,308 shares have been taken up, that there has been called up on 2,308 shares £10, and that the total amount received is £23,080. The total amount agreed to be considered as paid on 1,000 shares is £10,000. The names and holdings of the shareholders are:—

Exors of A. Cooper, 39, Cannon-street, E.C.... ...	10
Chas. Cooper, The Pagoda, Blackheath, gentleman	15
Ernest Cooper, 14, George street, Mansion House, chartered accountant	25
Francis Cooper, 14, George Street, Mansion House, chartered accountant	25
E. H. Fletcher, Stoneclough, Sidcup, chartered accountant	5
Randal Mercer, Kentish Bank, Maidstone, banker...	450
Samuel Mercer, Kentish Bank, Maidstone	700
W. F. Mercer, Boxley, Maidstone, banker	926
H. Tasker, Kentish Bank, Maidstone, banker ...	700
J. A. Wigan, Kentish Bank, Maidstone, banker ...	452
Total	3,308

———o———

GILLESPIE and MASON, Limited.

Registered 26th November, 1891, with a nominal capital of £50,000, divided into 5,000 shares of £10 each, to acquire and take over as a going concern the business of paper manufacturers, lately carried on by Thomas John Gillespie, of Newton-le-Willows, in the county of Lancaster. The first signatories to the company were: Thomas John Gillespie, Park House, Newton-le-Willows, paper manufacturer; Richard Barton, Blythsdale, Newton-le-Willows, papermaker; C. B. F. Borrow, Newton-le-Willows, glass manufacturer; Samuel Leather, Mill-lane, Newton-le-Willows, bookkeeper; John Bryce, Mill-lane, Newton-le-Willows, foreman; Edmund Walker, Mill-lane, Newton-le-Willows, foreman; John Broadbent, Hermitage Green, Newton-le-Willows, bookkeeper.

Thomas John Gillespie, Charles Bellford Borron, and Richard Barton were appointed first directors, and the number of the directors was not to be less than two nor more than six.

One agreement only is filed, and this is made between Thomas John Gillespie and the company, and refers to the purchase of the business by the company. The consideration paid consisted in part of the sum of £31,547 17s. 5d., satisfied by the allotment of shares and a payment of £7 17s. 5d. in cash. The remainder of the consideration for the transfer, was the satisfaction by the company of all debts, contracts, and obligations of the business.

The summary of the capital and shares of the company, dated 19th March, 1892, is as follows:

Shares taken up, 3189.
Called upon 35 shares, £350.
Total amount received, £350.
Agreed to be considered as paid on 3,154 shares, £31,540.

SHAREHOLDERS.

Thomas John Gillespie, Park House, Newton-le-Willows, paper manufacturer	3,154
C. B. F. Borrow, Newton-le-Willows, glass manufacturer	11
Richard Barton, Blythsdale, Newton-le-Willows, papermaker...	10
Samuel Leather, Mill-lane, Newton-le-Willows, bookkeeper	5
J. Bryce, Mill-lane, Newton-le-Willows, foreman ...	5
E. Walker, Mill-lane, Newton-le-Willows, foreman	3
J. Broadbent, Hermitage Green, Newton-le-Willows, bookkeeper	1

———o———

CARRON GROVE PAPER Co., Limited.

This company was incorporated under the Companies Acts of 1862 and 1867 as a limited liability company on the 31st May, 1877, and judging from its record contained in the Exchequer Office, Edinburgh, its shareholders have been few and confined to one circle. The company was established for the purchase of lands or otherwise, to acquire the Carron Paper Works, situated near Denny, in the county of Stirling, and the plant, machinery, and stock therein; the land adjoining to, or in the neighbourhood; the works and buildings including the Tamarce Weal Mill and Randolph Mill. The capital was £50,000, with power to increase it if such was deemed expedient, by the creation and issue of new shares, either ordinary or having such preference or priority and special privileges attached thereto, as might be determined by special resolution of the company. The capital of £50,000 was divided into 10,000 shares of £5 each, and the number of shares allocated on 5th October of the year in which the company was registered was 6,450. There was then called up on these shares £1 (one shareholder, Mr. James Johnstone, paid in £1,100), the total sum paid up being £7,550. The original subscribers to the company were David MacGibbon, architect, Edinburgh, 1,500 shares; Henry Moffat, C.A., Edinburgh, 500 shares; Thomas Ross, architect, Edinburgh, 100 shares; Alexander T. Niven, C.A., Edinburgh, 500 shares; R. Cameron Cowan, C.A., Edinburgh, 500 shares; James Johnstone, manager Esk Paper Mills, Penicuik, 400 shares. In addition to these shares were originally held by J. R. Mac Gibbon, Mayfield, editor, 500; Francis Black (of A. and C. Black, publishers), 200; Alexander P. Waddall, W.S., 4, Great Stuart-street, Edinburgh, 250; Charles William Cowan, Grange, Edinburgh, 100; Adam Beattie, 18, Grosvenor-street, Edinburgh, 200; John Russell, farmer. Saughton Hall, Mains, Edinburgh, 200. Total 6,450 shares. On the 10th January, 1879, there was no change in the number of shares issued, the company meantime working away on the capital subscribed. By this time, however, Mr. Niven had sold out 300 shares, 100 going to Mr. Russell and 200 to William Lambiel Moffat, architect, Edinburgh. According to the return made to the office of joint stock companies on 12th January, 1880, it seems that of the 10,000 shares of £5, the number taken up remained the same, but an additional call of 10s. had been made, the amount now subscribed being £11,275, and there were no unpaid calls. Mr. James R. MacGibbons shares were transferred to James Romanes, C.A., 42, Castle-street, Edinburgh, who got 400, and Mr. Francis Black added 100 to his existing interest in the company. By 1882 Mr. Romanes had increased his shares to 800, and Mr. Francis Black held altogether 600 shares. Mr. A. P. Waddell sold out, and others increased their interest in the concern slightly. In 1884 the company had 300 of its own shares, and the other changes consisted principally of transferences from one member of the association to another, David MacGibbon increasing his interest in the concern to 1,700 shares. In 1885 there was no material change in the share list, but in 1887 Mr. Mac Gibbon reduced his interest to 900 shares, and Mr. Johnstone, who was then manager of the company's mills, increased his to 1,050. In 1889 Mr. Thos. Muir, Mordington, Berwick-on-Tweed, as executor for Mr. Johnstone's trustees, was returned as holding these 1,050 shares. In 1890 there were added to the list of shareholders Mr. John Wilson, ex-M.P., Edinburgh, 250 shares; William Walker, manager at Carron-grove Mills, 350 shares, and the trustees of the late Mr. Johnstone reduced their interest to 400 shares. By 1891 £3 had been called up on each share issued, and then the subscribed capital amounted to £20,300, the total number of shares issued being 6,600. Only £300 of the calls had not been paid. One or two new shareholders were added in this year, including Mr. Gulland, paper agent, 6, Deangate-hill, London, who held 300 shares. By the 4th January, 1892, £4 10s. had been called up on the shares issued, and Mr. Gulland, in anticipation of a further call, paid his fully up, the total amount subscribed then being £31,855. Of the total calls £400 remained unpaid. In addition to those already mentioned as holding shares, the following were added to the list of shareholders as at 11th January, 1893, viz., Mrs. Wilhelmina Moffat, Upper Norwood, London, 200; Mrs. Barbara Ross, widow, Villa Beatrice, Naples, Italy, 150; John Johnstone, Post Cliffe, Peter-Culter, Aberdeen, papermaker, 800; James Alexander Learney, Arms Hotel, Torphins, Aberdeenshire, 20; John W. Johnstone. The Hollies, Sunny Gardens, Hendon, Middlesex, 20, the total issued at the date mentioned being 7,090. The registered office of the company is at 30, Queen-street.

JACKSON'S MILLBOARD AND PAPER CO., Limited.

The company was registered on the 24th July, 1891, with a nominal capital of £10,000, divided into 1,000 shares of £10 each, to carry on the trade or business of millboard manufacturers, paper manufacturers, wholesale stationers, and paper stock merchants in all its branches, and of dealers in the materials used in the manufacture of millboards and paper, and also of manufacturers of and dealers in any other article or thing of a character similar or analogous to the foregoing or connected therewith, or conveniently carried on in conjunction therewith; also to acquire by purchase, exchange, lease, or otherwise, real or other property, and any rights or privileges, patents, inventions, or trade marks necessary or convenient for the purposes of the company, and in particular any land, building, machinery, plant or stock-in-trade, and to erect works suitable for carrying on the business of the company, and to enter into an agreement with John Hezekiah Jackson and Frederick Jackson for the purchase of the business of millboard manufacture carried on by John Hezekiah, at Egham's Green, Wooburn, in the County of Buckingham, and of the business of wholesale stationer and paper stock merchant, carried on by Frederick Jackson, at 90, Upper Ground-street, London, and to do all things calculated directly or indirectly to enhance the value of the company's property or rights.

The subscribers to the articles of association were:—J. H. Jackson, Wooburn, Bucks, millboard maker; Frederick Jackson, Eghams Green, Wooburn, Bucks, wholesale stationers; Eliza Jackson (wife of J. H. Jackson); A. Smith, 90, Upper Ground-street, London, commercial traveller; Bernard Smith, 41, Wilson-road, Camberwell, commercial traveller; H. W. Mansel, 90, Upper Ground-street, London, mercantile clerk; Harriett A. Jackson (wife of Frederick Jackson).

The directors were not to be less than two in number, nor more than five. J. H. Jackson and F. Jackson were appointed first directors, their remuneration being decided in general meeting. The holding of £100 in shares is a director's qualification. F. Jackson was appointed first managing director for three years at a salary of £300 per year. The purchase price of the business carried on by J. H. Jackson was £4,905 12s. 1d., paid by 490 fully paid shares of £10 each, and the sum of £5 12s. 1d. in cash. F. Jackson received for his business the sum of £1,750 3s. 3d., paid by 175 fully paid shares of £10, and £8 3s. 3d. in cash. The last summary of capital and shares filed is dated 21st Sept. and is as follows:—Shares taken up, 667; called up on each of seven shares, £10; total amount received, £70; agreed to be considered as paid on 660 shares, £6,600. The shareholders names are:—

J. H. Jackson, Wooburn, Bucks, millboard maker... 247
F. Jackson, Egham Green, wholesale stationer ... 201
Mrs. Eliza Jackson 1
[illegible]ith, 90, Upper Ground-street, London, com[illegible]cial traveller 1
Bernard C. Smith, 41, Wilson-road, commercial traveller 51
W. H. Mansel, 90, Upper Ground-street, London, clerk 1
Harriet A. Jackson, Egham Green 1
J. Thomas, Wooburn, Bucks, papermaker 10
Miss Mary Comber, 18, Dorset-gardens, Brighton ... 118
W. Smith, 41, Wilson-road, Camberwell, cle k ... 36

PAPER & PULP MILL SHARES.

(Report received from Mr. F. D. DEAN, 36, Corporation Street, Manchester.)

Nominal Amnt	Amnt Paid	Name of Company	Last dividend	Price.
7	7	Bury Paper, ord.	nil	4¼—4¾
7	7	do. do. 6% pref.	6%	4¾—5
100	100	do. do. deb.	5%	103—106
10	10	Bath Paper Mill Co. Lim.	7½%	6—7
10	10	Bergvik Co., def.	15%	13½
100	100	do. do. 6% cum. pref.	6%	10⅞—11⅛
10	10	do. do. deb.	5%	105—110
5	3½	Burnley Paper Co.	3/-	77/6—80/0
5	3½	Darwen Paper Co.	10%	5½—6½
10	10	East Lancashire Co.	nil	4¼—4¾
10	10	do. do. 6% pref.	nil	6½—7
5	5	do. do. bonus	nil	1½—2
5	5	Hyde Paper Co.	4%	4½—5
5	4	North of Ireland Paper Co.	nil	2¼—2¾
10	5	Ramsbottom Paper Co.	17½%	12¼—12¾
5	4½	Roach Bridge Paper Co.	5%	3—3½
5	5	Star Paper Co.	10%	6—6½
5	3	do. do. 10% pref. cum.	10%	4¾—5¼
50	50	do. do. deb.	6%	55—56
5	2½	Kellner Partingt'n Pulp Co	—	62/0—£4/0

SUMMARY OF

IMPORTS & EXPORTS,

FOR THE WEEK ENDING TUESDAY LAST.

London, Liverpool, Bristol, Southampton, Hull, Fleetwood, Harwich, Folkestone, Newhaven, Dover, &c.

IMPORTS.

Paper	21961 bales	Pasteboards	14525 pkgs.
"	385 cases	Strawboards	12192 "
"	603 rolls	Stationery...... ...	40 cases
Millboards	9362 pkgs.	Tissues	147 pkgs.

EXPORTS.

BRITISH GOODS.			
		Waste	334 tons
Paper	1337 cwt.	Stock	139 "
Writing Paper ...	2812 "	FOREIGN GOODS.	
Printing Paper	3987 "	Paper	428 cwt.
"	£54 value	Writing Paper...	35 "
Cardboards	20 cwt.	Printing Paper...	471 "
Stationery......	£13893 value	Strawboards	241 "
Strawboard Cuttings	46 tons	Stationery	£574 value
		Parchment	£20 "
Parchment	£29 value	Wood Pulp	124 tons
Millboards	71 cwt.	Stock	4 "

Glasgow, Greenock, Port-Glasgow, Troon, Grangemouth, &c.

IMPORTS.

Paper	795 bales	Paper	9 cases

EXPORTS.

Printing Paper..	1905 cwt.	Millboards	74 cwt.
Writing Paper...	667 "	Bags	35 "
Wrapping Paper	430 "	Pasteboards	11 "
Envelopes	70 "	Stock	387½ "

Leith, Granton, Boness, Dundee, &c.

IMPORTS.

Paper	473 bales	Pasteboards	260 pkgs.
"	3 cases	Envelopes	57 "

PAPER EXPORTS.

FOR THE WEEK ENDING TUESDAY LAST;

	Printings.	Writings.	Other Kinds.
AUSTRALIA	3720 cwts.	1538 cwts.	576 cwts.
AFRICA	19 ,,	80 ,,	55 ,,
ARGENTINE ...	349 ,,	598 ,,	16 ,,
BELGIUM	— ,,	53 ,,	4 ,,
B. WEST INDIES...	6 ,,	6 ,,	3 ,,
B. GUIANA	— ,,	2 ,,	375 ,,
CHANNEL ISLES	2 ,,	— ,,	— ,,
CANADA	— ,,	3 ,,	2 ,,
CAPE COLONY ...	405 ,,	157 ,,	886 ,,
CHINA	133 ,,	40 ,,	45 ,,
DENMARK	43 ,,	— ,,	1 ,,
FRANCE	16 ,,	138 ,,	13 ,,
EGYPT	29 ,,	— ,,	— ,,
GERMANY	16 ,,	— ,,	— ,,
HOLLAND	4 ,,	— ,,	12 ,,
INDIA	442 ,,	315 ,,	86 ,,
JAPAN	44 ,,	15 ,,	2 ,,
MADAGASCAR ...	8 ,,	— ,,	— ,,
NEW ZEALAND ...	496 ,,	298 ,,	98 ,,
NORWAY	123 ,,	— ,,	— ,,
PORTUGAL	— ,,	2 ,,	— ,,
RUSSIA	— ,,	9 ,,	5 ,,
S. AMERICA... ...	— ,,	100 ,,	— ,,
SPAIN	4 ,,	41 ,,	— ,,
STRAIT Settlements	— ,,	5 ,,	— ,,
TURKEY	10 ,,	6 ,,	— ,,
U.S.A.	197 ,,	4 ,,	24 ,,
W. INDIES	— ,,	6 ,,	— ,,

———o———

PAPER IMPORTS.

FOR THE WEEK ENDING TUESDAY LAST:

AUSTRALIA ...	17 bales	GERMANY ...	[illegible]888 bales
BELGIUM ...	1200 ,,	,, ...	4 cases
,, ...	128 cases	HOLLAND ...	8405 bales
CHINA	28 bales	,, ...	85 cases
,, ...	21 cases	,, ...	30 rolls
DENMARK ...	70 bales	NORWAY ...	7754 bales
EGYPT	1 case	PRUSSIA ...	76 ,,
FINLAND ...	159 bales	RUSSIA ...	3 ,,
,, ...	7 cases	SWEDEN ...	2393 ,,
FRANCE ...	241 bales	U.S.A.	170 cases
,, ...	129 cases	,, ...	519 rolls

Including the Following:

Quantity	From	Importer	Port.
204 cases	Boston	B. Galloway	London
246 bales	Christiania	Christophersen & Co	,,
54 ,,	,,	J. Hamilton	,,
117 ,,	,,	F. G. Foulger	,,
173 ,,	,,	G. F. Green & Co	,,
21 ,,	,,	J. Spicer & Son	,,
6 ,,	,,	Lon. & Rhine S. Co	,,
24 ,,	,,	Alsing & Co	,,
17 ,,	,,	Hernu, Peron & Co	,,
9 ,,	Christiansand	J. Spicer & Son	,,
[illegible] ,,	,,	R. L. Lundgren	,,
117 ,,	Danzig	E. & E. Sabel	,,
34 ,,	,,	H. Huber & Co	,,
6 ,,	,,	E. B. Sabel	,,
17 ,,	Drammen	Hernu, Peron & Co	,,
290 ,,	,,	Crabb & Co	,,
74 ,,	,,	Alsing & Co	,,
25 ,,	,,	G. Smythe & Co	,,
31 ,,	,,	W. D. Edwards	,,
20 ,,	,,	J. Spicer & Son	,,
10 ,,	,,	Schenkenwald & Co	,,
[illegible] ,,	,,	G. F Green & Co	,,
[illegible] ,,	Gothenburg	Schenkenwald & Co	,,
50 ,,	,,	Hummell & Co	,,
24 ,,	,,	Alsing & Co	,,
22 ,,	,,	Simmons & Co	,,
5 ,,	,,	Sabel & Co	,,
[illegible] ,,	Helsingfors	Crabb & Co	,,
78 ,,	,,	J. Spicer & Sons	,,
7 ,,	,,	Townsend Son & Co	,,
30 ,,	,,	E. Byrne & Co	,,
8 ,,	,,	Spicer Bros	,,
135 ,,	,,	J. Holloway	,,
[illegible] ,,	,,	J. Hamilton	,,
102 bales	,,	G. E. Koenigsfeld	London
208 ,,	,,	W. D. Edwards	,,
165 rolls	,,	G. E. Koenigsfeld & Son	,,
41 bales	Marseilles	J. Pollock & Son	,,
85 ,,	Norrkoping	J. Spicer & Son	,,
2820 ,,	,,	Schenkenwald & Co	,,
100 ,,	Stettin	Becker & Ulrich	,,
43 ,,	,,	F. Dickinson & Co	,,
92 ,,	,,	J. Spicer & Son	,,
99 ,,	,,	B. Beer	,,
50 ,,	,,	W. Benscher	,,
3 ,,	St. Petersburg	W. Simpson & Co	,,
508 ,,	Uddevalla	Williams & Co	,,
415 ,,	,,	Osborne & Shearman	,,
164 ,,	,,	R. L. Lundgren	,,
522 ,,	,,	D. Gulland	,,
156 ,,	,,	Alsing & Co	,,

Printed and Published EVERY FRIDAY

AT 58, SHOE LANE, LONDON, E.C.,

By W. JOHN STONHILL.

ESTABLISHED 1878.

FRIDAY, OCTOBER 20, 1893.

A WORD more about that fluctuating St. Neot's Paper Mill. Mr. John McNish, the energetic chairman, is not happy. In March last the directors of the St. Neot's Paper Mill Co., Ltd., stated they had made arrangements for the entire re-modelling and re-equipment of the works. Nothing, however, has been done up to date. It would occupy too much space to go fully into the alleged causes of delay and the various changes of late. After a lapse of more than six months the reconstruction of the mill is once more to be considered. The notification (published in another column) records that the "landlord" will re-equip the mill. Generous landlord! Will he require debentures? We read that "the necessary new shares *and debentures* have been provided."

WOOD PULP importations continue to increase. Great Britain now draws large supplies from other countries as well as Scandinavia, as we pointed out, in commenting upon the Board of Trade returns, in our last issue. Perhaps it will be as well, however, to take the respective values for the nine months of 1893 and two preceding years :—

	1891	1892	1893
From Norway	£310,165	£346,259	£377,401
From other countries ...	285,841	324,518	437,757

The total in 1893 amounts to £815,158, against £596,006, surely evidence enough to condemn those *quidnuncs* who persistently maintain that wood pulp will never be appreciated in this country. It will be seen, however, that the value of the pulp from Norway has not increased so largely as from other countries. Comparing 1891 with 1893, Norwegian trade has increased 21½ per cent., and that of other countries 53 per cent.

PAPERMAKERS on the selected list compiled by the officials of H.M. Stationery Office will have the opportunity of tendering on Tuesday next for the various descriptions of paper specified in the schedule submitted to them. The total quantity amounts to some 52,275 reams.

ACCORDING to the *Droguisten Zeitung*, a patent has been refused in Germany for an invention consisting in the preparation of paper made with the ordinary raw materials to which asbestos and parchment size have been added. Any writing in ink on this paper may be removed by the application of a wet sponge. The paper pulp, after having been compressed by a roller, is submerged for a period of from 6 to 36 seconds, according to the thickness of the paper, in concentrated sulphuric acid of 20 degrees strength, diluted with from 10 to 15 per cent. of water. The paper is then pressed between glass rollers, and it is then successively tempered in water in an ammoniacal solution between rollers, and dried. It is said that the final product bears a complete resemblance to ordinary paper. Its sale has been prohibited, with a view to prevent the abuses to which it might easily be put.

PAPER and kindred articles are in growing request at Alexandria, judging from reports recently issued. Wonder is expressed that British participation is not larger, as exporters enjoy greater shipping facilities, and are able to compete in point of quality, and probably in price. In printings and writings there is a decided preference for British makes, and last year's trade amounted to £3,998, against £2,283 in the preceding year. This increase of 75 per cent. is very satisfactory, and it is to be hoped that further business will show a corresponding expansion.

IT is not often we grumble! By nearly every post, however, we get requests for data concerning not only trade matters and technical subjects, but affecting trade marks, shipping clauses, merchandise marks, customs queries, and innumerable subjects of a more or less money-saving character. We are always glad to be of service to our subscribers, for we recognise that they are the backbone of our influence, and that without them our efforts to thoroughly represent the paper trade would fall on desert soil and be

unproductive to our advertisers. But we feel aggrieved with numerous gentlemen who want something for nothing so frequently, coolly informing us when we put the query to them as to why they are not subscribers, that they read the *World's Paper Trade Review* at Mr. So and So's, an Upper Thames-street stationer, or see it filed at the offices of a dealer or shipping agent in Manchester, Glasgow, Berlin, Hamburg, Copenhagen, Drammen, Rotterdam, or Christiania, at the British Consuls, or elsewhere. It is very gratifying to have proof of the widespread interest and influence of our paper, but we must really notify to the gentlemen who do not pay that we cannot supply them with something for nothing in the way of replies to commercial queries. Concerning the products and appliances of our advertisers we are at all times pleased to answer enquiries.

The Belgian Consul-General at Philadelphia, in reporting upon the manufacture of wood pulp in the United States, says that from 1881 to 1891 the increase in production was about 500 per cent. It is estimated that at the present time this industry consumes 1,000,000 cords of wood annually, and meanwhile the production is still far from what it might be were it not for the fear of overstocking the market. The Consul states that newspapers and books absorb annually in the United States 1,000,000,000 lbs. of paper, and the wood pulp would certainly supply two-thirds of this quantity. The wood pulp industry is represented by 22 States, of which 13 are on the Atlantic coast, two on the Pacific coast, and seven in the interior. It is in New York that the largest number of factories are to be found; they were 75 in 1890, or one-third of the total figure, but they are probably more numerous at the present time, for the new tariff has increased the duties on wood pulp. It formerly paid 10 per cent., it is now taxed at 2·50 dolls. per ton (dry weight) for pulp produced mechanically, at 6 dolls. per ton (dry weight) for that produced chemically but not bleached, and at 7 dolls. per ton (dry weight) when it is bleached. Notwithstanding these increases, the imports only diminished by 2,196 tons during the fiscal year 1891-92, or 41,118 tons against 43,315, representing respectively a value of 1,820,143 and 1,902,680 dolls.

The Value of Copyrights in some of the balance sheets of limited publishing companies has, we are informed, lately had a rude shock. Private valuations of the properties recorded as very valuable assets have shown them to be decidedly losing properties, and therefore the inclusion as assets of extravagant value seems culpable negligence and misrepresentation amounting almost to dishonesty on the part of the directors.

There are numerous periodicals published in London which have lately barely covered out-of-pocket expenses, and certainly have shown no profit. Papermakers should act warily in allowing credit. The more frequent the publication the greater the loss. This may account for the unusual efforts which are now being made by partnership agents to obtain fresh capital. Even the daily papers contain such advertisements as the following:—

A HIGH-CLASS NEWSPAPER.—A Lady or Gentleman required to Buy a Share in an old-established Weekly of a high and influential standing; the paper does not yield any profits at present, but with additional capital would turn out an excellent property; principals only.

The frankness of the advertiser in admitting that "the paper does not yield any profits" is commendable. Sanguine, certainly.

Capitalists now are certainly being eagerly sought for by would-be publishers. Here is an example:—

WANTED, a Gentleman with £2,000 to Join the Advertiser in publishing a weekly periodical of great interest, and having good prospects of a wide circulation.

Nothing about profits! Why the omission?

Mr. Stead's latest proposal is an "ideal daily newspaper," with a capital of £130,000, to be supplied by 100,000 readers themselves, and to each of those yet-to-come subscribers Mr. Stead will give a debenture bond for £1, redeemable at his own option. He registers the company for £20, issued to himself, and truly the smallest capital ever proposed for a daily newspaper. His object in this is, in his own words, "not philanthropic nor generous; it is good business." The delusively named "debentures" are to carry 5 per cent. interest. Thus Mr. Stead avoids risk—to himself. The scheme is fully propounded in Mr. Stead's monthly, *The Review of Reviews.*

WORLD'S PAPER TRADE REVIEW OFFICE,
58, SHOE LANE, LONDON, E.C.
OCTOBER 19, 1893.

MARKET REPORT

and RECORD of IMPORTS

Of Foreign Rags, Wood Pulp, Esparto, Paper, Millboards, Strawboards, &c., at the Ports of London Liverpool, Southampton, Bristol, Hull, Fleetwood, Middlesborough, Glasgow, Grangemouth, Granton, Dundee, Leith, Dover, Folkestone, and Newhaven, for the WEEK ENDING OCTOBER 18.

From SPECIAL Sources and Telegrams.

Telegrams—"STONHILL, LONDON."

CHEMICALS. — The chemical market is still without activity, and new business is very limited. Manchester reports show that BLEACHING POWDER and SODA ASH have been sold fairly well for delivery over next year. The quotation for the former article at Newcastle is about £8, and £8 5s. soft wood casks on rail Lancashire. For 58% ALKALI figures vary from £5 7s. 6d. to £5 12s. 6d. There is a scarcity of CAUSTIC SODA; buyers, however, do not appear anxious to close contracts, doubtless owing to new competitive works about to be started up. The Tyne quotation for 77% is £11 5s. SODA CRYSTALS are firm at £3 5s. to £3 10s. barrels, and £3 to £3 5s. in bags. SULPHUR is quoted at from £4 to £4 2s. 6d.

Prices are nominally as follows:

Article	Package		Delivery	Terms	£	s.	d.
Alkali, 58%	tierces	...	f.o.r. works	2½%	5	10	0
,, 58%	bags	...	,, ,,	2½%	5	5	0
58%	...	...	f.o.b. Liverpool	2½%	5	12	6
Alum (Ground),	tierces	...	,, Liverpool	2½%	5	7	6
,, ,,	barrels	...	,, ,,	2½%	5	17	6
,, ,,	tierces	...	,, Hull	2½%	5	3	0
,,	,,	...	Goole	2½%	5	3	0
Alum (Lump)	,,	...	f.o.b. Liverpool	2½%	4	17	6
,, ,,	barrels	...	,, ,,	2½%	5	0	0
,, ,,	tierces	...	,, Hull	2½%	4	13	0
,, ,,	,,	...	Goole	2½%	4	13	0
,,	,,	...	London	2½%	5	5	0
,,	,,	...	f.a.s. Glasgow	2½%	5	5	0
Alumina Sulphate,	casks		f.o.b. Tyne		4	2	6
,, ,,	bags		,, ,,		3	17	6
Aluminoferric Cake,	slabs		Liverpool ...	...	2	15	0
,, ,,	tierces		,, ...	...	3	2	6
Alumina Cake,	slabs	...	Glasgow	...	2	15	0
,, ,,	tierces	...	,,	...	3	2	6
Aluminous Cake,	casks	...	Manchester	3½%	2	7	6
,, ,,	,,	...	Newcastle	2½%	2	10	0
,, ,,	,,	...	London	2½%	3	0	0
,, ,,	bags	...	,,	2½%	2	17	9
Blanc Fixe ...	...	...	f.o.b. Tyne	net	7	10	0
Bleach, 35%	...	...	,, ,,	net	8	0	0
,, (soft wood)		...	f.o.r. Lancs.	net	8	5	0
,, (hard wood)		...	f.o.b. Liverpool	net	8	10	0
...	...	...	landed London	2½%	9	0	0
Borax (crystals)	...	...	... ...	net	29	0	6
powdered	...	...	... ...	net	30	0	0
Caustic Cream, 60%		...	f.o.r. Lancs.	net	9	2	6
,, ,, 60%		...	f.o.b. Liverpool	net	9	7	6
,, Bottoms		...	,, ,,	net	6	15	0
,, ,,	...	...	f.o.b. Tyne	net	6	15	0
Chloride of Barium		...	f.o.b. Tyne	net	7	10	0
Caustic White 76-77%		...	f.o.r. Newcastle	net	11	15	0
,, ,, 77%		f.o.r. or	f.o.b. Tyne	net	12	0	0
,, ,, 74%		...	f.o.b. Liverpool	net	12	0	0
,, ,, 70%		...	,, ,,	net	11	0	0
,, ,, 70%		...	,, Hull	net	11	0	0
,, ,, 70%		...	f.o.r. London	net	10	15	0
,, ,, 70%		...	,, Lancs.,	net	10	17	6
,, ,, 60%		...	,, London	net	9	15	0
,, ,, 60%		...	f.o.b. Liverpool	net	10	0	0
Carbonat'd Ash 58%		...	,, ,,	net	4	10	0
48%		...	,, ,,	net	4	0	0
,, 58%		...	f.o.r. Widnes	net	4	7	6
,, 48%		...	,, ,,	net	3	17	6
Hypo-Sulphite of Soda...			f.o.r Tyne		5	15	0
,, ,,	10-ton lots		ex ship Liverp'l	net	6	10	0
Oxalic Acid ...	...	...	f.o.b. Liverpool	3½%	per lb		[illegible]
Salt Cake ...	...	...	,, works	net	1	10	0
Soda Ash, 52%	...	...	f.o.b. Tyne	net	4	0	0
,, 52%	...	...	ex ship Thames	1%	4	12	6
,, 52%	...	...	f.o.b. Liverpool	1%	4	5	0
Soda Crystals	...	...	,, Tyne	net	2	10	0
,, ,,	...	...	ex ship Thames	2½%	3	0	0
,, ,,	...	...	f.o.b. Liverpool	net	3	5	0
Sulphur, roll	...	...	f.o.r. works	2½%	7	17	6
,, flowers	...	...	,, ,,	2½%	9	10	0
,, recovered		...	,, ,,	2½%	4	2	6
Sulphate of Ammonia	,,		,, ,,	2½%	13	10	0
,, of Copper	...		,, Liverpool	5%	16	0	0

FOREIGN.—F.o.b. Continental port:

Article	£	s.	d.
Alkali, 58% 2-cwt. bags £4 10/0; 10-cwt. casks ...	5	0	0
Caustic Soda, 70-72%	10	12	6
Hypo-Sulphite of Soda 10-ton lots casks	6	0	0
Sulphate of Alumina 7-8 cwt. casks net c.i.f. Ldn	4	7	
Blanc Fixe (c.i.f. London)	7	12	6

ESPARTO.—A moderate enquiry for most descriptions, but generally at prices which sellers are unwilling to accept and business rather drags. Values are now at such a low point as to inspire importers with caution in taking heavy engagements.

Prices c.i.f. London and Leith, or f.o.r. Cardiff, Garston and Tyne Docks are nominally as follows:

Kind	Quality	£	s.	d.		£	s.	d.
Spanish—	Fair to Good ...	£5	5	0	to	5	10	0
,,	Fine to Best ...	5	10	0	,,	5	15	0
Oran —	Fair to Good ...	3	5	0	,,	3	10	0
,,	First Quality...	3	15	0	,,	3	17	6
Tripoli —	Hand-picked ...	3	15	0	,,	3	17	6
,,	Fair Average...	3	7	6	,,	3	10	0
Bona & Philippeville	...	3	15	0	,,	3	17	6

WEEK'S IMPORTS.

Quantity	From	Importer	Port.
1338 trusses	Aguilas	To order	Grangemouth
714 tons	Oran	Jacobs. Marcus & Co	Granton
578 bales	,,	To order	London
4474 ,,	Tripoli	I. Hassan	,,

CHEMICAL WOOD PULPS. — SULPHITE and SODA pulps are easier in price, owing to increased supplies coming into the market.

Prices, ex steamer, London, Hull, Newcastle, Leith and Glasgow are nominally as follows:

Kind	£	s.	d.		£	s.	d.
SULPHITE, Unbleached, Common	£10	15	0	to	11	0	0
,, Superior	11	10	0	,,	12	10	0
,, ,, 50% moisture, d.w.	11	10	0	,,	12	2	6
,, Extra	13	0	0	,,	14	0	0
,, Bleached, moist					16	10	0
,, Unbleached, English, del. Lancs. ...					10	15	0
,, ,, ,, No. 1, ex mills, Ldn.					10	10	0
,, ,, ,, No. 2, ,, ,,					9	15	0
SODA, Unbleached, Common ...	10	5	0	,,	10	10	0
,, ,, Extra... ...	10	10	0	,,	11	0	0
,, Half-Bleached	12	10	0	,,	14	0	0
SULPHATE, Unbleached, Common	10	10	0	,,	11	0	0
,, Extra	11	0	0	,,	12	0	0
,, Half-Bleached	13	10	0	,,	14	0	0
Bleached	15	0	0	,,	16	0	

MECHANICAL WOOD PULPS.—Pine pulp is extremely firm, and for early delivery there is scarcely any pulp available, whilst about 70% of the full output for 1894 is already sold, and those makers who have still any to sell are standing out for advanced prices.

Prices, ex steamer, London, Hull, Newcastle, Leith and Glasgow are nominally as follows:

Kind	£	s.	d.		£	s.	d.
MECHANICAL, Aspen, Dry ...	£7	10	0	to	8	0	0
Pine, Dry	6	12	6	,,	7	0	0
Pine, Moist	3	7	6	,,	3	10	0
Moist Brown	3	2	6	,,	3	5	0
Single sorted	2	7	6	,,	2	10	0
Dry Brown	6	5	0	,,	6	10	0

WEEK'S IMPORTS.

Quantity	From	Importer	Port.
1503 bales	Abus	Jensen & Glads	London
111 ,,	Abo	To order	Hull
779 ,,	Christiania	,,	,,
334 ,,	,,	,,	Grangemouth
406 ,,	,,	W. G. Taylor & Co	London
204 ,,	,,	Henderson, Craig & Co	,,
15 cases	,,	Johnsen & Co	,,
1318 bales	Drammen	W. Grant & Co	Leith
1200 ,,	,,	To order	Liverpool
4000 ,,	,,	,,	,,
2460 ,,	,,	Christophersen & Co	London
500 ,,	,,	W. D. Cook & Co	,,
150 ,,	,,	To order	,,
980 ,,	,,	M. G. Skramnes	,,
480 ,,	Drontheim	To order	Hull
282 ,,	Gothenburg	C. Salvesen & Co	Granton
450 ,,	,,	To order	Hull
476 ,,	,,	H. Pearsall	,,
1130 ,,	Helsingfors	To order	London
116 ,,	,,	P. D. Jones	,,
16 ,,	,,	Becker & Ulrich	,,
99 cases	Montreal	To order	Liverpool
120 ,,	Norrkoping	,,	London
380 ,,	,,	,,	Hull
300 ,,	Oporto	,,	London
250 ,,	,,	,,	Liverpool
400 ,,	Rotterdam	,,	Harwich
34 ,,	,,	,,	London
538 ,,	,,	,,	,,
70 ,,	Stettin	W. Friedlaender	,,
920 ,,	,,	To order	,,
325 ,,	Terneuzen	.	,,

Totals from Each Country:

CANADA ...	99 cases	NORWAY ...	15 cases
DENMARK ...	1503 bales	PRUSSIA ...	980 bales
FINLAND ...	1373 ,,	PORTUGAL ...	550 ,,
HOLLAND ...	1227 ,,	SWEDEN ...	1708 ,,
NORWAY ...	12823 ,,		

WEEK'S IMPORTS of WOOD PULP BOARDS.

Quantity	From	Importer	Port
78 bales	Gothenburg	To order	Hull
30 ,,	,,	,,	London

STRAW.—There is a good demand, but owing to short supplies prices remain high and firm.

WEEK'S IMPORTS.

(Purposes unspecified) at principal Ports From

DENMARK ...	3845 bales	HOLLAND ...	885 bales
FRANCE ...	503 ,,	NORWAY ...	17 ,,

STRAW PULPS.—Very little demand is experienced for Straw Pulp; prices are unchanged.

Prices, c.i.f. London, Hull or Leith:

Belgian, 25% moisture	£15 0 0 to 16 0 0
do. dry	16 0 0
German, 50 to 55% moisture	16 10 0
do. dry, ... No. 1 £18 10 0; No. 2	15 0 0

WASTE PAPERS.—Steady demand at well-maintained prices.

Cream Shavings ...	12/3	Small Letters	5/-
Fine ,, ...	9/6	Large ,, ...	7/0
Mixed ,, ...	2/0	Brown Paper	2/9
White Printings ...	8/9	Light Browns	2/9
White Waste ...	1/6	Books & Pamphlets ...	6/0
Wood Pulp Cuttings	3/6	Strawboard Cuttings	1/6
Brown Paper	3/0	Jacquards	2/6
Crushed News	2/0		

For Export: 25/- per ton extra.

JUTE.—Market firm, and prices of Cuttings show an upward movement.

Good White	£17 10 to 18	Common ...	£13 to £14
Good	£17	Rejections ...	£9 ,, £10
Medium ..	£15 to £16	Cuttings ...	£5 10 ,, £7

FLOCKS.—There continues a good steady demand for Cotton Flocks, preventing anything like an accumulation of stocks. Prices very firm—ranging from £3 10s. to £5 per ton, according to quality, delivered at mills.

FOREIGN RAGS.—The British demand for Foreign Rags is not very large at the present time. With continental mills, however, a steady trade is passing. Jute Bagging has been in strong request, and there is a growing enquiry for cheap rags, owing to higher prices of wood pulp.

WEEK'S IMPORTS.

Quantity	From	Importer	Port.
357 bales	Alexandria	To order	Liverpool
320 ,,	,,	,,	,,
36 ,,	Amsterdam	,,	Hull
37 ,,	,,	,,	Leith
14 ,,	Adelaide	,,	London
125 ,,	Bordeaux	,,	Liverpool
16 ,,	Boulogne	,,	London
5 ,,	Christiania	,,	Hull
394 ,,	Copenhagen	.	,,
162 ,,	Constantinople	,,	Liverpool
139 ,,	,,	,,	,,
54 ,,	Dunkirk	,,	London
3 ,,	Ghent	,,	Liverpool
74 ,,	,,	,,	,,
344 ,,	,,	,,	Leith
21 ,,	Harlingen	,,	Hull
32 ,,	Jersey	,,	Southampton
80 ,,	Jaffa	,,	Liverpool
170 ,,	Norrkoping	,,	Hull
43 ,,	St. Nazaire	,,	Newhaven
11 ,,	,,	,,	Liverpool
57 ,,	St. Malo	,,	Southampton
1 ,,	Wellington	,,	London

Totals from Each Country:

AUSTRALIA...	15 bales	HOLLAND ...	94 bales
BELGIUM ...	481 ,,	PALESTINE...	80 ,,
CHANNEL Isles	32 ,,	NORWAY ...	5 ,,
DENMARK ...	394 ,,	SWEDEN ...	170 ,,
EGYPT ...	677 ,,	TURKEY ...	301 ,,
FRANCE ...	306 ,,		

FRENCH RAGS.

Quotations range, per cwt., ex ship London, Southampton, or Hull; 2/0 per ton more at Liverpool, and 10/0 per ton higher at Newcastle, Glasgow or Leith.

French Linens, I ...	22/0	Black Cotton ...	4/0
II 18/6; III ...	14/6	Marseilles Whites, I	16/0
White Cottons, I ...	19/0	II 10/0; III ...	7/6
II 15/0; III ...	12/6	Blue Cotton	11/0
Knitted Cotton ...	11/0	Light Prints... ...	9/0
Light Coloured Cotton	8/0	Mixed Prints ...	6/0
Blue Cotton	9/6	New White Cuttings	23/0
Coloured Cotton ...	6/0	,, Stay ,,	21/0

DUTCH RAGS, f.o.r. Hull:

C.i.f. Thames; Hull 2/6 per ton more; ditto f.o.r. Leith c.i.f. Glasgow 4/-; c.i.f. Liverpool 4/-.

Selected Fines (free from Muslins) ...	17/0	Best Grey Linens ...	9/0
		Common ditto ...	5/6
Selected Outshots	9/9	White Canvas ...	15/0
,, Dirty Fines	5/9	Grey & Brown Canvas	9/9
Light Cottons ...	9/3	Tarred Hemp Rope	8/0
Blue Cottons ...	7/6	Ditto (broken) ...	5/3
Dark Coloured Cottons	2/10	White Paper Shavings	7/9
New Cuttings (Bleachd)	22/6	Gunny (best) ...	4/9
,, (Unbleached)	19/6	Jute Bagging ...	3/6
,, (Slate) ...	9/0	Ditto (common ...	3/0
Muslins	8/0	Tarpaulins	4/0
Red Cottons (Mixed)	5/9	Cowhair Carpets ...	2/9
Fustians (Light browns)	5/0	Hard ditto	3/0

GERMAN RAGS.

STETTIN: C.i.f. Hull, Leith, Tyne and London.

SPFFF and SPFF	18/0	LFB (Blue)	9/0
SPF	11/0	CSPFFF and CSPFF	14/0
FF	8/6	CFB (Blue)	7/6
FG	9/0	CFX (Coloured) ...	4/6
LFX	7/0		

HAMBURG: F.o.b.

NWC	22/0	FF Grey Linens ...	9/0
SPFFF	22/0	LFX Second ditto...	8/0
SPFFF and SPFF	18/0	CSPFFF	17/3
SPFF	16/0	CSPFF	11/3
SPF	12/0	CFB	8/0
CCC	5/6	Dark Blues (selected	11/9
CFX	4/6	Wool Tares... ...	8/0
White Rope... ...	8/0	Jute, No. I 6/0; No. II	5/6

BELGIAN RAGS.

F.o.b. Ghent. Freights: London, 5/0; Hull and Goole, 7/6 Liverpool and Leith, 10/0; Newcastle, 12/6; Dundee and Aberdeen, 15/0; Glasgow, 16/8.

White Linens No. 1	22/6	Fustians (Light) ...	6/0
,, ,, No. 2	16/0	,, (Dark) ...	4/0
,, ,, No. 3	13/0	Thirds...	3/0
Fines (Mixed) ...	12/0	Black Cottons ...	3/9
Grey Linens (strong)	9/6	Hemp Strings (unt'r'd)	3/0
,, ,, (extra)	14/0	House Cloths ...	4/9
Blue Linens... ...	8/6	Old Bagging (solid)	3/6
White Cottons S'p'fine	18/0	,, ,, (common)	2/6
,, ,, No. 2	15/0	NEW.	
Outshots No. 3 ...	10/0	White & Cream Linens	33/0
Seconds No. 4 ...	8/0	White Cuttings ...	22/0
Prints (Light) ...	8/6	Unbleached Cuttings	21/0
,, (Old)	4/6	Print Cuttings ..	3/0

BELGIAN FLAX and HEMP WASTE.

Best washed and dried Flax Waste, 10/0; Fair ditto 9/0
Flax Spinners' Waste (grease boiled out)... .... 12/0
Hemp Waste, No. 1 9/0; No. 2 ... ... 7/6
Flax Spinners' Waste, No. 1 (Flax Rove) 10/0: No. 2 8/6

NORWEGIAN RAGS.

C.i.f. London, Hull, Tyne, and Grangemouth.

1st Rope (tarred) ...	8/6-9/0	2nd Canvas ...	8/0
2nd ,, ,, ...	5/6-6/0	Jute Bagging	
Manilla Rope (white)	8/0-8/9	Gunny ...	3/0 3/6
Best Canvas ...	11/9-12/0	Mixed ...	2/6-2/9

RUSSIAN RAGS.

C.i.f. London. Hull, Newcastle or Leith.

SPFF	15/0	CC (Cotton	4/9
SPF	13/6	Jute I	3/6
FG	10/6	,, II...	2/3
LFB	9/6	Rope I	9/0
FF	8/3	,, II	5/3
LFX	7/3		

HOME RAGS.—LONDON: There is a better demand; prices of Country Thirds and White Manilla Rope are easier.—BRISTOL: Trade continues quiet, but no doubt there will be an improvement after the coal strike.—MANCHESTER: Enquiry is fairly good; prices unchanged. — EDINBURGH: The market is more active.—DUBLIN: Trade quiet.

LONDON:

New White Cuttings	21/6	Canvas No. 1	15/0
Fines (selected)	20/6	,, No. 2 ...	9/6-10/6
,, (good London)...	20/0	,, No. 3	5/6
Outshots (selected) ...	12/6	Mixed Rope	5/3
,, (ordinary) ...	11/0	White Rope	6/6
London Seconds	3/6-4/0	White Manilla Rope	8/0
Country do. ...	6/6-8/0	Coil Rope	9/0
London Thirds ...	1/9-2/0	Bagging...	1/6
Country do. ...	3/0-4/0	Gunny	3/0-3/6
Light Prints ...	7/0-8/0		

BRISTOL:

Fines	29/0	Clean Canvas ...	15/0
Outshots	13/6	Second Do. ...	9/6-10/6
Seconds	7/0-8/0	Light Prints ...	8/0
Thirds	3/6-4/0	Hemp Coil Rope	9/6-10/0
Mixed Bagging	3/6	Tarred Manilla	7/6

MANCHESTER:

Fines	15/0-16/0	Blues	6/6-7/0
Outshots (best) ...	11/6-12/0	Bagging...	4/0-4/3
,, (ordinary)	10/6-11/0	,, (common)	3/0-3/3
Seconds	7/0-7/3	W. Manilla Rope	10/0-10/6
Thirds	3/6-3/9	Surat Tares... ...	4/9-5/0

EDINBURGH:

Superfines	17/0	Black Cottons	2/9
Outshots	13/0	W. Manilla Rope ...	9/0
Mixed Fines...	14/0	Tarred Ditto	6/9
Common Seconds ...	8/0	,, Hemp Rope...	8/6
First do.	11/0	Rope Ends (new) ...	8/6
Prints	5/6-6/6	,, ,, (old) ...	6/0
Canvas (best)	16/0	Bagging...	2/0-3/0
,, 2nd	10/6	,, (clean) ...	4/3-5/0

DUBLIN.

White Cuttings ...	18/0	Mill Bagging	3/0
Fines	11/0	White Manilla	8/0
Seconds...	5/0	Tarred Hemp	8/0
Light Prints	3/0	Rigging	13/6
Black do.	2/0	Mixed Ropes	3/6
Bagging	2/0		

STARCH.—The market is rather dull; quotations firm.

F.o.r. London, less 2½%:

Maize—Crisp, £9 10/-; Powder, £9 15/-; Special £14.
Farina—Prime, £9 15/-; B.K.M.F., £12.

Delivered:

Rice—Special (in chests), £20 (net); Crystal (in bags) £19; Granulated (in bags) £18 less 2½%.
Dextrine—£15 to £16.

ROSIN.—Trade quiet.

Strained.		E.	F.	G.	K.	W.G.	W.W
Spot—	3/7½	4/0	4/3	4/6	6/9	9/9	10/3
To arrive—	3/2	3/5	3/7	3/9	5/6	9/0	9/6

SIZING.—Home demand keeps steady, but business with U.S.A. is quiet. B.A. pieces are firm at 31s. 6d. to 34s.

English Gelatines	per cwt.	70/0 to 140/
Foreign ,, ...	,,	70/0 ,, 140/0
Fine Skin Glues	,,	45/0 ,, 60/0
Long Scotch Glues	,,	45/0 ,, 60/0
Common ,, ...	,,	30/0 ,, 45/0
"Town" Glues	,,	26/0 ,, 34/0
"Bone" Glues	,,	20/0 ,, 30/0
Foreign Glues	,,	23/0 ,, 40/0
Bone Size	,,	4/0 ,, 10/0
Gelatine Size...	,,	5/0 ,, 10/0
Dry B.A. Pieces	,,	31/6 ,, 34/0
,, English Pieces	,,	22/0 ,, [illegible]
Wet ,, ,, ...	,,	5/0 ,, [illegible]
,, Sheep Pieces	,,	3/0 ,, [illegible]
Buffalo Hide Shavings	,,	20/0 ,, [illegible]
,, Picker Waste	,,	27/0 ,, [illegible]

COLOURS.—There is a fair enquiry; prices unchanged.

MINERALS.—CHINA CLAY is in fair demand, and stocks owing to a dry summer are not so heavy as they would otherwise have been. In FRENCH and ITALIAN CHALK prices show a slight fluctuation. MINERAL WHITE is in steady request, and a moderate business is passing in PATENT HARDENINGS.

Mineral White (Terra Alba), per ton f.o.r. or boat [illegible] works:

Superfine...	28/0 less 2½ %
Pottery Super.... ...	24/0 ,,
Ball Seconds	20/0 ,,
Seconds	15/0 ,,
Thirds	10/6 ,,

China Clay, in bulk, f.o.b. Cornwall, 14/0 to 27/6; bags [illegible] and casks 9/6 per ton extra; f.o.b. London, in casks 35/0 to 50/0 per ton.

Superfine Hardening, f.o.r. works, 40/0.

Patent Crystal Hardening, delivered at mills £3 to £3 1[illegible]

Patent Hardening (2 ton lots) f.o.r. Lancs., £3 5/0.
,, ,, (5 ton lots) f.o.b. Liverpool, £3 10/0.

Magnesite (in lump) 32/6 per ton.

Magnesite (containing 98% Carbonate of Magnesia), raw ground, £6 10/0; calcined ground, £12 10/0.

Albarine, £3. del. mills.

Asbestos, best rock, £18; brown grades, £14 to £15

Asbestine Pulp, £4 5/- to £5 c.i.f. London, Liverpool and Glasgow.

Barytes (Carbonate), lump, 90/0 to 95/0; nuts, 72/6 to 8[illegible]

Barytes (Sulphate), "Angel White," No. 1, 70/0; No. 2, 60/0 to 65/0; No. 3, 45/0. Souheur's Brands: A[illegible] 83/-; BF, 72/-; AB, 33/6; BB, 29/6; CB, 24/3.

French and Italian Chalk (Souheur Brand), per ton, in lots of 10 tons: Flower O, 63/6 c.i.f. London; Flower OO, 59/0, Flower OOO, 52/6. Swan White 58/0; Snow White, 80/0. Blackwell's "Angel White" Brand and "Silvery" 90/- to 92/6; prime quality, 90/- to 95/-; and superfine, 105/-.

Bauxite, Irish Hill Quality, first lump, 20/0; seconds 16/0; thirds, 12/0; ground, 35/0.

Pyrites (non-cupreous), Liverpool, 5d., 2 %.

Carbonate of Lime (Souheur Brand), Prima [illegible] Secunda 37/-.

LIME.—Bleach Lime is quoted at 12s. [illegible] per ton at works.

DIRECTORY.

Names and Addresses under this heading will be charged for at the rate of 50/- per annum (52 insertions) for each card of two lines or under. Each additional line £1 extra.

ALUMINOUS CAKE.

The ALUM, CHINA CLAY and VITRIOL Co., Lim., 63, Queen Victoria Street, London, E.C. Works: Rainham-on-Thames. Telegrams—"Chinnock, London.

ANALYTICAL.

WILLIAMS, ROWLAND, F.I.C., F.C.S., 28, Pall Mall, Manchester.

ARTESIAN WELLS.

BATCHELOR, Richard D., Artesian and Consulting Well Engineer, 73, Queen Victoria Street, London, E.C., and at Chatham. 5718

ISLER, C., & Co., Bear Lane, Southwark, S.E.

LE GRAND & SUTCLIFF, Magdala Works, 125, Bunhill Row, E.C.

BOILER COVERING.

LONSDALES, Boiler Coverers, Blackburn, will send a sample cask of their Patent Plastic Cork Covering to any Paper Mill in Great Britain—5 cwt. cask for 25/- (carriage paid).

CHINA CLAY.

The ALUM, CHINA CLAY and VITRIOL Co., Lim., 63, Queen Victoria Street, London, E.C. Mines: Ruddle and Colchester, St. Austell, Cornwall. Telegrams—"Chinnock, London."

ROGERS, J., & Co., Truro, Cornwall.—Agents: Taylor, Sommerville & Co., 83, Queen Victoria Street, E.C., and at 16, Princes Street, Edinburgh.

W. SINGLETON BIRCH & SONS, Lim., 15, Upton Street, Manchester. Mines: Roseveor, St. Austell, Cornwall. 2276

COLOURS.

CARDWELL, J. L., & Co., Commercial Buildings, 15, Cross Street, Manchester. Specialties: Mineral Black, Ven. Red, Ochres and Umbers. 5304

GEMMILL, W. N., & Co., Glasgow, Telegrams "Ruhe." Starches, Alumina, Antifroths, &c. All Paper Colours

COLOURS (Continued).

HINSHELWOOD, THOMAS, & Co., The Glasgow Colour Works, Glasgow. Colours and shades matched exactly.

MULLER, A. E., 9, Fenchurch Street, London, E.C.

ESPARTO.

IDE & CHRISTIE, Fibre, Esparto, and General Produce Brokers, 72, Mark Lane, E.C.

MINERAL WHITE or TERRA ALBA.

WINSER & Co., Portland Mills, Princess Street, Manchester. Also manufacturers of Aluminous Cake.

HOWE, JOHN, & Co., Carlisle. 3112

STEEL.

MAKIN, WM., & SONS, Sheffield. Established 1756. Roll Bars, Plates, Cutter Knives, Doctor Blades, &c. 5369

STRAW.

UNDERWOOD, E., & SON, Limited, Brentford, London, W. Press-packed Oat, Wheat, or Rye Straw, delivered to the chief British ports or railway stations.

TALC (French and Italian Chalk).

SOUHEUR, JEAN, Antwerp. All Minerals, Blanc de Silex, Barytes (superior and common), Carbonate of Lime, Blacklead, &c. British Agents: A. E. Muller, 9, Fenchurch Street, London, E.C. Agent for Liverpool and Manchester: G. H. Austin, Ditton, near Widnes.

RAGS.

CHALMERS, E., & Co., Lim., Bonnington, Leith.

MULLER, A. E., 9, Fenchurch Street, London, E.C.

WERTHEIM, A., & Co., Hamburg.

UMBER.

The ALUM, CHINA CLAY and VITROIL Co., Lim. 63, Queen Victoria Street, London, E.C. Telegrams—"Chinasock, London."

WOOD PULP.

FRIIS, N., & Co., 18, Carl Johans Gade, Christiania, Norway.

GOTTSTEIN, H., & Co., 59, Mark Lane, London, E.C., and at New York.

GRANT, W., & Co., 17, Baltic Street, Leith. Agents for best shippers, Sulphite and Sulphate, Mechanical, Pine, Brown, Aspen.

MATTHIESSEN, CHR., Christiania, Norway.

MULLER, A. E., 9, Fenchurch Street, London, E.C.

The SULPHITE PULP Company, Limited, 8a, Gordon Street, Glasgow.

WERTHEIM, A., & Co., Hamburg.

Special Prepaid Advertisements

IT IS IMPORTANT that Advertisements under any of the Headings mentioned below should reach us by the FIRST POST on WEDNESDAY Morning to INSURE INSERTION.

Charges for advertisements under the heading Situations Wanted are 1/- for twenty-four words, and One Penny per Word after, Minimum charge ONE SHILLING. Names and addresses to be paid for.

Advertisers by paying an extra fee of 6d. can have the replies addressed to the PAPER TRADE REVIEW under a number, and such replies will then be forwarded Post Free

Advertisements appearing under the following headings:

Tenders.	Mills Wanted or To Let.
Sales by Auction.	Machinery Wanted or For Sale.
Businesses Wanted.	Situations Vacant.
Businesses for Disposal.	

Miscellaneous.

The charges are 3/- for fifty words or under; 1s. extra for every line or portion after. Ten words to be reckoned for each line. Names and addresses to be paid for. Payment must be made in advance, except where the advertiser has a running account, in which case the cost can be debited thereto.

Legal and Financial Announcements: 1/- per Line.

Cheques and Post-office Orders to be CROSSED ——and Co., and made payable to W. JOHN STONHILL.

Situations Wanted.

ASSISTANT-MANAGER or Foreman desires an appointment in a sulphite pulp or paper mill in England or abroad; practical engineer and mechanic, fair knowledge of chemistry, speaks several languages, satisfactory references.—Address No. 5892, office of the WORLD'S PAPER TRADE REVIEW, 58, Shoe-lane, London, E.C. 5892

TO PAPERMAKERS.—Finisher requires situation; well up in shops and brown caps; good references.—Address W. H. Organ, 2, Aylmer Cottages, Watchet, near Bridgwater, Somerset. 5880

Machinery Wanted.

WANTED, a Set of Chilled Rolls, not less than 60 inches on face.—Address "A.B.," No. 5898, office of the WORLD'S PAPER TRADE REVIEW, 58, Shoe Lane, London, E.C. 5898

WANTED, second-hand Slitting and Cutting Machine, small size; must be cheap.—J. MacDougall, 6, Snowhill, London, E.C. 5895

Machinery for Sale.

ONE KOLLERGANG, new, Stones 51 inches by 14 inches, C.I. Pan, Scrapers, and Driving Gear.

ONE HYDRAULIC PRESS, second-hand, with Press Box 38 inches diam. by 32 inches deep, with wheels; all parts strong, Ram 2 feet 6 inches by 8 inches diam.

TWELVE REVOLVING STRAINER PLATES, second-hand, 18¾ inches by 21 inches, class B2, 3½ cut.

REFINING ENGINE, new, Conical Type; same as one working in a large printing mill.

Any reasonable offer will be considered by 5859

BERTRAMS LIMITED, SCIENNES, EDINBURGH

Mill to be Let or Sold.

TO be LET or SOLD, a Paper Mill at Stalybridge, called the Higher Mill, containing one large machine and room for another, steam engine and boilers, in good condition.—Apply for further information to the Caretaker on the premises. 2262

Patents, Designs & Trade Marks Acts, 1883-1888.

NOTICE is hereby given that CHARLES MORGAN, HERBERT JORDAN ADAMS, and THOMAS BENJAMIN BACON, all of 4, 6 and 8, Tabernacle Street, Finsbury, in the County of Middlesex, have applied for leave to amend the Specification of the Letters Patent No. 12,313 of 1892, granted to CHARLES MORGAN and THOMAS BENJAMIN BACON for "An Improvement relating to Envelopes."

Particulars of the proposed amendments were set forth in the Illustrated Official Journal (Patents) issued on the 11th October, 1893.

Any person may give notice (on Form G.) at the Patent Office, 25, Southampton Buildings, London, W.C., of opposition to the amendment within one calendar month from the date of the said Journal.

(Signed) *H. READER LACK*,
Comptroller-General.

5

GAZETTE.

Partnership Dissolved.

JACOB and NICHOLSON, rag, paper and metal merchants and dealers in waste paper, 86, Tooley Street, Southwark, S.E. March 28th.

The Bankruptcy Acts 1883 and 1890.—Notice of Intended Dividend.

STANYER, E. (trading as A. Stanyer and Son), Irk Mills, Long Millgate, and 210, Rochdale Road, Manchester, woollen and cotton rag merchant. Claims by October 28th to S. Tilzey, 79, Mosley Street, Manchester.

Notice of Release of Trustee.

LINSKILL, F. W., 77 and 79, Quarry Hill, Leeds, rag merchant. Trustee J. Bowling, 22, Park Row, Leeds, Official Receiver. Released Sept. 6th.

NEW PATENTS.

BRITISH.

APPLICATIONS.

18,519. Improved process for treating the black ash residium of wood pulp manufacture. L. S. Langville.

18,538. Improvements in and relating to the manufacture of paper. R. J. Lusby.

18,779. Improvements in and connected with pulp strainers. R. J. Hougee.

18,786. An improved process for recovering alkali from a waste product. J. B. Murray and M. S. Baird.

SPECIFICATIONS PUBLISHED.

(7½d. each. By post 8d.)

1892.

18,683. Papermaking machines. McNeill.

20,055. Bleaching powder, &c. W. J. and L. Fraser.

20,284. Chlorine. De Wilde and Ors.

1893.

5 694. Electrolytic decomposition of solutions of chlorine of sodium, &c. Richardson.

AMERICAN.

504,215. Apparatus for coating paper, &c. Frank W. Hayward, Alfred S. King and Alfred W. Loveland, Norwich, England. Patented in England, November 28, 1892, No. 21,724.

THE
United Asbestos Co.,
LIMITED.
DOCK HOUSE, BILLITER STREET, E.C.,
"SALAMANDER"
THE UNITED ASBESTOS COMPANY LIMITED · LONDON ·
INDESTRUCTIBLE
TRADE MARK
Pioneers
OF THE
Asbestos
Trade.
UNITED ASBESTOS
NON-CONDUCTING
COVERING
(For Steam Boilers & Pipes)
Best and Cheapest in the Market; Will not Injure Boiler Plates.
ASBESTOS
GOODS of ALL
DESCRIPTIONS
BELTINGS.
THE UNITED ASBESTOS Co., Limited,
PACKINGS.
UNITED ASBESTOS Co. LMD. LONDON
PURE ITALIAN MILLBOARD EXTRA QUALITY
A1
UNITED ASBESTOS
A1 MILLBOARDS
(ITALIAN)
Unequalled for Purity, Strength of Fibre, and Uniformity. For Dry Steam Joints it is admitted to be the cleanest, most durable and economical packing in existence.
UNITED ASBESTOS
SALAMANDER
Lubricating Cream & Oils,
SPECIALLY ADAPTED TO
PAPERMAKING MACHINERY.
DEPOTS:
MANCHESTER: 34, Deansgate; LIVERPOOL: 33, James Street; NEWCASTLE-UPON-TYNE: Quayside; GLASGOW: 54, Robertson Street; CARDIFF: 135, Bute Street; BRISTOL: Provident Buildings; HULL: Queen's Dock; ST. PETERSBURG: Gostinoe Dvor (Interior) No. 51.

Printed and Published by W. JOHN STONHILL 58, Shoe Lane, LONDON, E.C. October 20, 1893.

PAPER AND PRINT.

R. ROBINSON & CO., NEWCASTLE.

Large consumers of paper, who do business on sound commercial principles, are very welcome customers to papermakers. The demand for paper to meet the requirements of Messrs. R. Robinson and Co., of the Side and Clavering-place, Newcastle-on-Tyne, must be enormous. This paper and printing firm was the subject of an illustrated article in the *British and Colonial Printer and Stationer*, October 12th, and on the following pages we give two of the illustrations, showing the workshops as seen from the old castle, and the warehouses 56 to 66, Side. The business was founded so far back as 1818, by Mr. Robert Robinson. In 1830 Mr. Robinson added to his paper business the manufacture of paper bags and account books, and also provided himself with a plant which enabled him to undertake paper ruling. Without attempting to describe the enormous stationery stock held by this firm in their Side warehouse, perhaps some idea will be gained when we say that there are always over 500 tons of paper alone in stock, and something like six millions of envelopes, and an enormous quantity of other goods is also to be seen, the diverse character of which may be imagined when we say that the firm are wholesale stationers, paper merchants, bookbinders, paper bag makers, letterpress, litho, and chromo-litho printers, plain and fancy box makers, paper rulers, account book makers, relief stampers, and stationers' sundriesmen. With regard to the paper bag department, something like a million bags a year are manufactured on the premises, but this only comprises a comparatively limited proportion of their trade in these goods, as they buy largely from other manufacturers to the extent of several millions of bags annually.

THE CHURCH CONGRESS the other day at Birmingham denounced the honours to Zola, and all his works, also the reception by the Institute of Journalists and the co-operation of the Chief Magistrate of the City of London. But all the arguments in the world will not get over the little fact of which a well-known comedian sings nightly at a West-end theatre :—

Just for selling a novel of Zola's you know
To prison a publisher once had to go,
He pleaded for mercy—his worship said "No,"
And we paid no attention to that.

But the author himself who our guest's been of late
Was with honours received by the same magistrate
Who'd the publisher sentenced with felons to mate,
But he paid no attention to that.

MR. HENRY FROWDE may be complimented upon the elegance of the "Thumb Prayer Book," exquisitely printed in diamond type, upon remarkably opaque paper—which latter is a marvel of manufacture—and bound in that dainty style which is characteristic of the productions of the Oxford University Press.

R.ROBINSON
PAPER BAG MAK

Printed and Published by W. JOHN STONHILL, 58, Shoe Lane, LONDON, E.C. Oct. 20, 1893.

Telegrams: "STONHILL, LONDON." A B C Code. Registered at the General Post Office as a Newspaper.

Vol. XX. No. 17. LONDON, OCTOBER 27, 1893. Price 6d.

PULP STRAINERS.

TORRANCE & HOWELL'S PATENTS.

Some months ago Messrs. T. Torrance and J. H. Howell, of Bristol, took out a patent claiming certain improvements in strainers. These, according to the specification, consisted of a method of, and means for, the more perfectly and effectually dealing with all kinds of pulp used in papermaking, after leaving the beaters, and before entering upon the papermaking machine, than has been attained (according to the patentees) by any of the methods and means hitherto employed, at which period the pulp has always to undergo a process of straining for the purpose of removing therefrom "knots," or such particles of foreign matter as would be objectionable or detrimental to the desired texture and finish of the paper. Hitherto this has only been imperfectly attained by the employment of agitated flat sieve-like surfaces, over which the pulp has been caused to flow, and the slits or meshes formed in the sieves, and through which the pulp in its approved condition was desired to pass, have necessarily been of such infinitesimal dimensions, and the process of straining so slow and irregular, that the more or less clogging or choking of the slits has invariably resulted. With a view to overcome this difficulty, means have been resorted to for forming a vacuum beneath the sieve like surface, in order that the atmospheric pressure upon the upper surface of the pulp might push or force it through, but by reason of consolidation or coagulation arising from the irregular or intermittent passage through the said slits or meshes, the pulp, in this process gathered upon the under edges of these orifices, until dislodged by gravity, vibration or otherwise, which falling into the strained pulp would render this again in a more or less unsatisfactory condition. To overcome these difficulties and objectionable results is the object and purpose of Messrs. Torrance and Howell's invention, and satisfactory results are claimed to have been attained by providing in lieu of the sieve, a surface composed of a series of parallel rollers, rods or bars, of various shapes and dimensions in cross section, which are caused to rotate, oscillate, rise and fall or otherwise (in some cases or where convenient between stationary substances), so that the pulp when floated thereon is thereby kept in a continuous state of agitation, and by the employment of a novel adjusting mechanism the space between the rollers, or between the rods or bars, or between these and the stationary parts that accompany them, and through which the pulp is allowed to pass if in a proper and workable condition, may be gauged with the greatest precision, according to the width of the cut desired, while such "knotty" or combined portions of the pulp as would not pass through said spaces or divisions, would be conveyed by gravity or other means into suitable vessels or channels, through which it would be caused to pass by pumping or otherwise, to be again treated in a similar manner (in some cases after passing through auxiliary knotters) in combination with fresh pulp. By these means the patentees say they obtain a continuous unvarying delivery of the strained pulp without the slightest sign of consolidation or coagulation, and choking or clogging of the straining medium or waste of useable material becomes a matter of impossibility.

A number of modifications and additions have recently been made with the view of obtaining the following results:—(1) Economy in the cost of manufacture of the entire machine; (2) to obtain a more even distribution and agitation of the pulp while undergoing the process of straining; (3) to clarify the pulp before entering upon the papermaking machine, by removing the scum therefrom; and (4) to further provide a means for preventing the thick or knotty pulp after passing over the rollers, from mingling with the strained pulp that has passed between straining rollers, as compared with those shown in fig. 2 of the accompanying drawings.

Figs. 10 and 11 are part plan, and part sectional elevation respectively, illustrating certain improvements in the vortex chamber or receiver for the residue of the unstrained pulp.

Figs. 12 and 13 are vertical sections illustrating certain improvements in the chamber for the reception of the strained pulp.

Fig. 14 is a front elevation of part of a set of bearings illustrating an improved method of and means for rotating the rollers, in lieu of the worm shown in figs 1 and 2, fig. 15

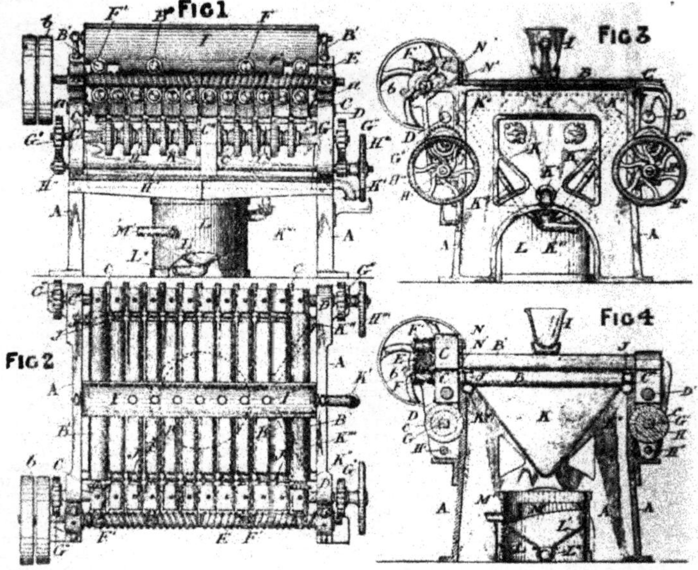

the rollers and ready for deposit upon the papermaking machine.

Figs. 1 and 2, and figs. 3 and 4 are front elevation, plan, side elevation, and vertical section respectively of a complete machine.

Figs. 5 and 6 are front and side elevation respectively of a portion of a series of bearings in which an improved method is claimed for adjusting the spaces between these, and the roller bars or plates borne thereby.

Figs. 7 and 8 are a perspective view and side elevation respectively of an improved method of constructing the spacing or adjusting wheels, the manner of using the wheels being shown in figs. 1 and 2.

Fig. 9 is a plan view illustrating certain improvements in the construction of the being a part sectional elevation, and fig. 16 a plan view.

Figs. 17 and 18 are views illustrating an alternative method of constructing the rollers, and improvements in connection therewith, while fig. 19 is a part section of same.

Figs. 20 and 21 illustrate further modifications in connection with the rollers, while fig. 22 is a part section of same.

The patentees now employ in connection with their previously patented apparatus, auxiliary or supplementary rollers B^{11}. They also claim in combination with the frame A, vat or hopper I, shafts D D^1, bearings C, C^1, C^{11}, carrying rollers B, B^1, B^{11}, rotated by a worm E, and worm wheels F F^1, receiver K and chamber L, the employment of shafts G and G_1, rectangular in cross section, carrying wheels or part wheels H, each provided with a graduated web or periphery c, occurring alternately with, and between lugs C^{111} on C C^1. The wheels or handles H^{111}, fixed upon front and back shafts H^1 borne by A, each carrying a pair of pinions H^{11} in gear with spur wheels G^{11} and G^{111}, mounted upon the ends of G and G^1, for imparting motions thereto and the wheels or part wheels H, for spacing the rollers B, B^1 B^{11}, shown by Figs. 1, 2, 3, and 4.

In substitution of the bearings and shafts,

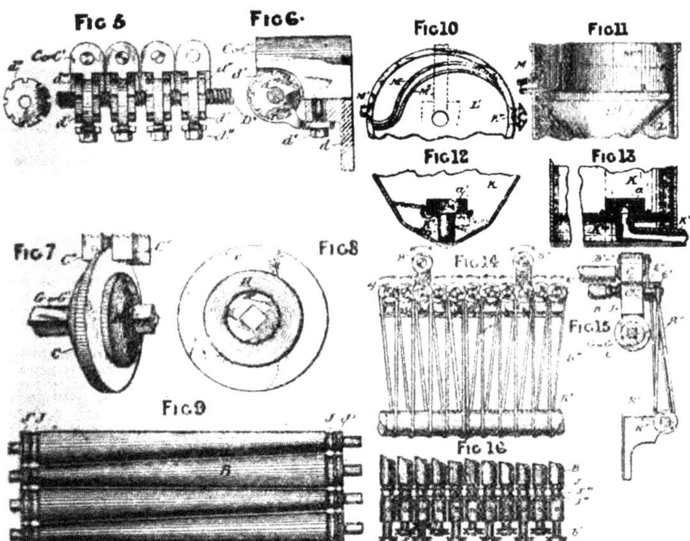

provision has been made for the employment of slotted shelves d, carrying bearings C C^1, each provided with a web d^1, connected to d by bolts or screws d^{11}, and borne upon threaded shafts D and D^1, passing through the webs d^1 or a suitable chuck therein, and carrying nuts d^{111} connected and operating for spacing the rollers B, B^1, B^{11}, and fixing them when so spaced, as shown by figs. 5 and 6.

Another modification shows, in combination with the apparatus previously set forth, but in substitution of the parallel rollers therein provided, the employment of tapered rollers B, provided at either or both ends with annular grooves J J^{11}, with or without recesses J^{111}, as shown by Fig. 9.

The patentees further claim the employment of a scum plate M^{11}, fixed vertically in the vortex chamber L, parallel with the wall of the trough M, as shown by Figs. 10 and 11; the employment of a scum trap in the chamber K, provided by extending inwardly and upwardly the outlet tube K^1, formed with a trumpet or funnel shaped mouth K^{111}, surmounted by an inverted bonnet a^1 (see Figs. 12 and 13); and in substitution of the worm E and wheel F F^1, the employment of an alternative method of rotating the rollers B B^1 B^{11}, by fixing upon the spindle ends thereof pulleys b^1 b^{11}, operated by cords, wires, straps or ropes R^{111}, engaging with a rotating drum or shaft R^1, carried by brackets R^{11} fixed to the frame A, shown by Figs. 14, 15, 16.

Messrs. Torrance and Howell also set forth, in combination, the alternate method of constructing the parallel or tapered rollers B, by forming at either or both ends thereof annular spaces J^{111}, and the employment therewith of inverted U shaped pieces S occupying the downward passage between the rollers provided by the grooves J, or the depending pieces T^{111} provided with heads T^{11}, sliding within the slot T^1 of a tube T, as illustrated by Figs. 17 to 22; further, the employment of a sprinkler for reducing the consistency of the pulp during filtration, consisting of brackets V, mounted upon the

[illegible] carrying adjustable plates [illegible] bearings [illegible] connected by [illegible] plate [illegible] preferably

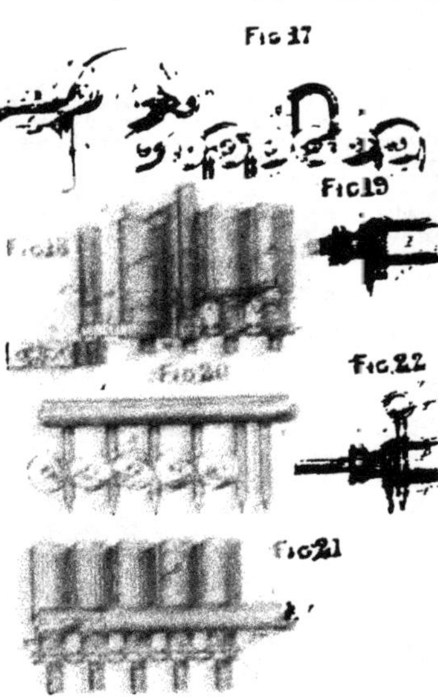

metallic heads W', carrying a slitted or perforated hollow tube W'', in connection with a water supply, shown by Figs. 17 and 18.

TRADE OF MALAGA AND DISTRICT.

The exports of esparto from Malaga for 1892 as compared with the two preceding years show a slight decrease: 1892, 1,106,830 kilos; 1891, 1,1[illegible],000 kilos; 1890, 1,300,850 kilos. During 1892 the shipments were: January, 200,000 kilos; February, 200,000 kilos; March, 206,000 kilos; July, 200,880 kilos; December, 300,000 kilos.

Paper was imported at Malaga as follows: 1892, 612,632 kilos; 1891, 892,826 kilos. In the former year the supplies were drawn from the following countries:

England	...	48,414 kilos.
France		51,8[illegible] ,,
Germany		221,443 ,,
Belgium		2[illegible]1,520 ,,
Holland	...	17 ,,
[illegible]		45,340 ,,

The [illegible] at Aguilas states that [illegible] tons of esparto were shipped to Great Britain, an increase of [illegible] [illegible]. Several new [illegible] have been established, and [illegible] will now be exported in larger quantities [illegible].

Some 20,000 tons of salt, [illegible] natural evaporation [illegible] left Almeria in 1892 for consumption in the Peninsula. The [illegible] neighbourhood (Baños de [illegible]) annually produce some 10,000 tons of [illegible], which is also chiefly consumed in the Peninsula and at Marseilles. [illegible] economic year of 1891-92 [illegible] issued by the Harbour Board [illegible] exported [illegible] tons of paper, and [illegible] of pasteboard were exported [illegible]. Some [illegible] tons of paper, [illegible] tons of pasteboard, and 4 cwts. of playing [illegible] were imported.

The quantity of esparto shipped from Cartagena in 1892 was 11,2[illegible] tons, [illegible] compared with the previous year, shows a decrease of 3,767 tons. The large drop in the amount [illegible] exported may be put down to the fact that esparto which in other years has been shipped from Cartagena has [illegible] at Aguilas by the Great Southern of Spain Railway, which has been partly opened for traffic. The whole of the shipments from Cartagena were made to England and Scotland.

From Garrucha the exports of esparto in 1892 amounted to 1,8[illegible] tons, of the value of £5[illegible],000. The esparto was shipped in British steamers to the United Kingdom, and the whole of the carrying trade is in the hands of the British shipowner, that is to say the foreign carrying trade, which is [illegible] permitted to vessels that are not under the Spanish flag. Were it otherwise, and the coasting trade open to foreigners, no doubt the whole of it also would be carried in British vessels to the manifest gain both to the merchant and consumer in a district where there are no railways, few roads, and where the excessive rates of freights coastwise caused by this exclusive monopoly often render impossible the carrying on of small industries altogether. Vessels discharging outward cargoes have a special advantage as to return freights, both dead weight, such as iron ore and bar-lead, and light cargoes of esparto are always procurable to the United Kingdom. The average rate of freight last year, for esparto in pressed bales, to the United Kingdom, was 12s. 6d. per ton.

ITALIAN TRADE.—The imports of paper and books at the various ports of the province of Cagliari were of the value of £2[illegible] in 1892, against £765 in the preceding year. The imports at Gallipoli of paper and books in 1892 were four tons of the value of £136; in 1891, 14 tons of the value of £543. Some 580 tons of rags left Leghorn in 1892, and of the 532 tons exported in 1891, three-quarters went to the United States, the remainder to South America and England. About 800 hands are employed in rag-picking in Leghorn, of whom seven-eighths are women.

LONSDALE'S Boiler Coverer and Paper Hair and Cork NON-CONDUCTING CEMENT.

Extract from the *World's Paper Trade Review*, August 2nd, 1889 :—

The "DAILY CHRONICLE" Mills ; "The Steam Mains are covered with a Non-Conducting Composition supplied by *LONSDALE BROS., of BLACKBURN*, which HAS BEEN FOUND TO ADHERE VERY WELL, and to EFFECT A CONSIDERABLE SAVING."

☛ "It has Stood the Test of an EIGHT YEARS' TRIAL." ☚

Improvement in Cork Covering. Patent No. 19,906, 1889. 2058

SOCIÉTÉ INDUSTRIELLE de MIOS,

MIOS, GIRONDE, FRANCE.

Bleached Chemical Pine Wood Pulp,

☛ *OF GREAT PURITY,* ☚

Especially Adapted for Use in the Manufacture of Fine Papers. 2646

TURNER BROTHERS,

SPOTLAND, ROCHDALE,

SPINNERS and MANUFACTURERS of

ASBESTOS,

IN ALL ITS FORMS.

SOLE MANUFACTURERS OF THE

"GRIPWELL"

SOLID WOVEN HAIR BELTING

FOR MAIN and OTHER DRIVING, 2336

SPECIALLY SUITABLE for PAPERMAKERS.

YATES & THOM

(Late Wm. & Jno. YATES),

BLACKBURN,

HIGH SPEED ECONOMICAL COMPOUND ENGINES. | MODERN MILL GEARING IN ALL ITS BRANCHES.

STEEL BOILERS with 2 and 3 FURNACES up to 200 lbs. WORKING PRESSURE

THE UNIVERSAL BARREL CO., LTD.

FIRST MEETING OF CREDITORS.

Yesterday (Thursday) the first meeting of creditors in the matter of the Universal Barrel Company, Limited, was held at 33, Carey-street, Lincoln's-inn, W.C.

In the summary of the statement of affairs the liabilities are returned at £8,642, of which £7,846 are unsecured, the whole of the assets being covered by debenture bonds. The total deficiency as regards contributories is £27,451.

According to the official receiver and provisional liquidator, Mr. George Stapylton Barnes, the winding-up order was made on a creditor's petition to the Court on the 28th July. The statement of affairs was made on the 29th September by two of the directors and secretary, and the books of the company appeared to have been properly kept.

The company was registered on the 6th September, 1888, and was promoted by Messrs. R. L. Jacobs, C. F. Barker, J. T. Thame, and H. Sanguinetti. The vendors agreed to sell to the company certain patents for the manufacture of barrels, etc., from pulp, the consideration being fixed at £14,000. Of this amount £11,000 was to be satisfied by the issue of fully paid shares.

The nominal capital of the company was £20,000 in £1 shares. Of these 19,607 have been issued—11,000 to the vendors as fully-paid, and to cash subscribers 8,607. The company had registered offices at Dashwood House, New Broad-street, E.C., and carried on business at Two Waters Mills, Boxmoor, Herts. According to the prospectus it was estimated that the cost of making the tests necessary to prove the value of the patents would not exceed the sum of £2,500. At the time the operations of the company commenced, however, the Directors proceeded to allotment on a subscription of £1,500 only. On the 7th May, 1889, a fire occurred at the mill, which necessitated almost the entire rebuilding of the premises, and from that date to the beginning of March, 1890, the company's operations appear to have been practically at a standstill. Very little business beyond experimental work appears to have been carried on by the company.

Certain arrangements were at one time pending for the formation of a larger company to acquire the business of the company and carry it on on a more extensive scale than had hitherto been done, but these negotiations do not appear to have been proceeded with. Two small issues of debentures were made, the first in September, 1891, and the second in November, 1892, but these debentures were subsequently redeemed by the company out of moneys raised by the issue in January, 1893, of first mortgage debentures amounting to £1,500, and in the following month of second mortgage debentures for £300. Both these issues of debentures were, in addition to being respectively a first and second charge upon the whole of the company's property, secured by the joint and several guarantee of some of the directors of the company.

A few days prior to the date of the winding-up order the vendors called upon the company to pay them the £3,000 due to them under the purchase contracts, to which demand the directors replied by stating that the company was not in a position to pay the amount, and that therefore they could not raise any objection to the vendors resuming possession of their patent rights under the agreements of the 3rd and 7th September, 1888. The directors further instructed the Secretary to communicate with the trustee, Mr. Brooks, to whom the patents had been assigned, to the effect that so far as the Company was concerned he was at liberty to hand over the patents to the vendors.

The proofs having been called over, the Chairman (Mr. Cully, assistant official receiver) commented upon the position of the company as set out by the official receiver's observations. He pointed out that the assets were valued at £788 9s. 1d., but inasmuch as they were all covered by the debentures, apparently there were no assets available for the payment of the unsecured debts, returned at £5,649. The deficiency account showed that although the gross sales from carrying on the business only amounted to £880, and at the date of the winding-up order the stock and materials in hand were only valued at £160, a sum of £3,406 had been expended in stores and materials, and the company had paid out £4,903 in salaries and wages. The contract for the purchase of the patents having fallen through, the patents had reverted to the vendors.

Mr. E. H. D'Avigdor, a director, pointed out that the difference in the purchases and sales of the stock and materials was entirely accounted for by the fact that the company was formed to experimentalize, and during the first two years the experiments did not prove successful, the result being that a large proportion of the stock was unsaleable. A further reason was that thousands of the barrels were given away as samples. The directors had never taken out any money from the company in the shape of fees or salaries, but had instead invested considerable sums with a view to making the undertaking a success. Negotiations were pending with a view to the reconstruction of the company, and if they proved effectual the directors hoped to shortly pay a substantial sum to the unsecured creditors.

The meeting resolved to leave the case in the hands of the official receiver, who will act as liquidator, and Messrs. Sanguinetti, Perry and True were elected as a committee of inspection to assist in the administration of the estate.

The contributories met later in the day, Mr. Cully again presiding, and a similar course was adopted as that resolved upon by the creditors.

NATIONAL UNION OF PAPER MILL WORKERS.

MEETING AT RADCLIFFE.

The members of the Radcliffe branch met at their Club House (Old Cross Inn), on Saturday night, 21st inst. Mr. Pemberton (branch president) took the chair.

The GENERAL SECRETARY of the Union (Mr. Wm. Ross) addressed the meeting. In commencing, he stated that the executive were unable to grant the application from the members of one mill in the branch for a special payment from the funds for repeated stoppages of work of less than nine consecutive days. Mr. Ross stated that even although they had adhered strictly to the "nine days' clause," they had already paid over £500 in unemployed benefit this year. He said that over £100 of that sum had been paid to members thrown idle by mills being shut for want of coal. He felt sure, however, despite that fact that they would all agree with him in wishing that the miners might be successful in maintaining their unquestionable right to a living wage, which was all they were asking for. He hoped that the example of united and heroic action being shown by the members of the Miners' Federation would serve to stimulate all paper mill workers to band themselves together. On concluding, Mr. Ross's explanation as to decision of the executive was unanimously accepted as satisfactory, and he was awarded a vote of thanks.

FENISCOWLES BRANCH.

The yearly meeting of the above branch was held at Feniscowles Hall on the 22nd inst., Mr. John Norse, president, presiding. After the usual branch business had been disposed of, the General Secretary, Mr. Wm. Ross (who had been requested to be present), was called on to give an address.

MR. ROSS spoke at some length on the general position of the Union, and stated that the experience of the past year had clearly shown the absolute necessity of raising the contributions to meet the heavy out-of-work expenditure. From what he knew of the feeling in the majority of the branches, he thought that the rates would be raised at the next annual meeting of the Union. Mr. Ross then briefly described the work done at the Belfast Trades Union Congress. He stated that the principal resolution he was instructed to move at the Congress was not reached, but that he had by desire of Executive just written to all the principal newspaper owners of the United Kingdom, and requested a reply as to their willingness to print the words, "Printed on paper made in the United Kingdom," on top of first page of their publication. He said that up to Saturday 30 replies had come to hand, and that no less than 20 of these were in favour of printing the declaration on all their issues. Mr. Ross said it was the intention of the Executive to publish a list of the newspapers willing to print the words suggested on the top of their issues, to all trade unions and similar bodies, and urge the members to only buy those newspapers that declared British paper only had been used in their production.

The meeting heartily approved of the action of the Executive.

A vote of thanks to Mr. Ross and the chairman concluded the business.

THE week's exports of paper at New York were:

B. West Indies	... 530 pkgs	South Africa	... 1 cases
" "	... 30 rms	Hull	... 16 "
B. Guiana ...	... 150 pkgs	London	... 224 "
Liverpool ...	... 31 "	New Zealand	... 21 "
Southampton	... 1 case	New Brunswick ...	20 "

MECHANICAL WOOD PULP.—During the year ended June 30th, 1893, the daily producing capacity of mills in the United States making mechanical wood pulp—excluding some pulp made and used at paper mills, for which no returns have been given—increased 26 per cent., compared with the year next preceding. The total daily capacity of the wood pulp mills, according to the New York *Paper Trade Journal*, is 2,142 7-10 tons.

DAILY PRODUCING CAPACITY (IN POUNDS) OF MILLS IN THE UNITED STATES MAKING WOOD PULP.

States.	1892.	1893.	Inc. or Dec.
California	20,000	20,000	...
Colorado	24,000	24,000	...
Georgia	16,500	16,500	...
Illinois	20,000	20,000	...
Indiana	189,000	181,000	†8,000
Kentucky	—	1,500	*1,500
Maine	332,000	591,000	*259,000
Maryland	20,000	20,000	...
Massachusetts	63,300	73,300	*10,000
Michigan	80,000	68,000	†12,000
Minnesota	20,000	20,000	...
New Hampshire	343,000	384,000	*41,000
New York	1 361,800	1,786,400	*424,600
North Carolina	15,000	9,000	†6,000
Ohio	20,000	20,000	...
Oregon	50,000	50,000	...
Pennsylvania	79,500	112,500	*33,000
Tennessee	2,000	4,000	*2,000
Vermont	265,200	277,200	*12,000
Virginia	12,000	12,000	...
Washington	12,000	12,000	...
West Virginia	90,000	90,000	...
Wisconsin	365,000	493,000	*128,000
Totals	3,400,300	4,285,400	*885,100

* Increase. † Decrease.

Since 1881 the percentage of gain in the producing capacity of the wood pulp mills has been 784 5-6 per cent., the total annual capacity being about 642,810 tons, the actual output being considerably short of this amount, and difficult to estimate approximately. There is also one other item of manufacture in the papermaking industry which exceeds the percentage of gain above stated, and that is wood pulp board, the gain in which for a corresponding period was 853 11-13 per cent.

THE new mill of the Poland Paper Company, Mechanic Falls, Me., will, it is said, be the most complete mill in the country. Two Hercules wheels on a horizontal shaft of 1,300 horse-power capacity have been put in to drive the beating and washing engines. These wheels were supplied by the Holyoke Machine Company.

THE Reed beating engine will be built for the American market by the Pusey & Jones Company, Wilmington, Del.

THE American paper trade does not show much improvement, and reports are not encouraging. Some mills are running full time, others half time, and some are shut down. The news mills seem to be the best off. The contest in the strawboard industry is greatly to the advantage of consumers, low prices being the order of the day.

DEATH OF MR. THOMAS VERNON.—The death is recorded of Mr. Thomas Vernon, the senior member of Vernon Bros. & Co., and one of the oldest men connected with the American paper trade. He died at Brooklyn on the 5th inst. Mr. Vernon was born in Devonshire, England, on the 20th August, 1818. He went to America when he was 20 years of age, and began business in the paper trade in a small way, and by energy and hard work developed a large trade.

GREAT FIRE IN NEW YORK.—A destructive fire, resulting in losses estimated at 3,500,000 dols., broke out on the 18th inst. at Messrs. William Campbell and Co.'s wall-paper factory, West Forty-first-street, New York. The whole of the building, with most of its contents, was burned out. The flames rapidly spread to Messrs. Haviland and Nevins's paper mills, and adjoining premises. The losses of Messrs. Campbell and Co. alone amount to 2,000,000 dols.

MR. CHAMBERLAIN recently went from New York to the Bahamas to look over the extensive sisal plantation on the island of Andros, which is under the management of his son, Mr. Nevile Chamberlain. Andros is the largest island in the Bahamas archipelago, and the soil there is said to be particularly suitable for the cultivation of sisal. Great preparations were made at Nassau to accord the Unionist leader a fitting reception, and no doubt the sisal industry will receive a fresh "boom" from the right hon. gentleman's visit.

MASCHINEN BANANSTALT GOLZERN (formerly Gottschald and Notzli).—The report for 1892-3 states that large orders last year enabled the company to make one of their best balances. After deducting general expenses, the gross profits amounted to M210,461. Of this sum M35,681 will be written off for various purposes, and M25,000 allowed against slowly coming in assets. The shareholders will receive 11 per cent. dividend (M99,000) M29,956 go as bonuses, M10,000 to reserve, M5,000 for benevolent purposes, M5,000 for gratuities, schools, &c., M596 will be carried forward. The general reserve fund amounts to M180,000, or 20 per cent. of the share capital, and the total reserve comes to M300,000, or 33⅓ per cent. of the share capital. The gross profit is M61,000 higher than last year.

WINTERSCHE PAPIER FABRIKEN, Wertheim, near Hameln.—Director H. Wedemeyer has retired, and Herr Ferd. Kuch has taken his place. The head office is now at Altkoster.

LIPSCHAU WOOD PULP WORKS, near Lorenzdorf, have been bought by Herr F. W. Rabenau, who has retired from the firm of Trapp and Munch, Berlin.

POMMERSCHE PAPIERFABRIK HOHENKRUG.—A gross profit of M70,887 has been made on a share capital of M650,000. The general meeting decided to write off M46,700, and pay a dividend of 2 per cent.

HERR LOUIS GRUNANER has taken over the firm of Engen Dietz, in Berlin, engineering and machinery works.

MR. LORENZ ECK, one of the members of the firm Joseph Eck and Sons, Dusseldorf, Germany, will be at the World's Fair (as we are informed by the German Machinery Commission) from October 12th to the close of it, in order to decide all pending questions in regard to their exhibit, personally, and to wind up the interests of their exhibit. Messrs. Eck and Sons made a splendid show in the German Section, Machinery Hall, consisting of super and friction calenders and embossing machines of very high finish and elegant construction.

AUSTRIAN CONSULAR REPORTS (ODESSA).—Paper has been imported 2,011q. in value of 118,369 rubels. Importations have remained for years on the same modest level. In 1890 2,000q., in 1891 2,300q. Austria only participates with about a third of the total; Germany does more. The sorts mostly capable of importation from Austria are certain kinds of luxus and fancy papers, also cardboards of best classes. In papers made from chemical pulp next to no importation can take place from Austria, because protective duties favour the Russian home production, particularly in Finland. The quality is not equal to the Austrian, but the price is so much lower that competition is impossible.

THE Finnish Senate has voted the sum of 200,000 marks towards the carrying out of railway works in the country during the coming year.

CHILI.—Paper of British manufacture to the value of £28,000, and foreign paper to the value of £1,300 were exported from the United Kingdom to Chili in 1892. In 1888 the respective values were £18,400 and £4,300.

WORLD'S PAPER TRADE REVIEW OFFICE,
58, SHOE LANE, LONDON, E.C.
OCTOBER 26, 1893.

TRADE NOTES.

PAPER MILL SHARES.—Dealings in paper mill shares during the past week have been very small, and, with the exception of Darwen and Ramsbottom which remain firm, show a downward movement. E st Lancashire have dropped ½. and a decline of ¼ is registered in Roachbridge shares. Kellner Partington's are weaker at 61s. to 63s. The scarcity of coal and high prices seriously affect some companies.

SALE OF BROUGHTON GROVE PAPER WORKS.—At the Mitre Hotel, Cathedral Gates, Manchester, on Tuesday last, Messrs. William Wilson and Son offered for sale the Broughton Grove Paper Works, and the estate adjoining, known as Fairy Hill estate, with residence, stables, &c., also twelve cottages. The whole of the property covering an area of 95,198 square yards, and subject to chief rents, amounting to £297 8s., realised £24,000.

HENRY'S CHEMICAL WORKS CO.—A petition, under the Cessio Acts, has been presented to the Sheriff of Lanarkshire, at the instance of William Tait and Co., 97, Fordneuk-street, Glasgow, pursuers, against Henry's Chemical Works Co., 145, Crownpoint-road, Mile-end, Glasgow, defenders; and the sheriff-substitute has ordained A. C. Henry, a partner of defender's firm, to appear for public examination within the chambers of Mr. Sheriff Birnie, County Buildings, Glasgow, upon the 8th of November, at which diet all creditors are required to appear.

THE CHEMICAL AND ELECTROLYTIC SYNDICATE, LTD.—The registration of this company has already been recorded in these pages. The patents to be acquired are those owned by Messrs. F. M. and C. H. M. Lyte, and Professor George Lunge. The patentees' representatives are Mr. W. Macnab, F.I.C., F.C.S., 14, Great Smith-street, Westminster, and Mr. H. K. Baynes, of 52, Gloucester-crescent, Hyde-park. These two gentlemen act as directors in conjunction with Messrs. W. E. B. Blenkinsop and Mr. N. H. Fenner. Mr. Baynes is chairman of Pyke, Harris and Co., Limited, electrical engineers, Westminster.

WILLIAM MUIR AND CO., MANCHESTER, LIMITED.—This company has been registered with a nominal capital of £80,000, in £5 shares. Objects: To acquire the business carried on by Charles Garnett, Alfred Muir and Herbert Garnett, at Strangeways, Manchester, and elsewhere, under the style or firm of William Muir and Co., and the works and property held therewith; to undertake the liabilities and engagements of the said firm, and to carry on the business of machinists, machine and engineering tool makers, mechanical engineers, iron and brass founders, workers in metal, gun and ordnance makers. There shall not be less than three nor more than five directors. The first are: Alfred Muir, Herbert Garnett and Francis H. Garnett. Qualification, £1,000 shares or stock. Remuneration, £100 per annum, to be divided as they themselves determine. Alfred Muir is the managing director. Remuneration as fixed by sale agreement.

MASSON, SCOTT AND CO., LTD.—At the meeting of debenture holders of Masson, Scott and Co., Ltd., engineers, York-place, Battersea, held on the 19th inst., in the London Tavern, Fenchurch-street, E.C., to consider the best means of dealing with the assets of the company in face of their large unrealised asset in Turkey, Mr. Scott gave a statement of the exact position of affairs, on hearing which the meeting resolved "to approve of the appointment of Mr. Robert Scott by the court as receiver, with the addition of five debenture holders to form a committee, such committee to advise with Mr. Scott as to the best means of realising the whole of the company's assets in the interests of the debenture holders and creditors." The following gentlemen were appointed to form the committe, viz.:—Mr. W. H. Willcox, of Messrs. W. H. Willcox and Co., 36, Southwark-street, London, S.E.; Mr. Alex. Glegg, of Messrs. Bowen and Co., brass founders, Clerkenwell, London; Mr. George Hatch, Crown Wharf, 5, Upper Thames-street, London; Mr. Henry Hendra, of Messrs. Wm. Hendra and Sons, founders, Battersea; Mr. John Harper, jun., of Messrs. Harpers, Ltd., Albion Iron Works, Aberdeen.

FORD PAPER WORKS, LIM.—On the 18th inst., at the Durham Quarter Sessions, the appeal of the Ford Paper Works, Limited, against the Sunderland Assessment Committee, was heard before Colonel Lloyd Wharton and other magistrates. The counsel for the appellants was Mr. Edward Boyle, of the South-Eastern Circuit, and Mr. Temperley, and for the respondents, Mr. Lawson Walton, Q.C., and Mr. Scott Fox. Among the witnesses for the Assessment Committee were Messrs. Hedley and Green, the union valuers, and for the company, Mr. Humphreys-Davies, F.S.I., Messrs. Cornett, Potts, Bertram, Menzies, and others. The case was stopped before all the appellants' witnesses were called. We are glad to report that the appeal was allowed with costs, and the old assessment of the company was reinstated. This is the second appeal this company have had to contest at Quarter Sessions during the last twelve months with uniform success.

THE RATING OF MACHINERY.—An important appeal, raising the whole question of the rating of machinery, was heard at Sheffield City Sessions, Friday, on Mr. Frank Lockwood, Q.C., M.P., Recorder. Messrs. Fairbrother and Co. (Limited), Crown Steel and Wire Mills, Sheffield, appealed against the assessment of their property on the ground that the machinery had been rated. Formerly the gross value was £466 and the rateable value £349. In October last the former was raised to £1,175 and the latter to £681. The Assessment Committee of the Sheffield Union, who were the respondents, alleged that previously the enhanced value of the property because of the presence of machinery in the buildings had not been considered. This consideration had now been given, and the property was not overrated. For the appellants it was argued that, though the committee were entitled to take into their consideration the presence of the machinery, they were not entitled to have it valued and then rate it, the course which had been pursued in this case. Mr. Edward Boyle was for the appellants, and Mr. Hugo Young for the respondents. After a long hearing, the Recorder reserved his decision until next sessions.

Short of Water.—The manufacturers at West Hartlepool have for six weeks been suffering from a scarcity of water, some large concerns running only part time. In consequence of the continued drought the gas and water company has sent out notices that the water supply for manufacturing purposes will be cut off. Most of the large works will soon be brought to a complete stoppage, and thousands of workmen thrown idle. No rain has fallen in the district for weeks.

Rag Importation. — Dr. Collingridge, medical officer of health for the port of London, in his half-yearly report just published, states that on January 21st the order of the Local Government Board requiring disinfection of rags from certain ports in Europe, Black Sea, Sea of Azof, and Turkey in Asia, was revoked for a period of two months, but during the three months following this period 3,777 bales of rags and clothing were disinfected, but this quantity might have been trebled without overtaxing the arrangements.

British Trade With South Africa.—A corrrespondent, having just returned from South Africa, finds that merchants out there were importing American manufactures from New York at a freight charge of seventeen shillings and sixpence per ton, whilst identical articles from England had to incur a freight of thirty-two shillings and sixpence per ton. The English and American manufacturers pay the same duty, but the extra cost on the carriage of the former seriously handicaps the English manufacturer in competition with his American cousin.

"Pura."—Mr. James Emmett, Reuben-street, Camp-road, Leeds, directs attention to his patent "Pura," a remedy claimed to be fully efficient and economical in dealing with pollution. The "Pura" is sent out in ½-cwt. blocks, and one is simply placed in an open conduit, and the discoloured and polluted water running over it carries away sufficient of the compound to effect purification after passing through settling tanks.

Alkali was exported from Great Britain to Italy in 1892 to the value of £79,975, a great increase compared with 1888, when the value was £59,000.

American Wood Pulp in Europe.—Another entire cargo of American wood pulp has arrived this week at Fleetwood by the vessel "Earnoch." This vessel which, like the preceding two cargoes, was shipped to this country by Messrs. A. Wertheim and Co., Hamburg, and carried the enormous quantity of 32,009 bales. The quality of the American wood pulp is said to have given great satisfaction, and it looks as if it will become a standard article in the European market.

The ceremony of unveiling a memorial to the poet William Drummond, of Hawthornden, took place on Saturday last in the churchyard of Lasswade, Mid Lothian. Amongst those who took part in the proceedings was Mr. John Cowan, of Beeslack.

From Tunis last year £92,668 of rags, esparto, etc., were received at United Kingdom ports. Compared with 1888 a great reduction is shown, the value at that period being £115,419.

The United States in 1892 imported British paper to the value of £71,562. In 1888 the value was £76,131. Great Britain in 1892 exported home rags to the value of £366,659, and foreign rags to the extent of £307,581. In 1888 the respective values were £435,941 and £385,152. Alkali was exported in 1892 to the value of £1,248,351, and in 1888, £871,606.

Scott's Evaporating Apparatus. — Messrs. F. W. Scott, E. G. Scott, and F. W. Scott, have recently introduced several modifications relating to apparatus for evaporating or concentrating saccharine juices, brine, and other liquids *in vacuo*, and to that class of such apparatus in which a valve or the like is employed for effecting the removal of the substances deposited during the evaporation or concentration without interfering with the operation of the apparatus. In using such an apparatus it is found that the recesses or troughs which receive the deposited substances after having discharged their contents become filled with air, which is carried back into the pan, and tends to reduce the vacuum. The object of the present invention is to prevent air from thus being introduced into the vacuum pan, and to this end the patentees provide for exhausting the air from such recesses or troughs. In carrying out the process they provide the following arrangement, that is to say, in that part of the casing of the cock or valve to which the troughs or recesses are opposite after they have discharged their contents and before they are again brought into communication with the interior of the pan they form an opening communicating by a pipe with the air pump or exhauster working in conjunction with the vacuum pan or with other suitable exhausting apparatus so that the air can be exhausted from the troughs or recesses in the desired manner. In practice Messrs. Scott find it advantageous to arrange a valve in the said pipe, which valve remains closed when a trough or recess is in communication with the atmosphere, and is opened at the required times by a cam rotated with the discharge valve.

RUSSIAN IMPORT DUTIES UP-TO-DATE.

PAPER, &c., STATIONERY, AND BOOKS.

TARIFF CLASSIFICATION.	TARIFF RATES OF DUTY.			ENGLISH EQUIVALE[NTS]	
		Rbls.	*cop.*		£
Papier mache and carton pierre, not manufactured, and cardboard of wood pulp ...	Poud	0	35	Cwt.	0
Pasteboard in sheets and rolls, not otherwise specified; tarred or untarred paper for roofing; pasteboard and paper impregnated with resin, sulphur, saltpetre, &c. ...	,,	0	60	,,	0
Articles of papier mache and carton pierre, except those mentioned below	,,	0	60	,,	0
Ditto - ditto, varnished or painted, imitating turned or carved wooden wares (except small wares)	,,	6	00	,,	[illegible]
Unsized paper, white or coloured, without ornaments; paper ruled for music and for embroidery, without pattern	,,	2	40	,,	
Sized paper, white or coloured in the paste, without ornaments; unbound copybooks; Bristol board and other surfaced and glazed cardboard; paper bobbins for winding thread; paper combined with coarse tissues; transparent and tracing paper ..	,,	4	00	,,	
Paper hangings, and borders for paper hangings...	,,	6	00	,,	
Writing paper, and paper for printers', bookbinders', lithographers', and confectioners' work, gilt, silvered, or ornamented with impressions, pastings, borders, crests, cyphers, pictures, &c.; cigarette paper, tissue paper, coloured paper not dyed in the paste	,,	9	54	,,	
Envelopes, lamp shades, artificial flowers, &c	,,	9	54	,,	
Prints, engravings, oleographs, lithographs, photographs	,,	8	00	,,	
Vegetable parchment	,,	8	00	,,	
Playing cards	Prohibited			Proh[ibited]	
Bookbinders' work, all kinds; office and copying books, bound; bindings for books and albums, imported separately	Poud	14	50	Cwt.	
Cardboard wares (except small wares) ...	,,	14	50	,,	
Pictures and drawings by hand, and manuscripts, unbound	Free			F[ree]	
Ditto - ditto, bound...	Poud	1	00	Cwt.	
*Music, maps, and plans, printed, lithographed, or photographed, and unbound	,,	4	00	,,	
*Ditto - ditto, bound	,,	5	00	,,	
*Books and periodicals in foreign languages, unbound	Free			[Free]	
*Ditto - ditto, bound	Poud	1	00	Cwt.	
*Books printed abroad in the Russian language, unbound	,,	3	00	,,	
*Ditto - ditto, bound	,,	4	00	,,	
Pens, pencils, &c.	Funt	0	40	,,	
Ink and ink powder	Poud	3	00	,,	
Sealing-wax	,,	2	65	,,	
Rags (except woollen)	Free				
Paper pulp:					
Pulp of wood chemically prepared (cellulose)	Poud	0	35	Cwt	
Ditto, not chemically prepared, and other paper pulp; also paper shreds	,,	0	20	,,	

* Subject to the Censor's regulations.

GREECE.

Paper was imported at Syra in 1892 to the value of £5,485, against £9,599 in the preceding year. The mineral resources of Milo, one of the Islands of the Cyclades, are very important, consisting principally of sulphur, manganese ore, gypsum, and argentiferous barytes. The quality, extracted in powder, is by far superior to that derived from Sicily (roll sulphur), which is imported into Greece. It is wholly sent to the Peloponnesus, where it is used chiefly in the treatment of the vines, against the oïdium. The annual output is 2,000 tons. This exploitation is very important. About 12,000 tons are annually exported to England and America, and from 3,000 tons to 4,000 tons to the Laurium smelteries. Though this mineral occurs in abundant and thick beds, chiefly associated with sulphur, the quantity disposed of is very limited, owing to the high price (6 dr. per quintal, or 44 okes) demanded by the Government, who reserve the rights of this and other exploitations in the island. The average annual extraction of gypsum is 220 tons, valued at £667. It is extensively used in the preparation of new wines. The exploitation of this rich mineral has not yet been taken in hand; but, according to a report recently issued, the results of the inquiries which were instituted by the Government, at a cost of 37,000 dr., exceeded the highest anticipations. The ores occur in different parts of the island, viz., Triades, Mirobilia, Pelonisa, Pikrodoun, Kastanàs, Bani, and Klima, but they are not all of the same importance. The masses of barytes have been estimated over 10,000,000 tons, and it is said the mineral contains, at different localities, a proportion of silver varying from 10-oz. to 350-oz. per ton. The salt pans are 10 in number, and a Government monopoly. About 150,000 okes of salt are yearly produced, exclusively obtained by evaporation from sea water. Though the millstones are of a very good quality, their use is very limited (chiefly in Greece, Turkey, Dalmatia, and Cyprus), owing to the little development of the industry. The value of the stones up to last year amounted to some 50,000 dr. annually. The quarries, however, from which the stones have hitherto been obtained are now nearly exhausted.

INLAND WATERWAYS.—Some interesting statistics touching navigable inland waterways have been published in Germany. It appears that China takes the lead in artificial waterways, having no less than 1,054 miles of canals. The United States come next with 666 miles. France follows with 630, and England with 625 miles, and then comes Germany with 264. Little Holland has 186 miles of canals, whilst big Russia has only 175. But canals by no means represent the whole of the inland waterways. Russia has 4,188 miles of navigable rivers, whilst Holland has only 68. France, again, has 1,080 miles of river navigation against England's 357, and Germany, with little more than half the mileage of canals in England and France, has a far larger extent of inland waterways than either of them, owing to the possession of 3,152 miles of navigable river. A country which does not possess a single canal has the longest inland waterways in the world, that country being Brazil, with no less than 4,442 miles of navigable rivers. Portugal seems to be the only European country without canals, contenting itself with its 94 miles of navigable river. In Spain there are 54 miles of canal.

A LOST OPPORTUNITY.—In connection with the appointment to the vacant Commissionership of Woods and Forests, the *Chronicle* laments that the Government has not taken the opportunity to appoint an expert in forestry. "We annually import," it says, "some 6,000,000 loads of timber, and as many of the sources of supply are contracting, we may, within an ascertainable period, be face to face with a timber famine. In other words, we are—or were a few years ago—spending some £13,000,000 sterling per annum on timber and timber products, while we have, according to the calculation of Mr. Schlich, the principal professor of forestry at Cooper's Hill, some 60,000,000 acres of waste land, which could, and should be laid down as forests. The bearing of this stupendous fact on the Labour problem is obvious enough. We are hearing much of the ever-present problem of the unemployed, and Mr. Fowler and his colleagues will hear much more of it before the winter is over. Mr. Schlich estimates that we might annually plant some 300,000 acres, employing at least 15,000 labourers, which would sustain a population of 75,000 souls. After forests had been created, and (say in some forty years) we had entered on our new possessions, we should be, says Mr. Schlich, in a position to employ regularly some 100,000 workers, or a population of a half a million people. It so happens that the opportunity for a national experiment in afforestation occurs at the very doors of the great Inferno of English poverty—the East-end. There is plenty of waste land obtainable between Barking and Pitsea, and Essex, especially that part of it which borders on London, is famous for the growth of English trees."

THE new harbour at Dover will have an extent of 56 acres. It will, no doubt, relieve the traffic of the overcrowded Thames. The heavy pilotage and constant risks of river navigation will induce other vessels to use the new port, in addition to which, vessels making short runs will be able to perform several extra voyages in the course of the year.

THE Lancashire paper trade does not look with a friendly eye upon the working of the Scandinavian combination of wood pulp producers, and their recent resolution to still further advance the price for deliveries during the forthcoming year. They are looking elsewhere for supplies of raw material.—*Manchester Examiner and Times.*

JAVA imported alkali from Great Britain in 1892 the value of £4,505; in 1888 the value was only £174.

Printed and Published EVERY FRIDAY
AT 58, SHOE LANE, LONDON, E.C.,
By W. JOHN STONHILL.
ESTABLISHED 1878.

FRIDAY, OCTOBER 27, 1893.

RIVER pollution is again troubling various Lancashire industrial concerns located on the Irk and the Irwell. One of the Manchester papers seems rather jubilant upon the subject, and heads the article regarding the officialism of the Mersey and Irwell Joint Committee as "Manufacturers Brought to Book." Manufacturers are worried enough by bad trade, foreign competition, the tricks of wholesale buyers, extra expenses owing to the coal strike and labour difficulties, without receiving intimation that they are offenders in the direction of river pollution, and that proceedings will be taken. A few of them luckily escaped with a notice to remedy the alleged defects within three months. The establishment of expensive filtration works in these times of depression is no light burden for the manufacturers, and in the opinion of many practical men it would be better for the rivers to run jet black rather than cause the stoppage of works, and the loss of work to thousands of men, whose wives and children would probably have to starve during the period of making the desired official "satisfactory progress" with costly filtration works. As a chain is only the strength of its weakest link, so also is an industry only capable of a certain amount of expenditure, and it may break down if unduly taxed at a time when money is scarcer to obtain than it has been at any period during the last quarter of a century. Local Government Boards, by needlessly harrowing manufacturers, are going the way to heavily increase local rates.

As the wood pulp industry develops various changes must inevitably follow. A Manchester paper says that Lancashire papermakers do not view with satisfaction the Scandinavian combination, and an American contemporary points out that "ground wood pulp is being shipped from Bangor to Europe in considerable quantities. Three cargoes, aggregating 3,500 tons, have cleared this season. The shipments were made by F. H. Clergue, the pulp all coming from the mills of the Moosehead Pulp and Paper Company, Solon, and Penobscot Pulp and Paper Company, Veazie." Of course, if Scandinavian mechanical wood pulp is well sold ahead at high and very profitable prices, manufacturers have nothing to complain of, and apparently the Union is at the present time stronger than ever. Quite recently the Union of South German Wood Pulp Makers was formed, comprising thirty-two firms. A central office has been established at Munich, which will entirely control the sales of pulp, and the members will have no direct relations with the consumers. The association, according to a circular issued, "trusts to meet with the goodwill of the papermakers, and assures them that their efforts will not go against the interests of the paper trade."

THE Manufacturers' Paper Co. (represented by Mr. Sidney Holt, London) are evidently developing a large business in wood pulp with this country. From latest reports to hand we notice a shipment of 25,693 bales from Portland, Me., on board the "Eleazer W. Clark," for Glasgow. Another large arrival is to the order of Messrs. A. Wertheim & Co., comprising 32,009 bales, from Bangor, Maine, landed at Fleetwood.

Although the funds of the National Union of Paper Mill Workers have been subject to heavy demands, owing to the stagnation of trade due to the coal strike and other causes, yet the spirit of activity seems to be as prominent as ever. The latest idea is to get the principal newspaper proprietors to use home manufactured paper, and to boldly proclaim the fact on the top of the first page as follows: "Printed on paper made in the United Kingdom." In response to the National Union's patriotic request some thirty replies have been received, of which twenty are favourable. It is doubtful whether our importations of foreign paper will be materially lessened, unless there be a universal application of the proposed system. Subsequently, perhaps, in the distribution of the necessary commodities of life consumers will insist upon having "paper manufactured in

Great Britain." We understand that trade unionists will be asked not to buy those newspapers which do not adopt "the top line," and considering the innumerable uses to which paper is put, they may, in carrying the principle further, refuse of merchants, tradesmen and others, both in matters commercial and domestic, any article where foreign has been substituted for "Paper of British manufacture." The idea sounds Utopian, but it is one way advocated by the Union of meeting foreign competition.

In reply to a correspondent, who asks us for particulars concerning the Russian import duties, we publish on another page a complete list of articles under the heading "Paper, &c., Stationery, and Books." It may be pointed out that the new tariff came into force in Russia in 1891, but by a decree of the 1st June last the Russian Government established a double customs tariff, consisting of maximum and minimum duties, thus adopting the principle upon which the tariffs of France and Spain are based. The maximum tariff is, under this *regime*, to be applied to imports from those countries which do not accord advantageous conditions to the importation and transit of Russian merchandise. It is based upon the 1891 tariff by the addition to the rates leviable under that tariff of a surtax amounting to 30 per cent. in the case of a number of articles, and of 20 per cent. in the case of some others. The 1891 tariff itself became the minimum tariff, but this has been modified in some not unimportant respects by the stipulations of the Franco-Russian Commercial Convention of June, 1893, and this modified tariff is applied to imports into Russia from the United Kingdom in virtue of the most-favoured-nation treatment to which we are entitled under our treaty with Russia. It may be mentioned in passing, that in consequence of the failure of commercial negotiations between Germany and Russia, a virtual tariff war is now proceeding between those powers. Not only does Russia at the present time apply her maximum tariff to German goods, but she has added a further 50 per cent. to the rates fixed by that tariff, and Russian dues on German shipping have also been increased. Comparing the present and former return it may be pointed out that a reduction of 10 per cent. in duty has been made on ornamental papers other than paper hangings, cigarette and tissue papers, envelopes and other paper wares. It may interest our readers to know that we have in course of preparation the tariff classification of Sweden, Norway, Denmark, Germany, Holland, Belgium, France, Portugal, Spain, Italy, Austria-Hungary, Switzerland, Greece, Roumania, and the United States.

Considerable verbosity has been introduced in the Mitscherlich-Ekman-Knosel controversy. Both Ekman and Mitscherlich claim to have been the first to introduce in Germany a practical sulphite pulp process, and statement after statement have been advanced to further the claims of the two disputants. They both, however, recognise that there has been a large amount of talk, and each endeavours to show the futility of of the other's observations by alleging absence of proof. It is easy to make assertions, but to substantiate them appears to be another matter altogether. Professor Mitscherlich, in his latest contribution on the subject, states there is nothing to show that sulphite was received in Germany in 1875 from the Bergvik works. He puts the date at the latter end of 1878, and is certainly not convinced by "proofs" that Mr. Ekman claims to have brought forward. The statement that Mr. Ekman was at one time in Mr. Francke's service is disputed, and Mr. Ekman says he has never seen Professor Mitscherlich, notwithstanding what has been said to the contrary.

The condition of the London unemployed is being very practically studied and reported upon by the *Evening News and Post*. The editor of our energetic contemporary knows well what he is doing, and observes that local authorities are doing practically nothing to alleviate the distress of the poorer classes in the metropolis, and objects to the absence of zealous interest in the workers in London by the organs which are so busy in assisting the miners in staying out on strike. The position of the lithographic trade is being examined this week by our contemporary, and the facts brought to light disclose difficulties in the life of the practical skilled workman of London which are appalling. We regret that space this week precludes us from reprinting and criticising the disclosures so graphically described, especially as regards the lithographic printing work for many of the religious and other public societies, which is needlessly "printed in Germany." The management of the so-called religious societies evidently forget the Scriptural injunction that "Charity should begin at home," thus helping to pauperise skilled labour in this country.

WORLD'S PAPER TRADE REVIEW OFFICE,
58, SHOE LANE, LONDON, E.C.
OCTOBER 26, 1898.

MARKET REPORT

and RECORD of IMPORTS

Of Foreign Rags, Wood Pulp, Esparto, Paper, Millboards, Strawboards, &c., at the Ports of London Liverpool, Southampton, Bristol, Hull, Fleetwood, Middlesborough, Glasgow, Grangemouth, Granton, Dundee, Leith, Dover, Folkestone, and Newhaven, for the WEEK ENDING OCTOBER 25.

From SPECIAL Sources and Telegrams.

Telegrams—"STONHILL, LONDON."

CHEMICALS.—The market is quiet. The tone is steady, due to the stoppage of works, and the consequent scarcity of supplies. A better business, however, is reported in shipping orders. BLEACHING POWDER is offered at £7 15s., and CAUSTIC SODA 77% is quoted at £11 10s. to £12. SULPHUR is firm at £4 2s. 6d to £4 5s. The continued low prices of SODA ASH are inducing buyers to contract over next year. SODA CRYSTALS remain at £2 10s. SULPHATE OF AMMONIA at £13, less 2½%, shows a drop of 10s.

Prices are nominally as follows:

Article			Terms		£	s.	d.
Alkali, 58%	tierces	...	f.o.r. works	2½%	5	10	0
" 58%	bags	...	" "	2½%	5	5	0
58%	...	...	f.o.b. Liverpool	2½%	5	12	6
Alum (Ground),	tierces	...	" Liverpool	2½%	5	7	6
" "	barrels	...	" "	2½%	5	17	6
" "	tierces	...	" Hull	2½%	5	5	0
"	"	...	Goole	2½%	5	5	0
Alum (Lump)	"	...	f.o.b. Liverpool	2½%	4	17	6
" "	barrels	...	" "	2½%	5	0	0
" "	tierces	...	" Hull	2½%	4	15	0
" "	"	...	Goole	2½%	4	15	0
" "	"	...	London	2½%	5	5	0
" "	"	...	f.a.s. Glasgow	2½%	5	5	0
Alumina Sulphate,	casks		f.o.b. Tyne		4	2	6
" "	bags		" "		3	17	6
Aluminoferric Cake,	slabs		Liverpool ...	...	2	15	0
" "	tierces		" ...	...	3	2	6
Alumina Cake,	slabs	...	Glasgow	...	2	15	0
" "	tierces	...	"	...	3	2	6
Aluminous Cake,	casks	...	Manchester	2½%	2	7	6
" "	"	...	Newcastle	2½%	2	10	0
" "	"	...	London	2½%	3	0	0
" "	bags	...	"	2½%	2	17	9
Blanc Fixe ...	...	...	f.o.b. Tyne	net	7	10	0
Bleach, 35%	...	...	" "	net	7	15	0
" (soft wood)		...	f.o.r. Lancs.	net	8	5	0
" (hard wood)		...	f.o.b. Liverpool	net	8	10	0
...	...	...	landed London	2½%	9	0	0
Borax (crystals)	...	...	... ...	net	29	0	0
powdered	...	...	... .	net	30	0	0
Caustic Cream, 60%		...	f.o.r. Lancs.	net	9	2	6
" " 60%		...	f.o.b. Liverpool	net	9	7	6
" Bottoms		...	" "	net	6	15	0
" "	...	...	f.o.b. Tyne	net	6	15	0
Chloride of Barium		...	f.o.b. Tyne	net	7	10	0
Caustic White 76-77%		...	f.o.r. Newcastle	net	11	15	0
" " 77%		f.o.r. or	f.o.b. Tyne	net	12	0	0
" " 74%		...	f.o.b. Liverpool	net	12	0	0
" " 70%		...	" "	net	11	0	0
" " 70%		...	" Hull	net	11	0	0
" " 70%		...	f.o.r. London	net	10	15	0
" " 70%		...	" Lancs.,	net	10	17	6
" " 60%		...	" London	net	9	15	0
" " 60%		...	f.o.b. Liverpool	net	10	0	0
Carbonat'd Ash 58%		...	" "	net	4	10	0
48%		...	" "	net	4	0	0
" 58%		...	f.o.r. Widnes	net	4	7	6
" 48%		...	" "	net	3	17	6

Article			Terms		£	s.	d.
Hypo-Sulphite of Soda...			f.o.r. Tyne		5	15	0
" "	10-ton lots		ex ship Liverp'l	net	6	10	0
Oxalic Acid ...	...	...	f.o.b. Liverpool	3¾%	per lb		½
Salt Cake ...	...	...	" works	net	1	10	0
Soda Ash, 52%	...	...	f.o.b. Tyne	net	4	0	0
" 52%	...	...	ex ship Thames	1%	4	12	6
" 52%	...	...	f.o.b. Liverpool	1%	4	5	0
Soda Crystals	...	...	" Tyne	net	2	10	0
" "	...	...	ex ship Thames	2½%	3	0	0
" "	...	...	f.o.b. Liverpool	net	3	5	0
Sulphur, roll	...	...	f.o.r. works	2½%	7	17	6
" flowers	...	...	" "	2½%	9	10	0
" recovered		...	" "	2½%	4	2	6
Sulphate of Ammonia	"		" "	2½%	13	0	0
" of Copper	...		" Liverpool	5%	16	0	0

FOREIGN.—F.o.b. Continental port:

Article	£	s.	d.
Alkali, 58% 2-cwt. bags £4 10/0; 10-cwt. casks ...	5	0	0
Caustic Soda, 70-72%	10	12	6
Hypo-Sulphite of Soda 10-ton lots casks	6	0	0
Sulphate of Alumina 7-8 cwt. casks net c.i.f. Ldn	4	7	
Blanc Fixe (c.i.f. London)	7	12	6

ESPARTO.—There is little change since last week in the market, which remains dull with a drooping tendency. Enquiry is limited, but at present rates there is not any encouragement to sellers to stimulate it.

Prices c.i.f. London and Leith, or f.o.r. Cardiff, Garston and Tyne Docks are nominally as follows:

		£	s.	d.		£	s.	d.
Spanish—	Fair to Good	£5	5	0	to	5	10	0
"	Fine to Best	5	10	0	"	5	15	0
Oran—	Fair to Good	3	5	0	"	3	10	0
"	First Quality...	3	15	0	"	3	17	6
Tripoli—	Hand-picked	3	15	0	"	3	17	6
"	Fair Average...	3	7	6	"	3	10	0
Bona & Philippeville	... ...	3	15	0	"	3	17	6

WEEK'S IMPORTS.

Quantity	From	Importer	Port.
625 tons	Almeria	H. Ottomann	Granton
709 "	Carthagena	R. H. Hay & Co	"
1884 "	Sfax	Bessich and Co	Leith

CHEMICAL WOOD PULPS.—There has been a better enquiry during the past week, but business has only been done on a small scale. The firmness of the best grades of SULPHITE hardly falls in with the views of buyers, and negotiations concerning contracts are consequently prolonged. SODA pulps are quiet.

Prices, ex steamer, London, Hull, Newcastle, Leith and Glasgow are nominally as follows:

	£	s.	d.		£	s.	d.
SULPHITE, Unbleached, Common	£10	15	0	to	11	0	0
" Superior	11	10	0	"	12	10	0
" " 50% moisture, d.w.	11	10	0	"	12	2	6
" Extra	13	0	0	"	14	0	0
" Bleached, moist					16	10	0
" Unbleached, English, del. Lancs. ...					10	15	0
" " " No. 1, ex mills, Ldn.					10	10	0
" " " No. 2, " "					9	15	0
SODA, Unbleached, Common ...	10	5	0	"	10	10	0
" " Extra.. ...	10	10	0	"	11	0	0
" Half-Bleached	12	10	0	"	14	0	0
SULPHATE, Unbleached, Common	10	10	0	"	11	0	0
" Extra	11	0	0	"	12	0	0
" Half-Bleached	13	10	0	"	14	0	0
Bleached	15	0	0	"	16	0	0

MECHANICAL WOOD PULPS.—The market is rather unsettled at the present time. Reports from Scandinavia are to the effect that prices have an upward tendency. Market quotations, however, are irregular, and this is attributed to American and Canadian pulp being shipped freely to Europe. There seems a desire on the part of several Scandinavian manufacturers to effect sales at present high prices, probably anticipating that they will not be maintained in the near future. Dry Pine is quoted £6 7s. 6d. and Moist Pine £3 5s.

Prices, ex steamer, London, Hull, Newcastle, Leith and Glasgow are nominally as follows :

MECHANICAL, Aspen, Dry ...	£7 10 0	to 8 0 0
Pine, Dry	6 7 6	,, 7 0 0
Pine, Moist	3 5 0	,, 3 10 0
Moist Brown	3 2 6	,, 3 5 0
Single Sorted	2 7 6	,, 2 10 0
Dry Brown	6 5 0	,, 6 10 0

WEEK'S IMPORTS.

Quantity	From	Importer	Port.
96 cases	Barcelona	F. Huth & Co	London
32009 bales	Bangor	G. Schjoth & Co	Fleetwood
269 ,,	Bergen	To order	Hull
1966 ,,	Christiania	,,	Grangemouth
1208 ,,	,,	,,	,,
41 ,,	,,	,,	London
4800 ,,	,,	H. B. Wood	Fleetwood
200 ,,	Christiansand	To order	Leith
500 ,,	Drammen	London Paper Mills Co	London
32 rolls	,,	Cookson & Co	,,
290 ,,	,,	Crabb and Co	,,
137 ,,	,,	Hernu Peron and Co	,,
184 ,,	,,	Alsing & Co	,,
680 ,,	,,	M. G. Skramnes	,,
70 cases	,,	Foulger & Co	,,
200 rolls	,,	Christophersen & Co	,,
660 bales	,,	G. Schjoth & Co	Fleetwood
563 ,,	,,	Raby and Mather	,,
1120 ,,	Drontheim	To order	Hull
201 ,,	Dusseldorf	,,	,,
608 ,,	Gothenburg	C. Salvesen & Co	Granton
650 ,,	,,	Henderson, Craig & Co	London
840 ,,	,,	Tough & Henderson	,,
68 ,,	,,	To order	,,
608 ,,	,,	,,	Hull
102 ,,	,,	Hummel & Co	London
20 ,,	,,	Smyth & Son	,,
6 ,,	,,	F. E. Foulger	,,
73 ,,	,,	To order	,,
43 ,,	,,	Bott and Co	,,
21 casks	Ghent	To order	,,
3051 bales	Halmstadt	,,	Hull
247 ,,	Helsingfors	,,	London
1191 ,,	Hambro	,,	,,
172 rolls	,,	,,	Leith
150 bales	Norrkoping	Johnston & Co	London
30 ,,	,,	Christophersen & Co	,,
132 ,,	Rotterdam	G. Gibson & Co	,,
27 ,,	,,	To order	,,
216 ,,	,,	,,	,,
503 ,,	Stettin	,,	Leith
514 ,,	,,	,,	London
245 ,,	,,	O. Herrlich	,,
69 ,,	,,	To order	,,
572 ,,	Skein	,,	,,
2600 ,,	,,	G. Schjoth and Co	Fleetwood
1564 ,,	,,	Blydt, Pans & Pace	,,
200 ,,	Trieste	To order	Hull

Totals from Each Country:

AUSTRIA ...	200 bales	NORWAY ...	70 cases
BELGIUM ...	21 casks	,, ...	1223 rolls
FINLAND ...	247 bales	PRUSSIA ...	1328 bales
GERMANY ...	1392 ,,	SWEDEN ...	3038 ,,
,, ...	172 rolls	SPAIN ...	96 cases
HOLLAND ...	375 bales	U.S.A. ...	32009 bales
NORWAY ...	18744 ,,		

WEEK'S IMPORTS of WOOD PULP BOARDS.

Quantity	From	Importer	Port
55 bales	Gothenburg	Salvesen & Co	Granton
16 ,,	,,	To order	London
20 ,,	,,	,,	Hull

STRAW PULPS.—There is only a small enquiry.

Prices, c.i.f. London, Hull or Leith :

Belgian, 25% moisture	£15 0 0	to 16 0 0
do. dry		16 0 0
German, 50 to 55% moisture		16 10 0
do. dry, ... No. 1 £18 10 0 ; No. 2		15 0 0

IMPORTS of STRAW PULP.

Quantity	From	Importer	Port.
83 bales	Hambro	To order	Hull
84 ,,	Rotterdam	,,	London
12 ,,	,,	,,	Leith

STRAW.—The supplies of straw are still scanty, and enquiries only moderate.

WEEK'S IMPORTS.

(Purposes unspecified) at principal Ports From

DENMARK ...	362 bales	U.S.A.	3 bales
HOLLAND ...	838 ,,		

FOREIGN RAGS.—The Continental market is quiet, except for the best grades and also in very cheap lines to replace wood pulp. Woollen rags are in good demand at well-maintained prices.

WEEK'S IMPORTS.

Quantity	From	Importer	Port.
31 bales	Antwerp	To order	Leith
99 ,,	Amsterdam	,,	Hull
10 ,,	,,	,,	Leith
38 ,,	,,	,,	Hull
28 ,,	Barcelona	,,	Liverpool
209 ,,	Bordeaux	,,	,,
30 ,,	Buenos Ayres	,,	,,
50 ,,	Bombay	,,	,,
35 ,,	Bremen	,,	Hull
323 ,,	Copenhagen	,,	,,
14 ,,	,,	,,	Leith
24 ,,	Dieppe	,,	Newhaven
68 ,,	Dunkirk	,,	London
44 ,,	,,	,,	Leith
87 ,,	Ghent	G. Gibson & Co	Leith
3 ,,	,,	To order	,,
151 ,,	,,	,,	Liverpool
11 ,,	Guernsey	,,	Southampton
23 ,,	Harlingen	,,	Hull
18 ,,	Hambro	,,	,,
40 ,,	Jersey	,,	Southampton
2 ,,	,,	,,	,,
4 ,,	Rotterdam	G. Gibson & Co	Leith
10 ,,	,,	To order	London
15 ,,	,,	,,	Hull
70 ,,	Rouen	,,	London
48 ,,	,,	,,	,,
37 ,,	St. Malo	,,	Southampton
22 ,,	,,	,,	,,
7 ,,	Stettin	,,	Hull
524 ,,	Stockholm	,,	,,
94 ,,	St. Nazaire	,,	Newhaven
200 ,,	Sydney	,,	London

Totals from Each Country:

ARGENTINA	30 bales	GERMANY ...	53 bales
AUSTRALIA...	200 ,,	HOLLAND ...	199 ,,
BELGIUM ..	272 ,,	INDIA ...	50 ,,
CHANNEL Isles	53 ,,	PRUSSIA ...	7 ,,
DENMARK ...	861 ,,	SPAIN ...	28 ,,
FRANCE ...	586 ,,		

GERMAN RAGS.

STETTIN : C.i.f. Hull, Leith, Tyne and London.

SPFFF and SPFF	18/0	LFB (Blue)	9/0
SPF	11/0	CSPFFF and CSPFF	10/0
FF	8/6	CFB (Blue)	7/6
FG	9/0	CFX (Coloured) ...	4/6
LFX	7/0		

HAMBURG : F.o.b.

NWC	22/0	FF Grey Linens ...	9/0
SPFFF	22/0	LFX Second ditto...	8/0
SPFFF and SPFF	18/0	CSPFFF	17/3
SPFF	16/0	CSPFF	11/3
SPF	12/0	CFB	8/0
CCC	5/6	Dark Blues (selected	11/9
CFX	4/6	Wool Tares... ...	8/0
White Rope... ...	8/0	Jute, No. I 6/0 ; No. II	5/6

DUTCH RAGS. f.o.r. Hull :

C.i.f. Thames ; Hull 2/6 per ton more ; ditto f.o.r. Leith c.i.f. Glasgow 4/- ; c.i.f. Liverpool 4/-.

Selected Fines (free from Muslins) ...	17/0	Best Grey Linens ...	9/0
		Common ditto ...	5/6
Selected Outshots	9/9	White Canvas ...	15/0
,, Dirty Fines	1/9	Grey & Brown Canvas	9/9
Light Cottons ...	9/3	Tarred Hemp Rope	8/0
Blue Cottons ...	7/6	Ditto (broken) ...	5/3
Dark Coloured Cottons	2/10	White Paper Shavings	7/9
New Cuttings (Bleachd)	22/6	Gunny (best) ...	4/9
,, (Unbleached)	19/6	Jute Bagging ...	3/6
,, (Slate) ...	9/0	Ditto (common ...	3/0
Muslins	8/0	Tarpaulins	4/0
Red Cottons (Mixed)	3/9	Cowhair Carpets ...	2/9
Fustians (Light browns)	5/0	Hard ditto	2/0

FRENCH RAGS.

Quotations range, per cwt., ex ship London, Southampton, or Hull; 2/0 per ton more at Liverpool, and 10/0 per ton higher at Newcastle, Glasgow or Leith.

French Linens, I ...	22/0	Black Cotton ...	4/0
II 18/6; III ...	14/6	Marseilles Whites, I	16/0
White Cottons, I ...	19/0	II 10/0; III ...	7/6
II 15/0; III ...	12/6	Blue Cotton	12/0
Knitted Cotton ...	11/0	Light Prints... ...	9/0
Light Coloured Cotton	8/0	Mixed Prints ...	6/0
Blue Cotton	9/6	New White Cuttings	25/0
Coloured Cotton ...	6/0	" Stay "	21/0

BELGIAN RAGS.

F.o.b. Ghent. Freights: London, 5/0; Hull and Goole, 7/6 Liverpool and Leith, 10/0; Newcastle, 12/6; Dundee and Aberdeen, 15/0; Glasgow, 16/6.

White Linens No. 1	22/6	Fustians (Light) ...	6/0
" " No. 2	16/0	" (Dark) ...	4/0
" " No. 3	13/0	Thirds...	3/0
Fines (Mixed) ...	12/0	Black Cottons ...	2/9
Grey Linens (strong)	9/6	Hemp Strings (unt'r'd)	2/0
" " (extra)	14/0	House Cloths ...	4/9
Blue Linens... ...	8/6	Old Bagging (solid)	2/6
White Cottons S'p'fine	18/0	" " (common)	2/6
" " No. 2	15/0	NEW.	
Outshots No. 3 ...	10/0	White & Cream Linens	35/0
Seconds No. 4 ...	8/0	White Cuttings ...	22/0
Prints (Light) ...	8/6	Unbleached Cuttings	21/0
" (Old)	4/6	Print Cuttings ..	3/0

BELGIAN FLAX and HEMP WASTE.

Best washed and dried Flax Waste, 10/0; Fair ditto	9/0
Flax Spinners' Waste (grease boiled out)... ...	13/0
Hemp Waste, No. 1 9/0; No. 2	7/6
Flax Spinners' Waste, No. 1 (Flax Rove) 10/0: No. 2	3/6

NORWEGIAN RAGS.

C.i.f. London, Hull, Tyne, and Grangemouth.

1st Rope (tarred) ...	8/6-9/0	2nd Canvas ...	8/0
2nd " " ...	5/6-6/0	Jute Bagging	
Manilla Rope (white)	8/0-8/9	Gunny ...	3/0 3/6
Best Canvas ...	11/9-12/0	Mixed ...	2/6-2/9

RUSSIAN RAGS.

C.i.f. London, Hull, Newcastle or Leith.

SPFF	15/0	CC (Cotton	4/9
SPF	13/6	Jute I	3/6
FG	10/6	" II...	2/3
LFB	9/6	Rope I...	9/0
FF	8/3	" II	5/3
LFX	7/3		

HOME RAGS.—Reports from London, Bristol, Manchester, Eninburgh, and Dublin state that trade appears to be gradually but slowly improving, and on the whole the outlook is rather brighter.

LONDON:

New White Cuttings	21/6	Canvas No. 1	15/0
Fines (selected)	20/6	" No. 2 ...	9/6-10/6
" (good London)...	20/0	" No. 3	5/6
Outshots (selected) ...	12/6	Mixed Rope	5/3
" (ordinary) ...	11/0	White Rope	6/6
London Seconds	3/6-4/0	White Manilla Rope	8/0
Country do. ...	6/6-8/0	Coil Rope	9/0
London Thirds ...	1/9-2/0	Bagging...	1/6
Country do. ...	3/0-4/0	Gunny	3/0-3/6
Light Prints ...	7/0-8/0		

BRISTOL:

Fines	19/0	Clean Canvas ...	15/0
Outshots	13/6	Second Do. ...	9/6-10/6
Seconds	7/0-8/0	Light Prints ...	8/0
Thirds	3/6-4/0	Hemp Coil Rope	9/6-10/0
Mixed Bagging	3/6	Tarred Manilla	7/6

MANCHESTER:

Fines	15/0-16/0	Blues	6/6-7/0
Outshots (best) ...	11/6-12/0	Bagging...	4/0-4/3
" (ordinary)	10/6-11/0	" (common)	3/0-3/3
Seconds	7/0 7/3	W. Manilla Rope	10/0-10/6
Thirds	3/6-3/9	Surat Tares... ...	4/9-5/0

EDINBURGH:

Superfines	17/0	Black Cottons	2/9
Outshots	13/0	W. Manilla Rope ...	9/0
Mixed Fines...	14/0	Tarred Ditto	6/9
Common Seconds ...	8/0	" Hemp Rope...	8/6
First do.	11/0	Rope Ends (new) ...	8/6
Prints	5/6-6/6	" " (old) ...	6/0
Canvas (best)	16/0	Bagging...	2/0-3/0
" 2nd	10/6	" (clean) ...	4/3-6/0

DUBLIN.

White Cuttings ...	18/0	Mill Bagging	3/0
Fines	11/0	White Manilla	8/0
Seconds...	5/0	Tarred Hemp	8/0
Light Prints	3/0	Rigging	13/6
Black do.	2/0	Mixed Ropes	3/6
Bagging	2/0		

WASTE PAPERS.—There is a moderate business passing in Waste Papers, at former quotations.

Cream Shavings ...	12/3	Small Letters	5/0
Fine " ...	9/6	Large "	7/0
Mixed " ...	2/0	Brown Paper	2/9
White Printings ...	8/9	Light Browns	2/9
White Waste ...	1/6	Books & Pamphlets ...	6/0
Wood Pulp Cuttings	3/6	Strawboard Cuttings	1/6
Brown Paper	3/0	Jacquards	2/6
Crushed News	2/0		

For Export: 25/- per ton extra.

JUTE.—Market steady. Cuttings are in fair request.

Good White	£17 10 to 18	Common ...	£13 to £14
Good	£17	Rejections ...	£9 " £10
Medium ..	£15 to £16	Cuttings ...	£5 10 " £7

STARCH.—Market quiet. Maize is rather lower, Crisp at £9 5s. and Powder at £9 10s. showing a drop of 5s.

F.o.r. London, less 2½%:

Maize—Crisp, £9 5/-; Powder, £9 10/-; Special £14.
Farina—Prime, £9 15/-; B.K.M.F., £12.

Delivered:

Rice—Special (in chests), £20 (net); Crystal (in bags) £19; Granulated (in bags) £18 less 2½%.
Dextrine—£15 to £16.

ROSIN.—Very little demand.

	Strained.	E.	F.	G.	K.	W.G.	W.W
Spot—	3/7½	4/0	4/3	4/6	6/9	9/9	10/3
To arrive—	3/2	3/5	3/7	3/9	5/6	9/0	9/6

SIZING.—Both home and foreign business is quiet. Prices of Buffalo Hide Shavings and Picker Waste are easier.

English Gelatines	per cwt.	70/0 to 140/0
Foreign "	"	70/0 " 140/0
Fine Skin Glues	"	45/0 " 60/0
Long Scotch Glues	"	45/0 " 60/0
Common "	"	30/0 " 45/0
"Town" Glues	"	26/0 " 36/0
"Bone" Glues	"	20/0 " 30/0
Foreign Glues	"	23/0 " 40/
Bone Size	"	4/0 " 10/0
Gelatine Size...	"	5/0 " 10/0
Dry B.A. Pieces	"	31/6 " 34/0
" English Pieces	"	22/0 " 24/0
Wet " "	"	5/0 " 6/0
" Sheep Pieces	"	3/0 " 4/0
Buffalo Hide Shavings	"	25/0 " 34/0
" Picker Waste	"	25/0 " 34/0

COLOURS.—Trade dull.

Mineral Black ...	cwt.	3/0	Ultramarine (pure)	
do. superior ...	"	5/0	... cwt.	40/0 to 45/0
Pure Ivory Black	"	12/0	PASTE COLOURS with	
Ochre	"	3/0	60% of colour, as follows:	
French J. C. Ochre	ton	55/0	Orange Pulp ... cwt.	40/0
Chrome (pure) ...	cwt.	40/0	Golden Yellow Pulp	36/0
Red Oxide	"	4/6	Lemon " " cwt.	36/0
Umber, Devonshire	"	50/0	Prussian Yellow ..	36/0
do. Turkish ...	"	40/0	Green (free of arsenic	36/0
Lamp Black ...		7/0-10/6	Paste Blue (20-45%)	
Cochineal	lb.	1/3-2/0	" ...	23/6-46/0

MINERALS.—The demand for CHINA CLAY of the best quality is fairly good, but lower grades are not in much request. FRENCH CHALK is steady at previous quotations. Trade in MINERAL WHITE, owing to the coal strike, is seriously handicapped; at the high rates now paid for fuel to keep works going it does not pay manufacturers to offer the lower grades. The demand keeps steady for PATENT HARDENINGS.

Mineral White (Terra Alba), per ton f.o.r. or boat at works:

Superfine...	28/0 less 2½ %	
Pottery Super.... ...	24/0	,,
Ball Seconds	20/0	,,
Seconds	15/0	,,
Thirds	10/6	,,

China Clay, in bulk, f.o.b. Cornwall, 14/0 to 27/6; bags 5/0 and casks 9/6 per ton extra; f.o.b. London, in casks 35/0 to 50/0 per ton.

Superfine Hardening, f.o.r. works, 40/0.

Patent Crystal Hardening, delivered at mills £3 to £3 15/0

Patent Hardening (2 ton lots) f.o.r. Lancs., £3 5/0.
,, ,, (5 ton lots) f.o.b. Liverpool, £3 10/0.

Magnesite (in lump) 32/6 per ton.

Magnesite (containing 98 % Carbonate of Magnesia). raw ground, £6 10/0; calcined ground, £12 10/0.

Albarine, £3. del. mills.

Asbestos, best rock, £18; brown grades, £14 to £15

Asbestine Pulp, £4 5/- to £5 c.i.f. London, Liverpool and Glasgow.

Barytes (Carbonate), lump, 90/0 to 95/0; nuts, 72/6 to 85/0.

Barytes (Sulphate), "Angel White," No. 1, 70/0; No. 2, 60/0 to 65/0; No. 3, 45/0. Souheur's Brands: AF, 83/-; BF, 71/-; AB, 33/6; BB, 29/6; CB, 24/3.

French and Italian Chalk (Souheur Brand), per ton in lots of 10 tons: Flower O, 63/6 c.i.f. London; Flower OO, 59/0, Flower OOO, 52/6. Swan White, 58/0; Snow White, 80/0. Blackwell's "Angel White" Brand and "Silvery" 90/- to 92/6; prime quality, 90/- to 95/-; and superfine, 105/-.

Bauxite, Irish Hill Quality, first lump, 20/0; seconds, 16/0; thirds, 12/0; ground, 35/0.

Pyrites (non-cupreous), Liverpool, 5d., 2 %.

Carbonate of Lime (Souheur Brand), Prima 43/-, Secunda 37/-.

LIME.—Bleach Lime is quoted at 12s. 6d. per ton at works.

BALING TWINE.—Prices:

		Thick.	Medium.	Car.
All Hemp	per lb.	4d.	4¼d.	4½d
All Jute		3¼d.	3½d.	4d.

DIRECTORY.

Names and Addresses under this heading will be charged for at the rate of 50/- per annum (52 insertions) for each card of two lines or under. Each additional line £1 extra.

ALUMINOUS CAKE.

The ALUM, CHINA CLAY and VITRIOL Co., Lim., 63, Queen Victoria Street, London, E.C. Works: Rainham-on-Thames. Telegrams—"Chinnock, London.

ANALYTICAL.

WILLIAMS, ROWLAND, F.I.C., F.C.S., 28, Pall Mall, Manchester.

ARTESIAN WELLS.

BATCHELOR, Richard D., Artesian and Consulting Well Engineer, 73, Queen Victoria Street, London, E.C., and at Chatham. 5712

ISLER, C., & Co., Bear Lane, Southwark, S.E

LE GRAND & SUTCLIFF, Magdala Works, 125, Bunhill Row, E.C.

BOILER COVERING.

LONSDALES, Boiler Coverers, Blackburn, will send a sample cask of their Patent Plastic Cork Covering to any Paper Mill in Great Britain—5 cwt. cask for 25/- (carriage paid).

CHINA CLAY.

The ALUM, CHINA CLAY and VITRIOL Co., Lim., 63, Queen Victoria Street, London, E.C. Mines: Ruddle and Colchester, St. Austell, Cornwall. Telegrams—"Chinnock, London."

ROGERS, J., & Co., Truro, Cornwall.—Agents: Taylor, Sommerville & Co., 83, Queen Victoria Street, E.C., and at 16, Princes Street, Edinburgh.

W. SINGLETON BIRCH & SONS, Lim., 15, Upton Street, Manchester. Mines: Rosevear, St. Austell, Cornwall. 2278

COLOURS.

CARDWELL, J. L., & Co., Commercial Buildings, 15 Cross Street, Manchester. Specialties: Mineral Black, Ven. Red, Ochres and Umbers. 5304

GEMMILL, W. N., & Co., Glasgow, Telegrams "Rube." Starches, Alumina, Antifroths, &c. All Paper Colours

HINSHELWOOD, THOMAS, & Co., The Glasgow Colour Works, Glasgow. Colours and shades matched exactly.

MULLER, A. E., 9, Fenchurch Street, London, E.C.

ESPARTO.

IDE & CHRISTIE, Fibre, Esparto, and General Produce Brokers, 72, Mark Lane, E.C.

MINERAL WHITE or TERRA ALBA.

WINSER & Co., Portland Mills, Princess Street, Manchester. Also manufacturers of Aluminous Cake.

HOWE, JOHN, & Co., Carlisle. 2112

STEEL.

MAKIN, WM., & SONS, Sheffield. Established 1736. Roll Bars, Plates, Cutter Knives, Doctor Blades, &c. 5389

STRAW.

UNDERWOOD, E., & SON, Limited, Brentford, London, W. Press-packed Oat, Wheat, or Rye Straw, delivered to the chief British ports or railway stations.

TALC (French and Italian Chalk).

SOUHEUR, JEAN, Antwerp. All Minerals, Blanc de Silex, Barytes (superior and common), Carbonate of Lime, Blacklead, &c. British Agent: A. E. Muller, 9, Fenchurch Street, London, E.C. Agent for Liverpool and Manchester: C. H. Austin, Ditton, near Widnes.

RAGS.

CHALMERS, E., & Co., Lim., Bonnington, Leith.

MULLER, A. E., 9, Fenchurch Street, London, E.C.

WERTHEIM, A., & Co., Hamburg.

UMBER.

The ALUM, CHINA CLAY and VITROIL Co., Lim. 63, Queen Victoria Street, London, E.C. Telegrams—"Chinnock, London."

WOOD PULP.

FRIIS, N., & Co., 18, Carl Johans Gade, Christiania, Norway.

GOTTSTEIN, H., & Co., 59, Mark Lane, London, E.C., and at New York.

GRANT, W., & Co., 17, Baltic Street, Leith. Agents for best shippers, Sulphite and Sulphate, Mechanical, Pine, Brown, Aspen.

MATTHIESSEN, CHR., Christiania, Norway.

MULLER, A. E., 9, Fenchurch Street, London, E.C.

The SULPHITE PULP Company, Limited, 83, Gordon Street, Glasgow.

WERTHEIM, A., & Co., Hamburg.

THE

World's Paper Trade Review.

SUBSCRIPTION, £1 PER ANNUM, Post Free to all Countries.

Workmen's Edition, 2/6 per Volume, or 5/- Yearly.

Printed and Published by

W. JOHN STONHILL, 58, Shoe Lane, E.C.

PAPER IMPORTS.

FOR THE WEEK ENDING TUESDAY LAST:

BELGIUM	... 765 bales		HOLLAND ...	... 61 rolls
,, ...	... 261 cases		INDIA ...	... 16 bales
DENMARK	... 321 bales		JAPAN ...	... 15 cases
FINLAND	... 481 ,,		NORWAY	... 4922 bales
FRANCE	... 90 ,,		,, ...	... 115 cases
,,	... 131 cases		,, ...	... 823 rolls
GERMANY	... 2167 bales		PRUSSIA	... 84 bales
,, ...	... 40 cases		SWEDEN	... 417 ,,
,,	... 13 rolls		U.S.A. ...	... 105 ,,
HOLLAND	... 5390 bales		,, ...	... 52 cases
,, ...	... 192 cases			

Including the Following:

Quantity	From	Importer	Port.
6 cases	Bombay	Berrick Bros	London
52 ,,	Boston	B. Galloway	,,
35 bales	Copenhagen	Becker & Ulrich	,,
18 ,,	,,	Becker & Ulrich	,,
5 ,,	Christiania	Christophersen & Co	,,
50 ,,	,,	Spicer & Sons	,,
40 ,,	,,	Crabb & Co	,,
76 ,,	,,	Lon. & Rhine S. Co	,,
44 ,,	,,	J. Hamilton & Co	,,
789 rolls	Christiansand	Lundgren	,,
30 cases	Marseilles	Williams, Torrey & Co	,,
1603 bales	Norrkoping	Schenkenwald & Co	,,
291 ,,	,,	Brooks Whf.	,,
1119 ,,	,,	Prop. Dowgate Dk.	,,
196 ,,	,,	J. Spicer & Sons	,,
19 ,,	,,	H. S. Lloyd & Co.	,,
390 ,,	,,	Tegner, Rice & Co	,,
30 ,,	Stettin	Becker & Ulrich	,,
42 ,,	,,	J. Spicer & Son	,,
5 ,,	,,	W. D. Edwards	,,
64 ,,	Skein	Christophersen	,,
225 ,,	,,	Lon. & Rhine Co	,,
19 ,,	,,	E. Saunders & Son	,,

———o———

PAPER EXPORTS.

FOR THE WEEK ENDING TUESDAY LAST;

	Printings.	Writings.	Other Kinds.
AUSTRALIA	6335 cwts.	853 cwts.	2217 cwts.
AFRICA	64 ,,	— ,,	170 ,,
ARGENTINE ...	— ,,	— ,,	14 ,,
ARABIA...	—	— ,,	1 ,,
BELGIUM	117 ,,	104 ,,	6 ,,
B. WEST INDIES...	4 ,,	4½ ,,	— ,,
BRAZIL	73 ,,	— ,,	25 ,,
B. GUIANA	20 ,,	14 ,,	979½ ,,
CEN. AMERICA ...	— ,,	14 ,,	— ,,
CANADA	91 ,,	25 ,,	— ,,
CAPE COLONY ...	252 ,,	128 ,,	237 ,,
CHINA	4 ,,	53 ,,	64 ,,
DENMARK	124 ,,	2 ,,	4 ,,
EGYPT	— ,,	42 ,,	3 ,,
FRANCE	333 ,,	128 ,,	9 ,,
GERMANY	— ,,	4 ,,	21 ,,
HOLLAND	18 ,,	— ,,	69 ,,
INDIA	871 ,,	507¾ ,,	42½ ,,
JAPAN	417½ ,,	— ,,	2 ,,
MAURITIUS ...	3 ,,	— ,,	— ,,
NEW ZEALAND ...	60 ,,	231 ,,	465 ,,
NORWAY	25 ,,	— ,,	— ,,
NEWFOUNDLAND	— ,,	1 ,,	— ,,
PRUSSIA	7 ,,	— ,,	— ,,
RUSSIA	— ,,	13 ,,	50 ,,
ROUMANIA	— ,,	10 ,,	1 ,,
SPAIN	— ,,	3 ,,	28 ,,
SWEDEN	— ,,	1 ,,	— ,,
TURKEY	— ,,	1 ,,	1 ,,
U.S.A.	10 ,,	68 ,,	49 ,,
W. INDIES	— ,,	3 ,,	— ,,

SUMMARY OF IMPORTS & EXPORTS,

FOR THE WEEK ENDING TUESDAY LAST.

London, Liverpool, Bristol, Southampton, Hull, Fleetwood, Harwich, Folkestone, Newhaven, Dover, &c.

IMPORTS.

Paper	13459 bales	Millboards	4005 pkgs.
,, ...	975 cases	Cardboards	393 ,,
,, ...	956 rolls	Pasteboards	7068 ,,
Parchment	3 pkgs	Strawboards	734 ,,
Stationery...... ...	54 cases	Paper Stock	1128 bales
Tissues	88 pkgs.	Leather Paper —	3 cases

EXPORTS.

British Goods.			
		Waste	600 tons
		Stock	83 ,,
Paper	2795 cwt.	**Foreign Goods.**	
Writing Paper ...	2074 ,,		
Printing Paper	7867 ,,	Paper	1470 cwt.
Stationery......	£11910 value	Writing Paper...	8 ,,
Cardboards	79 cwt.	Printing Paper...	252 ,,
Strawboards	275 ,,	Strawboards	100 ,,
Millboards	63 ,,	Stationery	£320 value
Strawboard Cuttings	20 tons	Cigarette Paper	£56 ,,

Glasgow, Greenock, Port-Glasgow, Troon, Grangemouth, &c.

IMPORTS.

Paper	660 bales	Envelopes	1 case
,, ...	8 cases		

EXPORTS.

Printing Paper..	709½ cwt.	Envelopes	47 cwt.
Writing Paper...	156½ ,,	Stock	27 ,,
Paper	195 ,,	Cardboards	6¼ ,,

Leith, Granton, Boness, Dundee, &c.

IMPORTS.

Paper	290 bales	Pasteboards	1045 pkgs.
,, ...	2 cases	Envelopes	170 ,,
,, ...	39 rolls		

PAPER & PULP MILL SHARES.

(Report received from Mr. F. D. DEAN, 36, Corporation Street, Manchester.)

Nominal Amnt	Amnt Paid	Name of Company	Last dividend	Price.
7	7	Bury Paper, ord.	nil	4½—4¾
7	7	do. do. 6% pref.	6%	4¾—5
100	100	do. do. deb.	5%	103—106
10	10	Bath Paper Mill Co. Lim.	7½%	6—7
10	10	Bergvik Co., def.	15%	13¾
100	100	do. do. 6% cum. pref.	6%	10⅞—11¼
10	10	do. do. deb.	5%	105—110
5	3½	Burnley Paper Co.	3/-	77/6—80/0
5	3¾	Darwen Paper Co.	10%	5¾—6¼
10	10	East Lancashire Co.	nil	4—4¼
10	10	do. do. 6% pref.	nil	6—6¼
5	5	do. do. bonus	nil	1½—2
5	5	Hyde Paper Co.	4%	4¾—5
5	4	North of Ireland Paper Co.	nil	2½—2¾
10	5	Ramsbottom Paper Co.	17½%	12½—17½
5	4½	Roach Bridge Paper Co.	5%	2¾—3
5	5	Star Paper Co.	10%	6—6½
5	3	do. do. 6% pref. cum.	10%	4¾ 5¼
50	50	do. do. deb.	6%	55—56
5	2½	Kellner Partingt'n Pulp Co	—	61/0—63/0

Special Prepaid Advertisements

☞ IT IS IMPORTANT that Advertisements under any of the Headings mentioned below should reach us by the FIRST POST on WEDNESDAY Morning to INSURE INSERTION.

Charges for advertisements under the heading Situations Wanted are 1/- for twenty-four words, and One Penny per Word after, Minimum charge ONE SHILLING. Names and addresses to be paid for.

Advertisers by paying an extra fee of 6d. can have the replies addressed to the PAPER TRADE REVIEW under a number, and such replies will then be forwarded Post Free

Advertisements appearing under the following headings:

Tenders.	Mills Wanted or To Let.
Sales by Auction.	Machinery Wanted or For Sale.
Businesses Wanted.	Situations Vacant.
Businesses for Disposal.	

Miscellaneous.

The charges are 3/- for fifty words or under; 1s. extra for every line or portion after. Ten words to be reckoned for each line. Names and addresses to be paid for. Payment must be made in advance, except where the advertiser has a running account, in which case the cost can be debited thereto.

Legal and Financial Announcements: 1/- per Line.

Cheques and Post-office Orders to be CROSSED ——and Co., and made payable to W. JOHN STONHILL.

Situation Vacant.

WANTED, Foreman, accustomed to tub-sized air-dried papers; must be thoroughly competent and well up in all the working details of a paper mill.—Apply by letter (stating salary, &c., age not to exceed 40) to W. and J. Sommerville, Bitton, near Bristol. 5900

Machinery Wanted.

WANTED, a Set of Chilled Rolls, not less than 60 inches on face.—Address "A.B.," No. 5898, office of the WORLD'S PAPER TRADE REVIEW, 58, Shoe Lane, London, E.C. 5898

WANTED, a Kollergang, about 8 ft. pan, runner stones 5 ft. 3 in. dia. × 16 in. broad; must be in good condition. State price and where to be seen.—Address No. 5899, Office of the WORLD'S PAPER TRADE REVIEW, 58, Shoe-lane, London, E.C. 5899

WANTED, in good working order, One Beating Engine to carry 400 lbs., and four 12 ft. × 5 ft. 6 in. × 2 ft. deep. State price, particulars, and where can be seen.—Address No. 5901, office of the WORLD'S PAPER TRADE REVIEW, 58, Shoe-lane, London, E.C. 5901

Machinery for Sale.

ONE KOLLERGANG, new, Stones 51 inches by 14 inches, C I. Pan, Scrapers, and Driving Gear.

ONE HYDRAULIC PRESS, second-hand, with Press Box 38 inches diam. by 32 inches deep, with wheels; all parts strong, Ram 2 feet 6 inches by 8 inches diam.

TWELVE REVOLVING STRAINER PLATES, second-hand, 18½ inches by 21 inches, class B2, 3½ cut.

REFINING ENGINE, new, Conical Type; same as one working in a large printing mill.

Any reasonable offer will be considered by 5859

BERTRAMS LIMITED, SCIENNES, EDINBURGH.

Mill to be Let or Sold.

TO be LET or SOLD, a Paper Mill at Stalybridge, called the Higher Mill, containing one large machine and room for another, steam engine and boilers, in good condition.—Apply for further information to the Caretaker on the premises. 2162

The Machinery Users' ASSOCIATION

Is a Combination of All Manufacturers for Promoting and Protecting their Common Interests.

Special Assistance is Rendered in cases of unjust and excessive assessment.

Full particulars on application to the Offices—

8, LAURENCE POUNTNEY HILL, CANNON ST., LONDON, E.C., AND 16, DEANSGATE, MANCHESTER.

NEW PATENTS.

BRITISH.

SPECIFICATIONS PUBLISHED.

(7½d. each. By post 8d.)

1892.

20,214. Electrolytical apparatus. Boult.

20,595. Evaporating apparatus. Scott and others.

1893.

15,768. Papermaking machines. A. M. Ende.

Money & Trade.

Published Every Wednesday Morning.

Annual Subscription, post free, 15s. in the United Kingdom. Ditto, 17s. to any part of the World.

Offices: Bishopsgate House, London, E.C.

"MONEY AND TRADE" is a fearless critic and exposer of all shams, frauds and swindles.

"MONEY AND TRADE" is THE JOURNAL for Investors, Speculators, Manufacturers and Traders.

"MONEY AND TRADE" is a thoroughly up-to-date Weekly Record of all Monetary, Trading, and Business matters. Bankers, Manufacturers, Merchants, Storekeepers, and Wholesale Buyers all over the World say it is indispensable.

"MONEY AND TRADE" is NOT subsidised by any financial association, clique, or syndicate, but is absolutely free, independent and honest.

BALANCE SHEETS of Assurance, Banking, Shipping, Trading, Manufacturing, and Trust Companies are fearlessly and impartially criticised in "MONEY AND TRADE."

"MONEY AND TRADE" enjoys a very large circulation, not only in Great Britain and Ireland, but also in all Foreign markets where English goods are sold; and as it goes direct into the hands of the wholesale and retail buyers, it offers unique advantages to advertisers.

THE MONTHLY FOREIGN AND COLONIAL EDITION is published on the last Wednesday in each month, and is forwarded direct to the Foreign Agents and Correspondents of all the leading English Merchants, and to all the large Wholesale Buyers and Storekeepers in the Colonies, India, China, Japan, South America and other countries.

☞ SPECIMEN COPY POST FREE. ☜

THE PAPER TRADE REVIEW is a widely informed and well-managed enterprise, of great value to exporters for its exact Market Reports and statistics of Raw Material.—*Central-Blatt fur die Papier-Fabrikation, Dresden.*

THE LATE MR. GEORGE WATERSTON.

The death is recorded of Mr. George Waterston, of Edinburgh. He was in the eighty-fifth year of his age, and the sixty-third of his connection with this important firm, served his apprenticeship with John Anderson, junr., a well-known bookseller and Stationer, whose premises were located at the Royal Exchange, Edinburgh, a very small shop in size as compared with those of the present day, but doing a large retail stationery business.

the business of which he has been for a long time the head partner, its specialty being sealing wax manufacture, the house being established as far back as 1752 by the late Mr. Waterston's grandfather. The deceased Mr. George Waterston, who was, as we have said, the head of

Leaving Mr. Anderson he joined his father's firm, the style of the firm being George Waterston and Son, and one of his first acts on obtaining a partnership was to add a stationery department to their already old established sealing wax, business.

THE
United Asbestos Co.,
LIMITED,
DOCK HOUSE, BILLITER STREET, E.C.,
"SALAMANDER"
THE UNITED ASBESTOS COMPANY LIMITED · LONDON ·
TRADE MARK
Pioneers
OF THE
Asbestos
Trade.
UNITED ASBESTOS
NON-CONDUCTING
COVERING
(For Steam Boilers & Pipes)
Best and Cheapest in the Market; Will not Injure Boiler Plates.
ASBESTOS
GOODS of ALL
DESCRIPTIONS
BELTINGS.
THE UNITED ASBESTOS CO., Limited,
UNITED
PACKINGS.
UNITED ASBESTOS Cº LMᵀᴰ LONDON
PURE ITALIAN MILLBOARD EXTRA QUALITY
A1
UNITED ASBESTOS
A1 MILLBOARDS
(ITALIAN)
Unequalled for Purity, Strength of Fibre, and Uniformity. For Dry Steam Joints it is admitted to be the cleanest, most durable and economical packing in existence.
UNITED ASBESTOS
SALAMANDER
Lubricating Cream & Oils,
SPECIALLY ADAPTED TO
PAPERMAKING MACHINERY.
DEPOTS:
MANCHESTER: 34, Deansgate; LIVERPOOL: 33, James Street; NEWCASTLE-UPON-TYNE: Quayside; GLASGOW: 54, Robertson Street; CARDIFF: 135, Bute Street; BRISTOL: Provident Buildings; HULL: Queen's Dock; ST. PETERSBURG: Gostinoe Dvor (Interior) No. 51.
2615

NEW COMPANIES.

"MEDICAL TIMES" CO., Ltd.

Registered with a capital of £4,000, in £5 shares, to acquire and carry on the *Medical Times and Hospital Gazette.* Registered without articles of association.

R. H. BAY and CO., Ltd.

Registered with a capital of £5,000, in £1 shares, to acquire or establish a newspaper, and to carry on business as newspaper proprietors, publishers, and printers generally. Table A mainly applies.

SCHOOL and COLLEGE PRESS, Ltd.

Registered with a capital of £5,000, in £1 shares, to acquire the copyright of, and to print and publish, the *Scholastic Globe*, and, with a view thereto, to enter into an agreement with Chas. H. Thomson. Registered without articles of association.

"LONG EATON ADVERTISER" COMPANY, Ltd.

Registered with a capital of £1,000 in £1 shares, to acquire and carry on the business of newspaper printers, publishers, and proprietors, carried on by Bewlay and Roe, Limited, at Long Eaton, Derbyshire. Registered without articles of association.

"THE EMPRESS," Limited.

Registered with a capital of £5,000 in £1 shares, to acquire a publication entitled the *Empress*, in accordance with an agreement, made September 20th, with Mrs. E. M. Stevens, and to carry on the same. Registered without articles of association.

MARCHANT, YOUNG and CO., Limited.

Registered with a capital of £4,000 in £1 shares, to establish and carry on the business of electrical and mechanical engineers. There shall not be less than two nor more than six directors. The first are B. J. Young, J. E. Marchant, and C. T. Young. Qualification not specified. Remuneration to be fixed by the company in general meeting.

PHILIP JOHNS AND CO., Ltd.

Registered with a capital of £2,000 in £1 shares, to acquire the undertaking of a printer and stationer, &c., hitherto carried on under the style of Philip Johns and Co., in accordance with an agreement expressed to be made between P. Johns of the one part, and this company of the other part, and to develop and extend the said business in all or any of its branches. Table A mainly applies.

"WORKMAN'S TIMES" CO., Limited.

Registered with a capital of £1,000 in £1 shares, to carry on, in all its branches, the business of printers and publishers, stationers, &c. The first directors are W. Cunliffe, H. C. D. Scott, Ben Billcliffe, A. H. Edmonds, T. Draper, J. Harker, C. W. Fraser, R. Anderson, and W. Hearnside, all of Manchester and suburbs. Qualification, one share. No remuneration specified.

JOURNALISTS' PRINTING and PUBLISHING CO., Limited.

Registered with a capital of £1,500, in £1 shares, to acquire and carry on a newspaper known as *The Journalist and Newspaper Proprietor*, belonging to John Bernard Atkinson; to enter into an agreement for that purpose, and to continue the business. The number of directors is not to exceed seven, nor be under three; qualification, 10 shares; remuneration, £2 2s. for each director every board meeting attended—or any other remuneration that may be determined upon.

COLONIAL PAPER CO., Limited.

Registered with a capital of £10,000 in £1 shares, to carry on business as paper manufacturers and merchants, stationers, &c. Table A mainly applies.

THE SONG OF THE COMPANY PROMOTER.

In Gilbert and Sullivan's new comic opera, *Utopia (Limited)*, at the Savoy, one of the characters is a company promoter, who, in the course of the proceedings, sings the following amusing song, which scores tremendously:—

Some seven men form an Association
(If possible, all Peers and Baronets),
They start off with a public declaration
To what extent they mean to pay their debts.
That's called their Capital: if they are wary
They will not quote it at a sum immense.
The figures immaterial—it may vary
From eighteen million down to eighteenpence.
I should put it rather low;
The good sense of doing so
Will be evidence at once to any debtor.
When it's left to you to say
What amount you mean to pay,
Why, the lower you can put it at the better.
When it's left to you to say, &c.

They then proceed to trade with all who'll trust e'm
Quite irrespective of their capital
(It's shady, but it's sanctified by custom);
Bank, Railway, Loan, or Panama Canal.
You can't embark on trading too tremendous,
It's strictly fair, and based on common sense;
If you succeed your profits are stupendous,
And if you fail, pop goes your eighteenpence.
Make the money-spinner spin!
For you only stand to win,
And you'll never with dishonesty be twitted;
For nobody can know,
To a million or so,
To what extent your capital's committed!

If you come to grief, and creditors are craving
(For nothing that is planned by mortal head
Is certain in this Vale of Sorrow—saving
That one's Liability is Limited),
Do you suppose that signifies perdition?
If so, you're but a monetary dunce—
You merely file a Winding-up Petition,
And start another Company at once!
Though a Rothschild you may be
In your own capacity,
As a Company you've come to utter sorrow:
But the Liquidators say,
"Never mind—you needn't pay,"
So you start another Company to-morrow.

ESCHER WYSS & Co.,

ENGINEERS.

ZURICH, SWITZERLAND.

New Patent STRAINER

OVER 100 AT WORK.

FACTS SPEAK FOR THEMSELVES.

The TORONTO PAPER CO.'S Experience: "They are durable and easily cleaned. We have had one in use for eighteen months, and it seems as good as new Once adopted not likely to be turned out."

FEATURES.

Superior to any other System for its Numerous Advantages as:

Large Production with any kind of Pulp.
No Stoppage for Cleaning.
Most Regular and Quite Noiseless Working.
Little room taken up on the Machine, &c.

AGENT:

ALPH. STEIGER, C.E.

16, MINCING LANE, LONDON, E.C.

NOW READY.

PAPER TESTING.

Being a DESCRIPTION OF PAPER TESTING as Carried out in the GERMAN GOVERNMENT LABORATORY at CHARLOTTENBURG. By

W. HERTZBERG,

Head Assistant in the Paper Testing Department.

TRANSLATED By

P. NORMAN EVANS, Ph.D., F.I.C., F.C.S.

W. JOHN STONHILL, 58, Shoe Lane, LONDON.

PAPER BAG

MAKING MACHINERY.

LATEST IMPROVEMENTS.

F. D. BUMSTED, L.E

Cannock Chase Foundry, Hednesford, Staffs

DAMPING MACHINES

On the most Improved Principle;
VENTILATION for all purposes;
Improved FANS or AIR PROPELLERS;
Patent SUSPENDING CLIPS to hold from one up to 50 sheets of paper or cardboard;
TURBINES; SMOKE CONSUMING APPARATUS;
Patent Life Protecting HOIST PLATFORMS;
New System of HYDRAULIC POWER for Lifts, Hoists, and Motive Power;
New Process of WIRE WEAVING by Steam Power

For particulars of all the above address 5812

E. BREADNER

(Ventilating Engineer to the Manchester Royal Exchange),
134, DEANSGATE, MANCHESTER.

NORWEGIAN PAPER AND PULP MILLS.

MAP DRAWN to SCALE.

By Chr. B. Lorentzen.

PRICE 2/6 EACH.

To be obtained of W. JOHN STONHILL,
Office of the PAPER TRADE REVIEW, 58, Shoe Lane, London E.C.

ABRIDGED PATENT SPECIFICATIONS.

14,968 (92).—Improvements in Machines for Counting, Feeding, and Folding, and Pressing Pa er in Sections.—WM. HOWARD and WM. JAMIESON. Accepted 19th August, 1893.

The object of this invention is to perform by mechanical means the folding of sections of paper for account books, for notepaper, and other purposes in which it is necessary to count off a given number of flat sheets, knock them up, fold in half, and press, the patentees describing their invention as capable of performing these operations by mechanical means.

14,763 (93).—Improvements in Embossing Machines.—ROBERT SCOTT ANDERSON and EDWARD WAKEFIELD BLACKHALL. Accepted 2nd September, 1893.

The patentees, who are already well-known in connection with labour saving machines, used by manufacturing stationers, state the object of their invention as being the production of a machine for embossing or stamping paper, particularly envelopes and other stationery, and that is simple in construction, accurate in operation, easy of manipulation, and that will permit of die stamping being executed at a high rate of speed.

[Judging from the drawings accompanying the specification, the apparatus appears to fulfil all that the patentees claim for it, it takes up but little floor space, is free from complication, and does not seem at all likely to get easily out of order.—ED.]

An envelope is made with two rows of perforations on the flap and underneath and between these and projecting from is fixed a thread or extra thickness of tape. These perforations and projections are placed so as to allow the person to open the envelope by pulling the projection.

21,173 (92).—Improved Letter Cards and the like.—M. JONES. Accepted 8th July, 1893.

Improvements are claimed to be effected upon those letter cards opened by tearing perforated strips. The principal improvement appears to be in leaving one edge free and unsecured (but at the same time secure from scrutiny by means of an internal flap), through which the finger can be inserted when opening the epistle.

5,528 (93).—Improvements in the Manufacture of Iridescent Fabrics and Papers.—F. VOLAND. Accepted June 17th, 1893.

The specification relates to the manufacture of iridescent fabrics and papers printing lines of different colours upon them (in a transverse, longitudinal, or oblique direction), and goffering the material by means of fluted or grooved rollers or other apparatus so as to produce flutes or ridges each containing one group of differently coloured lines.

13,095 (93).—Improvements in Memorandum Blocks or Pads.—G. W. BROWN. Accepted 5th August, 1893.

A memorandum book of such construction that the leaves can be swung vigorously, so that those that have been written upon may be readily displaced to expose the unused leaves, and can be readily detached and filed for reference.

ENVELOPE MACHINES.

Notwithstanding the acknowledged extent and importance of the trade, machines for envelope manufacture are anything but numerous, and the best known types, such as the Leader, the Reay, &c., scarcely number half-a-dozen all told. We have several times recorded the advent of a new machine, but seldom had, later on, to record its unqualified success. A new variety of envelope machine has, however, lately come to the front in the United States and Canada, and is shortly to be introduced here. We refer to the "Defiance" (Blackhall and Anderson's patent). This originally came out a year or so ago; but although an excellent machine of its kind, it was seen to be capable of still further improvement. This it has since received at the hands of the patentees—who have worked hard at it—and it is now offered to the trade as a perfect machine, and one worthy of every confidence. It is said to be capable of producing 5,000 envelopes per hour easily, perfect gumming (even on cockled or wavy paper) has also been secured—the arrangement being under the operator's control—and there is an automatic seal flap gummer. A new form of delivery device has been added, which makes waste almost an impossibility. Messrs. Anderson and Blackhall are also the patentees of a new bag and envelope machine, which will turn out special envelopes or bags of every description. A single machine will make three different sizes of bags, up to 6 by 10 inches. The blanks, plain or printed in large sheets, are first cut the required size with a die. One thousand or more are then placed in the elevator of the machine, and are separately carried into position, pasted, folded, pressed, dried, waxed, and delivered at a speed of over 5,000 per hour. The entire action is automatic. A waxing apparatus, for rendering the bags waterproof, is supplied separately; it is described as being very simple and easy to operate. Mr. Blackhall informs us that he intends to visit England very shortly with the view of introducing these machines and some others, particularly a new automatic embossing press.

Printed and Published by W. JOHN STONHILL, 58, Shoe Lane, LONDON, E.C. Oct 27, 1893.

Telegrams: "STONHILL, LONDON." A B C Code. Registered at the General Post Office as a Newspaper.

Vol. XX. No. 18. LONDON, NOVEMBER 3, 1893. Price 6d.

KNÖFLER & GEBAUER'S

Electrolytical Apparatus

FOR PAPER MILLS.

The following particulars relate to apparatus introduced by Dr. Oskar Knöfler and Mr. F. Gebauer, of Charlottenburg, Germany, for the technical electrolysis of solutions of all descriptions, especially aqueous solutions of chlorides of metals for the purpose of obtaining bleaching solutions, and it is so arranged as to occupy little room and require little electrical energy for its operation, so that it may be utilised in comparatively small plants, and enables high tension currents to be employed. It may, for example, be without any difficulty connected to any electric lighting plant however high the tension of current may be with which it is operated. It is also possible to employ a dynamo which during the night is employed for lighting, for operating the present apparatus for electrolytic purposes during the day, and it is mainly intended for establishments or factories where paper is manufactured or bleached, for the preparation of the required bleaching solution.

The apparatus mainly consists of electrodes in the shape of plates separated by insulated intermediate frames. These electrodes may be made of sheet-metal or consist of plates of carbon, maganese ore (brownstone), peroxide of lead, or the like, or they may be made of iron, preferably coated with hard rubber, or of ceramic material, such as clay, glass, &c., or of celluloid, impervious wood, or the like. The electrodes and frames are preferably of either round or angular shape, and when joined, form a series of closed divisions or chambers adapted to receive the solution to be treated by electrolysis.

The plates and frames are arranged in a supporting frame not unlike that used for filtering presses, and these frames and electrodes have lateral lugs or projections by means of which they are supported upon guide-rods or rails insulated by means of a lining or covering of hard rubber or the like. Two terminal plates and a spindle, similar to those used in filtering presses serve for compressing this series of electrodes and the joints between the frames and plates are made tight by means of india-rubber, asbestos, or the like.

Each of the frames is provided with a cock or tap through which the liquid to be electrolysed is admitted, and also with an outlet through which the liquid is discharged in corresponding quantities. A distributing pipe supplies all the divisions or compartments simultaneously with the fresh solution, while the liquid that has undergone electrolysis is conducted away by a channel provided for the purpose. The solution to be decomposed in this manner may also be circulated transversely, or in other words, it may be conducted from one compartment to another, and not discharged till it has passed the last compartment.

Instead of being arranged after the style of a filtering press the electrodes and frames may be also arranged in the shape of boxes, somewhat like Cruikshank's current generating batteries in which case the frames form one connected whole with the case or box. Instead of employing separate plates as before stated, each plate may be integral with its frame; the electrodes being in this case provided on both sides with a projecting edge so that by the simple juxtaposition of such plates a row of compartments, similar to those described above is formed. Or each electrode-plate may be on one side only rigidly connected with the frame, so that frames are obtained which are open on one side and closed on the other by its plate.

Whichever of the above mentioned arrangements is given the preference it is in all cases necessary that each electrode should combine both poles in its operation. Whether therefore it consists entirely of homogeneous material, or is composed of different materials, it must at all events act as an anode on one side and as a cathode on the other.

This feature is the chief improvement this apparatus offers, and in order to carry it out the electrodes are here arranged, not as they have been in the electrolytic decomposing apparatus hitherto used, viz., parallel to each other, but so as to be operated by tension, only the first and last plate of each series being connected each with one pole of the source of electricity. The current is thus conducted only through the liquid between the electrodes and throughout the whole surface of the latter, and in each case the sides turned towards the positive electrodes form cathodes, and the sides turned towards the negative electrodes, anodes. Thus each of the compartments formed jointly by the electrodes and frames and filled with liquid to be electrolysed forms an electrolytic decomposing cell, and in each electrolysis takes place according to Faraday's law.

The electro-chemical production or yield is in all cases the same, and will increase (assuming that the strength of current is the same for all cells) exactly in a predetermined proportion as the cells are in succession included in the circuit, *i.e.* according as the tension of current becomes more powerful. It will be understood that in one apparatus more than one series or row of electrodes may be operated by tension in the manner described, the two, three, or more additional rows being parallel to the first. The switching method above suggested offers the great advantage that tensions of any required magnitude may be employed while formerly the electrolytic process could only be carried out with a low tension, comparatively high tensions having only been serviceable in large plants, where a number of apparatus could be switched into the circuit in succession.

The described arrangement will prove particularly advantageous in the special case of platinum electrodes. It is a well-known fact that the attempt made to introduce platinum into general use as a material for electrodes has been frustrated by the enormous cost involved in the construction of apparatus with such electrodes. In consequence of the manner in which electrolytic apparatus have been operated hitherto, it was necessary that the electrode material should have a very large sectional area in proportion to its surface so that the current might be sent into the electrolyte without too considerable loss of tension. Other materials coated or lined with platinum have also proved failures. But in the present apparatus the whole of the surface forms the current-conducting area, and therefore platinum plates not exceeding one millimetre in thickness may be employed; plates in fact through which in the old arrangements only a small number of ampères could be sent, while here currents representing hundreds of ampères may be employed. One gramme of platinum with a surface of 100 square centimetres will on an average admit of the economical employment of 100 or more ampères.

The method of operating this apparatus also offers the advantage that all contact pieces are dispensed with, thus doing away with all the trouble connected with keeping them in repair. Even very large electrodes may, according to this invention, be readily composed of smaller ones which in the same way as large window panes have in former times, and not unfrequently are still, composed of a number of small glass plates. The idea is extremely simple in itself, but what has prevented its being carried out in practice hitherto is that in consequence of the old method of employing the current it was necessary for the different plates of say carbon, platinum or the like to be connected so as to form a conductor. It was therefore necessary to make the frames of metal or some other electrical conductor, and such material was generally very soon destroyed by the electrolysis.

The present method of operation admits of the frames connecting the different plates being made of non-conducting material such as hard rubber, celluloid, glass, clay, or the like, or it may be made of metal and covered or coated with some such material, so that their construction is greatly facilitated. For example the electrode may be set in a frame made of non-conducting material such as hard rubber, celluloid, clay, glass or the like, or of metal such as iron, copper, or the like covered or coated with such non-conducting material, somewhat after the style of a window; or a number of plates may be joined together by means of sulphur, cement, or the like, or by simple juxtaposition and subsequent framing so as to form one casement-like series or large plate.

Hitherto compartments have been devised without diaphragms, but apparatus can also be used in connection with diaphragms, and in that case the diaphragms may be arranged exactly in the same manner as the electrode plates.

BRITISH WEST INDIES.—Paper of British manufacture is being more appreciated in the British West Indies, an increased trade having been developed during the past five years. In 1892 the value was £19,759, and in 1888 £15,239.

PULP REGULATOR.

An appliance has been recently patented by Mr. G. McNeill, of Ballyclare Paper Mills, with the object of obviating thicks and thins, it being claimed by the improvements introduced that no matter how the consistency or density of the stuff in the chest may alter, the weight of fibre let off to the paper machine is always the same, thus keeping the paper regular at the desired weight.

The action of the appliance is as follows: The stuff cock at the inlet of the regulator is opened and allows more stuff to flow up through the cylinder than is required for the paper to be made. The surplus is conveyed back to the stuff chest by means of the other outlet. As the stuff passes through the cylinder the float is raised and kept in suspension, the float being kept at whatever level is required, by the weights which can be added to it. The float being attached to one end of the lever, and the sluice in the outlet to the paper machine being attached to the other end of the lever—as the float rises the sluice will close, and as it sinks the sluice will open. Therefore if the stuff should get thick or heavy, the float rises and the sluice is closed in proportion. If the stuff should get thin or light the float will sink, which will open the sluice and pass an increased volume, but always passing the same weight of fibre per hour.

In carrying out the invention as illustrated in sectional elevation Figure 1, elevation Figure 2, and plan Figure 3, of the accompanying drawings, Mr. McNeill employs an open cylinder A, which is provided with two outlets B, C, near the top, and one inlet D at the bottom as shown, so as to permit of the

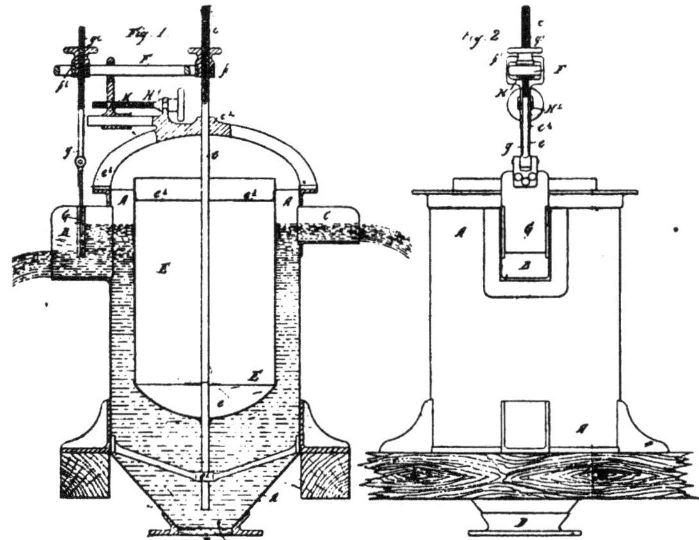

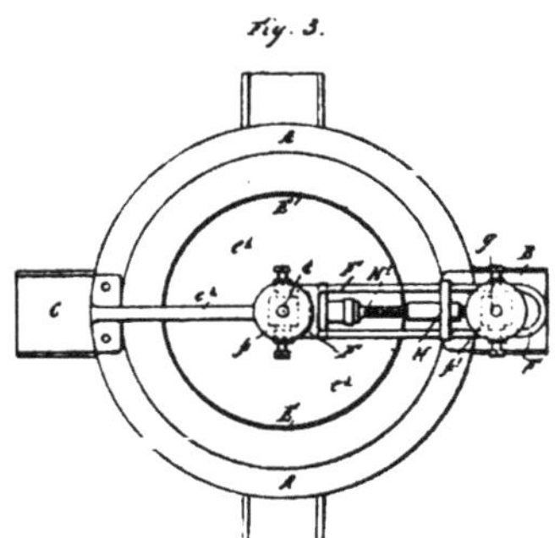

stuff being passed through the regulator to the machine by the outlet B, and the overflow passed back to stuff chests by the outlet C, which is arranged higher up than the outlet B as shown. There is mounted inside the cylinder a float E, preferably composed of a hollow metal casing having a central spindle *e*, which is guided at its lower end by means of a bridge bracket e^1, as shown more particularly in Figure 1, and at its top end by means of a saddle bracket e^2 as shown. The said float E is attached to a level F, preferably as shown, that is to say, the top end of the spindle *e* is screwed and is fitted into a screwed nut *f*, suitably mounted in the one end of the lever F, the other end of which is also provided with a screwed nut f^1, in which works the screwed end g^1 of the spindle *g* of the sluice G, which is suitably mounted in the outlet B so as to regulate the flow of stuff to the machine. The float E is adjusted and kept at its proper level in the stuff by means of suitable weights, which are placed on or taken off the platform e^3, according to the consistency or density of the stuff passing through the regulator. Also if desired the float E and sluice G may be adjusted relatively to each other by means of the screwed spindles *e* and *g*, and nuts *f* and f^1. The said adjustment being assisted by means of the sliding bracket H, which acts as a fulcrum for the lever F, and may be adjusted as desired by means of the handscrew H^1.

The whole arrangement thus forms an apparatus in which, on the float rising, owing to the stuff becoming thick or heavy, the sluice is proportionately closed, and when the stuff becomes thin or light the float will fall and the sluice will be proportionately opened, so as to always pass the same weight of stuff to the machine per hour.

PORTUGUESE importations of alkali in 1892 amounted to £16,756, and in 1888, £15,248.

BRITISH exports of alkali to Greece are of the average value of £9,500.

BRAZIL imported last year over £39,000 worth of alkali from Great Britain.

ALGERIA.—A large quantity of rags are exported to Great Britain from Algeria. The value in 1892 was £363,948, a decrease compared with 1888, when the value stood at £449,781.

PERSIA.—Reports dealing with the trade of Bushire shows that stationery was imported in 1892 to the extent of 352 packages of the value of £2,690; in 1891 119 packages of £2,129 value. The imports at Bunder Abbas during 1892 included 16 cases of stationery of £50 value; in 1891 15 cases, the value being £107.

CERTIFICATES OF ORIGIN FOR RUSSIA.—The following letter from the Foreign Office in reference to the issue of certificates of origin for Russia, and suggesting a change of port, has been received by the secretary to Liverpool Chamber of Commerce;—"With reference to the letter from this office of the 16th inst., I am directed by the Earl of Rosebery to inform you that Mr. Howard, her Majesty's Chargé d'Affaires at St. Petersburg, reports that he has made all possible representations to the Russian Goverment, but that they positively refuse to make any modification in the regulations relating to certificates of origin for goods sent to Russia through ports in Germany. Mr. Howard therefore suggests whether it might not be advisable for merchants to send their goods *via* non-German ports, and mentions Libau, which, from its being the nearest and most convenient port for the despatch of goods for ports and towns near the Russo-German frontier, would appear to be a suitable one. With reference to the particular difficulty in cases where goods have necessarily passed through the hands of several manufacturers, the Director of Customs said that the certificate of the last manufacturer who had manufactured the goods would be considered sufficient.—I am, &c., T. V. LISTER."

THE IMPORTATION OF MACHINERY INTO CHINA.—A curious correspondence is at present taking place between the foreign Diplomatic Body in Pekin, through its *doyen*, Colonel Denby, the United States Minister, and the Tsung-li-Yamên on the prohibition, by order of Li Hung Chang, of the importation of machinery into Shanghai. The question arose through the refusal of the Customs to allow the landing or transhipment of cotton-ginning machinery which had been imported from Japan, and it appeared that the prohibition extended to every description of foreign machinery for manufactories imported by foreigners or private Chinese. Colonel Denby remonstrated in a long despatch, pointing out that the prohibition was not only against plain rights guaranteed to foreigners by the treaties, but was also an infringement of the provisions against trade monopolies which are contained in many of the treaties, and especially in the French treaty of 1858. To this the Yarmên replies that the right of foreigners to manufacture native products at the treaty ports has never been admitted by the Chinese Government. Two instances in which foreigners sought to manufacture iron pans and silk stuffs in 1882 and 1883, and in which the Chinese intervened to prevent them, are mentioned, and reference is made to a letter of the Yamên in 1883 to all the foreign representatives, stating that such manufacture by foreigners was not allowed. The Yamên then states that the object of this prohibition was not to create a monopoly, but to "give protection to the means of livelihood of the common people . . . and thereby, correctly speaking, the practice of monopolies has been prevented." It is generally understood, however, that the welfare of the "common people" had little to do with the prohibition, the object of which is to protect the Shanghai cotton-spinning mill, which is a native official enterprise.

PUMPS AND PUMPING.

THE WESTINGHOUSE AUTOMATIC PUMP.

The gradual, yet steady, development of pumping machinery is one of the most remarkable features in the history of mechanical industry, and the change from such primitive appliances as those used, for instance, in some of the Cornish mines at the end of the last century, to the enormously powerful steam pumps now used in many Atlantic and other ocean liners, is as complete and decided as it could possibly be. The principle, however, notwithstanding all these changes, remains to a large extent the same, and the pump may in this respect be compared to the steam engine, with which it is generally connected; the mode of exerting power is almost precisely similar, but the means of economically producing and utilising that power have undergone almost complete revolution. It will be hardly necessary for us to dwell on the manifold uses to which pumps are put in paper mills and manufacturing premises generally; emptying and filling boilers, circulating water through condensers, creating vacuums, conveying "half stuffs;" heating and ventilating, the removal of sewage and liquid refuse, the disposal of waste water, &c. All these and many other necessary operations are largely, and in many cases, solely performed by means of pumps, which are thus indispensable auxiliaries not only to the paper manufacturer, but also to every machine owner. However numerous the purposes which pumps are made to serve, the variety of the pumps themselves is infinitely greater: air, vacuum, steam and water pumps, chain, bucket, and donkey pumps, and many other styles of pumps, all being

WATER PUMP WITH AIR VESSEL.

familiar to us. To attempt to describe them individually even in the briefest manner would be an impossible task within the limits of our space, so we must on this occasion content ourselves with pointing out the special features of one of the best known types, *i.e.*, the Westinghouse Patent Automatic Pump, manufactured by the Westinghouse Brake Co., Limited, Canal-road, King's-cross, N. The air compressor pump supplied by this firm is perhaps, from its intimate connection with railway rolling stock, more familiar to the general public than any other form of pump in existence. Millions of railway travellers who may never have used a power pump in their lives must be well acquainted with the peculiar sighing sound which announces the presence of an air compressor on the locomotive. The same description of pump is also used for a number of other purposes, its simple and practical character rendering it a very valuable accessory to a steam plant, especially in cases where compressed air is used. It can also be so fitted as to produce a vacuum if desired, although in the ordinary way separate vacuum pumps are supplied for this work. There is, however, but little difference in their construction, the pipe connections of the air cylinder in the compressor being reversed in the vacuum pump. The Westinghouse water pump is, however, the one in most general use, and the one that, by reason of its wide application, appeals most to papermakers. The upper part of this pump, *i.e.*, the steam cylinder, is similar in appearance, and is moreover constructed on the same principle as that of the air pumps. Steam is the motive power generally employed, although compressed air may be used with equally good results. If the latter mode of working be adopted, one of the firm's air pumps just referred to will be found the most convenient to use for the purpose. For general use these pumps are made in several sizes, having water cylinders from 3 to 6½ inches diameter, each size advancing half an inch. The cylinders are of the latest and most approved patterns, and each pump is fitted with the usual air vessel. If, however, the pump is to be used for feeding boilers, the air vessel is omitted, and a special form of water cylinder fitted, the design of which is more suited to the purpose. These boiler feed pumps are supplied in five sizes, commencing with the 2½-in. (diameter of water cylinder), the stroke of both these and the ordinary pump is nine inches. The efficiency of a pump of course lies to a great extent in the condition of its valves; if these are defective or leaky, and pass

WATER PUMP FOR BOILER FEED PURPOSES.

water or steam when not required to do so, a large part of the power expended in driving the pump is wasted, and this involves a corresponding loss of time and fuel, to say nothing of the inconvenience of stopping or disconnecting the pump for repairs. In the Westinghouse form of pump the valves are of indiarubber or gun metal, these being usually recognised as two of the best mediums to use for the purpose; in the boiler feed pumps the valves of course are of metal throughout. The suitability of these pumps for general pumping purposes, as well as for use as fire pumps, is apparent to all who have seen them ; they are small, portable, and compact, and may be readily fixed in any out-of-the-way position, such as on a post or column, or attached to a wall, a few bolts being all that is needed to fix them. Though unimportant in appearance, they are capable of developing much more power than might be expected from pumps of their

VACUUM PUMPS FOR CHEMICAL WORKS, &c.

size, and the practical form of appreciation that they have received in America is evidenced by the fact that the list of firms who have availed themselves of their advantages is a lengthy and constantly increasing one.

THE ALKALI exports to Denmark last year were considerably lower than at any period since 1888. In the latter year the value stood at £20,167, and in 1892 only £7,358.

BELGRADE.

AUSTRIAN CONSULAR REPORT.

Printing and writing papers are very saleable articles in Servia, in which a satisfactory business was carried out last year. The number of newspapers is increasing, so that there is a growing demand for printing paper. Unfortunately, when a political party gets out of office, its press experiences financial difficulties, so that the greatest caution should be exercised in giving credit. Printing and writing papers mostly come from Austrian and Hungarian makers among whom Schloglmuhl, Steyrermuhl, Hermanetz and Czerlan Paper Mills are the most important. Grey and blue packings and straw-papers come from Bohemia. Printing paper is sold in Servia in reams of 1,000 sheets with 3 per cent. discount for cash, writings in reams of 500 sheets against six to seven months acceptances. Ruled paper and commercial books and ledgers, which must be kept by merchants, according to Servian law, are throughout of Austrian manufacture. Cardboards and New Year's cards, birthday cards, &c., are still received from Germany, and if the style and taste may leave ample room for improvement, they are so very cheap that Austrian competition has no chance. The Servian State printing works make their purchases through dealers whom they invite to tender. The project of erecting paper mills in Servia has not been carried out. In writing paper with corresponding envelopes, sold in boxes, a change in favour of Austria has taken place. Whereas the lower sorts only came from Austria and better classes were imported from Germany, France and Great Britain, Austrian makers have now quite cut out their competitors. A Gratz manufacturer especially now does about 60 per cent. of the total business, and supplies a very good quality at so reasonable a price that non-Austrian competitors can no longer hold their own against him. Also mills near Vienna and Buda Pest have come in largely. Austrian makers of course have the great advantage ; the lower carriage is much in their favour against other countries at a much greater distance from Servia.

TRIPOLI.—Rags, esparto, etc., received by Great Britain from Tripoli, amounted in 1892 to £213,948; in 1888 the value stood at £310,214.

GUATEMALA imported last year paper from various countries as follows :—England, £1,173 ; Spain, £2,021 ; France, £2,116 ; Belgium, £599 ; Germany, £1,491 ; United States, £2,211 ; the total being £9,541.

THE SULPHITE PROCESS IN AMERICA AND CANADA.

BY GILEAD P. BECK.

PRODUCTION OF SULPHITE FIBRE QUANTITATIVELY.

At the beginning of 1890 the production of sulphite fibre in U.S. and Canada was a very small one indeed, probably less than 50 U.S. tons per twenty-four hours (100,000 lbs.), and of this small quantity none was A. No. 1, equal to good European fibre, and a good proportion was not at all merchantable and hardly fit to work into "news." To-day statistics are different. According to the most reliable sources of information there are 35 sulphite mills in operation in U.S. and 5 in Canada. For these the following production is claimed by the owners:—

American mills = 849,500 lbs. = 424¾ U.S. tons.
Canadian mills = 86,000 lbs. = 43 ,,

For reasons which will be obvious to those familiar with the pulp industry in these countries, and the irregular manner in which many of the mills are run, it is advisable to deduct say 25 per cent. from the above figures if an accurate estimate of the daily (24 hours) production of sulphite fibre is desired. This will make the figures as follows:—

Probable actual daily production.
American mills, about 319 U.S. tons.
Canadian mills, about 33 ,,

However, with respect to the Canadian mills (or rather to three of them), it is possible that their production may be quite up to the amount claimed for them, as they are under excellent management and very much of a success. It will be, therefore, safe to assume that the total daily production of the 40 mills referred to fluctuate from 352 U.S. tons to a maximum of say 468 tons. A number of new works are projected and in course of construction. These will be put into operation before long, and will, of course, largely increase the daily production.

Some sixteen mills are in this stage, the total *capacity* of which it is claimed will be 608,000 lbs. = 304 U.S. tons. The geographical distribution of the new plants is as follows: Three in Wisconsin, eight in New York State, two in New Hampshire, two in Maine, and one in Colorado.

ABANDONED MILLS.

Since the first experiments on the large scale were conducted, the following nine sulphite mills have been destroyed by fire or given up:

1. Bremaker-Moore Mill, Louisville, Ky.
2. Shawmut Fibre Co., Shawmut, Me.
3. Richards Paper Co., So. Gardner, Me.
4. Weymouth Pulp Co., Weymouth, N.J.
5. New Berne Pulp Co., New Berne, N.C.
6. Richmond Paper Co., Providence, R.I.
7. Carolina Fibre Co., Hartsville, S.C.
8. Kaukauna Fibre Co., Kaukauna, Wis.
9. Wisconsin Fibre Co., Monico, Wis.

Mills numbered 2, 3, 4 and 7 were organised under the auspices of the American Sulphite Co., of Boston, and used either the Ritter-Kellner or the Partington process. Mill 1 used a process and plant claimed to be devised by Mr. Chas. Bremaker; mills 5 and 6 were originally built for the Ekman process. That of the Richard Paper Co., just before commercial disaster forced them to shut down, made the finest bleached and unbleached sulphite pulp ever seen either in Europe or America, and it is history that Mr. Wheelwright, the manager, finally solved the problem, and had it not been for bad commercial management these works would no doubt to-day be turning out a magnificent product.

Mill 8 used the bronze digesters, and mill 9 lead lined digesters constructed according to the ideas of Mr. Wheelwright.

The total failures represented by a portion of the above-mentioned nine mills involved the loss of a very large amount of money. This, of course, was to a large extent inevitable with the pioneers of a new industry in countries where chemical engineering and applied chemistry was, and still is, in many cases conspicuous by its absence, and it would have seemed that those embarking into similar enterprises later on would have profited thereby, but this was not so, as the fiasco of, *e.g.*, the Manufacturing Investment Co. at Madison, Me., and Appleton, Wis., and of others has amply demonstrated.

PRODUCTION OF SULPHITE FIBRE QUALITATIVELY.

As mentioned above, some three years ago not a single mill in U.S. or Canada was making fibre equal to good European fibre. To-day there is certainly still a large amount of fibre produced which would find no sale at all in England, Germany, or Austria, and is difficult to sell here even for low grade "news." There has, however, been an appreciable improvement in quality all round, and some mills are turning out large quantities of very fair fibre regularly, and occasionally fibre which begins to approach that of Europe in regularity, brightness of colour, and proper reduction, as well as in length and silkiness of fibre. Of American mills the following may be mentioned as turning out very fair fibre indeed, some of which is excellent:

(*a*) Badger Paper Co., Kaukauna, Wis.
(*b*) Piedmont Pulp Co., Piedmont, W.Va.
(*c*) West Virginia Pulp Co., Davis, W.V.
(*d*) Louis Snider and Sons, Hamilton, Ohio.
(*e*) Dexter Pulp Co., Dexter, N.Y.
(*f*) Michigan Fibre Co., Port Huron, Mich.

(*g*) New England Fibre Co., Turner's Falls, Mass.

(*h*) Mount Tom Pulp Co., Mount Tom, Mass.

(*i*) Howland Falls Pulp Co., Howland, Me.

(*k*) Russell Paper Co., Lawrence, Mass.

(*l*) Alpha Fibre Co., West Carrollton, Ohio.

The mills marked *a*, *d*, *k*, *l*, consume their own fibre in making paper, and their product is but rarely seen in the market, and only in small occasional lots. The other mills supply the open market.

One reason why the sulphite mills have been, and still are, so slow in adopting themselves to turning out high grade fibre is that a common belief is prevalent that there is money in making large quantities of low grade fibre and selling it for any price it will fetch. Secondly, skilled help is few and far between and naturally commands high wages. It is frequently thought that any labourer who has worked around a steam plant or paper mill can be made into a skilled digesterman or liquorman by a few weeks' practice and some inaccurate instructions. The result is naturally a deplorable one. Finally, the management of sulphite mills here is usually in the hands of papermakers having no experience in making sulphite, or even in the hands of men who, while undoubtedly energetic, longheaded, and well-meaning, have no more knowledge of technical and chemical matters than a digester has of lunar theology. Thus, among the American mills there are five managed respectively by a dry goods man, a machinist, a railroad contractor, a paper salesman, and an insurance man. Another reason besides the absence of skilled specialists as managers lies in the fact that in America sulphite and paper mill chemists are considered as expensive and useless luxuries, and but little attention is paid to the many apparently minor details which have great influence on the quality of the product, and are not easily followed up and kept in sight by any except those having had just this kind of chemical experience in the same business. The same applies to economy of production, and the amount of sulphur, power, and fuel wasted in some mills would keep a European pulp mill expert in agonies until acclimatised. During the last few years special attention has been paid to sulphite pulp and paper manufacture by some well-known and skilful chemists and engineers, some of who are experts of international reputation, and these have introduced many economies and improvements. The principal among them are:

Professor Fisher, of Philadelphia.

Captain Ellis, of St. Catherines, Ontario.

Dr. Drewsen, of Dexter, N.Y.

Mr. Rademacher, of Lawrence, Mass.

Mr. Bonnevie, of Cumberland, M.A.

Mr. Schilde, of Port Huron, Michigan.

These names are known all through the country, and much credit is due to them for their share in the development of the industry. There is no finer wood in the world than the American and Canadian spruce, and it is low in price; pure, soft water for boiling and washing purposes is abundant, and water power is ample and well distributed. Lime supplies are good and cheap, sulphur and pyrites (the former from Japan and California, as well as imported from Europe) are obtainable at reasonable prices, and last but not least, an extensive and daily increasing market is right at hand. Surely these are very favourable conditions. Thus for example a statement published by Messrs. Howard Lockwood and Co. shows a gain in the capacity of American book and news mills of 16¼ per cent. over last year, and 254½ per cent. since 1881. If improvements in fibre making, tending to improvement of quality as well as to economy of production, anything like keep pace with the increasing production, there is no doubt at all that America as a market for European mills will lose much of its importance.

Methods of Manufacture.

As might be expected these differ widely in the various mills, and there are few plants that can be said to be constructed and operated on any definite "system" or "process," owing mainly to the tendency which is prevalent here of disregarding prior experience and altering plant or process for (or quite often without any) trivial causes. An interesting classification of processes may be based on the time used in cooking, and it is curious to note the difference between the number of plants operating on the "slow cook" (the so-called Mitscherlich) and "quick" process. Of the forty mills in U.S. and Canada now in operation only eight are run on the "slow-cook" process, which is based on the process invented by Professor Mitscherlich, and introduced into U.S. by Mr. Thillmany. They are the following:

1. Manufacturing Investment Co., two mills.
2. Alpena, Mich., mill.
3. Detriot, Mich., mill.
4. Port Huron, Mich., mill.
5. Goffstown Centre, N.H., mill.
6. Hull, P.Q., Canada, mill.
7. Dexter, N.Y., mill.

There is probably no mill in either U.S. or Canada which uses the "slow-cook" process as introduced from Germany, unless it be the two mills of the Manufacturing Investment Co., which have made such brilliant demonstrations of how *not* to do a thing. The process in question was found cumbersome and unable to compete with the quicker and more modern improvements of Dr. Kellner, and as the "quick" process pulp found more favour among the makers of better papers, the purchasers of licenses from the company which owned the Mitscherlich patents had no option but to introduce the Kellner improvements and ideas, and modernise their plant. Although Dr. Kellner would probably hold up his hands in holy terror if he saw some of the plants that are called by his name here, yet it is certain that the U.S. and Canada sulphite industry owes him a debt they can never repay. To speak further of the "quick" process with reference to digesters and general features, the Ekman process is not used in any mill at all now. Magnesite is very scarce and expensive. The rotary globular Partington digesters are now only used in the mill of the Barclay Fibre Co., at Sangerties, N.Y., that of the Russell Paper Co. at Lawrence, Mass., and in the mill of the Halifax Wood Fibre Co. of Sheet Harbor, N.S., Canada. They are cement lined. The bronze digester, although now out of date, is still used in the following mills:

1. Wilkinson Bros., Birmingham, Conn.
2. Eastern Manufacturing Co., South Brewer, Me.
3. Ypsilanti Paper Co., Ypsilanti, Mich.
4. Atlas Paper Co., Appleton, Wis.
5. Badger Paper Co., Kaukauna, Wis. (with Wagg's lining).
6. Marinette and Menominee Paper Co., Marinette, Wis.
7. Falls Manufacturing Co., Oconto Falls, Wis.

Kellner digesters, cement and tile-lined, are used at the following mills:

1. Cushnoc Fibre Co., Augusta, Me.
2. Lisbon Falls Fibre Co., Lisbon Falls, Me.
3. Mount Tom Sulphite Co., Mount Tom, Mass.
4. Hudson River Pulp Co., Palmer's Falls, N.Y.
5. Willamette Pulp Co., Oregon City, Ore.
6. Fall Mountain Paper Co., Bellow's Fall, Vt.
7. Toronto Paper Co., Cornwall, Ont., Canada.
8. Riordan Paper Co., Merritton, Ont., Canada.
9. Maritime Sulphite Co., Chatham, N.B., Canada.

Digesters lined with artificial stone blocks (Curtis and Jones' method) are used at the mill of the Howland Falls Pulp Co., Howland, Me., and also by the Orono Pulp and Paper Co., of Orono, Me.

The Salomon "natural crust lining" (Brungger) is found in the digesters of the

1. Susquehanna W. P. and P. Co., Conowingo, Md.
2. Yorkhaven Paper Co., Yorkhaven, Penn.
3. Kimberly and Clark Co., Kimberly, Wis.

The so-called Graham digester in which the lead is supposed to be "amalgamated" (?) to the boiler plate is used by the Hudson River Pulp Co., at Mechanicsville N.Y., and Louis Snider's Sons, Co., at Hamilton, Ohio, and the mill of the New England Fibre Co., at Turner's Falls, Mass., is believed also to be using a lead lining.

The Wagg method of lining is used by the Badger Paper Co., at Kaukauna, Wis., and the Cumberland Paper Co., at Cumberland, Md. The so-called Friend and Stebbin's lining, which is a Mitscherlich lining on a small scale, is used in the following mills:

1. Remington Paper Co., Watertown, N.Y.
2. Alpha Fibre Co., West Carrollton, Ohio.

The mills of the West Virginia Pulp Co., at Davis, West Virginia, and of the Piedmont Pulp Co., at Piedmont, West Virginia, use the so-called Pittsburg digester with cement lining. Of the sixteen mills which are in course of construction, two will have the Wagg lining in their digesters, viz., the Ashland, Wis., mill, and that at Appleton, Wis., of the Riverside Co. The Racquette River Co.'s mill at Potsdam, N.Y., has the Friend and Stebbin's digester. That at Denver, Colo., will have the Salomon Brungger digesters, while the new mills at Lincoln, Me., Berlin Falls, N.H. (Glen Manufacturing Co.), An Sable, N.Y., Fort Edward, N.Y., and Ticonderoga, N.Y., are reported to have decided on putting the artificial stone linings in. The following plants are, it seems, not yet decided on, or else the choice has not been made known:

1. Rumford Falls, Me.
2. Burgess Sulphite Co., Berlin Falls, N.H.
3. Wendler and Spiro, Forestport, N.Y.
4. High Falls Pulp Co., Potsdam, N.Y. (Probably Kellner digester with Russell cement lining.)
5. Warner, Miller and Co., Hinckley, N.Y.
6. Niagara Falls Paper Co.
7. Combined Locks Pulp Co., Combined Locks, Wis.

As to the liquor plants it is hopeless to attempt any classifications as one meets with too many vagaries. The best are undoubtedly the Kellner plants as used by the Riordon Mills and elsewhere. The Mitscherlich towers and various original and imitated Partington continuous apparatuses are also doing good work. Taking it all in all, great steps in advance are being made and in a few more years American and Canadian sulphite pulp may be common on the European market, although it will take some time before the sulphite industry is developed so as to keep pace with the older paper industry.

RAGS were exported from Italy to Great Britain in 1892 to the value of £7,137. In 1888 the value only stood at £143.

DANISH RAGS are not shipped so freely to England as in former years. In 1888 the value stood at £24,093, last year it dropped to £12,584.

TRIESNACHER PAPIERFABRIK.—It has been erroneously reported in German trade journals that this company has paid 15 per cent. dividend for the last two years. These mills have only lately been converted into a public company, and have therefore not yet been able to declare dividends.

THE MILLBOARD WORKS, WILHELM NITZSCHE in Ober Carsdorf i. S. have come into the possession of the widow of the late owner Frau Annetta Rossa Nitzsche, who has given procuration to her son, Herr Max Nitzsche. After being burnt down in June these works were re-built and re-opened on October 1st.

HOLZSTOFF LEDERPAPPEN UND PAPIERFABRIK, WASUNGEN.—No dividend has been declared for 1892-93. Of the clear profits M23,933 have been written off, M112 placed into reserve, and M2,752 carried forward into new account. The share capital of this company amounts to M600,000.

HOLZSTOFF UND HOLZPAPPEN, FABRIK LIMMRITZ, STEINA.—The general meeting will be asked to sanction the reduction of the capital from M1,200,000 to M587,000. These new shares are to be of M1,000 each, 516 to be preference and the remainder ordinary shares. The committee of inspection has to deposit five shares each. Of the clear profits five per cent. shall be put into reserve, until the reserve has reached 10 per cent. of the share capital. After this deduction the preference shares receive a dividend of 5 per cent.; 10 per cent. is paid to the committee of inspection, and the bonuses to directors, &c. The remaining balance is to be equally divided among all the shareholders, including the preference shares.

JULIUS SCHULTE'S PAPER MILLS, in Dusseldorf, were the scene of a fire on October 16th. The raw material stores and rag cutting implements were destroyed, but the prompt attendance and energetic action of the fire brigade prevented further damage, so that work at these mills will be resumed in a week or so.

HERR DOCTOR BOCK, the former partner of the firm of Korn and Bock, in Breslau, is reported to have bought the paper mills of Friedr. Schulte and Co., in Dusseldorf, with sixteen acres of land, for the sum of M400,000. His specialties will be printings and sugar papers.

VEREIN FUR ZELLSTOFF INDUSTRIE, IN DRESDEN.—The balance of 1892-93 shows a profit of M124,379 against M31,768 of the previous year. Considering that in the two last previous balances the writings off were but very small, the directors propose only to pay 1 per cent. dividend (M17,000), and to use the remainder for writing off and putting into reserve. The shareholders will be asked to sanction the buying back of M20,000 bonds and M70,000 shares, for which sufficient funds are in hand.

HERR ALBIN VON LENK, the managing director of the company, "Leykam," in Gratz (Austria), died recently after a long illness, in his 59th year.

THODESCHE PAPIERFABRIK ACTIEN-GESELLSCHAFT IN HAINSBERG.—The annual report for the year ending June 30, 1893, says that the hopes expressed in the last report have not been realised. Instead of showing better results than before, the enhanced prices of ground wood caused by the drought of the second half of 1892 on the contrary caused a loss in carrying out contracts previously taken. Ground wood often of a very inferior quality had risen 50 per cent., since the orders were accepted so that already on December 31st, 1892, a loss of M117,882 without any writing off was shown. The year 1893 commenced with sufficient orders, and only such classes of paper will now be made which are less open to competition. On a share capital of M2,700,000 a loss of M528,156 is shown. To make up this loss it is proposed to reduce the share capital to M1,350,000, by merging every two shares into one. The sum thus obtained will be used for writing off this loss and to reduce the value at which buildings, machinery, &c., are estimated.

PATENT PAPIERFABRIK ZU PENIG.—The report of 1892-93 states that the seven paper machines have been fully occupied. The production of paper at Penig and at Wilischthal rose from 8,652 meter tons to 8,837 meter tons, but the profit was only M475,681, against M543,677. This falling off was caused in the first place by the scarcity of water and consequent greater consumption of coal, and further by the heavier outlay for pulp, which particularly took place at Wilischthal. Home pulp makers being unable to carry out their contracts pulp had to be imported from Sweden at a higher cost, though the quality was inferior. If freight and duty are considered the rise comes to fully 50 per cent. Recently also chemical pulps and straw pulp have become dearer in consequence of increased American demand. The pulp production of the branch in Wolkenstein in the last year amounted to 247,302 kilos, against 473,517 kilos of the previous year. These figures show clearly the results of the scarcity of water. As these unfavourable conditions continue, steam power will be made use of in Wolkenstein. The wood production will thus become more independent and greatly increased and also a great part of the requirements of Wilischthal will be produced at these works.

EGYPTIAN RAGS were received at British ports last year to the value of £16,237. The value in 1888 was £23,812.

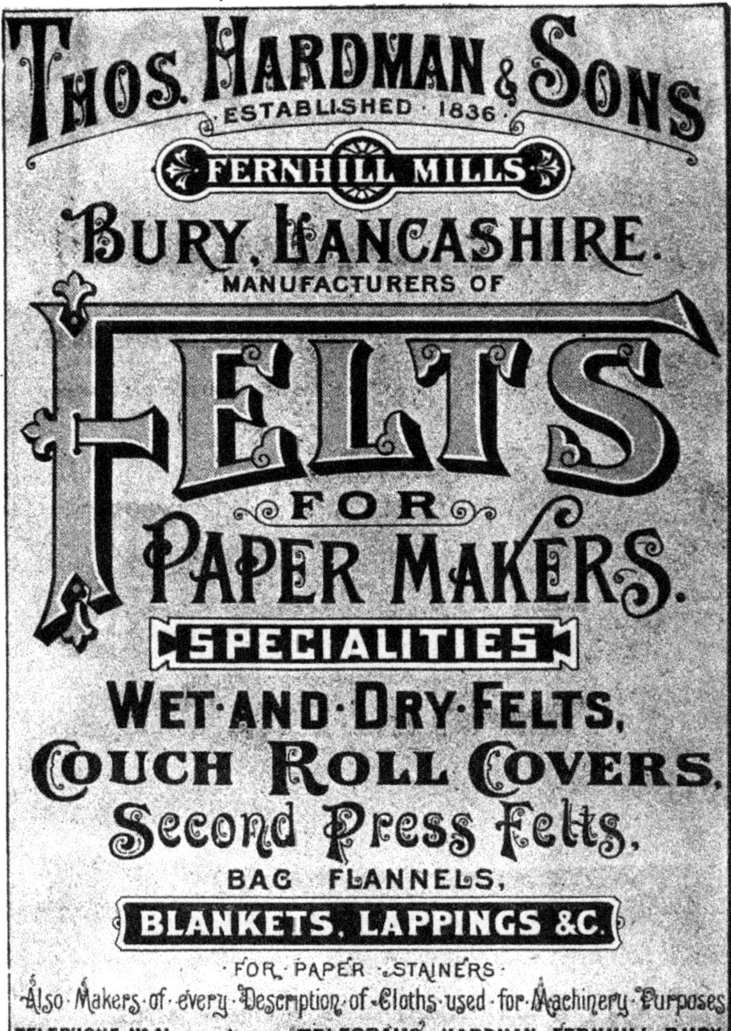
THOS. HARDMAN & SONS
ESTABLISHED 1836
FERNHILL MILLS
BURY, LANCASHIRE.
MANUFACTURERS OF
FELTS
FOR
PAPER MAKERS.
SPECIALITIES
WET AND DRY FELTS,
COUCH ROLL COVERS,
Second Press Felts,
BAG FLANNELS,
BLANKETS, LAPPINGS &C.
FOR PAPER STAINERS
Also Makers of every Description of Cloths used for Machinery Purposes
TELEPHONE Nº 41
TELEGRAMS. HARDMAN, FERNHILL, BURY.

D. N. BERTRAM'S
Patent REELER

The Special Features of the Machine are:

1.—**NO PART OF THE KNIFE BLOCKS** or knives, except the cutting edges, comes in contact with the paper, thus avoiding any damage to the web by narrow rings touching it.

2.—There **BEING NO BLOCKS** between the knives they can be instantly adjusted to any width without taking the spindle from its bearings.

3.—The **KNIVES ARE DRIVEN INDEPENDENTLY** of the paper at an increased speed ensuring clean cut edges.

4.—The **MACHINE IS DRIVEN** by belt pulley on drum shaft with fast and slow speeds, worked from front of machine by levers, so arranged that when the fast speed is put on the slow one disengages itself. The change from slow to fast is easily effected, and no jerking takes place.

☞ **THIS PATENT REELER is working in Several Well-known Paper Mills.**

IN THIS MACHINE the paper is slit into widths upon the spindle, which carries the finished webs, thus preventing irregularity of edges; the outside shavings being trimmed before the web passes to the winding-up spindle and slitting-knives.

THE KNIFE CARRIAGE is placed vertically over the web, and fitted with automatic raising gear, to compensate for the increase of web.

THERE IS ALSO AN ARRANGEMENT so that the operator can apply the slitting-knives with any given amount of contact that may be desirable, and it will retain the same position until the whole web is finished.

THE ACTION OF THE PRESSING ROLL on the top of the web ensures the reel being firmly and evenly wound, and there is a shackle at one side of the machine, with screw which can adjust pressing roll to a nicety on the drum upon which the slitting and winding apparatus is carried. This allows webs which may be slightly thicker at one side than another to be wound without creasing.

REFERENCES GIVEN ON APPLICATION.

BERTRAMS LIMITED

(Successors to Geo. & Wm. BERTRAM—ESTABLISHED 1821),

ENGINEERS,

ST. KATHERINE'S WORKS, SCIENNES, EDINBURGH.

WORLD'S PAPER TRADE REVIEW OFFICE, 58, SHOE LANE, LONDON, E.C.

TRADE NOTES.

McKENNA AND Co., LTD.—This company has been registered with a nominal capital of £15,000, in £10 shares, to carry on business as oil refiners, &c.

PEAT INDUSTRIES SYNDICATE, LTD.—The nominal capital of this company, recently registered, is £35,000 in £1 shares. The object is to acquire, develop, and turn to account patents and inventions relating to the use of peat, and to deal in all articles manufactured therefrom.

BERGVIK CO.'S SECOND DEBENTURES.—The numbers are announced of 26 five per cent. second debentures, amounting to £2,600, of the Bergvik Company (Limited), which have been drawn for payment at £105 per debenture on and after November 15th.

MESSRS. JULIUS SEYD, BISHOP, JOHNSON AND CO. (LIMITED), state that arrangements have been made whereby Messrs. Kelly and Co. (Limited), the well-known directory publishers, will take an interest in their business, which will in future be known as Seyd and Kelly's Credit Index Company (Limited). The business will be continued with the same managers as heretofore and all subscriptions to the "Credit Index" and otherwise taken out with the old company will be completed by the new.

MR. T. Y. NUTTALL, manager of the Darwen Paper Mill, whose brother, Mr. John Nuttall, recently died, has the sympathy of a large circle of friends in his still later bereavement—the death of his father, Mr. S. N. Nuttall, aged 65 years.

THE LORD MAYOR'S SHOW.—A feature of the show bearing upon paper and print will be a car representing Caxton in the act of submitting to King Edward IV., the Queen, the Princes, and the Lord Chamberlain the first products of his printing press. This last item has, we may suppose, some connection with the fact that the new Lord Mayor, Alderman Tyler, is a member of the exclusive semi-literary body, "Ye Olde Sette of Volumes," and Master of the Stationers' Company.

ABRIDGMENTS OF PATENT SPECIFICATIONS.—Class 96 (embracing paper, pasteboard, and papier mâche for 1877-83) just published at the Patent Office, contains short descriptions of over 300 inventions relating to the machinery, apparatus, and processes by which raw fibrous material is made into paper, &c. Most of the thirty or forty paper machines described belong to the Fourdrinier type. Amongst the inventions for machine details and processes the most numerous are those relating to rag engines or pulping engines, strainers, calendering, and sizing. The chief development of invention in the period appears to be in the preliminary treatment of the raw material before it is put into the pulping engine; this treatment, including boiling, bleaching, cutting-up and grinding, willowing and devilling, shredding, &c. There are no less than eighty specifications in which new fibrous materials are applied to making paper, including substances as diverse as slagwool, wood, esparto, sugar cane, and even straw manure and animal excrement, &c. There are a few cases relating to papermaking by hand, and a considerable number for making pasteboard and papier mâche.

TECHNOLOGICAL EXAMINATIONS. — We have received the 1892-93 report of the examinations department of the City and Guilds of London Institute. There were twenty candidates in 1893 who took up the subject of "Paper Manufacture," and only nine passed: Honours—1st, 2; 2nd, 1. Ordinary—1st, 1; 2nd, 5. The failures were one in "Honours," and ten in "Ordinary." In alkali manufacture four candidates presented themselves, and passed as follows: Honours—2nd, 1. Ordinary—1st, 2; 2nd, 1. Throughout the various London centres paper manufacture does not appear on the list of subjects upon which instruction is given. Amongst the prize winners were Mr. Joseph Macnaughton (Coatbridge Technical School)—1st H., £2 (Salters) and S. M., and Mr. Frank Southern (Manchester Technical School)—1st O., £1 (Salters) and S.M.

SALMON ANTI-FRICTION METAL CO.—The partnership has been dissolved between Messrs. W. H. Salmon, W. Salmon and E. S. Brace, metal mixers, Northfleet, under the style of the Salmon Anti-Friction Metal Co., so far as regards Mr. E. S. Brace.

PATENT BORAX CO., LTD.—This company has been registered with a nominal capital of £50,000 in £10 shares, to acquire the business hitherto carried on by Jesse Ascough, under the style of the Patent Borax Co., and to carry on in Great Britain, and in any part of the world, the business of manufacturers and preparers of and dealers in patent and other borax, and in boron, borate, boracic and other compounds, in all their forms and preparations therefrom of all kinds in which borax or boron, its principal element, is or can be used (whether for domestic, cleansing, purifying, disinfecting, food preserving, medical, sanitary or other purposes), manufacturers of starches, blues, soaps, washing powders, disinfecting powders, sodas, &c., candle makers, ink makers, papermakers, wholesale and retail grocers, and manufacturing or wholesale and retail chemists. Jesse Ascough, of the Grange, Handsworth, Staffs, is to be first managing director, at a salary to be fixed by the board.

MESSRS. SUTCLIFFE AND WADSWORTH, rag merchants, Pellon, Halifax, Yorks., have dissolved partnership, and all debts will be paid by Mr. J. Sutcliffe.

Vessels from Norway have experienced heavy weather in the North Sea during the past week. The "Odd" (s.), from Skein, slipped anchor and 30 fathoms of chain in Fleetwood Roads, and the "Thule" (Norwegian brig), from Fredrikshavn, and the "Marie" (Swedish schooner), are at Grimsted, where they will have to be repaired to stop leaking, &c.

Cholera at Susa.—An advice, dated October 28th, states that cholera has broken out at Susa and 25 deaths are reported. Four thousand of the inhabitants have fled, the majority proceeding to Tunis.

A New Portuguese Wood Pulp Mill.—A mill has recently been set up by an English company about 20 miles to the south of Oporto, for the manufacture of wood pulp for papermaking, from the "Pinus maritima," which grows in great abundance along the north coast of Portugal. The produce of this factory is steadily increasing, and besides being consumed in the country, is also sent abroad, and some of it even finds its way to the United States.

Canal Tolls and Charges.—The Board of Trade inquiry into the objections of traders to the schedule of rates and tolls proposed to be charged by the North Staffordshire Railway Company upon the Trent and Mersey Navigation was continued on Tuesday, at the Westminster Town Hall, before the Hon. T. H. W. Pelham. Evidence was given by Dr. Hewitt, a director of Messrs. Brunner, Mond, and Co., to the effect that the charges in respect to Wardle Lock would act and had acted as a hindrance to the traffic which the company desired to send over the canal, and this statement was confirmed by Mr. Thomas Moore, limestone merchant, of Northwich, and Mr. Durnford, of the Llanymymech limestone quarries. Mr. Harding, representing Messrs. Heath Sons, colliery proprietors and iron merchants, at Stoke-on-Trent, also objected to the exceptional charges, especially the bonus mileage proposed to be charged in respect of the Harecastle Tunnel. At that spot they had large ironworks, and were about to open a colliery which would produce 700 or 800 tons tons a week, and upon all that traffic they would be charged as for six miles when it only travelled two miles. Counsel for the traders addressed the tribunal, and Mr. Littler, Q.C., replied for the company, and the case was then concluded.

The Coal Crisis.—A special conference of the Miners' Federation is to be held at the Westminster Palace Hotel to-day (Friday), to consider and determine upon the course to be pursued at the joint conference with the coalowners to be held later in the day at the same place. It is understood that the miners' representatives will have no power to effect a settlement of the dispute which involves any reduction of wages, but if the employers withdraw their notices the federation will agree to the formation of a board of conciliation to consider future wage questions.

The Salt Union and Our Salt Trade.—Wednesday's *Liverpool Journal of Commerce* says that the decline in the salt exports from Liverpool to the East Indies still continues, and up to the end of October there is a falling off of almost 20 per cent. as compared with the ten months of last year. Hamburg is again in front of Liverpool with 12,000 tons against 10,000, while Middlesborough is booked for 3,000, and Bremen for 2,000 tons.

Liverpool is beginning to look concernedly upon Manchester as a seaport, and dock authorities and railway companies are urged to make sufficient concessions in the heavy dues and rates now charged to counteract the competition of the Ship Canal. It is felt that "much mischief is likely to accrue if a new tariff of landing charges in Liverpool and railway carriage thence is not speedily decided upon, and circulated as widely as the Canal tariff referred to."

Joss Paper.—The trade of Bangkok, Siam, shows that the Chinaman does not forget his religion in a foreign country, as the import of joss sticks and joss paper testify. The word "joss," it need hardly be explained, is "pidgin" English for a Chinese idol or god. Joss sticks are small scented tapers of sandal wood and oil, and the burning of these along with joss paper is a prominent feature of all religious ceremonies.

The death is announced of Mr. William Morrell Mentzel, a member of the firm of Mentzel and Sons, wholesale paper dealers at Baltimore, U.S.A., and president of the Mentzel Paper Co., Oella, Md. Aged 60.

PAPER & PULP MILL SHARES.

Very little business is being carried through in paper and pulp mill shares. During last week Ramsbottom Co. advanced ¼, and Kellner-Partingtons are 4s. better at 65s.-67s. 6d. United Alkali dropped a ¼ at 6¾-7¼ (ord.) and ditto 10¾-11¼ (pref.) A decline of one is registered on Brunner Mond ord. at 55-60; two in ditto at 37-40. Salt Union pref. have dropped a ¼ at 8¾-9¼.

(Report received from Mr. F. D. Dean, 36, Corporation Street, Manchester.)

Nominal Amnt	Amnt Paid	Name of Company	Last divi dend	Price.
7	7	Bury Paper, ord.	nil	4½–4¾
7	7	do. do. 6% pref.	6%	4¾–5
100	100	do do. deb.	5%	103–106
10	10	Bath Paper Mill Co. Lim.	7½%	6–7
10	10	Bergvik Co., def.	15%	13¾
100	100	do. do. 6% cum. pref.	6%	10½–11½
10	10	do. do. deb.	5%	105–110
5	3½	Burnley Paper Co.	3/-	77/6–80/0
5	3½	Darwen Paper Co.	10%	5½–6¼
10	10	East Lancashire Co.	nil	4–4½
10	10	do. do. 6% pref.	nil	6–6½
5	5	do. do. bonus	nil	1½–2
5	5	Hyde Paper Co.	4%	4½–5
5	4	North of Ireland Paper Co.	nil	2½–2¾
10	5	Ramsbottom Paper Co.	17½%	12½–12¾
5	4½	Roach Bridge Paper Co.	5%	2¾–3
5	5	Star Paper Co.	10%	6–6½
5	3	do. do. 6% pref. cum.	10%	4¾ 5¼
50	50	do. do. deb.	6%	55–56
5	2½	Kellner Partingt'n Pulp Co	—	65/0–67/6

THE CHICAGO EXHIBITION.

LIST OF AWARDS.

The following awards to exhibitors at the World's Fair are announced :—

GREAT BRITAIN.

Thomas Burch Ford, High Wycombe. Blotting paper.

Cotteril Bros., Bristol. Wall paper.

Jeffrey and Co., London. Three awards for artistic wall paper, embossed leather and leather paper.

Charles Knowles and Co., London. Art wall paper.

Woolamo and Co., London. Wall papers leather wall decorations.

F. B. Ford, London. Blotting paper.

Brunner Mond and Co., Northwich. Pure alkali, soda, ammonia, bleaching powder.

United Alkali Co., Ltd., Liverpool. Bleaching powder, salts, ammonia.

Lever Bros., Birkenhead. Soaps.

William Cleghorn, Dundee. Jute cloth and yarn.

Coombe, Barbour and Combe, Ltd., Belfast. Manufactured flax, sisal, jute, ramie, hemp.

Perkins, Bacon and Co., Ltd., London. Specimens of bank notes.

Religious Tract Society, London. Books, &c.

Sunday School Union, London. Text books, &c.

CANADA.

Rolland Paper Co., Toronto. Printing paper, writing paper, coloured paper.

John C. Watson, Montreal. Wall paper.

SWEDEN.

J. H. Munktells Paper Mills Co., Limited, Grycksbo. Filter paper in reams. Samples and pulp in large glass tube.

Munksjo Paper Mills Co., Ltd., Jonkoping. Samples of building and paper boards. Several kinds of wrapping paper.

Munksjo Paper Mills Lithographing Co., Jonkoping. Several kinds of wrapping paper.

Gustafsfors Manufacturing Co., Ltd., Gustafsfors. Wrapping paper.

Holmen Paper Mills and Manufacturing Co., Ltd., Norrkoping. Printing paper and paper for labels and match boxes.

DENMARK.

L. Levison, jun., Copenhagen. Paper in finest variety.

RUSSIA.

Russian Imperial State Paper Co., St. Petersburg. Paper.

Vargunin Brothers, St. Petersburg. Paper.

Imperial Russian State Manufacturing Co., St. Petersburg. Paper.

GERMANY.

Hofel and Co., Leipzic. Patented walking sticks made from paper tubes. Patent penholders made from paper tubes.

Louis Wertheim, Frankfurt. Asbestos paper, asbestos mill, board asbestonet (waterproof), asbestos papier maché.

T. Zuber and Co., Rishrim. Wall paper and decorations.

Zellstoffabrik, Waldhof. Writing paper for correspondence and commercial books.

Gebr. Leichtlin, Karlsruhe. Tracing paper and linen paper.

A. Schreiber & Co., Raschau. Paper and wooden stucco.

W. Schrober, Eurenfrierdorf. Stucco of paper and wood.

E. Spangenberg, Berlin. Paper furnishings, &c.

Verein Strohstoff-Fabrik, Dresden. Straw pulp in various shades.

C. L. Wust, Frankfurt. Cards.

Gebr. Pauli, Nuremberg. Armour paper, patent foil.

Hochstein and Weinberg, Berlin. Glazed paper and fine pasteboard.

Papier Fabrik, Sundern. Tissue paper, &c.

Gebr. Scherus Papier und Tapestenfabrik, Braumenthal. Panels of wall paper.

Apiam Bermiruitz, Leipzic. Cardboard, cards, &c.

Louis Wertheim, Frankfurt. Asbestos fireproof wall paper.

J. Zeuber and Co., Rexheim, Alsace. Decorated velvet wall paper, wall paper varnished in colours.

AUSTRIA.

Leykem Josephthal, Vienna. Paper pulp and paper stock.

Schlorgelmuehl, Vienna. Paper pulp and paper stock.

Neusical Stock Company, Vienna. Paper pulp and paper stock.

D. R. Pollak and Sohens, Vienna. Paper goods.

Christian Schutz, Vienna. Tissue paper.

Jac. Schnable & Co., Vienna. Tissue paper.

P. Piette, Freiheit-Pilsen. Writing paper.

Herman Braunert, Vienna. Paper, ornamental paper.

SPAIN.

Costas Marquillas, Barcelona. Cigarette paper, writing paper.

Tomas Hermanos, Barcelona. Papers for commercial books, lithograph and edition work.

Terres Morgat, Barcelona. Hand made cigarette paper.

Torras & Guerrera, Barcelona. Hand made cigarette paper.

Eugenia Guilbout, Barcelona. Propaganda envelopes.

THE exports from New York, according to the last weekly return to hand, included the following:—

B. W. Indies ...	767 pkgs	Southampton ...	1 case
London	340 cases	Australasia... ...	247 rolls
Honduras ...	96 pkgs	New Zealand ...	306 pkgs

ACCORDING to Mr. C. O. Harrington a paper mill is wanted at Carthage, Mo. He says the conditions are unusually favourable, there being good water, straw to be had at $2 per ton, lime, 11 cents. per bushel, and coal at $1.25 per ton delivered at the mill. The market and transportation are reported good.

THE sulphite mill at High Falls, N.Y., is nearly completed. The pyrites acid plant was recently started up by Mr. Julius Spiro.

IT is expected that the new plant of the United Indurated Fibre Company, Lockport, N.Y., will be started up by November 15. The buildings are constructed of stone, with roofs and flooring of the style known as "New England slow burning mill construction"; they will be supplied with Grinnel automatic sprinklers, hydrants and hose houses. The plant covers 10 acres.

MR. AUGUSTO VALENTINIS, manager of the Cartiera Keali paper mills, Italy, who recently visited Chicago and the World's Fair, has in a published interview the following to say about papermaking in Italy: "There is little to say about papermaking in Italy. It is in pretty good shape. Competition is great among us, and we cut prices as I suppose you do here. We have no combinations or deals to disturb us, but go on as merchants should do. At our mills we manufacture printing paper and wrapping. We use rags, wood and sulphite and straw. Wood pulp is now 18 francs (about 375 dols.) per 100 kilogs. (2,200 pounds). Italy exports quite a quantity of paper to the Orient, including writings and wrappings. Wages at our mill range from 2 to 4 francs a day, but the best and most skilled workmen can make more than that. Here, however, you pay better wages all round, and you appear to receive good service for it. I ought to say that your machines for the making of news paper are the largest and most complete I ever saw. Let me say that it is well worth a journey from Italy to visit the Exposition."

IT IS reported that the Rumford Falls Paper Company, Rumford Falls, Me., will put in a 50 horse power electric motor to haul out its logs above the upper dam, taking power from the electric light station, thus doing away with a steam engine and the trouble of carting fuel to the place where it would be located. The mill is now turning off about 35 tons of paper daily, but its ultimate capacity will be 60 tons.

SUMMARY OF
IMPORTS & EXPORTS,

London, Liverpool, Bristol, Southampton, Hull, Fleetwood, Harwich, Folkestone, Newhaven, Dover, &c.

IMPORTS.

FOR THE WEEK ENDING TUESDAY LAST.

Paper	7012 bales	Stationery..... ...	28 cases
,, ...	691 cases	Tissues	267 pkgs.
,, ...	436 rolls	Stock	1160 bales
Strawboards	17444 pkgs.	Millboards	6351 ,,
,, ...	60 brls.	Pasteboards	9968 ,,

FOR LAST MONTH:

Paper	67759 bales	Stationery	185 cases
,, ...	3884 cases	Pasteboards	34333 pkgs.
,, ...	4051 rolls	Strawboards	29243 ,,
Stock	2425 bales	Cardboards	1457 ,,
Tissues...............	552 pkgs.	Envelopes	25 ,,
Rags	38 ,,	Parchment	3 ,,
Millboards.........	25380 bales	Leather Paper...	3 cases
,, ...	190 cases		

EXPORTS.

FOR THE WEEK ENDING TUESDAY LAST:

BRITISH GOODS.			
		Rags..................	10 tons
Paper	2665 cwt.	Parchment	£121 value
Writing Paper ...	2740 ,,	Stock	323 tons
Printing Paper	6807 ,,	FOREIGN GOODS.	
Stationery......	£9768 value	Paper	641 cwt.
Strawboard Cuttings	63 tons	Writing Paper...	10 ,,
,, ...	208 cwt.	Printing Paper...	70 ,,
Cardboards	86 cwt.	Stationery	£101 value
Waste	120 tons	Millboards.........	£44 ,,
,, ...	476 cwt.	Parchment	17 cwt.
Millboards	134 ,,	Strawboards	101 ,,

FOR LAST MONTH:

BRITISH GOODS.			
		Rags..................	416 cwt.
Paper	7435 cwt.	FOREIGN GOODS.	
Writing Paper...	9301 ,,	Paper	2444 cwt.
Printing Paper..	23634 ,,	Writing Paper...	171 ,,
,, ...	£54 value	Printing Paper..	1224 ,,
Stationery	£49633 ,,	,, ...	£34 value
Stock	567 tons	Parchment	£320 ,,
Strawboard Cuttings.........	76 ,,	Strawboards	550 cwt.
Cardboards	220 cwt.	,, ...	£290 value
Millboards.........	176 ,,	Stationery	£1644 ,,
Parchment	£155 value	Millboards.........	64 cwt.
Waste	1289 tons	Wood Pulp	124 tons
,, ...	10 cwt.	,, ...	100 cwt.
Strawboards......	508 ,,	Stock	4 tons
Straw	5 tons	Cigarette Paper..	£56 value

Glasgow, Greenock, Port-Glasgow, Troon, Grangemouth, &c.

IMPORTS.

FOR THE WEEK ENDING TUESDAY LAST:

Paper	1035 bales	Paper	13 cases
,, ...	285 rolls		

FOR LAST MONTH:

Paper	3080 bales	Pasteboards	5 cases
,, ...	41 cases	Strawboards	6108 pkgs.
,, ...	280 rolls	Envelopes	1 case

EXPORTS.

FOR THE WEEK ENDING TUESDAY LAST:

Printing Paper..	87½ cwt.	Envelopes	66 pkgs.
Writing Paper...	517½ ,,	Millboards.........	£55 value
Paper	182 ,,	Rags..................	8½ cwt.
Stationery	£173 value	Tinfoil Paper ...	12½ ,,

FOR LAST MONTH:

Writing Paper...	3458½ cwt.	Rags	150 cwt.
,, ...	£146 value	Pulp Boards	£105 value
Printing Paper...	10208½ cwt.	Blotting Paper ..	76½ cwt.
,, ...	£164 value	Stationery	£458 value

Paper	859½ cwt.	Stock	702½ cwt.
"	51 rolls	Millboards	121 "
"	£22 value	Cardboards	6½ "
Envelopes	225½ cwt.	Wrapping Paper	430 "

Leith, Granton, Boness, Dundee, &c.

IMPORTS.

FOR THE WEEK ENDING TUESDAY LAST:

Paper	554 bales	Envelopes	431 pkgs.
"	7 cases	Strawboards	252 "
Tissues	30 bales		

FOR LAST MONTH:

Paper	1637 bales	Pasteboards	2061 pkgs.
"	33 cases	Printing Paper...	1 case
"	69 rolls	Tissues...............	7 bales
Envelopes	881 pkgs.		

PAPER IMPORTS.

FOR THE WEEK ENDING TUESDAY LAST:

BELGIUM ...	990 bales	ITALY	52 bales
"	243 cases	NORWAY ...	1175 "
FINLAND ...	873 bales	"	16 rolls
FRANCE ...	610 "	PRUSSIA ...	60 bales
" ...	70 cases	SWEDEN ...	1503 "
GERMANY ...	2100 bales	"	411 rolls
"	83 cases	U.S.A.	63 bales
" ...	9 rolls	"	48 cases
HOLLAND ...	1510 bales	"	285 rolls
"	168 cases		

Including the Following:

Quantity	From	Importer	Port.
20 bales	Danzig	H. Huber & Co	London
11 "	Gothenburg	Green & Co	"
8 "	"	Smyth & Co	"
314 "	"	Hummell & Co	"
44 "	"	R. L. Lundgren	"
387 "	"	Schenkenwald & Co	"
75 "	"	F. Sabel	"
10 "	"	Simmons & Co	"
175 "	"	D. Gulland	"
15 "	"	Aising & Co	"
1 case	New York	Hurst & Son	"
50 bales	"	H. Richards	"

LAST MONTH'S SUMMARY.

AUSTRALIA ...	17 bales	HOLLAND ...	142 rolls
BELGIUM ...	4384 "	INDIA	16 bales
" ...	1035 cases	ITALY	5 "
CHINA	18 bales	" ...	70 cases
" ...	21 cases	JAPAN	21 "
CANADA ...	5 "	NORWAY ...	16197 bales
DENMARK ...	1031 bales	" ...	216 cases
EGYPT	1 case	" ...	1448 rolls
FINLAND ...	1122 bales	PRUSSIA ...	717 bales
" ...	7 cases	RUSSIA ...	4 "
FRANCE ...	1402 bales	SWEDEN ...	4081 "
" ...	413 cases	" ...	654 rolls
GERMANY ...	9791 bales	SPAIN ...	6 bales
" ...	564 cases	" ...	8 cases
" ...	13 rolls	U.S.A.	875 bales
HOLLAND ...	22861 bales	"	411 cases
" ...	752 cases	"	997 rolls

PAPER IMPORTERS

WHERE NOT "TO ORDER."

E. & E. Sabel	W. D. Edwards
H. Huber & Co.	G. F. Green & Co.
Schenkenwald & Co.	Simmons & Co.
Hummell & Co.	Townsend, Son & Co.
Becker & Ulrich	E. Bryne & Co.
Aising & Co.	Spicer Bros.
Hundgrew	J. Holloway
Wooley & Cowley	G. E. Koenigsfeld
Rottman, Stone & Co.	J. Pollock
May Roberts & Co.	W. Benscher
J. Dickinson	Simpson & Co.
J. Spicer & Sons	Williams & Co.
B Beer	Osborne & Shearman
R. L. Lundgren	Cowan & Co.
D. Gulland	~. & C. Hooper & Co.
Christophersen & Co.	T. Swabey
J. Hamilton	E. Saunders & Son
F. E. Foulger	Berrick Bros.
G. F. Green & Co.	B. Galloway
J. Spicer & Son	Williams, Torrey & Co
Lon. & Rhine Co.	Brooks Whf.
Hernu, Peron & Co.	Prop. Dowgate Dk.
Grabb & Co.	B. S. Lloyd & Co.
G. Smythe & Co.	Tegner, Rice & Co.

PAPER EXPORTS.

FOR THE WEEK ENDING TUESDAY LAST;

	Printings.	Writings.	Other Kinds.
AUSTRALIA	3824 cwts.	458 cwts.	1437 cwts.
AFRICA	— "	49 "	130 "
ARGENTINE ...	— "	11 "	— "
BELGIUM	29 "	97 "	40 "
B. WEST INDIES...	— "	2 "	— "
B. GUIANA	— "	— "	477 "
CHANNEL ISLES	13 "	— "	— "
CANADA	— "	530 "	37½ "
CAPE COLONY ...	866 "	40 "	219 "
CHINA	42 "	50 "	45 "
DENMARK	12 "	1 "	— "
FRANCE	128 "	57 "	30 "
GERMANY	49 "	— "	5 "
HOLLAND	"	— "	28 "
INDIA	1031 "	997½ "	530½ "
JAPAN	6 "	21 "	2 "
MADAGASCAR ...	— "	1 "	— "
MAURITIUS ...	6 "	3 "	13 "
NEW ZEALAND ...	1031 "	745 "	431 "
NORWAY	— "	— "	37 "
RUSSIA	— "	16 "	— "
SPAIN	19½ "	2 "	— "
STRAIT Settlements	— "	— "	7 "
TURKEY	— "	20 "	— "
U.S.A.	60 "	50 "	1 "
W. INDIES	12 "	— "	— "

LAST MONTH'S SUMMARY.

AUSTRALIA	31610½ cwts.	INDIA	6230½ cwts.
ARABIA ...	9 "	ITALY	13 "
AFRICA ...	711 "	JAPAN	572½ "
ARGENTINE	1069 "	MAURITIUS	80 "
BELGIUM ...	407 "	MAD'GASCAR	24 "
B. W. INDIES	1064½ "	N. ZEALAND	3480 "
BRAZIL ...	356 "	NORWAY ...	189 "
B GUIANA ...	1551½ "	NEWF'NDL'D	1 "
CHANN'L Isles	46 "	PRUSSIA ...	7 "
Cen. AMERICA	40 "	PORTUGAL ...	2 "
CANADA ...	1220½ "	RUSSIA ...	89 "
CAPE COLONY	3469 "	ROUMANIA ...	11 "
CHILI	117 "	S. AMERICA	215 "
CHINA	1096 "	SPAIN	140 "
DENMARK ...	214 "	SYRIA	3 "
D. GUIANA ...	3 "	SWEDEN ...	1 "
D. E. INDIES	17 "	S. SETTL'M'TS	41 "
EGYPT	129 "	TURKEY ...	34 "
FRANCE ...	1729 "	U.S.A.	4344 "
GERMANY ...	119 "	W. INDIES ...	103 "
HOLLAND ...	205 "		

NEW PATENTS.

BRITISH.

APPLICATIONS.

19,396. A process for bleaching rags by bisulphites in the manufacture of paper. R. N. Redmayne.

19,542. Improvements in apparatus for the electrolytical decomposition of salt solutions. C. Kellner.

19,686. Improvements in dust collectors. P. Turner.

19,688. Improvements in safety appliances to be used in connection with electrical decomposing apparatus. J. C. Richardson.

19,699. An improved system and apparatus for removing impurities from the refined china clay. W. W. R. Nicholls and R. O. Daley.

19,807. Improvements in the process of bleaching fibrous materials. C. G. Hagemann.

Special Prepaid Advertisements

☛ IT IS IMPORTANT that Advertisements under any of the Headings mentioned below should reach us by the FIRST POST on WEDNESDAY Morning to INSURE INSERTION.

Charges for advertisements under the heading Situations Wanted are 1/- for twenty-four words, and One Penny per Word after, Minimum charge ONE SHILLING. Names and addresses to be paid for.

Advertisers by paying an extra fee of 6d. can have the replies addressed to the PAPER TRADE REVIEW under a number, and such replies will then be forwarded Post Free

Advertisements appearing under the following headings:

Tenders.	Mills Wanted or To Let.
Sales by Auction.	Machinery Wanted or For Sale.
Businesses Wanted.	
Businesses for Disposal.	Situations Vacant.

Miscellaneous.

The charges are 3/- for fifty words or under; 1s. extra for every line or portion after. Ten words to be reckoned for each line. Names and addresses to be paid for. Payment must be made in advance, except where the advertiser has a running account, in which case the cost can be debited thereto.

Legal and Financial Announcements: 1/- per Line.

Cheques and Post-office Orders to be CROSSED ——— and Co., and made payable to W. JOHN STONHILL.

Agencies.

WANTED.—AGENTS calling upon Paper Mills and Litho Printers to sell Damping Machines, Paper Suspenders, and P[illegible]ined Ventilating Apparatus; water purific[illegible] pollution scheme, &c. Good terms and soun[illegible]uld result.—Address, with full particulars, [illegible], Engineer and Commission Agent, 134, Deansgate, [illegible]'s Chambers, Manchester. 5903

Situations Vacant.

FOREMAN ENGINEER in Paper Mill.—Wanted at once, an Active and Experienced Man. Only first rate man having had charge of Paper Mill Machinery need apply.—Write, with full particulars and copies of references, to Thomas and Green, Limited, Soho Mills, Wooburn, near Maidenhead. 5902

WANTED, a Competent Mechanic, capable of erecting a Paper Machine.—Address, No. 5,910, office of the WORLD'S PAPER TRADE REVIEW, 58, Shoe Lane, London, E.C. 5910

Situations Wanted.

CHEMICAL PLUMBER desires Re-engagement; 5 years in Wood Pulp Mills; first class references.—Address, No. 5,907, office of the WORLD'S PAPER TRADE REVIEW, 58, Shoe Lane, E.C. 5907

ENGAGEMENT wanted as Assistant Manager or Foreman in a Sulphite Wood Pulp Mill; thoroughly experienced in the manufacture of chemical wood pulps; good practical engineering and chemical knowledge; satisfactory references.—Address No. 5,905, office of the WORLD'S PAPER TRADE REVIEW, 58, Shoe Lane, London, E.C. 5905

MANAGER, thoroughly competent in all classes of Paper Machinery; well up in the blending of fibres and mixing and matching of colours, desires Situation. Good testimonials as to character and ability.—Address, No. 5,908, office of the WORLD'S PAPER TRADE REVIEW, 58, Shoe Lane, London, E.C. 5908

WANTED, Situation as Machineman, accustomed to Tub and Engine Sized Writings and Fine Printings.—Address, "E.B.," No. 5,906, office of the WORLD'S PAPER TRADE REVIEW, 58, Shoe Lane, London, E.C. 5906

Wanted.

WANTED to PURCHASE, One hundred tons DRY WOOD PULP, good quality, f.o.b. Liverpool or Galveston, Texas.—Send samples and prices to Oak Cliff Paper Mills, Oak Cliff, Texas, U.S.A. 5871

Machinery Wanted.

WANTED—Second hand—Two Kollergangs, two Rag Boilers, and few Drying Cylinders about 86 inches on face by 4 feet diameter: also Single Sheet Cutter to cut 86 to 90 inches.—Address, No. 5,909, office of the WORLD'S PAPER TRADE REVIEW, 58, Shoe Lane, London, E.C. 5909

Machinery for Sale.

ONE KOLLERGANG, new, Stones 51 inches by 14 inches, C.I. Pan, Scrapers, and Driving Gear.

ONE HYDRAULIC PRESS, second-hand, with Press Box 38 inches diam. by 32 inches deep, with wheels; all parts strong, Ram 2 feet 6 inches by 8 inches diam.

TWELVE REVOLVING STRAINER PLATES, second-hand, 28½ inches by 21 inches, class B2, 3½ cut.

REFINING ENGINE, new, Conical Type; same as one working in a large printing mill.

Any reasonable offer will be considered by 5859

BERTRAMS LIMITED, SCIENNES, EDINBURGH.

Mills to be Let or Sold.

TO be LET or SOLD, a Paper Mill at Stalybridge, called the Higher Mill, containing one large machine and room for another, steam engine and boilers, in good condition.—Apply for further information to the Caretaker on the premises. 2162

MALDON, ESSEX.—TO BE LET on Lease or Sold, a Freehold Mill, with Engine, Boiler and 2 Water Wheels of 100 horse-power. The Property has an area of Five acres, with a Wharf giving facilities for carriage inland by river, or to London by sea, at the low rate of [illegible]s. 8d. per ton.—For further particulars apply to Fuller, Horsey, Sons and Cassell, 11, Billiter Square, E.C. 5904

Printed and Published EVERY FRIDAY
AT 58, SHOE LANE, LONDON, E.C.,
By W. JOHN STONHILL.
ESTABLISHED 1878.

FRIDAY, NOVEMBER 3, 1893.

In this issue we supplement our usual weekly statistical information dealing with imports and exports of paper and raw material by giving a summary of the figures which have appeared in our various issues during last month. The official data published could be materially improved upon if a better classification was made by the Customs authorities. Except for the Board of Trade Returns it would appear that no business was being done in the exportation of rags from this country. We hope that attention will be given to this matter in order that rags may be distinctly classified instead of being included under paper stock. Again, in regard to wood pulp there are no means of telling whether the material is chemical or mechanical. We also have reason to believe that straw pulp is often classed under the heading of wood pulp as a steady trade is being carried on with leading paper mills, both in Scotland and England, and therefore the absence of statistics showing importations of straw pulp may be attributed to the fact of inclusion under wood pulp.

Business in American and Canadian wood pulp is being rapidly developed. The Manufacturers Paper Co., of New York, who sell for the Hudson River Pulp and Paper Co., and Laurentide Paper Co., continue through their agent (Mr. Sidney Holt, 4, Queen Street-place, London, E.C.) to export largely to this country. Messrs. A. Wertheim and Co., of Hamburg, have chartered three vessels from America with pulp for Fleetwood. Messrs. Steinhoff and Co. are also identified with Canadian shipments. Judging from reports from Maine, U.S.A., the wood pulp industry there is bounding merrily along, and making progress by leaps and jumps. We are told that one of the large companies engaged in the manufacture of the material is now turning out the pulp at the rate of ten tons a day, and expects before long to increase the number of its machines from three to five, and later to ten. Other companies are also planning additions and contracting for more machinery. No less than 3,500 tons, in three separate cargoes, have been shipped during the summer from Bangor direct to European ports.

One thing favourable to an increasing American trade in wood pulp is the condition of the Scandinavian market. The Wood Pulp Makers' Association having sold more largely to other countries decreased supplies to the British market, and buyers have had to look to America. The output of pulp in Scandinavian is, however, being greatly increased, and no alarm is felt amongst Norwegian manufacturers concerning American competition in the European market. With low freights as at present the difference between sea freights from America and Scandinavia is not so very great, but when freights are high competition from America will be more difficult.

Objection was taken by interested parties concerning the criticism we passed upon the prospectus, proposed capital and patents, of the Millboard Manufacturing Co. Considering the wonders that were about to be effected by this company in the utilisation of spent hops, it is surprising that nothing has been made public of late. The vendors were Messrs. E. Davis and A. J. Woolrich (the latter having acquired a moiety of the patents from Mr. H. F. Harris), and the estimated profit was stated to be no less than 100 per cent. on the cost of production. Whilst there is an absence of demonstration on the part of the Millboard Manufacturing Co. at Burton-on-Trent, we find the subject of utilising hop waste is being considered in Germany. The oil in the hops, as a hindrance, has it is stated been overcome, and it is noteworthy that coping with this difficulty was one of the features so prominently set forth in the process of Messrs. E. Davis and A. J. Woolrich. In Germany the estimated profit on cost of production is only 50 per cent., not 100 per cent. as in England.

DR. O. KNOFLER and Mr. F. Gebauer's electrolytic apparatus is little known in this country. As will be seen from a description published on our front page, it consists of electrodes arranged like a filter press combining both poles, and consisting of plates of metal or other conducting material and insulating intermediate frames which are either separate from or united with the electrodes, and are composed of hard rubber, celluloid, clay, glass or other non-conducting material, or of metal covered or coated with non-conducting material, and when pressed against the electrodes form a series of closed divisions or chambers adapted to receive the solution to be treated, only the first and last plate of each series being connected each with one pole of the source of electricity. The patentees claim the substitution of compound electrodes, composed of several small plates of platinum carbon or other conducting material set in a frame made of non-conducting material, such as hard rubber, celluloid, clay, glass, or the like, or of metal covered or coated with non-conducting material somewhat after the style of a window, or joined together by means of sulphur, cement or the like, or by simple juxtaposition and subsequent framing. Also the insertion of compound diaphragms in the shape of plates composed in the same manner as the compound-electrodes of smaller plates of clay of similar porous material and arranged like the electrodes between the frames. It is stated that the apparatus has been designed for installation in paper mills.

A NEW series of illustrated abridgements of patent specifications are being published by the Patent Office, and when they are fully brought up to date will no doubt be found of great value. We refer to class 96, relating to paper, pasteboard, and papier mache, in a paragraph on another page. The patent laws of this country make no provision for an official search as regards novelty; consequently British patents are taken out at the risk of applicants, who are expected to cause a search to be made as to the novelty of their inventions, either before they make their applications or before they complete the same. It is to meet this want that abridgments have been completed referring to all specifications for the period A.D. 1877-83, and these, together with the abridgments in the Illustrated Official Journal from A.D. 1884 onwards (to which the annual indexes refer), will comprise a means for searching as to novelty as regards all living patents, and should enable the intending patentee to satisfy himself that he would not infringe existing patent rights. To complete a search, however, as to absolute novelty, a further exhaustive examination of technical literature would be necessary.

THE report of the technical examinations of the City and Guilds of London Institute for 1893, shows that in regard to paper manufacture there were 25 students in attendance. Twenty candidates presented themselves for examination, and nine passed. The report states that there were "16 class" and "4 external" candidates, and it is very probable that the majority of the class students are not actively engaged in papermaking, but belong to the allied trades. Technical instruction is being keenly developed on the Continent, and young papermakers who wish to take leading positions must seize every opportunity to supplement their practical knowledge, and the advantages of technological examinations held under the auspices of the City and Guilds of London Institute certainly deserve more consideration than has been given to them in the past. We congratulate Mr. J. MacNaughton, of Moffat Mills, and Mr. F. Southern (Manchester), upon their success, the former being first in the honours grade (Salters' Company's prize of £2 and silver medal), and the latter ordinary first (Salters' Company's prize of £1 and silver medal).

IN Germany the technical training of papermakers has reached a high standard; it is considered that the more complicated modern papermaking becomes the more indispensable is a most careful preparation of men for leading positions. One of the branches most necessary to study, is the testing of samples of paper, and therefore the various testing offices have been authorised to train so called volunteers, as far as they have room. Thus the Vienna office accepts 10 young men, and Charlottenburg 14. Besides these opportunities Herr E. Kirchner, the instructor of the technical academy in Chemnitz, has arranged special courses of lectures for papermakers, so that as time goes on the scientific part of paper-making receives more and more attention on the continent.

A VERY bold proposal has been made by M. Moskaleff, of St. Petersburg, concerning patent rights. He advocates a scheme for the suppression of all patent rights in Russia for foreign inventions, and recently submitted the proposal to the Administrative Council of the Russian Imperial Technical Society, amongst a section of which considerable indignation was aroused. The Society have to decide by vote at a fresh sitting whether or not the scheme shall be submitted to the approval of the Council of the Empire. The deliberations of the Technical Society on the subject are kept strictly secret in order to avoid the publication of reports in the Press.

ANOTHER semi-official warning is published that a speedy conclusion of the Russo-German commercial negotiations must not be expected, as the concessions which the Russian delegates are disposed to make are very far from satisfying the requirements of the German Commissioners. Meanwhile the council of commercial and industrial experts summoned by the Imperal Government has by an overwhelming majority expressed its full approval of the resolute attitude hitherto adopted and of the demands formulated for a reduction of the Russian duties.

THE excessive high charges made by the railway companies on certain classes of goods, and of the hindrances thrown in the way of the trade development of certain districts, owing to absurd anomalies in rates, occasionally call forth bitter complaints. A correspondent asks upon what principle can the railway companies justify the levying of practically the same tolls for the carriage of goods from the ports of the east coast of Lancashire towns, and for the carriage of the same kinds of goods from Widnes to the same places? Take for instance the rate on chemicals between Goole and Bury, and between Widnes and Bury. In the first place the distance is over fifty miles, and in the next case only twenty miles separate the two towns. It is scarcely credible that the rate for the twenty miles is no less than 9s. 6d. per ton, while the charges for the fifty miles only come to ten shillings per ton. The same thing holds good in regard to other Lancashire towns, and affords a striking instance of the way in which the trade of certain parts of Lancashire is being retarded, and in some instances ruined, by an inequitable system of rate discrimination. So keen is the German competition becoming in chemicals that the material from Hamburg can be placed on the Widnes market at less prices than those at which Lancashire manufacturers are willing to sell. With this alarming state of affairs it is hardly to be wondered that brokers and manufacturers are determined to renew their fight for a reduction of railway rates and charges.

Two statements in the triennial report of the Salt Chamber of Commerce will raise a smile of derision among all who know something of the matter. The first is that "the Salt Union has quite a dominant position, and is using it to regulate trade and prices with moderation and foresight." The other is that "the competition of German and Arabian salt has settled itself to its former subordinate position." Does the Chamber really believe these assertions? For our part we can simply stare at them and gasp in wonder at the boldness or the blindness of the men who make them. We have all seen instances of the moderation and foresight of the Salt Union. Taking that body all round, there are few combinations that have failed, and have deserved to fail, so miserably, and that have, moreover, worked so much irremediable injury to the salt trade of this country.

THE Chicago World's Fair closed on Monday. The ceremony was a solemn one, all festivities being omitted, owing to the murder of Mayor Harrison. When the accounts of the Fair are audited it will be found that there has been a colossal loss. But everything must be on a colossal scale in Chicago, and so the heavy financial failure of the exhibition only harmonised with the general condition of things. The Fair has had altogether since the opening 21,477,212 visitors who have paid for admission, and 2,052,188 who have been admitted without payment, making the total number of visitors 23,529,400. A list of awards appears on another page.

World's Paper Trade Review Office,
58, Shoe Lane, London, E.C.
November 2, 1893.

MARKET REPORT

and RECORD of IMPORTS

Of Foreign Rags, Wood Pulp, Esparto, Paper, Millboards, Strawboards, &c., at the Ports of London Liverpool, Southampton, Bristol, Hull, Fleetwood, Middlesborough, Glasgow, Grangemouth, Granton, Dundee, Leith, Dover, Folkestone, and Newhaven, for the WEEK ENDING NOVEMBER 1.

From SPECIAL Sources and Telegrams.

Telegrams—"STONHILL, LONDON."

CHEMICALS.—The market is quiet, and prices evidence a decline. CAUSTIC SODA 77% f.o.r. Newcastle is quoted £11 10s.; 74% f.o.b. Liverpool £12; 70% f.o.b. Liverpool £10 15s., and 60% £9 15s. BLEACHING POWDER is from £7 12 6d. to £7 15s., and SODA CRYSTALS are offered at £2 10s. f.o.b. Tyne and £2 17s. 6d. ex ship Thames. SULPHUR shows a rise at £4 5s. to £4 7s. 6d. SODA ASH is quiet. SULPHATE OF AMMONIA is quoted at £12 15s.; compared with last year an advance of 50s. is shown. SULPHATE OF ALUMINA, delivered Manchester, stands at from £4 15s. to £5. German SULPHATE OF ALUMINA remains at £4 7s. 6d.

Prices are nominally as follows:

Article		Terms		£	s.	d.
Alkali, 58%	tierces ...	f.o.r. works	2½%	5	10	0
,, 58%	bags ...	,, ,,	2½%	5	5	0
58%	... ...	f.o.b. Liverpool	2½%	5	12	6
Alum (Ground),	tierces ...	,, Liverpool	2½%	5	7	6
,, ,,	barrels ...	,, ,,	2½%	5	17	6
,, ,,	tierces ...	,, Hull	2½%	5	5	0
,, ,,	,, ...	Goole	2½%	5	5	0
Alum (Lump)	,, ...	f.o.b. Liverpool	2½%	4	17	6
,, ,,	barrels ...	,, ,,	2½%	5	0	0
,, ,,	tierces ...	,, Hull	2½%	4	15	0
,, ,,	,, ...	Goole	2½%	4	15	0
,, ,,	,, ...	London	2½%	5	5	0
,, ,,	,, ...	f.a.s. Glasgow	2½%	5	5	0
Alumina Sulphate,	casks	f.o.b. Tyne		4	2	6
,, ,,	bags	,, ,,		3	17	6
Aluminoferric Cake,	slabs	Liverpool ...	...	2	15	0
,, ,,	tierces	,, ...	...	3	2	6
Alumina Cake,	slabs ...	Glasgow	...	2	15	0
,, ,,	tierces ...	,,	...		2	6
Aluminous Cake,	casks ...	Manchester	3½%	2	7	6
,, ,,	,, ...	Newcastle	2½%	2	10	0
,, ,,	,, ...	London	2½%	3	0	0
,, ,,	bags ...	,,	2½%	2	17	9
Blanc Fixe ...	... ...	f.o.b. Tyne	net	7	10	0
Bleach, 35%	... ...	,, ,,	net	7	12	6
,, (soft wood)	...	f.o.r. Lancs.	net	8	5	0
,, (hard wood)	...	f.o.b. Liverpool	net	8	10	0
... ...	...	landed London	2½%	9	0	0
Borax (crystals)	... ...	... ...	net	29	0	0
powdered	... ...	... ...	net	30	0	0
Caustic Cream, 60%	...	f.o.r. Lancs.	net	9	2	6
,, ,, 60%	...	f.o.b. Liverpool	net	9	7	6
,, Bottoms	...	,, ,,	net	6	15	0
,, ,,	... ...	f.o.b. Tyne	net	6	15	0
Chloride of Barium	...	f.o.b. Tyne	net	7	10	0
Caustic White 76 77%	...	f.o.r. Newcastle	net	11	10	0
,, ,, 77%	f.o.r. or	f.o.b. Tyne	net	12	0	0
,, ,, 74%	...	f.o.b. Liverpool	net	12	0	0
,, ,, 70%	...	,, ,,	net	10	15	0
,, ,, 70%	...	,, Hull	net	11	0	0
,, ,, 70%	...	f.o.r. London	net	10	15	0
,, ,, 70%	...	,, Lancs.,	net	10	17	6
,, ,, 60%	...	,, London	net	9	15	0
,, ,, 60%	...	f.o.b. Liverpool	net	9	15	0
Carbonat'd Ash 58%	...	,, ,,	net	4	10	0
48%	...	,, ,,	net	4	0	0
,, 58%	..	f.o.r. Widnes	net	4	7	6
48%	...	,, ,,	net	3	17	6
Hypo-Sulphite of Soda...		f.o.r Tyne		5	15	0
,, ,,	10-ton lots	ex ship Liverp'l	net	6	10	0
Oxalic Acid ...	... ...	f.o.b. Liverpool	3½%	per lb		¼
Salt Cake ...	... ...	,, works	net	1	10	0
Soda Ash, 52%	... ...	f.o.b. Tyne	net	4	0	0
,, 52%	... ...	ex ship Thames	1%	4	12	6
,, 52%	... ...	f.o.b. Liverpool	1%	4	5	0
Soda Crystals	... ...	,, Tyne	net	2	10	0
,, ,,	... ...	ex ship Thames	2½%	2	17	6
,, ,,	... ...	f.o.b. Liverpool	net	3	5	0
Sulphur, roll	... ...	f.o.r. works	2½%	7	17	6
,, flowers	... ...	,, ,,	2½%	9	10	0
,, recovered	...	,, ,,	2½%	4	5	0
Sulphate of Ammonia	,,	,, ,,	2½%	12	15	0
,, of Copper	...	,, Liverpool	5%	16	0	0

FOREIGN.—F.o.b. Continental port:

Article	£	s.	d.
Alkali, 58% 2-cwt. bags £4 10/0; 10-cwt. casks ...	5	0	0
Caustic Soda, 70-72%	10	12	6
Hypo-Sulphite of Soda 10-ton lots casks	6	0	0
Sulphate of Alumina 7-8 cwt. casks net c.i f. Ldn	4	7	6
Blanc Fixe (c.i.f. London)	7	12	6

COMPARATIVE PRICES:

Alkali 58% tierces f.o.r. Works.	Nov. 1893	£5 10 0 2½%
	,, 1892	£6 15 0 2½%
	,, 1891	£6 15 0 2½%
Caustic White 77% f.o.r. Newcastle.	Nov. 1893	£11 15 0 nett.
	,, 1892	£11 15 0 nett.
	,, 1891	£12 0 0 nett.
Bleach 35% f.o.b. Tyne.	Nov. 1893	£7 15 0 nett.
	,, 1892	£7 10 0 nett.
	,, 1891	£7 5 0 2½%
Soda Crystals f.o.b. Tyne.	Nov. 1893	£2 10 0 nett.
	,, 1892	£2 15 0 nett.
	,, 1891	£3 3 6 nett.
Sulphur Recovered f.o.r. Works.	Nov. 1893	£4 2 6 2½%
	,, 1892	£5 0 0 2½%
	,, 1891	£6 10 0 2½%

CHEMICAL WOOD PULPS.—The best grades of SULPHITE keep firm, and judging from Continental advices the tendency of prices is still upward. British consumers, however, hold back from contracting in the belief that quotations will give way later on. Consequently business is not very extensive. SODA and SULPHATE pulps keep steady.

Prices, ex steamer, London, Hull, Newcastle, Leith and Glasgow are nominally as follows:

SULPHITE, Unbleached, Common	£10 15 0	to 11 0 0
,, Superior	11 10 0	,, 12 10 0
,, ,, 50% moisture, d.w.	11 10 0	,, 12 2 6
,, Extra	13 0 0	,, 14 0 0
,, Bleached, moist		16 10 0
,, Unbleached, English, del. Lancs. ...		10 15 0
,, ,, ,, No. 1, ex mills, Ldn.		10 10 0
,, ,, ,, No. 2, ,, ,,		9 15 0
SODA, Unbleached, Common ...	[illegible] 5 0	,, 10 10 0
,, ,, Extra... ...	[illegible]	11 0 0
,, Half-Bleached	12 10 0	,, 14 0 0
SULPHATE, Unbleached, Common	10 10 0	,, 11 0 0
,, Extra	11 0 0	,, 12 0 0
,, Half-Bleached	13 10 0	,, 14 0 0
Bleached	15 0 0	,, 16 0 0

MECHANICAL WOOD PULPS.—Scandinavian Mechanical Wood Pulps keep firm in price, although there is a feeling amongst British buyers that the large arrivals from America and Canada will subsequently cause a downward movement. Stocks held by the Union are reported to be very small, and next year's production is well contracted for.

Prices, ex steamer, London, Hull, Newcastle, Leith and Glasgow are nominally as follows :

MECHANICAL, Aspen, Dry	...	£7 10 0	to 8 0 0
Pine, Dry	... ...	6 7 6	,, 7 0 0
Pine, Moist	... ...	3 5 0	,, 3 10 0
Moist Brown	... ...	3 2 6	,, 3 5 0
Single Sorted	... ...	2 7 6	,, 2 10 0
Dry Brown	... ...	6 5 0	,, 6 10 0

COMPARATIVE PRICES :

Pine, Dry	Nov. 1893	£6 7 6	to	£7 0 0
	,, 1892	£4 12 6	,,	£5 0 0
	,, 1891	£5 0 0	,,	£5 5 0
Pine, Moist	Nov. 1893	£3 5 0	,,	£3 10 0
	,, 1892	£2 6 6	,,	£2 10 0
	,, 1891	£2 10 0	,,	£2 15 0

WEEK'S IMPORTS.

Quantity	From	Importer	Port.
1777 bales	Bergen	To order	Grangemouth
200 ,,	Cologne	,,	London
2770 ,,	Christiania	,,	Hull
739 ,,	,,	,,	Grangemouth
2800 ,,	,,	Goldsmith	London
1032 ,,	,,	G. Schjoth & Co	Fleetwood
373 ,,	,,	Christophersen & Co	,,
4200 ,,	Drammen	To order	London
906 ,,	,,	G. Schjoth and Co	Fleetwood
100 ,,	,,	Darwen Paper Mill Co	,,
254 ,,	,,	G. Schenkenwald & Co	,,
1250 ,,	,,	Raby and Mather	,,
420 ,,	Fiume	Brown, Stewart & Co	Glasgow
2040 ,,	,,	To order	Glasgow
1064 rolls	,,	A Guttmann	London
180 tons	Fredrikstadt	To order	Liverpool
440 ,,	Gefle	,,	London
408 ,,	,,	,,	,,
485 ,,	Gothenburg	C. Salvesen & Co	Granton
354 ,,	,,	To order	Glasgow
428 ,,	,,	Hummel & Co	London
74 casks	Ghent	To order	,,
3623 bales	Halifax	Steinhoff & Son	,,
425 ,,	Helsingfors	To order	Hull
24550 ,,	Hernosand	,,	London
810 ,,	Hambro	,,	,,
2810 ,,	Montreal	,,	Liverpool
600 ,,	Oporto	,,	London
25693 ,,	Portland	Mfg. Paper Co	Glasgow
267 ,,	Rotterdam	To order	London
2200 ,,	Skein	,,	,,
3870 ,,	,,	G. Schjoth & Co	Fleetwood
420 ,,	,,	H. Newall & Son	,,

Totals from Each Country:

BELGIUM ...	75 casks	ITALY	1064 rolls
CANADA ...	6433 bales	NORWAY ...	37242 bales
FRANCE ...	200 ,,	,, ...	180 tons
FINLAND ...	495 ,,	PORTUGAL...	600 ,,
GERMANY ..	810 ,,	SWEDEN ...	2105 ,,
HOLLAND ...	267 ,,	U.S.A. ...	25693 ,,
ITALY ...	2460 ,,		

LAST MONTH'S IMPORTS.

Where From:

AUSTRIA ...	303 bales	HOLLAND ...	986 rolls
BELGIUM ...	88 casks	,, ...	54 casks
CANADA ...	29062 bales	NORWAY ...	56152 bales
,, ...	774 rolls	,, ...	85 cases
,, ...	20 brls	,, ...	1223 rolls
,, ...	99 cases	PORTUGAL...	400 bales
DENMARK ...	1743 bales	,, ...	550 cases
FINLAND ...	3381 ,,	PRUSSIA ...	3949 bales
GERMANY ...	8119 ,,	SWEDEN ...	9141 bales
,, ...	347 rolls	SPAIN	96 cases
HOLLAND ...	3663 bales	U.S.A.	32009 bales

Port of Landing:

FLEETWOOD	69677 bales	LEITH... ...	347 rolls
GLASGOW ...	8705 ,,	,, ...	20 brls
,, ...	722 rolls	LONDON ...	1493 rolls
GRANG'M'TH	9953 bales	,, ...	452 casks
GRANTON ...	1786 ,,	,, ...	85 cases
HULL	[illegible] ,,	,, ...	50307 bales
,, ...	[illegible] rolls	LIVERPOOL .	9212 ,,
HARWICH ...	888 bales	,, ...	99 cases
LEITH... ...	2173 ,,	SOUTHAMP'N	900 bales

Importers (Where not "To Order"):

G. Schjoth and Co	E. J. and W. Goldsmith
Christophersen and Co	Alsing and Co
Blydt, Pans and Co	Tough and Henderson
Salvesen and Co	London Paper Mill Co
Green and Co	Ekman Co
Steinhoff and Son	C. Anderson
J. Currie and Co	British Xylonite Co
Jensen and Glads	J. Makin and Son
Taylor and Co	F. Huth and Co
Henderson, Craig and Co	H. B. Wood
Johnsen and Co	Crabb and Co
W. Grant and Co	Hernu Peron and Co
O. Herrlich	Foulger and Co
W. D. Cook and Co	Raby and Mathers
M. G. Skramnes	Hummell and Co
H. Pearsall	Smyth and Son
B. D. Jones	Bott and Co
Becker and Ulrich	G. Gibson and Co
W. Friedlaender	

WEEK'S IMPORTS of WOOD PULP BOARDS.

Quantity	From	Importer	Port
3 cases	Christiania	To order	Grangemouth
83 bales	Gothenburg	,,	Hull
85 ,,	,,	,,	Glasgow

MONTH'S IMPORTS WOOD PULP BOARDS.

Where From:

CHRISTIANIA	18 bales	GOTHENBURG	351 bales
,, ...	103 cases		

Port of Landing:

HULL	98 bales	SOUTHAMP'N	152 bales
LONDON ...	56 ,,		

Importers (Where not "To Order"):

Salveeen and Co

ESPARTO.—A somewhat better enquiry has been experienced for distant shipments, but without improvement in prices. The negotiation of business is very difficult and transactions go slowly through. Arrivals are still very moderate, and the figures would seem to justify sellers in adopting greater firmness.

Prices c.i.f. London and Leith, or f.o.r. Cardiff, Garston and Tyne Docks are nominally as follows :

Spanish—	Fair to Good ...	... ...	£5 5 0	to 5 10 0
,,	Fine to Best ...	... ...	5 10 0	,, 5 15 0
Oran —	Fair to Good ...	... ...	3 5 0	,, 3 10 0
,,	First Quality...	... ...	3 15 0	,, 3 17 6
Tripoli —	Hand-picked ...	... ...	3 15 0	,, 3 17 6
,,	Fair Average...	... ...	3 7 6	,, 3 10 0
Bona & Philippeville	...	... ...	3 15 0	,, 3 17

COMPARATIVE PRICES
("Fair to Good" Quality):

Spanish	Nov. 1893	£5 5 0	to	£5 10 0
	,, 1892	£5 10 0	,,	£6 0 0
	,, 1891	£5 15 0	,,	£6 0 0
Oran	Nov. 1893	£3 5 0	,,	£3 10 0
	,, 1892	£3 15 0	,,	£4 0 0
	,, 1891	£3 17 6	,,	£4 2 6
Tripoli	Nov. 1893	£3 7 6	,,	£3 10 0
	,, 1892	£3 12 6	,,	£3 15 0
	,, 1891	£3 17 6	,,	£4 0 6

WEEK'S IMPORTS.

Quantity	From	Importer	Port.
815 tons	Carboneras	Morris and Co	Granton

LAST MONTH'S IMPORTS.

Where From:

AGUILAS ...	800 tons	HOMOS ..	6174 bales
,, ...	1338 trus.	ORAN	925 ,,
,, ...	15085 bales	,, ...	1354 tons
ALMERIA ...	845 tons	SFAX	2419 ,,
ARZIO ...	2598 bales	SUSA	779 ,,
CARTHAGENA	743 tons	SKIRA... ...	280 ,,
,, ...	4472 bales	TRIPOLI ...	4474 bales

Port of Landing:

DUNDEE ...	860 tons	LIVERPOOL..	1734 tons
"	4736 bales	"	6174 bales
FLEETWOOD	3048 "	LONDON ...	35 tons
GRANG'M'TH	2338 trus.	"	9870 bales
GRANTON ...	3847 tons	LEITH... ...	1684 tons

Importers (Where not "To Order"):

Morris and Co	H. Blaik and Co
Guardbridge Paper Co	H. Ottomann
L. Jacobs, Marcus and Co	R. H. Hay and Co
J. Hassan	Ressich and Co

STRAW.—Trade quiet at high prices. Wheat and Oat Straw are quoted 75s. to 77s. 6d. per ton ex steamer London, and at Hull from 70s. to 72s. 6d.

WEEK'S IMPORTS.

(Purposes unspecified) at principal Ports From

DENMARK ...	106 bales	HOLLAND ...	605 bales
FRANCE ...	496 "		

MONTH'S IMPORTS.

Where From:

BELGIUM ...	105 bales	HOLLAND ...	17805 bales
DENMARK ...	7082 "	NORWAY ...	17 "
FRANCE ...	594 "	U.S.A.	17 "
GERMANY ...	130 "		

STRAW PULPS.—Fairly good demand.

Prices, c.i.f. London, Hull or Leith:

Belgian, 25% moisture	£15 0 0 to 16 0 0
do. dry	16 0 0
German, 50 to 55% moisture	16 10 0
do. dry, ... No. 1 £18 10 0; No. 2	15 0 0

WEEK'S IMPORTS.

Quantity	From	Importer	Port.
108 bales	Hambro	To order	London
10 "	Rotterdam	"	Hull

MONTH'S IMPORTS.

Where From:

HAMBRO ...	83 bales	ROTTERDAM	64 bales

Port of Landing:

HULL	83 bales	LEITH... ...	10 bales
LONDON ...	54 "		

FOREIGN RAGS.—Trade on the Continent continues dull.

GERMAN RAGS.

STETTIN: C.i.f. Hull, Leith, Tyne and London.

SPFFF and SPFF	18/0	LFB (Blue)	9/0
SPF	11/0	CSPFFF and CSPFF	10/0
FF	8/6	CFB (Blue)	7/6
FG	9/0	CFX (Coloured) ...	4/6
LFX	7/0		

HAMBURG: F.o.b.

NWC	22/0	FF Grey Linens ...	9/0
SPFFF	22/0	LFX Second ditto...	8/0
SPFFF and SPFF	18/0	CSPFFF	17/3
SPFF	16/0	CSPFF	11/3
SPF	12/0	CFB	8/0
CCC	5/6	Dark Blues (selected	11/9
CFX	4/6	Wool Tares... ...	8/0
White Rope... ...	8/0	Jute, No. I 6/0; No. II	5/6

DUTCH RAGS. f.o.r. Hull:

C.i.f. Thames; Hull 2/6 per ton more; ditto f.o.r. Leith c.i.f. Glasgow 4/-; c.i.f. Liverpool 4/-.

Selected Fines (free from Muslins) ...	17/0	Best Grey Linens ...	9/0
		Common ditto ...	5/6
Selected Outshots	9/9	White Canvas ...	15/0
" Dirty Fines	5/9	Grey & Brown Canvas	9/9
Light Cottons ...	9/3	Tarred Hemp Rope	8/0
Blue Cottons ...	7/6	Ditto (broken) ...	5/3
Dark Coloured Cottons	2/10	White Paper Shavings	7/9
New Cuttings (Bleachd)	22/6	Gunny (best) ...	4/9
" (Unbleached)	19/6	Jute Bagging ...	3/6
" (Slate) ...	9/0	Ditto (common ...	3/0
Muslins	8/0	Tarpaulins	4/0
Red Cottons (Mixed)	5/9	Cowhair Carpets ...	2/9
Fustians (Light browns)	5/0	Hard ditto	3/0

FRENCH RAGS.

Quotations range, per cwt., ex ship London, Southampton, or Hull; 2/0 per ton more at Liverpool, and 10/0 per ton higher at Newcastle, Glasgow or Leith.

French Linens, I ...	22/0	Black Cotton ...	4/0
II 18/6; III ...	14/6	Marseilles Whites, I	16/0
White Cottons, I ...	19/0	II 10/0; III ...	7/6
II 15/0; III ...	12/6	Blue Cotton	11/0
Knitted Cotton ...	11/0	Light Prints... ...	9/0
Light Coloured Cotton	8/0	Mixed Prints ...	6/0
Blue Cotton	9/6	New White Cuttings	23/0
Coloured Cotton ...	6/0	" Stay "	21/0

BELGIAN RAGS.

F.o.b. Ghent. Freights: London, 5/0; Hull and Goole, 7/6 Liverpool and Leith, 10/0; Newcastle, 12/6; Dundee and Aberdeen, 15/0; Glasgow, 16/8.

White Linens No. 1	22/6	Fustians (Light) ...	6/0
" " No. 2	16/0	" (Dark) ...	4/0
" " No. 3	13/0	Thirds...	3/0
Fines (Mixed) ...	12/0	Black Cottons ...	3/9
Grey Linens (strong)	9/6	Hemp Strings (unt'r'd)	2/0
" " (extra)	14/0	House Cloths ...	4/9
Blue Linens... ...	8/6	Old Bagging (solid)	3/6
White Cottons S'p'fine	18/0	" " (common)	2/6
" " No. 2	15/0	NEW.	
Outshots No. 3 ...	10/0	White & Cream Linens	35/0
Seconds No. 4 ...	8/0	White Cuttings ...	22/0
Prints (Light) ...	8/6	Unbleached Cuttings	21/0
" (Old)	4/6	Print Cuttings ..	8/0

NORWEGIAN RAGS.

C.i.f. London, Hull, Tyne, and Grangemouth.

1st Rope (tarred) ...	8/6-9/0	2nd Canvas ...	8/0
2nd " " ...	5/6-6/0	Jute Bagging	
Manilla Rope (white)	8/0-8/9	Gunny ...	3/0 3/6
Best Canvas ...	11/9-12/0	Mixed ...	2/6-2/9

RUSSIAN RAGS.

C.i.f. London, Hull, Newcastle or Leith.

SPFF	15/0	CC (Cotton	4/9
SPF	13/6	Jute I	3/6
FG	10/6	" II...	2/3
LFB	9/6	Rope I	9/0
FF	8/3	" II	5/3

WEEK'S IMPORTS.

Quantity	From	Importer	Port.
137 bales	Amsterdam	To order	Hull
97 "	"	"	"
46 "	Buenos Ayres	"	Liverpool
177 "	Bordeaux	"	"
54 "	Bremen	"	Hull
298 "	Copenhagen	"	"
14 "	Dieppe	"	Newhaven
29 "	Guernsey	"	Southampton
65 "	Ghent	"	Leith
34 "	Harlingen	"	Hull
219 "	Lisbon	"	Liverpool
370 "	Ostend	"	London
19 "	Rotterdam	"	Hull
10 "	"	"	"
49 "	St. Malo	"	Southampton
58 "	Stettin	"	Hull
25 "	St. Nazaire	"	Liverpool

Totals from Each Country:

ARGENTINA	46 bales	GERMANY ...	54 bales
BELGIUM ..	65 "	HOLLAND ...	297 "
CHANNEL Isles	29 "	PRUSSIA ...	58 "
DENMARK ...	298 "	SPAIN ...	219 "
FRANCE ...	635 "		

MONTH'S IMPORTS.

Where From:

AUSTRALIA	515 bales	INDIA	50 bales
ARGENTINE	30 "	NORWAY ...	86 "
BELGIUM ...	1037 "	PRUSSIA ...	134 "
CHANNEL Isles	140 "	PALESTINE...	80 "
DENMARK ...	1530 "	SWEDEN ...	250 "
EGYPT ...	677 "	SPAIN	258 "
FRANCE ...	1380 "	TURKEY ...	301 "
GERMANY ...	93 "	U.S.A.	14 "
HOLLAND ...	625 "		

Port of Landing:

HULL	2902 bales	LIVERPOOL.	2908 bales
LONDON ...	617 "	NEWHAVEN	485 "
LEITH... ...	789 "	SOUTH'MPT'N	336 "

Importers (Where not "To Order"):

G. Gibson and Co	J. Currie and Co

HOME RAGS.—Trade shows some improvement. There is a better demand for all grades, and prices in Seconds and Canvas are lower.

LONDON:

New White Cuttings	21/6	Canvas No. 1	15/0
Fines (selected)	20/6	,, No. 2 ...	9/6-10/6
,, (good London) ...	20/0	,, No. 3	5/6
Outshots (selected) ...	12/6	Mixed Rope	5/3
,, (ordinary) ...	11/0	White Rope	6/6
London Seconds	3/6-4/0	White Manilla Rope	8/0
Country do. ...	6/6-8/0	Coil Rope	9/0
London Thirds ...	1/9-2/0	Bagging...	1/6
Country do. ...	3/0-4/0	Gunny	3/0-3/6
Light Prints ...	7/0-8/0		

BRISTOL:

Fines	19/0	Clean Canvas ...	15/0
Outshots	13/6	Second Do. ...	9/6-10/6
Seconds	7/0-8/0	Light Prints ...	8/0
Thirds	3/6-4/0	Hemp Coil Rope	9/6-10/0
Mixed Bagging	3/6	Tarred Manilla	7/6

MANCHESTER:

Fines	15/0-16/0	Blues	6/6-7/0
Outshots (best) ...	11/6-12/0	Bagging...	4/0-4/3
,, (ordinary)	10/6-11/0	,, (common)	3/0-3/3
Seconds	7/0-7/3	W. Manilla Rope	10/0-10/6
Thirds	3/6-3/9	Surat Tares... ...	4/9-5/0

EDINBURGH:

Superfines	16/6	Black Cottons	2/3
Outshots	13/0	W. Manilla Rope ...	8/3
Mixed Fines...	14/0	Tarred Ditto	6/3
Common Seconds ...	7/0	,, Hemp Rope...	8/3
First do.	10/0	Rope Ends (new) ...	8/6
Prints	5/6-6/6	,, ,, (old) ...	5/0
Canvas (best)	15/6	Bagging...	2/0-3/0
,, 2nd	10/0	,, (clean) ...	4/3-6/0

DUBLIN.

White Cuttings ...	18/0	Mill Bagging	3/0
Fines	11/0	White Manilla	8/0
Seconds...	5/0	Tarred Hemp	8/0
Light Prints	3/0	Rigging	13/6
Black do.	2/0	Mixed Ropes	3/6
Bagging	2/0		

WASTE PAPERS.—There is a fair enquiry for Waste Papers at former figures.

Cream Shavings ...	12/3	Small Letters	5/-
Fine ,, ...	9/6	Large ,, ...	7/0
Mixed ,, ...	2/0	Brown Paper	2/9
White Printings ...	8/9	Light Browns	2/9
White Waste ...	1/6	Books & Pamphlets ...	6/0
Wood Pulp Cuttings	3/6	Strawboard Cuttings	1/6
Brown Paper	3/0	Jacquards	2/6
Crushed News	2/0		

For Export: 25/- per ton extra.

STARCH.—Prices:

F.o.r. London, less 2½%:

Maize—Crisp, £9 5/-; Powder, £9 10/-; Special £14.
Farina—Prime, £9 15/-; B.K.M.F., £12.

Delivered:

Rice—Special (in chests), £20 (net); Crystal (in bags) £19; Granulated (in bags) £18 less 2½%.
Dextrine—£15 to £16.

SIZING.—Enquiries are few; values unaltered.

English Gelatines	per cwt.	70/0 to	140/0
Foreign ,, ...	,,	70/0 ,,	140/0
Fine Skin Glues	,,	45/0 ,,	60/0
Long Scotch Glues	,,	45/0 ,,	60/0
Common ,, ...	,,	30/0 ,,	45/0
"Town" Glues	,,	26/0 ,,	36/0
"Bone" Glues	,,	20/0 ,,	30/0
Foreign Glues	,,	23/0 ,,	40/0
Bone Size	,,	4/0 ,,	10/0
Gelatine Size...	,,	5/0 ,,	10/0
Dry B.A. Pieces	,,	31/6 ,,	34/0
,, English Pieces	,,	22/0 ,,	24/0
Wet ,, ,, ...	,,	5/0 ,,	6/0
,, Sheep Pieces	,,	3/0 ,,	4/6
Buffalo Hide Shavings	,,	25/0 ,,	34/0
,, Picker Waste	,,	25/0 ,,	34/0

ROSIN.—The London market has been fairly active, with a good demand for spot rosin, prices for which may advance further as there is practically nothing afloat for this port, and very little stock here. Papermakers' qualities are scarce on the spot. At Liverpool prices have ranged somewhat lower for the low grades, and higher for the pale qualities than in London, with a fair trade doing. The American demand has been quiet, but prices have now commenced to harden. The present values of the various grades on the spot and ex ship to arrive, are as follows:

	London (on the spot).	Liverpool (on the spot).	C.i.f. net London or Liverpool.
B/C ..	4/0	3/7½	3/6
D ...	4/1½	3/9	3/7
E ...	4/3	3/10½	3/8
F ...	4/6	4/0	3/9
G ...	4/9	4/3	3/10
H ...	5/3	6/1½	3/11
I ..	5/9	5/9	4/9
K ...	6/6	6/3	6/0
M ...	7/9	7/6	7/0
N ...	9/0	8/9	8/10½
W G	9/6	9/6	9/6
W W	10/0	10/3	9/9

French Rosin: G, 5/3; H, 5/6; I, 5/9; K, 6/6; M 6/9; N, 8/0; W G, 8/6; W U, 9/6; Virgin, 11/0. Net c.i.f.

COLOURS.—Trade dull.

Mineral Black ...	cwt.	3/0	Ultramarine (pure) ... cwt.	40/0 to 45/0
do. superior ...	,,	5/0	PASTE COLOURS with 60% of colour, as follows:	
Pure Ivory Black	,,	12/0		
Ochre	,,	3/0		
French J. C. Ochre	ton	55/0	Orange Pulp ... cwt.	40/0
Chrome (pure) ...	cwt.	40/0	Golden Yellow Pulp	36/0
Red Oxide	,,	4/6	Lemon ,, ,, cwt.	36/0
Umber, Devonshire	,,	50/0	Prussian Yellow ..	36/0
do. Turkish ...	,,	40/0	Green (free of arsenic	36/0
Lamp Black ...		7/0-10/6	Paste Blue (20-45%)	23/6-46/0
Cochineal	lb.	1/3-2/0		

MINERALS.—CHINA CLAY is in better demand both for home and foreign consumption; there is little variation in prices. FRENCH CHALK arrivals are scarce at former quotations. MINERAL WHITE and PATENT HARDENINGS quiet.

Mineral White (Terra Alba), per ton f.o.r. or boat at works:

Superfine...	28/0	less 2½ %
Pottery Super.... ...	24/0	,,
Ball Seconds	20/0	,,
Seconds	15/0	,,
Thirds	10/6	,,

China Clay, in bulk, f.o.b. Cornwall, 14/0 to 27/6; bags 5/0 and casks 9/6 per ton extra; f.o.b. London, in casks 35/0 to 50/0 per ton.

Superfine Hardening, f.o.r. works, 40/0.

Patent Crystal Hardening, delivered at mills £3 to £3 15/0

Patent Hardening (2 ton lots) f.o.r. Lancs., £3 5/0.
,, ,, (5 ton lots) f.o.b. Liverpool, £3 10/0.

Magnesite (in lump) 32/6 per ton.

Magnesite (containing 98% Carbonate of Magnesia), raw ground, £6 10/0; calcined ground, £12 10/0.

Albarine, £3, del. mills.

Asbestos, best rock, £18; brown grades, £14 to £15

Asbestine Pulp, £4 5/- to £5 c.i.f. London, Liverpool and Glasgow.

Barytes (Carbonate), lump, 90/0 to 95/0; nuts, 72/6 to 85/0.

Barytes (Sulphate), "Angel White," No. 1, 70/0; No. 2, 60/0 to 65/0; No. 3, 45/0. Souheur's Brands: AF, 83/-; BF, 71/-; AB, 33/6; BB, 29/6; CB, 24/3.

French and Italian Chalk (Souheur Brand), per ton lots of 10 tons: Flower O, 63/6 c.i.f. London Flower OO, 59/0, Flower OOO, 52/6. Swan White, 58/0; Snow White, 80/0. Blackwell's "Angel White" Brand and "Silvery" 90/- to 92/6; [illegible] quality, 90/- to 95/-; and superfine, 105/-.

Bauxite, Irish Hill Quality, first lump, 20/0; seconds, 16/0; thirds, 12/0; ground, 35/0.

Pyrites (non-cupreous), Liverpool, 5d., 2 %.

DIRECTORY.

Names and Addresses under this heading will be charged for at the rate of 50/- per annum (52 insertions) for each card of two lines or under. Each additional line £1 extra.

ALUMINOUS CAKE.

The ALUM, CHINA CLAY and VITRIOL Co., Lim., 63, Queen Victoria Street, London, E.C. Works: Rainham-on-Thames. Telegrams—"Chinnock, London.

ANALYTICAL.

WILLIAMS, ROWLAND, F.I.C., F.C.S., 28, Pall Mall, Manchester.

ARTESIAN WELLS.

BATCHELOR, Richard D., Artesian and Consulting Well Engineer, 73, Queen Victoria Street, London, E.C., and at Chatham. 5713

ISLER, C., & Co., Bear Lane, Southwark, S.E

LE GRAND & SUTCLIFF, Magdala Works, 125, Bunhill Row, E.C.

BOILER COVERING.

LONSDALES, Boiler Coverers, Blackburn, will send a sample cask of their Patent Plastic Cork Covering to any Paper Mill in Great Britain—5 cwt. cask for 25/- (carriage paid).

CHINA CLAY.

The ALUM, CHINA CLAY and VITRIOL Co., Lim., 63, Queen Victoria Street, London, E.C. Mines: Ruddle and Colchester, St. Austell, Cornwall. Telegrams—"Chinnock, London."

ROGERS, J., & Co., Truro, Cornwall.—Agents: Taylor, Sommerville & Co., 83, Queen Victoria Street, E.C., and at 16, Princes Street, Edinburgh.

W. SINGLETON BIRCH & SONS, Lim., 15, Upton Street, Manchester. Mines: Rosevear, St. Austell, Cornwall. 2276

COLOURS.

CARDWELL, J. L., & Co., Commercial Buildings, 15, Cross Street, Manchester. Specialties: Mineral Black, Ven. Red, Ochres and Umbers. 5304

GEMMILL, W. N., & Co., Glasgow, Telegrams "Ruhe." Starches, Alumina, Antifroths, &c. All Paper Colours

COLOURS (Continued).

HINSHELWOOD, THOMAS, & Co., The Glasgow Colour Works, Glasgow. Colours and shades matched exactly.

MULLER, A. E., 9, Fenchurch Street, London, E.C.

ESPARTO.

IDE & CHRISTIE, Fibre, Esparto, and General Produce Brokers, 72, Mark Lane, E.C.

MINERAL WHITE or TERRA ALBA.

WINSER & Co., Portland Mills, Princess Street, Manchester. Also manufacturers of Aluminous Cake.

HOWE, JOHN, & Co., Carlisle. 2112

STEEL.

MAKIN, WM., & SONS, Sheffield. Established 17[illegible]. Roll Bars, Plates, Cutter Knives, Doctor Blades, &c. [illegible]

STRAW.

UNDERWOOD, E., & SON, Limited, Brentford, London, W. Press-packed Oat, Wheat, or Rye Straw, delivered to the chief British ports or railway stations.

TALC (French and Italian Chalk).

SOUHEUR, JEAN, Antwerp. All Minerals, Blanc de Silex, Barytes (superior and common), Carbonate of Lime, Blacklead, &c. British Agent: A. E. Muller, 9, Fenchurch Street, London, E.C. Agent for Liverpool and Manchester: C. H. Austin, Ditton, near Widnes.

RAGS.

CHALMERS, E., & Co., Lim., Bonnington, Leith.

MULLER, A. E., 9, Fenchurch Street, London, E.C.

WERTHEIM, A., & Co., Hamburg.

UMBER.

The ALUM, CHINA CLAY and VITROIL Co., Lim., 63, Queen Victoria Street, London, E.C. Telegrams—"Chinnock, London."

WOOD PULP.

FRIIS, N., & Co., 18, Carl Johans Gade, Christiania, Norway.

GOTTSTEIN, H., & Co., 59, Mark Lane, London, E.C., and at New York.

GRANT, W., & Co., 17, Baltic Street, Leith. Agents for best shippers, Sulphite and Sulphate, Mechanical, Pine, Brown, Aspen.

MATTHIESSEN, CHR., Christiania, Norway.

MULLER, A. E., 9, Fenchurch Street, London, E.C.

The SULPHITE PULP Company, Limited, 82, Gordon Street, Glasgow.

WERTHEIM, A., & Co., Hamburg.

☛ *NOW READY.* ☚

PAPER TESTING.

Being a DESCRIPTION OF PAPER TESTING as Carried out in the GERMAN GOVERNMENT LABORATORY at CHARLOTTENBURG. By

W. HERTZBERG,

Head Assistant in the Paper Testing Department.

TRANSLATED By

P. NORMAN EVANS, PH.D., F.I.C., F.C.S.

Price, 6/-. Post Free, 6/3.

W. JOHN STONHILL, 58, Shoe Lane, LONDON.

The SUBSCRIPTION to the

World's Paper Trade Review

is £1 per Annum.

Workmen's Edition, 2/6 per Volume, or 5/- Yearly.

☛ WOOD PULP—MECHANICAL and CHEMICAL.

FOR SALE

One of the FINEST & LARGEST WATER POWERS in Canada.

An ample supply of water and all the power required all the year round for the largest mill desired.

☛ Facilities for weekly shipments by steamer to Britain throughout the year are unsurpassed.

An INEXHAUSTIBLE SUPPLY of the BEST SPRUCE

close to the mill site is also a portion of this offer. This property offers advantages to be had nowhere in Scandinavia. Principals only dealt with.

Address "OWNER," No. 2692, Office of the WORLD'S PAPER TRADE REVIEW, 58, Shoe Lane, London, E.C. 2692

H. GOTTSTEIN & Co.,

59, MARK LANE, LONDON, AND AT NEW YORK.

PAPERMAKING MATERIALS, CHEMICALS, AND FOREIGN PRODUCE.

2582

THE
United Asbestos Co.,
LIMITED,
DOCK HOUSE, BILLITER STREET, E.C.,
"SALAMANDER"
THE UNITED ASBESTOS COMPANY LIMITED · LONDON ·
TRADE MARK
Pioneers
OF THE
Asbestos
Trade.
UNITED ASBESTOS
NON-CONDUCTING
COVERING
(For Steam Boilers & Pipes)
Best and Cheapest in the
Market; Will not
Injure Boiler Plates.
ASBESTOS
GOODS of ALL
DESCRIPTIONS
BELTINGS.
THE UNITED ASBESTOS CO., Limited,
UNITED
PACKINGS.
UNITED ASBESTOS Cº LMTD
PURE ITALIAN MILLBOARD EXTRA QUALITY
LONDON
A1
UNITED ASBESTOS
A1 MILLBOARDS
(ITALIAN)
Unequalled for Purity, Strength of
Fibre, and Uniformity. For Dry
Steam Joints it is admitted to be the
cleanest, most durable and economical
packing in existence.
UNITED ASBESTOS
SALAMANDER
Lubricating Cream & Oils,
SPECIALLY ADAPTED TO
PAPERMAKING MACHINERY.
DEPOTS:
MANCHESTER: 34, Deansgate; LIVERPOOL: 33, James Street;
NEWCASTLE-UPON-TYNE: Quayside; GLASGOW: 54, Robertson
Street; CARDIFF: 135, Bute Street; BRISTOL: Provident Buildings;
HULL: Queen's Dock; ST. PETERSBURG: Gostinoe Dvor (Interior) No. 51.

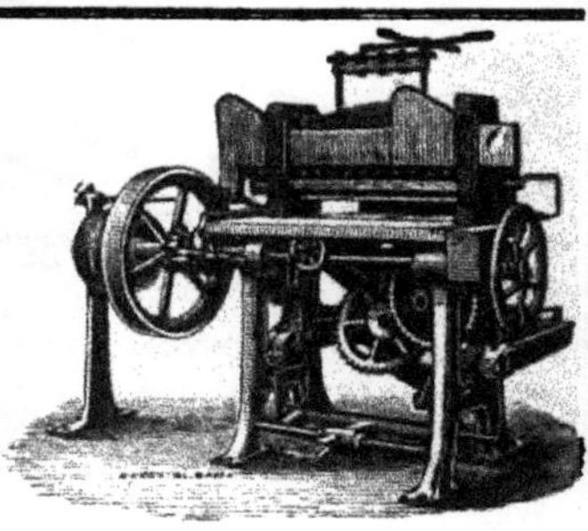

ESTABLISHED A.D. 1736.

WILLIAM MAKIN & SONS,

Attercliffe Steel Works, Sheffield, England.

3422

Illustrated Catalogue and Price Lists, in French and English, on demand.

E. CHALMERS & Co., Ltd.,

BONNINGTON, - - - LEITH,

RAG, ROPE, CANVAS AND WASTE PAPER

Merchants.

Telegrams: "GILES, LEITH."

Telephone: No. 465.

LINENS AND COTTONS, NEW AND OLD.

Bagging GRADED.

All CAREFULLY SELECTED.

ROPES OF All Classes, COILED AND BALED.

Woollen Rags.

HAND and PRESS BALED.

LARGE STOCKS KEPT.

PACKERS of EVERY GRADE of RAGS, &c., for PAPERMAKERS.

RICHARD ENGLAND, Brown Street, SALFORD.

(Successor to JAMES PARROTT.)

MAKER OF ALL TYPES AND POWERS OF STEAM ENGINES

Super Calenders, Friction Calenders, Emboss Calenders,

And CALENDERS of all descriptions for PAPER, COTTON, LINEN, WOOLLEN and SILK GOODS

CHILLED IRON, HARD-CAST IRON, STEEL, BRASS & BRASS COVERED ROLLS

Superior Cotton and Paper Bowls,

HAVING THE MOST POWERFUL PLANT IN THE WORLD FOR THEIR MANUFACTURE.

ROLL GRINDING MACHINES. ALL CLASSES OF ROLLS REGROUND.

HYDRAULIC PRESSES and PUMPS.

Printed and Published by W. JOHN STONHILL 58, Shoe Lane, LONDON, E.C. November 3, 1893.

A YEAR'S BANKRUPTCY.

Some very important statistics were submitted at the last weekly conference of the staff of our contemporary the *British & Colonial Printer & Stationer.*

POTORO said: The year 1892 was in every way a most unsatisfactory one for the trading community. During its whole length we suffered from great depression, which was rendered even more acute by certain domestic occurrences which not only destroyed the prospects of improvement which appeared to be opening up, but turned those very prospects into causes of additional losses in certain trades. Particularly was this the case in certain branches of the fancy goods trades, in which very heavy outlays had been incurred in anticipation of a more brilliant season under the spur of a royal wedding and other events. That outlay must have imposed a heavy strain upon wholesalers and manufacturers in particular. Looking at the matter in this light it would not have been matter for surprise if the returns had shown an increase of failures in the trades which come within our own particular cognisance. But singularly enough the number of stationers included in the list of receiving orders stands at exactly the same figure as in 1891, namely 21; printers and publishers show a decrease of five, from 28 to 23; the drapers show a decrease from 104 to 98; but dealers in jewellery, china and fancy goods show an increase from 59 to 77. There was an increase of 419 receiving orders made under the various trade divisions distinguished by the Board of Trade, and curiously enough the bulk of these increases belong to such trades as those of the grocer, the publican, the farmer, the bootmaker, the baker, the butcher, the provision dealer, the tailor, &c.

THE HEAVY INCREASE OF INSOLVENCY.

Alike under the heading of bankruptcy proceedings and under deeds of arrangement with creditors there were shown a considerable increase in numbers and in the amount of liabilities, concurrently with a decrease of assets in each case. There is this further agreement between the two classes of liquidations, that we have to go back to the years 1888-9 to find the numbers equalled or excelled, though the discrepancy between liabilities and assets is strikingly heavy in 1992 as compared with any former year, as the following tables will show:—

RECEIVING ORDERS UNDER THE BANKRUPTCY ACTS, 1883 AND 1890.

Year.	Number of Receiving Orders Made.	Estimated Liabilities.	Estimated Assets.
		£	£
1888	4,826	7,110,948	2,242,747
1889	4,520	6,328,293	1,990,160
1890	4,011	6,132,951	2,222,293
1891	4,216	8,562,941	3,152,419
1892	4,635	8,763,031	3,078,393
Increase	419	200,090	—
Decrease	—	—	74,026

DEEDS OF ARRANGEMENT.

Year.	Number of Deeds.	Estimated Liabilities.	Estimated Assets.
		£	£
1888	3,495	4,803,481	2,416,755
1889	3,237	4,773,947	2,718,721
1890	3,097	4,360,271	2,352,941
1891	3,008	5,092,448	3,106,755
1892	3,333	5,957,022	2,937,315
Increase	325	864,574	—
Decrease	—	—	169,440

Would it be reasonable, I may here ask, to assume that the all-round increase of liabilities and the decrease of assets indicates an increase of trading with a knowledge of insolvency? The difference as compared with last year is important enough to warrant such an inquiry. Summarised it shows the serious balance as against the creditor of £1,308,130 in increased loss over the year 1891. Thus:—

Increase of liabilities under the two heads	£1,064,664
Decrease in Assets	243,466
Total increased loss in 1892 ...	£1,308,130

The Inspector-General in Bankruptcy would seem to estimate the class of traders who carry on business with a knowledge of loss at five per cent. of the gross liabilities, but this does not cover the ground I have in view. Knowledge of trading at a loss is not the same thing as trading with a knowledge of insolvency. The general feeling of the trading community is that there is such an increase of trading after ascertained knowledge of insolvency, a feeling which found expression in the resolution proposed by the Bradford Chamber of Commerce in the recent gathering of the Associated Chambers of Commerce, namely, that "continuing to trade after clear knowledge of insolvency should be added to the offences punishable under the Debtors Act, 1869." There is no possibility of making any dependable deduction on the point from the report, but it is certainly worth the attention of those who have to deal with the administration of the Act. The Inspector-General labours to show that the *average* loss to creditors during last year under bankruptcy orders shows a decrease: this really conveys little comfort to the person principally concerned, that is the creditor, who will look rather to the aggregate loss than to the average. This aggregate loss is enormous, namely—

Under Bankruptcy Orders ...	£6,691,641
Under Deeds of Arrangement	3,998,812
	£10,690,453

This is the highest figure since the passing of the Deeds of Arrangement Act of 1887, as will be seen from the following comparison :—

1888	... ...	£8,753,428
1889	... ...	7,933,004
1890	... ...	7,388,019
1891	... ...	8,451,815
1892	... ...	10,690,453

There seems to be evidence of a disposition on the part of the insolvents and creditors still to favour settlements under the Deeds of Arrangements Act rather than under official control where assets are reasonably good, for if we cast up the last column of the first two tables given above we shall find that the assets of estates settled under arrangements reach the value of £13,532,487, as against £12,686,012 in the case of receiving orders. The *average* amount of liabilities, too, has increased in the case of deeds of arrangement from £1,692 in 1891, to £1,787 in 1892; whilst under the bankruptcy clauses the *average* liabilities have decreased from £2,031 to £1,890.

WHAT IS THE CAUSE OF THIS?

I think it resolves itself into two factors —the first, that solicitors strongly favour deeds of arrangement, and the second, that the costs of administration are lower than where bankruptcy proceedings are taken. It is perhaps not matter of common knowledge among our readers that the members of the Incorporated Law Society are as a body bitterly opposed to the present system of official liquidation. This is not the place to enter into the reasons for such opposition, but I may suggest that the circumstance that there is a steady movement downwards in the number of cases in which solicitors are employed may have something to do with it. It is but natural, therefore, that they should in advising clients favour deeds of arrangement. A comparison of the costs between the three classes of insolvencies —that is administration by official receivers, by non-official trustees, and under deeds of arrangement—is worth studying :—

PERCENTAGE OF COSTS TO GROSS ASSETS.

Value of Gross Assets.	Under Official Receivers.	Under Non-Official Trustees.	Under Deeds of Arrangement.
£500 and under £800	19·40	38·48	18·60
£800 ,, ,, £900	17·80	29·51	16·81
£900 ,, ,, £1,000	18·38	27·04	16·18
£1,000 ,, ,, £1,200	16·07	27·19	16·16
£1,200 ,, ,, £1,500	21·48	26·38	12·81
£1,500 ,, ,, £2,000	20·89	31·70	12·56
£2,000 ,, ,, £3,000	13·45	25·61	12·12
£3,000 ,, ,, £4,000	13·17	19·53	13·94

It will thus be seen that, as compared with administration by the official receiver the costs under deed of arrangement are sensibly lower, in some instances strikingly so. In comparison with those of realisation under a non-official trustee we have a very strong contrast indeed. To carry it further, I may give the following comparative statement of *law* costs under the three systems, for the sake of simplicity putting the costs of the petition and those of executing and registering the deed of arrangement on the same footing :—

	Law Costs of Petition.	Law Costs after Receiving Order.
Under Official Receivers.	4·53	1.36
Under Non-Official Trustees.	1·44	6·97
Under Deeds of Arrangement.	3·25	2·43

Here the percentage law costs to assets between deeds of arrangement and administration under official receivers is slightly in favour of the former, though the costs of the solicitor to the trustee after registration of the deed is much heavier than under the other system. In the case of the non-official trustee the after costs are disproportionately heavy.

PERCENTAGE OF REALISATIONS.

It now becomes important to see how the comparison stands between the three in the proportion of realisations to estimated assets. I give these in the following table :—

	per cent.
Under Official Receivers ...	71½
Under Non-Official Trustees ...	49
Under Deeds of Arrangement	71

To appreciate these percentages at their true value we must see what are the respective amounts of estimated and realised assets in the estates closed up to the end of 1892. They are as follows:—

	Estimated Assets.	Realised Assets.
	£	£
Under Official Receivers ..	501,755	359,924
Under Non-Official Trustees ..	1,151,585	568,031
Under Deeds of Arrangement	972,441	694,675

I have enlarged upon this comparison between official and non-official work, to bring out as strongly as possible a much disputed fact that administration by the official receiver is preferable to either of the others where circumstances are not exceptional. The proportion of realisations is highest, the cost compare favourably, and the official supervision counts for a good deal in favour of the creditor, for though his powers may not be greater than those of a non-official trustee, he is less likely to be hampered, and realisations are more speedy.

IMPROVEMENT IN THE SCALE OF COMPOSITIONS APPROVED.

A very noticeable feature in the annual return is the great improvement in the scale of compositions sanctioned by the courts since the passing of the Act of 1890. The Act of 1893 brought a better state of things within view, but the wisdom of the Act of 1890 is powerfully emphasised by a study of the following table, which I extract bodily from the Inspector-General's report:—

cent.; in 1890 56·66 per cent.; and in 1892 it was reduced to nil. This of course at once suggests the inquiry, How does the number of discharges compare with those of past years? The answer is unsatisfactory.

THE UNDISCHARGED BANKRUPT.

There has been a rapid falling off in the number of applications for discharge since the passage of the Bankruptcy Act of 1890. In that year the number of such applications was 1,408; in 1891 it fell to 998; and in 1892 it was only 795. This is by far the smallest number of applications since 1884, the number in 1885 (the year when the full effects of the provisions of the Act of 1883 as they affected discharge could be gauged) being 915. Here the difficulties imposed by the recent Act operates to prevent debtors applying for their discharge at all, which is quite understandable. The question is, What becomes of the undischarged bankrupt? Does he enter into trade again? The Luton Chamber of Commerce affirms that they do, and declares their increasing prevalence to be "a source of danger to the trading community." I am decidedly of opinion that once a debtor comes before the court under a petition in bankruptcy, the court should retain its hold upon him until he had passed through, that is obtained his discharge. The present system of permitting a debtor who is being pressed by his creditors and perhaps in danger of committal under the Debtors' Act to file a petition, pass his public examination, pay nothing in the pound, and then altogether sink out of sight is a scandal. No doubt a large proportion of

PROPORTION OF COMPOSITIONS APPROVED AT VARIOUS RATES.

	Under 1s.	1s. and under 2s. 6d.	2s. 6d. and under 5s.	5s. and under 7s. 6d.	7s. 6d. and under 10s.	10s. and under 15s.	15s. and under 20s.	At 20s.
ACT OF 1869.								
Average of 13 years from 1869..	19·64	26·25	28·54	11·79	8·77*	3·14	·59	1·28
1883 (last year of Act)	17·53	34·65	29·20	10·14	5.96	1·46	·58	·48
ACT OF 1883.								
1884	Nil	12·64	26·39	35·68	6·69	14·13	1·50	2·97
1885	Nil	7·24	28·96	34·14	12·76	12·07	2·76	2·07
1886	Nil	7·93	18·52	33·86	18·52	13·23	2·12	5·82
1887	Nil	3·15	18·11	41·73	15·75	14·17	2·36	4·73
1888	Nil	13·46	31·73	29·81	10·58	9·62	1·92	2·88
1889	Nil	4·0	22·67	29·33	16·0	21·33	1·34	5·33
1890	Nil	1·67	33·33	31·66	16·67	16·67	1·67	8·33
1891	Nil	Nil	Nil	2·27	52·27	34·09	—	11·37
1892	Nil	Nil	Nil	Nil	68·08	17·02	2·13	12·77

Under the old Bankruptcy Acts of 1869 the proportion of compositions under 10s. in the pound was (taking the average of 13 years) 94·99 per cent.; in 1884 it was 81·40 per cent.; in 1889 it had become 72·0 per

bankrupts do enter again into trade. But the greater proportion of the undischarged bankrupts are non-traders, who practically suffer no disadvantage from their position. The question of what should be done to remedy an indisputable evil is too wide for me to discuss here; I content myself with saying that the law should be amended on this point. Of the number of applications that were made, it is significant that the large percentage of 73·3 were suspended, 5·4 refused, and 10·6 granted or suspended subject to the fulfilment of certain conditions.

THE CAUSES OF INSOLVENCY.

In conclusion, I would quote the summary of the Inspector-General as to the causes of insolvency. He divides these under seven heads, as follows:—

1.—Insolvencies resulting from accidental circumstances beyond the control of the debtor, or from the fraud or failure of others. About 2 per cent.

2.—Trading concerns which have never been profitable, or which have gradually dropped into unprofitable conditions, and where the traders being apparently unable to face their position, continue to carry on at a loss, or whose personal expenditure is far in excess of their business income. About 5 per cent.

3.—Established businesses which are crippled and ultimately ruined by the sudden withdrawal of the partners' capital in consequence of death or otherwise. About 2 per cent.

4.—Traders who have created, inherited, or otherwise succeeded to a legitimate and profitable business, but who, owing to inexperience or in their haste to increase profits, are tempted into too rapid extensions, or into speculative ventures, or fields of enterprise of which they have no previous experience, frequently resorting to the use of accommodation bills. About 56 per cent.

5.—Traders who neglect their business either through dissolute habits or from love of horse-racing, betting, or other forms of gambling, or from operations on the Stock Exchange outside of their ordinary business. About 7 per cent.

6.—Persons not engaged in business, but who with substantial private means dabble on the Stock Exchange or in land and other speculative ventures upon credit, and who generally attribute their failure to "depreciation" in their property. About 7 per cent.

7.—Speculative and often fraudulent adventurers, who commence their career, as a rule, without any capital. About 21 per cent.

At the conclusion of Porono's remarks, the various members of the staff expressed their indebtedness to him for the pains he had taken to analyse the Bankruptcy Report for their advantage but no discussion worthy of the name and of publication took place.

THE BRISTOL INDUSTRIAL AND FINE ART EXHIBITION.

It may fairly be said of this Exhibition that it fulfils the purpose for which it was projected, viz., to illustrate the arts and crafts of Bristol in a thoroughly representative manner, and in operation:

MESSRS. STRACHAN AND HENSHAW, of Bristol, contractors for the Exhibition shafting, exhibit at No. 37, and in motion, a machine for making and printing triangular bags, which does its work well. The "Satchel" paper bag machine (at Messrs. Robinson's, see above) is also from the works of these engineers. Cutting machinery is also on show by them.

MESSRS. DOUGLAS BROS., at stand No. 120, of Kingswood Hill, Bristol, show machines and cutters for label cutting, also for punching and for eyeletting.

ALLEN DAVIES AND CO.—For a collection of high class machinery, as used in the different departments of Messrs. Allen, Davies and Co., Bristol (printers, stationers, and accounnt book manufacturers, &c.),—exhibit No. 20—there could scarcely be gathered one more thoroughly up-to-date and serviceable than that shown here. The "Wytorz" cylinder letterpress, the "Wharfedale" printing machine, and the new patent "Victoria" folding machines, by R. Cundall and Sons; a Crossland "Advance" paper cutting machine; Smythe book-sewing with thread, as well as a wire stitching machine; Gough's patent automatic relief colour stamping press, and Strong's newest pattern label puncher complete the array. Our readers will admit that the firm which will provide itself with such excellent servants can turn out the best work, and of that there is ample evidence in the specimens shown. Messrs. Allen, Davies and Co. have acquired the concession for the catalogue. Their "Files" and "Tallies" are well in evidence.

AN OIL MOTOR is shown at exhibit No. 26. The Daimler Motor Syndicate, Lim., 49, Leadenhall-street, London, E.C., have a striking exhibit here with their motor launch, actuated by a Daimler Petrol Motor. But our attention was mostly directed to the stationary motor, also on show but not working. The principle of this invention is in the application of petroleum instead of water or gas, as the motive agent. The oil is "vaporised," and this actuates the engine.

JAMES SPICER AND SONS are represented by a show case, exhibit No. 205. In papers for all the various purposes required by the stationer, the printer, the lithographer and fancy box maker, Messrs. James Spicer and Sons show a judicious selection.

A STANDARD SIZE FOR NEWS AND LIRRARY WORK.

Of making books there is no end, and of making sizes for books there is no end, as they all may be under the generic names of quartos, octavos, or duodecimos. The books may be octavos of anything from a foolscap sheet of 13½-in. by 17-in. to an imperial sheet of 22-in. by 30-in., ranging through the rising gradation of small post, 15¼-in. by 19¼-in.; crown, 15-in.

36-IN.

48-IN.

12 pages. 16 × 18

16 × 18

24 pages. 16 × 9

16 × 9

24 pages. 18 × 8

18 × 8

96 pages. 8 × 4½

96 pages. 8 × 4½

48 pages. 9 × 8

8 × 18

192 pages. 4½ × 4

4½ × 4

48 pages. 9 × 8

192 pages. 4 × 4½

4 × 4½

24 pages. 8 × 18

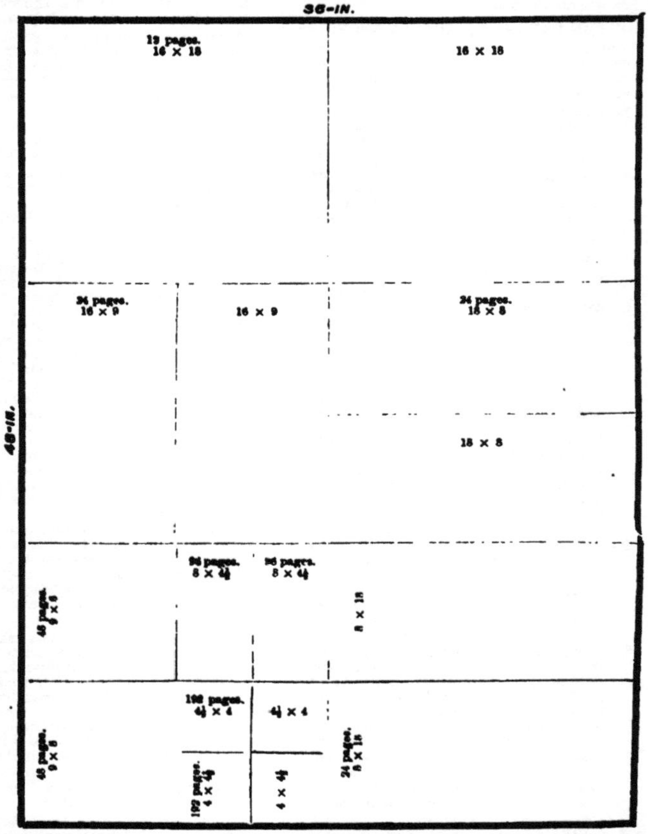

printers and paper dealers know to their cost from the various sizes of paper they have to keep in stock, and as every one with a library knows from the various sizes that appear on his shelves, although by 20-in.; large post, 16½-in. by 21-in.; demy, 19½-in. by 23½-in.; medium, 18½-in. by 23½-in.; royal, 20-in. by 25-in.; super royal, 20½-in. by 27½-in.; to imperial, 22-in. by 30-in. Here is diversity from which to

make quartos, octavos, or duodecimos with a vengeance, and out of these nine sizes, which are doubled or quadrupled as they are wanted for larger sheets, or more pages, there are only three that are even inches both ways. There is no method in the madness that has settled these sizes length and breadth, nor yet that representative of the middle class, medium, which is 24-in. by 19-in. in printing papers. But in drawing papers that size is called royal. There is a still greater difference between the names and sizes of drawing and printing papers, demy in drawings

36-IN.

48-IN.

8 pages to sheet.
24 × 18

24 × 18

32 pages.
12 × 9

12 × 9

18 × 12

16 pages.
18 × 12

9 × 6

64 pages.
9 × 6

256
4½×3

256
pages.

256
4½×3

256
pages.

128
6 × 4½

6 × 4½

from the foolscap to the imperial, although be it noted that the sizes with the regal names do not make "two bites of a cherry," or split inches, crown, royal and imperial being even inches, both in being 20-in. by 15½-in., but in printings 22½-in. by 17½-in.! It is quite evident, therefore, that what Whitworth did in fixing a standard system of measurement in the machine trade is wanted in the paper and printing trades, for it is evident that in fixing the sizes not even a rule of thumb, much less a mathematical system on the decimal, duodecimal, or octavo methods has obtained. Perhaps nothing better could be expected from a start from the "foolscap," although drawing papers have gone up in size and in dignity of title to the emperor, which is 72-in. by 48-in., in which there is some proportion between the scale used and the dimensions. There is in this size an evenness in feet as well as in inches—6-ft. by 4-ft., and the proportion is in thirds, the breadth being one third less than the length, or, to put it in another way, the length one half more than the breadth.

From the papermakers' point of view some method is needed, and from the adoption of the emperor size, with its double uniformity to the scale terms, and proportion in length and breadth, there is a systematising of the size and a simplification of the terms. The papermaker has begun the work, what has the printer done to relieve himself of these fractional measurements and unmethodical sizes, that began with foolscap, and now end with the emperor in drawings and in newspapers, as we find?

The printing sizes we have seen are various, and it is as true of newspaper and journal work as of ordinary book work. Newspapers have been of all sizes, beginning as they did in the earlier days of their existence with the foolscap, the contents of which sometimes led to the cropping of the ears of the proprietors, or their standing in public under conditions worse than those in which they stood on the school form with the fool's cap on head, made out of a sheet of foolscap, the letter paper of that time. In later times, as newspapers and journals have grown, a column has been added, or the columns have been lengthened, sometimes for an emergency, in other cases for so many days a week, and sometimes permanently, until the files of the same newspapers, that stand or lie in the catacombs of journalistic everyday life in the British Museum, are as many shapes and sizes as the sizes in paper quoted above. The file of a journal, made up in these methods of varying breadths or lengths, jars against the sense of the fitness of things, even where one journal is only filed and handled. What must the librarians and advertising agents, who keep files of no end of papers, think of the lack of proportion and sense of uniformity that there must be in the minds of the boasted and boasting teachers of the world, in everything except proportion, it seems? But all this is being changed. It was a matter of necessity and not of choice, of space and not of proportion, that led to what seemed to be the vagaries of an unbalanced mind, of men who had apparently not even the method of madness. In newspapers, the only methods of enlarging were by broadening or lengthening the columns, or adding one or two more, and this would go on until the enlargement got nearly to double the original size, and then the next enlargement became a return to the primitive sized page; but with eight pages instead of four. To meet these processes, due to natural growth and development, ultimating by careful cultivation into the doubling process, from the primitive single, as in some flowering plants, the inventor has stepped in, and machines are made, so that instead of enlargements by columns, until there can be the doubling of the sheet; there is an enlargement by pages, and the newspaper or journal begins by having an occasional supplement of one or two pages, which can be printed and pasted in with the other portion of the paper, and instead of going from six to eight columns, the newspaper comes out with a ten-paged instead of an eight-paged paper of six columns each page, no more type or paper being used in the one than in the other case; but the size of the pages is kept uniform. And so we have newspapers of eight, ten, twelve and sixteen pages, produced off the same machine, and all uniform in size, but varying in the number of pages. To that method all the papers must come at last, and they are coming fast.

Fixity of size is becoming necessary for each newspaper—as means are being found to meet their needs by machinists; and might there not be a fixed size for newspapers generally, to meet the needs of their readers, and those who find it necessary to file their papers? Why not if the requirements of newspapers can be easily met by a uniformity in the size of pages? The size should of course be handy, and if possible a standard that would have some simple and defined proportions to itself and to the scale of measurement used. These conditions have already been found, fixed, and adopted by the leading papermakers, newspaper proprietors, and machine makers. The emperor size of Whatman's drawing papers is just double the size of the *Times* newspaper sheet, and exactly the size of the first double newspaper machine made by Messrs. Hoe in this country, on which the breadth of the reel of paper was 72 inches, and the circumference of the cylinder, 48 inches. The *Times* page is 24 inches by 18 inches, and this is the size of the page of the *Newcastle Weekly Chronicle*, which is a sixteen-paged paper. This makes a good handy sized page, the size that newspaper proprietors usually at first adopt, when not driven by competition or pressure on space to go further; and it is likely to become the standard size for all standard journals, now that extensions can be easily made by pages, instead of by columns. Besides, a newspaper should not be so wide that it becomes tiresome to hold its open sheet. Indeed, the tendency is in these days of railway travelling to half that size for convenience of such reading, as we see by the sizes adopted by the penny evening papers in London, the *Globe*, the *Pall Mall Gazette*, the *St. James' Gazette*, the *Westminster Gazette*, and also by the *Morning Leader*. Above the *Times* size papers become unhandy, and as the tendency is to meet the needs of the people and add to the comfort and convenience of the readers, so we are getting our papers and periodicals of a handy size, and folded, stitched or pasted, and cut. The standard size of 48 by 36-in.—or the still simpler designation of 4-ft. by 3-ft.—appears thus to have been adopted by intent or chance by the representatives of the three great trades interested in the matter—papermakers, publishers, and machine-makers—and by the same accident or intent the same size has been adopted by some of the chief and most popular periodicals and other publications. A page half the size of the *Times* represents within a shade papers like the *Queen*, the *Million*, in its original size, the *British and Colonial Printer and Stationer*, and other journals. Fold the sheet once again and we get the *Family Herald* and the magazines with the largest circulations—no end of them with pages all within a fraction of 12-in. by 9-in. Another fold brings the size of the page down to monthlies like *Macmillan's Magazine*, and half that size again gives a class of books like Routledge's *World Library* and some railway time tables. Here is a diagram of sizes that could be made out of a sheet of 48-in. by 36-in., to a scale of 1 inch to a foot with the octavo fold. Using the 48-in. by 36-in. in the 12mo. fashion gives a greater variety, as will be seen by the accompanying diagram. Here we have square and oblong sizes to meet special publications, as maps and copy books specially, and out of the two methods of dividing the sheet almost any size can be got. By dividing this sheet and the 72-in. by 48-in. by thirds each way a still greater variety of sizes could be obtained, if these were required—although for the moment we are advocating a uniformity of sizes for libraries and newspapers, and a standard size of paper out of which the greater part of the work of the printing trade might be got, and so avoid the necessity of keeping all sizes, as well as all qualities of papers in stock. By a standard size, and that the largest that was most suitable, a further economy would be effected in the turn out, if a full-sized sheet—and a sheet the full size of the press—could be generally used. The French are great in such economies, and hence the binder in that country has often to cut his sheets and inset, and thus finds it impossible to use folding machines because of the pieces that have to be cut off and inserted. These complicated impositions and their insets and difficulties of folding are, however, not desirable, and not economical in the end. There is nothing like a good square fold, at right angles, running all through the sheet, and to this end the trade should work. Publishers should co-operate with printers and give the public what some of the leading caterers did for the public in newspapers and periodicals—see the need; and the public librarians, who represent the public and have become a class not to be despised by book publishers, should seek for the adoption of standard sizes in library work, a subject which their association has, we believe, had before them. And then for the benefit of all—papermakers, printers, machine-makers, publishers, and the public, a standard size for books and newspapers might be adopted, and the sin of waste in paper and time, and its unsightliness be avoided.

What, then, should the size be? A multiplication of the foolscap, so associated also with the "devil's own," or the emperor in full size or half size? Besides a fixed size for journalistic and magazine work would clear the way for many a printer to go in for a web machine of the fastest and simplest type, upon which he dare not speculate now, for almost every job is of a different size, and even if a machine will alter to sizes, the alterations are troublesome. We throw out these suggestions so that the trade may work intentionally in a direction they have apparently drifted, and for their own advantage as well as for that of the public. A standard size for newspapers and books would be of immense advantage also to our colonies in the ordering of paper and the getting of machines, and if they did not need the emperor size, rather unwieldy, they might take the "better half"—the empress, shall we call it—48-in. by 36-in., which would be a blessing at home and abroad.

Moreover, if there were a fixed or general size for publications of such long runs as newspapers and journals nowadays so often have, journalistic and magazine, and even book work, might be carried out in the same establishments, and on the same machines, and worked by the same agencies. This is, in fact, being done by some of the leading provincial newspapers, and *Tit Bits*, indeed, was years ago printed by the *Manchester Guardian* and run off on one of Farmer's rotary machines. This example has been followed by some of the most successful provincial papers. The Brothers Leng, both of whom have been knighted for their journalistic work, have at Sheffield and Dundee utilised their rotaries and the spare time of their machines for periodical work, as the *Times* has indeed done the same with publications or reprints of their own. But some of our newspaper proprietors might go even beyond these efforts, and instead of publishing a single number of a journal, publish a volume a week of some standard work, and with their machinery and staff of compositors, or shall we say now of composing machines, they could produce a volume at a fabulously low price compared with the price charged for many of the standard authors, or even as compared with the cheapest issues of some works that pretend to meet the needs of the mass of people, who are now able to read, and are ardent readers of almost anything that is placed before them. Why should not the best of our grand old standard English authors be published in this way, and at such a price as would place these works within the reach of every one in the land, and the poor man have his own library as well as the rich? Attempts have been made to meet these needs, and "popular libraries" have been issued, but often the standard works have not been up to the standard, for they have been abridgements, and the suppressed or abreviated portions have been those in which full information was most needed to the student if not to the general reader. Besides, our means of production has increased both in printing and engraving. Reproductions of the best engravings can be made as cheaply as the reproduction of the commonest specimen of engravings. So there is now everything ready for reproducing the high-priced literature of the past, and all that art has put on paper, at a price within the reach of all. The facilities are great, the field is large, who will enter upon this great educational work for the people?

Look what can be done in it. One single revolution of a machine that could print an emperor sheet, and one single sheet of that size would represent a volume of 128 pages, the size of the sixpenny edition of Kingsley's work, published by Messrs. Macmillan and Co. "Yeast" has only 102 pages, but "Hypatea" has 176 pages—a sheet would have printed the one and a sheet and a half the other, or three sheets of the Empress size—48-in. by 36-in. The cost of composition and printing and paper would be the chief items of expenditure, and what would the first be on an issue equal to the largest newspaper circulation in the world? There would be no highly paid writing and costly telegrams if there were no advertisements, as in the newspaper, in this weekly adjunct to a daily paper. Newspaper proprietors might thus also become the publishers of the best of novels, and even of other works, in a popular way, as many of them are to-day; but then not of weekly instalments of two or three chapters in their weekly papers, but of a whole volume every week, and at something like the price of some popular weekly newspapers. A penny or twopenny library for the people of the best Standard Works of the English people would have a world-wide circulation—a work, not necessarily a novel, complete in itself—and be one of the greatest educational agencies, for it would be all that is best and brightest in the literature of a nation that is leading the nations of the earth in everything that tends to the improvement of the race, and of a nation upon whose empire the sun never sets. Who will produce the Empress Library for the people of an empire of letters, that is guiding, ruling, and revolutionising the world? It would supplement and complete the educational work of our free national schools and public libraries, and let the English people know more about the literature of the land of their birth—a land of which they have reason to be proud, for its laws as well as its literature, and for its ingenuity and enterprise as well as its learning.

THE *Liberty Review* (quarterly) is about to be issued as a weekly journal, the first number of which is announced to appear on December 1st. It is to be a vigorous and uncompromising opponent of trades unionism.

MR. AUGUSTUS BIRRELL, M.P., has inaugurated a new political monthly, the *Liberal Magazine*, which is to be a supplement to the daily newspapers, systematising the analysis and collection of facts and figures likely to be permanently useful, and indexing the subjects treated at political meetings.

NEW GERMAN MERCHANDISE MARKS' ACT.—German manufacturers are greatly interested in the new bill, which is going to be introduced in the coming session of the Imperial Parliament. Experts of the various trades have been consulted beforehand, and it is therefore expected that the new legislation will be in every way satisfactory to honest people. It has been remarked that the growing competition has in many instances become dishonest, and that in fact it went very often very far indeed, though it did not transgress the letter of the law. The extension of the act is to give further protection to trade marks in so far that damages may not only be claimed against forgery of registered brands, but also against dishonest imitations of the style of packing, labels, etc., of any well known articles. Another point is the punishment of such employees as may divulge trade secrets to rival manufacturers. In this case damages are not considered a sufficient protection, and offenders will be made criminally punishable. As a further extention of the act protection is proposed against what is called dishonest advertisments. This evil has become very great, and the State is here invited to act, so to speak, as a guardian of that part of the general public which is not able to take care of its own interests. The subject of course is very important, and the debates no doubt will be very animated.

Printed and Published by
W. JOHN STONHILL, 58

Telegrams: "STONHILL, LONDON." A B C Code. Registered at the General Post Office as a Newspaper.

Vol. XX. No. 19. LONDON, NOVEMBER 10, 1893. Price 6d.

DUTCH PAPER, &c., IN THE BRITISH MARKET.

Holland takes the lead in sending paper to Great Britain. For the first nine months of the present year the value of Dutch paper amounted to about 29 per cent. of our total importations. Many people attribute the keenest competition to Germany, but her supplies only amounted to 23 per cent. of the total value. The following figures show the comparative value of foreign paper imported :—

	Jan.-Sept., 1893.
From Holland	£496,291
,, Germany	392,704
,, Other countries	809,538
	£1,698,533

The following figures relate to the trade of the past five years :—

Dutch Exports of Paper and Pasteboard to Great Britain.

1888	694,825 cwts.	£145,244
1889	802,920 ,,	468,622
1890	935,029 ,,	525,010
1891	1,037,211 ,,	548,853
1892	1,146,734 ,,	624,791

It is evident that trade is being enormously developed by Holland. Taking the figures given above there is an increase in value of over 40 per cent. since 1888.

Dutch Imports of British Paper.

1888	8,449 cwts.	£16,145
1889	9,788 ,,	19,295
1890	9,281 ,,	18,399
1891	12,572 ,,	21,777
1892	12,286 ,,	22,370

British paper shows a steady increase in value. It is surprising however that such enormous quantities of paper from Holland should find a market in Great Britain. It is true the various kinds must be of a very poor quality, as prices are extremely low.

Relative Prices.

	British Paper : Dutch Imports.	Dutch Paper : British Imports.
1888	38s. 2d. per cwt.	12s. 9¾d. per cwt.
1892	30s. 5d. ,,	10s. 10¾d. ,,

It may be pointed out that from January up to the end of September this year 900,780 cwts. of paper were shipped to Great Britain from Holland, out of which quantity 41,944 cwts. were entered as printings and writings.

THE MANUFACTURE OF BLEACHING POWDER.

Several improvements in the manufacture of bleaching powder, &c., are claimed by Messrs. W. J. and L. M. Fraser, engineers, Commercial-road, London. They employ a vertical chamber or tower made of suitable material fitted inside with an elevator (worked from the outside by a band or pulley), for the purpose of raising and distributing the lime or other material used in the process in such a manner that it takes up and absorbs more rapidly and efficiently and in larger quantities than hitherto the chlorine or other gases with which it has to be thoroughly incorporated.

The elevator is of the "bucket" principle, and raises the lime or other material continuously from the bottom of the chamber to the top, or thereabouts, and discharges it over fixed perforated inclined planes, from which it descends through the gas to the bottom of the chamber, and again ascends by the continuous operation of the elevator.

The chamber or tower is fitted with an inclined bottom and has a "discharging" door, and is also provided with a gas-tight feeding door. In connection with the chamber or tower a condenser or cooling apparatus consisting of earthenware or other pipes fixed to the outside of the chamber is employed, which condenser may be enclosed in a water trough for the purpose of cooling the gases as they become heated.

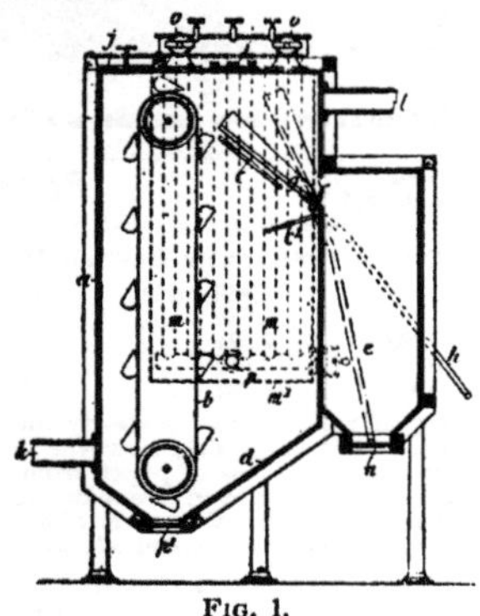

FIG. 1.

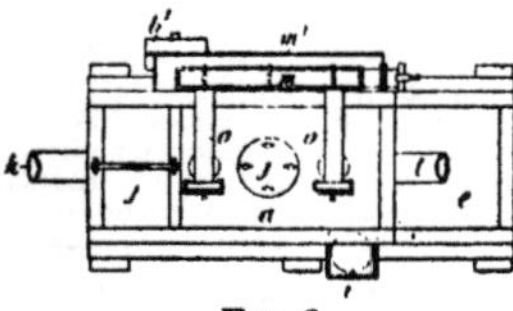

FIG. 2.

Fig. 1 is a vertical section, and Fig. 2 is a plan of the improved apparatus for the manufacture of bleaching powder and like compounds.

The letter *a* is a vertical tower, and *b* the elevator fitted therein. The elevator shown in the drawings is on the "bucket" principle, but it will be obvious that other kinds of elevators may be employed. It is worked from the outside by a pulley b^1 driven by a belt. *c*, c^1 represent two of the fixed perforated inclined planes or baffle plates over and through which the lime is discharged from the elevator *b*; *d* represents the inclined bottom of the tower and *e* a chamber in communication with the tower *a* by the opening *f*. *g* represents a hinged chute for the discharge of the finished powder, such chute being operated by the lever *h* outside the apparatus. *i* is the gas-tight feeding hopper of the tower *a*; *j*, *j* manhole doors; *l* the inlet for the gas, and *k* the outlet for the same. *m*, *m* represent the condenser or cooling apparatus fixed outside the tower *a*, which is advantageously enclosed in a water trough m^1. p^1 is a door for emptying the tower *a* when required.

The operation is as follows:—The lime or other material is fed into the tower through the hopper *i*, and the gas enters through the inlet *l*. The elevator *b* being set in motion, the lime will be continuously raised from the bottom of the tower and delivered on to the upper perforated baffle plate *c*, from and through which it falls on to the plate or plates c^1 below, and this is repeated until the lime has taken up and thoroughly absorbed a sufficient quantity of the chlorine or other gas in the tower. When the lime or other material has become thoroughly incorporated with the gas it is discharged by means of the hinged chute *g* (which is moved into the position shown in Fig. 1 of the drawings above the baffle plate *c*), into the chamber *e*, from which it can be withdrawn through the discharge door *n*. The hinged chute *g* is moved up out of the way into the position indicated by the dotted lines, except when the powder is to be discharged. The gas will be kept cool by passing through the condenser entering through the pipes *o*, *o*, and passing back into the tower through the pipe *p*.

TESTS OF SULPHITE PULP FOR MOISTURE.—A great deal of controversy is still going on in Germany between makers and consumers of sulphite pulp about the percentage of the moisture in certain parcels. If the pulp were sent out uniformly bone dry this would be a simple enough matter. Out of every hundred bales perhaps five bales need be tested, and the result would be convincing. As it is most makers leave from 5 to 15 per cent. moisture in the pulp, because they consider this necessary to give the quality greater softness and elasticity. The makers have various ways of testing the pulp, but they all agree in drawing samples from every bale and taking the average, which by most buyers is considered sufficient, the more so when they have to deal with makers who have given them sufficient proof that they know how to give satisfaction and whose honesty is well recognised. The trouble and time necessary for checking their calculations therefore is generally saved. But when a buyer wants to find fault it is easy for him in all cases to pick out samples either from a very wet bale or from a number of bales which he suspects, while extra dry bales are left alone. Such tests cannot agree with those of the maker, who in such cases generally goes to arbitration, and marks the buyer for future transactions.

ALLEGED POLLUTION BY PAPERMAKERS.

A special meeting of the Mersey and Irwell Joint Committee was held on Monday for the purpose of considering the cases of fourteen manufacturers upon whom notices of alleged river pollution had been served under part 3, section 6, of the Mersey and Irwell Joint Committee Act, 1892, and the case of eight other firms who had appeared before Committee on a previous occasion, and whose cases had been adjourned. Alderman Joseph Thompson occupied the chair. All the new cases dealt with were those of papermakers' works.

A letter was read from Sir Henry Roscoe, who was unable to be present. Sir Henry said: "I have not only seen and approved the analysis of the papermakers' effluents made by Mr. Scudder, but have looked at the samples themselves. With only one or two exceptions the whole of these are distinctly polluting liquids, and their entrance into the streams in this condition must be stopped. In many cases the greater part of the very considerable sediment consists of vegetable fibre (paper pulp) in a very fine state of division. It is quite possible, as I know from experience, to prevent almost entirely, by proper subsidence, aided by chemical precipitation, such solid matter passing into the streams. I therefore consider that it is absolutely necessary in the case of the papermakers on the stream to insist first on efficient tankage and suitable chemical precipitation, and second, that in the case of those works where soda is used for disintegrating the fibre, the liquors from the boiling pans, together with at least the first wash water, shall be evaporated and calcined, whereby the alkali is regained, and river pollution from this source prevented. It may be well to remind the committee that both these requirements are carried out very perfectly at certain works on other streams, and therefore it is clear that these means may properly be insisted on."

Members or representatives of the following firms appeared, and three months were allowed them in which to construct the necessary works and purify the effluent:—Messrs. Chadwick and Taylor, Ordsal-lane, Salford, J. W. Marshall and Co., Springfield Works, Bolton; C. Turner and Co., Bolton; T. Wilkinson, Lomax Bank, Little Lever; the Ramsbottom Paper Mill Co., Ramsbottom; Duxbury, Yates and Co., Heap Bridge, near Bury; John Wild and Sons, Radcliffe; Bibby and Baron, Limited, New Bridge Mills; W. Broadbent and Sons, Little Lever, Bolton; Grove Mill Paper Mill Co., New Mills, Cheshire; and Lancaster, Ferguson and Co., Harden Mill, Denton. The case of the Bury Papermaking Co., Ltd., Gigg Mills, Bury, was adjourned until December 4th.

Representatives of the East Lancashire Paper Mill Co., Radcliffe, attended, and were informed that on one occasion the effluent turned out by them was a bad one. The representatives assured the committee that the pollution of the effluent was due to an oversight, and the firm was warned against such oversights in future.

Mr. J. Hargreaves, paper mills, Collyhurst, to whom a notice had been sent, did not appear, and after hearing the analysis of the sample read, the committee ordered that application be made to the Local Government Board for permission to prosecute.

Persia.—A Consular report recently issued shows that paper was imported into Northern Khorasan, *via* Bombay, Bander Abbas, Kirman (or Yezd), during the year 1892-3 to the amount of 9,962 tumans (£2,549); books 5,600 tumans (£1,436). Paper was imported into Northern Khorasan from Russian territories to the amount of 11,194 tumans (£2,870). Paper was exported from Meshed to Afghanistan to the value of 100 tumans, or £26.

Rating of Machinery.—The interest in the rating of machinery seems to be moving from the House of Commons to the Law Courts. The Machinery Users' Association are advised that the time is ripe for obtaining a legal decision entirely favourable to their contention as to the interpretation of the Tyne Boiler judgment. Two appeals in which the expert advisers of the Association were engaged were contested at the recent Quarter Sessions. At Durham the Ford Paper Works appealed against a large increase in the valuation of their mills by the Sunderland Union Assessment Committee which professedly included machinery. This case was made specially interesting by the statement of Mr. Alderman Bell, the chairman of the Assessment Committee, that it was a test case, and if successful would mean that all the machinery in the borough could on appeal by the owners be relieved from taxation. Mr. Edward Boyle, of the South Eastern Circuit, was specially retained to lead for the appellants. Mr. Lawson Walton, Q.C., M.P., who appeared for the respondents, opened the case, but after a hearing lasting till late in the afternoon, the Bench stopped the case, after only a few witnesses had been called for the appellants, and allowed the appeal with costs. The other case was heard at the Sheffield Sessions, before the Recorder, Mr. Frank Lockwood, Q.C., M.P., being an appeal brought by Messrs. James Fairbrother and Co., of the Crown Steel and Wire Mills, and the question was raised as to how the machinery was to be taken into account in arriving at the gross value. Mr. Edward Boyle appeared here also for the appellants, and Mr. Hugo Young for the respondent. The case lasted the whole day, and at the close the Recorder reserved his decision. The Association is engaged in several other cases entered for Quarter Sessions at Aylesbury, Burton and Preston, and is also engaged in contesting increased assessments at Tiverton, Newcastle, Gateshead, Middlesboro' and elsewhere, and the committee are determined to resist attempts to rate machinery wherever made.

THE CHICAGO EXHIBITION.

The following list of awards is supplementary to that published in our last issue. The nature of the distinction has not at present been divulged:—

Group 89, Paper, Paper Goods, &c.

UNITED STATES.

American Paper Pail and Box Company, New York. Folding paper boxes.
Z. and W. M. Crane, Dalton, Mass. Writing paper; general exhibit; pasted boards.
Crosby Paper Company, Marion, Ind. Pulp-lined strawboard.
Crane and Co., Dalton, Mass. Note paper; bond paper; parchment paper.
Crane Brothers, Westfield, Mass. Linen paper; writing paper; ledger paper.
Denver Paper Mills, Denver, Col. Material for manufacturing paper.
Hurlburt Paper Manufacturing Company, South Lee, Mass. Writing paper in packages and boxes.
National Wall Paper Company, New York. Wall papers; Lincrusta Walton.
Paterson Parchment Paper Company, Passaic, N.J. Vegetable parchment paper.
Standard Paint Company, New York. Insulating; waterproof papers.
Western Paper Manufacturing Company, Dayton, Ohio. Roll paper.
Western Paper Bag Company, Batavia, Ill. Paper bags; paper in rolls.
Whiting Paper Company, Holyoke, Mass. Bond paper; envelopes and fine folded writing paper; bristol board.
Scott Paper Company, Philadelphia, Pa. Toilet paper.
Union Bag and Paper Company, Chicago, Ill. Automatic opening paper bags.
Fr. Beck and Co., New York. Wall papers.
Robert Graves and Co., New York. Wall paper.
Nevius and Haviland, New York, Wall paper.
H. Bartholomae, New York. Wall paper.
Warren, Fuller and Co., New York. Wall paper.
Tiffany and Co., New York. Fine stationery, writing paper, cards.

ITALY.

Reali Mills, Venice. Paper.
Pietro Milliani, Fabriano. Paper of all descriptions.

MEXICO.

Juan Benfield, City of Mexico. Cloth and filigree paper; cardboard.
Explorador y Georgnapia Com., Jalapa. Paper.
Emanuel Gutierrez Brothers, La Constancia. Cotton paper.
Manuel Oilman, Puebla. Blotters, paper holders.
San Rafael Fabrica, Chalco. Cardboard, paper.
José Ramos Sanchez, City of Mexico. Paper, cardboard.

JAPAN.

S. Tsukamoto, Okoyama. Paper.
T. Tamguchi, Kioto. Paper napkins.
Shidzuoka Leishi, Kaisha. Paper.
S. Iketai, Shizuka. Paper.
G. Yoshii, Kokichii. Paper.
Ichimatsu Oda, Osaka. Paper trunks imitating leather.
Printing and Engraving Bureau, Osaka. Paper (mark 17); paper (mark D); paper (mark G); Kiotsu paper, with watermark of Minister of Home Affairs and late Prime Minister; paper, with watermark.
Gouzaburo Yamaguchi, Nigata Prefecture. Japanese paper.
Bureau of Industry and Commerce, Tokio. Collection of envelopes, note paper, &c.
T. Haiada, Tokushima. Copying paper.
W. Haiada, Tokushima. Paper.
H. Osaka, Takushima. Paper.
B. Takumi, Tokushima. Copying paper.
K. Amenori, Osaka. Paper lanterns.
N. Asaka, Hiogo. Paper made of Edgeworthia papyrifera.
Banseisha, Saga. Paper.
S. Bessho, Nirja. Paper ware.
Tugiseishi, Tokio. Paper and paper material.
G. Goto, Gifu. Paper.
Idorgang Seishi Shia, Tokio. Paper.
Denguise Inonge, Kouchiken. Oil paper.
S. Ito, Tokio. Wall paper, imitation leather.
Tosa Shigio, Kiokai, Kochi. Paper.
M. Mizoda, Tokio. Wall paper.
K. Mauki, Tokio. Papier Maché.
E. Matsuhisa, Gifu. Paper.
Y. Mashiba, Hiroshima. Paper ware.
G. Nakamura, Nagoya. Paper goods.
A. Narita, Tokio. Lacquered paper ware.
N. Akamiya, Tokio. Paper umbrellas.
T. Sato, Tokio. Papers.
T. Suzuki, Nagoya. Paper goods, paper.
T. Tone, Tokio. Paper.
S. Takei, Gifu. Paper napkins, copying paper.
N. Teshikawara, Gifu. Paper ware.
K. Utsumie, Hiogo. Paper made of Edgeworthia papyrifera.
N. Nakamie, Hiogo. Paper and leather boxes.
T. Yasuda, Hiogo. Copying paper, paper napkins.
Yamakaseiank Naisha, Kumamoti. Paper umbrellas.
J. Abe, Osaka. Paper; wood fibre,
K. Tusayasu, Tottori. Paper.
M. Tukunishi, Nawa. Paper.
T. Tukunishi, Nawa. Paper.
T. Hagihara, Shizuka. Paper napkins.
J. Hinobo, Fukui. Paper.
I. Ikigaya, Shizuska. Material of paper.
L. Kwaisha, Shizuska. Tissue Paper.
T. Kubato, Shizuska. Blank visiting cards.
W. Kawato, Tottori. Paper.
Y. Konda, Kyago. Bleached Edgeworthia papyrifera.
K. Nishio, Tottori. Paper.
G. Ota, Shizuska. "Tikuki" paper.
O. Kamotoseishosha, Fukui. Paper.
Sanko Sha, Shizuska. "Tikuki" paper.
Shoshisha, Shizuska. "Tikuki" paper.
S. Shinedzu, Tottori. Paper.
Shuyosha, Fukui. Paper.
M. Takase, Shizuska. Tisuki paper.
K. Uchiyama, Shizusha. "Tengugio" paper.
T. Yoshioka, Tottori. Paper umbrellas.
Yoshuioshigio, Nawa. Paper.
Abe Paper Factory, Osaka. Japanese papers.

729

WHO'S WHO?

THE PERSONNEL OF THE PAPER, STATIONERY, PRINTING AND ALLIED TRADES.

Everyone must have observed that of late there has been a remarkable change in the style of a very large proportion of the oldest and largest paper, stationery, and printing concerns. The word "Limited" has become quite familiar as an integral part of their nomenclature. This affix was, as we all know, made obligatory by the provisions of "The Companies Act" (25 and 26 Vict. c. 89), which was passed in 1862. Our own Legislature, foreseeing the inconveniences which might be caused by the names of the acting responsible members of a firm not being given, provided for compulsory publication of the names of the shareholders in such companies. These returns are, as a rule, accurately and regularly made up and issued. But they are in a form which to the great majority of the public is quite unavailable. Not one person in a thousand knows "Who's Who" in a concern of even general repute. Yet for many reasons, and on divers occasions it is desirable to know the personnel of the company in question. This information we are about to supply. We shall do it from official and authentic data, and in no merely prying spirit. No reflection on the stability of any firm will be implied. The names of the parties constituting it will be given, and their shares in te capital stated, so far as official documents disclose them. The information we think will be both useful and interesting. Readers will know whom they have to deal with when transacting business with a limited liability company, and a contribution will be made to current trade history which the future annalist may greatly appreciate.

ST. NEOTS PAPER MILL CO.

In view of the changes about to be made in connection with St. Neots Mill, it may not be out of place to refer to the data furnished in the official returns. The particulars of registration, dated February, 1888, give prominence to gas manufacture as one of the objects of the company. According to the articles of association, all things needful were to be done for carrying out a "paper," "gas," "coal" and "electrical" programme, such as constructing works, buying and taking on lease premises and lands, &c. St. Neots Mill, when in the occupation of Messrs. Towgood Bros., had an excellent reputation for its productions. However, since the mill has been worked as a limited liability concern the even tenor of its ways, owing to various causes, has been frequently interrupted. At the date of registration the nominal capital of the company was £30,000, divided into 6,000 shares of £5 each. Now there are new shares and debentures. The first summary of the capital and shares, dated May 2, 1888, showed that 6,000 shares had been taken up, and there had been called up on each of these shares £2 15s., making a total of £16,500, the total amount of calls received, including payments on application and allotment, was put down at £15,949. and the calls unpaid amounted to £551. The returns for 1889, 1890, 1891, and 1892 (June 24th) state that 6,000 shares were still held, whilst the amount of the call on each share had been increased to £3 15s., the total amount received being £22,500. There are some 286 shareholders in the company, the principal holdings being as follows:—

Executors of F. C. Chapman, St. Neots, bank manager ...	209
C. R. Wade Gery, St. Neots, solicitor ...	140
J. McNish, St. Neots, brewer and miller ...	362
Joseph Wilcox, New-street, St. Neots, gentleman ...	295
J. Wilcox, 16, St. Helen's-place, London, merchant	140
A. C. McNish, St. Neots, brewer ...	50
Mary Paine, Neotsbury, Laton-road, Hastings ...	100
James Paine, Eynsbury House, St. Neots, gentleman	200
R. C. Meade, The Vicarage, St. Neots, clerk in holy orders ...	120
Sarah Leng, King's Head Inn, St. Neots ...	25
W. Emery, Bank, St. Neots, bank manager ...	104
W.H. Browning, 28, Grove-place, St. Cuthberts, Beds.	116
D. R. Thomson, St. Neots, bookseller ...	100
C. Fox, Avenue-road, St. Neots, schoolmaster ...	40
H. Harvey, Eynsbury, St. Neots, parchment manufacturer ...	45
G. Taylor, Eaton Socon, St. Neots, gentleman ...	100
A. W. Atkinson, St. Neots, merchant ...	21
W. Woolard, St. Neots, station master...	34
M. Gray, Bedford-street, St. Neots, clerk ...	26
A. C. Turner, Priory, St. Neots, surgeon ...	40
Jordan and Addington, St. Neots, merchants ...	40
Thos. Harwood White, Eynesbury, gentleman ...	50
J. Whitbread, St. Mary-street, Eynesbury, tailor ...	74
A. Pentelow, Papworth, St. Agnes; W. R. Giddings, Offord D'Arcy; E. Pentelow, News-st., St. Neots — Executors of gentlemen	60
W. Edwards, Luke-street, Eynsbury, baker ...	47
J. Lenton, Eynesbury, gentleman ...	50
G. Gray, Cambridge street, St. Neots, clerk...	46
W. Howard, Eaton Socon, smith ...	45
C. E. Malden, St. Neots, brewer...	50
F. Day, Priory, St. Neots, brewer ...	100
J. Basford, 8, Furnival's-inn, Holborn, journalist ...	30
H. Ackwich, Wintringham, St. Neots, farmer ...	100
W. Bower, Old Hall, St. Neots, farmer ...	200
Helen Paine, Upper Norwood, S.W. ...	30
R. D. Cooper, New-street, St. Neots ...	66
H. Lawrie, Avenue-road, St. Neots ...	80
Mary J. Skelton, Huntington-street, St. Neots, widow ...	80
J. Kirby, 52, Market-place, Leicester ...	30
Mrs. Alf. Papworth, Cockfield, Sudbury, Suffolk ...	207
W. F. Hide, St. Neots ...	30
Emily A. Day, Priory, St. Neots...	30
P. E. Tillard, Holmes, Godmanchester ...	80
Charles Sprigg, Gt. Barford ...	40
Sarah Strangward, St. Neots ...	60
G. Cranfield, Southoe, Huntingdon ...	40
Arthur O. Glossop, Sueyd Point, Bristol ...	50
J. Haynes, Stonely, St. Neots ...	30
G. Edey and others, New-street. St. Neots ...	40
Harriet S. Wade Gray, Fernhill, West Malvern ...	100
Lavina Lyon, 223, High-street, Exeter, Devon ...	30
H. C. Geldart, Huntingdon ...	50
Frederick Hide, Bank-street, Sevenoaks ...	45
James Murray, 103, High-street, Deptford ...	30
Mary Achurch, East-street, St. Neots ...	26
G. R. Doughty, Priory Cottages, St. Neots ...	50
C. Hull, Kimbolton, Hunts ...	50
Isaac Hall, Eynesbury, St. Neots, manager ...	79
Harriet Goodgames, Eynesbury, Hunts ...	100
Sarah E. Emery, The Bank, St. Neots...	100

In addition to the above there are 228 persons holding from 1 to 20 shares each.

—o—

LONDON & COUNTIES WASTE PAPER COMPANY, LTD.

INCORPORATED CAPITAL ...	£21,000
PAID-UP CAPITAL	570

Registered on the 16th November, 1892, with a nominal capital of £21,000 divided into 600 preference shares of £10, and 1,500 ordinary shares of £10. The objects of its incorporation were to enter into and carry into effect, with or without modification, an agreement between Frank Day and the company, and to carry on, as principals or agents, in England or elsewhere, the trade or businesses of paper stock merchants, and rag. rope and metal merchants, and for any of the purposes aforesaid; to acquire lands or any property, and machinery and plant, also patent rights and privileges. Also to carry on the business of carriers, forwarding agents, warehousemen, wharfingers, shipowners, charterers of ships, shippers, freight contractors, lightermen, and any other business which may conveniently be carried on in conjunction with any of the businesses aforesaid, or which may be extended, to be carried on for the purpose of developing and carrying on the business purchased by the company.

The names of the first signatories to the articles of association were :—J. W. Porteous, 18, Wilson-street, Poplar, E., merchant's clerk, 1 ; H. Beston, 11, Vincent-terrace, Islington, N., shipowner, 1 ; J. Bennett, 32, Guildford-street, Russell-square, W.C., marble merchant, 1 ; A. G. Culliford, 37, Walbrook, E.C., wine and spirit merchant, 1 : C. H. Keene, 13, Pensbridge-crescent, W., 1 ; J. T. Cropton, 37, Ulysses-road, Hampstead, accountant, 1 ; H. D. Milner, 160, Kennington Park-road, S.E., secretary to a public company, 1.

The state of the company upon the 31st August last, according to the summary of capital and shares filed on that date, was as follows :—Shares taken up, 50 preference and seven ordinary ; called up on each of the 50 preference shares, £10, total £500 ; called up on each of the seven ordinary shares, £10, total £70 ; making a complete total amount received of £570.

The names of the shareholders are those of the seven contributories to the articles of association, with a holding of one ordinary share each, together with the name of J. Halliday, of 2, Nelson-square, Blackfriars-road, S.E., rag merchant, who is credited with holding the 50 preference shares.

LAST MONTH'S PAPER TRADE.

IMPORTS, RE-EXPORTS, AND EXPORTS.

TOTAL IMPORTS.

Printings and Writings	1893	36,833 cwts	£40,078
	1892	37,315 ,,	44,297
	1891	25,900 ,,	31,971
Other Kinds	1893	212,288 cwts	£159,610
	1892	249,132 ,,	184,744
	1891	211,957 ,,	162,373

From GERMANY.

Printings and Writings	1893	6,517 cwts	£6,487
	1892	11,649 ,,	14,795
	1891	7,421 ,,	8,703
Other Kinds	1893	46,374 cwts	£39,525
	1892	52,983 ,,	50,807
	1891	51,883 ,,	42,704

From BELGIUM.

Printings and Writings	1893	4,240 cwts	£5,017
	1892	6,379 ,,	8,188
	1891	7,095 ,,	9,437
Other Kinds	1893	14,196 cwts	£20,988
	1892	11,419 ,,	18,471
	1891	12,340 ,,	17,551

From HOLLAND.

Printings and Writings	1893	5,035 cwts	£7,082
	1892	2,666 ,,	3,795
	1891	1,178 ,,	1,653
Other Kinds	1893	85,433 cwts	£42,758
	1892	115,056 ,,	54,412
	1891	81,719 ,,	42,575

From SWEDEN.

Printings and Writings	1893	10,827 cwts	£10,959
	1892	9,507 ,,	9,440
	1891	7,277 ,,	7,668

("Other Kinds" are not tabulated).

From FRANCE.

Other Kinds	1893	2,683 cwts	£6,499
	1892	2,592 ,,	6,925
	1891	2,161 ,,	6,859

From OTHER COUNTRIES.

Printings and Writings	1893	10,214 cwts	£10,533
	1892	7,114 ,,	8,079
	1891	2,929 ,,	4,510
Other Kinds	1893	63,602 cwts	£49,840
	1892	67,082 ,,	54,129
	1891	63,854 ,,	52,692

TOTAL RE-EXPORTS.

Printings and Writings	1893	1,254 cwts	£1,531
	1892	1,454 ,,	3,233
	1891	1,538 ,,	1,787
Other Kinds	1893	4,774 cwts	£4,670
	1892	6,936 ,,	5,401
	1891	10,340 ,,	7,088

TOTAL EXPORTS.

Printings and Writings	1893	57,378 cwts	£91,183
	1892	54,189 ,,	91,222
	1891	60,009 ,,	105,099
Other Kinds	1893	16,526 cwts	£24,865
	1892	16,166 ,,	25,807
	1891	20,068 ,,	32,572

To FRANCE.

Printings and Writings	1893	3,953 cwts	£7,262
	1892	2,961 ,,	6,555
	1891	3,475 ,,	6,213
Other Kinds	1893	841 cwts	£4,273
	1892	6875 ,,	3,485
	1891	1,121 ,,	4,659

To the UNITED STATES.

Printings and Writings	1893	815 cwts	£2,674
	1892	979 ,,	2,857
	1891	926 ,,	3,155
Other Kinds	1893	262 cwts	£913
	1892	905 ,,	2,896
	1891	906 ,,	3,419

WORLD'S PAPER TRADE REVIEW OFFICE, 58, SHOE LANE, LONDON, E.C.

TRADE NOTES.

TOVIL PAPER MILLS.—During the past week nearly the whole of the machinery at the above mills has been carted away. Whether the mills, which found employment for 300 persons, will ever again be opened for the manufacture of paper, is very doubtful. There is no truth in the rumour that the premises have been bought by Messrs. Lloyd and Company.

THE CLYDE PAPER CO. recently put in two boilers supplied by the well-known firm of Messrs. Penman and Co., Glasgow, who also supplied three boilers to the same mill about 18 months ago. They are all of one size, viz., 30-ft. long by 8-ft. diameter, and constructed on the duplex style, *i.e.*, with two furnaces joining a large back flue behind the fire bridge, which flue is fitted with 15 water circulating tubes. The plates are of Siemen's mild steel, and the boilers are constructed to stand a daily working pressure of 100 lbs. per square inch.

A CLAIM AGAINST A PAPERMAKER.—The case of Lord Balfour of Burleigh v. Weir, heard before Lord Low, in the Court of Session (Edinburgh), was an action by Lord Balfour of Burleigh against James Alexander Weir, papermaker, Forth Paper Mills, near Alloa, for payment of £500 casualty of one half-year's rent of the farm of Kilbagie, Clackmannanshire. The defender tenders £25 as the amount exigible. The case was sent to the Procedure Roll. Counsel for the pursuer—Mr. C. N. Johnston. Agents—W. and J. Cook, W.S. Counsel for the defender—Mr. Strachan. Agents—T. F. Weir and Robertson, S.S.C.

PROSECUTION UNDER THE TRADES UNION ACT.—At the Otley Police Court, on Friday last, Thomas Hurst, papermaker, of Ipswich, was charged, on the information of Alfred Austin, of Otley, with obtaining 12s. by false pretences at Otley on the 15th September. Mr. Gledstone, who prosecuted, said he appeared on behalf of the National Union of Papermill Workers, which was a trade's union society registered under the Trades Union Act, to prosecute this man for obtaining 12s. from the society under false pretences. It was one of the rules of the society that its members should be allowed so much per week during the time they were out of work, or when the mill at which they worked had to stop from lack of coal or other causes. When such a thing occurred a member had to get a certificate from the collector or foreman of the mill, and on this authority he was allowed so much per week during the time the mill was stopped. The prisoner had been working at Ipswich paper mill, and on the 16th of September he sent a certificate signed "J. H. Morris," the foreman of the mill, to the branch secretary at Otley, stating that in consequence of waiting for coal he had been out of work from the 25th of August to the 11th September. Prior to this Mr. Morris had signed certificates for the prisoner, and on the strength of this one, 12s. was sent to him. Inquiries were, however, made, and as a matter of fact it was found that the prisoner during the week ended September 11th, had worked 5¾ days, and that he had forged Mr. Morris's signature. Their worships had power to deal with the case by inflicting a penalty not exceeding £20. The costs incurred amounted to £7 5s. 7d., and as the society did not wish to unduly press the case they would be satisfied if the prisoner was fined and ordered to pay the costs. The prisoner having pleaded guilty to the charge, Mr. Barret (for the defence) said the prisoner had hitherto borne a good character, and had never been in trouble before. He had worked in paper mills all his life, and was formerly employed by Mr. Garnett. The mill at Ipswich was stopped on the dates named, and, although the prisoner was working that week, he was not at his regular trade, and thought that he was entitled to this 12s. As the society did not press the case he asked their worships not to inflict a heavy penalty, especially seeing that the costs were so very heavy. The Bench imposed a fine of 40s. and the costs.

MCNEILL'S PULP REGULATOR.—A description and illustration of this invention appeared in our last issue. We omitted to mention, however, that the sole makers are Messrs. James Milne and Son, Limited, Milton House Works, Edinburgh.

THE NEW LORD MAYOR.—On Wednesday, according to ancient custom and statute, the new Lord Mayor of the City of London, Alderman George Robert Tyler, was formally admitted into office at Guildhall. Before the ceremony of installation the outgoing Lord Mayor (Sir Stuart Knill) and the new Lord Mayor entertained at luncheon at the Mansion-house the Aldermen, the Recorder, the Sheriffs, and the high officers of the Corporation, together with the Masters, Wardens, and Courts of the Goldsmiths', Stationers', Plumbers', and Gold and Silver Wyre Drawers' Companies, to which they belong. The Lord Mayor, in proposing the health of his successor, referred to him as one whose intention it was to carry out the rights and privileges of the City, and in wishing him strength and happiness to discharge his arduous duties, he rejoiced that the mantle of chief magistrate fell upon one who was highly respected by all and would certainly make an excellent Lord Mayor. In the show on the following day was a car representing the visit of King Edward IV. to the Caxton Printing Press.

THE directors of Alsing and Co. (Limited) recommend a dividend of 10 per cent. per annum, tax free, for the year ended September 30th last, which is the uniform rate that has been paid since incorporation.

RAGS were exported from Cherbourg (France) in 1892 to the extent of 112 tons.

PRESSSPAHNFABRIK UNTERSACHSENFELD ACTIEN GESELLSCHAFT VORMALS M. HELLINGER.—The report for 1892-93 states that the improvement in the business was only temporary, because unsatisfactory customs and commercial treaties paralysed a natural expansion. In spite of these difficulties the last mortgage of M100,000 has been paid off. The land tenant has bought the agricultural inventory. Other accounts are but slightly changed, and creditors are next to none. After writing off M33,000 a clear profit of M66,950 remains, which is to be divided as follows: Transfer to reserve fund 5 per cent., (M3,347); to profit and loss account, M3,372; bonuses to committee of inspection and directors, M6,435; other bonuses, M3,500; 5 per cent. on share capital of M1,000,000 (M50,000); balance carried forward, M295.

HOLZSCHLEIFEREI UND HOLZPAPPEN FABRIK, LICHTENBERG.—According to the balance sheet issued on 30th June, 1893, this company paid M1,500 = 2 per cent. dividend —for 1891-92. This year the net profit was M1,077 on a share capital of M75,000.

COESLINER PAPIERFABRIK ACTIEN GESELLSCHAFT IN COESLIN. — Herr Alexander Tucholsky has retired from the board of directors, and Herr Fritz Stehle is now authorised to sign alone for the company.

NEUSSER PAPIER AND PERGAMENT FABRIK IN NEUSS.—On a share capital of M500,000 a profit of M167,374 has been made, of which M50,000 are placed into reserve, M1,956 written off for special purposes, M15,418 bonuses given, and M100,000 used as dividend, viz., M100 respectively, M200 for the share.

EUGEN DIETZ, ENGINEERING WORKS IN BERLIN,—Herr Louis Grunauer, the owner of these works, has admitted as partners the two civil engineers, Herren Georg Grunauer and Hugo Grunauer.

JOHANN HINTERSEBERS' ERBEN, papermakers in Imst in the Tyrol have gone into voluntary liquidation.

STEYRERMUHL PAPIERFABRIK UND VERLAGS GESELLSCHAFT.—In place of the late Doctor Max Franzos, Herr Alois Edler von Marquet, of Vienna has been elected as a member of the board of directors with powers of signing for the company.

GRANSHOLMS PAPPERSBRUK has put up a new paper machine which will commence work during this month.

HOLZSCHLEIFEREI UND HOLZPAPPEN FABRIK NAUNDORF.—The balance of June 30th, 1893, shows a dividend of 2 per cent. for 1891-92 on M50,000 share capital, M1,000 bonuses to directors, and a loss of M674 through various writings off.

DRESDENER PAPIERFABRIK.—The last year shows the highest production amounting to 2,200 tons, which is 84 tons more than the previous year. The amount realised, however, is M9,400 less. The gross profits came to M231,561. Net profits were M184,561, or M3,474 more than in the previous year. This satisfactory result is caused by increased production of more remunerative sorts, cheaper rags and economies in the management. Unfortunately business in general has not improved, and still suffers from excessive competition. After writing off bonuses to directors and staff with M22,421, and placing into reserve M80,000, and M2,000 to the pensions fund, a dividend of 7 per cent. will be declared on the share capital of M834,000. A balance of M1,759 is carried forward.

HERREN PAUL NEEF AND WILHELM HORZ have started lace paper works at Degerloch, under the firm of J. Neef and Co.

WURTTEMBERG CHAMBER OF COMMERCE.—In an annual report just published by this chamber, a wire sieve maker in Reutlingen describes the position of business as bad, sales difficult, prices going down, while raw and auxiliary materials remain stationary. In consequence of these various causes a restriction of the working hours has taken place. The new treaties of commerce have worked most unsatisfactorily. Biberach makers of the same article, who export to Belgium, Sweden, Norway, Finland, Russia, Switzerland and Austria consider the sales about the same as before, but prices are fallen, and since the passing of the new customs treaty with Austria exportation to that country has ceased. The united workshops of the Reutlingen Bruderhaus, making all kinds of machinery for paper mills, cranes, transmissions, colouring machines, calenders, perforating machines, &c., complain as in the previous year that foreign duties, particularly in Russia, France, and Austria, make business almost impossible. The sales remained almost unchanged, but prices made profits next to impossible. The higher duty in France and Austria makes itself greatly felt, there are many enquiries, but they very rarely lead to business. A maker of paper mill machinery and petroleum motors in Ravensburg reports very unsatisfactory business. Sales are more difficult and prices are bad, particularly out of Germany, where business is decreasing. Raw materials, however, have not become cheaper. The number of workmen has been reduced. The management of the infirmary and pension funds and the old age insurance leaves much to be desired, and ought to be more simplified in the interest of the manufacturers.

HERR W. TSCHUCK has not bought, but only rented, the Absamer Papierfabrik, which belongs to Herren Franz Taurer and Joh Ch. Fleischhacker.

RHEINISCHE ACTIEN GESELLSCHAFT FUR PAPIER FABRICATION in Neuss, proposes to pay a dividend of 5 per cent. for the year 1891-92.

THE Manufacturers' Paper Company has just closed a contract with the Chicago *News* to supply that publication with all its paper for the next three years.

THE affairs of the Eau Claire Pulp and Paper Company, Eau Claire, Wis., whose paid-up capital stock is $100,000, have been placed in the hands of a receiver. The action was brought by Mr. W. A. Rust, who held a note for $3,000, dated October 7th, and payable one day after that date, and on which judgment had been confessed. Complainant alleges the plant is worth $50,000, and material on hand $10,000; that various sums, the amount unknown, are due from debtors of the company in various States, and that the company owes $25,000. The company's mills were shut down some time ago, the warehouse being full and collections slow.

A CORRESPONDENT to the New York *Paper Trade Journal* comments upon the system of making contracts for the sale of paper, and asserts that in no other manufacturing business has the manufacture sunk so low as to accept such degrading terms. To substantiate his arguments, he publishes a memorandum of specifications, and a sample of settlement for paper used under contract. Further he points out that at the last meeting, in Saratoga, of the Papermakers' Association, the president, Hon. Warner Miller, stated that the makers of news had been running their mills as eleemosynary institutions, for the sole benefit of the consumers.

THE paper trade in the United States still remains in an unsatisfactory condition. Mills are running in a spasmodic way, shutting down for a time and starting up when sufficient orders have been accumulated. In this way some make three or four days a week, while some others more fortunately situated are doing better. Two Western mills, one making news and the other book and manilla, are reported in trouble. Two New York city paper staining establishments were burned out recently, and among the articles destroyed was a large quantity of paper. News mills are busy for the most part, but some paper is being sold at low figures. There is no particular change in writings, and manufacturers are not crowding the market at any material concession in values.

PAPER was exported from New York, according to the latest weekly list to hand, as follows :—

B. W. Indies ...	572 packages	B. Guiana ...	100 packages
London ...	104 cases	Liverpool ...	10 cases
Australasia ...	303 packages		

Printed and Published ***EVERY FRIDAY***

AT 58, SHOE LANE, LONDON, E.C.,

By W. JOHN STONHILL.

ESTABLISHED 1878.

FRIDAY, NOVEMBER 10, 1893.

THE BOARD OF TRADE RETURNS dealing with the importation and exportation of paper show a decreased business last month compared with the same period in 1892. The respective values were as follows:—

	IMPORTS.	RE-EXPORTS.	EXPORTS.
Oct., 1892	£229,041	£8,634	£117,029
,, 1893	199,688	6,209	116,048

There was a falling off in the imports of printings and writings to the value of £4,219, and other kinds £25,134. Re-exports decreased £1,702 and £731 respectively. A comparison of the exports of printings and writings show a diminution of £39 only, and £942 in other kinds.

FRENCH makers of tissues wish to curtail production. We recently recorded their decision to combine, but the idea is only to shut down for twelve hours on Sundays. A fine of 500 francs will be imposed upon any firm breaking the arrangement, and if the offence is repeated, a fine of 1,000 francs will be imposed. Sunday rest is a very mild restriction after all, in most countries 18 to 24 hours is generally considered the minimum.

LANCASHIRE papermakers, according to a Manchester daily paper, have a grievance against the Scandinavian Wood Pulp Makers' Association. It was alleged that the Association had decided to advance prices for deliveries of wood pulp during the forthcoming year. We may point out that no recent resolution has been passed for that purpose. The last meeting was held at Gothenburg, when, in view of the growing demand for mechanical wood pulp and the possibility of small supplies, the majority of the members expressed a desire not to further limit the output at the mills, feeling convinced that such a proceeding would not have an unfavourable influence upon prices; therefore, limitation of output for this year was suspended. At the same meeting the following prices for pine pulp were formulated: Moist white, kr.42 per ton; moist brown, kr. 42; dry white, kr. 85 to kr. 90; and dry brown, kr. 85 to 90, nett f.o.b. port of shipment. These prices are equivalent to £2 17s. 6d. for moist, and £5 17s. 6d. for dry c.i.f. England. As far as the Association is concerned the policy adopted seems to be a moderate one, although individual members may, however, seek to obtain higher prices on the ground of a scarcity of pulp.

CONFIRMING our remarks on the Scandinavian wood pulp market in our last issue, a correspondent writes:—"The recent comparison of official statistics published in the *World's Paper Trade Review*, showing less pulp from Norway than other countries, must be attributed to the fact that Scandinavia has not been able to supply the demands of Great Britain owing to other countries taking so much of its product. Consequently British buyers have had to turn to America, and in some cases have had to pay comparatively higher prices." Our correspondent also points out that the "increased production in Scandinavia will be readily taken up by buyers in this country, and that it will be a very difficult matter for American makers to supplant Norwegian manufacturers, especially when freights are higher."

A NOTEWORTHY feature in connection with the Chicago Exhibition was the extensive show made by Japanese papermakers. There were more exhibits from that country than any other; indeed the Japanese were in advance of the United States. No doubt this enterprise will have a beneficial influence in regard to Japanese paper and paper articles; at the same time it is rather surprising that American papermakers did not make a better show.

SEVERAL disturbing elements seem to have a serious influence upon the mechanical wood pulp industry in Germany. Notwithstanding the formation of combinations to regulate prices, makers view with alarm the possible competition of Scandinavia and the

United States, especially if those countries suffer from over production, fearing that the surplus would be sold at low rates to German papermakers. In surveying their position manufacturers state that they are forced to recognise that production by steam power is unprofitable unless prices are fairly high. During the drought of the past two summers they had to fall back on steam, which is now regarded as only an auxiliary motive power, and that for wood grinding to be on a profitable basis water power is indispensable.

WITH reference to labour time chaos may be said to exist in the German industry. Wood pulp and paper factories mostly work in day and night shifts and pay alike, changing every 12 hours. According to the statistics of the inspector of the district of Dresden, published under the heading of "Paper and Leather," seven factories work 11 hours per day, one 10½ hours per day, and four 10 hours. In the field of labour statistics Great Britain is also in advance of Germany. The German Empire does not possess any regular labour statistics made by the State. The fact will cause surprise that such a state of things can exist in a country in which for more than 10 years the Government has busied itself with nothing more eagerly than with social questions. It is only recently that the Imperial Government organised an institution for the development of regular statistics concerning labour. It is the "Commission for Labour Statistics." The law for insuring against sickness makes it compulsory on the authorities to decide on the so-called local average daily wages in all cities, *i.e.*, the wages for common labour. In this way a vast mass of statistics regarding the common labour wages of Germany has been collected, which show the greatest variety in the different parts of the country. In a few places the customary daily wages for adults, which comprise male labourers above 16 years of age, is less than 1 mark. How incredibly low the wages are in some places a few examples will prove. In the district of Schildberg, in the province of Posen (East), the wage for adult male labour is 75 pf.; in the province of East Prussia in the district of Gumbinnen, even in cities, small of course, and also in the province of West Prussia, a wage of 80 pf. occurs. Young working women in some East Prussian cities receive but 40 pf. and even 20 pf. daily. The income of skilled workmen may be approximately calculated by the Accident Insurance Fund of the German Empire. Manufacturers are obliged to insure their men against accidents and have formed into large corporations, which may be taken technically as a unity in insurance. For the purpose of calculating the amounts to be paid in case of accidents, the different trade societies have to estimate the usual wage in their respective branch of trade. The average yearly wages of those connected with paper manufacture is given at 572 marks, and the industries working up paper 682 marks.

THE Industrial Society of Copenhagen intends in January, 1894, to arrange a special Exhibition of such new inventions as may be considered likely to be used in Denmark, Norway, and Sweden, and specially such as it must be supposed will be of interest for the handicrafts and industrial establishments of these countries. The object of this special Exhibition, which will be held in the well-known, spacious and excellently situated premises of the Industrial Society, is partly to give native and foreign inventors and holders of patents an opportunity in a practical and economical manner to get their inventions made known in the three countries above mentioned, and partly to give mechanics, artisans, owners, and managers of industrial establishments, and others, a convenient opportunity to convince themselves of the nature of the inventions exhibited, as well as the latest advances in their special branches. In this manner the sale of a patent, or an agreement respecting the right to make use of it in one or more of the Scandinavian countries, will be most easily obtained, while, at the same time, such an Exhibition will doubtless give an impulse to the importation into and use in Scandinavia of such objects as may be adapted thereto. On the other hand, mechanics and artisans, the owners and managers of industrial establishments, and others, will thereby be enabled to acquire those inventions which are of special importance for them.

POLLUTION difficulties are harassing papermakers. On page 5 we give a letter received from Sir Henry Roscoe, and the views therein expressed no doubt will be insisted upon by the Mersey and Irwell Joint Committee. A number of papermaking firms are allowed three months to erect necessary works for purifying their effluent. Permission has been asked the Local Government Board to prosecute Mr. J. Hargreaves, of Collyhurst.

WORLD'S PAPER TRADE REVIEW OFFICE,
58, SHOE LANE, LONDON, E.C.
NOVEMBER 9, 1893.

MARKET REPORT

and RECORD of IMPORTS

Of Foreign Rags, Wood Pulp, Esparto, Paper, Millboards, Strawboards, &c., at the Ports of London, Liverpool, Southampton, Bristol, Hull, Fleetwood, Middlesborough, Glasgow, Grangemouth, Granton, Dundee, Leith, Dover, Folkestone, and Newhaven, for the WEEK ENDING NOVEMBER 8.

From SPECIAL Sources and Telegrams.

Telegrams—"STONHILL, LONDON."

CHEMICALS.—The market is dull, pending settlement of the coal strike. AMMONIA ALKALI has advanced in price. BLEACHING POWDER is quoted at about £7 10s. f.o.b. Tyne, soft wood £8 2s. 6d. and hard wood £8 10s. CAUSTIC SODA 77% f.o.r. Newcastle shows an advance at £11 15s.; 74% f.o.b. Liverpool stands at £11 15s.; and 70% f.o.r. Lancs. at £10 12s. 6d. SODA ASH is easier at £4 10s. ex ship Thames. SULPHATE OF AMMONIA is offered at £12 10s. and SULPHUR stands at from £4 5s. to £4 7s. 6d.

Prices are nominally as follows:

Article		Terms		£	s.	d.
Alkali, 58%	tierces ...	f.o.r. works	2½%	4	5	0
" 58%	bags ...	" "	2½%	4	0	0
58%	... ...	f.o.b. Liverpool	2½%	4	7	6
Alum (Ground),	tierces ...	" Liverpool	2½%	5	7	6
" "	barrels ...	" "	2½%	5	17	6
" "	tierces ...	" Hull	2½%	5	5	0
" "	" ...	Goole	2½%	5	5	0
Alum (Lump)	" ...	f.o.b. Liverpool	2½%	4	17	6
" "	barrels ...	" "	2½%	5	0	0
" "	tierces ...	" Hull	2½%	4	15	0
" "	" ...	Goole	2½%	4	15	0
" "	" ...	London	2½%	5	5	0
" "	" ...	f.a.s. Glasgow	2½%	5	5	0
Alumina Sulphate,	casks	f.o.b. Tyne		4	2	6
" "	bags	" "		3	17	6
Aluminoferric Cake,	slabs	Liverpool ...	...	2	15	0
" "	tierces	" ...	...	3	2	6
Alumina Cake,	slabs ...	Glasgow	...	2	15	0
" "	tierces ...	"	...	3	2	6
Aluminous Cake,	casks ...	Manchester	3½%	2	7	6
" "	" ...	Newcastle	2½%	2	10	0
" "	" ...	London	2½%	3	0	0
" "	bags ...	"	2½%	2	17	9
Blanc Fixe ...	... ...	f.o.b. Tyne	net	7	10	0
Bleach, 35%	... ...	" "	net	7	10	0
" (soft wood)	...	f.o.r. Lancs.	net	8	2	6
" (hard wood)	...	f.o.b. Liverpool	net	8	10	0
... ...	...	landed London	2½%	9	0	0
Borax (crystals)	... ...	... ...	net	29	0	0
powdered	... ...	... ...	net	30	0	0
Caustic Cream, 60%	...	f.o.r. Lancs.	net	9	2	6
" " 60%	...	f.o.b. Liverpool	net	9	7	6
" Bottoms	...	" "	net	6	15	0
" " ...	...	f.o.b. Tyne	net	6	15	0
Chloride of Barium	...	f.o.b. Tyne	net	7	10	0
Caustic White 76-77%	...	f.o.r. Newcastle	net	11	15	0
" " 77%	f.o.r. or	f.o.b. Tyne	net	12	0	0
" " 74%	...	f.o.b. Liverpool	net	11	15	0
" " 70%	...	" "	net	10	15	0
" " 70%	...	" Hull	net	11	0	0
" " 70%	...	f.o.r. London	net	10	15	0
" " 70%	...	f.o.b. Tyne	net	10	0	0
" " 70%	...	f.o.r. Lancs.,	net	10	12	6
" " 60%	...	" London	net	9	15	0
" " 60%	...	f.o.b. Liverpool	net	9	15	0
Carbonat'd Ash 58%	...	" "	net	4	10	0
48%	...	" "	net	4	0	0
" 58%	..	f.o.r. Widnes	net	4	7	6
" 48%	...	" "	net	3	17	6
Hypo-Sulphite of Soda...		f.o.r. Tyne		5	15	0
" "	10-ton lots	ex ship Liverp'l	net	6	10	0
Oxalic Acid ...	... ...	f.o.b. Liverpool	3½%	per lb		½
Salt Cake ...	... ...	" works	net	1	10	0
Soda Ash, 52%	... ...	f.o.b. Tyne	net	4	0	0
" 52%	... ...	ex ship Thames	1%	4	10	0
" 52%	... ...	f.o.b. Liverpool	1%	4	5	0
Soda Crystals	... ...	" Tyne	net	2	10	0
" "	... ...	ex ship Thames	2½%	2	17	6
" "	... ...	f.o.b. Liverpool	net	3	5	0
Sulphur, roll	... ...	f.o.r. works	2½%	7	17	6
" flowers	... ..	" "	2½%	9	10	0
" recovered	...	" "	2½%	4	5	0
Sulphate of Ammonia	"	" "	2½%	12	10	0
" of Copper	...	" Liverpool	5%	16	0	0

FOREIGN.—F.o.b. Continental port:

	£	s.	d.
Alkali, 58% 2-cwt. bags £4 10/0; 10-cwt. casks ...	5	0	0
Caustic Soda, 70-72%	10	12	6
Hypo-Sulphite of Soda 10-ton lots casks	6	0	0
Sulphate of Alumina 7-8 cwt. casks net c.i.f. Ldn	4	7	6
Blanc Fixe (c.i.f. London)	7	12	6

ESPARTO.—The market is without material change, but very little business is being done. Sellers' quotations are steady, nominally, at former figures.

Prices c.i.f. London and Leith, or f.o.r. Cardiff, Garston and Tyne Docks are nominally as follows:

		£	s.	d.		£	s.	d.
Spanish—	Fair to Good	£5	5	0	to	5	10	0
"	Fine to Best	5	10	0	"	5	15	0
Oran —	Fair to Good	3	5	0	"	3	10	0
"	First Quality...	3	15	0	"	3	17	6
Tripoli —	Hand-picked	3	15	0	"	3	17	6
"	Fair Average	3	7	6	"	3	10	0
Bona & Philippeville	... ...	3	15	0	"	3	17	6

WEEK'S IMPORTS.

Quantity	From	Importer	Port.
1864 trusses	Garrucha	To order	Grangemouth
644 tons	Oran	Henderson, McIntosh	Granton

STRAW.—Trade quiet. French Straw is not on offer. Oat ex steamer London is offered at 80s. per ton. Several lots of Danish Straw are about to be put on the market at rather lower prices.

WEEK'S IMPORTS.

(Purposes unspecified) at principal Ports From

HOLLAND ... ... 390 bales

STRAW PULPS.—In steady request.

Prices, c.i.f. London, Hull or Leith:

	£	s.	d.		£	s.	d.
Belgian, 25% moisture	£15	0	0	to	16	0	0
do. dry					16	0	0
German, 50 to 55% moisture					16	10	0
do. dry, ... No. 1 £18 10 0; No. 2					15	0	0

CHEMICAL WOOD PULPS.—The market keeps firm. There is a good enquiry for SULPHITE, at well-maintained prices. SULPHATE and SODA Pulps steady.

Prices, ex steamer, London, Hull, Newcastle, Leith and Glasgow are nominally as follows:

	£	s.	d.		£	s.	d.
SULPHITE, Unbleached. Common	£10	0	0	to	11	0	0
" Superior	11	0	0	"	11	10	0
" " 50% moisture, d.w.	11	0	0	"	12	0	0
" Extra	12	0	0	"	13	0	0
" Bleached, moist					16	10	0
" Unbleached, English, del. Lancs. ...					10	15	0
" " " No. 1, ex mills, Ldn.					10	10	0
" " " No. 2. " "					9	15	0
SODA, Unbleached, Common ...	10	5	0	"	10	10	0
" " Extra... ...	10	10	0	"	11	0	0
" Half-Bleached	12	10	0	"	14	0	0
SULPHATE, Unbleached, Common	10	10	0	"	11	0	0
" Extra	11	0	0	"	12	0	0
" Half-Bleached	13	10	0	"	14	0	0
Bleached	15	0	0	"	16	0	0

MECHANICAL WOOD PULPS.—Pulp for present delivery appears to be exceedingly scarce, and several makers are in arrears in regard to contract deliveries. Quotations for 1894 vary from £2 17s. 6d. to £3 for Moist and £5 17s. 6d. to £6 for Dry, delivered west coast.

Prices, ex steamer, London, Hull, Newcastle, Leith and Glasgow are nominally as follows ·

MECHANICAL, Aspen, Dry ...	£7 10 0	to 8 0 0
Pine, Dry	7 10 0	,, 7 15 0
Pine, Moist	3 10 0	,, 3 15 0
Moist Brown	3 2 6	,, 3 5 0
Single Sorted	2 7 6	,, 2 10 0
Dry Brown	6 5 0	,, 6 10 0

WEEK'S IMPORTS.

Quantity	From	Importer	Port.
160 bales	Abo	To order	Hull
279 ,,	Bergen	,,	,,
200 ,,	Christiania	Tough & Henderson	London
620 ,,	,,	Henderson & Co	,,
270 ,,	,,	Goldsmith & Co	,,
1970 ,,	,,	To order	Grangemouth
1860 ,,	,,	,,	Hull
324 ,,	,,	Goldsmith & Co	London
652 ,,	,,	Taylor & Co	,,
200 ,,	,,	G. F. Green & Co	,,
685 ,,	Copenhagen	To order	Leith
1015 ,,	Christiansand	J. Currie & Co	,,
80 ,,	Drammen	W. G. Taylor & Co	London
2000 ,,	,,	M. G. Skramnes	,,
1000 ,,	,,	Christophersen & Co	,,
500 ,,	,,	London Paper Mills Co	,,
250 ,,	,,	Ekman Co	,,
520 ,,	Drontheim	To order	Hull
2092 ,,	Fredrikshald	G. Schjoth & Co	Fleetwood
1725 ,,	,,	Hamer	,,
3092 ,,	Gefle	To order	London
23 cases	Ghent	,,	,,
100 ,,	,,	,,	,,
1612 bales	Gothenburg	,,	Hull
8 ,,	,,	,,	Liverpool
100 ,,	,,	,,	,,
643 ,,	,,	,,	Granton
30 ,,	,,	O. Konig & Co	London
141 ,,	,,	G. F. Green & Co	,,
404 ,,	,,	W. Pearsall	,,
400 ,,	Hambro	To order	,,
51 ,,	,,	,,	,,
1015 ,,	,,	,,	,,
108 ,,	,,	,,	Hull
204 ,,	,,	,,	,,
153 ,,	,,	,,	Leith
10 cases	Marseilles	,,	Liverpool
6460 bales	Montreal	,,	,,
400 ,,	Norrkoping	Christophersen & Co	London
320 ,,	Rotterdam	J. Currie & Co	Leith
80 ,,	,,	To order	Liverpool
108 ,,	,,	,,	Hull
44 ,,	,,	,,	London
418 rolls	,,	,,	,,
614 bales	,,	,,	,,
134 ,,	,,	,,	Liverpool
120 ,,	,,	,,	Grangemouth
91 ,,	,,	,,	London
400 ,,	,,	,,	,,
112 ,,	,,	,,	,,
260 ,,	Stettin	,,	,,
915 ,,	,,	,,	,,
121 ,,	,,	,,	Hull

Totals from Each Country:

BELGIUM ...	123 casks	HOLLAND ..	2523 bales
CANADA ...	6460 bales	,, ...	418 rolls
DENMARK ...	685 ,,	NORWAY ...	14367 bales
FRANCE ...	10 cases	PRUSSIA ...	1296 ,,
FINLAND ...	160 bales	SWEDEN ...	7090 ,,
GERMANY ..	1931 ,,		

WEEK'S IMPORTS of WOOD PULP BOARDS.

Quantity	From	Importer	Port
25 bales	Christiania	To order	Grangemouth
30 cases	,,	,,	Hull

WASTE PAPERS.—There is a moderate amount of business being done in Waste Papers at steady figures.

Cream Shavings ...	12/3	Small Letters	5/·
Fine ,, ...	9/6	Large ,, ...	7/0
Mixed ,, ...	2/0	Brown Paper	2/9
White Printings ...	8/9	Light Browns	2/9
White Waste ...	1/0	Books & Pamphlets ...	6/0
Wood Pulp Cuttings	3/6	Strawboard Cuttings	1/6
Brown Paper	3/0	Jacquards	2/6
Crushed News	2/0		

For Export: 2s/-per ton extra.

FOREIGN RAGS.—Continental advices state that there is very little business passing.

WEEK'S IMPORTS.

Quantity	From	Importer	Port.
11 bales	Amsterdam	To order	Hull
51 ,,	,,	,,	Leith
194 ,,	Alexandria	,,	Liverpool
8 ,,	Ascension	,,	London
208 ,,	Antwerp	,,	,,
43 ,,	,,	,,	Liverpool
78 ,,	Bordeaux	,,	,,
20 ,,	,,	,,	Hull
14 ,,	Buenos Ayres	Galand and Patterson	London
70 ,,	Bremen	To order	Hull
304 ,,	Copenhagen	,,	,,
61 ,,	Christiania	,,	,,
30 ,,	Cologne	,,	,,
3 ,,	Caen	,,	London
114 ,,	Ghent	G. Gibson & Co	Leith
94 ,,	,,	To order	Hull
104 ,,	Hambro	,,	,,
10 ,,	,,	,,	Leith
17 ,,	,,	,,	Hull
25 ,,	Harlingen	,,	,,
148 ,,	Konigsberg	,,	,,
14 ,,	,,	,,	London
14 ,,	Rotterdam	,,	Leith
44 ,,	,,	,,	Hull
25 ,,	Rouen	,,	London
34 ,,	,,	,,	Glasgow
2 ,,	Stettin	,,	Hull
45 ,,	St. Nazaire	,,	Southamptonn

Totals from Each Country:

ARGENTINA	14 bales	FRANCE ...	235 bales
ASCENSION	8 ,,	GERMANY ...	201 ,,
BELGIUM .	453 ,,	HOLLAND ...	143 ,,
DENMARK ...	305 ,,	NORWAY ...	61 ,,
EGYPT ...	194 ,,	PRUSSIA ...	164 ,,

GERMAN RAGS.

STETTIN: C.i.f. Hull, Leith, Tyne and London.

SPFFF and SPFF	18/0	LFB (Blue)	/0
SPF	11/0	CSPFFF and CSPFF	10/0
FF	8/6	CFB (Blue)	7/6
FG	9/0	CFX (Coloured) ...	4/6
LFX	7/0		

HAMBURG: F.o.b.

NWC	22/0	FF Grey Linens ...	9/0
SPFFF	22/0	LFX Second ditto...	8/0
SPFFF and SPFF	18/0	CSPFFF	17/3
SPFF	16/0	CSPFF	11/3
SPF	12/0	CFB	8/0
CCC	5/6	Dark Blues (selected	11/9
CFX	4/6	Wool Tares... ...	8/0
White Rope... ...	8/0	Jute, No. I 6/0; No. II	5/6

DUTCH RAGS. f.o.r. Hull:

C.i.f. Thames; Hull 2/6 per ton more; ditto f.o.r. Leith c.i.f. Glasgow 4/-; c.i.f. Liverpool 4/-.

Selected Fines (free from Muslins) ...	17/0	Best Grgy Linens ...	9/0
		Common ditto ...	5/6
Selected Outshots	9/9	White Canvas ...	15/0
,, Dirty Fines	5/9	Grey & Brown Canvas	9/9
Light Cottons ...	9/3	Tarred Hemp Rope	8/0
Blue Cottons ...	7/0	Ditto (broken) ...	5/3
Dark Coloured Cottons	2/10	White Paper Shavings	7/9
New Cuttings (Bleachd)	22/6	Gunny (best) ...	4/9
,, (Unbleached)	19/6	Jute Bagging ...	3/6
,, (Slate) ...	9/0	Ditto (common ...	3/0
Muslins	8/0	Tarpaulins	4/0
Red Cottons (Mixed)	5/9	Cowhair Carpets ...	2/9
Fustians (Light browns)	5/0	Hard ditto	3/0

BELGIAN RAGS.

F.o.b. Ghent. Freights: London, 5/0; Hull and Goole, 7/6 Liverpool and Leith, 10/0; Newcastle, 12/6; Dundee and Aberdeen, 15/0; Glasgow, 16/8.

White Linens No. 1	22/6	Fustians (Light) ...	6/0
,, ,, No. 2	16/0	,, (Dark) ...	4/0
,, ,, No. 3	13/0	Thirds...	3/0
Fines (Mixed) ...	12/0	Black Cottons ...	3/9
Grey Linens (strong)	9/6	Hemp Strings (unt'r'd)	2/0
,, ,, (extra)	14/0	House Cloths ...	4/9
Blue Linens... ...	8/6	Old Bagging (solid)	3/6
White Cottons S'p'fine	18/0	,, ,, (common)	2/6
,, ,, No. 2	15/0	NEW.	
Outshots No. 3 ...	10/0	White & Cream Linens	35/0
Seconds No. 4 ...	8/0	White Cuttings ...	22/0
Prints (Light) ...	8/6	Unbleached Cuttings	21/0
,, (Old)	4/6	Print Cuttings ..	8/0

FRENCH RAGS.

Quotations range, per cwt., ex ship London, Southampton, or Hull; 2/0 per ton more at Liverpool, and 10/0 per ton higher at Newcastle, Glasgow or Leith.

French Linens, I ...	22/0	Black Cotton ...	4/0
II 18/6; III ...	14/6	Marseilles Whites, I	16/0
White Cottons, I ...	19/0	II 10/0; III ...	7/6
II 15/0; III ...	12/6	Blue Cotton	11/0
Knitted Cotton ...	11/0	Light Prints... ...	9/0
Light Coloured Cotton	8/0	Mixed Prints ...	6/0
Blue Cotton	9/6	New White Cuttings	23/0
Coloured Cotton ...	6/0	,, Stay ,,	21/0

NORWEGIAN RAGS.

C.i.f. London, Hull, Tyne, and Grangemouth.

1st Rope (tarred) ...	8/6-9/0	2nd Canvas ...	8/0
2nd ,, ,, ...	5/6-6/0	Jute Bagging	
Manilla Rope (white)	8/0-8/9	Gunny ...	3/0 3/5
Best Canvas ...	11/9-12/0	Mixed ...	2/6-2/9

RUSSIAN RAGS.

C.i.f. London, Hull, Newcastle or Leith.

SPFF	15/0	CC (Cotton	4/9
SPF	13/6	Jute I	3/6
FG	10/6	,, II...	2/3
LFB	9/6	Rope I	9/0
FF	8/3	,, II	5/3

HOME RAGS.—Markets quiet. There is, however, a little improvement in some grades. Surat Tares are enquired for, and prices show an advance.

LONDON:

New White Cuttings	21/6	Canvas No. 1	15/0
Fines (selected)	20/6	,, No. 2 ...	9/6-10/6
,, (good London)...	20/0	,, No. 3	5/6
Outshots (selected) ...	12/6	Mixed Rope	5/3
,, (ordinary) ...	11/0	White Rope	6/6
London Seconds	3/6-4/0	White Manilla Rope	8/0
Country do. ...	6/6-8/0	Coil Rope	9/0
London Thirds ...	1/9-2/0	Bagging...	1/6
Country do. ...	3/0-4/0	Gunny	3/0-3/6
Light Prints ...	7/0-8/0		

BRISTOL:

Fines	19/0	Clean Canvas ...	15/0
Outshots	13/6	Second Do. ...	9/6-10/6
Seconds	7/0-8/0	Light Prints ...	8/0
Thirds	3/6-4/0	Hemp Coil Rope	9/6-10/0
Mixed Bagging	3/6	Tarred Manilla	7/6

MANCHESTER:

Fines	15/0-16/0	Blues	6/6-7/0
Outshots (best) ...	11/6-12/0	Bagging...	4/0-4/3
,, (ordinary)	10/6-11/0	,, (common)	3/0-3/3
Seconds	7/0-7/3	W. Manilla Rope	10/0-10/6
Thirds	3/6-3/9	Surat Tares... ...	4/9-5/0

EDINBURGH:

Superfines	16/6	Black Cottons	2/9
Outshots	13/0	W. Manilla Rope ...	8/9
Mixed Fines...	14/0	Tarred Ditto	6/6
Common Seconds ...	7/0	,, Hemp Rope...	8/3
First do.	10/0	Rope Ends (new) ...	8/6
Prints	5/6-6/6	,, ,, (old) ...	5/0
Canvas (best)	15/6	Bagging...	2/0-3/0
,, 2nd	10/0	,, (clean) ...	4/3-5/0

DUBLIN.

White Cuttings ...	18/0	Mill Bagging	3/0
Fines	11/0	White Manilla	8/0
Seconds...	5/0	Tarred Hemp	8/0
Light Prints	3/0	Rigging	13/6
Black do.	2/0	Mixed Ropes	3/6
Bagging	2/0		

ROSIN.—Demand fairly good at former figures.

	London (on the spot).	Liverpool (on the spot).	C.i.f. net London or Liverpool.
B/C	4/0	3/7½	3/6
D	4/1½	3/9	3/7
E	4/3	3/10½	3/8
F	4/6	4/0	3/9
G	4/9	4/3	3/10
H	5/3	5/1½	3/11
I	5/9	5/9	4/9
K	6/6	6/3	6/0
M	7/9	7/6	7/0
N	9/0	8/9	8/10½
W G	9/6	9/6	9/6
W W	10/0	10/3	9/9

Rosin: G, 5/3; H, 5/6; I, 5/9; K, 6/6; M, 6/9; N, W G, 8/6; W U, 9/6; Virgin, 11/0. Net c.i.f.

SIZING.—Enquiries scarce; prices unchanged

English Gelatines ...	per cwt.	70/0 to 140/0
Foreign ,, ...	,,	70/0 ,, 140/0
Fine Skin Glues ...	,,	45/0 ,, 60/0
Long Scotch Glues	,,	45/0 ,, 60/0
Common ,, ...	,,	30/0 ,, 45/0
"Town" Glues ...	,,	26/0 ,, 36/0
"Bone" Glues ...	,,	20/0 ,, 30/0
Foreign Glues ...	,,	23/0 ,, 40/0
Bone Size ...	,,	4/0 ,, 10/0
Gelatine Size... ...	,,	5/0 ,, 10/0
Dry B.A. Pieces ...	,,	31/6 ,, 34/0
,, English Pieces	,,	22/0 ,, 24/0
Wet ,, ,,	,,	5/0 ,, 6/0
,, Sheep Pieces ...	,,	3/0 ,, 4/0
Buffalo Hide Shavings	,,	25/0 ,, 34/0
,, Picker Waste	,,	25/0 ,, 34/0

STARCH.—Maize at £9 5s. (for crisp) and £9 15s. (for powder) shows an advance of 5s.

F.o.r. London, less 2½% :

Maize—Crisp, £9 10/-; Powder, £9 15/-; Special £14.
Farina—Prime, £9 15/-; B.K.M.F., £12.

Delivered :

Rice—Special (in chests), £20 (net); Crystal (in bags) £19; Granulated (in bags) £18 less 2½%.
Dextrine—£15 to £16.

MINERALS.—The demand for the best grades of CHINA CLAY is fairly good, but lower grades are not in much request. FRENCH CHALK is steady at previous quotations. There is a moderate trade doing in Finest WHITE SULPHATE. Business in MINERAL WHITE is quiet. PATENT HARDENINGS are in good request.

Mineral White (Terra Alba), per ton f.o.r. or boat at works:

Superfine...	28/0	less 2½ %
Pottery Super.... ...	24/0	,,
Ball Seconds	20/0	,,
Seconds	15/0	,,
Thirds	10/6	,,

China Clay, in bulk, f.o.b. Cornwall, 14/0 to 27/6; bags 5/0 and casks 9/6 per ton extra; f.o.b. London, in casks 35/0 to 50/0 per ton.
Superfine Hardening, f.o.r. works, 40/0.
Patent Crystal Hardening, delivered at mills £3 to £3 15/0
Patent Hardening (2 ton lots) f.o.r. Lancs., £3 5/0.
,, ,, (5 ton lots) f.o.b. Liverpool, £3 10/0.
Magnesite (in lump) 32/6 per ton.
Magnesite (containing 98% Carbonate of Magnesia), raw ground, £6 10/0; calcined ground, £12 10/0.
Albarine, £3. del. mills.
Asbestos, best rock, £18; brown grades, £14 to £15
Asbestine Pulp, £4 5/- to £5 c.i.f. London, Liverpool and Glasgow.
Barytes (Carbonate), lump, 90/0 to 95/0; nuts, 72/6 to 85/0.
Barytes (Sulphate), "Angel White," No. 1, 70/0; No. 2, 60/0 to 65/0; No. 3, 45/0. Souheur's Brands: AF, 83/-; BF, 71/-; AB, 33/6; BB, 29/6; CB, 24/3.
French and Italian Chalk (Souheur Brand), per ton in lots of 10 tons: Flower O, 63/6 c.i.f. London; Flower OO, 59/0, Flower OOO, 52/6. Swan White, 58/0; Snow White, 80/0. Blackwell's "Angel White" Brand and "Silvery" 90/- to 92/6; prime quality, 90/- to 95/-; and superfine, 105/-.
Bauxite, Irish Hill Quality, first lump, 20/0; seconds, 16/0; thirds, 12/0; ground, 35/0.
Pyrites (non-cupreous), Liverpool, 5d., 2 %.
Carbonate of Lime (Souheur Brand), Prima 43/-, Secunda 37/-.

LIME.—The production of Lime has been greatly effected by the scarcity and cost of fuel, consequently the supply is limited. The demand is good, and the present price is 12s. 6d. per ton f.o.r.

COLOURS.—Business quiet.

Mineral Black ...	cwt.	3/0	Ultramarine (pure)	
do. superior ...	,,	5/0	... cwt.	40/0 to 45/0
Pure Ivory Black	,,	12/0	PASTE COLOURS with 60% of colour, as follows:	
Ochre	,,	3/0		
French J. C. Ochre	ton	55/0	Orange Pulp ... cwt.	40/0
Chrome (pure) ...	cwt.	40/0	Golden Yellow Pulp	36/0
Red Oxide	,,	4/6	Lemon ,, ,, cwt.	36/0
Umber, Devonshire	,,	50/0	Prussian Yellow ,,	36/0
do. Turkish ...	,,	40/0	Green (free of arsenic	36/0
Lamp Black ...		7/0-10/6	Paste Blue (20-45%)	
Cochineal	lb.	1/3-2/0	.. ...	23/6-46/0

DIRECTORY.

Names and Addresses under this heading will be charged for at the rate of 50/- per annum (50 insertions) for each card of two lines or under. Each additional line £1 extra.

ALUMINOUS CAKE.

The ALUM, CHINA CLAY and VITRIOL Co., Lim., 63, Queen Victoria Street, London, E.C, Works: Rainham-on-Thames. Telegrams—"Chinnock, London.

ANALYTICAL.

WILLIAMS, ROWLAND, F.I.C., F.C.S., 28, Pall Mall, Manchester.

ARTESIAN WELLS.

BATCHELOR, Richard D., Artesian and Consulting Well Engineer, 73, Queen Victoria Street, London, E.C., and at Chatham. 5713

ISLER, C., & Co., Bear Lane, Southwark, S.E

LE GRAND & SUTCLIFF, Magdala Works, 125, Bunhill Row, E.C.

BOILER COVERING.

LONSDALES, Boiler Coverers, Blackburn, will send a sample cask of their Patent Plastic Cork Covering to any Paper Mill in Great Britain—5 cwt. cask for 25/- (carriage paid).

CHINA CLAY.

The ALUM, CHINA CLAY and VITRIOL Co., Lim., 63, Queen Victoria Street, London, E.C. Mines: Ruddle and Colchester, St. Austell, Cornwall. Telegrams—"Chinnock, London."

ROGERS, J., & Co., Truro, Cornwall.—Agents: Taylor, Sommerville & Co., 83, Queen Victoria Street, E.C., and at 16, Princes Street, Edinburgh.

W. SINGLETON BIRCH & SONS, Lim., 15, Upton Street, Manchester. Mines: Rosevear, St. Austell, Cornwall. 2976

COLOURS.

CARDWELL, J. L., & Co., Commercial Buildings, 15 Cross Street, Manchester. Specialties: Mineral Black, Ven. Red, Ochres and Umbers. 5304

GEMMILL, W. N., & Co., Glasgow, Telegrams "Rubie." Starches, Alumina, Antifroths, &c. All Paper Colours

OUR CATALOGUE
of Accessories
for the Transmission of Power, is
THE ONLY
Complete and Perfect
ONE IN THE WORLD.
BELT PULLEYS,
Belt Flywheels, Step-Cone Pulleys.
ROPE PULLEYS,
Rope Flywheels, Haulage Rope Pulleys.
GEAR WHEELS,
Gear Flywheels, Mortice Wheels.
SHAFTING,
Loose Collars, Fast Collars, Couplings.
PEDESTALS,
Horizontal, Angle, Vertical, Hanging.
FIXINGS,
Wall-Boxes, Hangers, Brackets, Stools.
HIGHEST CLASS.
REDUCED PRICES; FREE DELIVERY
throughout the Kingdom.
HARPERS LIMD., ABERDEEN.
Gladly sent to ANYONE on receipt of either Business or Private address.

PAPER IMPORTS.

FOR THE WEEK ENDING TUESDAY LAST:

BELGIUM ...	1101 bales	NORWAY ...	2983 bales
"	634 cases	"	9 rolls
DENMARK ...	55 bales	PRUSSIA ...	458 bales
FINLAND ...	677 "	RUSSIA ...	6 "
FRANCE ...	694 "	SWEDEN ...	3870 "
" ...	99 cases	"	1604 rolls
GERMANY ...	3060 bales	SPAIN	1 case
"	40 cases	U.S.A.	154 bales
HOLLAND ...	4732 bales	"	7 cases
"	52 cases		

Including the Following:

Quantity	From	Importer	Port.
514 bales	Christiania	E. & E. Sabel	London
20 "	"	Morgan & Co	"
20 "	"	Spicer & Son	"
104 "	"	C. F, Green	"
63 "	"	Crabb & Co	"
114 "	"	Alsing & Co	
25 "	"	Christophersen	"
12 "	"	Saunders & Son	"
12 "	"	Lon. & Rhine Co	"
33 "	"	Crabb & Co	"
11 "	"	J. Hamilton	"
23 "	"	Becker & Co	"
5 "	"	Christophersen	"
12 "	"	Lon. & Rhine Co	"
22 "	"	Hernu Peron & Co	"
11 "	"	Alsing & Co	"
21 "	Copenhagen	Becker & Ulrich	"
15 "	Drammen	Lon. & Rhine Co	"
10 "	"	R. L. Lundgren	"
12 "	"	J. Holloway	"
14 "	"	Hrenu, Peron & Co	"
16 "	"	Alsing & Co	"
110 "	"	Crabb & Co	"
97 "	"	H. Puckert & Co	"
138 "	"	R. L. Luudgren	"
72 "	"	Spicer & Sons	"
74 "	"	Alsing & Co	"
65 "	"	W. D. Edwards	"
15 "	"	J. Holloway	"
12 "	"	Spicer & Sons	"
8 "	"	Crabb & Co	"
3 "	Danzig	E. & E. Sabel	"
102 "	"	H. Huber	"
674 "	Gothenburg	Schenkenwald	"
1239 "	"	Hummell & Co	"
6 "	"	Brooks Whf.	"
300 "	"	R. L. Lundgren	"
211 "	"	E. & E. Sabel	"
2 "	"	J. H. Isaacs	"
38 "	"	Alsing & Co	"
4 cases	New York	Bell Punch Printing Co	"
1604 rolls	Norrkoping	Schenkenwald	"
76 bales	"	Brooks Whf.	"
420 "	"	Dowgate Dk.	"
10 "	Stettin	E. Lloyd, Ltd.	"
25 "	"	W. D. Edwards	"
65 "	"	J. Spicer & Sons	"
58 "	"	Becker & Ulrich	"
131 "	"	J. Spicer & Sons	"
22 "	"	W. D. Edwards	"

PAPER EXPORTS.

FOR THE WEEK ENDING TUESDAY LAST;

	Printings.	Writings.	Other Kinds.
AUSTRALIA	4727 cwts.	805 cwts.	789 cwts.
AFRICA	37 "	59 "	23 "
ARGENTINE ...	— "	64 "	15 "
BELGIUM	— "	103 "	89 "
B. WEST INDIES...	24 "	8 "	16 "
B. GUIANA	32 "	34 "	412 "
CEN. AMERICA ...	— "	— "	1 "
CANADA	9 "	69½ "	39 "
CAPE COLONY ...	557 "	195 "	222 "
CHINA	90 "	77 "	59 "
CHILI	16 "	33 "	— "
DENMARK	45 "	2 "	— "
EGYPT	— "	12	— "
FRANCE	235 "	38 "	34 "
GERMANY	3 "	— "	8 "
HOLLAND	— "	83 "	— "
INDIA	1151½ "	459 "	202½ "
JAPAN	2 "	— "	— "
NEW ZEALAND ...	401 "	179 "	183 "
NORWAY	24 "	— "	1 "
NEWFOUNDLAND	— "	15 "	— "
PORTUGAL	— "	9 "	— "
RUSSIA	— "	15 "	8 "
SPAIN	3 "	5 "	6 "
TURKEY	— "	— "	45 "
U.S.A.	64 "	90½ "	— "
W. INDIES	32 "	9 "	8 "

SUMMARY OF
IMPORTS & EXPORTS,

FOR THE WEEK ENDING TUESDAY LAST.

London, Liverpool, Bristol, Southampton, Hull, Fleetwood, Harwich, Folkestone, Newhaven, Dover, &c.

IMPORTS.

Paper	14469 bales	Stationery..... ...	40 cases
"	829 cases	"	30 pkgs.
"	1604 rolls	Strawboards	14706 "
Tissues	100 bales	Pasteboards	8413 "
"	15 cases	Millboards	9046 "

EXPORTS.

British Goods.		Strawboards	4 cwt.
		Foreign Goods.	
Paper	1688 cwt.	Paper	431 cwt.
Writing Paper ...	2132 "	Writing Paper...	55 "
Printing Paper	7353 "	Printing Paper...	44 "
Stationery......	£7462 value	Stationery	£858 value
Cards...............	54 cwt.	Wood Pulp	20 tons
Stock	165 tons	Strawboards	120 cwt.
Rags...............	4 "	Strawboard Cuttings	29 tons
Waste	177 "		
Millboards	3 cwt.		
Packing Paper...	£107 value		

Glasgow, Greenock, Port-Glasgow, Troon, Grangemouth, &c.

IMPORTS.

Paper	804 bales	Strawboards	6237 pkgs
"	2 cases	Stationery.........	1 pkge.

EXPORTS.

Printing Paper..	54½ cwt.	Stationery	£98 value
Writing Paper...	54½ "	Envelopes	7½ cwt.
Paper	98 "	Stock	12½ "

Leith, Granton, Boness, Dundee, &c.

IMPORTS.

Paper	671 bales	Stationery	6 cases
"	2 cases	Tissues	2 bales
"	9 rolls	Envelopes	270 pkgs.

NEW PATENTS.

BRITISH.

APPLICATIONS.

20,036. Improvements in obtaining useful products from the liquors resulting from the manufacture of cellulose or fibres by the sulphite process. C. D. Ekman.

20,116. Improvements in electrolytic cells. L. Lond and R. L. Mond.

20,132. Improvements in the preparation of caustic soda and in utilising products therefrom. G. E. Davis.

20,404. An improved process and means used therein for the production of caustic alkali. C. T. J. Vautin.

SPECIFICATION PUBLISHED.

(7½d. each. By post 8d.)

1887.

1,974. Caustic soda, etc. Mond and Hewitt.

THE PAPER TRADE REVIEW is a widely informed and well-managed enterprise, of great value to exporters for its exact Market Reports and statistics of Raw Material.—*Central-Blatt fur die Papier-Fabrikation*, Dresden.

Special Prepaid Advertisements

IT IS IMPORTANT that Advertisements under any of the Headings mentioned below should reach us by the FIRST POST on WEDNESDAY Morning to INSURE INSERTION.

Charges for advertisements under the heading Situations Wanted are 1/- for twenty-four words, and One Penny per Word after. Minimum charge ONE SHILLING. Names and addresses to be paid for.

Advertisers by paying an extra fee of 6d. can have the replies addressed to the PAPER TRADE REVIEW under a number, and such replies will then be forwarded Post Free.

Advertisements appearing under the following headings:

Tenders.	Mills Wanted or To Let.
Sales by Auction.	Machinery Wanted or For Sale.
Businesses Wanted.	
Businesses for Disposal.	Situations Vacant.

Miscellaneous.

The charges are 3/- for fifty words or under; 1s. extra for every line or portion after. Ten words to be reckoned for each line. Names and addresses to be paid for. Payment must be made in advance, except where the advertiser has a running account, in which case the cost can be debited thereto.

Legal and Financial Announcements: 1/- per Line.

Cheques and Post-office Orders to be CROSSED ——— and Co., and made payable to W. JOHN STONHILL.

Situation Vacant.

FOREMAN Papermaker required for a mill making browns and shops; must be young, active and thoroughly experienced.—Apply Masons Paper Mill Co., Limited, Ipswich. 592[illegible]

Situations Wanted.

ADVERTISER (21), having scientific education, and being about to complete his training in all departments of a first-class "white" mill, making fine printings and writings, desires to obtain the position of under-foreman in a good two-machine mill. References of the highest-class as to character and ability will be given by present principals.—Address No. 5913, office of the WORLD'S PAPER TRADE REVIEW, 58, Shoe-lane, London, E.C. 5913

CHEMICAL PLUMBER desires Re-engagement; 5 years in Wood Pulp Mills; first class references.—Address, No. 5,907, office of the WORLD'S PAPER TRADE REVIEW, 58, Shoe Lane, E.C. 5907

ENGAGEMENT wanted as Assistant Manager or Foreman in a Sulphite Wood Pulp Mill; thoroughly experienced in the manufacture of chemical wood pulps; good practical engineering and chemical knowledge; satisfactory references.—Address No. 5,905, office of the WORLD'S PAPER TRADE REVIEW, 58, Shoe Lane, London, E.C. 5905

MANAGER, thoroughly competent in all classes of Paper and Machinery, etc.; well up in the blending of fibres and mixing and matching of colours, desires Situation. Good testimonials as to character and ability.—Address, No. 5,908 office of the WORLD'S PAPER TRADE REVIEW, 58, Shoe Lane, London, E.C. 5908

WANTED, Situation as Machineman, accustomed to Tub and Engine Sized Writings and Fine Printings.—Address, "E.B.," No. 5,906, office of the WORLD'S PAPER TRADE REVIEW, 58, Shoe Lane, London, E.C. 5906

YOUNG Gentleman (31), 12 years' experience in first-class mills, wishes to hear of vacancy in good mill; capable of taking charge of counting-house, buying and selling, and commercial management generally under supervision of managing director or principal; limited liability experience; moderate salary; first-class references and testimonials.—Address No. 5912, Office of the WORLD'S PAPER TRADE REVIEW, 58, Shoe-lane, London, E.C. 5912

To Capitalists.

GENTLEMAN required with £3,000, (Partnership or otherwise) to take active part in Paper Mill abroad.—Address, No. 5,915, office of the WORLD'S PAPER TRADE REVIEW, 58, Shoe Lane, London, E.C. 5915

Agencies.

TO PAPERMAKERS, Envelope Manufacturers, &c.—A gentleman with extensive connection throughout the Provinces is prepared to negotiate with about half-a-dozen good firms making different classes of papers, &c., with a view to represent them. He would be willing also to take up any lines in kindred trades which can command a sale. Highest references. Principals only. —Address, "Juan," c/o Mr. Hewett, 4, Holywell Street, Strand, London, W.C. 5914

Machinery for Sale.

ONE KOLLERGANG, new, Stones 51 inches by 14 inches, C.I. Pan, Scrapers, and Driving Gear.

ONE HYDRAULIC PRESS, second-hand, with Press Box 38 inches diam. by 32 inches deep, with wheels; all parts strong, Ram 2 feet 6 inches by 8 inches diam.

TWELVE REVOLVING STRAINER PLATES, second-hand, 18½ inches by 21 inches, class B2, 3½ cut.

REFINING ENGINE, new, Conical Type; same as one working in a large printing mill.

Any reasonable offer will be considered by 5859

BERTRAMS LIMITED, SCIENNES, EDINBURGH.

Mills to be Let or Sold.

TO be LET or SOLD, a Paper Mill at Stalybridge, called the Higher Mill, containing one large machine and room for another, steam engine and boilers, in good condition.—Apply for further information to the Caretaker on the premises. 2169

MALDON, ESSEX.—TO BE LET on Lease or Sold, a Freehold Mill, with Engine, Boiler and 2 Water Wheels of 100 horse-power. The Property has an area of Five acres, with a Wharf giving facilities for carriage inland by river, or to London by sea, at the low rate of 2s. 8d. per ton.—For further particulars apply to Fuller, Horsey, Sons and Cassell, 11, Billiter Square, E.C. 5901

PAPER & PULP MILL SHARES.

(Report received from Mr. F. D. DEAN, 36, Corporation Street, Manchester.)

Nominal Amnt	Amnt Paid	Name of Company	Last dividend	Price.
7	7	Bury Paper, ord.	nil	4—4½
7	7	do. do. 6% pref.	6%	4½—4¾
100	100	do. do. deb.	5%	103—106
10	10	Bath Paper Mill Co. Lim.	7½%	6—7
10	10	Bergvik Co., def.	15%	13½
100	100	do. do. 6% cum. pref.	6%	10¾—11¼
10	10	do. do. deb.	5%	105—110
5	3½	Burnley Paper Co.	3/-	77/6—80/0
5	3¾	Darwen Paper Co.	10%	5¾—6¼
10	10	East Lancashire Co.	nil	4—4½
10	10	do. do. 6% pref.	nil	6—6½
5	5	do. do. bonus	nil	1½—2
5	5	Hyde Paper Co.	4%	4½—5
5	4	North of Ireland Paper Co.	nil	2½—2¾
10	5	Ramsbottom Paper Co.	17½%	12½—17½
5	4½	Roach Bridge Paper Co.	5%	2¾—3
5	5	Star Paper Co.	10%	6—6½
5	3	do. do. 0% pref. cum.	10%	4¾—5¼
50	50	do. do. deb.	6%	55—56
5	2¾	Kellner Partingt'n Pulp Co	—	65/0—67/6

HAMBURG

WOOD PUL

P's and Q's.

With the exception perhaps of the magic letters £ s. d., there are no signs in our alphabet more dragged into everyday life than the P's and Q's. These two letters are continually being recommended to the careful attention of everyone, not that they represent a state of helplessness which necessitates their being "minded," but they are considered as being peculiarly tricky, and should they be left out of sight during one's ordinary avocations, there is a very fair chance of something or other going wrong in consequence. "Mind your P's and Q's"—which originated in a warning to frequenters of taverns to see that their pints and quarts were correctly chalked up—is an admonition full of significance at the present time, and the trader at the commencement of each day does well to place these tricky symbols in full view and keep his eye upon them, so as to ensure as far as he can that his path be not crossed by untoward circumstances consequent upon either or both of them slipping away out of sight. A time of commercial depression is eminently favourable to the cultivation of these two tricky little symbols—the P's and Q's—which perhaps are not so tricky in themselves after all, but which may be taken in a sense to represent that attention to minutæ of detail, that care about apparent trifles which are apt only too frequently to be overlooked while in pursuit of big game. These apparently trifling details have been proved this year to have been of great importance in the conduct of many a business, with the result that every here and there one hears of the returns being fully up to, and in fact ahead of, previous years. Made up of what? Not of the big orders on the home and colonial markets—for such have not existed this year—but of a quantity of small items, finnicking little P's and Q's, which have at other times been too often passed by, if not with contempt, at least with a feeling that small fry must stand aside and give place to bigger items in the commercial culinary programme. When thinking of this raking together of commercial minutæ one is tempted to find an analogy in the allegorical chamber of the interpreter's house in the "Pilgrim's Progress," where was to be seen the man with the "muck rake" who, intent on gathering in a lot of insignificant rubbish, disregarded the crown, &c., held over his head. There is a slight difference in the condition of things between then and now. He (the allegorical gentleman) could have done better than he was doing, but our rake men of Fleet-street, Wood-street, and neighbourhood, had nothing much to speak of being held over their heads, unless, indeed, it were a species of Damoclean sword in the shape of prospective difficulties in big transactions. So they—at least some of them—have been handling their rakes to some purpose and, scraping the ground at their feet, have collected together the nucleus of a little pile out of what some people would term mere nothings. It is to be hoped that they will make their pile. There is another phase of the P and Q question which is very much *en evidence* this year, and of which an illustration is afforded by a custom which obtains amongst the French insurance companies, where a premium—of the P and Q genus—is either *portable* or *querable*, that is to say, the money has to be sent or be paid without demand, or demanded in the hopes of getting paid. Now it cannot fail to strike everyone very forcibly that, as far as accounts this year have been concerned, the letter Q has had by far the best of it. Money has been invariably *querable* or to be applied for. And applications have only in a very few instances been met in the spirit which was their due. In fact, the general verdict of both debtors and creditors may be said to be identical with the pithy money article of a certain financial editor who wrote: "Money is close but not close enough to reach." The Q's have it this time.

Told by the Door Plates.

It is gratifying when one comes across traces of national vitality, for the history of commerce told by the door plates in most, if not all, of our City thoroughfares points to the gradual extinction of the English merchant. Pass along the street, and while doing so endeavour to count up the number of English names on the door plates. Why! the difficulty is to find them. At any rate in certain classes of trade. The spaces are on the other hand filled with names more or less unpronounceable (correctly) by the untutored insular tongue, and at the end of the walk down the street one faces the conviction that times have changed, and the children of the soil are gradually and by no means slowly yielding up the commercial coigns of vantage to the pushing foreigner. Some day perhaps we shall awake from a too complaisant somnolence to find ourselves existing on tolerance where once we were masters.

WATER POWER.—The days of the old water wheel with its curved floats or buckets are over, for wherever water power is available the modern turbine is taking its place. About the best tried turbine is the "Victor," as supplied by Mr. F. Nell, of 16, Mark-lane, London, who has installed these turbines in numerous paper mills in Great Britain, Scandinavia, and Germany, whilst their use in the United States is believed to be greater than the makes of any other three firms in that country, where water power forms such an important factor in economical manufacture. Colonists who have at their elbows even a small fall of water would do well to consult Mr. Nell.

VERY SOCRATIC DIALOGUES UP-TO-DATE.

IV.

Dramatis Personæ—Two Greeks.

Cynicus.—Ah! my old friend Impecuniarius. Why, 'tis an age since we met. How are you, and how are you prospering?

Impecuniarius.—The gods have been good to me in my undertakings. And you?

Cyn.—Stumpy! Matters have gone crooked with me every way since I was lagged for that little indiscretion over Fitzboodle's investments. But you?—Let me see: when last we met I was coaching you in that matter of Pilulæ Crumbæ et Saponacæ, Limited, and had promised you some information as to the curious value of debentures. But as I hear that particular venture came to grief over a year since I am too late to serve you. Still the knowledge may be useful to you in some future contingency.

Imp.—It is never too late to learn; but it is sometimes late to attempt to impart to the grand-maternal progenitor instruction in the science and art of extracting the succulent contents from the ovarial deposit of the domestic duck.

Cyn.—Verily, the pupil hath surpassed the teacher! I would in turn sit at your feet and learn of you, O Impecuniarius: for selpmenever I haven't one red cent to rub against another. Give me, I pray you, the history of your doings with the Pilulæ Company. How did it pan out?

Imp.—Not badly, for a first attempt. But I had to give a lot away. The Pilulæ Crumbæ et Saponacæ Company, Limited, was duly registered, with a nominal capital of £40,000, with articles of association as long as a Chancery suit, and myself as sole governing director for a period of twelve months from date of formation, with provision for electing a board after that time. I gave away one share apiece to six "Greeks" of the first water whom you saw and approved: a pound apiece. The gluttons nearly crabbed my pitch the first week by hypothecating their shares for fours of sausage and mashed in the Borough. I redeemed them with my overcoat. It cost me two hundred shares to square the slang-whanging posh-papers—I mean a virtuous financial press. But that was a good investment, for they pitched a song that worked off quite ten thousand of my shares. Then we put in a lovely pilulæ plant, which relieved me of nearly another five thousand shares and five thousand debentures—second mortgage. I had to give away a few hundreds more to hurry in boodle and stuff on tick, but by the end of a year I had cleaned out my shares and resigned my directorate through ill-health induced by over-work.

Cyn.—But the pilulæ—did they sell?

Imp.—By the cart load.

Cyn.—Then you showed a divi?

Imp.—Well, hardly! Expenses of formation—installation of plant, heavy book debts—*you* understand! But I left it a flourishing industrial enterprise, with assets galore—not paid for. I went abroad for six months to recuperate, leaving my debenture bonds in good hands with a power of attorney. Then things began to go rocky with Pilulæ Limited, and my agent was forced to foreclose, as the trade creditors were acting in a stupid, ridiculous, and selfish manner.

Cyn.—It is a way the clamorous crew have: they are unreasoning and selfish, always pushing their own miserable claims to the front.

Imp.—But under the present dispensation, happily they do not get what they shout for. The ordinary creditor, my friend, is the silly working bee of the industrial hive. He gathers his honey—otherwise ooftish—and kneads his wax to feed and build houses and fortunes for the sovereign bee and the drone, which I take it are typified under the names of the company promoter, the speculative broker, the debenture demon *et hoc genus gravitallibus*. Without the working bee and his contributions the hive could not go on.

Cyn.—Most truly illustrated, my philosopher. These ordinary creditors are a greedy set who would, if permitted, eat the honey they have made. But as to the Pilulæ Company: what were its ultimate liabilities?

Imp.—Some fifty thousand pounds.

Cyn.—What a genius! And assets?

Imp.—Twenty-eight thousand, of which nearly eight thousand were book debts, estimated to realise about eight hundred.

Cyn.—And the ordinary creditors got—

Imp.—See here, my noble "Greek," it was my first venture, and probably I made some mistakes, but I was not such a galloot as to leave a shilling for the shareholders or the trade creditors. Not quite. I wanted all there was, and I got it. You advised me to go for the moderate sum of twenty thousand pounds. I reasoned that if it was good enough for that it was good enough to double the stakes. So I fixed the capital at forty thousand. I asked nobody publicly for a cent., but I handled the ducats for half of my shares all the same, and got together a reasonable amount of machinery and tangible assets with the remainder. I worked like a nigger to get goods and stock on credit and bills; fifty thousand pounds! Now do you think I was doing all this to let it slip through my fingers in the end, and go to feed the hungry maw of the ordinary creditor? You talk of the "curious value of debentures." When the time was ripe I put in my debenture claim, and scooped in the lot! If I had left a solitary quid for the others to fight for there might have been awkward inquiries.

CYN.—By the gods! ye are thick! My bright and wonderful pupil! While I, who thought I knew so much, was doing a stroke for a few hundreds with Fitzboodle and getting jugged therefor, you were raking it in to the tune of thousands and never a stain on you moniker. What did you make out of the deal?

IMP.—Only about thirty-eight thousand. But it led up to other good things. This game of company trading is a wonderful thing—knocks spots off any other swindle in the world.

CYN.—May it never be altered!

IMP.—Amen.

CYN.—You are my debtor for the suggestion. Can you do anything for me? I have a bad record, I know, through the Fitzboodle transaction, but—

IMP.—Not a bit against you that: an error of judgment, that's all. In this great commercial city we are above regarding such little peccadillos. The demand for directors is brisk just now, and I know quite a dozen shady concerns that would jump at you on your own merits; but with my recommendation, my boy, you can pick and choose. But why not go into business on your own account? Take any rotten thing that's going, and float it. If the company laws were not framed for such as you, I should like to know what they *were* framed for!

CYN.—But my soul trembles. Is there not a prospect of these laws being amended?—in which case an honest "Greek" may be made to suffer. "The burnt child dreads the water," as Sothernosius expresses it.

IMP.—As much prospect as there is of the National Debt being paid off. In this last case our senators would have to find a substitute for the investment of the national millions. In the former they would have to provide some other outlet for the energy and talents of the "Greeks," or there would be a new development of highway robbery and grand larceny. Fancy ten thousand unemployed "Greeks" thrown loose on the community—*id est*, ten thousand directors!

CYN.—You give me hope. I was not wont to be timid. I will follow your noble example, my Impecuniarius, and swindle and steal right and left under the shelter of the Companies Acts. It is the safest game.

IMP.—The gods prosper you!

ENVELOPE FOLDING MACHINE.—A self-feeding and self delivering envelope folding machine, that is made by Messrs. Joseph Richmond and Co., Ltd., 30, Kirby-street, Hatton Garden, E.C., is worth notice by our manufacturing stationery houses, as not only is it automatic in its feed and delivery, but it gums the flaps, counts in twenty-fives, and that too at the rate of 100 per minute, or 6,000 per hour.

THE
United Asbestos Co.,
LIMITED,
DOCK HOUSE, BILLITER STREET, E.C.,
"SALAMANDER"
THE UNITED ASBESTOS COMPANY LIMITED
LONDON
TRADE MARK
Pioneers
OF THE
Asbestos
Trade.
UNITED ASBESTOS
NON-CONDUCTING
COVERING
(For Steam Boilers & Pipes)
Best and Cheapest in the
Market; Will not
Injure Boiler Plates.
ASBESTOS
GOODS of ALL
DESCRIPTIONS
BELTINGS.
THE UNITED ASBESTOS Co., Limited,
UNITED
PACKINGS.
UNITED ASBESTOS Co. LMtd.
PURE ITALIAN MILLBOARD EXTRA QUALITY
LONDON
A1
UNITED ASBESTOS
A1 MILLBOARDS
(ITALIAN)
Unequalled for Purity, Strength of
Fibre, and Uniformity. For Dry
Steam Joints it is admitted to be the
cleanest, most durable and economical
packing in existence.
UNITED ASBESTOS
SALAMANDER
Lubricating Cream & Oils,
SPECIALLY ADAPTED TO
PAPERMAKING MACHINERY.
DEPOTS:
MANCHESTER: 34, Deansgate; LIVERPOOL: 33, James Street;
NEWCASTLE-UPON-TYNE: Quayside; GLASGOW: 54, Robertson
Street; CARDIFF: 135, Bute Street; BRISTOL: Provident Buildings;
HULL: Queen's Dock; ST. PETERSBURG: Gostinoe Dvor (Interior) No. 51.

Printed and Published by W. JOHN STONHILL, 58, Shoe Lane, LONDON, E.C. Nov. 10, 1893

766

The World's Paper Trade Review

A WEEKLY JOURNAL FOR PAPER MAKERS & ENGINEERS.

Telegrams: "STONHILL, LONDON." A B C Code. Registered at the General Post Office as a Newspaper.

Vol. XX. No. 20. LONDON. NOVEMBER 17, 1893. Price 6d.

THE ELECTROLYTIC CAUSTIC SODA AND CHLORINE TRUST, Ltd.

HOLLAND-RICHARDSON PROCESS.

The favourable reports read at the annual meeting of this company, held on Thursday last week, must have created amongst the shareholders a spirit of confidence in regard to the future of the undertaking.

The CHAIRMAN (Col. T. J. Holland, C.B.) referred to the development of the process, and also to the services of Mr. John Leith, manager since the latter end of 1892. The latter had made considerable quantities of caustic soda and bleach, and the chairman thought had fairly satisfied everyone interested in the subject that they were able to produce by electrolysis chemicals fully equal, if not superior, in quality to those daily used by paper and soap makers, oil refiners, bleachers, glass makers and others. They could manufacture possibly at a reduction of almost 75 per cent. on present processes. According to

MR. LEITH'S REPORT,

all the main difficulties hitherto impeding alkali manufacture by electrolysis had been overcome. With well situated works, both caustic soda and chloride of lime could be manufactured under the patents of the Electrolytic Company at a saving of £5 per ton. He estimated that by using the process a saving of one and a-half million pounds sterling a year could be effected alone in Great Britain. Mr. Leith paid special attention to the anodes which were now manufactured of carbon from gas retorts, ingeniously fitted. The anodes lasted about eight months continuous working. Amongst other improvements the resistance of the electrolytic tanks had been reduced from 6 volts to under 5 volts and the i.h.p. of the engine from 81 to 76. He thought that with a more modern fast running engine, as now specially made for dynamo driving, the h.p. could be reduced to 50-55. The report stated that one of the great advantages of the process would be its capability of being worked by manufacturers generally on their own premises.

THE VIEWS OF AN ANALYTICAL CHEMIST,

engaged with Mr. Leith since December, 1892, were very favourable. As compared with the Le Blanc process the electrolytic method had the following merits:—(1) Dispensing with the use of sulphur, pyrites, and manganese, it avoids the expense of these costly agents, and also the consequent production of noxious alkali "waste." (2) No corrosive acids are employed or produced in the electrolytic process, and no destructive acid fumes are emitted. No furnaces or fires are used, except for steam for driving the dynamo, and for boiling down the caustic. (3) The whole of the chlorine in the decomposed salt is utilised, whereas in the Le Blanc process at least 50 per cent. is lost. (4) The caustic soda produced is purer, being free from the sulphides and other sulphur compounds contained in the Le Blanc products. (5) The raw materials for the electrolytic process consist only of common salt or brine, lime and coal, the last being used only in the production of steam. As compared with the "ammonia-soda process:—"The electrolytic process has the advantage of producing a more valuable form of soda, without employing any such expensive re agent as ammonia. The caustic soda has a much higher commercial value than the carbonate. The electrolytic process, in addition, produces bleaching powder and liquor, which the ammonia-soda process does not, or at least not profitably." As compared with other electrolytic processes :—"The Holland-Richardson process has the advantages of simplicity and economy, dispensing as it does with the use of costly and defective diaphragms."

Critical Examinations of the Process.

Satisfactory reports, emanating from Mr. W. H. Massey, Mr. E. H. Liveing, Mr. James Swinburne, Professor John Hopkinson, F.R.S., and Mr. Tate were submitted to the shareholders. The chairman also said that Mr. Ludwig Mond, one of the ablest alkali chemists in Europe, visited the works, accompanied by Mr. Brunner. They carefully examined everything there taking away for analysis samples of caustic soda from the soda evaporating pans, and he believed chlorine from their chlorine absorbers, and chloride of lime from their lime chambers. Mr. Mond said that in his opinion the manufacture of caustic soda and bleach must be superseded by electrolysis, for the electrolytic process was more compact, more cleanly, more simple and more profitable to work. The following letter, received from Mr. Mond, was read at the meeting :—

"In answer to your question as to the impression I took away with me from my visit to Snodland, I have no hesitation in saying that it was extremely favourable. I only spent a few hours there, and had no opportunity of verifying the facts and figures brought before me; but I see that you have put up a substantial and well-constructed plant, of sufficient size to demonstrate the feasibility of your process, which has been at work for some time without showing any signs of wear. The figures given to me lead to the conclusion that the process can produce bleaching powder and caustic soda at a cost comparing very favourably with that of the Le Blanc and Weldon processes, by which these products are now almost exclusively produced in this country; while the consumers of these articles (such as papermakers) who used both in the form of solution, would derive great additional benefit from working your process thus, as they would save the considerable expenditure of solidifying the caustic, and handling the dry lime and bleaching powder, as well as the whole expense of packages. As far as I can judge, your arrangements are simple and inoffensive in working, and could easily be erected, and kept in working order by anyone conversant with chemical and engineering operations."

Dr. Hürter, chemist to the United Alkali Company, also visited the works, and critically examined the process throughout. He informed the chairman that they had tackled the very difficult problem of the decomposition of the chloride of sodium by electrolysis, and the production thereby of caustic soda and chlorine products in a thoroughly masterly, comprehensive, practical, and business-like manner, and as far as he could see had obtained excellent results.

Samples Please Papermakers and Others.

The company having settled all matters connected with the practical working and the validity of the patents, sent samples of their products to several well-known papermakers and eminent chemical analysts in the kingdom. Messrs. J. H. Walter and Co., of Taverham, acknowledged that from the cask of bleach sent them they had got as good results as they obtained from the bleach supplied by the United Alkali Co. The caustic soda was also very good. Messrs. Edward Cook and Co., of the East London Soap Works, Bow, said the soda was as good as any they had hitherto bought of similar strength. Messrs. J. R. Crompton Bros., of Elton Mills, Bury, submitted their analyst's report as follows :—

"I have examined the samples of caustic soda and bleaching powder manufactured by the Electrolytic Caustic Soda and Chlorine Trust, Limited, Snodland, Kent, with the following results :—The bleaching powder contains 34·8 per cent. available chlorine. The caustic soda contains 70·43 per cent. of soda (Na_2O) on the Lancashire Test; this is equivalent to 89·77 per cent. of pure sodium hydrate. It is a very good colour and dissolves quite clear, without any residue. I consider both articles quite equal to anything which can be made by the Le Blanc process, and well suited for use in a paper or bleach works."

Favourable testimonials were also received from the Glory Paper Mills, Wooburn Green, Maidenhead; Thomas and Green, Limited, Soho Mills, Wooburn; Horton Kirby Works; Messrs. Wrigley and Sons; Messrs. Henry Bruce and Sons, Midlothian; Thos. Owen and Co., Limited; Ford Paper Works, Limited; John Collins, Limited, Denny, N.B.; and C. Townsend, Hook and Co., Limited.

A Bright Future.

In conclusion, the chairman said he hoped before long they would be in a position to give further information which would cause all to congratulate themselves upon having put money into the shares of the company. He then proposed the report and balance-sheet be received and adopted, which was seconded by Mr. Vogan, and carried unanimously.

The retiring directors, Col. Holland, C.B., and Mr. Vogan were re-elected, and the usual vote of thanks terminated the proceedings.

BELGIUM.

The paper trade in Belgium is apparently at a rather low ebb just now, and manufacturers have been bestirring themselves with a view to remedying the existing state of affairs. Low prices form the chief grievance, and as this is considered to be caused by over production, it was suggested at a recent meeting of the Chambre Syndicate des Papier, at Brussels, to limit the home consumption of Belgium made paper to 60 per cent. of the total quantity produced, the remaining 40 per cent. to be exported. This proposition did not, however, meet with general approval, and ultimately the following resolutions were framed :

1.—Makers to bind themselves not to accept orders for less than 500 kilos, *i.e.*, half a ton, of paper of any given quality or description.

2.—For news paper in reams, weighing less than 45 grammes per square metre (about 1½oz., per square yard) the price will be augmented by at least one centime per kilo for each gramme less than the above weight.

3.—The cases will be invoiced at gross weights.

4.—The weights per ream will not be exactly guaranteed 2½ per cent. of margin being allowed in either direction The weight to include all retree sheets.

5.—For web news the minimum weight manufactured will be 48 grammes the square metre, with the same margin of difference as above

"LEAVES."

PROFESSOR P. L. SIMMONDS, F.L.S., gave an interesting lecture on Friday evening last, before the Science Class of the City of London College, of which he has long been a vice-president. The subject on which he discoursed was "Leaves: their Chemistry, Function, and Economic Uses." As was to be expected from his vast knowledge and long experience at International Exhibitions the subject was treated in a masterly manner. But the portions most instructive and interesting were the references to the industrial uses of leaves, in which he enumerated many of those used for food, for medicine, for dyeing and tanning, and for textile, manufacturing, and other useful purposes. Those for papermaking were specially dwelt upon, such as the palmetto, &c. But the following information is curious. Some leaves have been utilised in papermaking, especially those of the dwarf palms and the maize plant. The head leaves sheathing the cob or head of grain of maize were largely experimented on in Austria, some twenty years ago, for this purpose. Although paper made from it was strong, tough, and durable, it has not come into general use. The leaves of *Phonnium tenax* were also strongly suggested for this purpose, and a work was printed on paper made from it. Many leaves are still employed in India and elsewhere for writing on, a custom dating back more than 400 years. In tropical countries the leaves of trees have been, and are actually still used, as affording more convenient writing substances than other vegetable membrane. The great tribe of the palms yields nearly all the leaves so used, and they are written upon, not as paper and the various kinds of fibre have always been, with ink, but by cutting through the outer skin of the leaf; in fact by tatooing it. Without an acquaintance with these leaves, and the general prodigality of tropical nature, it might seem incredible that such a material and such a process should be adopted, even at the present day, for the commonest purposes to which writing paper is applied, and for the production of some of the most durable and highly finished specimens of book-making in the world. Yet such is the case, and it will be long before artificial paper will, for the purposes of common documents, entirely supersede these in such countries. The Hindoo and Bengalese books of this kind, which are preserved in the British Museum, the Indian Museum, the United Service Museum, and other repositories of Eastern curiosities, are highly worthy of attention, being comparable in every respect with the most delicate and elaborate mediæval missals. The pages and covers are regulated in shape by the natural production itself, and nearly resemble the staves of a cask, because they are cut out from between the radiating ribs of the great fan-like half of the talipot, or some other fan-palm, a single leaf of which might suffice for a considerable treatise; but for the production of these books twenty or thirty pages only are taken from the best part of the leaf. The smallness, regularity, and free ornamental flourishing of the delicate manuscript, engraved through the skin of the leaf, would hardly be credited without inspection, and as the skin dries of a paler brown tint than the interior, which is exposed by the penetration of the characters. They are thus rendered perfectly legible. In Angola often teachers and pupils make their own ink with certain leaves or berries, their own paper with banana leaves, and their own pens with the stalks of a tall strong grass. This art of writing on palm leaves in the East is very old, and the durability of the material was evidenced by leaves from a standard work in the library of His Highness the Maharaja of Mysore, shown at the Calcutta Exhibition in 1883, which dates from A.D. 1495. Leaves are still used for giving lessons in writing at schools in the interior of India, where paper is not easily procurable. They are supposed to impart the habit of moving the pen with the great delicacy of touch so often observed in natives; most of whom can write freely and rapidly, resting the paper on the thigh, while seated on the floor. The lecture was illustrated by numerous lantern slides, showing the various forms and uses of leaves.

CANADIAN NOTES.

THE Milton Pulp Company, Milton, N.S., have put in four four-pocket grinders, with 28 by 48 inch stones, three wet machines, a barker, pumps, &c., all supplied by the Lowville Iron Works Company, Lowville, N.Y.

THE E. B. EDDY CO., LTD., of Hull, report a brisk trade. In a recent interview Mr. Eddy stated that they had shipped during the 23 working days of October eighty-eight 10-ton carloads of goods from Hull alone, of which 58 cars were paper products and 30 cars matches, etc. Besides this they have 13 more carloads on order, and in addition to these carload shipments they made scores upon scores of shipments of less than carload lots, which amounted to a good many more carloads for the month. Neither at their mills in Hull, nor from any of their numerous branches and agencies all over Canada, had any complaint of dulness been heard.

RIVER POLLUTION IN LANCASHIRE.—The monthly meeting of the Ribble Watershed Joint Committee of the Lancashire County Council was held at Preston, on Monday, under the chairmanship of Mr. Lightbown, Darwen. It was decided that proceedings be taken against Colne Local Board. A further adjournment for three months was agreed to in the case of Rishton Local Board. It was also decided to give two months' notice to 24 manufacturing firms in East Lancashire to abate the pollution of water courses by liquid refuse, and that 19 paper manufacturers be invited to attend the next meeting of the Committee and explain their position as regards their pollution of streams.

[illegible] 36 hours' rest is un- [illegible] papermakers as a great [illegible] who think that [illegible] and a consequent saving [illegible] they could only ma- [illegible] rest to be limited [illegible] most 24 hours. The [illegible] difference of opinion and [illegible] ultimately be passed [illegible] it remains to be seen [illegible] will consider [illegible] proved. Some people [illegible] Government may [illegible] to save the paper trade [illegible] of over-production [illegible] exception from the [illegible] the paper trade may be [illegible] of paper firms.

[illegible] OF THE GERMAN [illegible] OFFICE.—It is well known [illegible] the normal papers the use of [illegible] has hitherto been prohibited [illegible] which are intended to [illegible] number of years, [illegible] any actual facts have been [illegible] against this useful [illegible] no absolutely convincing [illegible] been made in their favour. [illegible] the [illegible] arrangement [illegible] As these buildings are [illegible] enforced special arrangement [illegible] provided for treating [illegible] length of time under exposure [illegible] the light. [illegible] To this [illegible] will be solved definit[illegible] chemical wood fibre [illegible] and [illegible] Considering [illegible] increasing diffi[illegible] sufficiently extensive [illegible] the paper [illegible] those [illegible] become [illegible]

THE BOSTON PAPER TRADE ASSOCIATION.—The banquet of this association was held on the 1st November, Mr. Wheelwright presiding. Amongst those present were Col. Haskell, J. B. Forsythe, J. H. Rice, J. R. Carter, and others. Mr. Graham, in giving "The Paper Trade," referred to the various markets and also to the rapid development of mills all over the United States. The Hon. Wellington Smith, of Lee, remembered the time when news brought 20 cents. per lb., and now no one hardly knew the price. Other speeches were made dealing with tariff and other matters.

ACCORDING to the last weekly list to hand, the following were included in the exports of paper at New York :

B. W. Indies...	246 packages	London	184 packages
Australasia ...	114 ,,	B. E. Indies ...	13 cases
Southampton	1 case		

THE ASBESTOS PULP COMPANY, Gouverneur, N.Y., are shipping large quantities of ground talc to the papermakers of Europe. Over 300 tons have been shipped this month. The representative of the company is at present in Sweden.

THE REMINGTON PAPER COMPANY, Watertown, N.Y., recently obtained control of a very important and handy patented device for papermakers' use. It is a paper spool which, it is claimed, entirely supersedes the use of the old iron spools or tubes in winding and shipping paper. The difference in weight alone will make a large reduction in the cost of freight annually, while the additional advantages in handling and saving around large printing presses will easily be understood. All of the company's paper is shipped now on spools of this kind. The spools are made largely from sulphite fibre; the web passes first through a bath of adhesive sizing, and is then wound firmly to the desired thickness upon an expanding cylinder, after which it is pressed, then released and hung up to dry preparatory to use. The rigidity and evenness of the spools are improved by use, and the web of paper being wound firmly about them gives them accurate and permanent set. The chucks are patented as well as the winding machinery. It is understood that the company is ready to respond to inquiries for the spools, and that it will give any additional information necessary regarding them.

"SPOOK" PULP.—Mrs. Palmer is credited with being responsible for "Spook" pulp up in Maine. The properties of her mentality are said to be amazing. She had a piece of pulp given to her one day, and according to the *Lewiston Journal*, she held this in her hand a moment and then clearly explained its nature, the process of converting it from wood and the possibilities. She could see the formula used, but her perception went beyond that, even. A still different process was revealed to her—a process so strongly impressed that, woman though she was, with no inherent knowledge of wood pulp, she never lost sight of her discovery. She is somewhat of a chemist, and she at once set on foot some preliminary experiments. The results were surprising. The experiments were elaborated and extended, and the prospects grew still brighter. Mrs. Palmer laid the matter before some men of experience and good judgment in such matters and their opinion was expressed unhesitatingly and to such effect that action was promptly taken. Prominent men of well-known business capacity united with Mrs. Palmer in a stock company with a capital of $400,000. The formula has been patented in every country in the world. The claim is made for it that not only is the expense of manufacturing reduced at least fifty per cent., but further than that, only one-half as much time is required to make the pulp, and that it is unexcelled in quality. The final test is being conducted at the pulp mill at Great Works, Me. This experiment had been delayed somewhat because proper conditions for the test could not be found before. Mrs. Palmer and prominent members of the stock company are present at the scene of the experiments. Pulp manufacturers who have heard of the strange discovery are eagerly awaiting the result of the test.

THE LEFFEL TURBINE.—Another immense water wheel has just been shipped to Niagara Falls by Messrs. James Leffel and Co., Springfield, Ohio. The new wheel is a duplicate, and of nearly the same power as one which was shipped some six months ago to the Cliff Paper Company, and is intended for the same concern. The wheel is of the new type, on horizontal shaft, and is known as the James Leffel double discharge turbine, the entire weight being 30 tons. The water will be conducted to the wheel from a canal near the top of the cliff by an eight foot pipe, extending downward until it reaches the mill, located near the foot of the cliff. The water will enter the cylinder casing of the wheel from below, passing upward a few feet, filling the case, and thus obtaining the head pressure. The amount of head will be about 130 feet. The wheel being some 67 inches in diameter, a speed of 225 revolutions will be obtained, and almost or quite 1,200 horse power developed. The same firm has just completed a very original and unique design of wheel plant for another New York company. It comprises four wheels in one system, being a quadruple wheel of 1,000 horse power, to operate under a 40 feet head.

WRAPPING PAPER.—Since 1881 the capacity of the American mills running on wrapping grades has, according to the *Paper Trade Journal*, increased 76 2-5 per cent., or from a daily out-turn, according to figures of capacity, of 214¼ tons to one of nearly 377¾ tons. This includes all grades of wrappings and bogus, but excludes straw wrapping. It is estimated that the annual output of the mills making wrapping papers—straw wrapping excluded—and running under normal conditions, is about equal to 85,000 tons.

Foreign Import Duties on Paper, &c., Stationery and Books.

NORWAY:

Tariff Classification.	Tariff Rates of Duty.			English Equivalents.			
		Kron.	öre.		£	s.	d.
Pasteboard for sheathing and roofing purposes, etc.	Kilog.	0	01	Cwt.	0	0	6¾
Ditto, other kinds	,,	0	05	,,	0	2	10
Paper:							
Polishing and emery paper	Free			Free			
Cartridge, packing, blotting, or other similar coarse papers	Kilog.	0	02	Cwt.	0	1	1⅓
Gilt, silvered or glazed paper; also paper combined with cotton or linen tissues ...	,,	0	20	,,	0	11	4
Other kinds, including ruled paper	,,	0	10	,,	0	5	8
Envelopes and paper bags	,,	0	30	,,	0	16	11
Paper hangings and borders	,,	0	25	,,	0	14	1
Paper or pasteboard wares, not otherwise specified:							
Unlacquered	,,	0	50	,,	1	8	3
Lacquered, bronzed, gilt, or silvered ...	,,	2	00	,,	5	12	11
Prints, engravings, lithographs, or photographs, unframed...	,,	0	50	,,	1	8	3
Maps and Charts:							
With Swedish text—							
Loose or simply stitched	,,	1	50	,,	4	4	8
In boards, bound, or mounted on cloth...	,,	2	00	,,	5	12	11
Other kinds...	Free			Free			
Playing cards...	Pack	0	10	Pack	0	0	1⅓
Visiting cards, address cards, labels, forms for bills and accounts...	Kilog.	0	50	Cwt.	1	8	3
Books, printed:							
In the Swedish language, unbound... ...	Free			Free			
Ditto, bound:							
Bibles and psalters bound in paper or cloth covers, without gilding	Kilog.	0	50	Cwt.	1	8	3
Ditto, otherwise bound, or with gilding...	,,	2	00	,,	5	12	11
Other bound books in the Swedish language	Free			Free			
In foreign languages, bound or unbound ...	Free			Free			
Books, blank or merely ruled, bound... ...	Kilog.	0	35	Cwt.	0	19	9
Albums...	,,	2	00	,,	5	12	11
Ink:							
Writing	,,	0	10	,,	0	5	8
Printing	,,	0	07	,,	0	3	11½
Sealing-wax	,,	0	50	,,	1	8	3
Pencils, black-lead	,,	0	35	,,	0	19	9
Ditto, slate, with or without sheaths.. ...	Free			Free			
Pens	Kilog.	0	6	Cwt.	1	13	11
Rags	Free			Free			

SWEDEN:

Tariff Classification.	Tariff Rates of Duty.			English Equivalents.			
		Kron.	öre.		£	s.	d.
Paper:							
Sheathing or roofing paper; tarred or asphalted paper; glass, sand, slate, and emery papers; also descriptions of paper not otherwise specified	Free			Free			
Writing, drawing, and unruled music paper, and all paper suitable for writing or drawing purposes, white or coloured; varnished or oiled paper; parchment paper; also slips of paper for telegrams...	Kilog.	0	13	Cwt.	0	7	4

Tariff Classification.	Tariff Rates of Duty.			English Equivalents.			
		Kron.	ore.		£	s.	d.
Printing paper of all kinds, white or coloured; blotting paper; filtering paper	Free			Free			
Pasteboard, packing paper, cartridge paper, waste paper, press-boards	Free			Free			
Ornaments made of carton pierre	Free			Free			
Paper hangings	Kilog.	0	13	Cwt.	0	7	4
Crochet and embroidery patterns, pattern books, blank forms, labels, ruled paper, visiting cards, tickets, envelopes (including envelopes lined with tissue), shop paper bags, etc.; also paper with gauze or other applications, frames with or without glass, and lacquered pasteboard	,,	0	13	,,	0	7	4
Playing cards	Pack	0	08	Pack	0	0	107
Manuscripts, bank notes, bills, share certificates, etc.	Free			Free			
Paper, bound or stitched	Kilog.	0	27	Cwt.	0	15	3
Other articles of paper or pasteboard (except books), and of papier mache; also albums	,,	0	60	,,	1	13	11
Books, periodicals, newspapers, music, etc., not otherwise enumerated, illustrated or not, bound or unbound; also engravings and lithographs	Free			Free			
Maps and charts	Free			Free			
Ink, writing, and ink powder	Kilog.	0	10	Cwt.	0	5	7$\frac{3}{4}$
Sealing-wax	,,	0	46	,,	1	6	0
Pencils, black-lead, etc.	,,	0	35	,,	0	19	9
,, slate	Free			Free			
Metallic pens, including weight of cards or boxes	Kilog.	0	60	Cwt.	1	13	11
Rags	Free			Free			

DENMARK:

		Kron.	öre.		£	s.	d.
Paper:							
Common, waste, and packing paper; also glass, sand, emery, asphalt, and tarred paper	Pund	0	01$\frac{1}{24}$	Cwt.	0	1	2
Carton pierre and common ornaments, and articles thereof	,,	0	01$\frac{1}{24}$	,,	0	1	2
Other kinds of paper; also if coloured in the mass, varnished, oiled, and chalk paper, &c.	,,	0	05$\frac{5}{24}$	,,	0	5	11
Coloured, gilt, silvered, or embossed paper; engravings, lithographs, photographs, cards, tickets, labels, &c.; ruled paper, paper patterns, and pattern sheets, envelopes and other paper with linings, &c. on cotton or linen	,,	0	16$\frac{2}{3}$	,,	0	18	10
Other articles of paper and of papier mache, including paper with lining of silk or wool	,,	0	33$\frac{1}{3}$	,,	1	17	8
Playing cards...	Pack	0	04$\frac{1}{6}$	Pack	0	0	0$\frac{1}{2}$
Excise duty in addition...	,,	0	16$\frac{2}{3}$	,,	0	0	2$\frac{1}{4}$
Manuscripts, State papers, bank notes, etc...	Free			Free			
Books, printed, of all kinds, bound or unbound	Free			Free			
Sealing-wax	Pund	0	16$\frac{2}{3}$	Cwt.	0	18	10
Pencils, black-lead, etc.	,,	0	10$\frac{5}{12}$	,,	0	11	9
Steel pens	,,	0	33$\frac{1}{3}$	,,	1	17	8
Ink;							
Writing, and ink powder	,, Gross wt.	0	06$\frac{1}{4}$	,, Gross	0	7	1
Printing ink	,,	0	04$\frac{1}{6}$	,,	0	4	8$\frac{1}{2}$
Rags	Free			Free			

CRESCENT BRAND

ENTLE

Papermake

Pur

BURY, ne

Gu

EQUAL TO

'S IMPROVED RAG CUTTE

THE

Form

Econom

B

Refine

This Machine has now been Greatly Strengthened and Simplified, and its Outp Increased. It is Equally Effective upon the Strongest and Lightest Materia cut Every Class of Stock.

British Makers OF THE Coburn-T

FULL PARTICUL

JACKSON

gineers,

ANCHESTER.

RSHALL'S PATENT PERFECTING ENGINE.

BLE FOR ALL CLASSES OF STOCK AND EVERY QUALITY OF PAPER.

MADE IN THREE SIZES.

gine will produce a Better Fi... Stronger and More Even Sheet of Paper from materials than can be produced by any other Mechanical Process, and at the same time will REDUCE the TIME and POWER required for Beating.

supply these Engines on ... above results.

ine—NO WELL-EQUIPPED PAPER MILL SHOULD BE WITHOUT.

APPLICATION.

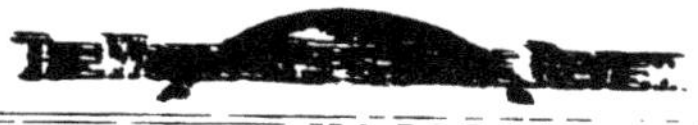

WALMSLEY & Co.,

LIMITED

…KS, BURY, NEAR MANCHESTER.

…Wrights,

Paper Machinists,

BRASS & IRON FOUNDERS.

PAPER BRUSH DAMPING MACHINE.

SPECIALTIES:

HIGH - CLASS STEAM ENGINES.

Simple, Double, Triple, and Quadruple Compound,
from 10 to 1,000 i.h.p., fitted with Automatic Cut-off Gears.

ALL TYPES OF PUMPING MACHINERY:

DEEP WELL PUMPS.	BOILER PUMPS.	PAPERMAKERS'
BORE HOLE PUMPS.	VACUUM PUMPS.	CHEMIC & CAUSTIC Pumps.
STATIONARY FIRE Pumps.	HYDRAULIC PUMPS.	STUFF & WATER PUMPS.

SOLE MAKERS OF

PARTINGTON'S Patent DUPLEX CUTTING MACHINE

...OOF PAPER ...ERIAL

... D... of ... Germ... for the manufacture ... ... a ... thereof, homogeneous ... through ... ... for the manufac... ... also for covering ... ... covering roofs.

... essentially in causing ... the prepared paper ... have become dry ... agglutinants and ... contained ... solidified by the ... in spiral con... roller in such a ... layers of paper ... another and are ... a counter pres... very strong homo... The intimate ... separate prepared ... strength of this ... two factors.

... paper are pressed ... resinous substance ... become dry, the ... ...mately with one ... of using separ... material.

... described manner of ... has for result a ... because there are ... layers of paper being ... time, but only one ... pressed at one time ... paper which have ... and thus rendered ... that they serve as an ... the still loose layer to be ... are only slighty less ... face of the roller itself. ... rollers acts only upon a ... paper at a time, and as it is ... thickness, the pressure is ... fullest extent. The pressure ... subsequent and as yet un... paper is pressed upon the ... that have already been united ... operation, is the same in all ... the result is a structureless or ... product of uniform strength or ...

...dinary gelatine, fish glue or isinglass, ...-glue, casein, oils, solutions of resin, solutions of caoutchouc, gutta percha, marine glue, and the like, may be employed as water-proofing substances and agglutinants, in carrying out the process.

Manchester Ship Canal.—According to the *Manchester Examiner and Times*, the authorities have confidence that the flooding of the canal will be commenced in a few days.

WORLD'S PAPER TRADE REVIEW OFFICE, 58, SHOE LANE, LONDON, E.C.

TRADE NOTES.

THE WOKING PAPER WORKS, LIM.—In the matter of Plomer and Schenkenwald v. the Woking Paper Works, Limited, Mr. Justice Chitty on the 10th inst. made an order, on the application of debenture holders and with the consent of the defendant company, appointing Mr. W. B. Keen receiver and manager.

STAR PAPER MILL CO., LIM.—The balance sheet for the past half-year, after allowing for depreciation and interest, shows a profit of £3,765 17s. 11d., which, added to the amount brought forward from the previous half-year, leaves a disposable balance of £6,771 18s. The directors recommend the payment of a dividend of 3s. per share on the preference, and 4s. per share on the ordinary shares of the company, and carrying forward the balance, £3,565 10s., to next half-year.

IMPROVEMENTS IN ELECTROLYSIS.—Mr. E. Andreoli claims several improvements in electrolysis. According to his latest published specification of patent (No. 12,662), his object is to provide an improved electrolytic apparatus in which a chloride of sodium or other solution is decomposed into its constituent parts, while circulating through positive and negative compartments formed by partitions made of asbestos or kieselguhr or other similar porous porcelain, closely situated between metallic or carbon cathodes and retort carbon anodes constructed in a very simple, economical, and efficient manner.

THE ASSESSMENT OF ESK PAPER MILLS.—Sheriff Blair, in the Edinburgh Sheriff Court, has issued an interlocutor in the appeal by Alexander Cowan and Sons, Limited, papermakers, against the assessment upon their mills by the North Esk Reservoir Company under their special act. He finds that in ascertaining the annual value of the appellants' mills on the banks of the Esk, near Penicuik, for the purpose of assessment, there falls to be deducted from the annual value of the mills, taken at the rent for which they might reasonably be expected to let, a sum which shall bear the same proportion to the annual value that the propelling power of the mills, other than water power, bears to the whole propelling power. He finds that the propelling power of the mills consists partly of water and partly, but to a much greater extent, of power other than water—viz., steam power—and that there has not been deducted from the annual value a sum bearing the same proportion to it that the steam power bears to the whole propelling power of the said mills. He therefore sustains the appeal, and before further answer remits to Mr. David Alan Stevenson, C.E., to fix the sum which falls to be deducted. In a note attached to the interlocutor, the Sheriff points out that the respondents contended that the construction of the proviso maintained by the appellants, and which he himself adopts, was manifestly inequitable and inconsistent with the other provisions of the Act, because it would lead to the result that a mill which did not use the water of the river as a propelling power, but employed it largely for manufacturing and similar purposes would escape assessment altogether, although benefiting from the water sent down from the company's reservoirs. The company may have other remedies against millowners who make such use of the water, but after carefully considering the clauses of the Act bearing on the matter, the Sheriff has come to the opinion that such millowners do not come within the scope of the assessing clauses of the North Esk Reservoir Company's Act. The Sheriff has also issued a similar interlocutor on a similar appeal by the Inveresk Paper Company, Musselburgh.

THE VALUE OF SPRINKLERS.—The recent fire at the Borough Paper Mills, Bradford, in the occupation of Messrs. James Shackleton and Son, paper merchants, would doubtless have assumed serious dimensions had not the operation of the patent sprinklers provided for each floor been at once effective. It was found that the fire had originated in the top storey of a new building, where a large number of bags of waste paper were stored. It had been kept fairly well in check by the sprinklers, but some difficulty was experienced in getting at the root of the mischief. When all the intervening bags had been removed, the flames were speedily subdued by the fire brigade. The sprinkler adopted at the Borough Mills is that known as the "Titan," the sole proprietors being Messrs. George Mills and Co., Globe Iron Works, Radcliffe, near Manchester. This firm recently received the following letter from Messrs. Shackleton and Sons:—"We send you by this post three sprinklers to repair, and we are glad to state that but for the three sprinklers our mill would have undoubtedly been destroyed by fire this morning. Please send us a few more in case something of the kind occurs again."

A ROYAL VISIT TO A NORWEGIAN PAPER MILL.—His Majesty King Oscar II, of Norway and Sweden, H.R.H. Prince Eugene and suite, on their recent tour to the highly-interesting Ulefos-Strengen-Canal, and the charmingly-situated town Skien in Norway (well-known to tourists who have visited Thelemarken), paid a visit to the Union Company's paper mill at Skotfos, close to the gigantic Lóveid Locks. The Skotfos wood pulp and paper mill is about the most extensive and complete industrial undertaking of its kind in Europe, and the Royal visitors were so highly interested in the process of papermaking that their inspection lasted over an hour. Machine No. I was at the time making "Standard" reel printing; No. II, "Lóveid" grease-proof paper; No. III, "Union" bag paper, and No. IV. "M. G." small hands. His Majesty and H.R.H. Prince Eugene pronounced their admiration

ST. NEOTS PAPER MIL[illegible] LIMITED.

It is rather surprising, consid[illegible]
large proportion of the shar[illegible]
St. Neot's Paper Mill Co., L[illegible]
near at hand, that only abo[illegible]
286 persons on the shareh[illegible]
the meeting called by the di[illegible]
Perhaps the flood of literatu[illegible] the
company's affairs during th[illegible] mount to
quenched to a great extent [illegible] balance.
may have had in the [illegible] appropriated
standing that the director[illegible] Borregard
circular dated the 6th of [illegible] have written
ments had been made [illegible] goodwill, &c.,
modelling and re-equipmen[illegible] a dividend
find it officially stat[illegible] of 7 per cent.
dated 27th September, [illegible] £12,391, carry-
of the mill buildings a[illegible] £1,647. The total
ing 'up-to-date' [illegible] therefore at the
the present time
and an appe[illegible] Y BILL.—The House
capitalists "[illegible] Wednesday resumed the
of debentur[illegible] Employers' Liability
out that [illegible] Tomlinson's proposed
The meeting [illegible] that where an em-
to Mr. J. M[illegible] workman on account of
of the [illegible] any person in the service
Thomas [illegible] such person may be made a
further [illegible] the suit, and the employer
plicit. [illegible] recourse upon him for damages
face of th[illegible] the plaintiff as if such person had
the shar[illegible] son sued. The amendment was
the [illegible] defeated by 162 to 61.—Mr.
[illegible] moved an amendment providing
[illegible] costs chargeable by the County
[illegible] issuing a summons, plaint, or writ
[illegible] Act should not exceed 5s. for a
[illegible] summons, and 10s. for hearing and
[illegible] fee.—Mr. A. J. Balfour pointed out
[illegible] amendment could only be regarded
[illegible] initial and governing step to a general
[illegible] of the present extravagant County
[illegible] fees. The difficulty in the way of such
[illegible] tion lay, he said, with the Treasury
[illegible] This amendment was agreed to, and
[illegible] others having been dealt with, the
[illegible] adjourned.

[illegible] AS FUEL.—The use of oil instead of [illegible] under the boilers at the World's Fair is [illegible] to result in the much greater use of [illegible] fuel by manufacturers than has been [illegible] case heretofore. The experiment at [illegible] cago has proved in almost every way a [illegible] satisfactory one. The oil has cost much less [illegible] coal for the same purpose would have [illegible], while there have been no ashes to [illegible] with, and the emission of smoke, a [illegible] essential point where cleanliness is so important as it is at the Fair, has been en[illegible] avoided. The heat, moreover, has [illegible] much more uniform than could have [illegible] obtained had coal been used. The [illegible] of the fuel has necessitated the em[illegible] of only about one-fourth as many [illegible] have been employed had coal [illegible] of oil. The experiment [illegible] argument for the use of [illegible] in large [illegible] and [illegible] is so [illegible] as to [illegible] high in price.—*Manufac-*

FINANCIAL.

Dealings in shares connected with paper and print show considerable fluctuations, some of which need explanation. H. Spicer and Co., Limited, have dropped considerably, the ordinary being freely offered at a fall of 10s. to £3 sellers, whilst the pref. £10 fully paid have fallen 5s., and are a difficult sale at 5½-6, while the debentures have fallen 3 to 60-70, a suggestively wide margin. Cassell and Co., Limited, have changed hands at 16[illegible], also at 16¼, falling to 16[illegible]. A few days ago S. Hildesheimer and Co., Limited, £5 fully paid were dealt in at 1½, and were freely advertised by a touting broker at £2 10s., but they are nominally quoted at 2-3. Townsend, Hook and Co., Limited, £10 shares, £5 paid, are being privately offered for sale at £4, ordinary £10 fully paid at £9 17s. 6d., although a 10 per cent. dividend has always been paid. R. Hornsby and Sons have fallen 2s. 6d. to 3¾-4, and Babcock and Wilcox 10s. lower to 9½-10½; also Bergvik 10s. to 5¼-6¼, and the ordinary 9½. Mason and Mason pref. have changed hands freely at 6 [illegible] and 6¼. The preference shares of Waterlow Bros. and Layton fell 10s. to 10½-11½ upon the announcement that the committee of the Stock Exchange have ordered to be quoted in the official list 5 per cent. preference shares, numbers 1 to 10,000, also the ordinary shares, number 1 to 10,000 in lieu of shares of the old company already quoted, whilst, curious to record, the ordinary rose 1 to 23-5. Waterlow and Sons, Limited, are £1 lower at 22-24. Angus and Co. are 5s. firmer at 11¾ and 12¼. Quite a small boom has occurred at Manchester in the Kellner-Partington shares, the £5 fully paid having advanced to £6-£6 10s. whilst the £2 15s. paid have been steadily rising to 3¾-¼. Chemical shares continue to fall, probably owing to the coal strike, and both the United Alkali and Brunner Mond and Co. are lower, and show a drooping tendency. A number of shares in other commercial companies are being offered, but are very difficult to dispose of. Mitchell's library deferred £1 fully paid are offered at 6s. 6d., and Linotype ordinary £5 fully paid at £1 3s. 9d., and £5 pref. fully paid £4 3s. 6d. Blackman's Ventilator £1 fully paid at 17s. 6d.; Greenwood and Batley ord. £1[illegible] fully paid at 4¼-5¼, and pref. at 6-7. London Stereoscopic £5 fully paid at 1¼-¾. Latest dealings may be recorded as follows: Babcock and Wilcox 9¾; Cassell and Co. 16¾; Mason and Mason, ord. 8¾; Waterlow and Sons, pref. 14[illegible]; and Waterlow Bros. and Layton 11½-12½ pref.

AT the Greenbank Chemical Works, at St. Helens, a fire broke out on Tuesday destroying the immense vitriol chambers.

IT appears that straw paper is usually imported into Turkey in bales of 50 kilogrammes (about 1 cwt. each, at least this is the legal weight, but in all probability it dries *en route*, as it sometimes only weighs 49 kilos on arrival, thus showing a difference of 2 per cent.

APPLICATIONS FOR TRADE MARKS.

RELATING TO CLASS 39.

174,567.—Paper and envelopes. An armorial device of a shield containing three crosses and a crescent, together with the words "Royal and Ancient" in Old English letter. William Ritchie and Sons, 16, Elder-street, Edinburgh, wholesale stationers. Applied for August 19, 1893. Date of publication, October 11, 1893.

174,673.—A newspaper. Title heading of *The Graphic*. H. R. Baines and Company, Ltd. The proprietors of *The Graphic* newspaper, 190, Strand, London, W.C., newspaper proprietors and publishers. Applied for August 24, 1893. Date of publication, October 11, 1893. Mark used by applicants and predecessors in business at least five years before August 13, 1875.

174,676.—A newspaper. The title heading of the *Weekly Dispatch*. Thomas Vernon and Company, Limited, the proprietors of the *Weekly Dispatch* newspaper, 20, Wine Office-court, London, E.C., newspaper publishers and proprietors. Applied for 24th August, 1893. Date of publication October 11th, 1893. Mark used by applicants and predecessors in business seventy-four years before the 13th August, 1875.

174,553.—A newspaper. Title heading of the *British Trade Journal*. William Agnew, 113, Cannon-street, London, E.C. newspaper proprietor. Applied for August 18th, 1893. Date of publication October 18th, 1893. Mark used four years and seven months before August 13th, 1875.

175,036.—A newspaper. The title heading of the *Hairdresser's Chronicle and Trade Journal*. Robert Hovenden and Sons, 30, 31, 32, and 33, Berners-street, W., and 91, 93, and 95, City-road, E.C., London, newspaper proprietors. Applied for September 14th, 1893. Date of publication October 25th, 1893. Mark used since eight years before the 13th August, 1875.

THE *Strand Magazine* for November is bright and entertaining. "The Adventures of Sherlock Holmes" are read with unflagging interest, and a feature in this number is the Royal Wedding from an Oriental point of view, a reproduction of a photo of the Duke and Duchess of York forming the frontispiece. The "Stories from the Diary of a Doctor," illustrated interviews, portraits of celebrities, and several short stories, profusely illustrated, go to make up the well-arranged contents. *The Picture Magazine* for this month keeps up its reputation for diversification, the illustrations, representing fine art, comic pictures, portraits, old prints, &c., are with one or two exceptions well printed. *The Million* and *Tit-Bits* are also included in the budget from George Newnes, Limited. The former publication contains a coloured portrait of the new Lord Mayor, and a sketch of the Guildhall by Val Prince. Several Christmas prizes are announced in *Tit-Bits*.

THE *English Illustrated Magazine*, published at 198, Strand, W.C., in its November number, gives a portrait of the late Surgeon-Major Parke, and Mr. Herbert Ward contributes an article on "Martyrs to a new Crusade," dealing with recent history of central African exploration. "Interesting Reminiscences of Balliol College," by Andrew Lang, illustrated by Holland Tringham, are published, and "The past and present of Lloyd's," gives the general reader some idea of the work of that institution. The various other well-illustrated contributions afford excellent reading matter.

A LITHOGRAPHER'S PAPER MATURING APPLIANCE.—Mr. J. P. Jennings, of Liverpool, has devised an apparatus for seasoning, maturing, drying, or shrinking, printing, lithographing and other papers either in sheet or in web—during the process of making—before the process of printing or lithographing the paper—and during the process of printing or lithographing the paper in one or more printings and colours, with the view of securing more accurate and exact register than is possible with paper not so matured for printing. The apparatus consists of a strong framework of wood or iron between the two uprights at each end, a number of rollers arranged one above another, and over these rollers a number of endless tapes are arranged, which are caused to travel by attaching to the driving wheel a belt connected with any motive power, or which may be turned by hand. A feed table is fixed near the top of the two front uprights, on this the paper if in sheet is placed and fed sheet by sheet by hand under the adjacent roller by which it is carried forward on the endless tapes, by which the paper is carried over each roller in succession, forwards and backwards from, and thereafter falls on to the sloping delivery table fixed near the bottom of the two front uprights. If the paper is in web the web is so fixed that the paper is run on to the tapes over the feeding board and re-reeled from the delivery table. The apparatus must be covered in on all sides so as to exclude dust and damp air, but more especially in order to get the full benefit from the warm dry air generated by an atmospheric gas stove or hot steam pipes placed underneath the machine, or in any other position from which a current of warm dry air can be directed so as to develop and act upon the paper during its process through the machine.

MESSRS. BROOK AND BRIGGS, rag merchants, Ossett, Yorks, have dissolved partnership.

as to the [illegible] fellow[illegible] stores [illegible] to State [illegible] the [illegible] employees.

[illegible] Co., [illegible] of [illegible] for [illegible] £1000 [illegible] for the [illegible] per [illegible] dividend [illegible] rate [illegible]

[illegible] supplies [illegible] years old. [illegible] card [illegible] wholesale [illegible] towns, who [illegible] Austria as [illegible] prices [illegible] foreign [illegible] expect [illegible] dealers are [illegible] object [illegible] the [illegible] agent [illegible] cases [illegible] firmly [illegible] mills are principally inter[illegible] trade, while Austria does [illegible] The over-pro[illegible] result is so great [illegible] improve[illegible]

[illegible] TRADE OF JAPAN.

[illegible] continues on a [illegible] was [illegible] of Japan [illegible] 1892 [illegible] The [illegible] Japan's [illegible] importation of [illegible] importa[illegible]

[illegible] increased [illegible] compared [illegible]

[illegible] the [illegible] place [illegible] value of [illegible] a little [illegible] the years

[illegible] from Japan [illegible] 1891 [illegible] 1892 [illegible] value, in [illegible] value of [illegible]

[illegible] PAPER Co., Rum[illegible] have three engines and [illegible] men at work piling logs. [illegible] feet of spruce are already [illegible] much more will be pulled out [illegible] which is to be converted into

PAPER EXPORTS.

FOR THE WEEK ENDING TUESDAY LAST:

	Printings.	Writings.	Other Kinds.
AUSTRALASIA ...	2847 cwts.	343 cwts.	588 cwts.
AFRICA	18 ,,	33 ,,	26 ,,
ARABIA	— ,,	2 ,,	— ,,
ARGENTINE ...	— ,,	35 ,,	17 ,,
B. WEST INDIES...	— ,,	66¾ ,,	2 ,,
B. GUIANA	— ,,	4½ ,,	— ,,
CHANNEL ISLES...	4 ,,	— ,,	— ,,
CANADA	499 ,,	215½ ,,	230¼ ,,
CAPE COLONY ...	40 ,,	88 ,,	558 ,,
CHINA	41 ,,	54 ,,	— ,,
DUTCH GUIANA...	1 ,,	— ,,	— ,,
DENMARK	42 ,,	2 ,,	— ,,
FRANCE	33 ,,	47 ,,	55 ,,
GERMANY	1691 ,,	72 ,,	11 ,,
HOLLAND	— ,,	— ,,	10 ,,
INDIA	912 ,,	728 ,,	139¼ ,,
ITALY	— ,,	20 ,,	— ,,
JAPAN	6 ,,	11 ,,	— ,,
MAURITIUS ...	— ,,	— ,,	1 ,,
NEW ZEALAND ...	389 ,,	77 ,,	243 ,,
NORWAY	12 ,,	2 ,,	— ,,
RUSSIA	— ,,	13 ,,	2 ,,
SPAIN	44 ,,	4 ,,	— ,,
STRAIT Settlements	6 ,,	1 ,,	2 ,,
S. AMERICA... ...	— ,,	7 ,,	8 ,,
TURKEY	— ,,	1 ,,	— ,,
U.S.A.	— ,,	94 ,,	— ,,
W. INDIES	268 ,,	8 ,,	2 ,,

PAPER IMPORTS.

FOR THE WEEK ENDING TUESDAY LAST:

AUSTRIA ...	602 bales	GERMANY ...	120 cases
BELGIUM ...	1375 ,,	HOLLAND ...	7184 bales
,, ...	333 cases	,, ...	173 cases
CHANNEL I. ...	15 bales	INDIA	26 ,,
DENMARK ...	266 ,,	ITALY	5 cases
,, ...	1244 rolls	NORWAY ...	956 bales
,, ...	59 cases	PRUSSIA ...	634 ,,
EGYPT	1 ,,	SWEDEN ...	853 ,,
FINLAND ...	218 bales	,, ...	2 cases
FRANCE ...	150 ,,	,, ...	2787 rolls
,, ...	41 cases	U.S.A.	228 bales
GERMANY ...	2627 bales	,, ...	280 rolls

Including the Following:

Quantity	From	Importer	Port.
44 bales	Copenhagen	Becker & Ulrich	London
15 ,,	,,	Schenkenwald & Co	,,
8 cases	Colombo	Berrick Bros	,,
2 ,,	Gothenburg	Duff & Co	,,
55 bales	,,	Hummell & Co	,,
109 ,,	,,	Sabel	,,
221 ,,	,,	Becker & Ulrich	,,
1004 rolls	,,	Schenkenwald & Co	,,
16 pkgs	,,	Spicer & Sons	,,
2 bales	Marseilles	L. Duforest	,,
100 ,,	New York	J. M. Richards	,,
151 ,,	Stettin	Becker & Ulrich	,,
7 ,,	,,	A. Rosedale & Son	,,
17 ,,	,,	W. D. Edwards	,,
68 ,,	,,	J. Spicer & Sons	,,
82 ,,	,,	M. Benscher	,,
50 ,,	,,	E. E. Sabel	,,
1 case	Suez	East Tel. Co	,,
82 bales	Stockholm	Hummel & Co	,,
11 ,,	,,	Horne & Co	
17 ,,	,,	R. Figg & Co	,,
1244 rolls	,,	Schenkenwald & Co	,,
602 bales	Trieste	Sabel & Co	,,
585 ,,	Uddevalla	C. Poulter	,,
456 ,,	,,	D. Gulland	,,
742 ,,	,,	A. L. Lundgren	,,

SUMMARY OF IMPORTS & EXPORTS,

FOR THE WEEK ENDING TUESDAY LAST.

London, Liverpool, Bristol, Southampton, Hull, Fleetwood, Harwich, Folkestone, Newhaven, Dover, &c.

IMPORTS.

Paper	13550 bales	Stationery.........	83 cases
,, ...	727 cases	,, ...	5 pkgs.
,, ...	5097 rolls	Strawboards	5083 ,,
Pasteboards	11 cases	Millboards	18043 ,,
,, ...	7592 pkgs.	Parchment	2 ,,
Tissues	76 cases		

EXPORTS.

British Goods.			
Paper	1615 cwt.	Strawboards	21 cwt.
Writing Paper ...	1420 ,,	Rags..................	10 tons
Printing Paper	4972 ,,	Parchment	£266 value
Stationery......	£7341 value	**Foreign Goods.**	
Millboards	75 cwt.	Paper	35 cwt.
Stock	36 tons	Printing Paper...	105 ,,
Cardboards	125 cwt.	Stationery	£96 value
Waste	172 tons	Strawboards	347 cwt.
		Wood Pulp	25 tons

Glasgow, Greenock, Port-Glasgow, Troon, Grangemouth, &c.

IMPORTS.

Paper	679 bales	Pasteboards	39 bales
,, ...	14 cases	Strawboards	5152 pkgs
,, ...	280 rolls	Stock	17 ,,

EXPORTS.

Printing Paper..	811 cwt.	Bags..................	6¾ cwt.
Writing Paper...	419 ,,	Pulp Boards	81 ,,
Paper	296½ ,,	Envelopes	9¼ ,,
Stationery	£62 value		

Leith, Granton, Boness, Dundee, &c.

IMPORTS.

Paper	680 bales	Envelopes	391 pkgs.
,, ...	8 cases	Millboards.........	83 ,,
Pasteboards	205 bales	Stationery	1 case
Tissues	14 pkgs.		

NEW PATENTS.

BRITISH.

APPLICATIONS.

20,525. Improvements in and relating to paper calender machines. C. Chalmers and J. Thomson.

20,575. A process for the production of tannic extract from the waste lyes obtained in the manufacture of sulphite cellulose. M. Honig and G. Spitz.

20,792. Improvements in and relating to machines for the manufacture of endless wire cloth or bands used in paper manufacture. P. Tourasse.

SPECIFICATIONS PUBLISHED.

(7½d. each. By post 8d.)

1893.

12,662. Electrolysis. Andreoli.

1890.

5,285. Bleaching vegetable fibres. Kellner. (Second edition).

1891.

5,999. Chlorine and sodium amalgam. Greenwood. (Second edition).

AMERICAN.

505,421. Machine for making paper hoops. Walter E. Frost, Lewiston, assignor of three fourths to Louis J. Cote, Waterville, Me.

505,483. Pulp strainer. D. Wellington Rounds, Dexter, N.Y.

505,895. Apparatus for the electrolytic production of soda and chlorine. Elisha B. Cutten, New York, N.Y.

505,970. Friction clutch. Peter Weber, Schenectady, N.Y.

505,982. Apparatus for applying colour to paper. William A Hall, Bellows Falls, Vt.

THE SWISS PAPER TRADE.

The Swiss paper industry dates the 15th century, for papermaking hand in hand with the early printing press in Basel and Zurich possessed one of the earliest and tant paper mills. Twelve paper at the beginning of the tury, but the mills were worked for home consumption last 20 or 30 years, however, place, and Swiss mills sales in east Up to the commencement war medium papers from Switzerland into papers came from Though Austria quite as good have always French taste, preference, papers find that importation qualities, which upon the This low abled the Austrian a good grade was

... NOVEMBER 17, 1893.

... the paragraph ... column be true, ... the title in the near ... and Mr. Stead and ... to their laurels, for ... merely playing with ... American lady, rejoicing ... Butler, has by the aid of ... evolved from her inner ... new method of making wood ... by a Yankee contem... "Pulp," and that, so it is ... made 50 per cent. cheaper ... present method, while it is, Oh! ... better. The lady is not a dis... Blavatsky, neither does she ... anything about the "fourth ... the astral fluids, but states ... discovery has been made more in ... with these theories than by mere ... or spiritualistic divina... Palmer possesses the power to ... with psychic power anyone's ... this too, irrespective of the ... at the time. Truly ... words," and knock the ... common professors of occultism ... hat, why, even a genuine ... is not in it with her. ... remember Irving Bishop, ... Slade, and Home (with his ... we are inclined to wait for more ... giving credit to what bears ... resemblance to a canard.

... shareholders of St. Neots Paper ... have agreed to a scheme of ... and the directors are author... the necessary steps to carry the ... So far back as April a ... was agreed to, but no advance in the matter was made. It is hardly fair to Mr. Edwin Thomas, who has been acting as managing director at the mill for the past few months, to blame him for the delay, although some of the shareholders at the recent meeting at St. Neots may feel inclined to do so, as the observations made were not sufficiently explanatory. Financial matters have been the chief cause, and owing to Mr. Thomas's propositions not being acceded to by the directors, he has now given up all connection with the concern. The present scheme is as follows:

1.—"When the new works are completed and Machinery erected as mentioned in the Report, the actual value of the property of the Company as a going Concern shall be ascertained by valuation and if the value as so ascertained, less the debts and liabilities of the Company then existing shall be less than the amount of the paid up Capital of the Company, then paid up Capital to the extent of the difference shall be cancelled as Capital lost or unrepresented by available assets, and the necessary steps shall be taken for this purpose, and the nominal amount of the issued shares and also the unissued shares shall be reduced accordingly. Or the amount may at the option of the Directors be placed to a suspense account, pending further instructions from the Shareholders."

2.—"When and as soon as the Capital lost or unrepresented by available assets shall have been cancelled or placed to suspense account as aforesaid, a call not exceeding five shillings per share is to be made on the Members in respect of their ordinary shares to the intent that one pound per share shall remain uncalled on such shares."

In the original scheme of reconstitution the actual value of the property of the company as a going concern was to be ascertained by an expert to be appointed by the company. In the present scheme it may be pointed out that the services of an expert are not stipulated.

THE Holland-Richardson electrolytic process is being steadily developed by the Electrolytic Caustic Soda and Chlorine Trust at their works at Snodland. At the recent annual meeting the shareholders were informed of the progress made, and independent testimony was quoted as to the difficulties overcome and the present economical advantages of manufacture compared with processes at present in use. At one time we were accused of giving too much prominence to electrolytical methods for the production of caustic soda and chlorine, but it is now evident their importance cannot be overestimated. Mr. Ludwig Mond, of Brunner, Mond and Co., Limited, and Dr. Hurter, chemist to the United Alkali Co., Limited, have carefully examined the Holland-Richard process and speak highly of the work accomplished. These gentlemen, it may be mentioned, are also associated with patents dealing with electrolysis. Apparently the Electrolytic Caustic Soda and Chlorine Trust, Limited, are in advance of other similar companies brought before the trade, inasmuch as they have submitted samples of their product to papermakers, and the testimonials received are highly satisfactory. The consensus of opinion given by scientific men must be very gratifying to the inventors and also to the shareholders. The future outlook may be considered one of great promise, and we understand since the meeting further reports have been made by Mr. Leith and Dr. Hopkinson, F.R.S. The latter says the company's latest electrolytic patents have further reduced the manufacture of caustic soda and bleach by another 33 per cent.

THE wide-spread and disastrous effects produced by the long continuance of the dispute in the coal trade was referred to by Mr. Gladstone in the House of Commons on Monday night, and the Government has now appointed Lord Rosebery to act as chairman at a Joint Conference to be held at the Foreign Office to-day, Friday. He has no official powers either as arbitrator or otherwise, to settle the question at issue, and will depend entirely upon his tact and influence, both of which, however, are great. Nevertheless, the step is one in the direction of Government interference in labour troubles, and it may lead to further developments in the same direction. If Lord Rosebery succeeds in bringing about a settlement, a precedent will have been established, which may be of the greatest service when another struggle of a similarly obstinate character, and affecting the well being of the community at large, turns up. It is to be hoped a speedy settlement will be effected as the air is full of rumours of mills being forced to shut down. It may be mentioned the East Lancashire Paper Mill, after having been at work only a fortnight, was again closed last week.

IN studying the Board of Trade Returns readers no doubt oftentimes notice certain incongruities. For instance, in our last issue reference was made to the British importations of paper from Holland, and according to the official statement for the first nine months of this year Holland supplied 29 per cent. and Germany only 23 per cent. of the total value of our foreign paper arrivals. It is obvious, considering the size of the two countries, and the competitive nature of the Germans, that a much larger quantity of paper would be received from Germany than from Holland. We may point out, therefore, that the latter country offers important advantages as a shipping centre, and the paper dispatched is frequently other than Dutch. The absence of any mention of this fact in the Board of Trade Returns greatly lessens the value which otherwise would attach to the figures compiled.

ON anther page we give the import duties of Norway, Sweden, and Denmark. In regard to Norway extensive modifications were made last year mostly by way of increase in rates of duty, and further additions were also introduced into the tariff last July. Some extensive alterations were made in the Swedish tariff in June, 1893, and the tariff is now in many respects less favourable to British trading interests than formerly. Machinery previously free now pays 10 per cent. *ad valorem*; leather belting formerly admitted free also pays 10 per cent. *ad valorem*. The alterations made in the Danish tariff have little or no material effect upon the paper and allied trades.

THE executive committee of the National Commission of the World's Fair has (according to *Reuter*) received a report from the special committee appointed to inquire into the complaints against the methods adopted by Mr. Thatcher, President of the Bureau of Awards, in judging the exhibits. The report supports the foreign exhibitors and censures Mr. Thatcher's action. It also appeals to the executive committee to extricate the premium list office out of the confusion into which it has been plunged.

Cheating the Gods! A correspondent of the *North China Herald*, writing from the interior of Kiangsu province, mentions that one of the industries there is the manufacture of mock money for offering to the dead. Formerly the Chinese burnt sham paper money, but in these days of enlightenment and foreign intercourse the natives of Soongkong, Hangchow, and other places have come to the conclusion that dollars are more handy to the ghosts than clumsy paper money; hence they now, to a great extent, supply their ancestors and departed friends with mock dollars. These are only half the size of real dollars, but there appears to be no more harm in cheating the dead than there is in cheating the living. Besides, the deceased are not supposed to know the difference, for many of them departed this life before silver dollars were imported into China.

[illegible]

MARKET REPORT

and RECORD of IMPORTS

Of Foreign Rags, Wood Pulp, [illegible] Paper Mill [illegible], &c., at the Ports of London, Liverpool, [illegible], Hull, [illegible], Middlesborough, Glasgow, [illegible], Dundee, Leith, [illegible], and [illegible] for the WEEK ENDING NOVEMBER [illegible].

From SPECIAL Sources and [illegible]

Telegrams—"[illegible], LONDON."

CHEMICALS. — The market is steady, and [illegible] f.o.b. Tyne shows a drop [illegible], and BLEACHING POWDER has advanced [illegible] £7 [illegible] SODA CRYSTALS are still [illegible] at £2 [illegible], and SULPHITE is about [illegible]. Exports of SULPHATE OF AMMONIA have slightly increased; it is offered at [illegible] 6d. to £[illegible] per ton.

Prices are nominally as follows:

					£	s.	d.
A.Rnk. [illegible]	[illegible]	—	[illegible] works	2½	4	5	[illegible]
„ [illegible]	[illegible]	—	„ „	2½	4	2	[illegible]
„ [illegible]	—	—	f.o.b. Liverpool	2½	4	[illegible]	[illegible]
Alum Ground, [illegible]	[illegible]	—	„ Liverpool	2½	5	[illegible]	[illegible]
„ „	[illegible]	—	„ „	2½	5	[illegible]	6
„ „	[illegible]	—	„ Hull	2½	5	5	2
„ „	„	—	[illegible]	2½	5	5	2
Alum (Lump)	„	—	f.o.b. Liverpool	2½	4	17	6
„ „	[illegible]	—	„ „	2½	5	2	0
„ „	[illegible]	—	„ Hull	2½	4	15	2
„ „	„	—	[illegible]	2½	4	15	0
„ „	„	—	[illegible]	2½	5	5	2
„ „	„	—	[illegible]	2½	5	5	2
Alumina Sulphate, [illegible]			f.o.b. Tyne		4	2	5
„ „	[illegible]		„ „		3	17	6
Aluminoferric Cake, [illegible]			Liverpool	—	2	15	3
„ „	[illegible]		„	—	3	2	6
Alumina Cake, [illegible]			Glasgow		2	15	0
„ „	[illegible]	—	„		3	1	3
Aluminous Cake, [illegible]		—	Manchester	[illegible]	2	7	6
„ „	„	—	Newcastle	2½	2	10	0
„ „	„	—	London	2½	3	0	2
„ „	bags	—	„	2½	2	17	9
Blanc Fixe	..	—	f.o.b. Tyne	net	7	10	0
Bleach [illegible]	—	—	„ „	net	7	15	2
„ (soft wood)	—	—	f.o.r. Lancs.	net	8	2	6
„ (hard wood)	—	—	f.o.b. Liverpool	net	8	10	0
... ...	...	...	landed London	2½%	9	0	0
Borax (crystals)	...	...	— — —	net	29	0	0
„ powdered		...	— —	net	30	0	0
Caustic Cream, 60%	..	..	f.o.r. Lancs.	net	9	2	6
„ „ 60%	..	..	f.o.b. Liverpool	net	9	7	6
„ Bottoms			„ „	net	6	15	0
			f.o.b. Tyne	net	6	15	0
Chloride of Barium	...		f.o.b. Tyne	net	7	10	0
Caustic White 76-77%			f.o.r. Newcastle	net	11	10	0
„ 77%	f.o.r. or		f.o.b. Tyne	net	12	0	0
„ 74%	..		f.o.b. Liverpool	net	11	15	0
„ 70%	..		„	net	10	15	0
„ 70%	..		„ Hull	net	11	0	0
„ 70%	...		f.o.r. London	net	10	15	0
„ 70	.		f.o.b. Tyne	net	10	0	0
„ 70%	..		f.o.r. Lancs.	net	10	12	6
„ 60%	..		„ London	net	9	15	0
„ 60%			f.o.b. Liverpool	net	9	15	0
Carbonate [illegible] 58%			„ „	net	4	10	0
„ 48%			„	net	4	0	0
„ [illegible]%			f.o.r. Widnes	net	4	7	6
„ [illegible]%			„ „	net	3	17	6
Soda [illegible]			f.o.r. Tyne		5	15	0
„ [illegible]			ex ship Liverpool	net	6	12	0

					£	s.	d.
[illegible] Acid	—	—	—	f.o.b. Liverpool	[illegible]	per lb.	
Salt Cake	—	—	—	„ works	net	1	10	0
Soda Ash, 58%	—	—	—	f.o.b. Tyne	net	4	0	0
„ 58%	—	—	—	ex ship Thames	1%	4	10	0
„ 58%	—	—	—	f.o.b. Liverpool	1%	4	5	0
Soda Crystals	—	—	—	„ Tyne	net	2	10	0
„ „	—	—	—	ex ship Thames	2½%	2	17	6
„ „	—	—	—	f.o.b. Liverpool	net	3	5	0
Sulphur, roll	—	—	—	f.o.r. works	2½%	7	17	6
„ [illegible]	—	—	—	„ „	2½%	9	10	0
„ [illegible]	—	—	—	„ „	2½%	4	5	0
Sulphate of Ammonia	—	—	—	„ „	2½%	12	10	0
„ of Copper	—	—	—	„ Liverpool	5%	26	0	0

FOREIGN.—F.o.b. Continental port:

		£	s.	d.
[illegible]	—	5	[illegible]	[illegible]
[illegible]	—	10	12	6
[illegible] Sulphate of Soda [illegible] casks ...	—	6	0	[illegible]
Sulphate of Ammonia [illegible] cwt. casks net c.i.f. Ldn		4	7	6
Blanc Fixe c.i.f. London	—	7	12	6

CHEMICAL WOOD PULPS. — The market is without material change, although there is a [illegible] tendency. SULPHITE keeps firm, and SODA Pulps steady.

Prices, ex steamer, London, Hull, Newcastle, Leith and Glasgow are nominally as follows:

	£	s.	d.		£	s.	d.
SULPHITE, Unbleached, Common	10	0	0 to		11	0	0
„ Superior — — —	11	0	0 „		12	10	0
„ „ 50% moisture, d.w.	11	0	0 „		12	0	0
„ Extra — — — —	12	0	0 „		13	0	0
„ Bleached, moist — —					16	10	0
„ Unbleached, English, del. Lancs. ...					10	15	0
„ „ No. 1, ex mills, Ldn.					10	12	6
„ „ No. 2. „ „					9	15	0
SODA, Unbleached, Common —	10	5	0 „		10	10	0
„ „ Extra —	10	10	0 „		11	0	0
„ Half-Bleached — —	12	10	0 „		14	0	0
SULPHATE, Unbleached, Common	10	10	0 „		11	0	0
„ Extra — — — —	11	0	0 „		12	0	0
„ Half-Bleached — —	13	10	0 „		14	0	0
„ Bleached — — —	15	0	0 „		16	0	0

MECHANICAL WOOD PULPS. — Nearly all arrivals are due on contracts, and few spot parcels are being offered except at high prices, although consumers are inconvenienced by the coal strike it does not hinder them from taking in supplies readily.

Prices, ex steamer, London, Hull, Newcastle, Leith and Glasgow are nominally as follows:

	£	s.	d.		£	s.	d.
MECHANICAL, Aspen, Dry ...	£7	10	0 to		8	0	0
Pine, Dry — — ...	7	10	0 „		7	15	0
Pine, Moist — — ...	3	10	0 „		3	15	0
Moist Brown — ...	3	2	6 „		3	5	0
Single Sorted — — ...	2	7	6 „		2	10	0
Dry Brown — — ...	6	5	0 „		6	10	0

WEEK'S IMPORTS.

Quantity	From	Importer	Port.
1516 bales	Christiania	To order	Hull
[illegible] „	„	„	Grangemouth
200 „	Cologne	„	London
300 „	Copenhagen	„	Leith
40 „	Drontheim	„	Hull
1[illegible] „	Drammen	Christophersen & Co	London
475 „	„	E. & W. Goldsmith	„
3048 „	„	E. Lloyd	„
[illegible] „	Gothenburg	To order	Granton
2535 „	„	„	Hull
203 „	„	Taylor & Co	„
6 „	„	Christophersen & Co	„
72 „	„	To order	„
643 „	Ghent	„	London
108 casks	„	„	„
204 bales	Hambro	„	Grangemouth
276 „	„	„	London
507 „	„	„	„
433 „	Helsingfors	„	„
200 „	Norrkoping	„	Hull
400 „	Rotterdam	„	Liverpool
1066 rolls	„	„	London
125 bales	„	„	Liverpool
630 tons	Skein	Brown, Stewart & Co	London
312 bales	Stettin	T. Ronaldson	„

Totals from Each Country:

BELGIUM	...	643 bales	HOLLAND	...	505 bales
,,	...	102 casks	,,	...	1066 rolls
DENMARK	...	300 bales	NORWAY	...	9418 bales
FINLAND	...	233 ,,	PRUSSIA	...	533 ,,
GERMANY	..	987 ,,	SWEDEN	...	4239 ,,

WEEK'S IMPORTS of WOOD PULP BOARDS.

Quantity	From	Importer	Port
6 cases	Christiania	To order	Hull
129 bales	Gothenburg	,,	,,

ESPARTO.—The market is unchanged. The enquiry is limited, and prices nominally without alteration.

Prices c.i.f. London and Leith, or f.o.r. Cardiff, Garston and Tyne Docks are nominally as follows:

Spanish—Fair to Good ...	... ...	£5 5 0 to 5 10 0
,, Fine to Best ...	... ...	5 10 0 ,, 5 15 0
Oran — Fair to Good ...	... ...	3 5 0 ,, 3 10 0
,, First Quality...	... ...	3 15 0 ,, 3 17 6
Tripoli — Hand-picked ...	... ...	3 15 0 ,, 3 17 6
,, Fair Average ...	... ...	3 7 6 ,, 3 10 0
Bona & Philippeville ...	... ...	3 15 0 ,, 3 17 6

WEEK'S IMPORTS.

Quantity	From	Importer	Port.
730 tons	Bona	To order	Glasgow

STRAW.—Stocks are low. There is an improved demand for Oat Straw which shows an advance of 5s., while Wheat Straw has been sold at a rise of 2s. 6d. to 5s. per ton.

WEEK'S IMPORTS.

(Purposes unspecified) at principal Ports From

BELGIUM	...	153 bales	GERMANY	...	20 tons
DENMARK	...	63 ,,	HOLLAND	...	1890 bales
FRANCE	...	2 ,,			

STRAW PULPS.—These is a moderate trade passing in Straw Pulp.

Prices, c.i.f. London, Hull or Leith:

German, 50 to 55% moisture £16 10 0
do. dry, ... No. 1 £16 10 0; No. 2 15 0 0

JUTE.—Cuttings are in steady request.

Good White	£17 10 to 18	Common ...	£13 to £14
Good	£17	Rejections ...	£9 ,, £10
Medium ..	£15 to £16	Cuttings ...	£5 10 ,, £7

FOREIGN RAGS.—The Continental rag trade has slightly improved with a better demand.

WEEK'S IMPORTS.

Quantity	From	Importer	Port.
65 bales	Amsterdam	To order	Leith
110 ,,	,,	,,	Hull
86 ,,	,,	,,	,,
47 ,,	Antwerp	,,	Leith
142 ,,	,,	,,	Liverpool
44 ,,	Bremen	,,	Hull
213 ,,	Bordeaux	,,	Liverpool
67 ,,	,,	,,	,,
50 ,,	Buenos Ayres	,,	,,
1 ,,	,,	,,	,,
334 ,,	Copenhagen	,,	Hull
44 ,,	Caen	,,	Newhaven
14 ,,	Ghent	G. Gibson & Co	Leith
20 ,,	,,	,,	,,
2 ,,	,,	To order	Liverpool
167 ,,	,,	,,	,,
279 ,,	,,	,,	,,
2 ,,	,,	,,	London
10 ,,	Guernsey	,,	Southampton
12 ,,	Hambro	,,	Hull
66 ,,	Jersey	,,	Southampton
41 ,,	,,		,,
7 ,,	Kobe	..	London
26 ,,	Konigsberg	..	Hull
40 ,,	Pernambuco	..	Liverpool
47 ,,	Rotterdam	,,	Leith
18 ,,	,,		Hull
60 ,,	,,	.	Leith
76 ,,	St. Nazaire	..	Newhaven
8 ,,	,,	..	,,
32 .	St. Malo	..	London

Totals from Each Country:

ARGENTINA		51 bales	FRANCE	...	440 bales
BELGIUM	..	504 ,,	GERMANY	...	56 ,,
BRAZIL ..	...	40 ,,	HOLLAND	...	386 ,,
CHANNEL Isles		284 ,,	PRUSSIA	...	19 ,,
CHINA	...	7 ,,	SWEDEN	...	26 ,,
DENMARK	...	334 ,,			

GERMAN RAGS.

STETTIN: C.i.f. Hull, Leith, Tyne and London.

SPFFF and SPFF	18/0	LFB (Blue)	/0
SPF	11/0	CSPFFF and CSPFF	10/0
FF	8/6	CFB (Blue)	7/6
FG	9/0	CFX (Coloured) ...	4/6
LFX	7/0		

HAMBURG: F.o.b.

NWC	22/0	FF Grey Linens ...	9/0
SPFFF	22/0	LFX Second ditto...	8/0
SPFFF and SPFF	18/0	CSPFFF	17/3
SPFF	16/0	CSPFF	11/3
SPF	12/0	CFB	8/0
CCC	5/6	Dark Blues (selected	11/9
CFX	4/6	Wool Tares... ...	8/0
White Rope... ...	8/0	Jute, No. I 6/0; No. II	5/6

DUTCH RAGS. f.o.r. Hull:

C.i.f. Thames; Hull 2/6 per ton more; ditto f.o.r. Leith c.i.f. Glasgow 5/-; c.i.f. Liverpool 4/-.

Selected Fines (free from Muslins) ...	17/0	Best Grey Linens ...	9/0
		Common ditto ...	5/6
Selected Outshots	9/9	White Canvas ...	15/0
,, Dirty Fines	5/9	Grey & Brown Canvas	9/9
Light Cottons ...	9/3	Tarred Hemp Rope	8/0
Blue Cottons ...	7/6	Ditto (broken) ...	5/3
Dark Coloured Cottons	2/10	White Paper Shavings	7/9
New Cuttings (Bleachd)	22/6	Gunny (best) ...	4/9
,, (Unbleached)	19/6	Jute Bagging ...	3/6
,, (Slate) ...	9/0	Ditto (common ...	3/0
Muslins	8/0	Tarpaulins	4/0
Red Cottons (Mixed)	5/9	Cowhair Carpets ...	2/9
Fustians (Light browns)	5/0	Hard ditto	3/0

BELGIAN RAGS.

F.o.b. Ghent. Freights: London, 5/0; Hull and Goole, 7/6 Liverpool and Leith, 10/0; Newcastle, 12/6; Dundee and Aberdeen, 15/0; Glasgow, 16/8.

White Linens No. 1	22/6	Fustians (Light) ...	6/0
,, ,, No. 2	16/0	,, (Dark) ...	4/0
,, ,, No. 3	13/0	Thirds...	3/0
Fines (Mixed) ...	12/0	Black Cottons ...	3/9
Grey Linens (strong)	9/6	Hemp Strings (unt'r'd)	2/0
,, ,, (extra)	14/0	House Cloths ...	4/9
Blue Linens... ...	8/6	Old Bagging (solid)	3/6
White Cottons S'p'fine	18/0	,, ,, (common)	2/6
,, ,, No. 2	15/0	NEW.	
Outshots No. 3 ...	10/0	White & Cream Linens	35/0
Seconds No. 4 ...	8/0	White Cuttings ...	22/0
Prints (Light) ...	8/6	Unbleached Cuttings	21/0
,, (Old)	4/6	Print Cuttings ..	8

BELGIAN FLAX and HEMP WASTE.

Best washed and dried Flax Waste, 10/0; Fair ditto 9/0
Flax Spinners' Waste (grease boiled out)... ... 10/0
Hemp Waste, No. 1 9/0; No. 2 ... ... 7/6
Flax Spinners' Waste, No. 1 (Flax Rove) 10/0: No. 2 8/6

FRENCH RAGS.

Quotations range, per cwt., ex ship London, Southampton, or Hull; 2/0 per ton more at Liverpool, and 10/0 per ton higher at Newcastle, Glasgow or Leith.

French Linens, I ...	22/0	Black Cotton ...	4/0
II 18/6; III ...	14/6	Marseilles Whites, I	16/0
White Cottons, I ...	19/0	II 10/0; III ...	7/6
II 15/0; III ...	12/6	Blue Cotton	11/0
Knitted Cotton ...	11/0	Light Prints... ...	9/0
Light Coloured Cotton	8/0	Mixed Prints ...	6/0
Blue Cotton	9/6	New White Cuttings	23/0
Coloured Cotton ...	6/0	,, Stay ,,	21/0

NORWEGIAN RAGS.

C.i.f. London, Hull, Tyne, and Grangemouth.

1st Rope (tarred) ...	8/6-9/0	2nd Canvas ...	8/0
2nd ,, ,, ...	5/6-6/0	Jute Bagging	
Manilla Rope (white)	8/0-8/9	Gunny ...	3/0 3/6
Best Canvas ...	11/9-12/0	Mixed ...	2/6-2/9

RUSSIAN RAGS.

C.i.f. London, Hull, Newcastle or Leith

SPFF	16/0	CC (Cotton	4/3
SPF	14/6	Jute I	3/3
FG	11/6	,, II	2/0
LFB	9/6	Rope I	8/6
FF	3/3	,, II .. .	5/0

HOME RAGS.—Reports from London, Bristol, Manchester, Edinburgh, and Dublin, state that the improved enquiry holds good; stocks are low and prices, without any material change, are firm.

LONDON:

New White Cuttings	21/6	Canvas No. 1	15/0
Fines (selected)	20/6	" No. 2 ...	9/6-10/6
" (good London)...	20/0	" No. 3	5/6
Outshots (selected) ...	12/6	Mixed Rope	5/3
" (ordinary) ...	11/0	White Rope	6/6
London Seconds	3/6-4/0	White Manilla Rope	8/0
Country do. ...	6/6-8/0	Coil Rope	9/0
London Thirds ...	1/9-2/0	Bagging...	1/6
Country do. ...	3/0-4/0	Gunny	3/0-3/6
Light Prints ...	7/0-8/0		

BRISTOL:

Fines	19/0	Clean Canvas ...	15/0
Outshots	13/6	Second Do. ...	9/6-10/6
Seconds	7/0-8/0	Light Prints ...	8/0
Thirds	3/6-4/0	Hemp Coil Rope	9/6-10/0
Mixed Bagging	3/6	Tarred Manilla	7/6

MANCHESTER:

Fines	15/0-16/0	Blues	6/6-7/0
Outshots (best) ...	11/6-12/0	Bagging...	4/0-4/3
" (ordinary)	10/6-11/0	" (common)	3/0-3/3
Seconds	7/0-7/3	W. Manilla Rope	10/0-10/6
Thirds	3/6-3/9	Surat Tares... ...	4/9-5/0

EDINBURGH:

Superfines	16/6	Black Cottons	2/9
Outshots	13/0	W. Manilla Rope ...	8/9
Mixed Fines...	14/0	Tarred Ditto	6/6
Common Seconds ...	7/0	" Hemp Rope...	6/3
First do.	10/0	Rope Ends (new) ...	5/6
Prints	5/6-6/6	" " (old) ...	5/0
Canvas (best)	15/6	Bagging...	2/0-3/0
" 2nd	10/0	" (clean) ...	4/3-5/0

DUBLIN.

White Cuttings ...	18/0	Mill Bagging	3/0
Fines	11/0	White Manilla	8/0
Seconds...	5/0	Tarred Hemp	8/0
Light Prints	3/0	Rigging	13/6
Black do.	2/0	Mixed Ropes	3/6
Bagging	2/0		

WASTE PAPERS.—In steady request.

Cream Shavings ...	12/3	Small Letters	5/0
Fine " ...	9/6	Large "	7/0
Mixed " ...	2/0	Brown Paper	3/9
White Printings ...	8/9	Light Browns	3/9
White Waste ...	1/6	Books & Pamphlets ...	5/0
Wood Pulp Cuttings	3/6	Strawboard Cuttings	1/6
Brown Paper	3/0	Jacquards	3/6
Crushed News	2/0		

For Export: 25/- per ton extra.

ROSIN.—The market is fairly brisk and prices steady.

	London (on the spot).	Liverpool (on the spot).	C.i.f. net London or Liverpool.
B/C	4/0	3/7½	3/6
D ...	4/1½	3/9	3/7
E ...	4/3	3/10½	3/8
F ...	4/6	4/0	3/9
G ...	4/9	4/3	3/10
H ...	5/3	5/1½	3/11
I ..	5/9	5/9	4/9
K ...	6/6	6/3	6/0
M ...	7/9	7/6	7/0
N ...	9/0	8/9	8/10
W G	9/6	9/6	9/6
W W	10/0	10/3	9/9

French Rosin: G, 5/3; H, 5/6; I, 5/9; K, 6/6; M, 6/9; N, 8/0; W G, 8/6; W U, 9/6; Virgin, 11/0. Net c.i.f.

STARCH.—Farina is firmer, and Prime is quoted at 9s. 6d. to 10s. per cwt., according to quality.

F.o.r. London, less 2½%:

Maize—Crisp, £9 10/-; Powder, £9 15/-; Special £14.
Farina—Prime, £9 15/-; B.K.M.F., £12.

Delivered:

Rice—Special (in chests), £20 (net); Crystal (in bags) £19; Granulated (in bags) £18 less 2½%.
Dextrine—£15 to £16.

SIZING.—Trade quiet; prices unchanged.

English Gelatines	per cwt.	70/0 to 140/0
Foreign "	"	70/0 " 140/0
Fine Skin Glues	"	45/0 " 60/0
Long Scotch Glues	"	45/0 " 60/0
Common "	"	30/0 " 45/0
"Town" Glues	"	26/0 " 30/0
"Bone" Glues	"	20/0 " 30/0
Foreign Glues	"	23/0 " 40/0
Bone Size	"	4/0 " 10/0
Gelatine Size...	"	5/0 " 10/0
Dry B.A. Pieces	"	31/6 " 34/0
" English Pieces	"	22/0 " 24/0
Wet " "	"	5/0 " 6/0
" Sheep Pieces	"	3/0 " 4/0
Buffalo Hide Shavings	"	25/0 " 34/0
" Picker Waste	"	25/0 " 34/0

MINERALS.—The market, as in all other industries, is feeling the effect of the prolonged coal strike, trade being dull and unsettled. CHINA CLAY is in moderate request at former quotations, FRENCH and ITALIAN CHALK (Souheur brand) has advanced all round, and there is an inclination for a still further rise which is occasioned by the ready sale and on account of the higher rate of wages paid to the miners. BARYTES are in good demand, and there is a fair amount of business being carried on in MINERAL WHITE and PATENT HARDENINGS.

Mineral White (Terra Alba), per ton f.o.r. or boat at works:

Superfine...	28/0 less 2½%
Pottery Super.... ...	24/0 "
Ball Seconds	20/0 "
Seconds	15/0 "
Thirds	10/6 "

China Clay, in bulk, f.o.b. Cornwall, 14/0 to 27/6; bags 5/0 and casks 9/6 per ton extra; f.o.b. London, in casks 35/0 to 50/0 per ton.
Superfine Hardening, f.o.r. works, 40/0.
Patent Crystal Hardening, delivered at mills £3 to £3 15/0
Patent Hardening (2 ton lots) f.o.r. Lancs., £3 5/0.
" " (5 ton lots) f.o.b. Liverpool, £3 10/0.
Magnesite (in lump) 32/6 per ton.
Magnesite (containing 98% Carbonate of Magnesia), raw ground, £6 10/0; calcined ground, £12 10/0.
Albarine, £3, del. mills.
Asbestos, best rock, £18; brown grades, £14 to £15
Asbestine Pulp, £4 5/- to £5 c.i.f. London, Liverpool and Glasgow.
Barytes (Carbonate), lump, 90/0 to 95/0; nuts, 72/6 to 85/0.
Barytes (Sulphate), "Angel White," No. 1, 70/0; No. 2, 60/0 to 65/0; No. 3, 45/0. Souheur's Brands: AF, 83/-; BF, 71/-; AB, 33/6; BB, 29/6; CB, 24/3.
French and Italian Chalk (Souheur Brand), per ton in lots of 10 tons: Flower O, 69/6 c.i.f. London; Flower OO, 62/0, Flower OOO, 55/6. Swan White, 63/0; Snow White, 95/0; Snow White XX, 89/0. Blackwell's "Angel White" Brand and "Silvery" 90/- to 92/6; prime quality, 90/- to 95/-; and superfine, 105/-.
Bauxite, Irish Hill Quality, first lump, 20/0; seconds, 16/0; thirds, 12/0; ground, 35/0.
Pyrites (non-cupreous), Liverpool, 5d., 2%.
Carbonate of Lime (Souheur Brand). Prima 43/-, Secunda 37/-.

COLOURS.—Very little business doing.

Mineral Black ...	cwt.	3/0	Ultramarine (pure)	
do. superior ...	"	5/0	... cwt.	40/0 to 45/0
Pure Ivory Black	"	12/0	PASTE COLOURS with 60% of colour, as follows:	
Ochre	"	3/0		
French J. C. Ochre	ton	55/0	Orange Pulp ... cwt.	40/0
Chrome (pure) ...	cwt.	40/0	Golden Yellow Pulp	36/0
Red Oxide	"	4/6	Lemon " " cwt.	36/0
Umber, Devonshire	"	50/0	Prussian Yellow ..	36/0
do. Turkish ...	"	40/0	Green (free of arsenic	36/0
Lamp Black ...		7/0-10/6	Paste Blue (20-45%)	
Cochineal	lb.	1/3-2/0	.. ...	23/6-46/0

LIME.—Demand good. The present price is 12s. 6d. per ton f.o.r.

BALING TWINE.—Prices:

		Thick.	Medium.	Cap
All Hemp ...	per lb.	4d.	4½d.	4½d.
All Jute		3½d.	3½d.	4d.

DIRECTORY.

Names and Addresses under this heading will be charged for at the rate of 30/- per annum (52 insertions) for each card of two lines or under. Each additional line £1 extra.

ALUMINOUS CAKE.

The ALUM, CHINA CLAY and VITRIOL Co., Lim., 63, Queen Victoria Street, London, E.C, Works: Erinham-on-Thames. Telegrams—"Chinnock, London.

ANALYTICAL.

WILLIAMS, ROWLAND, F.I.C., F.C.S., 28, Pall Mall, Manchester.

ARTESIAN WELLS.

BATCHELOR, Richard D., Artesian and Consulting Well Engineer, 73, Queen Victoria Street, London, E.C., and at Chatham. 5713

ISLER, C., & Co., Bear Lane, Southwark, S.E

LE GRAND & SUTCLIFF, Magdala Works, 125, Bunhill Row, E.C.

BOILER COVERING.

LONSDALES, Boiler Coverers, Blackburn, will send a sample cask of their Patent Plastic Cork Covering to any Paper Mill in Great Britain—5 cwt. cask for 25/- (carriage paid).

CHINA CLAY.

The ALUM, CHINA CLAY and VITRIOL Co., Lim., 63, Queen Victoria Street, London, E.C. Mines: Ruddle and Colchester, St. Austell, Cornwall. Telegrams—"Chinnock, London."

ROGERS, J., & Co., Truro, Cornwall.—Agents: Taylor, Sommerville & Co., 83, Queen Victoria Street, E.C., and at 16, Princes Street, Edinburgh.

W. SINGLETON BIRCH & SONS, Lim., 15, Upton Street, Manchester. Mines: Rosevear, St. Austell, Cornwall. 2276

COLOURS.

CARDWELL, J. L., & Co., Commercial Buildings, 15, Cross Street, Manchester. Specialties: Mineral Black, Ven. Red, Ochres and Umbers. 5304

GEMMILL, W. N., & Co., Glasgow, Telegrams "Rube." Starches, Alumina, Antifroths, &c. All Paper Colour

COLOURS (Continued).

HINSHELWOOD, THOMAS, & Co., The Glasgow Colour Works, Glasgow. Colours and shades matched exactly.

MULLER, A. E., 9, Fenchurch Street, London, E.C.

ESPARTO.

IDE & CHRISTIE, Fibre, Esparto, and General Produce Brokers, 72, Mark Lane, E.C.

MINERAL WHITE or TERRA ALBA.

WINSER & Co., Portland Mills, Princess Street, Manchester. Also manufacturers of Aluminous Cake.

HOWE, JOHN, & Co., Carlisle. 2112

STEEL.

MAKIN, WM., & SONS, Sheffield. Established 1736. Roll Bars, Plates, Cutter Knives, Doctor Blades, &c. 5366

STRAW.

UNDERWOOD, E., & SON, Limited, Brentford, London, W. Press-packed Oat, Wheat, or Rye Straw, delivered to the chief British ports or railway stations.

TALC (French and Italian Chalk).

SOUHEUR, JEAN, Antwerp. All Minerals, Blanc de Silex, Barytes (superior and common), Carbonate of Lime, Blacklead, &c. British Agent: A. E. Muller, 9, Fenchurch Street, London, E.C. Agent for Liverpool and Manchester: C. H. Austin, Ditton, near Widnes.

RAGS.

CHALMERS, E., & Co., Lim., Bonnington, Leith.

MULLER, A. E., 9, Fenchurch Street, London, E.C.

WERTHEIM, A., & Co., Hamburg.

UMBER.

The ALUM, CHINA CLAY and VITRIOL Co., Lim. 63, Queen Victoria Street, London, E.C. Telegrams—"Chinnock, London."

WOOD PULP.

FRIIS, N., & Co., 18, Carl Johans Gade, Christiania, Norway.

GOTTSTEIN, H., & Co., 59, Mark Lane, London, E.C., and at New York.

GRANT, W., & Co., 17, Baltic Street, Leith. Agents for best shippers, Sulphite and Sulphate, Mechanical, Pine, Brown, Aspen.

MATTHIESSEN, CHR., Christiania, Norway.

MULLER, A. E., 9, Fenchurch Street, London, E.C.

The SULPHITE PULP Company, Limited, 82, Gordon Street, Glasgow.

WERTHEIM, A., & Co., Hamburg.

Special Prepaid Advertisements

☞ **IT IS IMPORTANT** that Advertisements under any of the Headings mentioned below should reach us by the **FIRST POST** on **WEDNESDAY** Morning to **INSURE INSERTION.**

Charges for advertisements under the heading Situations Wanted are 1/- for twenty-four words, and One Penny per Word after, Minimum charge ONE SHILLING. Names and addresses to be paid for.

Advertisers by paying an extra fee of 6d. can have the replies addressed to the PAPER TRADE REVIEW under a number, and such replies will then be forwarded Post Free.

Advertisements appearing under the following headings:

Tenders.	Mills Wanted or To Let.
Sales by Auction.	Machinery Wanted or For Sale.
Businesses Wanted.	
Businesses for Disposal.	Situations Vacant.

Miscellaneous.

The charges are 3/- for fifty words or under; 1s. extra for every line or portion after. Ten words to be reckoned for each line. Names and addresses to be paid for. Payment must be made in advance, except where the advertiser has a running account, in which case the cost can be debited thereto.

Legal and Financial Announcements: 1/- per Line.

Cheques and Post-office Orders to be CROSSED ——and Co., and made payable to
W. JOHN STONHILL.

Situations Wanted.

ADVERTISER (21), having scientific education, and being about to complete his training in all departments of a first-class "white" mill, making fine printings and writings, desires to obtain the position of under-foreman in a good two-machine mill. References of the highest-class as to character and ability will be given by present principals.—Address No. 5913, office of the WORLD'S PAPER TRADE REVIEW, 58, Shoe-lane, London, E.C. 5913

BEATERMAN wants situation, thoroughly experienced in all classes, browns, shops, glazed casings, &c.; unexceptional references.—Mr. Hurst, 29, Fore Street, Ipswich, Suffolk. 5981

CHEMICAL PLUMBER desires Re-engagement; 5 years in Wood Pulp Mills; first class references.—Address, No. 5,907, office of the WORLD'S PAPER TRADE REVIEW, 58, Shoe Lane, E.C. 5907

MANAGER, thoroughly competent in all classes of Paper and Machinery, etc.; well up in the blending of fibres and mixing and matching of colours, desires Situation. Good testimonials as to character and ability.—Address, No. 5,908 office of the WORLD'S PAPER TRADE REVIEW, 58, Shoe Lane, London, E.C. 5908

MANAGEMENT Wanted by competent and experienced man of a chemical wood pulp mill; thoroughly up-to-date in all appliances, system of manufacture, economy and despatch, practical engineering and chemical training, thoroughly competent to manage and control workpeople; £500 guarantee if required.—Address No. 5919, Office of the WORLD'S PAPER TRADE REVIEW, 58, Shoe-lane, London, E.C. 5919

SITUATION Wanted as Machineman or Finisher, well up in shops and browns; good references.—Apply Walter Hobday, Richmond, Yorks. 5917

YOUNG Gentleman (31), 12 years' experience in first-class mills, wishes to hear of vacancy in good mill; capable of taking charge of counting-house, buying and selling, and commercial management generally under supervision of managing director or principal; limited liability experience; moderate salary; first-class references and testimonials.—Address No. 5912, Office of the WORLD'S PAPER TRADE REVIEW, 58, Shoe-lane, London, E.C. 5912

To Capitalists.

GENTLEMAN required with £3,000. (Partnership or otherwise) to take active part in Paper Mill abroad.—Address, No. 5,915, office of the WORLD'S PAPER TRADE REVIEW, 58, Shoe Lane, London, E.C. 5915

Machinery for Sale.

ONE KOLLERGANG, new. Stones 51 inches by [illegible] inches, C.I. Pan, Scrapers, and Driving Gear.

ONE HYDRAULIC PRESS, second-hand, with Press Box [illegible] inches diam. by [illegible] inches deep, with wheels; all parts strong. Ram [illegible] feet 6 inches by 8 inches diam.

TWELVE REVOLVING STRAINER PLATES, second-hand, [illegible] inches by [illegible] inches, close [illegible], [illegible] cuts.

REFINING ENGINE, new, Conical Type; same as one working in a large printing mill.

ONE COPPER ROLL, with ends, 6 feet [illegible] inch long by [illegible] inches diameter.

ONE C.I. HOLLOW ROLL, [illegible] inches diameter by [illegible] inches long.

ONE C.I. HOLLOW ROLL, [illegible] inches diameter by [illegible] inches long.

ONE C.I. CALENDER ROLL, [illegible] inches diameter by 7[illegible] inches long.

THREE C.I. SOLID ROLLS, [illegible] inches diameter by [illegible] inches long.

ONE PAIR BRASS PRESS ROLLS, [illegible] inches by [illegible] inches long.

TWO C.I. ROLLS for Paper Cutter, 9 inches and [illegible] inches diameter by [illegible] inches long.

ONE MAHOGANY COUCH ROLL, [illegible] inches diameter by [illegible] inches long.

TWO COPPER WIRE ROLLS, 8 inches diameter by [illegible] inches long.

ONE BRASS LEADING ROLL, 9 inches diameter by [illegible] inches long (old).

ONE BRASS TUBE ROLL, 4 inches diameter by [illegible] inches long (old).

ONE BRASS TUBE ROLL, 4 inches diameter by [illegible] inches long (old).

SEVEN BRASS TUBE ROLLS, 3[illegible] inches diameter by 72 inches long (old).

ONE BRASS TUBE ROLL, 3[illegible] inches diameter by [illegible] inches long (good).

FORTY-TWO BRASS TUBE ROLLS, 5 feet [illegible] inches long by [illegible] inches diameter.

THREE COPPER WIRE ROLLS, 5 feet [illegible] inches long by [illegible] inches diameter.

ONE COPPER GUIDE ROLL, 5 feet [illegible] inches long by 7 inches diameter.

ONE COPPER BREAST ROLL, 5 feet [illegible] inches long by [illegible] inches diameter.

TWO W.I. SHAKE BARS, Two C.I. Soles and Rocking Supports.

ONE DRYING CYLINDER CASTING, 48 inches diameter by [illegible] feet 3 inches long.

ONE INVICTA RAG CUTTER.

ONE RAG ENGINE TROUGH, [illegible] feet by 6 feet 6 inches by [illegible] inches and [illegible] inches deep.

TWO RAG ENGINE TROUGHS, [illegible] feet 6 inches by 7 feet 6 inches by [illegible] inches and [illegible] inches deep.

FIFTEEN ELBOW PLATES for Rag Engines, [illegible] inches by 7 inches by [illegible] inches deep, each having [illegible] Steel Bars.

ONE GRANITE STONE for Kollergang, chipped, 6 feet diameter by [illegible] inches broad.

ONE WROUGHT IRON H BEAM, [illegible] feet long by [illegible] inches by 7 inches.

☞ QUITE NEW.

EIGHT CHECK VALVES, 4 inches diameter.

ELEVEN C.I. COCKS, 4 inch bore, with brass plugs.

Any reasonable offer will be considered by 5[illegible]

BERTRAMS LIMITED, SCIENNES, EDINBURGH.

FOR SALE, one second-hand Beater and three second-hand Breakers, carrying [illegible] lbs. each.—Apply Pendlebury [illegible], Rishton Paper Mill, near Blackburn. 5[illegible]3

Machinery Wanted.

WANTED, Second-hand Rag Engine, size not less than 13 ft. 6 in. by 6 ft.; also spare Roll about 3 by 3 for smaller engine.—Address No. 59[illegible], Office of the WORLD'S PAPER TRADE REVIEW, 58, Shoe Lane, London, E.C. 59[illegible]

WANTED, a Revolving Knife Sheet Cutting Machine complete, with slitters to cut 54 in. to 60 in. wide.—Address Birmingham Waterproof Co., Ltd., Clevedon Road, Birmingham. 59[illegible]

WANTED, a Machine for making Waxed Tissue.—Full particulars to No. 59[illegible], office of the WORLD'S PAPER TRADE REVIEW, 58, Shoe Lane, London, E.C. 59[illegible]

Mills to be Let or Sold.

TO be LET or SOLD, a Paper Mill at Stalybridge, called the Higher Mill, containing one large machine and room for another, steam engine and boilers, in good condition.—Apply for further information to the Caretaker on the premises. [illegible]

MALDON, ESSEX.—TO BE LET on Lease or Sold, a Freehold Mill, with Engine, Boiler and 2 Water Wheels of 100 horse-power. The Property has an area of Five acres, with a Wharf giving facilities for carriage inland by river, or to London by sea, at the low rate of 2s. [illegible]d. per ton.—For further particulars apply to Fuller, Horsey, Sons and Cassell, 11, Billiter Square, E.C. [illegible]

The Machinery Users' ASSOCIATION

Is a Combination of all Manufacturers for Promoting and Protecting their Common Interests.

☞ *Professional Assistance is Rendered in cases of Unjust and Excessive Assessment, and on other matters prejudicially affecting manufacturers.*

Full particulars on application to the Offices—

8, LAURENCE POUNTNEY HILL, CANNON ST., LONDON, E.C., AND 16, DEANSGATE, MANCHESTER.

☞ NOW READY. ☜

PAPER TESTING.

Being a DESCRIPTION OF PAPER TESTING as Carried out in the GERMAN GOVERNMENT LABORATORY at CHARLOTTENBURG. By

W. HERTZBERG,

Head Assistant in the Paper Testing Department.

TRANSLATED By

P. NORMAN EVANS, PH.D., F.I.C., F.C.S.

Price, 6/-. Post Free, 6/[illegible].

W. JOHN STONHILL, 58, Shoe Lane, LONDON.

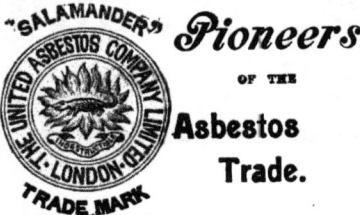

MR. W. T. EMMOTT. F.S.S.

Reproduced from a Photograph by Van der Weyde

... the popular ... Recently the ... Manchester Ex- ... acquired. ... Mr. W. T. Emmott, ... career. His ... houses men and ... published on ... was assured ... When success ... his interest, the ...

Mr. Emmott then determined to ... his quarters from 188, Fleet-street, to Manchester, his first printing offic... city being upon Blackfriars-bridge. ... the whole series of technical ... the list is wide enough in all conscie... would be impossible to select one that ... passes, and few that equal in any degree ... *Textile Manufacturer* for the general ... practical value of its contents. It is ...

Exterior View of Premises and Entrance Hall.

[illegible] journal of accom- [illegible] newspaper—but from its [illegible] present time its pages [illegible] original work—practical [illegible] designs for the weaver, [illegible] woollens and worsted; [illegible] silk; in printing, dyeing, [illegible] finishing, and the mechanics [illegible] greatest claim to favour [illegible] its bold originality. Its [illegible] from the advertisers' point of [illegible] be gathered from the statement [illegible] current number contains something [illegible] hundred folio pages of substantial [illegible] ments, embracing the most promi- [illegible] connected with the trade, and [illegible] far from being an exceptional number. [illegible] property to make one envious, alike [illegible] its reputation and its returns.

Another bold inception on the part of Mr. Emmott was that of the *Mechanical World*, [illegible] illustrated penny engineering journal. Mr. Emmott also produced the first number [illegible] *Tit-Bits*. In an interview with the representative of our contemporary, he said: "Mr. Newnes, who had probably scarcely been inside a printing office in his life, left the production of the first number to me, and as a matter of fact he hardly knew what it was going to look like until he saw a finished copy. . . . . . You can therefore imagine that it has been very amusing to me to read some of the published interviews with that gentleman—the fact being that he had little more to do with it than you had, beyond supplying the copy for it."

In 1884 Mr. Emmott entered upon another important enterprise in the form of a Sunday paper for the great northern counties, the result being the publication of the *Umpire*, which after twelve months had a circulation of 70,000 a week, and in little more than two years it had topped the 100,000. From that time progress has been steadily and undeviatingly upward. Whilst the *Umpire* was still young Mr. Emmott erected the present premises and took the printing into his own hands, it having previously been done at the office of the *Manchester Guardian*. Another journal which emanates from the establishment of Messrs. Emmott and Co. is *Good Health*.

As already stated Messrs. Emmott and Co., Limited, have just acquired by purchase the *Manchester Examiner and Times*—and have taken over the whole of the extensive plant, which has been transferred to their printing and publishing offices in Strangeways, from which the paper is now issued. The *Examiner and Times* has always maintained a high repute as a commercial intelligencer, and great weight has always attached to its opinions. The intention of the new proprietary of the *Examiner and Times*, however, is to greatly strengthen the financial features of the paper to make it indeed the first monetary organ of the

SODA ASH

(CHAPMAN'S PATENT).

POLLUTION of STREAMS, LOSS by LEAKAGE, and NUISANCE to the NEIGHBOURHOOD.

... 1893, the **Manager** of the **WOOLFOLD PAPER MILLS** says:—

... *our plant. The Evaporator has never worked ... our liquor for a month or two at 3½° ... a great deal of evaporation for little ash. ... (unless they saw) that we could treat so weak*

... QUADRUPLE EFFECT (CHAPMAN'S PATENT), ... Patent Incinerator, similar to that in use at ... Quadruple Effect (Chapman's Patent).

... March, 1893, the **Managing Director** of the **GIGG MILLS** says of this Incinerator:—

... at work several months, and find it very satis- ... we have recovered from 14 to 16 tons of ash ... small quantity just for starting up on a Mon- ... combustible matter. We can keep good fires all ... before stated, without any consumption of coal ... coal in the way indicated last week, and re-

FAWCETT, PRESTON & CO., LIM.,

ENGINEERS,

Phœnix Foundry Liverpool.

journal now being the property of Messrs W. H. and L. Collingridge, of the *City Press*. Mr. Emmott successfully projected several minor publications, and subsequently started the *Chamber of Commerce Chronicle*, which led to the birth in 1875 of the *Textile Manufacturer*. The success of the latter was instant, and in those days phenomenal.

MR. W. T. EMMOTT, F.S.S.

Reproduced from a Photograph by Van der Weyde

[illegible] most familiar to the popular [illegible] "the textile" office. Recently the [illegible] daily, the *Manchester Examiner* [illegible] *Times*, was acquired. [illegible] the firm, Mr. W. T. Emmott, [illegible] journalistic career. His [illegible] was the *Warehousemen and* [illegible] *Journal*, first published on [illegible]. When success was assured [illegible] parted with his interest, the

Mr. Emmott then determined to remove his quarters from 138, Fleet-street, London, to Manchester, his first printing office in that city being upon Blackfriars-bridge. Amongst the whole series of technical journals—and the list is wide enough in all conscience—it would be impossible to select one that surpasses, and few that equal in any degree, the *Textile Manufacturer* for the general and practical value of its contents. It is in no

Exterior View of Premises and Entrance Hall

sense a mere recording journal of accomplished events—a newspaper—but from its first number to the present time its pages have abounded in original work—practical suggestions and designs for the weaver, alike in cottons, woollens and worsted: hosiery, lace and silk: in printing, dyeing, bleaching, and finishing, and the mechanics of the trade. Its greatest claim to favour lies, indeed, in its bold originality. Its popularity from the advertisers' point of view may be gathered from the statement that the current number contains something like a hundred folio pages of substantial advertisements, embracing the most prominent names connected with the trade, and this is far from being an exceptional number. It is a property to make one envious, alike from its reputation and its returns.

Another bold inception on the part of Mr. Emmott was that of the *Mechanical World*, an illustrated penny engineering journal. Mr. Emmott also produced the first number of *Tit-Bits*. In an interview with the representative of our contemporary, he said: "Mr. Newnes, who had probably scarcely been inside a printing office in his life, left the production of the first number to me, and as a matter of fact he hardly knew what it was going to look like until he saw a finished copy. . . . . . . You therefore imagine that it has been very amusing to to read some of the published interviews with that gentleman—the fact being that he had little more to do with it than you had, beyond supplying the copy for it."

In 1884 Mr. Emmott entered upon another important enterprise in the form of a Sunday paper for the great northern counties, the result being the publication of the *Umpire*, which after twelve months had a circulation of 70,000 a week, and in little more than two years it had topped the 100,000. From that time progress has been steadily and undeviatingly upward. Whilst the *Umpire* was still young Mr. Emmott erected the present premises and took the printing into his own hands, it having previously been done at the office of the *Manchester Guardian*. Another journal which emanates from the establishment of Messrs. Emmott and Co. is *Good Health*.

As already stated Messrs. Emmott and Co., Limited, have just acquired by purchase the *Manchester Examiner and Times*—and have taken over the whole of the extensive plant, which has been transferred to their printing and publishing offices in Strangeways, from which the paper is now issued. The *Examiner and Times* has always maintained a high repute as a commercial intelligencer, and great weight has always attached to its opinions. The intention of the new proprietary of the *Examiner and Times*, however, is to greatly strengthen the financial features of the paper—to mak[illegible] indeed the first monetary organ of

North. In view of the completion of the Manchester Ship Canal, too, its columns will be made to reflect the shipping interest as

Machine Room Umpire Section.

[illegible] as may be. At the same time, under [illegible] of Mr. W. T. Emmott, it may be [illegible] to continue as it has begun, and to keep pace with the spirit of the times in every department.

The visitor to Messrs. Emmott and Co.'s works cannot fail to be struck by the fine proportions of the exterior of the buildings, which have imposing frontages to New

Bridge-street and Moreton-street. Heavily laden lurries are constantly discharging immense reels of paper intended for the

Machine Room – Examiner Section

Examiner and Times and the various other publications of the firm, or huge bales of paper in the flat for the *Mechanical World*, *Textile Manufacturer*, or other of the firm's publications. These are landed, weighed, and promptly warehoused, or lowered by a powerful Tangye's hydraulic hoist at each end of the building, which has an opening on the stage, into the machine room for im-

ESCHER WYSS & Co.,

ENGINEERS.

ZURICH, SWITZERLAND.

New Patent STRAINER

OVER 100 AT WORK.

FACTS SPEAK FOR THEMSELVES.

The TORONTO PAPER CO.'S Experience: "They are durable and easily cleaned. We have had one in use for eighteen months and it seems as good as new. Once adopted not likely to be turned out."

FEATURES.

Superior to any other System for its Numerous Advantages as

Large Production with any kind of Pulp.
No Stoppage for Cleaning.
Most Regular and Quite Noiseless Working.
Little room taken up on the Machine, &c.

AGENT:

ALPH. STEIGER, C.E.

MINCING LANE, LONDON, E.C.

"[The Paper] Trade Review is a widely informed and well-[conducted] enterprise, of great value to exporters for its [reports] and statistics of Raw Material."—[Centralblatt] für die Papier Fabrikation, Dresden.

NORWEGIAN PAPER AND PULP MILLS.

MAP DRAWN to SCALE.

By Chr. B. Lorentzen.

PRICE 2/6 EACH.

To be obtained of W. JOHN STONHILL, Office of the PAPER TRADE REVIEW, 58, Shoe Lane, London E.C.

DAMPING MACHINES

On the most Improved Principle;
VENTILATION for all purposes;
Improved FANS or AIR PROPELLERS
Patent SUSPENDING CLIPS to hold from one up to 50 sheets of paper or cardboard;
TURBINES; SMOKE CONSUMING APPARATUS;
Patent Life Protecting HOIST PLATFORMS;
New System of HYDRAULIC POWER for Lifts, Hoists, and Motive Power;
New Process of WIRE WEAVING by Steam Power.
SEWAGE TREATING.

For particulars of all the above address

E. BREADNER

(Ventilating Engineer to the Manchester Royal Exchange),
134, DEANSGATE, MANCHESTER.

Published by W. JOHN STONHILL 58, Shoe Lane, LONDON, E.C. November 17, 1[illegible]

Telegrams: "STONHILL, LONDON." A B C Code. Registered at the General Post Office as a Newspaper.

Vol. XX. No. 21. LONDON, NOVEMBER 24, 1898. Price 6d.

A THICKNESS GAUGE FOR PAPERMAKING MACHINES.

The accompanying illustrations relate to an apparatus (patented by Mr. O. W. Theodor Ende, of Bad Harzburg, Brunswick), for measuring the thickness of paper or pulp in a papermaking machine.

Fig. 1 represents a plan partly in section; Fig. 2 a side view; Fig. 3 a section on the line M N of Fig. 1; Fig. 4 part and elevation; Fig. 5, a section of the line O P of Fig. 1; and Fig. 6 shows the arrangement of the whole apparatus on a papermaking machine, and its position relatively to the measurement cylinder. The apparatus consists chiefly of a rectangular box, fitted first with a slide A which by means of a micrometer screw can be moved outwards or inwards. Second—with the divisions on the slide made to an enlarged scale for reading the thickness of the article to be measured. Third—with two copper wires a in the slide. Fourth—with a roller B suspended from arms C to the box by lever arms D. Fifth—with a copper plate b fixed to the plate E connecting the lower parts of the levers D. The copper wires a are connected with an electric battery and bell, in any suitable position, the bell being actuated at any desired moment determined by the apparatus, apprising the workmen that the prescribed thickness of the pulp or the paper has been reached.

The apparatus is so constructed as to measure thickness down to 11 m/m. and that it admits of being set to a degree of accuracy equal to $\frac{1}{100}$th of a millimetre. If finer measurements should be required, the length of the lever arm to the axis of the roller B is lessened, or a longer lever arm D may be used. The scale on the slide will in such case be proportionally increased. The slide A by means of its springs bearing against the ends of the bolts c is so far pushed out that the points of both the indicators e stand at zero on both scales. The slide A can be drawn horizontally into the box by means of the micrometer screw g working in the bar h which bears against stops i on both sides of the slide, the apparatus being thus set to any desired measurement. The true movement of the slide is ensured by the angle iron guides f. Both the lever arms D and along with them the copper plate b are connected with the slide A by springs k and pins l passing through a vertical slot of the springs, the arrangement being such that the front face of the plate b is kept away from contact with the points of the copper wires a a distance of 2 to 3 m/m by means of the springs k, but on a slight pressure against the roller B the plate b is brought in contact with the points of the copper wires a, thus closing a circuit and causing the bell to ring. The roller B will be acted on only when the pulp or the paper approximately reaches the desired thickness. The elasticity of the springs k is such that they will yield on the slightest pressure against the roller B allowing of contact of the plate b with the wires a, without the slide A being itself pushed back into the box. In graduating the slide A regard is to be had to the movement of the roller B in a circular path and to the variation of leverage at which the plate b touches the points of the copper wires a. In the apparatus shown a movement of the roller through 10m/m corresponds to a length of 39 millimetres on the slide A.

Except the connecting piece E, which is of wood, the apparatus is otherwise made of metal. It has to be mounted upon a firm stand, and if in a pulp machine, against the size cylinder as shown in Fig. 6, being bolted on to the framing by four bolts n which pass through slotted holes, it being so adjusted that the roller touches the size cylinder in the

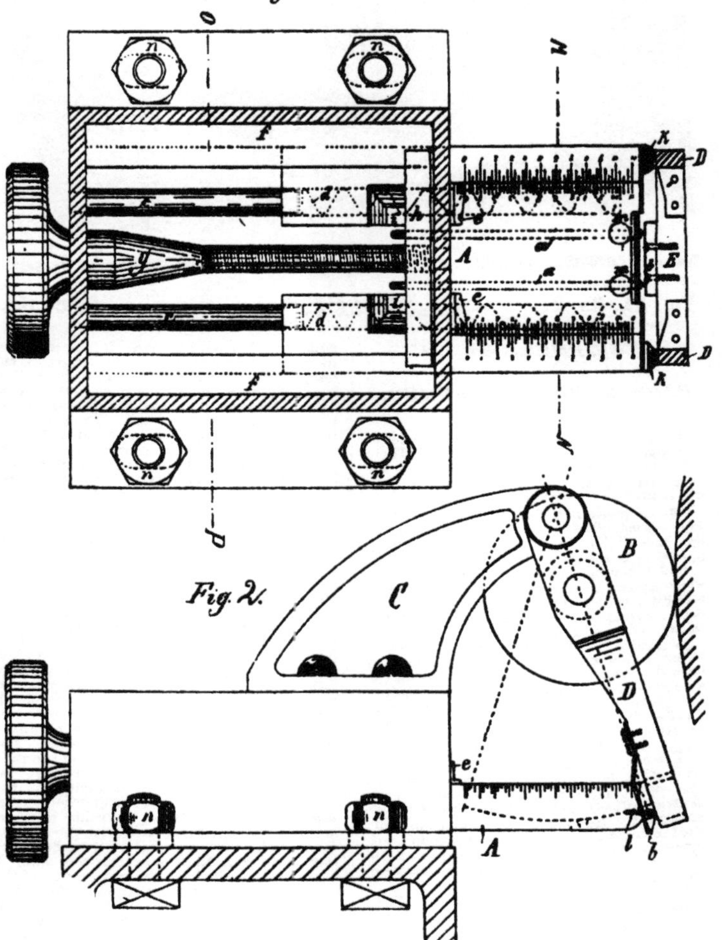

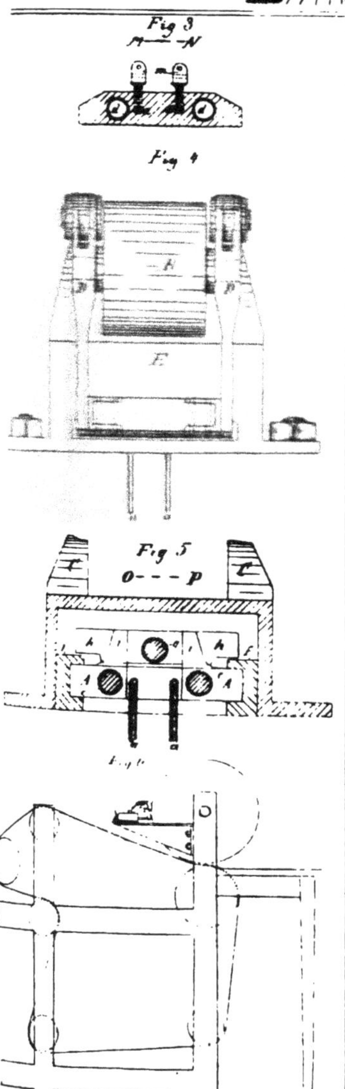

horizontal line passing through the centre of the cylinder, the copper plate *b* also touching the copper wires *a*, with the slide set to zero. In this position the electric signal would be heard, but then the slide is to be moved back by the micrometer screw, until the indicator *c* points to the required thickness for the pulp or paper.

ALEXANDRIA.

Last year's importation of writing paper for printing amounted in value to £36,140. Austria's supply amounted to £24,525; France sent paper amounting to £3,933; Italy, £3,637; Great Britain, £1,308, and other countries, £2,950. The total imports in the previous year amounted to £37,943.

A law on trade marks has for some time been in contemplation, but up to the present moment has not been promulgated. Although there is no legislation in Egypt respecting trade marks or patents, the Mixed Courts will (in cases between foreigners and natives or between foreigners of different nationalities) give damages against a person fraudulently using a trade mark which has been registered in any European country, it being necessary for this purpose to produce a certificate of such registration.

There is no doubt that inferior goods bearing the counterfeit trade marks of English firms are imported to a large extent, the imitation being sufficiently good to deceive the purchasers, especially when these are natives. In several cases English firms who formerly did business with Egypt to the extent of several thousands of pounds annually, have found their sales diminish to as many hundreds, while articles ostensibly bearing their trade mark are being sold to a larger extent than before.

The majority of these fraudulent imitations are said to proceed from Germany, and forged labels, corks, &c., are introduced into the country from the same source, and are employed to pass off as genuine spirits, poisonous decoctions, which are manufactured in Egypt.

Another unscrupulous device is adopted by certain traders. It is the practice of some continental firms to forward to their customers in Egypt two invoices, one of which is intended for the custom-house and bears a considerably lower value than the other. This trick is, of course, soon discovered, and the consignee is a marked man, but it is obvious that such conduct is calculated to injure honest traders, and to deprive genuine invoices of their proper value.

Rags were exported from Alexandria in 1892 to the value of £33,366, and in 1891, £24,836.

The imports of cigarette paper and writing paper were of the value of £108,104 in 1892, and £98,531 in 1891. Under the heading of "Printed Paper and Books" the imports at Alexandria were of the value of £26,257 in 1892, and £20,453 in the previous year.

RAGS were exported from Tunis to the value of £1,008 in 1892 and £867 in the previous year.

various descriptions. The wholesale stationery and papers firms were conspicuous throughout for their lavish decoration, and in Cannon-street that of Messrs. Grosvenor, Chater and Co. was much admired. The fine weather added greatly to the effectiveness of the display and the enjoyment of the crowds of spectators.

The invitation card for the Lord Mayor's banquet in the Guildhall, is a beautiful specimen of the colour printer's art. It is of an ornamental character (12 by 9 inches), the design carried out to a great extent is neutral tints, gives a pleasing *tout ensemble*; the intention being to produce, as nearly as possible, an imitation of water-colour work. The central portion is, as usual, reserved for the invitation wording; immediately above this are the armorial bearings, crest, and motto of the Lord Mayor beneath a garland of roses supported by two Cupids. To the left and right are the arms of the sheriffs; beneath which are seated youthful figures representing Music and Festivity. At the base, in the centre, are the arms of the City of London, with supporters. On the left is a view of the Lord Mayor Ward, Queenhithe, ·ooking from the river, with St. Paul's in ck-ground and on the right, views taken ·n the wards of the sheriffs, viz.—The ·ue of King William IV. (Candlewick d), and the Royal Exchange (Cornhill d). The designing and printing have been carried out by Messrs. Blades, East and Blades, fine art printers to the Corporation of the City of London, 23, Abchurch-lane, London, E.C.

We are indebted to the courtesy of Messrs. W. H. and L. Collingridge, the proprietors of our contemporary, the *City Press* for the loan of the blocks accompanying this brief description, the bulk of which has been gleaned from the columns of the same paper.

REDUCED COPY OF THE INVITATION CARD.

STRAW PULP.—We have received some excellent samples of straw pulp from the Vereinigte Strohstoff Fabriken, Coswig, Sachsen. The brands of this firm appear to be greatly appreciated by some of our largest mills in Scotland and England, and we are informed that in spite of the depression in the paper trade their bleached straw pulp is now in much better request than formerly. The V.S.T. brand has a good reputation as being largely suitable for finest writings, printings and tissues.

PAPER STOCK.—Mr. W. S. Stevenson, of the Liverpool Marine Store Co., Liverpool, England, who recently visited the States, complains that American orders for paper stock have stopped as suddenly as though there had been an earthquake, and paper mills swallowed up thereby. He never remembered anything during his thirty years experience like the present dead-lock in trade.

JACKSON

gineers,

ANCHESTER.

MARSHALL'S PATENT PERFECTING ENGINE.

ITABLE FOR ALL CLASSES OF STOCK AND EVERY QUALITY OF PAPER.

MADE IN THREE SIZES.

Engine will produce a Better Finished, Stronger and More Even Sheet of Paper from same materials than can be produced by any other Mechanical Process, and at the same time will REDUCE the TIME and POWER required for Beating.

We supply these Engines on approval subject to our accomplishing the above results.

chine—NO WELL-EQUIPPED PAPER MILL SHOULD BE WITHOUT.

APPLICATION.

Apparatus to Recover

SODA ASH

(CHAPMAN'S PATENT).

Avoiding POLLUTION of STREAMS, LOSS by LEAKAGE, and NUISANCE to the NEIGHBOURHOOD.

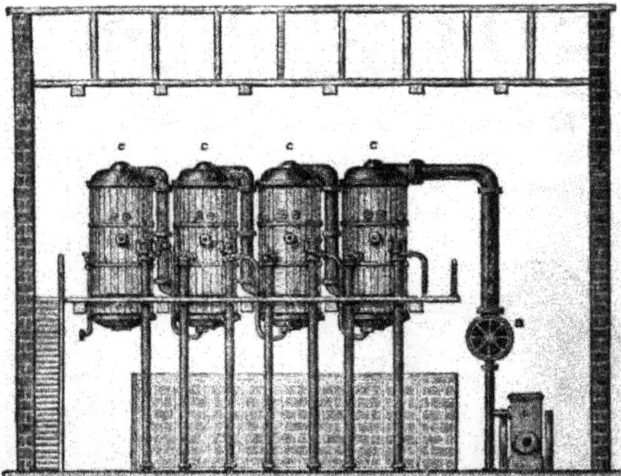

Writing on the 4th April, 1893, the Manager of the WOOLFOLD PAPER MILLS says:—

"We are getting very good work out of our plant. The Evaporator has never worked better than it is now doing. We have been treating our liquor for a month or two at 3½° Tw., and as you are well aware this means a great deal of evaporation for little ash. Many Papermakers would refuse to believe (unless they saw) that we could treat so weak a liquor profitably, but we can."

☛ *The Evaporator at Woolfold is a QUADRUPLE EFFECT (CHAPMAN'S PATENT), working in conjunction with a Thornley's Patent Incinerator, similar to that in use at Gigg Mills, where also the Evaporator is a Quadruple Effect (Chapman's Patent).*

Writing on the 6th March, 1893, the Managing Director of the GIGG MILLS says of this Incinerator:—

"We have now had your Incinerator at work several months, and find it very satis-
indeed. Since Christmas, for instance, we have recovered from 14 to 16 tons of ash
'he coal consumed being only a small quantity just for starting up on a Mon-
1. It is self-supporting for combustible matter. We can keep good fires all
This Mac- him constantly, and this, as before stated, without any consumption of coal
Increased. up. We only used 2 cwts. of coal in the way indicated last week, and re-
of ash."

Sole ETT, PRESTON & CO., LIM.,

ENGINEERS.

ix Foundry Liverpool.

THE
United Asbestos Co.,
LIMITED.
DOCK HOUSE, BILLITER STREET, E.C.,
"SALAMANDER"
THE UNITED ASBESTOS COMPANY LIMITED · LONDON ·
TRADE MARK
Pioneers
OF THE
Asbestos
Trade.
UNITED ASBESTOS
NON-CONDUCTING
COVERING
(For Steam Boilers & Pipes)
Best and Cheapest in the Market; Will not Injure Boiler Plates.
ASBESTOS
GOODS of ALL DESCRIPTIONS
BELTINGS.
THE UNITED ASBESTOS CO., Limited,
PACKINGS.
UNITED ASBESTOS Cº LIMᴰ LONDON
PURE ITALIAN MILLBOARD EXTRA QUALITY
A1
UNITED ASBESTOS
A1 MILLBOARDS
(ITALIAN)
Unequalled for Purity, Strength of Fibre, and Uniformity. For Dry Steam Joints it is admitted to be the cleanest, most durable and economical packing in existence.
UNITED ASBESTOS
SALAMANDER
Lubricating Cream & Oils,
SPECIALLY ADAPTED TO
PAPERMAKING MACHINERY.
DEPOTS:
MANCHESTER: 34, Deansgate; LIVERPOOL: 33, James Street; NEWCASTLE-UPON-TYNE: Quayside; GLASGOW: 54, Robertson Street; CARDIFF: 135, Bute Street; BRISTOL: Provident Buildings; HULL: Queen's Dock; ST. PETERSBURG: Gostinoe Dvor (Interior) No. 51.

Taylor's Patent

BEATING and REFINING ENGINE.

☛ THIS BEATER TAKES UP LESS FLOOR SPACE THAN ANY OTHER. ☚

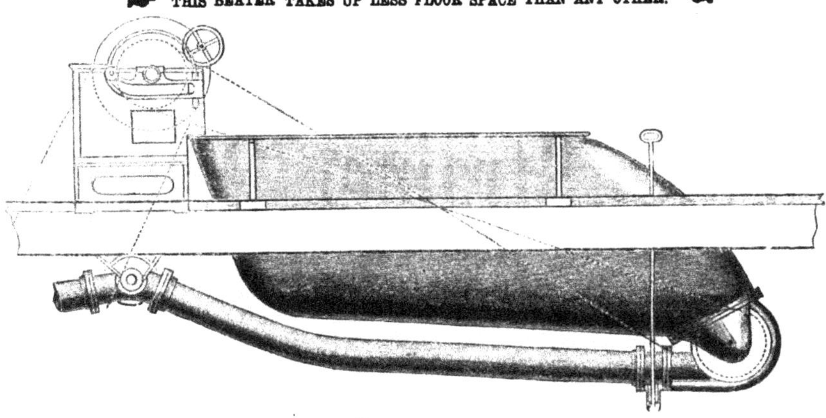

ADVANTAGES:

1.—**GREATLY INCREASED PRODUCTION** over that of the ordinary Beater in use.

2.—**GREAT SAVING IN POWER**, notwithstanding the increased production. This Beater has been proved to beat a given quantity of pulp with less than one-half of the power required by an ordinary beater of good modern construction.

3.—**COMPLETE AND PERFECT CIRCULATION**, which ensures complete uniformity in the length of the fibres.

For Full Particulars and Prices apply to

MASSON, SCOTT & Co., LTD.,

BATTERSEA, LONDON, S.W

Telegraphic Address: "BERTRAM—EDINBURGH," and "BERTRAM—LONDON." A B C and A 1 Codes.

D. N. BERTRAM'S

Patent SIMPLEX STRAINER

WITH INCLINED PLATES, ANGULAR SLITS, AND ABSOLUTE PREVENTION OF REFUSE PULP PROM COMING INTO CONTACT WITH STRAINER PLATES.

THIS STRAINER HAS BEEN DESIGNED so as to overcome the objections which hitherto have existed in all classes of strainers, whether they be the original ratchet, revolving, oscillating or ordinary diaphragm strainer. All these Strainers more or less cause the refuse matter to be kept in contact with the straining surface.

THIS NEW STRAINER entirely obviates the possibility of refuse matter lying on the plates, which are placed at an incline the narrow way of the Strainer. The apex is 6 feet long, and the plates 30 inches broad, the pulp thus only travelling the 30 inches, thereby coming in contact with the entire straining area, which is equally efficient all over.

THE SLITS IN THIS STRAINER, although parallel with the length of strainer, are angular to the flow of pulp, consequently the pulp cannot travel over the plates without coming in contact with the straining slits.

WITH A VERY LITTLE OVERFLOW to the Auxiliary, the refuse matter is carried into a double inclined channel at under end of plates, from which it can either be taken by the hand or discharged to an auxiliary Strainer as usual.

OUTLET FOR STRAINED PULP is the full length of the Strainer of ample area so that no undue pressure is caused in any part of the Strainer.

OPINION OF A PAPERMAKER WHO IS USING THE STRAINER.

HENDON PAPER WORKS CO., LTD.
SUNDERLAND, *1st November, 1893.*

D. N. BERTRAM, ESQ.,
EDINBURGH.

Dear Sir,

In reply to yours of yesterday, I am glad to inform you that the experimental Strainer you have fitted up here has been working continuously for the last fortnight, keeping No. 2 Machine going, passing 750 to 800 pounds per hour clean paper pulp through plates of half No. 3 and 2½ cuts.

This Strainer occupies very little space, and with its continuous overflow to the Auxiliary, I consider it to be one of the best in existence.

Had my strainer plant been less extensive I would have liked to apply it to all our machines.

Yours truly,
(Signed) THOS. GOODALL, MANAGER.

QUANTITY OF PULP PASSED.—Although the quantity, as named by Mr. Goodall, is very great, still we would draw the attention of the Trade to the fact that it can be made very much greater yet, were a longer stroke to be applied to the diaphragm, and plates of a wider cut employed. We would particularly request the perusers of this to note that the quantity which is referred to in the above letter is with a stroke of one-sixteenth full on the diaphragm. This stroke is undoubtedly less than is employed by any other strainers presently in use. From this fact it will be readily understood that the Strainer is thereby enabled to pass cleaner stuff than when a longer stroke is applied.

THE CONSTRUCTION of the Strainer throughout is of the simplest description, and most substantial.

WE COMMEND THIS STRAINER to the best consideration of the Trade generally, and offer any further information on the subject.

SOLE MANUPACTURERS:

BERTRAMS LIMITED

(Successors to GEO. & WM. BERTRAM—Established 1821),

ENGINEERS,

St. Katherine's Works, Sciennes, EDINBURGH.

GOLD and SILVER MEDALS.

London 1862.

Edinburgh 1890.

Edinburgh 1886.

MAKERS of ALL CLASSES of MACHINERY of the NEWEST and MOST IMPROVED CONSTRUCTION for the Manufacture of the Various Grades of Paper.

935

Telegraphic Address : "BERTRAM—EDINBURGH," and "BERTRAM—LONDON." A B C and A 1 Codes.

D. N. BERTRAM'S
Patent REELER

The Special Features of the Machine are:

1.—NO PART OF THE KNIFE BLOCKS or knives, except the cutting edges, comes in contact with the paper, thus avoiding any damage to the web by narrow rings touching it.

2.—There BEING NO BLOCKS between the knives they can be instantly adjusted to any width without taking the spindle from its bearings.

3.—The KNIVES ARE DRIVEN INDEPENDENTLY of the paper at an increased speed ensuring clean cut edges.

4.—The MACHINE IS DRIVEN by belt pulley on drum shaft with fast and slow speeds, worked from front of machine by levers, so arranged that when the fast speed is put on the slow one disengages itself. The change from slow to fast is easily effected, and no jerking takes place.

☞ **THIS PATENT REELER is working in Several Well-known Paper Mills.**

IN THIS MACHINE the paper is slit into widths upon the spindle, which carries the finished webs, thus preventing irregularity of edges; the outside shavings being trimmed before the web passes to the winding-up spindle and slitting-knives.

THE KNIFE CARRIAGE is placed vertically over the web, and fitted with automatic raising gear, to compensate for the increase of web.

THERE IS ALSO AN ARRANGEMENT so that the operator can apply the slitting-knives with any given amount of contact that may be desirable, and it will retain the same position until the whole web is finished.

THE ACTION OF THE PRESSING ROLL on the top of the web ensures the reel being firmly and evenly wound, and there is a shackle at one side of the machine, with screw which can adjust pressing roll to a nicety on the drum upon which the slitting and winding apparatus is carried. This allows webs which may be slightly thicker at one side than another to be wound without creasing.

REFERENCES GIVEN ON APPLICATION.

BERTRAMS LIMITED

(Successors to Geo & Wm BERTRAM—ESTABLISHED 1821),

ENGINEERS,

ST. KATHERINE'S WORKS, SCIENNES, EDINBURGH.

Printed and Published by W. JOHN STONHILL, 58, Shoe Lane, LONDON, E.C. Dec. 8, 189 .

The World's Paper Trade Review
A WEEKLY JOURNAL FOR PAPER MAKERS & ENGINEERS.

Telegrams: "STONHILL, LONDON." A B C Code. Registered at the General Post Office as a Newspaper.

Vol. XX. No. 24. LONDON. DECEMBER 15, 1893. Price 6d.

PULP WOOD.

About one-half the weight of wood consists of cellulose fibre, the remainder being principally water, mineral, resinous, and gummy matters. The amount of cellulose that a wood contains and the quantity obtainable on a practical scale are the main items that concern a pulp maker. By every process of manufacturing pulp a large percentage of cellulose fibre is lost. With the soda method the loss is greater than with the sulphite, owing to the fact that cellulose is more soluble in a hot solution of caustic soda than in a similar solution of sulphite of lime or magnesia. The following table gives the amount of cellulose fibre actually contained in a few of the common woods air dried. It will be seen that the difference in the real amount contained in them and the quantity obtained in practice is considerable (see table):—

Poplar	62·8	per cent.
Fir	57	,,
Willow	54·7	,,
Birch	55·5	,,
Pine	53·3	,,
Basswood	53	,,
Chestnut	52·6	,,
Beech	45·6	,,

The chemical composition of a few of the common woods will be seen from the analysis by Müller given in the following table:

	Birch.	Beech.	Lime.	Pine.	Poplar.
Cellulose ...	55·52	45·47	53·09	56·99	62·77
Resin	1·14	0·41	3·93	0·97	1·37
Aqueous extract	2·65	2·41	3·56	1·26	2·88
Lignin	28·21	39·14	29·32	26·91	20·88
Water	12·48	12·57	10·10	13·87	12·10

In the above table the mineral matter is not given, which averages about 0·5 per cent.

The table on page 2 gives a list of the various woods that are now employed for the production of wood pulp or fibre, also the average yield of air dry fibre obtained. By far the greater bulk of the chemical fibre now manufactured is derived from spruce, fir and pine, while poplar, spruce and aspen yield most of the mechanical pulp. Although almost every class of wood can be converted into pulp, it has been found by experience that the soft woods of the coniferous class are most suitable. For chemical pulp trees from 6 to about 18 inches diameter at the base are most suitable, and of about fifteen to twenty years growth. Within the last few years a great number of pulp mills have been started in the southern and western States of America and other parts of the world, which, in order to utilise the particular class of wood that grows in the vicinity, have adopted somewhat special methods, and we now find wood pulp being produced from a great variety of woods.

The great majority of pulp mills obtain their supply of wood in the form of round logs about 6 to 10 feet long, while many in the lumber cutting districts use edgings and other waste wood from saw mills. Board ends, battens, and even old packing cases and boxes are used for making pulp. Sawdust has also been experimented with for the purpose of producing chemical fibre, but owing to the difficulty of getting the digesting liquor to readily circulate through it, and other troublesome features, it has been found to be impractical. Shavings would be more suitable for converting into wood fibre, and are by some employed, although the bulkiness of them prevents any substantial weight being dealt with in each boilir· operation. They might, however, be m(

Common name.	Latin or Botanical name.	German.	French.	Used for.†	Average yield % air dry fibre.	Chiefly grown.
Norway Spruce	Abies excelsa*	Pechtanne [sprose]	Sapin de Norvege	M. So. Su.	35	Scandinavia & N. Europe
White Spruce	Abies alba	Weissen Sprose	Blanc sapin	"	35	U. States of America & Canada
Black Spruce	Abies nigra	Schwarzer Sprose	Noir sapin	"	35	" "
Red Spruce	Abies	Rothtanne	Sapin rouge	"	33	" "
Californian Spruce	Abies douglassi	——	Sapin de Californie	"	35	California and U. States
Canadian Hemlock	Abies canadensis	——	——	"	40	Canada and N. States
Fir or Var	Picea pectinata	Weisstanne	Bois de Sapin	"	38	N. Europe, America and Newfoundland
Scotch Fir	Pinus sylvestris	Fichte Kiefer	Ecossais Sapin Sauvage —	"	35	Europe
White American Pine	Pinus strobus	Amerikansche fichte	Blanc pin	"	33	America
Austrian Pine	Pinus austriaca	Fichte	Bois de Pin	"	35	Austro-Hungary, Germany.
Californian Pine	Pinus sabineanse	Californische fichte	Pin de Californie	M. So.	—	California
Red Pine	Pinus resinosa	Rothen fichte	Pin rouge	"	—	N. States and Canada
White Poplar	Populus alba	Zitterpappel	Peuplier tremblante	"	40	Europe and N. America
Aspen Poplar	Populas tremula	Aspen	Espe	"	41	" "
Grey Poplar	Populas canescens	Grauen Aspen	Espe gris	"	41	" "
Black Poplar	Populus nigra	Schwarzpappel	Peuplier noir	"	—	" "
Maple	Acer campestris	Ahorn	Erable	"	22	" "
Sycamore Maple	Acer pseudoplatanus	Bergahorn	Sycamore erfible	"	22	" "
Birch	Betula alba	Birke	Bonleav	"	41	" "
Beech	Fagus sylvatica	Buche	Hetre	"	38	" "
Cypress	Cupressus lawsoniana	Cypresse	Cypres	M.		" "
Cottonwood	Gossypium herbaceum	Baumwolle-holz	Cotonnier	M. So. Su.		Southern States
Basswood	Tilia Americana	Linden holz	Bois de Bass	M. So.		
Tamarac	——	Tamarak	Tamarac	M. So. Su.		
Balsam	——	Baumier holz	Bois de Balsamier	M. So.		

* Continental botanists name these Picea instead of abies.
† M. indicates mechanical pulp. So. indicates soda, and Su. sulphite pulp.

conveniently used if they were first put through some form of machine similar to a hay cutting mill, and reduced to small lengths of about half an inch. Obtaining a regular supply of the necessary quantity would probably be a difficulty.

WASHABLE WHITE AND SURFACE-COLOURED PASTEBOARDS.

Many attempts have been made, evidently with indifferent success, to prepare glazed cardboards so that they can be washed. A solution of shellac or of paraffin has been applied for this purpose. The coloured paste prepared by adding a known quantity of a solution of shellac or paraffin to blanc fixe, etc., forms a cheese-like but lumpy mass, immediately they are added together, which in no way possesses the necessary properties to allow it to be equally smeared over the surface of cardboards. It is practically unuseable.

Alois Dessauer has recently obtained a patent for a new method of doing this work. It consists in applying a specially prepared mixture of shellac in combination with other bodies which prevents the fluid from curdling, thus enabling it to be equally and more easily distributed over the surface of the paper.

The solution of shellac is made by dissolving it in water with borax or sal-ammoniac and then mixing this fluid with a decoction of althäa root (althäa werzel), prepared by digesting the root in water. About 20 lbs. of this shellac liquor are stirred into another liquor composed and made up of the following ingredients, viz., 10 pounds of hydrate of alumina (which should be slightly alkaline), $\frac{1}{10}$th of a pound of double sulphate of potash and chronium, 15 pounds of a solution of glue of specific gravity 1·05, and 2 pounds of water.

The colour paste used for covering the surface of the boards, etc., is made up as follows:—From 8 to 10 pounds of pure blanc fixe are added to 10 or 20 pounds of a solution of glue of specific gravity 1·05, and this mixture thoroughly incorporated with about half a pound of the above shellac solution.

Both the hydrate of alumina paste and the prepared blanc fixe paste should be squeezed through a very fine sieve before they are mixed together, and a quarter of a pound of glycerine finally added to them.

It is said that a beautiful paste is formed in the above way, which spreads itself equally over the surface of the paper, and which can be tinted or coloured to any desired extent with colour-lakes. When spread upon the surface of cardboard or lithographic papers, dried, brushed and glazed with zinc plates in the ordinary way it yields a very highly glazed surface, which can be washed, and to which printed and other impressions are easily communicated.

OWMAN, THOMPSON & Co.

LIMITED,

Lostock Alkali Works,

NORTHWICH.

RUDDER

BRAND.

RUDDER

BRAND.

MANUFACTURERS OF

HIGH-STRENGTH

BLEACHING POWDER.

Fine Quality Soda Crystals.

AMMONIA-SODA ALKALI.

96-98% Sulphate of Soda or Salt Cake.

Sulphuric and Hydrochloric Acids

(NON-ARSENICAL).

Hydrated Peroxide of Manganese.

943

Common name.	Latin or Botanical name	Ge[rman name]
Norway Spruce ..	Abies excelsa	.. Pecht
White Spruce ...	Abies alba ...	.. Wei
Black Spruce .	Abies nigra ..	. S
Red Spruce	Abies	.. Ro
Californian Spruce	Abies douglas	
Canadian Hemlock	Abies canadensis	
Fir or Var ...	Picea pectinata	
Scotch Fir	Pinus sylvestri	
White American Pine	Pinus strobus	
Austrian Pine .	Pinus austriaca	
Californian Pine ...	Pinus	
Red Pine	Pinus resinosa	
White Poplar	Populus alba	
Aspen Poplar ..	Populus trem	
Grey Poplar... .	Populus	
Black Poplar ...	Populus	
Maple.	Acer	
Sycamore Maple	Acer	
Birch	Betula	
Beech	Fagus	
Cypress .	Cupress	
Cottonwood... ...		
Basswood ...		
Tamarac		
Balsam ...		

conveniently through so... hay cutting lengths of regular ... would p...

WASH...

... crystalline form, which can be ... from its solution; or the bi-car... may be produced by other known ... and from this bi-carbonate of soda, ... may be produced in any known ... way.

... in a ... carbonate ... gen- ... to ... gen

... Williamson, ... patent, ... caustic soda ... sodium ... containing or ... solution ... causticised ... production of ... the same time ... of compara- ... or in other ... relatively rich ... and relatively ... manufacture or obtain- ... therefrom; which ... known way. In some ... the solution of car- ... subsequently to its pro- ... or sulphydrate of ... used for the manufac- ... soda, and soda ash

... treating sulphide of ... of sodium solution at ... temperature, with car- ... by passing the said ... solution, it is decom- ... converted into carbonate ... in solution, whilst the ... are relatively very rich ... twice as rich as those given ... usually practised in sul- ...

... the patentees place the solu- ... of sodium or sulphydrate of ... mixture thereof, in a suitable ... boiling point, or about boil- ... and then pass carbonic acid gas ... the effect of which is the direct ... of the sulphide or sulphydrate of ... to a solution of carbonate of ... by causticising in any suitable ... caustic soda. If it is ... carbonate ... the solution ... would be subsequently ... temperature, with car- ... converted to carbonate

Apparatus to Recover

SODA ASH

(CHAPMAN'S PATENT),

Avoiding POLLUTION of STREAMS, LOSS by LEAKAGE, and NUISANCE to the NEIGHBOURHOOD.

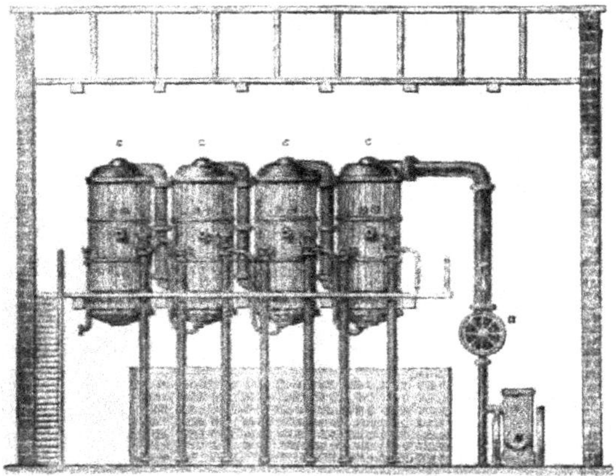

Writing on the 4th April, 1893, the Manager of the WOOLFOLD PAPER MILLS says:—

" We are getting very good work out of our plant. The Evaporator has never worked better than it is now doing. We have been treating our liquor for a month or two at 3½° Tw., and as you are well aware this means a great deal of evaporation for little ash. Many Papermakers would refuse to believe (unless they saw) that we could treat so weak a liquor profitably, but we can."

☛ *The Evaporator at Woolfold is a QUADRUPLE EFFECT (CHAPMAN'S PATENT), working in conjunction with a Thornley's Patent Incinerator, similar to that in use at Gigg Mills, where also the Evaporator is a Quadruple Effect (Chapman's Patent).*

Writing on the 6th March, 1893, the Managing Director of the GIGG MILLS says of this Incinerator:—

" We have now had your Incinerator at work several months, and find it very satisfactory indeed. Since Christmas, for instance, we have recovered from 14 to 16 tons of ash per week, the coal consumed being only a small quantity just for starting up on a Monday morning. It is self-supporting for combustible matter. We can keep good fires all the week and skim constantly, and this, as before stated, without any consumption of coal after starting up. We only used 2 cwts. of coal in the way indicated last week, and recovered 14 tons of ash."

FAWCETT, PRESTON & CO., LIM

ENGINEERS.

Phœnix Foundry Liverpoo

RIVERS POLLUTION PREVENTION (No. 2) BILL.

PROPOSED ACTION BY PAPERMAKERS.

The members of the North-east Lancashire Papermakers' Association, of which Mr. P. P. Peebles is chairman, and Mr. T. Y. Nuttall hon secretary, feel that some united action should be taken for opposing the progress of the above measure. The Bill has been passed by the Lords, and stands for second reading in the House of Commons.

A circular has been issued by the Association to papermakers, pointing out that the object of the Bill is to invest local authorities, including county councils and joint committees formed under the Local Government Act, with larger and more arbitrary powers than they are endowed with by the Act of 1876, which Act the present Bill proposes to repeal. For the attainment of this object the law affecting liquid manufacturing pollution is to be differently administered, and further, it is in effect proposed to make no allowance for the exigences of trade and industry in manufacturing localities. With reference to administration of law, at present the county court of the district has jurisdiction with a right of appeal to the High Court, but there is this valuable safeguard given by Section 6, that no proceedings can be taken against manufacturers without the consent of the Local Government Board, who are compelled in giving or withholding their consent to have regard "to the industrial interests involved in the case and to the circumstances and requirements of the locality." Nor can the Local Government Board give their consent to any proceedings against manufacturers unless they are satisfied, after due enquiry, that means for rendering harmless the polluting liquids are reasonably practicable and available, and that no material injury will be inflicted by such proceedings. By these means not only is a reasonably uniform interpretation of the Act secured, but manufacturers are properly protected in carrying on their various industries, and every part of the kingdom can appeal to one final and impartial authority.

Turning to the new Bill, it will be seen that it proposes to do away with the safeguards of the present Act. For instance, the first legal proceedings are to be taken before the local magistrates, with an appeal to Quarter Sessions. In a great many districts such a Court of Appeal would be most unsatisfactory. The degree of vigour in the application of the Act might, and probably would, vary considerably in different districts, not only so, but the fairness of the tribunal may well be questioned in view of the influence which members of the county councils or joint committee could exercise as justices at Quarter Sessions. It is specifically provided that they are not to be incapable of acting in that capacity in cases arising under this Act. Hitherto it has been an accepted principle, and one based on common sense, that in manufacturing localities the maintenance of a pure stream shall be subservient to existing legal rights, and to the welfare of the industrial community and manufacturing enterprises. In the new Act this policy is quite abandoned. By Clause 3 of the Bill the putting of any solid matter whatever into a stream is prohibited. The governing words which are in the present Act "so as to interfere with its due flow or to pollute its water" being omitted. This section alone will make every paper manufacturer in the kingdom an offender against the Act, for it is impossible to remove all solid matter from the effluent water of a paper mill. A further proposal is to the effect that the local authority shall have (by its inspectors) at all times free access to every part of any works or premises. The Act is not to apply to Scotland.

Manufacturers on the Irwell and Mersey watershed are already under the operation of a similar Act, specially obtained in the interest of the Manchester Ship Canal, but it is just possible that by the advantages proposed to those districts from this gigantic enterprise, the end may commercially justify the means. We hope it may be so. Without any such case for urgency or beneficent ground of action, the county councils now propose to extend the Irwell and Mersey Bill to the whole of England. Under these circumstances it is suggested that either through existing organisations, or by special combination for this purpose alone, English papermakers should try and exert their influence before it is too late. The North-east Lancashire Papermakers' Association will be glad to consider any suggestion made; and they are equally prepared either to convene a meeting or to co-operate with any other organisation that will provide the papermakers an opportunity of discussing this important measure, so as to prevent its becoming law in anything like its present shape.

PAPER & PULP MILL SHARES.

(Report received from Mr. F. D. Dean, 36, Corporation Street, Manchester.)

Nominal Amnt	Amnt Paid	Name of Company	Last dividend	Price.
7	7	Bury Paper, ord.	nil	4—4½
7	7	do. do. 6% pref.	6%	4¼—4¾
100	100	do. do. deb.	5%	103—106
10	10	Bath Paper Mill Co. Lim.	7½%	6—7
10	10	Bergvik Co., def.	15%	13¾
100	100	do. do. 6% cum. pref.	6%	10⅛—11¼
10	10	do. do. deb.	5%	105—110
5	3⅛	Burnley Paper Co.	3/-	77/6—80/0
5	3¾	Darwen Paper Co.	10%	6—6 years
10	10	East Lancashire Co.	nil	been sub-
10	10	do. do. 6% pref.	nil	
5	5	do. do. bonus		or by some
5	5	Hyde Paper Co.		dry sand the
5	4	North of Ireland Paper Co.		coal, but re-
10	5	Ramsbottom Paper Co.		very valuable,
5	4½	Roach Bridge Paper Co.		igh to be used as
5	5	Star Paper Co.		
5	3	do. do. o pref.		sily to all sorts of
50	50	do. do. deb.		
5	2¾	Kellner-Partingt'n		

LAST MONTH'S PAPER TRADE.

IMPORTS, RE-EXPORTS, AND EXPORTS.

TOTAL IMPORTS.

Kind	Year	Quantity		Value
Printings and Writings	1993	33,326	cwts	£36,344
	1892	27,624	,,	30,677
	1891	30,021	,,	37,346
Other Kinds	1893	230,028	cwts	£155,301
	1892	240,989	,,	179,180
	1891	190,444	,,	147,030

From GERMANY.

Kind	Year	Quantity		Value
Printings and Writings	1893	4,538	cwts	£4,779
	1892	5,466	,,	5,877
	1891	11,917	,,	13,388
Other Kinds	1893	39,486	cwts	£32,673
	1892	46,272	,,	42,137
	1891	41,309	,,	40,869

From BELGIUM.

Kind	Year	Quantity		Value
Printings and Writings	1893	5,245	cwts	£7,011
	1892	3,921	,,	5,557
	1891	6,973	,,	9,798
Other Kinds	1893	12,672	cwts	£16,319
	1892	11,233	,,	17,076
	1891	9,482	,,	15,295

From HOLLAND.

Kind	Year	Quantity		Value
Printings and Writings	1893	3,281	cwts	£4,339
	1892	3,550	,,	4,089
	1891	2,197	,,	3,244
Other Kinds	1893	113,094	cwts	£53,546
	1892	114,948	,,	60,734
	1891	99,173	,,	46,528

From SWEDEN.

Kind	Year	Quantity		Value
Printings and Writings	1893	7,016	cwts	£7,428
	1892	8,195	,,	8,217
	1891	7,316	,,	7,819

("Other Kinds" are not tabulated).

From FRANCE.

Kind	Year	Quantity		Value
Other Kinds	1893	3,261	cwts	£7,276
	1892	2,460	,,	6,283
	1891	2,527	,,	6,737

From OTHER COUNTRIES.

Kind	Year	Quantity		Value
Printings and Writings	1893	13,246	cwts	£13,287
	1892	6,492	,,	6,937
	1891	1,618	,,	3,597
Other Kinds	1893	61,515	cwts	£45,957
	1892	66,076	,,	52,950
	1891	46,953	,,	38,601

TOTAL RE-EXPORTS.

Kind	Year	Quantity		Value
	1893	1,629	cwts	£2,009
	1892	679	,,	1,054
	1891	454	,,	990
	[illegible]	4,959	cwts	£3,543
	[illegible]	6,464	,,	3,502
	[illegible]	4,051	,,	4,110

TOTAL EXPORTS.

Kind	Year	Quantity		Value
Printings and Writings	1893	51,815	cwts	£83,314
	1892	49,313	,,	84,776
	1891	61,174	,,	107,088
Other Kinds	1893	16,753	cwts	£25,671
	1892	15,320	,,	25,242
	1891	15,452	,,	26,923

To FRANCE.

Kind	Year	Quantity		Value
Printings and Writings	1893	3,122	cwts	£5,484
	1892	2,981	,,	5,977
	1891	3,078	,,	6,302
Other Kinds	1893	950	cwts	£5,217
	1892	879	,,	3,780
	1891	1,344	,,	4,753

To the UNITED STATES.

Kind	Year	Quantity		Value
Printings and Writings	1893	949	cwts	£2,144
	1892	786	,,	2,201
	1891	1,120	,,	3,496
Other Kinds	1893	680	cwts	£2,295
	1892	910	,,	3,049
	1891	868	,,	2,942

To SOUTH AFRICA.

Kind	Year	Quantity		Value
Printings and Writings	1893	3,191	cwts	£6,318
	1892	2,202	,,	4,144
	1891	2,590	,,	5,313
Other Kinds	1893	2,885	cwts	£2,762
	1892	2,881	,,	2,700
	1891	1,974	,,	2,304

To the EAST INDIES.

Kind	Year	Quantity		Value
Printings and Writings	1893	6,477	cwts	£11,256
	1892	8,337	,,	14,302
	1891	6,791	,,	11,348
Other Kinds	1893	1,399	cwts	£2,212
	1892	1,490	,,	1,976
	1891	1,728	,,	2,453

To AUSTRALASIA.

Kind	Year	Quantity		Value
Printings and Writings	1893	26,879	cwts	£34,454
	1892	24,895	,,	36,501
	1891	36,100	,,	55,884
Other Kinds	1893	6,707	cwts	£5,613
	1892	4,839	,,	5,755
	1891	6,390	,,	8,048

To BRITISH NORTH AMERICA

Kind	Year	Quantity		Value
Printings and Writings	1893	2,314	cwts	£4,207
	1892	2,277	,,	3,795
	1891	2,469	,,	4,687
Other Kinds	1893	610	cwts	£1,103
	1892	372	,,	722
	1891	472	,,	829

To OTHER COUNTRIES.

Kind	Year	Quantity		Value
Printings and Writings	1893	8,883	cwts	£19,451
	1892	7,835	,,	17,856
	1891	9,028	,,	20,058
Other Kinds	1893	3,522	cwts	£8,469
	1892	3,949	,,	7,260
	1891	2,676	,,	5,594

TOTALS FOR JAN.-NOV.

	Year	Quantity	Value
Imports..	1893	2,026,230 cwts	£2,090,866
	1892	2,822,609 ,,	2,164,763
	1891	2,339,958 ,,	1,918,267
Re-Exports	1893	72,159 cwts	£66,069
	1892	80,167 ,,	79,442
	1891	94,450 ,,	83,446
Exports..	1893	782,279 cwts	£1,224,894
	1892	796,807 ,,	1,310,094
	1891	855,223 ,,	1,421,905

RAW MATERIALS.

IMPORTS AND EXPORTS FOR NOVEMBER.

EXPORTS.

	Year	Quantity	Value
Alkali ...	1893	477,014 cwts	£134,640
	1892	543,747 ,,	185,848
	1891	547,185 ,,	199,895

	1891.	1892.	1893.
Russia	£11,434	£9,025	£4,782
Sweden and Norway	3,801	2,007	4,104
Germany	3,391	6,524	4,411
Holland	1,464	2,142	1,602
France	1,251	1,504	627
Spain and Canaries ...	11,130	8,554	7,038
Italy	4,775	5,770	4,882
United States ...	123,109	108,375	76,591
Australasia	5,756	4,868	4,330
British North America	6,258	9,183	6,155
Other countries ...	27,526	26,896	20,118

	Year	Quantity	Value
Bleaching Materials	1893	68,747 cwts	£28,575
	1892	131,747 ,,	53,338
	1891	151,738 ,,	54,223

	1891.	1892.	1893.
United States... ...	£38,560	£33,048	£11,976
Other Countries ...	15,663	20,290	16,599

	Year	Quantity	Value
Rags ...	1893	3,730 tons	£20,547
	1892	5,914 ,,	42,747
	1891	4,799 ,,	34,881

IMPORTS.

	Year	Quantity	Value
Alkali ...	1893	9,698 cwts	£9,174
	1892	6,633 ,,	4,640
	1891	6,099 ,,	3,678
Esparto	1893	8,095 tons	£38,180
	1892	13,591 ,,	71,169
	1891	17,981 ,,	85,439

	1891.	1892.	1893.
Spain	£37,961	£32,007	£15,832
Algeria	25,377	37,337	12,344
Other Countries ...	27,101	1,825	8,004

	Year	Quantity	Value
Wood Pulp	1893	19,366 tons	£99,126
	1892	17,229 ,,	90,220
	1891	13,382 ,,	84,838

	1891.	1892.	1893.
Norway...	£39,658	£45,792	£40,636
Other Countries ...	45,180	44,428	58,490

	Year	Quantity	Value
Rags ...	1893	1,096 tons	£10,601
	1892	250 ,,	2,841
	1891	3,425 ,,	34,209

TOTALS FOR JAN.-NOV.

EXPORTS.

	Year	Quantity	Value
Alkali ...	1893	5,407,924 cwts	£1,731,805
	1892	5,308,242 ,,	1,925,532
	1891	5,725,011 ,,	2,151,685
Bleaching Materials	1893	1,258,024 cwts	£522,058
	1892	1,363,669 ,,	547,510
	1891	1,394,214 ,,	478,764
Rags ...	1893	48,620 tons	£337,575
	1892	52,068 ,,	361,784
	1891	45,513 ,,	324,909

IMPORTS.

	Year	Quantity	Value
Alkali ...	1893	79,058 cwts	£71,603
	1892	50,406 ,,	37,125
	1891	70,174 ,,	45,358
Esparto	1893	168,676 tons	£794,719
	1892	190,538 ,,	919,363
	1891	200,640 ,,	969,864
Wood Pulp	1893	190,931 tons	£1,034,862
	1892	168,598 ,,	865,087
	1891	140,874 ,,	763,007
Rags ...	1893	19,659 tons	£187,484
	1892	22,075 ,,	206,132
	1891	29,625 ,,	288,693

EXPORTS OF PAPER HANGINGS.

	Year	Quantity	Value
Novemb'r	1893	3,372 cwts	£8,500
	1892	3,042 ,,	8,253
	1891	4,167 ,,	12,854
January to Novemb'r	1893	52,778 cwts	£130,266
	1892	53,761 ,,	137,684
	1891	62,765 ,,	165,738

THE AMSTERDAM POLICE AUTHORITIES warn foreign manufacturers of the following long firms: Willem Marie Cornelius Hoogendijk, alias Loon, Fraus Wauwenburg and Co., F. L. Heimel and Co., Frederik Godard Baron van Rede, alias Sinnige and Co., van Welzenius and Co., Frau Jansen Heijnings, J. H. van Hem, sen., alias Jeannot, alias Jean Baptiste, Hypolete Joseph Dehem, in Amsterdam Kinkerstraat pretends to be agent of the firm Chr Fonteijin and Co., 45, Kalverstraat, which latter firm, however, cannot be found under this address.

WOOD MINE IN TONKIN.—It is reported that a curious mine has been discovered in Tonkin about 20 or 30 feet below the ground. The inhabitants obtain wood from it in the same way as we exploit our coal mines. The origin evidently dates thousands of years back, when some forests have been submerged either by volcanic action or by some earthquake, but as the soil is dry sand the trunks have not decayed into coal, but remained intact. This wood is very valuable, and though not large enough to be used as timber, it adapts itself easily to all sorts of joinery and carving work.

WORLD'S PAPER TRADE REVIEW OFFICE, 58, SHOE LANE, LONDON, E.C.

TRADE NOTES.

BURY PAPERMAKING COMPANY.—This firm having promised to construct the necessary tank for the treatment of their effluent, the sub-committee have allowed an extension of time for three months to complete the same.

PAPER MILLS SUPPLY, LIMITED.—This company has been registered with a nominal capital of £2,000 in 5s. shares, to carry on a business under the style of the "Paper Mills Supply, Limited," for the purchase and sale of materials suitable for the manufacture of paper, pulps, etc.

INSTITUTE OF CHEMISTRY.—On the 8th inst. the new and very perfectly equipped laboratories of the Institute of Chemistry, Bloomsbury-square, were inaugurated in the presence of a considerable number of scientific men, who were welcomed by the president, Dr. W. A. Tyldin, F.R.S. After the view of the premises, Sir F. Abel spoke of the useful work of the institute in placing the profession of chemistry upon a thoroughly sound basis. At the present time there are nearly 200 students registered in the books of the institute.

WE understand that Mr. Jas. Beveridge, who has acted as managing chemist to the Ekman Pulp and Paper Co., Limited, Northfleet, Kent, for the past six years, is shortly severing his connection with this company. Mr. Beveridge is well known in connection with a patent beating and breaking engine, the sole makers of which are Bertrams Limited, Sciennes, Edinburgh, and also with a patent sulphite system of manufacturing wood pulp, which has been in active operation at Northfleet Mills for two-and-a-half years, giving results which are considered satisfactory.

RIBBLE JOINT COMMITTEE.—A meeting of the Ribble Joint Committee was held on Monday at the County offices, Preston, Mr. T. Fair in the chair. A deputation was received from the Briarfield Local Board, who asked that their summons might stand adjourned for 12 months. The Board had been in negotiations with the Corporation of Nelson to get them to treat their sewage, and a Local Government Board inquiry would be held into the question next week. It was ultimately decided to adjourn the summons for three months, dating from January next. Representatives of 18 paper mills attended before the committee, the mills being situated at Church, Rishton, Samlesbury, Horwich, Feniscowles, Simonstone, Darwen, &c. In the majority of cases it was stated that settling tanks, filtering beds, &c., were contemplated, and the committee granted periods varying from one to nine months for production of plans or completion of works.

PRESENTATION TO A PAPER MILL MANAGER.—Mr. David Pearson, who for the past eleven years has occupied a position of trust at the East Lancashire Paper Mill, and been manager during rather more than half that period, but who has now left, was a few days ago presented by the operatives with a silver tea and coffee service, consisting of tea-pot, coffee-pot, sugar basin and tongs, and cream jug. The teapot bore the inscription: "Presented to Mr. David Pearson by the employees of the East Lancashire Mill Company, Limited, Radcliffe. November 7th, 1893." Mr. Pearson personally has been very popular with the employees, and great regret has been expressed at his leaving. Owing to the fact that the mill is not working at present the presentation was not a formal one. Mr. Pearson has addressed to the operatives a letter, of which the following is a copy: "I am extremely proud to be the happy recipient of your valuable and handsome present, conveying as it does the best wishes and goodwill of the employees in a tangible form. I can assure you that I shall prize it as one of my most valuable possessions, especially so knowing the difficulties so many have to contend with, in consequence of the irregular employment caused by the exceptional depression in trade, largely due to the coal trouble. I cannot adequately thank you for your kindness in so handsomely remembering me at a time like the present, when so very many calls are made upon you, but I can assure you that when I look upon the beautiful articles when far away from Radcliffe, it will bring pleasant recollections of the eleven years I spent in your midst, and of the friendship and many expressions of good feeling I received during that period, and will, I trust, be a happy remembrance as long as I live. Accept my most sincere and heartfelt thanks, not only for the very handsome present, but also for the good wishes which prompted it; and I trust ere long brighter days may dawn, bringing prosperity and plenty to all.—Yours truly, D. PEARSON." Mr. Pearson, as recently announced in this paper, has accepted an appointment as manager of the mills of Messrs. Annandale and Sons, of Shotley-bridge, Durham.

DROUGHT THROUGHOUT SCANDINAVIA.—According to several Norwegian and Swedish correspondents, drought has necessitated a reduction in the output of several large Scandinavian wood pulp mills, and some of the smaller works have been temporarily closed.

THE LATE MR. J. M. GOODALL.—Probate duty has been paid on £162,936 5s. 8d. as the value of the personal estate of Mr. Josiah Montague Goodall, late of Linden House, The Grove, Highgate, and of the Camden Works, Camden Town, manufacturing stationer and card manufacturer.

THE MONARCH PAPER CUTTER.—The largest paper cutter ever made in America will soon be set up in the establishment of the Henderson Manufacturing Company, New York. It will be a 73½ inch Monarch cutter, made by the Seybold Machine Company, Dayton, Ohio.

PAPER EXPORTS FROM NEW YORK.—According to the last weekly list to hand the following are shown:—

B. W. Indies ...	305 pkgs	Australasia ...	44 cases
Hamburg ...	6 cases	New Zealand ...	19 cases
Bremen	29 pkgs.	S. Africa	1 case
Liverpool ...	9 cases	London ...	87 pkgs.
Copenhagen ...	2 cases	Hull	4 cases
Havre	29 pkgs.		

ASBESTOS PULP.—The Asbestos Pulp Company, Rochester, N.Y., recently closed the largest single contract for asbestos pulp for paper ever made. The amount to be supplied is 5,000 tons. It is reported that this quantity is going to Europe to one of the largest manufacturers of paper. The order was secured against opposition on this side entirely on account, it is claimed, of the superiority of the pulp manufactured by the Asbestos Pulp Company.

A CORRESPONDENT, writing from Appleton, Wis., refers to the gloomy prospect concerning the condition of the water power. It is stated that the autumn has been very dry, with scarcely any rain, and the country was long ago drained of all surplus water. Mechanical wood pulp is very firm, the lack of water power having contracted the supply. The average price is given as 90 cents, but 1 dollar 25 cents is now being asked. We are given to understand that the scarcity of pulp was one of the principal reasons for the recent shutting down of the two paper machines at the Kimberley and Globe mills of the Kimberley and Clarke Co., Neenah. When the production of the mammoth pulp mill at Little Chute is placed upon the market manufacturers expect that the price of ground wood will fall somewhat.

THE "PAPERMAKING EXHIBIT" AT CHICAGO.—The manufacturers represented in the papermaking exhibit, known as the Model Paper Mill, received first awards, consisting of medals and diplomas, as follows: Beloit Iron Works, paper machine; Downington Manufacturing Company (2), beating engines; Marshall Engine Company, refining engine; Farrell Foundry and Machine Company, calenders; Baker and Shevelin, screen; Williams Manufacturing Company (2), stuff chests; O. H. Jewell Filter Company, gravity filter; Cheney-Bigelow Wire Works, Fourdrinier wire and dandy roll; Western Screen and Plate Works, screen plates; Westinghouse, Church, Kerr and Co. (2), steam engines; Jeffry Manufacturing Company, conveyors; J. J. Manning, winders; M. J. Roach, metallic steam joint; Appleton Woollen Mills, papermakers' felts; Dodge Manufacturing Company, pulleys; Exhaust Ventilator Company, exhaust fans; Fairbanks, Morse and Co., trucks, scales, &c.; Gould's Manufacturing Company, pumps; W. Wenzel, pumps; C. Elmer Pope, slitter.

CHRISTIANIA.—A terrible storm raged on Friday and Saturday along the whole of the southern coasts of Norway from Christiania to Bergen. Eleven vessels are already known to have been wrecked at various points, and a number of lives lost.

ACTIEN GESELLSCHAFT FÜR PAPPEN-FABRIKATION, IN BERLIN.—It is reported that during the last half year sales were satisfactory, but prices low. If there should be but a slight improvement in the general position of business, it is expected the result of the whole year will be about the same as last.

MASCHINENFABRIK ACTIEN GESELLSCHAFT GEBRÜDER HEMMER in Neidenfels (Palatinate).—The profit on June 30, 1893, was M90,450, which is proposed to be used as follows:—M48,000 for an 8 per cent. dividend on the share capital of M600,000, M3,672 to be placed in reserve, bonuses' M12,119, balance forward, M26,659.

HERR DR. BOCK, having bought the paper mills of Herren Fr. Schulte and Co., in Düsseldorf, will reopen these works shortly under the firm of Dr. Bock.

RATHS DAMNITZER CELLULOSE UND PAPIER FABRIKEN ACTIEN GESELLSCHAFT have with a share capital of M1,000,000 only shown a clear profit for 1892-93 of M3,642. Of this M1,973 have been given away as bonuses and M1,669 carried to new account.

HERR MARZ has retired from the firm of Marz and Köhler in Gengenbach, in Baden, and Herr Köhler, has changed the style of the firm into that of Albert Köhler, Stroh and Zeugpappenfabrik Gengenbach. By making additions to the machinery, the daily turn out is expected to be five tons strawboards and 2½ tons grey millboards. The Stuttgart branch is given up.

LONG FIRMS IN EGYPT.—The consuls of various countries, particularly the French and Austrian, warn exporters to Egypt of a regular system of long firms, giving each other the best references, and advise no credit except on the recommendation of well known firms.

CELLULOSEFABRIK WARTHA—share capital M600,000. All the shares are in the hands of the following gentlemen, Herren Leopold Schoeller (in Breslau), Ewald Schoeller (in Roth Lobendau), Rudolf Schoeller (in Zurich), Arthur Schoeller (in Zurich), and Cæsar Schoeller (in Zurich). Dr. Armand Becker, in Wartha, is the managing director, and signs for the company.

NEW PAPER MILL IN CROATIA.—It is reported that a new paper mill is to be erected in Croatia, near Agram. The building arrangements are made for two paper machines, but for the present only one machine has been ordered and will produce 5 tons of fine paper during the 24 hours.

AMERICAN TARIFF.

THE NEW BILL.

The following table shows the paper, pulp, and book schedule as it now stands, and also as it is modified by the new tariff bill :—

	Proposed Rate.	Present Rate.
Mechanically ground wood pulp and chemical wood pulp, bleached or unbleached	10 p c	$2 50 to $7 & 10 p c
Sheathing paper	10 p c	10 p c
Printing paper, unsized, suitable only for books and newspapers	12 p c	15 p
Printing paper, sized or glued, suitable only for books and newspapers	15 p c	20 p c
Papers known commercially as copying paper, filtering paper, silver paper and all tissue paper, white or coloured, made up in copying books, reams or in any other form	15 p c	8c & 15 p c
Albumenized or sensitized paper	25 p c	35 p c
Papers known commercially as surface-coated papers, and manufactures thereof, cardboards, lithographic prints and photograph, autograph and scrap albums	25 p c	35 p c
Paper envelopes	20 p c	25c
Paper hangings and paper for screens or fireboards, drawing paper, writing paper and all other papers not specially provided for	20 p c	25 p c
Blank books of all kinds	20 p c	25 p c
Books, including pamphlets and engravings, bound or unbound, photographs, etchings, maps, charts and all printed matter not especially provided for	25 p c	25 p c
Playing cards	10c & 50 p c	50 p c
Manufactures of paper not specially provided for	20 p c	25 p c

Some items in other schedules are of interest to paper manufacturers, as, for example :—

	Proposed Rate.	Present Rate.
Alumina, alum, alum cake, patent alum, sulphate of alumina, aluminus cake alum in crystals or ground.	20 p c	6-10 c
Clays or earths, wrought or manufactured, china clay or kaoline	$1	$2
On blankets, hats of wool and flannels for underwear and felts for papermakers' use and printing machines, composed wholly or in part of wool, the hair of the camel, goat, alpaca or other animals, valued at not more than 30 cents per pound	25 p c	16½c & 30 p c
Valued at more than 30 and not more than 40 cents per pound	30 p c	22c & 35 p c
Valued at more than 40 cents per pound	35 p c	33c & 35 p c

Among the articles placed on the free list are these : Acids used for medicinal, chemical or manufacturing purposes ; gunny bags and gunny cloth, old or refuse, fit only for remanufacture. Paper stock, crude, of every description, including all grasses, fibres, rags (other than wool), waste, shavings, clippings, old paper, rope ends, waste rope, waste, bagging, old or refused gunny bags or gunny cloth, and poplar or other woods fit only to be converted into paper.

NEW PATENTS.

APPLICATIONS.

17,262. Taps and cocks. Partington and Bamforth.

22,842. Improvements in the manufacture of paper pulp or cellulose from wood, straw, and other vegetable fibres. M. Coulon and R. Godeffroy.

22,909. Improvements in reels, rollers, or cylinders for machinery for making and treating paper. J. White.

SPECIFICATIONS PUBLISHED.

(7½d. each. By post 8d.)

1893.

8,176. Electrolytic apparatus. Hanbury.

DEATH OF MR. BRYAN DONKIN.

The engineering profession has suffered a severe loss by the death, on the 4th inst., of Mr. Bryan Donkin, M.I.C.E., of Bermondsey, at the advanced age of 84 years. The deceased gentleman was the fifth son of Bryan Donkin, F.R.S. (the originator of the first practical, continuous, papermaking machine), and was born on the 5th April, 1809, in Bermondsey. He was educated at a school in Bromley, and at different schools near London, afterwards studying at Paris. He was apprenticed at an early age to his father, at the well-known engineering works, in Southwark Park-road, Bermondsey. He married Miss E. Day, of Isleworth, and had three children. He become Associate member of the Institute of Civil Engineers in 1835, and was elected member of the same in 1840. Mr. J. Forrest, the secretary of the institution, says he was by seniority, "The father of the institution." He took an active part in designing, superintending, and assisting his father in the construction of paper, printing, and other machinery; and, during his professional career, came in contact with many of the notable engineers of his day, amongst others — Isambard Brunel (of Thames Tunnel fame), Sir Henry Bessemer, Messrs. J. Penn, Maudsley, John Hall, J. Bramah, and J. Farey. He went to France in 1829 (at the time of the French Revolution, which he remembered well) to superintend the erection of paper and other machinery, near Nantes; and later, went to Spain to survey the River Ebro. After his father's death he became partner in the Bermondsey works, first with his brothers, John and Thomas Donkin and Mr. Farey, and later with his nephews, the present managing directors, Mr. Bryan Donkin, jun., and Mr. E. B. Donkin. In 1858 he went to St. Petersburg to supervise the erection of a large paper mill for the manufacture of Russian bank notes and the State papers, for which his firm had accepted a contract from the Russian Government. The works were on a large scale, with some 2,000 horse-power and 2,000 hands. In 1862 he witnessed the completion of this mill, in company with the Russian General Winberg. He retired from active business about the year 1881. For about 40 years he lived at Blackheath, but was often on the Continent. He was associated with the erection of St. Anne's Church, Bermondsey, and took a great interest in Bermondsey Parish Church Schools at Star Corner. During his business career, extending over 50 years, he took out several patents connected with papermaking machinery and steam engines. As a business man he displayed great energy and tact, and under his vigorous supervision and that of his partners, the works at Bermondsey were considerably enlarged. His kind and genial disposition was much appreciated by his employees, and all those who knew him. He was buried on Friday, the 8th inst., at Nunhead Cemetery.

Printed and Published EVERY FRIDAY
AT 58, SHOE LANE, LONDON, E.C.,
By W. JOHN STONHILL
ESTABLISHED 1878.

FRIDAY, DECEMBER 15, 1893.

THE co-operation of papermakers is urgently invited to offer a strong opposition against the Rivers Pollution Prevention (No. 2) Bill. As will be seen from an article published on another page, the matter is of serious importance to the trade. Now that the Papermakers' Association of Great Britain has pledged itself to an active programme, probably it will see its way to take up the question. A movement has already been commenced by the North-east Lancashire Papermakers' Association, and combination is highly desirable when the interests of our manufacturers are threatened.

THE moisture in wood pulp appears to be a very vexed question. "What is," asks the papermaker, "the right allowance for atmospheric moisture?" Considerable friction would be removed if some recognised standard was adopted. Perhaps the Papermakers' Association will do its best to facilitate this *desideratum*.

THE Board of Trade Returns for November show the following imports and exports of paper, excluding paper-hangings:

Imports ...	263,354	cwts.	£192,645
Exports ...	68,568	,,	108,985

Compared with the corresponding month of last year there was an increase in the importation of printings of 5,702 cwts. and £6,167, and in other kinds a decrease of 10,961 cwts. and £23,379. Notwithstanding that we exported 2,502 cwts. of printings and writings above the quantity in November last year, the value shows a comparative decline of £1,462; in other kinds the increased exportation amounted to 1,433 cwts., and the additional value only £429.

FROM the statistics, published on another page, relating to the importation of papermaking materials last month, it will be seen upon a comparison being made with the November figures of the previous year, that there was an increase in linen and cotton rags of 846 tons, giving an additional value of £7,760; a falling off in esparto of 5,496 tons and £34,969; and an increase in wood pulp of 2,137 tons and £8,906. It may be mentioned that the exports of rags show a decrease of 2,184 tons, the comparative drop in value being £22,200.

REDUCTION in the output of Scandinavian wood pulp! A drought is threatened throughout Norway and Sweden, the result of which will be a greatly diminished production of wood pulp and consequently a delay, or perhaps a partial stoppage of deliveries to England. We are informed that the production of several of the larger mills has already been considerably reduced, and some of the smaller mills have been compelled to temporarily close, whilst in the Skien district the mills have had to reduce their production 60 per cent. Under these circumstances the market generally cannot fail to be somewhat affected.

AMERICAN paper and pulp manufucturers on the whole appear to be fairly satisfied with the new tariff bill. Apparently reductions on most of the items in the schedule are not so radical as to create any serious injury, excepting possibly to one branch, that of copying and tissue paper. The real harm that the new tariff may do to the American paper industry will not be direct, but will be through the severe blows dealt to other industries. Col. Paine, of the New York and Pensylvania Co., says the paper and pulp industries have not been interfered with to any great extent. Mr. H. Atterbury, of Atterbury Bros., thinks the Bill pretty fair considering the fact that so much Free Trade has been shouted in the Democratic party. A representative of the Manufacturers Paper Co. and of the Hudson River Pulp and Paper Co., goes so far as to say that it would have been a matter of little consequence if the duty had been wiped out entirely. According to him the companies mentioned above "can produce and manufacture paper and pulp better and cheaper than any other paper and pulp mills on the face of the globe, barring none." He also claims to be doing a pretty big export trade.

In our list of imports of American mechanical wood pulp several shipments have been registered from Solon, Me., and judging from the sanguinary expectations of Mr. D. T. Mills, the general manager and one of the principal proprietors of the Moosehead Pulp and Paper Co., which operates a large mechanical wood pulp mill at Solon, increasing quantities are likely to come to hand. In a recent interview, Mr. Mills referred to the dull condition of the American paper market, but he was jubilant, as his company's mill was running full time. He said they started in 1891 "to make more mechanical wood pulp than any other mill in the world." They took the lead in shipping to Europe, sending 800 tons a month; further, they successfully competed with the Germans. He attributed this to the McKinley Bill, which put a duty of 2 dollars 50 cents per ton on foreign mechanical wood pulp. This stopped German business. He spoke lightly of the cheap labour in Germany, and complimented the Americans upon having better machines and better men, even if they had to pay more. He maintained that in the States they could grind four tons in twenty-four hours on a machine where the Germans only ground one. American machinery, although more costly, worked cheaper and turned out a better product. So with the men, their labourers got 1 dollar 50 cents a day against 50 cents in Germany. From the foregoing it will be seen Mr. Mills has a very high opinion of the existing conditions in the United States, but before he exhausted himself he said, in answer to a question as to how American pulp compared with that of European manufacture, that "we lead the world, and American pulp now ranks ahead of even the best Norway." Perhaps!

The advance in the prices of mechanical wood pulp in Germany is a matter that still occupies the attention of German papermakers. They have now to recognise that the normal price is 14 marks the metre cwt., and talk about raising the price of paper in consequence. The Germans pride themselves upon their pine wood being superior to the Scandinavian wood, and state that consequently their pulps are preferred. At one time it looked as if there would be a strong contentious feeling between papermakers and pulp makers, but now there seems more desire to work in a harmonious manner. It is maintained that the creation of wood pulp syndicates, instead of injuring papermakers, ought to be a lesson to them, which should be followed by syndicates among the various classes of papermakers. The more the latter concentrate their attention upon special kinds, the easier the formation of syndicates. A correspondent says that probably before long the makers of news will come to an understanding and it is only to be hoped that they may not lose too much time before they accomplish their object. No doubt it pays better, *e. g.*, to make news or printings at a profit than to try turning out half-a-dozen different kinds of paper, neither of which is of the best quality and leads to complaints and consequent loss. Concentration thus would seem to be one of the first steps for a general improvement of the German paper trade.

A Bill for the institution of Boards of Trade is about to be brought in by the so-called Imperial German Party, at the Berlin Reichstag. All trades are to be represented on these boards, which are to carry out a supervision and watch over their interests in every direction. They propose to regulate the admission of new members, and exclude any persons who do not possess the necessary knowledge and experience in the various trades, to arrange for apprentices, also to see that the work at the prisons is so manipulated as not to create a dangerous competition against legitimate trade.

It is stated that the Departmental Committee appointed by the Home Secretary to consider the conditions of labour in chemical works, and to suggest remedies for the dangers to life and health of the workpeople employed therein, have drawn up a series of special rules, the adoption of which will, they think, place things on a more satisfactory basis. Their report also contains a valuable statement of the whole case from the medical point of view.

The Consul-General of Guatemala announces that, according to a recent decree of his Government, dated November 2nd last, a reduction will be granted on payments of Customs duties—for all imports and exports—of 10 per cent., if the corresponding total amount be paid in United States or Guatemalan gold currency; of 9 per cent., if paid in sovereigns; and of 8 per cent., if such payment is made in gold currency of any other country belonging to the Latin Union.

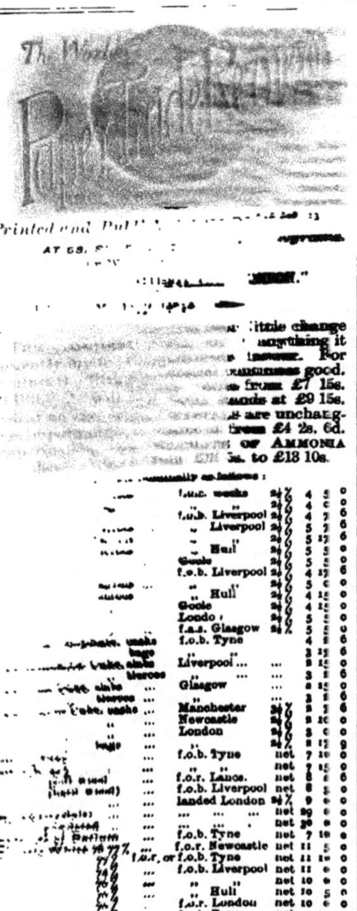

[illegible] 58%	...	...	f.o.b. Tyne	[illegible]	[illegible]
58%	...	...	ex ship Thames	[illegible]	[illegible]
58%	...	...	f.o.b. Liverpool	[illegible]	[illegible]
[illegible] Crystals	...	...	„ Tyne	[illegible]	[illegible]
„	...	...	ex ship Thames	[illegible]	[illegible]
„	...	...	f.o.b. Liverpool	[illegible]	[illegible]
Sulphur, roll	...	...	f.o.r. works	[illegible]	7
„ flowers	...	...	„ „	[illegible]	[illegible]
„ recovered	...	...	„ „	[illegible]	[illegible]
Sulphate of Ammonia	„		„ „	[illegible]	13
„ of Copper	...		„ Liverpool	[illegible]	10

FOREIGN.—F.o.b. Continental port

Alkali, 58% 2-cwt. bags £4 10/0; 10-cwt. casks [illegible]
Caustic Soda, 70-72% ... ... — — [illegible]
Hypo-Sulphite of Soda 10-ton lots casks ... [illegible]
Sulphate of Alumina 7-8 cwt. casks net c.i.f. [illegible]
Blanc Fixe (c.i.f. London) ... — — [illegible]

ESPARTO.—The enquiry for distant shipment is again rather better, and a fair amount of business is being done at steady prices. The November imports have been extremely limited, and early supplies are wanted on existing contracts.

Prices c.i.f. London and Leith, or f.o.r. Cardiff, [illegible] Tyne Docks are nominally as follows:

Spanish—Fair to Good ...	...	—	£5 5 [illegible]	[illegible]
„ Fine to Best ...	...	—	5 10 [illegible]	[illegible]
Oran — Fair to Good ...	...	—	[illegible]	[illegible]
„ First Quality ...	...	—	3 15 [illegible]	[illegible]
Tripoli — Hand-picked ...	...	—	3 15 [illegible]	[illegible]
„ Fair Average ...	...	—	3 [illegible]	[illegible]
Bona & Philippeville ...	...	—	3 15 [illegible]	[illegible]

WEEK'S IMPORTS.

Quantity	From	Importer	Port
4296 bales	Aguilas	H. Burrell	Grangemouth

STRAW.—Market dull.

WEEK'S IMPORTS.

(Purposes unspecified) at principal Ports From

DENMARK	... 1039 bales	HOLLAND	[illegible]
FRANCE	... 11 „		

STRAW PULPS.—Trade shows some improvement.

Prices, c.i.f. London, Hull or Leith

German, 50 to 55% moisture ... — — £[illegible]
do. dry, ... No. 1 £16 10 0; No. 2 [illegible]

WEEK'S IMPORTS.

Quantity	From	Importer	Port
58 bales	Hambro	To order	Hull
40 „	„	„	[illegible]
100 „	„	„	Hull

CHEMICAL WOOD PULPS.—Market unchanged; prices, however, are firm and likely to advance shortly.

Prices, ex steamer, London, Hull, Newcastle, Leith and Glasgow are nominally as follows:

SULPHITE, Unbleached, Common	£10	0	0	to	11	[illegible]	[illegible]
„ Superior	11	0	0	„	11	[illegible]	[illegible]
„ „ 50% moisture, d.w.	11	0	0	„	[illegible]	[illegible]	[illegible]
„ Extra	[illegible]	0	0	„	13	[illegible]	[illegible]
„ Bleached, moist					[illegible]	[illegible]	[illegible]
„ Unbleached, English, del. Lancs. ...					10	15	[illegible]
„ „ „ No. 1, ex mills, Ldn.					[illegible]	[illegible]	[illegible]
„ „ „ No. 2, „ „					9	15	[illegible]
SODA, Unbleached, Common ...	10	5	0	„	[illegible]	[illegible]	[illegible]
„ „ Extra	10	[illegible]	0	„	11	[illegible]	[illegible]
„ Half-Bleached	12	10	0	„	14	[illegible]	[illegible]
SULPHATE, Unbleached, Common	10	10	0	„	11	[illegible]	[illegible]
„ Extra	11	0	0	„	12	[illegible]	[illegible]
„ Half-Bleached	13	10	0	„	14	[illegible]	[illegible]
Bleached	15	0	0	„	16	[illegible]	[illegible]

MECHANICAL WOOD PULPS. — Stocks firmly held, and although one or two parcels on the spot seem to be begging, sellers apparently are not inclined to reduce prices. We are inclined to think that one parcel is being offered by more than one firm.

[illegible] London, Hull, [illegible], Leith [illegible]

WEEK'S IMPORTS.

Quantity	From	Importer	Port.
[illegible]	[illegible]	To order	Hull
[illegible]	[illegible]	[illegible]	London
[illegible]	[illegible]	[illegible]	Hull
[illegible]	[illegible]	[illegible]	Grangemouth
[illegible]	[illegible]	[illegible]	Hull
[illegible]	[illegible]	[illegible]	London
[illegible]	[illegible]	[illegible]	Liverpool
[illegible]	[illegible]	[illegible]	London
[illegible]	[illegible]	[illegible]	Hull
[illegible]	[illegible]	[illegible]	London
[illegible]	[illegible]	R. W. Lowe	[illegible]

Totals from Each Country.

AUSTRIA	[illegible]	HOLLAND	[illegible]
FINLAND	[illegible]	PRUSSIA	[illegible]
GERMANY	[illegible]	NORWAY	[illegible]
HOLLAND	[illegible]	SWEDEN	[illegible]

WEEK'S IMPORTS of WOOD PULP BOARDS.

Quantity	From	Importer	Port
135 bales	[illegible]	To order	[illegible]

HOME RAGS.—Prices unaltered, with a steady demand for most grades; not much business, however, [illegible] owing to stocktaking.

LONDON.

New White Cuttings	[illegible]	Canvas No. 1	[illegible]
Fines (selected)	[illegible]	„ No. 2	[illegible]
„ good London	[illegible]	„ No. 3	[illegible]
Outshots (selected)	[illegible]	Mixed Rope	[illegible]
„ ordinary	[illegible]	White Rope	[illegible]
London Seconds	[illegible]	White Manila Rope	[illegible]
Country do.	[illegible]	Tarred Rope	[illegible]
London Thirds	[illegible]	Bagging	[illegible]
Country do.	[illegible]	Gunny	[illegible]
Light Prints	[illegible]		

BRISTOL.

Fines	[illegible]	Clean Canvas	[illegible]
Outshots	[illegible]	Second do.	[illegible]
Seconds	[illegible]	Light Prints	[illegible]
Thirds	[illegible]	Hemp Tarred Rope	[illegible]
Mixed Bagging	[illegible]	Tarred Manila	[illegible]

MANCHESTER.

Fines	[illegible]	Blues	[illegible]
Outshots (best)	[illegible]	Bagging	[illegible]
„ (ordinary)	[illegible]	„ (common)	[illegible]
Seconds	[illegible]	W. Manila Rope	[illegible]
Thirds	[illegible]	Sacks, Linen	[illegible]

[illegible]

Superfines	[illegible]	Black Cottons	[illegible]
Outshots	[illegible]	W. Manila Rope	[illegible]
Mixed Fines	[illegible]	Tarred Ditto	[illegible]
Common Seconds	[illegible]	„ Hemp Rope	[illegible]
First do.	[illegible]	Rope Ends (new)	[illegible]
Prints	[illegible]	„ (old)	[illegible]
Canvas (best)	[illegible]	Bagging	[illegible]
„ 2nd	[illegible]	„ (common)	[illegible]

DUBLIN.

White Cuttings	[illegible]	Mixed Bagging	3 0
Prints	[illegible]	White Manila	3 0
Seconds	[illegible]	Tarred Hemp	3 0
Light Prints	[illegible]	Gunny	13 6
Black do.	[illegible]	Mixed Ropes	3 6
Bagging	[illegible]		

FOREIGN RAGS.—Very little change to report in the state of the Continental market. Supplies are scarce, and the demand somewhat restricted.

WEEK'S IMPORTS.

Quantity	From	Importer	Port.
[illegible]	Amsterdam	To order	Leith
[illegible]	[illegible]	[illegible]	Hull
[illegible]	[illegible]	[illegible]	Leith
[illegible]	[illegible]	[illegible]	Grangemouth
[illegible]	[illegible]	[illegible]	Hull
[illegible]	Antwerp	[illegible]	Leith
[illegible]	Bremen	[illegible]	Liverpool
[illegible]	[illegible]	[illegible]	[illegible]
[illegible]	Buenos Ayres	[illegible]	Hull
[illegible]	[illegible]	[illegible]	Liverpool
[illegible]	[illegible]	[illegible]	Hull
[illegible]	[illegible]	[illegible]	Liverpool
[illegible]	[illegible]	[illegible]	London
[illegible]	[illegible]	[illegible]	Leith
[illegible]	[illegible]	[illegible]	Hull
[illegible]	[illegible]	[illegible]	Liverpool
[illegible]	[illegible]	[illegible]	Hull
[illegible]	[illegible]	[illegible]	London
[illegible]	[illegible]	[illegible]	Leith
[illegible]	[illegible]	[illegible]	Hull
[illegible]	[illegible]	[illegible]	London
[illegible]	[illegible]	[illegible]	Liverpool
[illegible]	[illegible]	[illegible]	London
[illegible]	[illegible]	[illegible]	Hull
[illegible]	Rotterdam	[illegible]	Leith
[illegible]	[illegible]	[illegible]	Hull
[illegible]	St. [illegible]	[illegible]	Newhaven
[illegible]	[illegible]	[illegible]	Liverpool
[illegible]	[illegible]	[illegible]	Southampton
[illegible]	[illegible]	[illegible]	Hull
[illegible]	[illegible]	[illegible]	Liverpool

Totals from Each Country.

ARGENTINA	[illegible]	INDIA	[illegible]
BELGIUM	[illegible]	NORWAY	[illegible]
DENMARK	[illegible]	PRUSSIA	96
FRANCE	[illegible]	SPAIN	3
GERMANY	[illegible]	TURKEY	[illegible]
HOLLAND	[illegible]		

GERMAN RAGS.

STETTIN f.o.b. Hull, Leith, Tyne and London.

SPFFF and SPFF	[illegible]	LFB Blues	[illegible]
SPF	[illegible]	CSPFFF	[illegible]
FF	[illegible]	CSPFF	[illegible]
[illegible]	[illegible]	CSPF Blues	7/0
LFX	[illegible]	LFX Coloured	[illegible]

HAMBURG f.o.b.

SPFC	[illegible]	FF Grey Linens	9/0
SPFFF	[illegible]	LFX Second ditto	8/0
SPFFF and SPFF	[illegible]	CSPFFF	17/3
SPFF	[illegible]	CSPFF	11/3
SPF	[illegible]	LFB	8/0
[illegible]	[illegible]	Dark Blues (unbleached)	11/9
LFX	[illegible]	Wool Tares	8/0
White Rope	[illegible]	Jute, No. I [illegible], No. II	5/6

DUTCH RAGS c.i.f. Hull; [illegible] f.o.b. Leith [illegible] Liverpool [illegible].

Selected Fines free from Muslins	[illegible]	Best Grey Linens	9/0
Selected Outshots	[illegible]	Common ditto	5/6
„ Dirty Fines	[illegible]	White Canvas	15/0
Light Cottons	[illegible]	Grey & Brown Canvas	[illegible]
Blue Cottons	[illegible]	Tarred Hemp Rope	8/0
Dark Coloured Cottons	[illegible]	Ditto (broken)	5/3
New Cuttings Bleached	[illegible]	White Paper Shavings	7/9
„ Unbleached	[illegible]	Gunny (best)	4/9
„ [illegible]	[illegible]	Jute Bagging	3/6
Muslins	[illegible]	Ditto (common)	2/0
Red Cottons Mixed	5/9	Tarpaulins	4/0
Fustians [illegible]	5/3	Cowhair Carpets	2/9
		Hard ditto	/0

WORLD'S PAPER TRADE REVIEW OFFICE,
58, SHOE LANE, LONDON, E.C.
DECEMBER 14, 1893.

MARKET REPORT

and RECORD of IMPORTS

Of Foreign Rags, Wood Pulp, Esparto, Paper, Mill boards, Strawboards, &c., at the Ports of London, Liverpool, Southampton, Bristol, Hull, Fleetwood, Middlesborough, Glasgow, Grangemouth, Granton, Dundee, Leith, Dover, Folkestone, and Newhaven for the WEEK ENDING DECEMBER 13

From SPECIAL Sources and Telegra[illegible]

Telegrams—"STONHILL, LONDON"

CHEMICALS.—There has been littl[illegible] during the past week, but if any[illegible] has been in manufacturers' fav[illegible] ALKALI the home demand contin[illegible] BLEACHING POWDER varies [illegible] to £8 5s. CAUSTIC SODA stands [illegible] for 70%, and SODA CRYSTALS [illegible] ed. SULPHUR is scarce at fr[illegible] to £4 5s., and SULPHATE [illegible] shows a rise at from £13 5[illegible]

Prices are nominally [illegible]

Alkali, 58% tierces ... f.o.r. [illegible] ... 4/3
" 58% bags ... [illegible] ... 3/3
58% ... ... f.[illegible] ... 2/0
Alum (Ground), tierces ... " [illegible] ... 8/6
barrels ... " [illegible]mouth. ... 5/0
" " tierces ... [illegible] ... 8/0
" " " ... [illegible]
Alum (Lump) " ... [illegible] ... 3/0 3/6
" " barrels ... [illegible] ... 2/6-2/9
" " tierces
" " " ... [illegible] is a moderate [illegible] Papers.

Alumina Sulphate, ca[illegible]
Aluminoferric Cake, [illegible]
Alumina Cake, [illegible] tierces
Aluminous Cake, [illegible]

[illegible]mall Letters	5/[illegible]
[illegible] "	7/0
Brown Paper	2/9
Light Browns	2/9
Books & Pamphlets ...	6/0
Strawboard Cuttings	1/6
Jacquards	2/6

[illegible] per ton extra.

Blanc Fixe ...
Bleach, 35%
" (soft [illegible] to 18
" (hard [illegible] £17
[illegible] £16

[illegible]iet, with little offering [illegible] demand for Cuttings.

Common ...	£13 to	£14
Rejections ...	£9 "	£10
Cuttings ...	£5 10 "	£7

Borax (cryst[illegible]
Chloride of [illegible]
Caustic W[illegible]

Business quiet at previous [illegible]

[illegible] 3/0, 5/0, 11/0, 3/0, 55/0, 40/0, 4/0, 30/0, 40/0, 7/[illegible]-10/0, [illegible]

Ultramarine (pure) ... cwt. 40/0 to 45/0

PASTE COLOURS with 60% of colour, as follows:

Orange Pulp ... cwt.	40/0
Golden Yellow Pulp	36/0
Lemon " " cwt.	36/0
Prussian Yellow "	36/0
Green (free of arsenic	36/0
Paste Blue (20-45%) " ...	13/6-24/6

[illegible]—Prices:
[illegible] London, less 2½%.
[illegible] Powder, £9 [illegible] Special £12.
[illegible] B.K.M.F., £18.
[illegible]
[illegible] £20 (net); Crystal (in bags) [illegible] (in bags) £15 less 2½%.
[illegible]

Soda [illegible] fairly brisk; prices have [illegible]

		per cwt.	[illegible]
		"	7[illegible]
		"	45[illegible]
			45[illegible]
			3[illegible]

[illegible] steady; supplies of [illegible] scarce.

		Local (on the spot).	L[illegible]
	3 10 4 0 ...	3 9 ...	3 4[illegible]
	4 0 ...	3 10 ...	3 5
	4 6 ...	4 0 ...	3 7[illegible]
	4 [illegible] ...	4/1½ ...	3 9
...	5 0 ...	4/4½ ...	3 [illegible]
...	5 6 ...	5/0 ...	4/[illegible]
...	6 0 ...	6/0 ...	4 [illegible]
[illegible] ...	6 6 ...	6/6 ...	6/0
[illegible] ...	7/9 ...	7/6 ...	7/0
N ...	8/9 ...	8/9 ...	8/3
W G ...	9/6 ...	9/6 ...	9/3
W W .	10/0 ...	10/3 ...	9/9

French Rosin: G, 5/3; H, 5/4½; I, 5/7½; K, 6/3; M, 6/[illegible] N, 8/3; W G, 9/0; W W, 9/6; Virgin, 10/9. Net c.i.f.

MINERALS.—CHINA CLAY is in demand and contracts for next year are being closed at unchanged values. There is a good trade passing in FRENCH and ITALIAN CHALKS; prices are firm. BARYTES are scarce; quotations evidence no change. PATENT HARDENINGS and MINERAL WHITE are in moderate request.

China Clay, in bulk, f.o.b. Cornwall, 14/0 to 27/6; bags 5/[illegible] and casks 9/6 per ton extra; f.o.b. London, in casks 35/0 to 50/0 per ton.

Mineral White (Terra Alba), per ton f.o.r. or boat at works:

Superfine...	28/0 less 2½ %
Pottery Super.... ...	24/0 "
Ball Seconds	20/0 "
Seconds	15/0 "
Thirds	10/6 "

Superfine Hardening, f.o.r. works, 40/0.
Patent Crystal Hardening, delivered at mills £3 to £3 15/0
Patent Hardening (2 ton lots) f.o.r. Lancs., £3 5/0.
" " (5 ton lots) f.o.b. Liverpool, £3 10/0.
Magnesite (in lump) 32/6 per ton.
Magnesite (containing 98% Carbonate of Magnesia), raw ground, £6 10/0; calcined ground, £12 10/0.
Albarine, £3, del. mills.
Asbestos, best rock, £18; brown grades, £14 to £15
Asbestine Pulp, £4 5/- to £5 c.i.f. London, Liverpool and Glasgow.
Barytes (Carbonate), lump, 90/0 to 95/0; nuts, 72/6 to 85/0.
French and Italian Chalk (Souheur Brand), per ton in lots of 10 tons: Flower O, 69/6 c.i.f. London; Flower OO, 62/0, Flower OOO, 55/6. Swan White, 63/0; Snow White, 95/0; Snow White XX, 89/0. Blackwell's "Angel White" Brand and "Silvery" 90/- to 92/6; prime quality, 90/- to 95/-; and superfine, 105/-.
Barytes (Sulphate), "Angel White," No. 1, 70/0; No. 2, 60/0 to 65/0; No. 3, 45/0. Souheur's Brands: AF, 83/-; BF, 71/-; AB, 33/6; BB, 29/6; CB, 24/3.
Bauxite, Irish Hill Quality, first lump, 20/0; seconds 16/0; thirds, 12/0; ground, 35/0.
Pyrites (non-cupreous), Liverpool, 5d., 2 %.
Carbonate of Lime (Souheur Brand). Prima 43/-, Secunda 37/-.

LIME.—Demand good. The present price is 12s. 6d. per ton f.o.r.

BALING TWINE.—Prices:

	Thick.	Medium.	Cap.
All Hemp ... . per lb.	4d.	4½d.	4½d.
All Jute	3½d.	3½d.	4d.

DIRECTORY.

ALUMINOUS CAKE.

The ALUM, CHINA CLAY and VITRIOL Co., Limited, ... Street, London ... Works: ... Telegrams— ... London.

ANALYTICAL.

... all ... Manchester.

ARTESIAN WELLS.

... Richard ... Well Engineer, ... Queen Victoria Street, London ...

BOILER COVERING.

LONSDALES, Boiler Coverers, Blackburn ... sample ... Patent Plastic Composition ... Great Britain ...

CHINA CLAY.

The ALUM, CHINA CLAY and VITRIOL Co., Limited, ... Queen Victoria Street, London ... St. Austell, Cornwall. Telegrams— ... London.

ROGERS ... & Co., Truro, Cornwall — ... Street, Edinburgh.

... Lancaster ... Cornwall.

GAUGES.

... & Co., ... Manchester ...

GEMMILL ... & Co., ...

FRENCH RAGS.

Quotations range, per cwt., ex ship London, Southampton or Hull; 2/0 per ton more at Liverpool, and 10/0 per ton higher at Newcastle, Glasgow or Leith.

French Linens, I ...	22/0	Black Cotton ...	4/0
II 18/6; III ...	14/6	Marseilles Whites, I	16/0
White Cottons, I ...	19/0	II 10/0; III ...	7/6
II 15/0; III ...	12/6	Blue Cotton	11/0
Knitted Cotton ...	11/0	Light Prints... ...	9/0
Light Coloured Cotton	8/0	Mixed Prints ...	6/0
Blue Cotton	9/6	New White Cuttings	23/0
Coloured Cotton ...	6/0	,, Stay ...	21/0

BELGIAN RAGS.

F.o.b. Ghent. Freights: London, 5/0; Hull and Goole, 7/6 Liverpool and Leith, 10/0; Newcastle, 12/6; Dundee and Aberdeen, 15/0; Glasgow, 16/8.

White Linens No. 1	22/6	Fustians (Light) ...	6/0
,, ,, No. 2	16/0	,, (Dark) ...	4/0
,, ,, No. 3	13/0	Thirds...	3/0
Fines (Mixed) ...	12/0	Black Cottons ...	3/9
Grey Linens (strong)	9/6	Hemp Strings (unt'r'd)	2/0
,, ,, (extra)	14/0	House Cloths ...	4/0
Blue Linens... ...	8/6	Old Bagging (sol:d)	3/6
White Cottons S'p'fine	18/0	,, ,, (common)	2/6
,, ,, No. 2	15/0	NEW.	
Outshots No. 3 ...	10/0	White & Cream Linens	35/0
Seconds No. 4 ...	8/0	White Cuttings ...	22/0
Prints (Light) ...	8/6	Unbleached Cuttings	21/0
,, (Old)	4/6	Print Cuttings ..	8

BELGIAN FLAX and HEMP WASTE.

Best washed and dried Flax Waste, 10/0; Fair ditto	9/0
Flax Spinners' Waste (grease boiled out)... ...	10 0
Hemp Waste, No. 1 9/0; No. 2	7/6
Flax Spinners' Waste, No. 1 (Flax Rove) 10/0: No. 2	6/6

RUSSIAN RAGS.

C.i.f. London, Hull, Newcastle or Leith.

SPFF	16/0	CC (Cotton	4/[illegible]
SPF	14/6	Jute I	3/[illegible]
FG	11/6	,, II...	[illegible]
LFB	9/6	Rope I	[illegible]
FF	8/3	,, II	5/0

NORWEGIAN RAGS.

C.i.f. London, Hull, Tyne, and Grangemouth.

1st Rope (tarred) ...	8/6-9/0	2nd Canvas ...	3/[illegible]
2nd ,, ,, ...	5/6-6/0	Jute Bagging	
Manilla Rope (white)	8/0-8/9	Gunny ...	[illegible]
Best Canvas ...	11/9-12/0	Mixed ...	[illegible]

WASTE PAPERS.—There is a moderate trade passing in Waste Papers.

Cream Shavings ...	12/3	Small Letters	[illegible]
Fine ,, ...	9/6	Large ,, ..	
Mixed ,, ...	2/0	Brown Paper ...	
White Printings ...	8/9	Light Browns	
White Waste ...	1/0	Books & Pamphl[illegible]	
Wood Pulp Cuttings	3/6	Strawboard Cuttings	
Brown Paper	3/0	Jacquards ..	
Crushed News	2/0		

For Export: 26/- per ton extra

JUTE.—Market quiet, with little [illegible] on spot; fair demand for Cuttings

Good White	£17 10 to 18	Common .	[illegible]
Good	£17	Rejections	[illegible]
Medium ..	£15 to £16	Cuttings	[illegible]

COLOURS. — Business quiet [illegible] quotations.

Mineral Black ...	cwt.	3/0	Ultramarine [illegible]
do. superior ...	,,	5/0	[illegible]
Pure Ivory Black	,,	12/0	PA[illegible]
Ochre	,,	3/0	[illegible]
French J. C. Ochre	ton	55/0	Orange [illegible]
Chrome (pure) ...	cwt.	40/0	Golden [illegible]
Red Oxide	,,	4/6	Lemon [illegible]
Umber, Devonshire	,,	30/0	[illegible]
do. Turkish ...	,,	40/0	
Lamp Black ...		7/0-11/[illegible]	
Cochineal	lb.	[illegible]	

STARCH.—Pri[illegible]

Maize—Cr[illegible]
Farina [illegible]

SIZING.—Tr[illegible] upward tend[illegible]

English Gelatines
Foreign ..
Fine Skin Glues
Long Scotch Glues
Common ..
"Town" Glue
"Bone" Glue
Foreign Glues
Bone Size ...
Gelatine Size
Dry B A Pieces
,, English P[illegible]
Wet .. ..
,, Sheep Pie[illegible]
Buffalo [illegible]
.. Pi[illegible]

ROSIN [illegible]
Market [illegible]

B.C
D
E ...
F ...
G ..
H
I ..
[illegible]
M ...
N
W G
W W
French [illegible]
N[illegible]

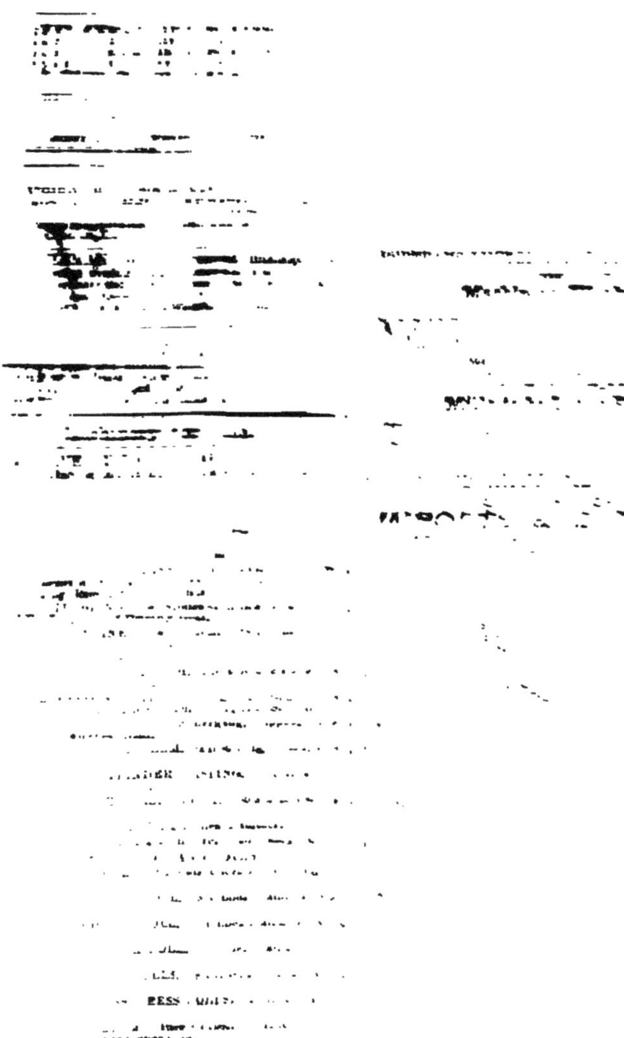

PAPER IMPORTS.

[illegible]OR THE WEEK ENDING TUESDAY.

[illegible]	17 bales	HOLLAND	139[illegible] bales
[illegible]	1149	..	8[illegible] cases
	2[illegible] cases	NORWAY	100[illegible] bales
[illegible]	11 bales	PRUSSIA	[illegible]
[illegible]	142 ..	SWEDEN	33[illegible] ..
[illegible]	1463 ..	..	5[illegible] rolls
[illegible]	664 ..	TURKEY	[illegible] bales
	446 cases	U.S.A.	2[illegible] ..
[illegible]MANY	2399 bales	..	[illegible] cases
	128 cases	..	[illegible] rolls

Including the Following:

	From	Importer	Port.
[illegible]	Boston	B. Galloway	London
[illegible]	Copenhagen	Becker & Ulrich	"
	"	G. R. Clark & Co	"
[illegible]	Fredrikstad	Christophersen	"
	"	Lou. & R. S. Co	"
[illegible]	Gothenburg	J. Hamilton	"
[illegible]	"	R. L. Lundgren	"
[illegible]	"	Schenkenwald & Co	"
	"	" "	"
[illegible]	"	" "	"
[illegible]	"	S.S.S. Co	"
[illegible]	"	Duff & Co	"
[illegible]	"	Schenkenwald & Co	"
[illegible]	"	Tegner, Price & Co	"
30	"	Brooke Wid.	"
10[illegible]	New York	J. M. Richards	"
[illegible]7	Stettin	Becker & Ulrich	"
12	"	M. Benecke	"
13	"	Becker & Ulrich	"
11	"	E. & E. Sabel	"

PAPER EXPORTS.

FOR THE WEEK ENDING TUESDAY.

	Printings.		Writings.		Other kinds.	
AUSTRALIA	4082½	cwts.	764	cwts.	809	cwts.
AFRICA	17	"	2	"	[illegible]	"
ARGENTINE ...		"	65	"	[illegible]	"
B. WEST INDIES ..	84	"		"		"
B. GUIANA		"	3	"	813	"
BELGIUM	46	"	53	"	4[illegible]	"
CANADA	80	"		"	11	"
CHINA	343	"	41	"	69	"
CAPE COLONY ...	597	"	177	"	95[illegible]	"
DENMARK	93	"	2	"	5	"
FRANCE	60	"	196	"	99	"
GERMANY	7	"	1	"	3	"
HOLLAND	84	"		"	43	"
INDIA	4301	"	548½	"	87[illegible]	"
JAPAN	176	"	10	"	20	"
MAURITIUS ...	—	"	4	"		"
MALTA...	14	"	—	"	15	"
NEW ZEALAND ...	1130	"	986	"	635	"
PORTUGAL	—	"	14	"	3	"
RUSSIA	42	"	11	"	8	"
SPAIN	155	"	54	"	1	"
STRAIT Settlements	12	"	—	"		"
SWEDEN	—	"	1	"		"
S. AMERICA... ...	13	"	—	"	43	"
TURKEY — ...	—	"	4	"	9	"
U.S.A.	382½	"	106½	"		"

[illegible] PAPER TRADE REVIEW is a widely informed and well [illegible] enterprise, of great value to exporters for its [illegible] Market Reports and statistics of Raw Material.—[illegible] für die Papier-Fabrikation, Dresden.

A. WERTHEIM & CO.,

HAMBURG,

SUPPLY ALL KINDS OF

Sulphite,

Soda and

Mechanical

WOOD PULPS.

OFFICES AT:

WERTHEIMO HAMBURG.

PAPER IMPORTS.

FOR THE WEEK ENDING TUESDAY

AUSTRIA
BELGIUM
CHANNEL I.
DENMARK
FINLAND
FRANCE
GERMANY

THE NEW JOURNALISM.

MR STEAD AND [illegible] PATENTS.

WHO IS LADY SIDNEY [illegible]?

[illegible] New Journalism [illegible] Mr W. T. Stead [illegible] Review of Reviews [illegible] The Daily Paper [illegible] a little sheet [illegible] of all [illegible] of all who [illegible] embraces the [illegible] from the [illegible] appearance of The Daily Paper is [illegible] to say [illegible]. The nearest [illegible] which we can trace in any publication of the day is to be found in the [illegible] magazines [illegible] for the various religious bodies. Indeed, it [illegible] inward and an outward [illegible] than a [illegible]. It is [illegible] from any ordinary [illegible] conception of a daily newspaper [illegible]. Fancy a [illegible] daily paper with one page devoted to editorial comment and [illegible] summary of [illegible] news! Picture the [illegible] with which the daily paper reader will turn to such items as [illegible] "Lesson for the day," "Hymn for the day," &c. Then, how [illegible] amid the hurry and [illegible] of commercial life in which one has scarce time to master the purport of the miscellaneous and multifarious contents of [illegible] daily papers, [illegible] a perusal of their [illegible] exciting [illegible] description [illegible] own correspondent [illegible] epistle [illegible] years or more ago. We may have [illegible] from [illegible] in our school [illegible] with what [illegible] we shall [illegible] the accounts of the [illegible] of [illegible] prize, from the [illegible] O. P. C. [illegible] account of the [illegible] or even the fearful [illegible] Eden, together with the [illegible] murderer. It is [illegible] items of intelligence as these [illegible] Reuter telegrams [illegible] a world's [illegible] and [illegible] into insignificance.

From the [illegible] personality of Mr Stead we [illegible] something [illegible] eccentricity [illegible] and [illegible] it. In the specimen [illegible] of The Daily Paper we [illegible] for that we must [illegible] as well as for the [illegible] upon which the high and exaggerated [illegible] Mr Stead's Ideal Paper are based. The Review of Reviews [illegible] contains [illegible] pages, of which [illegible] for The Daily Paper. The personality of the [illegible] veiled [illegible]

the pseudonym of "Jasper Sterling," not at all. "Professor," asks the daughter of Lady Sidney Nestor, the millionaire widow, "what do you know about Mr. Sterling?" "He is, I should say," replies the professor, "just a little mad—not too mad, you know, but just enough to keep his friends in a perpetual state of anxiety as to what he is going to do next. He is always breaking out in a new place, and he is often a greater affliction to his friends than his foes." It is to Lady Sidney that Jasper Sterling announces his intention of starting a daily paper. "Tell me," he says, "you say you have more money than you know what to do with. . . . Could you afford to throw a million of money into the sea?" "What would you do in my place?" asks Lady Sidney. "I would do what I believe the Apostle Paul would have done if he had lived in our generation." "What is that? Found a church, I suppose?" "No, the day for that has gone [illegible]. He would found a newspaper." [illegible] describes his [illegible] in prepaid subscriptions [illegible] of founding "without capital" a daily paper that shall [illegible] a world that [illegible]. But he [illegible] Lady Sidney's millions [illegible] The Daily Paper [illegible] a year [illegible] The English-speaking world [illegible] common [illegible] common ideas [illegible]—what wonder [illegible] Lady Sidney Nestor [illegible] millions with The Daily Paper [illegible] of the foundation of Mr Stead's [illegible] prepaid subscriptions. This Lady Sidney [illegible] millions. But [illegible] Mr Stead's [illegible] we may as well ask [illegible] Lady Sidney [illegible] the whole management of [illegible]

Now as to the [illegible] of this journalistic [illegible], and the methods of their accomplishment. They are set down in the third part of the Review of Reviews [illegible] [illegible]

... JOHN STONHILL, 58, Shoe Lane, LONDON, E.C. December 15, 1893.

tions before us, taking events in chronological order, the principal methods appear to be—(1) The institution of four-in-hand brake drives around London with sweet girl-graduates for guides and Ladies Mæcenas for whips; (2) the development of the Thames Embankment upon the lines of the Paris Boulevarde with kiosks and bands and cafés *al fresco*, and tho Thames rendered brilliant with gondolas and bunting galore; (3) the improvement of our living by the amelioration of our livers, to be brought about by dotting the face of the metropolis with cheap restaurants with irreproachable cuisine and unrivalled French chefs; (4) an Endowment of Charwomen; (5) the establishment of a National Theatre, and a Conservatoire of Music; (6) the encouragement and advancement of the Feister printing machine, with other patents handled by Mr. Byers; (7) the formation of an Amazonian Brigade of Widows; with some minor things, such as a Fellowship cult which shall guarantee everything and be called upon to pay for nothing, a Labour Bureau, a Civic Church, magic lantern exhibitions, a prison department; and over all *The Daily Paper*! We have been at pains to pick out these items, for we confess the strongest impression left upon our mind after struggling through the *Annual* was that set down under the sixth heading—the Feister machine and Byers' Patents, — *The Daily Paper* printed upon Feister machines by female operatives, and female carters clothed in Byers' ventilated waterproof garments—Feister and Byers' patents and Pegamoid, Pegamoid and Byers' Patents and Feister machines—the great Byers and the greater Stead. But how in the name of all that is sensible these things are going to regenerate a wicked world we don't know. We should like to learn more about the prospective millions. Having taken the world so far into his confidence, surely Mr. Stead might go a step further, and say who is the bright particular leader of wealth and fashion to whom his appeal is directed. It might greatly facilitate the subscription of the modest £130,000, which otherwise, we venture to think, is likely to hang fire, if not altogether miss fire. The name of W. T. Stead is well known; so is that of Byers' Patents; but another name still to back a bill for so large a sum is desirable.

Printed and Published by W. JOHN STONHILL 58, Shoe Lane, LONDON, E.C. December 15, 1893.

THE Rossendale Belting Co.,

ISAAC JACKSON, **GLOSSOP.** REPRESENTATIVE.

Telegrams—"FASTENER, GLOSSOP."

PATENTEES & SOLE MAKERS

Makers of PATENT EDGED

HAIR BELTING

ALSO PATENT

Cylinder and Beater Belts SPECIALLY PREPARED to RESIST WATER and ACIDS; Made in DIFFERENT PLIES to SUIT HEAVY and LIGHT RUNNING.

JACKSON'S

PATENT CONCAVE AND CONVEX PLATE FASTENER.

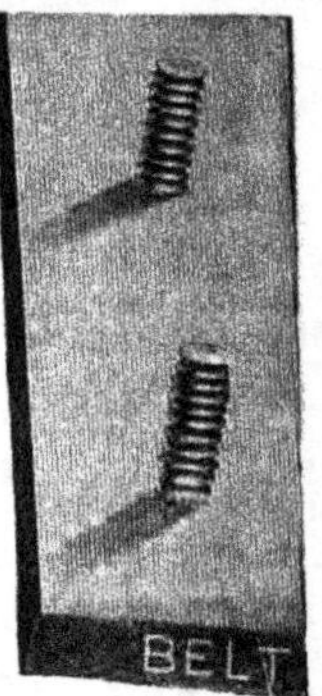

We Recommend JACKSON'S CONCAVE and CONVEX PLATE FASTENER for all BELTS in PAPER MILLS. 

THE COMPANY SWINDLERS' PROTECTION ACTS, 1862 TO 1890.

THE WORST BLOT ON THE STATUTE BOOK.

I

"On the whole it would be a difficult, if not an impossible task, to select out of the whole number of cases wound up by the court during the year a single case in which it could be said that the objects of the company were reasonable, that its promotion and management were honest, and that its failure was due chiefly to misfortune."

"The general conclusion to which an impartial observation of the facts leads, is that under the Companies' Acts a wide field has been opened up for the prosecution of objects of a more or less fraudulent character, which did not exist prior to the passing of these Acts, and which would be practically impossible in the the case of individuals, of private partnerships, or of unlimited companies."

The two paragraphs above quoted are among the most remarkable expressions ever uttered in an official quarter as to the effect and working of an Act or a series of Acts of Parliament. They emanate from the Inspector-General in Companies liquidation, and occur in his first (and at present only) published report under the Companies' Winding-up Act of 1890. It is not to be supposed that the official was telling any new thing: he was merely repeating what was broadly known to everyone engaged in commercial matters for twenty years or more—in fact ever since limited liabiilty was created, as distinct from the older joint stock companies. But it is the first time that so high an official has had the opportunity and the courage to speak out so emphatically in sweeping condemnation of the Acts he helps to administer. There is an almost brutal frankness in the two passages, a John Bull directness that almost prepares one for the subscription "John Smith."

Mr. Smith was dealing with the case of bankrupt companies whose affairs came under the supervision of the courts during the year ending December 31st, 1891. There was nothing particularly exceptional in the records of that year to distinguish it from any one of the dozen that preceded it, and when those of 1892 and 1893 are before us we expect to find no weakening in the logic of facts which go to support the Inspector-General's views, or anything that will modify the common knowledge that the Companies' Acts as they now stand afford the grossest protection to the swindler, not indeed by anything that is in them contained, but by the omission of all safeguards for the public.

WHAT ARE THE COMPANIES' ACTS?

The great parent Act, the Act that set up the principle of limited liability of shareholders, and practically absolved from liability a large and new class of bubble promoters, fraudulent debtors and incompetent directorates, is the 25th and 26th Vic., cap. 89, entitled "An Act for the Incorporation, Regulation, and Winding-up of Trading Companies and other Associations." It has been followed by quite a crop of amending Bills and Acts, of which the following have found their way to the Statute Book:—

27 Vic., cap. 19, "An Act to enable Joint Stock Companies carrying on business in Foreign Countries to have Official Seals to be used in such Countries."

30 and 31 Vic., cap. 131, "An Act to Amend the Companies' Act, 1862."

33 and 34 Vic., cap. 104, "An Act to facilitate Compromises and Arrangements between Creditors and Shareholders of Joint Stock and other Companies in Liquidation."

40 and 41 Vic., cap. 26, "An Act to Amend the Companies Acts of 1862 and 1867."

42 and 43 Vic., cap. 76, "An Act to amend the Law with respect to the Liability of Members of Banking and other Joint Stock Companies and for other purposes."

43 Vic., cap. 19, "An Act to amend the Companies' Acts of 1862, 1867, 1877, and 1879."

46 and 47 Vic., cap. 30, "An Act to authorise Companies registered under the Companies' Act, 1862, to keep Local Registers of their Member in British Colonies."

49 Vic., cap. 24, "An Act to amend the Companies' Acts of 1862, 1867, 1870, 1877, 1879, 1880, and 1883."

53 and 54 Vic., cap. 62, "An Act to give further Powers to Companies with respect to certain Instruments under which they may be constituted or regulated."

53 and 54 Vic., cap. 63, "An Act to amend the Law relating to the Winding-up of Companies in England and Wales."

53 and 54 Vic., cap. 64, "An Act to amend the Law relating to the liability of Directors and others for Statements in Prospectuses and other Documents soliciting applications for Shares or Debentures."

To examine the clauses of these various Acts, to note the particularity with which details are provided for and great principles entirely overlooked will form a useful and valuable study for our readers. In the present brief series of papers we aim to dissect the Acts, to demonstrate their weak spots, to show the protection that they afford to rogues and imbeciles, with some practical illustrations of the methods of each.

The Act 25 and 26 Vic., cap. 89, commonly spoken of as the Act of 1862, contemplated and authorised the formation of three distinct types of company, two with limited and one with unlimited liability. The broad purpose of the Act was to secure the proper registration of all trading or other associations, as set forth in Section 4:—

"No company, association, or partnership consisting of more than two persons, shall be formed, after the commencement of this Act, for the purpose of carrying on the business of banking, unless it is registered as a company under this Act, or is formed in pursuance of some other Act of Parliament, or of Letters Patent; and no company, association, or partnership, consisting of more than twenty persons shall be formed after the commencement of this Act, for the purpose of carrying on any other business that has for its object the acquisition of gain by the company, association, or partnership, or by the individual members thereof, unless it is registered as a company under this Act, or is formed in pursuance of some other Act of Parliament or of Letters Patent, or is a company engaged in working mines within and subject to the jurisdiction of the Stannaries."

Section 6 expresses that "any seven or more persons associated for any lawful purpose may, by subscribing their names to a memorandum of association, and otherwise complying with the requisitions of this Act in respect of registration, form an incorporated company, with or without limited liability." It therefore stands that whilst not less than seven persons are requisite to constitute a company under the Act, no body of persons exceeding twenty can trade as a company without registering under its provisions. Such companies may register with or without limit of liability, and the limit of liability may be fixed in either of two ways, as set forth in Section 7:—

"The liability of the members of a company formed under this Act may, according to the memorandum of association, be limited either to the amount, if any, unpaid on the shares respectively held by them, or to such amount as the members may respectively undertake by the memorandum of association to contribute to the assets of the company in the event of its being wound up."

The one system is widely known to the public, as of every-day adoption, and may be said to represent in the popular mind the "Limited Liability Company;" the other, the limit by guarantee, is scarcely recognised by them at all, and is best adapted as a basis for the class of associations contemplated by Section 21, that is, companies "formed for the purpose of promoting Art, Science, Religion, Charity, or any other like object not involving the acquisition of gain by the company or by the individual members thereof." Limit of liability by guarantee can afford no advantage to the speculative man, to the insolvent trader, to the fraudulent promoter. It offers no field for the fleecing of the public, or the general creditor, but does very well for the sanguine philanthropist, the politician, the socialist, and the crank who forms coteries to provide for indigent secretaries, to eat dinners, and to further Objects and to serve pet Interests. As such mild associations do not come within our present intent, we shall dismiss them from view. The limited liability company whose limit is fixed by share subscription is the one which interests the public mostly, and we will therefore examine the bearing of the Act of 1862 upon these first, and at length.

Considering the enormous change in our trading system which the introduction of the limited liability principle involved, it might be supposed that a body of 600 gentlemen, a large proportion of whom were recruited from the ranks of the great traders, would have been peculiarly alive to the necessity for hedging its privileges round to prevent its being made the instrument of fraud. How far this was done we shall see.

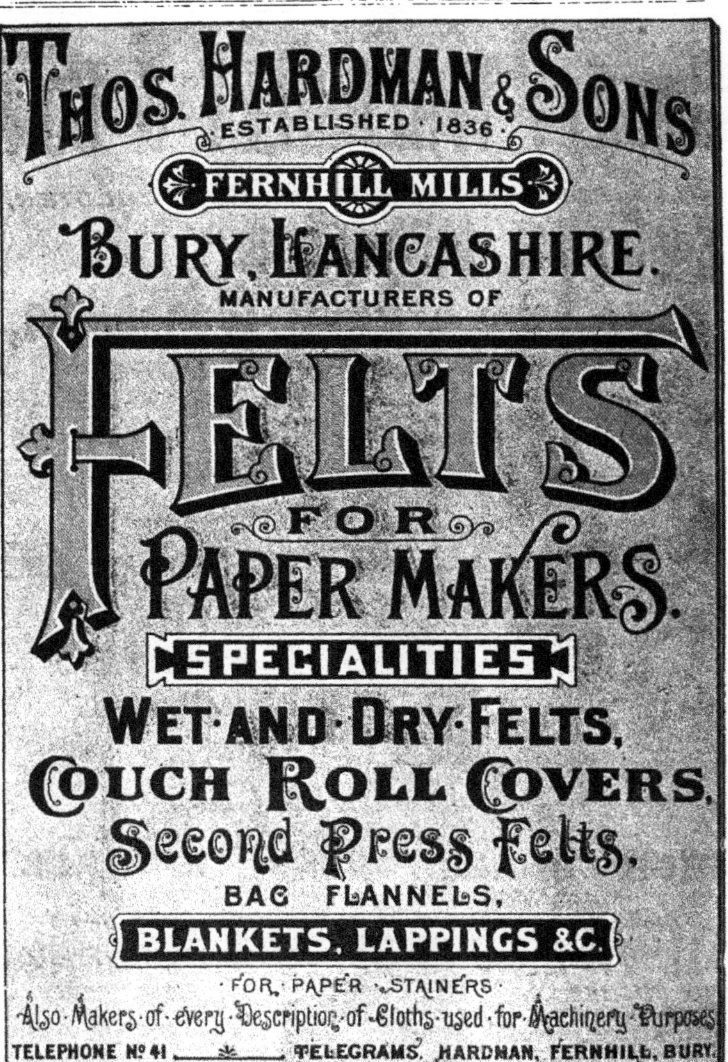

Printed and Published by W. JOHN STONHILL, 58, Shoe Lane, LONDON, E.C. Dec. 15, 189 .

Telegrams: "STONHILL, LONDON." A B C Code. Registered at the General Post Office as a Newspaper.

Vol. XX. No. 25. LONDON. DECEMBER 22, 1893. Price 6d.

Triple Expansion Engines

The illustrations given on the following two pages represent two distinct forms of triple expansion engines made by Messrs. Hicks, Hargreaves & Co., Bolton. The vertical triple engine shown is intended to develop 1,000-i.h.p., at 80 revolutions per minute, with a working steam pressure of 170 pounds. The sizes of the cylinders are 19-in., 20-in., and 46-in., and the length of stroke 48-in. It will be seen from the illustration that the cylinders are placed in the following order, namely, high, low, and intermediate, whilst the sequence of the cranks is also high, low, and intermediate. The cylinders are specially made, according to the firm's usual practice with such engines, and are each provided with four Corliss valves, two for steam and two for exhaust, the steam and exhaust being worked by separate eccentrics and gear to allow the most perfect distribution of the steam and ease of adjustment. All steam valves are provided with the "Inglis and Spencer" trip gear, that of the high pressure being actuated by the governor, whilst the others are adjustable by hand. The governing arrangements are all of the latest and most improved kind, and ensure practically perfect regularity of speed. The crank shaft is 12 inches in diameter, and built of Siemens-Martin steel, in the same way as is usual with marine engines. The crank and shaft pins are bored from end to end to avoid every possibility of defects. The crank shaft, crank pin bearings, and the guide blocks are lined with special white metal, and the guide bars are hollow and fitted for water for circulation. The most complete arrangements are made for lubricating. A novel indicating gear, suggested by Mr. Wilson, the superintending engineer of the firm, is also attached, which can be put in and out of gear while the engines are running. These engines are jet-condensing, a vertical acting air pump, 32 inches in diameter, and 16 inches stroke, as well as a feed pump being driven by levers off the low pressure engine.

An experimental trial, conducted with great care, by Mr. A. B. Wilson, a well-known consulting engineer and others, while the engines were doing their ordinary work and without special preparation, yielded the following interesting results:—The steam plant consisted of three Lancashire boilers 28-ft. long by 7-ft. 7-in. diameter; two flues, 2-ft. 11-in. diameter, with four cross tubes in each flue. Total grate surface = 96·25 square feet. Total weight of coal used, 5,096 lbs.; and as the duration of trial was 5¼ hours, the coal burnt per hour was 970 lbs. Steam pressure = 156 lbs. per square inch; vacuum 11·94 lbs. Temperature of injection water, 61·5 degrees Fah.; of overflow, 105 degrees Fah.; and of feed water from economiser (Green's 320 pipes), 258 degrees Fah. The temperature of main flue before economiser = 461·5 degrees Fah.; and after economiser 299 degrees Fah. The engines indicated 791·3 horse power.

The practical results of this test were as follows:—

Coal per i.h.p. per hour = 1·22 lbs.
Gross steam do. do. = 12·83 lbs.
Net steam do. do. after allowing for priming = 12·79 lbs.

These results show an exceptional economy, 12·79 lbs. of water per indicated horse power

VERTICAL TYPE OF TRIPLE EXPANSION ENGINE.

General View of 1,000 I.H.P. ENGINE,
BUILT BY
HICK, HARGREAVES & Co., BOLTON, ENGLAND.

HORIZONTAL TYPE OF TRIPLE EXPANSION ENGINE.

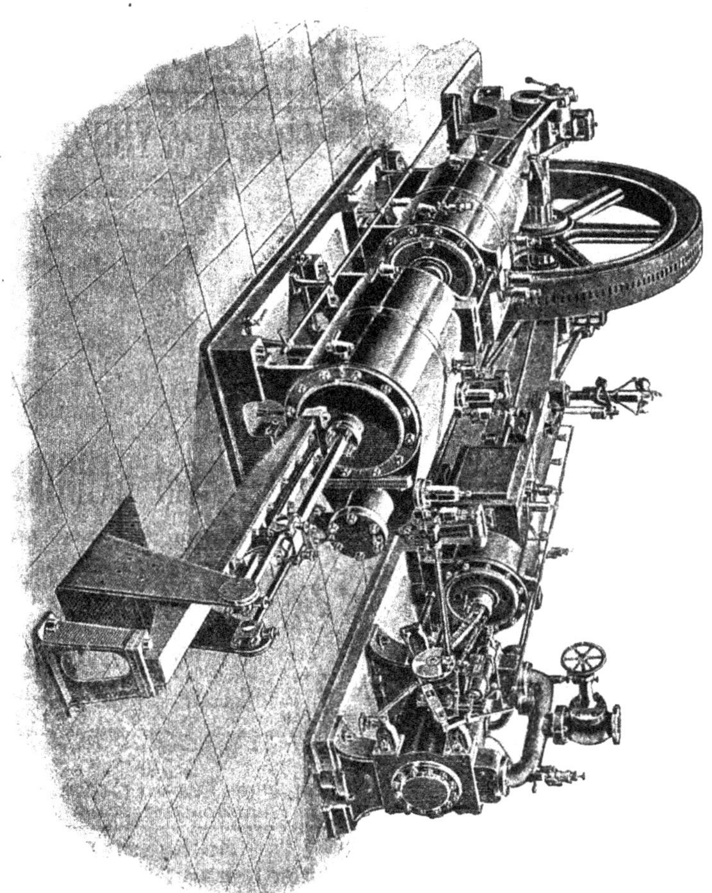

Genera View of LARGE POWER ENGINE,
BUILT BY
HICK, HARGREAVES & Co., Bolton, England.

per hour being considered lower than almost any other record for unjacketed triple expansion engines published in this country. The low quantity of coal, viz., 1·22 lbs. per indicated horse power per hour, is due, mainly, to the excellent quality used (Vivian's "Thro' and Thro'"), practically no ash being left during the trial. One pound of it evaporated 10·44 lbs. of water from temperature of feed to economiser.

The second illustration shows a set of horizontal, surface-condensing, triple expansion engines of the four-cylinder double tandem type, also made by Messrs. Hicks, Hargreaves and Co., Limited., to drive a textile mill in Sweden. The engine is intended to develop about 350-i.h.p., at 80 revolutions per minute, and with steam pressure at 160 pounds. The three cylinders are respectively 13-in., 20-in., and 21-in. in diameter; air pump, single-acting, 12-in.; circulating pump, also single-acting, 10-in.; and the cooling surface of condenser, which is of the marine type, is 640 square feet.

The high and one low pressure cylinder work on one crank, while the intermediate and the other low pressure cylinder work on the other crank. As in the case of the vertical triple expansion engine above described, the high pressure cylinder is fitted with "Inglis and Spencer" Corliss gear, but the intermediate pressure cylinder is provided with a piston valve, and the two low pressure cylinders with plain slide valves. All the cylinders are steam jacketed with steam at boiler pressure. In this particular set of engines the jackets are drained in series, the combined drain water from all passing into a receiver which, standing on the engine-room floor, and being provided with pressure and water gauges, gives the attendant a much better chance of keeping the jackets efficiently drained than where each jacket has its own trap placed out of sight under the floor, and too often out of mind. Very complete lubricating appliances are also provided, as also the necessary indicating gear for all the cylinders. The power of these engines is transmitted by a steel spur-wheel bolted to the fly-wheel, but which was not in position at the time the photograph was taken, from which the engraving is made. These engines have been in continual work for some time, and have proved to be exceedingly economical.

WHITE'S PATENT OSCILLATING STRAINER.

In one of our recent issues we reviewed a newly-patented form of pulp strainer introduced to the trade by Messrs. James Bertram and Son, Limited, of Leith Walk Foundry, Edinburgh. Since our first article this strainer has been greatly improved, and in its present state it appears to be one of the most efficient and powerful pulp strainers at present in the market. Some of the results obtained by it have, so far as we know, never been surpassed, if indeed they have been equalled by any other machine of like character.

The strainer, which we illustrate, is built on the rocking principle, that is to say, the cast-iron trough containing the brass plates, rocks slowly to and fro, which causes the shieve and unbeaten particles of pulp to find their way into channels at each side, from whence they are automatically carried away, instead of allowing them to settle down into the slits and stopping the passage of the pulp. It will be inferred at a glance that when this can be effectually accomplished by any strainer, it must necessarily pass a large quantity of pulp per given unit of plate surface during a given time; and it is found in practice that this is the case with White's patent strainer. The slits, being kept perpetually clean, the knots, &c., are washed, instead of being scraped away, as in other flat strainers, thus preventing coarse or dirty stuff passing to the machine with the fine pulp. The paper made is consequently much cleaner. In fact the rocking motion is said to give it all the advantages of the revolving strainer without any of its disadvantages, such as excessive power to drive, cost of up keep, and loss of stuff while changing sorts and washing up.

The strainer has a surface of 14 square feet, or measures 7-ft. by 2-ft., and when used for paper machine work is fitted with plates cut to No. 3 or No. 3½ (Watson's gauge), and on some machines this strainer is working with plates cut as fine as No. 2½ gauge. It has been demonstrated beyond dispute, that it will pass a maximum quantity of stuff of 1,000 lbs. per hour, and that on an average it will pass from 700 to 800 lbs. per hour, according to the quality of the stuff. Papermakers may probably be inclined to doubt this statement, but we understand Messrs. James Bertram and Son, Limited, are prepared to substantiate it by showing the machine at work. A well-known papermaker says that "the output from the paper machine working with *one* of White's patent strainers "averages 40 tons of paper per week, and "this fact alone proves that the stuff must "have passed through the strainer at an "average rate of 800 lbs. per hour." The stuff referred to was entirely esparto pulp.

It is also asserted that this strainer is equally successful when working on strong rag stuff. Messrs. R. and J. Couper, Millholm Paper Mills, near Glasgow, have had two of them working for a considerable time, making all qualities and weights of tub-sized rag papers, and are well satisfied with the results. They consider it a decided improvement over both the flat and revolving strainer, of the latest modern papermaking practice. The rocking motion—about 15 movements to and fro per minute—keeps the plate surface clean and effects a considerable saving in fibre. Other papermakers are also very decided in their praise of this machine. Messrs. Annandale and Son, Limited, of Polton Mills, experience no difficulty in passing 500 lbs. of pure rag pulp through it per hour using a 3½ cut, while at the mills of the Culter Mills Paper Co.,

Limited, similar work is done by it, and in other respects gives entire satisfaction.

For use with the press-pâte, White's patent strainer also appears a machine of the highest order. Messrs. Somerville and Co., Kevock Paper Mills, Lasswade, have worked one having plates 6-ft. by 2-ft. in connection with their press-pâtes for considerably over a year, passing 50 tons of esparto grass through it per week. The cut used is No. 4½, Watson's gauge. Messrs. Stewart and Co., of Bathgate, also pass through their strainer the pulp from 96 cwts. of esparto per hour.

The above are certainly startling facts connected with the straining of paper pulp, which we venture to think have not been exceeded by any other machine of its class. The mechanism of the strainer itself is simple and strong. As it is perfectly automatic in its action, it gives no trouble while at work, and because it is self-cleaning the flow of stuff through the slits is steady. The fact that one of these new strainers, with a plate surface 7-ft. by 2-ft., is capable of straining pulp for a single paper machine, and to do this regularly without inconvenience, is of itself a sufficient guarantee that it is a thoroughly capable and useful machine. At the present date there are 36 of these new strainers in active operation in England and Scotland.

The simplification of the straining machinery of a paper mill is a problem which has hitherto been imperfectly solved. We have, however, in the above arrived at a state as near perfection as it is possible to imagine, for this machine is comparatively noiseless, occupies small floor space, is simple to drive, takes little power, and above all is of large capacity in respect to what it will pass per hour, and is self-cleaning, allowing the stuff to flow steadily through the slits. The saving in pulp alone when washing up, compared with the old flat strainers is very considerable. Messrs. James Bertram and Son, Limited, of Leith Walk Foundry, Edinburgh, who are the sole makers, are prepared to supply any further information respecting it which their clients may desire.

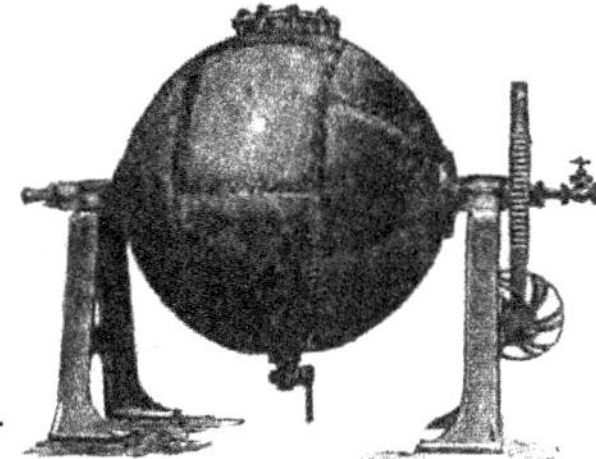

C. T. BAINBRIDGE & SON, LIM.

WINDING-UP PETITION.

A petition for the winding-up of the above company having been presented by Mr. Michael Fryer, of Middlesbrough, the 20th inst. was fixed for hearing the application before Mr. Justice Vaughan Williams. The company was registered on the 15th October, 1892, with a nominal capital of £25,000, divided into 2,500 shares of £10, with power to increase such capital if thought advisable. The company purchased from Mr. Michael Fryer, the Tees Side Paper Mills, at Yarm, which were carried on under the style of C. T. Bainbridge and Son, another business acquired also was that carried on at the Castle Paper Mills, Richmond, Yorkshire, under the style of M. Fryer and Co. Besides the conduct of these businesses, the company also took powers to undertake the carrying on generally of the business of papermakers, dealers and merchants in paper, the manufacture of paper bags, and envelopes, the business of stationers, printers, lithographers, stereotypers, photographic printers, engravers, die sinkers, bookbinders, machine rulers, numerical printers, cardboard manufacturers, advertising agents, electricians, and other trades.

The first members of the company were:—

*J. M. Livingstone, jun., Middlesbrough, brassfounder.
J. Gilchrist, Middlesbrough, accountant.
*Michael Fryer, Middlesbrough, paper manufacturer.
*Thomas Chapman, Middlesbrough.
*E. Thompson, Middlesbrough, gentleman.
*J. C. Bell, jun., Carlton Club, S.W., gentleman.
S. F. Thompson, Middlesbrough, solicitor.

Those marked above with an asterisk were appointed first directors, Mr. M. Fryer being the managing director.

At the time of their acquisition by the company, the buildings and other property connected with the businesses were subject to various liens and mortgages to certain persons, and these mortgagers received shares in the company for their liens upon the property in the proportions given below. The sum of £16,500 was the purchase price fixed, and this amount was distributed as follows:—

Allotment to M. Fryer, of 1,497 f.p. shares representing	£14,970
Allotment to J. C. Bell, of 50 f.p. shares representing	500
Allotment to J. Livingstone, jun., of 50 f.p. shares representing	500
Allotment to Edwin Thompson, of 50 f.p. shares representing	500
Allotment to T. Chapman, of 1 f.p. share representing	10
Allotment to J. Gilchrist of 1 f.p. share representing	10
Allotment to Frederick Thompson of 1 f.p. share representing	10

These names, it will be remembered, all appeared on the articles of association as first signatories to the company. The last annual return was made on the 1st March, 1893, when it appears that 1,600 shares only were taken up, representing *an agreed to be considered* paid up capital of £16,000. We notice that there is a difference between the number of shares allotted on the first place and those now held. The number of shares allotted upon the acquisition of the businesses was 1,650, whereas now only 1,600 shares are held.

The shares are held as follows:

M. Fryer	1,197
J. Livingstone, jun....	300
Edwin Thompson	50
Thomas Chapman	1
J. Gilchrist	1
S. F. Thompson	1
Thomas Stockdale, Sunderland, ship owner	50
Total shares	1,600

Mr. M. Fryer has, it will be observed from the above list, transferred 300 of the shares allotted to him, the shares in question now being held by J. Livingstone, jun., and Thomas Stockdale.

The petition came before Mr. Justice Wright on Wednesday, when his Lordship considered it necessary to postpone the hearing to a latter date as the matter was not in order.

THE first book printed on all wood paper has lately been sent to the Berlin Testing office for examination. It is a report of the meetings of the Silesian Forest Association of the year 1852, and contains a number of articles about the use of wood to replace rags in paper. Of course at that time chemical pulp was not yet known, and the book must have been printed on mechanical wood paper. The chief ranger Herr Pannewitz thought so much of this report, that he sent copies to the late king Frederic William IV. to interest him in a new industry, and also to some persons in high position. The test copy is one of these, and is very well preserved and appears to have been kept carefully packed up all these years. The sheets were of a yellowish cream shade and showed small yellow spots of the size of a pinhead or even of a pea. Probably some fungus is the cause, which, however, could not be definitely ascertained without spoiling the book. There were no brown marks on the outer margin of the leaves, nor did they at all vary in shade. The great softness of the paper first raised doubts, whether it really could be made from ground wood, but an examination by the microscope proved that it was made from pure wood alone probably by hand made process. The paper was unsized and in the ash showed 6·6 per cent. unburnt particles thus proving the absence of any mineral additions. On the test of strips of 100 m/meter length and 10 m/m. width on a Schopper Tester the medium bearing length was 1,860m., and the elasticity 1·4 per cent. From these tests the conclusion could perhaps be drawn, that ground wood paper after all will last longer than the general supposition has hitherto thought possible. However, it should not be overlooked that these copies have been carefully guarded from the influence of the light, nor would they be in the same state if they had been frequently read. Some strips were afterwards exposed for 20 hours to the direct influence of the sunlight, when the colour became first yellow and afterwards brown, thus unmistakably proving its origin.

WORLD'S PAPER TRADE REVIEW OFFICE, 58, SHOE LANE, LONDON, E.C.

TRADE NOTES.

OFFICIAL INQUIRIES UNDER THE BOILER EXPLOSIONS ACT.—A formal investigation was recently held at Nailsworth into the circumstances attending the explosion of a rag boiler at the Nailsworth Mills on the 18th October. No one was injured. The boiler was used for boiling rags and sacks, and steam was admitted into it for that purpose from a Lancashire boiler worked at a pressure of about 55-lbs. per square inch through an inlet pipe 1¼ inches in diameter. It was fitted with an outlet pipe 2 inches in diameter, and into this a cock had been inserted, very considerably reducing the area of the outlet. The boiler was not made for, nor was it intended by the owner to subject it to steam pressure, but the cock in the outlet pipe becoming choked with fluff given off in the process of boiling, steam accumulated in the boiler, and the explosion resulted. The court found that this was the cause of the explosion. They were of opinion that the owner, who had no training as an engineer, should not have designed the boiler without obtaining competent advice; that he should have had it examined by a competent person, and that it should have been fitted with a safety-valve in order to avoid risk, and for this neglect the court found him to blame. The owner was ordered to pay the sum of £15 towards the costs and expenses of the investigation.

MESSRS. ALSING AND CO. (LIM.), sole agents for the Klarafors cellulose mills, Sweden, makers of the well-known KK soda pulp, advise us that the mills, after having been shut down for some months for re-building and putting in new drying cylinders, have now commenced making again with one boiler, and expect to start with the other boiler by the end of the month.

ELECTROLYTIC APPARATUS.—The Société Outhenin Chalandre Fils and Cie, Paris, claim an improved electrolytic apparatus, which has been designed for the electrolysis of sea-salt or chloride of sodium, with a view to the simultaneous production of caustic soda in solution and of chloride of lime in the form of powder or liquid, and in the latter case free from sea-salt. A peculiar construction of the fluid-tight anode chamber with external fastenings is claimed. Also the use of tubular porous diaphragms, of any convenient form in transverse section, of porcelain, earthenware, or other suitable material, and characterised by the method of mounting the same, in which are placed the cathodes, and which, whilst permitting electrical communication, prevent the liquid in the anode chamber or compartment from passing into the outer or cathode tank or vat. A removable compartment is secured to the anode chamber, for the purpose of collecting the hydrogen, and a separate or independent tank or vat employed to maintain a uniform degree of concentration of the liquid in the anode chamber. The Société further claim the application of the electrolytic apparatus to the treatment of sea-salt or chloride of sodium for the purpose of producing, on the one hand, a solution of caustic soda, without admixture of the salt under treatment, and, on the other hand, products containing chlorine and oxygen directly applicable to the manufacture of hypochlorites of lime, chlorites, chlorates, and analogous compounds.

CHLORINE FROM SPENT LIQUORS.—A process has been jointly patented by Messrs. Cosnett, Bennison, Hayes and Smallwood, having for its object to obtain chlorine from the spent liquors produced in the manufacture of soda ash, by what is known as "Solvay's" ammonia soda process, or from brine or other similar substance, and to utilise such chlorine in the manufacture of chloride of lime. In accordance with the invention, a series of metal retorts are employed of an oval or other suitable shape, which are built into the roof of a furnace with their lower extremities projecting into the furnace so as to heat or warm the contents thereof. Into each of the retorts the patentees place the spent liquor, brine, or other substance to be treated with a solution of potassium permanganate in or about the proportions of one part of potassium permanganate to twenty parts of the spent liquor or brine or other substance, said solution being introduced through a suitable funnel and pipe. Through another funnel and pipe, a set of which is provided for each retort, there is introduced a quantity of sulphuric acid. By now applying a heat of about 90 degs. to 100 degs. Fahrenheit, a chemical action takes place in the retorts, chlorine being freely evolved, which readily escapes through pipes from the top of the retorts to a chamber, there to be converted into chloride of lime. In order to remove the bye products left in the retorts, a pipe or tube is provided from the bottom of each retort bent downwards and fitted with a cock or valve, and if desired, leading into a pipe arranged along the furnace for carrying all the bye products away to the front or side of the furnace. The chamber to which the gas is conveyed is of, by preference, rectangular construction, and is lined with lead and formed with apertures to admit of the gas. A layer of slaked lime is placed upon the floor of the chamber, which being exposed to the chlorine, absorbs the gas-producing chloride of lime. The chamber is fitted with a set of shutters closed and cemented during the converting action, but opened as soon as the action is complete to admit fresh air and allow of the removal of the lime. This latter is effected, by preference, through a trap door, hopper, or shoot in the bottom of the chamber.

COLLINS PAPER MILL CO.—The quarterly statement of accounts for the period ending November 30th shows, after allowing interest on loans and mortgages, and the usual depreciation, a loss of £386.

PAPER EXPORTS AT NEW YORK.—The last weekly list to hand shows the following, amongst other exports:—

B. W. Indies ...	582 reams	Australasia ...	5 cases
,, ...	212 pkgs	Hamburg ...	16 cases
Liverpool ...	32 cases	London	290 cases
Havre	4 pkgs	Hull	2 cases
B. Guiana ...	100 pkgs	Glasgow	50 pkgs
Newfoundland ...	23 b'ndls		

ONLY two machines out of five are now running at the mill of the Singerly Pulp and Paper Company, Singerly, Md.

BOILER EXPLOSION.—A large boiler at the American Strawboard Works, at Piqua, Ohio, recently exploded and wrecked the buildings, engines, and machinery, entailing a loss of from $20,000 to $25,000. The boiler crashed through three brick walls, and part of the machinery was hurled almost 200 feet in the air. Thirty men were at work when the explosion occurred, and all escaped serious injury.

PAPER STOCK IMPORTS.—The imports of rags and other papermaking fibres—jute butts excepted—at the port of New York during the month ended November 30, according to the *Paper Trade Journal*, amounted to 13,570 bales and 321 tons, the difference in quantities compared with the corresponding month of 1892 being an increase in rags of 2,496 bales, in old papers a decrease of 1,616 bales, and in manilla stocks a decrease of 2,087 bales. There was no wood pulp imported during November, and of chemical fibre 1,186 tons less than the October imports were brought in. The appended tabulation shows the quantities of papermaking materials of the kinds mentioned, which were reported as having been imported during the month of November during five years:

	1893.	1892.	1891.	1890.	1889.
Rags.........bales	6,733	3,237	12,404	10,698	11,937
Old Papers	379	1,995	677	748	1,537
Manilla Stocks..	6,548	8,545	35,521	7,310	11,863
Wood Pulp tons	--	—	—	—	—
Wood Fibre......	321	4,676	1,533	2,991	2,961

The arrivals from the different ports were as follows: Alexandria, 1,196 bales rags; Antwerp, 33 bales rags, 5 bales old papers, 1,118 bales manillas; Aspinwall 230 bales rags; Bremen, 229 bales manillas; Bristol, 114 bales manillas; Callao, 21 bales rags; Christiania, 55 tons chemical fibre; Dundee, 993 bales manillas; Glasgow, 58 bales manillas; Hamburg, 63 tons chemical fibre, 376 bales manillas; Hull, 52 bales rags, 75 tons chemical fibre, 280 bales manillas; Kobe, 4,541 bales rags; Leghorn, 350 bales rags; Liverpool, 21 bales old papers, 2,067 bales manillas; London, 310 bales rags, 353 bales old papers, 20 tons chemical fibre, 1,537 bales manillas; Newcastle, 694 bales manillas; and Rotterdam, 108 tons chemical fibre.

THE COMMERCIAL TREATY between Germany and Roumania, Servia and Spain after having been previously accepted by the committee of the German Reichstag was passed in the whole house by a sufficient majority in spite of very active propaganda on the part of the Agrarians. Thus the protective tendencies are checked for the present. It may also now be taken for granted, that if the Russian Commissioners now at Berlin can come to terms with the German Government the result of their deliberations will not meet with any very great opposition in Parliament, notwithstanding all the noise of the Agrarians.

ACTIEN GESELLSCHAFT FÜR BUNT PAPIER UND LEIMFABRIKATION and Actien Gesellschaft für Maschinen Papier Fabrikation, in Aschaffenburg (Bavaria).—Herr Philipp Dessauer, Privy Councillor, in consideration of his long and successful activity, has been appointed general director of both companies. He will, supported by the second director, Herr Otto Heckelmann, be at the head of both firms. The inspector of the Actien Gesellschaft fur Papier Fabrikation, Ernst Kuderling, has become the technical director of the same. Herr Ludwig Engelmeyer, late director of the chemical pulp factory of Niclasdorf, near Leoben, has been appointed director of the sulphite works of the company, and may sign for the company in the absence of the other directors. The same power is given to the head of the counting house, Herr Wilhelm Schmidt, who replaces Herr Carl Stadelmann, lately resigned.

VEREIN FUR ZELLSTOFF INDUSTRIE ACTIEN GESELLSCHAFT.—The report for 1892-93 has been issued. The scarcity of water in the autumn reduced production. The works in Wildhausen and Oberleschen were regularly employed. The works at Egelsdorf were stopped on August 17th, 1892, by order of the authorities, and the same happened to the Rietschen Works. The Liebau Works were voluntarily shut up. A law suit has been commenced for compensation against the community of Löwenberg. During the progress of this suit the Egelsdorf Works are kept up in working condition, and in case of an adverse verdict, which, however, is not feared, a special reserve fund has been created for buying up shares. The greater part of next year's production is already sold at better prices. Contracts for coal, wood, and chemicals are made long ahead. The total production of chemical and mechanical wood was 5,601 meter tons, against 6,823 tons of the previous year. The profit and loss account shows a profit of M124,399, though the actual sum is M156,769, but through the closing of Egelsdorf, and legal and technical expenses in connection therewith, a loss of M32,370 has been incurred. The committee of inspection decided to write off M66,653 for Oberleschen and Wildhausen, of the remaining M57,746, 5 per cent. to be placed in the reserve fund, with M2,887 and M10,000 to be written off extra on machinery at Wildhausen and Oberleschen, to place further, M26,000 into a special reserve fund, to pay 1 per cent. to shareholders with M17,000, and to carry forward M1,858 to new account.

Italian Imports and Exports.—From an official report we find that paper and books were imported into Naples last year to the extent of 880 tons, valued at £32,958. In 1891 the quantity amounted to 1,060 tons, of the value of £37,581. In the latter year 2,582 tons of paper and books, of the value of £41,316, were exported from Naples, against 2,103 tons of the value of £31,989 last year.

Characteristics of Labour Strikes in Germany.—The great majority of strikes in Germany are directly connected with the question of wages in one form or another. Before 1868 a large proportion of trade disputes was associated with a desire to assert the right of combination, which up to that time was not recognised by the majority of German Governments. After that year the strike movement was connected mainly with wages. Mr. Drage, in his late report, quoting a German writer, says the rise in prices after the Franco-German war made higher wages necessary, the favourable condition of trade made them possible, and the demand for labour brought with it the power to enforce it. Up to 1873 the strikes were, for the most part, successful. Wages rose 20 to 100 per cent., and working hours were reduced. "Strikes had become a terror to the country and a constant subject of public discussion." Then employers began to combine, the law of 1878 struck a blow at the Socialists, trade was depressed, and therefore between 1879 and 1882 there were scarcely any strikes. In the latter year the movement recommenced for the advance in wages, which had fallen during the bad years, and this period is characterised by the consolidation of labour organisations and the consequent decrease in the number of local strikes, and widening of the area of strikes when they do take place. Next to the desire to increase wages comes, as the source of strikes, that to reduce hours. Working hours in Germany are, as a rule, very long, and are subject to great fluctuations. The chief factory inspector of Bavaria says that in many factories the hours of labour are not the same every year, or even day by day, but are subject to manifold changes. Strikes are most frequent where Social Democracy is most powerful, and it does not appear that wages are especially low in the districts in which they are most frequent. They usually begin in the Spring, when the seasonal trades are making fresh adjustments of wages. Negotiations prior to the strike are usually fruitless; but about the second week both sides begin to give way; at the end of each successive week the number of men out diminishes, and when the strike funds give out both parties agree to a compromise. The membership of the local Socialists body usually shows a great increase just before a strike. This is the course of a typical German strike. As a rule, strikes are peaceably conducted.

Foreign Import Duties on Paper, &c., Stationery and Books.

FRANCE.

Tariff Classification.	Tariff Rates of Duty.			English Equivalents.			
		Frs.	cts.		£	s.	d.
Paper of all kinds, other than fancy paper:							
Machine made	100 kilos.	10	00	Cwt.	0	4	0¾
Hand made, imported in sheets with the four edges untrimmed	„	12	00	„	6	4	10½
Fancy papers, white or coloured, marbled, imitation Indian, goffered, stamped, or cut	„	30	00	„	0	12	2
Covered with metal of any kind, either in leaf or in powder	„	60	00	„	1	4	5
Paper hangings	„	10	00	„	0	4	0¾
Sulphurated paper	„	20	00	„	0	8	2
Albumenised photographic paper, not sensitised	„	100	00	„	2	0	8
Albumenised paper, sensitised with salts of silver or platinum; negative paper, so-called "*pelliculaire*" paper in sheets or rolls ("*strepping*" film, transparent film, ivory film)	„	200	00	„	4	1	3
Carbon tissue...	„	50	00	„	1	0	4
Paper, sensitised with salts of iron (ferro-prussiate, ferro-cyanate, gallate of iron) ...	„	30	00	„	0	12	3

TARIFF CLASSIFICATION.	TARIFF RATES OF DUTY.			ENGLISH EQUIVALENTS.			
		Frs.	cts.		£.	s.	d.
Cardboard:							
Rough, in sheets, weighing at least 350 grammes per square metre	100 kilos	10	00	Cwt.	0	4	0¾
Papier maché	,,	9	00	,,	0	3	8
Cut or shaped for boxes	,,	16	00	,,	0	6	6
In boxes, covered or not with white or coloured paper	,,	36	00	,,	0	14	8
Cylindrical and conical tubes, called "*busettes*," for use in spinning and weaving	,,	20	00	,,	0	8	2
Cardboard goods, ornamented with paintings, reliefs, stuffs, wood, plaited straw, or common metals	,,	70	00	,,	1	8	5
Articles of cardboard, or of cellulose:							
Moulded, compressed, or hardened, with or without reliefs	,,	16	00	,,	0	6	6
Lacquered or covered with a uniform varnish	,,	50	00	,,	1	0	4
Decorated with painting or incrustations	,,	200	00	,,	4	1	3
Books, in the French language...	Free			Free			
Books, in foreign or dead languages	Free			Free			
Scrap or drawing albums, black or in colours	100 kilos.	80	00	Cwt.	1	12	6
Newspapers and periodical publications ...	Free			Free.			
Engravings, prints, lithographs, chromos, labels, and designs of all kinds, including calendars, commercial advertisements, and interiors of photographic albums:							
Black, on paper or cardboard:							
Not glazed	100 kilos.	80	00	Cwt.	1	12	6
Glazed	,,	120	00	,,	2	8	9
Ditto, gummed on cardboard:							
Not glazed	,,	20	00	,,	0	8	2
Glazed...	,,	25	00	,,	0	10	2
In colours or gilt, on paper or cardboard:							
Not glazed	,,	200	00	,,	4	1	3
Glazed	,,	225	00	,,	4	11	5
Ditto, gummed on cardboard:							
Not glazed	,,	60	00	,,	1	4	5
Glazed	,,	75	00	,,	1	10	6
Photographs	Free			Free			
Prints of all kinds, other than those specified above, black or coloured	100 kilos.	40	00	Cwt.	0	16	3
Maps and charts	Free			Free			
Music, engraved or printed	Free			Free			
Pirated copyright books	Prohibited			Prohibited			
Playing cards...	Prohibited			Prohibited			
Pipes and tubes of bituminous paper... ...	100 kilos.	1	00	Cwt.	0	0	4¾
Pencils:							
Plain (not cased), stone...	Free			Free			
Common, cased in white wood, varnished or not, and carpenters' pencils cased in coarse wood	100 kilos.	50	00	Cwt.	1	0	4
Fine, cased in dyed or cedar wood:							
Of graphite or plumbago	,,	140	00	,,	2	16	11
Coloured	,,	180	00	,,	3	13	2
Fine, for pocket books or portfolios, with or without bone or metal tops	,,	300	00	,,	6	1	11
Pencil leads of graphite or plumbago... ...	,,	500	00	,,	10	3	3
Coloured pencils, not cased	,,	300	00	,,	6	1	11
Steel pens	,,	120	00	,,	2	8	9
Inks, writing, drawing, or printing	,,	20	00	,,	0	8	2
Sealing wax	,,	30	00	,,	0	12	2
Rags	Free			Free			
Cellulose-pulp:							
Mechanical, dried	100 kilos.	1		Cwt.	0	0	4¾
Ditto, moist	,,	0	00	,,	0	0	2¼
Chemical	,,	2	60	,,	0	0	9¾

DR. NORMAN EVANS.

It is with deep regret we record the death of Dr. Patrick Norman Evans, F.I.C., F.C.S. (third son of Sir John Evans, K.C.B., Nash House, Hemel Hempstead), who died at Reading, Berks, on Saturday week last, at the comparatively early age of 39 years. The deceased was educated at Harrow, and was early initiated into the art of papermaking at the works of Messrs. John Dickinson and Co., at a later period assisting in the management of the extensive card making industry at Apsley Mills. Having spent several years in South America, Mr. Evans on his return took up the science of chemistry, studying in Germany, and having become duly qualified, Dr. Evans became associated in the profession with Dr. Q. Wirtz, they holding, by appointment, the important position of Analytical and Consulting Chemists to the Papermakers' Association of Great Britain and Ireland. Several articles, of a technical and scientific nature, from the pen of Dr. Norman Evans have appeared in these columns, and it will be within the remembrance of our readers that the work on "Paper Testing," which was also published in the *World's Paper Trade Review*, was translated by Dr. Evans. His quiet and unobtrusive nature gained him many friends in the paper trade, and as an authority on technical subjects his loss will be severely felt. As a young man, Mr. Norman, as he was generally styled, was very popular amongst all classes of the community, being of a most genial disposition, and a great lover of cricket, in which game he often rendered valuable assistance to his side. The deceased was a grandson of the late John Dickinson, Esq., founder of the firm of that name, and leaves a widow to lament his loss.

SOUTH GERMAN PAPER MAKERS.

MEETING AT AULENDORF.

Under the auspices of Herr Güntter-Staib, the editor of the *Wochenblatt*, a meeting of South German papermakers took place at Aulendorf recently. It was, however, not so well attended as the previous one, as several members had been unavoidably prevented by illness or other causes.

The principal topic of conversation was the higher price of ground wood pulp, which now had to be taken into calculation as an accomplished fact. Several of the German syndicates are fixed for three years, one even for five years.

The Scandinavian Association having fixed prices, which would not allow pulp to be imported from Scandinavia into Germany Papermakers find the cost of producing printing papers raised by M4 the metre cwt., or £2 the metre ton. Under such circumstances it was decided to approach makers of printings confidentially with the view of forming a convention, and of fixing a minimum price of printing papers and news leaving a margin of profit. This appears all the more necessary, as chemical pulp has gone up as well. It is to be be hoped that these steps will have the desired result.

The remainder of the evening was spent with looking over an interesting collection of samples of various papers presented by Mr. Güntter-Staib. A pleasant dinner with humorous speeches wound up the proceedings, and the members separated with the confident expectation that the decision taken will meet with approbation on the part of papermakers all over the empire.

Printed and Published EVERY FRIDAY
AT 58, SHOE LANE, LONDON, E.C.,
By W. JOHN STONHILL
ESTABLISHED 1878.

FRIDAY, DECEMBER 22, 1893.

WE briefly mentioned in our last issue the advent of the Paper Mills Supply, Lim., with a nominal capital of £2,000 in 5s. shares. As one of our readers wishes for further particulars, we have it on official authority that the company has been formed "for the purpose of establishing and carrying on a business for the purchase and sale of materials suitable for the manufacture of paper, pulps, &c. Also for general development of papermaking and other kindred trades, to finance businesses, open branches or depots in the United Kingdom or abroad, for sale, manufacture, or storage purposes, also undertaking agencies for sale or purchase of other manufacturers and dealers in goods, and buying, selling, borrowing money, lending money, negotiating bills, issuing debentures, buying or selling land, and the doing of all other things incidental or conducive to the attainment of the above object." The registered office is at 39, Warwick-lane, London, E.C., and we believe Mr. Edward E. Plaistowe, paper agent, is the moving spirit.

MR. HORATIO BOTTOMLEY, well-known in connection with the Hansard Union, has adopted the profession of joint stock company expert. He has taken extensive offices in the city, which will be known as the Joint Stock Institute. Mr. Bottomley has, undoubtedly, had considerable practical personal experience of every possible application of the Companies' Acts, and we are told it will be his pride "to show how a real, genuine trust conducted upon prudent lines and under expert guidance can be honestly and lucratively carried on." He wants the shareholders in his past companies to accept something out of the profits of the Joint Stock Institute, and, we understand, there will be 500 bonds of £100 each, and their holders—preferably the shareholders of the Hansard Union and its kindred companies—will take half the profits, leaving Mr. Bottomley the other half.

THE proposed new American tariff, which provides for *ad valorem* instead of *specific* duties, does not please the New York *Paper Trade Journal*. Our contemporary states that this change is greatly to be deplored; it is in favour of foreign manufacturers, and will lead to frauds upon the customs, tempting men to become perjurers, and exciting a large amount of disputation and litigation. All experience has proved that specific duties are the most just, the simplest, and the most easily collected. Public opinion ought to, and probably will, says the *Journal*, prevent the adoption of the *ad valorem* system.

THE Canadians are demanding an export duty on pulp wood. According to Mr. O. B. Eddy, the Americans must obtain their wood from Canada, as the spruce of the Adirondacks does not half supply the pulp mills of New York, and as to the mills of Michigan and Wisconsin, they obtain 68 per cent. or 70 per cent. of their logs from Canada. Mr. Eddy points out that the Americans put up the duty on mechanical pulp from 1·25 dols. a ton to 2·50 dols., an increase of 100 per cent. The duty on chemical was 6 dols. a ton, but the Canadian could afford to sell it in spite of the duty. Mr. Eddy is very sanguine of the future, and asserts that spruce lumber is what will pay, and that pine is not "in it."

LANCASHIRE PAPERMAKERS are being worried concerning river pollution, and the difficulties of their position Mr. Peebles put very plainly before the Ribble Joint Committee the other day. He explained that his firm had spent £7,000 in the last two years, in putting down settling tanks, removing fibre and mineral water, &c., and he really did not see that they could do more at the present time, except get the local sanitary authorities to take their effluent, and that they were now endeavouring to do. In the present state of trade they might just as well withdraw their mills altogether, for there was now about half a million of money which was now absolutely lying idle in the paper trade, and the Lancashire paper trade was practically unremunerative.

THE first public journey along the entire length of the Manchester Ship Canal from Eastham in the Mersey Estuary to Manchester was taken on Saturday by a number of journalists from various parts of the kingdom. The journey was accomplished under steam in five hours and a half. The canal has occupied six years in construction, and has cost fifteen millions; the work has been attended with great difficulties, and has also involved great loss of life. The Manchester Docks have an area of water space of 114 acres, the area of quay space being 152 acres. At some future time it is proposed to construct a dock at Warrington with an area of 23 acres. With the use of electric light, steamers will be able to navigate by night as well as by day, and it is believed that the average length of the passage of vessels heavily laden with merchandise will be ten hours. The canal will be open for traffic on the 1st January, and warehouses and sheds for the storage and distribution of cargoes are in a forward state. There will be no formal opening on New Year's Day, the directors having decided to postpone rejoicings until more genial weather at Easter.

A VERY interesting article was recently published in the *Pall Mall Gazette*, "About Bank Notes." Bank paper is made at Portal's Mills, and, according to our contemporary, although this is a private firm its relations with the Bank have been so long and intimate that it may be regarded as a department of the great institution in Threadneedle-street. Although the term "watermark" is employed, what is meant is really a wire-mark, inasmuch as it is obtained by fixing wires twisted into the approved design on the face of the mould, so that when the pulp settles down it is of necessity thinner on the wire design than at any other part of the sheet. The crisp and crackling sound given forth at the touch by a bank note is the result of the employment of fine new linen in the mannfacture. Other makers could no doubt obtain the same quality if it were wanted, but there is no requirement for it anywhere else. It is admirably suited for its purpose, being so thin that an erasure is only made with much difficulty, and at the same time so strong that a note leaf with the addition of a single grain of size will support half a hundredweight without tearing.

OF COURSE, the notes are printed from engraved plates, and about these there are several things not known to the general public. For instance, few people could give, without inspection, the spelling of the words preceding the chief cashier's signature, "For the Governor and Company of the Bank of England." The word "company" is spelt "compa." Then the principal letters are differently formed in notes of different denominations. For example, the "L" in London is not the same in a £5 note as in a £10, or in a £10 as in a £20, or in a £20 as in a £50, and so on. Very few people recognise that a bank-note is a beautiful work of art. The figure of Britannia in the left-hand corner was designed by Maclise, and the original vignette from which it is reduced is still in the possession of the directors. If the engraving is carefully examined the features will be found to be full of dignity. It would not be proper to point out the many minutiæ by which the experts in the Bank can instantly detect a forgery. The general public may perhaps be excused for not being able to tell a forged note in all cases, but there can be no such excuse for the officials of the private and joint-stock banks; and yet they rarely detect a bad note, but pass it through, leaving the authorities in Threadneedle-street to make the discovery.

WHETHER it is due to the greater perfection to which bank-note printing has been brought, or to the increased vigilance of the police, or to both combined, there are comparatively few forged notes presented, and such as are are old productions. There are no gangs of bank-note forgers at work now. In former times the Bank suffered seriously from this class of crime. Putting on one side the memorable forgeries of "Old Patch," and the scarcely less remarkable imitations of John Nicholls, of Birmingham, at a later date, it shows the extent to which the crime was carried that in 1820 no fewer than 352 persons were convicted of forging small notes. There is kept at the Bank an album containing an interesting collection of forgeries. Some of them are on real Bank paper, which has been stolen from the mills; some are produced by the aid of photography; one is actually done with pen and ink, very skilfully, but not skilfully enough to deceive even a tyro in such matters; and in others the water-mark is a clumsy imitation made by the use of a stamp instead of by the application of wire in the pulp. In hardly any case is the engraving executed with sufficient skill to impose on anyone familiar with bank-notes. But no matter how cleverly the letters may have been formed, an expert official will detect a forgery directly it comes into his hands.

WORLD'S PAPER TRADE REVIEW OFFICE,
58, SHOE LANE, LONDON, E.C.
DECEMBER 21, 1893.

MARKET REPORT

and RECORD of IMPORTS

Of Foreign Rags, Wood Pulp, Esparto, Paper, Millboards, Strawboards, &c., at the Ports of London Liverpool, Southampton, Bristol, Hull, Fleetwood, Middlesborough, Glasgow, Grangemouth, Granton, Dundee, Leith, Dover, Folkestone, and Newhaven, for the WEEK ENDING DECEMBER 20.

From SPECIAL Sources and Telegrams.

Telegrams—" STONHILL, LONDON."

CHEMICALS.—Market dull. Consumers, on contract, appear to have covered their wants pretty fully for next year, regarding late prices as very favourable. For ALKALI the demand is steady at £4 to £4 5s. BLEACHING POWDER is easier at from £7 10s. to £7 15s., and SODA CRYSTALS stand at £2 5s. CAUSTIC SODA is on the basis of £9 5s. for 70%, f.o.b. Tyne. SULPHUR is offered at £4 2s. 6d. ALUM firm and unchanged. HYPO-SULPHITE OF SODA at £5 shows a drop of 5s. SULPHATE OF ALUMINA and BLANC FIXE remain unaltered.

Prices are nominally as follows :

Article		Terms		£	s.	d.
Alkali, 58%	tierces ...	f.o.r. works	2½%	4	5	0
" 58%	bags ...	" "	2½%	4	0	0
58%	... ...	f.o.b. Liverpool	2½%	4	7	6
Alum (Ground),	tierces ...	" Liverpool	2½%	5	7	6
" "	barrels ...	" "	2½%	5	17	6
" "	tierces ...	" Hull	2½%	5	5	0
" "	" ...	Goole	2½%	5	5	0
Alum (Lump)	" ...	f.o.b. Liverpool	2½%	4	17	6
" "	barrels ...	" "	2½%	5	0	0
" "	tierces ...	" Hull	2½%	4	15	0
" "	" ...	Goole	2½%	4	15	0
"	" ...	London	2½%	5	5	0
"	" ...	f.a.s. Glasgow	2½%	5	5	0
Alumina Sulphate, casks		f.o.b. Tyne		4	2	6
" "	bags	" "		3	17	6
Aluminoferric Cake, slabs		Liverpool ...	...	2	15	0
" "	tierces	" ...	...	3	2	6
Alumina Cake, slabs	...	Glasgow	...	2	15	0
" "	tierces ...	"	...	3	2	6
Aluminous Cake, casks	...	Manchester	3½%	2	7	6
" " "	...	Newcastle	2½%	2	10	0
" " "	...	London	2½%	3	0	0
" "	bags ...	"	2½%	2	17	9
Blanc Fixe ...	... ...	f.o.b. Tyne	net	7	10	0
Bleach, 35%	... ...	" "	net	7	10	0
" (soft wood)	...	f.o.r. Lancs.	net	8	2	6
" (hard wood)	...	f.o.b. Liverpool	net	8	5	0
... ...	...	landed London	2½%	9	0	0
Borax (crystals)	... ...	... ...	net	29	0	0
powdered ...	...	... .	net	30	0	0
Chloride of Barium	...	f.o.b. Tyne	net	7	10	0
Caustic White 76-77%	...	f.o.r. Newcastle	net	11	5	0
" 77%	f.o.r. or	f.o.b. Tyne	net	11	10	0
" 74%	...	f.o.b. Liverpool	net	11	0	0
" 70%	...	" "	net	10	0	0
" 70%	...	" Hull	net	10	5	0
" 70%	...	f.o.r. London	net	10	0	0
" 70%	...	f.o.b. Tyne	net	9	15	0
" 70%	...	f.o.r. Lancs.,	net	9	17	6
" 70%	...	" London	net	10	0	0
" 60%	...	f.o.b. Liverpool	net	9	0	0
Caustic Cream, 60%	...	f.o.r. Lancs.	net	9	2	6
" " 60%	...	f.o.b. Liverpool	net	9	7	6
" Bottoms	...	" "	net	6	15	0
" ...	...	f.o.b. Tyne	net	6	15	0
Carbonat'd Ash 58%	...	" "	net	4	10	0
48%	...	" "	net	4	0	0
" 58%	...	f.o.r. Widnes	net	4	7	6
" 48%	...	" "	net	3	17	6
Hypo-Sulphite of Soda...		f.o.r Tyne		5	0	0
" "	10-ton lots	ex ship Liverp'l	net	5	11	3
Oxalic Acid ...	... ...	f.o.b. Liverpool	3½%	per lb		[illegible]
Salt Cake ...	.. ...	" works	net	1	7	6
Soda Ash, 52%	... ...	f.o.b. Tyne	net	4	0	0
" 52%	... ...	ex ship Thames	1	4	10	0
" 52%	... ...	f.o.b. Liverpool		4	5	0
Soda Crystals	... ...	" Tyne		2	5	0
" "	... ...	ex ship Thames	2½%	2	15	0
" "	... ...	f.o.b. Liverpool	net	3	5	0
Sulphur, roll	... ...	f.o.r. works	2½%	7	17	6
" flowers	... ...	" "	2½%	9	10	0
" recovered	...	" "	2½%	4	2	6
Sulphate of Ammonia	"	" "	2½%	13	5	0
" of Copper	...	" Liverpool	5%	16	0	0

FOREIGN.—F.o.b. Continental port :

Article	£	s.	d.
Alkali, 58% 2-cwt. bags £4 10/0; 10-cwt. casks ...	5	10	0
Caustic Soda, 70-72%	10	12	6
Hypo-Sulphite of Soda 10-ton lots casks	5	10	0
Sulphate of Alumina 7-8 cwt. casks net c.i.f. Ldn	4	7	6
Blanc Fixe (c.i.f. London)	7	12	6

ESPARTO.—Moderate enquiry for all distant positions, and quotations steady at former currencies. The inconvenience of last month's short supply of African is beginning to be relieved by arrivals, and is expected to be entirely removed before Christmas. Freights easier.

Prices c.i.f. London and Leith, or f.o.r. Cardiff, Garston and Tyne Docks are nominally as follows :

		£	s.	d.		£	s.	d.
Spanish—	Fair to Good ...	£5	2	6	to	5	5	0
"	Fine to Best ...	5	7	6	..	5	10	0
Oran —	Fair to Good ...	3	5	0	..	3	10	0
"	First Quality...	3	15	0	..	3	17	6
Tripoli —	Hand-picked ...	3	15	0	..	3	17	6
"	Fair Average ...	3	7	6	..	3	10	0
Bona & Philippeville	...	3	15	0	..	3	17	6

WEEK'S IMPORTS.

Quantity	From	Importer	Port.
605 tons	Almeria	To order	Granton
167 "	Oran	Guardbridge Paper Co	Dundee
1022 "	"	To order	Southampton
4718 bales	Tripoli	"	London

STRAW PULPS.—Straw Pulps are in fairly good demand.

Prices, c.i.f. London, Hull or Leith :

German, 50 to 55% moisture £16 10 0
do. dry, ... No. 1 £16 10 0 ; No. 2 15 0 0

CHEMICAL WOOD PULPS. — SULPHITE keeps steady, and prices for best grades firm. SODA pulps quiet.

Prices, ex steamer, London, Hull, Newcastle, Leith and Glasgow are nominally as follows :

	£	s.	d.		£	s.	d.
SULPHITE, Unbleached, Common	£10	0	0	to	11	0	0
" Superior	11	0	0	..	11	10	0
" " 50% moisture, d.w.	11	0	0	..	12	0	0
" Extra	12	0	0	..	13	0	0
" Bleached, moist					16	10	0
" Unbleached, English, del. Lancs. ...					10	15	0
" " " No. 1, ex mills, Ldn.					10	10	0
" " " No. 2, " "					9	15	0
SODA, Unbleached, Common ...	10	5	0	..	10	10	0
" " Extra... ...	10	10	0	..	11	0	0
" Half-Bleached	12	10	0	..	14	0	0
SULPHATE, Unbleached, Common	10	10	0	..	11	0	0
" Extra	11	0	0	..	12	0	0
" Half-Bleached	13	10	0	..	14	0	0
Bleached	15	0	0	..	16	0	0

MECHANICAL WOOD PULPS.—The market is firm owing to reported drought in Scandinavia, which may affect deliveries. American pulp is quiet. Canadian arrivals are well maintained.

Prices, ex steamer, London, Hull, Newcastle, Leith and Glasgow are nominally as follows :

	£	s.	d.		£	s.	d.
MECHANICAL, Aspen, Dry ...	£7	10	0	to	8	0	0
Pine, Dry	6	0	0	..	7	0	0
Pine, Moist	3	0	0	..	3	10	0
Moist Brown	3	2	6	..	3	5	0
Single Sorted	2	7	6	..	2	10	0
Dry Brown	6	5	0	..	6	10	0

WEEK'S IMPORTS.

Quantity	From	Importer	Port.
49 bales	Bergen	To order	Hull
216 ,,	Cologne	,,	London
2412 ,,	Christiania	,,	Hull
1075 ,,	,,	,,	Grangemouth
200 ,,	Copenhagen	,,	Leith
280 ,,	Drammen	Taylor and Co	London
1100 ,,	,,	Skramnes	,,
3330 ,,	,,	G. Schjoth and Co	Fleetwood
254 ,,	,,	G. Schenkenwald & Co	,,
2200 ,,	Drontheim	To order	Hull
95 ,,	Fredrikstadt	,,	,,
166 ,,	Ghent	,,	London
1197 ,,	Gothenburg	,,	Hull
681 ,,	,,	,,	Leith
96 ,,	,,	Tough and Co	London
70 ,,	,,	G. F. Green & Co	,,
12 ,,	,,	F. B. Foulger	,,
90 ,,	,,	J. Spicer & Sons	,,
190 ,,	,,	To order	,,
203 ,,	,,	W. G. Taylor & Co	,,
4051 ,,	Gefle	To order	Hull
592 ,,	Helsingfors	,,	Liverpool
520 ,,	Norrkoping	,,	Hull
300 ,,	Oporto	,,	Leith
132 ,,	Rotterdam	,,	Liverpool
54 ,,	,,	,,	Leith
577 ,,	,,	,,	London
136 ,,	,,	,,	Liverpool
160 ,,	,,	,,	Leith
848 ,,	Stettin	,,	London
1016 ,,	,,	,,	,,
500 ,,	,,	,,	,,
2 ,,	,,	,,	Leith
100 ,,	Skein	Christophersen & Co	Fleetwood
106 ,,	,,	H. B. Wood	,,
680 ,,	,,	G. Schjoth & Co	,,
22000 ,,	Three Rivers	Darwen Paper Mill Co	,,
22000 ,,	,,	H. Newall & Son	,,

Totals from Each Country:

BELGIUM ...	4217 bales	NORWAY ...	10681 bales
DENMARK ...	100 ,,	PRUSSIA ...	2366 ,,
FINLAND ...	592 ,,	PORTUGAL ...	300 ,,
GERMANY ..	216 ,,	SWEDEN ...	2866 ,,
HOLLAND ...	1005 ,,	THREE Rivers	44000 ,,

HOME RAGS.—Trade is quiet, as is usual at this time of the year. A better business is anticipated after the holidays.

LONDON:

New White Cuttings	21/6	Canvas No. 1	15/0
Fines (selected)	20/6	,, No. 2 ...	9/6-10/6
,, (good London)...	20/0	,, No. 3	5/6
Outshots (selected) ...	12/6	Mixed Rope	5/3
,, (ordinary) ...	11/0	White Rope	6/6
London Seconds	3/6-4/0	White Manilla Rope	8/0
Country do. ...	6/6-8/0	Coil Rope	9/0
London Thirds ...	1/9-2/0	Bagging...	1/6
Country do. ...	3/0-4/0	Gunny	3/0-3/6
Light Prints ...	7/0-8/0		

BRISTOL:

Fines	19/0	Clean Canvas ...	15/0
Outshots	13/6	Second Do. ...	9/6-10/6
Seconds...	7/0-8/0	Light Prints ...	8/0
Thirds	3/6-4/0	Hemp Coil Rope	9/6-10/0
Mixed Bagging	3/6	Tarred Manilla... ...	7/6

MANCHESTER:

Fines	15/0-16/0	Blues	6/6-7/0
Outshots (best) ...	11/6-12/0	Bagging...	4/0-4/3
,, (ordinary)	10/6-11/0	,, (common)	3/0-3/3
Seconds	7/0-7/3	W. Manilla Rope	10/0-10-6
Thirds	3/6-3/9	Surat Tares... ...	4/9-5/0

EDINBURGH:

Superfines	16/6	Black Cottons	2/9
Outshots	13/0	W. Manilla Rope ...	8/9
Mixed Fines...	14/0	Tarred Ditto	6/6
Common Seconds ...	7/0	,, Hemp Rope...	8/3
First do.	10/0	Rope Ends (new) ...	8/6
Prints	5/6-6/6	,, ,, (old) ...	5/0
Canvas (best)	15/6	Bagging...	2/0-3/0
,, 2nd	10/0	,, (clean) ...	4/3-6/0

DUBLIN.

White Cuttings ...	18/0	Mill Bagging	3/0
Fines	11/0	White Manilla	8/0
Seconds...	5/0	Tarred Hemp	8/0
Light Prints	3/0	Rigging	13/6
Black do.	2/0	Mixed Ropes	3/6
Bagging	2/0		

FOREIGN RAGS.—Enquiry is rather quiet with the close of the year, owing to stock-taking, &c. Prices are without any noteworthy change, although for some grades the tendency is upward.

WEEK'S IMPORTS.

Quantity	From	Importer	Port.
38 bales	Amsterdam	To order	Leith
61 ,,	,,	,,	Hull
13 ,,	Antwerp	,,	Liverpoo
87 ,,	Alexandria	,,	London
48 ,,	Bordeaux	,,	Liverpool
46 ,,	Bremen	,,	Hull
10 ,,	Christiania	,,	,,
290 ,,	Copenhagen	,,	,,
14 ,,	Cherbourg	,,	Southampton
18 ,,	Dunkirk	,,	Leith
73 ,,	Dieppe	,,	Hull
40 ,,	Guernsey	,,	Southampton
13 ,,	Genoa	,,	Hull
241 ,,	Ghent	,,	Leith
22 ,,	Hambro	,,	,,
463 ,,	,,	,,	Hull
95 ,,	Harlingen	,,	,,
44 ,,	,,	,,	,,
18 ,,	Konigsberg	,,	Leith
6 ,,	,,	,,	Hull
200 ,,	Leghorn	,,	,,
15 ,,	Marseilles	,,	,,
5 ,,	Rotterdam	,,	Leith
27 ,,	St. Nazaire	,,	Newhaven
3 ,,	,,	,,	Hull
33 ,,	St. Malo	,,	Southampton
141 ,,	,,	,,	Hull
14 ,,	,,	,,	,,
37 ,,	,,	,,	Southampton

Totals from Each Country:

BELGIUM ...	254 bales	GERMANY ...	531 bales
CHANNEL Isles	40 ,,	HOLLAND ...	243 ,,
DENMARK ...	290 ,,	ITALY ...	213 ,,
EGYPT ...	87 ,,	NORWAY ...	10 ,,
FRANCE ...	423 ,,	PRUSSIA ...	24 ,,

GERMAN RAGS.

STETTIN: C.i.f. Hull, Leith, Tyne and London.

SPFFF and SPFF	18/0	LFB (Blue)	
SPF	10/0	CSPFFF	16/0
FF	8/6	CSPFF	10/0
FG	9/0	CFB (Blue)	7/0
LFX	7/0	CFX (Coloured) ...	4/6

HAMBURG: F.o.b.

NWC	22/0	FF Grey Linens ...	9/0
SPFFF	22/0	LFX Second ditto...	8/0
SPFFF and SPFF	18/0	CSPFFF	17/3
SPFF	16/0	CSPFF	11/3
SPF	12/0	CFB	8/0
CCC	5/6	Dark Blues (selected	11/9
CFX	4/6	Wool Tares... ...	8/0
White Rope... ...	8/0	Jute, No. I 6/0; No. II	5/6

DUTCH RAGS. f.o.r. Hull:

C.i.f. Thames; Hull 2/6 per ton more; ditto f.o.r. Leith c.i.f. Glasgow 5/-; c.i.f. Liverpool 4/-.

Selected Fines (free from Muslins) ...	14/0	Best Grey Linens ...	9/0
		Common ditto ...	5/6
Selected Outshots	9/9	White Canvas ...	15/0
,, Dirty Fines	5/9	Grey & Brown Canvas	9/9
Light Cottons ...	9/3	Tarred Hemp Rope	8/0
Blue Cottons ...	7/6	Ditto (broken) ...	5/3
Dark Coloured Cottons	2/6	White Paper Shavings	7/9
New Cuttings (Bleachd)	22/6	Gunny (best) ...	4/9
,, (Unbleached)	19/6	Jute Bagging ...	3/6
,, (Slate) ...	9/0	Ditto (common ...	3/0
Muslins	8/0	Tarpaulins	4/0
Red Cottons (Mixed)	5/9	Cowhair Carpets ...	2/9
Fustians (Light browns)	5/3	Hard ditto	/0

FRENCH RAGS.

Quotations range, per cwt., ex ship London, Southampton or Hull; 2/0 per ton more at Liverpool, and 10/0 per ton higher at Newcastle, Glasgow or Leith.

French Linens, I ...	22/0	Black Cotton ...	4/0
II 18/6; III ...	14/6	Marseilles Whites, I	16/0
White Cottons, I ...	19/0	II 10/0; III ...	7/6
II 15/0; III ...	12/6	Blue Cotton	11/0
Knitted Cotton ...	11/0	Light Prints... ...	9/0
Light Coloured Cotton	8/0	Mixed Prints ...	6/0
Blue Cotton	9/6	New White Cuttings	23/0
Coloured Cotton ...	6/0	,, Stay ,,	21/0

BELGIAN RAGS.

F.o.b. Ghent. Freights: London, 5/0; Hull and Goole, 7/6 Liverpool and Leith, 10/0; Newcastle, 12/6; Dundee and Aberdeen, 15/0; Glasgow, 16/8.

White Linens No. 1	22/6	Fustians (Light) ...	6/0
" " No. 2	16/0	" (Dark) ...	4/0
" " No. 3	13/0	Thirds...	3/0
Fines (Mixed) ...	12/0	Black Cottons ...	3/9
Grey Linens (strong)	9/6	Hemp Strings (unt'r'd)	3/0
" " (extra)	14/0	House Cloths ...	4/0
Blue Linens... ...	8/6	Old Bagging (solid)	3/6
White Cottons S'p'fine	18/0	" " (common)	2/6
" " No. 2	15/0	NEW.	
Outshots No. 3 ...	10/0	White & Cream Linens	25/0
Seconds No. 4 ...	8/0	White Cuttings ...	22/0
Prints (Light) ...	8/6	Unbleached Cuttings	21/0
" (Old)	4/6	Print Cuttings ..	8

BELGIAN FLAX and HEMP WASTE.

Best washed and dried Flax Waste, 10/0; Fair ditto 9/0
Flax Spinners' Waste (grease boiled out)... ... 20/0
Hemp Waste, No. 1 9/0; No. 2 ... ... 7/6
Flax Spinners' Waste, No. 1 (Flax Rove) 10/0: No. 2 8/6

RUSSIAN RAGS.

C.i.f. London. Hull, Newcastle or Leith.

SPFF	16/0	CC (Cotton	4/3
SPF	14/6	Jute I	3/3
FG	11/6	" II...	2/6
LFB	9/6	Rope I...	8/6
FF	8/3	" II	5/0

NORWEGIAN RAGS.

C.i.f. London, Hull, Tyne, and Grangemouth.

1st Rope (tarred) ...	8/6-9/0	2nd Canvas ...	8/0
2nd " " ...	5/6-6/0	Jute Bagging	
Manilla Rope (white)	8/0-8/9	Gunny ...	3/0-3/6
Best Canvas ...	11/9-12/0	Mixed ...	2/6-2/9

WASTE PAPERS.—There is a fair amount of business being transacted in Waste Papers.

Cream Shavings ...	12/3	Small Letters	5/0
Fine " ...	9/6	Large "	7/0
Mixed " ...	2/0	Brown Paper	2/9
White Printings ...	8/9	Light Browns	2/9
White Waste ...	1/6	Books & Pamphlets ...	6/0
Wood Pulp Cuttings	3/6	Strawboard Cuttings	1/6
Brown Paper	3/0	Jacquards	2/6
Crushed News	2/0		

For Export: 25/- per ton extra.

STRAW.—Business quiet.

WEEK'S IMPORTS.

(Purposes unspecified) at principal Ports From

BELGIUM ...	90 bales	FRANCE ...	143 bales
DENMARK ...	1920 "	HOLLAND ...	620 "

JUTE.—The high prices of cuttings precludes business.

Good White	£18 10 to £19	Common ...	£13 to £15
Good	£17 10	Rejections ...	£11
Medium ..	£15 10 to £16	Cuttings ...	£7 10 " £8

COLOURS.—Enquiry quiet; prices unaltered.

Mineral Black ...	cwt.	3/0	Ultramarine (pure)	
do. superior ...	"	5/0	... cwt.	40/0 to 45/0
Pure Ivory Black	"	12/0	PASTE COLOURS with	
Ochre	"	3/0	60% of colour, as follows:	
French J. C. Ochre	ton	55/0	Orange Pulp ... cwt.	40/0
Chrome (pure) ...	cwt.	40/0	Golden Yellow Pulp	36/0
Red Oxide	"	4/6	Lemon " " cwt.	36/0
Umber, Devonshire	"	30/0	Prussian Yellow "	36/0
do. Turkish ...	"	40/0	Green (free of arsenic	36/0
Lamp Black ...		7/0-10/6	Paste Blue (20-45%)	
Cochineal	lb.	1/3-2/0	.. ...	23/6-24/6

STARCH.—Prices:

F.o.r. London, less 2½%:

Maize—Crisp £9 0/-; Powder, £9 5/-; Special £14.
Farina—Prime, £9 10/-; B.K.M.F., £12.

Delivered:

Rice—Special (in chests), £20 (net); Crystal (in bags) £19; Granulated (in bags) £18 less 2½%.
Dextrine—£15 to £16.

SIZING.—Market, although quiet, is firm and higher prices likely.

English Gelatines	per cwt.	70/0 to 140/0
Foreign "	"	70/0 " 140/0
Fine Skin Glues	"	45/0 " 60/0
Long Scotch Glues	"	45/0 " 60/0
Common "	"	30/0 " 45/0
"Town" Glues	"	26/0 " 30/0
"Bone" Glues	"	20/0 " 30/0
Foreign Glues	"	23/0 " 40/
Bone Size	"	4/0 " 10/0
Gelatine Size...	"	5/0 " 10/0
Dry B.A. Pieces	"	33/6 " 36/0
" English Pieces	"	24/0 " 26/0
Wet " "	"	5/0 " 6/0
" Sheep Pieces	"	3/0 " 4/0
Buffalo Hide Shavings	"	25/0 " 34/0
" Picker Waste	"	25/0 " 34/0

ROSIN.—There is a good demand at former quotations.

	London (on the spot).	Liverpool (on the spot).	C.i.f. net London or Liverpool.
B/C ..	3/10½-4/0	3/9	3/4½
D ...	4/0	3/10	3/5
E ...	4/6	4/0	3/7½
F ...	4/9	4/1½	3/9
G ...	5/0	4/4½	3/10½
H ...	5/6	5/0	4/4½
I ..	6/0	6/0	4/10½
K ...	6/6	6/6	6/0
M ...	7/9	7/6	7/0
N ...	8/9	8/9	8/3
W G ...	9/6	9/6	9/3
W W ...	10/0	10/3	9/9

French Rosin: G, 5/3; H, 5/4½; I, 5/7½; K, 6/3; M, 6/9; N, 8/3; W G, 9/0; W W, 9/6; Virgin, 10/9. Net c.i.f.

MINERALS.—The demand for CHINA CLAY continues good, and prices are firm. FRENCH CHALK is also in request. BARYTES are scarce at unaltered figures. There is a fair amount of business passing in IRISH MOSS, and PATENT HARDENINGS and MINERAL WHITE are in request.

China Clay, in bulk, f.o.b. Cornwall, 14/0 to 27/6; bags 5/0 and casks 9/6 per ton extra; f.o.b. London, in casks 35/0 to 50/0 per ton.

Mineral White (Terra Alba), per ton f.o.r. or boat at works:

Superfine...	28/0 less 2½ %	
Pottery Super.... ...	24/0	"
Ball Seconds	20/0	"
Seconds	15/0	"
Thirds	10/6	"

Superfine Hardening, f.o.r. works, 40/0.
Patent Crystal Hardening, delivered at mills £3 to £3 15/0
Patent Hardening (2 ton lots) f.o.r. Lancs., £3 5/0.
" " (5 ton lots) f.o.b. Liverpool, £3 10/0.
Magnesite (in lump) 32/6 per ton,
Magnesite (containing 98% Carbonate of Magnesia), raw ground, £8 10/0; calcined ground, £12 10/0.
Albarine, £3, del. mills.
Asbestos, best rock, £18; brown grades, £14 to £15
Asbestine Pulp, £4 5/- to £5 c.i.f. London, Liverpool and Glasgow.
Barytes (Carbonate), lump, 90/0 to 95/0; nuts, 72/6 to 85/0.
French and Italian Chalk (Souheur Brand), per ton in lots of 10 tons: Flower O, 69/6 c.i.f. London; Flower OO, 62/0, Flower OOO, 55/6. Snow White, 95/0; Snow White XX, 89/0. Blackwell's "Angel White" Brand and "Silvery" 90/- to 92/6; prime quality, 90/- to 95/-; and superfine, 105/-.
Barytes (Sulphate), "Angel White," No. 1, 70/0; No. 2, 60/0 to 65/0; No. 3, 45/0. Souheur's Brands: AF, 83/-; BF, 71/-; AB, 33/6; BB, 29/6; CB, 24/3.
Bauxite, Irish Hill Quality, first lump, 20/0; seconds 16/0; thirds, 12/0; ground, 35/0.
Pyrites (non-cupreous), Liverpool, 4½d., 2½%.
Carbonate of Lime (Souheur Brand), Prima 43/-. Secunda 37/-.

LIME.—Demand good. The present price is 12s. 6d. per ton f.o.r.

BALING TWINE.—Prices:

		Thick.	Medium.	Cap.
All Hemp	per lb.	4d.	4½d.	4½d
All Jute		3½d.	3½d.	4d.

DIRECTORY.

Names and Addresses under this heading will be charged for at the rate of 50/- per annum (52 insertions) for each card of two lines or under. Each additional line £1 extra.

ALUMINOUS CAKE.

The ALUM, CHINA CLAY and VITRIOL Co., Lim., 63, Queen Victoria Street, London, E.C. Works: Rainham-on-Thames. Telegrams—"Chinnock, London.

ANALYTICAL.

WILLIAMS, ROWLAND, F.I.C., F.C.S., 28, Pall Mall, Manchester.

ARTESIAN WELLS.

BATCHELOR, Richard D., Artesian and Consulting Well Engineer, 73, Queen Victoria Street, London, E.C., and at Chatham. 5718

ISLER, C., & Co., Bear Lane, Southwark, S.E.

LE GRAND & SUTCLIFF, Magdala Works, 125, Bunhill Row, E.C.

BOILER COVERING.

LONSDALES, Boiler Coverers, Blackburn, will send a sample cask of their Patent Plastic Cork Covering to any Paper Mill in Great Britain—5 cwt. cask for 25/- (carriage paid).

CHINA CLAY.

The ALUM, CHINA CLAY and VITRIOL Co., Lim., 63, Queen Victoria Street, London, E.C. Mines: Ruddle and Colchester, St. Austell, Cornwall. Telegrams—"Chinnock, London."

ROGERS, J., & Co., Truro, Cornwall.—Agents: Taylor, Sommerville & Co., 83, Queen Victoria Street, E.C., and at 16, Princes Street, Edinburgh.

W. SINGLETON BIRCH & SONS, Lim., 15, Upton Street, Manchester. Mines: Rosevear, St. Austell, Cornwall. 2276

COLOURS.

CARDWELL, J. L., & Co., Commercial Buildings, 15, Cross Street, Manchester. Specialties: Mineral Black, Ven. Red, Ochres and Umbers. 5804

GEMMILL, W. N., & Co., Glasgow, Telegrams "Rube." Starches, Alumina, Antifroths, &c. All Paper Colours

COLOURS (Continued).

HINSHELWOOD, THOMAS, & Co., The Glasgow Colour Works, Glasgow. Colours and shades matched exactly.

MULLER, A. E., 9, Fenchurch Street, London, E.C.

ESPARTO.

IDE & CHRISTIE, Fibre, Esparto, and General Produce Brokers, 72, Mark Lane, E.C.

MINERAL WHITE or TERRA ALBA.

WINSER & Co., Portland Mills, Princess Street, Manchester. Also manufacturers of Aluminous Cake.

HOWE, JOHN, & Co., Carlisle. 2113

STEEL.

MAKIN, WM., & SONS, Sheffield. Established 1756. Roll Bars, Plates, Cutter Knives, Doctor Blades, &c. 5369

STRAW.

UNDERWOOD, E., & SON, Limited, Brentford, London, W. Press-packed Oat, Wheat, or Rye Straw, delivered to the chief British ports or railway stations.

TALC (French and Italian Chalk).

SOUHEUR, JEAN, Antwerp. All Minerals, Blanc de Silex, Barytes (superior and common), Carbonate of Lime, Blacklead, &c. British Agent: A. E. Muller, 9, Fenchurch Street, London, E.C. Agent for Liverpool and Manchester: C. H. Austin, Ditton, near Widnes.

RAGS.

CHALMERS, E., & Co., Lim., Bonnington, Leith.

MULLER, A. E., 9, Fenchurch Street, London, E.C.

WERTHEIM, A., & Co., Hamburg.

UMBER.

The **ALUM, CHINA CLAY and VITROIL Co.**, Lim. 63, Queen Victoria Street, London, E.C. Telegrams—"Chinnock, London."

WOOD PULP.

ALSING & Co., Limited, 27, Leadenhall Street, London, E.C. Sole agents for the well-known "K.K." Soda Pulp, also Sulphite and Mechanical.

FRIIS, N., & Co., Commission Agents, Christiania, Norway.

GOTTSTEIN, H., & Co., 59, Mark Lane, London, E.C., and at New York.

GRANT, W., & Co., 17, Baltic Street, Leith. Agents for best shippers, Sulphite and Sulphate, Mechanical, Pine, Brown, Aspen.

MATTHIESSEN, CHR., Christiania, Norway.

MULLER, A. E., 9, Fenchurch Street, London E.C.

The **SULPHITE PULP Company**, Limited, 82, Gordon Street, Glasgow.

WERTHEIM, A., & Co., Hamburg.

NOTICE.

TO MILL-HAND SUBSCRIBERS.

To prevent misunderstanding and needless correspondence, we wish to point out that we cannot undertake to send receipts for subscriptions received for the Mill-hand Edition of this journal. The regular continuance of the paper may be taken as a sign that the money has been received and credited.

The receipt of a copy in a COLOURED WRAPPER denotes the termination of a subscription, and subscribers who wish to preserve their sets unbroken should be careful to forward their subscription as soon as possible after the receipt of such a copy, as we cannot undertake to supply missing numbers when subscriptions are not sent until some weeks after they are due, all Subscriptions being Payable in Advance.

Special Prepaid Advertisements

IT IS IMPORTANT that Advertisements under any of the Headings mentioned below should reach us by the **FIRST POST** on **WEDNESDAY** Morning to **INSURE INSERTION.**

Charges for advertisements under the heading Situations Wanted are 1/- for twenty-four words, and One Penny per Word after, Minimum charge ONE SHILLING. Names and addresses to be paid for.

Advertisers by paying an extra fee of 6d. can have the replies addressed to the PAPER TRADE REVIEW under a number, and such replies will then be forwarded Post Free.

Advertisements appearing under the following headings:

Tenders.	Mills Wanted or To Let.
Sales by Auction.	Machinery Wanted or For Sale.
Businesses Wanted.	Situations Vacant.
Businesses for Disposal.	

Miscellaneous.

The charges are 3/- for fifty words or under; 1s. extra for every line or portion after. Ten words to be reckoned for each line. Names and addresses to be paid for. Payment must be made in advance, except where the advertiser has a running account, in which case the cost can be debited thereto.

Legal and Financial Announcements: 1/- per Line

Cheques and Post-office Orders to be CROSSED —— and Co., and made payable to

W. JOHN STONHILL.

Situations Wanted.

ADVERTISER (21), having scientific education, and being about to complete his training in all departments of a first-class "white" mill, making fine printings and writings, desires to obtain the position of under-foreman in a good two-machine mill. References of the highest-class as to character and ability will be given by present principals.—Address No. 5913, office of the WORLD'S PAPER TRADE REVIEW, 58, Shoe-lane, London, E.C. 5913

ADVERTISER, with good technical training and long experience in paper mills, is open for an engagement as Manager; thoroughly acquainted with the manufacture of pulp from straw, esparto, wood by sulphite and soda processes, and in the manufacture of medium quality papers; competent chemist and engineer. Good references. — Address No. 5937, Office of the WORLD'S PAPER TRADE REVIEW, 58, Shoe-lane, London, E.C. 5937

ADVERTISER, 20 years' experience as Foreman making E.S. writings, printings and news, desires situation; good references.—Address No. 5938, Office of the WORLD'S PAPER TRADE REVIEW, 58, Shoe-lane, London, E.C. 5938

A COLOUR MIXER or Dyer wants situation at mill; all coloured tissues, pulp dyeing, machine staining; all white copyings and buffs; pottery tissue, Indian Bible paper. Six years' reference from present employer; good reasons for leaving.—Address 5945, office of the WORLD'S PAPER TRADE REVIEW, 58, Shoe-lane, London, E.C. 5945

FINE GLAZED ROPES, BROWNS, &c.—Traveller, well-known to best buyers in the Midlands and the North, is open for engagement with reliable firm; has done good and safe business.—Address No. 5942, office of the WORLD'S PAPER TRADE REVIEW, 58, Shoe Lane, London, E.C. 5942

GENTLEMAN (40), at present manager of a superfine writing mill, desires a similar position; practical papermaker and good commercial buyer. Would go abroad if desired.—Address No. 5925, office of the WORLD'S PAPER TRADE REVIEW, 58, Shoe-lane, London E.C. 5925

MANAGER, thoroughly competent in all classes of Paper and Machinery, etc.; well up in the blending of fibres and mixing and matching of colours, desires situation. Good testimonials as to character and ability.—Address, No. 5,908 office of the WORLD'S PAPER TRADE REVIEW, 58, Shoe Lane, London, E.C. 5908

TO PAPERMAKERS.—Finisher requires situation; well-up in shops, browns and caps; good character.—Address No. 5944, office of the WORLD'S PAPER TRADE REVIEW, 58, Shoe Lane, London, E.C. 5944

THE INVENTOR and Patentee of one of the most economical and perfect systems of sulphite wood pulp manufacture is open to treat with a British papermaker for the introduction of the same into his works. This process can be proved beyond all question to yield excellent pulp.—Address, in first instance, to No. 5943, office of the WORLD'S PAPER TRADE REVIEW, 58, Shoe Lane, London, E.C. 5943

Machinery for Sale.

ONE STACK OF FIVE AMERICAN

CHILLED ROLLS,

comprising:

ONE ROLL 20 inches diameter,
TWO ROLLS 13 inches diameter,
ONE ROLL 14 inches diameter,
ONE ROLL 15 inches diameter,

All 7 feet 8 inches long on the body. The two 13 inch rolls bored for steam, and the 20 inch roll bored for clutch. These rolls are quite new and were supplied by a well-known American firm.

For price and further particulars apply to 2707

MASSON, SCOTT AND CO., LIM.,
YORK PLACE, NEW WANDSWORTH, S.W.

REFINING ENGINE, new, Conical Type; same as one working in a large printing mill.

TWELVE REVOLVING STRAINER PLATES, second-hand, 18¾ inches by 21 inches, class B2, 3½ cut.

SIX SPECIAL STRAINER PLATES, each plate 21 inches by 25⅞ inches, metal on body ⅛ inch thick, ribs 1⅛ inches deep, margin ⅝ inch all round, suitable for strainer 63 inches long by 25⅞ inches broad, No. 4 cut. These strainer plates are quite new and are offered for sale as the cut is rather wide for the special purpose for which they were made.

ONE HYDRAULIC PRESS, second-hand, with Press Box 38 inches diam. by 32 inches deep, with wheels; all parts strong, Ram 2 feet 6 inches by 8 inches diam.

ONE KOLLERGANG, new, Stones 51 inches by 14 inches, C.I. Pan, Scrapers, and Driving Gear.

ONE INVICTA RAG CUTTER.

ONE RAG ENGINE TROUGH, 12 feet by 6 feet 6 inches by 24 inches and 27½ inches deep.

FIFTEEN ELBOW PLATES for Rag Engines, 33 inches by 7 inches by 4½ inches deep, each having 22 Steel Bars.

ONE GRANITE STONE for Kollergang, chipped, 6 feet diameter by 18 inches broad.

ONE WROT IRON H BEAM, 24 feet long by 20 inches by 7 inches.

ONE DRYING CYLINDER CASTING, 48 inches diameter by 9 feet 3 inches long.

TWO M.I. SHAKE BARS, Two C.I. Soles and Rocking Supports.

EIGHT CHECK VALVES, 4 inches diameter.

ELEVEN C.I. COCKS, 4 inch bore, with brass plugs.

☞ SECOND HAND ROLLS.

ONE COPPER ROLL, with ends, 6 feet 0½ inch long by 6 inches diameter.

ONE C.I. HOLLOW ROLL, 20 inches diameter by 96 inches long.

ONE C.I. HOLLOW ROLL, 12 inches diameter by 82 inches long.

ONE C.I. CALENDER ROLL, 11 inches diameter by 78 inches long.

THREE C.I. SOLID ROLLS, 12½ inches diameter by 104 inches long.

ONE PAIR BRASS PRESS ROLLS, 16 inches by 120 inches long.

TWO C.I. ROLLS for Paper Cutter, 9 inches and 10 inches diameter by 92 inches long.

ONE MAHOGANY COUCH ROLL, 18 inches diameter by 104 inches long.

TWO COPPER WIRE ROLLS, 8 inches diameter by 104 inches long.

ONE BRASS LEADING ROLL, 9 inches diameter by 108 inches long (old).

ONE BRASS TUBE ROLL, 4 inches diameter by 52 inches long (old).

ONE BRASS TUBE ROLL, 4 inches diameter by 55½ inches long (old).

SEVEN BRASS TUBE ROLLS, 3½ inches diameter by 72 inches long (old).

ONE BRASS TUBE ROLL 3½ inches diameter by 92 inches long (good).

FORTY-TWO BRASS TUBE ROLLS, 5 feet 9½ inches long by 2½ inches diameter.

THREE COPPER WIRE ROLLS, 5 feet 10½ inches long by 4½ inches diameter.

ONE COPPER GUIDE ROLL, 5 feet 11½ inches long by 7 inches diameter.

Any reasonable offer will be considered by 2703

BERTRAMS LIMITED, SCIENNES, EDINBURGH.

Mills to be Let or Sold.

TO be LET or SOLD, a Paper Mill at Stalybridge, called the Higher Mill, containing one large machine and room for another, steam engine and boilers, in good condition.—Apply for further information to the Caretaker on the premises. 2162

NEW PATENTS.

APPLICATIONS.

23,357. Improvements in brackets for carrying dandy rolls. F. Webster.

23,436. Improvements in apparatus for electrolytically producing soda and chlorine. H. H. Lake.

23,478. Improvements relating to the electrolytic preparation of oxygen and the halogens, and to the simultaneous production of electrodes. A. Coehn.

23,502. An improved finely granulated paper and process of producing same. W. P. Thompson.

23,560. Improvements in apparatus applicable to paper-making or other machines for regulating the flow of pulp or liquids thereto. J. Makin.

PAPER & PULP MILL SHARES

(Report received from Mr. F. D. DEAN, 36, Corporation Street, Manchester.)

Nominal Amnt	Amnt Paid	Name of Company	Last dividend	Price.
7	7	Bury Paper, ord.	nil	4 – 4½
7	7	do. do. 6% pref.	6%	4¼ – 4¾
100	100	do. do. deb.	5%	103 – 106
10	10	Bath Paper Mill Co. Lim.	7½%	6 – 7
10	10	Bergvik Co., def.	15%	13¾
100	100	do. do. 6% cum. pref.	6%	10½ – 11¼
10	10	do. do. deb.	5%	105 – 110
5	3⅛	Burnley Paper Co.	3/-	77/6 – 80/0
5	3½	Darwen Paper Co.	10%	6 – 6¼ c.d.
10	10	East Lancashire Co.	nil	3¾ – 4
10	10	do. do. 6% pref.	nil	5 – 5½
5	5	do. do. bonus	nil	1¼ – 1¾
5	5	Hyde Paper Co.	4%	4¾ – 5
5	4	North of Ireland Paper Co.	nil	2¼ – 2¾
10	5	Ramsbottom Paper Co.	17½%	12½ – 12¾
5	4½	Roach Bridge Paper Co.	5%	2¾ – 3
5	5	Star Paper Co.	8%	5½ – 6
5	3	do. do. 0 pref. cum.	10%	4¾ 5¼
50	50	do. do. deb.	6%	55 – [illegible]
5	2½	Kellner Partingt'n Pulp Co.	1/11ps	3¼ – 3½xd

999

PAPER IMPORTS.

FOR THE WEEK ENDING TUESDAY.

BELGIUM ...	1489 bales	HOLLAND ...	226 cases
,, ...	61 cases	NORWAY ...	1165 bales
CHINA	29 ,,	,, ...	12 cases
DENMARK ...	238 bales	PRUSSIA ...	401 bales
FRANCE ...	77 ,,	SWEDEN ...	1932 ,,
,, ...	132 cases	,, ...	1844 rolls
FINLAND ...	322 bales	U.S.A.	177 bales
GERMANY ...	3775 ,,	,, ...	60 cases
,, ...	99 rolls	SPAIN	1 bale
HOLLAND ...	6290 bales		

Including the Following:

Quantity	From	Importer	Port.
70 bales	Drammen	F. H. Foulger	London
40 ,,	,,	Alsing & Co	,,
58 ,,	,,	Crabb & Co	,,
22 ,,	,,	Spicer & Son	,,
18 ,,	,,	J. Hamilton	,,
59 ,,	Gothenburg	Hummel & Son	,,
810 ,,	,,	Schenkenwald & Co	,,
126 ,,	,,	E. E. Sabel	,,
4 ,,	,,	C. Morgan & Co	,,
23 rolls	,,	Hunt & Son	,,
58 bales	,,	Phillipps & Graves	,,
12 ,,	,,	Brooks Whf.	,,
125 ,,	,,	Dowgate Dk.	,,
19 ,,	,,	J. Spicer & Son	,,
30 ,,	,,	Dunster & Co	,,
2 cases	,,	Townson & Co	,,
44 bales	,,	J. Hamilton	,,
107 ,,	Stettin	Becker & Ulrich	,,
99 ,,	,,	J. Spicer & Sons	,,
84 ,,	,,	Becker & Ulrich	,,
27 ,,	,,	J. Spicer & Sons	,,
49 ,,	,,	Gun Shot Whf.	,,
15 ,,	,,	H. Huber & Co	,,
50 ,,	New York	Acton Barmen	,,
426 rolls	Uddevalla	Gulland	,,
558 ,,	,,	R. L. Lundgren	,,
196 ,,	,,	Gulland	,,
457 ,,	,,	W. G. Wilkins & Co	,,
1161 ,,	,,	Osborne Shearman	,,

PAPER EXPORTS.

FOR THE WEEK ENDING TUESDAY.

	Printings.	Writings.	Other Kinds.
AUSTRALASIA ...	9750 cwts.	2037 cwts.	722 cwts.
AFRICA	142 ,,	70 ,,	88 ,,
ARABIA	— ,,	1 ,,	— ,,
ARGENTINE ...	600½ ,,	58 ,,	28 ,,
B. WEST INDIES...	69 ,,	— ,,	— ,,
B. GUIANA	19 ,,	27 ,,	— ,,
BELGIUM	84 ,,	53 ,,	7 ,,
BRAZIL	— ,,	2 ,,	— ,,
CANADA	— ,,	— ,,	49 ,,
CHINA	1329 ,,	236 ,,	14 ,,
CAPE COLONY ...	236 ,,	48 ,,	58 ,,
DENMARK	71 ,,	— ,,	— ,,
D. E. INDIES ...	— ,,	— ,,	8 ,,
FRANCE	34 ,,	15 ,,	81 ,,
GERMANY	46 ,,	— ,,	— ,,
HOLLAND	8 ,,	9 ,,	34 ,,
INDIA	724 ,,	608 ,,	144 ,,
JAPAN	8 ,,	— ,,	48 ,,
NEW ZEALAND ...	557 ,,	1212 ,,	635 ,,
NORWAY	36 ,,	— ,,	— ,,
PORTUGAL	— ,,	1 ,,	1 ,,
RUSSIA	— ,,	4 ,,	18 ,,
SPAIN	— ,,	19½ ,,	11 ,,
TURKEY	— ,,	1 ,,	— ,,
U.S.A.	826 ,,	43 ,,	10 ,,
W. INDIES	14 ,,	2 ,,	— ,,

SUMMARY OF IMPORTS & EXPORTS,

FOR THE WEEK ENDING TUESDAY LAST.

London, Liverpool, Bristol, Southampton, Hull, Fleetwood, Harwich, Folkestone, Newhaven, Dover, &c.

IMPORTS.

Paper	13498 bales	Millboards	9119 bales
,, ...	2962 rolls	Stock	182 ,,
,, ...	616 cases	Cardboards	400 ,,
Tissues	115 bales	Stationery...	14 ,,
Pasteboards	14060 ,,	,, ...	38 cases
Strawboards	8108 ,,		

EXPORTS.

BRITISH GOODS.			
		Strawboards	49 cwt.
		Waste	323 tons
Paper	1772 cwt.	FOREIGN GOODS.	
Writing Paper ...	2407 ,,		
Printing Paper	6053 ,,	Paper	150 cwt.
Stationery......	£7976 value	Writing Paper...	2 ,,
Stock	17 tons	Printing Paper...	358 ,,
Cardboards	112 cwt.	Strawboards	455 ,,
Pulp Boards	20 ,,	Stationery..... ...	£255 value
Pasteboards	76 ,,		

Glasgow. Greenock, Port-Glasgow, Troon, Grangemouth, &c.

IMPORTS.

Paper	467 bales	Strawboards	14720 bales
,, ...	3 cases		

EXPORTS.

Printing Paper..	274 cwt.	Envelopes	111 bales
Writing Paper...	1105¼ ,,	Millboards.........	23 ,,
Paper	222½ ,,	Bags..................	40 ,,
,, ...	£26 value		

Leith, Granton, Boness, Dundee, &c.

IMPORTS.

Paper	1585 bales	Tissues	3 bales
,, ...	219 rolls	Envelopes	2778 ,,
Pasteboards	4 bales	Millboards.........	2375 ,,
,, ...	6 cases		

THE
World's Paper Trade Review

PUBLISHED EVERY FRIDAY.

SUBSCRIPTION, £1 PER ANNUM, Post Free to all Countries.
Workmen's Edition, 2/6 per Volume, or 5/- Yearly.

W. JOHN STONHILL, 58, Shoe Lane, LONDON E.C.

LONSDALE'S Boiler Coverer & Paper Hair & Cork NON-CONDUCTING CEMENT.

Extract from the *World's Paper Trade Review*, August 2nd, 18[illegible] :—

The "DAILY CHRONICLE" Mills: "The Steam Mains are covered with a Non-Conducting Composition supplied by **LONSDALE BROS., OF BLACKBURN**, which HAS BEEN FOUND TO ADHERE VERY WELL and to EFFECT A CONSIDERABLE SAVING."

"It has Stood the Test of an EIGHT YEARS' TRIAL."

Improvement in Cork Covering. Patent No. 19,[illegible]06, 18[illegible].

J. & W. KIRKHAM, Renewals and Repairs to Revolving Strainers

LARK STREET BRASS WORKS, BOLTON, ENGLAND.

Executed on the Shortest Notice.

BRASS and PHOSPHOR BRONZE Castings, New STRAINER Plates, Old Strainer Plates Closed and Re-cut, Engine Mountings, Steam Traps & Reducing Valves.

Chr. Christophersen and Co.,

39, LOMBARD STREET, LONDON, E.C.

Sulphite, Soda & Mechanical WOOD PULPS.

TELEGRAPHIC ADDRESS: "ARBORARIUS, LONDON." 2142

HENDERSON CRAIG & Co. LIM.

WOOD PULPS	WET FELTS	CHEMICALS	ROSIN
RAGS	DRY FELTS	BLEACH	GELATINE
ESPARTO	MACHINE WIRES	ALUM	HIDE PIECES
STRAW PULPS	BELTING	STARCH	OILS

EDINBURGH: 10, PRINCES STREET — 116, Queen Victoria Street, LONDON, E.C. — *MANCHESTER: 18, OLD CORN EXCHANGE*

H. GOTTSTEIN & Co.,

59, MARK LANE, LONDON, AND AT NEW YORK.

PAPERMAKING MATERIALS, CHEMICALS, AND FOREIGN PRODUCE.

STRAW PULP

The VEREINIGTE STROHSTOFF-FABRIKEN (Dresden)

United Straw Pulp Manufacturing Co., Limited,

COSWIG, SACHSEN.

Recommend their First-class Bleached Dry STRAW PULP, Brands V S.T. and V.S.R. Unequalled in Whiteness and Purity. Strong and Felty. Warranted Free from clays and colours. Used by Leading Paper Mills in Europe and U.S.A.

For Samples, &c., please apply to

ROBERT H. HAY & Co., 26, GEORGE STREET, EDINBURGH, Sole Agents for Scotland, Ireland, and the Newcastle district of England; and

CHR. CHRISTOPHERSEN & Co., 39, LOMBARD STREET, LONDON, E.C., Sole Agents for England (except the Newcastle District).

THE WORLD'S PAPER TRADE REVIEW.

London 1862.
Edinburgh 1886.
Edinburgh 1890.

BAG & ENVELOPE MACHINERY.

ENVELOPE-MAKING machines are coming to the fore, and it is not surprising, because the quantity of envelopes used is enormous, and daily increasing, and fortunately the means of supplying them at a cost and at a rate to meet the ever-growing requirements of trade keeps pace with the demand. At first the machines were in the hands of a select few, but now they are getting into the hands of the many who do the stationery business. Anything new and good is welcome in these days of keen competition and ever-increasing demands, and the trade will be glad to find in Blackhall's new envelope-making machine, new features that will commend it to their notice. The particulars that have come over from Canada respecting it are highly favourable—and especially in regard to its capacity and quality of work, and ought to make it acceptable in this country. It can do, it is said, first-class work at the rate of 50,000 a day with one operator, who can band and box that quantity, and this represents a good day's work and shows how it is that envelopes can be produced and sold at a price that surprises people outside of the trade. The machine takes the blanks automatically from an advancing pile of paper, gums both flaps, forms the blank into an envelope, dries it, and counts it neatly into twenty-five's ready for banding. One machine can be constructed to make two sizes, and be changed from one size to another in half an hour, which would be an advantage in some trades. For light paper the machine has many advantages, as the gum box resting on the paper holds it firmly in position whilst it is being drawn into the machine by grippers. The best class of work can be done on it—wedding, and high grade envelopes at a fast speed, and the gumming imitates hand work to perfection, it is said, the action being light and gentle, and no pounding as with some makes of self-gummers. The drying chains—the serpent's skeleton in such machines—are twice the usual length, having 500 links, so that perfect drying is ensured even in damp weather.

Mr. Blackhall, who is a thoroughly practical man, thus puts his case in favour of making envelopes instead of buying them from a distance:—"A car load of paper consists say of twenty boxes or cases. Make this lot of paper into envelopes and it will increase it twenty times in size, so that it will take twenty cars to carry it, four hundred cases to pack it, and thousands of pasteboard boxes to hold it, to say nothing of the injury to the goods in transit. If this freight in car loads and packing cases were saved, it would show a large profit alone and save two handlings." This is a capital way of putting the case for the machine, and large buyers may think over this art of doing the work with a profit out of freightage, boxes, and handling. English makers will be glad to see the latest Canadian or Yankee notions. Mr. Blackhall hails from Buffalo as well as Toronto.

Messrs. Blackhall and Anderson's special bag and envelope machine is a new invention from the same firm, and working from blanks, can paste, fold, press, dry, and wax—coat with paraffin to keep the flavour in the bag or the damp out of it—at a speed of 5,000 per hour. One machine will make three sizes, up to 6-in. by 10-in. The seams are folded up the sides under the back fold, leaving a flat seamless surface on each side, a very desirable feature for printing. The price will bring the machine within the reach of many makers of bags of the type indicated.

Mr. Blackhall is the patentee, too, of two rotary perforators—one making a round hole perforation, and the other a slotted cut perforation, like a brass rule perforation—a kind of perforation in favour in Canada, and much used in their postal system. He is also the maker of ruling machines, and his double combination striker and sheet lapper appears to be a very complete machine. He has a system of change gearing for the striker, by which "seventy-two changes of size can be made on it by using six change gears, as each gear will give twelve sizes." Mr. Blackhall has another ingenious method of lapping and striking, without cogs or change gearing, by means of a wheel working on the sides of the disc, upon which the lifts and drops are placed, the wheel being moveable, so that according as it is near or remote from the centre of the disc, so are the revolutions of the disc increased or diminished according to the speed of the wheel operated by the worker. Great ingenuity and the application of old principles to new purposes mark the several machines with which Mr. Blackhall's name is identified, and we have only named a few. We can do with new machinery, the best our neighbours can give us; so that we may be able to compete with them with the least possible disadvantage, and with great advantage, if possible. It is better to import the worker, manual or mechanical, than the work; and that method of employing the unemployed will some day be more fully recognised than it is to-day, in circles in which it ought to be a cardinal doctrine in their labour creed.

WE are informed that Messrs. A. Sauvée & Co. are being kept busy with the erection of rapid newspaper machinery.

NEWSPAPER FOLDERS.

The newspaper machines we illustrate —manufactured by Messrs. Calvert and Tipping, Globe Ironworks, Avenham-street, Preston—are built upon Livesey's principle. They are now extensively used throughout the United Kingdom, and have been put down in some of the leading newspaper offices; three, for instance, are in the machine rooms of the *Weekly Dispatch*, and one in that of the *Dumfries and Galloway Courier*, whilst the *Cork*

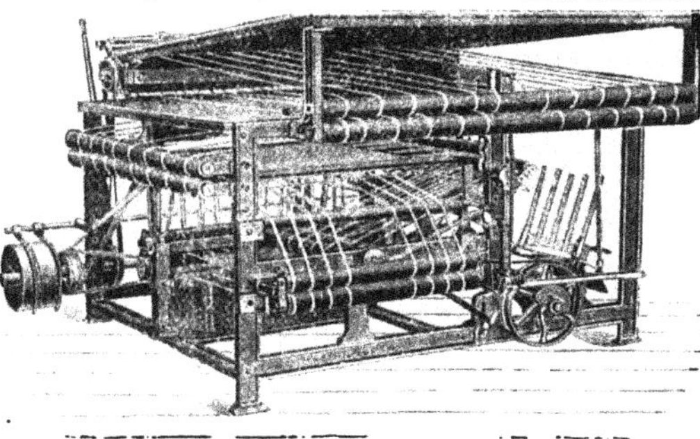

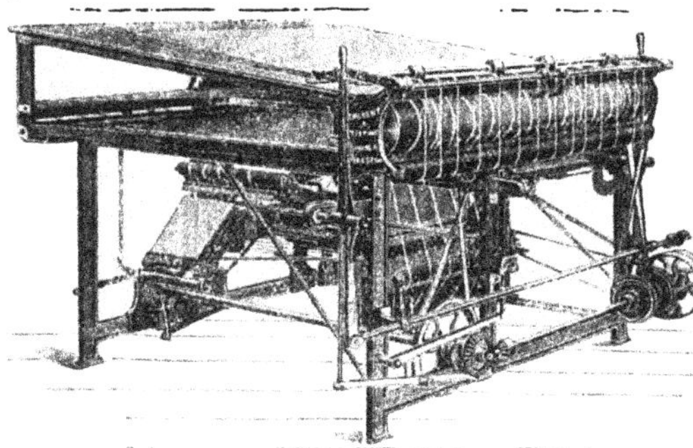

Examiner has two, Messrs. Judd and Co. two, a Lewes firm one, &c. The mechanism is of a simple and ingenious character. All the parts are easily accessible, and the apparatus works very smoothly even when running at a high speed. The general arrangement will be gathered from our illustrations, and we may add that the capacity of these folders is considerable at only a moderate speed of working. They are guaranteed to be able to fold from 2,500 to 3,000 per hour, in either one, two, three, or four folds.

COMMERCIAL INDICES.

Messrs. Eason and Son, of Dublin, have sent us a set of samples of the "Royal" commercial index series, which they have just brought out. These — six in number — are practically indexed books, ruled feint, but of superior quality, being made from fine azure laid paper, and very securely bound in flexible leather boards, covered with strong blue manilla paper. The front cover bears a label, on which space is left for a note of the subject to which the index is devoted, as well as the dates of its commencement and finish, a useful arrangement, which renders the indices valuable long after they are out of daily use. The index steps are double curved, a much better plan than the old one of having square corners, which quickly become "dogs-eared:" the letters are boldly printed in red and black alternately — one leaf to each letter. The sizes run from cap and third long quarto, 13-in. by 5¼-in., selling at 4s. 6d. per dozen trade (No. 6,741), to demy folio, 15-in. by 9½-in., and medium folio, 16¾-in. by 10½-in., priced respectively at 8s. 6d. and 10s. 6d. per dozen (Nos. 6,747 and 6,748). Special name labels are supplied free for an order of twelve dozen. Taking it as a whole, the series is certainly a very "commercial" one, consisting of plain, straightforward, and useful indices—nothing more or less.

The New Offices put up by Mr. George Newnes for the *Westminster Gazette* and the *Westminster Budget*, form a splendid block, and are quite palatial, located just near the Thames, overlooking the quiet cloisters of the Temple, and yet in the very centre of newspaperland. The solidity, and architectural forethought in design are evident at sight, and if the interior arrangements are as we anticipate, the printing machinery and office outfit will be of the very latest design, and the best and most complete attainable.

VERY SOCRATIC DIALOGUES UP-TO-DATE.

V.

DRAMATIS PERSONÆ { ASMODEUS—A demon let loose. CLEOPHAS—A student of humanity.

(With apoligies to the late Mr. Le Sage, of Vannes).

CLEOPHAS.—Well, Asmodeus, you've brought me all the way from Madrid—pray, what have you to entertain me with?

ASMODEUS.—I have no doubt we shall see quite as good entertainment here as in the Spanish capital. Humanity is much the same here as there—the same weaknesses, the same passions. But as this wonderful city of London is regarded as the commercial pivot of the world, we shall see a variation of their operations. Hence my reason for bringing you to the summit of St. Paul's.

CLEO.—What immense concourses are gathered together! I see none of the prevailing gaiety of the Spanish city, however. Everyone bears a sober and saddened aspect. Are they always thus dolorous in this island?

ASM.—Yes. This, you will understand, is the busiest period of the day. The hands of the public clocks are travelling hard on the meridian.

CLEO.—Upon what pursuit are all these gloomy-countenanced men engaged?

ASM.—Gain—lucre. In this commercial community scarce an honest bustler but would rob, ruin, and almost murder his neighbour for the sake of a few pieces of yellow metal.

CLEO.—Ah! then that explains the sad earnestness upon every face. Each man feels himself in imminent danger of having his throat cut. What a fearful community to live in! But have they no pleasures?

ASM.—Oh, yes. But even these they take sadly. I do not often visit this clime, for as you know my metier is not with such as you see below us. Uriel has the ear of the traders. But I have heard him remark that so far as this city is concerned his post is a sinecure, for they lie and cheat one another to the hilt without any manner of prompting. I declare—only never repeat it to him or he would be enraged, and being stronger than I, would certainly do me an injury: I declare, I say, that on one occasion I saw him blush to find how far some of these atomies surpassed himself in diabolic villainy.

CLEO.—Are you sure we cannot be seen of any of these wretches? I should tremble for myself if we were.

ASM.—You are quite free from observation. Do you see that little fat man getting into a two-wheeled vehicle? He is one of the financial princes of this wonderful city. He has just emerged from the offices of one of the great daily recorders of monetary intelligence. I will explain to you what his errand there has been. A week ago he visited this and other similar places, and by crafty and Mephistophelian hints and insinuations induced the publishers of the bourse intelligence to decry certain securities of which he held largely.

CLEO.—But that would be to his own injury surely, for the value of his securities would depreciate.

ASM.—True, and so would those of other holders, enabling him to buy them up cheaply. That is what is termed being a "bear." The operation was successful, and he has now become a "bull." That is to say, he has influenced the scribes to eat their words and work up the value of his securities to their original position, and perhaps higher still, when he will sell and reap an enormous profit.

CLEO.—But I understood that the men who guided public opinion, whether in politics or finance, did so with but the public or common weal in view; whereas this blowing hot and cold appears to benefit only the little fat man. What inducements could he offer the scribes or publishers to act thus? You place your finger to the left side of your nose and leer at me: I do not understand such signs and motions.

ASM.—Turn your eyes upon the building which the little fat man has just left, upon the first floor. Tell me what you see and hear.

CLEO.—I see a man at a desk, who holds in his hand a slip of paper. He writes something upon the back of this slip. He now rings a bell, and to a youth who enters his room he says, "Jennings, run round to the bank and pay this in, and send the Planet Paper Co.'s man in to me." I notice the slip of paper has the signature of "A. Littlefatman" on its front. The youth leaves the room, and now there enters a man with an oblong parcel in his hand, almost resembling a brick in size, but rolled in shiny cloth and fastened round with a band of indiarubber. The man at the desk seems to be in a rage and storms at the new-comer. The latter is very humble, and downcast. He says something which I can scarcely catch, so low are his tones, but I hear the words "directors—put pressure—mill can't go on—not a fraction of profit upon the transaction"—and so on. The man at the desk pulls out an oblong book from his pocket, containing similar slips to that he gave to the youth, and writes upon the front of one some words and figures, and then dashes two diagonal lines across it. He tears this out and gives it to the humble man, and says in domineering tones, "Tell your directors they'll have to come down to my price—another eighth lower—or I stop the orders. And I'll bring down the price of Planets to zero a week afterwards. You tell 'em from me." "But really," the depressed man says, "we are making this at a loss. You can't buy foreign paper at the price." "I know nothing about that. You tell 'em what I say." The visitor picks up his brick and departs, while the man at the desk says to himself, with a gloomy smile, "Littlefatman's cheque came in the nick of time."

ASM.—And what do you gather from this?

CLEO.—Why, I can only infer, upon what you tell me and what I have heard and seen, that the man and his publication are grossly venal, bought over by the little fat man to aid his schemes. I don't know which is the more villainous of the two.

ASM.—Oh, they are no worse than the average of the beings you see rushing about below.

ASMODEUS.—Do you see that short man bustling about with a small book and a few sheets of paper in his hand? See, he darts in and out of the various places where the art of printing is carried on. He styles himself a printing ink manufacturer, and he does a very considerable trade amongst a certain class without manufacturing a single pound of ink.

CLEOPHAS.—How say you? A manufacturer who does a large trade without manufacturing? Unfold me this riddle, I pray you.

ASMO.—Observe, I said he "calls" himself a manufacturer of printing ink. I will explain to you. You see that busy, narrow street below us on the left, and thronged with heavy conveyances? Well, in that narrow thoroughfare he has his place of business. It consists of two very small rooms. In the back room is set up a small ink mill, quite capable under pressure of making a dozen pounds of ink in a week. There he makes up his "samples"—that is, grinds up a few ounces of dry colours to submit to principals who flatter themselves that they select their own pigments.

CLEO.—All this is Syriac to me.

ASMO.—Probably, but you will soon grasp it. That is all the manufactory he has, and yet he sells several tons a month.

CLEO.—Whence does he procure that which he sells, since he does not make it?

ASMO.—From Germany, or anywhere else that he can buy cheaply. You must know that there are some factories in other countries than this, who turn out hundreds of tons of rubbish which they put on the market through the hands of such so-called manufacturers as Mr. Bam Boozler.

CLEO.—But you spoke of him selling to sample: if his samples are good, and his deliveries rubbish, how does he maintain his connections? His roguery must find him out in every instance.

ASMO.—You speak as one acquainted with the intricacies and customs of the trade. Understand that the final judgment as to values in ink does not rest with the employer, but with his servant. If Mr. Bam Boozler depended upon the former he would wait long before he got any profit. He covers one roguery by another one. When he wishes to supply inks to a firm, he first gets the goodwill of the servant by the easy process of bribing him in the present tense and holding out larger emoluments in the future tense. Let him send in the greatest rubbish imaginable after that, he is assured of retaining the connection—until somebody else outbids him. Hence his reason for buying as well as his ability to sell such inferior products of inferior manufactories.

CLEO.—But surely he must be exposed sometimes. He has competitors——

ASMO.—Who are too frequently as deep in the mud as he is in the mire, and therefore are afraid to incur the onus of exposing the dishonest traffic.

CLEO.—Then these practices are not confined to the pseudo-manufacturer?

ASMO.—By no means, but he is the grossest offender. Nor is it confined to ink, but extends far beyond it.

CLEO.—Paugh! Is there no honesty in this island? You laugh—is my question then so ridiculous? I have no love for looking continuously on villainy. Can you not show me, as an alternative, say an honest trader and an honest servant?

ASMO.—Undoubtedly. Mount a little higher in the air with me. Now look to the northward: there you will see a building with a smaller dome than this of St. Paul's, placed upon a great elevation. Just below it is a large building with more wards and dormitories than you could count in a half-hour. It is popularly named Highgate Workhouse. There you may find more than one honest tradesman mingling with the improvident and the reckless, the gamester and the riotous liver who have come to the same goal. For the incorruptible servant, look at that seedy figure passing from establishment to establishment around the street called Fleet, with want on his face and despair in his heart. He is an honest man seeking employment. Grown grey in one service, he has been superseded, and his honesty having stood in the way of his making provision for such a contingency, he will shortly perish from want.

CLEO.—Horrible! I feel sick and sad at the contemplation of such things. Pray show me something less lacerating to my feelings—something with a mingling of virtue and good fortune.

ASMO.—I will do my best, but virtue and I are *not* close acquaintances.

NEW COMPANIES.

VOLLER'S PRESS AGENCY, Ltd.

Registered with a capital of £1,000 in £1 shares, to carry on business as suppliers of news, shorthand writers, &c. Registered without articles of association.

COLBROOK PRINTING and PUBLISHING CO., Limited.

Registered with a capital of £2,000 in £1 shares, to acquire and carry on the business hitherto carried on at Savoy House, Savoy-street, Strand, under the title of the *Whitehall Review*. Registered without articles of association.

"ROCHDALE STAR," Ltd.

Registered with a capital of £2,000 in £1 shares, to acquire the business of newspaper proprietor, carried on by William Brown, at 10, Baillie-street, Rochdale, Lancs., and to carry on the business of newspaper proprietors, printers, lithographers, stationers, bill posters, and paper merchants.

WEEKLY PRESS SYNDICATE, Ltd.

Registered with a capital of £5,000 in £1 shares, to acquire the goodwill of the business now carried on by the Weekly Press Syndicate, Limited, and to carry on business as newspaper proprietors, printers and publishers. The first directors—to be not less than two nor more than five—are J. W. Poole and A. E. Willmer. Qualification £25. Remuneration £25 each per annum at least.

"IPSWICH JOURNAL" PRINTING and PUBLISHING CO., Limited.

Registered with a capital of £10,000 in £1 shares, to carry into effect an agreement, made September 29th, between F. C. Atkinson of the one part, and H. E. M. Bourke of the other part, the further object being sufficiently indicated by the title. There shall not be less than six nor more than nine directors. The first are E. Packard, jun., C. H. Berners, E. G. Pretyman, A. M. Bernard, H. Turner, and H. E. M. Bourke. Qualification, £25. Remuneration as voted by the general meeting.

THE firm of John Dickinson and Co., Limited, whose warehouse and head-quarters are at Old Bailey, London, and mills at Croxley, of a capacity and equipment second to none for all-round paper making, has lately made several fresh grades in most lines of manufacture, the variety of which is such that every requirement in the trade can be fulfilled from stock.

Printed and Published by W. JOHN STONHILL, 58,

The World's Paper Trade Review

A WEEKLY JOURNAL FOR PAPER MAKERS & ENGINEERS.

Telegrams: "STONHILL, LONDON." A B C Code. Registered at the General Post Office as a Newspaper.

Vol. XX. No. 23. LONDON. DECEMBER 8, 1893. Price 6d.

PROMINENT
Papermakers' Engineers.

BERTRAMS LIMITED, SCIENNES, EDINBURGH.

The name of Bertram, and the forefathers of those connected with the Sciennes, have been known in direct connection with the paper-making industry for the last 150 years, the family originally belonging to the side of the Esk, Midlothian, now so famous in the annals of papermaking history. St. Katherine's Works, Sciennes, although not the original establishment, have been long and honourably known in connection with the industry of papermaking machinery. In 1821, Mr. William Bertram, who had served his apprenticeship as engineer and papermaker at Springfield Paper Mills, commenced business on the opposite side of the street from that where the present and now famous St. Katherine's Works are situated, his father then being foreman papermaker at Springfield Mills. The start was made in a very primitive style, but from the fact of there being no man so well skilled in the construction of the then advancing ideas of papermaking machinery, he readily gained a good connection with papermakers. It may be explained that at that time the idea of producing paper otherwise than by the old hand-made system had taken root, and the idea found in Mr. William Bertram a ready and clever adaptor. Along with his father he produced the first automatic shake arrangement for imparting the shake to the mould by a mechanical motion. This machine consisted of a travelling band with moulds on it, which scooped up the pulp from the vats, produced the shake motion, and carried it along to the end, where it was delivered. This, however, was soon superseded by the invention of the Fourdrinier machine. At this time, his younger brother George, the father of the present acting director at the Sciennes, who was also a millwright in a paper mill, and papermaker, joined his brother William, and they, in conjunction with the late Mr. Fourdrinier, may be said to have introduced into Scotland at least the Fourdrinier papermaking machine.

With such an advancement the business very rapidly increased, and the establishment accordingly, until they found themselves hemmed in, and could not extend the premises to the extent required for the increasing business. They, therefore, removed to the present works, and although the site was a large one, yet they purchased the ground on which now stands certainly the largest and best-equipped papermakers' engineers' establishment in Britain at least. After Mr. George Bertram joined his brother William he took up the practical management, William then having more to do with the financial and commercial business. William retired shortly thereafter and died in November, 1860. At this time the late Mr. John Reid, brother-in-law of William and George Bertram, took the position of bookkeeper, &c., and no doubt many papermakers and others connected with the industry have a very pleasant recollection of the late Mr. John Reid, his genial, jocular, and kindly manner being greatly appre-

From a Photo by J. Davidson, Edinburgh.

MR. DAVID HARRIS,

Chairman, BERTRAMS LIMITED.

From a Photo by J. G. Tunny & Co., Edinburgh

MR. DAVID N. BERTRAM,

Acting Director, BERTRAMS LIMITED,

ciated. It is worthy of mention that his two sons, George and John, are head engineers in the employment of Messrs. A. Cowan and Sons, Valleyfield, and the Inveresk Paper Co., Musselburgh, respectively, where their services have been appreciated by their employers, and their quiet demeanour and ability lends a very agreeable contact to those who have to meet them on business matters.

Business at the Sciennes continued to increase rapidly, and with a free hand the works were extended accordingly. Even at this time it was no uncommon thing to see the late Mr. George Bertram starting at any time throughout the night with a staff of workmen in a van or other vehicle, bound for a mill near Edinburgh, to re-cog a wheel that had stripped, or to help the papermaker in some way or other. The amount of re-cogging work then required in the old mills was very great, as will be remembered from the fact that all the rag engines were driven by wheels cogged with timber, and old-fashioned, slow-running, water-wheels as motive power were largely employed. However, ere long, Mr. George Bertram was able to get relief by getting assistants, and among the earliest of his assistants may be mentioned Mr. James Walker, now senior partner, Messrs. James Walker and Son, Fountainbridge.

From a Photo by J. G. Tunny, Edinburgh.

MR. D. W. IRELAND, *Secretary.*

From a Photo by J. G. Tunny, Edinburgh.

MR. BENJAMIN THOM, *Works Manager.*

The Fourdrinier papermaking machine now assumed portentous dimensions, and even at this time the cylinders, which were about 30-in. in diameter, had to be turned with hand tools, a feat which nowadays would seem impossible; but still it is the case as was testified to by Mr. John Tod at a social meeting of the workmen and their wives recently held in Edinburgh. It may be said that there are few better qualified to speak on this than Mr. John Tod, he knowing full well the equipments of the works then, as he served his apprenticeship with Mr. Bertram as a millwright. Probably no one knows more of the intricacies and difficulties to be contended with in those days, the indomitable perseverance and success of the late Mr. George Bertram, than Mr. Tod—John Strathesk—who at all times expresses his great appreciation of the character of the late Mr. Bertram. The wonderful energy displayed by Mr. George Bertram brought to him many friends, among whom may be named the late Mr. Duncan of Denny, Mr. Alexander Cowan of Valleyfield, the late Mr. Robert Craig of Newbattle, Mr. Cameron of Springfield, Mr. Joynson of St. Mary Cray, the late Mr. Greig of Dartford

Creek, the Annandales of Shotley and Polton, Thomas Routledge of Ford Mills, the late Mr. Edward Lloyd of Sittingbourne, Mr. E. Collins of Kelvindale, the late Mr. William Tod of Polton, and many others, with whom he was closely identified in bringing the present papermaking machine into a very much more practical form than it had hitherto attained.

It may safely be said that at the present day the basis of the papermaking machine on the whole remains the same, with a few additions and alterations of detail necessary for fast running. In those days, however, the value of a papermaking machine would only approximately represent the present value of the calenders now necessary for a machine producing wide papers with a high-class machine finish. Still, to bring the machinery to this stage, many hours of toil and experiment had to be gone through, and it may be of interest to know that the late Mr. George Bertram, along with Mr. Cameron, of Springfield, was the original inventor of the revolving strainer, of which a very varied class is now made, the only difference, however, being in the style of suction apparatus.

Mr. Bertram's knowledge of papermaking was a thorough one, and as already mentioned, being brought up in a family of papermakers, not only was he able to conduct a papermaking machinery establishment, but he could also make paper to the satisfaction of his employers, he at one time having been foreman papermaker in the mills of Messrs. William Sommerville and Sons, Dalmore. Some of the older machinemen now alive may remember that after any alteration had been made on a machine, Mr. Bertram in a jocular way would present them with a ball of string, and when asked the reason would laughingly remark that a machineman never considered his machine in good working order until he had expended a ball of twine in tying up the various parts according to his ideas.

As time went on the sons began to assist their father, and the late Mr. William Bertram, nephew of the founder of the firm, became partner with his father, the business still continuing to increase and the works to grow in size. The firm, to identify itself from that of another name, was then styled "George and William Bertram." It is impossible in this article to give any adequate idea of the magnitude of the orders executed at the Sciennes, but it may be said that the enormous drying machines at Valleyfield were produced there in the earlier days, also those for St. Mary Cray, Springfield, etc., along with the complete plant for preparing the fibres, making the paper, sizing, etc. In 1875 the late Mr. Edward Lloyd entrusted the firm to build a machine for him 125-in. wide, this being really the first wide machine in the world, and the first machine erected in Sittingbourne Mills, which was constructed and delivered in about three months' time. It has given every satisfaction, and has run night and day since that time, producing we understand a very large quantity of paper. This machine was then considered a very heavy one for its time, and certainly it was a great departure from the usual or average width. Its comparative appearance is slim, but the speed at which it runs is a proof that a machine need not be so cumbersome in its parts to remain rigid at a high speed, provided

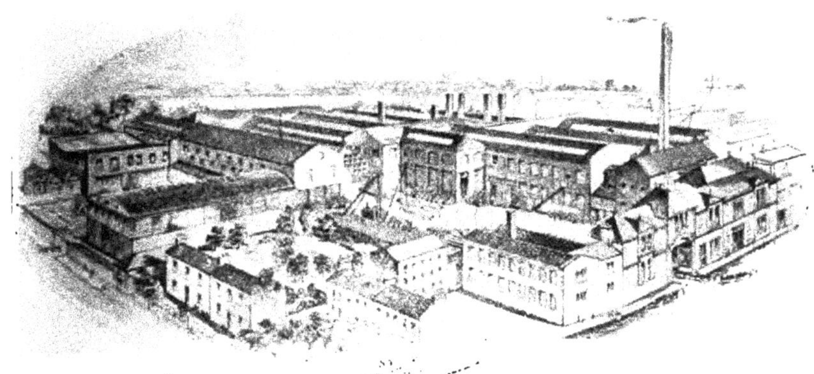

View of the whole Establishment, from which the magnitude of the works can be well seen

it is well constructed and put together. Before this many smaller machines had been made for all parts of the world, and after the construction of this machine it was seen that wider machines could be run with economical results, and produce a good sheet of paper. Consequently the Sciennes was greatly benefited by this venture, and have since then built on an average six or eight Hendon Paper Works Co., Limited, two machines; E. Lloyd, Limited, Sittingbourne, three machines; Clyde Paper Co., Dalmarnock; Pirie, Culter, Inverurie, Shotley, proprietors of *Daily Telegraph*, Spicer, etc., etc., have all two or more machines from this firm, and the preparing and finishing machinery has been largely supplied by the Sciennes also; in fact it is difficult to

Part of the yard in which are stored the general castings about to be treated by the various machines. In this yard there is a steam derrick crane which will lift anything up to 3 tons within a circle of 120 feet. There is also a very powerful hand crane which lifts many tons, and a special triangular crane for the shrinking of the shells over press and couch rolls.

machines every year. Such mills as the Guard Bridge Paper Co. received three machines from the Sciennes, all being large ones, and much other machinery besides; Messrs. E. Collins and Sons, Kelvindale, two machines; the Inveresk Paper Co., Musselburgh, two machines; Messrs. A. Cowan and Sons, Valleyfield, three machines; Mr. J. A. Weir, Forth Mills, two machines; the find any mill in Britain in which there is not a very considerable portion of the machinery from the Sciennes.

In 1877 Mr. George Bertram retired from the firm, leaving his three sons as partners, namely the late Mr. William Bertram, David, and John, with the late Mr. Patterson as manager, who was so long and honourably known in connection with

Messrs. J. Allen and Sons, Stowford Mills, Ivy Bridge. For family reasons the business was converted into a limited liability company in the end of June, 1888, the services of the late Mr. William and David being retained as joint acting directors. The chairman of the board of directors is Mr. David Harris, of Messrs. A. B. Fleming and Co., Caroline Park, Granton; Mr. John Turnbull, retired from his position as joint acting director with his brother David.

Scandinavians, owing to the low prices obtained for their pulp, determined in a very marked degree to convert it into paper, with the result that about three-fourths of the orders then given out came to the Sciennes. These orders were received by the acting director, Mr. David N. Bertram, during

General view of the Turning Department from the south. This department is complete in every respect, and equipped with the most modern class of tools throughout, those which are not entirely new having at least been modernised as much as possible. Some fine samples of modern shafting and pulley lathes, also boring and surfacing lathes are to be seen, and special lathes for drying cylinder ends, shell boring, and other work belonging to papermaking machinery and heavy engine work.

junr., consulting engineer, Glasgow, and several other well known professional and commercial gentlemen in the city of Edinburgh are directors, with Mr. D. W. Ireland as secretary. With such a business connection as the old firm were able to hand over, the limited company have continued to do good work. In 1890 Mr. William Bertram journeys made to Scandinavia for that purpose. Such machines are now running in the finest mills in Norway, Sweden, Russia and Finland, and those who have them at work have testified in a very laudable manner to the satisfaction which they have derived from their use. The acting-director is well known in Scandinavia, and it may be mentioned that after consultation with some of the foremost papermakers there, the Sciennes produced the now famous machines at Drammenselvens, Norway, and Gryckebo, Sweden, which are built in an altogether novel fashion with separate drives for almost every part of the machine on the cone system, and may be said to be a combination of American, German, and British ideas, and plete three-machine mill erected for the Titaghur Paper Co., the machines being erected one after another at intervals of about eight years out of the earnings of this now famous company. At present they are erecting a large three-machine mill, complete in every detail, for the Imperial Paper Mills Co., Ltd., near Calcutta, which is expected to be startedthis year. This mill, Bertrams

View of a part of the Turning Shop from the north, and in the foreground of this will be seen some of the rolls belonging to the large machine now being fitted up in the mills of Messrs C. T. Hook and Co., Limited, Snodland.

certainly possessed of the stability of the latter.

Eastern countries began to adopt papermaking machinery on a much larger scale, and the Sciennes has had the best share of such work, and it is worthy of note that out of about 11 machines in India which have

Limited have every reason to believe, will be a signal success, and certainly a "feather in the cap" of the Sciennes firm. The plans were produced in competition with the paper trade generally, and those laid before the Imperial Paper Company's representatives by Mr. David N. Bertram were accepted. modern and complete the crude material

engines, etc., from a higher building as the material passes along in its course of treatment, and the paper is finally discharged on to waggons at the opposite end to that at which the fibre enters. This order was executed in little more than six months, with the exception of piping, etc., a feat reflecting great credit on the management and resources of the establishment. The engines same firm two sets of compound main driving steam engines, one of 800 and one of 400 h.p. The Deccan Paper Mills Co.'s machine is also by the Sciennes firm, and the Bally Paper Mills Co. have received much machinery from them also, including a large 90-in. machine, which has given this company the greatest satisfaction. Hong Kong has recently received a complete mill from

General View of the Cylinder Department and Millwrights Shop. These Drying Cylinders, up to 10 feet diameter, are lifted with the greatest ease by the overhead travelling cranes.

for this mill were constructed from specifications issued from the Sciennes, and are 1,200 h.p., triple expansion. Everything else inside the mill has been supplied by the Sciennes, including felts, belts, and wires. The practical management of this mill will be under Mr. Thomas Tait Booth, recently manager at Messrs. Tait's, Inverurie, the commercial management being controlled by Mr. George Hall. The Raneegunge Mills were also redoubled by the Sciennes firm last year, and they also received from the the Sciennes firm, turning out about 40 tons per week, which has given its proprietors every satisfaction, as has previously been intimated in this journal. Japan has also received two complete mills from the same firm, and New Zealand one.

At the present time the firm are constructing several machines for Sweden, one very important one for the Kellner-Partington Paper Pulp Co., Limited, Barrow-in-Furness, London Paper Mills Co., &c., and have just fitted up the new mill for the Hull Chemical

Wood Pulp Co., and are presently completing the erection of the large 116-in. machine at Snodland. Their combined friction and rolling calenders are at work in many of the finest mills in Britain and foreign countries, repeat orders having been received from such firms as Messrs. A. Cowan and Sons, Valleyfield; Inveresk Paper Co., Musselburgh; Hendon Paper Works Co., Limited, Sunderland, &c., &c., in which some colossal machines are at work.

In proof of the advancement in the construction of calenders, it may be stated that several well-known papermakers about 15 years since considered it then possible to satisfactorily super-calender a sheet of paper 60-in. wide, but, as is known, this is now an exploded idea, as the Sciennes have produced calenders which are capable of finishing a sheet 100-in. wide, and presently are finishing webs 92-in. wide, either by friction or rolling. In Canada Messrs. Bertrams Limited have demonstrated by erecting large calenders there, that it is unnecessary to cut an ordinary width of paper into two widths before being super-calendered, such a calender being at work, along with a large paper-making machine, in the mills of the Royal Pulp and Paper Co., East Angus, sent out two years since. Large calenders are now being erected by the Sciennes firm in the mills of Mr. O. Tobiesen, Lysaker, near Christiania, the Randsfjord Traemasse and Papir Fabrik, Randsfjord, Norway, &c. Such calenders are made specially to suit thin wood pulp papers, it being well known that what will suit esparto is not so suitable for papers made from wood.

View of the Buffing Machine Shop and Strainer Department. These buffing machines are well known in the paper trade as turning out excellent work, and it may be stated that for the last three years they have practically run night and day buffing new rolls and re-buffing old rolls.

The acting director of the company, Mr. David N. Bertram, M.I.M.E., was born in Edinburgh in the year 1852, and served his apprenticeship with his late father, thereafter going to the works of Messrs. Randolph Elder, Glasgow, and returning to the Sciennes, where he was entrusted with the practical management of the establishment. Shortly after this he was assumed as partner along with his late brother William, and in the absence of his father and brother took the control of the establishment. When occasion required it he went with various squads of men to mills where machinery was to be fitted up, or repairs carried out. After the conversion of the firm into a limited liability company, he was assumed as joint acting director with his brother William, and on William retiring from the firm remained as sole acting director. He has advised the Board of Directors on the practical matters which are so very important in the quick and efficient out-turning of machinery, and as a result the Sciennes has in the last few years been greatly altered and enlarged, thus enabling the largest contracts to be handled with ease.

STEAM ENGINE & WEB CALENDER
ERECTING SHOP, LOOKING EAST
BERTRAMS LIMITED, SCIENNES, EDINBURGH

General view of the Calender and Steam Engine Fitting Shop, the engines shown in it being principally for driving papermaking machines. In these fitting shops there are six travelling cranes which will lift any article off the floor, and traverse it the complete length of the shop.

New tools on the combined English and American system have been added, and a system so far as papermaking engineering will allow has been introduced, in proof of which it may be stated that in 1890 the Sciennes firm turned out twelve papermaking machines, apart from the usual appurtenances such as Hollanders, calenders, steam engines, &c., there being at one time four machines on the floor and six never touched. Last year five complete new mills were constructed for India alone: that is, one three-machine mill and two single machine mills, as already referred to, beyond other machines, calenders, steam engines for Britain and foreign countries.

Since that period Mr. Bertram has advised his Board to make further improvements, and it may now be fairly said that the works are the most thoroughly equipped and largest in the papermaking engineering industry. Competition has been very keen in this branch of industry, but the Sciennes have been able to keep their works fully running, and with good results to the shareholders. Mr. David N. Bertram's name is identified as patentee of the reeling machine, now so favourably known in the papermaking trade, also in connection with his new strainer, which is an improvement on the patent flat system, of which so many hundreds have been turned out by the firm. In addition to the foregoing, his name is identified as joint patentee with Mr. David Pearson, of the refining engine, which has proved an undoubted success.

A very important department of this establishment, and one which during the past few years has been brought to a high state of perfection, is that devoted to the manufacture of strainers and strainer plates. The cutting and finishing of strainer plates involve skill, experience, and mechanism of the highest order, and the equipment of the shops devoted to this branch is sufficient evidence of their ability to deal with this class of work in the best possible manner. For quality of metals and workmanship the plates are all that can be desired; a special feature lies in the finishing of the slits, whereby the full strength of the ribs is maintained, and the slits are cut square out at each end, thus giving full benefit of the length of slits, and preventing as far as possible the liability to collect or create hanks, as

General view of the Calender and Rag Engine Fitting Shop.

is the case when crudely cut in the ordinary way. The plates are specially adapted, through the disposition of the metal and shape of the groove, for being reclosed. The superior finish and success of these plates is testified by scores of the large paper manufacturers from all parts of the world.

Passing from the exclusively papermaking machinery, we can only refer to one or two tion of the shafting in the machinery in motion section at the Exhibition, and is especially adapted for paper mills and fast running machinery. The high pressure cylinder is 16 inches diameter and the low pressure 28 inches, with a stroke of three feet. The working barrel of the high pressure cylinder is inserted into the outer shell and caulked at both ends with

View of one of the long Fitting Shops, in which many famous machines have been erected from 126 inches wide downwards, that seen in the shop meantime being the Snodland machine, which in itself is one of the largest in Britain.

other classes of machines in which this establishment does a large business. Foremost of these are the steam engines. At the International Exhibition at Edinburgh (1886) a horizontal compound steam engine was to be seen running, which elicited from engineers some very praiseworthy comments. The *Engineer*, which described and illustrated the engine, said:—"It has been running since the opening with great smoothness and regularity, and drives the large por- very soft charcoal iron wire ½ inch diameter. Two short valve chests, having suitable steam and exhaust branches are cast on. The cylinder is jacketed on the body, the jacket being proved to 100 lbs. hydraulic pressure. A blow through valve, 2¼ inches diameter, is fitted on this cylinder complete. The steam ports are 10 inches by 1½ inch, and exhaust port 10 inches by 2½ inches. The slide valves are box shaped with grid slots on the back connected to the eccentric rod, with guide complete, by a spindle working through a stuffing box, having adjusting nuts outside. The low pressure cylinder is jacketed, caulked and proved in all respects like the high pressure one. The ports are 15 inches by 1½ inch, and 15 inches by 5 inches for steam and exhaust respectively. The pistons are 6 inches deep, made of cast-iron, and fitted with Buckley's metallic packing and junk ring. The piston rods are of mild steel, arranged to work through both ends of the cylinder and secured to the piston nuts. The tail ends have cast-iron guides and slippers for supporting the weight of the piston. The noticeable smoothness of the working is due in some degree to the rigidity of the foundations ensured by the sole plate —which is of cast-iron of trunk and box section combined—being cast in one piece with guide channels, front cylinder ends and crank shaft pillow blocks. The crank shaft is double-throw, of malleable scrap, the journals being 7½ inches by 15 inches, and body 8¾ inches diameter swelled for the fly-wheel to 11 inches diameter. The fly-wheel is 12 feet diameter, cast in two pieces with rim of suitable width for 26 inch belt. The governor and cut-off gear—Turnbull's patent —are noteworthy features of the engine. A suitable air pump and condenser are provided, the pump 15 inches diameter and 16 inches stroke, being worked from the end of crank shaft by means of disc connecting rods, &c. The engine is beautifully finished in every respect, and deservedly attracts great attention at the Exhibition. A similar engine to the above was constructed for Messrs. Y. Trotter and Sons' paper works, capable of indicating 600-h.p., the sole plates of which weighed close upon 15 tons."

Messrs. A. Pirie and Son, Aberdeen, received 2 sets of engines, working in connection with turbines, for driving the complete beating and washing plant, which this firm erected for them, the rag engines being about 56 in number, and the combined power of the 2 steam engines being about 1,500-h.p. These were among the first of the inverted type of compound steam engines put into any paper mill, and are quite abreast of the times in details of construction, and are fitted with Dak's expansion gear; the Culter Paper Co. received 2 pairs of compound steam engines from them also; Messrs. J. Annandale and Sons, at Shotley Bridge, have also their main-driving steam engine from the Sciennes; the Horton Kirby Paper Works Co., Kent, have 2 heavy sets; Kelvindale and Ellangowan, each one set; and many others. In India, the entire main-driving power of the Titaghur Paper Co., near Calcutta, was constructed by Messrs. Bertrams Limited, consisting of 4 sets tandem compound engines with Turnbull expansion gear; the Raneegunge Mill have received 1 set of 350 and 1 set of 700-h.p. engines, the latter being of the Corliss type, with large main-driving rope-pulley fly wheel placed between the engine for transmitting the power to the mill shaft; the Aberdeen Paper Mills in Hong Kong were also fitted up with the Sciennes main-driving engine of 600-h.p.; and the large new mills for Messrs. Oro and Kurobe, in Japan, have a similar set of engines.

The coupled and single steam engines built by Bertrams Limited are specially suited for driving paper machines, calenders, etc., which are also made on the inverted type. For illustration and complete details of these engines the firm's catalogue should be consulted. Hydraulic and other pumps employed in paper mills are largely made at this establishment, and as engineers capable of reorganising and modernising paper mills, a more experienced firm could not be consulted. A feature, that must have a significant influence upon the success and harmony of this establishment, is to be found in the kindly manner in which the firm study the comfort and happiness of their employees. Modern manufacturing firms that are wise are beginning to see the value of studying the comfort and producing contentment among their workpeople, and few men are more just and generous in this respect than the head of this successful firm. Attached to the establishment is a workmen's club, with a large room comfortably fitted up, and capable of comfortably seating some 200 persons. Here the employees can obtain good refreshments, meals, &c., at a most reasonable charge. In the evenings they can amuse themselves at various games, or occupy their time in reading the newspapers, journals, books, &c., that are supplied. During the winter evenings lectures upon interesting subjects are delivered gratuitously to the workpeople and their friends, and the result of this attention to the welfare of the employees is contentment, harmony, and good will all round.

Mr. Benjamin Thom, works foreman, entered the firm's services about eleven years since, as foreman in the engine department, which is a very important one, as in it have been built many of the heaviest engines at work in paper mills in Britain, China, Japan, and India. Mr. Thom served his apprenticeship in the works of Messrs. Barclay, Kilmarnock, where he gained great experience in pumping engines. Afterwards he entered the mercantile navy, and qualified himself under the Board of Trade as chief engineer. On Mr. Mitchell Graham leaving the works he was elected principal foreman, and has filled this position to the entire satisfaction of the company. Mr. Thom's general experience is a very varied one, and with the tools in this well-equipped establishment at his command, good results have followed his endeavours. Mr. Thom has an assistant foreman, Mr. George Bird, who sees to all the details being brought forward. Mr. Bird will be remembered by many proprietors of paper mills as having erected their machinery.

In addition to the various parts of the Sciennes Works illustrated, there are pattern making departments, brass foundry, strainer plate manufacturing shops, plumber's workshop, all on the premises. The machinery is driven by two sets of compound high-pressure steam engines, working at a pressure of 120 lbs., the steam being supplied by a large Lancashire double flue boiler. The offices are replete in every respect, with a complete system of telephones throughout, so that the acting director can communicate from his room with any of the heads of departments.

The illustrations of works accompanying this article are reproductions by the Meisenbach process, and evidence the superior work of the Meisenbach Co., whose blocks are now widely used for commercial and artistic purposes.

PARKER'S ELECTROLYTIC APPARATUS.

According to the specification of patent just issued the following claims are made by Mr. E. T. Parker, electrician, of Wolverhampton :—

1. In the manufacture of chlorine and alkali by electrolysis, the passing of carbonic acid gas (carried in the form of bicarbonate) through the cathode compartment, whilst the electrolyte, or solution under treatment is subjected to heat.

2. Tanks, or cells, of iron, constituting the negative electrode, and anodes of chromium phosphide.

3. Subjecting a solution of a chloride to electric action in the presence of carbonic acid gas and with the application of heat, the current being conducted through the solution by means of a cathode of iron and an anode of chromium phosphide.

4. Subjecting a chloride to the action of an electric current of from 10 to 20 ampères per square foot of anode surface in the presence of excess of carbonic acid gas as bicarbonate, and with the application of heat.

5. Electrolysing a solution of a chloride in electrolytic cells, the employment of cells made of iron and provided with means for heating the solution, the cells being in communication with a carbonating apparatus into which the solution passes from the cells, and in which the solution is subjected to the action of carbonic acid gas under pressure, and from which it passes back to the electrolytic cells to be again subjected to electrolysis.

6. The manufacture of anodes for use in electrolysis by mixing anthracite coal (or coke made from anthracite coal), plumbago and pitch, and compressing the mixture with or without the application of heat.

7. The manufacture of anodes for use in electrolysis by mixing and compressing anthracite coal (or coke made from anthracite coal), plumbago and pitch, and applying heat whilst the anodes are embedded in plumbago.

MINERAL PRODUCTIONS OF MILO.

BARYTES.—The island of Milo, the most westerly of the Cyclades, has at all times been noted for its mineral resources; but it is only recently that general attention has been attracted thereto by the discovery among its mineral beds of large quantities of argentiferous barytes. The mineral productions of Milo were known even to the ancients, and alum stone, sulphur, plastic clay, and absidian, were used by them in different manners.

SULPHUR.—Sulphur occurs in thick and abundant deposits between Cape Provatà and Cape Apollonion. The existence of these mines were known even in prehistorical ages. The Phœnicians were the first to extract sulphur, subsequently the Greeks, Romans, and Byzantines, and many old borings are still to be seen. At present the mines are worked by the Hellenic Company of Public Works, established at Athens. The sulphur centres are situated on the eastern side at Firlingos, Paleoreoma, and Saint Theodore, in the first of which places an important exploitation is going on. Sulphur is found within the trachytes, and attains at times a depth of 10 metres on an area of more than 200 metres. About 20 per cent. or 30 per cent. of pure sulphur is contained in the masses. The company have this year commenced to export the sulphur to France, where it has been declared far superior to the Sicilian produce.

MANGANESE.—Manganese ores are to be found in many places, but more especially on the western portion of the island known as Chalaka. An extensive exploitation in open quarries is actually being carried on by the French company, "Serpieri et Cie," at Cape Vani. The Manganese occurs in alternate layers with liparite and baryta. The annual production amounts to 18,000 tons, of which 13,000 tons are sent to England, France and America, generally by English steamers; the rest, which is mostly of an inferior quality, is sent to the Laurium smelteries, used as a flux in the fusion of other minerals.

GYPSUM.—Gypsum is found on the southern side of the harbour, near Patrichià and close to Mount Damianos. This mineral occurs in crystalline masses in sedimentary and other tertiary layers, and generally of a white colour. The quality is the best to be found in Greece; the quantity disposed of is however limited.

THE AUSTRIAN PAPER INDUSTRY takes a great interest in the question of the Sunday rest in German paper mills. Austrian mills are in a similar position to the German; they also suffer from over-production, and most of them think that they would be greatly benefited if they would avail themselves of this opportunity for decreasing their production.

STRUCTURE OF PULP WOOD.

Structure of Wood.—A cross section or cut through the trunk of an ordinary tree, presents an appearance as represented in Fig. 1. In the centre is a small mass of substance, considerably softer than the surrounding wood, and which is termed the medulla or pith (M). In young trees and plants this is proportionally very large as in the elder shrub, but as the tree becomes matured it gradually shrinks up, and often entirely disappearing, leaving simply an empty channel, where decomposition or rot generally commences. Upon the outside of the trunk of rings the age of the tree can be told. The formation of these rings of woody fibre occurs during the summer, while in winter the growth is arrested, hence we get a break between successive rings. The growth or formation of each new ring takes place upon the inner side of the bast, and upon the outside of the wood, hence trees and plants growing in this manner have been termed by botanists Exogens, meaning outside growth. Plants such as rushes, ferns, and grasses grow by increasing in the centre, and are termed Endogens. Consequently in the ordinary trees, or exogens, the youngest wood is the outermost, while in palms and other trees of the endogen class the youngest wood is innermost. In addition to these

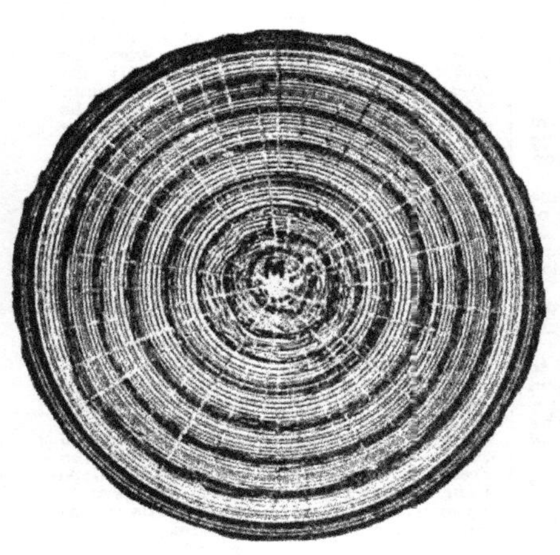

FIG 1.

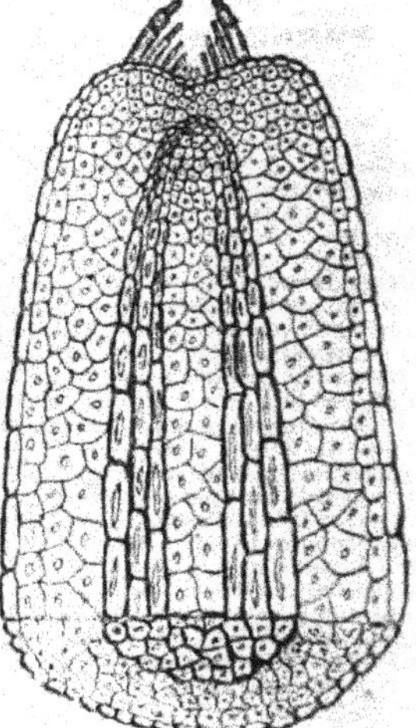

FIG. 2.

is the bark or cortex (B), which consists of three distinct parts or layers, the innermost of these is the bast, the middle is a soft growing cellular layer, while the outermost layer consists of the cork portion of the bark. It is from this outer layer of certain trees that the cork of commerce is obtained, and in ordinary trees it usually splits, and forms deep crevices as the tree enlarges, giving it a corrugated and rough surface. The inner or bast layer is renewed by growth annually, and in many plants this bast is of great value, as in the case of flax and hemp. The woody portion of the trunk is seen to be composed of a number of concentric rings, each of which represents a year's growth; by the number rings we also noticed lines radiating from the centre or pith to the bark, like the spokes of a wheel, these are known as the medullary rays. Although in section they appear as lines, they are in reality vertical plates or layers of soft tissue containing starch and other nutriment for supplying the wood during the winter. From the position they occupy it will be seen that they divide up the whole trunk into wedge shaped masses. In the oak these lines form what painters call the silver grain. We will now examine more minutely the structure of the wood and the manner in which it is formed. If, with the aid of a good microscope, we examine a portion of any young plant, we shall find that it is entirely composed of a great number of small somewhat rounded bodies termed vegetable cells. Each of these cells is composed of a thin closed transparent bag or cell wall, containing a simple cells throughout life, and such plants are consequently termed cellular plant, as mosses and algae or water plants, whereas in the higher forms of plants, the cells gradu-

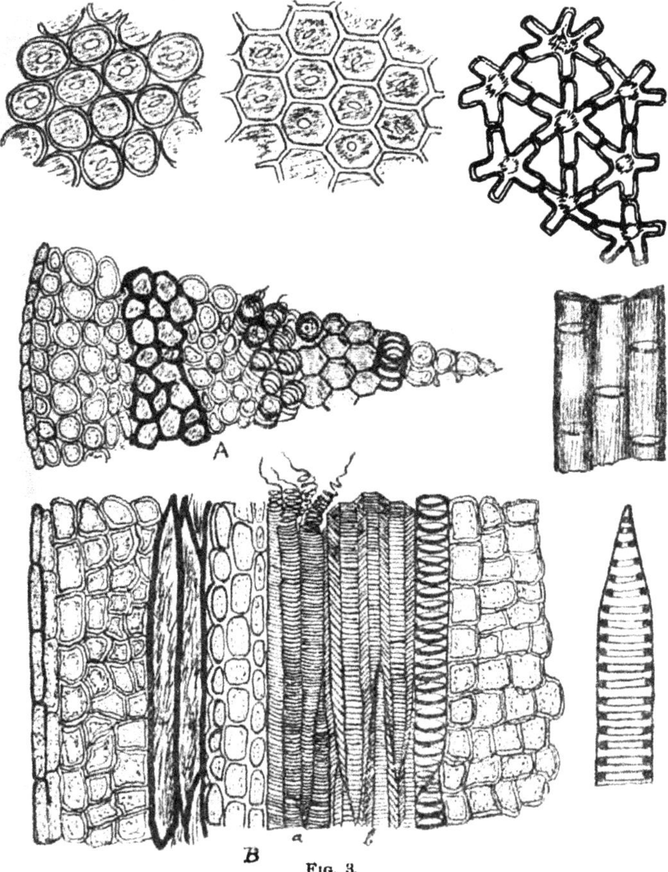

FIG. 3.

semifluid substance termed protoplasm. Fig. 2 represents a section of the growing point of the stem of a young plant, and is seen to be made up entirely of these cells. In the lowest forms of plants these cells remain as ally become changed or modified into totally different structures. In Fig. 2 it will be seen that the cells gradually become longer as we get further from the point of growth, or in other words as the cells get older they undergo greater changes. The nature of these modifications vary very considerably, producing the great variety of cells, vessels, and fibres that are met with in the various forms of vegetable life. The simple cell, which is originally somewhat spherical in form, Fig. 3, may become hexagonal, oblong, star shaped or greatly elongated, their size may vary from 1-500th to 1-50th of an inch in diameter.

The wall of the cell also thickens and hardens, as in the stone of the cherry or plum, where they consist of very regular twelve-sided cells, whose walls have been so thickened as to obliterate the central space. Very commonly the wall thickens only at certain regions, leaving thin places which appear as dots or pits. The thickening often takes place in the form of a spiral or screw thread, or in the form of distinct rings. The fibre of wood consists of greatly elongated spindle-shaped cells laid side by side, the walls are thickened by the growth upon the inner surface of a substance termed lignine. This thickening may take place in the various manners above described. In the cone-bearing trees, as pine and fir, the fibres are characterised by the presence of dots or pits, as shown in A, Fig. 4.

In Fig. 3, A represents a transverse, and B a longitudinal section of a portion of the woody part of a fern stem, the former shows the various forms of fibres, vessels, and cells cut across, while the latter represents the same lengthwise. In the figure *(a)* represents a spiral fibre and *(b)* fibres, which from their appearance have been termed scalariform or ladder-like. In Fig. 4, A represent a portion of two fibres from the pine tree very highly magnified; B, cotton fibres; C, flax fibre; and D, jute fibres.

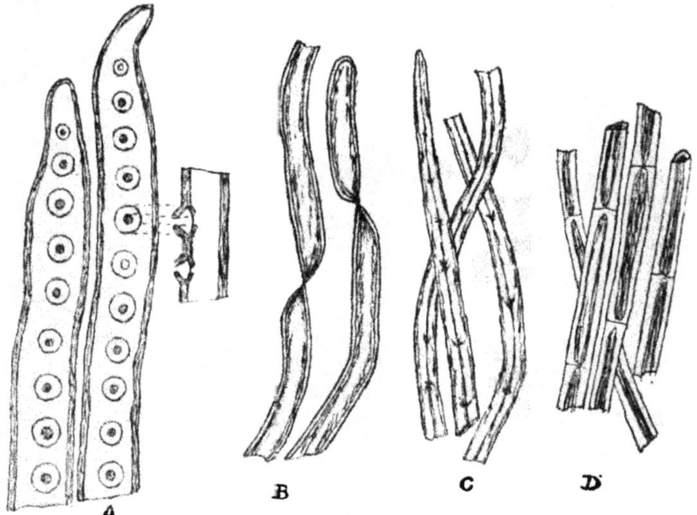

FIG. 4.

AUSTRIAN CONSULAR REPORTS. — The Consul at Sofia reports about the third quarter of 1893 as follows: The supply of paper was principally covered by Austrian mills, but Germany sent in 438 q. for the State printing office. Millboards were much in demand, but sales were not considerable as makers refused to contract ahead. Other articles coming from Austria, such as writing and cigarette papers, playing cards, &c., remained within the accustomed limits. A concession for a paper mill to be erected at Samakow has been demanded, but the Government has not yet taken a decision. A bill for the support of home industry is going to be put before the legislature.

MR. PEARSON, formerly manager at the East Lancashire Co.'s paper works, has now assumed the management of Shotley Grove Mills (Messrs. John Annandale and Sons).

COMING OF AGE OF MR. WILLIAM NIMMO TOD.

PRESENTATIONS.

Monday, the 4th inst., was the twenty-first anniversary of the birthday of Mr. W. N. Tod, son of Mr. John Tod, so well and widely known under the *nom-de-plume* of "John Strathesk," and in consequence great rejoicings took place at Lasswade, and many congratulations have been showered upon father and son. As is well known, Mr. John Tod is the senior partner of the old-established papermaking firms of Wm. Tod, junr., and Co., Springfield Mills, Polton, and Wm. Tod and Son, St. Leonard's Mill, Lasswade; in consequence, the workpeople of these mills have had a large share in being the donors and recipients of substantial tokens of mutual esteem between themselves and their employers. On Saturday afternoon last, the employees of St. Leonards Mill invited young Mr. W. N. Tod to meet them, when they presented him with a handsome dressing case in honour of his coming of age, and as a token of their personal regard for him. Mr. D. McMaster, general manager of the two mills, occupied the chair.

The presentation was made by the St. Leonard's manager, MR. G. DICKSON, who referred in excellent terms to the high respect in which Mr. Tod was held by all the employees at the mill, and conveying to him the sincere wishes of everyone, that in his future Mr. Tod should have all happiness and success. He had always found Mr. Tod a young man of sense and ability, and he had no doubt that these good qualities would be well used for the benefit of the mills and all employed therein.

MR. TOD, in accepting the gift, said he was quite at a loss to express his gratification at this unexpected token of kindly feeling towards him, and he trusted the good feeling might long be maintained between them; nothing would be wanting on his part to preserve and strengthen it. He desired them to accept his sincere thanks for their beautiful gift.

The Springfield workers also asked Mr. Tod to meet them at the close of the St. Leonard's meeting, Mr. D. McMaster again being in the chair. The chairman explained that they had met for the purpose of presenting a handsome gold albert, with a suitable inscription on the pendant, to Mr. Tod, and he called upon Mr. J. Blaikie, the Springfield manager, to make the presentation.

MR. BLAIKIE said they were met to convey to Mr. Tod their hearty congratulations on the occasion of his coming of age, and they all hoped he would have many years of usefulness and prosperity before him. Since Mr. Tod had come to the mills, they had all been well pleased with his conduct; he had been genial and kind to everyone, and had merited the confidence of every worker. He felt he spoke the sentiments of all when he said they wished Mr. Tod every blessing and success in the years to come.

MR. TOD, in reply, said he thanked all sincerely for the beautiful gift they had presented him with; it would through life be one of the most cherished articles in his possession. He felt their kindness very much, and he reciprocated it most heartily. He was interested in the welfare of them all, and he hoped the interest would long be maintained.

At the close of both the St. Leonard's and Springfield meetings, Mr. MCMASTER intimated that Mr. John Tod was at present making arrangements with the publishers with a view to presenting every worker at both mills with a nicely bound copy of his chief work, "Bits from Blinkbonny," in recognition of his son attaining his majority, an intimation which met with much pleasure.

DINNER.

In further honour of the occasion, Mr. Tod invited a large and representative number of the employees of both mills, including all the foremen and oldest servants, to meet him at dinner in Lasswade Hotel, in the evening of the same day. In addicion to those from the mills, the chief magistrates of the neighbouring villages were also invited, as also the Lasswade schoolmaster, Mr. Marshall; the carting contractors for both firms, Mr. Gibson, of Brunstone, and Mr. Armstrong, manager of Messrs. Annandale's Paper Mill, Polton. Through unavoidable reasons, the chief magistrate of Lasswade and the stationmasters of Lasswade and Polton were absent. The chair was occupied by Mr. John Tod himself, and Mr. W. Leonard Tod and Mr. D. McMaster were croupiers. The repast provided was excellent in quality and superabundant in quantity, and the "wine of the country" was not awanting. After dinner the usual loyal and patriotic toasts were honoured in a very enthusiastic style; and every man proceeded to enjoy himself in the highest of spirits. The presence of a chairman like Mr. John Tod is enough to enliven any meeting, however dull; but on this occasion the jovial "John Strathesk" was hilarity personified, and mirth of a high order filled the hours. To enumerate all the toasts given and replied to, and the songs sung, would take considerable space, and therefore an epitome of the three chief toasts of the evening must suffice.

The first of these was "Our Employees," by Mr. W. LEONARD TOD. He said he had the greatest pleasure in giving this toast, as he felt towards them the utmost cordiality. When the history of this age came to be written it would be found that the chief feature of it would be a record of industrial disputes, strikes, and warfare between capital and labour. This being so, he was all the more gratified in saying that nothing but the kindliest feelings had always existed between masters and men at these mills. He believed the workpeople there were a very fine class of men; he felt a personal interest in the welfare of them all, and he believed the attachment on their part was also strong.

The toast was duly honoured, and very suitably replied to by Mr. JOHN KETCHEN, who also gave another of the principal toasts, "The Members of the firms of Messrs. Wm. Tod, junr., and Co., and Messrs. W. Tod and Son." He conveyed to the masters the cordial feelings of all the workers; they held the members of the firms in the very highest esteem; the Messrs. Tod had ever been employers beloved by their employees, and the kindness they had experienced that night was sure to strengthen the bond of love. This toast was honoured with great enthusiasm.

MR. JOHN TOD replied in very kindly terms, and very touchingly referred to the losses in recent years the firms had sustained in the deaths of his brothers, Messrs. Andrew and William Tod; their memories were deeply revered and long would be fondly cherished. He thanked his workpeople for coming that evening, and he hoped and believed all would be the better for the friendly intercourse.

The toast of the evening, "The Health of Mr. W. Nimmo Tod," was proposed by Mr. D. McMASTER, who said that he had great pleasure indeed in giving it. Mr. Tod, the chairman, was to be greatly congratulated on the fact of his eldest son having arrived at his majority, and they all hoped young Mr. Nimmo would long live to be a credit to his father and to all. In entering into the conflict of life young Mr. Tod was well equipped, and he gave promise of becoming a man of many parts. In the first place he was possessed of splendid physical endowments, and in this respect was the envy of all young men. Secondly, he had had a thorough scientific and technical training as regards his business as a papermaker, and if he applied this as they all expected he would, the mills would greatly benefit and prosper. And lastly, Mr. Tod was eminently provided with the genial and enthusiastic nature of his worthy father, and in every way he gave promise of being a "chip of the old block." The toast was drunk amidst deafening cheers and musical honours.

In reply, Mr. TOD thanked all present for the splendid way in which the toast had been responded to; it was deeply gratifying to him, and he should do his utmost to always merit their best opinions. His feelings were too strong to permit him to say much, but he should not soon forget their kindness that night, and he hoped nothing should ever arise to mar the cordiality of his relationships with those present and all employed at the mills.

A highly successful gathering closed with a hearty vote of thanks and a prolonged round of cheering to Mr. John Tod for his hospitality. After singing "Auld Lang Syne" the meeting dispersed, all in the most jovial frame of mind.

"DECKLE-EDGE."

The mechanism illustrated has been patented by Mr. R. W. Moncrieff, general manager and engineer for the Sparre Patents Co., Limited. It has special reference to machines of the kind in which a series of laid or wove moulds are employed, the moulds being either hinged or connected together so as to form a continuous or endless chain of travelling moulds which successively receive the pulp from a pulp box or other source of supply, or being so carried one behind another as always to form a continuous set of contiguous moulds between the feed and the couch rolls.

As hitherto constructed these machines have been able to produce paper only in the form of a continuous sheet or web, because the sides of the successive moulds at the part of their travel where the pulp is received and the paper formed have butted closely against each other so as to constitute a continuous mould; the joints between the adjoining moulds have, moreover, been somewhat imperfect owing to the more or less uneven nature of the butting edges. The continuous sheet on leaving the mould has been conducted in the ordinary way to press rollers and then to a drying cylinder.

According to Mr Moncrieff's modifications, the machine is now constructed as to produce the paper in separate sheets with a true deckle edge on every side, and by a special arrangement of felts he provides for delivering these separate sheets successively so that they can be piled one above another immediately on leaving the machine. The sheets can therefore be "flat pressed," "parted," "loft dried," "sized," and otherwise treated precisely as vat made or hand made papers.

To either the leading side or the trailing side of each mould is attached a transverse strip of brass or other suitable metal or material of sufficient height to separate the pulp received by that mould from the pulp on the next adjoining mould, with the result that instead of the paper being produced in a continuous web it is produced in separate sheets. This metal strip preferably overlaps the edge of the adjoining mould, thereby avoiding all inconvenience from the unevenness of such edge.

Figure 1 of the accompanying drawings will serve to illustrate the preferred manner of constructing the moulds in order to produce the paper in separate sheets with a true deckle edge on every side as above described. The figure is a longitudinal section of a portion of the machine showing a mould *b* and portions of two other moulds *a* and *c*, these three moulds being hinged or connected together at *d* in any ordinary manner or carried one behind another. The body of each mould is shown as formed of bars *e e* constituting the mould sides, and of cross ribs *f f*, which may be about $\frac{1}{16}$th of an inch thick and about an inch apart, but any other suitable construction of mould may be adopted.

g h i represent the laid or wove wire surfaces of the three moulds *a b* and *c* respectively. *l* represents the ordinary deckle strap. *k k*¹ represent the transverse strips of brass or other metal which is soldered or otherwise fixed either to the leading side or the trailing side of each laid or wove wire surface so as to separate the pulp received by each mould from that on the next adjoining moulds; the strip *k* is for example fixed to the surface *h* so as to overlap the edge of the surface *g* and the strip k_1 is fixed to the surface *i* so as to overlap the edge of the surface *h*. Or the transverse separator may consist of two transverse strips attached piled on a table or otherwise; or they may be stripped off the first felt mechanically and deposited direct on the table.

Figure 2 represents diagrammatically the arrangement of felts as above described for delivering successively the separate sheets made upon the moulds. *m* is the couching roll to which the successive moulds carry their sheets. Around the couching roll an endless felt *n* passes; this felt takes up each successive sheet and conducts it to a guide roller *p*. At this guide roller the sheet meets a second endless felt *q* and it is carried between the two felts *n* and *q* to the press rollers *rr*. After leaving the press rollers the endless

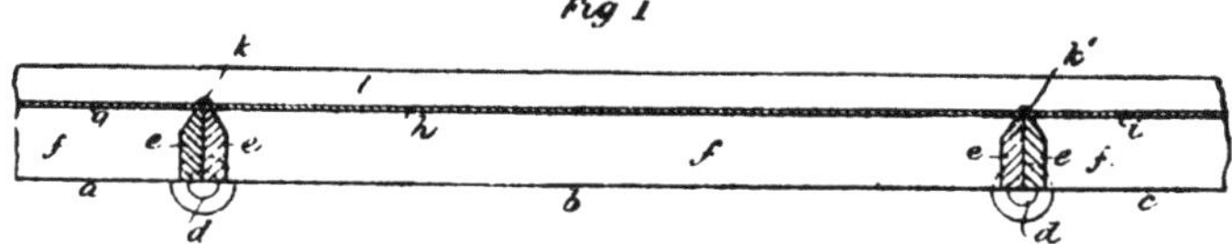

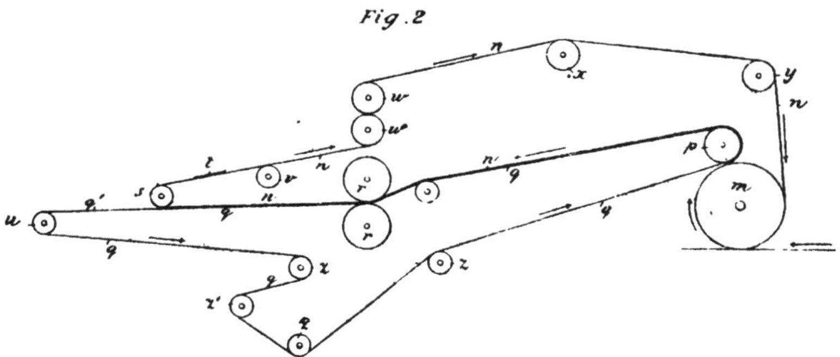

respectively to the meeting edges of adjoining moulds. The moulds carry the successive sheets formed under a couching roll, and on passing this roll each sheet is taken by an endless felt which conducts it to a guide roller. At this guide roller it meets a second endless felt, and it is carried between the two felts to the press rollers. After leaving the press rollers the first endless felt passes under a guide roller and begins to travel in an upward direction, the sheet adhering thereto while the other endless felt moves in a horizontal direction a certain distance. The successive sheets are stripped off the first felt by an attendant and deposited upon the horizontal portion of the other felt from which they are successively removed and felt *n* passes under a return guide roller *s* and begins to travel in an upward direction, the sheet which is indicated at *t* adhering thereto, while the other endless felt *q* travels in a horizontal direction as seen at *q*¹ to a return roller *u*. The sheets are successively stripped off the felt *n* at or about the point *t* and deposited upon the horizontal portion *q*¹ of the felt *q* from which they are successively removed and piled on a table or otherwise. The felt *n* after leaving the return roller *s* goes back to the couching roll *m*, passing on its way over various rollers, the arrangement shown, which however is not arbitrary, comprising a guide roller *v*, licking rollers *w w*, stretch roller *x* and conducting roller *y*. The felt *q* after leaving the return roller *u* goes back to the guide roller *p*, passing on its way over various rollers, the arrangement shown, which again is not arbitrary, comprising guide or conducting rollers *z z z* and a stretch roller z^1. The sides of the sheets where they were separated from the adjoining sheets by the transverse strips *k* (Fig. 1) have, it is claimed by the patentee, a true deckle edge, while the other sides of the sheets have also a deckle edge formed by the usual deckle straps *l*. And further, each mould may be divided either transversely or longitudinally by deckle wires so as to form any number and size of sheets desired, all having true deckle edges. Instead of the transverse strips *k* being sufficiently high to produce separate sheets as before described, they may be only high enough to produce transverse lines of thinness in what is in other respects a continuous sheet or web of paper, which can subsequently be readily torn or divided along such lines. In this case the continuous sheet on leaving the press rollers can be wound on a taking up roller.

STETTIN.—A consular report, just issued, on the trade of Stettin during 1892, points out that there was a decrease in the trade by sea compared with the previous year, both as regards number of vessels as well as the total tonnage. The freights for rags were 12s. 6d. to 14s. per ton, and cellulose, 14s. per ton. The regular steamers running between Stettin and London, Hull, Leith, Amsterdam, Rotterdam, and the Rhine, obtained fairly abundant cargoes, with the exception of in the hottest part of the summer, during which time the water in the River Oder was low and the arrivals in Stettin less. During the latter part of the year, a number of steamers from Norwegian and Swedish ports arrived in Stettin with cargoes of wood destined for inland manufactories, principally the cellulose and paper factories of Silesia. The export of rags to England and America ceased during the latter months of the year on account of the cholera. The chemical factory at Pomerensdorf and the Union Chemical Manufacturing Co. employ a large number of hands, and apparently are doing good work, each concern paying a dividend of 10 per cent. The paper mill at Hohenkrug is reported to have made no profits on their work during 1892. The pulp and cellulose factory at Alt-Damm declared a dividend of 11 per cent. Amongst the prominent industrial establishments may be mentioned the Vereinigte Stralsunder Spielkarten-Fabriken (The Stralsund Playing Cards Factory, Limited). The value of cards manufactured was 851,812 marks 85 pf., or £41,961 5s. The profits to be divided among the shareholders amounted to 127,430 marks 48 pf., or £6,277 8s.

CANADA.—A new line of pulp machinery is to be put in at the pulp mill at Milton, N.S.

THE PAPERMAKERS' ASSOCIATION.

According to a letter sent to British papermakers by Mr. Lewis Evans, chairman of committee, Mr. G. Humphrey-Davies, F.S.I., has been appointed honorary secretary of the above association on the resignation of Mr. McCaul, who has held the position of secretary for the last twenty-one years. Mr. Evans states it is the most anxious wish of the committee and of Mr. Humphrey-Davies to make the association thoroughly representative of so important an industry as the paper trade, and to neglect no opportunity of protecting and furthering the interests of the trade wherever it may be necessary and possible. The increasing tendency of the legislature to interfere with manufacturers in the conduct of their business, makes it more than ever necessary to support an association of this character, and papermakers will be only too well aware of the many directions in which its energetic and judicious action will be beneficial. The committee are at present engaged in considering in what direction the organisation of the association can be improved and its work more effectively carried out, and they especially desire that papermakers will favour them with their views and suggestions on these points. Arrangements have already been made for watching all bills introduced into Parliament, with the object of calling attention to any proposals likely to be inimical to the paper trade, so that if thought necessary they may be opposed or amended. It is also hoped shortly to complete arrangements by which members of the association can be advised on legal and other matters connected with their business. It is a subject of gratification to the committee that the long connection of Mr. McCaul with the paper trade will not be entirely severed, inasmuch as he will remain the secretary of the Papermakers' Club, the meetings and dinners of which will take place as heretofore. Dr. Wirtz, M.A., F.I.C., the honorary analyst of the association, will continue to place his valuable services at the disposal of members of the association. The appointment of Mr. Humphrey-Davies as honorary secretary, took effect from the 1st of December, from which date the offices of the association will be at 8, Laurence Pountney-hill, Cannon-street, E.C. Mr. Humphreys-Davies has also placed his Manchester offices (No. 16. Deansgate) at the disposal of members of the association, for meetings, whenever they may be found useful for the purpose.

WOKING PAPER WORKS, LTD.—In our remarks concerning the personnel of this company, under "Who's Who," in our last issue, we omitted to mention that Mr. R. L. Towgood, of St. Neot's, is one of the present directors, the other gentlemen on the Board being Messrs. Henry Rogers and G. Schenkenwald.

FOREIGN IMPORT DUTIES ON PAPER, &c., STATIONERY AND BOOKS.

GERMANY:

TARIFF CLASSIFICATION.	TARIFF RATES OF DUTY.	Mks.	pf.	ENGLISH EQUIVALENTS.	£	s.	d.
Paper and pasteboard:							
Unbleached or bleached half-stuff from rags, for papermaking	Free			Free			
Unbleached or bleached half-stuff of wood, straw, esparto, or other fibres, for papermaking	100 kilos.	1	00	Cwt.	0	0	6
Grey blotting and yellow rough straw paper	,,	1	00	,,	0	0	6
Pasteboard, except glazed pasteboard and leather-board; slate paper and tablets thereof not combined with other materials; emery and polishing paper ...	,,	1	00	,,	0	0	6
Unsized packing paper not otherwise specified	,,	3	00	,,	0	1	6¼
Sized packing paper	,,	3	00	,,	0	1	6¼
Glazed pasteboard and leather-board; press boards	,,	6	00	,,	0	3	0½
Printing paper, writing paper, blotting paper (other than coarse grey), tissue paper of all kinds, and paper prepared for accounts, labels, way-bills, &c. ...	,,	6	00	,,	0	3	0½
Paper lithographed, printed, or ruled; gilt or silvered paper; paper with gilt or silvered patterns; perforated paper; also strips or bands of these papers; artists' cardboard	,,	10	00	,,	0	5	1
Moulded work of carton pierre, combined or not with wood or iron, but not painted nor varnished	,,	4	00	,,	0	2	0½
Moulded work of carton pierre, painted or varnished...	,,	12	00	,,	0	6	1
Wares of paper, cardboard, or papier maché	,,	12	00	,,	0	6	1
Wares of paper, cardboard, papier mâché, &c., combined with other materials, provided they cannot be classified under the head of "Small ornamental wares" ...	,,	24	00	,,	0	12	2
Paper hangings, not gilt, silvered, bronzed, embossed, nor velveted	,,	18	00	,,	0	9	2
Paper-hangings, other than the foregoing	,,	24	00	,,	0	12	2
Playing cards (besides Excise duty)	,, Gross wt.	60	00	,, Gross	1	10	6
Paper manuscripts and books in all languages, bound or not	Free			Free			
Engravings, lithographs, photographs, maps, and charts; also music	Free			Free			
Pencils, all kinds	100 kilos.	20	00	Cwt.	0	10	2
Steel pens	,,	60	00	,,	1	10	6
Ink and ink powder	,,	3	00	,,	0	1	6¼
Printing ink	,,	3	00	,,	0	1	6¼
Sealing-wax	,,	3	00	,,	0	1	6¼
Rags	Free			Free			

MR. W. D. GROZIER, who for some time was with the Woking Paper Co., Ltd., has accepted an engagement at Catteshall Paper Mills, Godalming, Surrey.

MESSRS. FELBER, JUCKER AND CO., of 60, Peter-street, Manchester, advise us that Mr. John Wood has been appointed manager of their Glasgow House.

WORLD'S PAPER TRADE REVIEW OFFICE,
58, SHOE LANE, LONDON, E.C.

TRADE NOTES.

THE SCANDINAVIAN WOOD PULP UNION.—At the recent meeting of this association, held at Gothenburg, statistics relating to production was submitted by the secretary of the Norwegian department. These are referred to in our editorial notes. The association decided to fully maintain prices, which were fixed as follows:—Pine pulp, 50 per cent. moisture, £2 10s. per ton; dry pine, £5 5s. per ton f.o.b. Norway.

C. T. BAINBRIDGE AND SON, LTD.—A petition for the winding-up of this company was presented on the 1st December by Mr. Michael Fryer, of Johnson-street, Middlesbrough, and will be heard before Mr. Justice Vaughan Williams, in the High Court of Justice, on Tuesday, the 19th inst.

A RECEIVING ORDER in bankruptcy was made on November 24th against Mr. T. H. Bracken, of Gable House, Devonshire-place, Harrogate, Yorks, described as a papermaker's agent, and the debtor was adjudicated bankrupt on November 27th. The first meeting of creditors in this case will be held on the 11th inst., at 12-30 p.m., official receiver's office, 28, Stonegate, York. A meeting for public examination of the debtor will be held on January 12th, at 11 a.m., at the Courts of Justice, Clifford-street, York.

M'MURRAY *v.* M'FARLANE.—Judgment was given in the *Scottish Leader* case by Lord Stormonth-Darling, Edinburgh Court of Session, on the 2nd inst. The pursuer (James M'Murray, of the Royal Paper Mills, Wandsworth, Surrey) sued John M'Farlane, residing at Glenbourne, Oswald-road, Edinburgh, recently proprietor of the *Scottish Leader* newspaper, for payment of £5,055 17s. 4d., being the amount which pursuer had paid to the Commercial Bank of Scotland under a guarantee for an advance of £5,000 made by the bank to the defender. The defence was that repayment of the loan was to be made conditionally upon the *Scottish Leader* turning out to be a paying concern, and that that condition had not been purified in respect that the paper had turned out a failure in defender's hands. The Lord Ordinary assoilzied the defender from the conclusions of the action, with expenses.

FARRINGDON WORKS, LTD.—Registered with a capital of £40,000 in £10 shares, to carry on the business of engineers and ironfounders, millwrights, boiler makers, &c. The first directors—to be not less than three nor more than seven—are the Hon. S. C. Glyn, H. Barnard, W. Semmons, C. W. Barnard, G. C. Glyn, and L. Earle. Remuneration to be fixed by the company.

GALLOWAY, MATHEWS AND CO., LIMITED.—Registered with a nominal capital of £10,000, in £1 shares. Objects: To acquire and carry on the business of hemp, flax, jute, rope, twine, cordage and paper dealers, agents and manufacturers, carried on by Mathews and Co.

THE CARNTYNE CHEMICAL CO., LTD.—The objects for which this company has been established are:—To purchase, take over, and carry on the business of analytical and manufacturing chemists hitherto carried on by Messrs. Scott and Jack, at Carntyne Chemical Works, Old Edinburgh-road, Parkhead, Glasgow, in all its branches. Capital, £5,000, divided into 10 founders' shares of £40 each and 920 ordinary shares of £5 each.

A FIRE AT LONDON PAPER WAREHOUSES.—Early on Saturday morning a fire broke out in a block of seven-story buildings occupied by Messrs. Poulter, wharfingers, Upper Thames-street. Considerable damage was also done to the export paper warehouses of Messrs. Turner and Sons, facing Messrs. Poulter's premises. There were large quantities of paper awaiting shipment.

FIRE.—On Tuesday afternoon the brick building at Strath Paper Mills, Galston (Mr. William Gemmell's), used as a drying store, was destroyed by fire. Over two tons of millboard was in process of drying. The building, the property of the Duke of Portland, was fully insured.

THE SCOTCH COAL TRADE.—At a joint meeting of coal masters and miners' representatives of Mid and East Lothian, in Edinburgh, on Wednesday, the miners' representatives asked for an advance of 10 per cent. in wages to make the East of Scotland rates equal to an advance granted in the West of Scotland. After consultation, the coalmasters intimated that, in their opinion, no advance was warranted by the general state of trade, but, in view of the present enhanced value of coal, they would grant a temporary advance of 10 per cent. The men had lodged notices and intended to strike unless an advance was granted.

As one of the results of the coal strike, the remarks made by Mr. Mundella in the House of Commons, on Tuesday, may be of interest. He said the quantity of coal exported in the months of August, September and October of this year was 7,091,000 tons, as compared with 8,892,000 tons in the corresponding period of last year. A return just received from the Customs authorities showed that during the four months from August to November, inclusive, the quantity exported in the present year was 9,322,000 tons as against 11,455,000 tons in the corresponding period of last year. The bunker coal shipped for use of steamers in the same period in this year was 2,798,000 tons, as against 2,942,000 tons in the corresponding period of last year. The total decrease in the exports in the four months of 1898 was 2,310,000 tons.

THE FLASHING POINT OF MINERAL OILS.—At the second meeting of the session in connection with the Manchester Section of the Society of Chemical Industry, held on the 1st inst., with Dr. Schunck in the chair, a paper on the flashing-point of mineral oils was given by Mr. J. Carter Bell. The following motion was adopted:—"That in the opinion of this meeting the legal flashing-point of burning oil sold in this country is considerably too low, and that it should be increased to a standard of not less than 100 degrees Fahrenheit, Abel standard."

NATIONAL UNION OF PAPER MILL WORKERS.—The annual meeting of the Lancashire and Midlands District Council was held in the Crosby Hotel, Manchester, on Saturday, 2nd inst. The president, Mr. J. T. Blackledge, opened the meeting with a few earnest words of address to the delegates on the business before them. The minutes of previous meetings were then read by the district secretary, Mr. J. Diggle, and confirmed. Mr. Diggle submitted his quarterly and yearly statements, which, after some discussion, were unanimously adopted. The retiring officers of the Council were then unanimously re-elected for another twelve months. The general secretary, Mr. Wm. Ross, next addressed the meeting of delegates on the question of raising the contributions at the next annual meeting. At the conclusion of his address it was moved and seconded "that this District Council expresses its approval of the contributions being fixed, at next annual meeting at the rates of 2d. and 4d. per week, 6d. scale to remain optional, and benefits to remain as they are at present." An amendment that the rates of contributions be fixed at 2d. and 6d. per week, with week's suspension pay at end of six days was defeated, and the above motion carried almost unanimously. It was resolved to submit the above to the branches for discussion, also two suggestions as follows:—(1) "That £5 of funeral benefit be paid at the death of a member, such benefit to be paid by a 1d. levy on all members, at every death, and that all branches be asked to inform the general secretary as to the number of members they had lost by death during the last two years." (2) "That instead of the nine days' clause, one day's suspension pay be paid at end of seven days' suspension, and for each day following till work was resumed."

MESSRS. ERNEST SCOTT AND MOUNTAIN, LIMITED, of the Close Works, Newcastle, have received an order from the Coltness Iron Company, Newmains, Lancashire, for an electric light installation for their colliery, which will be one of the most complete plants in existence. The plant consists of a complete electric light installation for the colliery, consisting of a dynamo to run 200-16 C.P. lamps and about 180 lamps throughout the pit, both above ground and underground. The second is an installation for the lighting of 34 workmen's cottages, which are about 700 yards from the colliery, there being three lights placed in each cottage, or a total of 102 lamps in all. The third installation consists of a complete electric pumping plant, capable of delivering 100 gallons of water per minute from the river to the colliery. The dynamos for the lighting of the pit and the workmens' cottages are being specially constructed so that either dynamo can be utilised for either purpose, both machines being overcompounded so that the E.M.F. will remain constant at the cottages under variations of load. This installation is probably one of the first in which complete plant for pumping, lighting of a colliery and the lighting of workmen's cottages has been adopted.

MOGADOR.—A report on the trade of the district of Magador states that the exports of esparto were in 1892 very small. Importations of chemicals show an increase, especially from France. The imports of stationery (made up of wrapping paper, writing paper and "various") amounted to £985, or £127 less than the previous year. Adding cigarette paper, which is a new feature, a slight increase is shown. Wall paper is mostly supplied by Germany. In 1892 4-cwts. of books, &c., of the value of £14 were received against 30-cwts. of £90 value in 1891. Writing paper was imported last year to the extent of 4,600 reams of £505 value; in 1891 1,940 reams, of £510 value. Wrapping paper was imported in 1892 to the extent of 13,584 reams of £460 value; in 1891 18,360 reams, £512 value. Cigarette paper was imported last year to the value of £160 the quantity supplied being 10 cases. It may be mentioned that the production of esparto is very slight in the south, compared with that of the Mediterranean littoral, and although an Engliish merchant has a hydraulic press on purpose for baling it, the shipments only amounted to 80 tons.

PAPER & PULP MILL SHARES.

(Report received from Mr. F. D. DEAN, 36, Corporation Street, Manchester.)

Nominal Amnt		Last dividend	Price.
7	Bury Paper, ord.	nil	4—4½
7	do. do. 6% pref.	6%	4¼—4¾
100	do. do. deb.	5%	103—106
10	Bath Paper Mill Co. Lim.	7½%	6—7
10	Bergvik Co., def.	15%	13¾
100	do. do. 6% cum. pref.	6%	10½—11
10	do. do. deb.	5%	105—110
5	Burnley Paper Co.	3/-	77/6—80/0
5	Darwen Paper Co.	10%	5¾—6¼
10	East Lancashire Co.	nil	3¾—4
10	do. do. 6% pref.	nil	5—5½
5	do. do. bonus	nil	1½—1¾
5	Hyde Paper Co.	4%	4½—5
5	North of Ireland Paper	nil	2½—2¾
10	Ramsbottom Paper Co.	17½%	12¼—12¾
5	Roach Bridge Paper Co	5%	2½—3
5	Star Paper Co.	8%	5½—6
5	do. do. 6 pref. cum	10%	4¾—5¼
50	do. do. deb.	6%	55—56
5		1/11½	3½—3¾xd

PAPER EXPORTS AT NEW YORK.—The weekly list to hand shows the following :—

B. W. Indies ...	40 bales	New Zealand ...	243 cases
" " ...	544 pkgs.	Southampton ...	1 case
Liverpool ...	2 cases	B. Honduras ...	126 bales
Australasia ...	727 pkgs.	S. Africa	1 case
London ...	207 cases	Leith	133 pkgs.
Hull	50 pkgs.	Newfoundland ...	3 cases

PAPER TILES.—The Marseilles Paper Tiling Company, Marseilles, Ill., are about to engage in the manufacture of a new kind of tile, to be made from paper.

WOOD BOARD MANUFACTURE.—The paper mill of the Thomson Pulp and Paper Company, at Thomson's Mills, which is announced to start January 1st, will contain a machine capable of making the largest sheet of wood board in the world.

PAPER HOOPS.—Mr. Walter E. Frost, Lewiston, Me., is reported to have invented a machine to make hoops for orange boxes out of paper. It will make 200,000 hoops in one day.

NIAGARA FALLS PAPER CO.—The officers and directors of the Niagara Falls Paper Company, at a recent meeting at Niagara Falls, N. Y., decided to start up the three machines on January 1st if possible.

THE CHAMPION COATED PAPER COMPANY, of Hamilton, a branch of the Boston concern, has been incorporated by Messrs. Harlan Cleveland, P. G. Thompson, C. B. Mathews, Harry G. Pounsford and Adam Gray. The capital stock is 100,000 dols. Cardboard and coated papers will be manufactured.

THE "WORLD'S" CONTRACT.—The *Paper Mill* announces that the Glens Falls Paper Mill Company have secured this contract, calling for 16,000 tons of white paper, which is the yearly consumption of the morning *World*, the evening *World*, the Sunday edition, and Pulitzer's *Post-Dispatch*, published in St. Louis. This 16,000 tons is divided up in this manner: the morning and evening editions require 30 tons a day; the Sunday edition requires 100 tons a week, and the *Post-Dispatch* requires 1,500 tons a year. The morning and evening editions will be printed upon a grade of paper slightly better than that it is now using. The Sunday edition will be printed on a standard grade, similar to that used by the *Herald*. There is a difference of one cent. a copy between the prices of the *World* and *Herald*, on week days. Therefore, it is hardly to be expected that the *World* would use as fine a grade of paper as the *Herald*, but as the Sunday editions are all five cents., the *World* proposes to use as fine a grade of paper as the *Herald*. As far as price is concerned, the only reference made is that it is several thousand dollars more than was paid last year for the same quantity.

THE High Falls Sulphite, Pulp and Mining Company, Potsdam, N. Y., have started their new plant near Canton.

THE Washougal Land and Logging Company have secured a contract for 1,000,000 feet of hemlock logs from the Williamette Paper and Pulp Mill Company, of Oregon City, Ore.

THE Jeffrey Manufacturing Company are installing an entire new plant for the Rumford Falls Paper Company, Rumford, Me., from start to finish, for the economical hauling of logs from the river some hundreds of feet to a suitable place convenient to the mill, to be used as wanted. One of the objects is to provide a reserve for use in winter, when the adjacent river freezes solid, although provided for the quick handling of logs at any time.

THE ASHLAND SULPHITE FIBRE CO., of Ashland, Wis., have received $10,000 as a bonus] from the local authorities.

MASCHINENBAUANSTALDT GOLZERN (formerly Gottschald and Nötzli), in Golzern. —The accounts up to June 30th, 1893, show a profit of M211,232 on a share capital of M900,000, which is to be divided as follows:—Written off, M35,680; placed in reserve, M25,000; first dividend of 4 per cent., M36,000; bonuses, M29,956; super-dividend, 7 per cent., M63,000; suspension account, M10,000; benevolence fund, M5,000; gratifications, school fee, &c., M5,000; balance carried forward, M1,593. The total dividend comes, therefore, to 11 per cent.

THE NEUMMANN AND ESSER Engineering Works in Aachen, Rhen, Prussia, have come into the sole possession of Herr Oscar Peters.

HERREN I. L. LECHNER AND CO. have bought the ground wood factory, Beilhackmühle, in Prien-o/-Chiemsee, and will continue it under the firm, Holzschleiferei Beilhackmühle I. L. Lechner and Co. Herr I. L. Lechner will undertake the general management.

HERR LOUIS LEO, late partner of the firm, P. Lempenau and Co., in Höfen-o/-Enz, died lately at Stuttgart, in his 50th year.

THE AGRARIAN PARTY IN THE GERMAN PARLIAMENT is greatly opposed to free trade in any shape and form and uses every possible opportunity to create dissatisfaction with the existing commercial treaties. The lately concluded treaties with Austria and Italy are their special aversion. As they are not strong enough to force the Government to cancel them, they make the most of complaints, which some interested parties may raise here and there. Among others many papermakers grumble that Austrian paper is underselling theirs in Germany, while they themselves cannot find a market in Austria to make up for their loss. Some other trades have with more or less reason criticised these treaties, but of course the great point with the Agrarians is to prevent any importation of grain, and they now try to prevent a conclusion of a treaty with Russia, because this is the principal article which Russia exports to Germany. Whether they will ultimately succeed in their object, this much can safely be said that the chances of a free trade policy are not very strong in Germany at the present moment, though perhaps the present moderate duties will not be raised in spite of all this active propaganda.

Hasseröder Maschinen Papierfabrik, Hasserode-o/Harz. Herr Robert Jaeger has retired and Herr Rudolf Türk has been appointed a member of the board of directors.

Berlin Fair.—The project of holding regular fairs in Berlin appears to have been definitely adopted, as 400 firms taking an interest in the scheme met in Berlin lately, and arrangements have been made for holding a spring fair at the City Hotel. For later on a building is to be erected, and among 21 offers of a suitable site five have been taken into consideration. The plans show accommodation for 1,000 exhibitors, refreshment rooms, gardens, &c. The costs of this palatial building are estimated at 4½ million marks, of which a bank will advance 3 millions on mortgage. The remaining 1½ millions are expected to be taken up by a limited liabilily company, issuing shares of 1,000 marks each. There are to be two fairs per annum, one in spring and one in autumn. During the time of the year, when there are no fairs open, the locality is to be let out in small lots to manufacturers keeping stock in Berlin. It is expected that there will be a sufficient demand for the offered facilities.

Dorstener Papierfabrik Actien Gesellschaft, in Dorsten, with a share capital of M225,000, shows no profit in the balance 1892-93. For new buildings and new machinery M116,435 have been expended.

Papierfabrik Lomnitz Hoffmann and Schramm, has come into the sole possession of Herr Georg Hoffmann, who has placed the technical management into the hands of Herr Carl Eichhorn, formerly at Fockendorf, who signs per procuration.

Thodesche Papierfabrik Actien Gesselschaft, in Hainsberg.—The new rules of this company have been approved by the general meeting. The capital has been reduced from M2,700,000 to M1,800,000 in shares of M300 each, of which there are 6,000.

PAPER IMPORTS.

FOR THE WEEK ENDING TUESDAY.

BELGIUM ...	1163 bales	HOLLAND ...	149 cases
"	186 cases	"	1504 rolls
DENMARK ...	6 bales	NORWAY ...	1988 bales
FRANCE ...	1498 "	PRUSSIA ...	191 "
" ...	126 cases	SWEDEN ...	7189 "
GERMANY ...	1620 bales	" ...	170 rolls
"	54 cases	U.S.A.	243 bales
HOLLAND ...	5465 bales	"	60 cases

Including the Following:

Quantity	From	Importer	Port.
41 bales	Christiania	Alsing & Co	London
25 "	"	Christophersen & Co	"
46 "	"	E. Lloyd	"
127 "	"	Saunders & Son	"
151 "	"	J. Hamilton	"
39 "	"	J. Spicer & Sons	"
9 "	"	F. G. Poulger	"
127 "	"	Crabb & Co	"
108 "	"	C. Morgan & Co	"
13 "	"	R. L. Lundgren	"
43 "	"	Colley & Co	"
13 "	"	W. D. Edwards & Co	"
106 "	"	H. Puckert & Co	"
72 "	Christiansand	J. Spicer & Sons	"
56 "	Danzig	Huber & Co	"
799 "	Gothenburg	Schenkenwald & Co	"
14 "	"	D. Gulland	"
1196 "	"	Hummell & Co	"
10 "	"	O. Schotiz	"
792 "	"	Prprs. Dowgate Dk.	"
28 "	"	Brooks Whf.	"
80 "	"	Tegner & Co	"
200 "	"	C. Poulter	"
128 "	"	E. & E. Sabel	"
182 "	Helsingfors	J. Spicer & Sons	"
271 "	"	W. D. Edwards	"
49 "	"	Becker & Ulrich	"
29 "	"	Crabb & Co	"
18 "	"	Hummell & Sons	"
55 cases	New York	Maw, Son & Co	"
1664 bales	Norrkoping	Prop. Dowgate Dk.	"
171 "	"	J. Spicer & Sons	"
66 "	"	Brooks Whf.	"
134 "	Stettin	Becker & Ulrich	"
9 "	"	J. Dickinson	"
33 "	"	J. Spicer & Son	"

PAPER EXPORTS.

FOR THE WEEK ENDING TUESDAY.

	Printings.	Writings.	Other Kinds.
AUSTRALIA	892 cwts.	1909 cwts.	1045 cwts.
AFRICA	49 "	4 "	7 "
ARGENTINE ...	14 "	107 "	12 "
BELGIUM	3 "	— "	10 "
B. WEST INDIES...	— "	— "	5 "
B. GUIANA	55 "	37 "	4 "
CAPE COLONY ...	146 "	118 "	56 "
CANADA	10 "	1456 "	— "
CHINA	276 "	202 "	20 "
DENMARK	7 "	2 "	2 "
EGYPT	2 "	— "	127 "
FRANCE	15 "	135 "	22 "
GERMANY	— "	— "	50 "
HOLLAND	— "	1 "	19 "
INDIA	344 "	181 "	82 "
ITALY	— "	20 "	— "
JAPAN	— "	9 "	— "
NEW ZEALAND ...	95 "	453 "	125 "
NEWFOUNDLAND	— "	9 "	— "
NORWAY	— "	— "	5 "
PORTUGAL	— "	— "	35 "
SPAIN	8 "	351 "	82 "
S. AMERICA... ...	70 "	— "	— "
SWEDEN	— "	— "	4 "
TURKEY	2 "	12 "	— "
U.S.A.	— "	25 "	1 "
W. INDIES	— "	— "	17 "

Printed and Published EVERY FRIDAY

AT 58, SHOE LANE, LONDON, E.C.,

By W. JOHN STONHILL.

ESTABLISHED 1878.

FRIDAY, DECEMBER 8, 1893.

WE are glad to notice that there is now some likelihood of more activity and practical work on the part of the Papermakers' Association. Papermakers will have received a letter from Mr. Lewis Evans, the chairman of the committee, pointing out the objects and aims of the Association, and if these are prosecuted with energy the support of the trade will be merited, and our remarks on the lackadaisical condition of the past will not have been in vain. Mr. C. Humphreys-Davies has been appointed honorary secretary.

IT is pleasing to record, especially in these days of factious discontent, such amicable relations as were demonstrated between employers and employed at the celebrations in honour of the coming of age of Mr. William Nimmo Tod, at Lasswade, last week. From the report we publish on another page it will be seen that the workpeople were not slow to take advantage of the auspicious event to show their appreciation and respect. The remarks made and feeling shown by Mr. William Tod indicate him to be "a worthy son of a worthy sire." His father, Mr. John Tod ("John Strathesk"), is a most popular man amongst all classes, and many in the paper trade know well his genial and enthusiastic nature, and not a few have cause to remember his liberality and kindly advice. As Mr. McMaster aptly put it, the son gave promise of being a "chip of the old block," and, therefore, with such cordial relationships existing the workpeople at Messrs. Tod's mills comprise "a happy family."

SOME interesting statistics were furnished by the secretary of the Norwegian section of the Scandinavian Wood Pulp Union at the recent meeting held at Gothenburg. The whole production for 1893 was estimated to amount to 100,834 tons of pine pulp, calculated dry; against 87,815 tons in 1892. Of this year's production only 1,600 dry tons were unsold on the 1st of October, against 4,886 tons in 1892, and 5,398 tons in 1891. Of next year's production there was sold on the 1st October last 73,300 tons dry, against 33,000 tons dry on the 1st October, 1892, of this year's production. The prices agreed upon were £2 10s. for pine pulp, 50 per cent. moisture, and £5 5s. dry pine, free on board Norway. According to the information sent us by a correspondent several new mills are now being built in Norway as well as in Sweden, and we shall probably see a drop in prices for contracts over 1895. Before that time, however, we see no reason why prices should undergo much alteration. Frost has set in very early and should it continue, which seems likely, many mills may find it difficult to fulfil contracts for this and next year owing to scarcity of water.

THE American paper trade is still under the spell of depression, and failures are of frequent occurrence. Doubtless the future indicates an improvement, but progress is very slow indeed. The unsettled condition of trade has been severely felt by paperstock men, and the present spasmodic business is not at all exhilarating. According to Mr. F. G. Clergue, president of the Penobscot Pulp and Paper Co., Bangor, Maine, the lack of American demand resulted in shipments of wood pulp by his company to Europe. Personally he has no faith in continuous business owing to expenses of freight, &c. Mr. K. B. Fullerton, however, of the Manufacturers Paper Company, of New York, whilst deploring the small demand for mechanical in America, states the export call to be brisk and that his company were doing a good English trade. He further said they had enquiries from France, Germany and Spain, but he admitted the trouble of sending pulp to France in consequence of the duty on the weight, making no allowance at all for moisture, a condition naturally objected to as they had to pay a duty on 40 per cent., 50 per cent., or 60 per cent. of water. It must be remembered that the Manufacturers' Paper Company are authorised to sell for the Laurentide Paper

Company, Limited, a Canadian mill. Our imports certainly show more pulp from Canada than America, this week's list including 7,150 bales from Halifax, per s. Demara, for London, whilst no arrivals are registered from the States. We understand, however, that the Moosehead Pulp and Paper Company, of Solon, Me., are developing an export business with Europe.

AN emphatic declaration for modified free trade was made by President Cleveland in his message to Congress on Monday. Judging from his remark that "only the necessary revenue justifies the imposition of tariff duties," he apparently has faith in the principles of free trade. Naturally the interests of the American citizen come first, and the taxes to be taken off the raw material is because the "high tariff forbids to American manufacturers as cheap materials as those used by their competitors." In answer to the statement made by Mr. McKinley that the wages of the working classes will be reduced by the new tariff, Mr. Cleveland says:—"It is quite obvious that the enhancement of the price of our manufactured products resulting from this policy not only confines the market for these products within our own borders, to the direct disadvantage of our manufacturers, but also increases their cost to our citizens." What the fate of the Bill may be it is now impossible to conjecture, but it is probable that the Committee of Ways and Means will not finish their consideration until next week.

ALL classes of manufacturers in Germany view with satisfaction the proposed American tariff reform. As the duty is to be *ad valorem*, and probably lowered all round, they expect to benefit by the change, and hope the prosperous times, which ruled before the McKinley tariff, will be current again. Notwithstanding the active opposition of American wood pulp manufacturers, German producers of sulphite anticipate a greater demand for the States, and raw material merchants generally hope to be considerably benefited on the prospect of materials being admitted free.

THE Sunday rest question in Germany is still engaging general attention, and papermakers in particular are fighting about it. One section wants to extend the rest to 36 hours, but to this proposal there is considerable resistance, especially on the grounds that the day only consists of 24 hours, and that a longer period cannot very well be enforced. On the whole papermakers do not want to go below 12 hours, and the plea for total exemption is now not heard very much of. A restriction of production is, however, being advocated, but it is thought that this should be subjected to temporary requirements without permanently fixing the production at too low a figure. In the latter case, if the working hours were curtailed, the manufacturers would proceed to put up additional machinery and then the evil instead of being remedied would probably be accelerated. The wisdom of the Government in providing the needful rest for the workers is now admitted.

THERE is no end to exhibitions. Preparations are now actively being made for the Antwerp International Exhibition, 1894, by Mr. G. De Courcy Perry, the Commissioner General, and an influential committee. The promoters point out that the success of the Universal Exhibition of 1885 caused public attention to be directed to the old Flemish City as a trading centre, and that owing to its geographical position it is favourably situated for a large transit trade. There is also an International Workmen's Exhibition to be held in Milan next year. The committee have informed the Italian Chamber of Commerce in London, incorporated, that they will defray the cost of carriage of duly-admitted exhibits from the United Kingdom to the exhibition premises in Milan, and *vice versa*, provided such exhibits are sent through the carriers appointed by the committee, whose name will be communicated by the committee to exhibitors on application.

To find new markets was one of the suggestions given as a cure for the difficulty of want of employment by Mr. J. Chamberlain, M.P., to a deputatien of unemployed workmen which waited upon him on Monday last, at Westminster. He said our products were being excluded from the neutral markets by foreign competition, and at the same time were shut out from the markets of those competing Powers by their policy of protection.

World's Paper Trade Review Office,
58, Shoe Lane, London, E.C.
December 7, 1893.

MARKET REPORT

and RECORD of IMPORTS

Of Foreign Rags, Wood Pulp, Esparto, Paper, Millboards, Strawboards, &c., at the Ports of London Liverpool, Southampton, Bristol, Hull, Fleetwood, Middlesborough, Glasgow, Grangemouth, Granton, Dundee, Leith, Dover, Folkestone, and Newhaven, for the WEEK ENDING DECEMBER 6.

From SPECIAL Sources and Telegrams.

Telegrams—"STONHILL, LONDON."

CHEMICALS.—In chemicals speculation exists as to the effect on the trade owing to the changes proposed in the duties on chemicals in the United States; as yet the prices are unaffected. The demand for pure ALKALI continues good. BLEACHING POWDER is offered at from £7 15s. to £8, and CAUSTIC SODA 70% f.o.b. Tyne. shows a rise at £9 15s. SULPHUR evidences a lowering tendency at from £4 2s. 6d. to £4 5s. SODA CRYSTALS are dull at £2 5s.

Prices are nominally as follows:

Article	Packing	Terms	Disc.	£	s.	d.
Alkali, 58%	tierces ...	f.o.r. works	2½%	4	5	0
,, 58%	bags ...	,, ,,	2½%	4	0	0
58%	... ...	f.o.b. Liverpool	2½%	4	7	6
Alum (Ground),	tierces ...	,, Liverpool	2½%	5	7	6
,, ,,	barrels ...	,, ,,	2½%	5	17	6
,, ,,	tierces ...	,, Hull	2½%	5	5	0
,, ,,	,, ...	Goole	2½%	5	5	0
Alum (Lump)	,, ...	f.o.b. Liverpool	2½%	4	17	6
,, ,,	barrels ...	,, ,,	2½%	5	0	0
,, ,,	tierces ...	,, Hull	2½%	4	15	0
,, ,,	,, ...	Goole	2½%	4	15	0
,, ,,	,, ...	London	2½%	5	5	0
,, ,,	,, ...	f.a.s. Glasgow	2½%	5	5	0
Alumina Sulphate,	casks	f.o.b. Tyne		4	2	6
,, ,,	bags	,, ,,		3	17	6
Aluminoferric Cake,	slabs	Liverpool ...	...	2	15	0
,, ,,	tierces	,, ...	...	3	2	6
Alumina Cake,	slabs ...	Glasgow	...	2	15	0
,, ,,	tierces ...	,,	...	3	2	6
Aluminous Cake,	casks ...	Manchester	3½%	2	7	6
,, ,,	,, ...	Newcastle	2½%	2	10	0
,, ,,	,, ...	London	2½%	3	0	0
,, ,,	bags ...	,,	2½%	2	17	9
Blanc Fixe ...	... ...	f.o.b. Tyne	net	7	10	0
Bleach, 35%	... ...	,, ,,	net	7	15	0
,, (soft wood)	...	f.o.r. Lancs.	net	8	2	6
,, (hard wood)	...	f.o.b. Liverpool	net	8	10	0
... ...	...	landed London	2½%	9	0	0
Borax (crystals)	... ...	... ...	net	29	0	0
powdered	... ...	... .	net	30	0	0
Chloride of Barium	...	f.o.b. Tyne	net	7	10	0
Caustic White 76-77%	...	f.o.r. Newcastle	net	11	5	0
,, 77%	f.o.r. or	f.o.b. Tyne	net	11	10	0
,, 74%	...	f.o.b. Liverpool	net	11	0	0
,, 70%	...	,, ,,	net	10	0	0
,, 70%	...	,, Hull	net	10	5	0
,, 70%	...	f.o.r. London	net	10	0	0
,, 70%	...	f.o.b. Tyne	net	9	15	0
,, 70%	...	f.o.r. Lancs.,	net	9	17	6
,, 70%	...	,, London	net	10	0	0
,, 60%	...	f.o.b. Liverpool	net	9	0	0
Caustic Cream, 60%	...	f.o.r. Lancs.	net	9	2	6
,, ,, 60%	...	f.o.b. Liverpool	net	9	7	6
,, Bottoms	...	,, ,,	net	6	15	0
,, ...	...	f.o.b. Tyne	net	6	15	0
Carbonat'd Ash 58%	...	,, ,,	net	4	10	0
48%	...	,, ,,	net	4	0	0
,, 58%	...	f.o.r. Widnes	net	4	7	6
,, 48%	...	,, ,,	net	3	17	6
Hypo-Sulphite of Soda...		f.o.r Tyne		5	5	0
,, ,,	10-ton lots	ex ship Liverp'l	net	5	11	3
Oxalic Acid ...	... ...	f.o.b. Liverpool	3½%	per lb		[illegible]
Salt Cake ...	... ...	,, works	net	1	10	0
Soda Ash, 52%	... ...	f.o.b. Tyne	net	4	0	0
,, 58%	... ...	ex ship Thames	1%	4	10	0
,, 52%	... ...	f.o.b. Liverpool	1%	4	5	0
Soda Crystals	... ...	,, Tyne	net	2	5	0
,, ,,	... ...	ex ship Thames	2½%	2	15	0
,, ,,	... ...	f.o.b. Liverpool	net	3	5	0
Sulphur, roll	... ...	f.o.r. works	2½%	7	17	6
,, flowers	... ...	,, ,,	2½%	9	10	0
,, recovered	...	,, ,,	2½%	4	2	6
Sulphate of Ammonia	,,	,, ,,	2½%	13	0	0
,, of Copper	...	,, Liverpool	5%	16	0	0

FOREIGN.—F.o.b. Continental port:

Article	£	s.	d.
Alkali, 58% 2-cwt. bags £4 10/0; 10-cwt. casks ...	5	10	0
Caustic Soda, 70-72%	10	12	6
Hypo-Sulphite of Soda 10-ton lots casks	5	10	0
Sulphate of Alumina 7-8 cwt. casks net c.i.f. Ldn	4	7	6
Blanc Fixe (c.i.f. London)	7	12	6

ESPARTO.—The enquiry is again better both for spot and distant fulfilment, and a moderate business is being carried through at former quotations.

Prices c.i.f. London and Leith, or f.o.r. Cardiff, Garston and Tyne Docks are nominally as follows:

Description	£	s.	d.		£	s.	d.
Spanish—Fair to Good	£5	5	0	to	5	10	0
,, Fine to Best	5	10	0	,,	5	15	0
Oran — Fair to Good	3	5	0	,,	3	10	0
,, First Quality...	3	15	0	,,	3	17	6
Tripoli — Hand-picked	3	15	0	,,	3	17	6
,, Fair Average	3	7	6	,,	3	10	0
Bona & Philippeville	3	15	0	,,	3	17	6

WEEK'S IMPORTS.

Quantity	From	Importer	Port.
6951 bales	Aguilas	C. J. Turcan & Co.	Leith
1955 tons	Oran	To order	Liverpool
809 ,,	,,	Mackie, Koth & Co	Granton

STRAW.—Market quiet.

WEEK'S IMPORTS.

(Purposes unspecified) at principal Ports From

BELGIUM ...	130 bales	HOLLAND ...	1467 bales
DENMARK ...	391 ,,	U.S.A.	489 ,,

STRAW PULPS. — Moderate trade being transacted.

Prices, c.i.f. London, Hull or Leith:

German, 50 to 55% moisture £16 10 0
do. dry, ... No. 1 £16 10 0; No. 2 15 0

CHEMICAL WOOD PULPS.—Business is quiet, papermakers being slow to contract. SULPHITE, however, keeps firm, especially for the best grades. SULPHATE quiet.

Prices, ex steamer, London, Hull, Newcastle, Leith and Glasgow are nominally as follows:

Description	£	s.	d.		£	s.	d.
SULPHITE, Unbleached, Common	£10	0	0	to	11	0	0
,, Superior	11	0	0	,,	12	10	0
,, ,, 50% moisture, d.w.	11	0	0	,,	12	0	0
,, Extra	12	0	0	,,	13	0	0
,, Bleached, moist					16	10	0
,, Unbleached, English, del. Lancs. ...					10	15	0
,, ,, ,, No. 1, ex mills, Ldn.					10	10	0
,, ,, ,, No. 2. ,, ,,					9	15	0
SODA, Unbleached, Common ...	10	5	0	,,	10	10	0
,, ,, Extra... ...	10	10	0	,,	11	0	0
,, Half-Bleached	12	10	0	,,	14	0	0
SULPHATE, Unbleached, Common	10	10	0	,,	11	0	0
,, Extra	11	0	0	,,	12	0	0
,, Half-Bleached	13	10	0	,,	14	0	0
Bleached	15	0	0	,,	16	0	0

MECHANICAL WOOD PULPS.— The demand is rather quiet; prices, however, are well maintained. With an increased production in Scandinavia it is not anticipated that American pulp will gain a footing in Europe. Arrivals of Canadian pulp are frequently registered in our list of imports.

Prices, ex steamer, London, Hull, Newcastle, Leith and Glasgow are nominally as follows:

MECHANICAL, Aspen, Dry ...	£7 10 0	to 8 0 0
Pine, Dry	6 0 0	,, 7 0 0
Pine, Moist	3 0 0	,, 3 10 0
Moist Brown	3 2 6	,, 3 5 0
Single Sorted	2 7 6	,, 2 10 0
Dry Brown	6 5 0	,, 6 10 0

WEEK'S IMPORTS.

Quantity	From	Importer	Port.
618 bales	Bergen	To order	Hull
500 ,,	Christiania	,,	,,
1244 ,,	,,	,,	,,
2200 ,,	,,	H. B. Wood	Fleetwood
100 ,,	,,	Christophersen & Co	London
405 ,,	,,	Henderson & Co	,,
246 ,,	,,	Taylor and Co	,,
3656 ,,	,,	M. G. Skramnes	,,
695 ,,	Christiansand	J. Currie & Co	Leith
1500 ,,	Drontheim	To order	Grangemouth
360 ,,	,,	,,	,,
480 ,,	,,	,,	Hull
360 ,,	,,	,,	Grangemouth
710 tons	Drammen	,,	Liverpool
850 bales	,,	H. Newall & Son	Fleetwood
1207 ,,	,,	G. Schjoth & Co	,,
342 tons	Gothenburg	To order	London
2262 bales	,,	,,	Hull
936 ,,	,,	,,	Leith
101 ,,	Ghent	,,	London
7150	Halifax	,,	,,
400 ,,	Hambro	,,	,,
800 ,,	,,	,,	,,
500 ,,	,,	,,	,,
191 ,,	,,	,,	,,
1050 ,,	,,	,,	Leith
300 ,,	Norrkoping	Johnston & Co	London
160 ,,	,,	Christophersen & Co	,,
600 ,,	Oporto	To order	,,
52 ,,	Rotterdam	,,	Grangemouth
458 ,,	,,	,,	London
270 ,,	,,	,,	,,
172 ,,	,,	,,	Liverpool
2085 ,,	Sannesund	Kellner-Partington	Fleetwood
125 ,,	Stettin	To order	London
2400 ,,	Skein	Skramnes	London
28 brls	Terneuzen	To order	,,

Totals from Each Country:

BELGIUM ..	101 bales	NORWAY ...	710 tons
CANADA ...	7150 ,,	PRUSSIA ...	125 bales
GERMANY ..	2851 ,,	PORTUGAL ...	600 ,,
HOLLAND ...	952 ,,	SWEDEN ...	3658 ,,
,, ...	28 brls.	,, ...	342 tons
NORWAY ...	18915 bales		

WEEK'S IMPORTS of WOOD PULP BOARDS.

Quantity	From	Importer	Port
184 bales	Helsingfors	To order	London
179 ,,	,,	P. D. Jones	,,

HOME RAGS.—Market quiet, and no improvement is expected during the remainder of 1893. Surat Tares show an advance at the present quotation of 5s. to 5s. 3d.

LONDON:

New White Cuttings	21/6	Canvas No. 1	15/0
Fines (selected)	20/6	,, No. 2 ...	9/6-10/6
,, (good London)...	20/0	,, No. 3	5/6
Outshots (selected) ...	12/6	Mixed Rope	5/3
,, (ordinary) ...	11/0	White Rope	6/6
London Seconds	3/6-4/0	White Manilla Rope	8/0
Country do. ...	6/6-8/0	Coil Rope	9/0
London Thirds ...	1/9-2/0	Bagging...	1/6
Country do. ...	3/0-4/0	Gunny	3/0-3/6
Light Prints ...	7/0-8/0		

BRISTOL:

Fines	19/0	Clean Canvas ...	15/0
Outshots	13/6	Second Do. ...	9/6-10/6
Seconds	7/0-8/0	Light Prints ...	8/0
Thirds	3/6-4/0	Hemp Coil Rope	9/6-10/0
Mixed Bagging	3/6	Tarred Manilla	7/6

MANCHESTER:

Fines	15/0-16/0	Blues	6/6-7/0
Outshots (best) ...	11/6-12/0	Bagging...	4/0-4/3
,, (ordinary)	10/6-11/0	,, (common)	3/0-3/3
Seconds	7/0-7/3	W. Manilla Rope	10/0-10/6
Thirds	3/6-3/9	Surat Tares... ...	4/9-5/0

EDINBURGH:

Superfines	16/6	Black Cottons	2/9
Outshots	13/0	W. Manilla Rope ...	8/9
Mixed Fines...	14/0	Tarred Ditto	6/6
Common Seconds ...	7/0	,, Hemp Rope...	8/3
First do.	10/0	Rope Ends (new) ...	8/6
Prints	5/6-6/6	,, ,, (old) ...	5/0
Canvas (best)	15/6	Bagging...	2/0-3/0
,, 2nd	10/0	,, (clean) ...	4/3-6/0

DUBLIN.

White Cuttings ...	18/0	Mill Bagging	3/0
Fines	11/0	White Manilla	8/0
Seconds...	5/0	Tarred Hemp	8/0
Light Prints	3/0	Rigging	13/6
Black do.	2/0	Mixed Ropes	3/6
Bagging	2/0		

FOREIGN RAGS.—On the Continent the demand is fairly good. Supplies are not plentiful, and severe weather will interfere with transit; on the other hand stocktaking lessens buying. Prices keep firm.

WEEK'S IMPORTS.

Quantity	From	Importer	Port.
135 bales	Amsterdam	To order	Hull
99 ,,	,,	,,	,,
20 ,,	Antwerp	,,	Liverpool
16 ,,	,,	,,	,,
28 ,,	Bordeaux	,,	,,
311 ,,	Copenhagen	,,	Hull
1 ,,	,,	,,	Leith
57 ,,	Christiania	,,	Hull
10 ,,	Calais	,,	London
58 ,,	Cherbourg	,,	Southampton
12 ,,	Ghent	,,	Liverpool
199 ,,	,,	,,	Hull
76 ,,	,,	,,	Leith
4 ,,	Guernsey	S.W. Ry. Co	Southampton
28 ,,	,,	To order	,,
50 ,,	Harlingen	,,	Hull
31 ,,	,,	,,	,,
14 ,,	,,	,,	Leith
5 ,,	Hambro	,,	,,
5 ,,	,,	,,	,,
4 ,,	,,	,,	Grangemouth
21 ,,	Jersey	,,	Southampton
70 ,,	Konigsberg	J. Currie & Co	Leith
103 ,,	,,	To order	Hull
153 ,,	Lisbon	,,	Liverpool
26 ,,	Melbourne	,,	,,
292 ,,	Ostend	,,	London
139 ,,	St. Malo	,,	Southampton
5 ,,	Smyrna	,,	Liverpool
50 ,,	St. Nazaire	,,	Newhaven
37 ,,	,,	,,	,,
20 ,,	Stettin	,,	Hull

Totals from Each Country:

AUSTRALIA...	26 bales	HOLLAND ..	712 bales
BELGIUM ...	323 ,,	NORWAY ...	57 ,,
CHANNEL Isles	53 ,,	PRUSSIA ...	123 ,,
DENMARK ...	312 ,,	SWEDEN ...	70 ,,
FRANCE ...	614 ,,	SPAIN ...	252 ,,
GERMANY ...	14 ,,	TURKEY ...	5 ,,

GERMAN RAGS.

STETTIN; C.i.f. Hull, Leith, Tyne and London.

SPFFF and SPFF	18/0	LFB (Blue)	
SPF	10/0	CSPFFF	16/0
FF	8/6	CSPFF	10/0
FG	9/0	CFB (Blue)	7/0
LFX	7/0	CFX (Coloured) ...	4/6

HAMBURG: F.o.b.

NWC	22/0	FF Grey Linens ...	9/0
SPFFF	22/0	LFX Second ditto...	8/0
SPFFF and SPFF	18/0	CSPFFF	17/3
SPFF	16/0	CSPFF	11/3
SPF	12/0	CFB	8/0
CCC	5/6	Dark Blues (selected	11/9
CFX	4/6	Wool Tares... ...	8/0
White Rope... ...	8/0	Jute, No. I 6/0; No. II	5/6

DUTCH RAGS. f.o.r. Hull:

C.i.f. Thames; Hull 2/6 per ton more; ditto f.o.r. Leith c.i.f. Glasgow 4/-; c.i.f. Liverpool 4/-.

Selected Fines (free from Muslins) ...	14/0	Best Grey Linens ...	9/0
		Common ditto ...	5/6
Selected Outshots	9/9	White Canvas ...	5/0
,, Dirty Fines	5/9	Grey & Brown Canvas	9/9
Light Cottons ...	9/3	Tarred Hemp Rope	8/0
Blue Cottons ...	7/6	Ditto (broken) ...	5/3
Dark Coloured Cottons	2/6	White Paper Shavings	7/9
New Cuttings (Bleachd)	22/6	Gunny (best) ...	4/9
,, (Unbleached)	19/6	Jute Bagging ...	3/6
,, (Slate) ...	9/0	Ditto (common ...	3/0
Muslins	8/0	Tarpaulins	4/0
Red Cottons (Mixed)	5/9	Cowhair Carpets ...	2/9
Fustians (Light browns)	5/3	Hard ditto	3/0

FRENCH RAGS.

Quotations range, per cwt., ex ship London, Southampton, or Hull; 2/0 per ton more at Liverpool, and 10/0 per ton higher at Newcastle, Glasgow or Leith.

French Linens, I ...	22/0	Black Cotton ...	4/0
II 18/6; III ...	14/6	Marseilles Whites, I	16/0
White Cottons, I ...	19/0	II 10/0; III ...	7/6
II 15/0; III ...	12/6	Blue Cotton	11/0
Knitted Cotton ...	11/0	Light Prints... ...	9/0
Light Coloured Cotton	8/0	Mixed Prints ...	6/0
Blue Cotton	9/6	New White Cuttings	23/0
Coloured Cotton ...	6/0	,, Stay ,,	21/0

BELGIAN RAGS.

F.o.b. Ghent. Freights: London, 5/0; Hull and Goole, 7/6 Liverpool and Leith, 10/0; Newcastle, 12/6; Dundee and Aberdeen, 15/0; Glasgow, 16/8.

White Linens No. 1	22/6	Fustians (Light) ...	6/0
,, ,, No. 2	16/0	,, (Dark) ...	4/0
,, ,, No. 3	13/0	Thirds...	3/0
Fines (Mixed) ...	12/0	Black Cottons ...	3/9
Grey Linens (strong)	9/6	Hemp Strings (unt'r'd)	2/0
,, ,, (extra)	14/0	House Cloths ...	4/0
Blue Linens... ...	8/6	Old Bagging (solid)	3/6
White Cottons S'p'fine	18/0	,, ,, (common)	2/6
,, ,, No. 2	15/0	NEW.	
Outshots No. 3 ...	10/0	White & Cream Linens	35/0
Seconds No. 4 ...	8/0	White Cuttings ...	22/0
Prints (Light) ...	8/6	Unbleached Cuttings	21/0
,, (Old)	4/6	Print Cuttings ..	8

BELGIAN FLAX and HEMP WASTE.

Best washed and dried Flax Waste, 10/0; Fair ditto	9/0
Flax Spinners' Waste (grease boiled out)... ...	10/0
Hemp Waste, No. 1 9/0; No. 2	7/6
Flax Spinners' Waste, No. 1 (Flax Rove) 10/0: No. 2	8/6

RUSSIAN RAGS.

C.i.f. London, Hull, Newcastle or Leith.

SPFF	16/0	CC (Cotton	4/3
SPF	14/6	Jute I	3/3
FG	11/6	,, II...	2/6
LFB	9/6	Rope I...	8/6
FF	8/3	,, II	5/0

NORWEGIAN RAGS.

C.i.f. London, Hull, Tyne, and Grangemouth.

1st Rope (tarred) ...	8/6-9/0	2nd Canvas ...	8/0
2nd ,, ,, ...	5/6-6/0	Jute Bagging	
Manilla Rope (white)	8/0-8/9	Gunny ...	3/0 3/6
Best Canvas ...	11/9-12/0	Mixed ...	2/6-2/9

WASTE PAPERS.—The market is steady. and prices unchanged.

Cream Shavings ...	12/3	Small Letters	5/0
Fine ,, ...	9/6	Large ,, ...	7/0
Mixed ,, ...	2/0	Brown Paper	2/9
White Printings ...	8/9	Light Browns	2/9
White Waste ...	1/6	Books & Pamphlets ...	6/0
Wood Pulp Cuttings	3/6	Strawboard Cuttings	1/6
Brown Paper	3/0	Jacquards	2/6
Crushed News	2/0		

For Export: 25/- per ton extra.

JUTE.—Firmer, with a good trade at hardening prices. Cuttings are in request.

Good White	£17 10 to 18	Common ...	£13 to £14
Good	£17	Rejections ...	£9 ,, £10
Medium ..	£15 to £16	Cuttings ...	£5 10 ,, £7

COLOURS.—Business dull; prices unaltered.

Mineral Black ...	cwt.	3/0	Ultramarine (pure)		
do. superior ...	..	5/0	... cwt.	40/0 to 45/0	
Pure Ivory Black	,,	12/0	PASTE COLOURS with 60% of colour, as follows:		
Ochre	,,	3/0			
French J. C. Ochre	ton	55/0	Orange Pulp ...	cwt.	40/0
Chrome (pure) ...	cwt.	40/0	Golden Yellow Pulp		36/0
Red Oxide	,,	4/6	Lemon ,, ,,	cwt.	36/0
Umber, Devonshire	,,	50/0	Prussian Yellow ,,		36/0
do. Turkish ...	,,	40/0	Green (free of arsenic		36/0
Lamp Black ...		7/0-10/6	Paste Blue (20-45%)		
Cochineal	lb.	1/3-2/0	.. ...		23/6-24/6

SIZING.—There is no change in values, but the market is firm, and the outlook for the coming year fairly good; the tendency is certainly upwards.

English Gelatines	per cwt.	70/0 to 140/0
Foreign ,, ...	,,	70/0 ,, 140/0
Fine Skin Glues	,,	45/0 ,, 60/0
Long Scotch Glues	,,	45/0 ,, 60/0
Common ,, ...	,,	30/0 ,, 45/0
"Town" Glues	,,	26/0 ,, 36/0
"Bone" Glues	,,	20/0 ,, 30/0
Foreign Glues	,,	23/0 ,, 40/
Bone Size	,,	4/0 ,, 10/0
Gelatine Size...	,,	5/0 ,, 10/0
Dry B.A. Pieces	,,	33/6 ,, 36/0
,, English Pieces	,,	24/0 ,, 26/0
Wet ,, ,, ...	,,	5/0 ,, 6/0
,, Sheep Pieces	,,	3/0 ,, 4/0
Buffalo Hide Shavings	,,	25/0 ,, 34/0
,, Picker Waste	,,	25/0 ,, 34/0

STARCH.—There is a better demand for some grades and prices are easier. Maize crisp is quoted at £9, powder at £9 5s. Prime Farina is offered at £9 10s.'

F.o.r. London, less 2½%:

Maize—Crisp, £9 0/-; Powder, £9 5/-; Special £14.
Farina—Prime, £9 10/-; B.K.M.F., £12.

Delivered:

Rice—Special (in chests), £20 (net); Crystal (in bags) £19; Granulated (in bags) £18 less 2½%.
Dextrine—£15 to £16.

ROSIN.—There is a good demand at former quotations.

MINERALS.—CHINA CLAY is unaltered, contracts for 1894 being made at much the same prices as formerly. FRENCH CHALK is in good request and prices firm. MINERAL WHITE and PATENT HARDENINGS are in steady request. BARYTES quiet.

China Clay, in bulk, f.o.b. Cornwall, 14/0 to 27/6; bags 5/0 and casks 9/6 per ton extra; f.o.b. London, in casks 35/0 to 50/0 per ton.

Mineral White (Terra Alba), per ton f.o.r. or boat at works:

Superfine...	28/0	less 2½%
Pottery Super.... ...	24/0	,,
Ball Seconds	20/0	,,
Seconds	15/0	,,
Thirds	10/6	,,

Superfine Hardening, f.o.r. works, 40/0.
Patent Crystal Hardening, delivered at mills £3 to £3 15/0
Patent Hardening (2 ton lots) f.o.r. Lancs., £3 5/0.
,, ,, (5 ton lots) f.o.b. Liverpool, £3 10/0.
Magnesite (in lump) 32/6 per ton.
Magnesite (containing 98% Carbonate of Magnesia), raw ground, £6 10/0; calcined ground, £12 10/0.
Albarine, £3, del. mills.
Asbestos, best rock, £18; brown grades, £14 to £15
Asbestine Pulp, £4 5/- to £5 c.i.f. London, Liverpool and Glasgow.
Barytes (Carbonate), lump, 90/0 to 95/0; nuts, 72/6 to 85/0.
French and Italian Chalk (Souheur Brand), per ton in lots of 10 tons: Flower O, 69/6 c.i.f. London; Flower OO, 62/0, Flower OOO, 55/6. Swan White, 63/0; Snow White, 95/0; Snow White XX, 89/0. Blackwell's "Angel White" Brand and "Silvery" 90/- to 92/6; prime quality, 90/- to 95/-; and superfine, 105/-.

DIRECTORY.

Names and Addresses under this heading will be charged for at the rate of 30/- per annum (52 insertions) for each card of two lines or under. Each additional line £1 extra.

ALUMINOUS CAKE.

The ALUM, CHINA CLAY and VITRIOL Co., Lim., 63, Queen Victoria Street, London, E.C. Works: Mainham-on-Thames. Telegrams—"Chinnock, London.

ANALYTICAL.

WILLIAMS, ROWLAND, F.I.C., F.C.S., 28, Pall Mall, Manchester.

ARTESIAN WELLS.

BATCHELOR, Richard D., Artesian and Consulting Well Engineer, 73, Queen Victoria Street, London, E.C., and at Chatham. 5713

ISLER, C., & Co., Bear Lane, Southwark, S.E

LE GRAND & SUTCLIFF, Magdala Works, 125, Bunhill Row, E.C.

BOILER COVERING.

LONSDALES, Boiler Coverers, Blackburn, will send a sample cask of their Patent Plastic Cork Covering to any Paper Mill in Great Britain—5 cwt. cask for 25/- (carriage paid).

CHINA-CLAY.

The ALUM, CHINA CLAY and VITRIOL Co., Lim., 63, Queen Victoria Street, London, E.C. Mines: Ruddle and Colchester, St. Austell, Cornwall. Telegrams—"Chinnock, London."

ROGERS, J., & Co., Truro, Cornwall.—Agents: Taylor, Sommerville & Co., 83, Queen Victoria Street, E.C., and at 16, Princes Street, Edinburgh.

W. SINGLETON BIRCH & SONS, Lim., 15, Upton Street, Manchester. Mines: Rosevear, St. Austell, Cornwall. 2276

COLOURS.

CARDWELL, J. L., & Co., Commercial Buildings, 15 Cross Street, Manchester. Specialties: Mineral Black, Ven. Red, Ochres and Umbers. 5304

GEMMILL, W. N., & Co., Glasgow, Telegrams "Ruhe." Starches, Alumina, Antifroths, &c. All Paper Colours

COLOURS (Continued).

HINSHELWOOD, THOMAS, & Co., The Glasgow Colour Works, Glasgow. Colours and shades matched exactly.

MULLER, A. E., 9, Fenchurch Street, London, E.C.

ESPARTO.

IDE & CHRISTIE, Fibre, Esparto, and General Produce Brokers, 72, Mark Lane, E.C.

MINERAL WHITE or TERRA ALBA.

WINSER & Co., Portland Mills, Princess Street, Manchester. Also manufacturers of Aluminous Cake.

HOWE, JOHN, & Co., Carlisle. 5119

STEEL.

MAKIN, WM., & SONS, Sheffield. Established 1736. Roll Bars, Plates, Cutter Knives, Doctor Blades, &c. 5369

STRAW.

UNDERWOOD, E., & SON, Limited, Brentford, London, W. Press-packed Oat, Wheat, or Rye Straw, delivered to the chief British ports or railway stations.

TALC (French and Italian Chalk).

SOUHEUR, JEAN, Antwerp. All Minerals, Blanc de Silex, Barytes (superior and common), Carbonate of Lime, Blacklead, &c. British Agent: A. E. Muller, 9, Fenchurch Street, London, E.C. Agent for Liverpool and Manchester: C. H. Austin, Ditton, near Widnes.

RAGS.

CHALMERS, E., & Co., Lim., Bonnington, Leith.

MULLER, A. E., 9, Fenchurch Street, London, E.C.

WERTHEIM, A., & Co., Hamburg.

UMBER.

The ALUM, CHINA CLAY and VITROIL Co., Lim. 63, Queen Victoria Street, London, E.C. Telegrams—"Chinnock, London."

WOOD PULP.

FRIIS, N., & Co., 18, Carl Johans Gade, Christiania, Norway.

GOTTSTEIN, H., & Co., 59, Mark Lane, London, E.C., and at New York.

GRANT, W., & Co., 17, Baltic Street, Leith. Agents for best shippers, Sulphite and Sulphate, Mechanical, Pine, Brown, Aspen.

MATTHIESSEN, CHR., Christiania, Norway.

MULLER, A. E., 9, Fenchurch Street, London, E.C.

The SULPHITE PULP Company, Limited, 82, Gordon Street, Glasgow.

WERTHEIM, A., & Co., Hamburg.

NEW PATENTS.

APPLICATIONS.

22,183. Cleansing rhea fibre. W. Johnstone and J. B. Day.

22,415. Improvements in machines for making millboard or pasteboard from wood pulp. D. Westad.

22,463. Improvements in or relating to pulp strainers of papermaking machines. D. N. Bertram.

22,532. Improvements in apparatus for impregnating lime with chlorine to form bleaching powder. A. Campbell, A. Walker and J. W. Walker.

SPECIFICATIONS PUBLISHED.

(7½d. each. By post 8d.)

1893.

5,585. Decomposing chloride of sodium, &c. Holland.

Special Prepaid Advertisements

IT IS IMPORTANT that Advertisements under any of the Headings mentioned below should reach us by the FIRST POST on WEDNESDAY Morning to INSURE INSERTION.

Charges for advertisements under the heading Situations Wanted are 1/- for twenty-four words, and One Penny per Word after. Minimum charge ONE SHILLING. Names and addresses to be paid for.

Advertisers by paying an extra fee of 6d. can have the replies addressed to the PAPER TRADE REVIEW under a number, and such replies will then be forwarded Post Free.

Advertisements appearing under the following headings:

Tenders.	Mills Wanted or To Let.
Sales by Auction.	Machinery Wanted or For Sale.
Businesses Wanted.	
Businesses for Disposal.	Situations Vacant.

Miscellaneous.

The charges are 3/- for fifty words or under; 1s. extra for every line or portion after. Ten words to be reckoned for each line. Names and addresses to be paid for. Payment must be made in advance, except where the advertiser has a running account, in which case the cost can be debited thereto.

Legal and Financial Announcements: 1/- per Line

Cheques and Post-office Orders to be CROSSED ——and Co., and made payable to W. JOHN STONHILL.

Situations Wanted.

ADVERTISER (21), having scientific education, and being about to complete his training in all departments of a first-class "white" mill, making fine printings and writings, desires to obtain the position of under-foreman in a good two-machine mill. References of the highest-class as to character and ability will be given by present principals.—Address No. 5913, office of the WORLD'S PAPER TRADE REVIEW, 58, Shoe-lane, London, E.C. 5913

CASHIER and Book-keeper in paper mill is desirous of a change; experienced in making out costs and general mill work; good references.—Apply No. 5932, office of the WORLD'S PAPER TRADE REVIEW, 58, Shoe Lane, London, E.C. 5932

CHEMICAL PLUMBER desires Re-engagement; 5 years in Wood Pulp Mills; first class references.—Address, No. 5,907, office of the WORLD'S PAPER TRADE REVIEW, 58, Shoe Lane, E.C. 5907

GENTLEMAN (40), at present manager of a superfine writing mill, desires a similar position; practical papermaker and good commercial buyer. Would go abroad if desired.—Address No. 5925, office of the WORLD'S PAPER TRADE REVIEW, 58, Shoe-lane, London E.C. 5925

MANAGER, thoroughly competent in all classes of Paper and Machinery, etc.; well up in the blending of fibres and mixing and matching of colours, desires Situation. Good testimonials as to character and ability.—Address, No. 5,908 office of the WORLD'S PAPER TRADE REVIEW, 58, Shoe Lane, London, E.C. 5908

TO PAPERMAKERS.—A gentleman, with large country connection, is open for additional commissions in writings, printings and news. Highest references.—Address No. 5934, office of the WORLD'S PAPER TRADE REVIEW, 58, Shoe Lane, London, E.C. 5934

TRAVELLER desires engagement; well acquainted with the English ground. Good references.—Address No. 5933. Office of the WORLD'S PAPER TRADE REVIEW, 58, Shoe-lane, London, E.C. 5933

Machinery for Sale.

ONE HYDRAULIC PRESS, second-hand, with Press Box 38 inches diam. by 32 inches deep, with wheels; all parts strong, Ram 2 feet 6 inches by 8 inch in diam.

ONE KOLLERGANG, new, Stones 51 inches by 14 inches, C.I. Pan, Scrapers, and Driving Gear.

TWELVE REVOLVING STRAINER PLATES, second-hand, 18¾ inches by 21 inches, class B2, 3½ cut.

REFINING ENGINE, new, Conical Type; same as one working in a large printing mill.

ONE INVICTA RAG CUTTER.

ONE RAG ENGINE TROUGH, 12 feet by 6 feet 6 inches by 24 inches and 27½ inches deep.

TWO RAG ENGINE TROUGHS, 14 feet 6 inches by 7 feet 6 inches by 27 inches and 32 inches deep.

FIFTEEN ELBOW PLATES for Rag Engines, 33 inches by 7 inches by 4½ inches deep, each having 22 Steel Bars.

ONE GRANITE STONE for Kollergang, chipped, 6 feet diameter by 18 inches broad.

ONE WROT IRON H BEAM, 24 feet long by 20 inches by 7 inches.

ONE DRYING CYLINDER CASTING, 48 inches diameter by 9 feet 3 inches long.

TWO M.I. SHAKE BARS, Two C.I. Soles and Rocking Supports.

☛ SECOND HAND ROLLS.

ONE COPPER ROLL, with ends, 6 feet 0½ inch long by 6 inches diameter.

ONE C.I. HOLLOW ROLL, 20 inches diameter by 96 inches long.

ONE C.I. HOLLOW ROLL, 12 inches diameter by 80 inches long.

ONE C.I. CALENDER ROLL, 11 inches diameter by 78 inches long.

THREE C.I. SOLID ROLLS, 12½ inches diameter by 104 inches long.

ONE PAIR BRASS PRESS ROLLS, 16 inches by 120 inches long.

TWO C.I. ROLLS for Paper Cutter, 9 inches and 10 inches diameter by 92 inches long.

ONE MAHOGANY COUCH ROLL, 18 inches diameter by 104 inches long.

TWO COPPER WIRE ROLLS, 8 inches diameter by 104 inches long.

ONE BRASS LEADING ROLL, 9 inches diameter by 108 inches long (old).

ONE BRASS TUBE ROLL, 4 inches diameter by 52 inches long (old).

ONE BRASS TUBE ROLL, 4 inches diameter by 55½ inches long (old).

SEVEN BRASS TUBE ROLLS, 3½ inches diameter by 72 inches long (old).

ONE BRASS TUBE ROLL 3½ inches diameter by 92 inches long (good).

FORTY-TWO BRASS TUBE ROLLS, 5 feet 9½ inches long by 2½ inches diameter.

THREE COPPER WIRE ROLLS, 5 feet 10⅜ inches long by 4⅞ inches diameter.

ONE COPPER GUIDE ROLL, 5 feet 11½ inches long by 7 inches diameter.

ONE COPPER BREAST ROLL, 5 feet 11 inches long by 9½ inches diameter.

☛ QUITE NEW.

EIGHT CHECK VALVES, 4 inches diameter.

ELEVEN C.I. COCKS, 4 inch bore, with brass plugs.

Any reasonable offer will be considered by 5916

BERTRAMS LIMITED, SCIENNES, EDINBURGH.

Sale by Private Treaty.

PAPER MERCHANT'S Business, Manchester. Old established. Stock, plant, fixtures and goodwill under £1,000. Net yearly income (average for last five years) £400 (verified).—Apply, principals only, to "A.Z.," c/o Trevor, Pilling and Co., Chartered Accountants, Manchester. 5930

Mills to be Let or Sold.

TO be LET or SOLD, a Paper Mill at Stalybridge, called the Higher Mill, containing one large machine and room for another, steam engine and boilers, in good condition.—Apply for further information to the Caretaker on the premises. 2162

MALDON, ESSEX.—TO BE LET on Lease or Sold, a Freehold Mill, with Engine, Boiler and 2 Water Wheels of 100 horse-power. The Property has an area of Five acres, with a Wharf giving facilities for carriage inland by river, or to London by sea, at the low rate of 2s. 8d. per ton.—For further particulars apply to Fuller, Horsey, Sons and Cassell, 11, Billiter Square, E.C. 5904

OLDERFLEET (FORMERLY INVER) PAPER MILL, LARNE, FOR SALE.

TO BE SOLD BY PRIVATE TREATY, THE EQUITY OF REDEMPTION, after payment of a Mortgage, on foot of which £6,695 is due for principal and interest, in the OLDERFLEET PAPER MILL, LARNE, County Antrim, held partly by Lease, dated 3rd September, 1880, from James Chaine to Patrick Kennedy for 999 years, from 1st of November, 1879, at the yearly rent of £2 and, as to the remainder of said Premises by Lease, dated 9th August, 1889, from Alexander Williams and others, to the Inver Paper Company, Limited, for 99 years, from 1st of May, 1887, at the yearly rent of £3 10s. The Mill occupies a splendid situation, possesses an ample water supply, and is completely equipped with machinery of modern pattern, embracing the very latest improvements, for the production of paper.

A Schedule of Machinery and all further particulars can be had on application to JOHN M'CULLOUGH & CO., Chartered Accountants, Queen's Buildings, Royal Avenue, Belfast; or to L'ESTRANGE & BRETT, Solicitors, 9, Chichester Street, Belfast.

SUMMARY OF IMPORTS & EXPORTS,

FOR THE WEEK ENDING TUESDAY LAST.

London, Liverpool, Bristol, Southampton, Hull, Fleetwood, Harwich, Folkestone, Newhaven, Dover, &c.

IMPORTS.

Paper	16458 bales	Millboards	17028 bales
„	535 cases	„	24 cases
„	1674 rolls	Stationery	14 pkgs
Tissues	1515 bales	„	54 cases
Pasteboards	8161 „	Stock	19 bales
„	3 cases	Bags	38 cases
Strawboards	2070 „		

EXPORTS.

BRITISH GOODS.			
Paper	1864 cwt.	Cardboards	48 cwt.
Writing Paper	3583 „	Pulp Boards	34 „
Printing Paper	1966 „	Bags	65 „
Rags	34 tons	Strawboards	24 „
Stationery	£7816 value	**FOREIGN GOODS.**	
Stock	105 tons	Paper	33 cwt.
Waste	251 „	Printing Paper	50 „
Strawboard Cuttings	48 „	Writing Paper	15 „
Straw	80 „	Stationery	£219 value
		Strawboards	15 cwt.
		Parchment	30 „

Glasgow, Greenock, Port-Glasgow, Troon, Grangemouth, &c.

IMPORTS.

Paper	172 bales	Strawboards	8130 bales
„	2 cases		

EXPORTS.

Stationery	£579 value	Printing Paper	63¾ cwt.
Paper	108 cwt.	Writing Paper	332 „

Leith, Granton, Bo'ness, Dundee, &c.

IMPORTS.

Paper	667 bales	Tissues	6 bales
„	2 cases	Pasteboards	1967 „
Envelopes	640 bales		

LONSDALE'S Boiler Coverer AND Paper Hair AND Cork NON-CONDUCTING CEMENT.

Extract from the *World's Paper Trade Review*, August 2nd, 1889 :—

The "DAILY CHRONICLE" Mills, "The Steam Mains are covered with a Non-Conducting Composition supplied by LONSDALE BROS., OF BLACKBURN, which HAS BEEN FOUND TO ADHERE VERY WELL, and to EFFECT A CONSIDERABLE SAVING."

"It has Stood the Test of an EIGHT YEARS' TRIAL."

Improvement in Cork Covering. Patent No. 19,906. 1889. 2058

The LONDON GLUCOSE & FARINA Co.,

Telegraphic Address: "SNOWWHITE, LONDON." 72, MARK LANE, LONDON, E.C.

"AJAX" Brand (Registered.)

Importers of all Qualities of FARINAS, STARCHES, GLUES DEXTRINE, &c

Stock kept at all Important places in U.K. Contracts made for any period at Special Prices. 2638

PLANT AND MATERIAL—COMPLETE INSTALLATION FOR

ELECTRIC LIGHTING

TRANSMISSION OF POWER,

Electro-Plating, Depositing & Electro-Typing.

For Full Particulars Apply

ERNEST SCOTT & MOUNTAIN, LTD.,

CLOSE WORKS, NEWCASTLE-ON-TYNE.

SOCIÉTÉ INDUSTRIELLE de MIOS,

MIOS, GIRONDE, FRANCE.

Bleached Chemical Pine Wood Pulp,

OF GREAT PURITY,

Especially Adapted for Use in the Manufacture of Fine Papers. 2646

Postal Address: 98, ALBANY ROAD, LONDON, S.E. Telegrams: "Deckle, London." W. GREEN & SON'S

ARE THE BEST

2648

SPECIALTIES: DANDY ROLLS, PAPER MOULDS, MACHINE WIRES, &c., &c.

YATES & THOM

(Late Wm. & Jno. YATES),

BLACKBURN,

HIGH SPEED ECONOMICAL COMPOUND ENGINES. | MODERN MILL GEARING IN ALL ITS BRANCHES.

STEEL BOILERS with 2 and 3 FURNACES up to 200 lbs. WORKING PRESSURE

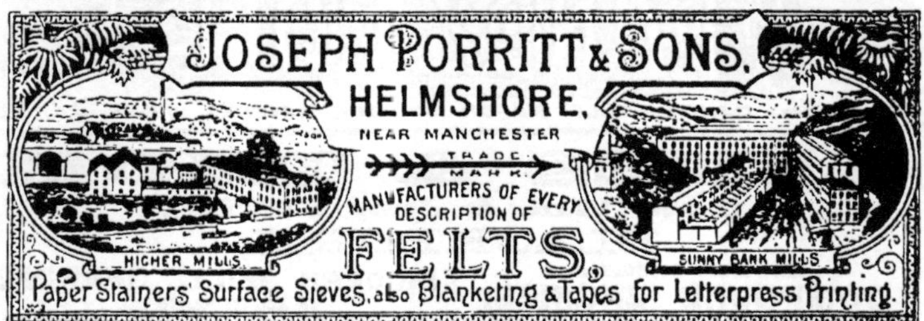
JOSEPH PORRITT & SONS.
HELMSHORE.
NEAR MANCHESTER
TRADE MARK
MANUFACTURERS OF EVERY DESCRIPTION OF
FELTS,
HIGHER MILLS
SUNNY BANK MILLS
Paper Stainers' Surface Sieves, also Blanketing & Tapes for Letterpress Printing.

JACKSON

ngineers,

IANCHESTER.

MARSHALL'S PATENT PERFECTING ENGINE.

SUITABLE FOR ALL CLASSES OF STOCK AND EVERY QUALITY OF PAPER.

MADE IN THREE SIZES.

chine—NO WELL-EQUIPPED ... SHOULD BE WITHOUT

APPLICATION.

Limited,
PACKINGS.
& Oils,
MACHINERY.

Taylor's Patent

BEATING *and* REFINING ENGINE.

THIS BEATER TAKES UP LESS FLOOR SPACE THAN ANY OTHER.

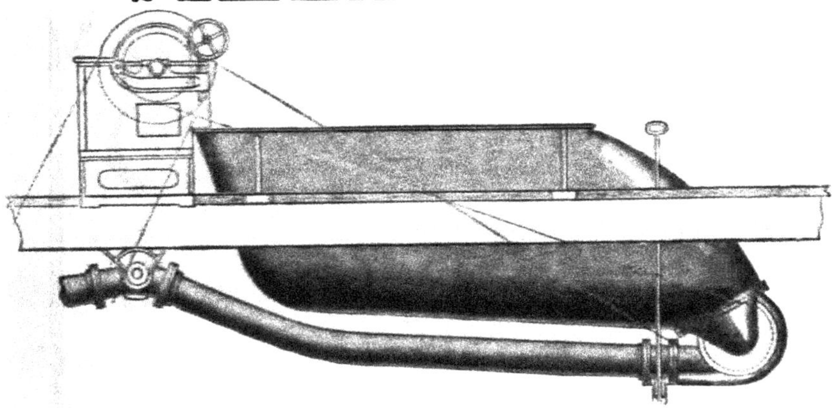

ADVANTAGES:

1.—**GREATLY INCREASED PRODUCTION** over that of the ordinary Beater in use.

2.—**GREAT SAVING IN POWER**, notwithstanding the increased production. This Beater has been proved to beat a given quantity of pulp with less than one-half of the power required by an ordinary beater of good modern construction.

3.—**COMPLETE AND PERFECT CIRCULATION**, which ensures complete uniformity in the length of the fibres.

For Full Particulars and Prices apply to

MASSON, SCOTT & Co., Ltd.,

BATTERSEA, LONDON, S.W

Lightning Source UK Ltd.
Milton Keynes UK
UKHW011842271118
333053UK00011B/860/P